SIKHISM : ITS PHILOSOPHY AND HISTORY

SIKHISM
ITS PHILOSOPHY AND HISTORY

With an Introduction by
CHOOR SINGH

Edited by
DALJEET SINGH
KHARAK SINGH

INSTITUTE OF SIKH STUDIES
959, SECTOR 59, S.A.S. NAGAR, CHANDIGARH, INDIA, 160 059

SIKHISM : ITS PHILOSOPHY AND HISTORY

Edited by

DALJEET SINGH

KHARAK SINGH

INSTITUTE OF SIKH STUDIES

959, Sector 59, S.A.S. Nagar, Chandigarh, INDIA, 160 059

ISBN : 81-85815-03-8

1997

Copies : 2,000

Price : Rupees 1200.00

Layout & Cover Design

by

Harjeet Singh

Laser Typeset by :

Computer World, 1806, Phase 7, Mohali, Phone 0172-679669

Published by Institute of Sikh Studies, 959, Sector 59, S.A.S. Nagar, Chandigarh, India, 160 059 and
Printed at Rashtra Rachna Printers, New Delhi

FOREWORD

It is a privilege to present this monumental work on Sikh religion and history, completed with the co-operation of a galaxy of distinguished scholars. The project was undertaken about two years ago at the instance of Justice Choor Singh of Singapore, by Sardar Daljeet Singh and Dr Kharak Singh in behalf of the Institute of Sikh Studies, Chandigarh. The project suffered a serious setback due to the unfortunate demise of Sardar Daljeet Singh in October 1994, after which the burden fell largely on Dr Kharak Singh.

The need for a single volume dealing with the salient features of Sikhism and its history had long been felt. This book, it is hoped, will fulfil this need adequately. It explains the cardinal principles of the Sikh religion, and surveys its history. It also deals with common misunderstandings or misrepresentation about Sikhs and Sikhism in world books and other media. In fact, this book is a mini-encyclopaedia and could be called 'all about Sikhism.' I wish to record my sincere appreciation of the hard work put in by the editors and the contributions made by various authors.

In behalf of the Institute of Sikh Studies, I am happy to present this book to readers, Sikhs as well as non-Sikhs, in the hope that it will not only lead to an appreciation of the tremendous contribution of Sikhism to religious thought, but also promote understanding among various faiths, essential for universal brotherhood of mankind.

November 12, 1996

Dr Kuldip Singh
President
INSTITUTE OF SIKH STUDIES
CHANDIGARH

PREFACE

Sikhism, founded in the fifteenth century by Guru Nanak Dev, is the youngest and the latest among world religions. With its emphasis on a single loving God, Who created the universe, and Who is the 'Father of us all'; Sikhism seeks to knit the entire mankind into one universal brotherhood. The Guru preached love, justice and equality, and condemned discrimination and exploitation — religious, social or political. God is the 'Ocean of Virtues.' The Sikhs or followers of the Guru are enjoined to imbibe these virtues without which no salvation is possible. God runs the universe with 'His Will' which is altruistic. A Sikh must understand His Will and carry it out to bring about the kingdom of God on earth. Sikhism is not a religion of passive spectators. It advocates active participation in the process of human evolution to superman.

Sikhism is a religion with a message of hope and optimism. It does not regard this world as a place of suffering, and human birth as a punishment. Rather, it is an opportunity given by God in His Infinite mercy, to practise righteousness and to realise one's destiny.

The brief history of Sikhism is a story of an inexorable battle in the cause of righteousness. During the last five centuries, the dauntless spirit of Sikhism has flourished in ups as well as downs. As early as the beginning of the eighteenth century the downtrodden people of North India, who had been subjected to inhuman treatment and exploitation by religious hierarchy and marauded by alien invaders for centuries, had succeeded in establishing their own empire in the entire North-West of the sub-continent of India. The Sikh Rule under Maharaja Ranjit Singh provided a model of governance. It is a remarkable and unique fact of history that during the half century of his rule, the Maharaja did not award death penalty to anyone, not even to those who had made attempts on his own life. Such was the benevolence of the Sikh rule. Unfortunately, the Sikhs lost their hard-earned self-rule. But the crusade for justice and equality continues and will continue. This is the way of life in Sikhism.

Since the beginning of the 20th century, Sikhs started migrating out of India, and due to their cosmopolitan nature and adventuresome spirit, they are today inhabiting virtually every corner of the world. They have stuck to their values as well as their external identity marked by full beard, unshorn hair and turban. They have no problem in maintaining this outward identity and fit into all societies, carrying with them the Guru's motto, 'No one is our enemy, nor is anyone a stranger. With all are we in accord.'

Their distinct appearance attracts attention and curiosity outside India. People want to know more about Sikhs and to understand their philosophy. The information about Sikhs and Sikhism, available in world books, is sketchy and often misleading. Coupled with that is the reality of some agencies deliberately indulging in misrepresentation of this great faith, which holds every promise of being a future religion of the world. In this situation, the need for a book explaining the origin and doctrines of Sikhism as well as the history of its followers, was keenly felt. It was in early 1994 that Justice Choor Singh of Singapore took the initiative for the project leading to the present volume. Besides initiative and inspiration, Justice Choor Singh organised the required financial support and has also contributed the Introductory chapter, which is no less than a summary of the book.

The book is divided into five sections. Section I deals with Sikh Ideology in which major doctrines of Sikhism are discussed. Sikhism is presented as a revealed religion, and a whole-life, independent, spiritual and socio-religious system, distinct from earlier Indian or other world traditions. For the sake of comparison, the earlier Indian traditions like Nathism, Vaisnavism and The Radical Bhagats, with which Sikhism is often erroneously confused, are discussed in Section II, to bring out the distinctive features of Sikhism. Section III deals with major institutions, while Section IV is a brief survey of Sikh history. The Gurus' period as well as other crucial periods in the history of Sikhs are briefly covered by authorities on the respective periods.

Finally, Section V has been added to enlighten the readers on some controversies regarding Sikhs and Sikhism that have surfaced in recent times. This is also necessary in view of the spate of misinformation let loose by certain groups with ulterior motives of damaging the image of Sikhs and Sikhism among the world Community.

We have tried to give as complete a picture of Sikhs and Sikhism as possible in a single volume. We are aware of the gaps left, as also of some overlapping which is inevitable in an effort involving such a large number of authors. But the very fact that so many eminent scholars have joined in lends a rare degree of importance to the work. I am sure that those who want to understand Sikhism and its colourful followers, will find the book extremely helpful.

It is my pleasant duty to express my gratitude to all those who have joined in this effort to produce this book. First among them is Justice Choor Singh who initiated the move, and as reported earlier, also organised the financial support. We are equally indebted to the Sikh Community of Singapore, who liberally contributed towards the project, represented by the following organisations :

CENTRAL SIKH GURDWARA BOARD
SINGAPORE SIKH EDUCATION FOUNDATION
BHAI MAHARAJ SINGH MEMORIAL SHRINE

Sikh Welfare Council
Sri Guru Nanak Sat Sang Sabha
Sri Guru Singh Sabha
Singapore Khalsa Association
Khalsa Dharmak Sabha
Pardesi Khalsa Dharmak Dewan
Gurdwara Sahib Yishun
Istri Sat Sang Sabhas
Sikh Sewaks Of Singapore
Sikh Missionary Society, Singapore
Sikh Moneylenders Association

We are highly indebted to all the authors who have contributed various chapters
to this volume. Since it is a co-operative effort, the book would have been incomplete
without contribution of any one of them. In fact, the joining together of so many highly
respected scholars, lends the book an authority, otherwise impossible. Special thanks
are due to Sardar Tharam Singh, who besides contributing two valuable chapters, took
keen interest in the publication throughout, and rendered invaluable assistance in editorial
work. Here, I must also acknowledge the help received from Col. Amrik Singh Khaira
and Sardar G.S. Sethi in going through the proofs and in the form of valuable suggestions.
Dr Hazara Singh, Adviser, Publication Bureau, Punjabi University, Patiala deserves
special thanks for his interest in the project and for his valuable assistance in production
of the book.

In the end, I must record my sincerest thanks to Dr Birendra Kaur and Ms Sumit
Kaur who have gone over the proofs time and again in order to eliminate errors, and to
Mr Akashdeep who laser-typeset the manuscript with a rare degree of patience, high
professional efficiency and uncommon devotion.

959, Sector 59, SAS Nagar,   Kharak Singh
Chandigarh, India - 160059.
November 12, 1996

CONTENTS

IV. SIKH HISTORY

V. CONTROVERSIES

INTRODUCTION

Who are the Sikhs ? And what is Sikhism ? It is not possible to understand the Sikhs or appreciate their religion, Sikhism, without studying their history and the circumstances under which Sikhism was born.

BIRTH OF SIKHISM

To answer the above questions, we must go back to the times of Guru Nanak Dev (1469 to 1539), the founder of the Sikh religion. Sikhism began with the preaching of Guru Nanak. He based his teachings on his personal experience of a *hukam* (command) received directly from God. Guru Nanak's simple monotheistic creed, supported by a set of humanitarian principles of conduct, and presented with humility and conviction, made a deep impact on the Indian population, then suffering under the heavy heel of the Mughal conquerors and the ritualised Hindu religious observances. Guru Nanak won a large number of adherents to his teachings. It was the beginning of a new religious fellowship, which, in course of time, developed into a well-defined new faith. Its chief doctrines were the unity of God, the brotherhood of man, rejection of caste, and the futility of rituals like idol-worship. Guru Nanak is, in fact, the revealer of a new gospel, the founder of a new faith, the perfect example of piety and deep devotion.

The new religion founded by Guru Nanak was nurtured by nine other Gurus who succeeded him in the holy office of Guruship in the following order :

1. Guru Nanak Dev   1469-1539 A.D.
2. Guru Angad Dev   1539-1552 A.D.
3. Guru Amar Das   1552-1574 A.D.
4. Guru Ram Das   1574-1581 A.D.
5. Guru Arjun Dev   1581-1606 A.D.
6. Guru Hargobind   1606-1644 A.D.
7. Guru Har Rai   1644-1661 A.D.
8. Guru Har Krishan   1661-1664 A.D.

    9. Guru Tegh Bahadur   1664-1675 A.D.

  10. Guru Gobind Singh   1675-1708 A.D.

The term "Guru" when applied to Guru Nanak and his nine successors means spiritual Enlightener. Thus, a Guru in this sense is one who delivers those who accept his teachings and discipline from darkness of materialistic illusion to spiritual enlightenment, from *samsara,* the cycle of rebirth, to the supreme spiritual bliss of union with God.

The term Guru in the Hindu tradition means a spiritual guide and instructor. In the Sikh scripture, however, the term Guru is often used by the Sikh Gurus and others in this sense as well as for God Himself. The role of the Sikh Gurus, however, was different from that of the Hindu gurus : instead of imparting knowledge of God based on the existing scriptures, they acted as revealers of truth, that is, knowledge of God. Their revelations formed the basis of Sikhism, and the Sikh Gurus became its founders. The Sikh Gurus did not claim to be incarnations of God, or God in human form. Sikhism does not believe in the theory of incarnation, because God does not take birth.

The Guru is a messenger of God sent to enlighten mankind. He is one who has realised God. Blessed by Divine Grace, he becomes perfect and capable of guiding mortals on the path to God. The disciple has to reflect on the Guru's teachings, be convinced of its truth in his mind, practise it in thought, word and deed, and pray for Divine Grace. He then obtains liberation from the cycle of birth and death while living a normal life. The Guru teaches the disciple how to link his own consciousness to Divine Consciousness. He makes the disciple see the vision of God within his own heart. The Sikh Gurus were ordinary human beings, but when they were blessed by Divine Grace, they became perfect and capable of guiding mortals on the spiritual path. The Sikh Gurus were treated with great reverence and people turned to them for instruction because of their wisdom and their moral piety.

Guru Nanak preached his new gospel in *dharamsalas.* In ancient times, *dharamsalas* were hostels for pilgrims. Guru Nanak's *dharamsalas* were different. Here his followers gathered to listen to his discourses on the new faith preached by him and to sing hymns taught by him. *Dharamsalas* played a very significant role in shaping and governing the life of the Sikhs. The first few *dharamsalas* were established by Guru Nanak Dev as centres of the new society with a new religious movement. More *dharamsalas* were created by the other Gurus who succeeded him and later on by Sikhs. These have been a source of strength and inspiration to the Sikhs, and have helped in maintaining the corporate life of the community. Guru Nanak Dev gave concrete expression to the ideas of unity, equality and fraternity by holding at these centres community prayers and community *langars* (meals from the community kitchen). In the words of Bhai Gurdas, "*dharamsala* is like Mansarovar (a sacred lake in the Himalayas) and the Sikhs flock there like swans." The great message of emancipation from invidious distinctions and caste prejudices was instilled into the hearts of the people, through these institutions of *sangat* (congregation assembled for worship) and *pangat* (line of devotees seated on the floor for a meal from the community kitchen), originally established at these centres.

Guru Nanak started the institutions of *dharamsala, sangat*, *langar* and *manjis* (seats of preaching). The succeeding Gurus further consolidated and extended these institutions.

Guru Amar Das systematized the institution of *manjis* and selected twenty-two centres for this mission. Persons of high religious calibre were nominated to these offices. They were in charge of the Guru's followers in an area and catered to their religious as well as temporal needs. They were the links of the organisation and the twenty-two channels of communication between the Guru and the *sangat*. They collected the offerings and passed the same on to the central treasury where they were used by the Guru for the purposes of the mission. Guru Arjun further regularised the collection of these contributions. He fixed the amount to be one tenth of one's income that every Sikh should set apart for the common cause.

The *dharamsalas* of the Sikhs not only helped to spread the gospel of the Gurus, but also served as meeting places for discussion of general problems concerning the welfare of the Sikh *Panth* and as training grounds for social service. Although there were then numerous Sikh *dharamsalas* all over the Punjab, he felt that there should be a central Sikh shrine to meet the growing needs of the Sikh *sangats,* where they could gather to celebrate jointly all Sikh religious festivals. Accordingly, he built Harimandar Sahib, the most sacred shrine of Sikhs, which has served as the heart of the Sikh faith and has played a crucial role in the consolidation of the Sikh *Panth.*

Guru Arjun Dev compiled Guru Granth Sahib, the sacred scripture of the Sikhs, consisting of the hymns of the Gurus and other saints. Guru Arjun Dev felt that there should be one Religious Book as the scripture and one central place — Harimandar Sahib — to be the rendezvous for the new religion and he accomplished both for the further development of the new faith.

Written in Gurmukhi script, Guru Granth Sahib became the nucleus of the Sikh way of life and of all religious observances of the Sikhs. The *Gurbani,* containing spiritual knowledge, became the object of the highest reverence for the Sikhs, as well as for the Gurus themselves. The word of Guru Granth Sahib is equated with the Guru himself. "The *Gurbani* is the Guru, and the Guru the *Gurbani"* sang Guru Ram Das. On August 16, 1604 A.D. Guru Arjun ceremoniously installed the sacred volume of Guru Granth Sahib in the centre of the inner sanctorum in the newly-built Harimandar Sahib. The high level of sanctity and reverence accorded to the Harimandar could not have been possible without Guru Granth Sahib enshrined in it.

Guru Arjun Dev, the compiler of Guru Granth Sahib, has very clearly and emphatically declared the independent position of Sikhism vis-a-vis Hinduism or any other religion :

"I do not keep the Hindu fast nor the Muslim Ramadan;
I serve Him alone who is my refuge
I serve the One Master; who is also Allah
I have broken with the Hindu and the Muslim,
I do not worship the Hindu way nor like the Muslim go to Mecca,
I serve Him alone and no other,
I will not pray to idols nor say the Muslim prayer
I shall put my heart at the feet of the one Supreme Being
For, we are neither Hindus nor Mussalmans."
                                                    (A. G. 1136)

With such an authoritative statement, from the pen of the compiler Guru of the sacred scripture of the Sikhs, it is not understood how non-Sikhs can keep asserting persistently that Sikhism is a sect of Hinduism.

Copies of Guru Granth Sahib were made, and in due course, installed in all *dharamsalas*. With the installation of Guru Granth Sahib in a *dharamsala*, it became a gurdwara (Abode of the Guru), and more so after Guru Gobind Singh, the tenth and last living Guru of the Sikhs, conferred Guruship on it. He ordained that after him, Guru Granth Sahib shall be the Guru of the Sikhs. He installed Guru Granth Sahib as his successor, thus putting an end to the line of living Gurus. After the conferment of Guruship on the Granth Sahib, it began to be addressed as Guru Granth Sahib. Guru Gobind Singh thus gave the institution of Guruship a permanent and abiding character by vesting in it the immortality of Guru Granth Sahib and in the continuity of the *Khalsa Panth* (Brotherhood of the Pure). It is of course not the book but its contents, the *Gurshabad* (the Divine Word) which is now the perpetual Guru of the Sikhs and shall remain ever so, for there is no longer any place in the Sikh faith for a new living Guru. It is for this reason that any attack on a gurdwara is considered by the Sikhs as an attack on their Guru, and a Sikh will not hesitate to lay down his life in defence of his gurdwara. A great part of Sikh history revolves around gurdwaras. In the daily Sikh prayer, an eloquent reference is made to the brave Sikhs who suffered martyrdom in protecting their gurdwaras. "The freedom of their gurdwaras has always been the measure of the Sikhs' freedom or prosperity", writes Teja Singh in *Essays on Sikhism*.

The gurdwara emerged as a new edifice on the Indian religious scene in the seventeenth century. Since then, this indestructible symbol of the Sikh faith has aroused intense and indefinable feelings in millions of Sikhs everywhere, as well as a longing to hear recitations from Guru Granth Sahib and the *shabads* (hymns) rendered in the robust and resonant voices of the *ragis* (hymn singers).

After the martyrdom of Guru Arjun Dev, his son Guru Hargobind took the seat of his father with two swords girded round his waist, one symbolising spiritual power and the other temporal authority. Seeing how peaceful resistance to oppression had proved abortive, he recognised recourse to the sword as a rightful alternative for self-defence. Opposite the Harimandar, he built the Akal Takht (The Throne of the Timeless God). In it, he sat on a throne and held court. He received envoys, settled disputes and administered justice. Ever since then, the Akal Takht has remained the seat of the spiritual and temporal authority of the Sikhs. During the eighteenth century, when, as a result of severe persecution, the Sikhs were forced to seek refuge in forests, it served as a rallying point. The meetings of the *Sarbat Khalsa* (a general meeting of all the Sikhs), were held here, usually on the Vaisakhi and Diwali festival days. It was from the Akal Takht, that the affairs of the Sikh community, thereafter began to be administered. The Akal Takht has ever since served as the supreme court of the Sikh faith. The Supreme spiritual and temporal authority of the Sikhs is enshrined in the Akal Takht. The importance of the Akal Takht to the Sikhs is hard to describe and impossible to exaggerate. It is also known as the *Akal Bunga* (Lord's Mansion).

The period of Guru Nanak's ministry was marked by the education and enlightenment of the people. Guru Nanak broke the first sod and cleared the ground for the building of the national character of the Sikhs. It was reserved for his successors to give them the lessons in obedience, service, self-sacrifice and other noble virtues. The final touch of perfection was given by the last prophet, Guru Gobind Singh, who, by founding the *Khalsa Panth,* completed the transformation of the Sikhs into a saint-soldier martial race imbued with spiritual qualities and with a distinct identity, which in time became a nation of warriors and conquered the whole of North India.

SIKH SCRIPTURE

The scripture of the Sikhs is contained in a volume of 1430 pages called Guru Granth Sahib. It contains a collection of the writings of their Gurus and some other *bhagats* (saints). Guru Granth Sahib contains the compositions of the first five Gurus, Guru Nanak Dev, Guru Angad, Guru Amar Das, Guru Ram Das, Guru Arjun Dev, and of Guru Tegh Bahadur (the ninth Guru), panegyrics of bards who attended on the Gurus and admired their character, besides hymns of medieval Indian Hindu and Muslim saints. The cardinal principle of the Gurus and *bhagats* whose writings find a place in the sacred book of the Sikhs, is the unity of God. This is inculcated everywhere in the Sikh sacred writings with ample and perhaps not unnecessary iteration, considering the forces, Sikhism had to contend with, in an age of ignorance and superstition.

Both the Gurus and Guru Granth Sahib inspire the reverence which they are accorded because of the *Gurbani* which they express, the word of Divine truth. Guru Arjun, the fifth Guru who compiled Guru Granth Sahib bowed before the collection which he had compiled and installed it in the newly built *Darbar* Sahib (Golden Temple) in 1604. In doing so, he was acknowledging the higher authority of *Gurbani* over his personal status as Guru.

The great Pandits and Brahmins of Hindustan communicated their instructions in Sanskrit, which they deemed as the language of the gods. The Gurus thought it would be of more general advantage to present their message in the local language of their age. When Guru Amar Das was asked the reason for this, he replied : "Well-water can only irrigate the adjacent land, but rain-water the whole world." On this account, the Gurus composed their hymns in the language of the people, and enshrined these in the Gurmukhi script, so that men and women of all castes and classes may read and understand it.

Contrary to the practice of the ancient Indian ascetics, the Gurus held that man can obtain eternal happiness without forsaking his ordinary worldly duties. All the Gurus and the *bhagats* whose writings find place in Guru Granth Sahib, emphasise that union with the Absolute should be the supreme object of man's devotion and aspirations. Merger in God is completely foreign to Sikh theology. Union or link with God but not merger is aspired, for merger involves loss of identity and can be possible only in a pantheistic creed and not in a theistic creed like Sikhism. In Sikhism, the goal of only personal salvation is excluded. God-centred activity in one's life and not salvation is the goal.

The Gurus emphasised the idea that God resides within the human heart and that the way to solve our problems and difficulties is to establish a relationship with Him. The presence of God in us has variously been described as *Naam*, Guru, Word, Light and Will. *Naam* is the Dynamic and Attributive Immanence of God, representing His *Hukm, Raza* or Will. In short, *Naam* is the essence of God. The goal in life for a Sikh is to link himself with *Naam*. Love, contentment, truth, humility and other virtues enable the seed of *Naam* to sprout. Our deeds alone bear witness unto our life. It is only the virtuous and altruistic deeds that lead one away from the life of *haumein* (self-exaltation, self-centredness) and towards the path of *Naam* or God-centredness.

In Guru Granth Sahib, through various ways, it has been emphasised that the path of virtuous deeds is the only discipline acceptable to God. In the hymn of *Dharam khand*, which lays down man's duties in life, Guru Nanak advises that man's assessment will be entirely according to his deeds and that final approval will be only by God's Grace.

Extreme humility is the dominant tone of all the Gurus' hymns. Throughout in comparison to God and even to others, they speak of themselves as the lowest of the low. The theological fundamentals and the doctrines of the Sikh religion are clearly and completely embodied in Guru Granth Sahib.

CREATION OF THE KHALSA PANTH

Guru Gobind Singh did not change the religion preached by the preceding nine Gurus. He had not only all their attributes, but also the power to mould *Nanakpanthis* (believers in Nanak's faith) into a nation and then to fire that nation with an ideal — the ideal of the *Khalsa* Commonwealth. His greatest achievement was the establishment of the *Khalsa* by the famous *amrit* ceremony on 30th March, 1699 by which he raised the *Khalsa,* and bestowed on them his blessings and the gift of valour in war. He bound them to a strict code of conduct *(Rahitnama),* and with unshorn hair, beard and turban, he gave the Sikhs a distinct identity. He ordained that they should uphold righteousness in every place and destroy evil in every form by all means available and should not submit to *zulum* (oppression and tyranny) but resist it, if necessary, by force. Guru Gobind Singh also made it explicitly clear that Sikhs were neither Hindus nor Muslims, and forbade worship of any of their idols or tombs; nor were they to follow the teachings of their holy books. Only Guru Granth Sahib was to be their Scripture. In a *Sawaiya* (religious text) composed by him, he states :

> *Pae gahe jab te tumre,*
>> *tab te kou ankh tare nahin aniyo.*
>> *Ram, Rahim, Puran, Quran anek*
>> *kahin mat ek na manio*
> *Simrat, Sastar, Bed Sabhai,*
>> *Baho bhed kahain, ham ek na janio*
> *Sri Aspan kirpa Tumri Kar, main na*
>> *Kahio, Sab Tohe bakhanio.*

(Chaupai, Dasam Granth)

(Lord, ever since I have fallen at your feet,
> I care not for anyone else,
> The different paths of Ram, Rahim, Puran and Quran, I do not accept.

The Simritis, Shastras, and the Vedas lay down many doctrines, but I recognise not
> any of them.

O Lord, I have composed these hymns by Your Grace, and it is all what You have
> taught me.)

(Ram here is the Hindu deity Ram of Ayodhya and Rahim refers to Prophet Mohammed of Islam).

Shortly before his death in 1708, Guru Gobind Singh declared to his assembled *Khalsa* that with his death the succession of living Gurus will terminate, and that thereafter the Guru will be mystically present within the sacred scripture and the corporate community, the *Khalsa Panth.* Some of the disciples who were present, Bhai Nand Lal, Bhai Mani Singh, Dhadi Nath Mall and the Court poet Sainapat have described in detail the ceremony by which the Guru conferred Guruship on Guru Granth Sahib. The Guru is reported to have informed his *Khalsa* that henceforth the divine authority of the Guru would be in the Guru Granth Sahib and the *Khalsa Panth,* and that all issues concerning belief or practice should be referred to them for guidance as and when necessary, for a final decision. The Guru is reported to have recited the following hymn composed by him :

Agya bhai Akal ki tabhi chalayo Panth,

Sab Sikhan ko hukam hai Guru Manyo Granth

Guru Granth ji manyo pargat Guran ki deh

Jo Prabhu ko milbo chahe khoj shabad men le

(Under orders of the Immortal Being, the *Panth* was created; All the Sikhs are enjoined to accept the *Granth* as their Guru, Consider the *Guru Granth* as representing the Guru's body. Those who wish to meet God can find the way in its hymns.)

(Hari Ram Gupta, *History of the Sikhs*, Vol. I, p. 327)

Thus started the doctrine of the *Guru Granth* and the *Guru Panth* which add up to the presence of the Guru in the world today.

BANDA ESTABLISHES FIRST SIKH STATE

Shortly before his demise in 1708 at Nanded in South India, Guru Gobind Singh sent Banda Singh Bahadur to the Punjab with a small army to carry on the Khalsa mission and conduct the final phase of the *Khalsa* struggle against the Mughal Empire. In May 1710, the *Khalsa* army under Banda conquered Sarhind province lying between the rivers Satluj and the Yamuna. Shortly afterwards, Banda extended the boundaries of the Sikh state to the Ganga in the East and up to the banks of the river Ravi in the West. He also conquered some parts of what is now West Punjab. Banda established the first ever independent Sikh state, complete with a royal seal, its own coin, and an efficient administrative system. Even though the first Sikh state was short-lived, its effect on the Sikhs was electrifying.

After the defeat of Banda Bahadur in 1716, the Sikhs were almost wiped out. The Mughal Emperor Faruk Siyar issued an edict according to which every Sikh was to be arrested and offered only one option, either Islam or death. This order was carried out with great zeal. With the death sentence on their heads, the Sikhs withdrew to the Punjab hills where they sought refuge in the jungles. Safe in these inaccessible jungles, they sang *Raj Karega Khalsa* (The Khalsa shall rule) for the fulfilment of their aspirations and bade their time.

SIKHS ESTABLISH THEIR KINGDOM

Tyranny does not have a long life and tyrants always perish under the weight of their own sins. Nine foreign invasions from the North by the dreaded Nadir Shah and his General

Ahmad Shah Durani, and one Maratha incursion, caused the gradual weakening of the Mughal rule in Punjab. When this happened, the *Khalsa* left the jungles and descended into the plains of the Punjab, carrying fire and sword everywhere. They humbled the Mughals and formed independent principalities known as *misls* on the ashes of the Mughal empire. They exercised sovereignty in the Punjab and sang *Raj Karega Khalsa* with every justification. In the words of Khushwant Singh, "Ranjit Singh hammered these Sikh factions (the *misls*) into a nation and made it strong and prosperous. The Sikh nation became not only the strongest Indian power, but also one of the most powerful sovereign States in Asia."

(*A History of the Sikhs*, Vol. 2, p. 3, Third Impression, 1981)

SIKH NATION RULES NORTH INDIA

Indians who now become irritated on hearing Sikhs claiming to be a nation, forget or choose to forget that the territories of the Sikh nation extended from the borders of China and Tibet in the North to the deserts of Sindh in the South, and from Afghanistan in the North-West to the river Ganga in the East. Present day Indians also forget that it was the Sikh nation which put an end to the perpetual foreign invasions of India from the North-West which had been going on for more than a thousand years. The Sikh nation sealed the Khyber pass. It was also for the first time in the history of India, that a military force from the East crossed the river Indus when the Sikh General Hari Singh Nalwa wrested the valley of Peshawar from the Afghans and made inroads into what is now Afghanistan. But for General Hari Singh's conquest of the Trans-Indus territory of Hazara and Peshawar and its annexation to the Sikh Kingdom, these fertile and strategic areas would not have been a part of the British Indian Empire, nor would Pakistan have inherited these areas at the time of the partition of India in 1947. For this, Pakistan owes a debt of gratitude to the Sikh nation. The Sikh nation, which possessed one of the most powerful and disciplined armies in the whole of Asia was highly respected even in Europe. Louis Philippe of France and King William of England sent presents to the Sikh monarch, Maharaja Ranjit Singh, all the way from Europe.

Ranjit Singh named his government, *Sircar-e-Khalsa*, but it was hardly the government of the *Khalsa Panth*. Ranjit Singh had so many non-Sikh Ministers, Generals and other non-Sikhs in positions of power, that in the end it was these non-Sikhs who brought about the dissolution of the Sikh *Raj*. The true standard bearers of the *Khalsa Panth*, reared from the beginning on a republican principle, were the *Khalsa misls*, who fought against the greatest conquerors of all time to save the *Panth* from extinction. Whereas Ranjit Singh showed great kindness to the British, almost to the extent of becoming subservient to them, the *misls* showed scant respect for the British.

Ranjit Singh not only unceremoniously liquidated all the *misls* in order to become an autocratic monarch, but also suspended all the institutions of the *Khalsa*, such as the *gurmatta*, the *Sarbat Khalsa* and the *Khalsa Dal*.

The *gurmatta* (the mind or intention of the Guru) was a resolution passed at a meeting of the *Sarbat Khalsa* (all the *misl* leaders and their followers) in the presence of Guru Granth Sahib. Such a decision was considered a decision of the *Guru Panth*, the corporate Guru of the Sikhs. During the period of the *misls*, the doctrine of the *Guru Panth* was elevated to a supreme authority, and it found its clearest expression in the *gurmatta* which was binding on all Sikhs. This practice of the *misls* of determining all important questions relating to the *Panth* by a *gurmatta* was abandoned by Ranjit Singh, who appropriated the decision making process as his sovereign right. The non-compliance with this doctrine of the *Guru Panth,* the supreme authority of the *Khalsa,* was probably the main cause of the fall of Ranjit Singh's kingdom, for, after his death, there was no corporate body or institution of the *Khalsa* to carry on the Sikh *Raj.* The effective control of the kingdom fell into non-Sikh hands, Dogras and Brahmins who were all intent on feathering their own nest. The doctrine of the *Guru Panth* was revived in 1873 by the Singh Sabha Movement.

Ranjit Singh surrounded himself with a coterie of sycophants comprising Dogras, Brahmins and Muslims, and forgot that it was on the strength of *Khalsa* arms that he came to power. The stalwarts of the *Panth,* such as General Sham Singh Atari, General Hari Singh Nalwa, Baba Sahib Singh Bedi of Una, a direct descendant of Guru Nanak and Akali Phula Singh, the Jathedar of the Akal Takht were all distanced away and tactfully, but without fail, eliminated from all effective voice in the councils of his government. He raised the alien hill Dogras, Dhyan Singh, Kushal Singh and Gulab Singh, almost from the gutter to positions of supreme authority in his government. The insignificant Purbia Brahmins, Tej Singh and Lal Singh, were granted such great influence that eventually they were raised to the supreme command of the *Khalsa* Army. By doing this and forgetting, that the Guru had bestowed the *Patshahi* (sovereignty) on the *Khalsa Panth,* "Ranjit Singh dug his own grave, the graves of his descendants and paved the way for the eventual enslavement of the Sikh people."

(Kapur Singh's *Parasaraprasna,* p. 239)

ANGLO-SIKH WARS

As long as Maharaja Ranjit Singh was alive, the British kept their distance. They coveted the territories of the Sikh nation, but although they had conquered the rest of India, they dared not move against the mighty Ranjit Singh.

After the death of Maharaja Ranjit Singh, the crafty British annexed Punjab through the treacherous and treasonable acts of Tej Singh, Lal Singh and the Dogra Gulab Singh, all of whom, for personal gain, betrayed the trust placed in them by the descendants of Ranjit Singh. But, in spite of the treachery and betrayal of the Dogras and the Purbias, it was no easy walk-over for the British. They had to fight eight bloody battles against the *Khalsa* army before they could annex the Sikh kingdom.

The battles fought at Mudki (18-12-1845), Ferozeshahr (21-12-1845), Aliwal (27-1-1846), Sabraon (10-2-1846), Buddowal (22-2-1846), Ramnagar (22-11-1848), Chellianwala (13-1-1849) and Gujrat (21-2-1849) were the bloodiest battles the British had fought in their entire history. British accounts of these battles, glorify the feats of their army but the truth is that the British were making no headway, so much so that in England, the aged Duke of Wellington threatened to come to India and take over the command of the British forces fighting the *Khalsa* army.

The supplies of arms and rations to the *Khalsa* army were cut off by a treacherous civil government at Lahore under Dogra Gulab Singh and the non-Sikh generals, Tej Singh and Lal Singh, treacherously sold their tactical plans and their lives to the crafty British. In the battle of Mudki, on 18th December, 1845, the *Khalsa* army was considered the loser, simply because their General, traitor Lal Singh, a Brahmin, after issuing attack orders, ran away with the munition stores, in accordance with a plan previously approved and agreed to by the enemy. In the battle of Ferozeshahr (formerly Pheru Shahr), on 21st December, 1845, although the Generals Lal Singh and Tej Singh shamelessly repeated their tactics of three days earlier, the *Khalsa* army who had gone without food rations and who had been deprived of their reserve munitions through treachery, inflicted such heavy crushing losses on the enemy that according to the admissions made by Sir Robert Cust, in his log book entry, dated 22nd December, 1845, the British Command had formally decided at night to "Surrender unconditionally" the next morning before the *Khalsa* army. Lord Hardinge, the British Governor-General, who took part in this battle, also thought that everything was over. After making his will, he handed it to his son, who was his ADC, together with his sword — a present from the Duke of Wellington and which once belonged to Napoleon, his Star of the Bath, and ordered him to escape in the night to Ferozepore, saying "if the day were lost, I must fall." The next morning, it was again the ignominious sabotage and treachery of Lal Singh and Tej Singh which saved the British Indian Empire when they deceived and persuaded the fresh reinforcements of the *Khalsa* army to refrain from pressing the previous evening's advantage by attacking the beaten enemy.

Before the Sabraon battle of 10th February, 1846, Gulab Singh Dogra, the *de facto* Prime Minister of the Sikh Government at Lahore, was already in treasonable communication with the British, and had promised to render all possible help and aid to the enemy to inflict a defeat on the *Khalsa* army with a view to facilitating occupation of Lahore by the British forces. Gulab Singh Dogra also had his private army of 40,000 Dogras standing by, ready to come to the aid of the British, in case they found difficulty in defeating the *Khalsa* army. While these battles were going on, Gulab Singh looted Ranjit Singh's treasury. "Gulab Singh Dogra carried off to Kashmir the accumulated treasures of Ranjit Singh. Sixteen carts were filled with Rupees and other silver coins, while 500 horsemen were each entrusted with a bag of gold *mohurs* (coins) and his orderlies with jewellery and other valuable articles." (Latif, *History of Punjab*, p. 507). Lord Hardinge, the British Governor-General of India, in a letter dated 2nd March 1845, to his wife, Lady Hardinge, wrote, "The man I have to deal with, Gulab Singh, is the greatest rascal in Asia." (Hardinge Family Papers, Penhurst, Kent).

Lord Gough, the British Commander-in-Chief, described the battle of Sabraon as the Waterloo of India, for had they lost it, that would have been the end of the British in India. But the battle at Chellianwala was even more ferocious and was the worst defeat suffered by the British since their occupation of India. Three thousand British soldiers and thousands of their native soldiers lay dead. The *Khalsa* fired a 21 gun salute to commemorate their victory. Lord Dalhousie, the new British Governor-General, made a candid admission of the true state of affairs in a private letter to the Duke of Wellington. He wrote, "In public I make, of course, the best of things. I treat it as a great victory. But writing confidentially to you, I do not hesitate to say that I consider my position grave."

The British realised that unless they won the next battle, they would have to leave India. They brought to Punjab reinforcements from the rest of India, fresh troops and more heavy guns. On the other hand, the *Khalsa* army, already depleted after so many battles, suffered from desertions brought about by the crafty British. The Dogras and Rohillas deserted the Sikhs and joined the British. In the last battle of Gujrat, fought on 21st February, 1849, the *Khalsa* army which had held the British power at bay with a stubborn skill hitherto unparalleled in Indian history, had to give way. The weight of numbers and armour decided the issue. The battle of Gujrat ended the Sikh resistance to the British.

On March 30, 1849, in full Durbar at Lahore, a proclamation was read which formally placed the land of the Five Rivers under the British sovereignty. The young Maharaja Dalip Singh was made to hand over the Koh-i-Nur diamond to the British Governor-General and to step down from his illustrious father's throne — never to sit on it again.

BRITISH ATTEMPTS TO HINDUISE SIKHISM

The first thing the British did after annexing all the territory of the Sikh nation was to take over control of all important Sikh shrines, including the Golden Temple. The uncanny British knew because of the ferocious defence put up by the *Khalsa* army during the Anglo-Sikh wars, that the military power of the Sikhs and their valour in war emanated from their religious zeal, which in turn was inspired by their ideology and their holy shrines. They made sure that the Sikh religious places were kept in hands that were hostile to the teachings of the Sikh Gurus. These hands also sought to direct them to the ritualistic maze of Hinduism. Accordingly, Hindu *mahants* and *pujaris* and others leaning towards Hinduism, were appointed to manage the Sikh gurdwaras, so as to be instrumental in the erosion of the Sikh faith. The British conferred proprietory rights on these *mahants*. As a result, Hindu rites were introduced and even Hindu idols were installed in sacred Sikh shrines including the Golden Temple.

The Sikhs resented the objectionable Hindu practices introduced with the connivance and support of the British. The resentment, in time, took shape in the form of the Sikh Gurdwaras Reform Movement, which had as its object the wresting of control of all gurdwaras from the hands of the corrupt Hindu *mahants*. A corps of volunteers, the *Akali Dal* was constituted for taking over gurdwaras from recalcitrant *mahants*. The *Akali Dal* became the spearhead of the struggle for the liberation of Sikh places of worship which were under the control of the *mahants*. The *Akali Dal* made great sacrifices during this passive struggle. The struggle went on for many years and many Akalis faced bullets and sacrificed their lives during the reform movement. There were Akali *morchas* (unarmed confrontations) at Guru Ka-Bagh, Muktsar and Jaito. Hundreds of Sikhs were killed. Finally, perturbed at the effect which these agitations were having on Sikh soldiers in the Indian Army, the British relented and the Sikh Gurdwaras Act of 1925, which met all demands of the Sikhs, was passed. It vested the control and management of the Golden Temple and all other historical Sikh shrines in Punjab in the Shiromani Gurdwara Parbandhak Committee, a representative body of the Sikhs, and the *Akali Dal* became the political party of the Sikhs.

PARTITION OF INDIA

At the time of partition of India in 1947, the leaders of the Indian National Congress, in particular Mahatma Gandhi and Pandit Nehru, assured the Sikhs that they would be given a semi-autonomous State in the Punjab. All the volumes of the "Transfer of Power Documents" reveal that the British did their best to persuade the Sikhs to ask for a separate independent state. Putting blind faith in the assurances of the Congress leaders, the Sikhs did not listen. They were led up the garden path by the Congress leaders only to be betrayed later. They had been assured, repeatedly, that the Congress would not let down the Sikhs in any constitutional arrangements for the independence of India.

For example, as far back as 1929, at the annual session of the Indian National Congress, held that year in Lahore, which was presided over by Jawaharlal Nehru, the following resolution was passed :

"The Congress assures the Sikhs that no solution in any future Constitution of India will be acceptable to the Congress that does not give them (the Sikhs) full satisfaction."

(A. C. Banerjee : *Indian Constitutional Documents*, Vol. II, p. 317)

Again in 1931, while addressing a meeting of Sikhs at the Sis Gang Gurdwara in Delhi, Mahatma Gandhi told the Sikhs :

"I ask you to accept my word and the resolution of the Congress that it will not betray a single individual much less the community of our Sikh friends. You have no reason to fear that it (the Congress) would betray you. For, the moment it does so, the Congress would not only thereby seal its own doom but that of the country too."

Mahatma Gandhi went on to say :

"Moreover the Sikhs are a brave people. They know how to safeguard their rights by the exercise of arms if it should come to that. What more can I say than this : let God be witness to the bond that binds me and the Congress with you. In case of betrayal, the Sikhs could in that case take their *kirpans* (sabres) in hand with perfect justification before God and man."

(*The Young India*, March 19th, 1931)

In 1946, at the Congress Committee session at Calcutta, Nehru said :

"The brave Sikhs of the Punjab are entitled to a special consideration. I see nothing wrong in an area and set-up in the North wherein the Sikhs can experience the glow of freedom. Redistribution of provincial boundaries is essential and inevitable. I stand for semi-autonomous units. If the Sikhs desire to function in such a unit, I would like them to have a semi-autonomous unit within India so that they have a sense of freedom."

(*New Cambridge History of India*, p. 205,
The Statesman, Calcutta, July 7, 1946)

In March 1946, when the British Cabinet Mission arrived in New Delhi, they met the Sikh leaders, Master Tara Singh, Giani Kartar Singh, Harnam Singh and Baldev Singh. Members of the Cabinet Mission asked the Sikh leaders to "specifically express their views on whether they favoured a united India, or its division, and in the case of its division, whether they would join India or Pakistan, or would they like to have a state of their own." The Sikh spokesman, Master Tara Singh, said that they were for a separate Sikh state with the right to federate either with India or Pakistan. Giani Kartar Singh elaborated the latter alternative as a "province of the Sikhs where they would be in a dominant position." The

Congress Working Committee on learning this, quickly passed a resolution assuring the Sikhs "of all possible support in removing their legitimate grievances and in securing adequate safeguards for the protection of their just interests in the Punjab." In response, the Sikhs abandoned their demand for a separate Sikh state and threw their lot with the Congress which resulted in Baldev Singh joining Nehru's interim Government as Defence Minister on 2nd September, 1946.

(New Cambridge History of India, pp. 176-177)

In a resolution moved by Nehru on 9th December, 1946, in the Constituent Assembly, Nehru said :

"Adequate safeguards would be provided for minorities in India. It is a declaration, pledge and an understanding before the world, a contract with millions of Indians and therefore in the nature of an oath we must keep."

(B. Shiva Rao : *Framing of the Indian Constitution — A Study*, p. 181)

Even as late as 5th January, 1947, at the Congress session, at Delhi, the Congress leaders again publicly repeated assurance of its support for minorities, particularly the Sikhs.

In April 1947, Mr. Jinnah, in consultation with certain most powerful leaders of the British Cabinet in London, offered, to the Sikhs, first through Master Tara Singh and then through the Maharaja of Patiala, a sovereign Sikh state, comprising areas lying to the west of Panipat and east of the left bank of the Ravi river, on the understanding that this state would confederate with Pakistan on very advantageous terms to the Sikhs. Master Tara Singh summarily rejected this attractive offer and the Maharaja of Patiala declined it after consulting Sardar Patel and Pandit Jawaharlal Nehru.

(Are Sikhs a Nation ?, p. 99)

On the 17th of May, 1947, Lord Mountbatten, Pandit Jawaharlal Nehru, Nawab Liaqat Ali Khan and Sardar Baldev Singh, flew to London on the invitation of the British Cabinet, in search of a final solution to the Indian communal problem. When the Congress and the Muslim league failed to strike any mutual understanding and Pandit Nehru decided to return to India, the British Cabinet leaders conveyed to Sardar Baldev Singh that if he stayed behind, arrangements might be made "so as to enable the Sikhs to have political feet of their own, on which they may walk into the current of world history." Baldev Singh promptly divulged the contents of this confidential offer to Pandit Nehru, and in compliance with the latter's wishes, declined to stay back. He flew back to India after giving the following brave message to the press :

"The Sikhs have no claims to make on the British except the demand that they should quit India. Whatever political rights and aspirations the Sikhs have, they shall have them satisfied through the goodwill of the Congress and the Hindus."

(Are Sikhs a Nation ?, p. 101)

Immediately after independence of India, the Sikhs were unashamedly betrayed by the Indian National Congress. They were deceived and denied the promised "Semi-autonomous Unit" in Punjab. The Congress reneged on their solemn promise which Nehru had described as "a contract" and "in the nature of an oath"; the promises on which the Sikhs had acted by opting for India and rejected Jinnah's very tempting offer of a sovereign

State federated with Pakistan. J. N. Sahni, the veteran editor of the *Hindustan Times* wrote, "The letting down of the Sikhs was not an act of carelessness on the part of the Congress leaders, nor even a blunder, but an act of gross and unpardonable betrayal."

In 1947, when the Sikh leader Master Tara Singh reminded Nehru of the solemn promises made to the Sikhs by Congress leaders, and of his speech in Calcutta a year earlier, Nehru replied, "the situation is different now." The Sikh leader was branded "an extremist" and imprisoned for demanding a measure of autonomy for the Sikhs.

Master Tara Singh was not the only one to clash with Nehru on the issue of an autonomous state for the Sikhs. Hukum Singh, who later became the Speaker of the Indian Parliament, was a member of the Constituent Assembly which drafted the Constitution of free India. He walked out of the Assembly when he found that the Congress leaders were going back on their assurances to the Sikhs, and later all the four Sikh members of the Constituent Assembly refused to sign the Assembly's Report. Hukum Singh had the guts to call Nehru a cheat. He is on record as having made the following statement :

"Pandit Nehru is, to say the least, the spearhead of militant Hindu chauvinism who glibly talks about nationalism, a tyrant who eulogises democracy and a Goebelian (i.e., like Goebels) liar — in short, a political cheat, deceiver and double-dealer in the service of Indian reaction."

(Amritsar, p. 38)

ROOT-CAUSE OF THE CRISIS IN PUNJAB

Sikhs who keep reminding the Congress leaders of their broken promises are readily branded as secessionists, traitors and troublemakers, when in truth it is the double-dealing Congress leaders like Nehru and Patel who are the real culprits who treacherously betrayed the Sikhs.

It is the reneging by the Congress leaders on solemn promises made to the Sikhs, followed by equally grave injustices, such as the diversion of Punjab's water and hydro-power resources to the neighbouring states — a death blow to Sikh farmers, which is the root-cause of the present trouble in the Punjab. The Indian Government has divided the Punjabis along communal lines and successfully carried out the propaganda that Sikhs are terrorists, anti-nationals and separatists. The Government's heavy-handed approach in dealing with the Sikhs which includes random killings and casual torture, has further deepened and solidified the division. This has made a unified and stable Punjab a remote possibility. The Punjab problem has been very accurately assessed by Dr Madanjit Kaur of Guru Nanak Dev University :

"The present generation of the Sikh community is facing a problem of discontent, and is in direct clash with the State which has been evading basic issues of the Punjab problem for decades and instead has been following a policy of tyranny, suppression and violation of human rights by introducing draconian laws, extra-judicial measures, illegal detentions in police custody, locking in jails without trials and eliminating the Sikh youth in false encounters."

(Professor Madanjit Kaur in *Co-existence in a Pluralistic Society*, p. XIV)

Sikhs can never tolerate injustice and tyranny. It is their ideology to fight the two.

They are the people who humbled the mighty Mughals and built a kingdom on the ashes of the Mughal Empire. Such being the case, in my view, they are not going to easily forget what is lawfully due to them. Hence, the struggle for an autonomous State will, I believe, go on and on until the promises made to the Sikhs are fulfilled. Time is on the side of the Sikhs. Knowing what the Sikhs are, I do not think there can be any peace in Punjab, until all the injustices committed against the Sikhs are addressed to their satisfaction.

SIKHS ARE A SOVEREIGN PEOPLE

As a result of two critical events in their history, the first in the middle of the nineteenth and the second in the middle of the twentieth century, the Sikhs have become a dispossessed nation, dispossessed of their territories through treachery, treason and deceit. In the first event, the Anglo-Sikh wars, the crafty British successfully promoted treachery and treason amongst the Generals and Ministers of the Sikh nation.

In the second event, the partition of India, the efforts of the Sikhs to obtain political control over a small part of their nation's former vast territories, were thwarted by deception on the part of Nehru and his colleagues in the Indian National Congress. Nevertheless, the lack of political control over any territory does not make the Sikhs a non-nation, for, they have all the other attributes of a nation, a distinct race with their own language, culture and religion, in addition to the undeniable historical evidence of their being the former rulers of North India. The Sikhs are one of the twenty or so nations that constitute present day India. After all, a nation is merely the crystallisation of a cultural ideal, the manifestation of a coherent personality usually based on race, religion and language. The Sikh nation provides the most conclusive evidence of this ultimate and abiding definition of nationhood. They are now in the same position in which the Jews were until the creation of Israel. They believe that it is their destiny to rule in their homeland. To others, this may appear to be blatant wishful thinking, but for the Sikhs, this belief is an affirmation of their faith in the words of their last Guru. At every *Ardas* (supplication), the recital by the congregation of *Raj Karega Khalsa* (the Khalsa shall Rule) echoes and resonates within the four walls of every gurdwara in the world.

In 1830, when asked by Capt. Murray, the British Charge-de-Affairs at Ludhiana, from what source the Sikhs derived their earthly sovereignty, for, by the rights of treaty or lawful succession they had none, Bhai Rattan Singh Bhangu, replied promptly and accurately :

> *Dhur dargaahon hum lei Patshaahi*
> *Sri Satgur ke mukh te pahi,*
> *Singh hoe raakhaon him kaan,*
> *Aerey gaerey ka sangeh furmaan.*

(The Sikhs' right to earthly sovereignty is based on the Will of God as authenticated by the Guru, and therefore, other inferior sanctions are unnecessary)

(Rattan Singh Bhangu in *Prachin Panth Prakash)*

There are those who accuse the Sikhs of living in the past, of trumpeting their past glory and of being oblivious of the present world. These are the people who gape with horror when they hear Sikhs singing *Raj Karega Khalsa* and it is they who are oblivious, to the Divine truth that sovereignty on this earth is by Divine sanction. They fail to realise the fallacy of identifying sovereignty with power. No matter how mighty a nation may be, it cannot stop or prevent what is ordained by God. The ghastly civil war in Yugoslavia demonstrates what happens when a federation fragments due to Divine intervention and old blood-feuds break out again. The French, Germans and Britons have fought in the two World Wars. Spain has been through a civil war, Italy fought both against the Germans and with them, and the Germans, French and British all lost their empires through defeat in battle or economics. All this happened in less than a century. And in very much less time, the mighty Russian empire, which straddled over most of Europe and Asia, has torn itself apart and disintegrated into sixteen independent sovereign States. When the time arrived, States which had been governed with an iron grip, became sovereign in a matter of days, in fulfilment of their destiny. All this is again undoubtedly, due to the result of Divine intervention.

So much has happened in the last hundred years. Who can predict what will happen in the next hundred ? In any case, what is a hundred years in the life of a nation ? Sikhs, especially the devout Khalsa, who revere the words of their last Guru as the revealed truth, firmly believe that the time will come when their *Raj Karega Khalsa* prayer shall be answered, their aspirations will be fulfilled and they will again rule the sacred land of their ancestors. Having experienced, enjoyed and exercised sovereignty over the whole of North India, following the benediction and prophecy of Guru Gobind Singh and with memories of the Sikh *Raj* not that distant, the Sikhs can never shed their sovereign nation mind-set which has become a pillar of their religious beliefs.

As the former rulers of North India, including most of present day Pakistan, and having been outwitted by Nehru of an autonomous Sikh state, the Sikhs have every right to aspire for political power in the Punjab, their ancestral homeland, by all lawful means. In view of the promises made to them, at the time of the partition of India, the Sikhs have a moral, indeed a lawful right to an autonomous Sikh State in the Union of India. With their proven bravery in war, such a State, on the northern border of India would be an asset to India, for it would be a formidable bulwark against any foreign invasion from the North. Happy and contented with their autonomous Sikh State, the brave Sikhs would defend it to the last man.

The Sikhs of the Punjab who are demanding justice, deserve sympathy and support, not condemnation as separatists and traitors. As pointed out by Sirdar Kapur Singh, it is time for those who govern India to realise, that "a satisfied and properly integrated-to-the-nation Sikh people can be an invaluable and lasting asset to any state, more so India, in the soil and tradition of which they are rooted, just as a frustrated and suppressed Sikh people can be an obvious weakness in the strength of the nation."

(Kapur Singh in *The Sikh Review*, August, 1992)

The Sikhs have not only a glorious past, but also, in my view, a bright future. Although they are now facing extremely adverse circumstances in the Punjab, they have not shown any despondency or given way to frustration. This is because they practise *charhdi kala* which means, in the words of Dr Baljit Singh Bagga, "the waxing mood and is the equivalence of a mind that never despairs, never admits defeat and refuses to be crushed by adversities." Abiding faith in their religion gives them solace, sustains them in their difficulties and keeps alive their aspirations, their desire and determination for the restoration of their rule in the Punjab. A people blessed with such an indomitable spirit cannot be suppressed forever and must, in my view, become sovereign sooner or later in fulfilment of their destiny. With the winds of change blowing all over the world, the denial to the Sikhs of their legitimate promised autonomous unit, may well result ultimately in their having an independent sovereign state. This is not impossible because even the most tyrannical government in the world, which enforced *apartheid* (segregation of the natives) at the point of the gun, has at last conceded the just rights of the natives who now govern the whole of South Africa for the first time in over 300 years. According to the great Tibetan sage, the Dalai Lama, "with optimism and great patience even the impossible becomes possible. But without optimism you cannot achieve even the simplest task." (Asia Magazine, 22nd May, 1994) Believing in *chardhi kala* the Sikhs are the most optimistic people on this earth, and as for patience, except for a few hot-heads, they have unlimited patience. Hence, it is inevitable that one day the Sikhs will again rule Punjab and "experience the glow of freedom."

SIKH RELIGION

For a precise account of the Sikh religion, we are indebted to Dr Kharak Singh of the Institute of Sikh Studies at Chandigarh. "Sikhism, a revealed religion, is the youngest among the major world faiths. This system, as preached by Guru Nanak, has a universal appeal and an eternal relevance. Some of its essential features may be briefly reproduced below :

(a) *Monotheism* : Guru Nanak believed in only One God as the Ultimate Reality. In the *Mul Mantra* he described Him thus; 'The Sole Supreme Being; of Eternal Manifestation; Creator; Immanent Reality; Without Fear; Without Rancour; Timeless Being; Unincarnated; Self-Existent.'

(b) *Reality Of The World* : Guru Nanak rejected the earlier view of the world being *mithya* or unreal or a place of suffering and human life a punishment. Since God is Real, he argued, so is His creation — 'the continents, the universe, the worlds and the forms ......' 'In the midst of air, water, fire and the nether regions, the world has been installed as a *dharamsal* or a place for perceiving and practising righteous actions.' 'This world is the abode of the Lord who resides in it.' 'Human life is a rare opportunity for spiritual fulfilment.'

(c) *Goal Of Life* : In Sikhism, the goal is not *moksha, nirvana* or personal salvation after death. The goal is to attain the status of *gurmukh* or *sachiara* or a godman in this life. A *gurmukh* is one attuned to the Will of God, who engages himself in the fulfilment of the Divine Will. There is no selfishness in his goal. He wants to liberate not only himself, but the whole world.

(d) *Methodology* : Guru Nanak did not accept the dichotomy between empirical and spiritual lives preached by earlier systems. Asceticism, which was considered essential for spiritual attainments, was described by the Guru as escapism and parasitism. He advocated a householder's life, with emphasis on hard work, honest means for a livelihood, and sharing of earnings with others in need. God loves His creation, and takes pleasure in looking after it. In fact, He is immanent in it. So, the godman must also love his fellow beings and carry out the Divine Will through altruistic deeds. Only thus, can one find the path to Him. Full social participation, and struggle against oppression, injustice and tyranny, in the cause of the poor and the weak, are an essential part of the Guru's system. While the need for worldly pursuits is recognised, there is a very clear warning against acquisitiveness, accumulation of wealth and indulgence or what is called consumerism. Ritualism is condemned. Instead the emphasis is on *Naam,* i.e., remembering God or keeping Him in mind or being conscious of Him always. This means a realization of His immanence in the entire creation, or living in His presence all the time. All this comes under *sach achar* or truthful living, which, the Guru says, is even higher than truth itself. Sikhism is, therefore, a system of noble deeds and moral conduct. It is the deeds in one's lifetime that determine whether one is close to or away from God.

(e) *Equality And Human Dignity* : Sikhism recognises no distinction between man and man on the basis of birth or otherwise. The Guru rejected the 3,000 year old caste system in India, and accepted and associated with the lowliest among them. His concept of equality for women can never be surpassed. 'How can she be considered inferior, when she gives birth to kings ?' he asked. He also preached a life of honour and dignity. 'He who lives with dishonour, does not deserve the food he eats', says the Guru.

(f) *Removal Of Inhibitions* : Apart from the caste system, which restricted one's right to spiritual pursuits and selection of occupation, there were several other restraints in the earlier religious systems in India. *Ahimsa*, celibacy, vegetarianism, and asceticism were considered essential in the practice of religion. He rejected all these and recommended a houseolder's life with emphasis on noble deeds, dignity of labour, service to humanity, and full social responsibility. Later, the Tenth Master confirmed this through his famous *Nash* Doctrine by which he completely broke away from all earlier traditions.

(g) *Development Of The Society* : Guru Nanak was not concerned with the individual alone. His concern covered the society as a whole. Based on the gospel preached by him, he founded a settlement towards the end of his mission at Kartarpur, which was open to all, and in which everybody worked and ate together. People crushed under the rigours of caste system, the oppressive alien rule and religious bigotry, could not be expected to take over the social responsibilities and adjust to the liberation offered in the new society, overnight. This infant society had to be nurtured for some time, and it had to spread geographically. So, the Guru introduced the system of succession under which nine Gurus carried the mission forward up to the time Guru Gobind Singh created the *Khalsa.* A practical demonstration of Guru Nanak's system had been given. A personal successor after the Tenth Lord was not considered necessary, and the guruship was conferred on the Adi Granth (Guru Granth Sahib), or the *shabad* or the 'Word' of the Lord.

(h) *The Scripture* : The Adi Granth, compiled by Guru Arjun Dev, with later addition of *bani* of Guru Tegh Bahadur, is the sacred scripture of the Sikhs. As pointed out above, the scripture was given the status of Guru by the Tenth Master. This appointment of the Scripture or the Word as Guru is unique to Sikhism. It simply means that in spiritualism the real Guru is the 'Word' or the command or *shabad* of the Lord, and not the human body.

Also, it is only in Sikhism that the Scripture was written and authenticated by the founder himself or his successors. In other religions, the scriptures were written decades or even centuries after the founders had left.

Besides the above, there are some other features that need to be mentioned. In contrast to earlier religious systems, Sikhism is a life-affirming faith with a positive attitude towards the world. It is a religion of activism, noble actions and altruistic deeds. It is a religion of hope and optimism with rich traditions of *charhdi kala* or ever-rising high spirits. Pacificism and pessimism have no place in Sikh thought. Sikh discipline is a conscious effort to live in harmony with nature and to carry out the altruistic Divine Will.

Macauliffe in his classic study *The Sikh Religion* (1910), summed up the moral and political merit of the Sikh Religion thus :

It prohibits idolatry, hypocrisy, caste-exclusiveness, the concremation of widows, the immurement of women, the use of wine and other intoxicants, tobacco smoking, infanticide, slander, pilgrimage to sacred rivers and tanks of Hindus; and it inculcates loyalty, gratitude for all favours received, philanthropy, justice, impartiality, truth, honesty and all the moral and domestic virtues known to the holiest citizens of any country.

On the originality of the Sikh religion, Macauliffe's conclusion was :

The illustrious author of *Vie de Jesus* asks whether great originality will again arise, or the world would be content to follow the paths opened by the daring creators of the ancient ages. Now there is here presented a religion totally unaffected by Semitic or Christian influences. Based on unity of God, it rejected Hindu formalities, and adopted an independent ethical system, rituals and standards which were totally opposed to the theological beliefs of Guru Nanak's age and country. And we shall see hereafter, it would be difficult to point to a religion of greater originality or to a more comprehensive ethical system.

The religion and the society founded by Guru Nanak grew steadily, and in the hands of his successors brought about a complete revolution in the minds of the people as well as in the social and political set-up in the north-west of India. His followers challenged the oppressive Mughal rule, overthrew it, and supplanted it with an empire of their own, based on egalitarian principles and freedom of religious practice, with real power in the hands of the common people, who had had nothing but oppression and exploitation at the hands of earlier rulers. The values taught by Guru Nanak are as relevant today as in the 15th century, when he started his mission. The world today needs this faith of hope and optimism that preaches *'sarbat da bhala'* (welfare of all). The Sikhs owe it to the world to share their rich heritage with the rest of mankind. Even more, they need to do this in their own interest in order to project a correct image of themselves.

(Dr Kharak Singh, in *Recent Researches in Sikhism*, p. 359)

"Sikhism is essentially a Religion of the Way, i.e. something that must be lived and experienced rather than something which may be intellectually grasped and declared. True, there can be no practice without the dogma. Sikhism, therefore, has its doctrines, its dogmatic stand, its view of Reality, its view of the nature of man, and their inter-relationship, but it lays primary stress on the practice, the discipline, the way which leads to the 'cessation of suffering,' as Gautam, the Buddha formulated it.

"A careful reading and understanding of the Sikh scripture reveals that the religion of Sikhism has three postulates implicit in its teachings. One, that there is no essential duality between the spirit and the matter. Two, that man alone has the capacity to enter into conscious participation in the process of the Evolution, with further implication that the process of Evolution, as understood by the modern man, has come to a dead-end and it, therefore, must be rescued by the conscious effort of man who alone is capable now of furthering this process. Three, that when man has reached the highest goal of Evolution, namely, the vision of God, he must not only remain in God, but must also remain earth-conscious so as to transform this mundane world into a higher and spiritual plane of existence."

(Kapur Singh, *Sikhism, an Oecumenical Religion*, p. 94)

MISREPRESENTATION OF SIKHISM

As pointed out by Dr Kharak Singh in a recent article, "Survey of Entries on Sikhism in 50 Major Encyclopaedias published in the West, has revealed gross misrepresentations. These include errors of fact as well as misinterpretations of Guru Nanak's system. The Guru has frequently been shown as a disciple of Kabir. Sikhism is invariably presented as a part of Hinduism, and its teachings are confused with the so-called *Sant Mat*. In several cases, the authors have failed to see the unity of thought of the Ten Masters, mistakenly referring to Guru Nanak's philosophy as pacificism, and that of Guru Gobind Singh as militancy. Another common misinterpretation is the theory of syncretism, which means that Sikhism is only an amalgam of elements drawn from Hinduism and Islam, denying any originality to Guru Nanak. Recognition of Sikhism as a revealed religion is rare. No wonder that the space given to Sikhism is extremely limited as compared with other major faiths of the world. Some of these publications make only a passing reference to Sikhism, while a few do not even mention it."

(*Recent Researches in Sikhism*, p. 364)

RECENT MISREPRESENTATIONS

The last two decades have seen the mounting of a regular campaign to misrepresent and blemish Sikhism. This was started by Dr W. H. McLeod, a former missionary in India, who has so far produced eight books relating to Sikhism in which he has, with insidious persistence, erroneously presented the Sikhs to the world as a sect of Hinduism. According to Dr Kharak Singh, who has studied McLeod's books, with some concern, McLeod's thesis revolves around the following main points :

(a) "It is misleading to call Guru Nanak the founder of Sikh religion, as he did not originate a new school of thought or set of teachings. What Guru Nanak offers us is the clearest and most highly articulate expression of the *nirguna sampradaya,* the so-called Sant tradition of Northern India, a system which he inherited, reworked according to his own genius and passed on in a form unequalled by any other representative of the tradition. It was the influence of Nath doctrine and practice upon Vaishnava Bhagti which was responsible for the emergence of Sant synthesis."

(b) "The ten Gurus never preached one set of religious doctrines or system, and particularly the Third Guru created new institutions on the old Hindu lines, the very thing Guru Nanak had spurned. From the Sixth Guru onwards the teachings of Guru Nanak were completely given up in favour of a militant pose in response to socio-political situations."

(c) "The arming of the *Panth* could not have been the result of any decision by Guru Hargobind, but because of Jat influx in the Sikh fold ...... The growth of militancy within the *Panth* must be traced primarily to the impact of Jat cultural patterns and to economic problems which prompted a militant response."

(d) "The traditional account about the founding of the Khalsa on the Vaisakhi day of the year 1699, (A.D.) cannot be accepted, as there are 'compulsive reasons for scepticism', and 'the traditions relating to the period of Guru Gobind Singh must be, in some considerable measure, set aside. The slate must be wiped clean and must not be reinscribed until we have ascertained just what did take place during the eighteenth century.'

(e) "The Sikh code of discipline, *Rahit Maryada,* and Sikh symbols were evolved during the eighteenth century as a result of gradual growth, though the tradition declares they were definitely settled by a pronouncement of Guru Gobind Singh and were a part of the Vaisakhi day proceedings in 1699 (A.D.)."

(f) "Though the Gurus denounced the caste system and preached against it, yet they did not seem sincere or serious in removing caste difference."

(g) "The succession of Guru Granth Sahib as Guru of the Sikhs, ending the line of living Gurus on the death of Guru Gobind Singh, was not because of an injunction of Guru Gobind Singh himself, but was a subsequent adaptation by the Sikhs, who were fighting for their existence, to meet the needs of the *Panth* for cohesion."

(h) "The authenticity of the current version of Guru Granth Sahib which is widely accepted and revered by the Sikhs, is open to question, since there are three manuscripts *(birs)* available which are not entirely identical."

(Recent Researches in Sikhism, p. 364)

Dr McLeod admits that his above mentioned assertions are mere conjectures, but he labels these as "informed conjectures at the present state." It would be more accurate to describe these as pure wishful and malicious speculation, for there is not an iota of evidence to support any of these fanciful formulations. They have all been answered and demolished by Sikh scholars in articles appearing in *Advanced Studies in Sikhism*, (1989, Institute of Sikh Studies, Chandigarh) and *Fundamental Issues in Sikh Studies*, (1992, Institute of Sikh Studies, Chandigarh).

ARE SIKHS HINDUS ?

The focus of this essay is on the issue whether or not there is any justification for labelling Sikhs as a sect of Hinduism. The chief proponent of the thesis that Sikhs are part and parcel of Hinduism is again Dr W. H. McLeod. Disregarding totally the research findings and opinions of Sikh scholars, Dr McLeod keeps harping on his favourite thesis that Guru Nanak Dev did not start any new system of religious doctrine. He commences Chapter II of his book *The Sikhs*, (1989, Columbia University Press) with the following statement, on p. 16 :

"Sikhism, we are often told, is a sect of Hinduism. Guru Nanak may have founded a new *Panth* or religious community within the larger Hindu fold, but he neither violated nor abandoned the Hindu tradition. Born a Hindu, he remained one until the day he died, and so too did his successors. The doctrines which he affirmed were already current in the North India of his own period and the message which he preached was entirely congenial to many of his Hindu audience. *Panths* are a regular feature of the Hindu experience, and Nanak, together with his followers, merely added one more. If we seek the origins of the Sikh tradition, the place to look is surely the wider area of Hindu tradition and specifically the teachings of the Sants. Nanak did not found "Sikhism," for this would have meant founding something which already existed."

And he adds, "This is one point of view." Yes, but whose point of view ? No authority is cited. This is his very subtle way of expressing his opinion, through an anonymous proxy. And yet on the very next page he states, "The proposition that Sikhism is a sect of Hinduism is beginning to look distinctly unsatisfactory." This is because his like-minded friend, Professor Wilfred Cantwell Smith, has pointed out to him that there is no such thing as Hinduism. McLeod accepts this and considers Hinduism as a basket of several Indian traditions such as Nathism, Vaishnavism, Vedanta and the Sant tradition of North India. McLeod then asserts that Guru Nanak was a practitioner of the Sant tradition like Kabir and Ravidas; that the Sant tradition "plainly derived fundamental features of its doctrine from Vaishnava belief' (Ibid., 25); that one must acknowledge Sants to be Vaishnava *bhaktas*" (Ibid., 27); that "the Sant doctrine has features derived from Vaishnava and Nath sources" (Ibid., 25) and that "Nath influences are also present in the works of Guru Nanak." (Ibid., 26). No examples are cited. McLeod goes on to concede that Guru Nanak did start a *Panth* (a community according to him), but it was, to use his own words, "within the larger context of the Hindu tradition and still remaining part of it." (Ibid., 24)

What a round-about way of saying that Sikhs are a sect of Hinduism. McLeod goes on to state that "subsequent developments may have transformed that later *Panth*, but it has never renounced its direct descent from the teachings of Nanak nor have its members effectively abandoned their place within the structure of caste society." In short, that Sikhs are part and parcel of Hinduism. All this has been debunked by Daljeet Singh in his book, *The Sikh Ideology*, (1990, Singh Brothers, Amritsar). By comparing Sikhism with the older Indian traditions named by McLeod, Daljeet Singh has clearly proved that Sikhism has nothing in common with any of the older ancient traditions; that Sikhism is an entirely new revelatory religion, totally unconnected with the Naths, the Sant tradition or Vaishnavism, and that it is different in its fundamentals, ideology, goals, methodology and world-view. Dr McLeod's failure to appreciate the revelatory source of Guru Nanak's *Gurbani* is a grave mischief in the face of overwhelming evidence in support of it, from the Guru's own pen, enshrined in Guru Granth Sahib.

Sikhism has been attacked even by persons who claim to be practising Sikhs. They have even gone so far as to commit blasphemy by attacking Guru Granth Sahib, the "Living Guru of the Sikhs."

First, in 1992, one Pashaura Singh submitted a Ph. D. thesis entitled "The Text and Meaning of the Adi Granth," to the University of Toronto, based on his work done under the guidance and supervision of W. H. McLeod. This work has attracted world-wide adverse criticism, and Sikhs have by and large reacted sharply to a number of misleading observations made in the thesis. Dr Kharak Singh gives five examples :

1. "Whereas McLeod accused the Sikhs of changing the basis of the *Adi Granth,* Pashaura Singh goes a step further, and says that the Fifth Master also made ideological and other changes in the *bani* of Guru Nanak Dev and that the Kartarpuri *bir* cannot be considered to be authentic in the sense that it is not a correct compilation of the *bani* of the First Master.

2. The *bani,* as proclaimed by Guru Nanak Dev and the other Gurus is not a revealed one, for later it can be changed, and has been changed by Guru Arjun Dev.

3. That Guru Arjun Dev made misrepresentations in so far as he passed on to the public his own *bani* as that of Guru Nanak.

4. That hymns which, for the Guru, were not true *bani (sachi bani)* are eulogised by the scholar to be true *bani* of Guru Nanak.

5. That *bhagat bani* was included later in the Adi Granth, by Guru Arjun Dev for mundane and political reasons, imputing to him the desire to gain a following amongst different castes."

(Dr Kharak Singh in *Abstracts of Sikh Studies*, January, 1993, p. 28)

Next, one Dr Piar Singh published a book entitled *Gatha Sri Adi Granth*. In the words of Dr Kharak Singh, "It is clearly a planned work undertaken with the singular object of attacking the authenticity of the holy *Granth* Sahib, and for that matter, the very foundation of the Sikh faith. It appears that the work has been taken up in association with those who share these objectives. One cannot fail to notice that so often the line of argument taken by the author, has been the same or similar to the one adopted by Dr W. H. McLeod and Pashaura singh who have attacked the authenticity of the *bir* at Kartarpur without examining the manuscript." (*Abstracts of Sikh Studies*, January 1993, pp. 29 & 40).

Piar Singh blames Guru Arjun Dev for changing *Gurbani,* and according to Dr Kharak Singh, his statements imply four acts of blasphemy :

(a) "That *bani* as compiled by Guru Nanak and other Gurus, is not a revealed one. For, later it can be changed and has been changed by Guru Arjun. Its revealed and unalterable character was thereby destroyed by the Guru himself.

(b) That Guru Arjun made theological changes in the *bani* of Guru Nanak.

(c) That Guru Arjun made misrepresentations in so far as he passed on to the public his *bani* as that of Guru Nanak.

(d) That the hymns which, for the Guru, were not true *bani (kachi bani)* are eulogised by the scholar to be true *bani* of Guru Nanak."

(Dr Kharak Singh in *Abstracts of Sikh Studies*, January, 1993 issue, p. 31)

Dr Piar Singh has recently appeared before the Akal Takht and retracted all the misstatements in his book. He has also undergone the punishment for this misconduct as prescribed by the Akal Takht.)

These blasphemous attempts by Dr McLeod and his like-minded group to destroy Sikhism by attacking the legitimacy of Guru Granth Sahib, "the living Guru of the Sikhs," has been thoroughly exposed and proved to be entirely groundless by Dr Kharak Singh in the January 1993 issue of *Abstracts of Sikh Studies.*

The truth is that many anti-Sikh elements have, and can afford to have, their knife in the back of Sikhism, because they know that Sikhs fundamentally believe in and daily pray for *sarbat da bhala* (May peace and prosperity come to all). Furthermore, the penalty which traditionally and invariably the Sikhs impose on any transgressor of their faith, no matter how serious the transgression, is the penalty of cleaning the shoes of the *sangat* (congregation), whereas in some other faiths, the penalty for blasphemy is death. And there have never been any battles in the courts for blasphemy, a criminal offence in all civilised societies, or for expunging false or other offensive slurs on the Sikh faith.

The *Jathedar* (Chief) of the Akal Takht, the lawful guardian and protector of the faith whose edict is binding on all Sikhs, was rather inactive in the 1980's due to frequent changes in the holder of the office.

This situation emboldened anti-Sikh elements who accordingly consider anti-Sikh rhetoric to be fair game for their attacks and other destructive salvos, either directly or through proxies. For, it is not difficult to find unscrupulous individuals in apparent Sikh form, who are willing to sell their soul for a few pieces of gold. This situation has recently changed, and a few of them have been hauled up before the Akal Takht and awarded *tankhah* or religious punishment. The Shiromani Gurdwara Parbandhak Committee being the supreme representative body of the Sikhs, should also respond to inaccurate statements and unfair allegations. No one should be allowed to flout, challenge and surreptitiously change the basic historical truths of the Sikh faith. Unless such mischievous conduct is restrained, it may well become a common occurrence, even political fodder, that could destabilise harmonious race relations and national unity. It is high time the Sikhs woke up and stopped people fooling around and taking liberties with their LIVING Guru.

Long before McLeod mounted his onslaught against the Sikh faith by producing eight books in a row in furtherance of his thesis that Sikhism is a sect of Hinduism, many other eminent writers had acknowledged the distinctiveness of the Sikh religion. These include Rev. H. L. Bradshaw, Edward Bittencourt, M. A. Macauliffe, Dorothy Field, Arnold Toynbee, Pearl S. Buck, Duncan Greenles, James Hastings, Professor Indubhushan Banerjee, Professor John Clark Archer, (who even took the trouble to personally examine the manuscript of the original Guru Granth Sahib dictated by Guru Arjun and engrossed by Bhai Gurdas, now kept at Kartarpur and commonly known as the *Kartarpuri bir),* Edward Geoffrey Parrinder, Sir Charles Elliot, Nirmal Kumar Jain, Dr Ishwari Prasad, Capt. J. D. Cunningham, M. Elphinstone, Dr R. C. Majunmdar and Sir Lepel Griffin. All these eminent writers, after carefully studying and researching the Sikh scripture, acknowledged that Sikhism indeed was and is a distinct religion like other great religions of the world, wholly new, original and genuinely monotheistic. And yet, McLeod persists in having the world believe that Sikhs are a mere sect of Hinduism. If McLeod was right, then it would appear that all the afore mentioned men and women of international fame, were gravely in error.

It is true that originally Sikhs sprung up from amongst the Hindus, because the local population was by and large Hindus. But right from its birth, Sikhism evolved into a separate and distinct religion from the different branches of Hinduism. There can be no better evidence of this fact than the words of the Sikh Gurus, the founders of the faith themselves.

Guru Nanak declared that he was neither a Hindu nor a Mussalman. To pointed questions at different places, he replied :

"I am not a Hindu nor a Mussalman.
   I accept neither the Ved nor the Quran."
"God is neither Hindu nor Mussalman.
   I follow God's right path."
"I accept the Path of Truth
   I reject all other ways."

(*Janam Sakhi,* Bhai Mani Singh)

Guru Nanak's replies clearly indicate his complete break with his Hindu past. Sikhism has been no part of Hinduism right from its birth. We have its founder's word for it.

Guru Arjun, the fifth Guru, left no doubt at all on the matter. He states :

"I do not worship with the Hindus
   nor like the Muslim go to Mecca."
"I serve Him alone and none other,
   For, we are neither Hindus nor Mussalmans."

(Guru Granth Sahib, p. 1136)

Guru Gobind Singh, the last human Guru of the Sikhs, who put the finishing touch of perfection to the Sikh faith, has emphasised the independence of the Sikh religion. He states :

"Ram, Rahim, Puran, Quran
   Anek Kahin mat ek na manio."

(*Sawaiya,* Dasam Granth)

(The different paths of Ram, Rahim,
   Puran and Quran, I do not accept.)

(Ram here is the Hindu deity of Ayodhya, and Rahim referes to Prophet Mohammed.)

It is abundantly clear to all right thinking men, that Sikhs are unquestionably a separate entity from the Hindus. They are clearly distinguishable from the Hindus, not only in outward form but also in religious, cultural and social outlook, concept of God and Gurus, mode of worship, language and contents of their scripture, and their idea of priesthood. In fact, Sikhism has controverted almost every fundamental trait of Hinduism.

The fundamental differences between Sikhism and Hinduism have been emphasised by Dr Gurdarshan Singh Dhillon in a recent article :

"At one stroke, Guru Nanak made revolutionary changes to the fundamental beliefs and traditions of the Hindus. Instead of the world being *mithya,* or a suffering, he called it real. He rejected monasticism, asceticism and withdrawal from life, and instead recommended total participation in life and acceptance of social responsibility. Instead of down-grading the status of woman in relation to spiritual life and recommending celibacy, he recommended a householder's life and equality of man and woman. Instead of the religious doctrine of *Varna Ashram Dharma* and consequent rules of caste, pollution, social segregation and professional immobility, he accepted equality of all men. He rejected *ahimsa* as an inviolable religious doctrine. Instead of life-negation, he recommended life-affirmation in all fields of life. In his ethical monotheism, Guru Nanak clearly denies the idea of *avtars* and their worship, including those of gods and goddesses. Instead of religion being a matter of personal devotion and salvation, Guru Nanak, because of his fundamental doctrine of combining the spiritual with the empirical, organised a society in which promotion or defence of righteousness became essential. Accordingly, Guru Nanak not only organised a society, but he also created a system of succession so as to develop it firmly on the lines of his thesis. Hence, the very wide differences between Hindu and Sikh societies, their value systems, their religious perceptions and social practices."

(*Recent Researches in Sikhism*, p. 228)

There is no evidence at all on which Sikhs can be presented to the world as a sect of Hinduism. In fact, the evidence points the other way. There is incontrovertible evidence that Sikhism is a world religion, separate and distinct from Hinduism or any other religion for that matter. No amount of misrepresentation of Sikh history and distortion of their holy scripture, can push the Sikhs into the Hindu fold. This is because in the words of Dr Harnam Singh Shan :

"The Sikhs profess one of the higher religions of the world, which is not only an original, distinct and independent faith, but is also an autonomous, complete and dynamic religion, born of a direct and definitive revelation like other major religions of the world. It is primary in its source and pure in its contents, as any other religion on this planet. The authenticity of its dogma, simplicity of its beliefs, exalted moral code, internal vigour, tenacity of purpose and sustained heroism together with the religious, spiritual energy, unshakable faith and indomitable spirit as well as the enterprising and self-sacrificing nature of its followers have kept it intact and firm on its ground in many a crisis, during its five hundred year old history, raising it up again with greater strength and better prospects after every attempt to annihilate it."

(*Fundamental Issues in Sikh Studies*, p. 29)

Finally, note what Dr Noel Q King, Professor of Religion, University of California, Santa Cruz (U.S.A.), has to say about Sikhism :

"Sikhism is a world religion : not only has it followers in the Punjab, all over India, in the United Kingdom, United States, East Africa and Oceania, and elsewhere, it spans the great divide between the so-called western religions (Judaism, Christianity and Islam) and the eastern (Hinduism and Buddhism) and Chinese classical ideologies (Confucianism and Taoism). It also has many features which go back to the primordial pre-Aryan religion of India. It has all these things, a personal God of love who is One and active in the cosmos, the idea of '*karma*', of *moksha*, it teaches an idea of balance and of reciprocal wholeness not unlike but not totally like *yin-yang*, yet in every case it presents these ideas on its own terms, in a way which makes it different from other religions. Again, it has a Book, but Sikhs are not just a people of a book, nor is the Book just an enliteration of the divine word : the *Guruship* is invested in the word enshrined in Guru Granth Sahib and in the

Khalsa past, present and future. This means that if properly understood and fairly presented in context and in full, Sikh Scripture and tradition have nothing to fear from any true criticism properly used. It has never lacked critical acumen of its own. In fact, we can say the first Guru was also the first relentless Sikh critic of all empty word-forms, of all religiosity, empty worship and blind acceptance of tradition. It has a living — native born and organic tradition of criticism. As for the newer types of criticism I mentioned above, a decade ago I found Sikh scholars at Chandigarh, Amritsar and Patiala deeply conversant with the latest in structuralism, semiotics, narratology and the newest literary criticism. Sikhism has nothing to fear, she has always welcomed scholars from wherever they come, but obviously this does not mean she should sit around and be overtaken by the outside world and by misunderstandings. She has to make sure the truth is established and be prepared to argue it out. She has to have everyone of her own people and well-wishers well informed. The ignorant are not enemies, but Sikhs must not miss a single chance to tell others the truth about their religion."

(Advanced Studies in Sikhism, p. 11)

SUMMARY OF SIKH RELIGION

For a summary of the Sikh religion we must go back to Dr Harnam Singh Shan :

"Sikhism is the youngest and the most modern of the world religions, being a wholly original and practical religion, having the whole humanity in view for its welfare and amelioration. It has been acclaimed by Bradshaw as the "Faith of the new Age" and *summum bonum* for the modern man. It has made valuable contribution towards the uplift of man and society in almost all spheres — thought, conduct, outlook, organisation and cultural pattern, etc.

"It arose, five centuries ago, as a new mode of humanitarian thought, heralding a new conception of the Ultimate Reality, a new vision of the Universal Man, a new altruistic ideal of a democratic state, and a new pattern of a casteless and classless society.

"Equating God with Truth and the Love of God with Service of Humanity, it urges self-realisation and recognition of the Creator through His creation. Exhibiting a just, catholic and tolerant temperament, it admits no discriminating distinction of any kind anywhere, and guarantees each individual his fundamental right and freedom of conscience. Envisioning a new cultural ethos and an ideal social order — mental, spiritual, physical, social and political — transcending all types of religious exclusiveness, formalism and ego-centric individualism, it brushes aside all claims of incarnations and intermediaries, and advocates direct communion with the Almighty.

"Sikhism gives optimistic hope of salvation for everyone, by Divine Grace, while leading a normal householder's life with virtuous conduct, remembering God, adoring nature, doing work, performing duties and sharing earnings with fellow-beings, as against pursuing enforced celibacy, barren asceticism and mortification of the human frame to attain it. It has set forth a strong moral force against the exploitation of man by man, who, by following its tenets and traditions, neither fears nor frightens, remains stable and steadfast in all eventualities, embodies the universal spirit of liberation and tolerance, and seeks God's blessings for the welfare of the whole humanity in his daily prayers. Its comopolitan outlook, liberal essence and glorious traditions have contributed thus, significantly for its age and limitations, towards human uplift and well-being by offering the message of good cheer for all mankind and by furthering goodwill, general happiness and collective moral values of society, both at home and abroad, for building a new and peaceful pluralistic world order."

(Abstract of a paper read by Prof. Dr Harnam Singh Shan at the 34th International Congress of Asian & North African Studies held from 22nd to 28th August, 1993 at the University of Hong Kong.)

There is no better way of closing this introduction than with Divine words from our holy scripture. The Sikh religion, as projected in the Guru Granth Sahib is concerned with the creation of a just social order, social equality and peaceful co-existence as proclaimed by Guru Arjun in the following words :

"Hun Hukum hua Meharvan da
pai koi na kisae ranjhan da
Sab sukhali wuthia
Eho hoa Halemi Raj jio!"

(Guru Granth Sahib, p. 74)

(The Gracious Lord has now promulgated His ordinance : None shall domineer over others or cause pain to them. All shall abide in peace and the governance shall be gentle and compassionate.)

1, Coldstream Avenue,   JUSTICE CHOOR SINGH (RETD.)
Singapore.
1st November 1996

I

IDEOLOGY

1

A METHOD TO STUDY RELIGION

Comparative studies of religion are essential both for the proper appreciation of any religion and its features, and more especially, for identifying the reasons for the wide varieties of religious doctrines and developments in the world. No doubt, the environmental situation and the social milieu in which a religion arises, do have their impact on its growth and the problems it seeks to tackle. Yet, it is very true that the perceptions, the internal strength, and the ideology of a religion are fundamentally the elements that give it substance and direction, and shape its personality.

Unless some definite principles are followed in making a comparative study of different religious systems, confusions, misunderstandings and misinterpretations are bound to occur, in the presentation thereof. The important thing, hence, is to identify the basic elements of religion and compare the fundamentals and the essentials of different systems. Otherwise, mere stress on similarities or dissimilarities only in the ancillary or peripheral features of the two or more systems could be very misleading, and give an entirely lopsided view of the traditions concerned.

The following could be the basic elements on which it is necessary to ascertain and compare the features of a system before arriving at any conclusion regarding its affinities, nature, class and stand.

1. THE METAPHYSICAL VIEW

While it is true that a religious system is not a philosophy, yet its metaphysical assumptions and its view about the nature of Reality, so often determine its other basic characteristics and its approach to the world. For example, in Yoga, Sankhya and Jainism, two kinds of Reality, material and spiritual, are assumed, and man is a combination of both. No one basic Reality, much less a creative Reality of God, is assumed. The logic of such dualism, therefore, involves the isolation of the spiritual monad from its connection or combination with the material element. Thus, in each case, the ideal is of withdrawal from the world and its activities, without any role for the ideal man. In the same manner, in the monistic system of Sankra, the world and its activities are *mithya* or unreal. Therefore, monasticism or the virtual turning of one's back to the world become necessary. Similarly, in a pantheistic system, moral life ceases to have a spiritual or primary value. Accordingly, the metaphysical assumptions of a religious system have a significant relevance for understanding a system and its character.

2. NATURE OF REALITY

The nature of Reality assumed by the tradition has also a crucial meaning. In case the Reality is attributive, world activity and moral life assume a primary and spiritual significance. Similar is the importance of the issue whether Reality is both Transcendent and Immanent. But, far more important is the assumption whether Reality is creative or not. For, in a materialistic or deterministic system, creativity and freedom have not much of a place, or scope.

3. REALITY OF THE WORLD

Answer to this issue makes all the difference between a system like Sankra's Vedanta where the world is *mithya*, or unreal, and a system like Sikhism or Islam, where the creation is not only real, but creative activity in the world is essential for the spiritual growth of man. The systems of the former kind recommend monasticism, involving withdrawal from life, whereas in the latter kind world affirmation becomes an essential feature.

4. IS WORLD WORTHWHILE ?

So far as approach to the world is concerned, this is a very important issue, dividing all systems into two categories, one of life-affirmation and the other of life-negation. For example, in Buddhism, world is a place of suffering. Salvation lies only in Nirvana through asceticism and withdrawal from life. Moral life could give one a better birth than before, but it could never lead to Nirvana. Similarly, in systems like Yoga, Nathism and some categories of Saivism, world is a place of misery. In Jainism, too, world activity, howsoever good or moral, is an involvement, and has to be given up. As against that, in Sikhism, Christianity and Islam, creative activity in the world, or activity in carrying out the Will of God, is of the highest spiritual significance. As such, the world is a meaningful place for spiritual endeavours. It is far from being a place of suffering or misery, which has to be given up, or from which release has to be sought. In fact, in systems like Sikhism, the entire growth of man and his spiritual stature are judged by the deeds performed by him in this world. Actually, divergent answers on this issue would place two systems entirely into widely varying categories of religions.

5. GOAL OF LIFE

For obvious reasons, the goal fixed in a religious system is of fundamental significance. For, this determines in many ways its entire direction and world-view, its values, and its methodology and discipline. Here, too, whatever be the apparent similarities between the two traditions, these would be meaningless, if the systems have opposing spiritual goals. In Sikhism, the goal is to carry out, through deeds, the attributive and creative Will of God. It can have nothing in common with a system, like Yoga or Sankhya, where no God is assumed, and where the goal is the isolation of the spiritual element from the material element. Actually, the spiritual goal in a religion determines not only its entire approach towards life, but also its ethics and the role of the superman. For example, religious systems in which the goal is isolation of the spiritual element, or merger in Reality, or even union, as an end in itself, have nothing in common with systems like Sikhism where human duty is ever to carry out the Will of God. In each case, the endeavour or activity is directed towards opposite ends. And this alone makes for a fundamental difference. It is the Yogic or Jainic goal of isolation of the spiritual monad, that make asceticism and monasticism distinct features and institutions of the Indian culture and history. And, it is these institutions that arose only in India, and are typically Indian contribution to foreign cultures like the Egyptian, Christian, etc. For, such asceticism was unknown to Babylonians or early Egyptians or Iranians. Hence, the importance of a goal in the study of different religions. The influence of the goal of isolation and of asceticism and monasticism as a sequel, has indeed, been profuse and fundamental. In contrast with it was the Vedic ideal of activity, heaven and sacrifices under which everything in this world, and even in the next, could be sought and obtained by the meticulous performance of rituals. Probably, as a compromise, the system of four Ashrams was devised early in the Upanisadic times. But, this compromise remained mostly a paper ideal, and the basic dichotomy of goals and approach continued not only to cause confusion, but also to affect adversely the religious growth, with attendant effects, sometimes quite adverse, on the moral, social and cultural developments. Hence the fundamental importance of the goal set in a religious system.

6. MYSTIC COMMUNION AND FACTOR OF FREEDOM

The issue of mystic communion has very great relevance for believers in and students of religion. Scholars, especially students of anthropology, sociology and history, believing only in deterministic and environmental philosophies and factors, are liable to make serious errors of understanding and interpretation, if they ignore this factor of freedom or mystic communion in relation to a religious tradition, movement, or development. Let us try to define this factor of freedom or mystic communion. Most of the traditional religions believe that there is a higher level of Reality, different from the empirical or phenomenal reality of which we are a part, and which works under a logic of cause and effect. All the same, under this logic, governing our entire rational thinking, we are unable to explain the First Cause or the Original Causeless Cause, the Creator, or the Transcendent Reality, which is ineffable and cannot be described in terms of "Is or Is not." We do not know the logic governing this Reality or Consciousness, and, therefore, call it Free or Creative, in so far as it introduces in human affairs a new element unexplained by the rational or scientific logic of man. Mystics or prophets like Buddha, Christ, Muhammad and the Sikh Gurus have not only asserted the existence of such a Reality, but have also claimed some kind of touch, link or communion with that Reality or consciousness. Christ clearly asserts his communion with God. Buddha too claims elevation to the state of Nirvana. The Sikh Gurus also repeatedly affirm that it is the Divine message that they have been delivering.

But, materialistic, deterministic or behavioural philosophies do not accept such statements or claims. This is understandable. But, it would be grossly naive to interpret the martyrdoms of Chirst and the Sikh Gurus on the deterministic basis and ignore altogether the element of freedom and creativity in human affairs. In fact, it is from the sacrifices of these men, that we understand and accept the value and validity of a free, moral or creative life. Otherwise, all talk of honesty, integrity and truth would be sheer hypocrisy and moonshine; since the realistic spectacle today is that the best of our teachers, scientists and academicians barter away their services, without any tangible compunction or protest, to their respective national states feverishly engaged in constructing engines of death and destruction for the rest of mankind. Against this background, it would be almost a perversion either to dub the statements and deeds of these great martyrs as actuated by hallucination, or determined by environmental causality. Therefore, in assessing or comparing a religious thesis, it is important to know whether the founder of the faith claims communion with the Creative Consciousness. While the role of men like Luther or other religious leaders could be understood or explained by the means of environmental, deterministic factors, such an explanation would be simply incongruous when applied to creative individuals like Christ, Buddha or the Sikh Gurus, who themselves claim touch with Higher Reality. Therefore, religious developments initiated by the creative individuals have to be viewed and appreciated very differently from the subsequent developments when that personality is off the stage of history. Hence, the importance of this issue and the claims of the prophet concerned.

7. THE PATH AND PRACTICES FOR THE ACHIEVEMENT OF THE GOAL

The discipline and methods suggested for attaining the spiritual goal in any system have an obvious relevance in any comparative study. Of course, the methods and practices prescribed are determined by the doctrines and ideals of the system, but these certainly clarify them, as also its basic tenets, structure and approach to social life. Religious leaders have prescribed a large number of practices and disciplines aimed at achieving the spiritual goal. For example, methods of Yoga, asceticism, one-point concentration, etc., varying in their rigour and duration, have been suggested. In Buddhism and Catholic Christianity, monasticism is a recognized mode of spiritual attainments. Side by side, celibacy and withdrawal from life are also prescribed. Ritualism and the potency and the mystic power of the recitation, or repetition of words and *mantras*, too, has been deemed spiritually efficacious. Deep religious devotion, including song and dance, and the invoking of ecstasy, are also religious practices. In a system like that of Naths and some other Saiva systems, extreme formalism in dress and odd living, celibacy, *ahimsa* and non-engagement in any work, are prescribed; and, alternatively, even sensual indulgence has been recognised. As against all these methods, the emphasis in some religions on moral deeds and carrying out the Will of God is deemed to be of primary significance and value in the spiritual progress. In Sikhism, the greatest stress is on moral deeds, on which alone human assessment is based. Evidently, different methodologies and spiritual practices are linked to different systems. For, celibacy, asceticism, ritualism and monasticism have no place in a system, where the stress is on moral deeds, leading to the spiritual development of man. So much so, that a system like Sikhism, prescribing the medium of moral deeds as the major vehicle of spiritual progress, clearly rejects or frowns upon methods of asceticism, ritualism or formalism. Such systems in their methodology and practices stand at opposite extremes without any meeting ground between them. That is so in the case of Sikhism and Nathism. Therefore, the principal modes of the discipline prescribed throw considerable light on the character, class, ideals, and affinities of a religious system.

8. ROLE OF THE SUPERMAN

Another major issue is the role of the superman. The goal, the philosophy, its discipline and its attitude to the world, are important distinguishing features in identifying and classifying different religious systems. Though largely depending on the other basic characteristics of a system, the role of the superman is a very significant point in differentiating between traditions, and understanding whether these are allied or not. For example, in the case of systems like Yoga, Sankhya, or Jainism, the superman, once isolated, is away forever from the world of man. He has, with extreme asceticism and discipline, sought and achieved his liberation from the world. He is, therefore, not going to re-involve himself in its entanglements. The Jain Tirthankra would not answer or respond to any prayers of men below. Similarly, in the Vedantic system, where 'I am Brahman' (*aham Brahm asmi*) is the final stage achievement, and involvement in the relative world of man is a fall. Once liberated, the question of return to a lower stage of development does not arise. Hence, in this system, the liberated person ceases to have any meaningful link with the world. In systems where the idea is merger in the Absolute, or bliss and tranquility of union with the Absolute as an end in itself, the superman has virtually no role to play. But, the position is very different in systems where the superman considers it his primary duty to carry out an attributive or creative role in life. For example, Guru Nanak's first words after his enlightenment were, "There is no Hindu, nor Mussalman." Further he says "A real superman is one who treats every person as his own and equal." In his system, the important thing is man. The superman is spontaneously benevolent, and "God showers His grace where the weak are helped." "He is the Shelter for the shelterless." So is the role of the superman. In such systems, the redemption of man is the primary concern. The sixth Guru stated that his sword is to deal with the tyrants. Obviously, where the ideology and methodology are very different, the role of the superman after his achievement is equally divergent in activity and direction.

9. SUPERMAN AND SOCIO-POLITICAL ACTIVITY

Different answers to this issue also sharply distinguish one religious system from the other. While socio-political activity on the part of the superman is the logical culmination in a system where the primary interest is in man and his future, in many religions such activity is virtually a taboo for the superman. Islam and Sikhism are the two systems where the responsibility of socio-political life is accepted as a religious duty. Probably, the case of Joan of Arc is the solitary example in the Christian world where a person of God has felt compelled to enter the political field. Except, regarding caste duties, all the Indian traditions (other than Sikhism), and to an extent even Christianity, are against it. It is for this reason that a person like Toynbee criticizes Prophet Mohammad for taking up socio-political activity. Similarly, Tagore, Gandhi, and J.N. Sarkar adversely comment on the role of Guru Gobind Singh. It is on account of the same background that McLeod has failed to understand the role of the sixth to tenth Gurus, and has to raise the prop or phantom of Jat infiltration in order to explain the militarization of the Sikh movement. The case of Buddhism and Sikhism will clarify the issue and the sharp differences in that regard. In Buddhism, world is a place of suffering wherein salvation could be only in Nirvana. Good deeds in this world could never lead to Nirvana, though these could give a better birth. So much so, that, once in Nirvana, further activity is stopped. It is only at the penultimate stage or *arhat*, that activity could be possible. Buddha was clearly requested to return to his kingdom, but he declined to do so. While there is no doubt that Buddhism has a strong ethical content, its doctrine of *ahimsa* and world being a suffering, almost place a bar against socio-political activity by the superman. As against it, in Sikhism, since man is the primary object of interest, as explained by the Sixth Guru to saint Ramdas, socio-political activity becomes a logical and moral duty of every religious person. It is on account of these fundamental differences of ideology that some historians have accused Buddhistic *ahimsa* to be the cause of India's political subjugation, and, on the other hand, others have criticized Sikh Gurus for wrongly diverting the pure stream of religion into the muddy fields of politics. But, it is these basic ideological differences that have led the two traditions to play distinctly divergent roles in history.

10. ETHICS

Just like the methodology and discipline, the ethics of a system is the projection and product of its basic doctrines and ideals. For, the value system of a religion has primarily been devised to serve, aid and help in achieving its goals. Accordingly, as there are variations in spiritual goals, there are differences in the ethical systems. Further, religions, which do not accept any social responsibility, or are other worldly, have ethics which is quite divergent from the one in which the love of man and love of God are almost synonymous. Both in Yoga and Nathism, no social responsibility is accepted. Each individual has to secure his own release from the bondage and misery of the world. In the individual's spiritual venture, he alone has to help himself. Not that truth and purity of conduct have no meaning, but these have no social relevance. Therefore, the ethical systems of religions like Christianity and Yoga-Sankhya are, in many ways, quite different. In Sikhism, God is the Ocean of attributes. Its ethics is basically social, because attributes have a meaning mainly in the social field. Where God is the succour of the helpless, the seeker has necessarily to accept social responsibility and consequently an ethics that is socially oriented. For example, the Sikh Gurus lay down the theological doctrine of the Fatherhood of God and also the logical ethical corollaries of the brotherhood of man and treating everyone as equal. Evidently, these corollaries are pregnantly and emphatically social in their content. All these three concepts form a unified and integrated doctrine. No part of it can be divorced from the other. Let us also take the example of Buddhism. According to Hinayana Buddhism, the fate of everyone is the result of his earlier deeds, One's blindness is due to one's own faults. It is a single line of ethical or moral responsibility. But, in the Mahayana, the ethical system is very different. It involves both aggregate and individual responsibility. This acceptance of social responsibility and consequent shift to a socially oriented ethics is evidently the result of the Boddhisatva doctrine. So much so, that the Mahayana Buddhists, with their socially oriented ethics, their Boddhisatva doctrine, and their concept of aggregate responsibility, call the ethics of Hinayana individualistic and selfish. And yet, with the goals set in the Hinayana system, its ethics is perfectly logical and consonant with its doctrines and system. Hence, the ethics of a religion, being intimately linked to its fundamentals, is very relevant and helpful in understanding its doctrines and goals.

11. THE UNITY OF PERCEPTION, IDEOLOGY AND ACTIVITIES

In rightly understanding a religious system, and in appreciating and placing its different doctrines in their proper perspective, it is essential to bear the unity of perception, ideology and activities in mind. Let us first explain what we mean by the unity of perception, ideology, and activity. Almost every religion owes its origin to the mystic or higher religious experience of some personality or prophet. Actually, it is this experience which forms the real fount of the entire ideology, mission and activities of the mystics. In this sequence, the first stage is the perception or the religious experience. At the second stage, the saint, naturally, tries to understand it, and reacts to it. This is the stage where thought appears or intervenes. This reaction constitutes both the ideology and the proposed plan of the saint for giving practical shape to the ideology. This ideology and plan are generally understood and interpreted by others from the words expressed, or other means of communication resorted to by the saint. The third stage is the life actually lived by the saint. This forms his real response to his higher religious experience, and reflects his ideology and the decisions made thereunder. For example, if the religious experience of a mystic is that God is all love, is Shelter for the shelterless and Help of the helpless, the mystic's ideology is that God is the Ocean of virtues and a God of attributes. In line with it, and as a reaction to this experience, he compulsively frames a plan of action of love and help to the poor and the needy. Accordingly, the activities undertaken and programmes initiated and executed by the saint are the true reflection and projection of his higher religious experience and the consequent ideology. The Fourth Sikh Guru explains the point in a beautiful and apt simile "While experiencing 'You', the 'I' is gone. The difference of 'You' and 'I' is obliterated. It is now only 'You' flowing." The activities of the saint are only the form and shape which his basic experience directs and takes. Such mystics rarely express in words the nature of their religious experience, it being generally ineffable. And, even if they do, the description is too inadequate to form the basis of a rational system. For the same reasons, even the utterances and statements of these persons are not always clear, or those are too brief and merely symbolic. In fact, these are not meant to be such; nor are these always aimed at laying a comprehensive religious philosophy. It is in the interpretation of these statements that students of religion and others make major errors of understanding and deduction. But, it is the deeds and activities of the person that portray truly and directly his higher religious experience and ideology. All we seek to stress is, first, the inalienable unity of experience, ideology and activity; and, second, the activities of the saint alone being the right key to the understanding and appreciation of his perceptions and message. So often, mere statements, taken in their isolation, have been wrongly interpreted, especially by those distant in time and space. Because, howsoever, sophisticated these may be, rational tools cannot rise above the prejudices and predilections of the person employing them.

Scholars, trained in a behaviouristic or mechanical methodology, have generally a tendency to trace one religious development from a preceding one. But, trying to build such a chain of ratiocination is a virtual denial of the validity, the very novelty, and the free character of the religious experience. Hence, the need for adhering to the principle of the unity of experience, ideology and activity, and of understanding and interpreting a religious message purely from the activities of its author. Otherwise, so often students of religion fall into the error of picking up seemingly common utterances of two religious pioneers and then of trying to relate them to a common source or a connecting bond. Mere words and statements unrelated to the deeds of their author are quite likely to be misunderstood and misinterpreted. Deeds alone are the true index of the ideology of the author.

12. THE WORLDVIEW

The worldview of a system is the best expression of its philosophy and appreciation of human destiny, of its aims and objectives, and of the direction in which men must move. The worldview represents the character and class of a system. Schweitzer, in his survey of different philosophical and religious systems, classifies them broadly in two distinct categories, the one with the worldview of life-affirmation and the other that is largely life-denying. In one case, creative and ethical participation in life is the spiritual goal. In the other case, withdrawal from the world for merger or union with Reality is the natural aim. The broad features of the two types of systems are quite characteristic and contrastive. In one case, moral life forms the chief fundamental of spiritual progress. For example, Guru Nanak says that the superman is he who treats all as his equals. In the other case, withdrawal from life, asceticism or monasticism forms an integral part of the religious discipline. Therefore, in appreciating the meaning and import of the doctrines and practices of a system, the context of its worldview has to be kept in view. For, each part not only reflects the other, but in turn also determines it.

Hence, for the intrinsic understanding of the features and class of any religious system, it is absolutely essential that the aforesaid principles, measures and methodology are constantly kept in view. Any varied approach is bound to lead to wrong conclusions. However, for obvious reasons, many of these principles may appear to overlap each other. This is so because, it is the components of an integrated whole that have to be taken up individually, and features of each part noted in isolation, so as to identify the same and the whole, in the light of the principles stated above.

2

PROBLEMS OF METHODOLOGY

DALJEET SINGH

It is a welcome sign that in the last few decades, interest in the study of Sikh religion, its institutions and history, has grown in India and abroad, both among Sikh and non-Sikh scholars. It is indeed a healthy development. But, partly because of the variant background from which scholars are drawn, and partly because of the methodologies of study followed by them, a few problems have to be faced and solved. In this brief article, we shall consider a few of them.

The first problem that has arisen concerns the methodology adopted in the study of Sikhism. This issue relates not only to the study of Sikhism, but also to the study of other religions, or of religion as such. In fact, the problem is ontological in nature. It is basic to almost every religion that there is a Spiritual Reality that is different from the empirical reality we perceive with our senses. Irrespective of the fact whether or not the phenomenal Reality is considered to be real or not, the Spiritual Reality is regarded as more real or true. It is the description and definition of this Reality by a religion that form the very basis of the study of that religion. Answers to questions whether that Reality is creative, attributive or otherwise, determine the structure of a religion, and furnish valid clues to its study and classification. For example, no student of Guru Granth Sahib can fail to understand that for the Gurus, God is not only creative and attributive, but He is also immanent, reveals Himself to man, and operates in history with His Will. The Gurus have repeatedly emphasized these aspects of God. Guru Nanak says, "O Lalo, I say what the Lord commands me to convey."[1] Similarly, the scriptures and the basic doctrines of every religion define Reality in their own way, and no study of any religion would be true or even valid, unless that definition is kept in view. It is, therefore, axiomatic to say that the study of the ontology or the spiritual base of a religion is essential to the proper understanding of it and its development. Yet, it is this very issue that raises the first problem.

Since the advent of science, and more particularly since the last century, materialistic philosophies have gained considerable relevance. In fact, in the fields of sociology, economics, political science, psychology and history, it is the materialistic interpretations that are, by and large, accepted as valid. Each of these social sciences has developed its own particular discipline and methodology of study. As all these studies relate to the phenomena of the empirical world, either taking little account of or denying the transcendent world, their world-views are, from the point of view of religion, partial or lopsided. Seen from the angle of social sciences, there is substance in the argument of these scholars of phenomenology, that the acceptance of the existence of transcendence is an uncalled for assumption that would knock off what they consider to be their scientific basis. The argument has a validity in the field from which it emanates. But, the confusion and the fallacy arise, when this argument is carried to the field of religion. For, by its very definition, the study of religion involves the study of the transcendent or the spiritual. Therefore, in the study of religion it would be an equally uncalled for assumption to accept that there is no transcendent element. For, many a religion believes that the transcendent is also immanent, and operates in history. Accordingly, religion has developed its own methodology and principles of study leading to a world-view which is holistic and comprehensive, instead of being limited and narrow. In fact, the denial of the spiritual element would not only vitiate the study of religion, but would also rule out the very meaning or need of such a study. It is in this context that we quote Dr Hannad Arenett, who after invoking the age-old view of Parmenides and Plato about the existence of the supersensual world, writes, "Meanwhile, in increasingly strident voices, the few defenders of metaphysics have warned us of the danger of nihilism inherent in the development; and although they themselves seldom invoke it, they have an important argument in their favour; it is indeed true that once the supersensual realm is discarded, its opposite, the world of appearances as understood for so many centuries, is also annihilated. The sensual, as still understood by positivists, cannot survive the death of the supersensual. No one knew this better than Nietzsche, who, with his poetic and metaphoric description of the assassination of God in Zarathustra, has caused so much confusion in these matters. In a significant passage in *The Twilight of Idols*, he clarifies what the word God meant in Zarathustra. It was merely a symbol for the supersensual realm as understood by metaphysics; he now uses instead of God the word 'true world' and says : "We have abolished the true world. What has remained? The apparent one perhaps? Oh no! with the true world we have also abolished the apparent one."[2] It is obvious that the study of religion, its institutions and history cannot be kept limited to the study of its phenomena, because such a study, in order to be complete, must essentially embrace the study both of its spiritual and empirical aspects. In this context Dr Huston Smith writes, "Ninian (Smart) approaches religion from the angle of phenomenology and the social sciences, whereas I, a philosopher, find phenomenology confining. Ontology is too central to be bracketed."[3]

This observation is particularly valid in the case of the study of a religion like Sikhism, in which the Gurus establish an inalienable link between the spiritual life and the empirical life of man. In fact, transcendence is fundamental. Every couplet in the over fourteen hundred pages in Guru Granth Sahib stresses that there is a higher level of Reality than the physical reality we perceive with our senses, and, unless we work in tune with that Reality, our problems of conflict, disharmony and war will remain unsolved. The Guru clearly envisages four stages in the progress of life after God had expressed Himself. "First, He manifested Himself; second, He created the individuality; third, He created multifarious entities; and fourth is the highest level of the God-conscious being who always lives truthfully."[4] And, it is this destiny of man, the Guru exhorts him to fulfil. "O man, you are supreme in God's creation, now is your opportunity, you may or may not fulfil your destiny."[5] This is the Guru's thesis in Guru Granth Sahib. According to it, real knowledge comes from the area of the transcendent. He is the Teacher who enlivens man's spiritual dimension and gives him a universal consciousness and a discriminatory vision. This realm is noetic. It was the knowledge thus gained that made Guru Nanak change radically almost every religious doctrine that stood accepted in the earlier three thousand years of Indian history. Against the world being illusory, delusive *(mithya, maya)* or a place of suffering or misery, he called it real and meaningful; against asceticism, monasticism and *sanyasa*, he accepted the householder's life and full social participation and responsibility; against celibacy and woman being considered sin-born, he gave religious sanctity to marriage and equality to women with men; against the rigidity of *Varn Ashram Dharma* and the institutions of caste and pollution, he stated that yoga lies not in one-point meditation but in treating all men as one's equal; against withdrawal from life and taking to renunciation and *sanyasa*, he stressed that he alone knows the true way who works and shares his earnings with others. For the social milieu of that period, this was a very radical thesis. And, yet, scholars employing the methodology and tools of social sciences say : Guru Nanak contributed no new religious thought; that Sikhism is hardly a religion; it is a combination of Vaishnaism and Nathism, two cults recommending celibacy and withdrawal from life, and accepting caste discrimination; or that it is a peasant faith. For the Guru, God is the source of truth, knowledge and energy; that way alone can we explain the revolutionary activities of Muhammad and Guru Nanak. That is why in Christianity, Islam and Sikhism, God is given the symbol of Light, and in Islam and Sikhism, He is called "Truth." For the man of faith, the door to truth is through the spiritual dimension of man. For the social sciences, the only reality is the physical world, and science constitutes the exclusive door to its secrets, the mystic world being just unexplored areas of darkness. But, for Guru Nanak, unless man wakens his spiritual dimension, he cannot know reality nor live a truthful and harmonious life in this world; for, spirituality forms the base of all moral life. Schweitzer, while surveying the entire field of Western thought, comes to the dismal conclusion that there is no trace of the ethical in the reflective thought of man. That is why, for the social sciences, morality is just 'a defence mechanism' or a 'reaction formation' in response to environmental impacts; religion too, being a similar behavioural phenomenon without any separate or independent roots.

It is in this context that William Nicholls feels that the culture and consciousness of the modern secular universities are unsuitable to interpret the culture and consciousness of the authors of Scriptures, "In so far as we adopt the culture of the secular university, we are systematically in opposition to the texts we are studying. In so far as we take our text seriously, and are successful in interpreting the intention of their writers, we are in opposition to the university and its culture."[6] Nicholls cites the following typical case of distortion by

Morton Smith, who js blind to the colossal spiritual energies generated by Christ and the phenomenal response he had over the centuries in shaping history and men. "A striking example of this limitation may be observed in the work of one of the most brilliant and respected of present-day scholars, Morton Smith. His recent book, *The Secret Gospel*, begins as a piece of literary detection which compels admiration, but it takes a startling nosedive at the point that it comes to the historical substance of the matter. On the basis of a second century source of doubtful provenance, which he prefers to more central sources, on no other apparent ground than that it was secret, Smith believes he has unmasked the truth about Jesus — he was really a magician, and perhaps one who used homosexual practices in his rites of initiation. The fact that this theory is shocking to the susceptibilities of the believer is not an argument against its truth. After all, many simple Christians will be most disturbed by the growing consensus of scholarship that Jesus was thoroughly Jewish, and had no thought of founding a new religion. What is more to the point is the total inability of such a theory to explain how such a person could also have been the originator of the lofty spiritual teachings to which both the Gnostic and ecclesiastical traditions bear witness."[7] What needs to be emphasised is that religious phenomena or history is intimately related to, if not the product and expression of, its spiritual base. Both components have to be studied together, one cannot be fruitfully studied in isolation of the other. No wonder Nicholls writes, "Thus, it can seem somewhat ludicrous to watch scholars in religious studies abdicating a function they alone can perform, and bowing down to the latest theories in anthropology, which seem unable to recognize in religion anything beyond a highly abstract code for ordering data and uniting and separating bits of information. Even if it has to be acknowledged that religions may perform such functions, to suppose that this exhausts their role, is to betray a crass failure to enter the outlook of other human beings, for whom religion was, and perhaps still is, a living reality opening doors on to the spiritual dimension and raising their existence to a higher level."[8]

We do not say that an anthropologist or sociologist should not study religion, but it would only be an anthropologist's or sociologist's view of religion by the use of his own methodology. Whereas the anthropologist is entitled to express his point of view about a religion, the reader is also equally entitled to know that the study is by an anthropologist by the use of an anthropologist's methodology. Because, from the point of view of the man of religion, such studies would be limited in their scope, partial in their vision, and inadequate as a study of man in the totality of his being and functioning, i.e., of his spiritual and empirical life. Perhaps, it is the limitation of the social science methodology, that scholars from this field have either scanty knowledge of the ideology of Guru Granth Sahib or are unwilling to take its contribution into account.

There is also another related point. In the study of religion it is not only necessary to know the methodology the author is using, but it is important to know who the writer is, and what is his own faith or training. Unlike as in science, religion is the study of the inner life of man. It is, therefore, relevant and necessary to know about the religious belief and background of the writer, i.e., whether or not he accepts the existence of the transcendent or the supersensual elements. It is in this context that Dr Noel Q. King writes, "One general conclusion which I draw from a long study of the critics, of which the above is a sketch, is that it is most important to remember the personality and circumstance of the critic. In a natural science like chemistry it may not be necessary to know anything about the human being who is writing. In any subject which entails human beings, the work must be put into a personal context. Accordingly, one feels that every such work of critical scholarship should have a government statutory warning that its consumption may be deleterious to the soul's health. If it is to do with religion, it should also have a statement of ingredients, including the religious standing of the writer. If he or she is a believer, it is necessary to know this, so that the critical reader can allow for bias. If he or she is not a believer, we should have some indication of that too, lest the disillusionment or enlightenment of a post-Christian, a post-Jew or a post-whatever should give the critic rosy-coloured spectacles or a jaundiced outlook."[9] Let us now quote C.G. Jung about objectivity of Sigmund Freud, "There was no mistaking the fact that Freud was emotionally involved in his sexual theory to an extraordinary degree. When he spoke of it, his tone became urgent, almost anxious, and all signs of his normally critical and skeptical manner vanished. A strange, deeply moved expression came over his face, the cause of which I was at a loss to understand. I had a strong intuition that for him sexuality was a sort of *numinosum*. This was confirmed by a conversation which took place some three years later (in 1910), again in Vienna. I can still recall vividly how Freud said to me, 'My dear Jung, promise me never to abandon the sexual theory. That is the most essential thing of all. You see, we must make a dogma of it, an unshakable bulwark.' He said that to me with great emotion, in the tone of a father saying, 'And promise me this one thing, my dear son, that you will go to church every Sunday.'"[10] It is strange that Freud, who was basing his theories on, and interpreting the dreams of others, including those of Jung, was, curiously enough, anxious to conceal his own and his private life. The motive for such concealment could hardly be academic or scientific. Jung writes, "Freud had a dream — I would not think it right to air the problem it involved. I interpreted it as best I could, but added that a great deal more could be said about it, if he would supply me with some additional details from his private life. Freud's response to these words was a curious look — a look of the utmost suspicion. Then he said, 'But I cannot risk my authority.' At that moment he lost it altogether. That sentence burned itself into my memory; and in it the end of our relationship was already foreshadowed. Freud was placing personal authority above truth."[11]

We quote the instance of another great man. It is well-known that the followers of Ramanuja, a philosopher of Bhakti, are very particular that the food they eat is undefiled. Therefore, the rule had been that if while cooking or eating food, another person cast a glance on it, the entire food was thrown away, and the food cooked again and eaten. This being the Vaishnava culture, let us record what Mahatma Gandhi, a protagonist of the Hindu tradition, writes, "...... but for years I have taken nothing but fruit in Mohammedan or Christian households ...... In my opinion, the idea that interdining and intermarrying is necessary for national growth is a superstition borrowed from the West. Eating is a process just as vital as the other sanitary necessities of life. And if mankind had not, much to its harm, made of eating a fetish and an indulgence, we would have performed the operation of eating in private, even as we perform other necessary functions of life in private. Indeed, the highest culture in Hinduism regards eating in that light, and there are thousands of Hindus still living who will not eat their food in the presence of anybody."[12] It is not our object to deride anyone, but we wish only to show that cultural or personal prejudices die hard, and that these consciously or unconsciously colour one's vision. It cannot, thus, be denied that in the study of a religion or another religion, objectivity of vision can, at best, be only limited. It is, therefore, essential to know of the background, beliefs and predilections of the author in order to enable the reader to assess and appreciate the value of his views and the slant of his vision. In scientific studies, the data and facts are mechanical, quantitative and spacial, that are generally measurable by fixed and accepted yardsticks. Even in that field, we have come to a stage where the observer's relative position in space and time affects his measurement and inferences. In the matter of religion, the difficulties of unbiased assessment are far too great, because here the field of study is primarily the emotional, the moral and the spiritual life of an individual or his society. An illustration would be relevant. Two ideas are intimately connected with the martyrdom of Chirst, namely, that of the act of redemption and of the resurrection of Christ. Howsoever one may view these ideas, it would, indeed, be impossible to understand and interpret the moral base and development of Christianity without accepting their validity, the deep faith and response they inspired, and the abiding influence they exercised on the early Christian society. In the same way, it is fundamental to the Sikh religion, as stated by Guru Nanak and the other Gurus in their hymns, that God had revealed Himself to them and that their hymns embody the commands of God. Therefore, in spiritual matters the genuineness of an idea is indicated by the spiritual and moral faith it evokes in the hearts of the people concerned. We do not urge that a sociologist or an anthropologist be debarred from evaluating religious matters and developments. But, the man of faith has also the right to know the writer's belief, i.e., whether he is an atheist, a materialist, an evolutionist, a Marxist or a sociologist. We shall specify our point still further. W.H. McLeod, while evaluating the originality of the religious thesis of Guru Nanak, writes that it is misleading to suggest that he originated a school of thought or a set of teachings.[13] As against it, Dr Muhammad Iqbal, the Muslim philosopher and scholar, finds in the entire panorama of Indian religious history only two tall persons, namely, Lord Buddha and Guru Nanak.[14] These contrasted assessments might be explained by the fact that whereas McLeod was for many years a part of a local Christian missionary organization in the Punjab, for Muhammad Iqbal, Guru Nanak is the only man of God in India, who like Prophet Muhammad, combined the spiritual life and the empirical life of man, and started a religion of 'deed', proclaiming and preaching the Oneness of God and the brotherhood of man. Another student of cultural history, H.S. Oberoi, views Islam and Sikhism in an altogether different light. "Sikh religion is first and foremost a peasant faith. Sociologists have often spoken of how Islam is an urban religion, Sikhism may be spoken of as a rural religion. When dealing with the beliefs, rituals and practices of the Sikhs, be they religious or political, it is always worthwhile to constantly remind ourselves that we are fundamentally dealing with the peasantry, and the world-view of this social class has historically always been very different from other social classes. A lot of knotty issues to do with Sikh studies would become easier to solve if we stop applying paradigms that have developed out of the study of urban social groups — merchants, middle-class or city workers — and deploy concepts that relate to the day-to-day life of the peasantry."[15]

In the above context, two points can hardly be overemphasised, namely, what is the methodology of study a scholar is using, and what are his personal belief and background, i.e., whether the study, examination or interpretation is under the discipline of sociology, anthropology or religion.

Next is the issue of breaking the dichotomy between the spiritual life and the empirical life of man. In most religions, for one reason or the other, this dichotomy exists; and it is more so in the Indian religions in which asceticism, monasticism, celibacy and *ahimsa* are almost the essential features of the religious life. In India, Guru Nanak was the first person to break this dichotomy, and proclaim a religion of life-affirmation, with emphasis on the moral life of man. Monasticism, asceticism and celibacy had become such essential symbols of religious life that the Naths questioned Guru Nanak how he was claiming to follow the religious path while living the life of a householder. Similar doubt was expressed by Sant Ram Das of Maharashtra, when he found the Sixth Guru riding a horse armed like a warrior. The Guru's reply was clear and categoric. He said that Guru Nanak had given up mammon but had not withdrawn from the world, and that his sword was for the defence of the weak and the destruction of the tyrant. In short, it is the Sikh doctrine of *miri* and *piri*, which looks odd to votaries of pacifist religions. Outside India, Moses and Prophet Muhammad broke this dichotomy and created religious societies that not only sought to tackle the socio-political problems of man, but also sanctioned the use of force for a moral purpose. On account of this difference between the pacifist and non-pacifist religions and the consequent differences in conditioning by the respective traditions, persons like Toynbee are critical of the socio-political activities of Prophet Muhammad, and Indians like Mahatma Gandhi, Rabindra Nath Tagore and Jadunath Sircar are critical of the militancy of Guru Gobind Singh. In contrast, we have already quoted the eulogy of Muhammad Iqbal in admiration of the lofty religious proclamation Guru Nanak made in India. Similarly, it was Pir Buddhu Shah, a Muslim Sufi saint, who was so inspired by Guru Gobind Singh, that he not only sent his followers and sons to fight for the cause of the Guru, but two of his sons actually sacrificed their lives while fighting in the army of the Guru. The annals of man hardly record another instance of this kind where a saint of a living religion should sacrifice his sons for the cause of a man of God of a different religious faith, especially while his co-religionist should be the ruling Emperor of the day. We, therefore, wish to emphasise that scholars drawn from the pacifist cultural background so often fail to understand that the Guru Nanak — Guru Gobind Singh combination, or the doctrine of *miri-piri* and the saint-soldier, logically follow from the ideology of Guru Nanak that combines the spiritual life and the empirical life of man. This is exactly the reason why, despite the ideological basis explained by the Sixth Guru himself, scholars, with pacifist background, try to find extraneous but fantastic reasons for militancy on the part of the Sikh Gurus while pursuing a righteous cause. This is what some Western scholars write, "The indigenous elements in Sikhism are largely those customs of the tribes of Jats, who made Sikhism their own, and the marginal elements are those of the Nath Yogi tradition, which with Vaishnava Bhakti was primarily responsible for the Sant synthesis."[16] "The teachings of Nanak do not have a direct causal connection with the later growth ...... which should be understood largely in terms of the historical events of the seventeenth and eighteenth centuries."[17] Little do these scholars realize or understand that tribal traits of character have never given rise to new religious ideologies. It is a significant fact of modern scholarship that whereas not a single Muslim scholar finds the least discontinuity between the ideology of the first Gurus and the later Gurus, it is only some scholars drawn from the pacifist traditions that discern any discordance between the ideology of Guru Nanak and that of Guru Gobind Singh. And, since both in India and the West most of the scholars are drawn from and are conditioned by the pacifist background and traditions, this is the second problem concerning Sikh studies. Of course, there are numerous scholars who are able to take an over-all view.

Partly related to the first two problems is the third issue arising from the increasing secularization of modern life. For the last over two centuries religion has been vitrually excluded from the socio-political life of the Western countries. The position in the Communist countries is also the same. Keeping the danger of secularism in view, the representatives of North American Churches suggested : "The American view was that there are three realities : Christianity, other religions, and secularism, and that these three realities can be either allies or enemies. It was argued that Christians had to choose whether they were to ally themselves with the other religions against secularism. The Americans, especially the Boston Personalists who were leading the debate at that time, took the view that secularism is a common danger for all religions and, therefore, there must be an alliance of all religions to fight secularism. European theologians, particularly Barth, Brunner, and Kramer, took a totally different view. They maintained that secularization, not secularism, is the primary process. It is a process in which some of the values of Christian faith have been put into a secular framework, bringing about a powerful force which is destroying all old ideas."[18] Unfortunately, this majority view still persists in the World Council of Churches.

The rise of the modern national state is something which Toynbee laments : "This transfer of allegiance from the Western Christian Church to parochial Western secular states, was given a positive form — borrowed from the Graeco-Roman Civilisation — by the Rennaissance." "On this political plane, the Rennaissance revived the Graeco-Roman worship of parochial states as goddesses." "This unavowed worship of parochial states was by far the most prevalent religion in the western world in A.D. 1956."[19] This has led to a contradiction. For, where there is a war between two national states, the churches of the opposing states pray to God for the victory of their own state, thereby bringing into ridicule the very institution of religion and the Church. We have already stated that in Sikhism the integral combination of the spiritual life and the empirical life of man has led to the doctrine of *miri* and *piri*. But, an outsider while reading a paper at an academic conference on Hindu and Sikh religions views the issue quite differently. He says, "Sikh scholars see the (*miri-piri*) concept as an inseparable whole in the religious order. Non-Sikhs have come to see a religion-politics linkage in Sikhism, and deduce (or adduce) the root cause of the current crisis in Punjab to this."[20] Another scholar is critical of Sikhs for their anxiety to maintain a separate religious identity. He writes : "But when it comes to the Indians belonging to religions which originated within India, such as Buddhists, Jains and Sikhs, many a Hindu regard them as downright unpatriotic or unspiritual or both, if they wish to maintain their distinct identity from the Hindus."[21] In a similar strain, another scholar questions the relevance and role of religion in the field of social reform or justice. He writes, "Untouchability has been abolished by political legislation. Government steps are persistently being taken to uplift the castes considered backward so far. As such, the very point against which original Sikhism had reacted, no longer remains a point of contention. Moreover, the problem of social inequality and the consequent demand for justice no longer remains a province of religious organization. It is the government agencies who have to look into the problem in order to eradicate social inequality and provide social justice. As such, the problem has shifted its locale from the religious to the political."[22]

We have given the above examples to indicate that men of religion feel that in view of the growing secularization of modern life and a consequent tendency to encroach on the religious field, it is not only necessary that religion should be studied with the tools of its own discipline, but that the funding and functioning of such academic studies should also be kept free from the influences of the modern state and its secular life.

REFERENCES

1. Guru Granth Sahib, p. 722.
2. Smith, Huston : paper entitled, *Another World to Live In*, Published in Religious Studies & Theology Vol. 7, Number 1, January 87, p. 54.
3. Smith, Huston : *Beyond The Post Modern Mind*, pp. 77-79.
4. Guru Granth Sahib, p. 113.
5. Ibid., p. 913.
6. Nicholls, William : paper entitled, *Spirituality and Criticism in The Hermeneutics of Religion*, presented at Annual Meeting of the Canadian Society for the Study of Religion, Guelph, Ont., May, 84, p. 4.
7. Ibid., p. 32.
8. Ibid., p. 22.
9. King, N.Q. : *Perspectives on Sikh Tradition*, edited by Gurdev Singh, pp. 46-47.
10. Jung, C.G. : *Memories, Dreams and Reflections*, p. 150.
11. Ibid., p. 158.
12. Baig, M.R.A. : *The Muslim Dilemma In India*, p. 60.
13. McLeod, W.H. : *Evolution of Sikh Community*, p. 5.
14. Muhammad Iqbal : *Bang-i-Dara*, p. 270.
15. Oberoi, H.S. : *Popular Saints, Goddesses, Village Sacred Sites : Re-reading Sikh Experience in the Nineteenth Century*, p. 28. Paper read at Conference at Berkeley in Feb. 87.
16. McLeod, W.H. : *Evolution of Sikh Community*, p. 67.
17. Juergensmeyer and Barrier : *Berkeley, Sikh Studies*, p. 19.
18. Paulos Markgegorios, in *Dialogue and Alliance*, International Religious Foundation Vol. I & II, 1987, p. 95.
19. Toynbee, A. : *An Historian's Approach to Religion*, p. 210.
20. *Theological and Social Issues in Hindu & Sikh Traditions*, Council of World's Religions — Seminar held at Srinagar in July, 88, paper by V.N. Narayanan, p. 5.
21. Ibid., paper by Ravi Ravinder, p. 7.
22. Ibid., paper by Basant Kumar Lal, p. 8.

3

SIKHISM : BASIC ELEMENTS

DALJEET SINGH

---

1. CONCEPT OF GOD

At the very outset we should like to say one thing. Obviously, it is not possible to deal with all aspects of Sikhism in this chapter. We shall, therefore, confine ourselves only to the essentials of Sikhism, and highlight only those aspects of it that clarify and underline the point of view which we wish to express.

The Sikh Gurus are uncompromising monotheists. In the very opening line of Guru Granth Sahib, God is described by Guru Nanak as "By the Grace of the Sole One, Self-existent and Immanent, the Creator Person, without Fear or Unconditioned, without enmity or Un-contradicted, the Timeless Person, Un-incarnated, Self-created and Enlightener." [1. p. 1]. God is never born. The becoming world is His creation, and not his emanation; nor is it identical with Him.

We shall first indicate, briefly, the kind of God that is envisaged in Sikhism. In their hymns the Gurus described God in numerous ways, referring to His social, political, aesthetic, metaphysical, ethical and other attributes. But a few aspects of God need particular mention. These will enable us to understand the significance, origin and objectives of the Sikh tradition, institutions and practices.

(i) *Creator* : God is the Creator. The universe is His creation. The very concept of a Creator-God implies a universe as different from Him. The universe is in time and space. It is changing and is governed by fixed laws. The Creator is different from the creation, which is limited and conditioned. As Creator, God is Free. He is not determined by any laws known to us. He is not the material cause of the universe. But, no independent *Prakriti* is assumed "God created the world of life, planted *Naam* (Immanent God) therein, and made it the seat of righteousness." [1. p. 930]. "He creates all, fills all, and is yet separate." [1. p. 937]. There are many hymns in Guru Granth Sahib which mention that God was there even before He created the universe, He being Transcendent. "He is the

Sole-creator. There is no second one." [1. pp. 11-12]. "God was by Himself and there was nothing else." "In the region of Truth, God creates perpetually, and watches His creation with a Benevolent eye. He is happy about it, and deliberates over it, directing it with His Will." [1. p. 8]. God is Ever-Creative.

This gives an idea of God, His creative activity, and the cosmological aspect of His creation.

(ii) *Transcendent and Immanent* : God is both Transcendent and Immanent. He is both in the universe and outside it. While time, space and change are features of the becoming universe, God is Eternal, Self-existent. He cannot be conceived or explained in empirical terms. He is beyond space and beyond time. The Gurus have cautioned us against the inadequacy of human logic to comprehend Him. He is Entirely Different, or 'Wholly Other.' "When there was no form in sight, how could there be good or bad actions. When God was in the Self-Absorbed state, there could be no enmity or conflict." [1. p. 290]. That state of God is to be envisaged in terms of spacelessness and timelessness. The nature of God transcends all known categories of thought. The Creator of these limited categories cannot be judged by them. The Gurus call Him Unfathomable, Indescribable and Ineffable. "The mind alone can know Him." [1. p. 612]. He is Transcendent.

The Immanent aspect of God has been variously described as His Will that directs the universe, His Word that informs the universe, and His *Naam* that not only creates the entire universe but also sustains and governs it. "God creates the universe, takes His abode in it and sustains it." [1. p. 788]. God creates the universe and becomes Immanent in it, being at the same time Transcendent. "He that permeates all hearts is Transcendent too." [1. p. 294]. "Having created the world, He stands in the midst of it and is separate too." [1. p. 937]. This Immanence of God is only a symbolic way of expressing God's connection with the world. When the world was not there the question of His Immanence did not arise. When "there was no form, the Word (Immanence) in essence abided in the Transcendent God." [1. pp. 945-6].

The Immanence of God is important. It emphasises the spiritual and meaningful character of the universe and life's capacity for relationship with God. His Immanence indicates God's Love for His creation. This Immanence gives relevance, authenticity, direction and sanction to the entire moral and spiritual life of man. It also emphasises God's capacity for revelation, His nearness to man and His deep and abiding interest in the world. All theistic systems assume His Immanence. For, where God is only Transcendent and unapproachable, all moral and spiritual life would become pointless.

God's being both Transcendent and Immanent, does not mean that there are two parts, stages, or phases of God. It is the Transcendent God who is everywhere in each heart, place and particle. It is He who is both Transcendent and Immanent. "The same God is *Sargun* and *Nirgun*, *Nirankar* and self-Absorbed (*Sun Samadhi*)." [1. p. 290]. "*Sargun* and *Nirgun* are created by *Naam*." [1. p. 387]. "He is the One, both *Nirgun* and *Sargun*." [1. p. 250]. The Gurus repeatedly emphasise that He is One and we only give Him different names. It would be highly inappropriate to confuse the Gurus' concept of *Sargun* and *Nirgun* (One Transcendent cum Immanent God) with the Vaishnava meaning of these terms or with the idea of *Ishvara*. These Vaishnava concepts of phases, or stages, have been clearly repudiated by the Gurus' concept of One God.

(iii) *God Of Attributes* : The Gurus call God the 'Ocean of Attributes, Values and Virtues.' This aspect of God is of importance in indicating the spiritual and moral trends and the character of Sikhism. A God of Attributes lays down the ideals for which man has to work. Its significance has often been missed. "He is always Benevolent." "You are my Mother, You are my Father, You are my Protector everywhere." "He relieves the sufferings of the downtrodden; He is the Succour of the succour-less." [1. pp. 263-4]. "God is eyes to the blind, riches to the poor, Nanak, He is the Ocean of Virtues." [1. p. 830].

This Attributive aspect of God not only links God with the universe, but it establishes beyond doubt the character and direction of God's Will. This leads to four important conclusions. First, attributes and values have relevance only in a becoming or relative world. Beacuse all perfection is static and all qualities are relative. A God of Attributes has, thus, a meaning only in relation to the changing world of man. Evidently, for the expression of attributes, a changing universe is essential and becomes an integral part of the creative plan of God. God and the universe are, thus, closely linked. It is impossible to think of a God of Attributes in the absence of a changing world. That is why when God was all by Himself, the question of 'Love and devotion or good or bad actions', [1. pp. 1035-6] could not arise. Secondly, and this is the most important inference, virtues and attributes emphatically indicate, apart from the standard of ethical values and moral life, the direction in which spiritual efforts should be made. These point out the purposes for which the Will of God works. Thirdly, it indicates the continuing interest of God in man and the universe. This gives authenticity to life and the universe which is as we shall see, decried or downgraded in many other religious traditions. In addition, there is the benevolent character of God. Not only is He the Creator and Sustainer of life. He nurtures and develops it with loving care. He has also been called the Enlightener (Guru or Guide) of man. "He rewards your efforts and acknowledges your deeds." "God rewards all efforts to become divine." [1. p. 859]. It gives a pre-eminent meaning to life, and optimism, hope and confidence to man in the achievement of his ideals. Man is given a clear direction in which he should move. In addition, he also knows that there is some one to guide and help him with love. Lastly, it gives primary validity and spiritual sanction to the moral life of man. For, in many other systems, it is deemed to be an entanglement. At best, some systems accept it as the preparatory method of purity for the spiritual life to be attained. But, in Sikh theology, this attributive aspect of God gives a clear priority, primacy and spiritual character to the moral life of man. This is the reason that in Sikhism moral life is of basic importance both for the seeker and the *gurmukh*. For, if God is the helper of the weak and the ocean of virtues, the spiritual person has to shape himself likewise.

(iv) *God Has A Will* : Everything is governed by His Will. "Everything happens within the ambit of His Will." [1. p. 1]. A God of Will naturally pre-supposes that He wants the universe to move not chaotically but in a system and with a purpose. Just like the Attributes of God, God's Will, too, can be exercised only in a changing world and towards a goal. The very idea of a Will implies a direction and an aim. This, too, re-emphasises the same points as stated in regard to a God of Attributes. The direction is governed by the Attributes of God and the purpose, as we shall see later, is to evolve a higher consciousness in man. This concept is central to Sikh theology. But, a God of Will does not at all mean a predeterministic world, because God is Creative and Free; and all movement in life is towards a creative freedom.

(v) *God Does Not Incarnate* : God has been mentioned as One who never takes birth, nor takes form. "May that mouth burn which says that God has incarnated." [1. p. 1136]. "God alone is the One who is not born of a woman." [1. p. 473]. The Gurus have definitely decried belief in the theory of incarnation. In order to dispel such ideas, they have stated that He created countless Brahmas, Sivas and Vishnus. "The Formless, One, alone, Nanak, is without fear; many are Ramas as the dust of His feet, and many Krishnas. Many are their stories and many are the Vedas." [1. p. 464] The idea that God never takes the human form has distinct implications. First, it shows that God is 'Wholly Other.' For a God that is Transcendent and unknowable, the question of His taking human form does not arise. Secondly, all pantheistic implications, as flowing from the idea of incarnation, are *ipso facto* repudiated. Besides, the concept has three other corollaries too.

The first is that man can never become God, and that God and man are not identical. Secondly, it indicates that the aim of spiritual effort is not merger in God, as under some other systems, but to be in tune with Him. This has a crucial significance in determining the human goal, and in showing that the entity of man is distinct from that of God. The two can never be one, though man can be His instrument. Thirdly, it, *inter alia*, shows that spiritual activity does not stop after the final achievement. The superman has a role to perform in carrying out the Will of God. Consequently, so long as the universe is there and the Will of God is in operation, the activities and duties of the superman continue endlessly.

(vi) *God Of Grace* : God has been called Gracious and Enlightener. A God of Will and a God of Grace have a meaning only in a becoming world, wherein alone, His Grace and Will can operate. These aspects of God also emphasise His Personal character. Grace implies that God's Will is free, undetermined by any outside law. In addition, it also stresses Love and Benevolence of God towards man. For, a Gracious Being can bestow His Grace only on something other than Himself. It has been repeatedly stressed that all final approval of man is an act of God's Grace. "O Nanak, the intellect is of no avail, one is approved only by His Grace." [1. p. 467]. A God of Grace dispels the idea that the world is deterministic. His activity is, therefore, incomprehensible except in terms of His Grace or Freedom.

(vii) *Naam* : The Sikh Gurus have given the word *Naam*, a distinct and significant meaning, which is far different from that of the mere '*Naam*' or psychic factors as understood in the traditional literature. "*Naam* sustains all regions and universes, all thought, knowledge and consciousness, all skies and stars, all forces and substances, all continents and spheres ...... He, on whom is His Grace, is yoked to *Naam* and he reaches the highest state of development." [1. p. 284]. "*Naam* is the Creator of everything." "*Naam* gives form to everything, and through *Naam* comes all Wisdom or Light." [1. p. 946]. *Naam* is the 'Nine Treasures' and nectar (*amrit*).

From the above verses it is clear that the Gurus do not use the word *Naam* in any restrictive or limited sense. They refer to it as the Highest Power : creating, informing, supporting and working the entire universe. The highest state of man is mentioned as the one when he lives and works in tune with God or *Naam*. Therefore, God and *Naam* are Real, Eternal and Unfathomable. It means that God and *Naam* are one and the same. *Naam* may be called the immanent or the qualitative aspect of God, working and directing the manifest world of force and form.

2. THE WORLD

Sikhism proclaims the dynamic reality and authenticity of the world and life. "God created the world of life and planted *Naam* therein, making it the place of righteous activity." [1. p. 930]. "God created the world and permeated it with His Light." [1. p. 1304] Since *Naam* has not only created the world but is also supporting, controlling and directing it, the same cannot be unreal or fruitless. His Immanence in this world guarantees its being a place of righteous action. "True are Thy worlds and Thy universe; true are the forms Thou createst. True are Thy deeds." [1. p. 463]. "True is He, True is His Creation." [1. p. 294].

The world being real, creative work and virtuous deeds are of fundamental importance. "The Guru contemplates God by word, thought and deed." "Earth is the true abode of righteousness." [1. p. 785]. "Truth and continence are true deeds, not fasting and rituals." [1. p. 841]. "Good, righteousness, virtue and the giving up of vice are the way to realize the essence of God." [1. p. 418].

The above quotations affirm unambiguosly the reality and significance of human life. Practices involving direct or indirect rejection of life have been denounced. There is a hymn in Guru Granth Sahib by Farid which would seem to suggest that the world is not real or is a place of suffering. While recording it in Guru Granth Sahib, the Fifth Guru has introduced, along with it, another hymn of his own. It is a clarification to dispel the contrary impression. He writes, "Beauteous, O Farid, are the garden of earth and the human body." [1. p. 1382]. The Guru further states, "Deride not the world as it is the creation of God." [1. p. 611].

This emphatic assertion about the reality of the world is a clear departure from the Indian religious tradition. The Gurus were extremely conscious of this radical and fundamental change they were making. That is why, both in their lives and in their hymns, they have been laying stress on this aspect of their spiritual thesis, lest they should be misunderstood on this basic issue. Living in this world is not a bondage for them but a rare opportunity. Not only is God benevolently developing and guiding the world in which He is Immanent, but each one of us is "yoked to his task and each is assigned a duty to perform." [1. pp. 736, 425,765]. The persistent interest of God in the creative movement is also obvious from the fact that the Gurus call Him Protector, Father, and a Just Administrator.

While discussing the concept of God of Attributes, Will and Grace, we have indicated its far-reaching implications about the reality of the world and the spiritual primacy of moral life therein. These aspects of God intimately connect Him with the world which is their only field of operation. Consequently, the Gurus' message and mission also relate to this world, wherein alone their mission could be fulfilled. No prayer has been expressed with greater depth and intensity than the one for the 'gift of *Naam*.' *Naam* being the

Benevolent Supporter and Director of the world, the gift of *Naam* to the devotee simply means an enlightened, loving and creative interest in the world and its development. How can one claim to be a devotee of God or *Naam* and ask for its gift and, yet decline to toe the line of God, namely, of nurturing and advancing the process of creativity and construction in the world ? It is for this reason that the Gurus have strongly condemned all ascetic and escapist practices. "One reaches not Truth by remaining motionless like trees and stones, nor by being sawn alive." [1. p. 952].

In India, generally, the householder's duties were not believed to be conducive to higher spiritual attainments. That is why one had to renounce worldly activities and take to the life of a hermit or *Sanyasin*. As against it, all the Sikh Gurus, excepting the Eighth Guru, who passed away at an early age, were married householders. Till the last days of their lives, they worked creatively and carried out their mission in the social and political fields. Seen in the context of Indian tradition, the ideals and institutions of Sikhism are entirely different. For the Gurus the world is a place of beauty. Man's struggle therein provides an opportunity for his progress. Hence the arena of man's and the mystic's work has to be in life and life alone. It is only the challenges of life that enable man to show and test his moral and spiritual fibre. It is his deeds in the world that alone form the basis of his spiritual assessment. The Guru, therefore, emphasises that "one gets not to God by despising the world."

3. HAUMAIN

The doctrine of *haumain* is basic to Sikh theology. The present state of man's consciousness, the Gurus say, is egoistic, i.e. it is governed by *haumain*. The Gurus call such a person *manmukh*. In this normal state of man, his self-will and animal propensities dominate. The ideal man, with the highest level of consciousness or God consciousness, is called *gurmukh*. This egoistic consciousness or *haumain* is the cause of all man's problems and limitations. This doctrine of *haumain* holds the key to the understanding of Sikhism.

Haumain is the "I" of the normal individual psyche. It is the director of all one's organs, including the nervous system and human reason. It is the self, the ego, or the centre of control of all working in every being or individual. The Gurus say that "the world came into being by individuation." [1. pp. 946, 466]. Evidently, for the growth of life, this creation of an individual self or *haumain* in every being was essential. There could be no animal life without there being in each organism a centre of consciousness. *Haumain* has, thus, enabled the evolution of life. Every man is equipped with many kinds of organs and faculties. These faculties, including his thoughts, are subservient to his individuality, self or ego. Throughout the evolution of life, this ego-centre, or *haumain* has been the instrument and guardian of his security, welfare and progress. Without a deep commitment to the interests, preservation and progress of the self, to the exclusion of every other being or self, life could never survive the battle against challenges from the environment. This ego, or *haumain*, has been the best means of securing the survival and the progress of life from amoeba to man.

But, what has been the very means of life's survival and progress, has now become "the great malady of man." [1. p. 1258]. The struggle against the elements and other species having been largely won, man still finds himself quite unequipped and helpless in dealing with the other members of his own species. The Gurus emphasise that this *haumain* has become the greatest problem of man both for his social life and future progress. Just as it is impossible for one's stomach or liver to digest food for another person; in much the same way, it is impossible for one's thought system, intellect or reason to be anything but self-centred, the same being basically subservient to the individual self or ego-consciousness. It is this organic condition of man that the Gurus call *haumain* or ego. Man's consciousness being self-centred, he is constitutionally incapable of looking to the interests of others. This is the root-cause of the entire conflict between man and man, between one society and the other, and between one nation and the other. Man is well equipped intellectually and materially, yet poverty, misery, and war remain his major unsolved problems. The altruistic tendencies developed in man as the result of cultural conditioning over the years are only superficial or conditioned. Spontaneous altruism is constitutionally and psychologically impossible in the egocentric or *haumain* governed man. The moment, the struggle for existence becomes keen, the basic self-centredness of man comes into play. Thus start all the conflicts of man, social as well as national and international.

According to the Guru in this state of *haumain* man has three limitations. He and his consciousness are alienated or unconnected with the Basic or the Higher Consciousness that is the source of all energy, virtues and goodness. "God created individuation but by forgetting *Naam* we come to grief." Secondly, he is unaware of his inalienable kinship with the other beings. Thirdly, ego-consciousness, by and large, works in a determined or mechanistic way. It is not creative or free. The Basic Reality or God alone is Free and Creative. God is the Causeless Cause or the Un-created Creator. We have already referred to two important aspects of God. He is Creative or Free, He is the Ocean of Values and Virtues. Man's egocentrism or *haumain* thus, constitutes his basic moral or spiritual problem. The fundamental question is, how to shed one's egoism and transcend one's present limiting state or development.

4. SOLUTION

The Gurus are not pessimistic about the world or this egocentric condition of man. They emphasise that man is not only capable of transcending this ego-consciousness, but is destined to do so. Their entire message is meant to solve this problem. Theirs is a crusade to enable man to rise above this present level and remove the hurdles that plague him and solve the problems that face him.

The Gurus indicate that there has been a continuing process of development, evolution and progress in the empirical world. They point out that progress from egoistic man to superman, or God-centred man is not only possible, but is in accordance with the purpose of God. Individuation was created by God. There has been gradual growth from small organisms to animals and finally to the animal-man with his subtle sense of discrimination and introspection. "For several births (you) were a mere worm, for several births an insect, for several births a fish or an animal." [1. p. 176]. "After ages you have the glory of being a man." "He endowed you with the light of reason, discrimination and wisdom." [1. p. 913]. "O man you are supreme in God's creation; now is your opportunity. You may or may not fulfil your destiny." [1. p. 913].

Further progress of this egoistic man depends entirely on the deeds of the individual. Till man had appeared on the scene, it was not possible for life to outgrow its animal character and alienation from God. So far, like other animals, man, too, has been living an animal life. But, the Gurus emphasise the opportunity available to man to grow into superman. They repeatedly address man to give up his egocentric activities and thereby to rise to his full stature. "After ages, this invaluable opportunity of human birth is available, but one loses it for nothing." [1. p. 1203]. "You have obtained the privilege of human birth, now is your only opportunity to meet God." [1. p. 12].

The remedy according to the Gurus is that man should develop a higher consciousness by linking his consciousness with God, *Naam*, or the Basic Consciousness. It is this solution which is the basis of their religious system and institutions. The Guru says, "*Naam* and *haumain* are opposed to each other. The two cannot co-exist." [1. p. 560]. "*Haumain* is a great malady. The remedy is to attune oneself to *Naam* by God's Grace." [1. p. 466]. It means that self-centredness should be substituted by God-centredness. "The man who is self-centred is far from God." [1. p. 235].

Let us explain the implications of these important hymns. In most other religions, worldly life is opposed to spiritual life. But, not so in Sikhism. Here it is egocentric life that is opposed to spiritual life and not worldly life as such. The Gurus consider the world to be real and accept full responsibilities in that regard. In fact, as God-centredness implies activity in the worldly life, the same is considered essential for the seeker and the God-conscious person. For, link with *Naam* means to be the agent of Dynamic *Naam* or God, the Ocean of Virtues. In fact, life and its activities alone reveal the distinction between a self-centred man and a God-centred one. Hence, "He who destroys evil becomes a perfect man." [1. p. 404]. "Love, contentment, truth, humility and other virtues enable the seed of *Naam* to sprout." [1. p. 955]. "Our deeds alone bear witness unto our life." [1. p. 1383].

These hymns indicate that the way to higher achievement lies in being altruistic or moral instead of being self-centred. Except for some conditioned or calculated moral activity, a self-centred person cannot be spontaneously altruistic. The solution really consists in transferring the control of the mind and body from narrow ego-consciousness to *Naam* God or God-consciousness. And being linked to *Naam* involves neither inactivity nor withdrawal from life. Perforce it must lead to spontaneous altruistic deeds because this consciousness is aware of its kinship both with every other being and with the Basic Reality, the Ocean of Virtues. Therefore, this consciousness accepts total responsibility and is as active as the Creative Reality. Just as *haumain* and *Naam* are opposed to each other, in the same manner God-centredness and inactivity are a contradiction in terms.

We shall explain why there is so much emphasis on moral life in Sikhism. A self-centred person has virtually a determined psyche. He is neither free, nor creative. The progress from self-centredness to God-consciousness, is progress from a virtually determined or a mechanistic state to a free and creative state. A moral act involves voluntary decision on the part of one's consciousness. We never call a material thing to be moral or immoral, since it is governed by the laws of physics and its movement is determined. But, a moral act on the part of a person is the result of his free will or decision or choice. It is, thus, a clear step on the path from being determined to being free; it is an effort to rise from the state of *haumain* to the state of God-consciousness or creative freedom. It is, indeed, a spiritual act. Hence the fundamental importance of moral life in Sikhism, since it is the only spiritual means leading towards God-consciousness. "One cannot be a Yogi by mere wishing. Real Yoga lies in treating all beings alike." [1. p. 730]. "Let all be called high, to me none appears low; One Potter has fashioned all vessels and One Light pervades the whole universe." [1. p. 866]. Real spiritual life involves the acceptance and practice of the idea of the Fatherhood of God and the brotherhood of man in one's actual living. The Gurus stress that God pervades all hearts and one can attune oneself to Him and develop a new state of higher consciousness. While we are in the normal ego-state, we are unconscious of this Immanence of God in us. "Where there is egoism, God is not; where there is God, there cannot be any egoism." [1. p. 1092]. "God unites the seeker with Himself." "God pervades the heart and one gives up ego and evil." [1. pp. 32, 30, 35, 49]. "By His Grace God comes in body and mind." It means that the entire psyche of such a person is guided by God-consciousness. "By *Naam* is the mind illumined." [1. p. 82]. *Naam* is dynamic and attributive.

These hymns emphasise that the way to solve our problems and difficulties is to establish a relation with God. This presence of God in us has variously been described as *Naam*, Guru, Word, Light and Will.

It is virtuous deeds alone that lead one away from the life of *haumain* and towards the path of *Naam* or God-centredness. But, ultimately it is only God's Grace that unites one with *Naam*. By this union a new and higher centre of consciousness is gained, called God-consciousness. With God's Grace is the ultimate insignia of approval conferred on man." [1. p. 7]. It is a state when the human consciousness becomes free and spontaneously moral and altruistic.

Guru Nanak puts the question as to, "How can the wall of falsehood intervening between us and Reality be removed", and gives a categoric reply. "It can be removed by carrying out God's Will." [1. p. 1]. And God's Will is Attributive, Creative and Gracious. This explains the pre-eminent importance of moral life in Sikhism.

5. GOAL

The next issue is as to what is the goal in Sikhism. In this field the Gurus have made a completely radical departure from the general religious tradition, more especially from the Indian tradition. Many misunderstandings about the ideology, growth and history of Sikhism arise because of the fallacious assumption that the goal in Sikhism is the same as in the other Indian religions.

The Gurus have explained their views about the spiritual goal of man by enunciating five principles. All of them point to the same conclusion about the ideal life.

(a) *Righteous Deeds Alone The Basis Of Man's Spiritual Assessment* : In the first hymn of Cosmography, Guru Nanak states what should be the role of man on earth, which has been declared to be a place for the practice of righteousness. The assessment of man, Guru Nanak says, will be made on the basis and character of his deeds. This idea has been repeated in numerous hymns like. "With God only the deeds one does in this world, count."

[1. p. 1383]. "Through virtue is one enlightened."

(b) *Higher Than Truth Is Truthful Living* : Guru Nanak states, "Everything is lower than Truth, but higher still is truthful living." [1. p. 62]. It is just a symbolic way of emphasising that the ideal is to live the active life of truth and not only to know Truth as an end in itself. The goal is to live an active and creative life. "True living is living God in life." [1. p. 684].

(c) *Carry Out The Will Of God* : Guru Nanak specifically raises the question as to how one can be a true human being, or an ideal man. Then he himself provides the answer : "By carrying out the Will of God." The Gurus conceive of God as a God of Will, Dynamic, Attributive and Creative. God is always nurturing the world with a benevolent eye. For man, the ideal life is to carry out His Will. The goal is not only to establish union with God, not only to know his Will, but after having done that, to carry it out. The ideal is not blissful union as an end in itself, but union in order to be God's instrument or agent in the world. Therefore, in Sikhism it involves a life of continuous moral activity.

(d) *God-Conscious Man* : On the question of *haumain*, we came to the conclusion that the Gurus lay down God-consciousness as the ideal. Because of his new consciousness he is spontaneously virtuous. All exhortations to man are to achieve his ideal by the practice of virtues. "Make the body the soil; put therein the seed of good deeds; with *Naam* Divine irrigate it. Let thy mind be cultivator, and raise crop of God's devotion." [1. p. 23].

(e) *Link With Naam* : *Naam* is Creative and Attributive. *Naam* is working in the world with Benevolence and Love. A very large number of hymns in Guru Granth Sahib request for the individual to be linked to *Naam*. "He reaches the highest stage whom God graciously galvanises to His *Naam*." [1. p. 284]. "Pray, link me to God."

Accordingly, the ideal of Sikh Bhakti is to be yoked, attuned or linked to *Naam*. *Naam* being the opposite of egoism, and the Ocean of Virtues and Values, to be linked to *Naam* simply means to become His instrument and share the responsibility of a creative and virtuous development in the world.

The Gurus have laid down these five principles prescribing the goal in Sikhism. Whether it is the ideal of God-consciousness, or of carrying out the Will of God, or of the gift of *Naam*, in essence all of them prescribe the same goal or spiritual truth. Again, whether it is the ideal of righteous deeds or of truthful living, the discipline and direction are exactly the same. We, therefore, come to the conclusion that in Sikhism, the goal is to develop a higher consciousness and lead a life of creative and moral activity. It means that spiritual life and moral life are virtually synonymous and coextensive. One inevitably leads to the other.

It is in this context that the Gurus describe themselves as the "servants" of God and His "soldiers." The Gurus pray that their lives may be devoted to the service of God. "May I have millions of hands to serve Thee." [1. p. 781]. "The service is the way to cross the hurdles of life." "Be ever alert in the service of God. Serve God every moment and relax not." [1. p. 77]. As the world is the authentic creation of God, supported by His Immanence, the service of God means the service of His creation. "Service in the world leads to approval in the Court of God." [1. p. 26]. This is the goal of Sikhism.

6. GURMUKH OR THE IDEAL MAN

The Gurus describe the qualities of the *gurmukh* and the role he is expected to play in life. These draw a clear picture of the ideal life in Sikhism. The lives of the Gurus are another indication of the kind of life, the seeker and the *gurmukh* are supposed to lead. Bhai Gurdas calls Guru Nanak a *gurmukh*. A *gurmukh*, being the instrument of God, exhibits in his life all the qualities attributed to God. Because on the one hand he is in touch with God who is All Love, and on the other hand he is conscious of his close kinship with every other living being.

(i) *He Is Godly, And Has All Virtues* : "He (*gurmukh*) is the ocean of virtues, pure and truthful." [1. pp. 905,1000,1175]. "He deals in the virtues of God." "He is shelter for the shelterless." "God is Compassionate, Merciful and Support of the earth; and so is the nature of saints." [1. p. 1017]. "The *gurmukh* saves all and removes pain." [1. p. 232]. "He becomes like Him with whom imbued." [1. pp. 411, 1021]. "He practises good spontaneously; he is the fountain spring of benevolence." [1. p. 273]. Being God-conscious, he is not alienated from his relationship with other beings.

(ii) *He Carries Out His Will* : God has a Will. The ideal man carries out that attributive Will. His mind is filled with *Naam;* true mind is imbued with Word, he serves truth, practises truth and earns truth. "Imbued by His Will, he carries it out." [1. p. 1423]. "The soldiers of God act just as He Wills." "Wonderful is His Will; one knows it only if one walks in His Will. Then alone one knows how to lead the life of truth." [1. p. 940]. The Guru emphasises, that he who carries out His Will alone knows it; and he who knows it must carry it out. A Will known is essentially a Will carried out. "They who know His Will carry it out." [1. p. 991].

(iii) *He Is The Servant Of God And Man* : They "dedicate life to Him"; he is "a combatant in the cause of God"; [1. pp. 74, 281] he is "the servant of God." The Guru calls himself as "the slave of all creation." [1. pp. 254, 377, 844]. The Guru prays : "The world is sick, O save it by any means you please." [1. p. 853]. This hymn is of classic significance. The Guru prays for the entire humanity. He does not want God to help men only through him. He makes no claim to exclusive prophethood. He wants everyone to be saved by any means God may be pleased to use. Nothing could be more expressive of the anonymity and humility of the Guru and his deep concern for the entire humanity.

(iv) *He Partakes Actively In All Fields Of Life* : Unlike the *Jivan Mukta* in other systems, where the goal is union or merger as an end in itself, the *gurmukh's* aim is not salvation for himself alone. He works for all, nor does he compromise with evil. For, "God's chosen is one who fights for the oppressed." [1. p. 1105]. His responsibility is total. As the instrument of God, he works for others and in all fields of life. Just as is the area of his responsibility, the *gurmukh's* sphere of activity too is unlimited.

(v) *He Aims To Make All Others God-Centred* : "He unites himself with God and unites others too with Him." "The servants of God salvage all." [1. pp. 8, 3, 944, 295]. "His self is emancipated and he emancipates others." The emphasis on this ideal of making everyone God-centred is so great that the Guru says that "God established the earth for the sake of God-centred persons." [1. pp. 965, 941]. This, in essence, means that the creation or evolution of the superman on earth is the purpose of God towards which all life is moving, and the *gurmukh* works for it.

7. METHODOLOGY

The Gurus have prescribed three modes of discipline. (a) company of God-centred persons, (b) moral life or service of man, and (c) remembering God and prayer. It is a code of conduct the seeker has to practise throughout the entire course of one's life.

(a) *Company Of God-Centred Persons* : The society of the ideal man is of great value to the seeker, both as a model and as a guide. His influence is the best for shaping man's growing personality and giving him strength and direction in times of doubt and difficulty. "Just as the *harind* (castor plant) imbibes the fragrance of the *chandan* tree, the fallen are emancipated by the saints." "In good company one becomes good." "God sends saints to reveal God's concern for man." [1. p. 929].

(b) *Moral Life And Service* : Guru Nanak says that the earth is a place for the practice of reighteousness. In Sikhism, moral activity is a step towards freedom and creativity. Hence, the highest importance of moral activity in the spiritual training and system of the Gurus. Spiritual discipline aims at enabling man to face life in a righteous and creative way. As such, a householder's life is an essential moral responsibility of man. The seeker's training has to take place during the course of a moral life and not in a monastry. It is important to understand that the Gurus never created any monastic system or a place for the training of a few. The psyche can be properly conditioned only when it is subject to the stresses and strains of the social environment of man. One can learn to swim only inside the pool and not outside it. This is exactly the reason why the Gurus excluded ascetics from the Sikh fold [4. p. 86] and condemned all ritualistic, yogic and other-worldly practices and austerities. In Sikhism, moral activity is the basis of all spiritual growth, and this activity can be done only in the social field. For, such activity alone is the way to eliminate egoism, and test the seeker's progress. Keeping in view the character and role of the *gurmukh* it is obvious that progress is possible only through moral life. "Singing and dancing in ecstasy are no worship; love and the giving up of ego are the ways of real worship." [1. pp. 159, 465] "Drive out selfishness and one is fulfilled." "Where the weak are cared for, there is showered God's mercy." [1. p. 750]. "Evil separates, good deeds unite." "Service in the world is the way to be fulfilled." There is, indeed, no spiritual progress without active moral functioning. The service of God is a synonym for the service of man. Moral activities have the highest priority in Sikhism, these being the best means of training.

The use of human rationality and a sense of discrimination (*babek budhi*) have a distinct place in moral life. Sikh theology being non-deterministic, man has a distinct moral freedom and responsibility in the choice of his actions. It is this exercise of right choice that determines his spiritual progress. "By use of discrimination or intellect one serves God." [1. p. 1245]. God's concern for the moral development of man can be gauged from the fact that it is "His innermost nature to help the erring." "With self-control and discipline, we forsake vice and see the miracle of man becoming God." [1. pp. 343, 347].

For the moral life of man two virtues, namely, humility and love, find the highest priority in the Guru's ethical system and the discipline prescribed for the seeker.

(c) *Remembering God And Prayer* : In Guru Granth Sahib, there is considerable emphasis on remembering God. But, the remembering of God is by itself not enough to link oneself with Him. This contemplation does not mean yogic practices for the achievement of the so-called bliss as an end in itself. We are unaware of any hymn in Guru Granth Sahib recommending yogic practices or any tradition in this regard. Nor are we aware of any hymn in Guru Granth Sahib which, apart from recommending prayer and keeping the fear of God always in one's mind, directs the practice of day-long meditations in seclusion, and away from the day's work. There are clear hymns against the use of such a course as a means of spiritual advancement. "Every one repeats God's name, but such repetition is not the way to God." "With guile in heart, he practises guile but mutters God's name. He is pounding husk and is in darkness and pain." [1. p. 656]. The Gurus deny the utility of any mechanical means of worship or mere repetition of words or hymns. But remembering can be a way to keep in mind one's basic ideals. Evidently, remembrance of God is a kind of preparation for the virtuous activities to be undertaken in the social life. It is actually the character of the subsequent deeds that will be the test of man. This remembering is like keeping the fear of God in mind and moving in life strictly on the moral path. It does not mean mechanical repetition every day or morning. That is why the Guru says that "it is only one out of *crores* who remembers God." [1. p. 1428].

Prayer as in any other theistic system, finds a place of eminence in Guru Granth Sahib. Prayer, expresses the humility and insignificance of the devotee. It is a mode of seeking God's Grace. It is a humble attempt to draw upon God's strength so as to restore one's sagging energies and will in the moral struggle of man. "My energies are exhausted and I am helpless. But O God, with Thy Grace nothing is difficult for me to accomplish." [1. p. 1429]. Such a prayer is not a repetitive formula or practice, nor is it an end in itself. It is really a preparation for the moral activity to be undertaken in the world. In fact, it is inalienably linked with the subsequent activity. Without its external operation, the internal activity remains invalid. The very fact that the Gurus started no monastic system shows that they never advocated either prayer or any other meditational system as an independent mode of spiritual training. "One is emancipated while laughing and playing in life and living a full life." [1. p. 522]. "The God-centred lives truth while yet a householder." [1. p. 661].

8. SIKH BHAKTI AND SOCIETY

We have already come to the conclusion that in Sikhism moral activity is the chief method of spiritual growth. This raises two issues. The first concerns the approach of the *gurmukh* towards social institutions and making changes in them. The Gurus, and more especially Guru Nanak, have been sharply critical of the evil socio-political institutions and customs of the times. About prejudices regarding caste and against women (which had recieved almost religious sanction), the Gurus say, "The Vedas make a wrong distinction of caste, colour, heaven and hell." [1. p. 1243]. "No one should take pride in caste; foolish man be not proud of caste; this pride leads to innumerable evils. They make distinction of four castes, but all are born of God." "The whole world is made of the same elements. Then why make distinctions ?" [1. pp. 1128]. "They talk of pollution and warn others not to

touch their food, lest it should be defiled. But their own bodies are impure." [1. p. 472].
"Why call woman impure when without women there would be none." [1. p. 473]. Evil
social practices and customs have been denounced. God-consciousness consists in treating
all as equals. The idleness of yogis and ascetics, hypocrisy of priests and Brahmins, and
inequalities in the economic field and the amassing of wealth have been condemned. "God's
riches are for all but men try to grab them for themselves." "God's bounty belongs to all,
but in the world it is maldistributed." [1. p. 1171]. "Man gathers riches by making others
miserable." [1. p. 889]. "Riches cannot be gathered without sin and these do not keep
company after death." [1. p. 417]. " O yogi, are you not ashamed of begging from door to
door for your food?" [1. p. 886]. "The man incapable of earning a living, gets his ears split
(to become a yogi) or becomes a mendicant. He calls himself a guru or saint but begs for
food from door to door. Never look up to such a person or touch his feet. He knows the
right way who earns his living by hard work and shares his earnings with others."
[1. p. 1245]. Similarly, in the political field, the oppression of the rulers, the tyranny of the
invaders, and the corruption of the officials have been deprecated.

   Two important things should be understood in regard to this criticism. This criticism
is the direct consequence of the Guru's ideas about God and the reality of the world. Their
world-view is clearly of life-affirmation. The brotherhood of man is the basis of their socio-
spiritual approach. Hence their three-pronged attack on all kinds of socio-political evils
and inequalites, on downgrading the socio-religious status of women, and on idleness,
renunciation and withdrawal from the world. Secondly, this condemnation was not a mere
verbal exercise, it was an essential step to educate the people, change their ideas and build
up fresh motivations. For, an important function of religion is to create and "establish
powerful, pervasive and long lasting moods and motivations in men." [5. p. 75]. Further
change in social institutions could never have been brought about unless this calculated
change in the moods and the minds of people had been brought about before that.

   The second issue concerns the remoulding of social institutions and organisations,
and the means to be adopted for the desired purposes. The Gurus describe God not only as
the Helper of the weak, the shelterless and the supportless, but also the Destroyer of the
oppressor. The Sixth Guru clearly stated that his sword was both for the help of the oppressed
and the destruction of the tyrants. It evidently implies that the Gurus contemplate
reconstruction and creation of alternative moral institutions. Naturally, alternative human
institutions can come up only by the substitution, remoulding or destruction of the old and
unwanted organisations. The lives of the Gurus are a clear pointer that, in their system,
change of environment to improve the moral climate in all fields is clearly envisaged and
sanctioned. In any system where moral life has an independent validity and an importance
of its own as a desirable end, the making of environmental and organisational changes for
that purpose would *ipso facto* be justified. The Gurus accordingly envisage a change in
environment and the remoulding of social organisations.

   An allied important issue is the means to be adopted for bringing about the desired
institutional and other changes. In God's world all form and progress are the product of
force; since no change is possible without the use of force. Again, as all encroachment on

the rights of others involves aggression, the same cannot be undone except by the use of an equal and opposite use of force. In fact, all action and activity, howsoever good, involve the use of force, because action and force are synonymous. Action not involving the use of force is a contradiction in terms. Therefore, except by some miracle, it is impossible to bring about a change in the social or institutional environment without the use of requisite force. It is significant to note that in the entire Guru Granth Sahib there is no miracle attributed to a Guru. In the Guru's system, only the miracle of deeds are performed. Logically, it is impossible to construct anything without destroying or remoulding the existing structure. Of course, the force used should not seek to serve any selfish or egoistic purpose.

In the background of the Indian tradition this issue about the use of force as the means for a moral end needs some clarification, since a lot of confusion among some scholars has arisen on this score. The alternative to the use of force or killing and meat-eating is the doctrine of *ahimsa*. *Ahimsa* has been advocated by most Indian religions, as was also done by Bhagat Kabir. But, it is of significant importance that it is Guru Nanak who opposed this doctrine. "Men discriminate not and quarrel over meat-eating. They know not what is flesh and what is non-flesh, and in what lies or does not lie a sin." [1. p. 1289]. In his hymns, the Guru details his views concerning the issue of means and the cant about meat-eating. He chides the Brahmins for their pretence about meat-eating. He describes how the ways and processes of life involve the transformation and the use of the flesh. He also explains that life is present in every grain of food and even in the fire-wood and the cow-dung which the Brahmins use for the purpose of purification. The Guru exposes the fallacy that life, much less a moral deed, is possible without the use of force. He means that immorality does not lie in the use of force, which is inevitable for all living, whether moral or immoral, but it lies in the direction or the purpose for which force is used. The significance and thrust of these hymns have often been missed. Evidently, from the very start Guru Nanak contemplated a change in the socio-moral atmosphere and institutions. The doctrine of *ahimsa* was a serious hurdle in disturbing or demolishing the *status quo*. Therefore, as a prophet of a new religion, he once and for all made it plain that, so long as one worked in the midst of social life, all arbitrary prejudices against meat-eating or the use of force as such were wrong and meaningless. It is very significant to note that the religious systems that insisted on *ahimsa* were either ascetic or monastic, or suggested withdrawal from the world. The Radical Bhagats were neither monastic nor ascetic, but they never considered social involvement to be a duty or a field of spiritual training and growth. Kabir deems the world to be a trap from which deliverance has to be sought. His attitude towards woman is exactly like that of monastic or ascetic religions. While referring to the Bhakti cults of India, Ray says that these had completely surrendered to the *status quo* and the socio-political establishment of the day. All we wish to emphasise is that no religious system that suggests the love of man as an essential part of the love of God can accept or suggest the limitation of *ahimsa* for work in the moral or the social field. *Ahimsa* is inevitably linked with religious systems that have a world-view of life-negation and are unconcerned with socio-political changes. It is, in fact, an ascetic tool, being the product or a part of an ascetic or monastic methodology.

It may be argued that great pacifists like Mahatma Gandhi successfully employed non-violence as the means of bringing about socio-political changes. But, it is now well-known that when the Mahatma had to face the major challenge of his life, he found himself helpless. The Mahatma being the greatest exponent of non-violence in modern times, when the Second World War broke out, the pacifists of the world looked up to him for a lead. But the Mahatma could furnish or suggest no non-violent or effective remedy. *Ahimsa* could be of little help to him in stopping the holocaust. The situation became so frustrating for the Mahatma that he even thought of committing suicide so that if he could do nothing to stop the destruction, he would at least not live to see the misery caused by it. [2. p. 34]. The two occasions when he had to discard *ahimsa* as a tool are quite well-known, namely, when he agreed to the Congress accepting the responsibility of the war effort, and, again, when in 1947, he had no objection to the entry of Indian forces in Kashmir for its defence. Another great pacifist, too, had to take a contrasted stand when faced with a crucial issue. During the First World War Bertrand Russel opposed the idea of war and violence to the point of being arrested in pursuance of his pacifist beliefs. But, later, after the Second World War, Russel himself suggested an attack against Soviet Russia before it became a major atomic power and a threat or menace to the entire world. [3. pp. 53-57].

The issue needs some further clarifications. Reasons and force are two tools available to man for work and progress in the socio-political sphere. Without the use of both these means, it is impossible to bring about any social change. In fact a high sense of reason or discrimination is the chief faculty that distinguishes man from other animals. We have seen that the Gurus clearly indicate reason to be a good instrument of religious progress. "By the use of discrimination of intellect one serves God. By discrimination one is honoured. By intellect and study one understands things." "It is the sense of discrimination that makes one charitable. This is the right way, rest is all wrong." [1. p. 1245]. "Man is blessed with the light of reason and discrimination." "One in fear of God and discriminating between good and bad, appears sweet to God." [1. p. 763]. Yet in the history of civilisation human reason or intellect has also been used as the greatest instrument of oppression and destruction. Human rationality has been called a convenient and clever cloak to cover man's bestiality. Does it imply that we should altogether discard reason as a useful tool for religious progress. We have already noted what is the answer given by the Gurus on this point. The fact is that both reason and force are neutral tools that can be used both for good and evil, for construction and destruction. The Gurus unambiguously accept the use of both of them as the means of religious functioning and progress. In doing so they made major departure from the earlier Bhakti and religious traditions. This break with the past was the direct result of their new religious methodology and goals and consequent social involvement and objectives.

All consciousness or life is nothing but a centre of perfection, deliberation, activity and organisation. The Gurus accepted life, the world and its responsibilities in toto. "Despise not the world for it is the creation of God," says the Guru. As the instruments or the servants of God, they had to carry out God's Will in helping the weak and destroying the oppressor. Their spiritual system, therefore, involved the use of all the available tools, including reason and force, for the purposeful progress of man and his organising consciousness. According to the Guru, the malady is not the use of reason and force, which can both be used and abused, but the egoistic consciousness of man, which is narrow and inadequate in its perception and partial in its outlook and functioning, because it stands alienated from the Basic Reality. Therefore, the way out is the development of a higher consciousness in order to become a whole man or superman with a sense of kinship and total responsibility towards all beings. The higher the consciousness, the truer its perception and the greater its capacity for organisation and functioning in order to execute God's mission. Man's greatest problems today are poverty, disease and wars. Undoubtedly, these need the greatest organisational effort in the socio-political field. The diagnosis of the Gurus is that the egoistic man has neither the perception nor the vision nor even the organisational, moral and spiritual capacity to solve the problems of man. It is only the religious man with a higher consciousness, who alone can fulfil God's mission of creating the Kingdom of God on earth. The Guru indicates the path of progress or evolution : "God created first Himself then *haumain*, third *maya* and fourth the state of poise and bliss." [1. p. 113]. And in the second and third stages man's development is only partial. The aim is the achievement of the fourth stage. In Sikhism, the development of union with God is not an end in itself. The goal is the development of a higher consciousness, so as to discharge the total responsibility devolving on man in order to create a world of harmony and happiness.

The Gurus say that human problems cannot be solved at the third stage of man's development. These can be dealt with adequately only at the fourth stage. And, this development of a higher consciousness is for a religious purpose. That purpose or mission is epitomised in the lives of the Gurus. Guru Hargobind in his talk with Saint Ramdas made it clear that what Guru Nanak had given up was mammon and not the world, the enrichment of which, in accordance with the attributive Will of God, was the mission of the Gurus, as also of every God-conscious man. In such a righteous world alone the problems of poverty, misery, disease, war and conflict can be solved. The development of superman is, therefore, the spiritual purpose for which life has been striving.

REFERENCES

1. Guru Granth Sahib.
2. Maulana Abdul Kalam Azad : *India Wins Freedom.*
3. Russel, Bertrand : *Unpopular Essays.*
4. Hari Ram Gupta : *History Of The Sikh Gurus.*
5. Juergensmeyer, M., (Ed.) : *Sikh Studies.*

4

NAAM IN SIKHISM

DALJEET SINGH

1. INTRODUCTORY

Every religion has its world-view on which are based its concepts about Reality, the place of man in the universe, ethics and human goals. All students of Sikhism know that the concept of *Naam* is fundamental to the gospel of Guru Granth Sahib and the entire structure of its theology. In fact, Sikhism has often been called the *Naam Maarg* or the way of *Naam*. It is in this context that we shall endeavour to trace the salient features and implications of this concept, which we believe, holds the key to the understanding of the message of the Sikh Gurus, their religious and social ideas and their world-view.

At the outset, we should like to make one point clear about the language and the various traditional terms used by the Sikh Gurus. Since they were conveying their message to the mass of the people, both Hindus and Muslims, with a view to evoking a response in the very depths of their hearts, they have, for obvious reasons, used in their hymns the then current words and symbols from Indian, Persian and Arabic languages. And yet, one thing is patent even from a cursory study of the Guru Granth Sahib that the Gurus have, as was essential for the proper understanding of a new gospel, made the meaning of each concept, symbol and term employed by them, unambiguously clear. Many a time the meaning of such words is entirely their own. Accordingly, we have refrained from tracing the meaning of *Ncam* to its traditional usage and background. In fact, such an exercise could be even misleading and wasteful. We shall, therefore, base our arguments and inferences about *Naam* on the hymns in Guru Granth Sahib and the accepted facts about the lives of the Sikh Gurus.

2. DEFINITION

Let us now try broadly to indicate how *Naam* has been used in Guru Granth Sahib, where it appears in a majority of hymns. The Sikh Gurus have given the word *Naam*, a distinct and significant meaning which is far different from that of mere 'Name' or 'psychic factors' as understood in *Naam-Roopa* in traditional literature. [5. p. 169]. The basic definition of *Naam* as contained in *Sukhmani* and other hymns in Guru Granth Sahib is given below :

(i)   '*Naam* sustains all regions and universes, all thought, knowledge and consciousness, all skies and stars, all forces and substances, all continents and spheres. *Naam* emancipates those who accept it in their heart. He, on whom is His Grace, is yoked to *Naam,* and he reaches the highest state of development.' [1. p. 284].

(ii) '*Naam* is the Creator of everything. To be divorced from *Naam* is death.' [1. p. 603]. 'All is created by *Naam*.' [1. p. 753]. '*Naam* gives form to everything and through *Naam* comes all Wisdom or Light.' [1. p. 946].

(iii) '*Naam* extends to all creation. There is no place or space where *Naam* is not.' [1. p. 4].

(iv) '*Naam* is the 'Nine Treasures' and Nectar (*amrita*). It permeates the body.' [1. p. 293].

(v)   '*Naam*, the immaculate, is unfathomable. How can it be known? *Naam* is within us. How to get to it ? It is *Naam* that works everywhere and permeates all space. The perfect Guru awakens your heart to the vision of *Naam*. It is by the Grace of God that one meets such an Enlightener.' [1. p. 1242].

From the above verses it is clear that the Gurus do not use the word *Naam* in any restrictive sense, of its being a psychic factor or mere consciousness, but refer to it as the Highest Power, creating, informing, supporting and working the entire creation. In short, *Naam* is the Reality, supporting and directing the created worlds or the entire cosmos. There are numerous verses in Guru Granth Sahib where *Naam* and God have been described synonymously. Both *Naam* and God have been mentioned as "the Creator of the Cosmos", "the Sustainer of the Universe", "Permeating and informing all things, beings, space and interspace", "the Treasure of virtues, values", "the Support of the helpless", "the Giver of peace and bliss", "Eternal", "Perfect", "Unfathomable", "Friend", "Master" and "Emancipator." The highest state of man is mentioned as the one when he lives and works in tune with God or *Naam*, often called God's *Naam*. We, therefore, find that God and *Naam* are real, eternal and unfathomable. The Sikh Gurus have repeatedly emphasized, as is also stated in the very opening verse of Guru Granth Sahib, that God is one, *Ek Oamkaar*, and no second entity, as in the case of the *Sankhya* system, is at all postulated. The Guru says, "My Lord is the only One. He is the only One, (understand) brother, He is the only One." [1. p. 350]. This unambiguously leads us to conclude that God and *Naam* are one and the same, and the latter may be called the immanent or qualitative aspect of God, since God has been described both as unmanifest (*nirguna*) and the Creator, and Ocean of values.

In view of the above, we should define *Naam* as the Dynamic Immanence of God or the Reality sustaining and working the manifest world of force and form. It is on the basis of these fundamentals that we should like to trace and understand some important concepts and conclusions, ideas and institutions, trends and traditions in Sikhism and its socio-religious way of life.

3. NAAM AND COSMOLOGY

The Guru writes, "the self-existent God manifested Himself into *Naam*. Second came the Creation of the universe. He permeates it and revels in His creation." "God created the world of life, He planted *Naam* in it and made it the place for righteous activity." [1. p. 463].

Thus, according to the concept of *Naam* and the hymns quoted earlier in this regard, God created the world and in His immanent aspect, as *Naam*, is informing and working it. Only one entity, namely, God, is envisaged and the world, in time and space, is His creation, the same being supported and directed by *Naam*. Let us see if this cosmological view is also supported by other verses in Guru Granth Sahib.

In the very opening verse of Guru Granth Sahib, God is described as the Sole-One, His *Naam* as Real, Creator-Lord, ... Timeless Person, One that is not born, Self-existent. [1. p. 1]. The Gurus have stated at a number of places that there was a stage when the Transcendent God was by Himself; and it is later that He started His Creative Activity. In *Sidh Gosht*, in answer to a question as to where was the Transcendent God before the stage of creation, Guru Nanak replied, "To think of the Transcendent Lord in that state is to enter the realm of wonder. Even at that stage of *sunn* (void), He permeated all that void." [1. p. 940]. The Guru, in effect, means that to matters that are beyond the spacio-temporal world, it would be wrong to apply the spacio-temporal logic, and yet man knows of no other logic or language. Perforce, He has to be explained, howsoever inadequately or symbolically, only in terms of that language. That is why the Guru has cautioned us against the pitfalls and inadequacy of human logic and language to comprehend the Timeless One. All the same, the Guru has mentioned the state when the Transcendent God was all by Himself and there was no creation. The Gurus say, "When there was no form in sight, how could there be good or bad actions? When God was in the Self-Absorbed state, there could be no enmity or conflict. When God was all by Himself, there could be no attachment or misunderstanding. Himself He starts the creation. He is the Sole-Creator, there is no second One." [1. p. 290]. "For millions of aeons, the Timeless One was by Himself. There was no substance or space, no day or night (i.e., no time,) no stars or galaxies; God was in His Trance." [1. p. 1035]. "God was by Himself and there was nothing else ...... There was no love or devotion, nor was His Creative Power in operation ...... When He willed, He created the Universe." [1. p. 1036]. The same idea is expressed in these words, "When He willed, the creation appeared." [1. p. 18]. Again, in answer to the question of the Yogis, "When there was no sign and no form, where was the Word (Logos) and how was He identified with Truth?" [1. p. 945]. The Guru replied, "When there was no form, no sign, no individuation, the Word in its essence abided in the Transcendent God; when there was no earth, no sky, (time or space), the Lord permeated everything. All distinctions, all forms then abided in the Wondrous Word. No one is pure without Truth. Ineffable is this gospel." [1. pp. 945-6].

In short, the Gurus say that before He created form, He was Formless; before He was Immanent, He was Transcendent only : and yet, all immanence, expression, creativity were inherent in Him, and so was His Word, in essence.

In the *Jap(u)*, where a picture of the realm of creativity is given, the Guru writes, "In the region of Truth is God, where He perpetually creates and watches the universe with His benevolent eye, deliberating and directing according to as He Wills." Further, it is stated, "In the region of Creativity (*Karam*), only God's Power or Force is at work." [1. p. 8]. Again, "Of the region of construction or effort, the medium of expression is form. Here most fantastic forms are fashioned, including consciousness, perception, mind and intellect." Further still, "Innumerable creations are fashioned, myriads are the forms, myriads are the moons, suns, regions." [1. pp. 7-8]. These hymns also indicate how the process of creativity or a becoming world started, and is being sustained and directed by Benevolent God.

In all the above quotations from Guru Granth Sahib, the same idea is expressed, namely, that God is the Sole Entity, Who in His Creative Urge, has produced the Cosmos, which He, in His immanent aspect, *Naam*, is sustaining vigilantly and directing benevolently according to His Will. In the created world no other entity, like *Prakriti* in Sankhya and other dualistic systems, is assumed. While the world is real and is directed by Immanent God, at no stage is the separate independent existence of matter accepted directly or by implication.

4. METAPHYSICAL IMPLICATION OF NAAM

We have seen that according to the concept of *Naam* and the hymns already quoted in this regard, God created Himself and *Naam*, and at the second place was created the universe. Further, this universe is being sustained and directed by God as *Naam* or His Immanent Aspect. This concept of God being the Sole Entity and being the Creator God (*karta purakh*) is so fundamental in the Sikh theology, that it is mentioned in the very opening line (*Mool Mantra*) of Guru Granth Sahib and in the beginning of almost every section and sub-section of it. Both the doctrine of *Naam* and *Mool Mantra* clearly point out the theology of Sikhism being monotheistic. Let us, therefore, try to see whether this conclusion of ours is correct and whether many of those hurriedly-begotten views about Sikhism being pantheistic, Vedantic, Sankhyic, Yogic or Buddhistic have any validity. A few of the reasons supporting our conclusion are as under :

(i)   Throughout the hymns of Guru Granth Sahib, nothing is more significant than the acceptance of the Creator-creature relation between God and man. Invariably, God has been addressed as 'Thou', 'Mother', 'Father', 'Brother', 'Beloved', 'Lord', or 'Husband.' In fact, a majority of the hymns in Guru Granth Sahib are in the form of prayers addressed to God. In the Sikh tradition, two things are firmly established, having the sanction of the Gurus. First, every ceremony, religious or social, ends with an *Ardas* or supplication to God, invoking His Grace. Secondly, at the time of initiation ceremony (*amrit),* a Sikh is enjoined upon to recite or hear daily *Jap(u)*, *Jaap(u)*, ten *Sawayaas, Sodar(u), Rahiras* and *Sohila*, besides reading or hearing of Guru Granth Sahib (Sikh Rahit Maryada, Shiromani Gurdwara Parbandhak Committee, Amritsar, 1970, p. 35). We thus see that both in the hymns of Guru Granth Sahib, and the Sikh tradition and practice, this Creator-creature relation is never forgotten. So much so that the Guru calls himself as "the lowliest of the low," [1. p. 15] and never does he mention another person as 'That is Thou.' According to tradition, the Fifth Guru declined to include in Guru Granth Sahib a hymn by a contemporary saint, Bhagat Kaanhaa, saying, "I am He, O, I am the same," because this hymn was felt by the Guru to be evidently contrary to the Sikh thesis that man is not and can never be God, though he can be His instrument.

(ii) The arguments advanced to show the Creator-creature relation in Sikhism and the importance of prayer, *mutatis mutandis*, apply also to God having a Personality. We need hardly state that this idea of Personality in Theism is not analogous to the idea of limited personality in man, who is a finite being. In the very opening line of Guru Granth Sahib, God is mentioned as the Creator Person, the Timeless Person (*karta purakh, akaal moorat*). In fact, in all devotional and mystic religions, the idea of Personality of God is inherent, since devotion involves God and a devotee.

In Sikhism, the idea of Will (*hukam, razaa*) of God in relation to the created world is as fundamental as in other theistic religions like Christianity and Islam. In fact, both the words *hukam* and *razaa* used in Guru Granth Sahib are Arabic in origin. The idea of Will is inalienably linked with the idea of Personality of God, the Creator, Who alone can have a Will. In reality, we know that Will and *Naam* are virtually synonymous, both being the Immanence of God. While this point will be elaborated later on, it is well-known that in Sikhism the highest ideal for man is to 'carry out the Will of God' [1. p. 1] or to link oneself with *Naam*.

Another fundamental characteristic of Sikhism showing the Personality of God is His Grace. One of the chief points made out in Guru Granth Sahib is that nothing happens without God's Grace. While it is stated in the hymn of *dharam khand*, which lays down man's duties in life, that man's assessment will be entirely according to his deeds, it is clearly mentioned that 'final approval will be only by God's Grace.' [1. p. 7]. The idea of Personality, Will and Grace of God being basic to Sikhism, too, underlines its theistic character.

(iii) The verses quoted earlier mention nature as the Creation of God, and not His Emanation or Extension. Obviously, nature is a changing or becoming world, limited by space and time, and cannot be eternal like God, who is beyond time (*akaal moorat*). Whereas God is Self-Existent or Self-created (*swai bhang*), nature is the creation of God. While everything in nature is changing, i.e., is born and dies, God is never born (*ajooni*). This is the reason why in Sikhism the doctrine of incarnation (*avatarhood*) or God taking the human form is strictly denied, and is considered heretical; so much so that Guru Gobind Singh described any person holding such an idea as accursed, he being only a servant of God. [2.]. This is also in line with the hymns in the *Jap(u)* quoted earlier. Here, the world is up to the Region of Creativity (*karam khand*) initiated through the medium of energy or power (*jor*). As indicated in the hymns of *saram khand* and *gyaan khand*, a fantastic multiplicity of forms, shapes and things, including the moulding of consciousness, sense perceptions, mind, intellect, etc., are described. Everyone knows that in Sikh theology, the highest form of being is the mystic (*bhagat*). In *Japji*, the Guru distinctly mentions, or rather limits the presence of these God-conscious or God-filled beings (*jin main Raam rahiaa bharpoor*) only up to the Region of Creativity, but never beyond it, i.e., not in the Region of Truth or God (*sach khand vase Nirankaar*). The Universe is the creation of God but not identical with God, which is the basic distinction between monotheism and Indian monism or pantheism.

(iv) At a number of places in Guru Granth Sahib have the Gurus described symbolically the state of God when the creation was not there. All this indicates that God is Transcendent as well, and that He is not co-terminus or identical with His creation. Not only does the creation not exhaust God, but He is both prior to and Transcendent to His creation. And God's transcendence could be envisaged only under a monotheistic system and never in pantheism.

(v) An argument has been raised in favour of the supposed pantheistic character of Sikhism because of the Gurus', frequent mention of the immanent character of God in the created world. The Gurus have clearly emphasized the transcendental character of God by saying that the world was created in time and space, and the Transcendent God had been there while the world was uncreated, and, for that matter, God's immanent character was unexpressed. We refer to the hymn quoted earlier in this regard. It is also stated that the Word was in God when there was no universe or form. The expression of *Naam* was prior to the creation of the universe, i.e., 'God manifested into *Naam,* and at the second place the world was created.' As stated already, *Naam* is mentioned as the Creator and Director of the world. It is true that the Guru quite often mentions God as informing the universe. But in no scripture has the distinction between the Transcendent and the Immanent aspects of God been made more clear than in Guru Granth Sahib, because God's Immanence has been given separate names, i.e., of *Naam*, Will and Word. Evidently, all immanence can be expressed only in relation to the realm of creation; i.e., when God's immanence as *Naam* creates, sustains and moves the world of name and form; when God's immanence as His Will controls and directs the becoming world; when His immanence as His Word informs and supports the created universe. In other words, in Guru Granth Sahib both the transcendent and the immanent aspects of God are clearly specified and distinguished so as to avoid any confusion or hasty conclusion that Sikhism is pantheistic. We have already seen that in Sikhism the immanence of God in relation to the becoming world does not exhaust God and that is why God's immanent aspect has almost invariably been called His *Naam*, His Will, His Word. True, at a number of places, the Guru describes God as informing the river, the fish, the boat, and everything. Perhaps, it is such verses as these that have led some to the superficial conclusion of Sikhism being pantheistic. But, all these verses are only a symbolic or another way of expressing the immanence of God. In modern monotheistic theologies, including Christian and Islamic, God's Transcendence and His Immanence in the created world are accepted. Even in Islam, God's Immanence is referred to as, "Is He not closer (to you) than the vein of the neck." [6.]. Such verses as these do not at all indicate anything beyond the immanence of God, or anything contrary to the doctrine of *Naam*. Obviously, God's immanence (His *Naam* and Will) is manifested and exercised only in relation to the created and becoming world. This description of His immanence and its operation, metaphoric as it is, can mislead no one to any erroneous inference, especially because the Gurus have clearly stated that the immanent God in the universe does not exhaust God, and He is transcendent too. "He that permeates all hearts (i.e., Immanent) is Unmanifest too." [1. p. 939]. "He is pervading every where (Immanent) and yet He is beyond everything, beyond pleasure and pain (Transcendent)." [1. p. 784]. "He informs everything and yet is separate too." [1. p. 294]. "Having created the world, He stands in the midst of it and yet is separate from it" [1. p. 788].

(vi)   One of the chief objections to any pantheistic theology in the West is the lack of any ethical content and impact in any such view of the universe. Pantheistic philosophies, whether in the East, as in the case of *Upanishads*, or in the West, as in the case of Spinoza and Schopenhauer, lead to pessimism and fatalism, and lack of moral effort and responsibility on the part of the individual. The disasterous ethical consequences of pantheistic doctrines, including monism that downgrades the reality of the phenomenal world, are too well-known to be detailed here. In this context, we may like to see what is the ethical content and impact of the doctrine of *Naam*. In no religious system is the emphasis on ethical conduct greater than in Guru Granth Sahib, where "truthful living or conduct has been declared higher than Truth itself." [1. p. 62]. In *Jap(u)*, the Guru says that man's final assessment and approval before God will depend entirely on his deeds in this world. [1. p. 7]. Further, 'egoistic conduct' has been called 'the opposite of *Naam*', [1. p. 560] which, as we find, involves selfless and virtuous conduct, *Naam* being the treasure of all virtues. Similarly, moral living is stressed, since the ideal in life is 'to carry out the Will of God', God's Will and *Naam* being virtually synonymous. Judged from the emphasis on virtuous life (the matter will be detailed while dealing with the subject of goal, ethics, etc.) and moral responsibility in Sikhism and its anti-deterministic view, we should evidently conclude that Sikhism is monotheistic and not pantheistic.

(vii)   There is a philosophic controversy whether or not mysticism of all kinds is monotheistic or pantheistic. Sikhism is undeniably based on a mystical experience. But so are religions like Christianity and Islam which are fanatically monotheistic. It is well-known that many of the great Christian and Muslim mystics have been dubbed as heretical, because their description of their mystical experiences could be misconstrued to support a pantheistic view of God, even though these mystics were devotedly religious and deeply reverential to their respective Prophets. Hence, the controversy hardly affects our argument.

True, some symbolic descriptions in Guru Granth Sahib, which, when seen out of their context, and not seen against the overall background of Sikh theology and the overwhelming scriptural evidence to the contrary, could be misconstrued to suggest pantheistic inferences. But, such a view would obviously be not only far-fetched, but also opposed to the general thesis of the Gurus, which they themselves actually lived and demonstrated for 240 years, and the concept of *Naam*. The metaphysical implication of the doctrine of *Naam* clearly gives a monotheistic import to Sikhism, which view we find is unmistakably in accordance with the accepted concepts in Guru Granth Sahib.

5. NAAM AND THE REALITY OF THE WORLD AND INTEREST IN LIFE

The greatest implication of the doctrine is in its proclaiming the dynamic reality and authenticity of the world and life. "God created the world of life and planted *Naam* therein, making it the place of righteous activity." [1. p. 463]. "God created the world and permeated it with His Light." [1. p. 930]. Since *Naam*, God's Immanence, has not only created the world, but is also supporting, controlling and directing it, the same cannot be unreal or illusory. In fact, *Naam's* immanence in this world guarantees its being a place of righteous activity, and not being a fruitless, unwanted or capricious creation. In one form or the other, this idea about the reality of the world gets repeated expression and emphasis in Guru Granth Sahib. "True are Thy worlds, true are Thy universes, true Thy forms Thou createth. True are Thy doings. This world is the Abode of the True One and He resides in it." [1. p. 463]. "True is He, True is His creation." [1. p. 294]. "Human body is the Temple of God." [1. p. 952]. "Beauteous, O Farid, are the garden of earth and the human body." [1. p. 966]. "Deride not the world, it is the creation of God." [1. p. 611].

It naturally follows from this doctrine that the world is real and God is greatly interested in it, since He has created it. He 'revels in His creation' [1. p. 463] and is sustaining and directing it. In *Japji,* God is described as 'perpetually creating the world and benevolently nurturing His creation.' [1. p. 8]. 'God is the One, Who works through winds, waters and fire.' [1. p. 930]. This emphatic assertion about the authenticity of the world is a clear departure from the Indian religious tradition, and is, for that matter, radical in its implication. The Gurus were extremely conscious of this fundamental change they were making, and that is why, both in their lives and in their hymns, they have been laying great and repeated stress on this aspect of their spiritual thesis, lest they should be misunderstood on this issue. Living in this world is not a bondage (*bandhan*) for them, but a great privilege and opportunity. Not only is God benevolently directing the world in which He is immanent, but each one of us is 'yoked to His task and each is assigned a duty to perform.' [1. p. 736]. All this clearly indicates God's or *Naam's* plan and purpose in His creative activity.

This idea is also clear from the Gurus' reference, again and again, to God's Will working in this becoming universe. The very idea of a God of Will clearly presupposes and implies a direction, and a goal in the creative movement. The persistent interest of God in the creative movement is also obvious from the fact that the Guru calls Him 'the Protector' (*raakhaa*), 'Father' (*pita*), 'King-emperor' (*Padshah*) and a 'Just Administrator' (*adlee*). In *Japji* also, the Guru emphasizes the idea that God adjudges each according to his deeds in this world.

Naam has been described as the 'Treasure of Virtues and Qualities.' As a loving God with social and other attributes, He has been referred to as 'Father and Mother' (*maataa, pitaa*), 'Brother' (*bharaataa*), 'Friend' (*mittar*), 'Helper of the poor' (*gareeb nivaaz*), 'Shelter of the shelterless' (*nithaaviaan daa thaan*), 'Help to the Helpless' (*nidhariaan di dhar*), 'Remover of suffering and pain' (*dukh bhanjan*), 'Merciful' (*raheem*), etc. God with attributes leads to three inferences. First, qualities have a meaning only in relation to spacio-temporal world, since all perfection is static and all qualities are relative, capable of expression only in a changing universe. We have already seen that when God was by Himself and the world was not there, the question of good or bad, saved or saviour, love or devotion did not arise. *Naam*, being the source of all virtues, the world becomes an essential and integral part of the plan of *Naam*; since without a world for expression there could be no Will and no attributive aspect of God. Thus, *Naam* and the world are conjoint. Secondly, qualities in *Naam* indicate clearly — and this is the most important aspect — the direction of the progress and the ideal to be pursued by man in this world. Thirdly, all this ensures a logical and deep interest of *Naam* in the empirical world, since its attributive expression can be made only in it. That is also exactly the reason why the Gurus call the world real. Consequently, their message and mission also relate to this world, wherein alone these can be fulfilled. For the same reason, the Sikh Gurus' deep interest in all aspects of life, including socio-political aspects, can be directly traced to *Naam*, whose devotees they were. No feeling or prayer is expressed with greater depth and intensity than the one for the 'gift of *Naam*.' Now, *Naam* being the Benevolent Supporter and Director of the world, what can be the gift of *Naam* to the devotee, except that of an enlightened, loving and creative interest in the world and in its development. How can one claim to be a devotee of *Naam* and ask for its gift or link with it, and yet, decline to toe the line of *Naam*, namely, of nurturing and furthering the process of creativity and construction in the world rather than becoming an ascetic or a drop out. That is why the Gurus have strongly condemned all ascetic and escapist practices. They say, "One reaches not Truth by remaining motionless like trees and stones, nor by being sawn alive." [1. p. 952]. "In vain are yogic practices, without *Naam* life is a waste." [1. p. 905]. "All yogic austerities, rituals, trance, etc., are in vain; real yoga is in treating alike all beings. " [1. p. 730]. "O Yogi, you are sitting in a trance, but you discriminate and have a sense of duality. You beg from door to door, are you not ashamed of it ?" [1. p. 886]. "Jainic ascetism", or "even if the body is cut into bits, does not efface the dirt of ego." [1. p. 256].

What kind of life the Gurus recommended will be detailed while dealing with the subject of goal, but it would be pertinent to quote here the Guru's dictum that "by despising the world one gets not to God." [1. p. 962].

In Buddhism, *nirvana* and *samsara* are opposite entities. [7.]. In fact, in all Indian traditions, except in the case of the saints of the Radical Bhakti movement, worldly life had normally to be given up in order to pursue the spiritual ideal. But according to Guru Granth Sahib, it is not *Naam* and *samsara* that are opposed, but *Naam* and *haumain* (egoism); [1. pp. 560,1092] it is not worldly activity, as such, that has to be given up, but it is only egoistic and selfish activities that have to be shed. [1. pp. 522, 1246, 661]. Otherwise, belief in a God of attributes, which involves expression in the world of man, becomes meaningless.

The best undestanding of the kind of interest in life the Gurus recommended for their disciples is gained from the lives they lived themselves. We shall revert to this point in detail while dealing with the issue of goal. Suffice it to say here that the Gurus, in harmony with the ethics of *Naam*, went in for full participation in life. For them it would have been incongruous on one hand to call life as real and on the other hand to fight shy of taking up the challenges of the socio-political life of their times.

All this was an ideological, deliberate and clear departure from the Indian religious tradition and the Gurus gave a firm lead on this new path. While eulogizing the role of the Sikh Gurus in this regard, N. Ray laments the abject surrender to the vicious status quo on the part of the saints of the Bhakti movement. [4.].

6. NAAM AND ETHICS

On one hand, *Naam* being (a) the Sustainer and Director of the universe, (b) opposed to egoism (*haumain*) and (c) treasure of all qualities, lays down the standard of its ethics and on the other, points out that the universe is the plane and place where the qualities of *Naam* have to be expressed, so as to counteract and remove the vices of egoism and the practice of a sense of duality. Egoism involves separatism, selfishness, and individualism leading to the vices of greed, anger, pride, passion, conflict, wars, etc. 'The removal of duality is the way of God,' [1. p. 126] *Naam* being the opposite of ego, the same has been indicated as the only remedy for egoism, pain and frustration. [1. p. 1205]. In the same context, the Gurus have mentioned two sets of people — one, the self-faced (*manmukh*) or egoistic, following the ethics of egoism and selfishness, and the other, the superman or God-faced (*gurmukh*), following the ethics of *Naam* in all phases of human activity. The ethics of *Naam* chooses its duties, virtues and value-system as consonant with the standard of *Naam* or a unitary view of life. Following are some of the verses in Guru Granth Sahib condemning egoism and duality and instead recommending the virtues and spirit of *Naam* so as to avoid and eliminate the vices of egoism :

"In the grip of *maya*, we grab what belongs to others." [1. p. 715].

"Man gathers riches by making others miserable." [1. p. 889].

"Human passions, ego, duality lead us away from God." [1. p. 647].

"God does not come near a person hard of heart and with a sense of duality." [1. p. 751]. "Some people shun meat, but devour men." [1. p. 1289]. "With God, only the deeds that one does in the world are of any avail." [1. p. 1383]. "Goodness, righteousness, virtue and the giving up of vice are the ways to realize the essence of God." [1. p. 418]. 'God's riches belong to all, and it is the world that makes distinctions." [1. p. 1171].

Thus, the entire progress of man is from being an egoist to being a man of *Naam* by shedding egoism and accepting the ethics of *Naam,* i.e., from being self-centred to being God-centred.

7. NAAM AND HUMAN GOAL

It is in the field of human goals that the world-view of *Naam* and its logic make a basic departure from the traditional Indian view on the subject. On this problem, the Gurus' views have not only been made clear and precise in their doctrine of *Naam* throughout Guru Granth Sahib, but these have also been emphasized and exemplified by their lives, which embody an unambiguous lesson on the issue. We shall, therefore, attempt to consider the subject from all the three angles, namely :

(a) the doctrine of *Naam*,

(b) other tenets and principles *laid* in Guru Granth Sahib,

(c) the lives that the Gurus led so as to lay down the ideal for others to follow.

(a) The Doctrine Of Naam :

Naam, the Ever-Creative Immanence of God, is engaged in directing the universe, which is real, to become a qualityful world. Every student of Guru Granth Sahib knows that the theme of a large number of prayers and hymns therein is a longing for the gift of *Naam*, or to be linked with *Naam*, e.g., "I am beholden to Him who enlightens me with *Naam*." "My Guru makes *Naam* permeate me." [1. p. 40]. "Let me not forget *Naam*, rest is all greed." [1. p. 1247]. "I beg from You the gift of *Naam*." [1. p. 289]. "He reaches the highest stage whom God benevolently yokes to His *Naam*." [1. p. 284]. "To ask for any boon other than *Naam* is to invite pain." [1. p. 958]. "To be imbued with *Naam* is the essence of true living." "Pray, link me to God." [1. p. 701].

Accordingly, the highest ideal under the *Naam Marga* is to be yoked or linked to *Naam* in order to take the world of man to a qualityful goal. In this context, the significance of a God of attributes has already been explained. *Naam* being the opposite of egoism, this progressive movement is towards an ideal in which selfishness and egoism disappear and qualities of *Naam* are practised. And to be linked to *Naam* only means being its instrument and sharing the responsibility of this creative and qualityful development in the world. One imbued with *Naam* not only takes part in the world without a sense of duality and selfishness, but also strives to create a beautiful world of harmony and quality. Egoism is the cause of all pain, suffering and conflict, which hinder progress towards the goal. As against it, the practice of *Naam* and its ethics, namely, the unitary view of life, is both the ideal and the sovereign remedy for all ills and evils (*sarab rog kaa aukhad Naam*), and the way to human development. "Destroy evil and you become a perfect man." [1. p. 404]. "Give up evil, do right and you realise the essence of God." [1. p. 418].

(b) Other Tenets And Principals In Guru Granth Sahib :

Let us see if the same ideal is prescribed under the other doctrines of Guru Granth Sahib. In answer to a specific question as to how to remove the wall of falsehood obstructing man's progress to become an ideal or a true man, the Guru gives a categoric reply : "By working according to the Will of God." [1. p. 1]. Again the same ideal of deeds (not of words, rituals, ascetism or even of yogic discipline) is prescribed in the hymns of cosmography quoted earlier about the role of man on earth. It is pointed out that "all assessment is made in accordance with the deeds and doings of man ...... By His Grace only the righteous get the insignia of God's approval." [1. p. 7]. In Sikhism, God is the Creator of the Universe and invariably the prayer is to be of service to Him. "May I have millions of hands to serve Thee. Service is the way to cross the hurdles of life." [1. p. 781]. "Be ever alert in the service of God. Serve God every moment and relax not." [1. p. 647-8]. This in effect means to be of service in the universe, which is the authentic creative activity of God, who is directing it towards a goal and with a purpose. This service in the universe is really the selfless and qualityful service of all who have to be looked upon alike. [1. p. 77]. The Guru says, "Where there is egoism, God is not; where God is, there cannot be any egoism." [1. p. 1092].

In *Sidh Gosht*, Guru Nanak has very clearly specified his mission and goal and thrown full light on the issue as to how he would lead his followers across. He says, "With the help of other God-conscious persons, I shall help man to remove his alienation from *Naam* and God and assist him to cross the difficult hurdles in life." [1. p. 939]. Guru Nanak has thus clarified as to what he means by 'carrying out His Will' and executing God's mission of creating a society of God-centred men. The Guru says, "The God-man achieves the goal and makes all others do so." [1. p. 125]. That is exactly the reason why the Gurus have likened themselves to a 'servant of God,' 'a soldier in God's Legion,' or 'a wrestler in the cause of God.' The world being the authentic creation of God, supported by His immanence, the service of God means the service of His creation, namely, the world, this life and man. It is in this light that the Guru's hymns in *Sidh Gosht* and elsewhere have to be understood.

Here we may lay stress on two very important and relevant points : (i) The Gurus have repeatedly indicated a continuing process of development, evolution and progress in the empirical world, and (ii) they clearly point out that further progress from animal-men or egoistic men to supermen or God-centred men is not only possible, but is also aimed at. In the hymns of cosmography, already quoted, an ascending order of creation, form, or evolution is indicated. The Gurus have stated that individuation was created by God and 'slowly there has been growth from small organisms, insects, etc., to animals, and finally to the present animal-man, with his subtle sense of perception, discrimination, reason, introspection.' [1. pp. 946, 466]. "For several births (you) were a mere worm, for several births an insect, for several births a fish, animal, ... after ages have you the glory of being man." [1. p. 176]. " ...... after passing through myriads of species, one is blest with the human form." [1. p. 631]. "God created you out of a drop of water and breathed life in you. He endowed you with the light of reason, discrimination and wisdom ...... From a sinner He made you virtuous and the lord of all beings. Now it is up to you to fulfil or not to fulfil your destiny." [1. p. 913]. Further progress of man or animal-man, as stated in the hymn of *Dharam khand*, depends entirely on the deeds of the individuals. Till man came on the scene, it was not possible for life to outgrow its animal existence and alienation from God. So far, like other animals, man too has been living an animal existence. But, the Guru emphasizes the opportunity available to man to become a superman, the highest ideal in the world of creation, and thereby be the humble but active agent of the Creative God, as indicated in the hymns of *Sidh Gosht* quoted above. "Man with his egocentric individuality is basically an animal, with all animal limitations" [1. p. 267] and alienation from *Naam* or God. But, he has the invaluable capacity to come into his own by breaking this alienation and establishing a link with *Naam*.

The Guru again and again addresses man to give up his egocentric activity and instead to rise to his full stature and avail himself of this one opportunity. "After ages, this invaluable opportunity of human birth is obtained, but one loses it for nothing; one loses a ruby in exchange for a piece of broken glass." [1. p. 1203]. "Among eighty-four lakhs of species, man is assigned the supreme position, whosoever misses the opportunity, suffers the pain of transmigration." [1. p. 1075]. "Human birth is the epitome of fruitful effort, but man loses it for a trifle." [1. p. 1179]. "Human birth is precious." [1. p. 751]. "You have obtained the privilege of human body, now is your one opportunity to meet God." [1. p. 12]. This is how we understand Guru Nanak's statements that his mission is, with the help of other God-conscious persons, to assist man to grow into superman, so as to cross egoistic obstacles in the sea of life, and thereby to help the process of evolution and creativity to supermanship, flowering into a beautiful world. Hence, the ideal is not only to be a superman oneself, but with the help of other supermen to convert everybody into supermen. [1.p.295]. And this physico-spiritual ideal, laid down in Guru Granth Sahib, can be reached only in this world by removing human alienation caused by ego (haumen) which is opposed to Naam, and which can be removed only by creative and altruistic living.

Already we have looked at this issue from another angle and concluded that Naam is conducting a qualityful movement expressible and aimed at fructifying in the world of man. In the background of Indian religions, this is the way to emphasize the importance of creative living in the world, as also of what one may call, this-worldly interest of God. To say that God has moral qualities does not mean an anthropomorphic description of God, but it is a metaphoric way of expressing the essentiality of virtuous conduct which alone secures progress as against the egoistic and individualistic activity of the selfcentred man (manmukh), who generates forces of separatism, conflict, war and chaos. That is why the Guru also describes the God-centred man (gurmukh), the ideal in Sikhism, as having qualities of spontaneous beneficence, love, help to the poor, etc., essentially the same qualities as of God. In short, in the case of God-centred man, his love for God is in fact transformed into God's love for man.

It needs to be clarified here whether the ideal in Sikhism is linkage with God or merger in God. According to the Gurus, man, because of his individualism and selfishness, stands alienated from God's immanence. Instead of serving God of attributes, man, in his ignorance and myopic vision, starts serving his own self and fails to rise to his full height of being a conscious and humble instrument of God's creative functioning in the world. In His Transcendence, God's Being is all by Himself in a Self-absorbed state, without sign of any visible form, devotion, love or creative activity. In that state, God's Will, Naam or attributes are not expressed, since these can work only in the created world.

Second is the state when God's Naam and Will are expressed and creative functioning in the universe goes on. To talk of merger in God in this state involves virtually a reversion to the first state of God being Self-absorbed. This is, therefore, a contradiction in terms, because while God is engaged in His Creative Activity, there can be no question of the cessation of this dynamic activity or merger of man in the Self-absorbed state. Besides, such an opposite process would be evidently counter to the expressed creative Will of God. True, there are some hymns in Guru Granth Sahib where merger with God appears to be indicated, but this merger or joining means only a link, as quoted earlier, with the Creative Immanence of God, because merger involves loss of identity and can be possible only in a pantheistic creed and not in a theistic creed like Sikhism.

Below are quoted a few of the hymns which clarify the issue :

(i)   "His body and mind are imbued entirely with the hue of Naam and he lives always in the company of God; as one stream of water intermingles with another, in the same manner his light merges in the light of God." [1. p. 278].

(ii)   "The gurmukh is all admiration for the attributes of God; and he remains merged in

God." [1. p. 942].

(iii)   "*Brahmgyaani* looks solely to God for all support." "God lives by the side of *Brahmgyaani*." "*Brahmgyaani* is himself God." [1. p. 273].

(iv)   "He devotes himself to God with his whole being and remains merged in his God." [1. p. 286].

All these and similar other hymns are significant, because the idea of the superman's identity being different from that of God appears in the same hymn as containing, side by side, the idea of his apparent merger in God. Evidently, the Gurus would not give two contradictory concepts in the same breath. Therefore, the seeming symbols of merger only signify a link between the superman (*gurmukh*) and *Naam*, especially as in all these and other such hymns, the superman has been indicated as a functioning and separate identity.

We further amplify to show that the interpretation stated above is the only one that can be accepted :

(i)   The Gurus do not lay two kinds of ideals for their disciples, i.e., one of link with the Creative *Naam* or His Will and expressible only in the created world, and the other of one's merger in the Self-absorbed state of God, even while the created world exists and is being dynamically worked by His Immanence. Nowhere in Sikhism is there the least evidence or suggestion of two alternative ideals or duality of goals. Such a thing is contrary to the very fundamentals of Sikhism as expressed profusely in Guru Granth Sahib and in the entire Sikh tradition, which is not only anti-ascetic and anti-withdrawal from life, but stands for active participation in the world. Merger in the anonymity of Brahman may be the ideal in other Indian systems or salvation religions, where the world is either an illusion or of a lower category, or where participation in *samsara* is anti-spiritual, but it cannot be so where God is the Creator of this beautiful world, which is the only field of His Will and Creative Activity. The goal is not heaven or salvation but love of *Naam* : "Heaven cannot equal God's *Naam*. The God-faced has no desire for salvation." "I seek not power, nor salvation; pray, give me the love of God." [1. pp. 1078, 534].

(ii)   In *Dharam khand,* the Guru has clearly laid down that for every one on this earth, the only ideal is of virtuous activity and deeds, which alone meet God's approval. The same direction is given in the Guru's dictum : 'Higher than truth is truthful conduct or living.'

(iii)   In the Hymn of Cosomography, as discussed earlier, the superman is limited only to the Region of Creativity. He is not merged in His Immanence, much less in His Transcendence, where the question of the separate identity of the devotee does not arise. Any such suggested merger would even be contrary to the clear denial of incarnation of God (*avatarhood*) in Sikh theology. For, a corollary of man's merger in God would be God's incarnation as man.

(iv)   Merger of the superman with God, without being His creative instrument, would inevitably involve the re-absorption of the Immanence or Will of God. This would virtually be a request for winding up all God's creative activity. Such an ideal might be logical in religious systems where human existence is not considered real and authentic, or is a bondage, or in dualistic creeds where the separation of the spiritual element from the material element (*prakriti*) is sought. That is why in such systems, self-immolating asceticism and calculated other worldliness or austerities have a logical and recognised spiritual sanction, but not so in Sikhism, where all such practices have not only been considered to be useless and superfluous, but are deemed positively harmful and un-spiritual, especially when the Guru's God is Creative and Attributive, and wants His supermen to be the instruments of His Will and of His Progressive Creativity. This makes one point clear. The Guru's language being symbolic, link, merger, or joining can never mean fusion, or loss of human identity of the superman, and, thus, his ceasing to be a creative instrument of God's Will, plan and purpose in the created world. The ideal of simple merger or *nirvana* (not Bodhisattvic) would not be the service of God or *Naam* or action according to His Will, but would rather be an anti-creative annihilation or spiritual suicide almost egoistic in its content.

(v) The ideal of merger in God would be quite foreign to a monotheistic creed like Sikhism, which in all its aspects, is anti-pantheistic and casts on the individual the responsibility of taking up God-centred activity instead of self-centred indulgence. Harmony with the Will of God does not mean absorption into it but free co-operation with it. 'Our wills are ours to make them Thine.' In other words, 'identification with the Divine Will on man's part really signifies an act of faith and freedom by which he makes the Divine End, his own end; it is not the recognition of the actual identity of his will with God's Will,' writes Galloway. [3.].

We conclude that the superman, towards whom the evolutionary progress is directed, becomes the instrument of, or linked to *Naam*. This is the meaning of the ideal of one's being linked with *Naam* or doing the Will of God or being given the boon of *Naam*. The role of the God-faced is not only to be ever-creative and altruistic himself, but also to make the entire social fabric creative and virtuous. In Indian religious life, it involves a radical shift from personal piety and salvation to service of man in general, whose uplift becomes the first and the highest love and priority in spiritual endeavour. Everyone is to be raised to the level of the superman and treated as equal. This we have seen is the thesis of Guru Granth Sahib. Since all these ideals can be pursued by the superman only in the spacio-temporal world, it is obvious that any supposed ideal of merger, as in some other religions, is both foreign and contrary to the thesis of *Naam*. Just as in the case of the art of swimming, no training or test of it is possible outside the pool, similarly, whether a person is self-centred or God-centred, qualityful or otherwise, can be tested and authenticated only in this world of ours, and that also from one's deeds and activities during his participation. The aim is to be the instrument of God and to fulfil the object of evolving supermen and making this world into a beautiful and qualityful place of supermen, i.e., to create God's kingdom on earth.

(c) The Lives That The Gurus Led So As To Lay Down The Ideal For Others To Follow :

Having come to the conclusion that according to the doctrine of *Naam,* as laid down in Guru Granth Sahib, complete participation in life is the ideal, we may see what kind of life the Gurus lived. The lives of the ten Gurus are the best pointer to the goal of human life set in Guru Granth Sahib, since these constitute the clearest interpretation of their teachings. In the Guru Granth Sahib, all kinds of social and political qualities have been attributed to God and the Superman. Accordingly, it was the demand of the doctrine of *Naam* that the Gurus take full share in the life of their times. And we see that this is, as it should have been.

Apart from the eternal problems of man, with which the Gurus dealt in detail, students of history know that in the Gurus' times there were two malignant growths — the caste and the tyrannical political system. The Gurus never bypassed them as being too mundane to concern them. Regarding both these matters, the Gurus' role has been revolutionary. In their hymns, they have forcefully condemned these institutions : "The pride of caste leads to multifarious evils." [1. p. 1128]. "Distinction of high and low caste and colour, hell and heaven introduced by the Vedas are misleading." [1. p. 1243]. "Kings are like tigers and courtiers like dogs, and they prey upon peaceful citizens. The Kings' employees tear up innocent persons, and the dogs lick up the blood that is shed." [1. p. 1288]. "The Mughals are made the instrument of death. The people have suffered intensely, O God, art Thou not moved? ...... If the strong mauls the strong, I grieve not. If the lion attacks the sheep, the master of the flock must answer." [1. p. 360]. Their protest against these evils did not rest at that. In the social institutions which the Gurus organised, caste had no place. Four of the five Beloved Ones (*panj piaraas*) of the Guru, who were to lead the entire community of the Sikhs were from the Sudras. After the political execution of the Fifth Guru, the Sixth Guru started regular military training and preparations in order to fight the challenges of the oppressive political system. The execution of Guru Tegh Bahadur intensified the socio-political struggle against Mughal misrule. Two of the sons of Guru Gobind Singh sacrificed their lives in war, while the remaining two were bricked alive. The Tenth Guru also laid down his own life in this struggle. It is not our object here to go into historical details or to assess the political impact of the Sikh movement. We need only to stress that as the result of their own thesis laid down in Guru Granth Sahib, the Gurus felt a spontaneous spiritual compulsion to organise and raise a revolt against the oppressive socio-political system.

Obviously, the lives of the Gurus reinforce the conclusion we have already reached, namely, that Guru Granth Sahib stands for complete participation in all creative and constructive aspects of life.

8. WAY TO NAAM

Now, we come to the last question as to how to establish link with *Naam*, how to become God-centred from a self-centred person, and what method of training to adopt on this path. Just as the attributive God must work in the world, the training and transformation must also be in the world itself, and not outside it. In Guru Granth Sahib the following five modes of training have been referred to :

(a) remembering God *(Naam)*;
(b) keeping good company;
(c) developing a sense of discrimination;
(d) doing virtuous activities in the sense explained already;
(e) avoiding vices.

It is not our object here to elaborate on these except (i) to clarify an ambiguity which, we feel, exists about remembering *Naam* and (ii) to give a few statements of the Gurus on each of these modes.

(a) *Remembering God (Naam)* : There is considerable misunderstanding as to what constitutes the remembering of *Naam*. True, in Guru Granth Sahib there is laid great stress on remembering *Naam* (*Naam Japanaa*) and praise of God (*sift saalaah*). Accordingly, it has been said by some that this remembering, or what Trumpp calls "muttering", is by itself enough for one to link oneself with God. This remembrance is sometimes also understood to mean yogic practices for the achievement of the so-called bliss as an end in itself. We are not only unaware of any hymns in Guru Granth Sahib recommending such yogic practices or any tradition in this regard, but there are clear hymns against the use of such practices as means to spiritual achievement or as ends in themselves. In the very first hymn of *Japuji*, mere one-point meditation is considered pointless, the way to be a *sachiara* is to work according to His Will. True, there are numerous verses in Guru Granth Sahib eulogizing *Naam* and Its remembrance. But there are also innumerable verses denying the utility of any mechanical means or mere repetition of words or hymns, e.g., "Every one repeats God's Name, but by such repetition one gets not to God." [1. p. 491]. "With guile in heart, he practises guile, but mutters God's Name. He is pounding husk and is in darkness and pain." [1. p. 1199]. "One mutters God's Name, but does evil daily in this way the heart is not purified." [1. p. 732]. The important thing is the motivation behind praise and remembrance. Flattery, sycophancy and hypocritical utterances cannot be considered praise, because the motive of such utterances is self-interest. Real praise involves admiration, love and devotion accompanied by an honest desire to follow as an ideal or imbibe the qualities of the one who is praised, God in this case. Such praise is a pining for what we are not, with a humble desire to move in the direction of the ideal. Praise, thus, is a spontaneous acknowledgement of the Glory of God and the desire to please Him, not by mere words but by qualityful deeds. Similarly, remembrance or repetitive utterances can be mechanical, magical, or ritualistic in nature. As against it, remembering can be a way to keep in mind one's basic ideals so that the frail human psyche does not falter or deviate from one's chosen direction and ideals. That is why, in the hymns of Guru Granth Sahib, the reference is not at all to any mechanical repetition but to keep God in mind. Hence, the words used for the purpose are, *Naam* 'being or living in one's consciousness' (*man vasai,* or *kare nivaas*), 'enlightening one's being' (*kare pargaas*), 'imbued' (*ratte*), etc. This remembrance is like keeping the fear of God in one's mind while embarking on any activity or making any decision. It is not an end in itself and seeks no magical or compulsive effects, but it is a way of reminding oneself to take heart and courage to do the right thing. Just as in the case of 'doing the Will of God' and 'being yoked to *Naam*', 'remembering' is also inalienably linked with the subsequent decision to be made and activity to be undertaken. 'By dwelling on the Word, mind flows to serve others.' In short, the praise and remembrance of *Naam*, or keeping '*Naam* in heart' is just the means to recall the lesson and the ideal suggested by Attributive *Naam*. It is an humble attempt to seek the Grace and Light of the Guiding Star of *Naam*, to show to the weak and wavering psyche the path one has to tread and the direction in which one has to move in life. The conclusion is the same, namely, that all deeds and activities have to be in life, which is the sole test of the earlier training, remembrance and preparation.

(b)   *Company Of God-faced Men* : The Guru writes : "Just as castor plant imbibes the scent of the adjacent *sandal* wood, similarly, even the fallen are emancipated by the company of true ones." [1. p. 861]. "In good company, we become true and develop love for *Naam*." [1. p. 58]. In good company, one becomes good." [1. p. 314].

(c)   *Use Of Reason And Sense Of Discrimination* : In the Gurus' system, use of human rationality and sense of discrimination have a distinct and important place. Man's faculty of reason is without doubt an asset which other animals do not possess. Sikh theology being non-deterministic, man has a distinct moral freedom and responsibility in the choice of his actions and thereby to bring about his transformation. The Guru writes, "By use of discrimination or intellect one serves God. By discrimination one is honoured. By discrimination and study one understands things. It is the sense of discrimination that makes one charitable. This is the right way, rest is all wrong." [1. p. 1245]. "Man is blessed with the light of reason and discrimination." [1. p. 913]. "One, in fear of God and discriminating between good and bad, appears sweet to God." [1. p. 768]. "We know right from wrong and yet fall into the well with torch in hand." [1. p. 1376].

(d)   *Ethical And Creative Activities* : We have concluded already that only moral deeds in all fields of human activity are acceptable to God. God's interest in this development of man can be gauged from the fact that "He takes cognizance of and rewards even an iota of good deed," [1. p. 784] it being "His innermost nature to help the erring." [1. p. 828]. A few of the Guru's hymns on the issue are given below : "Love, contentment, truth, humility and other virtues enable the seed of *Naam* (vision of basic unity and reality) to sprout." [1. p. 955].

(e)   *Avoiding Vices* : Side by side with the above positive step it is equally important to avoid vices, "With self-control and discipline, we forsake vice and see the miracle of man becoming God." [1. pp. 343-4]. "Drive out lust and anger, be the servant of all, and see the Lord in all hearts." [1. p. 866]. Control your evil propensities and you become a perfect man." [1. p. 404]. "Good, righteousness, virtue and giving up of vice are the way to realize the essence of God." [1. p. 418]. "Control cravings, and the light of wisdom will come; then fashion this wisdom into deeds." [1. p. 878].

We need hardly amplify the point except to say that the entire approach and the method of training have to be interconnected and simultaneous. The remembrance of God, good company and use of human rationality have to be the means to help man to undertake and do right kind of action and deeds, involving productive work, sharing of profits, and looking upon and treating all alike. "The man incapable of earning a living gets his ears split (for wearing yogic-earrings), or one becomes a mendicant. He calls himself guru or saint, but begs for food from door to door. Never look up to such a person or touch his feet. He alone knows the way who earns his living by hard work and shares his income with others," [1. p. 1245] i.e., the training of man has to be in life and for life. "My whole being, body and consciousness are imbued with *Naam*. True living is living God in life." [1. p. 684]. In the Guru's system, the entire development has to be integrated, good actions leading to change in emotions and attitudes, and change in motives and approach resulting in good reactions and deeds. According to the Guru, "without good deeds no worship is possible." [1. p. 4].

Here is an important word of caution. We are not at all denying the basic sanctity of the mystic approach and experience, or that the ultimate link with *Naam* involving the highest spiritual or suprasensory experience is an act of God's Grace. All we suggest is that according to the Sikh Gurus, the seeker's way to invite God's Grace is through virtuous and non-egoistic deeds in life, and that after the mystic experience, the compulsion for such deeds is even greater than before, since one is the creative instrument of the Attributive *Naam*, dynamically directing and sustaining the world.

9. CONCLUSION

We recapitulate briefly our conclusions :

(i)   The Transcendent God expressed Himself in *Naam* that created the world.

(ii)   *Naam* is the Creative and Dynamic Immanence of God, supporting and directing the becoming universe towards (a) a qualityful goal and (b) the emergence of a society of supermen.

(iii)   The Gurus' system is monotheistic, since God is both Transcendent and Immanent, and the world is His creation.

(iv)   The world is proclaimed as authentic and the sole sphere of *Naam's* deed, interest and activity. It is not illusory or of a lower category of reality.

(v)   Accordingly, all human actions have a reality and validity, and are immoral or moral, destructive or constructive, self-centred or God-centred, to the extent they contribute or not to the ethics of *Naam* or a unitary view of life.

(vi)   The superman is both the knower and the executor of God's Will. After enlightenment, his duties and responsibilities, as the agent of *Naam*, increase and become more purposeful. He cannot be a silent spectator of this world, or a mere enjoyer of bliss; his bliss lies in being yoked to God's purpose, giving meaning to life, and hope and optimism to man, i.e., in Sikhism, the test, expression and goal of all mystic and spiritual endeavour is life and life alone.

(vii)   The way to establish link with *Naam* is through virtuous participation and deeds in all aspects of life, which is the sole arena and test of spiritual and mystic activity both for men and supermen. It is not possible to have link with God by ritualistic, ascetic or escapist practices or even so-called salvation or merger.

The doctrine of *Naam* gives a clear clue to the understanding of Sikh theology and Sikh history. It also explains vividly the ten Gurus' attack on the socio-political institutions of their times, their martyrdoms and military preparations and struggle with a view to creating new socio-political organisations and institutions, and how all these were the logical consequence of a single spiritual thesis and the continuous unfolding of a planned process, uninfluenced by local, social or political circumstances or the exigencies or accidents of history.

REFERENCES

1. *Guru Granth Sahib.*
2. *Bachitar Natak*, part A-6 (33).
3. Galloway : *The Philosophy of Religion,* Edinburgh, 1915, p. 654.
4. See, Niharranjan Ray : *The Sikh Gurus and The Sikh Society*, Punjabi University, Patiala, 1970.
5. Sharma, I. C. : *The Ethics of Buddhism*, Ethical Philosophies of India, p. 169.
6. Smith Huston : *The Religion of Man*, New York, 1959, p. 214.
7. Stace, W. T. : *Mysticism and Philosophy*, p. 126.

SIKH THEORY OF EVOLUTION : HAUMAIN AND PROBLEM OF HERMENEUTICS

DALJEET SINGH

I

THEORY OF EVOLUTION

The Sikh theory of evolution is a distinct and unique contribution of Guru Nanak to the religious thought of man. We shall attempt to outline this theory of evolution from a *manmukh* (ego-conscious being) to a *gurmukh* (God-conscious being), and how it is necessary to interpret the revelation or spiritual experiences of the Gurus in relation to their lives, or their historical role, which is a product of their revelation; and why persons drawn from pacificist or dichotomous religions have difficulty in understanding the system of the Gurus.

Spiritual Experience Of The Gurus : Every prophet builds the structure of his religious system on the foundations of his spiritual experience of the Basic Reality or God. It is these perceptions of the prophet that govern his understanding of the world and approach to it. Guru Nanak's spiritual experience highlights four facts about the Basic Reality. First, He is the Creator, and is both transcendent and immanent, but He does not incarnate. Second, He is the Fount of all values. Third, He, being Love, is interested in the evolution and progress of the world, and is its Guide and Enlightener. Fourth, in view of the first three qualities of God, the goal of the spiritual man is to be the instrument of such a God or Reality.

Individuation, Ego And Man : This being the perception, the Gurus envisage a clear evolutionary growth in the organic constitution or consciousness of man. The Gurus say that, "The world came into being by individuation." [1] Evidently, for the growth of life, creation of an individual self or *haumain* (I-am-ness) or ego in every being was essential. For, there could be no animal life without there being in each unit a centre of consciousness or autonomy, which could be both the guardian and guide of the individual being. It is this centre of individuation that has enabled the evolution of life from the smallest being to the extremely complicated biological structure of man. The Gurus describe the evolution thus : "For several births (you) were a worm; for several births an insect; for several births a fish and an antelope."[2] "After passing through myriads of species, one is blessed with the human form."[3] "After ages you have the glory of becoming a man."[4] These statements of the Gurus make it clear how from the smallest speck of life, man has evolved after millions of years and myriads of births. Second, although man is mainly an animal, he is distinctly superior to other animals. His superiority lies in his two attributes which the other animals do not possess. First is his sense of discrimination, i.e., his awareness of his own thinking process and his capacity to deliberate over his thinking. The Guru makes a clear statement that man has, apart from his other potentialities, a superior sense of discrimination. "God created you out of a drop of water, and breathed life into you. He endowed you with the light of reason, sense of discrimination and wisdom."[5] This clearly emphasises that man has the sense of making judgement and choice, i.e., a moral sense to distinguish right from wrong. For, this light of discrimination is an additional weapon with man to cope with the problems of life. The Gurus' perception is basically different from the view of modern psychology, which believes that man is virtually a determined being, and that his development and evolution are governed by the environment, following a struggle for existence and survival of the fittest. The Gurus differ completely. For, they emphasise that man should use his sense of discrimination or his freedom of choice in making a correct decision. This freedom forms the base of his moral life, which is beyond the ken of an animal. They, thus, completely repudiate the view that moral life is just a 'defence mechanism', or a 'reaction formation' for survival to battle against the impact of environment. The Gurus state unambiguously that a social or a civilised life is not possible unless man develops his internal discipline or moral life, which alone can make for progress of man in social life, or in a multi-national society.

The second superior attribute of man is that, although he is at present at the egoistic state of development, he has also the capacity to develop a link with the Universal Consciousness, the Basic Reality of God. True, presently man is at the *manmukh* (egoistic) state of consciousness, but he has the capacity to be linked with the Universal Consciousness, or to be a *gurmukh* who works in line with the Fundamental Reality by being its instrument. The Gurus say, "You have obtained the privilege of human birth; now is your opportunity to meet God."[6] "O man, you are superior in God's creation; now is your opportunity; you may fulfil or not fulfil your destiny."[7] The Gurus stress that not only is there hope for man and an opportunity open to him, but it is also his destiny to rise above his egoistic instincts, so as to become a superman or a *gurmukh*. And it is this spiritual progress of man, which Benevolent God is helping with His Grace.

The Malady Of Haumain : The Gurus repeatedly state that at the *manmukh* stage, man's greatest malady that blocks his progress is his egoism or *haumein* consciousness. The struggle against the elements and environment having largely been won, man finds himself incapable of dealing with his own species. All his rational capacities and talents are still the equipment of the egoistic man, and for that matter, are governed by his ego-consciousness. His intellectual capacities being subservient to his ego-consciousness, cannot be used for the benefit of another person. Just as a man's lungs cannot breathe for the benefit of another human being, in the same way, his rational capacities cannot help being selfish, since they are directed by his ego-consciousness. It is this organic condition of the present-day man, that holds out little hope for his ever being able rationally to solve the problems of conflict, clash and war, at the individual, social or international level. It is true that during the period of man's civilised life, certain cultural conditioning for moral ends has taken place, but the change is very superficial. The moment there is anything threatening man's personal entity or interests, his basic self-centredness is unmasked and works with unabashed vehemence and violence. This is the spectacle we witness everyday in dealings between man and man, one society and another, and one nation and another. And this, despite all pretensions to the contrary. The twentieth century has witnessed the worst massacres, butchery, holocausts and wars in the history of man. Not only have there been large-scale killings, but we have had the worst rulers who have not refrained from killing millions of their own innocent citizens. It is a fact that our Einsteins, Oppenhauers, and Sakharovs have been just the instruments of the tyrants who have staged Auschwitz and other crimes, and destroyed Nagasaki and Hiroshima. The fact remains that greater the instruments of violence science has supplied to our rulers, the greater has been the threat to the security of the people and the environment of the planet. For, the ape in man, or his egoist consciousness, continues to drive the vehicles of violence that science has placed at his disposal. And he knows of no other use of it, except to cater to his egoism and pride. Hence, the warning the learned authors of *Limits of Growth* gave to the present day man : "The outcome can only be disastrous, whether due to selfishness of individual countries that continue to act purely in their own interest, or to a power struggle between the developing and the developed nations. The world system is simply not ample enough, nor generous enough, to accommodate much longer such egocentric and conflicting behaviour of its inhabitants." Unfortunately, despite about a quarter of a century having elapsed since this warning was given, neither human behaviour, nor the behaviour of nations has changed materially to curb the drive towards destruction. In fact, the gap between the rich and the poor nations has been widening as also between the rich and the poor of a nation.

Schweitzer, who made a survey of the entire field of Greek and Western thought and philosophy, came to the dismal conclusion that there is no trace of the ethical in the working of the world, or any sound basis for ethics in the present-day thought of man. He could discover nothing of purposive evolution in the material world or our thinking by which our activities could acquire a meaning. Nor is the ethical to be found in any form in the world process. We can only describe more and more minutely the phenomena of the world. But neither science nor thought has been able to find any meaning, purpose or direction in the world process, except a drive towards death and meaninglessness.[9] Schumacker also sounds the same plaintive note saying that nothing is more in disarray than the ethical thought of man.[10] Consequently, both the working of man in the present century and his present day thought do not hold out any hope for mankind.

The Gurus' Solution And The Theory Of Spiritual Evolution : It is in the above context that the Gurus not only hold out hope of progress for man, but also lay down the path of human evolution. That path is through a moral life. This is so for two reasons. First, God alone is the Source of all morality. This is, for the Gurus, not a mere assumption, but a truth which they have intuitively or mystically perceived. We find that in the processes of the world and its thought and science, there is no trace of the ethical. As against it, the Gurus emphasise that the Basic Reality is not only ethical and the Ocean of Values, but is working the world towards a life of morality, harmony and love. They repeatedly stress their spiritual experience about the Fatherhood of God, the consequent brotherhood of man and the direction of the Universal Consciousness to create and evolve the superman or the *gurmukh*, who being linked to the Universal Consciousness, will work according to its direction. The Gurus, thus, explain that there is no midway between ego-consciousness and *Naam* or God-consciousness. They state, "There is conflict between *Naam* and *haumein*; the two cannot be at one place."[11] The necessity of the goal of progress from *manmukh* to *gurmukh*, or ego-consciousness to God-consciousness or link with Universal Consciousness, is the spiritual thesis of the Gurus laid down in Guru Granth Sahib, and they lived and demonstrated it for a period of about 240 years. This thesis of evolution, the role prescribed for the superman, and the methodology of progress, have been clearly stated by the Gurus. They say, "God created first Himself, then *haumein* (sense of individuation), third *maya* (multifarious beings and entities), and at the fourth place, *gurmukh*, who always lives truthfully."[12] This hymn clearly conveys the Sikh theory of evolution, and meaning, direction and hope for man. The concept that the world has been made for contemplated evolution of the superman (*gurmukh*), and for the practice of truth or righeousness, is fundamental to the Sikh thought. This emphasises that God has made the earth for a serious purpose and with a specific goal. On one hand, it lays down that it is essential to have an integral combination between the spiritual and empirical dimensions of man, for, this will break his alienation from the Basic Reality, the only source of love, strength and knowledge. On the other hand, it will ensure his link with the Fount of Love, Energy, Freedom and Creation, thereby giving him an optimistic and whole-life world-view, and eliminating his sense of loneliness, frustration and sorrow. Instead, it will give him strength and confidence to strive and sacrifice to serve God as His meaningful instrument. In answer to a question of the Sidhas, Guru Nanak clearly replies. "It is for the God-conscious beings (*gurmukhs*) that our True God has established the earth."[13] Repeatedly, the Guru stresses that the earth has been created for the sole purpose of practising truth or righteousness. In his very first long hymn, called *Japuji*, Guru Nanak records : "In the midst of fire, water, nether regions, nights, seasons, dates and days, the earth has been established as a place for the practice of righteousness."[14] Again, the Guru repeats : "He created the earth, the Abode of Righteousness."[15] The same thought about the purpose of creation is stressed in, "God created the world, He planted *Naam* in it, and made it the place for righteous activity."[16] Hence, in Guru Nanak's spiritual experience, the theory of God's purpose in creating the earth, of the evolution of the *gurmukh*, and of the earth being a place for the practice of truth or righteousness is fundamental. The entire thesis of the Gurus is a superstructure on this base, and the lives of the Ten Gurus are a demonstration of the system. The second part of the thesis is the role of the superman. Guru Nanak, while indicating the uselessness of some ascetic disciplines, clearly concludes that to be a *sachiara* or a superman, one has to work according to the Will of God, which he calls Altruistic. In their *bani,* the Gurus profusely indicate the innumerable attributes of

God, including help and shelter to the weak, and destruction of the evil-minded. The Guru says, "Friends ask me what is the mark of the Lord. He is all Love, rest He is ineffable."[17] It is in this light that Guru Nanak says, "If you want to play the game of love, come with your head on your palm, and waver not."[18] It means that life is a game of love; God being All Love, He is working the world with His Altruistic Will. That is also why Guru Nanak emphasises. "Truth is higher than everything; higher still is truthful living."[19] Further, the Guru says, "Love, contentment, truth, humility and other virtues enable the seed of *Naam* to sprout."[20] "With self-control and discipline, we forsake vice, and see the miracle of man becoming God."[21] "Good, righteousness, virtues and the giving up of vice are the ways to realize the essence of God."[22] "God created the world of life and planted *Naam* therein, making it the place for righteous activity."[23]

The quotations above and the thesis of the Gurus, lay stress on four points. First, that moral conditioning apart, at the present stage of man, he is imperfect, being only ego-conscious, which is his greatest limitation, and is also the cause of his conflict, wars, poverty and other problems. Second, that although, like the animals, his working is largely determined by the processes of cause and effect, he has, unlike other animals, the capacity to gain freedom of functioning through a moral life. Third, and this is their fundamental spiritual experience, that the Basic Reality is not only Loving and Altruistic, but is also the only Source and Guide of altruism. Fourth, accordingly, man can be free, creative and altruistic, only through a moral life, which alone, through His Grace, can link him to the Universal Consciousness, and, for that matter, bring him peace, blissfulness, and harmony with his environment, physical, social and political.

Here we should like to explain one point. It is not suggested that the Gurus do not stress the value of meditation, remembrance or *simran* of God. But these, they do not indicate as an end in themselves. These are important means to enable man to pursue the goal of working according to the Altruistic Will of God. This point stands stressed both in their *bani* and their lives over a period of about two and a half centuries. The Guru says, "It is by our deeds that we are judged in His court."[24] "It is by our deeds that we become near or away from God."[25] "Truth and continence are true deeds, not fasting and rituals."[26] "True living is living God in life."[27] "Through virtue is one enlightened."[28] "Imbued with His Will, he (*gurmukh*) carries it out."[29] "Wonderful is His Will. If one walks in His Will, then one knows how to lead the life of Truth."[30] "They who know His Will, carry it out."[31] The above quotations, the hymn of evolution of *gurmukh*, and the lives of the Ten Gurus, unambiguously emphasise that since God is immanent in the world, and is working it, the only spiritual path is to be the instrument of His Will. And, that is why the Gurus say that they are His soldiers or wrestlers. Thus, both the *gurmukh* and the seeker have to "live truthfully." This is the Gurus' system of spiritual evolution, as embodied in Guru Granth Sahib, and as lived by the Ten Gurus.

Religious Implications Of The Guru's System : The most fundamental implication of the Gurus' spiritual system is an inalienable combination between the spiritual life and the empirical life of man. They have stressed that there can be no spiritual progress of man, unless spirituality is expressed in life and deeds. This is essential, because God Himself is informing and working the world, and the spiritual man can neither remain indifferent to, nor step aside from, the mainstream of life. Its necessary implication is that there can be no progress in empirical life, unless it is linked to the Spiritual Base, which is the Source of all values and morality. This is the fundamental or the singular base of the Gurus' religious system. This also explains all the departures in principles and doctrines the Gurus made from the thousand year old systems and traditions that had been in vogue in their times. Dichotomy between the empirical and the religious life with emphasis on personal salvation has been the basis of all the Indian systems like Buddhism, Jainism, Vaishnavism, Vedanta, etc. The logical implications of these religions were the institutions of asceticism, monasticism, *sanyasa*, celibacy, downgarding of women, and *ahimsa*. In the Hindu system, caste divisions in the social life had the religious sanction, but it was a discriminatory system, far from being just, fair or moral. Spiritual and empirical progress having been declared inter-linked and inter-dependent, the other corollaries of the Gurus' system follow so logically. First is the rejection of asceticism, monasticism, *sanyasa* and celibacy, and instead, the acceptance of a householder's life, and the necessary creation of a society concerned with the socio-political problems of man. The Gurus say, "One gets not to God by despising the world." "One becomes liberated even while laughing and playing."[33] "The God-centred lives truthfully while a householder."[34] The second corollary is the brotherhood of man, and equality between man and woman as well. This was a logical step following from the Gurus' fundamental thesis, but it was unknown so far as the Indian contexts were concerned. For, equality between man and woman in the religious or social field was nowhere prescribed in the religions of the world. But this was emphasised by Guru Nanak. The Guru says, "Spiritual path can be trodden not by mere words and talk, but by actually treating all humans alike and as one's equals. Yoga does not lie in living at cremation grounds, doing one-point meditation, roaming all over places, or visiting places of pilgrimage, but in remaining balanced and God-centred, while conducting the affairs of the world."[35] "Why call women impure, when without women there would be none ?"[36] The Third Guru, when he created centres of religious organisations, appointed women, too, to head some of them.[37] The third implication of the system is doing work in order to sustain life. Guru Nanak says, "The person incapable of earning his living gets his ears split (turns a *yogi*), and becomes a mendicant. He calls himself a guru or a saint. Do not look up to him, nor touch his feet. He alone knows the way, who earns his living, and shares his earnings with others."[38] In this and some other hymns, the Gurus not only emphasise the necessity of work and sustaining life, but they also stress the necessity of fair distribution, saying, "God's bounty belongs to all, but men grab it for themselves."[39] "Man gathers riches by making others miserable."[40] "Riches cannot be accumulated without sin, but these do not keep company after death."[41] Fair distribution of wealth, and censure of its exploitative accumulation are clearly implied. Guru Nanak's acceptance of the invitation of Lalo, a poor carpenter, and rejection of the hospitality of Malik Bhago, the local rich landlord, also stress the same point. Fourth, as total participation in life and social responsibility in all fields are desired, Guru Nanak condemned injustice and oppression in the social and political fields by the rulers, invaders and others. He even complained to God for allowing the weak to be oppressed by the strong.[42] This clearly implies that in the Order of God, justice, fairness and equality are the rule, and for that matter, it is essential for the seeker, the God-man and his society, to confront and remove injustice and oppression. It is for this reason that Guru Nanak stressed two points. First, that God was the Destroyer of the evil,[43] the Punisher of the demoniacal,[44] and the Slayer of the inimical.[45] Second, as a corollary of the above, he rejected *ahimsa* or pacificism,[46] as prescribed in the other Indian systems. It is both important and significant that this fundamental principle of combination between the spiritual life and the empirical life of man was enunciated by Guru Nanak, as also the four corollaries thereof. Not only that, Guru Nanak himself laid down the foundations of the institutional structures that were necessary to implement his thesis. He led a householder's life, worked as a peasant, and organised a society, eating together from a common kitchen, and at a common platform. Second, since he felt that the organisational structure had still to be completed and nurtured, he started the institution of succession, and in selecting Guru Angad, a householder, as the second Guru, he left out his son, Baba Sri Chand, who was of an ascetic bent of mind. He gave Guru Angad instructions to organise and lead the *Panth*.[47] Third, Guru Nanak rejected *ahimsa* and described his God as the Destroyer of the evil. Consequently, Guru Hargobind's statement to Sant Ramdas of Maharashtra, that his sword was for the destruction of the tyrant and for the protection of the weak,[48] only reiterated what Guru Nanak had defined as the attributes of God, who was both the Protector of the weak and the Punisher of the evil, and who showered His Grace where the weak were helped.[49] Since the entire system of the Gurus was against the tide of times and traditions, thousands-of-years-old, Ten Gurus had to work and demonstrate for about 240 years their thesis according to the targets laid down by Guru Nanak. This explains the necessity of the uncommon steps the Ten Gurus took, the new institutions they created, and the long period they spent in training, motivating and conditioning their followers to tread the path laid down by Guru Nanak. In the Indian context the Gurus' system was so revolutionary that many a people, including scholars, conditioned by their own thought and background, have failed to understand the essentiality of the measures the Sikh Gurus took, and the spiritual fundamentals of the Sikh thought.

An important implication of the Sikh theory of evolution is that the Gurus attribute faults and evil in the society to the imperfections of man. They repudiate the concept of a Fall, Satan or Devil. Nor do they accept the doctrines of Atonement or Sacrifices for the sins or salvation of man. All such myths or concepts are rejected. In fact, they declare that God is benevolently helping with His Will and Grace the process of human evolution, and the *gurmukh* has to be the instrument of that Will. The concept of Grace is fundamental to the Gurus' thought, because it repudiates all systems of determinism, mechanical or environmental evolution, and the empirical logic of cause and effect. For, Grace implies freedom, choice and creativity. As such, it is the source of morality. Thus, the ideal of individual salvation as an end in itself is not there.

The concept of incarnation is also denied. Of course, immanence of God in the world and man is accepted. Another major implication of the Sikh thesis is its universalism. The Gurus do not assert exclusivism. For, they pray to God to save the anguished world by any means. He may be gracious enough to do.[50] In fact, they clearly contemplate co-operation with other systems or God-conscious men. For, Guru Nanak declared that his mission was, with the help of other God-conscious men, to ferry people across the turbulent sea of life.[51] It is in this light that we have to understand the hymns of some other saints in Guru Granth Sahib. Considering the exclusiveness of some other religions, Guru Nanak's system is unique in its universalism.

The Gurus also make another logical but significant change. As God's Will is pervasive in the entire world, the spiritual man's participation and responsibility extend to the entire field of life and human functioning. Since injustice, oppression and evil are a fact of life, and since these are the greatest in the socio-political field, the man of God has neither to withdraw from any field nor to remain neutral. In fact, in order to discharge his socio-moral responsibilities, he has to confront, resist and undo injustice. Hence, Guru Nanak's organisation of a *Panth*, rejection of *ahimsa* and the inevitable use of minimum force to undo injustice.

In short, whereas *ahimsa*, monasticism, withdrawal, celibacy, ritualism and sacrifices are logical and essential in a dichotomous system, Guru Nanak at one stroke rejected all of them. Because with his perception of an Immanent God, who is a Destroyer of the evil, he created a whole-life system with the acceptance of total responsibility to sustain life, and move towards a spiritual goal.

CONCLUSION

In sum, the Gurus' theory of evolution from the present stage of *manmukh* (ego-conscious man) to the higher stage of *gurmukh* (God-conscious man) is a unique contribution to the spiritual thought of man. For, it repudiates all concepts of the fall of man or his moral degradation from an era of *satyug* to *kalyug*. Simultaneously, it gives the seeker optimism and hope. For, God is interested in his destiny, future and progress. There is no obsession with sin, nor any system of sacrifices to atone for one's moral lapses. On the other hand, it has been stated that man at present is at the stage of imperfection; and hence, like the infant, he has to be helped to move and run, and not to be obsessively punished for not being able immediately to gain speed. The fledgeling cannot be expected to fly. All the same, it has been repeatedly emphasised that God alone is the Source of all spirituality and morality, and man's empirical life cannot rid itself of its present conflicts and wars, until it learns to draw spirituo-moral sap and support from Him.

Further, since Sikhism is universal in its approach, it claims no exclusiveness for its system, and is eager and willing to co-operate with every other religious system that seeks or aims to give succour to man and ferry him across the troubled sea of life, so as to reach the level of man's chartered destiny, proclaimed by the Gurus.

II

PROBLEM OF HERMENEUTICS

Multifarious have been the reasons for the inability of some scholars or others to understand the spiritual thesis of the Gurus, and their theory of the spiritual evolution of man.

Revelation : One hurdle has been, especially with the so-called 'modern scholars', the issue of revelation. All the world over, religious systems and mystics accept the reality of revelation, in one form or the other. In their ontologies, practically all of them believe in the existence of a Fundamental Reality, transcendent to the physical world. Many of them also conceive of its operation in the material world, and its perception by supermen. It is this intuitive perception of the Reality by prophets of the world that has been called revelation. The hymns of the Gurus repeatedly emphasise this truth, which forms the basis of their entire spiritual system. Guru Nanak says, "O Lalo, I express what the Lord conveys to me to speak."[52] The other Gurus also emphasise the same truth, "Nanak says the word of Truth. He expresses only the Truth; it is time to convey the Truth."[53] "I have recited Thy Name only when You made me say it."[54] "I have no voice of my own; all that I have said, is His Command."[55] "Guru's words are divine nectar; these quench all spiritual thirst."[56] "Consider the *bani* of the *satguru* the words of Truth. O Sikhs, it is the Lord who makes me convey them."[57] "The Word is the Guru; my consciousness is the follower and listening to the ineffable account of the Lord, I remain untainted by *maya*."[58] "The *bani* is the Guru, and the Guru is the *bani*; all spiritual truths are enshrined in it."[59] Following their spiritual experiences, the Gurus declare, first, that there is a Higher Reality than the becoming material world, which is His creation, and, second, that the Reality informs the world, and graciously reveals itself to one who thereby attains the final level of evolution; i.e., becomes a *gurmukh*. Equally emphatic is the Guru's statement that the superman, once in contact with this Basic Reality, compulsively follows the Direction and Will (*hukam*) of that Reality. Consequently, there can be no peace or harmony in the physical world, unless man evolves to the final stage of development; and, in tune with the Reality, moves in line with its Direction and Order.

Revelation of, contact with, or order from the Basic Reality, has been claimed by Prophets Moses, Mohammad and Christ, as also by mystics like Eckhart and Hallaj. The lives of the prophets are the best evidence of revelation. Their activities are the outcome of their spiritual experience. Toynbee, the celebrated historian, observes, "They are not the product of their social milieu; the events that produce them are encounters between the human beings and the Absolute Reality that is in, and at the same time, beyond the phenomenon of Existence, Life and History; and any soul may meet God at any time or place in any historical circumstances. Nevertheless, an examination of the social milieu will help us to understand the nature, as well as the rise of religions in which this experience of meeting God is communicated and commended to mankind as the inspiration for a new way of life."[60]

Significantly, in Sikhism, the claim of revelation has repeatedly been made by the Gurus themselves, and it stands authenticated in the Scripture compiled by the Fifth Guru. In every other case, the scripture was prepared by the devotees, decades or even centuries, after the demise of the prophet. It is a unique feature of the Gurus' system, and shows the great care they took to define their system, so that its purity is maintained, and it is not misunderstood or misconstrued. Hence, the yardstick which we apply to assess the claims of the followers of other religions cannot be used in the case of Guru Granth Sahib. Very sagaciously, the Guru has excluded the relevance of any textual criticism, form criticism or redaction criticism and the like. Even if the authenticity and validity of revelation is not accepted, it can certainly be understood and logically deduced from its evident spiritual, moral and empirical consequences. Unfortunately, in modern times, the burden of social science methodology is so heavy that even persons believing in the Transcendent Reality and the intervention of revelation are not able to shake it off. Some of them tend to relate prophetic or revelatory systems to empirical or environmental causes. To do so, is a contradiction in terms. Anything which is revelatory, is from the realm that is free, and is ungoverned by empirical or the mechanical laws of the world of cause and effect. The Transcendent, by its very definition, is beyond the empirical logic, it being a world of Freedom and Grace. For, His Will and Grace have no causal relation with a world that is determined. It is, therefore, pathetic to find persons having faith in God or the Transcendent, explaining basic religious developments by social or environmental causes. Major social and historical developments have been the product of a revelation or a spiritual event. For, by its definition, a revelation or a spiritual event cannot be the result of a social development, although it could be the cause of it. In view of the *bani* in Guru Granth Sahib, it is essential to interpret it and the history of the Guru period in the light of the spiritual phenomena and culture, of which these are the product. For, God described by the Guru has an Altruistic and Gracious Will, which operates in the world. He is the Ocean of Values, and for that matter, the Fount of all morality and ethics. Because, morality has a significance only if man has the freedom of choice, and his moral activity is undetermined.

Materialistic Explanations Examined : Following the empirical method of cause and effect, some scholars suggest that Sikhism is a syncretism, or a growth occurring under the impact of *bhakti, shakti,* Christian, Islamic or environmental influences. First, let us take the Hindu systems, especially its *bhakti* sects. Guru Nanak rejected almost every principle of these sects, i.e., their faith in the *Vedas* and *Upanishads* as the sole scriptures, in *sanyasa,* in *ahimsa,* in the efficacy of rituals, *mantras,* fasts, pilgrimages, and sacrifices, in meditation and yogic methodology as an end in itself, in celibacy and downgrading of women, in the theory of incarnation and personal salvation, in the religiously sanctioned hierarchical division of the caste ideology, etc. In fact, no Hindu, except a *sanyasi* or *bairagi,* could be without a caste tag. Even in the liberal *bhakti* system of Chaitanya, the priests were Brahmins.

Second, we come to the system of radical *bhagats,* like Kabir and Namdev. They were all believers in personal salvation, in *ahimsa,* and even in withdrawal and other-worldliness. Serious prejudice against woman and marriage was there. Bhagat Kabir has been considered a misogynist,[61] and Bhagat Shankradeva, a contemporary of Guru Nanak, said, "Of all the terrible aspirations of the world, woman's is the ugliest. A slight side-glance of hers captivates even the hearts of celebrated sages. Her sight destroys prayer, penance and meditation. Knowing this, the wise keep away from the company of women."[62] Murthi writes about him that "to trouble about the improvement of social conditions seemed to him as little profitable."[63] Whereas none of the *bhagats* ever sought to organise a society, or to appoint a successor for the purpose, it was Guru Nanak, who at the very outset, not only created a society with a common kitchen, but also started the chain of successors, so that his socio-spiritual mission could mature and fructify. In fact, both Hindu sects and the radical *bhagats* belong to the dichotomous category of religions, in which *ahimsa* (pacificism), withdrawal, *sanyasa*, and celibacy or downgrading of women, are religious values. In a whole-life system, all those are rejected, and socio-moral responsibilities are accepted, and minimum use of force to discharge them is approved. For, the very goal of life, ethics, and methodology in Sikhism, on one hand, and those in the above two cases, on the other, are different, and, to an extent, contrasted.

The position of Christianity with its pacificism, monasteries and nunneries, and goal of personal salvation, is no different. The syncretic argument, thus, is very thin. Since Jeremiah, for six hundred years there were pacificist and other-worldly sects in Judaism like Essenes, Kabbalists and others, and yet Christ's originality has not been in doubt. But, in a country with a dichotomous and pacificist tradition of over 2,000 years, Guru Nanak's whole-life system cannot rationally be called a syncretism, or a part of the *bhakti* systems.

If we consider Sikhism a *bhakti* system, we can never explain how it was that in 1975, when Indira Gandhi imposed Emergency Law and abrogated all civil liberties, it was only the Sikhs who organised from the precincts of the Golden Temple, Amritsar, a peaceful and continuous protest for years, involving the imprisonment of 40,000 volunteers, while in the rest of India of 750 millions, no social group, much less a religious group, organised, or sent even two scores of volunteers for protest.

In fact, Vinobha Bhave, the spiritual successor of Mahatma Gandhi, called the Emergency a good diciplinary measure. Mrs. Vijayalakshmi Pandit, sister of Jawaharlal Nehru, paid a handsome tribute to the Akalis for their brave resistance to the Emergency. She said, "Punjab which had always been in the forefront of resistance of oppression, kept its colours flying during the Emergency also. It was in Punjab and Punjab alone, that a large scale resistance was organised against it. The worst thing that happened during the Emergency was that a brave nation was frightened into submission, and nobody spoke, except in hushed tones. In Dehra Dun, where I was, I hung my head in shame, and wondered if this was the Bharat for which we, the freedom fighters, had suffered. Even those, not actually in prison, were no less than in jail. Only in Punjab, the Akalis organised a *morcha* (protest) against this. Punjab's lead in such matters should continue."[64] The contrast between the socio-religious ethos of Hindu religious sects and that of Sikhism is evident. Similarly, James Lewis, who made a detailed analysis of the syncretic theory, writes : "From this perspective, it is reasonable to hypothesize that the syncretism appellation probably originated with English missionaries or some other group of colonial officials who regarded the Sikh religion as spurious."

"If someone were to argue that 'syncretism' has lost its negative, judgemental connotations, we can ask, why, then, are the major religions of the West never described as 'syncretisms?' In other words, there is basically nothing wrong with the observation that both Muslim and Hindu influences are evident in the Sikh religion, as long as one does not fail to note that the same state of affairs exists in other religious traditions. Christianity, for examaple, was shaped by Judaism, Mithraism, Neoplationism, and other Hellenstic religions.

And, not just during the period of their birth, but also over the course of later contact with other peoples, all of the major world traditions have been influenced, to some extent, by other religions. Why, then, is it appropriate to refer to Sikhism as a 'syncretism', but not appropriate to thus refer to other religions? In other words, if a faith like Christianity cannot appropriately be called a 'syncretism,' then what term would apply to Christianity's particular blend of influences that could not apply to Sikhism?

"With a little reflection, it should be apparent that there is no clear criterion for distinguising Sikhism from other religious traditions on this point. The covert judgement, and here we are finally in a position to state the evaluation implicit in this seemingly neutral term, is that Sikhism can be understood entirely in terms of its constituent religions, whereas other traditions are somehow 'more,' or that they somehow 'transcend,' the religions from which their costituents are derived. To restate this value-judgement as bluntly as possible, the founders of other traditions were somehow able to provide a special (creative? revealed?) element to their new spiritual synthesis that was somehow missing in the case of Guru Nanak."

"I am, of course, exaggerating the point, but it needs to be made perfectly clear that the characterization of the Sikh tradition as a 'syncretism' is a holdover from the days when all of the other world religions were compared with Christianity for the purpose of demonstrating Christianity's superiority. Although I recognize that present-day scholars do not consciously intend to pronounce such a judgement against Sikhism, the fact that 'syncretism' continues to be used differently to describe some religions but not others, indicates that this judgement has not ceased to shape interpretation of the Sikh tradition."[65]

"Given the popularity of this state of affairs, it would not be inappropriate to postulate some kind of unconscious repression-projection mechanism at work that might explain the scholars' lack of even-handedness. One does not have to be a psychoanalyst to perceive that the guilt about the gap between one's ideals and one's behaviour can be pushed out of the light of full awareness only to re-emerge as a projection. In lieu of a better explanation of the one-sided treatment of the Sikh religion by Westerners, it appears to the present writer that the relevant scholars are uncomfortable with the contradictions between the theory and practice of their own traditions, but have repressed the problem and have projected the contradiction on to Sikhism, a tradition that apparently (but not actually) contains the same contradiction. Thus, their condemnation of Sikh militancy is really a projection of their own (unexpressed, repressed) condemnation of the Christian tradition. The point here is not to criticize Christianity, but rather to once again point out the different treatment that the Sikh religion has received at the hands of Western scholars. These kinds of evaluative statements would have been less objectionable, had similar criticism been levelled against other religious traditions as well."[66]

The argument about the influence of Islam is equally without substance. For, not only are its ideas of Fall of man, Satan, Sin, exclusivism, Prophet Mohammed being the Seal of Prophets, and acceptance of slavery, variant from the Sikh concepts, but Sufism, the face of Islam in India, was itself a system of withdrawal and personal salvation. It never accepted any social responsibility, much less did it think of confronting Moghal oppression in the state. In fact, like Christianity in the British colonial period, Sufism took advantage of the prestige and protection Muslim rule gave to it. It is on record that the Head of Nakshabandi Sect of Islam congratulated Emperor Jehangir on the execution of Guru Arjun Dev. But the greatest contrast is that while Sikhism raised the level, both social and moral, and the sense of self-esteem of the lowest sections of the society, Indian converts to Islam continued, by and large, at the low level at which they had lived earlier. Niebuhr, a distinguished Christian theologian of the century, had argued, "that because of the evil in man and in society, Christian political action called not only for love but for an attempt to give each group within society enough power to defend itself against exploitation by other groups. Although relations between individuals might be a matter of ethics, relations between groups were a matter of politics."[67] In the religious and political history of man, it is a remarkable achievement of the Sikh Gurus that the socio-moral and political status of the lowest classes has nowhere else been raised to a higher level than that in the Sikh society.

Apart from the contrasted ideological position of Sikhism with the contemporary systems, one major fact alone demolishes the environmental arguments, namely, Guru Nanak's religious stand about equality of man and woman. In the religious or social systems of the world, there was not an iota of evidence to give rise to the radical approach of the Sikh Gurus on this issue of socio-spiritual equality of man and woman; or of social justice, as a whole, in the caste-ridden society of India. Not only Shudras like Kalals, Ranghretas and Ramgarhias became leaders of the Sikh Community, but the Third Guru appointed women to head some of the religious districts, when he constituted 22 of them in the country.[68] Shankara calls woman, "the gateway to hell."[69] For Ramanuja, woman is sin-born. The position of women in other religious systems of the world, including that of radical *bhagats*, as mentioned earlier, is certainly not of equality with men. It ranges between her being considered a temptress and being regarded as second rate. No environmental theory can explain this radical change Guru Nanak made. The only explanation for it, as stated by him, is his revelation, or what he calls the Will of God, and His immanence (*Naam*).

Singularity Of Spiritual Experience Which Is Noetic : William James, who made a detailed study of the religious experiences of mystics, clearly records that those are also noetic in character, i.e., they give knowledge.[70] This knowledge, as stated by Plato, is true and not a matter of opinion. Its authenticity accounts for the certitude of mystics who are willing to lay down their lives pursuant to its call or logic. Both Christianity and Islam give God the symbol of Light. Guru Nanak, in the very opening line in Guru Granth Sahib, calls Him Enlightener and Gracious. While the Gurus clearly recommend the use of reason and one's sense of discrimination for moral purposes, they repeatedly emphasise that the real knowledge and guidance come from His Will (*raza*). In fact, they call Him the final and the ultimate Source of all knowledge and direction. Collingwood in his book, *Idea of History*, states, "It would be nearer the truth to say that in religion the life of reflection is concentrated in its intensest form, and that the special problems of theoretical and practical life all take their special form by segregation out of the body of religious consciousness, and retain their vitality only so far as they preserve their connection with it and with each other in it."[71]

Toynbee also concedes that "the historians' point of view is not incompatible with the belief that God has revealed Himself to man for the purpose of helping man to gain spiritual salvation."[71] Of course, there is a difference in the concept of salvation as between Christianity and Sikhism. A Christian like Saint Augustine believes that salvation is an other-worldly event, and he did not expect "the world to get better"; or "that the spread of Christianity would ensure political and economic improvement. The earthly city of self-will would continue to exist amidst the rise and fall of states and empires.[73] We have already stated that Guru Nanak's thesis was whole-life, and envisaged the expression of spirituality in the empirical life of man as well.

It is evident, as has been recorded by many students of religion, that there is variation in the spiritual experiences of different mystics or prophets. The Gurus stress that the historical expression of their lives is in pursuance of the spiritual direction and knowledge the Will of God supplies. The Gurus say, "They who know His Will, carry it out."[74] "Wonderful is His Will; if one walks in His Will, then one knows how to lead the life of Truth."[75] Bergson, too, expresses a similar opinion, "The ultimate end of mysticism is establishment of a contact, consequently of a partial coincidence, with the creative effort which life itself manifests. This effort is of God, if it is not God Himself. The great mystic is to be conceived as an individual being capable of transcending limitations imposed by its material nature, thus continuing and extending the divine action. Such is our definition."[76]

Importance Of History In Sikh Hermeneutics, And Unity Of Perception, Ideology And Deed : For the proper understanding of a religious system, and in appreciating its different doctrines in their proper perspective, it is essential to bear the unity of perception, ideology and activities in mind. Let us explain what we mean by the unity of perception, ideology and activity. Almost every religion owes its origin to the mystic or religious experience of some prophet. Actually, it is this experience which forms the real fount of the entire ideology, mission and activities of the mystic. In this sequence, the first stage is the perception or the religious experience. At the second stage, the saint, naturally, tries to understand and absorb it, and reacts to it. This is the stage where reflective thought appears. This reaction constitutes both the ideology and proposed plan of the saint for giving practical shape to the ideology. This ideology and plan are generally understood and interpreted by others from the words expressed, or other means of communication resorted to by the saint. This forms his real response to his religious experience, and reflects his ideology and decisions made thereunder. For example, if the religious experience of a mystic is that God is Love, is the Shelter of the shelterless, and the Helper of the helpless, the mystic's ideology is that God is the Ocean of virtues and a God of attributes. In line with it, and as a reaction to this experience, he compulsively frames a plan of action of love and help to the poor and the needy. Accordingly, the activities undertaken and the programmes initiated and executed by the saint are the true reflection and projection of his religious experience and the consequent ideology. The activities of the saint are only the form and shape which the basic experience directs and takes. Mystics can rarely express in words fully the nature of their experience, it being generally ineffable. And even if they do, the description is so often interpreted variously. For the same reason, even the statements of these persons cannot always be very clear, being sometimes too brief or merely symbolic. It is in the interpretation of these statements that students of religion and others make major errors of understanding and deduction. But it is the deeds and activities of the person that portray truly and directly his or her religious experience and ideology. All we seek to stress is, first, the inalienable unity of experience, ideology and activity; and, second, the activities of the saint alone being the right key to the understanding and appreciation of his or her perceptions and message. So often, mere statements, taken in isolation, have been wrongly interpreted, especially by those distant in time and space. Because, howsoever sophisticated these be, rational tools cannot rise above the prejudices and predilections of the person employing them.

We have, therefore, to re-emphasise the very special position of Sikh hermeneutics. We have no access to the actual spiritual experience of the Gurus, nor can we be aware of the deliberations consequent to the experience in the consciousness of the prophets. We are aware only of the activities and the expression of their decisions. This expression is either in the form of words or deeds. Here comes a major difference. In the case of almost every other system, the Scripture is a post-facto man-made construction, recorded decades or even centuries later. The debate has continued as to how far the record could be true, considering the known human weakness to remain subservient to personal or social influences. This handicap does not exist in the case of Guru Granth Sahib, which stands authenticated by the Guru himself. The second point is that expression in the form of deed has always been considered clearer than the word. This is for two important reasons. The expression in words can at best be general or theoretical in nature. For, this expression must seek to cover all possible eventualities that may arise in the future, and which possibilities can never be anticipated or guessed completely. In short, word is the penultimate step in the expression of spiritual perceptions, of which deed is the concrete, unambiguous and final step in a comparatively specific flux of events. For this reason, it is easier to understand and less liable to misinterpretation than the word.

The second point about the word is that it is a secondary mode of expression, and, for that matter, it can never be as clear and concrete as the deed. Language, at any rate, is always a pre-existing vehicle of communication. It has its own changing nuances, and many a time, its roots extend to a distant cultural past. Obviously, language, being a second hand vehicle of expression, its truth is more liable to misinterpretation than that of deed which is not only particular to the author, but is also clearly related as a response to known or identifiable set of events. For this reason, apart from being accurate and direct, it is simpler and easier to comprehend. Hence, our emphasis that by losing sight of the historical perspective and hastening to go by a literal interpretation, we may so often miss the real meaning of the *bani*. For this reason, the lives of the Gurus are of fundamental importance, to enable us to understand the real import of the words of the Gurus. For example, in *Asa de Var*, the Guru sings :

> "Sache tere khand sache brahmand,
> Sache tere loe saache akar."[77]

and again :

> "Koor raja koor parja koor sabha sansar."[78]

To a casual reader, these hymns would appear discrepant, which they are not, if one keeps in view, how the Gurus led their lives. The first hymn stresses the reality of the world, so that we do not withdraw from it, and instead, ensure responsible participation. The second hymn, while referring to life's evanescence, deprecates lust for power and wealth, and describes it as vain. For, in the *Japuji*, Guru Nanak clearly prescribes that the goal is to work in life, in line with the Altruistic Will of God. The truth of the hymns becomes explicit, when we keep in mind, how in their lives the Gurus worked, struggled and suffered their martyrdoms. The Tenth Nanak, almost from his childhood, had to face a most intense strife, which, for any ordinary human being would have been impossible to bear, because of its pressures, anguish and tragedies. This being the context, it is impossible to conclude that the Gurus considered life to be false and illusory. In the absence of a close study of the lives of the Gurus, it is not possible to be clear about the subtleties and depths of the *bani*. Hence, the fundamental importance of the exemplary lives of the Gurus in Sikh hermeneutics. The *bani* says that those who know His Will, carry it out. It was the Altruistic Will of God that the Gurus were following in their lives.

In the above context, let us see what the Guru did for us to remove all possibilites of misunderstanding or misinterpretation. In the case of the Word, the Guru himself authenticated it. As to the clearly understandable expression of the deed, Guru Nanak lived for us in ten lives for 240 years. He lived, worked, struggled, organised a *Panth*, sacrificed self and family, while facing all sets of events, eventualities and milieus, social and political. The above are the two unique steps Guru Nanak has taken to make his system clear to us, and to solve our problems of interpretation. Hence, the fundamental importance of the history of the Guru period in Sikh hermeneutics.

Sikhism And Its Historical Role : Revelation does not mean that the students of religions should not seek to synchronize the historical events with the spiritual thesis of the mystic. In fact, our emphasis is that Sikh history is a product of the Sikh thesis, which is a revelation. In this short essay, it is not possible for us to portray all the historical events that have followed from the Gurus' spiritual view of life. But we shall refer to only two points.

(a) Social Responsibility: Guru Nanak prescribed four empirical responsibilities for the spiritual man, namely, to secure the brotherhood of man, second, the importance of work and sustenance of life, third, fair distribution of wealth and the bounties of nature, and fourth, justice in society and confrontation with the unjust and the oppressor of the weak. Hardly a prophet or *bhagat*, in the statement of his thesis, has so clearly enumerated the faults of the contemporary socio-political life, as did Guru Nanak. These four components of empirical life, provided the structural foundations of related new institutions, so that his successors could develop them to fructify. Although the evolutionary processes in socio-political life and conditioning have always been extremely slow, yet progress in the four fields has been visibly significant. Equality in the Sikh society has been distinctly at a comparatively higher level. It was a fraternization unknown on the Indian soil. Apart from bringing about improvement in social equality and human relations, the very moment Banda gained political power, he undertook distribution of land among the peasantry so as to raise the economic level of the lowest people in the state. And, it is well-known that the

Sikh masses constitute the real strength of the Sikh community.

The second achievement is the work habit among the Sikhs, for which they are well-known the world over. That the Green Revolution was first brought about in Punjab, whereas the wherewithal and pre-requisites for it were as well available elsewhere in India and Asia also demonstrates their zest for work and life. Further, it is significant that a very tiny section of the community in the country, Punjab, not only suffered and survived extreme persecution and destruction, but also was able to supplant a mighty Empire and repulse, once and for all times, the thousand-year wave of invasions from the north-west of India. And, compared to his contemporary rulers in Maharashtra and elsewhere, Ranjit Singh's rule was far more fair and humane. He made available all opportunities arising in his administration, civil, political or military, to every section of the community without any communal, religious or other discrimination. The ethos of his functioning was such that neither was there any attempt at conversion, nor was there the least feeling of revenge or discrimination against the Muslims for the persecution the Sikhs and their Gurus had suffered during the Moghal rule. This is evident from the fact that in the Anglo-Sikh wars, the Muslim soldiers fought with the same loyalty, zeal and valour as did the Sikhs. And the bard, who sang the swan song of the tragic fall of this benevolent Administration, was a Muslim. This is what Gardiner writes about Ranjit Singh, an unlettered man thrown up by the masses who represented the Sikh ethos : "The Maharaja was one of those masterminds, which only require opportunity to change the face of the Punjab. The Punjab was not the same, semi-starving, terrified, looted by the rulers and poorly clothed during his reign. It was a prosperous, homogeneous and peaceful state with all the communities, Hindus, Muslims and Sikhs, fully satisfied, partners in the Government, in the civil and military administration, and it was the happiest state communally in Asia. The Maharaja visited Hindu, Sikh and Muslim places of pilgrimage. It was the only state in India, which was the most prosperous, the most flourishing and the most contented."[79] In contrast, in the Hindu Poona of Sivaji, only Brahmins were the Ministers, Hindu codes were followed strictly and Sudras could not appear on the streets before 9 AM and after 3 PM, for their shadows defiled the higher castes, especially the Brahmins.

(b) Sikhism And Militancy : The second point relates to militancy and political objectives. Without a close study of the spiritual thesis of the Gurus, there have been lazy suggestions mostly by scholars drawn from dichotomous or pacificist religions, or from believers in the environmental evolution of man, that militancy in the Sikh religion was the result of social or environmental factors.

Let us examine this view, piece by piece. First is the ideological factor about the use of force for a righteous cause. Dichotomous religions apart, there is no religion, except Christianity, which, while recommending a householder's life, does not accept use of force, as the last resort, to discharge one's social responsibility. For, in them, withdrawal or *sanyasa* is never a value. It is so in Judaism, Islam and Sikhism. For outsiders, it has sometimes not been easy to understand the position of Exodus or Torah in the Old Testament, the Sermon on the Mount in the New Testament, and the Just-War theory of Later Christianity. In the revelation of Moses, God clearly goaded Jews to attack and drive out the Canaanites, saying, "My angel goes before you, and brings you to the Amorites, the Hittites, the Perizzites, the Canaanites, the Hivites and the Jebusites, and I will annihilate them; you shall not bow down to their gods in worship and follow their practices, but shall tear them down and smash their pillars to bits."[80] Out of the commandments prescribed for war, one is, "Eye for an eye, tooth for a tooth," etc.[81] Six hundred years later, Prophet Jeremiah suggested pacificism against the Babyloanian attack. Later, followed the pacificist cults of Essenes and others. It is true that Christ's emphasis on pacificism in the Sermon on the Mount is unambiguous, and forms the fundamental basis of Christian theology. However, since Christianity has become a state religion, the concept of a just-war has appeared. Dr Walsh says that at present it is virtually the accepted doctrine by most sections of Christianity, except the Anna-Baptists and a few others.[82]

Evidently, pacificism and a whole-life system cannot go together. As suggested by theologian Niebuhr, Liberation theologians and other noted Christians, the use of political action for a righteous cause becomes inevitable, if social responsibility has to be discharged. Let us examine the position of two noted pacificists of the century. Pacificist philosopher Bertrand Russel, who had courted arrest during the First World War, suggested, after the Second World War, that in order to avoid the appalling disaster of a Russian victory, threat of force, or, if necessary, actual use of force should be made against the USSR so as to impose on it the rule of a democratic world government.[83] Pacificist Mahatma Gandhi cut an equally sorry figure. At the beginning of the Second World War, pacificists of the world wrote to Mahatma Gandhi for guidance and advice. He felt distressed and baffled, but had hardly an answer. Maulana Azad writes that more than once he thought of committing suicide, saying that if he was helpless to avoid it, he would at least not be a witness to the holocaust.[84] But, as is well-known, later he became prepared to join the war effort, provided India was given autonomy; and again he approved of the sending of Indian forces into Kashmir to maintain Kashmir Maharaja's accession to India and to repel the Pakistan-backed tribal intrusion.[85] The greatest constitutional lawyer of India, H. M. Seervai, has examined the Mahatma's principle of non-violence and come to the conclusion that "there is little doubt that Gandhi used non-violence as a political weapon, and was prepared to support, or connive at violence to secure political goals."[86] All this exposes the bankruptcy of pacificism in human affairs, especially when a religion seeks to solve socio-political problems. The logic is clear in a system that accepts social responsibility and seeks to provide succour for the poor, the downtrodden or the oppressed. Injustice and oppression being the greatest in the socio-political field, in no way can these be resisted or undone, except by the use of force by an organised society. Hence, the sanction for it in Judaism, Islam and Sikhism.

There is a common misunderstanding that a doctrine of love, *ipso facto* implies non-violence. The logic of love points just the other way. How can one remain neutral and unconcerned, or shirk using minimum force, if the very person or the cause one loves is in jeopardy, or under attack ? Social responsibility, or succour to the oppressed, is an essential counterpart of love of your neighbour. Inevitably, love or social responsibility and pacificism cannot always go together.

Pacificism is consistent only where the ideal is individual salvation and/or withdrawal from life, which is considered a suffering, *mithya* or an avoidable entanglement. In fact, whole-life religions have regarded the approach of withdrawal as escapist or self-centred.

In this context, we have to see what is the stand of the Gurus on the issue. Guru Nanak has defined God as the Director of the World, the Helper of the weak and the oppressed, and Destroyer of the evil. For him, oppression of the weak and injustice are not consonant with the Order of God. This implies that the God-conscious man, who has to be His instrument, must resist and undo injustice. Since political injustice can be undone only by a society, by the use of force, if necessary, it was he who rejected *ahimsa*, initiated the organisation of his *Panth*, and started the institution of succession, so as to develop and direct its growth and to enable it to achieve the targets fixed by him.

Sikhism And Its Socio-Political Role : Some outsiders feel that the first five Gurus were pacificists. But, facts do not support this contention. Guru Nanak himself directed Guru Angad that he had to lead a *Panth*. The Third Guru, in order to expand the organisation of the Sikh society, created 22 districts of socio-religious administration, with a head at each Centre, covering almost the entire expanse of India from Dacca to Kabul. He created new institutions to develop an independent sense of Sikh consciousness and identity. The Fourth Guru founded Amritsar as a religious as well as business centre. The role of the Fifth Guru showed unambiguously what part the future Sikh society would play. Contemporary evidence of Mohsin Fani, the Emperor himself and others is clear. He prescribed the system of *daswandh* or 10% contribution of one's earnings by every Sikh,[87] and strengthened the institution of *masands* for its collection. These collections were used for religious as well as political purposes. This made it plain to everyone that a parallel religio-political society with deep motivation was being created. The *masands* also dealt with temporal problems of the Sikhs. In fact, since Guru Nanak, as stated by Bhai Gurdas, the Gurus were called *Sacha Padshah*, and their followers looked up to them for solution of their problems, mundane or spiritual. Mohsin Fani records that the Fifth Guru erected lofty buildings, kept horses, and even elephants, and maintained retainers.[88] He also organised trade of horses and commerce. On his own behalf, and otherwise, he sent Sikhs to Central Asia to procure and trade in horses. Gupta, the distinguished historian, writes that the Guru had, in every respect, created a 'state within a state.'[89] According to Khulasat-ul-twarikh (Persian), the Guru successfully interceded with Emperor Akbar for reduction in the land revenue imposed on the hard-pressed peasantry.[90] The Guru's compiling the Granth was an obvious declaration of the ideological independence of the Sikh society. It is because of the Guru's religio-political status that Chandu Shah, a senior official of the Moghal Administration, offered the hand of his daughter to Hargobind. But the crucial event was his help to Khusro. Mohsin Fani records that the Guru blessed Khusro, the rebel Prince, after Jehangir's accession to the throne. Indian historians like Jadunath Sircar, Latif and Beni Parsad, record that monetary assistance was also given to the Prince. Beni Parsad in his *History of Jehangir*, puts the amount at Rs. 5,000/-.[91] Both because of the temporal status and political potential of the Sikh society, and the Guru's help to the rebel Prince, claiming the throne, the incident came significantly to the notice of the Emperor. Jehangir, in his autobiography, records that for three or four generations, the Sikh Gurus had been successfully creating a society, and thereby misleading the common folk, Hindus and Muslims. He, therefore, felt that it was time that he put a stop to it, and, accordingly, ordered the execution of the Guru, as also the imposition of a fine and confiscation of his property.[92] The Dabistan records that the unpaid fine was demanded even from the Sixth Guru. It is inconceivable that an Emperor in Delhi would take notice of a peaceful religious group, or order such a drastic action as he did, or consider the event of such importance as to record it in his autobiography, unless the development and aims of the Guru and his *Panth* had been considered by him of serious socio-political potential and proportions. Had the Guru's activities been felt to be purely of a salvation or a quietist saint, there could never be any question of an Administration and the Emperor having taken note of the organisation, assessed its likely effects on the polity, and ordered its being nipped in the bud. That the development was both significant and well-known, and had invited jealousy, is also evident by the reaction of the politically important Head of the Naqshabandi Sect of Islam at Sirhind, who conveyed his delight and congratulations at the Emperor having eliminated the Fifth Guru.[93]

The other part of the story is equally clear. Obviously, the Guru envisaged confrontation with the Empire. He could never be unaware of what would be the result of his help to the rebel Prince, who was moving with his army, and had claimed the throne. Simultaneously, it is also on record that Guru Hargobind, even in the time of the Fifth Master, had been having military training, and joining hunting parties.[94] All evidence makes it plain that Guru Hargobind knew clearly from his father as to what course had been followed by the Sikh society, and what were its future plans or aims. Otherwise, it is impossible to conceive that Guru Hargobind, on the very first day of his Guruship, should equip himself with two swords, and don a military dress. All this makes it clear that the socio-political objectives of the Sikh society had become clearly visible, even from the time of the Fifth Guru. The Guru's martyrdom was, from his own angle, a voluntary step, taken to prepare his people for the struggle initiated by Guru Nanak. On the part of the Emperor, his order was a necessary step to stop the growth of the Sikh movement. In a whole-life ideology, martyrdom is not an act of suicide, sacrifice or atonement, but it is a calculated step to stop aggression, if that could be possible, and simultaneously an essential lead to prepare and strengthen the will of the people for the struggle and sacrifices required to lead a religious life.

Guru Hargobind's military activities are well-known. He created a fort at Amritsar, and the institution of the Akal Takht, the symbol of the *miri-piri* system of Guru Nanak. It is clear that the Guru took to the militant path as a positive step, and not under any social or political pressure, or for personal defence. The Guru had openly declared his policy to punish the tyrant and protect the weak.[95] He kept 700 horses and fought six battles with the Moghal Forces, several thousand strong. In one of his successful battles at Gurusar, he lost 1,200 men.[96] He even recruited mercenaries to train his people and to create a regular army.

The Seventh Guru, who on all accounts was personally of a very compassionate temperament, maintained an army of 2,000, which was quite a sizeable force. Another political move of the Guru was extremely significant. When Dara, a rival to the throne, was moving with his army, he met him and offered military assistance.[97] Just as Jehangir never forgot Guru Arjun's aid to rebel Khusro, Aurangzeb did not fail to note Guru Har Rai's offer of assistance to his elder brother claiming the throne. Significantly, the Seventh Guru took this step knowing fully well that his grandfather's assistance to Khusro had led to his martyrdom. Evidently, had the policy of the Sikh Gurus been to avoid confrontation with the Empire, or to give up militancy and socio-political objectives, the Seventh Guru would never have offered military help to Dara. In the socio-political growth of the Sikh society, the part played by the Ninth Guru is very meaningful and ideologically important. Governor Timur Shah, son of Ahmed Shah Abdali, writes in his *Hakikat-i-Bana-wa-Uruj- Firqa-i-Sikhan*, that it was reported to Aurangzeb that the Guru was creating a new nation, and was making military preparations. On this, the Emperor conveyed to the Guru that if he gave up his political and military role and confined his acitivities to preaching and prayers, he would be given state grants for that purpose. The Guru declined the offer, and his consequent martyrdom[98] at the hands of the Emperor is the second major event in the Sikh confrontation with the Moghal Administration so as to inspire and steel his men for the final confrontation.

The Tenth Guru's militant role and his armed confrontations with the Empire were protracted, long and decisive. From his very boyhood, he strengthened his military preparations, fortified Anandpur, and proclaimed an independent political status. His clash with the local Hill Princes, thus, became inevitable. He, too, recruited mercenaries for his army. After the great event of his creating the Khalsa, he invited the Hill Princes to join him in his liberation struggle against the Empire. Owing to fundamental ideological differences, they did not accept the Guru's suggestion.[99] Instead, they joined the Imperial forces against the Guru. In this struggle, he lost all his four sons and his mother, but he continued the confrontation uninterrupted and undismayed. It was he who deputed Banda to mount an attack on Sirhind,[100] and sent *hukamnamas* to his Sikhs to join and support him. The message which his spouse Mata Sundri, later conveyed to the Sikhs, made two things clear. First, that Banda's mandate was to supplant the Moghal Administration, and second, that political sovereignty was to be with the Sikh *Panth*.[101]

Sikhism : A Miri-Piri System : The above facts should enable us to understand Sikh history as the product of Sikh ideology. For, unless we grasp the intimate relation between the two, problems of interpretation arise. Sikhism is a whole-life, *miri-piri* or *sant-sipahi* religion. The three terms are synonymous and convey a single concept, and not a combination of two concepts. For, the Guru's concept of God (True Emperor) or spirituality is incomplete or partial without an essential and inalienable combination of the spiritual life with the empirical life. Spirituality and its attributes have to be expressed in and to enrich the latter. Empirical life, without drawing moral sap from the former, remains egoistic, chaotic and barren. In Guru Nanak's system, God Himself is engaged in the socio-spiritual development of man. He does not want the spiritual man to withdraw to Him, but wants him to be the agent of His Altruistic Will. Man has not been left alone by God to fight lone battles with Satan. He is a Benevolent Helper, enabling man to remove and shed his imperfections resulting from his egoism at the present level. The spiritual man, as stated by Guru Nanak, has to ferry others across the turbulent sea of life. The concept of personal salvation, as in some other religions, by withdrawing from the empirical life is distinctly denied. A dichotomous system or the modern concept of secularism, governing empirical life, leaves the society to devise its own ethics. Thus, secularism has led to the appearance, in the twentieth century, of the biggest ruling monsters civilised history has known. For, the Frankenstein of military power, modern science has placed with the state or its ruler, virtually makes it impossible for the downtrodden or the weak to defy him or dislodge him from his self-chosen path, howsoever evil or disastrous it may be.

It is a whole-life or a *miri-piri* thesis that Guru Nanak has laid down in Guru Granth Sahib; and the Ten Gurus or the Ten *gurmukhs* have demonstrated for 240 years how to live it under all combinations of circumstances. It is because of the completely radical nature of their religion that they took so long to show in life how to live every aspect of their system, and thereby, to motivate and condition the Sikhs in their faith. The lives of the Gurus for over 240 years are a lesson in interpretation or hermeneutics.

Guru Granth Sahib stresses that all the Gurus express a single unified thesis, representing the same spirit.[102] Guru Gobind Singh has stated that they are all a unity, and express the same spiritual ideology. In fact, he emphasises that unless this is realised and recognised, there can be no success in understanding the Sikh thesis, and that it would be foolish to believe otherwise.[103] That is also the reason that in the entire Guru Granth Sahib, only the word 'Nanak' has been used to convey the authorship of all the hymns and messages of the Gurus therein. This emphasis is not without meaning.

A superficial reading of the hymns of the Ninth Guru would suggest to an outsider that he was a pacificist. But, historical evidence of Governor Timur Shah, quoted earlier, that the Guru declined to stop his military and political activities, as desired by the Emperor, disproves that opinion. By his confrontation and the consequent martyrdom, the Guru prepared his people for the final role the Tenth Guru had to play. Evidently, he could not be unaware of the consequences of the rejection of the Emperor's offer. And yet, as in the case of the Fifth Guru, he, in order to help Kashmiri Pandits,[104] sought martyrdom as a part of his socio-political struggle, and to inspire and strengthen the people's faith in the mission.

Creation Of Khalsa — An Epitomic Event : The creation of the Khalsa was the epitomic achievement of Guru Nanak's mission. Guru Gobind Singh prescribed five *kakkas* for the Sikhs, including a *kirpan*. Quite often the significance of the *kirpan* (sword) as an essential wear of the Sikhs has been missed. But, it emphasises two important principles, which the Guru wants the Sikh to remember, namely, his duty to confront injustice and oppression, and second, to stop him from escape into withdrawal and monasticism. It is in this context that one has to understand the outstanding role and contribution of the Sikhs in fighting the Moghals and the invaders in the 18th century, for Indian Independence in the 20th century, and during the encroachment on all human rights and liberties following the imposition of Emergency Laws in 1975. Can any historian or sociologist explain why in history no other political, social or religious section of India rose to struggle or protest ?

Our conclusion is plain. Neither Sikh ideology in Guru Granth Sahib nor Sikh history can be understood in isolation. It is impossible to grasp one without the other. For, each historical event, social development or institution is part of a multi-dimensional process, which, in turn, is an essential and positive empirical projection of the ideology of Guru Nanak and Guru Granth Sahib. As such, Sikh history is the best explanation and index of the Sikh ideology.

Sikhism — A System Of Evolution : Sikhism is an evolutionary theory about the spirituo-empirical development of man. We can never understand the human process, its psychology and its spirituality, by experimenting with and dissecting the lower animals or examining material processes. Our scientific tools cannot yield any information about what is not discernible in the life of animal or the state of matter. The sufferings, trials, tortures and martyrdoms through which the moral man or the spiritual person can go without flinching, cannot be understood by any principle of cause and effect, or egoism, which is the present level of man. But the *gurmukh* is as spontaneous in his altruistic activities and sacrifices, as the normal man is egoist in his thought and deed. For, the latter cannot rise above his organic or constitutional level, which is governed by his ego-consciousness. In the same way, the *gurmukh* with his universal consciousness cannot help or refrain from being altruistic, which is his compulsive mission. Freedom, creativity, spirituality or morality are virtually synonymous terms expressing a higher level of consciousness. Somewhat similar thought is suggested by a modern thinker, "The inner world seen as fields of knowledge (......) is the world of freedom, the 'outer world' (......) is the world of necessity." "'It is dying to oneself', to one's likes and dislikes, to all one's egocentric occupations. To the extent one succeeds in this, one ceases to be directed from outside, and also ceases to be self-directed. One has gained freedom, or one might say, one is then God-directed."[105] The only difference with the above thought is, that although the two levels have been clearly brought out, one cannot be partially God-directed and partially self-directed. For, that would be a contradiction in terms. The Gurus say, "Ego-consciousness and God-consciousness are contrary; the two cannot be at one place."[106] For, the moment universal consciousness is achieved, ego-consciousness disappears. In the case of a *gurmukh*, while earth-awareness is necessary, the driving force is his universal consciousness.

The radical and revolutionary changes the Gurus made can be understood only on the assumption of their revelation and universal consciousness. No rational, mechanical, empirical or environmental logic can explain the originality of their thought, their mission and activities. An important fact to bear in mind is the die-hard burden of the prevalent, religiously sanctioned and divisive caste ideology. There was nothing in the contemporary life of Hinduism, Islam or Christianity to give rise to an ideology which instead of assuming a Fall from *satyug* to *kalyug*, or from the Garden of Eden to Earth, suggested an ideology of evolution.

It is in this context that we feel that any theory of syncretism or sociological, environmental, religious or empirical influences would appear to be superficial and naive. Sikh ideology or Sikh history has to be understood and interpreted on its own terms. It has been explained in Guru Granth Sahib, and has been lived and demonstrated by the Gurus.

An argument is sometimes advanced that whereas the Torah, the Old Testament, and the Quran, alongwith enunciating spiritual principles and revelations, also prescribe civil duties, rules concerning war and rituals, Guru Granth Sahib lays down no such specifications, and hence, it cannot be taken to be a scripture recommending any role in the socio-political life of man. The argument is invalid and even casual. Any detailed study of Guru Granth Sahib would show the Gurus' wisdom and vision. For, while they clearly and repeatedly lay down every spiritual and moral principle, and man's responsibility concerning the religious, social and political life, they scrupulously avoid any injunction about civil, cultural or social matters, which, by their very nature, are always dated. We are all aware that many of the civil rules or *shariat*, provided in other scriptures or holy books, sometimes become a problem for the devotees. Because socio-political practices and matters, being always evolving and changing, rigid adherence to them in a future context could become an embarrassing and avoidable limitation. Hence, just as the Fifth Guru, by authenticating the Scripture, excluded all possibility of confusion or controversy about the purity of the text and the principles prescribed, the Gurus have not included in the Scripture anything that could be dated. But, it should not be understood that they have, on that ground, kept their followers without guidance. Guru Granth Sahib not only lays down every spiritual principle that is universal and eternal, but also all the major responsibilities, moral and social, which the seeker has to shoulder and discharge, i. e. , regarding brotherhood of man and equality, fair distribution of wealth, sustenance of life, assistance to the downtrodden, and struggle against injustice and aggression. In addition, the more important lessons are the demonstrations and the lead which the Ten Gurus have given over a period of about two and a half centuries in respect of almost every eventuality that could arise in the socio-political life of the individual and society. It is for setting examples of conduct for the religious man regarding every aspect of life that the Ten Gurus guided the Sikh society from its infancy to its maturity.

CONCLUSION

Thought, as stated by Iqbal, is the internal and integral component of the deed, which is its external part. In the case of mystics and prophets, unity between thought and deed is a logical certainty, because the two are not the product of ego-consciousness, but these are the expression of the fundamental or universal consciousness. There is no intervention of the ego-consciousness to distort the fundamental unity and harmony of life. Hence, the deeds of the Gurus are the truest interpretation of their thesis and the *bani*. The Tenth Guru has stressed that no success in understanding the Gurus' system can be achieved, unless the unity of their spirit is accepted. He says, "Those who recognised them (all the Gurus) as one, were successful on the spiritual plane." This reveals the basis on which the Gurus themselves worked, and how firmly and strongly they believed in the unity of spirit, thesis and goal of all the Gurus. Therefore, what is of fundamental importance is the spirit, faith and understanding of Guru Nanak's thesis emphasised by his successors, who were considered spiritually the most competent contemporaries who laid down their all for it.

In the matter of interpretation or hermeneutics, Sikhism has a unique advantage, which is not available to other religions. Here, we have nine successors who have uniformly lived and interpreted the system of Guru Nanak. Three points indisputably emerge from the above. First is the belief and understanding of the nine successors about his thesis. Second, they being the most competent contemporaries and executors of Guru Nanak's thesis, their understanding and interpretation of it is of far greater value and importance than the *post facto* views of those who have a subjective commitment to a dichotomous religion or a social science discipline or any other system, which, at best, is only limited in its vision and scope. Third, the Gurus have lived, acted and proclaimed the unity of that thesis. Consequently, the logical method of interpretation is to accept the unity of their spiritual experience, deliberation and deed, and to approach the understanding of their spiritual thesis from the end of the deed. We have no ground to think otherwise.

There is a major difference between the Sikh Scripture and other scriptures, which were constructed by human beings, decades, even centuries after the concerned prophet had left the scene. Of the Christian Gospel, John Hick states, "Our modern historical awareness is that Christian doctrines should not be regarded divinely formulated and guaranteed propositions, but rather as human attempts to grasp the religious meaning, primarily of the Christ event, and in the light of this, of our human situation as a whole. The history of Christian theology is thus a part of the history of human thought." In the case of Sikhism, it is entirely different. Guru Granth Sahib is not only the authentic *bani* of, or revelation to Guru Nanak, but it is also the authentic record of the understanding and interpretation of his five spiritual successors. They are not human records of understanding, but true statements of unsurpassed spiritual value and authenticity.

By their living and deeds, the Gurus themselves have explained how to understand and interpret their *bani* or system. Guru Nanak laid down that the goal of man is to carry out His Will. The hymns quoted above say that those who know His Will, carry it out, this being a spiritual compulsion, and that only when one walks in His Will, does the Truth comes to be known. These wonderful statements give us a true glimpse of Sikhism and Sikh hermeneutics. This emphasises the primary importance of the lives and deeds of the Gurus. Consequently, in Sikhism, the unity of the spiritual experience of the Gurus, their deliberations of thinking, and their deeds, has to be accepted in order to grasp or interpret their *bani* or thesis. This is what they have stressed in their hymns quoted earlier.

The best, and the only way to truly interpret the thought of the Gurus is to understand and trace it from their deeds to the other end of their spiritual experience. For, the Gurus emphasise that His Will has compulsively to be followed, and only after following it, one comes to know of the Truth. Accordingly, so as to interpret their system, their deeds have to be understood and given priority. Otherwise, any attempt to understand their thought by ignoring their deeds will only keep us entangled in debates about what is the correct linguistic paraphrase of their *bani*. This is like putting the cart before the horse. It is this egoistic failing of the scholars that often results in numerous interpretations of the same writings. For example, the Vedas and Upanishads have been interpreted differently by scholars like Kumarila Bhatt, Sankara, Ramanuja, Nimbarka, Madhava, Vallabha, Swami Dayanand, and others. Many a time, a scholar's interpretation is just a piece of self justification, as has happened in the interpretations of the variant Parnalis of Udasis, Nirmalas, Gyanis and others. For the Gurus, there was not only complete unity of spiritual experience and thought, but they were all pursuing uniformly the same thesis, aims, objectives and goals during the

240 years of their lives. Hence, all talk of multiple or different levels or methods of approach and interpretations is faulty *ab initio*. The Gurus themselves emphasise that the sure method of understanding and interpretation of their thesis is to start with deeds as the basis, which would give one a clue or glimpse of their spiritual experience. Otherwise, we shall have the same crop of confusion as that of this Parnali or that Parnali, Western Parnali or Eastern Parnali; and most of these would be products of egoistic self-justification or personal prejudices.

For the true interpretation of the Sikh religion, there are five unique events which cannot be ignored. The first is that Guru Nanak's system is a revelation. Second, that the revelation has been recorded by the Guru or the prophet himself. Third, that both Guru Granth Sahib and the Gurus emphasise the impeccable unity of their thesis, and that failure to understand its unity and integrity means failure to comprehend and interpret its depths and truths. Fourth, that the thesis has been lived and demonstrated with love and humility by the Ten Gurus for 240 years, thereby leaving no scope for ambiguity. These demonstrations have been made by them as the unquestioned heads of a society dealing with all kinds of problems, and under variant social and political circumstances. Fifth, as is the clear lesson from the Gurus' lives, the *kakka* or *kirpan* prescribed by the Tenth Guru, stresses not only that Sikhism is a whole-life or *miri-piri* system, and that Sikhs should live truthfully, discharging all their social responsibilities in all fields of life, but also that they should never withdraw into the isolation of asceticism or monasticism.

REFERENCES

1. Guru Granth Sahib, p. 946.
2. Ibid., p. 176.
3. Ibid., p. 631.
4. Ibid., p. 176.
5. Ibid., p. 913.
6. Ibid., p. 12.
7. Ibid., p. 913.
8. *Limits of Growth* : Report for the Club of Rome. Project on the Predictament of Mankind, pp. 191-192.
9. Schweitzer, Albert : *Civilization and Ethics*, pp. 9.11-13.
10. Schumacher, E.F. : *Guide to the Perplexed*, p. 132.
11. Guru Granth Sahib, p. 560.
12. Ibid., p. 113.
13. Ibid., p. 941.
14. Ibid., p. 7.
15. Ibid., p. 1033.
16. Ibid., p. 463.
17. Ibid., p. 459.
18. Ibid., p. 1412.
19. Ibid., p. 62.
20. Ibid., p. 955.

21. Ibid., pp. 343, 347.
22. Ibid., p. 418.
23. Ibid., p. 463.
24. Ibid., pp. 1383, 9.
25. Ibid., p. 8.
26. Ibid., p. 730.
27. Ibid., p. 684.
28. Ibid., p. 931.
29. Ibid., p. 1423.
30. Ibid., p. 940.
31. Ibid., p. 991.
32. Ibid., p. 962.
33. Ibid., p. 522.
34. Ibid., p. 1376.
35. Ibid., p. 730.
36. Ibid., p. 473.
37. *The Panjab Past and Present*, Oct., 1976, Punjabi University, Patiala, p. 468.
38. Guru Granth Sahib, p. 1245.
39. Ibid., p. 965.
40. Ibid., p. 889.
41. Ibid., p. 417.
42. Ibid., pp. 417-418, 360.
43. Ibid., p. 1208.
44. Ibid., p. 224.
45. Ibid., p. 145.
46. Ibid., pp. 1282, 472.
47. Bhalla, Sarup Das : *Mehma Parkash*, p. 326.
48. Gupta, H.R. : *History of Sikh Gurus*, p. 114.
49. Guru Granth Sahib, p. 915.
50. Ibid., p. 853.
51. Ibid., p. 939.
52. Ibid., p. 722.
53. Ibid., p. 723.
54. Ibid., p. 566.
55. Ibid., p. 763.
56. Ibid., p. 35.
57. Ibid., p. 308.
58. Ibid., p. 943.
59. Ibid., p. 982.
60. Toynbee, A. : *An Historian's Approach to Religion*, Oxford University Press; 1957, p. 75.
61. Juergensmeyer, M. : *Sikh Studies*; Berkeley Religious Studies Series, Graduate Theological Union, Berkeley, California, 1979, p. 83, 88.
62. Murthy, H.V.S. : *Vaishnavism of Sankaradeva and Ramanuja*, pp. 201-202.
63. Ibid., p. 203.
64. *The Tribune,* Chandigarh, March 13, 1977.
65. Mann, J.S. & Saraon, H.S. (Eds.) : *Advanced Studies in Sikhism*; The Sikh Community of North America, Irvine, California, USA, 1989, pp. 270-271.
66. Ibid., p. 274.
67. Dowley, Tim : *Eerdman's Handbook to the History of Christianity*; reprint 1987, Eerdman Publishing Company Michigan, pp. 597-598.
68. *The Panjab Past and Present,* Oct. 1976, Punjabi University, Patiala, p. 468.

69. Jain, N.K. : *Sikh Gurus and Indian Spiritual Thought*, Punjabi University Patiala, p. 168.

70. James William : *Varieties of Religious Experience*, pp. 370-373.

71. Collingwood, R.G. : *Idea of History*, Oxford University Press, 1980, p. 178.

72. Toynbee, A. : op. cit., p. 132.

73. Dowley, Tim. : op. cit., p. 5.

74. Guru Granth Sahib, p. 991.

75. Ibid., p. 940.

76. Smullyan *et al*: *Introduction to Philosophy*, pp. 358-363.

77. Guru Granth Sahib, p. 463.

78. Ibid., p. 468.

79. Diwan Singh : *Revolution of Guru Nanak,* Peoples Publishing House, Chandigarh, 1993, p. 227.

80. Torah : *A New Translation of the Holy Scripture* (first Section), The Jewish Publication Society of America, Philadelphia. 2nd edition. 1981, p. 141.

81. Ibid., p. 135.

82. Ibid., p. 139.

83. Russell, Bertrand : *Unpopular Essays*, pp 53-57.

84. Azad, Maulana, A.K. : *India Wins Freedom*, Orient Longman, Calcutta, 1959, pp. 33-34.

85. Daljeet Singh : *Sikh Ideology*, Singh Brothers, Amritsar, 1990, pp. 48-49.

86. Seervai, H.M. : *Constitutional Law Of India, 3rd edition,* Sweet and Maxell Ltd., London, 1988, pp. 143-147.

87. Gupta, H.R. : *History of Sikh Gurus*, U.C. Kapoor & Sons. Delhi, 1973, p. 92.

88. Ibid., p. 92.

89. Ibid., p. 93.

90. Ibid., p. 93.

91. Ibid., pp. 100-101.

92. Ibid., pp. 101-102.

93. Ibid., p. 104.

94. *Gur Bilas Patshahi Chhevin*, pp. 84-85.

95. Gupta, H.R. : op cit.. pp. 114-19 and *Pothi Panj Sakhian*.

96. Ibid.

97. Ibid., p. 130.

98. Anonymous : *Haqiqat-i-Bana-wa Uruj-i-Firqai-Sikhan*, 1784 AD, pp. 3-6. *The Sikh Review*, Calcutta, Feb. 1990, p. 22.

99. Gupta, H.R. : op. cit.. p. 177.

100. Ibid., p. 234.

101. Rattan S. Bhangoo : *Sri Guru Panth Parkash*, Ed. Jit Singh Sital, SGPC, Amritsar, p. 189.

102. Guru Granth Sahib : p. 966.

103. Macauliffe, M.A. : *The Sikh Religion*, Vol. V, p. 295.

104. Gupta, H.R. : op. cit., pp. 139-140.

105. Schumacher, E.F. : *A Guide to the Perplexed*, pp. 134-135.

106. Guru Granth Sahib, pp. 560, 1092.

6

THE SIKH THOUGHT

KAPUR SINGH

The basic problems of Sikh thought are naturally the same as those of other world religions and, as may be expected, their treatment by Sikhism is, in the main, on the lines of the Hindu and Buddhist speculative thought. Wherever Sikhism differs or departs from these lines of thought, it does so, as a rule, not by introducing new terms or concepts but by underlining an already familiar concept, or by amplifying or interpreting it otherwise. This is, as it should be, for, thus alone is it possible to effect a new advance of expansion in the cultural and religious horizon of mankind, and it is thus that all great cultures and civilizations have emerged and developed.

THE UNIVERSE

In Sikh thought, the final duality between the Matter and Spirit is denied. The basic Sikh thought is strictly monistic :

"From One the Many emanate, and finally into the One the Many submerge."[1]

All that exists, whether in the form of phenomena and appearances, as Becoming, or as Numenon and Reality, as Being, is, in fact, the Spirit and the Mind. The individual mind, the numerous forms of life and the inanimate matter are all Spirit in different forms. Out of its own impulse and initiative of the Spirit a process of involutions occurred for some limited purpose, the precise nature of which is beyond human comprehension. All we can say is that such is its nature and such its pleasure. The fraction of the universe in its initial form, which the modern theorists, such as Abbe Lamatre call, the Primaeval Atom, resulted from the involutionary impulse of the Absolute Spirit, God. In this Primaeval Atom was originally concentrated, in a super-dense state, that which expanded and disintegrated, through an antithetical evolutionary impulse, for thousands of millions of years of the human mind, and finally into the universe as it is today. This eruptive, fissionary impulse, whereby the Primaeval Atom has issued into the innumerable forms constituting the universe, has reached its highest point, up-to-date, in the creation of man, and man, therefore, is the point in creation from where the inverse movement of evolution may take a further leap towards the Spirit. These two processes of involution and evolution, *apasarpani* and *upasarpani* as the profound ancient Jaina thought speculated, constitute a double but simultaneous movement, and thus creation of the universe is an involution-cum-evolution process, a descent and an ascent. The universe, thus, is nothing but God-in-Becoming. "The Formless has become all the innumerable forms, Himself. He, that is beyond the attributes, inheres. Nanak declares the doctrine of the One Absolute Being, that is Becoming, for, the One indeed is the Many."[2]

The main doctrines of Sikh theology are grounded in this view of the Ultimate Reality and its nature.

GENESIS

With regard to the coming into being of the Primaeval Atom, the Sikh doctrine is that the process was instantaneous, caused by the Will of God. "The forms become in consequence of the Divine Will. Comprehension fails at this stage of understanding of the Divine Will."[3]

After thus stating this beginning of the Becoming, the further statements made in the Sikh scripture about the creation and evolution of the universe, are remarkably akin to the picture which has now been adumbrated by scientific speculation after considering the data revealed by the recent advances in Observational Astronomy and probes into the heart of Matter. One of the basic hymns in the Sikh scripture, which may be called, the Hymn of the Genesis, says :

"For millions upon millions, countless years was spread darkness,
    When existed neither earth nor heaven,
    But only the limitless Divine Ordinance.
Then existed neither day or night, nor sun or moon;
    The Creator into unbroken trance was absorbed.
Existed then neither forms of creation, nor of speech;
    Neither wind nor water;
    Neither was creation, or disappearance or transmigration.
Then were not continents, nether regions, the seven seas,
    Nor rivers with water flowing.
Existed then neither heaven or the mortal world
    or the nether world.
Neither hell or heaven or time that destroys."
      ......

    "As it pleased Him, the world He created;
    Without a supporting power the expanse He sustained."
      ......

    "None His extent knows.
Of this from the Master, perfectly endowed comes realisation."[4]

MAN

Paul Tillich identifies man's basic predicament as existential estrangement from his essential being, estrangement which is expressed in anxiety about meaninglessness of life, gnawing awareness of alienation and incurable lack of wholeness, as his existential dilemma : "my bedstead of anxiety, strung with strings of pain and my cover quilt of alienation is my existential predicament. O, my God, take note of it and have mercy upon me."[5]

Paul Tillich, the modern Western man, was not aware that in the Sikh scripture, not only the human predicament has been noted, but the way to its cure has also been pointed out : Let man take refuge in God and proceed to cure his incurable sickness through identifying himself with God's purposes; "How else can man secure abiding peace and wholeness except through refuge in and communion with God ?"[6]

Man being the highest-yet point in the process of creation, where the evolutionary impulse has apparently near-exhausted its initial momentum, it is man on whom now the responsibility rests for consciously revitalising this impulse for a further evolutionary leap.

"Thou art the very essence of God. Therefore, know thyself as such."[7]

"You have received this gift of the human body and it is from here that the further upward movement towards God-realisation starts. Therefore, now make an all-out effort to reach the Goal and do not waste human life in frivolities."[8]

It is the involution-cum-evolution which is responsible for the creation of the universe, and which after reaching the point of human consciousness, has reached a stasis, and the man is thus a voluntary diminution of the infinitude of God, for some obscure but limited purpose, as, indeed, all forms of existence, represent a diminution of God. Since God is truth, knowledge, bliss, light, harmony and immortality, the involuted forms of creation are so much less of all these. Man being the stage at which the evolution has emerged into self-consciousness, man is capable of knowing that he has reached a particular stage of the creative process, and he is capable, volitionally, of taking steps to evolve upwards to the next stage. This is the stage of the *brahmajnani*, or the God-conscious man, and it is this notion of evolution, the premonition of which finds expression in the later 18th and early 19th century West European literature in the form of the concept of 'the Superman.' "Lo, I preach to you the Superman; Superman is the meaning of the earth," said Nietzsche. Again, "Man is a rope stretched between the animal and the Superman ...... what is great in man, is that he is a bridge, and not a goal."[9] Sikhism agrees with this except, that Sikhism declares that 'the meaning of the earth' reaches far beyond the stage of the Superman, and Superman is only an interim stage 'a bridge and not a goal.' Sikhism endorses Neitzsche that the sphere of the activity of the Superman, and of the higher-still goal of the evolution, is 'the earth', in the sense that it is on this earth that a perfect human Society of God-conscious men, a psycho-social perfection, is the ultimate objective of the impulse of God, which has originally given rise to the process of creation. In contradistinction to all those and previous philosophies and religions, which taught that the ultimate goal of man was either absorption into God, or entry into a supramundane Kingdom of God, wherein there is abiding propinquity to God, Sikhism urges man to divinize the whole of humanity on this earth by transforming mind, life and matter, through a conscious effort and will, and with the aid of the spiritual technique of the Namyoga, which is capable of taking along the whole psyche of man to a level of existence, undreamed of before, where pure knowledge, limitless harmony and divine bliss would prevail. This indeed would be a Society of god-like-beings, and the ultimate purpose of the divine impulse of creation is the establishment of this Society of human deities in the terrestrial spheres of the universe. It is the teaching of the Sikh Gurus that the supreme duty of man is to make an all-out effort towards this divine goal, and the Sikh Gurus not only point out this goal, but also reveal the way towards it. "Hail, the Guru, a hundred thousand times, hail, for, He reveals the secret of transforming mankind into deities, and that, too, in an instant."[10]

GOD

The Sikh concept of the Ultimate Reality is more akin to the Judaic notion of an Almighty Person than to the Aryan concept of an immanent neutral Principle. The basic formula of Sikh dogma is the opening line of the Sikh scripture which characterised the Ultimate Reality as follows :

"The One Becoming-Being. Truth. Numenon. Creator. Person. Without fear of another. Without animosity towards another. Beyond Time. Form. Unborn. Self-expression. Light. Contacted by human mind through (His) Grace.[11]

MAYA

The doctrine of *maya* has been basic to the Hindu and Buddhist speculations from the very beginning. The best known work, apart from the omniscient, *Mahabharta*, in which the term, '*maya*' (relative truth) is employed as a philosophical concept, is the metrical treatise, *Karika*, by Gaudpad, where-in, unlike the *Mahabharta* (*Bhagwadgita* XVIII. 61), the term is not taken for granted, but is explained and defined. Since this name, Gaudpad, was borne by the teacher of the famous philosopher of Hindu monism, Samkara, the author of the *Karika* may be the same person who might have lived at the end of the 7th century. This work, *Karika*, is usually printed with the *Mandukya-upanisad*, and for practical purposes, is regarded a part of it. In language and thought, both, it bears a remarkable resemblance to Buddhist writings of the *Madhyamik* School, and the criticism of the Hindu orthodoxy that the monism of Samkara, in which the doctrine of *maya* is embedded, is, in reality, crypto-Buddhism, is not without substance.[12] In the *Karika*, the world of appearances is compared to the apparent circle of fire produced by a whirling lighted torch. This striking image first occurs in the *Maitrayana Upanisad* (VI. 24). It also occurs in the Buddhist Mahayan scripture, the *Lankavtarsutra*, which purports to be an account of the revelation of the true Religion of Gautama, the Buddha, when he visited Ceylon and there gave discourses to the King of the island, Ravana, and his wife, Mahamati. This represents a well matured phase of speculation in Buddhism, as it criticises the Hindu schools of philosophy of the Samkhya, *Pasupat*, as well as other schools. It includes a prophecy about the birth of Nagarjuna, the great Buddhist savant of the 4th century A.D., and it mentions the advent of Guptas which marks the renaissance of Hinduism in India. It also alludes to the fresh incursions of the Hunas into northern India, which incursions destroyed the Imperial Gupta dynasty at the end of the 5th century A.D. Throughout the Hindu speculative and religious literature ever since, this doctrine of *maya* is admitted as in some way an independent principle of the process and ontological structure of creation. True, the subtle Samkara asserts that the principle of *maya* is *aniravacani*, that is, it can neither be said to exist nor not to exist. A is neither A, nor not A. Whatever else this statement may mean, it does concede that *maya* has a positive existence. Sikhism denies the doctrine of *maya*, thus conceived. As ignorance and nescience have no positive existence, they merely being the aspects of the self-limited involuted Spirit, likewise, *maya*, as such, has no positive existence. It is merely a way of saying that the individual consciousness perceives the Reality only in the form of partial knowledge, which is there on account of involution. As the darkness is merely a negative aspect of the light of the sun, similar is the case with ignorance and nescience.

"What is there positive to which we can give the name of *maya* ? What positive activity is the *maya* capable of ?"

The human soul is subject to the pleasure and pain principle in its very nature, as long as it operates on the individuated plane of consciousness.

Again, "*Maya*, in the form of a snake, entwines to render human mind immiscible with the real, and the more it is accepted at its face value, the more it misguides. Rare indeed is such a man who overcomes and casts it away." Further, "what is *maya* except a befooling magic trick ? Yea, a dry blade of grass afire, a passing shadow of a summer cloud, a momentary flooding after a tropical rain, for him who is out of communion with God."[13]

What do these dissertations on *maya*, in the Sikh scripture mean ?

Maya is the antithesis of *moksha* in Hindu thought. But *maya* is not the antithesis of the Absolute Reality. There is no incompatibility between the *brahma* and *maya*, for the former is not opposed to the Many. It is *advanda*, non-dual, that is, it has no opposite being outside all classification. To be precise, 'classification' is exactly *maya*. *Maya* noun of Sanskrit is derived from the root *matr*, 'to measure to form, to build, to lay out a plan', the same root from which Graeco-Latin words, 'metre' 'matrix', 'material' and 'matter' are obtained. The fundamental process of measurement is division. Thus, the Sanskrit root, *dva*, from which we get 'divide', is also the Latin root of 'dus', and the English, 'dual.' To say, then, that the world of 'facts' and 'events' is *maya* is to say that the words, 'facts' and 'events' are terms of measurement rather than the real itself, *per se*. 'Measurement' is setting up bounds of all kinds, whether by descriptive classification or by screening. Thus, the 'facts' and 'events' are as abstract as lines of latitude or feet and inches, metres and centimetres. This is not to be confused with the "Idealism" or "Monism" of the Western philosophy, for all concrete things are not, in reality, illusion, unreal, or just, the One. They are not unreal and illusory, because *maya* is not non-existence; it is a wrong mode of apprehension. It is not 'One', because 'One' is a thing, a mode of measurement and, therefore, itself *maya*. To join the 'many' into 'one' is as much *maya* as to separate the many from one. The world, as we perceive it, is made up of surfaces and lines, of areas of density and vacuity, but the '*maya*' concept of the Sikh scripture says that these forms and appearances, these things and events have no "own-being", *svabhava*; they do not exist in their own right, but only in relation to one another, like "the spark of a dry blade of grass", or like "the fleeting shadow of a summer cloud." Concretisation and formalisation is *maya*, when the human mind attempts to comprehend and control that which impinges upon his consciousness. This is the unreal world of Buddhism, the world of 'name and form', *nama-rupa*. When the Sikh scripture says that "*maya* is a snake which entwines human consciousness, and whosoever takes it at its face value, him *maya* misleads and confuses", it means that man confuses his measures with the world so measured, of identifying money with wealth, fixed convention with fluid reality. The Sikh doctrine of *maya* points out the impossibility of grasping the actual world in the verbal net of man's mind and the fluid character of those very constructions he thus artifacts. This world of *maya* escapes both the comprehension of the philosopher and the grasp of the pleasure-seeker, like water from a clutching fist, "like the fleeting shade of a summer cloud."

This interpretation of the concept of *maya* in Sikh terminology has far-reaching consequences in so far as it pulls the Hindu mind out of the slough of indolent introspective pre-occupation, and subjectivism, generated by the belief that the whole world of the appearances in which man is born to pursue his socio-political life, is no more real than a phantasmagoria in the minds of the gods above. By giving a foundation of solid reality to the world of appearance, this re-interpretation of the concept of *maya* conforms to a sense of reality, a feeling of urgency and an objectivity to the whole frame of mind of man, which is necessary for the all-out effort to speed up the evolutionary process through the human will, and this is the core of the precepts of Sikhism, as a way of life.

ETHICS

The fact that religious experience, *per se*, is non-moral, has been known to Hindu thought from the very beginning. In the West, it has been recognised clearly only in recent times. It was Dr Otto who in his *Idea of the Holy,* about a quarter of a century ago, made this point finally clear. In the Judaic religious tradition, for all practical purposes, religious life and ethical conduct appear to have been made identical. The ten Commandments of Moses are ethical precepts. In the Koran, it is these ethical commands which are presented as the essence of religion. Western scholars are sometimes shocked at the stories narrated in the ancient Hindu texts, of the conduct of gods that does not conform with strict ethical standards, and about which the narrator of the story expresses no moral horror and passes no censorial judgement. From this, the Western reader erroneously concludes that ethics has no place in the Hindu religious practice and tradition. This is far from the truth. From the very beginning, it has been recognised that ethical conduct is the very foundation on which the life of a religious man must be based. The rules of conduct of the Buddhist *sharamans*, the formulary of conduct of Jain *bhikshus*, the daily rules regulating a Brahmin's life, bear ample testimony to the fact that the relation of ethics to religious experience is well recognised and established, though a man with secular sovereign status is exempted from moral censure.[12] This moral exemption, however, is more a juridical rule rather than a moral precept. The case of non-human gods, though is obviously on a different law. In Sikhism, while it is recognised that the religious experience belongs to a category of values which has a unique status and ontological structure in its own right, it is, nevertheless, insisted that without strictly ethical purity of conduct there is no possibility of any advance in the religious experience. A religious life, not strictly grounded in ethical conduct, or a religious discipline which ignores the ethical requirements, is considered as a highly damaging error. "The seed of the teachings of the Guru cannot germinate except in the field of ethical conduct, constantly irrigated by the waters of truth."[15] "A man of religion is ever characterised by ethical deeds, honest living, sincerity of heart, and a fearless passion for truth."[16] "Nanak maketh this emphatic declaration, let all men ponder over it. Ethical conduct is the only true foundation of human life on earth."[17] Sikhism, thus, lays a stress on morality which raises the moral law to a higher and absolute status such as was not so in the Hindu and Buddhist thought.

The Buddhist and Brahminic systems appear to assume tacitly that morality is a means to felicity and that it is not obedience to a law which exists in its own right as demanding obedience, what Immanual Kant called, the Categorical Imperative. It is true that by them moral conduct is regarded as governed by the cosmic law, called, the law of *karma*, which means that good deeds bring good results and evil deeds bring evil results. "The evil deeds I did in past lives have now become impediments and misfortunes for me."[18] Sikhism, however, raises ethical conduct to a higher and more independent, absolute status, and makes it as the true expression of the harmony of human personality with the Will of God. All ethical conduct, therefore, is not merely conducive to good results such as happiness, but it is primarily, an act of establishment of concord between the human personality and the Person of God. Since this concord is the highest end and the goal of human existence and endeavour, it is, therefore, the basic ingredient of the highest activity of man which is religion. Thus, Sikhism while recognising that the order of Reality which is revealed as numenon to the human experience does not fall under the category of ethical experience, it unequivocally emphasises that the two cannot be divorced or separated, and that the nature of the numenon is such that its realisation is impossible without ethical conduct. The ethical category and the numenal category are distinct, but are structurally and inseparably joined.

In this way, the Sikh thought fuses the Hindu thought and the Semitic tradition on the subject of ethics and religion.

FREE WILL

European philosophy and theology have been much exercised on the subject of the 'free will', while the Hindu tradition has considered this subject as of minor importance. The explanation for this lies in the analytical understanding of the concept by both the traditions. In European thought, an individual is conceived of as a permanent fixed entity, basically separate from the rest of the world which is his universe. It is argued that without freedom of will there is no moral responsibility, there can neither be guilt nor punishment, either in society or hereafter, before the throne of God. This problem has not much troubled the Hindu thought which considers that there is no such thing as a completely free and stable entity, called, 'the individual', and secondly, the Hindu argues, that if the human will is not free then what does the term, "freedom", mean ? What instance shall we bring forth with which to contrast the supposed determination of human will ? Our notion of "freedom" is inalienably derived from our own experience to which we give the name of "will." Whatever, therefore, we may mean by "freedom", it is ultimately in the terms of our own 'will', that we give meaning to it. Thus interpreted, to say that human will is free, is an axiom, as well as a tautology. There is no meaning in the thesis that human will is not free, for, "free" is that which is like unto the human will. The trouble, however, arises when we give to the expression, "free will", a meaning which we have not derived from our experience of our 'will', but which have been superimposed by our intellect. Thus, we like to think that, "free will" is that power of volition of the human individual which is totally uncaused and unconditioned. The concept of 'self-caused inevitability' and 'freely chosen determinism' would appear as puzzling, if not altogether non-sensical to the Western mind. A little reflection, however, will show that such a "freedom" does not, and cannot, in fact, exist, and further, that, if it did and could exist, it will destroy all foundations of 'moral responsibility', 'sense of guilt', and justification for 'punishment' either here or hereafter. To begin with, there are the facts of heredity, the environment, and the subconscious mind. There is not much doubt that the individual is the product of his heredity, the inner mechanism of which the science of biology has discovered recently in the fertilized germ-cells and its genes, which make all the organic cells that make up the body including the brain and the nervous system. This pattern we inherit from our parents and our ancestors and it is certainly a determination of the choices that we make in our lives from time to time. Psychology has revealed to us that subconscious layers of human mind as the seat of instincts, emotions, and intuitions, for those who faithfully follow the dogma of the Church Council of Constantinople (553 A.D.) which anathematised the doctrine of transmigration, in the race during evolution of millions of years; or, accumulated, for those who hold the doctrine of metempsychosis as fundamental, accumulated in the course of untold numbers of previous births and rebirths of the individual. They are certainly a determinant throughout a man's life in the matter of his choice and the conduct that follows it. Again, from outside, the social environment is active in continuously influencing and moulding the individual's mind, and thereby his power of choice and conduct. These three factors, the physical, the environmental and the hereditary, are there as a fact, and their powers of influencing the human power of choice cannot be denied. In this sense, there cannot be a 'free will', as an uncaused and unconditioned factor which solely determines as to what choice, in a given situation, an individual will make. But, even if there were such a "free" will, it will entail disastrous consequences. If a man's actions are not free, when they can be shown to be casually chained to his character, the sum total of his heredity, past experiences and environment, then the only circumstances in which it would be proper to call a man "free", would be those in which he acted independently of his received character, that is, of his habits, desires, urges, and perspective on life, and all the rest. But, if this agent of 'free' action, is not to be equated and identified with that which is subject to particular desires and urges, which is circumscribed by a given environmental and circumstantial set-up, which is devoid of character, motives, persistent interests and the like, then who is this agent of 'free' choice, the 'he ?' Such a notion of 'free' will completely dissolves the agent of action; a person with such a 'free' will is a completely disembodied and unidentifiable entity. Such an entity can neither be blamed nor praised. Indeed, such an entity would be truly like the "Superman" of Nietzshe, "beyond good and evil." Nor can such an entity be held responsible for what it does, for, it would be clearly unreasonable to hold an individual responsible for his actions, if we did not think there was a cause and effect connection between his character and his conduct. When we can show that there is no such connection, as, for instance, an act is committed as a result of coercion, we do not normally hold him responsible. The reason is not that the one act is 'uncaused' and 'free', while the other is 'determined.' In one case, the cause lies in the character of the individual over which he has, in some sense, control while in the other case, he has no such control. As we gain new knowledge about the kinds of causes that affect conduct, we change our mind about the kinds of behaviour for which we should hold men responsible. The recent shifts of stress in the science of Penology in the modern world, and the ancient wisdom of the East and West, which iterated that an individual is ultimately responsible for nothing, must be appreciated in the context of this analysis, and not in the superfine frame of reference of 'determinism' and 'free will.' "A man reaps only what he sows in the field of *karma*,"[17] declares the Sikh scripture. It simultaneously says, that, "Say, what precisely is it that an individual can do out of his free choice ? He acteth as God Willeth."[20] And the *Bhagvadgita* asserts that, "God sits in the heart of every creature with the consequence that all revolve in their set courses, helplessly tied to the wheel of *maya*."[21] That man is free to choose and act to some extent, and to the extent that he is so, to that extent alone he is morally responsible and subject to praise and blame, is a true statement. That there is no such entity, and no such entity is conceivable, which is wholly 'uncaused' and 'undetermined', and further that in the ultimate analysis, the whole area of individuality can be linked to a cause of causes which are supra-individual, is also a true statement, and these two true statements are not self-contradictory or incompatible with each other, constitutes the Sikh doctrine on the subject.

This brings us back to our immediate experience that seems to carry its own certitude with it, that, in some sense, we are 'free', for, we have the notion of 'freedom' as the core of this experience. Sikhism, while implicitly taking note of the three factors which determine the powers of human choice, lays stress on this fourth factor, perpetually present and operative in the human mind, which possesses the autonomous power of choice. This autonomous power is the divinity in man, according to Sikhism, and it is this core around which the whole human personality is built. It is, at heart, "the source of all human misery, as well as the panacea of all his ills."[22] "How may man demolish the wall of nescience that separates him from God ? By being in tune with the Will of God. And how shall we know the Will of God. Nanak answers : It is embedded in the very core of human personality."[23] It is this autonomous power of free choice which is given to every human personality, and by virtue of which the effects of the other three determining factors of human choice are interfused, and, thus, the act of free human choice gives birth to a new event, which is not wholly determined, and which is not a mere combination and aggregational consequence of all these four factors, but which is a new event, unique in nature, and potently capable of giving rise to other similar events in the future. It is this power of free choice that is included in man's original heritage, which has the capacity to go beyond this heritage, and thus, within the limits given, a human being is free to shape his own destiny. Nor are the other three factors, his received character, the environment and the subconscious mind, merely accidental and fortuitously superimposed upon the individual, for, they too are the fruits of his past *karma* of uncounted previous births, and thus, they are self-determined, self-caused, result of free choices earlier made. When and why and how did an individual make the first free but wrong choice ? This question relates to the First Things, and, therefore, *exhypothesis*, the individual comprehension fails at this point : "the son observeth and knoweth not the birth of his father."[24]

KARMA

The doctrine of *karma* is not the same as the doctrine of pre-destination of the Christian theology. *Karma* is, in a sense, fate, self-caused inevitability, not pre-destination, for, within the limits given, (and these limits constitute the *karma* inherited from the previous births), a man is free. This *karma* is not 'fate', because all the time we are making our own *karma* and determining the character of our further status and births. The doctrine of *karma* as understood in higher Hinduism, and as expounded in Sikhism, merely teaches that our present limitations are traceable to our acts of autonomous choice in our past lives, and as such, our *karma* is a source of rewards and punishments which we must enjoy and endure, but this idea differs from the idea of 'fate', as commonly understood in European thought, in as much as it is not inexorable, for all the time we are making our own *karma* within a context, the core of which is always free and autonomous.

EVIL

The existence of evil, it might be said, is the main reason for the keen interest in religion, and, therefore, the explanation of evil is the chief problem of theologies and religious philosophies. Whether it was God who created evil, and whether evil is due to misuse of the gifts of free will, are problems which constantly occur and recur in almost all religions of the world. But, the presence of evil, as a de-tranquilliser and disturber of the composure of the human mind, cannot be ignored or argued away, so much so that perceptive minds regard it as the preponderant characteristic of the existential human situation.[25]

The main trend of Hindu thought on this problem is that since the world itself is unreal, the existence of evil in it is not of greater concern to the individual than the world itself. He asserts that the proper course for the human soul is to seek *mukti*, liberation or unison with God by renouncing and discarding this vain show of appearances, called, the world. The Hindu, thus, is not very much concerned to prove that evil does not really exist in the world, or to explain why God allows it to exist. Since the world itself is no more than a phantom and an insubstantial dream, the evil itself cannot be of a more enduring substance, and, at any rate, it is of no direct concern to the man of religion.

Sikhism cannot and does not adopt this view, because Sikhism does not accept the ultimate dichotomy of matter and spirit, and does not accept as an independent entity, the principle of illusion, *maya*. Since Sikhism postulates that religious activity must be practised in the socio-political context of the world, the problem of evil is very much a real problem to Sikhism as it is to the European thinker. Sikhism, therefore, returns almost the same answer to the problem of evil which the European pantheist gives, namely, that since God is all things and in all things, evil is only something which is a partial view of the whole, something which appears as such, when not seen from the due perspective. Sikhism asserts that there is no such thing as the independent principle of evil, as some theologies postulate, although there are things in this world which are evil. This antithesis of evil and good, according to Sikhism, is a necessary characteristic of the involution syndrome involved in the process of creation of the world. Evil and good appear at one stage of this involution-cum-evolution and they disappear when the process of evolution culminates into the unitive experience of God, just as the white ray of light splits into its variegated spectrum while passing through a prism, and again gathers these multichromatic hues into its all-absorbing whiteness, when it becomes itself again. In the final stage of things, "all evil transmutes itself into good, and all defeat into victory." When a complete perspective is granted to man by the Grace of God, all evil melts into its source which is All-Good.[26] There is no independent principle of evil in the universe because God is All-Good and, "nothing that proceeds from All-Good can be really evil, and there is naught, which proceeds from any other source but God."[27]

But this Sikh metaphysical speculation on the ontological status of evil, does not supply a clear cut answer to the problem of evil as man encounters it in his everyday experience and life.

Ours is a time of upheaval political, social, religious, and moral; our most urgent problem is to forestall the catastrophe that menaces us, catastrophe of total destruction, and unprecedented unrest and violence. The causes of the present troubles and future dangers can all be traced back to the lack of any root-principles, generally agreed in philosophy, religion and politics. Everywhere, old class structures of society have been undermined by the advent of democracy. European hegemony and overlordship in Asia and Africa have yielded place to independence or partnership. In religion, the simple faith in the ancient theologies, and in their sacred writings as the explanation of the universe and as the foundation and sanction of morals, has been shaken by the impact of modern science. Civilisation has been disadjusted, and confusion prevails. General consensus is that the present age is mostly concerned, not with the world of ideas, but with the world of things, material things that we make and use, sell and buy. Though physical sciences, technology and economics are of immense value to mankind, it is not anywhere in that world that we may hope to find the solution to our problems, and that solution, whatever it might be, lies in the world of ideas. Men's actions are determined by their ideas and not vice versa, as fanatical Marxists fondly hope and obstreperously assert. Right ideas are those that lead to good actions, and good actions are those that are known to lead to welfare. Wrong ideas are those that lead to opposite results, suffering and disaster. Welfare means everything worthwhile, material, intellectual, moral and spiritual welfare.

To discover wherein welfare consists, and to find ways to attain it, constitute a continuous enquiry, discussion, study, meditation and argument. Thus, the ancient problem of evil is reopened, and the explanation of it that monotheistic theologies give, namely, to argue it away at the transcendental level, appears unsatisfying : the two world-wars of our times, for instance. If God is omnipotent and benevolent, why are there wars ? The answer that the ontological status of evil is negative and non-existent, or the answer implicated in the Book of Job, constitute an impressive argument and a magnificient poem, respectively, but in the face of the concrete evil, the latter appears a sterile philosophy and the former an evasion, but no straight answer. In the case of a dualistic theology that concedes two real and positive opposing powers, good and evil, it would appear that if God has created a maleficent power, the power of evil, of negation and denial, then God is not all Benevolent, but if this power is co-equal and co-existent then God is not All-powerful. The problem of evil may be a mere abstraction, but there are problems of evil everyday in tangible and concrete situations, and they raise not merely the philosophical questions about the status and origin of evil, but also what is the moral imperative for man, in dealing with evil situations, in day-to-day life.

Sikhism takes direct and full cognizance of this aspect of the problem. While it denies evil an ultimate status in the structure of Reality, it squarely faces the concrete existence of evil in the day-to-day life of man, as well as the agents of evil in human affairs.

"The cannibals say ritual prayers of Islam, and the assasins strut about as practising Hindus ...... All concern for human decencies and respect for ethical conduct has disappeared and the evil rules supreme."[28]

Sikhism calls upon all men of moral perception and spiritual awakening to oppose the agents of evil, the evil-doers and their aides singly, through appropriate organisation, to oppose relentlessly, till the end, till this evil is destroyed or contained. The Light of God, that shone through the Sikh Prophets, to guide mankind is unambiguous and uncompromising on this point : "O, God of Benedictions, this blessing above all, we do ask of You : the will and tenacity to tread the path of good promoting actions and fearlessness in opposition to the agent of evil."[29] "The Light of Sikhism is for the supreme purpose of urging men to destroy and extirpate evil-doers."[30]

But, since according to Sikh metaphysics, the evil is just a passing phase, a phenomenal occurrence, neither there in the beginning nor there at the end, and, therefore, having no substance or real existence, why should any man of understanding bother to oppose it or to destroy or contain it ?

Sikhism answers this question. The ancient Hindu insight into the scientific laws governing character formation, tells us that, "what a man does, what he attitudinises, that he becomes."[31] To tolerate evil, to co-exist with it, and not to confront it, is to accept and compromise with it. Such acceptance and compromise are antivirtuous passivity and negative life style, and the destiny of ethical and spiritual negation is hell. A negative personality is a naked personality. In the absence of a proper covering of virtue and merit, there is no more frightful fate that can overtake man : "On its predestined march towards hell, a naked soul looks truly frightful."[32]

Jacob Boehme in his, *Signatura Rerum*, tells us, "What is evil to one thing, that is good to another. Hell is evil to the angels, for they are not created thereunto, but it is good to the hellish creatures. So also heaven is evil to the hellish creatures, for, it is their poison and death."

Emmanuel Swedenborg (1688-1772) wrote in his, *Heaven and Hell* :

"No punishment is from the Lord, but from Evil itself; because Evil is so joined with its own punishment that they cannot be separated."

By co-existence and non-confrontation with evil things, man is utterly degraded from his essential humanity, and becomes a hellish creature, and thus, his punishment is great.

"Fall and rise, rawness and ripeness are known and seen hereafter in the next world."[33]

NUMENON AND SAMSAR, OR THE REALITY AND APPEARANCE

Samsar is the principle of change, which determines the world of phenomena, and in Hindu thought and in some other systems of metaphysics, it has been argued that on this account it is unreal. It is presumed as axiomatic that the real must not be infected with change. The basic formula of Sikh dogma, with which the Sikh scripture opens, is proceeded by the exegetic statement that "all change, all evolution, all that is characterised by the time-process, is ultimately real."[34]

The numenon, the order of Reality, which is revealed to the human mind through gnosis, therefore, is not something which is fundamentally different and away from the phenomenon, altered in the gnosis is not that what really is, but it is the mode of perception and the quality of prehension of the individual, which is transformed, thus revealing the vision of the numenon. It is this very mundane and the material world and the phenomena which is fresh and differently prehended and cognised by the human consciousness, a consciousness that is enlarged and uplifted. Sikhism, therefore, is in agreement with the aphorism of the great Buddhist philosopher, Budhagosa who declared that, "*yas-samsaras tan-nirvanam*", that is, "the flux and the Absolute are the same." "This world of fleeting appearances that you see, is, in fact, the true face of God, and as such, it is revealed to the consciousness of emancipated man."[35]

REFERENCES

1. *Ikkas te hoio ananta, Nanak ikkas mahi samae jio.* — Majh, p. 131.
2. *Nirankari akar apu nirgun sargun ek, ekahiek bakhanano Nanak ek anek Gauri, Bavan akheri,* p. 250.
3. *"Hukmi hovan akar hukam na kahia jai."*, p. 1.
4. Guru Granth Sahib, pp. 1035-36.
5. Ibid., p. 1379.
6. *"Har nah na miliai sajanai kat paiay bisram ?"*, G.G.S., p. 133.
7. *"Man tu jotsarup hain apna mul pachhan."* — Asa di var, G.G.S., p. 441.
8. *"Bhai prapat manukha dehuria, gobind milan ki eho teri baria, saranjami lagu bhavajalu tarankai, janamu birtha jat rangi mayakei."* — Asa di var, G.G.S., p.12.
9. *Thus spake Zarathustra.* I. 4.
10. *Balihari gur apne diohari sadvar, jini manas te devte kie karat no lagi bar.* — Var Asa, G.G.S., p. 462.
11. *"1. Onkar, Satu, Namu, Karta, Purukhu, Nirbhau, Nirvaira, Akal Murti, Ajuni Saibhang, Gur Prasadi."* G.G.S., p.1.
12. *Mayavadam asachhastram, prachhannam bauddham.* — Padam-purana.
13. *"Maya kisnau akhiye ? kia maya karam kamai ? dukh sukh iha jio baddh hai haumai karam kamai."* G.G.S., p. 67.
    "Maya hoi nagani jagati rahi laptae, is ki seva jo kare tisi hi ko phir khae, gurmukh koi garadu tini mali dali laee pae." G.G.S., p. 510.
    "Mai maya chhal; trin ki agan, megh ki chhaya Gobind bhajan binu had ka jal." — G.G.S., p. 717.
14. *Samrath ko nahin dos gusain.* — Tulsi, Ramcaritmanas.
15. *Amal kar dharti bij sabdo kar sace ki ab nit deha pani* — Srirag, G.G.S., p. 24.
16. *Sac karni sac taki rahit, sac hirdai sac mukhi kahit* — Sukhmani, G.G.S., p. 283.
17. *Bhanat Nanak bujhe ko bicari, isi jag mahi karni sari* — Sorath, G.G.S., p. 599.

18. *Purva janamam kritam papam byadhi rupen pidatam* : Sarvadarsan Samgrah.
19. *Jeha bijai so lunai karma sandra khet* — Baramaha, G.G.S., p.134.
20. *Kahu Manukh te kia hoe ave ? jo tisi bhave soi karaye.* — Sukhmani, G.G.S., p. 277.
21. *Ishvrah sarvbhutanam brideso Arjun, nishtoti, bhramayan, sarvabhutani yantrasudhani maya.* — XVIII. 61.
22. *Haumain diragh rog hai daru bhi is mahi.* —Var Asa, G.G.S., p. 466.
23. *Kiv saciara hoiai kiv kude tuttai pal ? hukamrajai callana, Nanak likhia nal.* — Japu, G.G.S., p.1.
24. *Pita ka janam kai janai put* — Sukhmani, G.G.S., p. 284.
25. Therefore, since the world has still
      Much good, but much less good than ills
      And while the sun and the moon endure
      Luck's a chance but trouble is sure
      I'd face it as a'wise man should,
      And train for ill and not for good. — Houseman, A.E.
26. Guru Granth Sahib; p. 1302.
27. *Isu te hoe su nahi bura, orai kahahu kinai kachhu kara.* — Sukhmani, G.G.S., p. 294.
28. *Manas khane karahi nivaj churi vagayin*
      tin gal tag ...... saram dharam ka beda dur,
      Nanak kud rahiya bharpur. — Var Asa, G.G.S., p. 471.
29. *Deha siva bar mohi ihai subh karman te kabahun*
      na taraon, na daraon, ari sio jab jae laraon. — Dasamgranth
30. *Eha kaj dhara ham janamam ...... dust sabhan kau mul ukparan.* — Ibid.
31. *Yatha kari yatha cari tatha bhavati.*
32. *"Nanga dojak calia ta disai khara draona."* — Asa Var, G.G.S., p. 471.
33. *Kacc pakai othe pai, Nanak gaia jape jae.* — Japu.
34. *Adi sacu, jugadi sacu, hai bhi sacu, Nanak, hosi bhi sacu.* — Japu, G.G.S., p.1.
35. *Ihu visu sansar tum dekhde ehu hari ka rup hai, harirup nadri aia.* — Ramkali., G.G.S., p. 922.

7

THE SIKH WORLDVIEW

DALJEET SINGH

INTRODUCTION

In order to understand the Sikh worldview, it is necessary to answer a number of questions, namely, (1) what is the spiritual experience of the Gurus about the Fundamental Reality ? (2) what are the logical implications of that religious experience ? (3) how do these implications or ideas differ from those in other religions ? (4) did those ideas govern the course of Sikh religion ? and (5) what future does the Sikh worldview hold for man ? In answering these questions, we shall confine ourselves entirely to the *bani* in Guru Granth Sahib and historically accepted facts about the lives of the Gurus. Many of the misrepresentations about Sikhism arise from the failure of writers to understand Sikhism on the basis of its thesis, or to define Sikhism in terms of doctrines in Guru Granth Sahib. Obviously, in this short paper, we shall only give an outline of the Sikh worldview. We shall start with a definition of the Fundamental Reality or God in Sikhism.

GOD IN SIKHISM

The Reality or God has been profusely defined in Guru Granth Sahib. Guru Nanak calls Him "*Karta Purkh*" or "Creator Person", the world being His creation. Apart from being immanent in the world, He is the Ocean of Virtues, i.e., He is a God of Attributes. In defining the fundamental nature of God, the Guru says, "Friends ask me what is the mark of the Lord. He is all Love, the rest He is Ineffable."[1] Thus, the key to understanding the Sikh worldview is that God is Love. And Love has four clear facets : It is dynamic; it is the mother of all virtues and values; it is directive or has a will; and it is benevolent towards life in which He is immanent; i.e., it generates neither a dialectical movement, nor a class war, nor suicidal competition or struggle.

COROLLARIES OF 'GOD IS LOVE'

This spiritual experience leads to five corollaries. First, it *ipso facto* gives status, meaning and reality to the world and life, because Love and God's Attributes can be expressed only in a becoming universe. For, when God was all by Himself, the question of love and devotion did not arise. In unambiguous words, the Guru says, "True is He, and true is His creation."[2] Second, it clearly implies that the religious man has to lead a life of creativity and activity. Consequently, a householder's life is accepted and monasticism is spurned. Third, it gives spiritual sanction to the moral life of man, indicating thereby that it should be of the same character as the loving nature of God. For, "Love, contentment, truth, humility and virtues enable the seed of *Naam* (God) to sprout."[3] This clearly prescribes the methodology of deeds. Fourth, it unambiguously points out the direction in which human effort should move, and the yardstick with which to measure human conduct. This sets the goal for the seeker, or Godman. Fifth, it shows the gracious interest of God in human affairs and activities. An important attribute of God is that He is 'Guru' or Enlightener who gives both knowledge and guidance, i.e., spiritual experience is noetic. The Guru's God being a God of Will, one feels confident that one is working in line with His altruistic Will. For, God is perpetually creating and watching the world with His Benevolent Eye.[4] And, He rewards every effort to become divine.[5] For that matter, it gives man hope, strength and optimism.

IMPLICATION OF 'GOD IS LOVE'

Here it is necessary to stress that the definition that God is Love, is extremely important for determining the category of Sikh religion. For, all systems in which God is Love, are life-affirming, and there is an integral combination between the spiritual life and the empirical life of man. And, as in the case of Abu Ben Adam, love of one's fellowmen, is the primary and essential counterpart of the love of God. But, in life-negating systems, there is a clear dichotomy between the empirical life and the spiritual life of man. And *sanyasa*, asceticism, monasticism, withdrawal from life, pacifism or *ahimsa* and celibacy are the normal modes of the spiritual path. Sikhism, Judaism, Islam and Christianity belong to the first category. Jainism and most other Indian systems belong to the second category.

In fact, differences in approach to life are due to the basic difference in the spiritual experience. In the second category of systems like Vaisnavism and Vedanta, God has been defined as *sat-chit-ananda* (truth-consciousness-bliss). This is far from being a dynamic concept. Stace has made a detailed survey of the description various mystics give of the nature of their spiritual experience of the Ultimate Reality. They all give blessedness, tranquility, holiness, unitary consciousness and ineffability as the nature of their spiritual experience.[6] No mystic mentions love as the characteristic of that experience. The distinction is not arbitrary, but real. Huxley says, "The Indians say, the thought and the thinker and the thing thought about are one and then of the way in which this unowned experience becomes something belonging to me; then no me any more and a kind of *sat-chit-ananda* at one moment without *karuna* or charity (how odd that the Vedantists say nothing about love) ...... I had an inkling of both kinds of *nirvana* — the loveless being, consciousness, bliss and the one with love, and, above all, sense that one can never love enough."[7] He also says, "Staying in this ecstatic consciousness and cutting oneself off from participation and commitment in the rest of the world — this is perfectly expressed today in powerful slang, in the phrase 'dropping out.' It completely denies the facts, it is morally wrong, and finally of course, absolutely catastrophic." "Absolutely Catastrophic."[8] Hence, the religious system laid down by the Gurus is radically different from the earlier Indian systems.

CONSEQUENT DIFFERENCES WITH OTHER RELIGIOUS SYSTEMS OF INDIA

As it is, the Guru's concept of God is quite different from the concept of many of the quietist mystics, or from the Indian concept of *sat-chit-ananda*. We find that Guru Nanak's system follows strictly his spiritual experience and his view of the Attributes of God. And as a Godman, he seeks to follow the line of expression of God's attributes in the world of man. Consequently, in the empirical life, this concept has important implications which stand emphasised in the *bani* and life of Guru Nanak. Hence, Guru Nanak's system and its growth are entirely different from his contemporary religious systems and their growth.

First, it means, as already pointed out, the reality of the world and the life-affirming character of Sikhism. For, God is not only immanent in the world, He also expresses His Love and Attributes in the empirical world, and casts a Benevolent Eye on His creation. But in Vedanta and other Indian systems, the world is either *mithya*, an illusion, a misery, or a suffering. Second, Sikhism being life-affirming, this, inevitably, involves an integral combination between the spiritual life and the empirical life of man. This constitutes the foundation of the *miri-piri* doctrine laid down by Guru Nanak in his *bani*. In other words, Guru Nanak's system is a whole-life system like Islam and Judaism, which also combine the spiritual and the empirical lives of man. Third, in consequence of it, monasticism, *sanyasa*, asceticism, pacifism and withdrawal from life are rejected, and a householder's life is accepted as the forum of spiritual activities and growth. Logically, monasticism and celibacy go together, and Guru Nanak categorically rejected both of them. Obviously, God's qualities of being 'Shelter to the shelterless', 'Milk to the child', 'Riches to the poor', and 'Eyes to the blind',[9] can be expressed by the Godman only by being a householder and participating in all walks of life, and not by withdrawing from them. The fourth difference follows as a corollary to this and to the rejection of celibacy, namely, equality between man and woman.

In contrast, we find that in life-negating systems, and more especially in the Indian systems, the position on all these four points is essentially different. For them, life is far from real or an arena of spiritual endeavours. The spiritual path and the worldly path are considered separate and distinct. Whether it is Vedanta, Jainism, Buddhism, Vaisnavism or Nathism, asceticism, monasticism, *ahimsa*, *sanyasa* or withdrawal from life into *bhikshuhood* is the normal course. In consequence, celibacy is the rule, and woman is deemed to be a temptress. Dighambra Jains believe that a woman cannot reach *kaivalya* (spiritual summit), and has first to achieve male incarnation.[10] In Buddhism, woman *bhikshus* are deemed second grade compared to male *bhikshus* who are considered senior to them.[11] A male *bhikshu* is not supposed to touch and rescue a drowning woman, even if she were his mother.[12] Sankara calls woman 'the gateway to hell.'[13] Both Ramanuja and Shankaradeva (a liberal Vaisnava saint) would not admit a woman to be a Vaisnava.[14] The latter stated, "Of all the terrible aspirations of the world, woman is the ugliest. A slight side glance of hers captivates even the hearts of celebrated sages. Her sight destroys prayer, penance and meditation.

Knowing this, the wise keep away from the company of woman."[15] *Bhagat* Kabir, we know, is considered a misogynist and calls woman 'black cobra', 'pit of hell' and 'the refuse of the world.'[16] It is well-known that even today in Catholic Christianity, a woman is not ordained as a priest. Against this, Guru Nanak not only sanctioned a householder's life but stated as to, "How can a woman be called impure, when without woman there would be none."[17]

All this has been explained to stress that the basic perceptions about the nature of the spiritual experience and the ontological Reality being different, the spiritual paths, under the two categories of systems, become automatically divergent.

Further, the acceptance of a householder's life has important empirical and socio-political implications. Except for Guru Harkrishan, who died at an early age, every Guru married and led a householder's life. By way of demonstration, this step was essential, otherwise, the entire Indian tradition being different, Guru Nanak's system would have been completely misunderstood and misinterpreted. We are well aware that it is the Naths who questioned Guru Nanak as to how incongruous it was that he was, wearing the clothes of a householder, and at the same time claiming to follow the religious path. Guru Nanak's reply was equally cryptic and categoric, when he said that the Naths did not know even the elementaries of the spiritual path.[18] For this very reason, the Guru did not make his son, Baba Sri Chand, a recluse, his successor.

Regarding the fifth important difference about the goal of life of the religious man, Guru Nanak has made the position very clear in his Japuji. After putting a specific question as to what is the way to be a *sachiara* or a true man, the Guru, while clearly rejecting the method of observing silence, coupled with continuous concentration or meditation, replies that the right method and goal are to carry out the Will of God.[19] And, God being Love and the Ocean of Virtues, His Will is Altruistically Creative and Dynamic. The Sikh goal of life is, thus, to be active and live a creative life of love and virtues. The goal is not personal salvation, or merger in Brahman, but an ever active life of love. It is in this context that Guru Nanak gives the call, "If you want to play the game of love, then come to my path with your head on your palm; once you set your foot on this way, then find not a way out and be prepared to lay down your head."[20] For him, life is a game of love. It is significant that the same advice was given by Guru Arjun to Bhai Manjh who was then a Sakhi Sarvarya and wanted to be a Sikh of the Guru, "You may go on with the easy path of Sakhi Sarvar worship, because Sikhism is a very difficult path, and unless you are willing to be dispossessed of your wealth and to sacrifice your very life, it is no use coming to me."[21] Exactly, the same call for total commitment and sacrifice was given by Guru Gobind Singh on the Baisakhi Day, 1699, when he created the Khalsa and administered *amrit* to the *Panj Piaras*.

The goal being different, the sixth implication is as to the method to achieve that goal. In Sikhism, the emphasis is on the methodology of deeds. Guru Nanak has made this point very clear when he says in *Japuji* : "Man's assessment in His court is done on the basis of one's deeds",[22] and "It is by one's deeds that we become near or away from God."[23] In order to stress the fundamental spiritual importance of deeds, Guru Nanak says, "Everything is lower than Truth, but higher still is truthful living."[24] In fact, when the Guru defines the *gurmukh* or the superman, he calls him : 'One who always lives truthfully."

ESSENTIALS OF SIKH LIFE AND ITS DIFFERENCES WITH OTHER SYSTEMS IN MATTERS OF
SOCIAL RESPONSIBILITY

The basic difference between a whole-life system and a dichotomous system is that in the former, every field of life of operation of God, is also the field of operation and responsibility of both the Godman and the seeker. This is the broad approach. Having defined the nature of God and the goal of man, the important issue is what are the essentials of the religious life. In the context explained above, Guru Nanak has fixed specific duties and responsibilities of the religious life. The first is of accepting equality between man and woman. Guru Nanak clearly states, "Why downgrade woman, when without woman there would be none",[25] and "It is she who gives birth to great persons."[26] When the Third Guru created *manjis* or districts of religious administration, women were appointed in charge of some of them.[27] The second responsibility is of maintaining equality between man and man. This was a direct blow to the social ideology of *Varn Ashram Dharma* which gave scriptural sanction to the hierarchical caste system. Guru Nanak found fault with that ideology saying, "The Vedas make a wrong distinction of caste",[28] and "One cannot be a Yogi by mere wishing, real Yoga lies in treating all alike."[29] He demonstrated the primary importance of treating all as equal by taking, after his enlightenment, Mardana, a low caste Muslim, as his life companion. This meant a total departure from the then existing religious prejudices, not only against lower castes, but also against Muslims who were regarded as *malechhas*. He made it clear that any one wanting to join his society, had, at the very start, to shed all prejudices against inter-religious or inter-caste dining and social intercourse. The revolutionary character of this step could be gauged from the fact that a Ramanuja would throw the entire food as polluted, if any one cast a glance on it while he had been preparing or eating it.[30]

The third social responsibility, Guru Nanak emphasises, is the importance of work. This too, we find, was something opposed to the then prevalent religious practice. Evidently, other-worldliness, *sanyasa* and monasticism excluded the religious necessity of work and sustaining the society. In fact, the Naths who were then the principal religious organisation in Punjab took a vow never to engage themselves in any work or business.[31] But Guru Nanak says, "The person incapable of earning his living gets his ears split (i.e., turns a Nath Yogi) and becomes a mendicant. He calls himself a Guru or saint. Do not look up to him, nor touch his feet. He knows the way who earns his living and shares his earnings with others."[32] The Guru deprecates the Yogi who gives up the world, and then is not ashamed of begging at the door of the householders.[33] The fourth social responsibility Guru Nanak stresses is about the sharing of wealth. He states, "God's bounty belongs to all, but men grab it for themselves."[34] "Man gathers riches by making others miserable."[35] "Wealth cannot be gathered without sin, but it does not keep one's company after death."[36] All this clearly condemns exploitative collection of wealth. The story of Guru Nanak rejecting the invitation of Malik Bhago, a rich person exploiting the poor, but accepting the hospitality of Lalo, a poor labourer, illustrates the same point as stressed in his *bani*.

Thus, the twin ideas about the brotherhood of man and the sharing of wealth to eliminate poverty and maintain equality in society are stressed by Guru Nanak. Even after his missionary tours, Guru Nanak took to the role of a peasant for the last 18 years of his life. It is significant that till the time of the Sixth Guru, when social and military duties of the leadership and organisation of the Sikh society became quite heavy and absorbing, every Sikh Guru had been doing a vocation or business to support his family.

The fifth social responsibility, where Guru Nanak radically departed from all the contemporary religious systems, including Sufism, Santism and Christianity, was his approach towards injustice and oppression of all kinds in society. He made a meticulous study of injustice and corruption, aggression and incongruity in every field of life. He pointed out the greed and hypocrisy of Brahmin priests and Mullahs, the 'blood thirsty corruption' and injustice by lower and higher-rung officials in the administration, the misrule, oppression and irresponsibility of the local rulers, their inability to give security, fairplay and peace to the people, and brutal and barbaric butchery of the people. All this was not just idle rhetoric, but a diagnostic assessment of the prevailing turmoil and conditions in the society, which the Guru felt, needed to be changed. It needs to be emphasised that in Guru Nanak's ideology, there was nothing like private or personal salvation. Just as God of Love is benevolently looking after the entire world, in the same way, the Godman's sphere of activity and responsibility is equally wide, and is unhedged by any self-created barriers. This is, as we shall see, a fundamental difference between a salvation religion catering for individuals, and a universal religion catering for the spiritual well-being of society as a whole.

Here it is very relevant to give, as recorded by Bertrand Russell, the contrasted approach of St. Augustine, one of the greatest exponents of the Christian gospel and author of *City of God*. Russell concludes : "It is strange that the last men of intellectual eminence before the dark ages were concerned, not with saving civilization or expelling the barbarians or reforming the abuses of the administration, but with preaching the merit of virginity and the damnation of unbaptized infants. Seeing that these were the preoccupations that the Church handed on to the converted barbarians, it is no wonder that the succeeding age surpassed almost all other fully historical periods in cruelty and superstition."[37] Whereas Guru Nanak meticulously points out every dark spot in the religious and socio-political life of his times, St. Augustine is simply unconcerned with socio-political conditions of his period. For, "Augustine's *City of God* (426) attacked both Christians who expected the world to get better and pagans with a cyclic view of history. Augustine did not believe that the spread of Christianity would ensure political and economic improvement. The earthly city of self-will would continue to exist amidst the rise and fall of states and empires."[38]

Another important fact is Guru Nanak's criticism in *Babar Vani* of the brutalities and massacres perpetrated and misery caused by the invaders. He condemns them in the strongest terms and complains to God for allowing the weak to be trampled upon by the strong.[39] This hymn has an extremely important lesson, which many of us have missed. For, anything which is within the sphere of His creation and the responsibility of God, is certainly within the sphere of responsibility of the Godman. The hymn has four implications; first, that injustice and oppression are violative of the Order of God; second, that as the Master and God of Love, harmony has to be maintained by His Will; third, that, as the instrument of

God, it is the spiritual duty and responsibility of the Godman to confront all kinds of injustice; and, fourth, that, as such, resistance to oppression was a task and a target laid down by the Guru for the religious society he was organising. Because, it is Guru Nanak who defines God as 'Destroyer of the evil-doers',[40] 'Destroyer of demoniacal persons',[41] 'Slayer of the inimical',[42] and 'Protector of the weak.' Such being the God of Guru Nanak, it is equally the responsibility of the Godman, *gurmukh*, or the Sikh to carry out His Will which is just and altruistic.

In short, in Guru Nanak's system to ensure equality and fair play and to react against injustice and aggression, become the religious duty and responsibility of the Sikh. Since the dawn of civilisation, the greatest oppression and injustice have undeniably been done by the rulers, the State, or the Establishment who have possessed all the instruments of power and coercion. It is impossible for idividuals to confront such power. This leads to two important inferences. First, that in a whole-life system like Sikhism, which combines spiritual life with the empirical life of man and accepts the *miri-piri* doctrine, the religious man must, as a religious duty, resist and confront injustice, wherever it takes place. Second, that such a religious man should not only be cognizant of such injustice, but also organise a society that should be in a position to face the challenge of such injustice and oppression. This follows logically both from Guru Nanak's *bani* and his system. This also explains why from the very beginning of his mission, he started organising the Sikh societies at places which he visited and how the societies were logically linked and developed by his successors into the *Panth*. These aspects are very significant and important about his society and religion. It is obvious to every student of the Adi Granth that so far as the ideology is concerned, it had been completely laid down in the *bani* of Guru Nanak. But what was lacking was the presence of a properly motivated and responsible society that should be in a position to successfully discharge the responsibility of reacting against injustice and oppression prevalent in his times.

There is another important and related issue. Having cast on his society the responsibility of confronting injustice, again it is Guru Nanak who eliminates the hurdle of *ahimsa* or pacificism that stood as a bar against the religious man or a religious society trying to confront socio-political aggression. Among Vaisnavas, Jains, Buddhist Bhikshus, Naths, or Radical Sants like Kabir, *ahimsa* is deemed to be a cardinal virtue and meat eating is a prohibition. These religious persons are all from life-negating systems, with personal salvation as the ideal. But a society that has to accept the social responsibility of confronting injustice cannot remain wedded to the hurdle of *ahimsa*. For, reason and force are both neutral tools that can be used both for good and evil, for construction and destruction. That is why Guru Nanak says, "Men discriminate not and quarrel over meat eating, they do not know what is flesh and what is non-flesh, or in what lies sin and what is not sin",[43] and that "there is life in every grain of food we eat."[44]

ROLE OF LATER NINE GURUS

In a country, which for over 2,000 years had been trained in religious systems involving clear dichotomy between spiritual and empirical life, and which had accepted *ahimsa* as a fundamental value and individual salvation as an ideal, it was no easy task to create a mature society with the new motivation of religious responsibility of always fighting injustice and oppression in all spheres of life.

It is very significant that Guru Nanak laid the foundations of every institution that was later developed and matured by his successors. By starting the institution of *langar* (common kitchen) and taking Mardana as his life companion, he gave a heavy blow to the divisive institution of *Varn Ashram Dharma*, pollution and caste. He created a separate Sikh society with their own *dharmasalas* as centres of religious worship and training. He sanctified the role of the householder as the medium of religious expression and progress, and made it plain that work was a necessity of life, and idleness a vice. He emphatically made it clear that to fight injustice and oppression is an essential duty of the religious man and the religious society. For that end, while he created a new society with a new ideology, he also removed the hurdle of *ahimsa*, so that his society could discharge its socio-religious responsibility without any unwanted inhibitions and impediments in its path. And since the new society had not yet been fully organised and developed, and had yet to be properly oriented to enable it to discharge its responsibilities, he also created the institution of succession. It is very significant of the social and societal aims of Guru Nanak that after passing the succession to Guru Angad, when he found him to be living a somewhat solitary life, he reminded him that he had to be active since he had to organise a society or *Panth*.[45]

In the time of the Second, Third and Fourth Guru, four important steps were taken. Through the creation of 22 *manjis* or districts of religious administration, the Sikh society was organised into a separate religious *Panth*. But, the most important and difficult part of the task was the creation of new motivations and the acceptance of the new life-affirming religious ideals of Guru Nanak. For, these were radically new in their approach, implications and goals. The stupendous nature of the task of the Gurus can be judged from the fact that even today great Hindus, like Jadunath Sarkar, Rabindra Nath Tagore and Mahatma Gandhi, and Christians like McLeod, Cole, Toynbee and the like, all coming from pacifist traditions and conditioned by them, find it difficult to understand the spiritual role of the Sixth and the Tenth Master.

The Third Guru created new institutions which had the dual purpose of weaning the Sikhs away from the old Hindu society and of conditioning them in new values, ideals and practices. For example, while Guru Nanak had bypassed his recluse son, Sri Chand, for the same reasons, the Second and the Third Guru avoided persons of ascetic tendencies from entering the Sikh fold. The institution of *langar,* with the dual purpose of feeding the poor and of eliminating the caste and status prejudices and distinctions, was strengthened. Finally, the important religious centre of Darbar Sahib and the town of Amritsar were founded and developed for the periodical meetings of the Sikh society and visits of the Sikhs to the Guru. The object of all this was to establish a separate historical identity of the Sikhs and to wean them away from the traditional society, its centres of pilgrimage, and its religious practices and rituals. Not only had they to be trained in the essentials of a new religious system, but they had to be taken out of the strangle-hold of the Brahmin priests claiming to be the sole medium of religious growth, practice and interpretation.

Then came the stage of the Fifth Guru who created and installed the Sikh Scripture as the revealed and final doctrinal authority. The system of *daswandh* (giving 10% of one's earnings for the cause of the community) was organised. Sikhs were initiated into trading in horses, so that the transition to the next stage of militancy could become smooth. As the instrument of God on earth, the Sikhs called their Guru, 'True Emperor.' In the time of the Fifth Guru, the Sikh society had become 'a State within a State',[46] and had developed a social identity which had caught the eye of the Emperor, who considered it an unwanted socio-political growth. By his martyrdom, the Guru not only strengthened the faith and determination of the community, but also sought confrontation with the Empire, leaving instructions to his son to begin militarisation of the Sikhs. In the process, the Sixth Guru even recruited mercenaries to train his people. This phase of martyrdom and confrontation with the Empire was continued by the subsequent Gurus till Guru Gobind Singh did, as recorded by his contemporary Kavi Sainapat, the epitomic work of starting the institutions of *amrit* and the Khalsa.[47] Having felt that the *Panth* had become mature and responsible enough, the Guru created the Khalsa in 1699, and requested the *Panj Piaras* to baptise him.[48] It is significant that at that time all the Guru's sons were alive, meaning thereby that Guru Nanak's mission had been completed and thereafter the succession was not to be continued. And, finally, the Guru made Guru Granth Sahib the Everlasting Guru of the Sikhs.[49]

Let us have a rapid look back to find out if the five tasks indicated by Guru Nanak had been accomplished. First, the Sikhs had been formed into a distinct new religious society with a Scripture of its own, being the full repository and complete and final guide of the Sikh ideology and its way of life. This separateness was made total by Guru Gobind Singh's *Nash* doctrine of five freedoms — *Dharam Nash, Bharam Nash, Kul Nash, Karam Nash* and *Kirt Nash*.[50] This means freedom from the bonds of old religions and traditions, of earlier superstitions and prejudices, of earlier acts and of restrictions in choice of trade or calling, or in professional mobility. The Tenth Master made a complete break with the earlier traditions and societies. Second, it was a society of householders, rejecting all kinds of otherworldliness, idleness and monasticism. Third, it was a casteless society with complete fraternity among its members. Men from the lowest and Sudra castes rose to be its leaders. The contrast is evident from the fact that while the Sikhs have never had Brahmin leaders, in India after Independence in 1947, the Prime Minister and practically every Chief Minister was a Brahmin. Four, it was a society which was fully earthaware; and habits of work, production and service became ingrained among its members. Begging was considered a disgrace in its social ethos. The fifth social responsibility discharged by the Sikhs was to free the country from the curse of a thousand-year wave of invaders from the North-West. Though the Sikhs were subjected over the years to the worst persecution in Indian history, yet they suffered it and emerged triumphant. And, finally, they were able once and for all to stem that tide. They have been trained to react against wrong, injustice and oppression. A society has been created with the ideal of a *Sant-Sipahi* (Saint-Soldier).

MANMUKH TO GURMUKH : THE GURU'S CONCEPT OF EVOLUTION OF MAN

Here, it is necessary to state the *manmukh-gurmukh* concept, which is essential for understanding the Sikh worldview. As the Gurus say, over millions of years life has evolved into man from a tiny speck of life. The Guru says, "For several births (you) were a mere worm, for several births, an insect, for several births a fish and an antelope", "After ages you have the glory of being a man."[51] "After passing through myriads of species, one is blest with the human form."[52] "God created you out of a drop of water and breathed life in you. He endowed you with the light of reason, discrimination and wisdom."[53] "O man, you are supreme in God's creation; now is your opportunity, you may fulfil or not fulfil your destiny."[54] At its present stage of development, man is, without doubt, better equipped than other animals, in so far as he has a higher sense of discrimination. But, as an ego-conscious being, he is still an animal, being a *manmukh*. This implies that whatever be human pretensions, man is basically and organically a self-centred being. His psyche is governed by an egoistic consciousness, that being his centre of awareness, control and propulsion. Because of his present inherent limitations of ego-consciousness, it is virtually impossible for man to avoid conflict, aggression, and wars. But the Gurus clearly hold out hope for man. There are four stages of evolution or development. The Guru says, "God created first, Himself, then *haumain*, third, *maya* (multifarious things and beings) and fourth, the next higher stage of the *gurmukh* who lives truthfully."[55] The Gurus clearly say that it is human destiny to reach the fourth stage and to meet God, or to be a *gurmukh*, or one who is in tune with the fundamental Reality or Universal Consciousness, God, *Naam*, or Love. His ideal is not merger in God or salvation, or union as an end in itself. Being the instrument of, or in touch with God's Altruistic Consciousness, he is spontaneously benevolent, compassionate, creative and loving. It is very important to note that the *gurmukh* or superman is not a quietist , he 'lives truthfully.' He lives as did the ten Gurus. For, Guru Nanak was called just a *gurmukh*. This is the next higher stage of evolution towards which life is striving and not towards darkness and death as materialist scientists would have us believe. Nor does Sikhism accept any concept of the basic sinfulness or fall of man from grace. It only indicates the constitutional weakness, immaturity or imperfection of man at his present stage of the evolutionary process or development. Hence, it gives us an ideology of optimism and hope, invoking and exhorting us to make moral effort.

SURVEY OF HIGHER RELIGIONS

Before we draw our conclusions, let us make a brief survey of some religious ideologies of the world and find the place of Sikhism among them. There are four clear religious ideologies that are current today.

DICHOTOMOUS RELIGIONS

First is the category of religious systems like Buddhism, Jainism, Nathism, Vaisnavism and Vedanta, in which there is clear dichotomy between the spiritual life and the empirical life. Monasticism, *sanyasa*, otherworldliness, celibacy, yogic meditation and *ahimsa* are the common but important features of this category. They hold out no hope for man, except by withdrawal from life and yogic or one-point meditation. In each case, it is a path of personal salvation without any involvement in the socio-political affairs of man. Practically, all the Indian religions, except Sikhism, belong to this category.

JUDAISM

Second is Judaism which has a long and chequered history. Basically, it is a system in which there is no dichotomy between the religious life and the empirical life of man. Prophet Moses who got the revelation, was both a religious and political leader. His Torah or Commandments and Laws prescribe and govern the entire gamut of the spiritual and temporal life of the Jews. It is a system that prescribes rules governing the conduct of prayer, rituals, sacrifices and their socio-political life. The renowned Hillel when asked to explain the 613 commandments of the Torah, replied, "Whatever is hateful to you, do not do to your neighbour. That is the entire Torah. The rest is commentary, go and learn it."[56] In short, it is basically a life-affirming system. It makes no distinction between the spiritual and the socio-political life of man. The Torah governs every aspect of it. As to the means of resistance, Judaism recommends the use of force by saying, "Eye for an eye, tooth for a tooth", and indicates rules for a righteous fight.[57] But, over its long history including the period of the prophets, this aspect of its principle has, to an extent, been altered, or changed at least by some sects of the community. At the time of the Babylonian attack (Sixth Century B.C.) on Palestine, Prophet Jeremiah strongly recommended non-resistance or pacificism. He asserted that the attack was God's punishment to the Jews for their non-observance of His Laws.[58] His assertion was something like Mahatma Gandhi's statement that the Bihar earthquake was a punishment to the Hindus for their practice of untouchability. However, over the centuries thereafter, many religious sects of Jews like Essenes, Kabbalists, Hasidists, Therapeutics,[59] and even some Pharisees accepted the principle of non-resistance, pacificism, withdrawal and otherworldliness. Even monastic and celibate cults appeared among Jews, discarding both the world and the use of force. This important change, in a basic religious principle, we believe, came about in this religion in later parts of its history, when Judaism was unable to cope with challenges from the socio-political environment, and their religious fervour had been exhausted. Practically, all these otherworldly sects appeared after the destruction of the First Temple and the fall of Jerusalem, when thousands of Jews were driven out as exiles and slaves to Babylonia. We wish to stress that these fundamental changes in Judaic ideology, including otherworldly or monastic sects, appeared only during the lean period of Jewish history. This happened about eight centuries after the revelation of Moses, and after the heydays of Jewish life in the times of David and Solomon. But, it is very significant that despite the presence of somewhat pacifist or otherworldly cults and sects in Judaism, and despite about 2500 years of suffering and travail, the idea of Zionism, a virtual revival of earlier non-pacifist ideals, strongly reappeared in Judaism in the last century. And it is an important fact that Einstein, who says that his life was spent 'between politics and equations' was a staunch Zionist. So much so, that when Israel was formed he was offered its presidency.[60] However, apart from this apparent doctrinal ambivalence in its ideology, Judaism is a highly exclusive religion, not quite universal in its character, affinities and approach.

CHRISTIANITY

The Judaic heritage of Christianity is undoubted. As in Judaism, in Christianity, too, there is, in principle, no dichotomy between the spiritual life and the empirical life of man. For, Christ emphasises both loving God with all one's heart, and loving one's neighbour as oneself.[61] But like Buddha, he also emphasises the pacifist principles, 'resist not evil' and 'turn the left cheek if hit on the right.' Religious history demonstrates that pacifist religions almost invariably become otherworldly, even if they were life-affirming in the beginning. Because of their religious pacificism, the Christians declined to take up service in the Roman army. In fact, historians like Gibbon and Sir James Frazer have mentioned Christian otherworldliness as one of the major causes of the fall of the Roman Empire.[62] It is obvious that Christianity, which, like Judaism, was a religion of householders, showed, by the beginning of the 4th century A.D., clear monastic trends.[63] Increasingly, monasteries and nunneries appeared as a significant development in the Christian religion. This life of monasticism, asceticism and nunneries led, on the one hand, to otherworldly quietist mysticism, and, on the other hand, to corruption and malpractices in the Catholic Church.

Consequent to this schism in the life of the Christian Church, ultimately arose the Reformation, causing a major blow to the supremacy of the Church and its role as the guiding moral force in the life of the Christian society. Lutheran and Calvinist reforms not only shattered the universal character of the Church, but also brought about its subordination to the national State. In addition, because of Luther's leanings towards the feudal princes, he took a very hostile and feudalistic stand against the rights of the peasantry. This landslide in the fortunes of the Church caused its gradual waning as a major moral influence in the socio-political life of the Christian societies. After the rise of science, which was considered to be the new elixir, it came to be believed that it would, in course of time, cure most human ills. The net result is that in the last 300 years, Renaissance, scientism, empiricism and secularism have virtually eliminated religion from the moral life of man in the West.

Toynbee says, "This transfer of allegiance from the Western Christian Church to the parochial Western secular state was given a positive form borrowed from the Graeco-Roman civilization by the Renaissance." "This unavowed worship of parochial states was by far the most prevalent religion in the Christian society."[64] Since the loss of supremacy of religion in the Christian society, Western life has lost its moral moorings. Nationalism, communism and individualism have been the unstable offsprings of this broken home. "Together with Darwinism, secularism and positivism, they have dehumanised the Western culture, reducing liberalism to a self-serving, highly competetive individualism."[65] By relegating religion to the background and having lost the moral springs of the Western culture, either utilitarian ethics has been accepted as an expedient substitute or a reductionist search has been made to find appropriate ethical elements in the life of the animals, or in the material base of man which is considered to be its fundamental constituent. And this search has finally come to the dismal conclusion that all ethical life is 'a defence mechanism' or a 'reaction formation' to the impacts of the environment. After the Second World War, a third of the population of the world was living under the Communist system. As the century is closing, these countries find that despite the myth of dialectical movement and synthesis, the system has been unable to make any synthetic values or devise a system of ethics which is able to maintain cohesion within these societies. And it is the existence of this moral vacuum that made the Foreign Secretary of the Soviets proclaim that 'universal values should have priority over class, group or other interests.'[66] The warning remained unheeded, and the Russian Empire has collapsed, purely because of its inability to build internal cohesion. At the ethical plane, this decries, in a way, the validity of Darwinism, and its struggle for existence, and Marxism with its dialectical movement of class struggle. It involves equal condemnation of economic wars, cut-throat competition, consumerism and increasing disparities in capitalist societies.

From the point of view of internal cohesion, the position in the capitalist countries of the West is no better. Mounting number of divorces, broken homes, drug addiction, alcoholism, and individualism have created such a situation in North America, which made the Christian Church raised a strong voice saying that secularism was a common danger and needed to be eliminated as a social force, and that Christianity should seek the co-operation of other religions to combat its evil influence. Christianity had given to the empirical life in the West its cohesion, strength and elan; the divorce of religion from politics and the empirical life, has left secularism a barren institution without any hope of a creative future. This is the tragedy both of communism and capitalism. It is this tragedy with its dark future that the North American Churches wanted to avoid. But in the temper of the times, this voice of sanity was drowned in an exhibition of suicidal egoism of the European Churches who felt that "Secularization, not secularism, is the primary process. It is a process in which some of the values of Christian faith have been put into a secular framework, bringing about a powerful force which is destroying all old ideas. Hence, secularization is an ally, because it will destroy Hinduism, Islam and other forms of what they considered to be superstition. So, we should ally ourselves with secularization and see it as the work of God." Later, it was again repeated : "We do not feel that we have anything lacking. And so we are opposed to dialogue unless it is for the sake of testifying to Jesus Christ." "That was it. Then they passed a resolution saying that under no circumstances should multi-religious dialogues be undertaken because multi-religious dialogues put Christianity on the same level as other religions, and this is unacceptable. So, because the European Christians had that point of view, the World Council of Churches has not been able to engage in multi-religious dialogues for quite some time."[67]

This is the state of affairs of the moral life of man in Western countries that lead the dominant culture of our times. Recently, however, some priests in Latin America have raised a voice for an integrated and composite culture of Liberation Theology, invoking the Bible in support of a revolutionary struggle to help the poor. Father C. Torres states, "The Catholic who is not a revolutionary is living in mortal sin."[68] Theologian Moltmann says, "Political theology wants to awaken political consciousness in every treatise of Christian theology. Understood in this way, it is the premise that leads to the conclusion that, while there may be naive or politically unaware theology, there can be no apolitical theology." He concludes, "The memory of Christ crucified compels us to a political theology."[69] But these are still minority voices in the Christian world.

ISLAM

Islam started with a full-blooded combination between the spiritual life and the empirical life of man. It is this combination that swept everything before it and created an epoch which is unrivalled in its achievements. It is a religious system and culture, which is, in many respects, more comprehensive and unified than the parochial culture of the city states of Greece. It is hardly complimentary to the Christian world of the West that while today it seeks to fashion many of its cultural institutions on the basis of Greek classical models, yet these, but for the interlude of the Islamic epoch which preserved most of the Greek thought, would have been lost to posterity. Never was the concept of human brotherhood advanced, in thought and deed, on a scale as during this epoch. It speaks volumes for the liberalism of Islamic culture that the heydays of the Judaic literature, philosophy and thought synchronise with the countries and periods of Islamic rule. Not only were some of the Jewish classics written, but Maimonides, the king of Judaic philosophy, also flourished and wrote during the Muslim rule. As against it, under Christian rulers, the Jews suffered periodical massacres, persecution and the segregated life of the ghetto. Admittedly, the Muslim rulers were, by comparison, quite liberal towards the followers of other religions. Islamic contribution to the scientific thought of the day was significant. But far more important is the contribution of men like Al Qushairi, Al Ghazali and Arbi to the religious thought of man.

There is, however, little doubt that mystic quietism and otherworldliness of Sufis is a growth that appeared during the time of later Caliphs, when they indulged in luxurious and un-Islamic living. It has happened in the case of Judaism and of Islam, both whole-life religions, that in times when religiously sensitive souls found it difficult to face the social or socio-political challenges, they withdrew themselves into the shell of quietism, otherworldliness, monasticism and asceticism. Sufi sects appeared all over the Muslim world, but they never posed a challenge to the oppression and misrule of the Muslim emperors or kings. In this respect, the Jewish prophets were quite bold in their criticism of Jewish rulers, including David and Solomon.

It is very significant, and shows the lofty spiritual status of the Sikh Gurus and the basic ideological affinity between the two religions, that a Sufi saint like Pir Buddhu Shah fought and sacrificed two of his sons for the cause of Guru Gobind Singh.[70] But it was the Sikh Gurus and not the Sufis who challenged the growing Mughal tyranny. This instance demonstrates that although as an organisation, Sufis had become otherworldly and failed to confront the major challenge of societal oppression in the Muslim empires, yet when the Sikh Gurus had actually taken up the challenge and the ideological struggle was on, the Sufi saint made it clear that, considering the tenets of Islam, on which side should be the sympathies of a pious person.

There are, however, some scholars like Iqbal and Abdus Salam who believe that like the otherworldliness of the Christians, as in the case of the Roman Empire, Sufis also became a significant cause of the decline of the Muslim cultural supremacy in the world. For, there is considerable truth in Dr Mohammad Iqbal's couplet : "Whether it be the facade of a great republic, or the domain of a glorious empire, if its polity is divorced of the religious component, the system is reduced to sheer Changezian barbarity and tyranny." Thoughtful and saner elements in the Muslim world seem to be disillusioned with the bankrupt Western Secularism, and are trying to revert to a reformed and composite culture of Islam.

RELIGIOUS HISTORY AND CREATION OF THE KHALSA

In our brief survey, we have indicated four categories of religious systems. The Indian systems are all dichotomous. To the second category belongs pacifist Christianity which, though it originally suggested the love of one's neighbour as oneself, has gradually but ultimately reduced itself to sheer Secularism, Individualism and Consumerism, bereft of any religious component. To the third category belong Judaism and Islam which started with a full-blooded combination of the spiritual life with the empirical life, but ultimately, under pressure of circumstances, bifurcated, on the one hand, into otherworldliness or mystic quietism, and, on the other hand, into the pursuit of worldly gains and sheer animal survival.

Sikhism belongs to a different or a fourth category of the religious systems. For the purpose of understanding, clarity and comparison, it will help us if we recapitulate the salient features of Sikhism. The Gurus say that the Basic Reality is creative and free. It has a Direction and a Will. It is the Ocean of Values, Destroyer of evil-doers, Benevolent and Beneficent. That Reality is Love and we can be at peace with ourselves and the world only if we live a life of love and fall in line with the Direction of that Reality. Though ego is God created and man is at present at the ego-conscious *(manmukh)* stage of development, it is his destiny to evolve and reach the stage of Universal or God-consciousness and work in line with His Altruistic Will, i.e., achieve the *gurmukh* stage of development, when alone he can 'be spontaneously moral' and 'live truthfully.' At the present, or the egoistic stage of his development, man cannot avoid conflicts and suicidal wars. It is a futile search to try and find the moral base of man either in the animal life or in the material constituents of man. Nor can reason, which is just a tool of the egoistic psyche, like any other limb of the individual, devise and give man a helpful ethics. God or the Basic Reality, which is Love, can alone be the source of the moral life of man. Ultimately, it is only God or *Naam*-consciousness, involving link with the Basic Fount of Love, that can lead to truthful living. That is why the Guru says, "*Naam*-consciousness and ego-consciousness cannot go together."[71] The two are contradictory to each other. It is a hymn of fundamental significance. For, ego-consciousness means man's alienation from the basic Force of Love. And, greater the alienation or isolation of man from his spiritual and moral source, the greater would be his drive towards destruction. Secularism as an institution represents that egoistic isolation. This trend, the Guru says, is inconsistent with the path towards link with the Universal Consciousness, the spring of moral life. The Gurus have given a lead to man in this field. Ten Gurus or ten *gurmukhs*, lived the life of God-consciousness. In one sense, it is the life of one *gurmukh* completing a demonstration and furthering the progress of life and its spiritual evolution and ascent. Guru Nanak's thesis involved the integration of the spiritual life of man with his empirical life. This integration has to enrich life and society. Because of the earlier cultural and religious tradition, it took ten lives for Guru Nanak, the *gurmukh* or *Sant-Sipahi*, to demonstrate his thesis and role, and discharge his social responsibilities.

These socio-spiritual responsibilities involved not only the creation of a society motivated with new ideas, but also the completion of the five tasks Guru Nanak had indicated as targets before himself and his society. With every succeeding Guru, the ideal of *gurmukh* or *Sant-Sipahi*, as laid down and lived by Guru Nanak, unfolded itself progressively. It is a path of love, humility, service, sacrifice, martyrdom and total responsibility as the instrument of God, the basic Universal Consciousness moving the world.

A question may be asked as to why there have been ten incarnations of Guru Nanak in Sikhism, while in other religions there have generally been only one prophet. To us, four reasons appear quite obvious. First, in a society in which dichotomous religions stand deeply embedded and established for over three thousand years and which claims to have contributed asceticism and monasticism to the cultures of the rest of the world, it was not easy for a whole-life religion with its *miri-piri* concept to be acceptable and take firm roots in one generation. Second, the Sikh ideology did not involve individual salvation, or a *gurmukh* just living truthfully; but it also involved compulsively the creation of a society motivated with new aspirations and ideals. And this new orientation and conditioning could be done only by the process of creating a new ideology, embodying it in a new scripture, organising new institutions, socio-religious practices and centres of the new faith, and inspiring people, by the method of martyrdoms, into accepting a new ethical standard or morality and values. For, as Ambedkar[72] and Max Weber have stated, the Hindu society cannot be reformed from inside, and rid itself from the unjust system of caste and untouchability, because the *Varn Ashram Dharma* has the sanction of *Shashtras* and scriptures; and a Hindu while making caste distinctions and exhibiting caste prejudices never feels any moral guilt or abhorrence. Instead, he feels a real sense of religious and moral satisfaction that he is observing his *Dharma* and *Shastric* injunctions. Hence, the inevitable necessity of creating a new ideology and Scripture with a new religious and socio-moral code of conduct. Third, even if the ideology and institutions had been there, the Sikh society would, like some reformed societies, soon have reverted to the parent society, if it had not successfully achieved the social targets discussed above, including those of creating a fraternal society of householders, of dislodging the political misrule, and sealing the North-Western gate of India against the invaders.

The fourth reason appears to be very important. Our survey of the major religions of the world shows that revealed systems which start with a combination of the spiritual life with the empirical life and even with clear social objectives, over a period of time, either shed their social ideals and become pacifist, otherworldly, or a salvation religion, or become dichotomous, bifurcating, on the one hand, into monasticism, and, on the other hand, into either political misrule and tyranny or sheer secularism. Sikhism does not stand any such danger of ideological decline or bifurcation, because of its gradual and firm ascent and unfolding. It shows the prophetic vision of Guru Nanak that he not only profusely and clearly defined all aspects of his life-affirming and integrated ideology, but also detailed the targets his society had to achieve. He laid the firm foundations of the institutions and the socio-religious structure his successors had to develop and complete. Guru Nanak defined his God not only as the Ocean of Virtues, but also as a *Sant-Sipahi* or the Destroyer of the evil-doers; and the ideal he laid down for the seeker was to be the instrument of the Will of such a God. Guru Arjun gave instructions to his son to militarise the movement and thereafter, as was explained by Guru Hargobind to Sant Ramdas,[73] his sword was for the protection of the weak and the destruction of the tyrant. While Guru Arjun, the first martyr of the faith, had confrontation with the empire and gave orders for militarisation, the subsequent five Gurus manifestly proclaimed and practised the spiritual ideal of *Sant-Sipahi*. So, whatever some votaries of pacifist or dichotomous ideologies or other outsiders may say, to students of Sikhism or a seeker of the Sikh ideal, there can never be any doubt as to the integrated *miri-piri* or *Sant-Sipahi* ideal in Sikhism. Because in the eyes of a Sikh, any reversion to ideas of pacificism, personal salvation or monasticism would be a manifest fall from the spiritual ideology laid down by Guru Nanak, enshrined in Guru Granth Sahib, and openly, single-mindedly and demonstrably lived by the ten Gurus, culminating in the creation of the Khalsa, with *kirpan* as the essential symbol for resisting injustice and oppression. The *kirpan* essentially signifies two fundamental tenets of Sikhism, namely, that it is the basic responsibility of a Sikh to confront and resist injustice, and that asceticism, monasticism, or escapism, of any kind is wrong. Thus, the *kirpan*, on the one hand, is a constant reminder to the Sikh of his duty, and, on the other hand, is a standing guard against reversion to pacificism and otherworldliness. The extreme sagacity and vision of the Sikh Gurus is evident from the thoughtfully planned and measured manner in which they built the structure of their ideology and the Sikh society, epitomised in the order of the Khalsa. That is also the reason that so far as the ideology and ideals of the Sikh society are concerned, there cannot be any ambiguity in that regard. Hence, considering the manner in which the lives of the ten Gurus have demonstrated the Sikh way of life, the question of its bifurcation or accepting pacificism or otherworldliness does not arise. And this forms, we believe, the fourth important reason for there being ten Gurus and the closure of succession after the Khalsa was created.

CONCLUSION

The summary of the Sikh ideology, in the background of the religious history of some higher religions, makes the viewpoint of the Sikh Gurus and the Sikh position very clear. The Gurus emphasise that at the *manmukh* stage of man's development, man is constitutionally incapable of avoiding injustice, wars and conflicts. Because, man is basically egocentric and stands alienated from the Fundamental Force (God) which is Love. So long as he does not link himself with the Flow of Love and fails to work in unison with it, his problems of clash, disharmony and tensions will continue. The diagnosis of the authors of *Limits of Growth* is also the same, namely, that unless man is able to shed his egocentrism, there appears little hope for peace and happiness in the world.[74]

The state is an instrument devised by man to curb the basic egocentrism or wickedness of individuals and power groups. But, politics divorced from the Fundamental Spiritual Force, or moral brakes creates the situation that the State or Establishment is seized by individuals and groups, who openly use and employ all the enormous means of the modern state for the satisfaction of their egocentrism, working to the detriment of the masses and the poor. And the more backward or poor a country, the greater the oppression uninhibited secularism can do with the power machine of the state. The result, logically and unavoidably, is that the gap between the downtrodden masses and the oppressive elites goes on widening. This happens both within a state, and among the various national states. We wonder if anyone who is acquainted with recent history, can contradict this observation.

Rationally speaking, secularism is incapable of reversing the present trend, or finding a solution of the existing malady. The causes for this failure have been stressed by the Gurus. Reason being a tool or limb of the egocentric man (*manmukh*) and being unconnected with the Universal Consciousness or spirituo-moral base of man, it can never make the individual spontaneously altruistic. Hence, any search for a humanitarian ethics through empiricism, communism or secularism is doomed to failure. The hopes which science in the first decades of the century had raised, stand tragically shattered.

To us, materialism and morality seem a contradiction in terms. Similarly, dichotomous or life-negating religions are equally amoral in their social impact. It is because of the Indian religions being dichotomous that the unjust secular institution of *Varn Ashram Dharma* and caste could continue in the Indian society, and also have the approval of its scriptures. The study of the three Western religions of Judaism, Christianity and Islam also furnishes the same lesson. The moment any of these societies became otherworldly, or showed dichotomous tendencies, the moral strength of the society to face the challenges of life became minimal. Or vice versa, the society became dichotomous, when it failed to face effectively the challenges of life. And, ultimately it is the moral stamina of a people or culture that by and large determines its survival. This is evident from the known history, both of Judaism and Islam. But for the subordination of religious institutions to the national state, following the Reformation, the triumph of secularism and scientism to erode the Christian ethical base from the Western life would never have been possible. The ethical field today is in complete disarray.[75] Since religion is the only source which could furnish the moral sap to maintain social cohesion, and Christian elan being at its lowest ebb, the twentieth century has witnessed the worst slaughter and butchery of tens of millions, both at the international and the national levels. Hitler, Stalin and Hiroshima are phenomena of the twentieth century secularism. The nations of the world are spending on arms a thousand billion dollars each year. It is this dismal spectacle that had, on the one hand, forced the Soviets to talk of the 'priority of universal values over the class or group values', and, on the other hand, led the North American Churches to suggest co-operation with other religions in order to fight the common danger of secularism. For the present, either out of their ignorance, or for other reasons, the European Churches have overruled the American view. But, the problem remains and stands highlighted by thinking persons. Decades back, Collingwood wrote : "The discovery of a relation is at once the discovery of my thought as reaching God and of God's thought as reaching me; and indistinguishable from this, the performance of an act of mine by which I establish a relation with God and an act of God's by which He establishes a relation with me. To fancy that religion lives either below or above the limits of reflective thought is fatally to misconceive either the nature of religion or the nature of reflective thought. It would be nearer the truth to say that in religion, the life of reflection is concentrated in its intensest form, and that the special problems of the theoretical and practical life all take their special forms by segregation out of the body of religious consciousness and retain their vitality only so far as they preserve their connexion with it and with each other in it."[76] This statement presents the view that unless reason and religion are combined, or the spiritual life is combined with the empirical life of man, his problems will remain insolvable. Reason is incapable of devising or creating a moral force. Hence, the inherent incapacity of secularism to create any worthwhile values, much less universal values. The fall of the Russian Empire has made this clear.

Five hundred years ago, Guru Nanak emphasised that unless the spiritual component enriches the empirical life, man's problems of conflict, war and disharmony will remain. The solution lies in working in consonance with God's Will or the Basic Force of Love and Altruism. The brotherhood of man cannot be a reality without accepting the Fatherhood of God. For the Gurus, the Fatherhood of God or Force of Love or Universal Consciousness is not an assumption, but a reality. For them, it is a true and most indubitable experience, spontaneously leading to activity. It is an experience far more real than the sensory perception of external phenomena or the construction of a pragmatic or utilitarian ethics, or the assumption of a dialectical movement raised by human reason. The Gurus exhort man to follow the path of altruistic deeds to reach the next evolutionary stage of *gurmukh* or God-man. It is a worldview of combining the spiritual life with the empirical life of man, thereby breaking the alienation from which man suffers. It is a worldview of total responsibility towards every sphere of life, the God-man's sphere of responsibility being co-terminus with the sphere of God. At a time when most of the higher religions have either become dichotomous, or are withdrawing from the main fields of social responsibility, and human reason feels frustrated, the Sikh Gurus express a comprehensive worldview of hope and eternal relevance. At the same time, it is important to state that, far from being exclusive, Sikhism is universal in its approach, always anxious and willing to serve and co-operate with those who aim at harmony among beings and welfare of man. For, the Guru's prayer to God is that the world may be saved by any way. He may be Gracious enough to do.[77] And, Guru Nanak proclaimed that his mission was, with the help of other God-men, to steer man across the turbulent sea of life.[78] This fundamental ideal stands enshrined in the final words of the daily Sikh prayer, "May God bless all mankind."

REFERENCES

1. Guru Granth Sahib, p. 459.
2. Ibid., p. 294.
3. Ibid., p. 955.
4. Ibid., p. 8.
5. Ibid., p. 859.
6. Stace, W. T. : *Mysticism and Philosophy*, pp. 131, 133.
7. Huxley, Aldous : *Moksha*, p. 175.
8. Ibid., pp. 222, 223.
9. Guru Granth Sahib, p. 830.
10. Zimmer, H. : *Philosophies of India*, pp. 222-223.
11. Journal of Sikh Studies, Vol. VII, February-August, 1980, p. 38.
12. Ibid.
13. Jain, N. K. : *Sikh Gurus and Indian Spiritual Thought*, p. 168.

14. Jaiswal, Suvira : *Origin and Development of Vaisnavism*, pp. 116-118.
15. Murthy, H. V. S. : *Vaisnavism of Shankradeva and Ramanuja*, p. 232.
16. Juergensmeyer, Mark : *Sikh Studies*, pp. 83-88.
17. Guru Granth Sahib, p. 473.
18. Bhai Gurdas, Var 1.
19. Guru Granth Sahib, p. 1.
20. Ibid., p. 1412.
21. Macauliffe, M. A. : *The Sikh Religion*, Vol. III, pp. 7-8, 419.
22. Guru Granth Sahib, p. 7.
23. Ibid., pp. 8-9.
24. Ibid., p. 62.
25. Ibid., p. 113.
26. Ibid., p. 473.
27. Panjab Past and Present, October, 1976, p. 468.
28. Guru Granth Sahib, p. 1243.
29. Ibid., p. 730.
30. Wilson, H. H. : *Religious Sects of Hindus*, p. 19.
31. Briggs, G. W. : *Gorakhnath and Kanphata Yogis*, p. 32.
32. Guru Granth Sahib, p. 1245.
33. Ibid., p. 886.
34. Ibid., p. 1171.
35. Ibid., p. 889.
36. Ibid., p. 417.
37. Russell, Bertrand : *History of Western Philosophy*, p. 362-363.
38. Dowley, Tim (Ed.) : *Eerdman's Handbook to the History of Christianity*, p. 5.
39. Guru Granth Sahib, pp. 360, 417-418.
40. Ibid., p. 1028.
41. Ibid., p. 224.
42. Ibid., p. 145.
43. Ibid., p. 1289.
44. Ibid., p. 472.
45. Bhalla, Sarup Dass : *Mehma Prakash*, p. 326.
46. Gupta, H. R. : *History of the Sikh Gurus*, p. 110.
47. Saina-Pat : *Gur Sobha*, pp. 21, 32.
48. Bute Shah : *Tawarikh-i-Hind*, pp. 405-406.
49. Gurdev Singh : *Sikh Tradition*, pp. 183-227.
50. Cunningham, J. D. : *History of the Sikhs*, p. 64.
51. Guru Granth Sahib, p. 176.
52. Ibid., p. 631.
53. Ibid., p. 913.
54. Ibid., p. 913.
55. Ibid., p. 113.
56. Hertzberg, Arthur (Ed.) : *Judaism*, p. 98.
57. Zvi Cahn : *Philosophy of Judaism*, pp. 503-504.
58. Smart, Ninian : *The Religious Experience of Mankind*, pp. 356-358.
59. Zvi Cahn : op. cit., p. 504 Roth. Cecil : *Short History of the Jewish People*, pp. 45-52, 57.
60. Hawking, Stephen : *A Brief History of Time*, pp. 177-178.
61. Bible : John, p. 15, Mathew, p. 22.
62. Toynbee, Arnold, J. : *Christianity and Civilisation*, pp. 14-17.
63. Dowley, Tim (Ed.) : op. cit., pp. 204-207.
64. Toynbee, Arnold, J. : *An Historian's Approach to Religion*, p. 210.

65. Dowley, Tim (Ed.) : op. cit., pp. 570-571.
66. The Tribune : July 12-13, 1990.
67. Dialogue & Alliance : A Journal of International Religious Foundation, Summer 1987, Vol. 1, pp. 94-96.
68. Dowley, Tim (Ed.) : op. cit., p. 610.
69. Moltmann, J. *et al* : *Religion and Political Society*, pp. 19, 46.
70. Panikkar, K. M. : *Hindu Society at Cross Roads*, p. 18.
71. Guru Granth Sahib, p. 560.
72. Ambedkar, B. R. : *Annihilation of Caste*, (an undelivered speech edited by Mulkh Raj Anand).
73. Gupta, H. R. : *History of the Sikhs*, Vol. 1, p. 163.
74. *Limits of Growth* : A report for the Club of Rome's Project. pp. 191-192.
75. Schumacher, E. F. : *A Guide to the Perplexed*, p. 132.
76. Collingwood, R. G. : *Idea of History*, pp. 314-315.
77. Guru Granth Sahib, p. 853.
78. Ibid., p. 939.

8

SIKHISM : A MIRI-PIRI SYSTEM

Kharak Singh

I. Introduction

1.1 On the *miri-piri* concept in Sikhism a lot of literature has appeared, both in English and Punjabi. The Department of Guru Granth Sahib Studies, Punjabi University Patiala, devoted a whole issue of its journal in order to emphasise that this concept is fundamental to Sikhism. Since then, however, articles have appeared in some papers and journals that seek to confuse the issue. Therefore, a reiteration of the basic character of this concept of Sikhism will not be out of place. Before that, however, it seems necessary to briefly recount some other fundamental beliefs that underlie this doctrine :

(a) Concept Of God In Sikhism : In every spiritual system the concept of God or the Spiritual Reality determines its worldview and its structure. In the hymns of the Japu ji, Guru Nanak calls Him the Creator Person, Self-existent, Eternally True and Guru. As Guru, He is both Enlightener and Guide. Further, He is called the Master, the Emperor who is benevolent and directs the world with His Will. He is not only the Creator Person, but is also immanent in the world and is the Fount of all values and virtues. This is how Guru Nanak describes Him.

(b) Spiritual Experience : The spiritual experience of the Guru further highlights that 'He is All Love, and the rest He is ineffable.'[1] The important aspect of this spiritual experience is that the Basic Reality, apart from being the Master of the creation, is guiding it with love. It is this spiritual experience of the Guru, which determines the Sikh world-view : that the world is real, and not an illusion or *mithya*. The *bani* says, "True is He; True is His Creation." "True are Thy continents, and true Thy universes. True are Thy worlds and the forms created by Thee."[2] A consequential implication of a Loving God is that He expresses His love and all virtues in this world. This further fortifies the inference about the reality and meaningfulness of the universe. It also implies that the universe is not a purposeless mass of confusion, but is directed with a Will which is Altruistic. Also, the Fundamental Reality is deeply interested in guiding the world in all its spheres. As Emperor and Master

of the world, He guides both the *piri* and the *miri* aspects of the universe. In fact, as its Benevolent Guide, He hardly makes as division between these two aspects, which are just man-made distinctions or splittings. It gives spiritual sanction to moral life of man, because the Basic Reality is the Fount of all virtues and values.

(c) Goal of Life : It is in this background of his description of the Basic Reality and his Spiritual Experience, that Guru Nanak lays down the goal of man in the very beginning of Guru Granth Sahib. He categorically rejects the ascetic path of withdrawal, remaining silent, one-point meditation or the like, and lays down that the path for the spiritual man is to move and work according to His Will.[3] This is the emphatic goal in Sikhism. As compared to the earlier Indian systems, it completely changes the very basis and direction of pursuit of religion. The failure of many scholars to grasp the radical departures Guru Nanak makes, is due to the lazy notion that Guru Nanak was just a quietist Sant, or a part of the *Bhakti* movement. Keeping in view the spiritual experience of the Guru the changes he made were both natural and essential. For, where God, the *Miri-Piri* Master, is deeply interested in the world, and in guiding all spheres of life with His Altruistic Will, for the spiritual seeker to drop out or be interested in only a part of it, would be incongruous, if not defiant and self-contradictory. Thus in Guru Nanak's system, for a Sikh to be a disinterested onlooker of the world and life, is out of the question. In short, Guru Nanak lays down a fully life-affirming goal for the spiritual man without any aspect of it being taboo for him.

(d) Methodology : It is in the background of his spiritual experience and his concept of God, that Guru Nanak lays down the methodology of his system which, as we shall find, is so logically necessary. Its first corollary is that withdrawal, monasticism and asceticism are rejected; and instead, the householder's life is accepted. He condemns the yogis for "being idlers, and not being ashamed of begging alms at the very door of the householder whose life they spurn." He declares that "liberation is possible even while playing and laughing" and that "the God-centered lives truthfully, while a householder."[4] Every earlier Indian system accepts monasticism, asceticism, or *sanyasa*. In fact, asceticism is considered to be the Indian contribution to the world culture. Yet, straight away Guru Nanak rejects all such worldviews, as directly or indirectly give credence to these institutions. It is important to grasp that there is nothing like half life-affirmation or half life-negation. Life is one composite whole. It has no non-essential compartments, that can be ignored or rejected. God is the Gracious Master of the entire universe and life, and for that matter, faith in Him leaves the seeker no choice to select some aspects and leave others. This is the fundamental spiritual fact which has to be grasped, so as to understand the revolutionary changes in goals, direction, ethics and methodology Guru Nanak makes. Thus the first corollary of his system is to accept every aspect of life and share its responsibilities.

1.2 The equality that Guru Nanak prescribes, is not only between man and man, but also between man and woman. The second part is a major departure from earlier religious thought and a monumental contribution to spiritual advancement of mankind. Guru Nanak was the first man of God to lay down this principle and bring about the change. All the Hindu systems including the Vedic and Vedantic systems, Vaishnavism, Upanishadic and *Nath* sects, had approved of the sanctity of caste. Some *bhagats* and mystics in India and abroad, did support and accept the equality of man. Yet, none of them had accepted the equality of man and woman which Guru Nanak emphasised. Scholars have failed to realise the implications of this major change. Neither Buddhism and Jainism, nor Islam and Christianity, gave full equality to woman. The reason for it is obvious. In these systems monasticism and withdrawal remain approved religious practices, and celibacy is a virtue. In this background, by implication, woman became essentially a temptress. Thus, neither Hindu systems, nor Christianity and Islam, could give equality to woman. Withdrawal from life and downgrading of women, have indirectly been approved by even the *bhagats* or *sants*. K. Schomer and W. D. Flaperty call *Bhagat* Kabir ascetic in his views and a misogynist.[5] But in a life-affirming system, complete equality of man and woman is a must, as also the sanctity of a householder's life. In order to emphasise this principle, not only Guru Nanak but every Sikh Guru, except Guru Har Krishan, who died at a very early age, led a married householder's life. Otherwise, this aspect of his system would have been misunderstood, especially in the Indian context. So much so, that the Sikh Gurus later avoided inclusion in the Sikh society of those who believed in ascetic practices.[6] Guru Nanak emphasises that the spiritual man has to partake in the whole of life, and that he cannot shirk any of the responsibilities of a householder. Hence, the revolutionary significance of Guru Nanak's principle of equality, which embraces both man and woman. This principle, which is so logical considering his system, is in the religious background of man entirely new.

1.3   The corollary of rejecting monasticism is that the seeker has to express his sense of spirituality in virtuous activity and deeds. The stress is that in ultimate analysis all spirituality has to be lived in the form of human conduct and work. The *bani* says : "Man's assessment in His Court is done on the basis of his deed." "It is by one's deeds that we get nearer to or away from God." "Everything is lower than truth; higher still is truthful living." "Gurmukh always lives truthfully."[7]

1.4   This is the second fundamental of Guru Nanak's methodology. He calls life a game of love, and says, "If you want to play the game of Love, enter my lane with your head on your palm, and, once on this path, then sacrifice your head ungrudgingly."[8] This principle he has unambiguously and repeatedly emphasised in his hymns in the Japu ji and elsewhere. For, a follower of God's Will cannot remain a bystander in life. He has to work according to his capacity. Thus, Guru Nanak's system is not only a whole-life spiritual venture, but also a life of continuous love and altruistic activity. Further, the responsibilities of the spiritual man, prescribed by Guru Nanak, logically follow from this. He stresses the need of productive work, which involves sustenance of man and life. He clearly deprecates the idleness of yogis and ascetics, and recommends a life devoted to virtuous deeds.

1.5   Here it would be relevant to state that while *bhagats* like Namdev and Ravidas favour withdrawal from life, the Guru says : "The person incapable of earning his living, gets his ears split (turns a Nath Yogi) and becomes a mendicant. He calls himself a guru or a saint. Do not look up to him, nor touch his feet. He alone knows the way who earns his living and shares his earnings with other."[9] In this regard Machwe writes : "The conflict between a rightful performance of duty and all-absorbing love of God, has existed at all times and in all countries. But it seems that the saints of this period were inclined in the latter rather than in the former direction, and exhibited an all-absorbing character of God realisation. God indeed is an all devourer, and it seems from examples of these saints, that He devours also the performance of one's own natural duties."[10] Nihar Ranjan Ray writes : "They had no other social purpose in view than to make better individuals from out of the groups that assembled around them. Their aim seems to have been the individual, not the society in any significant sense." "These leaders seem to have been individuals working out their own problems and towards achieving their personal religious and spiritual aims and aspirations.[11] The responsibility about sharing is equally important, Guru Nanak and the other Gurus recommend sharing of the Lord's wealth and bounties, and deprecate grabbing and accumulation of wealth. The *bani* says : "God's bounty belongs to all, but men grab it for themselves." "Man gathers riches by making others miserable."[12]

1.6 Another responsibility, which is so natural and logical in Guru Nanak's system, but which is new in the Indian context, is the spiritual man's responsibility to resist and confront injustice and oppression. Here again, what Guru Nanak did was, in the Indian religious tradition, absolute radical. In India all earlier religions and systems accepted the value of *sanyasa*, withdrawal, monasticism, celibacy and *ahimsa*. The Kshatriya alone was asked to fight but that only as a part of his caste duties. Any departure from the duties of one's caste, was frowned upon in the *Bhagwat Gita*[13] and other Hindu scriptures. But Guru Nanak, being very conscious of this background and having laid for the seeker the responsibility of resisting injustice and oppression, took a number of tangible steps to clarify the issue. First, unlike most saints and *bhagats*, he criticised in detail all the faults in the social, administrative, religious and political life of his times. He deprecated the hypocrisy, greed and evil ways of *pundits* and *mullahs*, the social discrimination and practices of pollution following the caste prohibitions, the corruption, bribery and blood sucking practised by public functionaries in the Administration, the luxurious life lived by the rulers, their oppression of the people and their failure to give security of life to their subjects, and the tyranny, cruelty and butchery indulged in by the invaders. Few saints, prophets or mystics have so clearly described the faults and dark spots in the socio-political life of the times, as did Guru Nanak. The second step he took in this direction is manifest in his hymn in which he complains to God for allowing the weak to be trampled upon by the strong. It is a hymn of crucial significance and implications. It is in fact a corollary of the *miri-piri* system which he followed. The first implication of this hymn is that in the Order of God, oppression of the weak and the downtrodden is an aberration. The second inference is that this being so, it is primarliy the duty of the spiritual man, as an instrument of God's Will and Order, to undo and resist oppression and injustice. The third inference is that, as such, it is the duty of his disciples and the Sikh society he was creating, to face and tackle all problems of injustice and oppression. And the fourth one is that, in this context, a society with necessary wherewithal had to be created, which should be in a position to undo injustice. In order to shoulder this spiritual responsibility and accomplish the task, again it is Guru Nanak, who initiated three steps. First, he started the organisation of a Sikh society or *sangats* which could carry on his mission and discharge its responsibilities. And, it was at the time of

Guru Nanak that such organisations were created at different places he visited. The second step which he took was to discard the institution of *ahimsa*. This was an essential step for any society that had to confront the might of tyrants, oppressors and the unjust. This is a particularly significant step, because all the religious Indians, including the *bhagats*, were devoted votaries of *ahimsa* as a creed. Guru Nanak stated that people did not understand what was sin, and were confused over issues like vegetarianism and the use of force.[14] Guru Nanak clearly saw that no society that had to undo injustice and oppression, could remain fettered with impediments like *ahimsa*. And the third important step which Guru Nanak took was that, since the society he was creating was still in its infancy, and could not be motivated overnight to face the gigantic problems of injustice and oppression in the conditions then prevailing in India, and since it was to be a great long-drawn task to train and condition people to accept the responsibility of undoing injustice, he started the institution of appointing a successor, so that the succeeding Gurus could accomplish the targets and tasks of his mission. From the above it is evident that the *miri-piri* thesis is a part of the spiritual experience of Guru Nanak, and that it is also he who in his own lifetime took all the necessary and basic steps, theoretical as well as organisational, to implement and continue his spiritual mission. This explains the uncommon system of appointing a successor which no other *bhagat* or prophet adopted, but which Guru Nanak considered essential for the continuance and completion of his mission.

II. GROWTH OF MIRI-PIRI TRADITION

2.1 Now we have to look at the development of the *miri-piri* tradition initiated by Guru Nanak, during the period of the subsequent Gurus. We have explained that a whole-life or a *miri-piri* system is fundamental to Guru Nanak's spiritual perception and the mission he started. Guru Nanak had taken clear and firm steps to lay the foundations of the *miri-piri* structure. The measures he took in his life-time and the system of succession he introduced, cannot be explained otherwise, than as a consequence of his whole-life system and his desire to develop it further through his successors. In fact, the introduction of the idea of succession, becomes un-understandable, unless it is seen as a clear, conscious, and specific step toward building a *miri-piri* structure and society. For, so far as the ideology was concerned, it had been laid down in Guru Nanak's hymns in Guru Granth Sahib completely, very succintly and emphatically. The subsequent Gurus made no addition to or alteration in the thesis of Guru Nanak. Their role can thus be understood primarily as development, demonstration and implementation of Guru Nanak's mission in the socio-spiritual field. It is not at all meant that other aspects of his system were not carried out. But, because of the need of the subject under discussion, in the subsequent paragraphs, we shall confine our narration of events to the development of the *miri-piri* aspect of Guru Nanak's mission. For that reason our statements may sometimes look unavoidable selective.

2.2 It is on record that when Guru Nanak visited Guru Angad at Khadur Sahib, shortly after the latter's appointment as Guru, he found him leading a somewhat secluded life. He, therefore, reminded him that he was expected to organise and lead a mission and that, as such, further extensive steps had to be taken. Guru Angad took three tangible measures which indicate that Sikhism was to develop as a socio-spiritual growth and society.

He strengthened the institution of *langar*, which Guru Nanak had initiated. Its social role was expanded. The Guru's wife (*Mata Khivi*) was put in charge of it. This institution, as a measure of attack against caste distinctions and of providing free food for the indigent, was apparently well-known in the area, and finds mention in Guru Granth Sahib. Second, he made it clear that recluses could not be welcome in the Sikh society, since their otherworldly ideology was incongruous with Guru Nanak's system.[16] Third, the Guru promoted the physical well-being of the members of the society through physical training and health activities. A gurdwara called Mal Akharan at Khadur Sahib, where the Guru patronised and personally supervised wrestling and other sports, is a monument to this measure adopted by him.

2.3 The third Guru, Amar Das shifted the venue of his activities to Goindwal which was on the bank of the river Beas and a known place of crossing the river. Guru Amar Das took an unusual step to emphasise the institution of *langar*. No one, big or small, could join his *sangat*, until he had given evidence of his anti-caste and anti-pollution views by eating on a common platform of food from the Guru's common kitchen, where no distinction of high and low, Brahmin or non-Brahmin, was made, and where food was cooked by any of the Sikhs irrespective of his or her caste. The significance of the measure is tremendous, considering the fact that in the Hindu temples, Nath monastries, or other religious places of Vaishnavas, food is cooked by Brahmins alone.[17] The republican and anti-caste character of this measure can also be guaged from the fact that, even in the twentieth century, a statue of a Brahmin unveiled by the then Deputy Prime Minister of India, was considered to have been defiled, because of the touch of the Minister, who belonged to a low caste, and had later to be purified with waters from the Ganges. The hold of the caste structure is so pervasive, that even Mahatma Gandhi in this century felt that unfettered entry of untouchables into the Hindu temples was not possible because of the religious injunctions, which evidently he was not willing to disturb or violate, because of his faith in the existing Hindu structure. In fact, the best he suggested was that in some temples the untouchables could go during fixed hours only, and thereafter the temple could formally be purified by the prescribed method for undoing the pollution or defilement caused by the visit of low castes.[18] The second major organisational step the Third Guru took was the creation of 22 districts for preaching Sikhism and administering and organising the Sikh society. The area covered was almost from Kabul to the East of India. The number of districts was the same as the number of political provinces in the country. These districts catered to the religious as well as temporal needs of the Sikh society. Sikhs, women as well as men, were appointed to head these districts. It is also reported that for the first time separate organisations called *pirhis* of women were also created, which were headed by women only. Third, in order to establish separate indentity of the Sikh society, to create a consciousness about their independent social standing, and to dissociate the Sikhs from the Hindu practices and places of pilgrimage, he created a *bauli* at Goindwal as an alternate place for the biannual religious visits, gatherings, education and regeneration of the Sikhs. In short, by this time the Sikh society had reached a new stage of awareness not only of their ideological identity, but also of their distinctive role as a cohesive social group. They developed motivations to achieve the new goals set for them. The ministry of the Fourth Guru lasted only for seven years. But he, too, made the momentous decision of founding Amritsar as the sacred centre of the new community and developing it as a new township, which has since then played a crucial role in Sikh history. It has become the Vatican of the Sikhs, and, in fact, their throbbing heart. The history of the Guru period and the subsequent periods shows that enemies of the Sikhs have always believed that subduing Amritsar would mean the decline of Sikhs and their ethos.

2.4   The role of the Fifth Guru is extremely important as the leader of a *miri-piri* society. The earlier Gurus had created a formal and well-knit organisation socially and religiously cohesive and ideologically committed. Guru Arjun also accomplished the momentous work of compiling and authenticating the Sikh Scripture, thereby making the ideological break with the traditional form of Indian society complete. It is in his time that the Sikh society was taken by his contemporaries and historians to be a 'state within a state',[19] in which the Guru was formally taken by the Sikhs to be the real emperor or the *sacha patshah* of *piri* and *miri*. He was the first Guru to introduce the system of *daswandh*, namely, that every Sikh contributed a tithe or one tenth of his earnings towards the cause of the society. In fact, nothing could be more regal than the introduction of this collection and reorganising the system of *manjis* and *masands*. They were not only supposed to make collections for the Centre, but also to cater to the spiritual and temporal needs of the local Sikh society. In fact, the Fifth Guru openly and visibly created a socio-religious organisation, which, if seen in the background of the religious history of man, finds hardly a parallel. Neither Buddha nor Lord Mahavira, nor Moses, nor Christ created a comparable organisation of the size and structure developed by the Fifth Guru. As we have said, the work of motivation and conditioning had continuously been done to give the Sikhs their cohesion and direction. It is at this stage, that the Fifth Guru with his supreme vision took some other organisational steps. He finalised the Sikh Centre and the town of Amritsar. He created a similar town and gurdwara with a large tank at Tarn Taran in the heart of the Majha area. The Guru constructed a number of tanks at other places, too, as public works, because in those days Punjab suffered from scarcity of rains, and famine conditions frequently prevailed. He dug a tank at Santokhsar by raising contributions from far and near. The Amritsar tank was widened and deepened. The Guru dug another tank called Gangsar and started the township at Kartarpur. A *bauli* was also constructed at Lahore. Similarly he dug a well which could feed six Persian wheels, the place being called Chheharta on this account. Not only that, the Guru persuaded Emperor Akbar, when he visited him to remit or reduce the revenue demand as relief to the famished peasants of the area. The significant point is the distinct measures taken by the Gurus to relieve the sufferings of the people during the time of famine and distress.[20] Further, providing free food at every Sikh Centre has, since Guru Nanak, always been a Sikh social practice. And the steps which the Guru took were exactly those which any good administration would take to relieve the sufferings of the people. All we seek to stress is that in the Sikh concept of *miri-piri*, adequate care of temporal needs of the people is also necessary. Otherwise, few religious leaders have undertaken such large scale construction of townships and tanks for water supply. Mohsin Fani who was a contemporary of the Guru, recalls that in the time of the Fifth Guru there was tremendous increase in the number of Sikhs all over, and that in most of the towns of the entire country, Sikhs were definitely found. Gupta, the distinguished historian writes that the Guru advocated spiritual life and worldly living as two aspects of a single reality.[21] In fact, Mohsin Fani reports that 'the Sikhs had already become accustomed to a form of self-government within the Empire.' The belief that the world was *maya,* had no place in the Sikh thought and society.[22] The Guru erected lofty buildings at Amritsar, procured horses from Central Asia, kept elephants and engaged retainers for them.[23] It is his temporal status that induced a senior functionary of the Mughal Administration to offer the hand of his daughter to the Guru's son, Hargobind.

2.5   Another important fact which portends the coming events, is the Guru's inducements to the Sikhs to enter trading in horses from Central Asia. This trading he did himself, and encouraged his Sikhs to follow it. The step had evidently profound meanings. It suggested that the Guru had a clear vision of the future role of the Sikh Society in which both training in horse-riding and procurement and supply of horses would be necessary. It is well-known that earlier the Sikhs were mostly either petty traders, peasants or small functionaries. This distinct turn to a new profession given by the Guru himself, is meaningfully suggestive of the coming confrontation with the Empire of the day. Lastly, another great act of the vision of the Guru is that after having made his assessment, he initiated a new period of Sikh history. For, he felt that from the point of view of organisation, motivation and size of the community, it was ready for the struggle ahead. The important fact is that the landmark of that struggle was created by the Fifth Guru with his own martyrdom.

2.6   Jehangir came to the throne at Delhi, Khusro, his brother, who was considered to be of better temperament, training and aptitude, rebelled against Jehangir. His army did not make much headway, and he retreated to reorganise towards Lahore. There was a meeting between Khusro and the Guru. The Prince sought help and blessings, and both were given. Beni Parsad in his *History of Jehangir* records that the Guru gave Rs. 5,000/- to the Prince as help for his journey and the army.[24] Seen in the existing context the monetary help was very sizeable. The significance of the step, while it was never lost on Emperor Jehangir, has so often been missed by some historians. It is unthinkable that the Guru did not realise what would be the implications of this step, as naturally understood and actually interpretted by Jehangir. Another significant fact is that whereas the Guru gave such a large sum to the rebel Prince from the common treasury of the Guru, he refused to give even a penny from it by way of fine to save his own life, when it was imposed on him by the Emperor. In fact, he forbade even the Sikhs to make the payment to save his life. It is extremely meaningful to understand that while he considered the five thousand Rupees he gave to Khusro to have been well spent, he would not give even a penny for his own self. It is, therefore, naive on the part of some historians either to misunderstand or to minimise the implications of a step, the meanings of which were clear to Jehangir. The Emperor in his autobiography distinctly expressed his ire at the event, and recorded that Sikhism was certainly a growth which he wanted to nip in the bud.[25] Few Emperors are concerned with quietist saints, and Mughal Emperors were always fond of Sufi *Pirs* and sought their blessings. Jehangir's going out of the way to punish the Guru and, for that matter the growing Sikh society, was a distinct measure to curb the evident political potentials of the Sikh society. It is also evident that Sheikh Ahmed Sirhindi, the head of the Naqshabandi Order, a revivalist of Islamic orthodoxy, who was in a position to judge the growing influence and expansion of the Sikh society, urged the Emperor to curb the development of the Sikh society in the area.[26] That a heavy fine was imposed on the Guru, is testified by Mohsin Fani who records that Guru Hargobind was sent to Gwalior as a prisoner for his father's non-payment of the fine imposed on him.[27] Before his execution Guru Arjun sent a message to his son that the time for starting open military preparations had come and that he should do so. Here it is significant to state that in the time of the Fifth Guru, Guru Hargobind as a boy had been joining hunting parties involving requisite use of arms.

2.7 Beni Parsad, the renowned historian of Jehangir, declares that Guru Arjun's was a political execution.[28] The events of the time of the Fifth Guru, and the positive steps and the tangible measures he took, make it plain that Guru Arjun raised a visible structure on the *miri-piri* foundations laid by Guru Nanak, and that the Sixth Guru only continued further development thereof. As stated earlier, the conditioning and motivation about the socio-political and ideological independence of the Sikhs, had been developed by the first four Gurus. What is of profound significance is that Guru Arjun started the next stage in the growth of the Sikh society, and by his confrontation and martyrdom, he strengthened the faith, determination and cohesion of the Sikhs for the struggle ahead.

2.8 From the time of the Sixth Guru the *miri-piri* complexion of the Sikh society became visible and tangibly clear. On the very first day of his Guruship the Sixth Guru used two swords as symbol of the *miri-piri* aspect of the Sikh society. The very significant fact is that in Sikh symbolism even for the *piri*, sword is the necessary insignia and not a rosary. For, it clearly defines and stresses that in Sikh ideology *miri* is an essential component of the Sikh spiritual system, and not that two separate concepts have been combined. The Sixth Guru took a number of positive steps in the *miri-piri* development of the Sikh society. Evidently, in the initial stages he could not find men from among the Sikhs to impart training in the military arts. He, therefore, recruited mercenaries for the purpose. His two other steps were the construction of the Akal Takht with an additional flag on the premises of Harimandar Sahib, showing thereby that, whereas the activities appeared to be different, their integral fusion as a common source was essential. He also built a regular fort at Amritsar.

2.9 As stated above, the Guru was imprisoned at Gwalior for his father not having paid the fine imposed on him. He was later released, but he continued with his military preparations and ventures. Henceforward, he instructed his Sikhs to don a sword and keep horses. He partook in hunting parties, and he gave, as before, full freedom for use of non-vegetarian diet. The Sikhs, as reported by historian Gupta, squarely established themselves as 'a state within a state.' Necessary recruitment of soldiers was done, and requisite wherewithals for an army were created. The first opportunity for a significant military venture of the Guru came soon after his release from Gwalior, when he helped Dharam

Darbar Sahib, Amritsar, (Punjab)
Popularly known as Golden Temple, stands in the middle of the "Pool of Immortality."
Entrance on four sides represents universal access, and its low domes symbolise humility.

Akal Takht Sahib, or the "Throne of the Timeless"
Established by Guru Hargobind as the seat of temporal and spiritual authority,
at Amritsar, (Punjab).

Takht Kesgarh Sahib, Anandpur Sahib, (Punjab)
The birthplace of the Khalsa (1699 CE).

Takht Damdama Sahib, District Bathinda, (Punjab)
Established by Guru Gobind Singh as an academic centre.

Banda Singh Bahadur (1670-1716 CE)
The first Sikh General commissioned by Guru Gobind Singh,
who established Sikh Rule in North India.

Maharaja Ranjit Singh (1781-1839 CE)
The founder of the Sikh Commonwealth in North India with capital at Lahore.

Dalip Singh (1837-1890 CE)
The last Ruler of the Sikh Commonwealth

Khalsa College Amritsar
Premier educational institution of the Sikhs established in 1892 CE.

Chand, a Prince of the Nalagarh Hindu state to regain his throne.

2.10   Before we go to the other military encounters of the Guru, let us record a clarification given by the Guru himself about the ideology of Guru Nanak. Goswami Ramdas, a saint from Maharashtra, happened to meet Guru Hargobind and expressed his surprise as to how he, who was riding a horse, keeping an army and wearing a soldier's garb, could be a sadhu or a good successor to Guru Nanak. Guru Hargobind's reply was clear and categoric, saying that Guru Nanak had never renounced the world, and that his sword was to protect the poor and to destroy the tyrant.[29] The importance of this statement is that it is an authentic elucidation of Guru Nanak's thesis and spiritual man's responsibility in the field of injustice and oppression, as laid down by the First Guru, and as understood by his spiritual successor. In fact, it is a reiteration of what Guru Nanak had himself laid down in his hymns. Here again it needs to be stressed that Guru Hargobind's understanding of Sikhism as defined by Guru Nanak, is perfectly authentic. For, it is Guru Nanak who in his hymns describes God as 'the Destroyer of the evil', 'the Saviour of Saints', 'the Slayer of the inimical' and 'an Annihilator of the demonical.'[30] As we are aware, the Naths were also surprised at the spiritual role of Guru Nanak, while he continued to wear the garb of a householder. Persons brought up in the Indian tradition like Sant Ramdas of Maharashtra, always express their surprise at the *miri-piri* thesis of Guru Nanak. Guru Hargobind started military preparations in right earnest. Mercenaries were employed and thousands of Sikhs trained as soldiers. On the basis of the organisational steps taken by the earlier Gurus, a sizeable and an independent socio-political system had been created. Gupta writes : "The Sikhs came to occupy a kind of separate state within the Mughal state, the position of which was securely established by the fiscal policy of Guru Amar Das and Guru Arjun and his armed system."[31]

2.11   It is in this context that the confrontation with the Empire, initiated by the Fifth Guru, was continued, and six battles with the Empire were fought by the Sixth Guru. The battle of Jallo clearly suggests the climate and approach in the Sikh society towards the Empire. Jadunath Sircar writes that during a hunt the Sikhs clashed with the Imperial Forces about the possession of a falcon claimed by them "and that in the end Imperialists were beaten off with slaughter."[32] The Sikhs declined to return the bird, because according to the rules of the game, it had legitimately come into their possession. The important fact is that they refused to accept the claim, or superiority of the claim of the Imperial troops on the basis of their soverignty. It is a clear case where Sikhs, because of their own sense of political independence, declined to accept the sovereignty of the Mughal Administration. Two statements are significantly indicative of the Sikh self-understanding of their stand and their socio-political status. A contemporary of Guru Gobind Singh, Konkan, later wrote about this incident saying that the Imperialists were claiming the bird (*baj*), but that they should forget about it, since the Sikhs were out to have the crown (*taj*) also from them (the Mughals). Another writer reports that this statement about snatching the crown was made by the Guru himself, when a Muslim tried to intercede and suggested to the Sixth Guru that he would have the matter settled and the issue closed.[33] The incident and the consequent battle at Jallo are very significant of the politico-military defiance of the Guru. He not only refused to accept Mughal hegemony, but also openly started to prepare his people for clash with the Empire.

2.12   Later, more battles with the Mughal Forces from Lahore and Delhi, were fought by the Guru. According to Mohammad Latif, Mukhlis Khan who attacked at the head of 7,000 troops, was repulsed, defeated and killed. It is during this period that the town of Sri Hargobindpur sprang up, where the Guru built a mosque, evidently for his Muslim subjects and soldiers to offer their prayers. As in the case of the falcon, the Guru sent Bidhi Chand to recover his horses wrongly appropriated by the Mughal Governor. On this the Governor Khalil Begh mounted an attack on the Guru. The Governor was defeated.[34] Another major battle with the Imperial Forces took place at Gurusar near Lakhi jungle, between Ferozepur and Bhatinda. In this battle alone, which the Guru won, 1,200 Sikhs lost their lives.[35] In view of these continuous clashes with the Imperial Forces the Guru selected a site in the hilly area of Kehloor state and settled there.

2.13   From the history of the times Gupta clearly concludes : "After 600 years of slavery he (the Guru) was awakening his fellow contrymen to the realisation that, irrespective of consequences, which were quite obvious, the people should rise against a cruel government to get their wrongs redressed." "Guru Hargobind had a clear conception of the changing circumstances and had realised the necessity of playing an active role in the political life of the community." "He certainly inaugurated a policy which was to lead the most downtrodden people slowly but assuredly to political and military advancement. The Guru created a revolution in the life of the Sikhs. Along with recitation of hymns they were taught the practical lesson of *dharamyudha* or holy war." "In reality Guru Hargobind rendered a unique service to this country in showing the true path of deliverance from political bondage."[36]

2.14   The large scale military preparations and organisation he created, his battles with the Mughal Forces, and, what is more important, the thought of political independence or sovereignty he promoted in the Sikh society, especially in the context of the Akal Takht, and the independent standard he raised at Harimandar Sahib, make it abundantly clear, that the Guru visibly and calculatedly furthered, both in theory and in practice, the *miri-piri* concept of Guru Nanak. But, as historians have recorded, he could do so only because of the foundations laid, conditioning done, and structures built already by the earlier Gurus. This preliminary work of motivation and education of the Sikh society was very essential. Because in the over 2,000 year old Indian tradition *ahimsa*, withdrawal, monasticism and celibacy had been established and accepted as basic religious values. It was, therefore, a colossal task indeed to discard them and make people accept, and make sacrifices for, the idea that it is the spiritual man's responsibility to undo injustice and oppression even in the political field.

2.15   The Seventh Guru maintained an army and continued military preparations. When the struggle for succession between Aurangzeb and Dara Shikoh started, the latter gathered his force for the contest. Dara who was considered to be a person of liberal and tolerant views, called upon persons who were likely to support him. Dara was defeated by Aurangzeb, and he retreated to Punjab, the area of his Viceroyalty. The Guru met him at the head of a few thousand Sikh troops, and offered help. Dara, however, it seems, was demoralised and despaired of his success, and gave up the contest.[37] But Aurangzeb, like Jehangir, never forgot the offer of help made by the Guru to Dara. It is significant that the Guru took a positive and voluntary step, when he knew full well that it was a contest for royalty, and as to what had been the result of a similar assistance rendered by his grandfather to Khusro, the then contestant for the throne. Yes, it is evident that the Guru did so in full consciousness of the likely consequences of the offer. And this could never have been done, if the Guru had eschewed political objectives. It is important to note that invariably the Gurus sided with the political party that in comparative terms stood for some semblance of fairness and tolerance.

2.16   As soon as Aurangzeb was secure at his throne, he called Guru Har Rai to Delhi. The latter sent his son Ram Rai. It is then that Ram Rai wrongly quoted a hymn from Adi Granth to the Emperor, and the Guru discarded him for ever. Later, Guru Har Rai passed away in 1661. Similarly, the Eighth Guru was also sent for by the Emperor. But before any meeting between the Guru and Aurangzeb could take place, the Guru passed away, while still at Delhi. The period of the Ninth Guru is very eventful. Aurangzeb intensified his bigoted activities of intolerance against non-Muslims. Large scale demolition of Hindu temples, execution of opponents and conversion of Hindus to Islam, particularly in Kashmir, took place.[38] Two facts about the period of the Ninth Guru are important. The Emperor was informed that the Ninth Guru was creating a new nation with the object of a rebellion against the Empire. Thereafter, the Emperor conveyed a message to the Guru that if he gave up his political activities, he would get Government grants for his prayers and preachings.[39] The political implications of the rejection of this offer, were too obvious to the Guru, and yet he did so. The Guru toured Punjab in order to relieve peoples' suffering and raise their moral. In fact, when the harassed Kashmiri *Pundits* approached him for advice and help, he gave them a solemn assurance.[40] The subsequent story of his being called to Delhi, and of his execution is well-known. These two facts make it plain that not only political objectives and help to the oppressed people were within the religious purview of the Gurus' system, but they actively, militarily and otherwise, always pursued those interests with a view to confronting injustice and oppression. And for this purpose they staked everything and organised and led the *Panth* to do so. The above is the story of Guru Har Rai and Guru Tegh Bahadur, allegedly pacificist Gurus, who not only made military preparations, but distinctly and openly made political moves that provoked intense hostility towards their persons and the *Panth*.

2.17   The pontificate of the Tenth Guru is a period of open, continuous and mounting military activities and clash with the Empire, the Mughal Governors and their associate Hill Princes. In all he fought about twenty battles involving the loss of thousands of his men, his four sons and his mother besides extreme personal hardship and suffering. He accomplished in his lifetime the epitomic work of creating the Khalsa and its organisation, with the clear objective of fighting injustice and oppression. This he declared in his speech at the time. Facts and events clearly point to political objectives also, which were involved, because of the oppressive Mughal policy of the period. The Guru built a sizeable military force, recruited mercenaries, and invited the Hindu Hill Princes to join him in the struggle to overthrow the oppressive Empire. Because of the liberating policies of the Sikh *Panth*, the caste-ridden Hindu Princes not only declined to side with him,[41] but also invited and fought on the side of the Mughal armies against him. That the objectives of the Guru were religious and just, is clear from the fact that a Muslim *Pir*, Budhu Shah, sided and fought on his side, involving the loss of his two sons and hundreds of his Muslim followers.[42] This marvellous event makes it glaringly clear that, while the struggle of the Guru was political, it was considered by all good persons just and fair, and in the interest of the people as a whole.

2.18 Even after the demise of Aurangzeb, the Guru did try to help Bahadur Shah, on an understanding that he would prove a fair ruler. But when the Emperor's conduct belied his hopes, he deputed Banda for the expedition in Punjab. He gave his blessings to Banda Bahadur, sent five of his trusted Sikhs as Advisors with him,[43] and issued messages and directions to the Sikhs in the state to support the revolution. The significant fact is that the Guru's attack was against the Mughal Administration, and not against any particular person. The Guru's disappointment was with the Emperor, who according to historian Gupta, had been playing a double and deceptive game and was involved in the murderous attack on the Guru. For, he clearly felt that the Guru's move of sending Banda and his army to the North was an assault against the Empire. Significantly, for seven weeks the Emperor did not shift his headquarters from Nanded further down, to subdue his brother, until the demise of the Guru, an event which, he felt, would frustrate the Sikh attack, and enable him to safely continue his march to the South.[44]

2.19 The political objectives of the Guru are also evident from the statement of his spouse, *Mata* Sundri, when she stated that the Guru had bestowed *patshahi* (sovereignty and rule) upon the *Panth*, and that Banda had only been entrusted with the task of doing this service to the *Panth*. (*Bande ko khijmat dei, dei patshahi nahi; Dei patshahi panth nij ap sache patshahi*).[45] This makes the objective of sending Banda, his advisors and army to the Punjab very explicit. This is also supported by Bhai Nandlal's record of thd Guru's emphatic statement in his *Tankhahnamah*, saying, "Listen, Nandlal, to this truth. I shall clearly manifest self-rule of sovereignty."[46] It is significant that after the success of Banda in the Punjab and his declaration of self-rule there was no difference of opinion or policy as between Banda and his deputed advisors and Sikhs. The differences arose only when Banda was considered to have departed from Sikh practices, meaning thereby that whereas establishment of self-rule was a part of the Guru's mandate and within the ambit of his policy, it is Banda's supposed departure from Sikh practices that led to the schism.

2.20 The above is a brief record of the *miri-piri* development in Siklhism in the Guru period. But the most important fact is the insignia the Tenth Guru finally prescribed for every *amritdhari* Sikh as an essential part of his wear. The *kirpan* constantly reminds the Sikhs of three things. First, of his responsibilities to confront injustice and oppression in the political field, both as an individual and as a member of the Sikh society. Second, that use of force, to the extent necessary, is permitted. The third reminder is equally significant, namely, that the Sikh society should never shirk its socio-political responsibilities, nor decline into monasticism, withdrawal or asceticism. The prescribing of this insignia, virtually a *hukamnama* (command) by the Guru is indeed an act of deep historical insight and vision. For, it has been a historical experience that religious societies that started with clearly accepted socio-political responsibilities, later in their leaner periods, declined into pacificism, withdrawal and monasticism, forgetting their social responsibilities. And, it is this responsibility that Guru Nanak emphasised while taking to the life of a householder, and combining spiritual life and empirical life.

III. GURU PERIOD : AN OVERALL LOOK FROM THE MIRI-PIRI ANGLE

3.1 Let us have a look at the Guru period from the angle of *miri-piri* concept the Gurus introduced. Earlier in India religion unmistakably involved withdrawal, *sanyasa*, ascetic practices, *ahimsa*, celibacy, and the consequent downgrading of women and householder's life. Guru Nanak's colossal task was to change this over-2000-years-old religious tradition. He could very well have been misunderstood, if he had started abruptly, crudely or just theoretically. The primary question which the Naths raised with the Guru, was as to how he claimed to be leading a religious life, while retaining the garb of a householder. Such die-hard prejudices and practices could not be removed overnight. Guru Nanak spent almost a whole life time, preaching far and wide the essentials of his system. Hardly any religious leader of his or earlier times travelled so extensively. Yet, he also laid the firm foundations both of its entire theory in his hymns and of its structural and organisational framework on the ground. People had to be weaned away from their old ideas and habits. The basic task was not only to create a new ethos, but also to convince the people that the path he led was indeed spiritual in its true sense. Accordingly, in the time of the first four Gurus, the emphasis was on conditioning and education of the Sikh society in the new mission and goals.

3.2 The period of the Fifth Guru is clearly the one when the march on the highway of the *miri-piri* course became visible. Muslim contemporaries like Mohsin developed a political potential, and posed a serious threat to the Imperial policies. For, the Fifth Guru started collection of *daswandh* and used it for political organisation and objectives. The Fifth Guru's periodical Sikh gatherings were considered regal in their size and operation. He initiated confrontation with Delhi, and by his martyrdom reinforced the will of the Sikh society to struggle and sacrifice. The Sixth Guru's militancy and battles were open enough. The Seventh Guru never faltered when the opportunity came to offer help to Dara, nor did the Ninth Guru give up his military and political activities, even when the Imperial offer came and the risk in declining it was evident. Each time the road to martyrdom was chosen voluntarily. The Tenth Guru not only made his military confrontation open and continuous, but he also made two monumental landmarks. By his *amrit* system he finalised the structural framework of the *Panth*, ensuring that it would not slip back into withdrawal and pacificism. Second, by his dispatch of Banda expedition to Punjab, he finally mounted a full-fledged assault on the Empire.

3.3 Yet, how difficult it is for persons with a pacificist religious background, or bent of mind, to accept the ideology of Guru Nanak, is evident from the fact that not only *Naths* and Sant Ram Das, but even today persons given to the pacificist or soft life of the time, or impervious to poverty and distress, are disinclined to accept the bold *miri-piri* logic of the Gurus. On the other hand, the Gurus have been very outspoken and clear about it. Guru

Nanak emphasises that the only path of spirituality was the one of love and, if once chosen, one should waver not. The same is the clear message the Fifth Guru gave to *Bhai* Manjh, when he asked him if he should follow *Sakhi Sarvar* or be a Sikh of the Guru. The Guru replied that he better continue with the soft life of a *Sakhi Sarvaria*, because as a Sikh his whole wealth and life would be at stake.[47] And, exactly the same message was given, and the undertaking obtained, when the Tenth Guru administered *amrit* to the Five Beloved Ones or *Piaras*. In each case the path was of love, and the commitment demanded was total. And what total commitment means, has been amply demonstrated by the Gurus themselves in their sacrifices, deeds and martyrdoms, which hardly have a parallel in human history. It is just naive to say that the last over 140 years of the Guru period were just incidental or accidental. In fact, they record the most indelible imprints of the Guru period and an incontrovertible interpretation of the Sikh thesis which Guru Nanak had completely embodied in his hymns and the Fifth Guru had finally compiled in the Adi Granth in 1604 A.D. The subsequent tempestuous 104 years of the lives of the Gurus, which were full of sufferings, and creation of the Khasla, become evidently incongruous, if any other interpretation of the Sikh thesis is suggested.

IV.   SOME CRITICISMS ANSWERED

4.1   There have been a number of criticisms of the historical view presented in this essay. A major criticism, mostly from scholars with a pacificist or dichotomous religious background, is that a doctrine of love of God cannot be reconciled with the use of force or war. This mental inhibition is understandable from votaries of dichotomous or pacificist religions. Jadunath Sircar, Mahatma Gandhi and Tagore have been critical of the role of the Tenth Guru. Similarly, Toynbee frowns upon the work of Prophet Mohammed for his militancy. These scholars ignore that actually it is the doctrine of love that provides the compulsion to confront injustice. Evil is a fact of life. The question is how to undo it, and who is responsible for doing so. In a whole-life religion the answer is clear. Since God is himself the Destroyer of the evil and the demonical, the seeker, as His instrument, must make every effort to fight oppression, as a religious responsibility. Injustice, as is well-known, is greatest in the political field. The man of religion, imbued with love, cannot remain indifferent or step aside, when injustice is done within his social sphere. The next issue is whether that confrontation should remain confined to the use of pacificist means only or should include resort to the use of force as well. The twentieth century has made the answer to this question quite clear. After the start of the Second World War, votaries of pacificism sought the advice of Mahatma Gandhi, the apostle of non-violence. But he had no answer and felt so frustrated and baffled, that he even thought of committing suicide.[48] Later he himself suggested participation in war for the Allies, in case Britain agreed to grant autonomy to India.[49] It is also well-known that after 1947 he blessed the dispatch of Indian forces to Kashmir to repel Pakistan-backed intrusion by tribals. H. M. Seervai, the greatest constitutional lawyer of India, concludes, "There is little doubt that Gandhi used non-violence as a political weapon, and was prepared to support or connive at violence to secure political goals."[50] Bertrand Russell has been another known pacificist who even suffered imprisonment for his views during the First World War. But after the Second World War the same Russell suggested that in order to avoid the appalling disaster of a possible Russian victory, threat of force, or even the actual use of force, should be employed against the U.S.S.R., before it could develop a big stockpile of atom bombs, and become a threat to the West.[51] In short, this shows the bankruptcy of pacificism in human affairs, if injustice and oppression have to be confronted. Pacificism is all right where the objective is individual salvation, and goes well with all systems of withdrawal.

4.2 Some scholars are fond of quoting the hymn of the Guru, *"Rajna chahon mukt na chahon man preet charan kamlare."* Invariably the meanings and message of the hymn are distorted. What is rejected are power, pelf and the pride and the glamour thereof. Guru Nanak declared that Sikhism is a path of love, and the Gurus for over hundred years waged a war against oppression and the intolerant state, involving death of thousands of Sikhs and their own martyrdoms. They were certainly following the compulsions of the path of love. Bergson has clearly stated that in the case of a mystic of activity, his love of God is transformed into God's love for all men.[52] It is the love of God and man both that compels the *gurmukh* to fight for a righteous cause. Similarly, the story of Abu Ben Adam demonstrates that in God's system the love of man is synonymous with his love for God. True, scholars from pacificist religions have their own compulsions. But, as stated above, love of man, help to a neighbour under attack, and confrontation with evil on the one hand, and pacificism, in the face of injustice or oppression, on the other hand, are a contradiction, and cannot often go together. It is also incongruous to suggest that this interpretation of the hymn, while it can justify struggle with oppression, means that after the oppressor is eliminated, the religious man should withdraw from the field and leave another *manmukh* to occupy the seat of power. The history of the Guru period does not suggest any such withdrawal from social responsibility. In fact, during the last hundred years the Sikh Gurus not only were administering large scale economic and socio- political organisations, and punishing wrong-doers, like *masands*, but were undertaking every kind of social responsibility almost impossible to discharge in a lifetime.

4.3 Another ideological objection that has been raised is the couplet in *Bachitar Natak* '*Babeke Babarke Dou, ap kare parmesar sou, Deen Sah inko pehchano, duni pat unko anmano.*' This is interpreted as the Guru virtually saying, "Render unto Caeser what is Caeser's." First, as in known, the authenticity of the verses is in doubt. It is unbelievable that the Tenth Guru who all his life confronted the Mughal Administration, fought twenty battles, invited the Hindu Hill Princes to join his struggle to supplant the intolerant rule of Aurangzeb, and dispatched Banda to Punjab, could ever write such a couplet conceding temporal authority to him. Second, even the interpretation and translation of the words as explained by Kapur Singh and Jagjit Singh,[53] have been incorrectly done. The couplet is just a factual statement that both the house of Babar and the house of the Guru are the creation of God. There is nothing in it to suggest that the Guru directed the Sikhs to recognise the house of Babar as such, while all his life he himself had been fighting that house. It is just a couplet to mean the omnipotence of God as the Creator of everything. The translation of the word '*pehchano*' to mean 'recognise' is obviously incorrect. The word means only a statement of the position of the two houses as it was, and does not at all imply any recognition thereof.

4.4　It has also been suggested that the Guru sent Banda with the Advisors and the Sikh Army only to negotiate with or to subdue and punish Wazir Khan, Governor of Sirhind. The suggestion is a bit naive. Sending the army with Banda and messages to the Sikhs to rally round him, can hardly be considered consistent with Banda's role as a negotiator. The Guru had himself tried to negotiate with Bahadur Shah, who alone was in a position to make a settlement, and had come to the conclusion that he was not inclined to do so. The circumstances following the negotiations and the step taken by the Guru are clearly indicative of their failure. On his part the Guru sent Banda to launch the attack in Punjab. Bahadur Shah obviously, resented the Guru's move and deceptively tried to send the Pathans to assassinate the Guru.[54] It is just absurd to suggest that Wazir Khan was in a position to negotiate anything, or that, if subdued or destroyed, the Emperor would remain unconcerned; or that Banda or the Guru would later take orders from Bahadur Shah to appoint a new Governor of Sirhind after Wazir Khan's elimination. Hence, as also confirmed by *Mata Sundri*, Banda had been deputed to establish the *Raj* of the *Panth*.

4.5　It has also been suggested that although the Gurus kept armies, and fought battles for over hundred years, they never carved out any area for themselves, and had no political consideration in view. The suggestion appears quite meaningless. The entire Punjab was under Mughal rule. The question of carving out a principality for the Guru could arise either by supplanting the Mughal rule or by accepting their suzerainty. The question of the second possibility could not arise, and it is to undo the unjust, intolerant and oppressive Mughal rule, that the Gurus had been fighting throughout.

4.6　Another scholar has argued that the use of force permitted by the Guru is only for the purpose of defence. Confusion about the meaning of defence in human and military affairs is common. The basic question is about oppression and injustice, and how to undo them. What has to be defendend is peace, freedom and justice. Thus, military activity of every kind in support of justice is defence. As such, the question of defence or offence is irrelevant, the form of operation being just a matter of strategy. The maintenance of thousands of soldiers, including employment of mercenaries, waging of scores of wars by the Gurus, and the dispatch of Banda to Punjab from Nanded can in the common terminology hardly be called defensive, except in the sense that all such operations were in defence of righteousness. It can never be suggested that the Gurus waged the wars and made the attacks to save their person of property. It is simply unthinkable that the Gurus kept army just for any personal or parochial purpose and not to secure justice and peace for the people, and to save them from oppression or conversion, as had been explained by the Sixth Guru to *Sant* Ram Das.

4.7　It has also been argued that as Guru Granth Sahib never lays down any rules for civil or political administrator like *Shariat* in Islam, it means that the Gurus never contemplated any political role for the Sikhs. The argument is far from sound. As noted already, the Gurus themselves had been creating and managing large scale socio-political organisations and armies. That they conducted their administration with love and justice, is evident from the extreme devotion they inspired from the Sikh as well as non-Sikh forces.

It is this sense of fairness and spiritual purity in their conduct and objectives that led Budhu Shah to join the Guru's forces, involving the loss of his sons and men. The second part of the issue is that civil rules and practices are always dated, and never universal or eternal. These demand adjustment to ever changing socio-economic conditions. Therefore, for a spiritual man to prescribe rules of civil life can, quite often, become an embrassing handicap for his followers. We are well aware that rules of the *Shariat* and similar practices that had been laid down in Judaism and Islam, both whole-life religions, have sometimes become a limitation or incongruous in changed circumstances. It shows, indeed, the vision and wisdom of the Gurus that while they clearly laid down basic principles of ethics and morality to be followed by the Sikh society, they avoided laying down civil rules that could in the course of time become restrictive or a hurdle.

4.8 In modern times persons with background of social sciences are very fond of suggesting environmental or social factors as the cause of religious or historical developments. It has been argued that since *Jats* of the area became followers of the Guru, and since *Jat* are known for a militant temperament, it is concluded that militancy in the Sikh society was the result of their infiltration in the Sikh ranks. Jagjit Singh in his book *The Sikh Revolution* has dealt with the subject at length, and exploded the entire basis of this argument.[55] Factually the position was that at the time Guru Hargobind took to militancy, the *Jats* were in a minority in the Sikh society. Among the prominent Sikhs listed by Bhai Gurdas, the *Jats* formed a small fraction.[56] It is well-known that Baba Budha, a *Jat*, and Bhai Gurdas, the two topmost Sikhs, remonstrated with the mother of the Guru to dissuade him from the risky path. But since in the Sikh society final decisions had to be made by the Guru, he not only continued with his policy, but what is most significant, he even recruited numerous Muslim mercenaries to train the Sikhs in military arts. In fact, the adversaries of the Guru ridiculed the strength of the Guru's army, because most of its constituents belonged to low castes despised by the Muslim adversaries who were proud of their own race and competence in the art of war and militancy.[57] It is understandable that later the *Jats* joined the Sikh fold because of the military needs and leadership of the Gurus. It is, thus, ridiculous to suggest that the Gurus took to militancy because of *Jat* entry among the Sikhs. The fact is that, the Guru had to employ mercenaries, because of paucity of available recruits in his own ranks.

4.9 Social science scholars also sometimes give syncretic explanation of militancy is Sikhism. For, they are disinclined to accept ideological reasons for it. The syncretic explanation has been discussed and discarded both by Jagjit Singh[58] and James Lewis.[59] The suggestion is that the militancy was accepted because of prevalence of Shaivism and Devi worship in the Hill areas or because of Islam. So far as Devi worship in the Shivalik Hills is concerned, the argument has obviously no basis. Guru Hargobind raised his army, fought all his six battles and built the Akal Takht and Lohgarh Fort at Amritsar in the Plains of Punjab, long before he retreated to the Hills. And, Devi worship and Devi temples were too insignificant in the plains of the Punjab so as in any way to influence the Guru or the Sikhs. In fact, because of the Sikh ideology and their conditioning, the Sikhs had hardly any faith in the validity of Devi or Shiva worship. It is also well-known that the Hindu Hill worshippers of the Devi declined to join the Guru in his struggle against the Empire. Rather, they supported the Mughal forces against the Guru. Similarly, the influence of Islam is out of question, because Sufism, the principal missionary wing of Islam, was itself non-militant and never raised any voice, much less an organisation, to oppose the oppression of the Mughal Administration.

V.   ACHIEVEMENTS OF *MIRI-PIRI* SYSTEM

5.1   The achievements of Guru Nanak's *miri-piri* system are in many human fields revolutionary, monumental and abiding. Jagjit Singh in his three books, *The Sikh Revolution*, *Perspectives on Sikh Studies*, and *In the Caravan of Revolutions*, has dealt with the subject at length, and shown that, although burdened with the tradition of life-negating ideology and caste-ridden social structure and ethos of the Indian society, the Gurus assiduously weaned away the Sikh society from it by creating among them a new set of values and goals.

5.2   *Equality/Egalitarianism* : First is the sense of equality and fraternity the Sikh Gurus brought about in the social field. By the essential institution of *langar* they broke all barriers and discriminations arising from the caste ideology and the concept of pollution. In the Guru period and even later in the eighteenth century, the elimination of all restrictions concerning commensality and social intercourse stood removed. The supremacy of the two higher castes was completely rejected as also the stigma against the lower castes concerning mobility of profession. Upto the eighteenth century there was hardly any prominent Sikh leader except from the two lower castes, and Sikhs from the so-called higher castes willingly accepted their leadership. The first Sikh leader who struck a coin was Jassa Singh, a Kalal considered to be a very low *Sudra* subcaste, who never felt shy of proclaiming his caste on the coin he introduced. Even from the other *Sudra* castes there were respected and distinguished leaders in the Sikh society, like Jiwan Singh and Jassa Singh of Ramgarh. The lowest castes were recruited to the Sikh forces without any stigma or discrimination. The self-respect of these lower castes was raised to a level that left no sense of inferiority vis-a-vis the higher castes. It is by no means a small contrast that, unlike Hindus, the Sikhs have never been led by Brahmins either in socio-political or intellectual fields.

5.3   *Socialisation* : The greatest measure of socialisation was the step Banda took after his victory, namely, the distribution of land among the peasants and elimination of the *zamindari* and *jagirdari* systems. He created a bold peasantry. It is this great step of socialisation which raised permanently the sense of self-respect, self-confidence and self-reliance among the masses in the Sikh society. Neibuhr, the distinguished Christian theologian of the century writes : "Because of evil in man and in society, Christian political action called not simply for love, but for an attempt to give each group within society power to defend itself against exploitation by other groups. Although relations between individuals might be a matter of ethics, relations between groups were a matter of politics."[60] What the Christian theologian suggests as the necessary corollary of love, was meaningfully done by the Sikh religion to check human tendency towards exploitation and oppression of the poorer sections of society. Similarly, Jagjit Singh in his book *In the Caravan of Revolutions* has stated that whereas the French Revolution never changed the class structure, nor raised the power or social level of the lower strata, the Fourth Estate of the Christian society, and power continued to be in the hands of the upper middle sections of the French society, it is only the Sikh religion that permanently broke in the Punjab the social stratification in order to raise the level of the lowest classes in the social structure.[61] The status of women was improved, and they became leaders and heads of *manjis* and *misls*. In the history of man such a large scale change in the social and power structure has hardly ever taken place. In fact, many of the social and political developments and problems in the Punjab and the Sikh society, can be understood only in the context of such achievements of the Sikh religion.

5.4 *Earth Awareness* : It is Guru Nanak, who condemned the idleness of the *yogis*, their vow to shun economic activity, and the general habit of withdrawal. The Gurus by their ideology and personal example and leadership, created the work and sustenance habit in the Sikh society, which has since then become its established feature. Accordingly, in the Sikh society not to do any productive work or to live on begging is considered parasitism and a stigma. It is this cultural trait that enables the Sikhs to adjust and live gainfully as acceptable migrants in most foreign societies. It is because of their work habit and sense of adjustment, innovation and pragmatism, that not only were they the first in the East to accept and adopt the wherewithal of the Green Revolution, but today they regularly produce each year enough grain to contribute over 60% of the food reserves procured by the India Government for distribution among deficit areas of the country.

5.5 *Reaction Against Injustice And Oppression* : Guru Nanak is the first man of God in India, who introduced the concept of resistance against injustice as a moral value for a man of religion. It was by their martyrdoms and leadership that Guru Nanak and his successors created, among a stagnant pool of population, a new spirit, cohesion and zeal that enabled them to supplant in Punjab a mighty Empire, and to stop once for all a thousand-year wave of invasions from the North-West of India. Individual leaders have been galore in India and elsewhere, but rarely have the masses been fired with such a spirit for justice and liberty, as was created by the Sikh Gurus. The marvellous work of Guru Gobind Singh against tyranny has been epitomised in a single couplet of contemporary Sufi mystic Bulleh Shah, who sang his tribute to the Tenth Guru, "I neither speak of the past, nor do I speak of the future, but I speak of the present : but for Guru Gobind Singh, all the Hindus would have been circumcised i.e. converted to Islam."[62]

5.6 Despite a price on each Sikh head, and repeated reports that all of them had been eliminated, the Sikh masses rose, on the one hand, to uproot the oppressive administration in the area, and on the other hand, to repel the invaders periodically swarming India, for loot and booty, from the North-West.

5.7 What is important is the acceptance in the society, of a new set of values, and to cultivate its capacity to make sacrifices and suffer for the cause of justice. The role of the Sikh society in the fight for liberty in the eighteenth century is well recognised. Their contribution to the cause of freedom is equally outstanding in the 20th century. The first two rebellions against the British, the *Kuka* Rebellion and the *Ghadar* Rebellion, were almost wholly manned by the Sikhs. While the Sikhs form only 2% of the Indian population, during the struggle for Indian Independence, of the 121 persons hanged, 2,644 imprisoned for life, and 1,330 massacred in the Jallianwala Bagh protest meeting, 93, 2,047 and 799, respectively, were Sikhs. Again, of the soldiers who in the early forties, fought under Subhash Chandra Bose in the Indian National Army, 60% were Sikhs. In 1975, when the Prime Minister, Indira Gandhi imposed the Emergency Law, curtailing all human rights and liberties, the Sikhs were the only people who organised, sustained and managed from the Golden Temple, Amritsar, a peaceful struggle against this invasion on all human freedoms. It involved imprisonment of over 40,000 Sikhs, when in the rest of India, not even one third of that number offered, as a protest, voluntary arrest.[63] It is necessary to state that movements initiated by the Sikhs against the state were executed from the precincts of Darbar Sahib, Akal Takht, wherefrom they drew their inspiration and strength. It is regarding this struggle of the Sikhs that Ms. Vijayalakshmi Pandit, sister of Jawaharlal Nehru, said, "Punjab which has always been in a forefront of resistance of oppression, kept its colours flying, during the Emergency also. It was in Punjab and Punjab alone, that a large scale resistance was organised against it. The worst thing that happened during the Emergency was that a brave nation was frightened into submission, and nobody spoke, except in hushed tones. In Dehra Dun, where I was, I hung my head in shame, and wondered, if this was the Bharat for which we, the freedom fighters, had suffered. Even those, not actually in prison, were no less than in jail. Only in Punjab the Akalis organised a *morcha* (protest) against this. Punjab's lead in such matters should continue."[64]

5.8 *Sikh Ethos* : A very important fact is the ethos the Sikh society and its leaders displayed, when they were in power. Qazi Nur Mohammed, an official reporter who came with the invading armies of General Abdali, reports that while the valour of the Sikh soldiers and their courage are undisputedly outstanding what is extremely significant about the Sikhs is their conduct towards the vanquished. For, the Sikh soldiers neither loot, nor fire upon or attack a fleeing soldier.[65] In fact, the self-discipline and ethical level of the victorious Sikh soldiers have not been achieved even in modern times.

5.9 An equally significant fact is the magnanimity displayed by the Sikh Administration during the time of Ranjit Singh. Even though Sikhs had suffered the severest persecution at the hands of the Muslim Administration, in the 18th and early 19th centuries, the Sikh Rule never showed any discrimination for recruitment in the army or civil administration against them. In fact, they enjoyed, both in the army and the ministries, the highest and most trusted positions. It is, due to this unrivalled conduct of Ranjit Singh that in the Anglo-Sikh Wars the Muslim soldiers fought the British with the same zeal as the Sikhs.

5.10 It was because of caste discrimination, acute caste consciousness, and professional immobility that the contemporary Rajput and Mahratta rulers could never develop any sense of cohesion or nationalism among their people as a whole. In these administrations, feudal and *jagirdari* systems continued, and caste ideology and its exploitative and other manifestations were upheld. The social stratification was so strong that a Rajput scorned to work on land, because if he did so, he was denigrated in social status. In Maharashtra apart from the fact that the Ministers were Brahmins, there was prohibition against the entry of untouchables on the roads during most of the day, lest their shadow should pollute the higher castes.[66] It was a standing state order that caste and

Shastric regulations should be adhered to in the administration of justice as between different sections of the people and that no innovation or departure should be made in their enforcement.[67] It is also well-known that pogroms against Jews and ghettos were a regular feature in contemporary Christian states in Russia and Europe.

5.11 As against this, Ranjit Singh gave ample grants to Muslim and Hindu religious places, and there were no communal tensions or clashes in his State. It is also significant to state that Ranjit Singh spent about 10% of his revenue for beneficent causes and religious grants.[68] No attempt at religious conversions was ever made. His beneficence went to the extent that he never gave a death sentence to anyone including those guilty of attempts on his own life.[69]

5.12   What we seek to emphasise is that although change in ethical values of the masses is a very slow process, especially in traditional cultures, it is in this field that the Sikh society showed a distinct and radical change, both in its external and internal behavior, moral discipline, social conduct and sense of responsibility for maintenance of human rights and justice, and towards other contemporary societies. The important fact is that the change was significant at the mass level.

VI.   CLASSIFICATION OF RELIGIONS

6.1 One of the major reasons for misunderstanding and misinterpretting Sikh ideology is the ignorance of some scholars, especially those drawn from the field of social sciences, about the basic classification of the religions of man. Broadly speaking, religions may be divided into two categories, namely, life-negating, and life-affirming. In the case of life-negating religions, the world is deemed to be *mithya* (unreal or an illusion) or a place of suffering, or man is considered an unwanted combination of the spiritual and the empirical elements, which has to be disentangled. In all these cases the institutions of withdrawal, *sanyasa*, asceticism, celibacy and the downgrading of women are ideologically accepted and recommended methods for pursuing the spiritual path. In such religions, for that reason, monasticism, nunneries and pacificism appear. The salient fact displayed by the religious history of man is that practically all these institutions, and values, being correlated, go together. The goal is personal salvation (*moksha*), union with or merger in the Absolute, or an eternal life of the soul.

6.2   In the second category, evil in life is considered a problem, and the man of religion, while taking full participation in life, seeks to battle with the forces of evil. In these cases God is considered to be Altruistic and Immanent, and to have a Will directing the world. The goal of the man of religion is, thus, to live and work as an instrument of God's Will, and in that pursuit to accept total social responsibility. The seekers are supposed to live the virtues described as attributes of God. They do not withdraw from, or reject life or any part of it. For them life is a single whole, and cannot be compartmentalised. In these religions the emphasis is on family life and social responsibility which includes confrontation with evil. As such, love, moral life, freedom, justice, and equality of man, become primary values for the spiritual man, and simultaneously, what is contrastingly significant, the institutions of withdrawal, *sanyasa*, celibacy, monasticism and *ahimsa* are rejected.

6.3 Jainism and most other Indian systems are typical of the first category, in which the related values and institutions mentioned above, are fully accepted. Once the seeker reaches the final stage of spiritual goal, *kavilya*, there is no return to life with which connection is permanently served. Similarly, the *videhi-mukta* has no role to play in the world.[70] The important fact is that, except in the case of Sikhism, which belongs to the other category, all these methods and values, accepted and used in the first category of religions, have been an integral part of the Indian cultural and religious heritage for the last over 2,500 years.

6.4 Judaism, Islam and Sikhism belong to the other category. The revelation of God to Moses straightaway directs him to make an attack on the land of Canaanites. Moses and his men were reluctant to move, but God revealed, "My angel goes before you and brings you to Amarites, Hittites, Perizzites, Canaanites, Hivites, and Jevusites, and I annihilate them."[71] "So God led the people roundabout by way of the wilderness at the Sea of Reeds." "The people may have a change of hearts, when they see war and return to Egypt."[72] Further, the Law of Punishment revealed to Moses says, "The penalty shall be life for life, eye for eye, tooth for tooth, hand for hand, foot for foot, burn for burn, etc.."[73] The Torah, apart from prescribing the rules of war and civil life, lays down the Ten ethical Commandments, as also regulations for sacrifice and rituals. David and Solomon were celebrated kings of their times, and the Jewish prophets saw to it that they worked according to the ethics prescribed in the Torah. The Torah is an integral part of the Bible. The important fact is that the ethical commandments laid down over three millennia back embody certain fundamental laws of morality, which are valid even today. In short, it is an ethically sound *miri-piri* system that sanctions the use of force of war for a righteous cause, or for the purpose of God. It is obvious that withdrawal, monasticism, celibacy, etc., are nowhere prescribed. Torah continues to be the spiritual guide of the Jews, and from the time of Moses to the sixth century B.C., no variation was suggested by the prophets, or was practised.

6.5 It is for emphasis that every religious system has its logic and corollaries which lead to congruous institutions and values. Another important fact is that in revelatory religions basic ideology is laid down at the very start, and consequently, it is in the early part of the religion that foundations of the system are laid and proclaimed. The history of Judaism and Islam makes this point very explicit. Further, all whole-life religions accept the family system, and are social in their constitution and character. Being life-affirming, the emphasis is on a life of love and virtue, and not on adopting ascetic practices, or creating monastic institutions. Pacificism is rejected. Significantly, while the acceptance of certain values and institutions is natural and necessary, simultaneously the rejection of contrary institutions is also considered equally natural and desirable. An important corollary of the whole-life religions is the institution of martyrdom.

6.6 Here it is extremely necessary to understand that it is Guru Nanak who calls spiritual life a 'game of love', organises a society, and rejects asceticism, withdrawal, celibacy and *ahimsa*. In fact, the words *hukm* and *raza* meaning the Will of God, were taken by him from the Muslim terminology. Similarly, the Arabic word *shahid* (martyr) in Sikhism had hardly an equivalent in the Indian languages, because withdrawal, *sanyasa* and *ahimsa* being celebrated religious institutions, the question of martyrdom could not arise. Whereas quietist mystics or *bhagats* appeared in all ages and all countries, nowhere have they ever organised a society or a people, because their objective invariable has been just personal salvation of a few. But, in contrast, Guru Nanak is the first man of God in India to proclaim a new ideology, and create the entire structural framework of his system in his own lifetime. At one stroke, and from the very start, he unmistakenly accepted and implemented the elements of a whole-life or *miri-piri* system, and rejected all the essentials of the earlier over 2,500-years-old dichotomous religious tradition. The contrast is that this old tradition, particularly its caste system, the society is not willing to change even today. At the risk of alienating the entire *Sudra* population, forming almost one fourth of India. Mahatma Gandhi stoutly stood for the maintenance of its discriminating religious system of worship, and temple entry and management.[74] Social leaders like G. D. Birla and the religious Shankracharyas justify it, and A. Coomaraswamy, the distinguished modern scholar, calls *Manu Smriti* a book of Hindu Utopia.[75] In this background, for Guru Nanak to reject the dichotomous Indian systems, and instead, proclaim and practise a whole-life system, means two things. First, that his system, as asserted by him, was the result of his revelation, since there was nothing in the social environment to influence him into making the revolutionary change; second, that he introduced a full-blooded whole-life system, including equality of man and woman, of which there was no trace in the then religious or cultural life of the world.

6.7   Among religions of man the above are the two principal kinds of religions that have appeared in the East or the West. It is not suggested that there have not been intermediate or subsidiary and sectional developments. The greatest proliferation of sects has been in India. But all of them have been dichotomous and otherworldly, catering only for personal salvation. As concluded by Maitra in his *Hindu Ethics*, a common feature of all Hindu systems and their doctrines of the ideal life is "the conception of the ideal as a negation or at least as a transcendence of the empirical life proper and that this state is thus a super-moral spiritual ideal rather than a strictly moral idea."[76] "It is a transcendental state of deliverance from all struggles of life."[77]

6.8   *Christianity* : In the Western world and the Middle East, Christianity is the third major religion. It has a chequered history. While a whole-life system, it does present features like pacificism which normally belong to the life-negating systems. It is, therefore, necessary to indicate a brief outline of developments in that system. It is well-known that following the call of Jeremiah not to resist the Babylonian attack of the sixth century B.C., many pacificist of monastic cults like Essenes, Kabbalists, etc., appeared in Judaism. It has been suggested, on the basis of some Jewish manuscripts, including the Dead Sea Scrolls, that Jesus Christ belonged to one of those pacificist groups. We do not contribute to this theory, but there is a strong belief that Jesus Christ never wanted to start a new religion, and desired only to reform Judaism.[78] Because of the short period of his ministry and paucity of early records about his religion, it is not easy to be categoric about its history. The Bible was compiled only in the early fourth century A.D. During this period Christianity became a cohesive societal religion, and underwent extreme sufferings, persecutions and martyrdoms. In these centuries, except for its pacificism, Christianity exhibited all the features of a whole-life religion. In fact, many pacificist Jewish sects had existed already, and except for the independent revelation of Christ, Christian principles were not significantly different from theirs. The close ideological affinity of the two religions is apparent from the fact that Torah and the Old Testament are a part of the Bible, which is a man-compiled scripture. It is important to bear in mind that God's revelation to Moses, which suggests the use of force for a political or a societal purpose, is an integral part of the Bible. The variation is prilimary with regard to rituals. It is, thus, apparent that Christianity, like Judaism, is a whole-life religion, with many doctrinal principles common with the pacificist sections of Judaism. Except for the schism and subsequent tensions that followed in the two religions consequent to the crucification of Christ, they have a common heritage and cultural history.

6.9   After Christianity became the state religion in the fourth century A.D., the incongruity between pacifism and political rule came to the surface. It was virtually a marriage of convenience. For the Roman Emperor Christianity was a good cloak, on the one hand, to maintain the old Roman position of the monarch being the representative of God, and, on the other hand, to be supplied with a cohesive people or force for the expansion of his empire. Christians who in the early period had, because of their pacificism, declined to join the army, started entering the forces of the Roman Empire. Christianity gained political prestige and relief from suffering. But the position thus developed, became an ideological incongruity. The period of persecution being over, it is in this period that Christian philosophers turned attention to framing its ideology. Many of them gave it a completely otherworldly trend, suggesting that their religion did not have much to do with the empirical world. The renowned St. Augustine in his famous treatise, *City of God*, attacked both Christians who expected the world to get better as well as the pagans with a cyclical view of history. He did not believe that the spread of Christianity would ensure political and economic improvement. The earthy city of self-will would continue to exist amidst the rise and fall of states and empires.[79] We shall refer to this development later as well, but this much is evident how a whole-life religion, once it adopts pacificism, slowly and necessarily becomes otherworldly. For, the heightened moral sense of the religious man, when it is unable to guide and influence the working of socio-political life, refuses to co-operate with it, and turns towards monasticism and celibacy. Significantly, it is no chance that monastries and nunneries also started appearing in the Christian life only round the close of the third century A.D. As is usual, these believers of monasticism and celibacy not only became otherworldly, but increasingly emphasised Christian eschatology of heavenly gains after death and the redemptive role of Chirst. Without going into a detailed account, it may be noted that the ambivalence between the whole-life original character of Christianity and its later stress on otherworldliness and monasticism has continued in its long history. For, in the later centuries not only priests and the Pope led the crusades, but Joachim of Fiore applied Christian doctrines to secular affairs. "He had a millenarian vision of a future age of the holy spirit, when love and justice would prevail on earth." So much so, that this theologian of the twelfth century A.D. is considered to be the forerunner of modern Christian ideas. "Most of the secular ideas about the future in modern times are derived from Joachim's interpretations of the role of Christianity."[80]

6.10   It is also well-known that Luther's reforms led to another major change, and incongruities of the Christian ideology became more significant. True, Chruch life improved, its monastic tendencies slowed down, and there was greater interest in the empirical life. The Reformation gave a distinct fillip to empirical life or what Weber calls 'worldly asceticism.' But, unfortunately the Church came under the control of the national states instead of being their master. Since Luther had the support of the princes, this became unavoidable. The ambivalence continued, and while the Calvinists approved of the use of force for a righteous cause, Luther himself sided with the princes. He opposed the peasants who rose for their rights, calling them mad dogs. But following the Enlightenment and the rise of science, religion was ultimately sidetracked, and Secularism became the ideology, claiming to devise its own ethics for the empirical life. Rousseau believed that Christ had created a spiritual empire, separating religion from political systems. For Hobbes, the state was supreme in all matters. Kant had faith in the power of reason, and thought that it would bring about a just political order. All these factors strengthened the power of the national states over religious institutions and the Churches.

6.11 This ambivalent ideological trend in Christianity has continued upto the present century. But the rise of two secular rulers, Hitler and Stalin (they and their methods and systems are not in disgrace), and the two world wars have led religious men to rethink about the ethical life of man, which is in disarray.[81] The present position is that whereas the Churches of North America suggest that Secularism is a danger to religion, and that it is time they co-operated with other religions to combat it, the majority in the World Council of Churches believes that Secularism is a God-sent growth which embodies and owns Christian values, and would be eminently helpful in destroying superstitious ideologies like Islam and Hinduism.[82] Of course, non-Christian religions have evidently a very different view of the moral role of the Christian West and its national states, and uphold the minority view of the North American Churches. For, wars, tyranny, massacres, ghettos, inquisitions, and large scale pogroms and persecutions, and consequent expulsions and migrations from one country to another, have continued to be a part of the political life of the national states in the West.

VII. PACIFICISM IN JUDAISM AND ISLAM

7.1 We have seen that both Judaism and Isalm are from the very beginning empathically *miri-piri* systems. But in both of them at later stages of their history, withdrawal or pacific sects have appeared. It is, therefore, necessary to record the circumstances of their emergence.

7.2 After the settlement of Jews in Canaan, Judaic kings appeared, the more famous of them being David and Solomon. Their period of rule has been eulogised in history for its justice and wisdom. A significant fact of Jewish history is that simultaneously with their kings, there lived respected Jewish prophets, distinguished for their piety and upholding of ethical values. They were always critical of kings, if at any time they faltered in their behaviours or in the administration of justice and the Law. This shows that not only the kings were obliged to be fair and just, but there was also the institution of religious prophets who guided their functioning, and were strongly critical, if the kings went astray. In short, this combination of the religious life and the empirical life brought about a healthy social atmosphere for the people. It needs to be stated that the king was not considered the representative of God, but he was supposed to run his administration according to the ethical Laws of his religious system, and for that reason, was always subject to criticism, in case he failed to uphold the prescribed values.

7.3   But in the sixth century B.C., the situation changed. This followed the major calamity of the Babylonian attack on Jerusalem, which involved the destruction of the Temple and the compulsory migration of the Jews as slaves to Babylonian territories. It is at this time that Prophet Jeremiah for the first time gave a call that the Babylonian attack should not be resisted, since it was a punishment to the Jews by God for their violation of the Laws prescribed in the Torah and their covenant with God. Not many Jews were left in Jerusalem. Socio-political circumstances and pressures were such that men of religion took to withdrawal and pacific and monastic cults. Political confrontation had failed, and it was thereafter that many pacific sects like the Essenese, Kaballists and others came into existence. They continued side by side with the mainstream Jews who accepted the basic combination between the religious life and the empirical life. From then onwards Jewish history has mostly been centuries of suffering, massacres, migrations, and consequent diaspora. In the subsequent periods of Roman, Muslim and Christian rule, Jews continued to be oppressed. It is during the Roman rule that Christ was crucified. As revealed by the Jewish writings, manuscripts and the Dead Sea Scrolls, it was a time when there were present many pacific or monastic cults. After their uprooting from Jerusalem area, the Jews continued to be a minority in every European state, and persecution, pogroms, refugee camps and ghettos remained their dismal lot.

7.4   Ultimately, in the nineteenth century the concept of Zionism, a homeland for Jews, became a growingly settled Jewish goal. Einstein was a vocal Zionist. After the creation of Israel, it is the original religious philosophy of Judaism that has been sought to be implemented. Rabbis invariable state that in Judaism, the ideal person is a strong religious man, something of a *sant-sipahi* who is not a votary of non-violence. In short, the presence of a society and the combination of religious and empirical lives is an integral part of Jewish philosophy and heritage. What is significant is that despite their lean periods of extreme suffering of about 2,000 years, when the opportunity has arisen, the Jews have reverted to their original goal, which ideologically they never disowned, or shed.

7.5   The position in Islam has not been very different. Sufism in Islam is not an original development. It appeared, as authorities like A. J. Arberry have stated, when luxurious living and corruption became a part of the life of the Muslim rulers. While the Qoran is a complete guide to the socio-political and civil life of the Muslims, men of religion felt disgusted with the ways of their kings, and Sultans. It is at this time that Sufism, a system of withdrawal and monasticism, with the attendant institution of *khankahs* arose and continued. It became in a certain sense a system of personal salvation. While Sufis lived a married and pious life, and did the missionary work of Islam, unlike the Jewish prophets, they never became very critical of the Muslim rulers, nor confronted them. It is significant, however, that because of the basic Islamic ideology, Sufi *pirs* like Budhu Shah made major sacrifices on the battlefield, when Guru Gobind Singh took up cudgels against the Muslim

Empire in Punjab. But as a religious group they never, in any manner, sought to oppose the tyranny or misrule of the kings. It is in this context, that Islamic scholars like Dr Iqbal and the Nobel laureate Abdus-salam attribute the decline of Muslim culture and Muslim life to the dichotomous institution of Sufism which on a large scale diverted the religious zeal and energy to ends of pacificism or personal salvation. It is obvious that despite the vicissitudes of life, both Jews and Muslims now uphold their basic *miri-piri* ideologies.

VIII. PRESENT IDEOLOGICAL THINKING IN THE CHRISTIAN WORLD

8.1   The glaring symptoms of internal contradictions, as reflected in the socio-political life and events of the twentieth century in the world, have set many Christian theologians to rethink and reinterpret Christian ideology, the fulcrum of which is Christ's martyrdom on the Cross. The second major development has been the fall of the Russian Empire. Ideas of Darwinism, Evolutionism, Marxism and Materialism had given rise to a very confident euphoria and hope that Secularism and Communism would create a humanistic force that would improve the life of man. While Marxism on the hand, rapidly expanded the Communist hold over countries, both in the West and East, on the other hand, it deeply influenced the thinking of many social scientists to suggest that all human developments, whether social, political, cultural, or economic, were basically governed by the means of production and consequent socio-economic relations. It is in the above context that we shall briefly indicate the ideological and theological thinking in the Christian West, especially the one that has followed the experiences of the Second World War, and the events before and after it. The main trend in the new thinking is the attack on unbridled Secularism and the Western divorce of religion from politics, or the tendency of the national states to develop their own, what are called, "patriotic civil religions", and to reinterpret the Christian theology, especially the fundamental event of Christ and the Cross.

8.2   As Toynbee laments, the last 250 years have been the period of Secularism and national states in which, as in the Greco-roman thinking, the goddess to be worshipped is the State, which also lays down the values of social life. Secularism, by its very definition, has to devise its own ethical system, or what is called the 'civil religion.' The result is that the twentieth century has not only created two major World Wars, but over hundred national wars, involving brutal killings of more people in one century than those killed in the entire earlier history of wars of man. What is most dismal and disgusting, is that it has produced political monsters that have put into shade tyrants like Chengese Khan. Hiroshima, Nagasaki, and Auschwitz are its unprecedented features. The future of man and the planet is at stake. This is the dark background that has led to search for salvage of man from the deep moral crisis in which he finds himself. Both, the Churches of the world and its thinking men, have been deeply concerned about it. It is a healthy feature that new thinking about Christian ideology has appeared not only in the dark areas of Latin America and Germany, but also in North America. Latin America has come out with its 'Liberation Theology.' It was a reaction to the church life, in which on Sundays the persons who had for six days of the week suffered acute tyranny of the strong and the rich, sat on the hind benches, while the 'respectable rich' who had done the oppression, occupied the front benches. The priest could hardly do anything to alleviate the pain and persecution of the poor. It is in this context that arose the Liberation Ideology. Catholic Archbishop, Holder Camara asserts that "the violence of the rich against the poor, and the violence of the developed countries against the underdeveloped, is more worthy of condemnation than the revolutionary violence that they create."[83] In North America the Churches came to the conclusion that Secularism was a danger to human values, and should be opposed with the co-operation of other religions of the world. The World Council of Churches did not accept this view.

8.3   Similarly, the reaction in the Church was strong in Germany which had in one sense suffered the worst during the secular rule of Hitler. Instead of burdening our essay with the views of large number of thinking men on the issue, we shall give, by way of a sample, the thought of only a few theologians and thinkers. Theologian Hurgen Moltmann in his essay, *The Cross and Civil Religion*,[84] brings out with emphatic clarity that "The crucifixion is a single public political act in the life of Jesus." "Many have accused the Cross of enshrining resignation, indifference to history or surrender to circumstances. Such views of the Cross could never found a theology of hope or a political theology." "Jesus indentified himself with those who were abandoned, and challenged the status quo." "Christ's eschatological message attacks every state's claim to absolute loyalty. Functionally, Christ was seditious. Functionally, his crucifixion was a regnant government's repression of an alternate ultimate value that would relativise its own claims to be absolute. Functionally, the Christ's was the initial rejection by the Church, of all political structures seeking to become religions. In this sense, the Cross represents divine rejection of political and civil religions." This author criticises the efforts of modern nation states to develop 'patriotic civil religions.' But Secularism and National States consider it their right to create and lead their men to accept and believe in it. Moltmann sees this tendency in America today, as it was in Germany in the time of the Third Reich, when German ideology affirmed the separation of spiritual and temporal realms, and developed the theme of 'political morality.' He asserts, "Today, the destiny of man is, as they saw, less and less dependent on natural environment, and more and more dependent on technical civilisation, urbanisation, social milieu and politics." "Theology that wants to be responsible today, must consider self- critically the psychological and political implications of its words, images and symbols. It can no longer view the Church's institutional task as merely given and neutral, thereby opting out in indifference. It must scrutinise each discourse about God : Does the Church supply with religious opium or a real ferment of freedom ?" He adds, "Political theology wants to awaken political consciousness in every treatise of Christian theology. Understood in this way, it is the premise that leads to the conclusion that, while there may be a naive and politically unaware theology, there can be no apolitical theology." "Politically theology in our opinion no longer implies only theology and politics; church and state. Rather, responsible theology must become aware of an inherent political dimension in itself and in Church life." "The old theology of natural order could be understood as sanctioning the social *status quo*." He reminds us that the early Christians, conflict with the Roman state was because of its state religion, and they were punished and persecuted as atheists, "godless and seditious followers of Christ." For him, early Christian martyrology was the theology of the Cross.

8.4 Moltmann places "Crucifixion at the centre of Christian conflict with the Empire," and add that "Jesus' eschatological message of freedom was implicitly a total attack on the very existence of the religious state. In this sense, his crucifixion had political implications; it was not merely fortuitous." Even Hegel saw these implications, when he wrote, "When the cross has been elevated to the place of a banner, and is made a banner in fact, the positive content of which is at the same time the Kingdom of God, inner feeling is in the very heart of its nature detached from civil and state life, and the substantial basis of the latter is taken away, so that the whole structure has no longer any reality."[85] Moltmann feels that "The Christological starting point is that Jesus was condemned as a blasphemor by Israel's law." "Those who recognise God in the crucified one, see the glory of God only in the face of Christ, and no longer in nature, reason or political achievement. Glory no longer rests upon the head of the mighty. For believers, Christ crucified was made the righteousness of God, and for them political authority was deprived of its religious sanction." "Modern political theology considers the mortal conflict of Jesus with the public powers of his day to be central." While condemning withdrawal, he pleads for positive action and approach, "Emancipation from idolatry requires a new motivation, a new direction to life. Hence, stoic equanimity makes little sense as a replacement for idolatry. Such equanimity may remove man's aggressiveness, but it makes him hard-hearted, able to live neither in fear nor in hope. All things are alike to such a man, for he has become incapable of love. If idolatry consist in absolutising a relative good, still its abolition must not lead to stoic indifference. Selfish love is overcome in love of another; superstition is removed only by a faith which, freeing, makes possible selfless love, otherwise an 'enlightened' man becomes all too quickly a wisened old man. Self-justification always includes righteousness, but in a perverse form. Idolatry always includes faith, but in a despairing and hybrid form. Selfish love is love, but love that destroys the life it so desperately wants to preserve. We can cast down the idols, man continually fashions, so that they do not arise again. A God who guides man to the Lordship of creation, who justifies those who are unable to justify themselves, who makes possible selfless love for those whom He loves. For theology to work out the practical significance of these ideas, it must relate itself to the Enlightenment program of critical reason aiming to effect the liberation of mankind." "This means that the Church's task of liberating men from idolatry through faith must deal with social, economic, political and racial alienation as well as with religious alienation. Churches must be shaken to their foundation, and become institutions of socio-political freedom (as Metz has demanded). It is, however, impossible to eliminate religious idolatry, while one is aligned with a political or an economic idolatry. Conversely, it is impossible to criticise political or economic idolatry when religious alienations remain untested." He concludes, "Therefore, the theology of the Cross is the theology of hope; and the theology of hope is the theology of the cross." "According to its Biblical traditions the Chruch everywhere has to be with those for whom there is neither state, nor status. The Christian faith founded on the Cross must begin again to demythologise the state in which it lives. This will succeed only if it concomitantly analyses the religious situation of those, who according to the present order of things, have no status. Christianity was not founded as a national religion. Its 'Deus Crucifixus' is a

'Stateless God.' But even though its God is stateless, Christianity did not originate as a private religion, and its God is not an 'apolitical God.' From the beginning of Israel's history, Yahweh was known as the God of the poor. This tradition runs through Israel's history, despite its covenantal and national institutions : 'For Thou art God of the lowly, Helper of the oppressed, Upholder of the weak, Protector of the forlorn, Saviour of those without hope' (Judith 9 :11). In order to clarify his revolutionary position he adds, "It would be a misunderstanding to think that the promise given to those who have nothing in this world, means their compensation after death, and their riches in heaven. Quite the opposite is true. The poor do not go to the Kingdom of God, rather the Kingdom of God comes to the poor. The Kingdom of God begins in this world with the poor; the justice of God comes justifying those who are suffering from injustice. The new feature promised by God begins not in the 'beyond' but in the appearance of the Son of Man among the neglected. This new feature of God is not some 'vanguard of social progress and cultural development', rather, it belongs to those who are in the dark and, therefore, overlooked. With the Cross, the future of God allies itself with those whom a self-satisfying and a conformist society has reduced to nothing. The oppressed are no longer the object of charity of the rich, nor recipient of aid in the developing nations, but are themselves custodians of Law and redeemers of the rich. The rich do not save the poor, the poor save the rich. How can this happen ? Only the poor know the oppression of exclusion from riches. Only the humiliated know the pain of humiliation. Only the hated know the wretchedness of hatred. Conversely, the rich, the oppressors, and the haters are unknowing and blind, they unconsciously live in terms of an objective communal delusion, and despite their own effort and critical theory they manage to remain blind to the way things really are. The oppressed hold in their hands the key for the liberation of mankind from oppression." Quoting Christ, he refer to Black Theology, "What you have done to the least of my brethern, this you do unto me; who visits them visits me." "The Christian church is not co-extensive with the Church of Christ, as long as it cannot express the twofold brotherhood. The Church would be false, if in the spirit of triumphantalism, it represented only the risen Lord, and claimed to be the Kingdom of God. The Church, because of Christ crucified, should search out and identify with those, whom by his sufferings and death he took as brothers. It can only credibly preach the Gospel as a call to freedom, if it utters the cry for freedom of those reduced to silence. Is there some justice in J. Cone's contention in Black Theology that it should be theologically possible in the 20th century to see Christ as black, as it was in the 1st century to see him as Jew." He reiterates his ideas in his conclusions, "Liberation from the idolatry of a nation's political religion, introduces people to the universal Kingdom of God in fellowship with the others." "The freedom of Christian faith transforms a nation's self-justification into solidarity with the victims of its political religion; Christian faith seeks to act as the representative of those who are victimised. Ecclesiastical institutions cannot persist in their socio-political neutrality, nor can they leave social responsibility to individual Christians alone. Moreover, because Churches have a certain public respectability and influence, they cannot develop into institutions that exercise genuine social criticism. Only if the Churches bind themselves completely to the lives of the 'others', will they free themselves from their alliance with the dominant society, and its religious need for self-justification." "A Christian political theology wants to bring Christians to a point of solidarity to the place where Christ awaits them. In the sufferings of the outcast on this earth Christ awaits his own. Christian hope focuses not simply on a better future, but on the future of the hopeless." Finally he concludes, "The thesis of this treatise is : the Cross is our political critique, the Cross is our hope for politics of freedom. The memory of Christ crucified compels us to a political theology."

8.5   Johann Baptist Metz warns Christians against working and running into the groove of sectarian mentality, "Traditionalism could never be a theological characteristic of the missionary church of Jesus Christ; traditionalism is a characteristic of the sect. This gives us a catchword for what will occupy us in the second orientation, namely, the danger of sectarianism." "The danger of sectarian mentality appears in a more theological way in my opinion in the notion of a 'pure theology', a new elitist gnosis that articulates the aristocratic side of the sectarian mentality." He questions, "For, how could a church which became a sect in the theological sense, still be the church of Jesus Christ ? It would be the completely assimilated religion of a secularised society. Ultimately what remains is the dead, stifled residue of a hope that was once vital and courageous and liberating for all, a hope to which there is no alternative, either purely within the history of attempts to create freedom or purely outside of (i.e., in isolation from) that history."[86] Metz's above observation reminds us of the unfortunate and somewhat parochial approach of the majority in the World Council of Churches, particularly of Barth, Brunner and Kramer, when they rejected the laudable approach of the North American Churches for co-operation with other religions in order to fight the looming danger of Secularism. The European theologians maintained, "that secularisation, not Secularism, is a process in which some of the values of Christian faith have been put into a secular framework, bringing about a powerful force, which is destroying all old ideas. Hence secularisation is an ally, because it will destroy Hinduism, Islam or what they consider to be superstitions. So we should ally ourselves with secularisation and see it as the work of God." That was Bon Hoffer's, Barth's and Kramer's point of view, writes Metropolitan P. M. Gregorios. Unfortunately, until today the above view prevails, saying "We do not feel that we have anything lacking. And so we are opposed to dialogue unless it is for the sake of testifying to Jesus Christ."[87] Metz considers that "The Christian hopes not in just any open future, but precisely in that future which is shaped by God's sovereignty and brings justice to the oppressed. Our memory of Jesus constantly forces us to transform ourselves in order to do justice to this future. This memory breaks through the dominant consciousness of our age, a one-dimensional way of looking at things, which hides the fact of oppression and injustice from us."[88]

8.6   Other theologians, too, hold the view that Church and politics cannot remain isolated. Neibuhr, the distinguished theologian of the century, in his major work, *Moral Man and Immoral Society*, argues, "Because of the evil in man and in society, Christian political action called not simply for love, but for an attempt to give each group within society enough power to defend itself against exploitation by other groups. Althouth relations between individuals might be a matter of ethics, relations between groups were a matter of politics."[89] Theologian Gutierrez also asserts that salvation means "to struggle against misery and exploitation and involves all men and the whole of man."[90]

8.7 Aldous Huxley who continued making spiritual experiments, categorically spoke against a life of isolation, or of spiritual bliss alone. In his letter to Humphery Osmond he wrote : "The Indians say, the thought and thinker and the thing thought about are one and then of the way in which this unowned experience becomes something belonging to me; then no me anymore, and a kind of *sat-chit-ananda*, at one moment without *karuna* or charity (how odd that the Vedantists say nothing about love) ...... I had an inkling of both kinds of *nirvana* — the loveless being, consciousness, bliss, and the one with love, and, above all, sense that one can never love enough."[91] About staying in bliss, he answers : "You can immobilise it, but it isn't the real thing. You can remain for eternity in this thing at the exclusion of love and work." Such ecstatic withdrawal he called making the greatest 'Ice Cube' of a 'Flowing River' of love. He calls it "a temptation to an addiction of even higher order; the addiction of being in the Light and staying there." But he considers : "Staying in this ecstatic consciousness and cutting oneself off from participation and commitment to the rest of the world — this is perfectly expressed today in the powerful slang in the phrase 'dropping out.'" He emphatically asserts, "It completely denied the facts : it is morally wrong; and finally of course, absolutely catastrophic 'Absolutely Catastrophic.'" "These two words", his wife writes, "he said with the most earnest and profound conviction," and adds that "these remain sculptured on the soul of anyone who hears it. It is a definitive statement : One cannot isolate oneself from one's fellow and environment, for, there is no private salvation; one might 'get stuck' in even Pure Light instead of infusing it in 'Love and Work', which is the direct solution of everyone's life, right here and now. Love and Work — if I should put in a nutshell, the essence of Aldous's life. I could not find a more precise way of saying it."[92]

8.8 In Sikhism all conflicts of man are believed to be due to human egoism, and for that reason, are basically moral, this being a religious problem. Hence divorce between religion and life or any aspect of it, is a contradiction in terms. For, neither reason, nor economics, nor politics can help to solve the human problems. They can be instruments but not solutions.

8.9 In the field of thought Kant expounded the *a priori* existence of morality as a 'categoric imperative.' His emphasise on reason and his assumption that human reason would ultimately lead to social emancipation, hardly solves the problem of man. For, if human interest or desires have to be fulfilled and each man menas to fulfil his own desires, it remains an anamoly and a question how in a democratic set up, the ruler will deny the opportunity available to him to fulfil his own desires and will instead pursue the desires of others to the exclusion of his own.[93] It is the same old objection as raised by Thrasmachus before Socrates, that justice ultimately reduces itself to be the 'interest of the strong.' Russell concedes that while materialism explains the source and structure of things and life, it has failed to account for the source or existence of values.[94] Merely stating that values are a matter of feeling or 'reaction formation', and a part of the 'defence mechanism' of man in order to react against the social and other environment, explains nothing. It merely begs the question. On two scores Russell contradicts the Marxian view of human affairs being a play of the means of production. For "the social circumstances, of which account must be taken, are as much political as economic; they have a lot to do in the game of power, of which wealth is only one form. Further, even social causation largely ceases to apply as soon as a problem becomes detailed and technical."[95]

IX. LESSONS OF RELIGIOUS HISTORY

9.1 We have outlined that religions can safely be divided into two broad categories, dichotomous religions and whole-life or *miri-piri* religions. They have also been called life-negating and life-affirming religions. Each of these categories has clear and distinguishing characteristics that are in matters of goals, ideology, methodology and institutions, opposed to each other. The history of man shows that in practice and operation one category becomes a religion of personal salvation, and the other accepts social participation, and full responsibility and expression in all fields of life. Further, we have seen that in their long history, in periods of their sufferings, even whole-life religions tend to accept withdrawal, monasticism, celibacy and pacificism. However, whenever opportunity arises and reconstruction or revival is possible, whole-life religions, as in the case of Judaism and Islam, seek to regain their earlier moorings in order to practise their original system in its purity. It is significant that Judaism and Islam, in which withdrawal and pacificism appeared in their lean periods, clearly indentify that development or phase, as the cause of its decline or lack of vigour. In fact, ideologically the pacific sects, even though in existence, are never looked upon as leaders of the community. For, the ideological contradiction between the original system and the pacific variants is obvious. Actually, serious tensions have often arisen between the Church of the religion and the monastic mystics. Whereas the original Church is whole-life, and leads the entire community, the pacific variants remain unconcerned with it, excepting for the salvation of their small group. Obviously and logically, they cannot be the ideal or represent the community, especially because of their departure from the line of the original prophet.

9.2 The case of Christianity stands apart. For, while it is a whole-life religion, accepting the role of family and society, it has, because of the Sermon on the Mount, from the very start been pacific. In order to understand the position, we have tried to indicate developments in its history in somewhat greater detail than in the course of other religions. The facts reveal that from the very beginning, because of its basic ideology of love of its neighbour, it not only was demonstrably a societal religion, but for that reason, straightaway came into conflict with the Roman State, where the Emperor claimed to be the representative both of God and the temporal life. Hence the clash between the 'state religion' and the 'universal religion' of the Christians, as in the case of Christ himself, became inevitable. Thus followed centuries of suffering, persecution and martyrdoms.

9.3 Early in the fourth century, marked changes appeared in the Christian life. For, Christianity became a state religion. The same developments took place as in the case of some other whole-life religions, when they had lost their zeal and elan to battle with the problems of life in accordance with their original systems. Two features of this change become clearly identifiable. First, it is towards the end of the third century A.D., that monastic, ascetic, or withdrawal trends started appearing in Christianity. From the fourth century arose quietism and large scale organisation of monastries and nunneries. Just as in the case of Sufism, the number quietist mystics and saints these institutions have produced, is very large and galore. The system and its institutions slowly gained respectability and acceptance. Celibacy and the consequent stigma against women also appeared, with the result that priests were barred from marriage, and women could not become priests. This limitation in the Catholic Church continues even today. The social results of this change became increasingly visible. First, the man of religious devotion receded from the empirical life towards which he felt no responsibility, and his moral influence ceased to enrich it. Second, the religious leadership, thus, became depraved and enfeebled, and, this gave rise to growing corruption in the Church which ultimately led to the Reformation. Conversely, the moral tone of the Christian society, its political management and its capacity to face political challenges, showed a worsening decline. This is evident from the subsequent history of Christian society. With corruption in the Church and increasing political struggle and tensions between the kings and the popes, fall in the ethical standards was natural and distinct. Cruel inquisitions, massacres, pogroms and ghettos became almost a constant feature of the Christian socio-political life. That we are not exaggerating the faults of the Christian political life, should be clear from the contrasted level of conduct and tolerance shown by the Muslim rulers in Europe towards other religions, including Jews and Christians.

9.4   The second feature of the above development was a change in approach from life-affirmation to otherworldliness. This change is obvious both from the ideas of Christian theologians and the understanding of scholars about Christian history. Saint Augustine, as quoted earlier, believed that Christianity would not improve the political or secular life, which would continue to exist as before. In short, Christianity had hardly anything to give to the life of the common man. It is also well-known that Christian ideology in its formation derived very heavily from neo-Platonism, which was a religious development that, apart from being a system of complete withdrawal, appeared at a time when Greek life was at it lowest ebb, and its days of vigour had long since been over. Plotinus, recommended contemplation alone, without leading to any activity,[96] which in a way was considered a fall. Since the days of Christ's confrontation with the Empire and his crucification, Christianity remained under serious pressure and persecution. It could hardly produce a theologian of note, and even the Bible could not be finally compiled until after the beginning of the fourth century A.D. Hence, ideologically neo-Platonism was the only handy and respectable system which its scholars found available to model its ideology upon. The Kingdom of God became, thus, an entirely otherworldly affair. And, as happens under such circumstances, ritualism and formalism gained primary importance, and became the essential features of the system. The following words of Bertrand Russell graphically represents the position of the socio-religious life of the community : "It is strange that the last men of intellectual eminence before the dark ages were concerned not with saving civilisation, or expelling the barbarians, or reforming the abuses of the Administration, but with preaching the merit of virginity and the damnation of unbaptised infants. Seeing that these were the preoccupations that the Church handed over to the converted barbarians, it is no wonder that the succeeding age surpassed almost all other fully historical periods in cruelty and superstition."[97] The subsequent history of the Church and the Christian monarchs, and life of the people show the havoc otherworldiness can cause in a whole-life system of love that recommends social responsibility towards the downtrodden. The promise was for a good life in heaven, but not on earth. Historians like Gibbon and Sir James Fraser, clearly record that the otherworldliness of the Christian society enervated it, and was one of the major causes of the fall of the Roman Empire,[98] and the success of the barbarians.

9.5 Thus from the fourth century onwards corruption in the Church, serious fall in the public morale and socio-political life, and the otherworldy structure of its ideology, became notable features of Christianity. The Reformation, while it brought about a distinct improvement, both in the Church and public life, gave a major blow to the Church Universal and its supremacy over political rulers. With the rise of national states, the Church in each state increasingly became its handmaid. True, it gave rise to what Weber calls 'worldly asceticism', but side by side, it also prepared the ground for the ultimate rise of Secularism, Individualism and Consumerism. It is also true that Enlightenment, Science and consequent Industrialisation and Technology, hastened these trends, but the marginalisation of religion was the potent cause which ultimately loosened the internal moral brakes of the Western life. There was a time when it was considered that Science and Technology would, in not so distant a future, bring about a major improvement in human life. But the happenings of the twentieth century have dispelled all such hopes. Toynbee writes : "After having been idolized for a quarter of a millennium as the good genius of mankind he has now suddenly found himself undeservedly excreated as an evil genius who has released from his bottle a *jinn* that may perhaps destroy human life on earth. The arbitrary change in the technicians onward fortunes is a severe ordeal, but his loss of popularity has not hit him so hard as his loss of confidence in himself : Till 1945 he believed without doubt that the results of his work were wholly beneficial. Since 1945 he has begun to wonder whether his professional success may not have been a social and a moral disaster."[99] For the last about three hundred years the national state has been supreme, and the twentieth century has seen Secularism completely in the saddle. It is in this context that we have to understand the wars of the century, its large scale killings and its monster rulers who never hesitated to kill millions of their own citizens.

9.6 It may be argued that we are only picturing the dark side of otherwise promising developments. But the anomalies of the modern life are too obvious to be ignored. Not that there have never been contradictions in human affairs, but their gravity has been growing both for man and the planet. Over a quarter century back the secular authors of the Club of Rome's report, *Limits of Growth*, gave a serious warning that human and national egoism has to be curbed seriously, if disaster for man has to be avoided, saying, "The world system is simply not ample enough nor generous enough to accommodate much longer such egocentric and conflicting behaviour by its inhabitants."[100] This warning was given over a quarter century back. It remains unheeded, and the annual expenditure on militarisation has reached the level of a thousand billion dollars per annum. In the Third World the population explosion, which in the present political climate appears impossible to curb, continues unabated. The fall of the Russian Empire, because of causes mostly internal, has given rise to some serious introspection.

9.7 After the Second World War serious rethinking has taken place the world over, especially in the field of Christian theology, which is, by and large, the religion of the dominant countries of the world. The rise of Science and Technology had also given a serious fillip to the eminence, and to an extent even to arrogance, of social sciences which tended almost to monopolize the explanation of all developments and movements in human affairs. Willi Oelmuller in his well-known essay, *The Limitations of Social Theories*,[101] brings out major gaps in their understanding and methodology. On the point of search for truth he states : "Today, decision making procedures in the sciences and in all research dependent on the economy and the state, operate not according to any logic which arises out of a pure scientific interest in the truth. Rather, they are widely dependent on extra-scientific, military and national interests. Critical rationalism has not, to the present time, developed adequate criteria for identifying and diagnosing this set of relations." While we are planning everything, there is no answer to the question : "Whether the science and research which seek to plan everything that can be planned, and done, is really serving social progress, i.e., is really serving the removal of hunger, the overcoming of oppression and the prevention of war." On the other hand, we find that our Einsteins, Oppenhaeurs and Sakharovs, serve and further the interest of the national state. The danger is that "Scientific reason is increasingly instrumental, society increasingly governed by technology, and individuals increasingly powerless and susceptible to manipulation. Emancipation through revolution and reform is ever more difficult. In this situation, it is imperative to insist that freedom from tyranny of nature and the domination of man over man, means more than socio-technical progress or blind revolutionary action; similarly that progress means more than constantly increasing needs, production and consumption." It is a fact that under well organised and heavily militarised national states the common man remains a helpless tool, subject to subtle and corrosive influences on his thinking and life. The growing tendency is that Social Sciences in their anxiety to gain scientific status have increasingly become in principle determinate in their conceptions of the human person, the goal of human life and the phenomenon of negativity.[102] This in a way either eliminates or marginalises the role of values in life. This, we believe, is the major problem that the twentieth century and its tragic developments have posed before man. For, life in shown to be a determined flow of events without goal or hope.

9.8 It is in the above background that we find a serious ferment and thinking in the Christian theological world. Christ's life on the Cross is the fundamental spiritual event that gives rise to a universal call to men of religion to struggle for the Kingdom of God on earth and give relief to the downtrodden and the hungry.

X. CONCLUSIONS

10.1 In the above context let us have a look again at the religions system and the role of the Gurus. Theirs is a thisworldy system calling upon man to live a life of love and hope, and zealously to struggle against evil, and for the creation of the Kingdom of God on earth. It is Guru Nanak who gave the call for a life of love, and to waver not from making every sacrifice in the struggle against evil. In their Scripture compiled and authenticated by the

Gurus, they not only laid down distinct spirituo-ethical principles of life and the responsibilities of man, but also demonstrated in their personal lives extending over almost two and a half centuries how to live a true socio-spiritual life. They trained, conditioned and motivated an organised society led by them to struggle against all forces that impede the socio-spiritual progress of man. The history of the Guru period is a demonstration of how sufferings, and martyrdoms and fight in every field of life become necessarily a part of the responsibility of the spiritual man and the seeker. Here it is relevant to recall the criticism of Bertrand Russell of the Christian life of the Middle ages, and to state the contrast shown by Guru Nanak in first recounting every dark spot in the socio-political and religious life of his time; and then to plan, and devise ways and institutions to bring about improvement in every field, religious, social, and political. To the extent possible it is this organised society that took care not only to stop a 1,000 year wave of invaders and to supplant the oppressive political rule of the times, but, as facts show, also to bring about a distinct improvement in the socio-moral life and sense of responsibility of the common man. The basic thesis of the Gurus is that values are the sustaining sap of life and that God or the Basic Reality is the Flowing Immanent Source of it. That life is a venture of hope, provided man links himself with that, Altruistic Flow, works in line with His Will or Direction, and draws his strength and zeal from that Gracious Fount. Two important conclusions emerge from the Gurus' thesis. First, that ours is not a determined or a dismal world, nor are, for the matter, values a meaningless 'deffence mechanism.' On the other hand, values have a distinct and a basic role to promote a life freedom, harmony and creativity, which is enriched by linking oneself with that Fundamental Flow of Love, and falling and working in line with it. Dichotomy or what Huxley calls making Ice Cubes of a Flowing River, is wrong, and responsible participation in unison with His Current is essential for the progress and emancipation of man. Evil or negativity is due to the imperfection and egoism of man, but the future is not without hope. Reason and other instruments of life are at best limbs of the individual psyche, and, while they can be used for a good end, they become a hurdle and a handicap, unless used for the purpose of the Flow.

10.2   We have already indicated some of the historical impacts and features of this *miri-piri* system. Apart from its achievement against the invaders and the oppressive Empire, the rule of Ranjit Singh shows, that in contrast with all the contemporary rulers of the world, his treatment of all subjects, including Muslims, was fair and liberal. No attempt whatsoever was made at conversion of anyone to Sikhism, nor were his administration and time sullied by communal riots, massacres, migrations or pogroms.

10.3   The significant fact has been that *miri-piri* thinking has brought about a transformation and regeneration of man in his thinking, motivations and approach towards life of the common man in the Sikh society. It is this distinct change in the ethos and moral of the masses and the Sikh society which drives them, on the one hand, to make maximum sacrifices for the freedom of man, and, on the other hand to create the wherewithal for promotion of production, and sustenance of life in general. It is also shown how difficult and slow is this process. It is most important that this change in ethos can be brought about only by the man of religion who has faith in the originality of values and their Source.

10.4 Let us recapitulate the notable features of and the lessons from our brief survey of the religions of the world. Without going into the historical background, it is a fact that all Indian religions except Sikhism, have been dichotomous and continue to be so for the last 2,500 years. Without the presence of this dichotomy between the spiritual life and the empirical life, the discriminatory institutions of caste and pollution could neither survive nor be continued till today. Some Indian thinkers like Mahatma Gandhi have tried to curb or change it. However, it is also a fact, as Dr Amebedkar, the framer of the Indian Constitution, explains, that the Mahatma made every effort to maintain its structure intact. As Weber and Ambedkar have explained, reform of the Hindu society from within, is virtually impossible,[103] because of scriptual sanctions to the institutions of caste. Most Indian thinkers lament the fall in values and ethos in the socio-political life of the country today. The values, professed by Gandhi and Nehru, have simply disappeared, as if they had lived and laboured in some other society.

10.5 The history of the two *miri-piri* systems, Judaism and Islam, has clearly shown that pacificism and withdrawal with their attendant features, have appeared in those two systems, only when socio-political life of the people became lean, so that they were unable to meet the challenges of life. It is only when the spirituo-moral fibre of a people fails to cope with the battles of life, that its religious men tend to recede from the mainstream into monasticism, asceticism, celibacy and pacificism and the system of personal salvation. It is not necessary for us to say that pacificism and withdrawal contribute towards decline of social morale and vigour of life, or that these features and institutions appear, when the socio-political life suffers defeat and decline. In any case the two positions are contemporaneous. And when ever opportunity has arisen, these societies have again harked back to the original call of their prophets. The thinkers of the two communities have openly attributed the decline to the dichotomy, and for that reason have suggested reversion to the original theses of their systems.

10.6 The religious history of Christianity has been extremely chequered. May be, changes or ambivalence in its later ideological expression has been due to the very short ministry of Jesus, its crowing event being the crucifixion. We have indicated that neither during the time of Jesus Christ, nor during the early centuries of martyrdoms and persecutions, was there any sign of bifurcation or otherworldliness. But major changes in interpretation and theology followed, when after the beginning of the fourth century, on the one hand, appeared monastries, nunneries and withdrawal, and, on the other hand, started the decline in the socio-moral life of the people and their institutions. Protestantism curtailed the supremacy of the Church, leading, in the subsequent centuries to the slow and undisputed rise of Secularism, which seeks to devise its own ethics, value system or civil religion, and for that matter, accounts for the marginalisation or virtual elimination of the role of religion in life. After the Second World War a distinct disillusionment with the secularist philosophies has started among some sections of the thinking and religious men of the West. Solynstein who almost predicted the fall of the Russian Empire, was critical of the West for its liaison with it. Civil religion, whether of the Communist society or of the Free Market society, cannot be sustained. That is why men of religion have criticised it. Important sections of the Christian religious world, as noted earlier, clearly interpret the crucifixion of Christ as not only the landmark of a universal struggle, but also as a continuous clairon call for the elimination of oppression, and relief to the downtrodden through political means. Hence the call of Father Camilo Torres that "the Catholic who is not revolutionary, is living in mortal sin," and the willingness of priests in South America to endorse the use of force.

10.7   Dr Walsh's statement appears fairly representative of the modern thinking, when he says that the present theological thinking in Christianity is that "The question of Jesus and/or Christianity's pacificism, however, remains hotly debated, as it has been for centuries. In general, the Just War Tradition has won out with its conviction that there are occasions when it is legitimate and appropriate for the Christians to take up arms. Peace Churches have generally been in a minority, e.g., Annabaptists and Mennonites." In the same survey he observes that "Sikhism's major contribution to the world has been its sense of responsibility in the world, emphasis on spiritualising what have been viewed as secular spheres of life," and that "in Sikhism salvation is not another-worldly event, but is directly related to our actual life on earth, it being a religion of responsibility, a religion of ethics." In short, the conclusion of numerous Christians theologists the world over and thinkers like Huxley is clearly for the acceptance of a whole-life system, and for active socio-political participation and sense of responsibility towards the oppressed, wherever they are. Christology and the Cross are the basis to invoke this interpretation. There are understandable reservations regarding the use of force, but the majority opinion is certainly for its minimum use. With the fall of Russia the damage done by Secularist philosophy has been exposed, and analysis done about the inherent limitations of the social science theories, especially in the field of values, has been brought out.

10.8   There is an unmistakable lesson of our survey based on the historical role of the world religions, namely that when the *miri-piri* systems like Judaism, Islam and Sikhism, have participated in the socio-political sphere, the resultant administrations of rulers like David and Solomon in the Middle East, of Muslim rulers in Europe, and of Ranjit Singh in North India, have been far more fair and humane than the administrations of rulers following dichotomy in the socio-religious field. Not that an utopia was brought by anyone of them, but the ethos of the times created by the religions concerned, was such that both cohesion and internal moral brakes of the system were strong enough to restrain those who wield power from indulging in tyranny and oppression.

10.9   This being the broad history of the major religions of man, the validity of the various elements of Sikhism, a *miri-piri* system, laid down by the Sikh Gurus, has to be seen in the light of that experience. Apart from others, two lessons of this religious history are clear. And, the Gurus took pains to devise ways and means to ensure that the pitfalls, that could arise from certain ideological and other developments, were avoided. First is the necessity for the clarity of canon, the essential elements and doctrines of a religious system. The world over their late compilation into the concerned scriptures has so often given rise to variation in interpretations and consequent confusion or even schisms in society. To avoid this the Gurus themselves compiled the Scripture, so as to set at rest for all times any doubts about its asuthenticity. Second to avoid any confusion in interpretation of the Scripture, as has happened in other systems, the Gurus themselves lived and demonstrated in their lives the principles of their system over a period of 240 years. And, this they did in response to all social, environmental and political challenges of the times. Another important thing is that having finally organised the Sikh society started by Guru Nanak, Guru Gobind Singh prescribed certain symbols continually to remind the Sikh of his socio-religious responsibilities, and the fundamental canon of the Sikh system. The *kirpan*, as explained earlier, has been prescribed for regular wear of the Sikh, so that he remains constantly aware of the three fundamentals of the Guru's system, and his responsibilities, as a member of a *miri-piri* society. To recapitulate, the three principles are : first confrontation with oppression and injustice; second, permission to use only minimum force; and third, not to withdraw into monasticism or *sanyasa*. The importance of these three steps the Gurus took, speaks volumes for their sense of history and their vision of the future in order to ensure the continuity and purity of their system.

10.10 We have attempted to explain the *miri-piri* character of Sikhism and to stress that this character is a fundamental part of its structure and concepts. But here it appears necessary to indicate three features which Sikhism does not share with the other whole-life systems. These features are their exclusivism, consequent reluctance to co-operate on terms of equality with other systems, and, a zealous missionary tendency for conversions. Without going into detail it is known that these three features of whole-life or societal systems, have not been uncommon, and for that reason have attracted criticism from religious thinkers. For, the features are regarded as corollaries of the systems themselves. It shows the foresight and vision of the Gurus that they themselves took steps to avoid the possibility of any such developments in Sikhism. The concepts of 'chosen community', 'seal of prophets', or 'salvation only through their prophet' are known signs of exclusivism. But while Guru Nanak created a new religious society, it was also he who laid down in his hymns that his mission was to elicit the co-operation of other God-men in order to ferry people across the turbulent sea of life.[104] It was an emphatic statement against exclusivism, and for ready co-operation with other religious men or societies. Thus he imparted universal character to his system. Second is the point about salvation only through a particular system or prophet. Against this, there is a clear hymn of the Guru in Guru Granth Sahib praying for His Gracious intervention to save the burning world by any means or path (door),[105] He may be benevolent enough to do. This not only concedes that there are or could be other valid religious systems, but also clearly warns against exclusivism, saying that the creation of the Path, rests with Him and not with any human, howsoever high he may be. A prophet can at best be His instrument to help the wavering, on to that Path or Door. This universalism is also evident from the daily prayer of the Sikhs which seeks from God the blessings for all, the world over. The third feature relates to large scale coercive conversions, often indulged in by whole-life systems. For ideological and other reasons, this has never happened in the history of Sikh religion. The reason for it is the lead given by the Gurus themselves. Sikhism, as Guru Nanak stated, and as for that matter any religious path, is a most difficult path. For, Guru Nanak in his very first call stressed that the game of love involves total commitment and sacrifice, and that, once man treads on this path, he should waver not from sacrificing his all for it. The same total commitment to sacrifice everything was desired by the Tenth Guru, when he chose the Five *Piaras* to administer *amrit* to them. The very nature of the sacrifices contemplated and demonstrated in Sikhism, and the lead given by the Gurus, make it plain that the commitment demanded to tread the Sikh path is total. Therefore, converting people by coercion to this path is hardly relevant or necessary. Because by the very nature of the system, forced conversion becomes a contradiction in terms. This explains why in the period of the Sikh rule, the Sikhs remained in a minority in Punjab, for there was never any organised system for conversion, much less for forced conversions. Of course, people did become converts of convenience to gain prestige, and they reverted to their old faith as soon as political benefits became scarce. On the other hand, in Guru Granth Sahib itself, the Gurus ask men of other religions to follow truly the path of their own religions, and that instead of adhering to ritualism they should lead a moral life of virtues and values.

10.11   It is obvious that Sikhism, accordingly to its concept, doctrines, institutions and history, is fundamentally a *miri-piri* system, started by Guru Nanak. While its ideological as well as social fundamentals, were laid down by Guru Nanak himself, over a period of time, it surely and gradually developed into a whole-life or *miri-piri* system, unaffected by the accidents, exigencies, or influences of the milieu or history. It is important to understand that every system has its own logic, and so have *miri-piri* systems and the dichotomous systems. Each of them creates, develops and fructifies into its own characteristic institutions, and plays a role that is germane, natural and necessary to it. Basically, whole-life or *miri-piri* systems are societal from the very start, whereas dichotomous systems are invariably for personal salvation, unconcerned with the society as a whole. Any study in depth regarding the essentials, corollaries and history of a system leaves no room for confusion in distinguishing one system from the other. It is, however, true that scholars do sometimes display misunderstanding in identifying the role and character of Sikhism. Many a time it is due to their ignorance of the basic system of classification of religions, or their personal predilections and conditioning by the system or milieu to which they belong, or sometimes their inability to shed the burden of the un-dimensional social science methodology, which, as we have explained, is either too simplistic or fails to take into account the role of religion and its institutions, history and values. Otherwise, as explained by us, Sikhism on account of its ideology embodied in Guru Granth Sahib, its institutions and the history of the Guru period is unambiguously a *miri-piri* system.

REFERENCES

1. Guru Granth Sahib : p. 459.
2. Ibid., pp. 294, 463.
3. Ibid., p. 1 (Japuji).
4. Ibid., pp. 522, 886, 1376.
5. Juergensmeyer, Mark : *Sikh Studies*, Berkeley, pp. 83-88.

6. Mann, J.S. & Kharak Singh : *Recent Researches in Sikhism*, Punjabi University, Patiala, 1992, p. 24.
7. Guru Granth Sahib : pp. 7, 8-9, 62, 113.
8. Ibid., p. 1412.
9. Ibid., p. 1245.
10. Machwe, Parbhakar : *Namdev*, pp. 59-60.
11. Nihar Ranjan Ray : *Sikh Gurus and the Sikh Society*, pp. 61-62, Punjabi University Patiala.
12. Guru Granth Sahib : pp. 889, 1171.
13. Annie Besant : *English Translation of Bhagawat Gita*, pp. 252-54. Jaiswal, S. : *Origin and Development of Vaishnavism*, pp. 111-12.
14. Guru Granth Sahib : p. 1289.
15. Bhalla, S.D. : *Mehma Parkash*, p. 326.
16. Mann, J.S. & Kharak Singh : op. cit., p. 24.
17. Daljeet Singh : *The Sikh Ideology*, p. 94.
18. Ambedkar, B.R. : *Writings and Speeches*, Vol. V, pp. 340, 388.
19. Gupta, H.R. : *History of the Sikh Gurus*, p. 110.
20. Ibid., p. 93.
21. Ibid., pp. 92-3.
22. Ibid., pp. 92-3.
23. Ibid., p. 93.
24. Ibid., pp. 100-1.
25. Ibid., pp. 101-2.
26. Ibid., p. 104.
27. Ibid., p. 111.
28. Ibid., p. 104.
29. Ibid., p. 114.
30. Guru Granth Sahib : pp. 145, 224, 1028.
31. Gupta, H.R. : op. cit., p. 110.
32. Jadunath Sircar : *A Short History of Aurangzeb*, p. 156.
33. Gur Bilas Patshahi Chhevin, p. 29.
34. Gupta, H.R. : op. cit., p. 110. Mohammad Latif : *History of Punjab*, p. 256.
35. Ibid., p. 119.
36. Ibid., p. 125-6.
37. Ibid., p. 130.
38. Ibid., pp. 135, 136, 139, 140.
39. *Haqiqat-i-Bana-u-Uruj-i-Firqa-i-Sikhan* (1783), p. 3-6. Quoted in *The Sikh Review*, Calcutta, Feb. 1990, p. 22. Banerjee, A.C. *Journal of Sikh Studies*, GNDU Amritsar, Feb. 1976, p. 61.
40. Gupta, H.R. : op. cit. p. 139-140.
41. Ibid., p. 177.
42. Ibid., p. 155.
43. Ibid., p. 233-34.
44. Ibid., pp. 35-36, 239-40.
45. Bhangoo, Rattan Singh : *Panth Parkash*, (Jit Singh Sital), p. 189.
46. Piara Singh Padam : *Rehat Name*, Tankhahnama Bhai Nand Lal, p. 47.
47. Macauliffe, M.A. : *The Sikh Religion*, Vol. III, pp. 7-8, 419.
48. Azad, A.K. : *India Wins Freedom*, p. 34.
49. Ibid., p. 108.
50. Seervai, H.M. : *Constitutional Law of India*, p. 143-47.
51. Russell, Bertrand : *Unpopular Essays*, pp. 53-7.
52. Smullyan *et al* : *Introduction to Philosophy*, p. 367.
53. Jagjit Singh : *The Sikh Revolution*, pp. 286-87.
54. Gupta, H.R. : op. cit., pp. 231-240.
55. Jagjit Singh : op. cit., pp. 261-279.
56. Bhai Gurdas : Var 11, *Dabistan*, translation by Dr Ganda Singh, *Panjab Past and Present,* Vol. III, (1969), p. 53.
57. Macauliffe, M.A. : *The Sikh Religion*, Vol. IV, pp. 107, 197.

58. Jagjit Singh : op. cit., pp. 278-280.
59. Lewis, James : *Advanced Studies in Sikhism*, edited by J.S. Mann & H.S. Saraon, pp. 269-271. *Recent Researches in Sikhism*, edited by J.S. Mann & Kharak Singh, Punjabi University, Patiala, 1992, pp. 291-295.
60. Dowley, Tim (Ed.) : *Eerdsman's Handbook to the History of Christianity*.
61. Jagjit Singh : *The Sikh Revolution*, pp. 205-12.
62. Gupta, H.R. : op. cit., pp. 148-49.
63. Mann, J.S. & Kharak Singh : op. cit., p. 54. Rajinder Puri : *Rediscovery of India*, p. 21.
64. Vijayalakshmi, Pandit : *The Tribune*, Chandigarh, March 1970.
65. Nur Mohammad, Qazi : *Jang Namah* (1765). English Trans. Ganda Singh, Amritsar (1939), pp. 58-59.
66. Ghurye, G.S. : *Caste and Race in India*, pp. 11-12.
67. Sardesai, G.S. : *The New History of Mahrattas*, p. 52.
68. Mann, J.S. & Kharak Singh : op. cit., p. 367. *Sikh Rule and Ranjit Singh* by G.S. Dhillon.
69. Osborne, W.G. : *The Court and Camp of Ranjit Singh*, p. 94-5.
70. Swami Sivananda : *Spiritual Experiences*, pp. 242-44.
71. *Torah*, The Jewish Publication Society of America, Philadephia, USA, P. 141.
72. Ibid., p. 122.
73. Ibid., p. 150.
74. Ambedkar, B.R. : *Baba Saheb Ambedkar's Writings and Speeches*.
75. Coomaraswamy, A.K. : *Buddha and the Gospel of Buddhism*, p. 214.
76. Maitra, S.K. : *The Ethics of the Hindus*, p. 244.
77. Ibid., p. 265-266, 263.
78. The Bible : New Testament, St. Mathew, 5.17.
79. Dowley, Tim : op. cit., p. 5.
80. Ibid., p. 5.
81. Schumacher, E.F. : *A Guide to the Perplexed*, p. 132.
82. Dialogue & Alliance, A Journal of International Religions Dialogue, 1987, pp. 94-95.
83. Dowley, Tim : op. cit., p. 637.
84. Moltmann *et al* : *Religion and Political Society*. Institute of Christian Thought, Harper and Row Publications, New York, London, pp. 12-47.
85. Hegel, C.W.F. : *Philosophy of Religion*, New York, Humanities.
86. John Baptist Metz : *Religion and Political Society*, Harper and Row Publishers, New York, London, pp. 195-203.
87. Dialogue & Alliance : op. cit., pp. 94-95.
88. John Baptist Metz : op. cit., p. 204.
89. Dowley, Tim : op. cit., pp. 595-597.
90. Ibid., p. 610.
91. Huxley, Aldous : *Moksha*, p. 115.
92. Ibid., 222-223.
93. Russell, Bertrand : *History of Western Philosophy*, p. 744.
94. Ibid., p. 788.
95. Ibid., p. 751.
96. Smullyan : op. cit. p. 363.
97. Russell, Bertrand : op. cit., pp. 362-363.
98. Toynbee, A. : *Christianity and Civilization*, Burge Memorial Lecture, Oxford; Pendel Hill, Wallingford, Pennsylvania, pp. 12- 17.
99. Toynbee, A. : *An Historians Approach to Religion*, pp. 233-34.
100. Club of Rome Report : *Limits of Growth*, pp. 191-192.
101. Oelmuller, Willi *et al* : *Religion & Political Society*, A Harper Forum Book, pp.121-170.
102. Moltmann *et al* : op. cit., Joan Lockwood, p. 125.
103. Ambedkar, B.R. : *Annihilation of Caste*, Ed : Mulk Raj Anand.
104. Guru Granth Sahib : p. 939.
105. Ibid., p. 853.

9

POLITICAL IDEAS OF GURU NANAK

GURTEJ SINGH

A brief appraisal of the opinions of historians of the Sikhs and prominent writers about the political concerns of Guru Nanak may form a proper beginning of the present undertaking.

Early historians of the Sikhs generally refused to read a political content in the message of Guru Nanak.[1] It is not a coincidence that they were also the supporters of the contemporary British Empire.[2] It appears that Cunningham was the first to doubt the veracity of such observations and speaking of Guru Arjun wrote, "he was that first who clearly understood the wide import of the teachings of Nanak, or who perceived how applicable they were to every state of life and to every condition of society."[3]

Indubhushan Banerjee while agreeing that "the future Sikh nation grew on the foundations provided by Nanak", would not agree with Cunningham that "Guru Nanak had some original distinctiveness which alone could provide the basis of the nation."[4] This position runs counter to the underlying thesis of his book and can, in part, be legitimately attributed to his desire to save Guru Nanak for Hinduism as a reformer within its fold.

Arnold Toynbee held Guru Hargobind responsible for violating the "spiritual trust" of his predecessors by entertaining "vulgar worldly ambitions" and for transforming the "embryonic church into embryonic state."[5] It is however apparent that he was under a compulsion to fit Sikh history into a framework he had contrived for it. It is now fairly well established that his views in this regard are inadequate as well as untenable even within the framework of his own formulations.'[6] For instance, he clubs Sikhism with Kabirism in his *Study of History*, but is not able to explain why Kabirism, which shunned "vulgar worldly ambitions", did not progress as it should have done according to his formulation. It never made any impact on society and history as Sikhism did.

Generally it is true to say that those who were able to distinguish "that Sikhism should be regarded as a new and separate world religion rather than as a reformed sect of Hindus"[7] are the same who also could appreciate "something positive and realistic" about Guru Nanak's work which is indicative of "a religion and a state."[8] The religion preached by Guru Nanak originated in a clearly perceived whole-life system which was absolutely fresh and hence beyond the comprehension of those who were used to other systems which were mostly dichotomous in varying degrees.

Sikh literati, including men of history, literature, philosophy and theology have always been more explicit and have all along discerned pronounced political currents in the thought of Guru Nanak. Ganda Singh considers him to be "the founder of the militant church of Sikhism."[9] Along with Teja Singh, he is of the opinion that during the entire period of development, there was "no break, no digression in the programme of Sikh life."[10] Mohan Singh, studying the writings of the Gurus, could discern only "difference of accent" from Guru Nanak to Guru Gobind Singh.[11] Sita Ram accepts *Babarvani* verses to be the "first ...... voice against oppression."[12]

Sher Singh dealing with the philosophy of Sikhism, opines that inspite of the development of two hundred years, the basic doctrinal truths, which had been preached by Guru Nanak, remained the same.[13] Kapur Singh observes about the formation of the Khalsa that "it was a logical development and entelechy of the teachings of Guru Nanak."[14] Kartar Singh sums up the generally held view about the political concerns of Guru Nanak when he says that he would have reacted to oppressions, sword in hand like Guru Gobind Singh, if he likewise had the nation at his back.[15]

Any analysis of Guru Nanak's views must begin by first noting his emphatic claim to prophethood. Disclaiming a worldly preceptor, he accepted God as original and true Guru to be his sole Teacher.[16] Claiming direct and intimate touch with Reality, he asserted that he had been specifically commissioned by God to disseminate knowledge of the Divine.[17] While emphasising direct inspiration, he goes on to say, "I have been given a permanent revenue free grant by God himself and others, who lay tall claim to high spiritual status, are like mere temporary tenants."[18] Everything that he uttered was, therefore, directly inspired and explicitly sanctioned by God.[19] It could hardly be otherwise, for, "One may speak of Him if one has seen the Unseeable One, or else preaching is to no purpose."[20] His mandate to interpret the Will of God was upheld and his status of a prophet was insisted upon by the succeeding Gurus[21] and Sikh theologians including Bhai Gurdas and Mani Singh.[22] "The Truth which filled his mind was not borrowed from books; it came to him as illumination of his entire life", and while scholars wrangle loudly over the questions of influences, "so says Nanak, is the burden of his songs."[23]

Political views of the Guru are also intimately connected to his acceptance of this world as real and a legitimate sphere of activity for a man of religion. He realised that the "Omnipresent One lives in His creation and pervades it in all directions."[24] Wherever he looked, he "found the Merciful One whose very shadow the earth is."[25] His teachings are, therefore, grounded in the basic concept that God is Love and that He is intensely interested in human destiny or Godward journey. He cares and lovingly directs human beings in their evolution from the ignorant, ego-oriented *manmukh* to the enlightened and liberated *gurmukh*. It is his belief that spiritual progress is possible only in society. The Guru, therefore, denounced asceticism and advocated the fulsome life of a householder setting the example himself by, in addition, accepting the professions of a civil servant and an agriculturist. His concern for the material world was as great as his preoccupation with the spiritual one and he essentially sought to secure the next by worthwhile social and political activity in this.[26] "Those who serve others in this world are respectfully received in the next."[27] The Guru reproached Bhangarnath for having renounced the world and told him that life in society was a precondition for spiritual attainment.[28] His favourite expression for ideal balance is that one must live unsoiled by the dross, but in the midst of everything, as the swan lives in water without getting wet.[29]

In relation to activity in this world, the most significant and frequent description of God by Guru Nanak is in a vocabulary befitting an emperor.[30] He consistently addresses Him as "my King, true King, and King of Kings, He has his court, His throne and His palace. He is the sole Sovereign and sole Wazir. He has his eight-metal coin, the Word. To Him belongs real command; all power and praise belong to Him alone ...... Indeed to find honour in His court is the aim of human life."[31] God is the only Sovereign entitled to the allegiance of mankind.[32] True Sovereign performs truely sovereign functions of destroying the evil-doers[33] and of promoting the good.[34] He dispenses even-handed justice. Together, these constitute the aim of all earthly political activity.

One significant factor that the Guru stresses in this connection is the soul's innate and intense desire to know God and to become one with Him. There are several passages of the Guru describing this yearning.[35] Those who feel no such yearning are termed as animals wrapped in human skin.[36] As a Guru, the knower of Reality, he prescribes that for successful catering to this divine inclination of the soul, a seeker must here and now attain the status of a liberated one. Every human being is expected to incessantly strive to become a *gurmukh*. In terms of individual personality and psyche, the exercise seeks the complete and absolute transformation of both. The process is variously expressed by Guru Nanak as that of "rust being turned into gold,"[37] of "ghosts and animals being transformed into angles"[38] and of "crow becoming a swan."[39] This miracle according to the Guru is to be attained by successfully imbibing attributes which the knowing Guru has revealed to be those of God. For a human being that is the only method of living in God. The unusual metaphor describing the state is, "companions of the Guru have become philosopher's stone on coming in contact with philosopher's stone."[40] There are further references like the suggestion that by contemplating on the Fearless One, one becomes fearless. The culmination is to become like the One you serve.[41]

There is much in Guru Nanak which establishes that the vital process must remain a dead letter unless political conditions conducive to it prevail. According to the Guru, this all important spiritual journey cannot even be started by a politically oppressed person. Victims of Babar's invasion, for instance, are in no position to serve God.[42] The opportunity is also denied to those groaning under an alien culture.[43] The Guru is emphatic that no religious activity under such circumstances is possible at all. It is obviously the duty of a God-oriented man to take effective measures so that such contingency never arises. Significantly, he rules out divine intervention for the purpose.[44] The obligation to perceive evil and to engage it in battle with a view to eradicating it, is solely that of a man of God. The Guru is not averse to the use of force for the purpose and advocates active armed resistance; he deplores the lack of any preparation of the Lodhi rulers to repel the sinning hordes of the invader Babar.[45]

Those who are called upon to rule also have their obligations. Nothing comes to anyone as a result only of his individual striving, by performing penances or by observing rituals, but in accordance with His Will (*hukm*) and by His Grace (*nadr*). He creates everyone;[46] elevates as well as degrades.[47] Rulers must be spiritually wide awake persons, who constantly live in values derived from revealed attributes of God, otherwise they are base pretenders.[48] Firm commitment to justice and equity alone makes a rule legitimate. The exercise of sovereign power must also be free of evils pointed out by the Guru. There are loud and strong suggestions in Guru Nanak's *bani* which indicate that a ruler loses the right to rule when he fails to comply with the above requirements.[49] God does not tolerate deviation on such vital matters and decrees the lapse of the mandate. This loss of mandate is to be taken seriously by men of religion, who must execute the command to remove a rejected ruler.

It is in the context of the above discussion that some of the most poignant political comments of Guru Nanak must be interpreted. He has mentioned martyrdom in war amongst the accepted modes of attaining salvation.[50] He is certain that under certain circumstances it is more honourable to resist and die than to just continue living passively.[51] Most significantly he recommends dying for a cause of God, stating that a person who dies thus, attains acceptance at His Court.[52] In an oft repeated couplet, he requires a lover of God to be ready to sacrifice his head on the path of love.[53]

In an ideal political set up, grave duties are cast upon a man of God. He must fully appreciate the conditions under which a mandate to rule is granted. It is his pious religious duty to discern when it has been violated. There is also no doubt that the attainment of *summum bonum* by him squarely depends upon his promptness and willingness to execute the command of God withdrawing the mandate. No sacrifice is to be considered too great for the purpose. If one shirks one's duty in this regard, one is no man of religion, does not live in the light of God and exists only at the animal level, wasting the unique opportunity for salvation.

From his utterances, it is possible to precisely enumerate some of the evils that the Guru would like the people to resist. Denial of justice, oppression, arbitrary curtailment of right to life, dishonouring of women, plunder, undermining the accepted social norms of a cohesive group are amongst the specific forms of evil the Guru abhors. Many of the above are mentioned in the *Babarvani* verses.[54]

CONCLUSIONS

The most significant single factor in the political thought of Guru Nanak is the firm belief that an individual cannot tread the spiritual path alone, that eventually salvation outgrows the bounds of personal relationship of the individual with God and must take the society, social and political organisations into account. His teachings, which make life in society a pre-condition to spiritual fulfilment, exclude the possibility of regarding the highest worldly position as incompatible with the purest spiritual life. In fact, it is possible to suggest that Guru Nanak considers politics to be the ultimate test of faith.

For Guru Nanak, the sole aim of individual existence on earth is the attainment of the highest spiritual status or consciousness. Consequently, the ultimate aim of social and political activity as envisaged by him is to facilitate its attainment. Accordingly, for him, such activity becomes meaningful and relevant if it seeks the spiritual welfare of the people and is beneficial only in proportion to the extent it serves to bring it about.

He, however, denies to the state the power to regulate matters of spirituality or conscience. He resents such interferences by the contemporary state and some of his most vehement denunciations of it are in this context.[55] He advocated that the primary allegiance of a man of God must be to righteousness, truth and conscience and denied the claim of the state exclusively to rule over the souls of its citizens. His ideal appears to be a sovereign individual in the image of God he worships and imitates as a matter of religious discipline. Constituted as it was, political authority is consistently disregarded by him and is held directly responsible for many ills of the contemporary society. On emerging from the river Vein after his commission to prophethood, he made a statement repudiating allegiance to a temporal power. The messengers came and said, "Nanak the Khan has summoned you" and Baba Nanak replied, "he is your Khan, what do I care for him."[56] It was perfectly in line with his pronouncement : "he who stands in the presence of God, needs to bow to no other."[57]

From heartfelt laments about violation of other people's culture by powerful aliens, which abound in the Guru's *bani*, it is legitimate to conclude that the Guru's concept of basic political organization revolves around the cultural cohesiveness of a people. He would have society as a conglomeration of such units with inviolate autonomy existing freely and so regulated as to be without an inclination or an opportunity to violate any other similar unit. Guru Nanak is imbued with the concept of intrinsic worth of human personality. He believes that an individual, with the help of God, can transcend his baser self. He is certain that by right conduct, incessant striving, rigorous discipline and God's grace, an individual can lift himself to divine status. Such a desirable status is defined as that of a *gurmukh*, a *sadh*, a *jiwan mukta* and that of a ruler or *panch* — in a word the ideal man of Guru Nanak and Guru Granth Sahib.

God as love stands for peace and harmony in His creation. It is His Will that those who love him must not await a miracle to restore peace. It is the knower of the Will, the *gurmukh*, who must execute it and restore normalcy. He must. be the shelter of the shelterless, a refuge for the weak, as God showers His grace where the weak are supported.

REFERENCES

1. For instance, Sir Charles Gough accuses other writers of Sikhs of telling "more than they knew." And though he himself wrote less than a page and a half on Guru Nanak in a book relating to Sikh Wars, still he ventured an opinion that the Guru founded a "sect entirely religious without any political aim or organization."
  Gough, Sir C. and Arthur D. Innes : *The Sikhs and The Sikh Wars*, A.D. Innes & Cov., London 1897, V. 18.
  Payne, who did not understand Guru Granth Sahib found it unreadable, and had no access to Guru's Word, nevertheless observed that Guru Nanak did not "profess to be the founder of a new nation, his purpose was ethical, not political."
  Payne, C. H. : *A Short History of The Sikhs*, Thomas, Nelson and Sons, London, pp. 29, 25.
  Same could be said of others of the above category including General J. H. Gordon : *The Sikhs*, Blackwood & Sons, London 1904, p. 24 and of W. L. M. Gregor : *The History of The Sikhs*, Vol. I, James Madden, London 1846, pp. 39, 44.
2. Some modern historians of the Sikhs like Reverend W. H. McLeod also fall in this category.
3. Cunningham, Joseph Davey : *A History of The Sikhs*, John Murray, London 1849, p. 53. This position appears to have been taken hesitantly, as it is also observed by him that the Guru had no clear views on "political advancement." Ibid., p. 48.
4. Indubhushan Banerjee : *Evolution of The Khalsa*, A. Mukherjee & Co. (Private) Ltd., Calcutta (2nd Edn.) May 1963, p. 19.
5. Cf. Toynbee, Arnold J. : *Study of History*, 10 Vols., Oxford University Press, 1935-54, Vol. V, pp. 187, 665-67, 673, Vol. VII, pp. 414-415, Vol. VIII, p. 466.
6. Cf. Singh, Kapur : *Parasaraprasna*, Guru Nanak Dev University, Amritsar 1988, pp. 197-206.
  See review by Daljeet Singh : "The Sikhs — History, Religion and Society" by W. H. McLeod : *The Panjab Past and Present*, Punjabi University, Patiala, April 1989, pp. 250-59 for discussion on position of Sikhism on the issue.
  Also Cf. Grewal, J. S. : *Toynbee's Interpretation of Sikh History*, Punjab History Conference, Patiala 1969, pp. 304-10.
7. Field, Dorothy : *The Religion of The Sikhs*, 1901 (Reprint) Ess Ess Publications, Delhi 1976, pp. 10, 60.
8. Archer, J. C. : *The Sikhs in Relation to Hindus, Moslems, Christians and Ahmadiyas*, Princeton University Press, 1946, pp. 60-61.
9. Singh, Ganda : "The Maratha-Sikh Relations," *The Panjab Past and Present*, Punjabi University, Patiala, October 1967, p. 311.
10. *A Short History of The Sikhs*, Orient Longmans Ltd., Bombay, 1950, p. 14.
11. *An Introduction to Panjabi Literature*, Amritsar 1951, pp. 65-66.
12. "Nanak Bani Vich Phalsafa," *Madh Kalin Punjabi Sahit*, (Pbi.), Bhasha Vibhag, Patiala 1970, p. 64.
  Singh, Lal : "Guru Nanak da Shahkar," *Shabdarath Bani Guru Nanak Dev Ji*, (Pbi.), Bhasha Vibhag, Patiala 1970, 31 comment on *Babarvani* verses is that they represent a revolutionary call ...... sharpened on the spiritual sharpener to become a sword's edge."
13. *Gurmat Darshan* (Pbi.) Shiromani Gurdwara Prabandhak Committee, Amritsar, 1962, p. 47.
14. Cf. Preface to *Parasaraprasna*, Hind Publishers Ltd., Jullundur 1959, p. 12.
15. *Life of Guru Nanak Dev*, Lahore Book Shop, Ludhiana, 1958, p. 231 f.n.
16. *Sorath*, Guru Granth Sahib, p. 599 :
  Aprampar parbrahm parmeshar Nanak gur milia soi jio.
  also, Ramkali, Guru Granth Sahib, p. 878 :
  Gur Parmeshar Nanak bhetio sache sabad nibera.
17. *Var Majh*, Guru Granth Sahib, p. 148 :
  Hau dhadi bekar kare laiya. Rat dihai kai var dhurhu farmaiya. Dhadi sache mahal khasam bulaiya. Sachi sift salah kapra paiya.
18. Guru Granth Sahib, p. 1286 :
  ਮੈ ਮਹਿਮੁਦ ਲਿਖਾਇਆ ਖਸਮੈ ਕੈ ਦਰ ਜਾਇ॥
  ਦੁਨਿਆ ਕੇ ਦਰ ਕੇਤੜੇ ਕੇਤੇ ਆਵਹਿ ਜਾਇ॥
19. *Tilang*, Guru Granth Sahib, p. 722 :
  Jaisi mai avai khasam ki bani taisra kari gian ve Lalo.
  also *Wadhans*, ibid., p. 566 :
  Ta mai khaiya kaihan ja tujhai kahaiya.
20. *Gauri*, Ibid., p. 222 :
  Adist disai ta kahia jae.
  Bin dekhe kaihna birtha jae.

21. *Gauri* M. IV, Ibid., p. 308 :
    Satgur ki bani sat sat kar janhu gursikhu
    har karta ap muhhu kadhae.
    Gauri ki Var M. IV, Ibid., p. 306 :
    Ih akar tin akhia jini jagat sabh upaia.
    Sorath M. V. Ibid., p. 628 :
    Dhur ki bani aae tin sagli chint mitai.
22. *Bhattan de Swaiye*, Ibid., p. 1395 :
    Ap narayan kaladhar jag mahi parvario.
    Ibid., p. 1408 :
    Jot rup ap Guru Nanak kahaio.
    Varan Bhai Gurdas Ji, (Pbi.), Shiromani Gurdwara Prabandhak Committee, February 1952, Var I,
    Pauri 35 :
    Ik baba akal rup.
    Mani Singh, Bhai : *Sikhan di Bhagatmala*, (Pbi.).
    Khalsa Samachar, February 1955, p. 90.
    Jis nirnakar da vichar devte brahmadik nahin pai sakde so Guru Nanak ji hain.
23. Seshagiri Rao, K. L. : "Guru Nanak and The Hindu Heritage," *The Journal of Religious Studies*,
    Punjabi University, Patiala, September 1969, p. 48.
24. *Srirag*, Guru Granth Sahib, pp. 83-84 :
    Kudrat kar ke vassia soi.
    Jeh dhir dekha teh dhir mauzood.
25. *Maru*, Ibid., p. 1038 :
    Jaih dekha taih din dayala ......
    Jag tis ki chhaya jis bap na maya.
26. *Ramkali*, Ibid., p. 952 :
    Karni bajhon bhist na pai.
27. *Srirag*, Ibid., p. 26 :
    Vich dunian sev kamaie ta dargah baisan paie.
28. *Varan*, Bhai Gurdas Ji, op. cit. p. 20.
29. *Sidh Gosht*, *Ramkali*, Ibid., p. 938 :
    Jaise jal meh kamal nralamu murgai naisane.
30. For an almost complete compilation of such terms see Sekhon, Sant Singh : *Madh Kalin Punjabi*
    Sahit, (Pbi.), Bhasha Vibhag, Patiala 1970, pp. 118-26.
31. Grewal, J. S. : *Guru Nanak in History*, Panjab University, Chandigarh 1969, pp. 148-49.
32. *Suhi*, Guru Granth Sahib, p. 729 :
    Ja kau mahal hajur dujaia nivai kis.
33. *Maru*, Ibid., p. 1028 :
    Asur Sangharam ram hamara.
34. *Gauri*, Ibid., p. 224 :
    Daint sanghar sant nistare.
    Sri Rag, Ibid., p. 59 :
    Sukh data dukh metno satgur asur sanghar.
    cf. also *Gauri*, Ibid., pp. 224-25.
35. One such passage is found in Rag Wadhans, Ibid., pp. 557-58.
36. *Malhar*, Ibid., p. 1284 :
    Pasu manas chum plete androh kalia
    Suhi, Ibid., p. 751 :
    Mul na bujhan apna se pasua se dhor jio.
37. *Maru*, Ibid., p. 990 :
    Bhaia manur kanchan phir hovai je gur mile tineha.
38. *Parbhati*, Ibid., p. 1329 :
    Satgur paaiai pura navan pasu prethu dev kare.
39. *Srirag ki Var*, Ibid., p. 91 :
    Jo tis bhavai Nanka kagu hans kare.
40. *Basant*, Ibid., p. 1172 :
    Paras bhet bhae se paras Nanak har gur sang thiai.
41. *Gauri*, Ibid., p. 223 :
    Bhai rach rahe so nirbhauhoai,
    Jaisa seve taiso hoai.
    Ramkali, Ibid., p. 931 :
    Jin jata so tis hi jeha.

Ibid., p. 936 :
    Tin hi jaisi thee rahan jap jap ridai murar.
Sidh Gosht, Ibid., p. 943 (cf. also *Freedkot Wala Teeka*, Bhasha Vibhag, Patiala 1970, p. 1940) :
    Anhat sunn ratte se kaisai
    Jis te upje tahi hi jaisai
42. *Rag Asa*, Ibid., p. 417 :
    Ik na wakhat khuhaieh ikna puja jae ......
    Ram na kabhu chetia hun kahni na milai khudai.
43. *Ramkali*, Ibid., p. 903 :
    Kal puran Kateb kuran.
    Pothi pandit rahe puran.
    Nanak nao bhaia rahman,
    Basant, Ibid., p. 1191 :
    Ad purakh kau allah kahiai sekhan aai vari.
    Deval devtian kar laga aisi kirat chali.
Dhanasari, Ibid., p. 662 :
    Thaanast jag bhrisht heo dubta iv jag ......
    Khatrian ta dharam chhodia malechh bhakhia gahi.
    Srisht sabh ik varan hoi dharam ki gat rahi.
44. *Rag Asa*, Ibid., p. 360 :
    Eti mar pai kurlane tain ki darad na aaiya
cf. also ...... pp. 417, 418.
45. *Rag Asa*, Ibid., p. 360 :
    Ratan vigar vigoai kutti muia sar na kaai.
Ibid., p. 417 :
    Aggo de je chetie ta kait mile sajaai.
    Saha surat qwaiah tangg tamasai chaai.
46. *Japji*, Ibid., p. 7 :
    Jor na raj mal man sor.
Wadhans, Ibid., p. 566 :
    Sarbai samana ap tuhai dhande laiya.
    Ik na tujh ki kiai rajai ikna bhikh bhavaiya.
Asa, Ibid., p. 472 :
    Ik nihali pai savan ikna upar rahan kharai.
47. Ibid., p. 472 :
    Nadr upathi je karai sultana gha karaida.
48. *Japji*, Ibid., p. 3 :
    Panch parvan. Panch pardhan,
    Panchai pavhi dargahai man,
    Panchai sohai dar rajan.
49. *Asa*, Ibid., p. 417-18 :
    Jis no ap khuvai karta khus laai changiai ......
    Jin ki chiri dargahi phati tinha marna bhai ......
    Jai tis bhavai dai wadiaai jai bhavai dai sajai.
50. *Var Asa*, Ibid., p. 467 :
    Lakh surtan sangram ran mahi chhutai pran.
51. Ibid., p. 142 :
    Je jivai pat lathi jai
    Sabh haram jeta kichh khaai.
52. *Wadhans*, Ibid., pp. 579-80 :
    Mahli jaai pavhu khasmai bhavhu rang sio ralian manei ......
    Maran Maansa suria haq hai marn parvano.
53. *Slok Varan te Wadhik*, Ibid., p. 1412 :
    Jau tau praim khailan ka chau,
    Sir dhar tali gali more ao.
54. Popularly known as *Babarvani* verses are four in number. Three have been composed in *Rag Asa* by Guru Nanak and one is in *Rag Tilang*. Altogether they add up to ninety-nine lines.
In greater part of these verses, the Guru describes the woes of an unequal contest.
He sees it as potentiality of the evil to triumph and perpetuate itself if inadequately resisted. He ridicules the efforts of those who pretended to provide supernatural support against the offenders, and advises that being adequately prepared to resist is better preparation against such an eventuality. He exhorts the victims not to be overawed by the barbarian hordes, as their

success, being in violation of God's Will, is ephemeral. They would soon reap what they had sown if resisted effectively by the God-oriented.

Brutal violation of a people, their culture and religion agitates him much. A third part of the verses is devoted to depicting the sad plight of women which has particularly moved him. He considers it to be the consequences of evil being given a free hand. The victims have not made adequate preparation, have been lured to life of wanton luxury, and material pursuits, lived in ignorance of God's Will, so they must share the responsibility for what is happening to them.

The Guru prefers a people capable of protecting the honour of their women-folk and maintaining their religious, political and cultural heritage inviolate.

God is unequivocally accepted as the final arbiter in political power, as in everything else.

55.   *Rag Asa,* Guru Granth Sahib, p. 470 :
> *Kal main bed atharban hua nam khudai aallah bhaiaa ......*

      Var Malar, Ibid., p. 1288 :
> *Hansan baajan te sikdaran ehna apria nao.*
> *Fadkhi lagi jat fahain agai nahi thao.*

      Dhanasari Ibid., p. 662 :
> *Thanst jag bhrisht hoe dupta iv jag.*

56.   *Puratan Janamsakhi* Bhai Vir Singh (ed)., Khalsa Samachar, Amritsar 1971, p. 43. See also Bhalla, Sarup Das : *Guru Nanak Mahima,* (Pbi.) (Reprint) Bhasha Vibhag 1970, p. 34.

57.   *Rag Suhi,* Guru Granth Sahib, p. 729 :
> *Ja Kau mahal hajur dujai nivai kis.*

10

SAINT-SOLDIER

KHARAK SINGH

I. THE BACKGROUND

To grasp the significance of the ideal of 'saint-soldier', it would be helpful briefly to refer to two most prominent features of the religious tradition of India before Guru Nanak. These are :

(a) Dichotomy between spiritual and empirical life, and

(b) The Caste system.

While the former was common to practically all systems of religious thought, the latter constituted the very foundation of the diversity of faiths included in Hinduism.

DICHOTOMY BETWEEN SPIRITUAL AND EMPIRICAL LIFE

In a monistic system like Sankra's Vedanta, the world is unreal or *mithya*. In dualistic systems like Yoga, Sankhya and Jainism, two kinds of Reality are assumed — spiritual and material. And man is a combination of both. In Buddhism the world is a place of suffering in the endless cycle of birth, life and death. Goals vary from a realisation of the self to deliverance from transmigration, or *nirvana* or *mukti* or merger with the Ultimate Reality. The effort of the individual is directed towards a selfish end of personal salvation with little or no regard for, or even at the cost of, society and fellow-men. Worldly activities were considered incompatible with, and a hindrance to spiritual progress. Renunciation or withdrawal from the world, asceticism, celibacy, and *ahimsa* were essential components of the spiritual discipline prescribed. There was little scope or need for altruism or moral deeds. Dichotomy between spiritual and empirical life was complete. In Nathism, which was the predominant faith at the time of Guru Nanak, the initiate had to take vows of following no occupation, living on alms, celibacy and *ahimsa*. Although living as a parasite on society, the Naths looked down upon householders, and any concern with society was considered irreligious and beneath the dignity of a religious man. Some of the practices endowed with religious merit have been recounted by Guru Arjun Dev :

Despite recitation of holy texts, study of Vedas and praxis of bowels and the
Kundalini,
>From the five agents has not come parting of company,
And more and more in egoistic thinking is one bound.
Cherished one ! by such devices comes not union —
>Innumerable are the means I have adopted.
Tired of all such, at the Lord's Portal I threw myself,
>Praying, 'Grant me discriminative understanding.'
Vows of silence I observed; on my bare hands received food,
>And unclad in forests wandered;
>I wandered over water-edges and holy spots over the earth —
>Still has duality not dropped off.
At holy water-edges I resided where desires are fulfilled.
Had the saw placed over my head;
>Yet thus is not impurity of mind washed off, despite a million devices.
Gold, maids, horses, elephants — thus charities of various kinds I dispensed;
>Gave away grain, clothing, land —
>Still found I not the Lord's Portal.
To offerings before deities, sprinkling sandalwood paste,
>folding of hands,
>Lying prostrate, and to the six ritual acts have I remained devoted.
Still, by egoism in bonds am I fallen —
>Not by these devices is the Lord met.
Eighty-four poses of Yoga-praxis too to exhaustion I performed;
>Lived to a great age, yet found not union with the Lord,
>And into transmigration fell.
Royal display of glory, the pomp of kingship I had,
>And exercised absolute authority;
>I lay in elegant couch, applied to my limbs
>sandalwood and attar — all these are gateway to terrible hell.
Divine laudation in holy company is the supreme act of piety.
Saith Nanak : This to such comes as by primal writ are this destined to receive.
In such joy of devotion is Thy servant absorbed.
By grace of the Shatterer of suffering of the humble,
>To Divine laudation is my mind devoted.[1]

CASTE SYSTEM

The Indian caste system is a unique institution evolved by the Hindu society, and has no parallel anywhere in the history of the world. The fundamental assumption of the caste ideology is that[2], "Men were not — as for classical Confucianism — in principle equal, but for ever unequal." They were so by birth, and "were as unlike as man and animal." The whole society is divided into four major castes : Brahmins, Kshatrias, Vaishyas and Sudras. The number of sub-castes, however, exceeds 3,000, all of which are meticulously arranged in a hierarchical social pyramid in which the social grade of each group was fixed permanently by birth. Each layer in this social pyramid was superior in caste status (i.e. virtually in social status) to all layers below it, and lower in caste status to all the others above it, irrespective of their political or economic position. The privileges, disabilities, obligations and duties, i.e., practically all aspects of social behaviour of each sub-caste were regulated by fixed rules and codes. At the top were the Brahmins enjoying every conceivable privilege, and at the bottom were the Sudras, mostly untouchables, doomed to perpetual serfdom doing all the dirty and disagreeable jobs required of them, with no hope of ever moving up along the social ladder. The system had religious sanction of the Vedas, and was confirmed by the *avtars* of Vishnu, incarnated as Lord Rama and Krishna. One was born as Sudra as a punishment for sins of one's previous birth, and nobody could, therefore, change it. Every *varna* could perform only the specific functions allotted to it. Only Brahmins could preside over religious ceremonies. Wearing and use of arms was the monopoly of Kshatrias. Vaishyas could not do anything except farming and trading. It was a grave offence for a Sudra to attempt anything other than his menial jobs. Lord Rama, known as Maryada Purshotam, is said to have cut off the head of a Sudra for the sole crime of indulging in religious rites not allowed to his caste. Lord Krishna was supposed to have asserted that he was the creator of *Chaturvarnya*.

It is obvious that religious requirements or creeds of different castes were different. Guru Nanak draws attention to this anomaly :

> The Yogi's creed in seeking enlightment is expressed.
>
> The Brahmin's in following the Vedas.
>
> The Kshatria's creed is heroism; the Sudra's service of others."

The Guru, however, does not approve of this. He goes on :

> "Should one, however, realise this secret,
>
> One creed all should inspire.
>
> Nanak is a slave to one with such realisation.
>
> In him is manifest the immaculate Lord.[3]

II. THE CONSEQUENCES

Rigid enforcement of the caste system ensured internal stability of the society and control of the Brahmins for almost three thousand years. The life-negating pacific religious beliefs also helped in this. But an unjust and exploitative system cannot sustain itself indefinitely. The vast majority of the population had been deprived of education, and had been disarmed. The shabby and cruel treatment meted out to the Sudras and even the Vaishyas did not inspire or encourage any feelings of sympathy or loyalty to the higher castes. So when the Muslim invaders started their attacks from the North and West, they met no formidable resistance. Mahmud Ghaznavi is known for his seventeen invasions on India. It was almost a sport with him. He would come anytime he liked and return with as much loot as troops could carry. He desecrated temples, killed people by the thousands and took countless men and women as slaves. His official reporter records that while his troops were plundering the famous temple at Somnath and breaking the idols, people from the surrounding 300 villages collected and sat chanting mantras, and did not offer any resistance. Bakhtiar Khilji is believed to have crossed into India with only 300 horsemen, and trampling vast territories, reached as far as Nalanda, where he demolished the famous university, killing 1,000 teachers and about ten thousand students, besides destroying over 100,000 valuable manuscripts. Such examples of wanton destruction by invaders could be cited by hundreds from the Indian history. Muslim invaders were able to establish their empires in India without much difficulty. Indian pacificism was no match for the life-affirming approach of the invading armies. The Muslim rule in India lasted for almost a thousand years, only to be replaced by another foreign power, the British.

Guru Nanak was himself a witness to the attack of the founder of the Mughal Empire in India. In his famous composition, *Babarvani*, he gives a very vivid account of the atrocities committed by Babur's armies on innocent people, including women and children. He calls Babur's army a "horde of sin." At the same time he takes to task the local rulers for their unpreparedness. He points out the need for forethought to escape chastisement, as well as the futility of spells for dealing with the Mughal invaders, or any other aggressor.

III. THE CONCEPT OF SAINT-SOLDIER

We have seen that religious thought of the pre-Guru period was oriented towards development of the individual, in respect of some selected traits or qualities, rather than his entire personality and the society. The popular couplet *'Janani jane to bhagat jan, kai data, kai sur'* indicates the prevalent values of the times. The ideals sought were *bhakti* or generosity or heroism. One of these was considered enough. It never occurred to religious leaders that emphasis on a single quality would lead to lop-sided development of the individual, and emaciate the society. Guru Nanak, on the other hand, wanted balanced and fullest development of the individual, covering every aspect of his life, physical, temporal, moral and spiritual. Himself perfect, he set out to create a perfect society of perfect individuals, basing his philosophy on the unity of God, the Sole Loving Creator. This is amply testified by Dr Mohammad Iqbal in his reference to Guru Nanak thus :

> Phir uthi Tauhid ki awaz ik Punjab se,
> Mard-i-kamal ne jagaya Hind ko phir khwab se.[4]

Then arose from the Punjab the call of Unity of God;
    And the perfect man (Guru Nanak) shook Hind from its slumber.

Guru Nanak's religion derives its origin from his mystic communion with the Sole Loving Creator. He wanted all human beings to develop in God's image and to carry out His Altruistic Will.

> 'Harijan aisa chahie Hari he jaisa hoe' (Kabir)

God's servant should be each as God Himself.

One should, therefore, cherish the attributes of God, some of which are mentioned in the *Mul Mantra* of Guru Nanak as 'truthfulness', 'creativity', 'to be above fear or rancour', etc. God's image is not cast in sanitly virtues alone. Guru Arjun hints at the fullness and versatility of His image as follows :

Among kings art Thou reputed as the Supreme King;

Among possessors of land also Supreme.

Among lords art Thou Supreme Lord;

Among the castes Thine is the pre-eminent caste.

My father is the great Master, inaccessible.

Lord Creator, what can we utter of Thy praise ?

In wonder are we beholding all.

Among masters of joy art Thou also supreme;

Supreme Bestower among those that bestow gifts.

Among masters of glory art Thou All-glorious;

Among hedonists the Supreme Hedonist.

Among heroes art Thou Supreme Hero;

    among enjoyers of pleasures pre-eminent.

Among householders art Thou Supreme Householder;

    among yogis the Supreme Yogi.

Among doers art Thou Supreme Creator;

    among upholders of traditions the Supreme Traditionalist.[5]

The Guru's system differs radically from earlier religious traditions in its goals. The Guru did not approve of any selfish goal of personal salvation through asceticism and withdrawal from life, flourishing on parasitism. The Guru saw God as All Love. He loves His creation, and has a Will that is Altruistic. So the goal for the Guru's ideal man or *gurmukh* is to carry out the Altruistic Will of God. The devotion of the Guru's disciple expresses itself as love for His creation in the form of service and sacrifice. For, love without sacrifice is meaningless. In fact love and sacrifice are closely linked complimentary qualities. Love of a cause inevitably leads to sacrifice or heroism. The Guru's religion, therefore, rejects pacificism of the earlier salvation systems, and prepares the seeker to be a saint *as well as* a soldier, and not a saint *or* a soldier. He says :

Shouldest thou seek to engage in the game of love,

    Step into my street with thy head placed on thy palm.

    While on to this stepping, ungrudgingly sacrifice your head.[6]

Guru Arjun repeated the same thing, when he said :

Accept first death as inevitable, and attachment to life discard;

Turn dust of feet of all — thereafter to us come.[7]

Sikhism is a whole-life system combining spiritual life with empirical life. The *sant-sipahi* ideal is thus logically and morally essential. For, love of one's fellow-men becomes meaningless, and even hypocritical, if one is not willing to sacrifice and secure for them sustenance, equality, safety and justice in all spheres of life. Hence in Guru Nanak's system the ideal of *sant-sipahi* is spiritually and naturally a necessary culmination. It is, therefore, neither incidental nor accidental that while the first four Gurus organised, motivated and developed the Sikh society, and Guru Arjun created a state within a state, the later five Gurus maintained a regular army and wielded the sword, when necessary.

It must be emphasised that while a Sikh is expected to acquire the skills of a soldier, he is permitted to use his sword only for a noble cause, to resist oppression and tyranny, and to secure justice and equality for humanity. Guru Gobind Singh gave a clear sanction to the use of force, when he said :

When all other means (to secure justice) fail,
It is righteous to take the sword in hand.

On the other hand, fighting for selfish ends, self-aggrandisement and lust for power, is condemned in clear terms. The Guru says :

Call not these heroes that in pride die and bear sufferings :
Blind, not realising the self, in duality are they absorbed.
In extreme of wrath they wage battles.
In this life and the next sufferings.
Declare the scriptures, pride pleases not the Lord.
Those dying in pride, of liberation shall be deprived
And in the cycle of death and birth shall ever move.[8]

Guru Nanak condemned the invasion of Babur in strongest words, since his exploits were not only devoid of saintliness, but were actually opposed to it. Dr Iqbal expresses similar sentiments, when he says :

Be it the pomp of monarchy.
Or the show of democracy,
Separate (nobility of) religion from politics,
What remains is the sheer tyranny of Jenghese.[9]

Guru Arjun stressed the need for saintliness in heroes, when he said :

In this age such alone are designated as true heroes,
As in the love of Lord are dyed.[10]

In numerous hymns the Gurus have urged upon the heroes to inculcate saintly qualities. Using metaphor of wrestling, the Guru refers to the fight with the evil forces thus :

The Lord's champion am I;
After meeting the Master is my tassel held high.
The tourney of champions assembled.
The Lord Himself is witnessing.
Trumpets and drums are playing;
Champions in the arena are moving around :
Five wrestlers have I overthrown;
The Master my back has stroked.[11]

The ideal of saint-soldier is the practical expression of the whole-life approach preached by the Gurus, who categorically rejected renunciation which is usually associated with saintliness. Guru Arjun says :

Saith Nanak : By contact with the Master is the true device of living perfected.
In a life of smiling playfulness, enjoyment of wear and food,

Is attained liberation.

......

My self ! in joy abide by endeavouring and working in the way of God.
By meditation obtain union with the Lord :
Thus, saith Nanak, shall thy anxiety be removed.[12]

IV. FOUNDING A SOCIETY OF SAINT-SOLDIERS

Guru Nanak was not content to merely state his doctrines. He knew that, in the background of the long Indian tradition, these would be forgotten, unless he could create a motivated and well-knit society, wedded to his principles and willing to fight for them. With this idea in mind he had been organising *sangats,* wherever he went. Towards the end of his tours he created the nucleus of a Sikh society and centre at Kartarpur, in the form of a colony, in which everybody including the Guru himself, worked and ate together, attended the daily congregations, and imbibed the spirit of the Master and his religion. The members of this community were the humble and the lowly people who had suffered for centuries under the Draconian *Varna Dharma* and the tyrannical rule of foreign invaders. The infant society had to be nurtured, until it grew in size and conviction, and developed full consciousness of the strength of its cause and potentialities. All this could not be achieved overnight or even in one generation. So the Guru introduced the institution of succession, passing on the torch to his worthiest disciple, Lehna, giving him the name of Angad, i.e., a part of his own self. This succession continued, until it reached the tenth guru, Guru Gobind Singh. Each Guru made rich contribution to the cause of advancing towards the goal of an organised society of saint-soldiers. The first five Gurus created the necessary infrastructure like the institution of *sangat* and *pangat,* creation of headquarters at Amritsar, compiling of the Scripture, organisation of districts for efficient administration, starting the institution of *daswandh,* developing physical strength of the individual and the society as a whole, etc.

The Sixth Guru, under instructions of his great father, took the next step to implement the doctrine of *miri-piri* by donning two swords at the time of his coronation. He took up in real earnest the training of his followers in the military skills and warfare. It needs to be noted that the symbol for *piri* or spiritualism was also a sword, and not a rosary, signifying that even spiritual obligations cannot be discharged fully without *shakti* or sword. In the initial, stages even mercenaries were employed to impart training. For, the earlier disciples of the Guru, thoroughly grounded in the Sikh doctrines, required training in the arts of soldiery. The goal was to create a society of saint-soldiers, properly trained, equipped and willing to fulfil their social responsibilities to fight and even die for the cause of justice and defence of the poor and oppressed. History records that the army of Guru Hargobind fought four pitched battles with the forces of the local Mughal Chiefs, and won. The following three Gurus also maintained armies, approximately thirty thousand strong, and continued preparing their followers for the ensuing struggle. The ninth guru, Guru Tegh Bahadur, who died a martyr for resisting the forcible conversion of Hindus to Islam, championing the cause of freedom of faith, is also famous for his slogan of the saint-soldierly concept.

Frighten not; fear not.[13]

The first part shows a saint, and the second a soldier.

V. THE EPITOME

The revolutionary movement launched by Guru Nanak, culminated in the creation of the Khalsa by Guru Gobind Singh on the Vaisakhi day of 1699, when he dramatically selected the *Panj Piaras*, the most devoted of his Sikhs or disciples, who had offered their heads to the Guru for the saintly cause, to form the nucleus of the Khalsa *Panth*. Around this nucleus under the inspiring leadership of the Guru and the example of his unparalleled sacrifices, grew a society of saint-soldiers, with strong convictions of the spiritual realities of life, wedded to the highest moral values, trained in the arts of soldiering, and ever willing and prepared to fight for the cause of justice, in defence of the poor, the oppressed and the downtrodden. The exploits of the Khalsa are too well-known to need mention in this brief paper. Suffice it to say that it was this organisation of saint-soldiers, that stemmed the spate of invasions from the North-West that had plagued India for nearly a thousand years, and introduced an era of peace, stability, freedom and human dignity after centuries of tyranny, destruction, slavery, humiliation and indignity.

VI. THE SAINT-SOLDIER IN HISTORY

The history of Sikhs after creation of the Khalsa is the story of an unending series of martyrs and saint-soldiers, who staked their lives for the cause of justice and resistance to oppression and exploitation. It is beyond the scope of this paper to go into details of such heroic deeds and near miracles performed by the Khalsa. One of the numerous examples, recorded by Rattan Singh Bhangoo in his *Panth Parkash*, is the attack on Kasur, on the complaint of a Brahmin whose wife had been forcibly taken away by the ruling Pathans. The attack was undertaken against heavy odds, with a meagre 24,000 soliders against an enemy over a *lakh* strong, involving tremendous risk. With conviction of the righteousness of the cause, and with faith in God, the attack was launched, because the Khalsa could not resist the call to duty as saint-soldiers. A mere saint of earlier traditions, would have paid little attention to the Brahmin's request, and would have advised him to accept it as the will of Providence. And a mere soldier would see no need or justification for such a risky operation. But the saint-soldiers of the Guru did not shirk their responsibility and succeeded in rescuing the Brahmin's wife at a heavy cost in terms of loss of life.

"Every page of Sikh history burns with a hundred star-like names; one name is enough to thrill a whole life in us with the noblest spirit of heroism. The names of Guru Arjun Dev, Guru Tegh Bahadur, Guru Gobind Singh, his Four Sons, the five Beloved Disciples, and of the Sikh martyrs and devotees, the heroes of war and peace, provide the Sikh with an inexhaustible and intense past which few races in history can provide in its life-giving, death defying powers of inspiration to serve the Master and His ideals!"[14] Among the countless heroes, mention may also be made of the Forty Muktas, Baba Banda Singh Bahadur, Baba Dip Singh, Bhai Mehtab Singh, Bhai Sukha Singh, Nawab Kapur Singh, Maharaja Jassa Singh, Akali Phula Singh and others. Outstanding among the more recent saint-soldiers are the names of Bhai Sahib Randhir Singh and Baba Waisakha Singh, who spent their lives in jail for resisting the oppression of the British rule in India in response to the inner call for action as disciples of the Guru.

The spirit of saint-soldiers lives and will live for ever. The Akali Movement of the early twenties furnished ample evidence of this spirit. Professor Puran Singh makes a touching reference to this as follows :

The awe-inspiring scenes of the "Akalis" in their present somewhat confused struggle, however misled and misguided from certain points of view — counting death like moths, the Sikh women coming and garlanding their husbands before the Akal Takht to go and bare their breasts to bullets if need be, in the name of the Guru; mothers and fathers putting with their own hands the flaming crown of martyrdom on their young sons' heads and praying that the Guru may grant them the honour of death in His Name; people laying themselves down on railroads before the rushing railway engines, carrying a trainful of their brethren as prisoners, as an appeal for stopping the train to let them who are out of prison to feast those who are going in; thousands dressed in yellow and black, vying with each other to be the first to form the groups of five hundred or a thousand martyrs that are sent to face prison, torture and even death in the name of the Guru; and the universal diffusion of this one feeling of service and sacrifice throughout the Sikh masses — these make one wonder if one is living in an age of rank materialism as the present one, or in the age when under the direct inspiration of the Tenth Guru the Sikhs were taking the vows of absolute self-surrender to the Ideals of the Khalsa.[15]

VI. CONCLUSION

The concept of saint-soldier is clearly traceable to Guru Nanak, who made a radical departure from the earlier pacific and personal salvation-oriented religious thought. Guru Nanak preached a positive approach to the world, and a whole-life religion, with emphasis on altruistic activity and righteous deeds, based on the highest moral values. He wanted a balanced development of the individual to create a perfect man or 'the man in all men' that he himself was.

The Guru's vision went far beyond the individual. He wanted to create a perfect society, and took positive steps towards that end. He envisaged a society of God-men living as householders in the midst of the social milieu, engaged in pursuits of daily life, discharging with a sense of responsibility their social and political functions, committed to carry out the Altruistic Will of the Loving Creator, and willing and ever prepared to resist oppression and fight injustice. That was his concept of the Ideal Man combining spiritual and empirical values, the saint-soldier, and a perfect society of such individuals. Under his successors the idea flourished and advanced towards the most fitting epitome of the creation of the Khalsa under Guru Gobind Singh. That was indeed the final event, on the Vaisakhi of 1699, the greatest day in the history of mankind. For, the socio-spiritual ideal of saint-soldier is the highest ideal that has ever been given to mankind.

REFERENCES

1. Guru Granth Sahib : Mahila-5, pp. 641-42, (Trans. Talib).
2. Jagjit Singh : *Perspectives on Sikh Studies,* p. 14, Guru Nanak Foundation, New Delhi.
3. Guru Granth Sahib : *Asa di Var*, M-1, p. 469.
4. Mohammad Iqbal : *Bang-i-dara.*
5. Guru Granth Sahib : *Gujri* M-5, p. 507.
6. Ibid., p. 1412.
7. Ibid., *Var Gauri*, M-5, p. 1102.
8. Ibid., *Var Maru*, M-3, p. 1089.
9. Mohammad Iqbal : *Bang-i-dara.*
10. Guru Granth Sahib, *Dhanasari*, M-5, p. 679.
11. Ibid., *Siri Rag*, M-5, p. 74.
12. Ibid., M-5, p. 522.
13. Ibid, Sloka M-9, p. 1427.
14. Puran Singh : *Spirit of the Sikh,* Part I, p. 9.
15. Ibid., p. 8.

SIKHISM : AN ORIGINAL, DISTINCT, REVEALED AND COMPLETE RELIGION

HARNAM SINGH SHAN

The word 'Sikh', as we know, is the Punjabised form of the Sanskrit word *shishya*, meaning a disciple or a learner, especially a seeker of truth. It came to be used for the disciples of Guru Nanak Dev and his nine spiritual successors who graced humanity from 1469 to 1708 A.D. in the Indian subcontinent. Thus, their religion, called Sikhism, literally means the path of discipleship and the new way of life taught by them.

Their faith is the youngest and the most modern of the world's religions. It originated in Punjab, the land of Five Rivers, about five centuries ago, during the Muslim rule of Lodhis followed soon after by that of the Mughals in India.

II

Soon after the passing away, in 1708, of the Tenth Master, Guru Gobind Singh, the Mughal Emperor, Bahadur Shah, issued an imperial ordinance on the 10th of December 1710 from Delhi to "kill and finish them (the Sikhs) wherever they were found,"[1] ordering thus their wholesale destruction. That royal proclamation, outlawing the Sikhs and seeking their complete annihilation, was repeated by Emperor Farrukh Siyar, and it remained in force for three long years in all parts of the Mughal Empire. "According to it, every Sikh or Nanakpanthi, wherever seen, was to be immediately arrested. He was to be offered only one alternative, either Islam or the sword. He was to be executed there and then without any hesitation or loss of time. A schedule of valuable rewards was proclaimed. For every Sikh head Rs. 25/- were to be given, and for a Sikh captive a sum of Rs. 100/- was to be awarded. Their pretty girls were to be reduced to concubines, and others were to be made maid-servants. When a Muslim died, his grave was to be dug by the Sikhs or their Hindu sympathisers. For *begar* (unpaid labour), in place of cobblers, Sikhs were to be employed. The Emperor's orders were strictly obeyed. The Governors of Sarhind, Lahore and Jammu tried to surpass one another in persecution of the Sikhs in order to win the goodwill of Farrukh Siyar."[2] Later, in 1746, according to Syed Mohammad Latif, "The Governor (of Punjab), Yahya Khan, issued a proclamation for a general massacre of all Sikhs, wherever they could be found. Death was to be the punishment of all persons who invoked the name of Guru Gobind (Singh), and a reward was offered for the heads of Sikhs. Thousands were put to death daily, and their heads brought before the Subedar of Lahore for reward."[3] It was reported, on three occasions, to the authorities that the Sikhs had been exterminated root-and-branch. The Afghan invader, Ahmad Shah Abdali, during his invasion of India in 1762 and his continued campaign of the Sikhs' extermination, killed about twenty five thousand of them[4] in a single day's battle.[5] Besides, he ransacked their capital (viz. Amritsar), blew up their Harimandar (the Temple of God, better known as Golden Temple), and desecrated its *Sudhasar* (sacred pool) with blood, bones and entrails of cows, etc., and had it filled up with debris.[6]

With the establishment, in 1849, of the British rule in Punjab, Dr Ernest Trumpp, a German missionary, appointed by Her Majesty's Government to translate the sacred Sikh scriptures, asserted in 1877 that "Sikhism is a waning religion that will soon belong to history."[7] Joginder Nath Bhattacharya rather prophesied in 1896 that "Under British rule, Sikhism is fast losing its vitality and is drifting towards amalgamation with the Hindu faith. In the course of a few more generations, Sikhism is likely to be superseded by one of those forms of Vaishnavism which alone have the best chance of success among a subject nation in times of profound and undisturbable peace."[8] Max Arthur Macauliffe also apprehended such a danger of amalgamation or absorption, when he observed, first in his essays and papers (1881-1906),[9] and later in his *magnum opus* (1909) : "Truly wonderful are the strength and vitality of Hinduism. It is like the boa constrictor of the Indian forests. When a petty enemy appears to worry it, it winds round its opponent, crushes it in its folds, and finally causes it to disappear in its capacious interior. In this way, many centuries ago, Hinduism on its own ground disposed of Buddhism which was largely a Hindu reformation; in this way, in a pre-historic period, it absorbed the religion of the Scythian invaders of Northern India; in this way, it is disposing of the reformed and once hopeful religion of Baba Nanak. Hinduism has embraced Sikhism in its folds; the still comparatively young religion is making a vigorous struggle for life, but its ultimate destruction is, it is apprehended, inevitable without state support."[10] Gokul Chand Narang posing a self-prophetising question and answering it himself in a self-righteous manner, stated in 1912, "What is their (the Sikhs) future ? It is anything but dark. However, it is apparent that the best days of the Khalsa are altogether behind."[11]

During the all-out crusade of extermination against its adherents (who are easily recognizable by their strikingly distinctive appearance sporting unshorn hair and colourful headgear) immediately before and after the partition of India and the creation of Pakistan on the 15th August 1947, thousands of them (the Sikhs) were killed at sight. The rest were uprooted, *en masse*, from their homes, lands and historic shrines; and were deprived of all other belongings in an unprecedented way.[12]

The horrendous holocaust reduced nearly half of their thriving community to a homeless, landless and seething refugee population. So much so that of all other persons, one of its own followers, Khushwant Singh, while prefacing his first book about them and their faith, observed in 1953 : "The chief reason for my writing an account of my people is the melancholy thought that contemporary with my labours are being written the last chapters of the story of the Sikhs. By the end of the century, the Sikhs themselves will have passed into oblivion. Before that happens, it is proper that some estimate of their religion, history, traditions and political and cultural achievements should be made by someone identified with them by faith and association."[13] Gokul Chand Narang, a staunch Arya-Samajist, came out in 1960 with another self-fulfilling statement asserting that the "Sikhs have no political future as an independent community."[14] Fourteen years later, another highly learned Sikh, Kapur Singh, stated while concluding his speech on 7th of October 1974 at Vancouver : "While as Canadian citizens, the Sikhs may look forward to a hopeful and bright future; in India, their historic homeland, they now face the basic problems of their identity and existence, since the control of their own history has been snatched out of their own hands and their historical potential has been submerged and throttled. And I add that the Sikhs want to live, as all living things do not want to die."[15]

Only ten years after that last pronouncement, the Sikhs had to face still another holocaust in 1984, only thirty-seven years after the independence of India; for the attainment of which their sufferings, sacrifices and contribution far exceeded their numerical strength in their motherland.[16] This too involved not only a multi-pronged attack on their historic shrines and institutions,[17] but also a genocidal campaign to slaughter thousands of innocent Sikhs, disgracing their women and burning their properties all over India, not accounted for to this date.[18]

But in spite of such recurrent persecution and treacherous onslaughts perpetrated on this religion by the rulers and the foreign invaders as well as the ongoing challenges and intimidating prophesies about its absorption, assimilation or disappearance, Sikhism has stood its ground and withstood all tests of the time. All nefarious efforts made from time-to-time to suppress, subjugate or exterminate it have gone up in smoke. All prophets of doom who predicted its extinction had to bite the bullet and their prophesies have proven totally wrong. Even "the boa constrictor has failed to swallow it,"[19] The fact remains that it has not only survived, but is very much here to stay. Its followers are flourishing now in even larger numbers, not only in Punjab, its home-land, and in all other parts of India, but also in every part of the world. Despite various limitations, such as their 'stateless status' — the Sikhs have achieved a far greater success in all walks of life, contributing a lot to the progress of the communities they live in and wielding "an influence much in excess of their numerical strength"[20] everywhere in the world. So much so that according to the renowned historian Arnold Toynbee, "they are the burliest men on the face of the planet, tough and capable, and slightly grim. If human life survives the present chapter of man's history, the Sikhs for sure, will still be on the map."[21]

III

This is so and shall remain thus; because the Sikhs, in spite of being about 2% of the population of India, their country of origin, profess one of the 'higher religions' of the World which is not only an original, distinct and independent faith, but is also an autonomous, complete and dynamic religion, born of a direct and definitive revelation like other major religions of the world.   It is primary in its source and pure in its contents.

The authenticity of its dogmas, simplicity of its beliefs, exalted moral code, internal vigour, tenacity of purpose and sustained heroism together with the religious zeal, spiritual energy, unshakable faith and indomitable spirit as well as the enterprising and self-sacrificing nature of its followers have kept it intact and firm on its ground in many such crises during its 500 plus year-old history, raising it up again with greater strength and better prospects after every attempt to annihilate it.

IV

Those who have not been able to study Sikhism properly or objectively, or have been unable to understand rightly its nature, origin, essence, psyche and spirit, have often described it wrongly or misleadingly.

Some of them, like Estlin Carpenter, have considered it not an original and distinct, but an eclectic and 'composed' religion, maintaining that "the movement of Nanak which culminated in the formation of a kind of church nation, was fed from two sources and attempted to establish a religion combining the higher elements of Hinduism and Islam alike."[22] According to Rev. F. Heiler, too, it is "a pure and elevated religion in which the best of Hinduism and the best of Islam unite ...... Many elements of the religion ...... come near the central truths of Christianity, though these glimpses of revelation are indeed blurred by the strong influence of Vedantic pantheism and Islamic fatalism.   Above all, the element which robs the teaching of the Granth (its sacred scripture, Guru Granth Sahib) of any creative power is its eclecticism, its continued oscillation between theism and pantheism."[23]   In the words of Khushwant Singh, "Sikhism was born out of a wedlock between Hinduism and Islam."[24] It is "a synthesis of these two faiths."[25]   According to Bhattacharya, it may be described briefly as a Hinduized form of Mahomedanism or a Mahomedinized form of Hinduism, ... is a mixture of Hinduism and Mahomedanism minus circumcision and cow-killing, and plus faith in the Sikh Gurus.   Even in outward appearance, a Sikh with his short trousers, flowing beard, forehead free from paint and neck without beads, looks more like a Mohamedan than a Hindu.   The only visible sign by which he may be distinguished is the iron ring which he wears on the wrist."[26] The Time magazine has recently described him as "a member of a casteless religion that combines elements of Hinduism and Islam, but .scorns the caste system of the Hindus and the historical expansionism of the Muslims."[27]

Some others, like Frederic Pincott, have also tried to identify Sikhism with

Muhammadanism. According to him, "the religion of Nanak was really intended as a compromise between Hinduism and Muhammadanism, if it may not even be spoken of as the religion of a Mohammadan." Concluding his article on Sikhism, included in the *Dictionary of Islam*, he observed, "It is enough for the purpose of this article to have established the fact that Sikhism, in its inception, was intimately associated with Muhammadanism; and that it was intended as a means of bridging the gulf which separated the Hindus from the believers in the Prophet."[28] Tara Chand has even gone to the extent of asserting that "Nanak took the Prophet of Islam as his model and his teaching was naturally deeply coloured by this fact."[29]

Sri Rajagopalachari has described the Sikhs as "no better than uncircumcised Mussalmans."[30] Ascribing the theistic character of Sikhism to the influence of Islam, Monier Williams has stated, "Nanak was partially Islamised, to the extent at least of denouncing idolatry."[31] G.T. Battany has also mentioned this religion "having been largely influenced by the growing Mohammadanism."[32] But the Muslim writers, like Maulvi Insha Ulla Khan,[33] Maulvi Muhammad Ali,[34] Khawaja Hasan Nizami,[35] and Shaikh Muhammad Yasuf,[36] have gone a step further even by claiming Guru Nanak as a great Muslim Fakir who, according to them, taught a religion which in itself was a form of Muhammadanism.[37]

On the other hand, according to Ernest Trumpp, "Sikhism has only an accidental relationship with Muhammadanism. It is a mistake if Nanak is represented as having endeavoured to unite the Hindu and Muhammadan idea about God. Nanak remained a thorough Hindu according to all his views."[38] "Although precipitated by Islam," asserts Gokul Chand Narang, "Sikhism owes nothing to that religion. It is, on the other hand, a phase of Hindu religious revival, and has in consequence retained all essential features of real Hinduism."[39] Mahatma Gandhi has even claimed that the "Sikhs are a part of the Hindu community. The Granth Sahib is filled with the Hindu spirit and the Hindu legends, and millions of Hindus believe in Guru Nanak."[40] Gandhi, records Archer, "acknowledged that he had met some Sikhs who held themselves distinct from Hindus, but intimated that he would be pleased to find that the separate tendency is confined to only a very few Sikhs and that the general body regard themselves as Hindus,"[41] thus paving the way for Sikhism to be labelled as an off-shoot of Hinduism.

There are still others who, like Muhammad Akbar, have even denied the distinct identity and separate entity of Sikhism by asserting that "Guru Nanak did not enunciate any new religion, but only wanted to reform Hinduism."[42] According to Guru Datt also, it is difficult to say whether Sikhs have any separate or distinct religion of their own. The faith they profess is the basis of the present-day Arya-Samaj.[43] Nirad C. Chaudhuri has also identified Sikhism with Hinduism and has described it as one of its different forms.[44]

According to some others, like Marian Smith, Sikhism is a religious synthesis. She "finds a similarity between the reforms of Guru Nanak and those of Martin Luther. She calls Sikhism a religious synthesis, pointing out that Guru Nanak offered a doctrinal synthesis which answered the challenge of Islam, and aimed at the foundations of the top-heavy Brahminical social structure."[45]

V

But those who have studied Sikhism and have understood its origin, growth and gospel have proclaimed, in the words of Duncan Greenlees, the celebrated author of the *World Gospel Series*, that "Sikhism is no disguised Hindu sect, but an independent revelation of the Truth of all sects; it is no variant of Muslim teaching ...... It too is a distinct religion like the other great religions of the world ...... The Sikh is not a Hindu or a Muslim; he is the disciple of the one Eternal Guru."[46] According to Edward Bittencourt, "Sikhism is a wholly new, original and genuinely monotheistic religion. It is an independent religion which naturally may be said to have a background of Hinduism and Islam, much as Christianity has a background of Judaism, and Judaism has a background of Akhnatonism and Zoroastrianism and previous Semitic Paganism."[47] M.A. Macauliffe, who devoted thirty long years to its study and research and produced a six-volume monumental work about its prophets, scripture, tradition, etc., had already stated, while introducing to the West this religion and its founder as follows : "Guru Nanak was not a priest either by birth or education, but a man who soared to the loftiest heights of divine emotionalism, and exalted his mental vision to an ethical ideal beyond the conception of Hindu or Muhammadan. The illustrious author of *Vie de Jesus* asks whether great originality will again arise, or the world be content to follow the path opened by the daring creators of ancient ages. Now there is here presented a religion totally unaffected by Semitic or Christian influences. Based on the concept of the unity of God, it rejected Hindu formulations and adopted an independent ethical system, ritual, and standards, which were totally opposed to theological beliefs of Guru Nanak's age and country."[48] Hence, he asserted, "It would be difficult to point to a religion of greater originality or to a more comprehensive ethical system."[49] According to R.C. Majumdar too, the founder of this new and distinct religion, "cut himself adrift from all associations with prevailing sectarian religions."[50]

It even fell away from allegiance to their respective codes, and developed its own, as observed by Sir Lepel Griffin in 1870 : "The Sikhs had abandoned the Hindu faith, and with it the system of law which is the basis of the faith and which was inseparable from it. For a hundred and fifty years they had been governed, as far as chiefships were concerned, by another code altogether, and it was as reasonable for them to refer to *Manu* and the *Shastras* as the source of legal authority, as it would have been for Muhammadans who had embraced Sikhism to appeal to the *shariat*."[51] So much so, that, in the words of Prof. Indubhushan Banerjee, it "forged its own weapon, hedged itself behind newer forms and customs, in short, developed individuality of its own."[52]

And this is what Guru Arjun Dev, the holy compiler of its sacred scripture, Guru Granth Sahib, has himself stated in unambiguous terms as long back as in 1604 A.D. :

" I observe neither fasting (like a Hindu),
    nor the month of austerity (like a Muslim).
    For I serve God alone,
    Who saves all at the last.
    Gosain of the Hindus and Allah of the Muslims are one to me.

I have broken free from Hindus as from Muslims.
Neither I go to Mecca to perform Hajj (like Muslims),
nor I perform worship at pilgrim places of Hindus.
I serve only the sole Lord (i.e., God) and no other.
I neither perform the Hindu worship,
nor say the Muslim prayer.
I bow to the One Formless Lord in my heart.
We are neither Hindus nor Musalmans,
Our body and soul belong to the One Supreme Being,
Who alone is both Ram and Allah for us."[53]

A contemporary historian, Mobid Zulfiqar Ardistani (popularly known as Shaikh Mohsin Fani), who happened to stay with his son and successor, Guru Hargobind, at Kiratpur Sahib, and who had been the first non-Sikh writer to record an account of the Sikhs and Sikhism of those days, and that too based on first-hand information, has recorded his statement in his famous work on comparative study of religions, entitled *Dabistan-i-Mazahib*, compiled in 1654 A.D. Opening his chapter on the subject, Mohsin Fani observes : "the Nanak Panthis who are known as the Sikhs of the Gurus, have no faith in idols and temples of idols."[54] Proceeding further, he states "They do not read the *mantras* of the Hindus. They do not venerate their temples or idols, nor do they esteem their *avtars*. They have no regard for the Sanskrit language, which, according to the Hindus, is the speech of the angels."[55] Indicating Guru Nanak's own attitude towards *avtars* and divinities, he tells that Guru Nanak did not believe in divinities and incarnations. "Just as he praised the Mohammadans, so has he praised the incarnations and the gods and goddesses of the Hindus. But, he considered them all to be the created (*makhluq*) and not the Creator (*khaliq*). He denied the doctrines of *Halool* (i.e. direct descent from or incarnation of God), and *Ittihad* (i.e., direct union of the All-pervading God with any particular body)."[56]

Bhai Gurdas, the amanuensis who wrote the Holy Granth at the dictation of Guru Arjun, was himself a great scholar and writer, and his ballads and couplets are regarded as the 'key' to the understanding of the Sikh scriptures, tenets, practices, etc., has categorically stated : The Guru's *Panth* is distinct. And cannot be mixed with others.[57]

Basing his conclusion on numerous references and statements contained therein, Owen Cole has, therefore, observed, "Hinduism at all levels is rejected and replaced by the practices which have come to be the essential part of Sikh ceremonial use of the Adi Granth and celebration of the anniversaries of the Gurus (*gurpurbs*)."[58]

Qazi Nur Muhammad who came to India from Baluchistan in the invader's train to record the events of the seventh (dt. 1764) invasion of Ahmad Shah Abdali, and who completed his "invaluable"[59] *Jang Namah* in 1765, has also expressed similar views which are based upon his personal observations and close contacts. Speaking of the religion of the Sikhs against whom the said expedition had been organised, Nur Muhammad tells us that religiously they were absolutely separate from Hindus :

"The Sikhs are the disciples of the Guru, and that august Guru lived at Chak

(Amritsar). The ways and manners of these people received their impetus from Nanak who showed those Sikhs a separate path (i.e., taught them a distinct religion). He was succeeded by Gobind Singh from whom they received the title of 'Singh.' They are not from amongst the Hindus, and have a separate religion of their own."[60]

J.D. Cunningham (1812-1851), who happened to be the first-ever Westerner to write and publish in 1849 the first full-fledged history of Sikhism after fighting fierce and decisive battles with its followers, therefore, observed in 1849 : "The last apostle of the Sikhs did not live to see his own ends accomplished, but he effectually roused the dormant energies of a vanquished people, and filled them with a lofty, although fitful, longing for social freedom and national ascendancy, the proper adjuncts of that purity of worship which had been preached by Nanak. Gobind saw what was yet vital, and he relumed it with Promethean fire." The result of the miracle that the Tenth Master wrought, tells Cunningham, is that, "A living spirit possesses the whole Sikh people, and the impress of (Guru) Gobind (Singh) has not only elevated and altered the constitution of their minds, but has also operated materially and given amplitude to their physical frames. The features and external form of a whole people have been modified, and a Sikh Chief is not more distinguishable by his stately person and free and manly bearing than a minister of his faith is by a lofty thoughtfulness of look which marks the fervours of his soul, and his persuasion of the near presence of the Divinity." Asserting that the people marked by such high spirits and changed features belonged to a distinct faith, altogether different even from that of their other countrymen, Cunningham added : "Notwithstanding these changes, it has been usual to regard the Sikhs as essentially Hindus, and they doubtless are so in language and everyday customs, for Gobind (Singh) did not fetter his disciples with political systems or codes of municipal laws; yet in religious faith and worldly aspirations they are wholly different from other Indians, and they are bound together by a community of inward sentiment and outward object unknown elsewhere. But the misapprehension need not surprise the public nor condemn our scholars, when it is remembered that the learned Greeks and Romans misunderstood the spirit of those humble men who obtained a new life by baptism. Tacitus and Suetonius regarded the early Christians as a mere Jewish sect, they failed to perceive the fundamental difference and to appreciate the latent energy and real excellence of that doctrine which has added dignity and purity to the modern civilization."[61] Sir Charles Elliot acclaimed it, therefore, as "a religion of special interest (to mankind), since it has created not only a political society, but also customs so distinctive that those who profess it, rank in common esteem as a separate race.'[62] Guru Gobind Singh's "ordinances", he added, "were successful in creating a nation."[63]

Recognizing and acclaiming this amazing fact of history, the Sage-Scholar of Pondicherry, Sir Aurobindo, has similarly observed : "A more striking instance was the founding of the Sikh religion, its long line of Gurus and the novel direction and form given to it by Guru Gobind Singh in the democratic institution of Khalsa."[64] Explaining it earlier, he has stated : "The Sikh Khalsa was an astonishingly original and novel creation, and its face was turned not to the past but to the future."[65] Nirmal Kumar Jain has likewise asserted that those who consider this religion as an off-shoot of Islam "are as mistaken as those who think Sikhism to be an off-shoot of Hinduism. Like every original religion, it is born of a direct revelation. It is not based on any scripture. As it does not derive from any established creed, it does not fight any preceding religion."[66] In the same vein, maintains Ishwari Prasad that "Guru Nanak declared that there was no Hindu or Mussalman. He set aside the Vedas and the Quran, and asked his followers to repeat the name of God."[67] Hence, said Dorothy Field, "Pure Sikhism is far above dependence on Hindu ritual. A reading of the Granth strongly suggests that Sikhism should be regarded as a new and separate world religion, rather than a reformed sect of the Hindus.[68]

It is similarly not a sect or a form of Muhammadanism. It is neither a mixture of both nor a compilation of good points selected from the Hindu and Muslim faiths. It has not been formed, as alleged above, by combining some rational and acceptable rituals, beliefs and dogmas of the Hindus and Muslims. "The teachings of Guru Nanak have," says Geoffrey Parrinder, the eminent author of the *World Religions*, "commonly been represented as a syncretic blend of Hindu tradition and Muslim belief. This is a gross simplification, and when expressed in terms of a mixture of Hinduism and Islam, it must be totally rejected. The teachings of Guru Nanak do indeed represent a synthesis, but the elements which constitute the synthesis can never be defined, however loosely, as Hinduism and Islam."[69] Thus, Sikhism can, in no way, be termed as an eclectic religion, composed of selections made from various systems, doctrines, sources, etc.

The order of the Khalsa "from its very birth has claimed the status of a new Way of Life, the Third *Panth*, a separate community, and distinct people from the two Ways of Life, already known and largely practised by the peoples of East and West and the inhabitants of India : the Way of the Aryans, represented by Hinduism and its heterodox forms, Buddhism and Jainism; and the Semitic Way of Life, represented primarily by the Christians and the Mussulmans."[70] "That such was the unambiguous claim made for his new order of the Khalsa by the Guru (Gobind Singh) himself, cannot be in doubt, as the Guru's own assertions on this point amply support the testimony of the contemporary non-Sikh historians and writers."[71]

This is also quite clear from the proclamation he made in the great gathering of the Sikhs at Anandpur Sahib soon after initiating the first five members of the Order of the Khalsa, knighting them as Singhs and calling them his Beloved Ones, on the historic Vaisakhi day of the 30th March, 1699. "According to the Persian historian Ghulam Muhi-ud-Din, the newswriter of the period, sent to the Emperor (Aurangzeb) a copy of the Guru's address (which) is dated the first of Vaisakh Samvat 1756 (A.D. 1699), and is as follows"[72] :

> "I wish you all to embrace one creed and follow one path, rising above all
> differences of the religions as now practised. Let the four Hindu castes, who
> have different rules laid down for them in the Shastras, abandon them
> altogether, and adopting the way of mutual help and co-operation, mix freely

with one another. Let no one deem himself superior to another. Do not follow
the old scriptures. Let none pay heed to the Ganga and other places of
pilgrimage which are considered to be holy in the Hindu religion, or worship
the Hindu deities such as Rama, Krishna, Brahma and Durga; but all should
cherish faith in the teachings of Guru Nanak and his successors. Let men of the
four castes receive my baptism (of the Double-edged Sword). Eat of the same
vessel, and feel no aloofness from or contempt for one another."[73]

The newswriter of the Mughal Court who was present there on the occasion, when
forwarding this proclamation to his master, submitted his own report : "When the Guru
had thus addressed the crowd, several Brahmins and Khatris stood up, and said that they
accepted the religion of Guru Nanak and of the other Gurus. Others, on the contrary, said
that they would never accept any religion which was opposed to the teachings of the
Vedas and the Shastras, and that they would not renounce at the bidding of a boy, the
ancient faith which had descended to them from their ancestors. Thus, though several
refused to accept the Guru's religion, about twenty thousand men stood up and promised
to obey him, as they had the fullest faith in his divine mission."[74] About eighty thousand
men, say Ahmad Shah Batalia and Bute Shah, received the Baptism of the Double-edged
Sword and joined the Order of the Khalsa during the first few days.[75] Their names were
changed, and "they were given one family name 'Singh' for thenceforth their father was
Gobind Singh (so renamed after his own baptism), their mother Sahib Devan, and their
place of birth Anandpur. The baptism symbolised a rebirth, by which the initiated
renounced their previous occupations (*krit nash*) for that of working for God; severed
their family ties (*kul nash*) to become the family of Gobind; rejected their earlier creeds
(*dharma nash*) for the creed of the Khalsa; gave up all rituals (*karam nash*) save that
sanctioned by the Sikh faith; and stopped beliving in superstition (*bharam nash*) for
belief in One God. Five emblems were prescribed for the Khalsa. They were to wear
their hair and beard unshorn (*kesh*); they were to carry a comb (*kangha*) in the hair to
keep it tidy; they were always to wear a knee-length pair of breeches (*kach*), worn by
soldiers of the times; they were to carry a steel bangle (*kara*) on their right wrist; and
they were to be ever armed with a sabre (*kirpan*). In addition to these five emblems, the
converts were to observe four rules of conduct (*rahit*) : not to cut any hair on any part of
their body; not to smoke or chew tobacco, or consume alcoholic drinks; not to eat an
animal which had been slaughtered by being bled to death, as was customary with the
Muslims, but eat only *jhatka* meat, where the animal had been despatched with one blow,
and not to molest the person of Muslim women. At the end of oathtaking, the Guru
hailed the converts with a new form of greeting :

Waheguru ji ka Khalsa

   Waheguru ji ki Fateh

"Hail the Khalsa who belongs to Lord God !

   Hail the Lord God to Whom belongs the victory !"[76]

The very first ordinance issued by the Founder of the Khalsa to the Sikh
congregations throughout the subcontinent, Kabul and Ghazni confirms the above,[77] and

his definition of the Khalsa corroborates all that further as under in his own words :

"He whose mind dwells, night and day,

On the Ever-effulgent Light,

And never swerves from the thought of one God;

He who is full of love for God and faith in Him,

And believes not, even mistakenly,

In fasting and worship of the graves of Muslims

Or sepulchres of Hindus;

He who recognises the one God and not another,

And does not believe in pilgrimages,

Ceremonial acts of mercy

And charity, penances and austerities;

And he whose heart is illumined within

By the Light of the Perfect One,

He is to be recognised then

As a pure member of the Order of the Khalsa."[78]

All that ushered in a complete break with the past of all those who joined the Order of the Khalsa. It also marked "the culmination which had crowned Guru Nanak's revelation."[79] It also pronounced the complete independence and distinctiveness of the Sikh religion. "That such has been the stout belief, and the basic impulse of the Sikhs and their history can be readily ascertained by any dispassionate person who would take pains to enquire with an open mind."[80] He or she would surely come to a similar conclusion.

Further authentication to this stance has been duly provided by John Clark Archer, who, after conducting a critical and comparative study of the Aryan and Semitic religions and recognising the separate entity and identity of Sikhism, has maintained that, "Indeed Sikhism in itself reveals something of what in the last analysis religion is ...... " It is "an independent and conspicuous order of its own, with a character worthy of comparison with that of Hinduism and Islam, and with Christianity in particular ...... The five centuries of Sikh history provide many lessons in human thought and action which are of more than passing value ...... Sikhs may stand, therefore, as symbols and examples of all who search for God and Truth ...... They preserve among themselves a hardy tradition of religious and political activity, and enjoy among Hindus, Moslems, Christians and other peoples, an extraordinary prestige."[81] The dispassionate enquirer would also find like an American convert, Ralph Singh, that the followers of this distinct faith "have their own Prophets who brought a new divine revelation to earth which is enshrined in their own sacred scripture, Guru Granth Sahib, regarded as the living Word of God."[82] But, a biased enquirer, like Hew McLeod, who has, according to Justice Gurdev Singh "attacked most of the Sikh traditions, institutions and beliefs, questioned their validity and striven to create doubts about others,"[83] would, on the other hand, maintain on flimsy props and erroneous conclusions that "Sikhism does not deserve much consideration as it is only a rehash of a minor effete Hindu creed" and that Guru Nanak was not the founder of this religion "as he did not originate a new school of thought or set of teachings." McLeod has even gone to the extent of choosing not to accept the aforesaid account of the birth of the Khalsa and the five emblems and rules of conduct prescribed for it by Guru Gobind Singh himself on the Vaisakhi of 1699, "not because he finds any evidence to falsify it, but by simply refusing to believe it," saying, "Our knowledge of this (18th) century is still limited. Traditions abound, but so too do compulsive reasons for scepticism. What we do know, however, indicates that traditions relating to the period of Guru Gobind Singh must be, in some considerable measure, set aside. The slate must be wiped clean and must not be reinscribed until we have ascertained just what did take place during the eighteenth century."[84]

VI

But the history and tradition of a religion cannot, and should not be "set aside," "discarded" or "wiped clean" on the mere suspicions or unjustified scepticism of an ex-employee of a Christian Mission. Such scepticism is unwarranted particularly in the case of a religion, viz. Sikhism, which was born just about five centuries back and which has survived so gloriously through this eventful period of the modern world in full gaze of history. More so, when it has been duly recognised not only as an original and distinct, but also as an independent and autonomous higher religion of the world.

Besides, as already stated, this is a prophetic religion. It is born of a direct and definitive revelation like all other great and 'higher religions' of the world, "Instead of drawing authority and inspiration from any revealed scripture, such as the Hindu *Puranas* and *Smritis*, Guru Nanak depended on his own mystical experience."[85] The revelation did not also come to him as an 'external inspiration' (called *wahi zahir*) which "was used for the production of Quran" during whose process "the mind of Muhammad was passive and the message, an external one, was brought to him by Gabriel."[86] On the other hand, "It seems certain," says Duncan Greenlees, "that his (Guru Nanak's) views welled up from the deeps of inspiration in his own heart and owed little or nothing to what he received from others, either through books or through their words."[87] Guru Nanak himself vouchsafed this fact and has himself recorded those experiences and revelations, received directly from God Himself, in his own *bani* or revealed word, preserved till today in its original and undefiled form, singling out his religion, thereby, "from, most other great theological systems as regards the authenticity of its dogmas."[88] He has defined this as *Khasam-ki-Bani* ("Word of the Lord") in one hymn, and *Eh Bani Mahan Purakh Ki*, ("This Word of the Supreme Being") in another.[89]

The spiritual and religious truths which Guru Nanak preached, had been revealed to him "through a direct encounter with God at some level of consciousness", and he preached what he had been told and taught by God Himself. He conveyed only those words to the world which God had wished him to give forth as His divine message, as stated by him in verses such as the following :

"As the Lord's Word descends to me
So I express it, Lalo !"[90]

"I have uttered only what You, O' Lord !

Have inspired me to utter."[91]

Guru Nanak has also mentioned in another hymn that he was an ordinary minstrel who was commissioned and blessed by God with His service. Describing his first audience with the Supreme Being, the Guru sang aloud thus :

"I was an idle bard,

God assigned to me a rewarding task,

And commanded me to sing His praises night and day.

He summoned me to His Eternal Mansion,

Bestowed on me the robe of holy laudation,

And feasted me on the holy Name ambrosial ......

The Supreme Being is attained, says Nanak,

By laudation of the holy Eternal."[92]

As is well-known to students of comparative religion, contents of revealed religion are conveyed to the people by the Supreme Being through His special messengers, either by calling them to His presence, as in the case of Moses, or by communicating His messages to them, as in the case of Prophet Muhammad. As regards Sikhism, God is stated to have been pleased to use direct ways to convey His Words, Laws and Commandments, to its founder,[93] as stated above by the first Sikh Prophet, Guru Nanak, himself in his own words.

His successors in the Apostolic Lineage have not only endorsed this fact, but have also recorded their own experiences and audiences, as under, in their respective writings, compiled in 1604 by the Fifth Master in Guru Granth Sahib, and preserved intact to this day :

I. BY COMMUNICATION :

1. As stated by Guru Amar Das, the Third Master :

"God is Sole and Supreme,

None is His equal.

I speak as and when He makes me speak,

My utterance is directed by Him."[94]

2. As confirmed by Guru Ram Das, the Fourth Master :

(i) "To Nanak the Truth was revealed by the Lord.

So he relates mysteries of the Divine Portal."[95]

(ii) "Know the utterance of the holy Preceptor to be pure and true. Disciples of the Master :

For, the Lord-Creator Himself makes him utter it."[96]

(iii) "The Lord has appointed me, the unsophisticated, to His task."[97]

3. As affirmed repeatedly by Guru Arjun Dev, the Fifth Master :

(i) "Inaccessible, unperceivable, my eternal Lord, Nanak speaks as Thou inspire him to speak."[98]

(ii) "By myself I do not know what to say;

I have stated all by His command."[99]

(iii) "This servant of the Lord while Conveying the Divine Word,
      Speaks as the Lord directs him."[100]
(iv) "What can I utter ? I know nothing to utter;
      As the Lord Wills, so He makes me utter."[101]

II. BY AUDIENCE :

    1. As stated by Guru Ram Das, the Fourth Master :
      "I, a minstrel of the Lord-God,
      Came to the Divine Portal,
      The Lord inside listened to my supplication,
      And called me into His Presence.
      Addressing me, He asked,
      'What brings you here, My Minstrel'
      I prayed, 'Confer on me, O, Gracious Lord;
      The boon of your ever-abiding Name Divine.'
      The Bountiful Lord granted my prayer,
      Conferred on me meditation on the Name
      And blessed me with a robe of honour."[102]
    2. As affirmed by Guru Arjun Dev, the Fifth Master :
      "As I have attained the sought-after Lord,
      Illumination and joy have filled me ......
      I have been fully blessed by the Perfect Lord
      Who has come, in His grace; to His servant."[103]
    3. "The Lord-God called me into His Mansion
      Wherein I consumed nectar (of Immortality)."[104]

Such important disclosures, solemn statements, persistent affirmations and firm conviction, in the existence and beneficence of God, prove beyond doubt that Sikhism is a revealed religion. It is so, because it has been directly revealed by God through a line of Ten Prophet-teachers, who, after receiving its contents directly from Him, presented it to mankind in word and deed. They reproduced it in exactly the same original form; and also recorded it in their sacred writings. It is so, because it still remains primary in its source, and pure in its contents. It is neither selective or elective in its nature; nor secondary in its source; nor adulterated in its content. Hence, says M. Mujeeb, "the revelation that came to Guru Nanak, must have been as direct and immediate, and as independent of history and social circumstances, as the religious literature of the Sikhs show it to be."[105]

That being so, Sikhism can in no way be called an admixture or juxta position of various doctrines gathered from this religion or that theological system by its Prophet-teachers who were genuine messengers of God. Its tenets and teachings have been borrowed neither from Hinduism nor from Islam, nor from any other such source, as has been alleged by those who have not been able to study or understand its essentials properly or dispassionately. It is true, in the words of R.C. Majumdar, that "his was the first and also the last successful attempt to bring together the Hindus and Muslims in a common fold of spiritual and social brotherhood."[106] The first words he uttered when called to take up the mission of his life after the aforesaid Audience with God were :

"Nah ko Hindu Nah Mussalman."

"There is no Hindu, there is no Mussalman."[107]

On the face of it, this cryptic phrase was "a simple announcement, and yet a significant one in the context of India of his day.[108] To a society torn by conflict,[109] he brought a vision of common humanity — a vision which transcended all barriers of creed and caste, race and country. He reminded men of their essential oneness. The terms, 'Hindu' and 'Mussalman', included Jainas, Buddhists, Jews, Christians and so on. Guru Nanak was asking men of all faiths and denominations to look beyond external divisions and distinctions to the fundamental unity of mankind. In proclaiming the unity which lay beyond particularisms, Guru Nanak was not overruling any existing religious designation or tradition. His intention was more radical : "he wanted to point men beyond their accepted condition to a new possibility — a human community with a true spirit of fellowship and justice, with that deep ethical and spiritual commitment which expresses itself in concern for fellowmen. Nor was he seeking a syncretistic union between Hinduism and Islam, or striving to achieve in his teachings a judicious mixture of elements from both to be acceptable to all. His equal attention to Hindu and Muslim identities and use of some of their religious vocabulary have led some to depict him as the reconciler of the two faiths, and to see Sikhism as 'a deliberate mingling of Hindu and Muslim practices. To do so will mean missing much of his individual genius and misinterpreting the historical development issuing from his revelation.'"[110] The beginnings of the Sikh faith, in fact, go back to this revelation which Guru Nanak brought to light around 1496 A.D., soon after his enlightenment and just before his departure for his preaching odysseys in India and abroad.

VII

Sikhism is, above all, a complete religion in all respects like all other original and revealed religions of the world.

1.   It is *Ahl-al-Maqam*,[111] having its own spiritual and political Capital, viz., the holy city of Amritsar (as Mecca is for Islam), with its world famous Harimandar (Golden Temple) and Akal Takht which are its focal point, and for its followers the highest seat of spiritual and temporal authority, besides being "the centre of a World religion, meeting ground of the various facets of the human-spirit, and a profound symbol of future confluence of the World cultures into a universal culture for mankind."[112]

2.   It is *Ahl-al-Kitab*,[113] possessing its own holy book, viz., Guru Granth Sahib, (as Quran is for Islam), which is not only the Guru Eternal of its adherents, but is also unique among the world's sacred scriptures. It has been acclaimed as "the only non-denominational scripture,"[114] the "scripture of universal religion" and "part of mankind's common spiritual treasure," which, according to Arnold Toynbee, "should be brought within the direct reach of as many people as

possible" and which also "deserves close study from the rest of the world."[115]

3.   It is *Ahl-al-Milla*[116] being a true religion revealed by Guru Nanak and having its own fellowship of faith and a cohesive community, called *sangat* and *Panth*. The Turkish and Persian connotations of the word will mean a 'nation', a 'people' and a 'state.'[117] Sikhs are a casteless democratic society, assuring equal status and respect for all. It is for this society that Guru Gobind Singh, while expressing his great love and respect for it, declared :

"Whatever is available in my house, my wealth,
      My body, my mind, even my head
      Are ever at the disposal of my people."[118]

Paying his tribute to their selfless services, contributions and achievements, he also stated without any reservation that :

"It is through their favour that
      I have won my battles,
      And have gifts been bestowed.
      It is through their favour that
      I have overcome my troubles
      And my stores are filled.
      It is through their favour that
      I have acquired knowledge
      And have smothered my enemies.
      It is also through their favour that
      I am exalted and have attained this position;
      Otherwise, there are millions of
      Humble persons like myself going about."[119]

After administering *Khande di Pahul*[120] to the First Five, knighting them as Singhs,[121] and proclaiming them as his *panj piare*,[122] the inaugurator of that 'self-abnegating, martial and casteless' Fellowship of Faith, Guru Gobind Singh, himself besought to be initiated by them in the same way as he had initiated them. Having been initiated and admitted as such to their brotherhood, called Khalsa,[123] he later announced that he had created the Khalsa in his own image under the direct command of God, the Timeless Being :

"The Khalsa is my alter ego, my own image,
      The Khalsa is my embodiment.
      In it I have my being.
      The Khalsa is my beloved ideal."[124]

Hence, there was to be no difference between him, the Guru and the Khalsa, as created and initiated by him in his own image. All this is unheard of in the annals of the religious and spiritual history of the world.

4.   It is *Ahl-i-Kalam*,[125] having firm faith in the doctrine of the *Shabad*[126] the holy Word, and the *Shabad-Guru*, i.e., the Word is Guru and Guide.[127]

"God permeates the celestial music of the Word."

"The Word is the essence of all meditation and discipline."[128]

"God's Name is cherished in One's heart by means of the Word.

The supreme state, realization and liberation is attained by means of the Word."[129]

"The Word alone can ferry us across the Ocean of Existence."[130]

"The holy Word is the true Preceptor,

The Guide, the Mystery profound and inscrutable.

And it is the Word, the absence of which

Results in spiritual confusion."[131]

5.   It is *Ahl-al-Zaban*, having its own language, viz., Panjabi (as Arabic is for Islam), with its own specific script called Gurmukhi, in which its scripture, annals and chronicles, etc., stand recorded right from the beginning.

6.   It is *Ahl-al-Nishan*, having its own distinct flag or banner, called *Kesri Nishan Sahib*, with *Khanda* (the Khalsa emblem) inscribed and or installed thereon (as the *parcham* is for Islam). It keeps on waving over all Sikh temples, called gurdwaras.

7.   It is *Ahl-al-Shahad,*[132] cherishing a long and unique line of great martyrdoms, like those of its two prophets (viz. the Fifth, Guru Arjun Dev and the Ninth, Guru Tegh Bahadur), the Sahibzadas (Babas Ajit Singh, Jhujar Singh, Zorawar Singh and Fateh Singh) and their followers (such as Bhai Mati Das and Bhai Mani Singh).

8.   It is *Ahl-al-Shamshir*, possessing the ceremonial sword called *kirpan*, as a symbol of power, sovereignty and weapon of defence and justifiable offence in time of need. This specific weapon is a significant part of the required uniform of a member of the Khalsa Brotherhood, being one of the Five Ks or symbols of the Sikh faith, obligatory for him to always keep on his body. "Since a member of the Khalsa Brotherhood is pledged not to accept any alien restrictions on his civic freedom, he is enjoined to insist on and struggle for his unrestricted right to wear and possess arms of offence and defence."[133] According to a quotation attributed to Guru Gobind Singh :

"The political power and the State rest on armaments.

And without political sovereignty,

the good way of life cannot securely prevail in society."[134]

As he created the Khalsa "to establish the ever-persisting community of saint-soldiers," who could assist in the fulfilment of Guru Nanak's revelation and mission, it was considered essential to equip them with an "instrument of offence and defence and as an emblem of power and dignity which India had lost and which Guru Gobind Singh wanted to restore."[135]

At the same time, he approved and allowed recourse to the sword as 'the last resort of a reasonable man for settling conflicts when all other means have failed in due course. In his letter to Emperor Aurangzeb, he, therefore, made it quite clear that,

"When an affair is past every other remedy,

It is just and righteous to draw the sword."[136]

It is obvious that the creator of the Khalsa created this new metaphor of the sword "to give a new orientation to the minds of men given to passivity."[137]

9.   It is *Ahl-al-Sunnah*[138] as well, having its own usages, customs and a distinctive code of conduct recorded in its scripture, compositions of Bhai Gurdas and Bhai Nand Lal, various Rahitnamas[139] and Rahit-Maryada.[140]

Describing the Sikh way of life, these works cover not only the spiritual discipline and moral code, but also the social behaviour of the community whose members "are required to observe a distinctive code of conduct, one which specifies normative behaviour, outward appearance, and social obligation."[141]

VIII

Sikhism is, thus, a complete and perfect religion, not only because of its having such prominent features, elements and essentials of a 'higher-religion', but also because it was established, as its Founder stated, to carry out a specific command of the Lord-God Who Himself is, as proclaimed by him in the following couplet, All perfection or perfection-incarnate :

"All that the Perfect One has made is perfect.

There is nothing lacking or excessive in its making."[142]

It is dynamic, stable and eternal, too, as, according to the holy compiler of its sacred scripture,

"The holy Preceptor has laid the immutable foundation of the faith

That never and in no way shall shake."[143]

Rather, it becomes firmer and firmer with the passage of each day, as stated below :

"The eternal foundation laid by Guru Nanak, Is ever-ascendant."[144]

According to the following assertion of the contemporary bards, Rai Balwand and Satta,

"Guru Nanak founded the True Dominion of God.

He raised the citadel of Truth on firm foundations."[145]

On these foundations was raised a glorious spiritual and temporal edifice by Guru Gobind Singh who imparted his "stern Olympian air" to the followers of his, who are recognizable till today by their distinctive appearance and are distinguished by their everpresent high spirits, particularly in a period of adversity and crisis. That is so because "His impress not only elevated and altered the constitution of their minds, but contrary to the experience of ethnological experts, it also operated materially and gave amplitude to their physical frames. They came to be regarded as models of physical beauty and stateliness of manner. A tremendous change was affected in the whole tone of their national character. Even those people who had been considered as dregs of humanity were changed, as if by magic, into something rich and strange. The sweepers, barbers and confectioners, who had never so much as touched the sword, and whose whole generation had lived as grovelling slaves of the so-called higher classes, became, under the stimulating leadership of Guru Gobind Singh, doughty warriors who conquered fear, and who were ready to rush into the jaws of death at the bidding of their Guru."[146]

IX

This revealed, distinct and complete religion of such self-sacrificing saint-soldiers is a universal world faith with an all-embracing appeal and elevating message for all mankind. "It is the faith of the New Age," says Rev. Bradshaw, "It is the *summum bonum*[147] for the modern man. It completely supplants and fulfils all the former dispensations of older religions. The other religions contain Truth, but Sikhism contains the fullness of Truth. The older faiths were good in their day, but that day is now past; and we are living in the dispensation of Guru Nanak. Just as we appreciate the discovery of modern living and do not want to exchange our modern jet airlines, automobiles and electricity for the horse-drawn carriages and candles of the past, we do not want to exchange the New Age Faith of Guru Nanak for any of the old age systems and their antiquated philosophies. The Sikh faith is the universal religion for the present space age. The Sikh religion is truly the answer to the problems of the modern man."[148] And it "is the only living faith," according to Bittencourt, "that gives the healing outlook on life."[149]

As regards its potential and prospects in the religious domain of the world, it was Macauliffe, who, while addressing the Quest Society in 1910 at London, stated : "The Sikh religion (as compared to other religions) presents no mysteries, and embraces an ethical system such as has never been excelled, if indeed it has ever been equalled. It offers fewer points of attack than any other theological system, and if patronized and cherished, as its religious and political importance deserves, by a powerful government, it might become one of the first religions on this planet."[150]

Dorothy Field observed as follows in 1914, "Sikhism is capable of a distinct position as a world religion, so long as the Sikhs maintain their distinctiveness. The religion is also one which should appeal to the Occidental mind. It is essentially a practical religion. If judged from the pragmatical standpoint, which is a favourable point of view in some quarters, it would rank almost first in the world. Of no other religion can it be said that it had made a nation in so short a time. The religion of the Sikhs is one of the most interesting at present existing in India, possibly indeed in the whole world. That it should have transformed the outcaste Indian — a notoriously indolent and unstable person — into a fine and loyal warrior is little short of a miracle." [151] It was Arnold Toynbee again who prophesied, therefore, as recently as in 1960 : "Mankind's religious future may be obscure; yet one thing can be foreseen. The living higher religions are going to influence each other more than ever before in the days of increasing communication between all parts of the world and all branches of the human race. In this coming religious debate, the Sikh religion, and its scripture, the Adi Granth, will have something of special value to say to the rest of the world."[152]

This will indeed be so, because it will have the opportunity of sharing the sort of

experience which the Nobel-laureate Pearl S. Buck had gained when she observed, after
going through the 4-volume English translation (by Dr Gopal Singh) of Guru Granth
Sahib : "I have studied the scriptures of other great religions, but I do not find elsewhere
the same power of appeal to the heart and mind as I find here in these volumes. They are
compact in spite of their length, and are a revelation of the vast reach of the human heart,
varying from the most noble concept of God to the recognition and indeed the insistence
upon the practical needs of the human body. There is something strangely modern about
these scriptures and this puzzled me, until I learned that they are in fact comparatively
modern, compiled as late as the 15th century, when explorers were beginning to discover
that the globe, upon which we all live, is a single entity divided only by arbitrary lines of
our own making. Perhaps this sense of unity is the source of power I find in these
volumes. They speak to persons of any religion or of none. They speak for the human
heart and the searching mind."[153] And they do speak in verses such as these which,
indeed, indicate that unique concept of unity and universality :

> "The One Lord is our Father,
> We all are His children."[154]

> "None is our enemy,
> Nor is anyone a stranger to us.
> We are in accord with all..
> The one God is pervasive in all creation
> At the sight of which Nanak is in bloom of Joy."[155]

These and many other hymns contained in Guru Granth Sahib, clearly visualize
and preach a religion which knows no ethnical, racial or regional limitations; recognises
no distinction on account of birth, sex, caste, creed or colour, embodies universal respect
and concern for all, and regards all as equals. This is testified by its first and last
prophets, Guru Nanak Dev and Guru Gobind Singh, in the following words :

> "There is Light among all
> And that Light is God's Own.
> Which pervades and illuminates everyone."[156]

> "Some one by shaving his head
> Becomes a *sanyasi*, another a *yogi*,
> And yet another passes for a monk or ascetic.
> Some call themselves Hindus,
> Other claim to be Muslims;
> Among these some are *Shias* and some are *Sunnis*.
> Recognise all as belonging to the one race of humanity
> God as Creator (for the Hindus) and God as Good (for the Muslims)
> God as Sustainer and God as Merciful
> Is all one and the same God.
> Recognise not another even in error or in doubt.
> Worship that One alone,
> As He is the Supreme Lord of us all.

It is only His form, His Light

That is diffused in one and all."[157]

Hence, the followers of this universal faith conclude their daily prayer to that One
God, in the name of their founder, Guru Nanak Dev, with the following couplets :

" May Your holy Name,

be ever in ascendance.

May peace and prosperity

come to all !!

In Your Will

By Your Grace !!"[158]

They, thereby, ask for God's blessings in favour not only of their own community,
but also of the entire humanity, for the maximum good of each and every creature in the
world.

X

Thus, apart from being such a distinct monotheistic faith, Sikhism is also a social
and fraternal religion, standing equally for the common Fatherhood of God and universal
Brotherhood of Man, guaranteeing equal status to all human beings and asserting that
normal family life, lived with virtuous conduct and firm faith in God, surely leads to the
path of salvation.

"Contemplation of the True Lord brings illumination,

Which enables one to remain unattached in the midst of evil.

Such is the greatness of the True Preceptor

(that through His grace and guidance)

One can attain fullness

while living with one's wife and children."[159]

Hence, it is the religion of our time, modern in outlook, scientific in analysis,
rational in approach and practical in adaptability; suited to the needs, aspirations and
conditions of the modern man and his social set-up. It is a religion which is concerned
with the creation of a just social order, and is committed to social equality and peaceful
co-existence, as proclaimed by its Fifth prophet, Guru Arjun Dev, in the following verse :

"The Gracious Lord has now promulgated His ordinance;

None shall dominate over others or cause pain;

All shall abide in peace and happiness.

As the governance shall be gentle and affectionate."[160]

Sikhism enjoins on its followers social responsibility involving both social service
and social action :

"He who does dedicated service in the world

gets a place at His Portal."[161]

"They alone understand the right way

Who eat the bread of their labour,

And share it with others."[162]

The above directives of Guru Nanak, (couched in his own pithy aphorisms : *Nam Japo, Kirt Karo, Vand Chhako*) are indeed "the foundation of a spiritually oriented, dynamic social life." [163] His frequent exhortations to follow the under-mentioned six-sided discipline cultivates and follows the virtues associated with it, and leads further to the enrichment and fulfilment of such an ideal life :

  Naam : Devotion to the Divine Name.
  Daan : Giving to others, particularly to the needy.
  Isnan : Purity of mind, body and environment.[164]
  Seva : Service of mankind.[165]
  Simran : Contemplation and remembrance of God.[166]
  Satsang : Fellowship or company of true believers : Association with holy men.[167]

XI

Sikhism is thus based on humanistic and universal values of the purest form. Human freedom and dignity, self-realization and self-confidence, service and sacrifice have been the essential elements of its ethos.

The history and heritage of this religion, whether in its principles, doctrines and sacred pronouncements, or in the practical lives of its founders and followers, "has been one of exhortation to liberation from all kinds of degrading bondage, mental, spiritual and social. Long before the modern idea of social freedom was evolved in the West, Sikhism had brought to mankind the message of freedom. In its social aspects, it was a movement of freedom from feudalism and caste tyranny. While socially, it brought to man liberation from feudalism and caste tyranny, spiritually it brought to man freedom from suppression and those false beliefs which enslaved man to a selfish or ignorant priest-craft, whether the priest was called Brahmin, Yogi or Mullah." The founder of the holiest Sikh shrine and the compiler of the Sikh Scripture, Guru Arjun Dev, has himself recorded the impact of this unique movement in the following verse :

  "The eggshell of doubt has shattered,
    And the mind is illumined;
  The Master has freed us from bondage
    By cutting off fetters from our feet."[168]

This is the verse which Macauliffe, while recognizing its lasting significance, reproduced on the title-page of each of the six volumes of his *magnum opus*, *The Sikh Religion*, published in 1909 by the Oxford University. This is also the verse on the basis of which Banerjee stated, seventy years later : "The fetters of ritualistic religion were cut off and the captives were ...... freed; and the foundations of the Spiritual Empire were laid. On these foundations was raised an imposing structure of Temporal Empire, blessed by Guru Gobind Singh's never-to-be forgotton utterance : RAJ KAREGA KHALSA."

NOTES AND REFERENCES

1. Its operative clause, in the original, reads as follows : *"Nanak prastan ra har ja kih bayaband ba-qatal rasanand."* Akhbar-i-Darbar-i-Mualla (cf. *A Brief Account of the Sikh People*, by Prof. Dr Ganda Singh, Amritsar, 1956, reprint, Delhi, 1971, p. 29).

2. Gupta, Prof. Dr Hari Ram, *History of the Sikhs*, Vol. II, 3rd revised edition, New Delhi-1978, p. 39. See also Browne, James, *History of the Origin and Progress of the Sikhs* (India Tracts), London-1788, Vol. II, p. 13; M'Gregor, W.L., *The History of the Sikhs*, London-1846, Vol. I, pp. 113-114.

3. Latif, Syed Mohammad, *A History of the Punjab from the Remote Antiquity to the Present Times*, Calcutta-1891, p. 213.

4. Miskin, Tahmas Khan, Tazkirah-Tahmas Miskin, also called Tahmas Namah, MS. No. 1918 of British Museum, London, dated 1779-80 A.D., Forster George, *A Journey from Bengal to England*, London - 1798, Vol. I, p. 319.

5. That fearful bloody carnage which occurred on 5th February, 1762 at Kup, near Malerkotla, is known as *Dooja Wadda Ghalughara*, i.e., the Second great Holocaust.

6. Nur-ud-Din, Husain Khan, Sayyed, *Tarikh-e-Najib-ud-Daulah*, also called *Ahwal-i-Najib-ud-Daulah*, MS. No. 24410 of B.M., London, f. 57a (cf. English Translation by Sir Jadu Sarkar in the Islamic Culture, 1933-34); Khushwaqt Rai, Tawarikh-i-Sikhan, also called *Kitab-i-Tawarikh-i-Punjab*, MS. No. Or. 187 of B.M., London, dated 1811, f. 95.

7. Trumpp, Dr Ernest; *The Adi Granth*, London-1877, p. vi.

8. Bhattacharya, Joginder Nath, *Hindu Castes and Sects*, Calcutta-1896, p. 511; reprint-1968, p. 404.

9. Macauliffe, M.A., *The Sikh Religion under Banda and its Present Condition* in the *Calcutta Review*, Calcutta-1881, Vol. CXLV, p. 168; *The Sikh Religion and its Advantages to the State*, Simla-1906, p. 28; *How the Sikhs became a Militant Race* ? Simla- 1906, pp. 26-27.

10. Macauliffe, M.A., *The Sikh Religion, Its Gurus, Sacred Writings and Authors*, Oxford-1909, Vol. I, p. Lvii.

11. Narang, Dr Sir Gokul Chand, *Transformation of Sikhism*, Lahore-1912; 2nd. ed. Lahore-1945, p. 350.

12. For details see *Muslim League Attack on Sikhs and Hindus in the Punjab* by Prof. Gurbachan Singh Talib, Amritsar-1950; *Divide and Quit* by Mr. Penderal Moon. London-1961; *The Partition of Punjab* by Dr Kirpal Singh, Patiala-1978.

13. Khushwant Singh, *The Sikhs*, London-1953, p. 7.

14. Narang, *Transformation of Sikhism*, op. cit., p. 350.

15. Kapur Singh's speech entitled, *Sikhs and Sikhism*, Vancouver, 7th October 1974, p. 26.

16. "Of the total number of persons martyred during the Independence Movement, 75% were Sikhs; of the number sent to gallows, 81% were Sikhs; and those exiled and deported to Andamans, a deadly and uninhabitated island in the Bay of Bengal in the Indian Ocean, 80% were the Sikhs." (cf. *Sikhism* by Prof. Dr Ujagar Singh, Washington-1988, p. 22).

17. Under 'Operation Blue Star', stated to be "the biggest and the most significant army action against its own countrymen ever taken in the world," and used as the "Code name for the Indian army's move into Punjab against the Sikhs" during the first week of June 1984. (Gurmit Singh, Dr, *History of Sikh Struggles*, Vol. III, p. 1). "On 5th June 1984, the Indian army began its attack on the complex at Amritsar which housed the two most sacred shrines of the Sikh Community, the Golden Temple and the Akal Takht ...... tanks were ordered in and the Akal Takht was virtually reduced to rubble." (Mark Tully & Satish Jacob, *Amritsar : Mrs. Gandhi's Last Battle*, Delhi-1985, p.i.). For some details see Report to the Nation : *Oppression in Punjab* by Citizens for Democracy, Bombay-1985.

18. *History of Sikh Struggles*, op. cit., Vol. III, pp. 28-29, 34- 39. For some details refer to the Reports to the Nation published under the auspices of the People's Union for Democratic Rights; People's Union For Civil Liberties (entitled *Who Are The Guilty* ?, New Delhi-1984) and the

Citizens For Democracy (entitled *Truth About Delhi Violence*, Delhi-1985); *Army Action in Punjab : Prelude and Aftermath*, New Delhi-1984 : Report of the Citizens' Commission : Delhi-31st Oct. to 4th Nov. 1984, New Delhi-1985.

19. Banerjee, Prof. Dr Anil Chandra, *Guru Nanak : The Teacher of Man*, Chandigarh-1979, p. 23.
20. Parrinder, Prof. Geoffrey, *World Religions from Ancient History to the Present*, New York-1983, p. 260.
21. *The Hindustan Times*, New Delhi-2nd June, 1957. See also Kapur Singh, *Sikh and Sikhism*, op. cit., p. 3.
22. Carpenter, J. Estlin, *Theism in Medieval India*, London-1921, p. 489.
23. Heiler, F., *The Gospel of Sadhu Sunder Singh*, London-1927, pp. 35-36.
24. Khushwant Singh, *The Sikhs Today*, New Delhi-1959; reprint, 1969, p. xiii.
25. Khushwant Singh, *A History of the Sikhs*, Princeton-1963, Vol. I, p. 17.
26. Bhattacharya, *Hindu Castes and Sects*, op. cit;, Ist. ed., pp. 497, 510; reprint, pp. 393, 403.
27. Time, New York, dated 12th November, 1989, p. 53.
28. Picott, Frederic, *Sikhism in the Dictionary of Islam* by Rev. T.P. Hughes, London-1885, p. 583 & 594.
29. Tara Chand, Dr, *Influence of Islam on Indian Culture*, Allahabad-1946, p. 169.
30. Rajagopalachari, Sri, Vaishnava reformers of India.
31. Williams, Monier, *Brahmanism and Hinduism*, London-19, p. 64.
32. Battany, G.T., *Encyclopaedia of World Religions*, London-19 ......, p. 246.
33. cf. Insha Ulla Khan, Maulvi, *Sikhon aur Mussalamanon Ke Ruhani Tualqat*, Lahore-1909.
34. cf. Muhammad Ali, Maulvi, *The Founder of Sikhism*, Lahore-1919.
35. cf. Nizami, Khawaja Hassan, *Sikh Qaum aur unke Bani ki nisbat Mussalamanon ki Muhabbat-amez Rai*, Batala-1919.
36. cf. Muhammad Yusuf, Sheikh, *Baba Nanak Ka Mazhab*, Qadian-1919.
37. Quadiani, Mirza Ghulam Ahmed, *Satya Bachan*, Batala 2nd. ed. 1902, pp. 4377-4504.
38. Trumpp, E., *The Adi Granth*, op. cit., ch. III, p. ci.
39. Narang, *Transformation of Sikhism*, op. cit., p. 379.
40. Gandhi, M.K., *Young India*, May-1924, p. 829. Ahmadabad.
41. Archer, Prof. Dr J.C., *The Sikhs, in Relation to Hindus, Moslems, Christians and Ahmadiyas : a Study in Comparative Religion*, Princeton-1946, p. 301.
42. Ibid., p. 302; Akbar, Dr Mohammad, *The Punjab Under the Mughals*, Lahore-1943; reprint, Delhi-1979, p. 187.
43. Kenneth, W.J., *Journal of Asian Studies*, transl. in *Singh Sabha Patrika*, Amritsar-January, 1974, pp. 92-94.
44. Chaudhuri, Nirad C., *The Autobiography of an Unknown Indian*, London-1951, pp. 492-3.
45. Smith, Marian W., *Synthesis and other Processes in Sikhism* in the *American Anthropologist*, Vol. 50, No. 3, Pt. I, July-September, 1948, pp. 457-62; Marenco, Ethne K, *The Transformation of Sikh Society*, New Delhi-1976, p. 24.
46. Greenlees, Duncan, *The Gospel of the Guru Granth Sahib*, Madras-1952, p. 216.
47. Bittencourt, Dr Edward A.de., in his 'Foreword' to the *Sikh Way of Life* by Ranbir Singh, New Delhi-1968, p. vi.
48. Macauliffe, M.A., *The Sikh Religion*, op. cit., Vol. I, p. Liv.
49. Ibid., Vol. I., Introduction, p.l.v. Lv.
50. Majumdar, Dr R.C., *The History and Culture of the Indian People*, Vol. VI, Bombay-1960; 2nd.-1967, p. 569.
51. Griffin, Sir Lepel, *Rajas of the Punjab*, Lahore-1879, p. 338.
52. Banerjee, Prof. Indubhushan, *Evolution of the Khalsa*, Calcutta-1936, Vol. I, p. 182.
53. Arjun Dev, Guru, Guru Granth Sahib, Amritsar-1604 A.D., Rag Bhairo, M.5, p. 1136.
54. Mohsin Fani, Shaikh, (Ardistani, Mobid Zalfiqar), Dabistan-i-Mazahib, dated 1654 A.D. - 1904, p. 223.

55. Ibid., p. 233.
56. Ibid., p. 223. See also Ganda Singh, Prof. Dr, *Nanak Panthis*, extracted, translated and edited with notes, Amritsar-1940, pp. 4, 5, 10, 11.; *Nanak Panthis or The Sikhs and Sikhism of the 17th Century*, in the *Journal of Indian History*, Vol. XIX, pt. 2.
57. Gurdas, Bhai, *Varan*, composed around 1600 A.D., Var no. 3, pauri no. 5.
58. Cole, W. Owen, *Sikhism and Its Indian Context* (1469-1708), New Delhi-1984, p. 251.
59. "For the history of the Sikhs in particular, and a knowledge of the country and people in 1764", according to Sir Jadu Nath Sarkar in his 'Foreword' to the *Jang Namah*, (fn. no. 58).
60. Nur Muhammad, Qazi, *Jang Namah*, Gunjaba-1765, ch. XLI, pp. 156-159 edited and translated into English by Dr Ganda Singh, Amritsar-1939, pp. 158-59 (of the text), pp. 59-59 (of the English rendering).
61. Cunningham, Capt. J.D., *A History of the Sikhs from the Origin of the Nation to the Battles of Sutlej*, London-1849; reprint, Delhi-1985, pp. 75-76. See also Elphinstone, M., *History of India; Rise of the British Power in the East*, Vol. II, London-1887, pp. 561-564.
62. Elliot, Sir Charles, *Hinduism and Buddhism*, London-1921, Vol. II, p. 267; reprint-1954, p. 272.
63. See also Malcolm, Lt. Col., *Sketch of the Sikhs : A Singular Nation who inhabits the Provinces of the Punjab*, London-1812, pp. 129, p. 148; Burnes, Alexander, *Travels into Bukhara*, London-1834, Vol. p. 285, Vol. II, p. 39; Barth, A., *Religions of India*, Paris-1882; London-1906, pp. 242 & 249.
64. Aurobindo, Sri, *The Foundation of Indian Culture*, Pondicherry, 1959, pp. 150-151.
65. Aurobindo, Sri, *A Defence of Indian Culture, Religion and Spirituality*, published in *The Arya*, Vol. VI, No. I-1920.
66. Jain, Nirmal Kumar, *Sikh Religion and Philosophy*, New Delhi- 1979, p. 1.
67. Ishwari Prasad, Dr, *The Mughal Empire*, Allahabad-1974, p. 30.
68. Field, Dorothy, *The Religion of the Sikhs*, London-1914, p. pp. 34, 10.
69. Parrinder, Edward Geoffrey, *World Religions, from Ancient History to the Present*, 1983, p. 251.
70. See *Bachitar Natak* by Guru Gobind Singh, Anandpur Sahib-1696, cont. VI; *Chaubis Avtar*, Verses 2-27, 2488; etc.. (*Ramkali Var Patshahi Daswen ki*, dated 1700 A.D. (?), Stanza No. 16). See also *Panth Parkash* by Giani Gian Singh, Delhi-1880, ch. 85.
71. Kapur Singh, *Parasarprasna or The Baisakhi of Guru Gobind Singh* (An Exposition of Sikhism), Jalandhar-1959, pp. 8-9; 2nd. ed., *Parasarprasna*, Amritsar-1989, p. 4.
72. Macauliffe, M.A., *The Sikh Religion*, op. cit., Vol. V, p. 93.
73. Bute Shah alias Ghulam Muhay-ud-Din, *Tawarikh-i-Punjab*, MS. Ludhiana-1848, pp. 405-406; Macauliffe, M.A., *The Sikh Religion*, op. cit., Vol. V, pp. 93-94; Teja Singh, Prin. & Ganda Singh, Prof., *A Short History of the Sikhs*, Bombay-1950, pp. 68-69; Kapur Singh, *Parasarprasna*, op. cit., pp. 2-3.
74. Macauliffe, M.A., *The Sikh Religion*, op. cit., Vol. V, p. 94.
75. Batalia, Ahmad Shah, *Tawarikh-i-Hind*, MS. dated 1818; Bute Shah, *Tawarikh-i-Punjab*, op. cit., 406.
76. Khushwant Singh, *A History of the Sikhs*, Princeton-1963; 7th impr.-1987, Vol. I, pp. 83-84.
77. See Saina Pati, *Sri Guru Sobha*, Anandpur Sahib-1711, Chs. V & VII; Santokh Singh, Bhai, *Sri Gurpratap Suraj Granth*, Kaithal-1843, III. 21.
78. Gobind Singh, Guru, 33 Swaiyyei, Sw. no. 1. in the *Dasam Granth*, op. cit.
79. Harbans Singh, Prof., *The Heritage of the Sikhs*, New Delhi-1983; 2nd. ed., 1985, p. 95.
80. *Baisakhi of Guru Gobind Singh*, op. cit., p. 9.
81. Archer, *The Sikhs in Relation to Hindus, Muslims, Christians and Ahmadiyas*, op. cit., pp. 1, v, viii.
82. Ralph Singh, *Sikhism*, New York-1988 (c.), p. 1.
83. Gurdev Singh, Justice, *Perspectives on the Sikh Tradition*, Patiala-1986, pp. 5, 8-9, See McLeod, W.H., *Guru Nanak and the Sikh Religion*, Oxford 1968; *The Evolution of the Sikh Community*, Delhi-1975; *Early Sikh Tradition*, Oxford 1980. 22-23.
84. McLeod, W.H., *The Evolution of the Sikh Community*, op. cit., pp. 16-18; Gurdev Singh,

Perspectives on the Sikh Tradition, op. cit. pp. 22-23.

85. Banerjee, *Guru Nanak, The Teacher of Man*, op. cit. p. 44.

86. Hastings, James, *Encyclopaedia of Religion and Ethics*, New York-1914; latest ed. 1971, Vol. VII, p. 354.

87. Greenlees, *The Gospel of Guru Granth Sahib*, op. cit., p. 37.

88. Macauliffe, M.A., *The Sikh Religion*, op. cit. Vol. I, p. iii.

89. Guru Granth Sahib, op. cit., *Rag Tilang*, M.I., p. 722 and Rag Ramkali, M.I, p. 935.

90. Guru Granth Sahib, op. cit., *Rag Tilang*, M.I., p. 722.

91. Ibid., *Rag Wadhans*, M.I., p. 566.

92. Ibid., *Rag Majh*; M.I., p. 150. See also p. 148.

93. This has been duly mentioned by the earliest chroniclers of Sikh religion; such as by Bhai Gurdas (1551-1629) in his var no. 1 pauri no. 24; *Puratan Janamsakhi* (1634 c.), pp. 17-18; Sodhi Meharban (1581-1640) in his *Sachkhand Pothi* (dt. 1620 c.), pp. 88-89; Bhai Nand Lal (1633-1741) in his *Ganj Namah*, ch. I, verses 48-50.

94. Ibid., *Raga Sri*, M.3, p. 39.

95. Ibid., *Raga Gauri*, M. 4, p. 308.

96. Ibid., *Raga Gauri*, M. 4, p. 308.

97. Ibid., *Raga Asa*, M. 4, p. 449.

98. Ibid., *Raga Suhi*, M. 5, p. 743.

99. Ibid., *Raga Suhi*, M. 5, p. 763.

100. Ibid., *Raga Sorath*, M. 5, p. 629.

101. Ibid., *Raga Sarang*, M. 5, p. 1203.

102. Ibid., *Raga Sri*, M. 4, p. 91.

103. Ibid., *Raga Sarang*, M. 5, p. 1237.

104. Ibid., *Raga Wadhans*, M. 5, p. 562.

105. Mujeeb, Prof. M., *Guru Nanak's Religion, Islam and Sufism, in Guru Nanak : His Life, Times and Teachings*, ed. by Prin. Gurmukh Nihal Singh, New Delhi-1969, ch. VII, p. 116.

106. Surendra Nath Banerjee, as quoted in *The History and Culture of the Indian People*, Vol. IX (ii), Bombay-1977, p. 481, and Majumdar, Prof. R.C., Ibid., Vol. VI, Bombay-1960; 2nd. ed. 1967, p. 569.

107. For a detailed account see *Guru Nanak : The World-Teacher (Jagat Gurubaba)*, Chandigarh-1979, pp. 30-32; and *Teachings of Guru Nanak*, Chandigarh-1984, pp. 31-32 — both by Dr Harnam Singh Shan.

108. According to Dr Mohan Singh, "No teacher of the populace had uttered words of that import and significance, since the time of Upanishads. Those few words at one stroke felled the giant structures of caste, credal, sectional and religious differences." (cf. *Sri Guru Nanak Dev and Nation Building*, Tarn Taran-1934, p. 8.

109. Harbans Singh, Prof., *Berkeley, Lectures on Sikhism*, New Delhi-1983, pp. 9-10 : That terrible conflict grew from the fact that the "impact of Islam on north-western India in the 11th century had been through military conquest and sword, and this had created reactions in the proud and sensitive Hindu mind such as resulted in impassable barriers of hatred and prejudice between the two World-culture currents, and their mutual contacts have, therefore, left irritating and unfortunate monuments of bigotry and misunderstanding, spiritual and historical, that still mark the Indian scene. The Sikh Prophets, the Nanaks, desired to level down these barriers with a view to discover and provide a common spiritual ground for the two, Hinduism and Islam, where Hinduism gets over its injured superiority and sense of exclusiveness, and Islam, its arrogance and self centricity born out of military superiority. The Nanak V declared : Let Muslims rediscover the truth that the true essence of religious practice is compassion and its goal, the purification of soul, and that political utilitarianism and expedience is not basic to Islam as such, and let the Hindus concede that Islam, thus understood, is as respectable and ceremoniously pure as the flowers, the silk, the deerskin and the butter-fat." (Guru Granth Sahib, op. cit. Rag Maru,

M. 5, p. 1084; *The Golden Temple : Amritsar*, a paper read by S. Kapur Singh at Guru Nanak Dev University, Amritsar, on 24 Oct. 1977, p. 2).

110. Harbans Singh, Prof., *Berkeley, Lectures on Sikhism*, New Delhi-1983, pp. 9-10.

111. *Ahl* in Arabic originally meaning those who occupy the same tent, thus family inmates. Therefore, *ahl-al-bait* means the household of the Prophet Muhammad, his descendents. But this word is often connected with other notions, meaning so much as sharing in a thing, belonging to it or owner of the same, etc. (see *The Encyclopaedia of Islam* ed. by M.Th. Houtsma & others, Leyden-1913, Vol. I, p. 183. *Maqam* means place or glorious station. (see Quran, ch. 17, V. 81).

112. *The Golden Temple : Amritsar*, op. cit., p. 3.

113. "*Ahl-al-kitab*, the people of the Book. Muhammad calls so the Jews and Christians, in distinction from the heathens, on account of their possessing divine books of revelation, (Tawrat = Torah; Zabur = Psalter; Indjil = Gospel)." See Ibid., p. 184, "According to T.P. Hughes, it is a term used in the Quran for Jews and Christians, as believers in a revealed religion." (See his *Dictionary of Islam*, London-1885, p. 12).

114. Khushwant Singh, *The Sikhs*, Varanasi-1984, p. 21.

115. Toynbee, *UNESCO's Selections from the Sacred Writings of the Sikhs*, op. cit., p. 9.

116. *Milla* in Arabic means religion, rite, "In, Kur'an the Prophet speaks of Abraham's *Milla*, by which he means the original revelation in its purity ...... with the article, *al-milla* means the true religion revealed by Muhammad and is occasionally used eliptically for *ahl-al-milla*, the followers of the Muhammadan religion." (See *Shorter Encyclopaedia of Islam*, ed. by H.A.R. Gibb & J.A. Kramers, Leiden-1953, p. 380). According to the *Kitab t-Tarifat*, "it is expressive of religion as it stands in relation to the Prophet, as distinguished from *Din*, which signifies religion as its stands in relation to God., from *Mazhab* which signifies religion with reference to learned doctors." (See *Dictionary of Islam*, op. cit., pp. 348-349).

117. See Glasse, Cyril, *The Concise Encyclopaedia of Islam*, Francisco-1989, p.269.

118. *Khalsa Mahima, Swaiyya* no. 3, p. 717.

119. Ibid., *Swaiyya* No.2, p. 716.

120. That is, Baptism of the Double-edged Sword.

121. That is, the lions, used as surname by all male followers of Sikhism.

122. That is, the Five Beloved Ones, Three out of them belonged earlier to the so-called low castes (viz. Muhkam Chand, washerman from Dwarka; Himmat; a cook from Jagannath; Sahib Chand, a barber from Bidar, the fourth (viz. Daya Ram, a Kshatriya or Khatri by caste, from Lahore), the fifth (viz. Dharam Das, a Jat from Delhi).

123. 'Khalsa' means the pure baptised and initiated Sikhs; Sikh brotherhood. The aim of Guru Gobind Singh in founding the Khalsa was to build up a nation of the purified Ones who would be free from the evils of religion and society. (Teja Singh & Ganda Singh, *A History of the Sikhs*, op. cit., p. 72).

124. See *Sarab Loh Granth*, ch. *Khalsa Parkash*.

125. *Kalam* in Arabic means word; speech. "The first technical use of *Kalam* seems to have been in the phrase *Kalam Allah* meaning either the *Kuran* or Allah's quality (*Sifa*) called speech." (See *Short Encyclopaedia of Islam*, op. cit., p. 210, *Dictionary of Islam*, op. cit., p. 260).

126. "The majesty of the mystic *Sabda (Shabad)* which we come across in the Sikh scripture," tells Dr R.K. Arora, hardly finds any parallel in its fullness ...... It has been associated with God without attributes ...... As the Guru is the repository of all spiritual jewels, so, in him enshrines the *Sabda* and he also imparts it to the devotee. *Sabda* is the means by which one gets wisdom and the knowledge of the Lord. 'By the *Sabda* of the Guru one recognises the abode of the Lord within.' (Guru Granth Sahib, p. 364) ...... He is one with *Nama* and *Sabda*, the two most profound concepts in the Sikh faith." (See *The Sacred Scripture : Symbol of Spiritual Synthesis*, New Delhi-1988, pp. 35, 45, 103, 109).

127. Guru Granth Sahib, op. cit., Raga Asa, M.1, .p. 351.

128. Ibid., *Raga Dhanasari*, M.1, p. 661.

129. Ibid., *Raga Parbhati*, M.1, p. 1342.

130. Ibid., *Raga Ramkali*, M.1, p. 943.

131. Ibid., *Raga Sorath*, M.1, p. 635.

132. *Shuhada* in Arabic means testimony, evidence and martyrdom. The meaning martyr is not found for *Shahid* in the *Koran*. It is only later commentators that have tried to find it in the *Sura iv*. The development of the meaning of *Shahid* to martyr took place under Christian influence ...... The martyr who seals his belief with his death, fighting against the infidels. *Shahid* through out the Hadith literature and the great privileges that await him in heaven is readily depicted in numerous Hadiths ...... In the book of Djihad, martyrdom is praised quite in the style of the Hadith ...... The praise of *Shahada* (martyrdom) led to a real longing to meet a martyr's death and even Muhammad and 'Omar longed for it.' (see *The Dictionary of Islam*, op. cit., p. 571; *Shorter Encyclopaedia of Islam*, op. cit. p. 515; *Encyclopaedia of Islam*, op. cit., Vol. IV, p. 259-60. Penrice, John, *A Dictionary and Glossary of the Quran*, New Delhi-1978, pp. 79-80).

133. Kapur Singh, *Parasaraprasna*, op. cit., p. 108.

134. As stated by Bhai Santokh Singh, in his *Gurpratap Suraj Granth*, Kaithal-1844 ain 7, ansu 36; *Parasarasprasna*, op. cit., p. 41.

135. Teja Singh, Prin., *Sikhism : Its Ideals and Institutions*, 322, Amritsar-1938, reprint-1978, p. 34, *Essays in Sikhism*, Lahore-1941; reprint-1988, p. 168.

136. Guru Gobind Singh, *Zafarnamah*, Dina Kangar-1706, Verse No. 22.

137. *Heritage of the Sikhs*, op. cit., p. 90.

138. *Sunna* or *Sunnah* means "custom, use and wont, statute." (see *Another Encyclopaedia of Islam*. op. cit., p. 552)" According to H.P.T. Hughes, "lit. a path or way; a manner of life. A term used in the religion of the Muslims to express the custom or manner of life. Hence, the tradition which records either the sayings or doings of Muhammad. Consequently, all traditional law is divided into (1) what Mohammad did; (2) or what Muhammad enjoined; (3) or that which was done or said in the presence of Muhammad and which was not forbidden by him." (see his *Dictionary of Islam*, op. cit., p. 622).

139. By *Rahit* we mean the distinctive Sikh code of conduct or discipline which is "feature of fundamental importance to the life of the *Panth*," that is, the Sikh religion. The manuals in which this code is recorded are called *Rahitnamas*.

140. That is, the *Sikh Code of Conduct* compiled by a committee appointed in 1931 by the Shiromani Gurdwara Parbandhak Committee, Amritsar, with Prin. Teja Singh as convenor. It was approved by it in 1945 and has since been accepted as an authoritative manual, and regarded as the standard guide for the whole community.

141. McLeod, Dr W. H., *Textual Sources for the Study of Sikhism*, Manchester-1984, pp. 3, 73.

142. Guru Granth Sahib, op. cit., *Slok Varan te Vadhik*, M.I, No. 33, p. 1412.

143. Ibid., *Raga Sarang*, M.V., p. 1226.

144. Ibid., *Raga Gujari*, M.V., pp. 500-501.

145. Ibid., *Ramkali ki Var*, Rai Balwand tatha Sattei Dum akhi st. 1, p. 966.

146. *A Short History of the Sikhs*, op. cit., pp. 71-72.

147. That is, the chiefgood, especially as the end on the ultimate determining principle in an ethical system.

148. Bradshaw, H.L., *Sikhism*, in the Sikh Review, Calcutta.

149. Bittencourt, *The Sikh Way of Life*, op. cit., p. vi.

150. Macauliffe, M.A., The Sikh Religion : A Lecture, London-1910, p. 25.

151. Field, The Religion of the Sikhs, op. cit., p. 9, 34-55.

152. Toynbee, A., *UNESCO's Selections from the Sacred Writings of the Sikhs*, 'Foreword', pp. 10. 11.

153. Buck, Mrs. Pearl S., in her Opinion as published in Vol. I of Sri Guru Granth Sahib, English Version by Dr Gopal Singh, Delhi-1960, p. xiv.

154. Guru Granth Sahib, op. cit., Raga Sorath, M.V., p. 611.

155. Ibid., *Raga Kanara*, M.V., p. 1299.

156. Ibid., *Raga Dhanasari*, M.I., p. 663.
157. Guru Gobind Singh, *Akal Ustat* in *Sri Dasam Granth*, op. cit., *Kabit* no. 15/85.
158. See *Ardas*, that is the Sikh congregational prayer to God which is a basic religious activity in Sikh religion. Its version is available in various *Gutkas* (i.e., anthologies of hymns meant for daily and occasional prayers etc.) and *Sikh Rahit Maryada*, q.v.
159. Guru Granth Sahib, op. cit., Raga Dhanasari, M.I., p. 661.
160. Ibid., *Rag Sri*, M.V., p. 74.
161. Ibid., M.I. *Rag Sri*, p. 26.
162. Ibid., Rag Sarang, M.I., p. 1245.
163. Mujeeb, Prof. M., in his 'Foreword' to *Guru Nanak in His own Words* by Dr Harnam Singh Shan, Amritsar-1969, p. xiii.
164. Guru Granth Sahib, op. cit., Rag Maru, M. 5, p. 1002.
165. Ibid., *Rag Asa*, M.I., p. 419.
166. Ibid., *Rag Asa*, M.I., pp. 354, 468.
167. Ibid., *Rag Asa*, M.I. p. 9, Rag Ramkali, p. 944.
168. Ibid., p. 72; Rag Sorath, p. 598.

12

SIKH IDENTITY AND CONTINUITY —
A PERSPECTIVE FROM ETHICS

AVTAR SINGH

One of the most difficult areas of human knowledge relates to the comparative studies. There is a significant increase in the quantum of tension when this happens to be the area of contemporary religions and history of the societies where such religions have emerged. The questions about Sikhism are, in a way, not very different in this respect from the identical questions about the historical identities of Christianity, Islam, or the faiths of the Aryans before and after their entry into the land, now known as India. Buddhism and Jainism have experienced no less confusions about their identities at the hands of the lay and somewhat over-zealous interpreters. We are, therefore, approaching the subject matter of our present paper without any illusion of its final acceptance. The debate shall, perhaps, continue.

We may notice an important aspect of the comparative study before we proceed any further in this direction. There are two broad aspects of the work to be done in this area. We may name them as the micro approach or the macro approach to the subject matter. In terms of ease, the macro approach is to be preferred and is, in fact, preferred by many people. The macro approach is generally visible in the work of some of the scholars who are either themselves 'outsiders' or approach the subject of their study as outsiders. The conclusions arrived at are often so general that they appear to be fair and easy to grasp and accept. A significant thrust of this methodological approach lies in viewing or portraying the subject matter of their study as syncretic in character. They fuse the earlier-side-end in the history of the tradition, but under pressure to explain the distinctness, they plant the departures in the mid-point or the end-side point in the history of the tradition.

The micro approach has to be adopted with great patience and care. It requires hard work and a good amount of objectivity and regulation of emotion. The scholar has to overcome the temptation to magnify the trivial and the insignificant. Although the insider is generally gifted with greater possibilities of understanding his tradition, yet the amount and intensity of differences among the insiders should warn us that everything need not be final even in the work of insiders. The micro approach can of course be adopted by the 'outsiders' with satisfactory results, if they were not to lose sight of inner experience and the tradition based on it. The 'availability' of the material 'proof' or its 'non-availability' is not made the sole ground of belief in the growth of the illumination in a certain direction.

Apart from the above two paths, there can also be a fairly good combination of the two approaches. The results differ from each other in the gestalts resulting from these compounds and mixtures. Most of the synthesis stories display this approach.

We have set out this brief analysis of the three approaches to the comparative study of the religions in general and of Sikhism in particular. The purpose of this early submission is two-fold. First, we have sought to hint at the tensions involved in the comparative study and the possible way out adopted by scholars. Second, it is sought to highlight the fact that two approaches may lead to different results because of the difference in the approach itself.

Herein, we shall seek to adopt a path somewhat akin to the micro-analysis approach. This will, hopefully, enable us to keep in view the dynamics of the inner impulse and thus maintain the authenticity of the work. The paper is rather brief and seeks to analyse and interpret the main theme of the argument. We may begin first with the main frame of the Sikh theology.

Sikh theology is another area of Sikh religion which has received continuous attention and has been a subject for interpretation or re-interpretation. This statement may appear to be contrary to the superficial notion that Sikh theology has not received attention over the past five centuries or so. It is not unusual to come across even a few laments who feel sad that the twentieth century displays a singular lack of awareness of the need for expounding the Sikh theology. A still more interesting observation was presented during a conference held abroad. The learned scholar appeared to be obsessed. by the idea that now there were not many interpreters of Sikhism. The only persons acknowledged by this scholar as authentic seekers of knowledge in this area were those who were trained well away from the country of origin of Sikhism, and who tended to follow a certain methodological approach to the interpretation of Sikh history, or the extended application of the Western models of anthropological interpretation to the Sikh religion. The conceptual model of the tribal rituals and rites-de-passage were made applicable to the Sikh society without recognising the inappropriate consequences which follow from this stretched and stressed approach. This historical, as well as anthropological, approach does not appear to even notice the evolutionary process in the value experience or the praxis of the people they seek to study and analyse. Many of the Hindu practices which were continued by some convert families for some time even after initiation into Sikhism have been taken by these anthropologists and historians as 'Sikh rites', thus displaying a singular lack of the understanding of the Sikh society, its values, religion and theology.

There are two noticeable characteristics of the normative imperatives and ideals.

The normative cannot be established in terms of the actual conduct or the practical. The anthropoligist, the historian, or scholars of the like studies are pretty close to their discipline as long as they follow this rule of the game. They may, however, go astray from their course when they infer the normative from the actual. The normative is the critique in terms of which the actual is analysed and evaluated. It does not permit us to establish the normative from what we may tend to believe as being perceived by us. Such a difficulty may become multiplied manyfold when the normative to be so construed is several centuries away from the times of the inference by the anthropologist, sociologist, historian or persons of the like disciplines. One may, to some extent, attempt a history of the morals in this case but the compiler must, in this, clearly distinguish between the moral values and the history of the events including the personal or social conduct. Such a distinction is very crucial for both the scholar of the normative or the social sciences. In recent years some historians or anthropologists appear to have overlooked this, and thus either involuntarily or perhaps by choice, have created an illusion whereby the actual conduct of some individuals or groups on their way of change or conversion have been presented as the normative. Often such inferences are made in the face of the injunctions to the contrary. For example, we are aware of the injunctions by the Gurus in Guru Granth Sahib against various practices based on superstitions. We are also aware of the often cited incident where the Gurus have tested the awareness of their followers against superstitions. But all this has not deterred some scholars from creating the illusion that the Sikh society has consisted of or consists of worshippers of goddesses and graves. Unfortunately, some scholars appear to be greatly impressed by the empirical dimensions of the generalisations made by them. The human finitude has often impelled people to seek strength or success through superstitous actions. But this does not reflect the values and normative teachings of the traditions to which they belong. There need be no theoretical confusion on this score.

We have a modest programme in this brief paper. Its objective is to direct the attention of keen students of the Sikh religion, theology and ethics to take notice of the various and sustained efforts to interpret Sikh theology. Let us begin by stating the nature and scope of Sikh theology before discussing its main contents.

The word theology is often used to refer to various kinds and aspects of knowledge relating to God. It may refer to "knowledge of God and the supernatural; religious knowledge and belief, especially when methodically formulated." It is also used for "the critical, historical, and psychological study of religion and religious ideas", or it may signify "a system of religious theory or observance." While this may be the general outline of the subject referred to as theology, there is a wide variation in the actual contents of the various doctrines described as theology of different religions or of the sects within a religion. It is rather difficult to pronounce which statement of each religion or each sect within a religion is theology proper. However, we may seek to limit our inquiry to the exposition of Sikh theology, and within Sikhism, the attempt will be to deal with the mainstream statements.

Historically, the tradition of interpreting the revelation or the Word of God in

Sikhism is as old as the tradition itself. The companions of Guru Nanak and the subsequent Gurus may have been called upon by themselves, or by those around them, to interpret and explain as one whole the elements of the revelation and their intra coherence. The existence of the different levels of the seekers of knowledge must also have made this process of interpretation a continuous one. The added need for this continuous interpretation could have been the departure of the new doctrines from the traditionally accepted social codes of morals and ethics. As theology also illumines the personal and social conduct of the related individual, the new frontiers of the theology also invariably influence his ethical perceptions and actions. Thus, although there may be ethical conduct which may not be consciously grounded in theology, yet the converse does not appear to be true. And, where the new religious revelation has directly aimed at social and moral ends, the need for a continuous interpretation is obvious.

Sikhism is directly grounded in the revelation received by Guru Nanak. His subsequent journeys in India are said to have been made in the company of Bala or Mardana. Even apart from these companions, Guru Nanak is recorded to have met many saints and religious leaders during this phase of his life. In a dialogue recorded as the *Sidha Gosht* in Guru Granth Sahib, he is asked by the *Sidhas* to expound his doctrine. The dialogue is rich in the theological exposition of Guru Nanak. We encounter the simple and the complex as the two ends of the dialogue in the *Sidha Gosht*. The seemingly simple question asked by the Sidhas about the doctrinal identity of Guru Nanak is answered by the latter in a step-by-step ascending manner of the exposition of God's nature and the knowledge of His nature. Towards the higher and the complex end of the dialogue, the esoteric seems to speak to the esoteric. It is a very fine and illuminating example of the exposition of the Sikh theology which conveys the profundity of the revelation through the symbols of everyday use.

The second Guru, Angad, the third Guru, Amardas, and the fourth Guru, Ram Das had respectively spent time with their earlier preceptors and companions. The exposition of the religious knowledge and belief by the former for the latter is easy to imagine and understand. A typical Eastern style of describing this process is like 'the lamp lighting the lamp.' There is no break or darkness in between the lighting of the two lamps in succession.

The role of the fifth Guru, Arjun Dev, is worthy of special mention in any understanding of the history of Sikh theology. Apart from being himself a Guru, he brought to fruition a tradition of compiling Guru Granth Sahib. It is often said that Guru Granth Sahib is the only Scripture of a major world religion which was composed and established during the life-time of the founders themselves. This has obviated the possibility of any subsequent interpolation. Guru Arjun Dev got the whole Guru Granth Sahib finally compiled and his trusted scholarly companion, Bhai Grudas, was the principal scribe for the first edition of Guru Granth Sahib. The present form is of this origin and authenticity.

Bhai Gurdas has also authored some compositions of his own. His writings have often been termed as the 'key' to Guru Granth Sahib. His long association with the fifth

Guru has led people to believe that he is the first theologian of Sikhism, other than the Gurus. His personal status is that of a highly authentic expositor of the Sikh theology. His *Vars* are a close reflection of the present authentic scripture.

A similar claim is often made in respect of the second scribe of Guru Granth Sahib, namely Bhai Mani Singh. His compositions are also attempts at the reflection and exposition of the Sikh theology as in Guru Granth Sahib. He is said to have worked directly under the guidance of the tenth Guru, Gobind Singh. He is the last important link in the chain of the major Sikh theologians who were contemporary to the Gurus.

The Sikh theologians who have followed after the cessation of the chain of ten Gurus in Sikhism in 1708 A.D., have proceeded in various directions in their exposition of the Sikh theology. Let us briefly notice two main streams, both of whom have sought to remain close to the Sikh traditions.

The Nirmalas had emerged as the important theologians of the Sikh religion during the recent past. They have expounded the Sikh religious knowledge and belief both substantively as well as analogically. The latter has been done by using the notions of the earlier schools of Indian philosophy and religion. It appears to have been significant for them to explain the originality of the revelation received by the Sikh Gurus by calling Guru Granth Sahib the fifth *Veda*, as the status of divine revelation (*Sruti*) was being conceded by the people at large in respect of the *Vedas*. The Nirmalas did not call Guru Granth Sahib as the fifth *Veda* as a scripture continuous to the earlier four *Vedas*. The use of the figure 'fifth' is more with a view to stressing the analogy so as to drive home the view that Guru Granth Sahib is an independent and original revelation. The use of this analogy has, however, been sometimes misinterpreted.

The Giani tradition of the Sikh theologians has proceeded towards its goal in a somewhat traditional manner wherein its closeness to the Sikh mainstream has remained strong for a longer time. Some of them have claimed to continue the Bhai Mani Singh tradition. There are, however, other developments also in this area. Bhai Vir Singh is a very outstanding theologian whose mainstream acceptability is of an outstanding status. His contribution to the Sikh intellectual literature and exposition of the theology proper is of a very significant nature. The mystic quality of his poetry, as well as his famous epic *Rana Surat Singh*, (1905 A.D.), which has been described as "the sole epic in Punjabi with a religio-ethical theme" is very impressive. By this time Bhai Vir Singh was "already famous as an exponent of the teachings of Sikhism through his exegetical writing no less than his historical novel *Sundari*." The Sikh penchant for intermingling the theological with the social, as observed by us earlier, is continued in *Rana Surat Singh* also. It has been pointed out that "*Rana Surat Singh*, a deeply religious work in spirit, enshrines also a powerful social message." In it, the Rani is "exhorted to shed her own despondency and to find a new path of ascent to a fulfilment that is both spiritual and ethical." Anyone interested in knowing the Sikh attitude towards theology has to keep in view the Sikh perception of the concern of God with the social and the ethical. The theological cognition is not without the ethical impulse and ideal. The ethical is the meeting point of God-His Knowledge-Man axis. This fundamental nature of the Sikh theology is seen in Guru Nanak's *Sidha Gosht* as well as the lay, but devout, expression in *Rana Surat Singh* of Bhai Vir Singh. The often quoted saying of Guru Nanak that "Truth is higher than everything but higher still is true conduct" is an expression of the dynamic nature of the theos which is the subject-matter of theology. It is partly because of this new, but unmistakable, dimension of Sikh theology that Sikh theology is what it is.

Guru Nanak has, in the very first creedal statement with which Guru Granth Sahib begins described the 'One' as *Sat Nam, Kárta Purukh*. It is a reference to God and He is described as *Karta Purkh*. He is also, both in the Scripture, as well as at the common and lay level, referred to as *Kartar*, the 'Doer.' The Gurus have sought to convey their experience of the revelation in a somewhat unusual manner. Our efforts to comprehend the uniqueness of this revelation will have to take due and proper notice of this underlined nature of Sikh theology. The usual and the conditioned response will not do the required job. It is here that most of the Western, as well as the Eastern, scholars have failed to understand what must be comprehended. The creedal statement, popularly called *Mul Mantra* in Guru Granth Sahib, has only at a later stage referred to God as *Akal Murat*. The current use of *Akal Purakh* is historically of much later usage. The word *Waheguru* is also very often used by scholars as well as lay Sikhs to refer to God. One of the recent Western attempts at the expounding of the Sikh theology appears to have underlined only *Akal Purakh* and *Waheguru* as the core concepts. Such an attempt often leads to the fusion of the Sikh dyanamism into the quiescence of the theology and ethics prior to Sikhism. Once the *Karta* in the *Karta Purakh* is conveniently or unintentionally lost sight of, two distortions emerge almost immediately. First, Guru Nanak has repeatedly stressed the dynamic and the active nature of God as an example for humankind to follow. This is a very significant and crucial identity of Guru Nanak's message in the fifteenth century. The *Karta Purakh* is described as *Nirbhau* (free from fear). Any scholar who fails to notice this identity in the fifteenth century is bound to feel puzzled by the dynamic ethics of the subsequent Gurus. Such an error can be both intentional as well as unintentional. The latter can be corrected when the scholar comes across the literature written on the original lines. But when some scholars, even when aware of this position, remain persistent in their claims that Sikhism has suddenly deviated from the path of the earlier Gurus during the later Gurus, we may not be entirely wrong in doubting the bonafides of their unwarranted conclusion. We are all aware of the logical difficulties of the theory of *Karma* prior to Sikhism. It is the revealed authority of the Guru's imperative that one ought not shun or escape from the duty of ethical actions. Such ethical actions, Guru Nanak and other Gurus have told us, do not bind the person into the cycle of transmigration. This is in very sharp contrast and total departure from the earlier held view of *Karma*. This departure is a complete discontinuity with the earlier tradition and is the shaping of a new ethical identity. Second, the non-acceptance of the sacred thread as initiation into the privileged three upper castes is a very significant ethical co-relate of the theology of *Karta Purakh*. Nearly all the philosophers acquainted with the Indian Philosophy are aware of the doctrinal implications of this identity.

However, many anthropologists and historians seem to either not notice it or reject it for reasons best known to themselves.

The absolute and the continuous identity of the ethical teaching from Guru Nanak's *upar sach achar* to Guru Gobind Singh's *Shubh Karman te Kabhu na taru* is easy to see and understand. The founders of the Sikh religion were, obviously, stressing the continuity of the ethical chain. And this was being done in defiance of the earlier notion that even the good actions or *shubh karman* bind the self to the *sansara* and, therefore, ought to be renounced or abjured. The Gurus have totally departed from the earlier Indian ethics in this respect. The law of *Karma* in the earlier Indian systems was the mainspring of the *Varnasharama dharma*, which provided support to the institution of caste and the impulse for withdrawal from social participation. The earlier social ethics was developed on an entirely different model. The Gurus, from Guru Nanak to Guru Gobind Singh, gave up this model and instead developed the new structure of the ethics which universalised the participatory role of action rather than restriction and withdrawal. This is an extremely important development in Sikh ethics which has influenced the general Indian society subsequent to its emergence. Even the general Indian society has gradually imbibed the teachings of the Gurus and there are many who may be seen today to have rejected the earlier doctrine of *Varnashrama dharma*. A significantly large number of contemporary Indian scholars and social leaders have derived remarkable inspiration from the teachings of the Gurus on this score. Bal Gangadhar Tilak, Tagore, Vivekananda, and Radhakrishnan are only a few names which may be mentioned but the list is large and impressive. The values of the social ethics propounded by the Sikh Gurus have provided the impulse for many ideals of social concern and service as witnessed by us in modern India. The insistence of the Gurus on freeing the social ethics from the caste imperatives may not be so well appreciated in the changed social situation today, but its emergence and open advocacy by the Gurus is the first and very modernising attempt to proclaim the freedom of man in the Name of God. Freedom of the self is made the foundation of social freedom. Some of the ideals of freedom proclaimed by the Western society in the nineteenth and twentieth centuries are very clearly perceived in the teachings of the Gurus in the fifteenth to the eighteenth century India. This freedom is based on the spiritual and social equality of human beings.

We may pause here and make a submission. In recent times some persons have sought to interpret this love of Sikhism for freedom and equality as a struggle for some particular class of people. However, their teaching for participation in the social life, as well as their ideal of freedom and equality, should not be interpreted merely in material terms. The Gurus have always held the spiritual as higher than the material. They taught us to regulate the material by the spiritual. Any effort for equality without inspiration by the spiritual may tend to generate tension and conflict. But the Gurus have inspired freedom and equality from the mainsprings of the spiritual which may initiate and sustain the progress towards the ideal of harmony and equipoise. The Gurus have taught us that the basis for judging the issue are moral and spiritual. If an act is wrong, then it is wrong regardless of whosoever has done it. Similarly, if it were right, then it is so regardless of whosoever is involved in it. The tradition of holding even a colleague to be wrong, or serving water even to your enemy is a teaching which is grounded in the spiritual principle. The issues are not judged on partisan lines but are evaluated entirely on the moral and the spiritual grounds. In all this lies the strength and identity of Sikh ethics.

13

THE SIKH PANTH

Jagjit Singh

In view of their ideology, the Sikh Gurus could not rest content merely with preaching their doctrines and leaving it at that. Their worldview impelled them to accept the challenges which the unjust caste order and the religious and political domination posed. To solve these problems, it was imperative to organize people. Institutions like the caste system and the oppressive political state could be replaced only by creating parallel institutions. There was no alternative to taking steps in this direction. Ignoring the challenges would not have solved any of the problems, nor contributed to universal humanism. It was a very difficult mission both to build new institutions, and at the same time maintain the spirit of universalism in the mass organisation.

Idealism has, except as a source of inspiration, limited social utility if it is not properly organised for social ends. This is amply illustrated by the negligible social impact of the Radical Bhakti ideology on the caste society. If idealism is to be yoked to achieving social aims, it has got to be institutionalised. In the process, it cannot escape assuming a certain distinctiveness and identity of its own. And greater the resistance to the social change, the greater has to be the emphasis on the separate identity and organisation of the new ideology.

1. DISTINCTIVENESS

The universal and non-sectarian gospel of Guru Nanak in itself became the first step in differentiating the Sikh mission from the older creeds. In his time, the Indian atmosphere was surcharged with hatred between Hindus and Muslims. They were further torn by extreme sectarian rivalry within their own ranks. Religious votaries were pigeon-holed into one sect or the other. It was not common to rise above narrow sectarian considerations. It was in this milieu that Guru Nanak declared that he was neither a Hindu nor a Mussalman. To pointed questions at different places, he replied, "I am neither a Hindu, nor a Mussalman. I accept neither the *Vedas*, nor the *Quran*."[1] "If I say I am a Hindu, I am lost altogether; at the same time, I am not a Mussalman."[2] He advised the yogis to rise above sectarianism and regard the whole humanity as their own.[3] Besides his numerous hymns, there is the evidence of the *Janamsakhis* that the contemporaries of Guru Nanak were impressed by his universal humanitarian approach. When he visited the tomb of Sheikh Baha-ud-Din Zakria in Multan, the Muslim priest observed, "We know you do not discriminate between Hindus and Muslims."[4] Guru Nanak advised a Muslim saint named Wali Kandhari not to discriminate between *Sunnis* and *Rafzies*, because all sects belonged to God.[5] The Pathan Ubare Khan recognised that the Guru was above Hindu or Muslim sectarianism.[6] When Guru Nanak settled at Kartarpur, both Hindus and Muslims used to visit him.[7] Bhai Gurdas, a near contemporary of Guru Nanak, wrote : "Hindus and Muslims, forsaking their sectarianism, began to worship Baba (Guru Nanak)."[8] Coming under the influence of Guru Nanak, 'Hindus and Muslims shed off their sectarianism.' At his death, Hindus and Muslims both claimed the right to perform his last rites.[9] His image in the mind of the masses is reflected by the popular saying : 'Nanak Shah *fakir* is *Guru* to Hindus and *Pir* to the Muslims.'

Although the universalism of Guru Nanak lent its own distinctiveness to his message, the real reason which made this differentiation deep and lasting, was that his gospel cut at the roots of some of the most cherished faiths of both the Hindus and the Mussalmans. The Guru repudiated all claims to exclusive religious authority by any prophet or scripture. The Sikh Gurus accepted no authority other than that of God. "God being ineffable, Brahma and Vishnu have not found His limits; ...... He made millions of *Indars* and *Bawans*; He created and destroyed Brahmas and Shivas."[10] Secondly, "In His court, there are hundreds of thousands of Muhammads, Brahmas, Vishnus and Mahesh (Shivas)."[11] As regards scriptures, Guru Nanak says : "The drum of the Vedas resoundeth for many a faction. Remember God's Name, Nanak, there is none but Him."[12] We have it on the authority of Dabistan that Sikhs "do not read the mantras (i.e., the Vedic or other scriptural hymns) of the Hindus, they do not venerate their temples of idols, nor do they esteem their *avtars*. They have no regard for the Sanskrit language which, according to the Hindus, is the speech of the angels."[13] It has been seen that the demand for exclusive allegiance to religious source-heads was one of the major causes of cleavage between the Hindus and the Mohammadans. The gospel of the Sikh Gurus struck at this foundation on which the super-structure of the then existing religious sectarianism had been raised.

The grounds for the differentiation of the Gurus' message from that of the caste ideology and the caste society were far more basic. The caste ideology was the anti-thesis of humanism, and the caste society was extremely parochial in its outlook. To belong to it, it was necessary to be born within it. The land where the *Varna Ashrama Dharma* was not established, was regarded impure;[14] and the Aryavarta, the pure land, was at one period circumscribed within the limits of the river Sindh in the north and the river Carmanvati in the South.[15] The Sikh Gurus rejected almost all the cardinal beliefs of the caste society. They repudiated the authority of the Vedas and allied scriptures, discarded the theory of *avtarhood*, disowned all its sectarian gods, goddesses and *avtars*, and condemned idol worship, formalism, ritualism, and ceremonialism.

The ideology of the Sikh Gurus, thus, stood differentiated by its own logic. Its universality and humanism were compatible neither with Muslim exclusiveness, nor with the caste-ridden and sectarian orthodox Hindu society.

2. SEPARATE IDENTITY

Mere ideological distinctiveness was not enough. The greatest social hurdle in the way of humanism was the inequitous caste system. It could not be reformed from within. For, social inequality and hierarchism were in-built in its very constitution and mechanism. The anti-caste movements could survive only if these divorced themselves from the caste society. Buddhism organised a monastic society outside the caste ranks. But, it left its laity to remain in the caste fold. The result was that, when Brahminism reasserted itself, the lay followers of Buddhism imperceptibly moved into their caste moorings, leaving the order of monks, high and dry, in its isolation. Kabir was far more vocal than Basawa, but the Lingayats established a far more separate identity than the Kabir-panthis; because their deviations (e.g., widow remarriage, burying the dead and admission of all castes) from the caste usages were very radical. Later, the Lingayats tried to tone down their radicalism. But, inspite of this, they are, perhaps, more an appendage of the orthodox society than its integral part; because even the toned down Lingayatism is not wholly adjustable in the caste order.[16] Chaitanya, who was more radical with regard to caste restrictions than the Maharashtra Bhaktas, had both low caste Hindus and Muslims as his disciples. In the Kartabha sect, which branched out of the Chaitanya School, there is no distinction between Hindus, Muslims and Christians. A Muslim has more than once risen to the rank of a teacher. The members of the sect eat together once or twice in a year.[17] But, the main body of the followers of Chaitanya reverted to the caste society; and even its Kartabhai section, like the Lingayats, does not assert a distinct entity apart from the caste society. The creed of Kabir attained the stage of only a *Mata* (religious path), although of all the denouncers of caste considerations, he was the most unequivocal and vocal. The Kabir-panth remained a loose combination of those who were attracted by Kabir's religious appeal, or were attracted by some other considerations (e.g., *julahas* [weavers], who constituted the majority of the Kabir-panthis, were attracted to Kabir because he was a *julaha*).[18]

These instances leave no doubt that anti-caste movements, like those of Kabir and other Bhaktas, whose departure from the caste ideology had been confined only to the ideological plane, remained still-born in the field of social achievement. And, those like the Lingayats and the followers of Chaitanya, who, under the influence of a teacher, did adopt certain anti-caste usages, but either they did not want to break away completely from the caste society, or did not pursue their aim consistently enough, remained tagged to the caste order in one form or the other. The Buddhist monks alone could escape being swallowed by the caste society, because they had made a complete break with the caste order, both ideologically and organizationally. Accordingly, in the mediaeval period, the chances of success of any anti-caste movement were in direct proportion to the separate identity it established outside the caste society, both at the ideological and the organizational levels. And the foremost prerequisite for this purpose was a clear perception of this aim, a determined will and a consistent effort to pursue it.

The separate identity of the Sikh *Panth* and the Sikh movement is such a patent fact of history that it is hardly questioned. This by itself is a clear indication of the fact that the Sikh Gurus had a definite aim of giving their message a distinct and new organizational form. Otherwise, it is hard to explain why the Sikh movement should not have met the same fate as that of Lingayats and the followers of Kabir and Chaitanya. The Sikh Gurus realised, which the others did not, that, in order to give battle to the caste order, it was imperative to build a social system and organise people outside the caste-society. This process of establishing a separate society (the Sikh *Panth*) started with Guru Nanak himself.

Guru Nanak began his career as a teacher of men with the significant utterance that "there is no Hindu and no Mussalman." The Guru thereby wanted to emphasise the eternal unity and brotherhood of man. For the Guru, everybody was primarily a man and not a Hindu or a Mussalman. The same *Janamsakhi*, which gives the above story proceeds to say : "Then Guru Baba Nanak gave all his earthly belongings and went to join the company of fakirs (i.e., Muslim recluses) ...... Then people asked him, 'Nanak, earlier you were something else, i.e., Hindu, now you have become different. There is the one path of the Hindus, and the other that of Mussalmans; which path do you follow ?' Then Guru Baba Nanak said, 'There is no Hindu, no Mussalman; which of these paths can I follow ? I follow God's path. God is neither Hindu nor Mussalman. I follow God's right path.'"[19]

Guru Nanak's reply clearly indicates his complete break with his Hindu past. Guru Nanak clarified unambiguously that he was rejecting both the Hindu and the Muslim paths, and instead, was following God's right path, because God was neither Hindu nor Mussalman. In other words, the Guru rejects the Hindu and the Muslim paths, not because of the shortcomings of their followers, but mainly because God is non-sectarian.

We have seen that the Radical Bhaktas were not Hindu reformers. If all that they rejected is taken out of Brahminism, there is nothing of substance left that the orthodox religion could claim as exclusively its own. This applies doubly to Guru Nanak's ideology, because he was even more vehement in his criticism of Brahminism and its scriptures and practices.

The *Janamsakhis* also make it clear that Guru Nanak's mission was non-sectarian, and in the context of the times, a new path. "God sent (Nanak) to start a *panth* (religion)."[20] "Nobody could make out whether he was a Hindu or a Muslim."[21] Two *Qazis* who came to see him, came to the conclusion that he was the *pir* of both Hindus and Muslims. "You carry conviction with (both) Hindus and Muslims."[22] "Then it became a current topic of discussion among Hindus and Muslims ...... What is his religion ? He does not follow any one of the paths of *Yogis, Sanyasis, Tapasvis, Qazis, Mullahs, Hindus, Muslims, Vedas* and *Katebs* ......"[23] A Hindu Khatri complained to the Delhi Sultan that "he does not recognise the authority of either *Vedas* or *Kateb*."[24]

He went to preach his message in Muslim countries, and was warned of the hazards to his life for doing so. If he had been a mere Hindu reformer or a sectarian, there was no point in his going to far off lands, because no Hindu could ever contemplate converting Muslims to Hinduism. In addition, we have the evidence of Bhai Gurdas who wrote : "(Guru Nanak) vanquished the Sidhas in discussion, and made a separate *Panth* of his own."[25] "Opening the Book, (they) asked who is better, Hindu or Mussalman ?"[26] "(Guru Nanak replied) They (Hindus and Mussalmans) quarrel with each other, (but) Ram and Rahim are on the same footing."[27] "Nanak struck his own coin in this world, and created a pure *Panth*."[28]

Further, Guru Nanak took clear organizational steps in shaping a Sikh society on separate ideological lines. He established *dharmsalas* in far-flung places inside the country and outside it.[29] These *dharmsalas* became the centres where his followers could meet together, practise the *dharm* of his concept, and spread his message to others. In addition, he appointed select persons (*manjis*) for the purpose of furthering his mission.[30] In his lifetime, his followers came to be known as Nanakpanthis, and they had their own separate way of saluting each other (*Sat Kartar*).[31]

The greatest single organizational step that Guru Nanak took was to select, by a system of tests, a worthy successor to lead and continue his mission. He was named Angad, i.e., a limb of Guru Nanak himself. It is recorded in Guru Granth Sahib that the change-over from Nanak to his successors meant only a change of bodily forms, otherwise, the same light shone in them and they followed the same course.[32] Bhai Gurdas also writes that Guru Nanak established a pure *Panth*, blended his light with that of Angad, and nominated him in his place as the Guru of that *Panth*.[33] Guru Nanak directed his successor Guru Angad not to remain absorbed wholly in meditation, but to devote his time to the shaping of the *Panth*.[34] The same instructions were passed on by Angad to his successor Amar Das,[35] and this mission was continued by the later Gurus.[36] This evidence is of great value because it embodies an altogether new tradition. This could be true only of the Sikh Gurus, because nowhere else in the Indian religious tradition were social objectives given preference over personal spiritual bliss.

Guru Nanak had started the institution of *dharamsalas* (religious centres), *sangat* (congregations of his followers), *langar* (common kitchen and *manjis* (seats of preaching). The succeeding Gurus further consolidated and extended these institutions. Guru Amar Das systematised this institution of *manjis*, and created twenty-two centres for the extension of the mission. Persons of high religious calibre were nominated to these offices. They were in charge of the Guru's followers in an area, and catered to their religious as well as temporal needs. They were the links of the organization and two-way channels of communication between the Guru and the *sangat*. They collected the offerings, and passed the same on to the central treasury, where these were used by the Guru for the purposes of the mission. Guru Arjun regularised the collection of these contributions. He required every Sikh to set apart one tenth of his income for the common cause. When Guru Nanak settled at Kartarpur after completing his missionary tours, the place became the central *dharamsala*, the focal meeting place for his followers. Guru Amar Das made Goindwal the centre of his mission. He fixed two occasions when the Guru's followers should come from far and near for general meetings of the *Panth*. Guru Ram Das and Guru Arjun extended these centres to Tarn Taran and Amritsar. In the course of time, the latter place became to the Sikhs what Mecca is to the Muslims.

In addition to the consolidation of these institutions initiated by Guru Nanak, Guru Angad invented the Gurmukhi script and Guru Arjun compiled the Sikh scripture. These two steps went a long way in establishing the separate identity of the Sikhs. With a distinct organization, separate religious centres, a separate script, and a scripture of their own, they became an entirely separate church and a new society. It is not our purpose to go into the details of the organizational steps taken by the Gurus, but it may be mentioned that the militarisation of the movement, as will be seen, only added a new dimension to this development. Even before this militarisation, the Sikh movement had established a firm and a separate organizational identity known as the Sikh *Panth*.

3. IDENTITY AND UNIVERSALITY

While repudiating claims of others to exclusive religious authority, the Sikh Gurus did not advance any such claim on their own behalf. Guru Nanak calls himself "lowest of the low."[37] Guru Ram Das describes himself to be the meanest of the whole creation[38] and Guru Gobind Singh regards himself as "the slave of the Supreme Being."[39] Of the ten Sikh Gurus, the hymns of seven have been recorded. In not a single hymn do they indicate any claim to exclusive religious authority. It was Guru Gobind Singh, the creator of the brotherhood of the Khalsa — a body devoted to the service of humanity — who specifically made it clear that the Hindu temple and the mosque, are the same; and that the whole humanity is to be regarded as one.[40]

The single greatest step that the Sikh Gurus took to prevent religious authority becoming the source of sectarianism was to detach ideology from the person of the ideologue. It was the eternal spirit, the doctrine, the tenet, or the principle, which was made supreme over and above the person or the teacher, the Guru or the prophet. When Guru Nanak nominated Angad as his successor, he (Nanak) laid his head at the feet of Angad as a mark of homage.[41] It is significant that Guru Nanak did not bow before Lehna (i.e., the disciple who was not yet perfect), but bowed before Angad, the person who had then become the head and represented the spirit of the mission. As soon as the same spirit was enshrined in both, the distinction between the Guru and the disciple was obliterated. Satta and Balwand, in their hymns recorded in Guru Granth Sahib, and Bhai Gurdas, have made this point absolutely clear, "The light was the same, the system was the same, the only change was a change of bodies."[42] "Nanak blended his light with his (Angad's light), (and in this way) the Satguru Nanak transformed his form."[43] Not only the distinction between one Guru and the other Guru disappeared, but the distinction between the Guru and all those Sikhs who had imbibed in toto the Guru's spirit, also disappeared. Guru Hargobind touched the feet of Bhai Budha to pay him homage.[44] And by conferring Guruship on Guru Granth Sahib, Guru Gobind Singh emphasised two points. First, that the Guruship was not embodied in any person but in the principle and the spirit he enshrined; and second, that it was the ideology that mattered, and not its source, because, the hymns of the Bhakti saints incorporated in Guru Granth Sahib were to be as sacred to the Sikhs as the hymns of the Sikh Gurus.

The Sikh tradition is replete with instances showing the cosmopolitan spirit of the Sikh Gurus. "The Hindus reject Muslims, and the Muslims reject the Hindus. God has ordained me (Nanak) to act upon the four *Katebs*. The merit does not lie in reading or hearing them, but lies in living them in life."[45] Guru Amar Das sent Prema to a Muslim saint for getting himself cured,[46] and made Alayar, a Muslim, one of his priests, who drew no distinction between Hindus and Muhammadans.[47] Guru Arjun incorporated in Guru Granth Sahib the hymns of two Muslim saints, Farid and Bhikan, thus giving them equal status with the hymns of the Gurus. He got the foundation stone of the premier Sikh temple laid by the famous Sufi saint, Mian Mir. Guru Hargobind, who was the first to raise the standard of armed revolt against the Mughals, and fought six battles against them, built, on his own, a mosque when he founded the new township of Hargobindpur.[48] It was Guru Gobind Singh who created the Khalsa to wage a relentless struggle against the religious and political tyranny of the Mughal empire, but his hymns leave no doubt about his cosmopolitan approach : "What is a Hindu or Muslim to him, from whose heart doubt departeth."[49] At a period when Muslim sentiment against the Sikhs had crystallised, many a noble spirit among the Muslims recognised the non-sectarian character of the Guru's mission. Budhu Shah was a known Muslim divine. He himself, his brother, his four sons and seven hundred disciples fought for the Guru. During the struggle, two of his sons died fighting,[50] and he himself was tortured to death by Osman Khan for having sided with the Guru.[51] Saiyed Beg, one of Aurangzeb's generals, who was in command of five thousand men, changed his mind at a critical moment in the course of the battle, and "threw in his lot with the Sikhs, and contributed all his wealth towards their struggle against the Muhammadans ......"[52] Later, Saiyed Beg died fighting for the Guru in another action.[53] Another general, Saiyed Khan, sent by the Emperor Aurangzeb to subdue the Guru, also left the imperial forces, and voluntarily submitted himself to the Guru.[54] By far the best instance of the cosmopolitan spirit of the movement is the story of Kanahiya, who, during the critical battle at Anandpur, used to offer water and assistance with absolute impartiality to the wounded both among the Sikhs and the enemy forces. When questioned, Kanahiya quoted the Guru's own instructions that one should look on all men with an equal eye. The Guru complimented him for displaying the true spirit of a Sikh.[55] The author of *Hakikat* attested to it in 1783 (i.e., after the Sikhs had passed through the severest persecution at the hands of the Muslim rulers) that, "In his (Nanak's) religion, there is very little prejudice against the Muslims, nay, they have practically no prejudice against any nation."[56]

It is important to understand that this cosmopolitan Sikh tradition could not be born either out of Muslim exclusiveness, or the caste ideology of the Hindus. Only the Radical Bhaktas shared this outlook, but they never ventured in the social or organizational field. The Bhaktamala, the only earlier record of their lives, does not mention the shaping of any such tradition. Therefore, the very existence and persistence of the Sikh tradition is a strong indication of the universal character of the Sikh movement.

The really important point to be noted is that for the practice of their universal humanism, the Sikh Gurus established the forums of the Sikh *Panth*. Their universalism had distinct social aims. This was their major difference with the Radical Bhaktas who never tried to institutionalise their ideology. The Sikh Gurus were deeply committed to achieving practical social goals. It was the inner compulsion both of their religion and universalism that prompted them to create a new path and a *Panth*, so as to give practical shape to a programme that directly militated, on the one hand, against the caste ideology and, on the other, against the *Shariat* of the ruling Islam in India. Just as in the case of the doctrine of *ahimsa*, they did not make a fetish of universalism so as to allow it to be used as a cover for inaction, and for ignoring their avowed social goals. The Gurus never wanted the Hindus to remain as Hindus in a manner which left the caste system and its anti-humanism intact. Similarly, they did not want the Muslims to remain as Muslims in a manner which led to Shariatic exclusiveness and, its corollary, the religious domination over non-Muslims. All that Guru Nanak wanted was that Hindus should be Hindus of his concept, and that Muslims should be Muslims of his concept. His hymns leave no doubt on this issue. For these clearly commend the acceptance of values and virtues instead of the formalism and ritualism of the old religions. "Make kindness thy mosque, sincerity thy prayer carpet; and what is just and lawful thy Quran. Modesty thy circumcision; civility thy fasting; so shall thou be a Musalman."[57] "A Musalman is he who cleaneth his impurity."[58] "(A Muslim) dwells on the *Shariat*. But, they alone are perfect who surrender their self to see God."[59] "He who instructeth all the four castes in the Lord's Wisdom, Nanak, such a Pandit I salute for ever."[60] "Yoga is neither in the patched coat, nor in the yogi's staff, nor in besmearing oneself with ashes ...... If one looketh upon all the creation alike, he is acclaimed as a true yogi."[61] This meant pure and simple humanism and the abolition of all those institutions which were unjust or aggressive. The creation of parallel institutions to replace the anti-humanistic ones, e.g., the caste society and the tyrannical state, was an indispensable prerequisite. It was for this purpose that the Sikh Gurus organised the Sikh *Panth*. But, they scrupulously maintained the spirit of humanism and universality in that organisation. The universalism of the Sikh Gurus was not of that hue which is self-satisfied in remaining in an amorphous state and does not aspire institutionalisation for a humanitarian purpose. At the same time, the Sikh *Panth* was not created just to add another sect; it was established to serve an egalitarian cause.

REFRENCES

1. *Janamsakhi, Bhai Bala*, p. 292.
2. *Janamsakhi, Bhai Mani Singh Wali (Janamsakhi Prampra,* edited by Kirpal Singh, Antka, p. 333).
3. Guru Granth Sahib, p. 6.
4. *Janamsakhi Meharbanwali*, edited by Kirpal Singh, p. 439.
5. *Janamsakhi, Bhai Bala*, p. 270; *Janamsakhi Prampra*, Antka, p. 307.

6. *Ibid.*, p. 293.
7. *Jąnamsakhi, Walaitwali, Sakhi Guru Angad ji nun Guriayee*; *Janamsakhi, Meharbanwali*, p. 517.
8. Bhai Gurdas, *Var One*, Pauri 34.
9. *Janamsakhi,Walaitwali, Sakhi Guru Angad ji nun Guriayee*; *Janamsakhi Prampra*, Antka, pp. 57, 401.
10. Macauliffe, Vol. V, p. 262.
11. *Janamsakhi, Bhai Mani Singh Wali (Janamsakhi Prampra*, Antka, p. 334.)
12. Macauliffe, Vol. I, p. 369.
13. *Dabistan*, trans. by Ganda Singh : *The Panjab Past and Present* (1969), p. 51.
14. Max Weber, p. 7.
15. *Alberuni's India,*Vol. II, p. 134.
16. Tara Chand, p. 117.
17. Ibid., pp. 219-220.
18. Rose, Vol. II, p. 419.
19. *Janamsakhi, Meharban Wali*, pp. 10-12.
20. Ibid., p. 89.
21. *Janamsakhi Prampra*, Antka, p. 174.
22. Ibid., p. 204.
23. Ibid., p. 200.
24. *Janamsakhi Bhai Bala*, p. 279. *Latif*, p. 245.
25. Bhai Gurdas, *Var One*, Pauri 31.
26. Ibid., Pauri 33.
27. Ibid.
28. Ibid., Pauri 45.
29. *Janamsakhi Prampra*, Antka, pp. 124, 125, 127,174, etc.
30. *Ibid.*, pp. 44, 48, 259, 268.
31. *Ibid.*, pp. 106, 110, 121, 124, 127, 131, 133, 132, etc.
32. Guru Granth Sahib, p. 966.
33. Bhai Gurdas, *Var One*, Pauri 45.
34. *Mehma Parkash*, I, p, 326; II, p. 9.
35. Ibid., II, p. 57.
36. Ibid., pp. 95, 103, 233, 358.
37. Guru Granth Sahib, p. 15.
38. Ibid., p. 1295.
39. Macauliffe, Vol. V, p. 300.
40. Ibid., pp. 275-6.
41. *Janamsakhi Walaitwali*, Sakhi Guriayee Guru Angad.
42. Guru Granth Sahib, p. 966.
43. Bhai Gurdas, *Var One*, Pauri, 45.
44. *Gurbilas Chhevin Patshahi*, p. 341.
45. *Mehma Parkash*, I, p. 217.
46. Ibid., II, p. 246.
47. Macauliffe, II, p. 77.
48. *Gurbilas Chhevin Patshahi*, pp. 337, 340.
49. Macauliffe, Vol. V, p. 308.
50. Macauliffe, Vol. V, pp. 33, 37, 38, 42.
51. Ganda Singh : *The Panjab Past and Present*, Oct., 1975, p. 446.
52. Macauliffe, Vol. V, pp. 153-154.
53. Ibid., p.162.
54. Ibid., p. 163.
55. Ibid., pp. 173-174; Koer Singh, *Gurbilas Patshahi Das*, pp. 189-190.

56. *Indian Historical Quarterly*, March, 1942 sup., p. 3; Rose, I, p. 688.
57. Macauliffe, Vol. I, p. 38.
58. Ibid., p. 339.
59. Guru Granth Sahib, p. 465.
60. *Ibid.,* p. 274.
61. Ibid., p. 730.

II

SIKHISM AND EARLIER INDIAN TRADITIONS

14

NATHISM

DALJEET SINGH

As the words Nath yogis indicate, Nathism is a Saiva cult employing fundamentally Yogic ideology and methodology.

1. HISTORY OF THE SECT

Saivism's combination with yoga has probably the longest religious history in the country. Seals of Shiva in a yogic pose have been found in the Indus valley or Harappan excavations. Shiva is generally believed to be a pre-Rig Vedic and non-Aryan god. [3. pp. 13-15, 2. p. 259]. He is also mentioned as a god in the Vedas, Upanishads and the Mahabharata. [3. p. 115]. He is a feared god in the Rig Veda. [5. p. 106]. Lord Krishna acknowledged his greatness and got a boon from him. The Nath yogis belong to an ascetic group of Saivism. [5. pp. 112-15]. Asceticism as a spiritual tool to gain supernatural powers, has been accepted by all the old systems like Jainism, Yoga, Saivism and the Vedic religion. In the Rig Veda, the hairy Muni in ecstasy is extolled when he drinks poison with Rudra. [3. pp. 15-19, 2. pp. 210-11, and AB Keith, 'Rig Veda', Vol. II. p. 402]. The oldest Saiva system is the Pasupata. It has been mentioned in *Atharvasiras Upanishad* and the *Mahabharata*. [3. pp. 115-16, 5. pp. 112-15]. The Nath yogis are not only directly connected with it, but are also a part of the group called Lakula that has directly developed from the parent Pasupata. This group includes the Kanphata yogis, the Kala Mukhas, the Kapalikas, Aghorpanthies, etc. [2. p. 218]. In this group, four elements are basic and common, namely, asceticism and renunciation of the world, yogic methodology with emphasis on Mantra yoga and Hath yoga, the combination and worship of male and female deities, and the goal of gaining powers, liberation from the world, and merger with Shiva. [3. pp. 128, 133, 2. pp. 112-15]. The Kapalikas are the precursors of Gorakhnathis. Rather, there is no material difference between the two except that Gorakhnathis are comparatively a little moderate in their practices.

In all these systems there is emphasis on the combination of male and female energies, Shiva and Shakti, *linga* and *yoni*, *Purusa* and *Prakirti*, etc. [2. pp. 163-64, 171-73]. The female part is represented by Uma, Parvati, Durga and Shakti. The group is noted for its wild, erotic and abhorrent practices and blood sacrifices. [2. pp. 116, 171-72].

As is well-known, all yoga, especially Hath yoga, is generally done in order to gain miraculous physical and psychical powers. It is a very old belief that the yogi can do anything and is the master of nature. [2. pp. 270-71, and Radhakrishnan Indian Philosophy, Vol. II, p. 336].

The four elements mentioned above have been present in these systems from the earliest times. The worship of *linga* and *yoni* was there in the Lakula Group including Kanphatas. The Kapalika system, which is nearest to the Naths, has been mentioned in the Upanishads. [2. pp. 171-73]. The sect existed before the Christian era and the time of Kena Upanishad. [3. pp. 117-18]. The Kanphata line started with Machhendra Nath, who is the first historical Nath. Gorakhnath is probably the third Nath, though some say that six Naths intervened between the two. [2. pp. 229-30]. It is generally believed that Gorakhnath appeared any time between the 11th and the 14th century. But according to Briggs, who has considered all evidence on the point, he lived in the 12th century A.D. [2. p. 249].

2. LEGENDARY HISTORY

It is common in India that whenever a cult breaks away from the parent sect, the devotees of the new cult create numerous legends about its author by giving him both the highest spiritual status and maximum antiquity. The legendary history of Gorakhnath is very variant. One legend says that he is the original deity and Shiva, Brahma and Vishnu are his disciples; another version calls him the *avtar* of Shiva, who appears in all *Yugas*. In the *Satyuga*, he appeared at Tilla in Jhelum district, Pakistan. [2. p. 228]. But, the generally accepted legend about the Nath is that once Shiva was imparting to Parvati the secret mantra for spiritual realization, Machhendra Nath, who was lying as a fish near by, heard and grasped the mantra. [2. p. 231]. Though Lord Shiva is supposed to be the first Nath (Adinath), [2. pp. 228-30, 98]. Machhendra Nath is the first human Nath. [2. pp. 230-31]. In that lineage, Gorakhnath is probably the third or the ninth Nath to get the secret mantra. [2. pp. 231-49]. In the course of time, this mantra, it is believed, was received by Janeshvara, the famous commentator of the Gita, Chatanya and Tukaram. [2. pp. 234-35]. It is this secret mantra which is possessed by Naths of this cult.

3. THE METAPHYSICAL VIEW AND APPROACH TO THE WORLD

Saivism has a variety of metaphysical views regarding the world. In the Pasupata system, the parent system of Naths, Ishwara and Pradhana are the cause of everything. Pradhana produces the world, or effects (*karya*), including souls. The effects are of three kinds, the soul (*pashu*), 'cognition' and 'organs.' The 'effects' are dependent on Shiva, who is the cause of everything. But the effect, the created soul, is eternal. Shiva is the original cause, on which the effects depend. [5. pp. 121-123]. In the Pasupata system, the chief aim is to gain powers. The world, though real, is considered to be in fetters, from the bondage of which release has to be sought. In essence, thus, the Naths accept the philosophy and approach of yoga, which is dualistic and seeks the liberation of *purusha* from the meshes of *prakriti*. [5. pp. 121-23]. In Nathism, too, the world is deemed to be a place of misery which has to be renounced as an entanglement. Irrespective of the fact whether Nathism is dualistic or monistic, its approach to the world remains the same as that of yoga. It is said that Shiva being fed up with creation, cut off his organ. [3. pp. 114-16]. That is why the yogis are ascetic and are associated with cremation grounds. The ashes on the body of the Nath represent cremation ashes. Shiva is called *maha yogi* and has been shown in the garb of a yogi. The Nath yogis, too, take a vow of celibacy and altogether shun the world of man.

4. THE GOAL

Being basically akin to yoga, Naths have a goal which, even though slightly variant in its description, is in essence, the same as in yoga. In yoga, the goal is three fold, to gain power, to be liberated from the world, and to seek isolation. In Nathism, the first two objects of the goal are the same. [3. p. 114, 2. pp. 137-8, 258-64, 270-73, 324, 343]. The final state is called Kaivalya or isolation of *purusha* in a state of mindless unconsciousness. In Nathism, too, the final goal is of complete dissociation from the world, involving a wholly passive and blissful union with, or merger in, Shiva. [3. pp. 116-18]. The difference in the goals is in name only. In both cases, it is a state of complete inactivity. In one case, the *purusha* shines in its own light; in the case of Nathism, the soul shines in the eternal light of Shiva. In both cases, the primary object is to gain powers and seek liberation from the oppression of the world. [2. pp. 261-64, 269-71, 324].

5. ORGANISATION, METHODOLOGY AND DISCIPLINE

Let us now give the rationale, the routine and the practices of the religious life of the Naths and the physical and spiritual discipline observed by them.

(i) *The Organisation* : The Nath system being ascetic and monastic, they have a number of monasteries all over the country. The important centres are Tilla (Jhelum district, Pakistan), Hinglaj (Baluchistan), Dhinodhar (Kuchh), Gorakhpur and Devi Pattan (U.P.), etc. [2. pp. 102-5]. All yogis are members of one monastery or the other, and each monastery is headed by a *pir* or guru. Since even Muslims are accepted in the faith (at one time there were over 38,000 Muslim Naths), the heads of the centres at Hinglaj and Tilla, which are situated in the Muslim areas, are called *pirs*. Actually, the head of the important monastery at Hinglaj was a Muslim, and the complaint was that visitors to that centre were converted to Islam. [2. p. 106]. Every person initiated among the Naths is accepted by a guru of some monastery, of which the new entrant becomes a member. There are twelve sects of *kanphatas*. Each was organised by a disciple of Gorakhnath. [2. p. 62].

The disciple has to take three important vows. He has to be a celibate. Further, he undertakes not to engage himself in any business, employment or profession and has to sustain himself by begging for his food. Thirdly, he has to observe *ahimsa*. [2. p. 28]. The yogi is advised to live in a place where the area is not disturbed, the king is good and alms are freely available. There, he has to choose a solitary place for his meditation and yoga. [2. pp. 1-5, 28]. After the yogi is accepted as a probationer, he is supposed to walk on both sides of the river Narbada. The period of probation may extend to anything from one year to a much longer period. When the person is finally accepted as a yogi, his ears are split. By it a mystic channel or Nadi is opened up. [2. pp. 5-6, 30]. The yogi travels barefooted. Except for the four rainy months, the yogi is on the move to different Nath monasteries and other Hindu places of pilgrimage. He wears the scantiest of clothes and goes almost naked. He rubs ashes on his body and wears earrings in his split ears. The *mudras* should preferably be of the horns of a rhino. The yogi wears a necklace of Rudraksha beads and also a special thread. In addition, he carries a whistle. These three items are called the *saili*. The loss of any of these items involves stoppage of the eating of food till it is replaced. [3. p. 134]. The daily routine involves begging, and at that time he wears kerchiefs round his arms. The *mudra* is so important that if the same is broken, the yogi would not take food; nor can he perform religious rites or talk to his fellow yogis till the same is substituted. [3. pp. 8-9]. The Naths bury their dead.

(ii) *Monasteries And Places Of Worship* : It is of religious significance and merit to visit Nath monasteries, particularly, Tilla, Hinglaj, Dharmodhar, etc., and sacred Hindu rivers and places of pilgrimage like Haridwar, Prayag, Ganga, Godawari, Benaras, Ajudhia, Brindaban, Badrinath, Kedarnath, Pushkar, etc. At the monasteries, there are temples, images and pictures of Hindu gods and religious presonalities like Dattartreya, Krishna and *gopies*, Ram Chandra, Hanuman, Lakshman and others. Shiva in the form of Bhairon is worshipped. [2. pp. 78-86, 3. p. 137]. Homage is paid to Hindu gods. Dattatreya and Hanuman are also worshipped by the *kanphatas*. In Bengal, the Naths worship both Shiva and Vishnu. At their centres, blood sacrifices are done at the Bhairon temple and at some tombs. [2. pp. 94-96].

(iii) *Caste And Social Distinctions* : In theory, only twice born are initiated as Naths. At Tilla, the recruits are only from the first three castes. But, elsewhere, all castes, except some very low castes like Meghwalis and Dheds, are accepted. [2. pp. 26-27]. Women are generally not initiated except widows. [3.p.133] Hindu Naths do not eat with Muslim Naths. [2. p. 27]. Nor do Naths go for begging to Muslim houses or houses of lower castes. [2. p. 45]. "None but a Brahmin ascetic can cook the meals and serve them at any of the ascetic centres extant today, whether Saiva or Vaishnava. Likewise, the worship of the deity remains his privilege and preserve." [3. p. 228]. At Dhinodhar monastery, the higher castes are given uncooked food. The other castes are fed at the monastery hall, but lower castes and Muslims get food outside the monastery in the open. [2. p. 45, 3. pp. 27, 47]. Naths do not sit and eat with their womenfolk, nor even with women Nath-panthis. Many Naths do marry, but the married lot are held in contempt by others. The other Naths do not smoke with them till they have paid a penalty. [3. p. 139].

(iv) *Religious Discipline* : The Nath yogis have four prominent elements of their discipline : (a) asceticism, (b) ritualism, (c) yogic methodology, and (d) the combination of male and female energies and the raising of the *kundalani* with the view to attain union with Lord Shiva. In order to understand these features, we shall briefly trace the history of each of them and indicate the Nath practices. It is relevant to understand that despite the lapse of time and the modern environment, the Naths have not even slightly modified their practices which continue as of old. [3. p. 139].

(a) *Asceticism* : Asceticism is a typically ancient Indian institution. It is believed to be an Indian contribution to world cultures, since asceticism was unknown to the ancient Iranian, Babylonian or Egyptian cultures. It appears to belong to the pre-Aryan or the Sramanic tradition. [3. pp. 1-3]. Harappan seals represent Shiva in an ascetic pose. Jainism particularly extols the power and value of *tapas* (hard discipline and austerity) [3. p. 18-19]. In the *Rig Veda*, too, the force and merit of *Tapas* have been recognised. The *Satpatha Brahmana* says that God created the earth through *Tapas*. The epics and the *Upanishads*, too, accept the significance and supernatural powers of asceticism. This is especially so from the time of Kena Upanishad. Manu has prescribed the conditions and rules for the austere life. [2. pp. 208-10]. In the *Rig Veda*, the hairy *muni* in ecstasy is praised as having divine power who could drink with Rudra from a poison cup. [2. pp. 210-11]. Svetaketu was an Upanishadic philosopher, law-giver and Jnani, a contemporary of Yajnavalkya. [3. p. 30]. He, too, was an ascetic. Sanaka, whom libations are offered as a Vedic sage, was a *brahamacharya*. There were many other ascetic Hindu sages. [3. pp. 27-30]. Even before the time of Buddha, the theory of four *ashramas* provided that half the period of life should be devoted to ascetic living. Dattatreya, deemed to be an incarnation of Vishnu, was a celibate. Even Yajnavalkya says that wise men, without becoming householders, straightaway take to the life of mendicants. It was considered the right and proper course for spiritual endeavour and self-realisation. [3. p. 24]. Chandogya goes a step further, calling "Such *brahmacharya* as not only one of the pillars of rigtheousness, but as a state that ensures Brahma—realisation." [3. pp. 24-25]. Mundaka Upanishad, too, recommends *sanyasa* for final salvation. Even Yajnavalkya says, "Having known Him, one becomes a *muni*, sage or wise one. Desiring the same end, recluses renounce the world. For that very purpose, wise men of old used not to desire progeny." "With this thought, they used to take to the life of mendicancy." "For, desire for progeny is desire for goods." "Brahmins having known Him, practise the life of mendicants." "There are schools of asceticism which have raised the physical part of it to be an ideal in itself, whether as a contortive activity or as the esoteric Hath yoga." [3. pp. 24-32].

It is thus clear that both in the Pre-Aryan Sramanic tradition and the Vedic-Upanishadic tradition, asceticism, celibacy and otherwordliness have been taken to be the principal means of salvation and knowledge. Buddha did strike a mean path; but with him, too, world was a *dukkha* and monasticism became a basic part of his system for nirvana. It is this tradition of asceticism and liberation from miseries of the world the Nath yogis accept as an integral part of their system. Because the vows of Nath yogis provide for celibacy and non-engagement in any business or employment, Shiva, who is called the *maha yogi*, is always associated with wilderness and cremation grounds. That is why the Nath yogis have the ritual of rubbing ashes on their bodies, representing thereby death to worldly connections. [2. pp. 16-17].

(b) *Ritualism And Formalism* : Ritualism has a definite place and value in the system. Certain months, December to April, are considered auspicious for initiation into the system. [2. p. 27]. At initiation, the disciple sits in a particular posture and faces north. Mantras are read at the time of initiation and splitting the ears. These are supposed to have distinct potency and value in preventing pain and bleeding in the process. Rhino horn earrings are preferred because it is a sacred animal. [2. pp. 8, 32-33]. The splitting of the ear has great potency and makes a person immortal. [2. p. 6]. In case the split ear is mutilated, the Nath is excommunicated. In earlier years, he either died or was buried alive. [2. p. 8, 3. pp. 134-35]. If a *mudra* is lost, the yogi must substitute it before he can take food, perform religious rites or talk to his fellow yogis. [2. p. 8].

As we shall mention under the sub-head yoga, Mantra Yoga has a definite value in achieving spiritual advancement. Belief in the mystic potency of words and letters and their repetition is an integral part of the system. This is so especially regarding the word *Om*.

Fasting is considered very efficacious. It removes sins. Fasting on Shivratri is particularly meritorious and makes a person immortal. [2. pp. 142-43]. May be because of the black colour of Bhairon, black buck, black snakes and even black dogs are venerated. Nag Panchami is celebrated by the Naths. [2. pp. 132-35].

Animal and blood sacrifices at the temples of Bhairon and some tombs are a common feature. At the annual fair at Devi Pattan, 20 buffaloes, 250 goats and 250 pigs were sacrificed on a single day. The fair opens on the arrival of the Nath *pir* from Nepal, who presides over the function. The mark of the blood is applied to the devotees. [2. pp. 94-96]. Kalaki Purana, which is a scripture of the *saktas*, has a chapter on human sacrifices. [2. p. 168]. The Gorakhnathis have some practices similar to this group. Naths serve as *pujaris* at the *Sakti* temples. Gorakhnath is said to have substituted animal sacrifice for human sacrifice. [2. p. 141].

At Hinglaj, *linga-yoni* mark is put on the visiting yogis. [2. pp. 17, 172]. Visits to Nath monasteries and Hindu sacred places are regarded as of distinct religious benefit. A visit to Hinglaj monastery is necessary to make a person perfect. [2. p. 108].

The Naths accept and recognise Hindu beliefs in gods and goddesses, good and bad spirits, auspicious and inauspicious days and many other superstitions. [2. p. 125].

(c) *Yogic Practices* : Saivism and yoga have an ancient bond or combination. Harappan seals show Shiva in yogic pose. Both are a part of the Sramanic tradition. Das Gupta writes that yoga arose as the means of deliverance of the hermits from the oppressive environment and the misery of the world. Its theory envisages that, as in the case of Jainism and Sankhya, the combination of the material and spiritual elements is a bondage, and release from the world has to be sought by breaking this combination. Another object is a state of eternal quiet, isolation and bliss.

The basic yogic discipline is the one detailed by Patanjali in the period about 300 A.D. For yoga, celibacy is essential. This discipline is eight-fold, involving *yama, niyama, asana, pranayama, pratyahara, dharna, dhyana* and *samadhi*. It includes use of the word *Om*, fasts, concentration, one-point meditation and stoppage of mental processes, creating unconciousness. As from the ancient times, the general and primary aim of yoga is to gain miraculous powers. The yogi is the master of three worlds and can control the evolution of '*gunas*' of *prakriti*. [2. pp. 265-71]. Such powers are called *siddhis*. Yogis, who have attained those powers, are called Siddhas. Naths are closely associated with Siddhas, whose principle aim is to gain power. For, Gorakhnath is not only one of the nine Naths, but he is counted as one of the eighty four Siddhas. He is supposed to be their teacher. [2. pp. 136-38].

Das Gupta enumerates four kinds of yoga : Raj Yoga, Mantra Yoga, Laya Yoga and Hath Yoga. Raj Yoga deals with mind and its psychic powers and the intellectual processes. Mantra Yoga employs the repitition of sacred texts, words and letters. This yoga almost enters the realm of magic. [2. pp. 272-73]. Laya Yoga is quietist. It involves elimination of mental processes and of inducement of trances and unconsciousness, leading to the final state, ending in permanent quiet of mind. The fourth is Hath Yoga or Kundalani Yoga. The method is mainly physical and in practice it uses Pranayana. The aim is the same, namely *samadhi*, isolation or union with Shiva. The practice of Kundalani Yoga also employs other yogas including Mantra and Laya Yoga. In fact, the practice of any one of the yogas also involves the use of the methods of the other yogas. The general methods used are the ones indicated by Patanjali. The difference is only of emphasis. For, no kind of yoga is exclusive in its character. The Naths mainly stress upon Mantra Yoga and Hath Yoga. [2. pp. 272-74].

The three most important religious texts of the Naths are *Goraksastaka, Goraksa — Paddhati* and *Hath Yoga Pradipika*. The first of them is the most revered work of Naths. It is attributed to Gorakhnath himself. It suggests 84 postures and six stages of yoga and gives 100 verses by the knowledge of which the highest state is attained. It prescribes *asanas* and gaze between the eyes and on the tip of the nose. There are nine doors and those are presided by five deities. During the yogic practice, *linga* and *yoni* are mentioned to appear, accompanied with great light. By seeing this light, death is overcome. [2. pp. 284-88, 3. p.132]. According to the discipline, the Nath must repeat 1008 names of God everyday. The yogi sees 72,000 *nadis* below the navel. In Goraksastaka the *Nadis, Ida, Pingala, Susumana, Gandhari,* etc. and their courses are indicated. [2. pp. 288-91]. The Prana is connected through *Ida, Pingala* and *Susumana.* The repitition of the word *hamsa* is prescribed. By the repitition of the mantra 21,600 times a day, the yogi gains liberation in a year's time or so. By the practice of yoga, even poison can be digested. The secret of Mahanrudra practice should not be told to anyone. He who knows *Khetari Mudra* is not troubled by death. The *Bindu* is of two kinds, white (semen) and blood red (menstrual fluid). *Bindu* is Shiva and *Rajas* is Shakti. By uniting the two, the highest state is achieved. *Om* is the supreme light in which three worlds, three Vedas, three accents and three gods are situated. In *Om* is three-fold knowledge, Shakti, etc. *Om* is the light in the elements of which the world, *bhuh, bhavah, soah* and the three divinities of sun, moon and fire exist. *Om*, the seed should be repeated and uttered. Whether pure or impure, whoever repeats it is not affected by sin. Pranayama, while meditating on the sun and moon, is recommended. In this text, the yogic system, involving Pranayama, six circles, three channels and *kundalani* and *nada* and *bindu*, is detailed. The ten chief *Nadis* are *Ida, Pingala, Susumana, Gandhari, Hastijihoa, Pusa, Yasasvani, Alambusa, Kuhus* and *Samkhini*. These terminate in ten openings. The first three *nadis* are the important ones in raising the *kundalani*. *Susumana* extends to the tenth opening. It is the path of enjoyment and bliss in which male and female elements unite. *Kundalani* is raised through the six *chakras*. *Indra, Brahma* and *Kali* with four-hands, a staff, wine, skull and spear are involved in *kundalani* symbolism. The final goal of *kundalani* is to reach the top of the head at *Sahasrara*, the place of final bliss and union with Shiva. There is *Sunya*, the place of Ishvara, the abode of Brahma. The union of Rajas and Bindu (Shiva and Shakti) is the aim of yoga. The thrills of the physical reaction in the process of yoga are called religious experiences. [2. pp. 293-322].

The aims of yoga are immobility of body and mental process, the ecstatic experiences of union of Rajas (*kundalani*) and Bindu (Shiva) at the various levels and the six *chakras* in the body, supernatural powers, and final release and bliss. All these are secured by *Asanas, Mudra, Bandha, Pranayama*, retention of breath and *bindu*, breath control, cleaning of *nadis* and miscellaneous practices. The other physical yogic methods adopted are *Dhoti, Basti, Neti, Trataka, Mauti, Kapala Bhati*, etc. By Pranayama, *kundalani* is directed to *Susumana*. During the process, one hears internal sounds (*Anahata nad*) in a year's time. Mental processes are brought to a stand still. There are many varieties in the use of *Mudra, Asana, Pranayama*, etc. By this yoga, all physical, psychic and mystic powers are gained and finally Shiva is enjoyed in eternal bliss. If in wrath, the yogi can move the three worlds. The union of *Bindu* and *Rajas* in the throat yields supernatural power. It is the gateway to final release. The *Sahasrara* is the true world, there one has the highest bliss. Mind is dissolved and unconsciousness follows. It is the fountain-head of all creation where *kundalani* enjoys *Paramatman* and bliss. This is the yoga prescribed in the Nath system. It involves all kinds of yogas, but the stress is on Hath Yoga and Mantra Yoga. [2. pp. 326-33].

The question now is whether Hath Yoga is a later innovation, or it is basically a variety of the old and original yogic system. We find that Hath Yoga, in its fundamental form, including the system of *Nadis* and *kundalani*, is very old. It was known to the Chandogya Upanishad which says that the soul departed through the *chakras* gains immortality. [3. p. 130]. Not only is there a reference to *Susmana Nadi*, but the theory of *Nadi* and its spiritual value is given also in the Maitri Upanishad. Tessitore writes : "The close alliance of Kanphata system to the yoga both of Patanjali and of the Upanishads is visible from the prominent part given to the yoga praxis as well as to the mystical theory, to the circles in the body (*chakra, kausala*), arteries (*nala*), vital air (*pavana*) and breaths (*hamsa*)." [3. p. 130]. Similarly, Svetasvatara mentions the great gains of Pranayama. All this only shows that the yoga variety practised by the Nath yogis is nothing new. The system, in its essentials was known in the ancient and the Upanishadic times. There is nothing fundamentally Tantric about it. In fact, the Tantric systems assume the basis of Hath, Mantra, and Raj Yogas. Even the non-Tantric Vaishnava works detail the Hath

Yoga. [3. p. 30-33]. After his survey, Ghurye also concludes that Hath Yoga, in all its essentials, is an ancient or an Upanishadic system. [3. p. 132].

(d) *The Combination Of Male And Female Forces* : The fourth element of Nath fundamentals is the emphasis on the union of male and female energies, Shiva and Shakti, so as to achieve liberation.

Both in the Hath Yoga Pradipika and Goraksa Paddhati which are Nath texts (the former is attributed to Gorakhnath), it has been stated that the highest state can be attained both by asceticism and restraint as well as by sex indulgence. Some of the methods prescribed for achieving eternal bliss or *siddhi* are *Vajroli, Sahjoli* or *Amroli*. These sex practices, conducted in the company of a woman, lead both to *moksha* and enjoyment. *Mudras* and *bandhas* are similar to *asanas* in their efficacy. Great powers are obtained by such like practices. Gheranda names 25 methods, including *Vajroli*, which confer magic and spiritual powers. By Khetari Mudra, one gets ecstatic experiences beyond the range of senses; one becomes deathless and Karma becomes inoperative. The mind and Prana are dissolved in Samadhi. In fact, Raj Yoga, Unmani, Manomani, Asunga, Amaratva, Laya Tatvas, Paramapada, Idvaita, Sahaja, Niranjana, Miralamba, Jivan Mukti and Turiya denote the same or the final state of being or achievement. [2. pp. 333-43]. It means bliss, isolation, union or merger with Shiva or the Absolute. This is the final state in all yogas, including *Kundalani* yoga. [2. pp. 343-47]. "By this yoga, Shiva appears as the vast ocean of bliss and knowledge, destroying the misery of the world, and the end is the state of the unmoving flames of light in the inner soul, a body of bliss and knowledge." [2. pp. 347-48]. While *tapas* (hard discipline and austerity) have their place in the system, many of the practices are concerned with sex functions and experiences. Drugs also induce ecstatic states and there are methods for it. Both *Rig Veda* and Patanjali are aware of their use and utility. Patanjali says, "Perfections proceed from both, or from drugs, or from spells, or from self-castigation or from concentration." [2. p. 346]. There are three classes of practitioners; Pasu, the one seeking self-control; Vira, the one who has gained self-control and powers; and Divya, the one who has reached the final state. He is then free from all rules of virtue and vice. He can do anything and indulge in anything he likes. [2. pp. 281-83].

About the system of Naths, Briggs concludes, "The essence of the Hath Yoga is physical exercise and manipulations, quite mechanical. If it is charged against the exposition found in the preceding pages that it is overburdened with interpretations on too low a plane, it must be said in reply that both the practice and the outlook of the yogis confirm this point of view."

"The historical background of the cult of Gorakhnath points in the same direction. The high religious value to man-woman relations was insisted upon. The first Chatanaya Sahajya movement confirms this point, as does Gorakhnath's early affiliation with Vajarayana Buddhists." "While Vaishnavite movement emphasises love in the consort of the divine, the Saivite lays stress on her power of energy." [2. pp. 349-50].

(e) *Antiquity Of Nathism* : We are not inclined to agree with the view that this aspect of Nath Yoga arose under Tantric influence and led to Nada-Bindu combination.

Even Briggs concedes, while referring to the times of Vedas, "that it is clear that from ancient times, drugs and sex stimulations were used for the same ends of ecstasy and trance." [2. pp. 216, 347]. The view of Tantric influence has arisen largely because of a suggestion that, before being converted to Nathism by Matsyendra Nath, Gorakhnath was a Vajrayana Buddhist. Apart from the fact that the suggestion is far from confirmed, this view displays quite an ignorance of the history of yogic methods and Nathism. We have already seen that *kanphatas* are a part of the Lakula group of the Saivas of the Pasupata system of which Aghoria Kalamukhas and Kapalikas are a part. In fact, Kapalikas are the nearest to *kanphatas*, the essentials of the two cults being the same and similar. As such, this development of the Naths has to be traced to the Pasupata and the earlier systems which are much older than Tantric Buddhism.

Harappan seal and other sources testify celibacy of Shiva [3. pp. 13-15] and his asceticism is vouchsafed. [3. p. 115]. Shiva-yoni worship is mentioned in the *Atharva Veda*. Burnett found a reference to *Saiva Yogis* or *Vratyas* occuring in the Atharva Veda. "He travels in a bullock cart, with a harlot, a musician, two carriers, and two footmen, and professes Saiva magic with great fluency." [3. p. 116]. Harier says that these *Vratyas*, followers of Rudra Shiva and yoga, stand included in the Brahmanic system and are mentioned in the *Atharva Veda*. These persons like yogis stand erect for a year and go over the country (like later yogis) cursing and blessing the people. They are accompanied by a woman. The couple represent the male god and female goddess, Shiva and Shakti. These wandering persons appeared in 800 B.C. before the birth of Buddha. [2. pp. 212-13]. Bhandarkar draws pointed attention to the fact that Shiva, in the form of Lakulisa, is portrayed with his organ erect. And it is in this form of Lakulisa that he is the tutelary deity of the Pasupatas. Bhandarkar further connects this portrayal of Shiva with a similar seal-armlet discovered at Mohanjedaro. [3. p. 13]. Thus, this sex symbolism and combination of male and female forces is both Vedic and pre-Vedic. And, in all its erotic manifestations, is continued in the Kapalikas. This group is referred to in the works of the Ist century A.D. Bhandarkar believes that the sect is mentioned in the *Keno* and *Maitri Upanishads* and is older than them. In the old Soma sect, Shiva is represented as always with his consort Uma. The Kapalikas are known for their methods of sense indulgence for spiritual advancement. [3. pp. 115-17].

In a dramatic skit of the 7th century A.D., Kapalika and Kapalini ridicule the systems of a Jain *muni* and a Buddhist *bhikhshu* and extol their method of spiritual attainment through enjoyment of wine and women. Ultimately, the Jain and the Buddhist are converted to the ways of the Kapalika. [3. pp. 118-19]. This shows that the Saiva systems hardly needed Buddhist influence for accepting erotic practices. It could rather be the other way round. The parent Pasupata system of this group is the oldest Saiva system, being mentioned in the *Atharva Veda, Mahabharta* and *Atherasiras Upanishad*. [3. p. 115]. Till recently, at the Amarnath temple, Nath yogis danced naked, and women wore only a single garment. [2. p. 98].

Another important point is that Dattatreya is one of the chief deities worshipped by the Naths. He is a Hindu deity, who is an *avatara* of Vishnu and is mentioned in more than one list of his incarnations. He was a celibate with miraculous powers and gave self-realising knowledge to great persons like Alarka and Prahlada. He is referred to in the *Upanishads* and is considered to be a *Jnani* and a *Paramahamsa*. Dattatreya is the only incarnation who has a cult following him and has temples devoted to his worship. All through, the Puranic account "depicts him as always in ecstasy, surrounded by women, drinking wine and indulging in sex." In one Puranic account, "he demands flesh and wine in a human skull." And he is one of the chief deities whom Nath yogis worship. [3. pp. 34-5].

The Hindu works also recognise that the highest achievement can also be made through wine and women. Hindu Tantra is supposed to be the 5th Veda of Kalyuga. [2. pp. 275, 280-8]. Infact, Tantric systems themselves depend on Raj, Mantra and Hath Yogas, which are older systems. The Mantra Yoga as is known, is closely allied to the Vedic theory [3. p. 21] that words, verses, letters and symbols have mysterious powers, and that man and the world are subject to their influence.

Ghurye has collected a mass of evidence to dispel the suggestion of Tantric influence on the Nath Panthis. He writes, "As Tantric literature is fairly recent, it may be supposed by our readers that the yogi order is of recent origin. This impression must now be countered." "Fundamentally, the yogis represent the oldest school of Indian asceticism." [3. p. 115]. "The yogis are the residue of the ancient Saivite Sects." [2. p. 218].

Zimmer also, in his broad survey of Tantric systems, concludes, "and in the deep philosophy of the Tantric, we have again signs of the resurgence of the religiosity of the non-Aryan, matriarchal tradition of Dravidian times." [4. p. 569].

Another significant fact which clearly shows the link of Gorakhnathis with the ancient Pasupata or Saiva system is the wild and abhorrent nature of the two sects. The author of the *Dabistan* writes that Gorakhnathis use filtered excreta. He himself saw a Gorakhnathi eating the rotten flesh of a corpse. This practice is deemed meritorious. [2. p. 227].

Two other factors also show the lack of the Nath connection with Tantric Buddhism and its antiquity as a system. It is admitted that Gorakhnath introduced some moderation in the Naths, both in regard to blood sacrifices and sex practices, compared to the extremes of the older Saiva sects like the Kapalikas and Kalamukhas (though Aghorpanthis, also followers of Gorakhnath, are very extreme in their practices). Had he really the Vajarayana background, which according to Briggs is one of the most degraded religious groups, the Naths would have been more licentious and erotic in their practices than the Kapalikas. This they are not. Hence, the improbability of Gorakhnath's being originally a Vajarayana.

Secondly, old religious systems like Hinduism, in order to maintain a semblance of continuity, developed a number of internal contradictions. Because, while attempt is made to accept and absorb new developments, the older beliefs are not shed. This feature of contradictory practices is typically present among the Naths. Gorakhnathis, while they take a vow of *ahimsa*, also indulge in blood sacrifices at their monasteries. Many of the

Naths eat meat except pork and beef. On the one hand, there is a vow of asceticism and all concern with the world is given up by rejecting all business and employment, on the other, the chief aim is to gain power over the forces of the body, nature and the world. While the Nath takes a vow of celibacy, sex-symbolism, erotic practices and licensed indulgence are recognised as the path of spiritual achievement. And the person who has reached the spiritual height is above virtue and vice, being free to indulge in anything forbidden to the seeker. Such strong contrasts in Nath beliefs and practices clearly indicate an old tradition that has developed over a long period of time. It is not a new cult with a unified system of doctrines and disciplines.

There is, thus, overwhelming evidence to conclude the direct lineage of the Nath cult from the oldest pre-Vedic and Vedic traditions through the Saiva system of Pasupata and Kapalikas, with both of which all its essentials are common. All the world over, ascetic or monastic systems, whether Hindu, Saiva, Vaishnava or Buddhist, at one point or the other, lead to male and female symbolism and consequent erotic practices, ultimately recognising sensual indulgence as a means to salvation. We should also like to emphasise that where creative energies are not yoked to life-affirming, constructive and virtuous deeds, sects insisting on celibacy or adopting sex symbolism almost always degenerate into accepting erotic, licentious or abhorrent practices. This has happened both inside and outside India. On this issue, we agree with Briggs that whereas female divinities have arisen all over and in all ages, no where in the world has male and female symbolism been able for long to keep itself on a high plane. [2. pp. 350-51].

6.   SOCIAL RESPONSIBILITY AND THE WORLDVIEW OF THE NATH YOGI

The yogi, whether liberated or otherwise, has no social responsibility. By his very basic vows, he cuts himself off from the world. The liberated person is either above virtue and sin, or stops all physical and psychical processes entering a state of mindless unconsciousness. His mystic union involves eternal bliss and rest. The question of any consequent activity does not arise. He has no social responsibility towards his fellow beings. [2. pp. 351-52]. The yogi is under a vow that he will not earn his living and will instead beg for his food — that being a part of his routine at the monastery. For his meditation, he is enjoined to select a place which is not socially disturbed and where alms are freely available. [2. pp. 2-3, 326]. Evidently, this worldview is categorically life-denying and negative. It is wholly opposed to the worldview of life-affirmation. The world is a place of misery, release from it can be sought by completely dissolving all physical and psychical processes of life. Applying the test of the unity of perception, ideology and activity, the entire system and life of the yogi unmistakenly point towards a worldview of withdrawal from life. While the Nath yogi expects the social system to provide him with abundant alms and an undisturbed solitude and socio-political environment and security, he, on his part, feels altogether no responsibility towards the society on which he depends. In short, in its approach to the world, its ethic, methodology, discipline and its goals, it is typically a worldview of what Schweitzer calls life-negation. According to the classification adopted by us, Nathism is a mysticism of rest, merger, or inactivity.

SIKHISM AND NATHISM : A COMPARISON

We find that the answers of Nathism and Sikhism to the twelve issues indicated by us are mostly opposed in their implications. Sikhism is monotheistic, Nathism being a Saiva cult, also claims to be such, but leans more towards, pantheism. In both cases the world is taken to be real. But, here ends the apparent similarity. As we probe further, sharp divergences appear. The two systems have entirely different methodologies, goals and worldviews. In Nathism, the world is a misery, and liberation from it has to be sought by vows of celibacy, *ahimsa*, and non-participation in the affairs of man. The Nath cuts himself off from the world as far as he can, because his goal is liberation from it. Once liberated, the superman merges in Shiva in peace and bliss. The discipline to reach the goal is all formal, ritualistic and yogic.

The Sikh Gurus, goal is very different. They say, "by despising the world one gets not to God." They consider the world "a *dharamsal* — a beautiful place for all spiritual endeavours." As such, participation in the activities of man becomes essential. The responsibilities of the householder's life are freely accepted. God being the Ocean of Virtues, He shows His deep interest in the world and man. Therefore, in Sikhism, the superman has to be the instrument of God in alleviating man's sufferings and solving his problems. God's Will is attributive and man's goal is always to carry it out. The Sikh prayer is not for liberation from the world but for being given millions of hands to serve Him. For God showers His Grace where the weak are helped. As to the spiritual discipline, there is only one method, the way of good deeds and deeds alone. The Gurus do not believe in *ahimsa* nor do they preclude the use of force when quite utterly necessary. By applying the test of the unity of perception, ideology and activities, this is the only inference we could draw from the lives of the Gurus.

Accordingly, we conclude that the two systems hold diametrically opposite views.

Not only is the contrast between the two systems glaringly evident, but every student of Guru Granth Sahib knows that Nathism is one of the few systems, in which the approach, the methodology, the formalism and the goal have been strongly criticised by the Gurus. There are numerous hymns in which the ways and the ideals of the Naths have been denounced and the right ways and approach indicated. For example, in the following hymns, the Gurus reject the practices of the Naths and instead recommend that virtues should be cultivated and practised.

"Instead of wearing *mudras* and necklace of beads, carrying a beggar's bowl and staff and scrubbing ashes on the body, one should cultivate contentment and self-respect, strive and always keep God in mind." [1. p. 939]. "One has to control one's mind, keep away from vices, treat all beings as of one class and salute Him alone." [1. Japuji]. Again, "The spiritual path (yoga) does not lie in wearing *mudras* in ears and necklace of beads, nor does it lie in keeping a staff and a horn, nor in rubbing ashes on the body and making a close shave of head. Real yoga (spiritual way) is to remain tranquil and balanced amidst the distracting turmoils of the world." [1. p. 730]. "The spiritual path can be trodden not by mere words and talk, but by actually treating all men alike and as one's equals. Yoga does not lie in living in cremation grounds, doing one-point meditation or in roaming all over the land or visiting places of pilgrimage, but in remaining balanced and God-centred while conducting the affairs of the world." [1. p. 730].

The yogic methods have also been clearly rejected, including *Neoli* and other yogic exercises. The only worthwhile thing is the love of God and man, and to keep Him in one's mind. The rubbing of ashes on the body and other rituals have no meaning unless vice and egoism are given up and the heart is in tune with Him. The Gurus lay down that "no worship of God is possible without the practice of virtues." [1. p. 4]. "Good, righteousness, virtues and giving up of vice are the ways to realize the essence of God." [1. p. 418].

In the Guru's system, "he who earns his living through honest means and shares the fruit of his labour with others, knows the (Godly) way." [1. p. 1245]. Parasitism in every form is deemed most despicable. The Guru deprecates "the yogi who gives up the world and then is not ashamed of begging from door to door." [1. p. 886].

In the Nath system celibacy is essential. Woman, as in many other Hindu systems, is deemed to be a temptress, because the Naths would not sit and eat with even Nath women. But in the Guru's system, downgrading the woman has been denounced and she is deemed to be an equal partner in man's spiritual venture. When the Third Guru created districts of religious administration, women too were selected to head them. All this was wholly contrary to the entire Indian tradition in which women had been given only a secondary place and generally considered to be an impediment in the spiritual path. In all ascetic and monastic systems, woman has been dubbed as evil to be shunned. That is so even in systems that renounce the world either on account of *bhakti* or devotion or for other reasons. But in the Guru's system, her role is significant and equal to that of man.

The Gurus emphatically reject the otherworldly approach of the Naths. They deprecate renunciation of the world as well as one who does not earn his living. In all the hymns of the Gurus, the emphasis is on the shedding of vice and on virtuous living. "Love, contentment, truth, humility and other virtues enable the seed of *Naam* (God) to sprout." [1. p. 955]. "With self-control and discipline, we forsake vice and see the miracle of man becoming God." [1. p. 343].

A confusion has arisen in the minds of some students of religions, because the Gurus have used some words in their hymns which have also been employed by the authors of other religious books, but with a different meaning and import. For example, the Gurus say that at the final stage of spiritual achievement, one gets the bliss of *Anhad Sabad* or unstruck music. But this *Anhad Sabad*, as the Gurus call it, has nothing to do with the "*Anhad Sabad*", as used by the Nath Yogis. In the Nath Yoga "*Anhad Sabad*" is a sound which the Yogi hears when the *kundalani* is raised through the *nadis* and the *chakras* in the body. This is a process which occurs at a far lower stage than the final one of bliss when the union of *kundalani* takes place with Shiva at the *Sahassare* in the top of the head. As such, the "*Anhad Sabad*" of the Naths, as Dr Jodh Singh has also stated, has nothing to do with the *Anhad Sabad* of the Gurus, which indicates the bliss one attains at the time of the final spiritual achievement. [6. pp. 214-220]. In fact, the

Gurus have described this ultimate state also with many different terms like *Nirbana*, *Turya*, *Mukti*, etc. But these words have quite different import and meanings in the other religious systems, where too, these terms have been used. A close study of Guru Granth Sahib makes clear the real content and meaning of these terms. These are the Gurus own, and are quite variant from the way other systems use them. For example, Buddhist *nirvana* is entirely different from what the Gurus conceive and convey by this term. They only mean union with *Naam*. Sometimes, the Gurus' use of these terms is only metaphoric. Therefore, the use of some words, also employed by the Nath yogis, does not mean that the Gurus accept the Nath yoga approach. In fact, the Gurus definitely denounce it. Though McLeod has been misled by such terms, yet even he concedes that Guru Granth Sahib does not mention the system of *Ida*, *Susumana* and *Pingla*, which is fundamental to the Nath Yoga methodololgy. Guru Granth Sahib clearly records Bhagat Namdev saying, "I shall sing and imbibe the name of God and achieve the highest stage, I reject the methods of *Ida*, *Pingla* and *Susumana* and of the union of the sun and the moon (as in Nath Yoga, the sun representing Shiva and the moon, the *kundalani*). I shall reach Him otherwise." [1. pp. 972-3].

There is one more point of contrast. In Nathism, the method of sense indulgence is accepted as an alternative discipline for spiritual attainments. In Guru Granth Sahib there is not the faintest suggestion of this kind. Rather Nath celibacy and its ill effects are denounced. "He carries a beggar's bowl by giving up the world and women. But overpowered by passion he is infatuated by women of others."

In short, Nathism and Sikhism present opposite worldviews. It is the compulsions and implications of each worldview that lead the two systems to give opposing answers practically to all of the various issues raised by us. The fundamental difference is that Nathism rejects the world and life as misery, whereas Sikhism accepts them as spiritually meaningful. Therefore, in Nathism withdrawal from the world, asceticism, celibacy, the downgrading of women, solitude, yogic methodology, etc., become naturally essential. Similarly, in Sikhism, God being Attributive, virtuous participation in the world, accepting a householder's life and responsibilities, the consequent raising of the status of women, and the love and service of man in all spheres of his life become logically necessary. Because, here the key test of spiritual growth and stature is in the deeds of a person and whether or not the person earns his living through his own honest endeavour, shares his income with others, and treats everyone as his equal. In one case, the goal is merger or union with Shiva, involving eternal peace and bliss without any role for the superman. In the other, the goal is always to carry out the Attributive Will of God and a continuous virtuous endeavour to solve the problems of man. There is hardly a meeting ground between the two systems.

REFERENCES

1. Guru Granth Sahib.
2. G.S. Briggs : *Gorakhnath and Kanphata Yogies*.
3. G.S. Ghurye : *Indian Sadhus*.
4. H. Zimmer : *Philosophies of India*.
5. R.G. Bhandarkar : *Vaisnavism and Saivism*.
6. Jodh Singh : *Gurmat Nirnain*.

15

VAISNAVISM

DALJEET SINGH

Vaisnavism is far from being a unified or an integrated religious system. The reason for it is that it has not grown from the religious experience or the inspiration of a single personality or prophet. It is a grouping together of cults and creeds that are at times mutually quite at variance in their doctrines and essentials. Even the name Vaisnavism was given to this group only during the later period of its growth extending over two thousand years. In order to understand Vaisnavism and its various modes of worship of the Lord, we shall first have briefly to trace its long and chequered history.

The ancient systems of India were either dualistic, involving a multiplicity of *purushas* without the concept of God in the theistic sense, or were ritualistic (Vedic), without the concept of a Commander issuing the Vedic commands. In the Upanishadic system, Brahman was conceived primarily in the monistic or in the pantheistic sense. In this system, there was naturally no place for devotion or a system of love as contemplated in a theism. For, in the Vedic system, everything including heaven could be obtained by the performance of rituals and sacrifices. In this context, the growth of a system of worship and devotion could appear only by the inflow of a side-stream and not as indigenous to the Vedic or the other orthodox systems. Having been accepted in the Brahminical fold originally, only as an alternative method of *moksha*, it later grew into an independent religious system, with doctrines and a philosophy of its own. This happened mainly in the post-Sankara period, especially when the Alwar saints in the south and other Vaisnava saints came up in the north, the east, and the west of India. Let us see, how the content and the thought of the Vaisnava system developed and crystallised during its long history which may be divided into three phases; the first of the pre-Gita period, and the second of the period between the Gita and the emergence of the Alwar saints. In the third phase, *bhakti* was deemed to be the major, if not the sole, means of salvation. This is mostly in the post-Sankara period.

THE FIRST PHASE

(a) It is now commonly believed that originally four streams of thought mingled to form the early Vaisnava system of the pre-Christian era when it was incorporated in the Gita. Probably, the oldest of them was the worship of Vasudeva, who was the god of a tribe called *Vrsni* or *Satvatas*. One of the earliest references to it is in a Buddhist text, where the worship of Vasudeva is mentioned alongwith over half a dozen other minor systems of worship, including the worship of a cow, a horse, an elephant, a crow, etc.[1] Vasudeva was a historical figure. The system of his worship with other accretions was called the Bhagavata system. This cult, which later involved the worship of Vasudeva-Krishna, had many non-Aryan and non-Vedic elements.[2]

(b) The second stream of thought was connected with the name of Narayana, who had been mentioned as a god in the Vedic times. Nara, Narayana, Hari, sons of Dharma, are referred to as forms of the Supreme. But, apart from reference to them as gods and the ritualistic use of the related hymns, there was no system of their separate worship. For, in the Vedic period ritualism was supreme. It is later that the worship of Narayana began. Narayana was originally a tribal god.[3] Later still arose the worship of Hari as a side or subsidiary growth. In course of time, both these streams, of the worship of Vasudeva and of Narayana and Hari, appear to have joined each other, though their complete mingling had not taken place even up to the time of the Bhagavad Gita.

(c) The third stream of thought arose from the Upanishads themselves. The Upanishads and the Bhagavad Gita are believed to be mere compilations of variant and unreconciled religious thoughts.[4] In the Chandogya Upanishad occurs the name of Krishna, which name was later associated with Vasudeva as Krishna-Vasudeva. In the Upanishads, especially the later Upanishads, the idea of a Controller of the universe had appeared. But, it is there entirely in the context of the monistic or pantheistic Brahman, the Vedic ritualism, and the caste. In fact, the caste divisions had not only been accepted by the Upanishadic thought as a part of their overall ideology, but the system had been well formed in the Upanishadic period.

(d) Though Vishnu was also a Vedic deity, the theory of his incarnation had not been advanced in the Vedic times. All the same, his worship constituted the fourth stream that formed the system of Vaisnavism.

These four streams contributed to the thought of the Bhagavad Gita, which, being an eclectic compilation, also drew heavily on the religious systems of *Sankhya*, yoga, Vedic Ritualism, and the Upanishads.

Originally, the worship of Narayana, Vasudeva and Visnu became associated with the religion of ritualistic sacrifices. This is probably the price these cults had had to pay for being accepted in the Brahminical fold. Till the time of the Gita, neither the complete identification of Vasudeva and Narayana had taken place, nor had his being the incarnation of Visnu been accepted. Thus, Pancaratra or Bhagavatism, we find, is the original and the chief source of Vaisnavism. The Gita had no organic connection with this earlier system which had been there since almost the fifth century B.C.

In the beginning, *bhakti* meant only favour, fondness or kinship. Gods had *bhakti* for men, just as men had *bhakti* for gods. *Bhakti* meant merely a form of adoration.[5] The view, has also been expressed that the theistic worship of Narayana, and later even the theory of the incarnations of Visnu, arose under the influence of Buddhism. Because, it was the Mahayana that introduced the doctrine of Boddhisattva and the idea of an Ambitabha and a Buddha who took birth in order to save mankind. As a consequence, also appeared the idea of devotion towards such a compassionate saviour of mankind.[6]

THE SECOND PHASE

It is practically a settled view that the Gita is of composite origin.[7] Admittedly, it suggests different doctrines. The path of *Jnana* or knowledge, the path of ritualism or *Karman* and the path of modified *Sankhya* are recommended as different means for the achievement of the goal. In addition, the path of worship is suggested as an alternative method of *moksha*. It is not the type of worship or emotional *bhakti* which we find in the Bhagavata Purana, or as described and defined by Sandilya more than ten centuries later. The worship prescribed in the Gita is a mere form of adoration.

Let us first consider the place of theistic thought in the Bhagavad Gita. For this purpose we shall state briefly the contents of the Gita and the systems it suggests. The path of knowledge is from the *Sankhya* and of *Karma* (Yajnas) from the Rig Veda. In the *Sankhya*, all desires and actions are the activities of Prakriti. Hence the way to liberation is a realisation by the '*Purusa*' that no activity is his. To dissociate oneself from that activity, is the aim of life. The so-called method of unattached action, a 'psychological impossibility',[8] is, thus, simply another way of expressing the same idea of disentanglement of *Purusa* from Prakriti. Man should not, be attached to actions in the world. He should, instead, withdraw himself (the *Purusa*) from all activities, which are only the phases and forms of *prakriti* with which *Purusa* should remain unconcerned. In addition, Gita gives religious sanction to the path of worship or *bhakti*. In the Mahabharata the prominent gods are Shiva and Visnu. It is stated in Chapter IV that 'those who know the incarnations and the celestial deeds of Bhagavata are released from the body and are not born again'; that '*Yajna* of knowledge is the best .' The system of rituals and sacrifices is also fully rationalised and recognised. *Sankhya* and *Yoga* are linked with *Sanyasa* and *Karam* yoga or meditational ritualism. By following either, one gets the fruits of both. It suggests that all worship and austerities should be devoted to God. By yoga practices one gets tranquility in Bhagavata. The devotees of Lord are of four kinds. Of these, the *Jnani* is the best. He who dies while remembering Lord Krishna attains to this condition. By yoga practices, concentration and meditation, and by uttering *Om* and remembering Krishna, one gets *Moksa*. There is no return from that stage. Those who die while the sun is in the northern course go to Brahman. Those who die while the sun is in the southern course, go to the moon from which the soul returns. Through yoga practices one reaches *Aksara* (Brahman), the highest goal. By meditation on the syllable *Om*, the soul hits the target of Brahman. The system is made theistic by Brahman being called Bhagavata. Those who perform sacrifices and rituals, attain heaven thereby. The value of rituals is, thus, recognised. One who adores Krishna single-mindedly, becomes holy even if one were wicked earlier. The Vaisyas, the Sudras and women can worship Bhagavata. Those who meditate on Bhagavata reach him quickly. Those who meditate on Brahman reach there but with difficulty. If one cannot meditate and concentrate on Bhagavata, nor can remember him, one should do disinterested deeds. But, to this method the third place is given in the order of preference as a mode of salvation.

Modern research discloses that this concession to women and Sudras for admission to the path of *bhakti* was given as a result of Buddhist influence, because Buddhist monasteries had been opened to Sudras, Vaisyas and women without any distinction.[9] It is also believed that this opening of the path of *bhakti* to women and Sudras was far from being a new thing or a concession. In the local or non-Aryan tribes, there was no religious prejudice against women or others. Therefore, for Brahminism, the acceptance of the *status quo* became necessary for bringing these tribes under its authority. This is also suggested by the fact that, as time passed, the religious prejudice against women and Sudras instead of wearing out became hardened. For, both Ramanuja and Sankaradeva (a very liberal saint), would not initiate women to the Vaisnava path.[10] The former virtually confirmed the religious distinction between Sudras and others by opening only *Prapatti* to the low castes and closing the path of *bhakti* to them.

The metaphysical position in the Gita is somewhat puzzling, as both pantheistic and dualistic views are indicated. As also stated in some of the Upanishads, God divides himself and forms the various beings of the world. In this sense, souls are considered identical with God. At the same time, the dualism of *Sankhya* and co-eternal *prakriti* are recognized. The goal is an eternal life of bliss. All changes, qualities and actions belong to *prakriti*, which is the cause of all of them, while *Purusa*, who is inactive, suffers. In this body is '*Purusa*', the Supreme Soul. By meditation one can see it and withdraw *Purusa*. The final stage can be attained both by *Sankhya-yoga*, and by *Karam-yoga*. Others can do so by meditation. The *Sankhya* system and all the details of the working of *prakriti* are fully accepted. But the mention of the atheism of *Sankhya* is avoided. It is also accepted by implication that since *Purusa* does not take part in the activities of *prakriti*, man is absolved of all moral responsibility. Hence the emphasis is on concentration, meditation, mechanical remembering, withdrawal, ritualism and knowledge, but not on ethical conduct as the foremost path to salvation.

The diet taken and the modes of worship, sacrifices and austerities practised by one differ according to one's faith and nature, which are of three kinds, featured by goodness, activity and knowlege. This would seem to suggest differences of even diet among higher and lower castes. It is laid down that the duties of a man vary according to his caste. In the Gita there is a major emphasis on confirming and consolidating the caste system. Not only has it been stated that the Lord made the four castes but it has twice been stressed that the doing of the caste duties of another caste, howsoever well done, or well meant, is not as good as the doing of one's own caste duties, even though without quality and worth. "Of Brahmanas, Kshattriyas, Vaishyas and Shudras, O Parantapa, the duties have been distributed according to qualities born of their own natures." "Ploughing, protection of kine, and trade are the Vaishya duty, born of his own nature.

Action of the nature of service is the Shudra duty born of his own nature." "Better is one's own duty though destitute of merits than the well-executed duty of another. He who doeth the duty laid down by his own nature incurreth not sin." "Congenital duty, O son of Kunti, though defective, ought not to be abandoned."[11]

On the side of all phenomenal change, the *Sankhya* system and its twenty-four principles of change are accepted; so are yoga principles and its meditation. It is the contemplative union with God that we find in the Gita, and the transition to it from the state of yoga concentration is not difficult to understand. The earlier literature does not emphasize the emotional element in devotion. The kind of emotional *bhakti* or love, which appeared in the post Sankara-Ramanuja period, is simply not there. In the times of the Gita, and those of Ramanuja, all that is meant by *bhakti* or devotion is '*upasana*', or meditation and concentration on God. The ideas of the worship and the grace of God are there. But the same were present, though in a faint form, even in the Upanishads like the Brhadaranayaka, the Katha and the Mundaka.

It is necessary here to indicate the mode of worship of the Bhagavata system which became, in conjunction with streams from the other schools of thought, the chief base of the worship of the deity. *Pancaratra Samhita* is the book on which is based the method of worship. The system is somewhat ritualistic and prescribes mantras variously arranged. Many rites are also indicated in the *Satvata-Samhita*. Shankaracharya details the following methods of worship : (1) Going to the temple with mind fixed on the deity, (2) collecting materials for worship, (3) actual worship, (4) the muttering of mantras, and (5) yoga or meditation. By worship in this manner for a hundred years all sins are destroyed. As to the method of worship of Hari, there are six steps : (1) Remembering Him, (2) the uttering of His Name, (3) salutation, (4) resorting to His feet, (5) constant worship with devotion, and (6) the surrender of the soul.[12]

It is significant that all, modes of worship are devotional, ritualistic and formal without any reference to social and moral conduct. In fact, in the Bhagavata system, *bhakti* or worship was done in order to gain religious merit rather than as an expression of love for the deity.[13]

It is clear that the Bhagavad Gita gave few new religious ideas. In fact, it records all kinds of divergent systems within one compilation. The overall system and approach remains, by and large, orthodox and traditional. The duality and co-eternal character of *Purusa* and *prakriti* are accepted, as also the priority of the system of meditation, yoga and concentration. It is clearly mentioned that the Lord came to fulfil the law and not to supplant it. The rigidity and the immobility of the caste system are confirmed, sanctified and stressed, in so far as one must do one's own caste duties and not those of other castes.

Further, the sacrificial system is also regarded as a valid path. What is suggested is the worship of Bhagavata. This system had existed already. Except for the purposes of worship, the status of Sudras and women, put in the same class, is kept where it was in the Brahminical system. The worship recommended is also of a formal nature in the sense that even remembrance at the time of death absolves one of all sins and ensures salvation.

Ramanuja defines devotion (*bhakti*) as "un-broken contemplation of God. It is this contemplative union with God that we find in the Gita. In fact, the word *bhakti*, as in the system of the Upanishads or of Ramanuja, only means mere meditation (*Upasana*) and not the loving devotion or love, Self-surrender in the Gita does not mean an ideal of love or of personal relationship. It is the ideal of contentment, non-attachment and self-control. It is the idea of the old yoga of Patanjali, where also this discipline of self-surrender has been suggested.

It is, therefore, important to understand that the system of love, as in the case of Mahayana or of Sufism or of the *bhakti* saints like Kabir, Namdev and others, is simply not there in the Gita, either as an idea or as a basis for future development. It is much later in the Bhagavata Purana that the different forms of emotional *bhakti* are mentioned. In fact, the *bhakti* system of love or mystic intuition through love did not exist before Sandilya. The Gita tended only to consolidate and bring in one compilation variant systems like the worship of Bhagavata, the ritualism and caste duties of the Vedic religion, the dualism of Sankhya-Yoga and its mode of isolation of *Purusa* from the activities of the *prakriti*, the meditation of yoga, and the monism and pantheism of the Upanishads. Das Gupta also refers to the syncretic character of the Gita where he says that it is a compromise "between the worldly life of allotted duties and the hermit's life of absolute renouncement." "On the one hand we purify our minds by non-attachment, and yet, on the other hand, we continue to perform all the ritualistic and other duties belonging to our particular caste or stage of life, i.e. the prescribed stages of four *ashrams*."[14] The Gita laid down different paths of *moksha*. But, the systems had existed already. While it gave priority to the path of *Jnana* and the meditational processes of yoga, and accepted the ritualistic mysticism of the Vedas, it also approved of the formal and meditational devotion of the Bhagavata system.

In the Gita the ideal, by the very nature of things, was merger or salvation from the empirical world with the object of never returning to it. In life all one had to do was to perform one's caste duties that had been assigned under the Vedic and orthodox scriptures. Their authority was fully recognised as also of the overall social structure these prescribed.

In the course of time, the four streams of Vasudeva, Visnu, Narayana and the Upanishad idea of a Supreme Soul combined to form one religion. To this was added the fifth stream of Gopala Krishna from the Ahir race.

The Theory Of Incarnation

This theory is a basic fundamental of Vaisnavism. It portrays faithfully both the genesis and the growth of Vaisnavism as well as the variety of its trends and thoughts. It also explains the evident conflict in some of its principles and theology, and the main thrust and objectives of the system. Simultaneously, with the consolidation of Vaisnavism as a separate system, the theory of incarnation of Visnu came to be formed. The idea, believed to have arisen under Buddhist influence, is that God takes the human form in order to save man. This theory gave an impetus to the attempt at the integration of various religious systems and modes of worship, even though very divergent in their historical origin, creeds, or aims. The only thing common among them was the general acceptance of the Vedic scriptures and *status quo* in the social order. Slowly Visnu rose from a minor to a major god. This cult served a triple purpose. On the one hand it gave recognition to the non-Aryan or local gods and included them in the Hindu pantheon. On the other hand, it brought within the Brahminical fold many of the local and foreign tribes,[15] and thirdly this enabled the Brahminical priests to impose on these new entrants not only their authority and caste ideology, but also their ritual and religious practices. All *avtars* are supposed to be the different forms of Visnu. The theory has become a noteworthy feature of Hinduism. It enables it to absorb other creeds by declaring their gods or prophets as the manifestations of the Supreme God or Visnu. In the Gita, Lord Krishna says that those who worship other gods also worship him, though imperfectly. The number of *avtars* of Visnu rose from time to time, including the boar, the man-lion, the dwarf, Rama, swan, tortoise, and Vasudeva-Krishna. In the Bhagvata Purana this number rose to twenty three. The mythical Kapila, the author of the dualistic *Sankhya* system without a god, is included as an *avtar*, as also the Rsabha, the first Trithankra of the Jains who do not believe in God. By the eighth century A.D., Buddha was also accepted in the list of *avtars*. It appears that, in Vaisnavism, the integrity of the theistic doctrine was hardly the concern of any one. Similarly, in the apparently synthetic attempt of the Bhagavad Gita, the elements of the dualistic systems like the *Sankhya* and yoga were included both for meditational purposes and for explaining changes in life as the activity of co-eternal *prakriti*. Among the *avtars*, authors of the non-theistic systems of Buddhism, Jainism and *Sankhya* were also included. Evidently, to the authors of Vaisnavism, the only concern was to accept and to show Visnu as the Supreme God. They were unconcerned with the unity or purity of its doctrine and theology, or of the modes of worship and the prescribed religious practices. In fact, heterogenous doctrines and authors of heterodox, non-theistic and dualistic systems were owned. It is, therefore, important to understand that, as against the equality and brotherhood of man and the fatherhood of God, almost inherent in any monotheistic system, the grading of the caste system and the social and religious segregation of the Sudras were kept intact, duly sanctioned and approved. One thing is significant. In the Buddhist theory of incarnation, Buddha has been taking birth even in the house of lower castes in order to save mankind. But, there is no *avtar* of Visnu who took birth in the house of a low caste.[16] This would suggest that, while in the metaphysical or the theological stands, there could be considerable variation, relaxation or diversity,· there could be no compromise on the social ideology of caste. In addition, Vedic ritualism and the authority of the Vedas and the Brahmin priests were accepted by the new entrants. All this was maintained not only in the earlier Vaisnava systems, but also in the Vishist Advaita of Ramanuja and the later Vaisnavism.

Lord Rama was taken to be an *avtar* porobably in the early centuries of the Christian era, though there was then no separate cult in his name. It was later, near the 11th Century A.D. that the cult of Lord Rama actually came into existence. Here, too, there are manuals giving the mode of worship of the deity, by means of mantras, formulae and magic circles, quite like those prescribed in the Satvata-Samhita for the worship of Vasudeva.[17]

THE THIRD PHASE

Next we come to the period of Sandilya and Bhagavata Purana in the 11th century A.D. The *bhakti* these two describe is not the worship of or meditation on God as in the Gita. Nor does it involve formal singing. It is a deep affection for God. According to Vallabha, God invokes love in man. It is a favour bestowed by Him (*pusti*). In the emotional type of *bhakti*, the devotee feels a sense of spiritual intoxication and joy. Like Chaitanya, the devotee 'sings, laughs, dances and weeps.' He is no longer a person of the world.

It is in the Bhagavata Purana that we first find the idea of devotion as the supreme source of bliss. *Bhakti* becomes by itself the goal. It substitutes the place of wisdom or philosophical knowledge. Such *bhakti* is believed to destroy all the past sins of man. Thus, *bhakti* becomes a mantra or a type of magic. But, in all this, no moral action is stressed. The *bhakti* of Bhagavata Purana is not the old contemplative meditation of God. It is the upsurge of feelings and emotions of love for God. The Bhagavata Purana mentions nine modes of worship. Each of these can lead to *moksha*.[18] These include listening to the praise of God, the reading of sacred books, the repeating of God's Name, remembering Him, etc. The repeating of God's Name can bring deliverance. All these modes are ritualistic and magical. The important thing is that no moral activity is prescribed or emphasised. Idol worship is accepted. The Bhagavata Purana is aware of the three methods of salvation, namely, that of knowledge, of work, and of devotion. It not only accepts their validity, but also the Vedic scriptures and the prescribed social system. The point of importance is that the goal of life and the role of the *jiwanmukta* remains otherworldly.

Sandilya's definition of *bhakti* not only prescribes it as the only mode of worship, but also distinguishes it from the types of worship prevalent earlier to this period, including *bhakti* as indicated in the Gita. These old modes of worship, like the offerings of flowers (as mentioned in the Gita), indicate only *shraddha*, or faith. This new *bhakti* is a loving affection. It is neither knowledge nor action. Sandilya and his commentator, Svapnesvara, attack the Vedanta doctrine that liberation or salvation arises from knowledge of the soul. This *bhakti* has been described as follows. "The true method is 'bhakti', or devotional faith, directed to the Lord. This is the immediate cause of salvation. Knowledge is an auxiliary to *bhakti*, and may become useful by washing away the filth of unbelief. But it will not by itself abolish the veil which exists between the soul and the Supreme." "In the highest form, it (*bhakti*) is affection fixed upon the Lord. Affection is its essence."

"*Bhakti* is not an action (a 'work'). It does not depend, as knowledge does, upon an effort of the will. Hence, as it is not an action, its fruit (beatitude) is endless. Every action, on the other hand, ultimately perishes." "The means are knowledge, concentration, etc. The end is *bhakti*."

"*Bhakti* (or faith) is not *shardha* (or belief). Belief may be merely subsidiary to ceremonial works, not so faith. Belief is a preliminary or subsidiary to faith, but is not faith."[19] This is Sandilya's definition of *bhakti*.

Further, development of Vaisnavism started in the South, far away from the earlier centres. Dr Tara Chand feels that this development took place as a reaction to the impact of Islam. But, this issue is not relevant to our purpose since we are mainly concerned with the nature and content of this development. A chain of Alvar saints appeared, extending over a long period of time.

In the following pages, starting with Ramanuja, we shall briefly indicate the systems and views of the chief exponents and saints of this new Vaisnava *bhakti* movement.

Ramanuja : The successful crusade of Sankara in favour of his Advaita, under which the world was *mithya* or illusory, gave an ideological set-back to the need and importance of all devotional systems. For Sankara, Brahman alone was real. By this onslaught, the basis for the cult of idol and devotional worship was being eroded. This was also the period of the Alvars who constituted two classes, the saints, who composed the devotional songs, and the Acharyas, who were the philosophers and teachers of the doctrine. Ramanuja, on the direction of his guru, took upon himself the task of tracing from the scriptures, and the Brahma Sutras, the justification and basis for this religion of worship prevalent in his time. According to him, the world is real and there are three eternal principles of Brahman, God (*Ishvara*), individual souls, and the world (*prakriti*). The individual soul and the insensate world are deemed to be the attributes or body of Brahman, just as the soul has a human body. The three elements are different but the embodied parts, though different, are one. These three parts are inseparable and eternal. Before creation, the body of the Supreme Soul is in a subtle form. At that time, matter and souls are in Him, in an unmanifest form. After creation, He has them in His body in a manifest form. Thus, Brahman or God is both the material and the efficient cause of the world and controls it from within. The soul and the world are a mode of the Supreme, eternal but dependent on Him. Man is identical with God. As in the Gita, the system of changes of *prakriti* for the creation of *Ahankara*, activity, etc., is the same as in *Sankhya*, except that God is there to guide it.[20]

Ishvara has a wonderful celestial body with *Lakshmi* as His consort. *Ishvara* appears in five forms : (1) as Narayana or Para-Vasudeva, he lives, adorned with ornaments and gems, in Vaikuntha on a throne surrounded by Sesa (serpent), Garuda and other delivered souls; (2) as his four forms in the world, including that of Vasudeva to enable men to worship Him, (3) as the ten *avtars*, fish, tortoise and others; (4) as present in each being even when one goes to heaven or hell; and (5) as in the idols kept in the houses. For Ramanuja, the ritualism of the Vedas and the Brahma Vidya of the Upanishada are equally important. Rituals are not for a lower class of people, nor do they give a lower truth. He thinks that rituals prescribe the method of worship. These he accepts fully, as also the caste system. The doctrines relating to Brahman (Brahm Vidya), and that about rituals form one system. These are not addressed to different categories of persons as is believed by Sankara. For Ramanuja, *Karam Marga* includes the Vedic rituals, the worship of idols, and the repeating of mantras.

Souls are of three kinds : (1) the bound ones, (2) the delivered ones, and (3) the eternal souls like Garuda. Of the bound ones, some seek wealth and others seek heaven. Some of them are devotees of Bhagavat and some worship other gods or *avtars*. Of those who desire deliverance, some seek the consciousness of the pure soul *(kevalin)* and others strive for eternal bliss. Of the latter, some seek God through *bhakti*. For them the study of Vedas and the philosophy of sacrifices and rites is necessary. But, this *bhakti* is open to the three higher castes only and not to *Sudras*. The caste system and Vedic ritualism are fully maintained.[21] In fact, the dietary rules made and practised by this sect are very rigid and exclusive. Every one has to cook one's own food. And if per chance another person casts his glance on the food while the disciple is cooking or eating it, the entire victuals have to be thrown away or buried as having been polluted.[22]

But the Sudras can resort to 'Prapatti', or surrender to God, after renouncing the world. For the efficacy of *bhakti*, *Karma Yoga* and *Jnana Yoga* are essential. The first involves the performance of all prescribed acts, rituals, sacrifices, ceremonies, pilgrimages, and the worship of idols. *Jnana Yoga* means the gaining of cognitive knowledge of one's being separate from *prakriti* and being an Attribute of God. These two preparatory steps lead to *bhakti* which consists in meditations, accompanied by the yoga practices of *Yama*, *Niyama*, etc. Thus, for Ramanuja, the preliminary knowledge of *Jnana* and *Karma yoga* is necessary for *bhakti*. These methods include : (1) the use of un-polluted and unprohibited food, (2) chastity, (3) constant practice, (4) performing the rites and sacrifices according to one's means, (5) virtuous acts of truth, compassion, *ahimsa*, uprightness, (6) hopefulness and (7) absence of elatedness. *Bhakti*, as done by these seven means, leads to one's seeing God.

As against it, 'Prapatti' involves complete self-surrender. In the *Padma-Purana* seven other modes of worship are also suggested. They are all ritualistic and formal, e.g. (1) the imprinting of marks on the body and the forehead, (2) the repeating of mantras, (3) the drinking of water used for washing the feet of the idol of Hari, (4) the eating of the cooked food offered to the idol, (5) the service of devotees, (6) the observing of fasts on the fixed days of the lunar month, (7) the laying of Tulsi leaves on the idol; etc.[23]

This *bhakti* has no ethical bias or emphasis. It is *bhakti* of a formal nature without the kind of love that fructifies into a moral life for the service of man. On the basis of the study of Alvar saints, Hooper asserts that there is no necessary connection between *bhakti* and moral character. In this regard, he particularly cites the example of one Alvar saint, Tirumangai.[24] Maitra, who has discussed the problem of Hindu ethics and the problem of ideal life in all Hindu schools of orthodox philosophy, including that of the *Vaishesika*, the *Purva Mimansa*, Sankara, Ramanuja, Madhava and Vallabhacharya, comes to the conclusion that a common feature of all these doctrines of ideal life or *moksha* is "the conception of the ideal as a negation, or at least as a transcendence, of the empirical life proper, and that this state is thus a super-moral spiritual ideal rather than a strictly moral ideal."[25] And after achieving the state of *moksha*, there is hardly anything to be done. It is a negative and quietist ideal without any activity, except that in the case of Ramanmuja's system one has to do unconditional scriptural works like the daily rituals, bathing in the Ganges on the day of lunar or solar eclipse, etc. As such, in Vaisnavism, the otherworldly ideal or goal has been accepted. It is a transcendental state of deliverance from all the struggle of life. It is generally and essentially a state of quiescence.[26] In all these systems, including that of the Vishnu Purana, release from the bondage of the world is sought.

Ramanuja's *bhakti* does not mean boundless love; it only involves Upasana or meditation. It is a doctrine of identity. Upto the end of life, one must carry out all ritualistic duties and duties of one's station in life, i.e. the caste duties.

Like the Bhagavad Gita, Ramanuja's Vashisht Advaita or theism is also syncretic and incorporates the chief elements of the *Sankhya* and yoga, and of Vedic ritualism. The world and souls are the body of Brahman both in their manifest and unmanifest forms. On the metaphysical side, the system is broadly pantheistic, God being the material cause of the world, and, *Ishvara*, the souls and the material world being the constituents of Brahman. In a way, the system is also pluralistic, as souls and *prakriti* are eternal. The socio-religious sanctity of the caste system is fully accepted and confirmed. The continuance of the Brahminical system for the worship of images is justified. For *bhakti*, the world has virtually to be given up and celibacy maintained. Full sanction is given to faith in the scriptures and the observance of Vedic rites and other prescribed pilgrimages and fasts. The worldly activity, including all moral life, is considered to be a movement of the eternal *prakriti*, from the bondage of which release is sought by resort to *bhakti* and meditational methods. As in all the yogic systems, virtues are practised entirely with a view to preparation and discipline for meditation. Virtuous acts, as such, have no social content or ends. They serve purely as aids to meditation. In the social fields one has to do one's caste duties, and the word *karma* includes all Vedic rituals, idol worship, and other ceremonies.[27]

The deal is the attainment of *Narayana*, the enjoyment of bliss and deliverance from the world. The system of training is the *karma* yoga, the *Jnana yoga* and the *bhakti yoga* (meditation). Though the householder could follow the path of salvation, the Sanyas Ashram prescribed in the Upanishads leads to speedy salvation. The tendency is towards otherworldliness. The person who has made the final achievement, is also obliged to perform all the prescribed purificatory rituals (*karma*), like fasting and baths.

Madhava : In Madhava's system the separate existence of God, souls and material world is assumed. Though God is the efficient cause of the world, all movement in it is due to the eternal *prakriti* which is its material cause. The system is thus dualistic with a plural number of souls. As in the Gita, in substance, the *Sankhya* system is accepted, except for the addition of a Personal God. Madhava believes that God is a substance. The doctrine of incarnation is accepted. In his qualities and actions, the *avtar* is identical with God. Lakshmi is distinct from God but is dependent upon Him. She is co-extensive or co-eternal with God. Souls are of three kinds : (a) those fit for attaining bliss, (b) those eternally undergoing transmigration, (c) those fit for darkness only.

Creation begins when God disturbs the equilibrium of Prakrit. *Moksha* can be attained through devotional service but only by a soul fit for it.[28]

There are eighteen methods that help salvation, including (a) *Vairagya* or renunciation of the world and its pleasures, (2) self-control, (3) self-surrender, (4) acquaintance with the lore, (5) attendance on the guru, (6) knowledge got from the guru or a Vaisnava, and reflection on it, (7) devotion to God, (8) sympathy for inferiors and love for equals, (9) the performance of vedic rites without the desire for fruit, (10) the avoidance of prohibited acts or sins, (11) the knowledge of Visnu being the highest, and of the distinctions between God and the world, *prakriti* and *Purusas*, God and the individuals, etc., (12) worship or Upasana, the hearing of Sastras, meditation, etc. These steps lead to the direct knowledge of God which is cognitive. The followers of Madhava use special marks, created sometimes even by heated metal, leaving permanent scars on the body.[29]

The presence of the two classes of souls, that are not redeemable and are doomed to misery and perdition, is something extremely incongruous in a theistic system. For it virtually limits the scope of human freedom and divine grace. As no progress is envisaged for these souls, the system is partly deterministic.[30] The ideal is the attainment of bliss. For liberation, the knowledge of God and self-knowledge are obtained through the study of scriptures. For achieving such knowledge, meditation and reflection under a guru are necessary. Like Ramanuja, Madhava accepts the necessity of doing caste and ritual duties and feels that these should be done throughout life. The performance of any worldly duties or moral acts by the spiritually enlightened person is unnecessary. In short, here too the ideal of salvation is otherworldly. One has no socio-political role. The goal is achieved by doing scriptural duties, the study of scriptures and meditation.

Nimbarka : Nimbarka's system is monistic and also, in a way, pluralistic. He feels that the world, souls and God are both distinct and identical (*Bheda-Abheda*). The first two have no independent existence, but are dependent on God. His recommendations for the modes of *bhakti* are practically the same as those of Ramanuja. He believes that Brahman had in it the rudiments of the world. By manifestation, Brahman becomes the material cause of the world. The souls are numberless. By contact with *maya* or *prakriti*, the form of the soul is distorted. The nature of soul can be known by the grace of God. In this system, the Vedic ritualism, the theory of incarnation, the caste system and *Sankhya* are accepted. The approach is otherworldly. The object is for the soul to know its own nature. This is achieved by dissociation from *prakriti* and by the grace of God. The worship recommended is that of Radha-Krishna. This worship is more devotional than that in the case of Ramanuja, but the approach to life remains otherworldly. Since the individual soul is distorted by its contact with *prakriti*, naturally the system involves ascetic withdrawal from life.

Ramananda : All religions or *bhakti* systems prior to Ramananda excluded the *Sudras* from their fold. They had to do the duties prescribed for their low castes and rise in status so as to be born as Brahmins. Then alone they could tread the path of the Vaisnava *bhakti*. Ramananda's reform extended to the effect that lower castes, if admitted to the Vaisnava fold, could dine with the other disciples. For the rest, the system is the same as of Ramanuja. Ramananda was originally a follower of Ramanuja and observed all the dietary rules prescribed for the sect. Once when he had returned to the *Math* after a tour of the north, his co-disciples objected to his laxity in the strict observance of the prescribed dietary rules. On the matter being reported to the head of the *Math*, the guru agreed with the objection and sided with the critics. In sheer disgust, Ramananda left the order of Ramanujas and formed a new sect with the only difference that the strict dietary rules were partly relaxed.[31] Ramananda's deity was Rama with Sita as his consort.

Tulsidas : Though a disciple of Ramananda, Tulsidas's philosophy leans towards spiritual monism. Like other saints of Vaisnavism, he accepts the rigidity of the caste system, even though his guru Ramananda had, to an extent, relaxed it for admitted Vaisnavas. He is conservative and otherworldly. In his system there is no emphasis on socio-moral conduct.

Vallabha : In Vallabha's system, the devotee can continue to be a house-holder. He first took an ascetic vow but later became a householder. He says that God has Himself become the world and the individual souls, because the Supreme Soul was not happy while all alone. He decided to become many. The system, is, thus, pantheistic.

Salvation is only through *bhakti*. Though one need not give up the householder's life, the method of worship is entirely ritualistic, formal and ceremonial. Apart from the devotion of singing and praising God, the devotee should rise early, drink the water in which the feet of the idol has been washed, utter the names of Goverdhana and others, remember the river Yamuna, etc. Similarly, at other times of the day, there should be image worship and the feeding of the deity, accompanied by other ceremonies, like *aarti*, the ringing of bells, the blowing of the conchshell, bathing, dressing and the feeding of the idol.[32]

There are no public temples, but each guru, who is a householder, maintains a private temple at his own house. At eight fixed intervals during the day, the devotee should visit the temple of the guru. The best stage of salvation is that of joining the sport of Krishna and Radha in the highest place of heaven, called Goloka. Vallabha's system is not known for any new ideas except that he has excessively ritualised *bhakti* and made it open to householders. It is believed that Vallabha's devotion appears more dramatic than real.

Chaitanya : Born in Bengal, Chaitanya was a devotee of Radha and Krishna. He developed the emotional side of the *bhakti* of Krishna and his consort. He composed songs, did fervent singing and ecstatic dancing. This was his mode of approach to God. His disciples included persons of all castes and even Muslims. For him the deeply emotional singing of the praises of God (Radha-Krishna) was the only method of *bhakti* and salvation. While singing, the devotees would laugh, weep, jump and embrace each other in a state of emotional outburst. Chaitanya became an ascetic and a *sanyasi*. His loud singing became so charged with feeling that he even swooned under the intensity of his emotion. For Chaitanya, Krishna is the highest god who is so beautiful that he excites love in the hearts of all. He remained too busy in his emotional singing, dancing and ecstasies to have any social involvement. Like Nimbarka, Chaitanya believes in identity with a difference between the soul and God (*Bheda-Abheda*). God Krishna, can be approached by love alone. Through continuous love, the soul becomes one with God, it becomes unconscious of its individual existence, and is absorbed in Him. In spirit the soul is one with God and God appears in finite spirits. The goal of life is the bliss of union in which the soul loses its consciousness. But actually they remain distinct. In practice, most of the 'Advaitas', followers of Chaitanya, observe caste distinctions, but those who are recluses or Bairagis do not do so. At the time of taking meals, caste distinctions are generally observed and the cook is always a Brahmin.[33] The teachers of this system are all celibates.   The life of Chaitanya illustrates the type of *bhakti* recommended by the *Bhagavat Purana*. Chaitanya mentions different kinds of love : (a) love with awe and reverence for His greatness; it is the peaceful, calm and tender love (*Shanta*); (b) love with the submission of the heart like that of a servant's (*Dasya*) for his master; (c) the love of God as a friend (*Sakhya*); and (d) the deepest love as of the wife for her husband (*Madhura*). The last kind is the sweetest and the deepest as for a beloved. Chaitanya suggests the last kind.

THE SENSUAL METHOD

There is another feature of Vaisnavism. The worship of male and female gods has led to erotic symbolism and ultimately to Tantric methodology. Ghurye has collected ample evidence to suggest that the method, as an alternative spiritual path of *moksha*, has ancient and Puranic sanction. We may emphasise that devotional systems like Vaisnavism that lay emphasis on celibacy, and involve worship of a female deity and erotic symbolism, without human energies being channelised into moral and creative activities, almost invariably end up as advocates of the sensual path for spiritual achievement. This leads to unfortunate results and practices. This has happened in Buddhism, and in fact all the world over. This change has taken place in Vaisnavism too.[34] Even a modern Vaisnava saint too has recognised the sensual method as a valid, though a difficult and risky, spiritual path.[35] We may also here refer to the case of Dattatreya, the spiritual teacher of Prahlada and Alarka. The Puranic accounts "depict him always in ecstasy, surrounded by women, drinking wine and indulging in sex." "He demands flesh and wine in human skull."[36] The Tantric Shastras have also been called the fifth Veda of Hinduism.

CONCLUSION

We have made a brief survey of Vaisnavism which prescribes *bhakti* as one of the methods of *moksha*. Let us now draw our conclusion about its thesis, trends, methodology and direction.

1. *The Fundamentals* : Vaisnavism has four fundamentals. Its basic scriptures are the Vedas and the Upanishads which also form the foundations of the extereme ritualism of the original Vedic system (Purva Mimansa), the monism of Sankara, the downgrading of the world as illusory, and the otherworldly and meditational mysticism of the Upanishads. While each sect puts its own interpretation of the Vedas and Upanishads,

there is implicit faith in their scriptural authority and all that they stand for. Having accepted the authority of the Vedas, Upanishads and the Gita, it could not ignore their social ideology and related injunctions. For the first time, the Gita included the heterodox Bhagvatism in the Hindu fold and linked its system of worship to the scriptural authority of the Vedas. The result was that the Vedic caste structure was wholly accepted by this system of *bhakti*. Actually, this social system and its ideology became the second fundamental of Vaisnavism to which it adhered completely. Ramanand's modifications in the dietary regulations were, perhaps, made, only as a personal reaction to his own conduct having been subjected to severe criticism by his colleagues and his Guru for his having violated some dietary rules. This slight change in the rules about eating only involved a virtual *post-facto* justification of his own conduct, without in the least affecting the basis or the rigidity of the caste system. Evidently, this change neither formed an important, nor an integral part of Ramanand's religious system. This is also clear from the fact that Tulsidas, the chief disciple of Ramanand, strictly believed in the sanctity and the rigid observance of the caste system. Even now among Ramanand's ascetics, only the higher three castes are freely admitted. Sudras and untouchables if and when admitted have to maintain and worship in separate temples. In the temples of the first three castes, they alone are allowed to enter. In actual practice only Brahmins cook food and serve the deity.[37] The theory of *avtarhood*, the third fundamental of Vaisnavism, was, as we have seen, only an omnivorous method of absorbing all kinds of divergent and heterodox systems in the Hindu fold. The ritualism of the Vedic religion became its fourth fundamental. In fact, *bhakti* itself was completely formalised and ritualised. The method of worship almost became a system of mantras. This devotion towards the deity never turned towards love of one's fellow beings. In fact, the fundamental acceptance of the inequity of the caste system and the formalism of *bhakti* stood as a complete bar to any transformation of the love of God into the service or love of man and suffering humanity. That is also the reason that good conduct never involved any act of social morality or any activity to solve the difficulties and problems of one's fellow beings. Moral life, at best, meant only a sense of ritualistic or formal piety, without the least reaction to any social evil, injustice or cruelty, much less to any political oppression or tyranny. Accordingly as was observed by Hooper, Vaisnava *bhakti* never involved any change in the moral character or values of the devotee.

2. *The Worldview* : No doubt the world is deemed to be real. But, in view of the *Sankhya*-yoga background and the ideal of *moksha* or liberation from *Samsara*, the entire approach and the attitude are otherworldly. In Vaisnavism, the clear preference for celibacy and renunciation and its attitude towards women also confirms this view. The overall metaphysical view is either pantheistic or dualistic, where co-eternal *prakriti* is assumed. In the former case the world and souls are the body or qualities of Brahman. Brahman is both the material and the efficient cause of the world. In the latter case, it is virtually the *Sankhya*-yoga system with the addition of *Ishvara* as a Personal God. The soul forms a part of Brahman. Even if the ideas of worship between man and God, and creature and the Creator, are mentioned, there is basic identity between the soul and

Brahman, the former being a part of the latter. Generally speaking, in theism, the world is the creation of God, it is not co-eternal with Him. Hence, whatever name one may give to the Vaisnava system, it is not theistic in the normal sense of the word; because even personalities like Kapila, Rasaba and Buddha, who held atheistic views, were declared as *avtars*. Sharp divergence in the metaphysical views of its philosophers like Ramanuja, Nimbarka, Madhava and Vallabha is also clearly symptomatic of its assorted and syncretic character. In fact, none of its scriptures or its philosophers even attempted to reconcile its variant and conflicting thoughts, or give it a unified ideology or methodology. Evidently, this was really not possible, because its authority and theology are based on the Upanishads and the Bhagavad Gita which are admittedly eclectic compilations expressing different thoughts and doctrines.

3. *Doctrine of Ahimsa* : Though in its early phase Vaisnavism could not emancipate itself from the religion of sacrifices, yet later it accepted and stressed the observance of *ahimsa*. Possibly, this change, too, occurred under Buddhist influence. The Visnudharmottara Purana, while it permits sacrifice for religious purpose, prohibits the destruction of even an insect or a fly, saying that there is nothing so sinful as eating meat.[38] It is quite significant that the Puranas state that the four forms of Narayana had *ahimsa* as their mother. In fact, *ahimsa* later became a cardinal principle of Vaisnavism. Both Ramanuja and Sankradeva insisted upon it and did not allow meat-eating. However, Vaisnavism did not stop the kings from waging a war.[39]

4. *The Goal* : The goal is *moksha*. It means the return of the soul for merger in Brahman, or a state of bliss and union with God, without involvement in the world of man. The aim is not the service of God or man, nor is it the carrying out of His Will in the world. None of these matters receives any priority, the ideal being liberation from the tangles of the world. In life, the *jiwanmukta* has no social role to play, except that he is still obliged to follow all the prescribed ritualistic duties. As such, there is no stress on the moral life except for purposes of personal purity and as an aid to meditation.

5. *Kind Of Bhakti* : Another characteristic feature of the system is its changing concept of *bhakti*. This change reveals both the growth and the goal of the system. Originally, *bhakti* involved only a sense of favourable consideration, affinity, relationship or adoration between the *Bhakta* and the deity; it was indeed a sense of shared kinship. In the second phase of its history, the gap between the deity and the devotee widened, and devotion took the shape of a system of formal worship, including ritualistic and idol worship. This was the period when *bhakti* was only an alternative method of *moksha*, and the preliminary aid of *Jnana* and *Karam Margas* was essential for treading the path of *bhakti*. This position continued even upto the time of Ramanuja. It was only in the third phase of its development that the feeling or the emotional element became prominent and central to *bhakti*. It became virtually the sole path of liberation. This emotional *bhakti* developed in two distinct directions. In the case of Vallabhacharya, it became quite dramatic and ritualistic, accepting, to an extent, erotic symbolism. This trend naturally led to some unsavoury developments. In the case of Mira Bai and Chaitanya, it took the form of extreme and ecstatic emotionalism, absorbing completely

the entire being and the personality of the devotee. While dancing and singing, Siri Chaitanya remained so much surcharged with the intensity of his feelings, that he had hardly any time or willingness for anything else. The goal of life is to lose one's consciousness under the intensity of the joy of union. It is believed that he lost his life while in an ecstatic trance of such a union Chaitanya suggested the *madhura* (as between wife and husband) kind of love which he considered to be the deepest and most intense. But Sankradeva recommended the *dasya* type of love (as between the servant and the master) because the results of the *madhura* type of love, he felt, could be disastrous for the devotee.[40]

In all these various forms of *bhakti* one thing is common and significant. This *bhakti* remained only a relation between man and God and never flowed into the field of social responsibility or moral deeds. It was a *bhakti* which isolated the devotee from the world as much as was done by asceticism or renunciation. Whether this insulation and otherworldliness were due to the acceptance of the caste ideology, or to Vaisnavism's preference for celibacy and its attitude towards women, or to its faith in excessive formalism or ritualism, is beside the point. But, the broad fact is that this *bhakti* remained unresponsive to and unconcerned with the social and moral problems of man. It did not accept the principle of the equalilty and the brotherhood of man, as is normally done under a theistic system.

6. *Social Ideology* : In Hinduism, caste divisions had become established and well-formed during the Upanishadic times.[41] Either because of Buddhist influence, or because of the need for absorption of non-Aryan tribes, or because of any other reason, the Bhagavad Gita for the first time admitted Sudras and women to the path of *bhakti*. But, otherwise the Bhagavad Gita emphatically upheld the social ideology of caste. Lord Rama, too, severed the head of a Sudra for doing rites not allowed to his caste under the Vedic injunctions.[42] Such being the social approach of two of the incarnations of Visnu, Vaisnavism, thus, fully endorsed the social philosophy of Brahminism. Even now among the Vaisnava Sadhus only Brahmins can cook food. In addition the worship of the deity is the sole preserve of the Brahmins. Even Ramanuja, who opened the system of *Prapatti* to Shudras, in a way confirmed the system of caste-divisions by closing the gates of Vaisnava *bhakti* to Sudras and instead permitting them only to the system of self-surrender.

Systems that are ascetic or monastic have generally a harsh attitude towards women. There is little doubt that the ancient religious traditions of India were largely ascetic. Asceticism is considered to be a typically Indian contribution to the world, since this trait was un-known to the ancient cultures of Egypt, Babylonia and Persia.[43] In the early Indian tradition, woman had been looked upon as a temptress and an impediment in the spiritual life of man. In the course of time, the emphasis on monasticism and celibacy increased in Vaisnavism. Accordingly, the position of women worsened in the social and religious fields. In *Bhagavad Bhasya*, Ramanuja writes, "By putting trust in me, even women, the Vaisyas or the Sudras, though sin-born, do yet go to the supreme state."[44] Both Ramanuja and Sankradeva, otherwise liberal religious teachers, did not permit women to join the Vaisnava order. Ramanuja denied the facility of Vedic study to women.[45] They were not permitted to mix with men for devotion, nor were they allowed to give up household duties and become nuns. The ideas of Sankaradeva on this issue were even more rigid. He stated, "Of all the terrible aspirations of the world, woman's is the ugliest. A slight side glance of her's captivates even the hearts of celebrated sages. Her sight destroys prayer, penance and meditation. Knowing this, the wise keep away from the company of women."[46] He did not allow women to join the religious functions of men. They did their chanting only in the courtyard, and that too not simultaneously with men. He never accepted women as his disciples, nor gave *Nama-mantra* to a woman; nor allowed them to be nuns. Except on certain days, even uptil now, women are not allowed to enter the *Kirtanghar* of the sect.

In such a climate the growth of the ideas of the equality and brotherhood of man could hardly be possible.

All the same, some of its saints like Sankaradeva relaxed, to some extent, the Brahminical social injunctions against the Sudras. However, food cooked by a Sudra was not taken by a Brahmin even though a Vaisnava.[47] Vaisnavism, which to start with, was a religion of the wealthy and the elite, became quite popular among the masses. The chief reason for its acceptance by them was the simplicity of its methods of worship compared to the expensive and elaborate Brahminical system of sacrifices and rituals.

It has been considered a meaningful coincidence, that the Bhagavad Gita, while it accepted women and Sudras to the path of worship, simultaneously gave religious sanction to the rigidity of the social system. The result was that Vaisnava *bhakti* remained intimately linked with the social ideology of the caste, including, as we have seen, its attitude towards women. Even an outstanding saint philosopher like Ramanuja, while admitting Sudras to *Prapatti*, considers women and Sudras to be sin-born. It meant that Vaisnavism, except for religious purposes, always approved of the social ideology of Brahminism. That is also why, even though Vaisnavism laid stress on the doctrine of *ahimsa* and non-meat eating, it permitted the kings to wage wars and sacrifice animals for ritualistic ends.

In short, Vaisnava *bhakti* remained a system completely at ease with the social divisions and distinctions of the times and found nothing inconsistent between its deep devotion towards the deity, and the social discrimination against the lower castes and women. Therefore, in classifying Vaisnava *bhakti* it cannot be ignored that in this religious system and its worldview the hierarchical or the graded social ideology became an integral part of it.

Let us apply the test of unity of perception, ideology and activity and trace the ideology and religious perception of the Vaisnava *bhakti*. The major objective activity of Vaisnava *bhakti* has been the maintenance of the caste system. Accordingly, its religious ideology, as reflected in the social field or its social activities as giving a clear clue to its religious ideology, point towards the same conclusion, namely, that its worldview, or its theism was not only congruous with the caste system but gave full religious sanction to it. For, even a liberal saint like Sankaradeva was never bothered about making any social change; his concern was only with affording religious fellowship. "He saw his vocation only in establishing religious freedom and fellowship rather than social overhaul. To trouble about the improvement of social conditions, perhaps, deemed to him as little profitable."[48]

As revealed in its theory of incarnation, the aims and ideals of Vaisnava *bhakti* have been quite clear and consistent during the long course of its history. The reason for it is its faithful acceptance of the scriptural and religious authority of the Vedas, Upanishads, the Bhagavad Gita and the Sastras. And Dattatraya, too, with all his Puranic descriptions, was regarded a Paramhansa and an incarnation of Visnu.

We therefore, conclude that Vaisnava *bhakti* is a class by itself. It is not easy to find its parallel either in the Indian tradition or outside it.

SIKHISM AND VAISNAVISM : A COMPARISON

Our survey and the history of the system show that Vaisnavism is in every way a part and parcel of the Brahminical tradition and its complex of systems. As of all other Hindu systems, Vedas and Upanishads are its scriptures. The answers of Vaisnavism on the twelve issues are opposed to those given by Sikhism. Vaisnavism accepts the four fundamentals of Hinduism indicated earlier. In addition, it has faith in the mystic potency of words and mantras. The theory of the *avtars* of Visnu is, in fact, a Vaisnava creation and not a part of the earlier Vedic system. Probably, because of its faith in the Vedic system, *bhakti* in Vaisnavism is basically formal and ritualistic, without its ever fructifying into virtuous deeds in the social field. The Vaisnava *bhakti* remains confined to meditational practices, and formal and devotional idol worship in the temples.

But, Sikhism clearly denies the four principles of Vaisnavism. Not only is the scriptural authority of the Vedas and Upanishads repudiated, but the Gurus are critical of the Vedic injunctions. "The distinctions of high and low, castes and colour, hell and heaven, introduced by the Vedas are misleading."[49] There are numerous hymns clearly denying the *avtar* character of all Vaisnava gods.

Having rejected the fundamentals of Vaisnavism, the question of any similarity between the two systems does not arise. While Sikhism is strictly theistic, Vaisnavism is, broadly speaking, pantheistic. In Vaisnavism, the emphasis is merely on formal devotional methods divorced from deeds. And this devotion involves an otherworldly life, leaning towards *sanyasa* and celibacy. In Sikhism, the path is entirely different. Sheer devotional dancing is considered to be of no consequence.[50] It is the virtuous deeds that are of essence in Sikh spiritual life. "With God, only the deeds one does in the world are of any avail.[51] "Without good deeds no formal worship is possible."[52] "Vice is our enemy and virtue the only friend."[53] "It is by our deeds that we become near or away from God."[54]

The Vaisnava saints were too preoccupied with formal devotion to enter the social field. Not even one of them did so, nor did their devotional system permit it, much less prescribe it.

As against it, the Gurus insist on virtuous deeds so as to seek the Grace of God. The Guru Nanak started the organisation of the Sikh *Panth*. The Fifth Guru invited the wrath of contemporary Mughal ruler, Jahangir, for having blessed the rebel prince Khusro. Instead of paying the heavy fine, he preferred to face martyrdom at the hands of the Mughal authorities. The Sixth Guru fought battles with the Imperial forces. The Seventh Guru attempted to come to the military aid of Dara,[55] the rebel against the then Emperor. The Eighth Guru died very young. Aurangzeb suggested to the Ninth Guru not to dabble in the socio-political field. But, he rejected this suggestion[56] and sought martyrdom by openly coming to the aid of the Kashmiri Pandits in defiance of the imperial policy of religious persecution.[57] The Tenth Guru's creation of the Khalsa and confrontation with the Empire is well-known.

There is another major difference between the two. Vaisnavism accepts the sensual path as an alternative spiritual approach, but Sikhism rejects it outright.

The conclusion is evident that there is an obvious contrast between Vaisnavism and Sikhism on all the essentials of the two systems and the issues stated by us. The worldview of Sikhism is life-affirming and ethical. The worldview of Vaisnavism involves a virtual withdrawal from the world.

REFERENCES

1. Bhandarkar, R.G. : *Vaisnavism and Saivism*, p. 3.
2. Jaiswal, Mrs. S. : *The Origin and Development of Vaisnavism*, p. 64.
3. Ibid., p. 211.
4. Zaehner, R.C. : *Mysticism Sacred and Profane*, Bhandarkar : op. cit., p. 1, Hiriyanna M. : *Essentials of Indian Philosophy*, p. 53.
5. Jaiswal : op.cit. p. 111-112.
6. Ibid., p. 119.
7. Hiriyanna, M. : op.cit. p. 53.
8. Ibid., p. 55.
9. Jaiswal, op.cit. pp. 214-215.
10. Murthy, H.V.S : *Vaisnavism of Shankradeva and Ramanuja*, pp. 201-202.
11. Annie Besant : *Bhagavad Gita* (English Translation) : pp. 252-254.
12. Bhandarkar : op.cit. p. 40-41.
13. Jaiswal, op.cit. p. 114.
14. Das Gupta : *Hindu Mysticism*, pp. 117, 38-42.
15. Jaiswal, op.cit. pp. 155, 119, 132.
16. Ibid., pp. 214-15.
17. Bhandarkar, op.cit. p. 47.
18. Spencer, S. : *Mysticism in World Religions*, p. 49.
19. Cowell : J.R.A.S., p. 1907.
20. Bhandarkar, op.cit. pp. 52-54.
21. Ibid., pp. 54-55.
22. Wilson, H.H., *Religious Sects of Hindus*, p. 19.
23. Bhandarkar, op.cit. p. 55.
24. Spencer, S., op.cit. p. 58.
25. Miatra, S.K., *The Ethics of the Hindus*, p. 244.
26. Ibid., pp. 263, 265-266.

27. Bhandarkar, op.cit. p. 54.
28. Ibid., pp. 58-60.
29. Ibid., p. 61.
30. Hiriyanna, M., op.cit. p. 192.
31. Wilson, *Religious Sects of Hindus*, p. 24.
32. Bhandarkar, op.cit. p. 80.
33. Ibid., p. 86, Ghurye, p. 171.
34. Briggs, G.W., *Gorakh Nath and Kanphata Yogis*, pp. 350-51.
35. Zimmer, H., *Philosophies of India*, p. 590.
36. Ghurye, G.S., *Indian Sadhus*, pp. 34-35.
37. Ibid., p. 171.
38. Jaiswal, op.cit. pp. 115-118, 212.
39. Ibid., pp. 116-118.
40. Murthy, op.cit. p. 232.
41. Ibid., p. 194.
42. Senart, E., *Caste in India*, p. 100.
43. Ghurye, op.cit. p. 1.
44. Murthy, op.cit. p. 196.
45. Ibid., pp. 201-202.
46. Ibid., pp. 201-202.
47. Ibid., pp. 201-202.
48. Ibid., p. 203.
49. Guru Granth Sahib, p. 1243.
50. Ibid., p. 465.
51. Ibid., pp. 1383, 26.
52. Ibid., p. 4.
53. Ibid., p. 577.
54. Ibid., p. 11.
55. Gupta, H.R., *History of the Sikh Gurus*, p. 130.
56. Banerjee, A.C., in *Journal of Sikh Studies* Vol. 111, (Feb, 1976) p. 61.
57. Gupta, H.R., op.cit. p. 140.

16

THE RADICAL BHAGATS

DALJEET SINGH

1. INTRODUCTORY

The Radical Bhagats constitute another school of *bhakti*. This group has also been called, though erroneously, the *Nirgun Bhagats*, or even the *sant* tradition. They have been given a separate name because discerning observers feel that there is a wide gap between their doctrines and those of Vaisnavism. Similarly, there is an equally wide gap, if not wider still, between the Radical *bhakti* and the Sikh *bhakti*. This raises three issues. How is this system different from Vaisnavism, what are the special features of this group and how is it variant from Sikhism ? The last issue we shall examine after considering the first two which will be dealt with now.

Unfortunately, not very much is known of the lives of these saints. A considerable part of the available material is replete with the stories of miracles performed by them. It does not give their precise views, nor does it give a helplful account of their biographies and socio-religious doctrines. Neither can the compilations of their hymns, made mostly about 150 to 200 years after the demise of the concerned saints, be deemed to be entirely authentic. Therefore, the need for some caution and sifting is there so as to make a realistic appreciation of the religious views of these *Bhagats*.

In this study, we shall mainly deal with Bhagat Kabir and refer very briefly to saint Nam Dev. The reasons for taking up Kabir are three. He is, without doubt, not only a pioneer in the field but is also the tallest of them. Secondly, he is typically representative of the group. Thirdly, comparatively, his hymns are probably the largest in number and have some authenticity, because these form the religious guide of the *Kabir-panthis* and *Dadu-panthis*. For this study, we shall refer mainly to the *Bijak*, which is known as the Eastern or the *Kabir-panthi* version of the saint's *bani*, and also to the hymns in the Guru Granth Sahib and the Kabir *Granthavli*, the *Dadu-panthi* or the Rajasthani version.

2. RADICAL BHAKTI AND VAISNAVISM

Vaisnavism, we find, stands on four pillars, namely, the scriptural sanctity of the

Vedas and the doctrines these prescribe, the theory of avtarhood of Visnu, the social ideology of caste, and the formalism and ritualism of its methodology and its devotional and idol worship. Kabir emphatically repudiates all these fundamentals.

As to the Vedas, he says : "The Vedas and the book are two spread nooses; realise that thou are snared therein."[1] "Nine *bhaktis*, Vedas, the Book, these are the cloaks of falsehood."[2] "The four Vedas are fictitious stories."[3] "Heed not the sayings of the world or Vedas."[4] "O, thou, that knowest Brahman, be not led astray by the Vedas and the world."[5] "Renounce the Vedas and the book, O' Pandit; these are fictions of the mind."[6] "O' brother, these Smrities are the daughters of the Vedas, but these have come with chains and ropes to bind us. The chain behaves like a female serpent and devours the entire world. Under our eyes this has plundered the whole world." Says Kabir, "I have released myself from this chain of Smriti."[7] "The Vedas and Puranas are the mirror of the blind, what does the spoon know of the taste of the delicacies."[8] In *"Pipaji ki Bani"* (Pipa is another saint of this group), the author says that if Kabir had not lived in the *Kali-yuga*, the Vedas in conspiracy with *Kali-yuga* would have thrown *bhakti* to the underworld.[9]

True, there are some hymns of Kabir which speak well of the Vedas, but his rejection of them is too categorical to suggest that he had considered them as reliable guides for the spiritual path.

Kabir is equally emphatic in denying the theory of incarnation or the spiritual character of Vaisnava *avtars* or gods. In fact, he denounces the very idea of incarnation : *"maya* has sprung from the mind, the ten *avtars*, Brahma and Visnu passed away deluded."[10] "There was no Mahadeva, no Krishna, no Mohammad, nor any fish, tortoise or Rama, etc. Dattatreya did not know the secret, he was vainly entangled in his appetites."[11] Kabir mentions the *avtars* of Visnu only to show that they all are of no consequence or of any spiritual status. "Many the Ramachandras, so austere, who preserved the world; Many the flute-bearing Krishnas, but none reached the Whole;[12] They took the form of fish and tortoise and boar, they took the name of dwarf; many were the Buddhas, the stainless, but none reached the Whole."[13] "On one side stand gods, men and 'munis', on the other, she (*maya*) alone. Indra and Krishna are standing at her door, their eyes hungry with longing."[14] "She (*maya*) ran in pursuit of Shiva and Brahma and made both her captives."[15] He calls Visnu to be the author of *maya*. "Casting the angle of action, he has caught the whole world. I can annul his dominion and speed the soul across this ocean. I can make you fearless, test this mintage."[16] He considers Brahma to be guilty of offence and thefts.[17]

Kabir's tirade against caste is very out-spoken. He says that all men have been created from one Light and from the same clay and blood. The same blood runs in the veins of the Sudra and the Brahmin. How can the Brahmin claim superiority, when they are all born the same way.[18] "They live from age to age who renounce all caste and pride of race."[19]

Kabir's condemnation of all kinds of ritualism and the formal worship of idols and gods is also quite severe. "Devotion, sacrifice and rosary, piety, pilgrimage, fasting and alms; ...... these are cloaks of falsehood."[20] "By all his worship, not one sin is removed; by singing his praises one is drowned in the world."[21] "O, Kabir, all spoiled *bhakti* by laying stones and pebbles."[22] "If by repeating Rama's name, the world is saved, then by repeating the word "Sugar", the mouth should become sweet."[23]

Kabir's denunciation of Vaisnavism as a system is quite unambiguous. For, he says that it is devoid of the real *bhakti* of God. He even calls all kinds of earlier *bhaktis* as cloaks of falsehood. Kabir's views are diametrically opposed to all the basic doctrines of Vaisnavism. He and his group of saints completely reject Vaisnava scriptures. Not only is the *avtar* theory denied, but Lord Visnu and his *avtars* are clearly disregarded. Caste ideology, dietary rules and ritual observances formed the basis of the social system of Vaisnavism. These were so much an integral part of the system that, though Vaisnavism subscribed to the doctrine of *ahimsa*, it permitted kings and Kashatriyas to wage a righteous war. In fact, Arjuna was goaded by Lord Krishna not to shirk his caste duty of fighting for a just cause. Ramanuja, the chief exponent of Vaisnavism, was extremely strict in the observance of caste and dietary rules. In order to maintain purity, "all the Ramanujas cook for themselves; and, should the meal during this process, or whilst they are eating, attract even the looks of a stranger, the operation is instantly stopped and the viands buried in the ground."[24] We have seen that Ramananda, who was originally a follower of Ramanuja, was censured by his co-disciples and the guru for suspected laxity in the strict observance of these dietary rules. Ramananda was enraged and this led to his break with Ramanuja and the *Math*. As against the graded social system and allied formalism being a sanctified part of the religious structure of Vaisnavism, Kabir and his group swore by the principle of 'the fatherhood of God and the brotherhood of man.' In fact, many of the Radical Bhaktas belonged to the low castes who could normally not be admitted as equals in the Vaisnava socio-religious system. May be, owing to its Vedic heritage, ritualism, mantras and all kinds of formalism in worship have a distinct value and validity in Vaisnavism. The Radical Bhaktas not only discarded all that but ridiculed it. In fact, they attacked Vaisnavism and Vaisnava *bhakti* as a whole. Evidently, the two systems are so much apart, and even opposed to each other, that there is hardly a meeting ground between them.

3. KABIR

Before we draw any inferences, we shall give a brief description of the life and system of Kabir.

(i) *Life* : There is little doubt that Kabir was an abandoned child who was lifted and adopted by a poor Muslim couple of the weaver class. Kabir's connection with the Sufis in the early years of his life appears quite probable, if not conclusively established.[25] All the same, it is plain from Kabir's hymns that his search for and union with the Eternal are purely a personal achievement. He was not linked to either a Hindu saint or a Sufi *pir*. Kabir married and had children. A hymn of Kabir would suggest that he married twice. He calls his first wife ugly and the second one beautiful. He says, "It is just and proper that my first wife is dead."[26] To us it appears that the relevant lines only refer to Kabir having given up the way of the world and adopted the way of God.

Kabir did not leave his home, nor joined a hermitage or a *khankah*. But his hymns show that both his mother and wife complained that he was little interested in his profession; and that while his family remained poor and without even adequate food, he neglected his work and remained busy in the company of saints. No wonder the author of *Dabistan* describes him as a *bairagi*. Undoubtedly, both Kabir's life and his hymns show a strong ascetic trend.[27] But, we shall detail this point while considering his approach to the world.

Both Bhandarkar and Mohan Singh have given ample chronological and other evidence to show that Kabir was not the disciple of any living saint. There is hardly any reference to a living guru in his hymns. This negative evidence is of great significance when we know that he believed in the sanctity and the importance of the institution of guruship. As in the case of Guru Nanak, the word 'Guru' in Kabir's *bani* refers to God. This view is also supported by Mohan Singh.[28]

(ii) *Cosmology* : Kabir's views about the creation of the world are somewhat his own, though to an extent mythical. God created Niranjana who created the world. In the beginning was *Sabad*. There is an impress of Word on all creation.[29] Desire was made in the form of a woman. Niranjana created this woman or *maya*.[30] Everything grew from her. Brahma, Vishnu and Mahesh were born to her. She also created three daughters for this trinity. Later, the world and all forms were created through them.[31] Ultimately, everything will be reabsorbed in Him.

(iii) *Idea Of God* : As is usual with non-ascetic saints, Kabir's description of God could lead both to theistic and pantheistic inferences. "He is all created things." "And the Lord Himself taking form."[32] "From one egg of *Onkar*, all world is formed." "Himself God, Himself the leaf that is offered." He also calls God, Absolute and Attributeless.[33] His description is quite paradoxical. For, he calls Him both with and without Attributes, Personal and Impersonal, Transcendent and Immanent.[34] Kabir being essentially a *Bhagat*, many of his hymns clearly point to a loving adoration of a Personal God. He calls Him "Father" and "Mother." He says, "Kabir has found the Elixir of love."[35] And love can be expressed only towards a Personal God. "I play with God and there is no separation."[36] "There is no one Liberal like you and sinner like me."[37] Kabir's metaphysical thoughts, like those of the Sufis, would appear to be pantheistic, but like the Sufis, he too believes in a personal and loving relationship with Him. In one of his *Ramainis*, he takes a clear theistic stand. For, he rejects that there is identity between man and God at the final stage, as suggested by Chandogaya Upanishad in its phrase "That thou art."[38] From the overall point of view, the monotheism of Kabir and other Radical Bhagats appears clear. The reason for the seeming ambiguity is that descriptions of mystic experience, which is non-sensory, can at best be symbolic. And, such symbolic descriptions, being inadequate are liable to be misunderstood or misinterpreted.
Kabir states that God is immanent and is present in all hearts. As such, it is possible to have a personal relationship of union with Him.[39] This is the only worthwhile goal for man. Kabir so often claims such a blissful union.

(iv) *Goal* : For Kabir, the goal of life is to have a blissful union with God. In this union, the personality almost disappears. Kabir says, "I have attained the Supreme State." Even after the union, the identity of the mystic remains separate. "I am a fish in God's water."[40] It is an intuitive realisation, a union of soul and God. It is a love as of wife for her husband.

Kabir's cosmogenic utterances show similarity with both Muslim and Hindu thought. But, his description of the ascent to God is distinctly of the Sufi character and resembles that given by Hallaj. "Abandoning the actions pertaining to humanity (*nasut*), one sees the sphere of angels (*Malakut*), then leaving even the sphere of Majesty (*Jabarut*) one gets the vision of divinity (*Hlabut*); but when these four are left behind, then comes "*Lahut*", where there is no death or separation and where Yama (God of death) finds no entrance. Humanity (*Nasut*) is darkness, *Malakut* is angelic, in *Jabarut* shines the Majestic Light (*Nurjalal*), in *Lahut* one finds Beautiful Light (*Nurjamal*) and in *Habut* is the dwelling place of Truth (*Haq*)."[41] Kabir's four stages of *bhakti* have also been compared to the four stages of Sufi *Ibadat* i.e. of *Shariat, Tarikat, Haqiqat and Marfat.*[42] It is without doubt that many of Kabir's views are identical with Sufi thought and practices.

(v) *Approach To The World* : Kabir's approach to the world is very revealing of his religious thought. Here too his views about the reality of the world are ambiguous. There are many statements of Kabir that suggest that the world is not real. "Nothing in the world is true and real. It is all illusory."[43] He calls it a dream or a hallucination. "The play is false. The player is true."[44] "This world is but a trafficking in phantoms. At the end, there is nothing at all."[45] "It is the shadow of a cloud."[46] Once when asked whether or not the world was real, he replied, "Can Rajaram cook cakes of ice ? Can man in his senses eat them ? Can a lion seated in his den prepare betel ? Can a mammoth rat serve it when made up ? Can a mouse sing a song of rejoicing from house to house ? Can a tortoise blow a shell ?, etc."[47] This reply and many of his other statements would show that the world is not real. But, we have already quoted many of Kabir's pantheistic statements like, "He is all created things." Such an ambiguous approach towards the world is not peculiar to Kabir; it is so with the Sufis and also many quietist mystics like Eckhart.

But, there is one point on which Kabir is very vocal, repetitive, and emphatic. There are numerous hymns which suggest that the world is a trap laid for man to divert him from the true path of union with God. Kabir thinks the world to be *maya*, but his idea of *maya* is different from that of Sankara. He repeatedly likens *maya* to a woman whose role is to entice man on to the wrong path. Kabir never looks upon the activities of the world to be worthwhile. In fact, he finds the world almost a place of misery and a vale of tears. "The guru of this Kalyuga is full of viles; by the robbery he practices, he slew the whole world."[48] As stated earlier, Kabir deems Niranjana, whom he also calls *Kal* and *Kal Purash*, to be the creator of the world.[49] *Kal* and *maya*, he says, separate man from God, and both strive to mislead man and *bhagats* away from God. It is Niranjana who created a woman or *maya*, and both try to entangle man in the vicious ways of the world.[50] Kabir virtually attributes to *Kal* and *maya* the same role as is attributed to Satan, who is out to entice and mislead man. Kabir says, "First desire was made in the form of a woman, Gayatri."[51] "One woman (*maya*) deludes and devours all men." "One woman has spread her net, fear overcomes all men."[52] "There is a roof of falsehood; it spreads over the earth and sky. In all the religions it has beset the soul."[53] "I kill, I burn, I devour, my name is Niranjana."[54] "Having a serpent noose within her, she has plundered and devoured all the world."[55] "*Maya* sportingly plays the temptress, the whole world she has taken captive."[56] "God men, *munis*, deities, Gorakh, Datta and Vyas, Sanaka and *Sananda* lost at the game, what hope have others ?"[57] "I shall escape from the world untrammeled."[58] "*Maya* is mad ...... and she goes forth to hunt for the prey. The wise and polished she chose and slew. She has not spared the ascetic, the yogi, deep in his meditation, the Jangam in the jungle. Swami doing worship, Machhindarnath and others."[59] "*Maya* is the serpent wife that preys on the world." "The woman's (*maya's*) husband knows not the shame."[60] "On one side stand gods and *munis*, on the other side is she alone."[61] "The three worlds are a cage, virtue and vice, a net, all souls become a prey, there is one hunter, *Kal*."[62] "I saw the whole world burning, each one in his own fire."[63] "Never did I meet the man with whom I might link myself."[64] "Liars keep company with liars, and robbers deal with robbers. The three worlds are full of such persons. There is no one to be trusted."[65] Kabir remains a very solitary person. "In the whole *Brahmand* (universe), Kabir is the only swan, the rest are crows with open beaks."[66]

The very significant and important thing is that, in Kabir's view, *maya* deliberately entices and bewitches man on to sinful ways. The world is a phantom play and *maya* stands between man and God. All his statements suggest that there is virtually a conspiracy deliberately to lure the simple man into false and evil ways and to destroy him. Repeatedly, Kabir warns man to escape from the bondage and the destructive tentacles of the world. Kabir has almost contempt for it. Though, at times, Kabir condemns ascetic methods, but all his above statements show a very strong ascetic bias and an excessive otherworldly approach. Hence his repeated warnings to others to escape from the grip of *maya*. Such being the views of Kabir, no wonder he neither took any step to organise any religious institution, nor evinced any interest in the social affairs around him. Such views are, indeed, quite akin to those of Sufis. His attitude is almost like the "*tauba*" of Sufis which involves abstinence, renunciation and solitariness. Like the Sufis, Kabir married, but like them he remained cut off from the mainstream of life.

(vi) *Methodology* : Kabir believes in self-surrender and God's *bhakti*. The *Kabir-panthis* follow a life of singing the praises of God, prayers and a simple and pure life of devotion. Kabir recommends ceaseless singing of God's praises.[67] He virtually suggests withdrawal from the world. He is against all ritualistic and ascetic methods as means to salvation. It is true that Kabir refers to some yogic terms in describing the meditational and mystic methods of the yogis. But, there is no ground to suggest that he himself recommends the yogic path. In fact, far from recommending yoga, he is quite strong in condemning ascetic or yogic methods, and says that yogis, in their meditations, become prey to *maya*. The point will, however be considered further while comparing Radical *bhakti* with Nathism.

The moral tone is quite strong in Kabir's hymns. "Kabir deck thyself with garments of love. To them is given honour whose body and soul speak the truth."[68] "The ruby of goodness is greater than all the mines of rubies, all the wealth of three worlds resides in the goodness of heart. When the wealth of contentment is won, all other wealth is as dust."[69] "Where there is mercy, there is strength, where there is forgiveness, there is He."[70] "The man who is kind and practises righteousness, who remains passive in the affairs of the world, who considers creatures of the world as his own self, he attains the immortal Being; the true God is ever with him."[71] Kabir suggests inward worship and remembrance of God. For him, true worship is only inwards. "Put on the rosary inward. By counting beads, the world will be full of light." He clearly suggests moral discrimination between good and bad deeds. "What can the helpless road do, when the traveller does not walk understandingly."[72] "What can one do, if, with lamp in hand, one falls in the well."[73] "Or goes astray with open eyes." "Discern ye now between good and evil."[74]

Kabir is a firm advocate of *ahimsa*. His doctrine extends even to the non-destruction of flowers. "The life of the living you strike dead and you say your slaughter makes it dedicated. It is blood haunting you and those who taught you."[75] "They fast all day, and at night they slaughter the cow; here murder, there devotion; how can this please God ? O' Kazi, by whose order doth thou use thy knife."[76] "When you declare the sacrifice of an animal as your religion, what else is sin ? If you regard yourself a saint, whom will you call a butcher ?"[77] "The goat eats grass and is skinned, what will happen to those who eat (goat's) meat ?"[78] "Do not kill poor *jiva*, murder will not be forgiven even if you hear a million *Puranas*."[79] Among the fifty commandments laid down for the followers of Kabir, vegetarianism is one of them.[80] For Kabir, moral life involves adherence to *ahimsa*.

In common with all monastic, ascetic or otherworldly sects, Kabir does not think well of women. There is almost a tirade against them in the hymns of Kabir. Woman is characterised as "a black cobra", "the pit of hell" and the "refuse of the world."[81] She is considered to be a hurdle in the path of the spiritual progress of man. He spoke, "Woman ruins everything when she comes near a man; Devotion, salvation and divine knowledge no longer enter his soul."[82] Schomer and O' Flaherty find a misogynist bias in the hymns of Kabir.[83] His views, about woman are also evident from all his vehement attacks against *maya*. Almost everywhere he likens *maya* to a woman who is out to entice and entrap man, and destroy his spiritual life. Such views about woman from a married person are, indeed, quite uncommon.

(vii) *Kabir's Worldview* : The cosmological views of Kabir give a clear clue to his worldview. He finds Niranjana to be the creator of the world; *maya* or woman. And this woman stands between man and God. She is there to entice him away from Him.

These views clearly affect Kabir's stand about the reality of the world and his consequent approach to it. He finds the world to be a trap, a cleverly laid trap, from which escape has to be sought. This also explains Kabir's attitude towards woman, his stress on *ahimsa* and his strong ascetic bias. All these features, involving virtual withdrawal from life, are common to all monastic or ascetic religious systems.

Similarly, Kabir's goal of liberation from *maya* and union with God as an end in itself, too, is otherworldly. For, Kabir, after his achievement, never took any initiative either to start a religious organisation or movement, or to accept any social responsibility. The inequality in the world he seems to ascribe to one's own acts. "To one man God has given silks and satin and a niwar bed, others have not even a ragged coat or straw in the house to lie upon. Indulge not in envy or bickerings, O' my soul, do good deeds and gain their reward."[84] In this background, no wonder, Kabir never took any interest in the social or temporal affairs of his times. Obviously, such activity was not in line with his system. In the whole *Bijak*, there is hardly a categoric reference to God's Will working in the world. No doubt, Kabir calls all men to be the children of God, but it is equally true that for him the world is far from being a field of spiritual training and test. There is no direction for, much less emphasis on, carrying out the Will of God. Generally, his description of God is of one without Attributes and is Absolute. Mystics who are disinclined to enter the social field generally describe God as Absolute and Attributeless.

Apart from the popular hymns of Kabir, most of them either deal with subjects that are abstract, esoteric or mystic, or are couched in a language that is seemingly paradoxical. Many of his hymns are in the form of riddles to be solved. In fact, Kabir is aware of it, because, at the end of some hymns, he invites persons to indicate their meaning, saying he who could understand them would be a master of religion.[85] It is undoubted that Kabir, like the Hinayana, addressed only the elite. His lack of interest in creating a separate religious movement is also obvious from the fact that he appointed no successor, and after him his disciples divided into Hindu *Kabir-panthis* and Muslim *Kabir-panthis*, each group owing allegiance to its own respective tradition as well.

Therefore, whether seen from the point of view of his goal, his approach to the world, his ideas about the reality of the world, his attitude towards women, his insistence on *ahimsa* and other factors mentioned above, it is apparent that Kabir holds the world-view of withdrawal from life.

4. NAM DEV

Nam Dev is another pioneer of the Radical *bhakti* School. Though he appeared a century earlier than Kabir, his religious and social views are very much like those of Kabir. He unambiguously repudiates all the four fundamentals of Vaisnavism. Though in his devotional approach, he is clearly a monotheist, he makes many pantheistic statements too, e.g., every thing is God; there is nothing but God; consider the world and God to be one; the foam and the water are not different. Chaturvedi writes : "*Sant* Nam Dev seemed to believe both in transcendence and immanence, in pantheism and nondualism. His devotion was purely of the non-attributional absolute."[86] But, he also considers God to be immanent, everywhere, in all hearts, and the Creator of everything. Like Kabir and the Sufis, Nam Dev is very otherworldly. For, he says, "The strength of contempt of the world should be in the body an unchanging companion. One should lay aside differences between oneself and others, and feel no anxiety for things of the world."[87] Ranade also writes : "He (Nam Dev) tells us that it is impossible that the pursuit of God can be coupled with a life of *Samsara*. If it had been possible for a man to find God while he was pursuing *Samsara*, then *Sanaka* and others would not have grown mad after God. If it had been possible for him to see God while carrying on the duties of a householder, the great Suka would not have gone to the forest to seek God. Had it been possible for people to find God in their homes, they would not have left them to find out. Nam Dev has left all these things, and is approaching God in utter submission (Abhg. 83)."[88]

Nam Dev's cosmogenic views are also orthodox. He says that God created *maya* and "*maya* is the name of the power that placeth man in the womb."[89] Indirectly, he is neither happy with the world, nor with the human birth. For him, shop, shopkeeper, men and everything are unreal excepting God.[90] In this background he seeks release from the world and suggests renunciation : "...... Nam Dev gave up trade, and devoted himself exclusively to the worship of God ......"[91]

The world being a play of *maya* and not being a worthwhile field of spiritual endeavours, Namdev's goal is to have union with God through devotion and singing His praises. He says, "I perform worship, sing God's praises and meditate on Him for eight *pahar* in a day[92] i.e, round the clock. At the same time, he suggests good conduct and purity of life. For, God created all men alike. Though he holds every person responsible for his acts, he clearly does not believe in a world rigidly governed by *karma*. Because he says : If everything were determined by *karma*, who created *karma* originally ?[93]

Nam Dev not only claims union with God, but, like Kabir, also states that more than once God miraculously intervened on his behalf to reveal Himself to him, or help him. Without doubt, Nam Dev's approach remains otherworldly both before and after his achievement. At one time, he even gave up work so as to remain absorbed in his worship and meditations. He never initiated any religious institution or movement. His was a solitary search for God, without creating any social or religious organisation.

We find that in his repudiation of Vaisnava doctrines, in his metaphysical ideas, methodology and goal, and more particularly in his otherworldly approach to the world and society, Namdev's views are quite identical with those of Kabir.

5. GENERAL

We have considered the doctrines and thoughts of two pioneers who are distinctly typical of the Radical School. Other saints like Pipa, Dhanna, Ravidass, Tuka Ram, Trilochan, too, have similar views both in regard to Vaisnavism, the mode and ideals of *bhakti* and their approach to the world. Almost all of them claim union with God and are guided purely by their individual mystic experience which is their final authority. All these saints, many of whom belonged to the low castes, accepted the fatherhood of God and the brotherhood of man. They believed in the heart-whole love of God and moral living, shorn of all formalism and ritualism.

6. WORLDVIEW OF RADICAL BHAGATS

From the above description, let us draw some general conclusions about them. While, as seen by us, they are radically different from the Vaisnava Bhaktas, they are, as a class, equally distinct from the Sikh Gurus.

From the metaphysical point of view, Radical *bhakti* is theistic, though the theistic picture is a little blurred, because at times pantheistic statements have also been made by the *Bhagats*. It cannot be denied that both in regard to their theism and the reality of the world their views are, to an extent, ambiguous. It is necessary to understand that ambiguities on these two issues are almost common to all quietist mystics, including Christian and Buddhist mystics and the Sufis, with which group they are nearest in their doctrines and practices. Pantheistic systems generally have two features. Their worldview is life-denying, and the moral tone is weak since everything is the working of the Basic Reality. Man being a part of Reality, the goal is a return to the original state, God head or Brahman which is Attributeless or *Nirgun*. In the Radical *bhakti*, the moral sense is clear enough to denounce the inequalities of caste, but it is not strong enough to fight its logical challenges. So, the pantheistic streak in Radical *bhakti* does make it indifferent to social interests and functioning.

In addition, the Radical Bhagats have two other characteristic features. Everyone of these saints had a clear otherworldly attitude. Secondly, none of them accepted any social responsibility or started a movement, institution, or organisation in the religious field, much less in the social field. Ranade writes, "Mystics of this period show an all-absorbing love of God, which would not allow a rightful performance of one's duties before God-absorption." "The conflict between a rightful performance of duty and all absorbing love of God has existed at all times and in all countries. But it seems the saints of this period were inclined to lean in the latter rather than in the former direction and exhibited an all-absorbing character of God-realisation. God indeed is an all-devourer, and it seems from the examples of these saints that He devours also the performance of one's own natural duties."[94] Let us also quote a few relevant conclusions of Ray which he expressed regarding the radical saints, "I do not find any evidence to indicate that any of them ever attempted to institutionalise their faith and followers." "They had no other social purpose in view than to make better individuals from out of the groups that assembled around them. Their aim seems to have been the individual, not the society in any significant sense." "These leaders seem to have been individuals, working out for their own problems and towards achieving their personal religious and spiritual aims and aspirations."[95]

It is, indeed, a glaring fact that the saints of the Radical School felt no social interest or concern for the affairs of man. There is no evidence whatsoever, that any of these saints initiated an activity or step in the social field. Like all quietist mystics, they led a solitary and otherworldly life, because it was their firm belief that temporal life was inconsistent with the religious path.

All this evidence makes it plain that the worldview of the Radical group was virtually of life-negation, since all of them led and recommended a life of withdrawal from the world and unconcern with the society in general. For them, religious life was only a matter of personal concern and pursuit for union with God.

7. SAINTS AND NATHS

Let us examine if there is any affinity between Saints and Naths. Kabir is severely critical of most of the Nath practices and injunctions. He says, "With shaven head you sit swollen with pride, rings in your ears, within a cave, your body you have besmeared with ashes, but within, you rob the house. In your village dwells a proud mendicant, filled with self, with pride and lust."[96] Naths are Saivites and Machhindernath and Gorakhnath are the founder Naths or the Nath Gurus. Kabir derides all of them. He rejected the ritualism, spells, blood sacrifices and horrid practices of Naths as inconsistent with his simple spiritual methods. "I was inclined neither towards *yoga* nor towards *Dhyana,* but I am certain that by *Vairagya* (renunciation) *maya* cannot be discarded."[97] "Brahma, Shiva and *Sanaka* know Him not. Recite the name of Ram."[98] Two points need to be kept in view in interpreting hymns of Kabir. When he refers to some of the yogic methods of meditation, it does not mean that he accepts their adoption or system. He only means that the achievements claimed by the yogis are achieved by him by his own methods of *bhakti.* "I have smashed Shiva and Shakti and have enlightened my soul with *Sahaj* of the thousand petalled *Kamal.*"[99] This hymn is clearly derisive of Lord Shiva who is the god with whom the Nath seeks final union of bliss. Secondly, in many cases, the meaning of words used by Kabir is his own. With Naths, *Sahaj* means only a righteous temperament. Naths also used this term quite differently from its use by *Siddhas,* with whom *Sahaj* indicates natural abstinence and the medium through which they experience *Maha-Sukha.* But, for Kabir *Sahaj* means the final state of union with God through his own devotional systems.[100] So, this caution is necessary while interpreting Kabir.

Kabir not only criticises all ascetic life, methodology and practices, but he almost ridicules Shiva, the Lord of Naths, Machhindernath and Gorakhnath, the two pioneers of the system. "Mahadev wasted his life with Uma." "Dead are Gorakh, Dattatreya." "Many *Siddhs*, *Sanyasis* and Gorakh found not the end." "Brahma, Shiva and Sanaka know Him not." "There was no Mahadeva." "Gorakh could not retain the breath for all his vaunted devices of devotion. By multiplying their mystic rites and ceremonies, they did not know *Parbrahma*." "Machhindernath was overwhelmed by *maya*."[101]

In fact, Nam Dev is quite categoric in rejecting the Hath Yoga method of Naths, when he says that he follows the path of *Nam* and disregards the yoga of *Ida, Pingla* and *Susmana.* "I shall sing and imbibe the Name of God and achieve the highest stage; I reject the methods of *Ida, Pingla* and *Susmana,* and of the union of the sun and the moon (as in Hath Yoga where the sun represents Shiva and the moon *Kundalani*); I shall reach Him otherwise."[102]

It would, indeed, be idle to suggest that mystics who reject the Nath methodology and who are quite derisive while describing their chief god, the pioneers or the gurus of the Naths, would in practice own or follow *Hath Yoga* or their system of methodology.

SIKHISM AND RADICAL BHAGATS : A COMPARISON

The common point between Sikhism and the *sants* is their theism. It cannot be denied that, despite some of their pantheistic statements, the *sants* are, broadly speaking, theistic. In their rejection of the fundamentals of Hinduism and their denouncement of the caste ideology of the Brahminical society, the two systems, are quite similar. But, divergences start in regard to most of the remaining issues raised by us. The overall worldviews presented by the two systems are wholly different.

The views of the *sants* about the reality of the world are somewhat ambivalent. The *sants* clearly led a life of withdrawal from the world and non-involvement in its affairs. For the Gurus, activity in the world is the measure of one's spiritual progress. For Kabir, the world is a snare. But, for the Gurus, "The world is in bloom like a garden." For them, rejecting the world and its responsibilities is wrong, because it is the meaningful field of spiritual training. Activity therein alone shows whether or not a person has shed his ego. Between the two systems, there is a fundamental contrast in their approach to the world. This basic difference explains the contrast in the goals, in the methodologies, in the roles of the superman, and the worldviews of the two systems.

Whereas among the *sants*, the goal is to have union with God as an end in itself, in Sikhism, the *gurmukh's* objective is to carry out the Attributive Will of God in the world. In Sikhism, man's assessment and his nearness to God depend on the deeds of the seeker. But, in the *sant* methodology, the emphasis is on singing the praises and love of God. Among the *sants*, there has never been any social concern, much less social involvement in the problems of the community and humanity, since withdrawal from the mainstream of society is a part of their methodology. As against it, in Sikhism, since God is the Protector of the weak and the helpless, and Destroyer of the tyrant, the God-conscious person has a perpetual role to play in all fields of life. The result of all these differences is that, whereas the Sikh worldview is life-affirming, that of the *sants* is life-denying. Let us explain this point about life-affirmation or activity.

In this context, it is fundamentally important to bear in mind how this thesis of life-affirmation and activity was lived, what was its impact on society, and how it flowered. Guru Nanak's very first words, after his Enlightenment were, "There is no Hindu, no Mussalman." For, without any distinction of creed or colour, he saw only man everywhere, and his primary interest was in man alone. Of this principle of the brotherhood of man, Gupta writes, "Like Rousseau, Nanak felt 250 years earlier that it was the common people who make the human race." The marvel is that this principle was proclaimed and practised in a society, where, for over two thousand years, the divisive rigidity of the hierarchical caste had not only been strictly observed, but the same had also received complete religious, ethical and social sanction. In furtherance of their thesis, the Gurus purposely organised and created an egalitarian society outside the social system governed by the caste ideology. No other religious or liberal movement, whether Buddhistic, Vaisnava, Saiva or of the Radical Bhagat, ever made an attempt in this direction; much less organise it. This calculated organisation and socio-political direction of the movement inevitably led to a clash with the establishment and the martyrdoms of the Gurus themselves and hundreds of their followers. For the first time in history, there arose an idealistic revolution, a pleople's movement constituted by all sections of society, but led by the so-called lowest of them, including *Kalals*, *Sudras* and *Ranghrettas*. The deep significance of these features and the ethos that gave rise to them can be gauged from the fact that in 1947 when India won independence, the Prime

Minister and the Chief Ministers of practically all the states belonged to the Brahmin caste. Again, the elan of this movement was such that it not only suffered and survived persistent attempts of the Moghul Empire to exterminate it, even by placing a price on the head of every Sikh, but it actually supplanted the very Empire that sought to uproot and destroy it. No wonder, Dr Gupta calls this saga of martyrdoms, sacrifices and a successful struggle nothing short of a miracle. It is of this revolution that he says, "He (the Guru) thus enunciated a hundred years earlier the principles of liberty, equality and fraternity which formed the bedrock of the French Revolution."

A question arises why there is such a contrast between the essentials and the activities of the two systems when both of them are theistic. This point takes us back to the issue raised by us initially, namely, the unity of perception, ideology and activity. In that regard, we came to the conclusion that the best clues to the ideology and basic perceptions of a religious system are its activities. Otherwise, simplistic or merely academic definition or classification of a religious system could be very misleading. Quietist mystic systems or theistic saints like the *sants* have appeared in all times and in different countries. And, yet, none of them have ever shown social concern and responsibility as did the Sikh Gurus. It would, therefore, be very wrong to class both the activist and the quietist mystics in the same category, or to assert that the ideologies and perceptions of these two kinds of saints are the same, even though their activities in life are wholly divergent.

The answers of the *sants* and the Sikh Gurus regarding most of the essentials of their religions being different, evidently the religious perceptions and experiences of the *sants* and the Gurus are different. For obvious reasons, evidence on this issue can, by and large, be only inferential. However, before we examine this issue further, we shall consider the views of two mystics on this matter.

Abdul Qadus of Gangoh, while referring to the active role of Prophet Mohammad, said, "Mohammad of Arabia ascended the highest heaven and returned. I swear by God that if I had reached that point I should never have returned."[103]

It is no mere coincidence that centuries later, Baba Wasakha Singh, a Sikh saint, emphasised the same point saying, "What kind of *bhakti* is that in which one remains absorbed in one's meditations and the poor suffer all around us. This is not *bhakti*. A Guru's Sikh must work and serve the poor."[104] In Sikhism, the highest stage is not to remain enthralled in the mystic union, but, simultaneously, to work for the welfare of suffering humanity." The same point he stressed in different words, "You know how difficult it is for an ordinary person to give up the worldly pleasures and possessions and instead to follow the path of God. It is even more difficult for the *bhagat* to come out of his intense and tranquil bliss in order to serve man and do the Will of God. But, brother, it is the highest kind of *bhakti* to serve the poor and the downtrodden and yet remain in union with Him."[105]

Bergson, who has considered the issue from the point of view of philosophy, goes to the extent of saying that the religious experience of the quietist mystics, like Plotinus or Buddhists, is not full-fledged. According to him, complete mysticism inevitably involves "the establishment of a contact, consequently of a partial coincidence, with the creative effort which life itself manifests. This effort is of God, if it is not God Himself. The great mystic is to be conceived as an individual being, capable of transcending the limitations imposed on the species by its material nature, thus continuing and extending the divine action." He, therefore, considers Greek, Indian and Buddhist mysticisms to be incomplete, because these give up activity. Plotinus, the Greek mystic, says that, "action is a weakening of contemplation." But, in complete mysticism, after the union, the mystic soul yearns to become His (God's) instrument. "Now it is God who is acting through the soul." The mystic is all activity. It is not now "the love of man for God, it is the love of God for all men" that works. It is this love which the mystic expresses in life. It coincides with "God's love for his handiwork." These mystics are the instruments of God so as to "lift humanity up to God and complete the divine creation so that it could reach its end." To such a God-conscious man, the creation appears to be "God undertaking to create creators, so that he may have besides Himself, beings worthy of His love."[106] The views of Hocking too are very similar. For him also, a *bhagat* of the active kind "not only establishes a communion with God and develops a higher spiritual consciousness, but also becomes, in the domain of life the divine organising vehicle of the Transcendent Reality. In all humility, he seeks to translate into activity the Will of God. This forms his continuing mission."[107] Such has been the perpetual, creative, constructive, and organising role of the Sikh Gurus.

Centuries before Bergson and Hocking defined activity or prophetic devotion to God and distinguished it from quietist devotion, the Sikh Gurus had not only clearly and emphatically expressed their views on the subject of their prophetic or activity religion, but they had actually lived according to the principles of active *bhakti* laid down by them.

Another question arises as to why there should be such vast difference in the ideology and the activities of the two kinds of devotees or *bhagats* of God. These differences, we feel, are entirely due to the difference in the perceptions of the two kinds of saints. Stace has collected a mass of evidence about the nature of the religious experiences of numerous mystics and saints of the world, including those from India, the Middle East, Europe, England and Greece. He describes this experience as unitary, ineffable, paradoxical, blessed, blissful and tranquil. The entire evidence Stace has collected, relates to saints who in their lives were quietists. In his description, Stace does not mention love as being an element in the religious perceptions of those saints or mystics.[108] Like Stace, William James had also recorded the nature of religious experiences. He too does not mention love to be an essential part of that experience.

But Bergson considers love to be the chief ingredient of the mystic experience of the activity mystics. Let us see what the Guru says in this regard. "Friends, ask me what is the chief mark of the Lord. He is all Love, rest He is ineffable."[109] For the Guru, the fundamental feature of the religious experience is love. That is why Guru Nanak says, "He who wants to play the game of love should come with his head on his palm",[110] and Guru Gobind Singh declared, "Let everyone know that he alone is approved by the Lord who loves."[111] And love is dynamic, creative, cohesive, directive and virtuous. Such is also the Attributive Will of God. The Guru says, "He who knows His Will, carry it out."

In Sikhism, both the seeker and the *bhagat* have to live the life of continuous activity for the service of man. With the quietist *bhagats*, the position is entirely different both in theory and practice. Hence the wide differences between the two systems, their religious perceptions and their activities.

REFERENCES

1. Ahmed Shah, *Bijak of Kabir*, p. 111.
2. Ibid., pp. 147-148.
3. Machwe, P., *Kabir*, p. 33.
4. Ahmad Shah, op. cit. p. 220.
5. Ibid., p. 117.
6. Varma, R.K., *Kabir Biography and Philosophy*, p. 37.
7. Ibid., p. 37.
8. Ahmad Shah, op. cit. p. 69.
9. Varma, op. cit. p. 7.
10. Ahmad Shah, op. cit. pp. 88, 220.
11. Ibid., pp. 105-6.
12. Ibid., p. 138.
13. Ibid., pp. 103-104; Juergensmeyer, M., *Sikh Studies*, p. 70.
14. Ibid., p. 175.
15. Ibid., p. 174.
16. Ibid., p. 149.
17. Ibid., pp. 60, 104.
18. Ibid., p. 82, *Guru Granth Sahib*, p. 324.
19. Ibid., p. 116.
20. Ahmad Shah, op. cit. pp. 147-149.
21. Ibid., pp. 95, 158.
22. Ibid., pp. 209-210.
23. Ibid., p. 114.
24. Wilson, H.H., *Religious Sects of the Hindus*, p. 19.
25. Tara Chand, *Influence of Islam on Indian Culture*, p. 148.
26. Varma, op. cit. p. 22.
27. Ibid., pp. 19, 50.
28. Machwe, op. cit. p. 19, Bhandarkar, R.G., *Vaisnavism and Saivism*, p. 69.
29. Ahmad Shah, op. cit. pp. 41-42.
30. Ibid., pp. 41-43.
31. Ibid., p. 7.
32. Tara Chand, *Influence of Islam on Indian Culture*, p. 154.
33. Machwe, op. cit. p. 23; Varma, op. cit. p. 94; Ahmad Shah, op. cit. pp. 58, 68.
34. Tara Chand, op. cit. p. 154; Machwe, p. 24.
35. Varma, op. cit. p. 94.
36. Ibid., p. 118.
37. Ibid., p. 118.
38. Bhandarkar, op. cit. p. 71.
39. Macauliffe, *The Sikh Religion*, Vol. 6, p. 160; Tara Chand, op. cit. p. 150.

40. Varma, op. cit. p. 118.
41. Tara Chand, op. cit. pp. 161-162.
42. Ahmad Shah, op. cit. p. 37.
43. Ibid., pp. 38, 81.
44. Ibid., p. 132.
45. Ibid., p. 163.
46. Ibid., p. 163.
47. Macauliffe, op. cit. Vol. 6, p. 199.
48. Ahmad Shah, op. cit. p. 111.
49. Ibid., pp. 41-42.
50. Ibid., pp. 38-43. 63.
51. Ibid., p. 52.
52. Ibid., pp. 87, 96-97.
53. Ibid., pp. 148-149.
54. Ibid., p. 63.
55. Ibid., p. 96.
56. Ibid., p. 174.
57. Ibid., p. 174.
58. Ibid., p. 165.
59. Ibid., pp. 166-167.
60. Ibid., p. 170.
61. Ibid., pp. 170-175.
62. Ibid., p. 186.
63. Ibid., p. 216.
64. Ibid., p. 216.
65. Ibid., p. 136.
67. Bhandarkar, op. cit. p. 73.
68. Ahmad Shah, op. cit. p. 200.
69. Ibid., p. 225.
70. Ibid., p. 225.
71. Tara Chand, op. cit. p. 160.
72. Ibid., p. 202; *Guru Granth Sahib*, p. 1376.
73. Macauliffe, op. cit. Vol. 6, p. 141.
74. Ibid., p. 179.
75. Ahmad Shah, op. cit. pp. 134-135.
76. Ibid., p. 71.
77. Varma, op. cit. p. 31.
79. Ahmad Shah, op. cit. p. 204.
80. Ibid., p. 44.
81. Juergensmeyer, op. cit. p. 83.
82. Ibid., p. 84.
83. Ibid., pp. 83-88.
84. Macauliffe, op. cit. Vol. 6, p. 204.
85. Ahmad Shah, op. cit. p. 144, Varma, p. 122.
86. Machwe, P., *Namdev*, p. 61.
87. Macauliffe, op. cit. Vol. 6, p. 27.
88. Machwe, op. cit. pp. 74-75.
89. Macauliffe, op. cit. Vol. 6, p. 48.
90. Ibid., p. 75.
91. Ibid., p. 65.
92. Ibid., p. 43.

93. Ibid., p. 60.
94. Machwe, pp. 59-60.
95. Ray, N., *The Sikh Gurus and the Sikh Society*, pp. 61-62.
96. Ahmad Shah, op. cit. p. 164.
97. Varma, op. cit. p. 73.
98. Juergensmeyer, op. cit. p. 70.
99. Varma, op. cit. pp. 43-44.
100. Ibid., pp. 55-56.
101. Ahmad Shah, op. cit. pp. 78-79, 104, 138-140.
102. Guru Granth Sahib, pp. 972-973.
103. Iqbal, M., *Reconstruction of Religious Thought in Islam*, pp. 124, 197-98.
104. Daljit Singh, *Sikhism*, p. 298.
105. Ibid., p. 297.
106. Smullyan and others, *Introduction to Philosophy*, pp. 363-66.
107. Spencer, S., *Mysticism in World Religions*, p. 173.
108. Stace, W.T., *Mysticism and Philosophy*, pp. 131-133.
109. Guru Granth Sahib, p. 459.
110. Ibid., p. 1412.
111. *Swayyas Patshahi Das* (Tenth Guru).

III

INSTITUTIONS

17

THE KHALSA

JAGJIT SINGH

One of the objectives of the Sikh movement was to capture political power for a plebeian mission. The Khalsa was the instrument created and used both to overthrow the Mughal, and to capture political power for achieving plebeian objectives. The significance of the Khalsa, and the role it played in the revolutionary struggle, are of the highest importance, because the Khalsa was the climax of the Sikh movement.

1. REVOLUTIONARY MISSION ENSHRINED

Describing the attributes of God, Guru Gobind Singh says, "Thou bestowest happiness on the good, Thou terrifiest the evil, Thou scatterest sinners, I seek Thy protection."[1] "God ever cherisheth the poor; saveth saints, and destroyeth enemies."[2] He speaks of God as "Compassionate to the poor, and Cherisher of the lowly."[3] Guru Nanak also identifies himself with "lowliest of the lowly, the lowest of the low-born ......, for, where the weak are cared for, Thy Mercy is showered."[4] Thus, 'cherishing the poor' and 'destroying the tyrant' are, according to Sikhism, God's own mission. In the Guru's own words, "his father (Guru Tegh Bahadur) suffered martyrdom for the sake of religion." It was in the pursuance of His mission that God sent Guru Gobind Singh to this world. In the Guru's own words the mission was :

"Go and spread my religion there,
And restrain the world from senseless acts."[4a]

Guru Gobind Singh bestowed sovereignty on the Khalsa for plebeian objectives. This was how this Sikh revolutionary mission was consecrated. It was God's own mission.

2. WAHEGURU JI KA KHALSA

Waheguru ji ka Khalsa;
Waheguru ji ki Fateh.

It means, 'The Khalsa belongs to God, and so does Victory belong to Him.' When

Guru Gobind Singh conferred leadership on the Khalsa, he ended his address with this expression. It became a motto of the Khalsa. It is repeated on all occasions and ceremonies, especially the *amrit* ceremony, and as a form of daily greetings among Sikhs. Guru Nanak had told Daulat Khan Lodhi that he recognised no other authority than that of God. Guru Arjun had declared, 'I am a worshipper of the Immortal God ...... There is no monarch save Him.' Guru Gobind Singh said in his hymn : 'Since I embraced Thy Feet, I have paid regard to none besides.'[5] The same lesson was impressed on the mind of the Khalsa by the repeated expression of the above motto. The Khalsa owed allegiance to God, and to none else. In its social implications, it meant loyalty only to the Khalsa mission which had been sanctified by God Himself. Forster narrates a personal experience. Once he travelled in the company of a Sikh horseman for some days. 'His answer, when I asked him very respectfully in whose service he was retained, seemed strikingly characteristic of what I conceive to be the disposition of the Nation. He said, in a tone of voice, and with a countenance which glowed and was keenly animated by the warm spirit of liberty and independence, that he disclaimed an earthly master, and he was the servant only of his Prophet.'[6] This is a glimpse of the Khalsa spirit as it had survived even in the post-revolutionary period. This motto also generated a spirit of everlasting optimism and humility — optimism because the revolutionary cause, being God's cause, was bound to succeed sooner or later; and humility because all victory was God's Victory and by His Grace. It involved no credit for the participant.

3. OPEN DECLARATION OF REVOLUTION

When the head of Guru Tegh Bahadur was brought to Guru Gobind Singh at Anandpur, he asked, how many Sikhs had sacrificed themselves along with the Guru ? He was told that only two Sikhs sacrificed themselves. The Guru remarked, 'But the Sikhs are many in number ?' The answer given was, 'All turned their back to the faith. All slipped back in the populace. There was no distinguishing mark for a Sikh to prevent that from happening.' This provoked the Guru to say, 'I shall assign such distinguishing marks to the Sikhs that a Sikh would be recognizable even among thousands."[7] Guru Gobind Singh proceeded to create the Khalsa, an armed body of revolutionaries, who were to carry out the revolution 'by the open profession thereof.' On being initiated as a member of the Khalsa, a Sikh become a Singh (male) or Kaur (female). A Singh or Kaur has to carry fixed distinguishing marks, especially hair, which he/she cannot discard, so long as he/she want to remain a Singh or Kaur. So he/she is recognizable even among thousands, by friends and foes alike. Thus, each and every Singh or Kaur is made not only an instrument of the declared revolution, but also its standard bearer.

It was in 1675 A.D. that the Guru expressed his intention of assigning distinguishing marks to the Sikhs. He gave it a practical shape by creating the Khalsa in 1699, 24 years later. This shows a long-term plan and preparation. Guru Hargobind's battles had not been in vain. These inspired 'the Sikhs with self-confidence, and gave them an exalted sense of their own worth.' Guru Har Rai and Guru Tegh Bahadur had kept regular forces, but that remained primarily a period of truce. And, there was now a radical change in the political situation. Aurangzeb confronted non-Muslims with an undisguised religious and political challenge. He started undermining even the position of his loyal Rajput allies. This challenge could be met only by a direct confrontation and by pitching against the power of the state the power of the masses. Guru Gobind Singh, therefore, made an open declaration of revolution and started arming the general body of the Panth[7a] with a view to creating a large force of revolutionaries. As Bhangu has rightly put it, the Guru 'first increased the number of the Khalsa, and then started the revolution.'[8]

4. KHALSA AS AN INSTRUMENT OF REVOLUTION

Guru Gobind Singh invited the hill Rajas to join him in his struggle against the Mughals. For a short time, he even succeeded in persuading some of them to make common cause against the Mughal rulers. But, the attitude of the hill chiefs was not consistent. They were guided primarily by their feudal interests and made war or peace with the Mughals accordingly. Another basic point of difference was that they were governed by caste considerations. When invited by the Guru, they refused even to entertain the idea of working side by side with the so-called low caste followers of the Guru. Had the Guru been guided by the consideration of only meeting the Mughal challenge, he might have come to terms with the hill Rajas. But he did not. This is very significant. His basic objective was to raise the level of the poor and the downtrodden. He wanted these very people to capture political power for themselves. For that end, the Guru had to embark upon his project from humble beginnings. He made arrows with his own hands[9] and trained people who had been denied the use of arms by the caste ideology. He did not follow the easier course of depending upon the hill chiefs who had arms and martial tradition. For, this would have been at the cost of his fundamental religious and social principles and objectives.

Guru Gobind Singh gathered together the Sikhs and gave them the call, 'Take up arms and defeat the Turks (Mughals).' He devised the plan for initiation of the Khalsa. On the annual Vaisakhi gathering of the Sikhs, the Guru came out of a tent with a drawn sword in his hand and demanded from the congregation the head of a Sikh for sacrifice. There was great consternation, but one Sikh got up and offered himself to the Guru. The Guru took him inside the tent. Soon after he came out with a blood-stained sword in his hand and again demanded a second head. This time the consternation was greater than before, but undaunted, another Sikh offered himself. Five times the Guru made the same demand. Every time a Sikh offered himself. This showed that the community had attained the level at which it was ready to stake its all for the cause. Finally, the Guru brought out from the tent the *Panj Piaras* (Five Beloved Ones), hale and hearty. First he initiated them and then got himself initiated by them. Thus was created the Khalsa, ready for the mission. The Guru said :

'They will destroy the (established tyrannical) rule,
And establish their own everywhere ......
Khalsa will become the image of God,
With His own attributes.
They will acknowledge no authority,

Other than that of the True Lord.'[10]

Gursobha testifies that 'The Khalsa is created to destroy the evil-doer ('*asur*' and '*durjan*').'[11] Koer Singh writes that after the initiation ceremony, the Guru gave instructions to the following effect :

'Destroy the Mughal forces ...... (and you) rule for ever.'[12]

Later Sikh literature records the same tradition. 'Khalsa is one who fights in the front line ...... Khalsa is one who protects the poor ...... Khalsa is one who crushes the tyrant (*dushat*).'[13] 'Where the (Singhs) fight the Turks for upholding *dharma* and the Sikh ideals and to help others, there my presence will be felt among the Sikhs.'[14] 'Khalsa is the army of God.'[15] It was ordered : "You should now wear weapons, and value steel; and love it, because this will lead you to a high status."[15a]

Guru Gobind Singh addressed his two sons at the battle of Chamkaur thus : 'My sons, you are dear to me. You are born to destroy the Turks (tyrants). Only if you sacrifice yourselves in the battle, can the tyrants be eliminated. There can be no better opportunity than the present one. Both of you go and join the battle.'[16] And, when his eldest son died fighting there, the Guru said, 'Today he has become the chosen Khalsa in God's court.'[17] Thus, to sacrifice oneself for the revolutionary cause was the fulfilment of the Khalsa ideal and it was sanctified by the religion.

The acceptance of the Khalsa ideology naturally meant becoming whole time revolutionaries. An important part of the Sikh discipline was the dedication of one's all — body, soul and belongings (*tan, man, dhan,*) — to the Guru or God. "By dedicating body, mind and possessions to the Guru, and abiding by His Will does one reach God."[18] This ideal demanded extreme self-sacrifice. The Guru said, "As the elephant suffers the goad, and the anvil the stroke of the smith, so should one surrender one's body and mind to the service (of God)."[19] When Banda expressed his desire to become a disciple of Guru Gobind Singh, the Guru cautioned him that in order to become a Sikh, he would have to surrender and stake everything for the mission."[20] To regard one's body and possessions as belonging to the Guru or God was the Sikh way of creating a commune. With the militarization of the Sikh movement, this ideal was orientated towards dedication of one's all to the revolutionary cause. The Khalsa is God's own (*Waheguru ji ka Khalsa*). Therefore, dedication of oneself to the Khalsa was dedication to God. A Sikh's dedication of body, soul and possessions to the Khalsa has to be complete. Guru Gobind Singh has himself made this point explicit. "All the wealth of my house with soul and body is for them (Khalsa)."[21] "Khalsa is my own image; I abide in the Khalsa; Khalsa is my body and life; Khalsa is the life of my life; I belong to the Khalsa and the Khalsa belongs to me; the way the ocean and the drop are one.'[22]

Thousands of Sikhs lived upto this standard. Even at a very late stage of the struggle, those who joined the Khalsa Dal (an organisation of combatant volunteers) had, according to the demands of the mission, to cut off virtually all their connections with their families. Those, who without permission, visited their families even for some urgent reason, had to pay the prescribed penalty.[23] When the *Khalsa Dal* was reorganised into five divisions (*jathas*), one of these divisions was of shaheeds, viz., those who had dedicated themselves completely to the revolutionary cause and vowed not to shirk martyrdom, when necessary. The Nihangs and Akalis were quite sizeable in numbers and played a notable part in Sikh history. *Nihangs* and *Akalis*, like the *shaheeds*, were those volunteers who had dedicated their lives to the armed service of the Panth. Maybe, they were a part or an offshoot of the *shaheeds*. They cut off for life all worldly connections, spent their entire lives in the *jathas*, remained always armed to the teeth and were ever ready to lay down their lives for the Panth. They were to the Sikhs what the *Jannessears* were to the Turks, with the difference that the *Nihangs* and *Akalis* were honorary volunteers and not organised or paid by the state. The *Nihangs* were a dedicated and inspired lot, highly conscious of the Sikh mission and its revolutionary ideals. Theirs was an armed commune and continues to be so to this day. In other words, they institutionalized the ideal of dedicating '*tan, man, dhan*' to the Sikh revolutionary cause. It is for this reason that they are held in high esteem in the Panth. They were at one time its conscience keepers. When the movement entered its lean period and split up into different fighting corporations (*misls*), one of the *misls* was of the *shaheeds*. They held no territory of their own and were provided food and shelter by the Panth. The *Shaheeds* and *Akalis* provided the rallying point for the *misls* to co-ordinate in order to meet a common danger to the Panth. At such a time, the resolution (*gurmatta*) to meet such an eventuality (e.g. at the time of threatened danger from Abdali's invasion) would be sponsored by the *Akalis*. All the *misls* would honour the resolution.[24] Even Ranjit Singh respected them and was afraid of offending the *Akalis*. They were the dominating factor in the Khalsa army committees.[24a] Scott compares the *Akalis* with Cromwell's Ironsides. 'The *Akalis* would represent the 'Fifth Monarchy Men', stern and uncompromising, firmly believing in the righteousness of their cause, insisting on the right to equality for all, guided by the decisions of the *Panch*, or Committee of Five, than by their nominal leaders, and watching those leaders with the jealous eyes lest they should assume absolute power.'[25]

5. AS CUSTODIAN OF ETHICAL VALUES

The Sikh movement, as already pointed out, had a twofold objective. It aimed at raising man above his ego-centredness and thus produce an ideal man, and it wanted to change the social and political environment which hindered such development. Guru Gobind Singh, no doubt, bestowed political sovereignty on the Khalsa, but it was to be the Khalsa of his definition. The Guru had said that 'Khalsa was his own image ...... his perfect Guru.'[26] Accordingly, great emphasis was laid on the maintenance of the ethical standards set for the Khalsa. 'He who shuns the company of the five evils, loves to associate with noble men, owns *dharma* and compassion, gives up ambition; ...... He is the Khalsa of the *Waheguru*.'[27] One day before his death, when the Sikhs asked Guru Gobind Singh as to who was to be his successor, he replied :

'Khalsa is my image, I abide in the Khalsa;
From beginning to end, I reveal myself in the Khalsa.'[28]

Bhai Nand Lal, a close associate of Guru Gobind Singh, writes :

'Khalsa is one who does not speak ill of others;

Khalsa is one who fights in the front ranks.
Khalsa is one who conquers the five evils;
Khalsa is one who destroys doubt.
Khalsa is one who gives up ego;
Khalsa is one who keeps away from woman, not his wife;
Khalsa is one who looks upon all as his own;
Khalsa is one who attunes himself with God.'[29]

In the *Rahitnama* of Bhai Prahlad Singh, it is written, 'He who lives up to the Sikh ideals, he alone is my Sikh.'[30] Guru Gobind Singh's uncle Kirpal Singh and some other leading Sikhs expressed their concern to the Guru that it would not be possible to maintain the sense of discrimination between good and evil in the revolutionary struggle he wanted to initiate. And, if that discrimination is lost, the Sikh ideals would be nowhere. The Guru's reply was that the true Sikhs would not lose that discrimination; only those would go astray who join the revolution from ulterior motives.[31] In fact, in the literature of the revolutionary period, there is great emphasis on the observance of ethical values by the Khalsa. For his overall development, the Sikh was asked both to maintain the highest moral standards and to faithfully pursue the socio-political objectives of the Khalsa.

Sikhism regards *haumain* (ego or individualism) as the greatest human failing. It is this which leads to acts of encroachment and aggression. It is for this reason that they have laid great stress on the elimination of individualism. The Sikh ideal is : "Neither frighten anyone, nor fear anyone."[32] "The *gurmukh* is powerful, yet humble in spirit"[33] The sublimation of ego was not only a theological ideal, but also a social ideal of Sikhism.

The Gurus had all along been identifying themselves with Sikhs or the Sikh Panth. The Tenth Guru made it clear that the corporate movement was of greater significance than any individual, howsoever highly placed he may be. All his achievements, he says, he owed to the Khalsa. "Through their favour I am exalted, otherwise, there are millions of lowly men like me."[34]

When the so-called *Nawabi* was offered to Kapur Singh, a humble person who did service at the daily gatherings, he said he would accept it only after it was touched to the feet of five Singhs.[35] This episode leads to four inferences. That honour was considered by the Khalsa as the reward of humble service. This was the reason for selecting Kapur Singh. Secondly, there was, till then, no craving for personal power. That is why *Nawabi* was acceptable to no one and had to be imposed by the Khalsa on an unwilling Kapur Singh. Thirdly, the objective was not personal power (*Nawabi*), but to be a humble servant of the Khalsa, from which everyone drew his strength. Fourthly, it showed that all power vested in the corporate body, the Khalsa. When the first mud fort of the Khalsa was built, 'the Singhs were their own brick-layers and labourers; (they) themselves ground corn and prepared food; the more one served, the bigger he grew as a leader. Whosoever put in more labour, blessed was the life of that Singh. It was said that nobody bore ill will to another; nobody gave air to his personal difficulties.'[35a]

6. COMPLETE BREAK WITH THE SOCIAL PAST

It was the basic inequality of the caste society that the Gurus wanted to eradicate. However, the sole recruiting ground for the Sikh movement was the caste society. The Gurus had hitherto furthered the objectives of their movement in a cautious manner so as not to break this life-line. But, the Khalsa had to be the instrument of capturing political power for a plebeian mission. It was, therefore, necessary that the membership of the Khalsa be restricted to those who were not only alive to the objectives of the movement, but were also willing to make major sacrifices for it. At the time of the initiation, each entrant to the brotherhood of the Khalsa gained five freedoms; freedom from the shackles of (a) earlier religions, (b) earlier deeds (*karam*), (c) caste, clan and race, (d) earlier taboos and customs, and (e) superstitions, rituals, etc.[36] These freedoms ensured the complete severence of the Khalsa from the caste society. Those who were baptised into the Khalsa were also said to be reborn. But, unlike the *Upananya* ceremony, they were not re-born into Aryan-hood. They were reborn because, by being baptised, they shed off all stigmas attached to them or their status by the caste society. Not only that; there became a clear distinction between Singhs and Sikhs. Those Sikhs who did not become Singhs, i.e., did not join the Khalsa, came to be known as *sahejdhari* Sikhs. This term is meaningful. These *sahejdharis* were in a way in the evolutionary process of becoming Singhs. They had accepted the main ideology of Sikhism, but were, for some reason or other, not ready to follow it to its logical end.

At the time of the creation of the Khalsa, there was a rift on ideological grounds all along the line in the Sikh ranks. Some people expressed their inability to forgo traditional usages and customs. But this cleavage did not sever the life-line of the movement from its source of recruitment. The *sahejdhari* Sikhs served as a buffer to absorb the shock which the creation of the Khalsa was bound to cause to the caste society. Also, by being baptised at the hands of the *Sudras* (*Panj Piaras*), the Guru had symbolically made them his Guru. This was unthinkable for the caste ideology and the caste society. Many Sikhs drawn from the higher castes dissociated themselves from the movement, 'Khatris and Brahmins remained aloof.'[37] The second cleavage shows clearly that the creation of the Khalsa meant a complete break with the caste society. Those who could not go whole hog with the anti-caste drive of the movement, parted company or remained as *sahejdhari* Sikhs.

7. LEADERSHIP

The leadership of a movement has always an important bearing in determining the direction of the movement. The way the question of the leadership of the Khalsa was tackled shows that Guru Gobind Singh wanted to preserve the plebeian character of the movement.

Writing about the significance of the initiation ceremony of the Khalsa, Gokal Chand Narang states : 'Of the five who offered their heads, one was a *Khatri*, all the rest being so-called *Sudras*. But the Guru called them *Panj Piaras*, or the Beloved Five, and baptised them after the manner he had introduced for initiation into his brotherhood. He enjoined the same duties upon them, gave them the same privileges, and as a token of newly acquired brotherhood all of them dined together.

'The Guru's views of democratic equality were much more advanced than the mere equality among his followers could satisfy. In his system, there was no place even for the privileges of the chief or the leader. No leader, he believed, could be fit to lead unless he was elected or accepted by the followers. History shows that individuals or classes enjoying a religious or sacerdotal superiority, have been only too loth to forgo even a particle of their privileges. But the Guru, regarded by his faithful followers as the greatest of prophets, was made of a different stuff, and had too much political insight to stand on an exclusive eminence apart from his followers. Therefore, when he had initiated his first five disciples, his Beloved Five, he was initiated by them in turn, taking the same vows as they had done, and claiming no higher privileges than those he allowed them. Soon after, he called a meeting of all his followers and announced his new doctrine to them.'[38]

The Guru did this not only because he 'was made of a different stuff', but also because he wanted to ensure that the leadership of the movement remained in the hands of the Khalsa, who had a plebeian mission. The Beloved Five (of whom four were *Sudras*) were made the nucleus of the leadership of the Khalsa, and this was done when the Guru's sons were alive. More than that, by accepting initiation at the hands of the Beloved Five, he accepted them as his own leaders. Again, at the battle of Chamkaur, when the Sikhs requested him to leave the place so that he might reorganise the Khalsa, 'the Guru circumambulated them three times, laid his plume and crest in front of them, offered them his arms and cried out, '*Sri Wahguru ji ka Khalsa! Wahguru ji ki Fateh.*'

The fact that the leadership of the movement devolved on the Khalsa Panth as a whole, became an article of living faith with the Sikhs. In this connection, the episode of Banda's nomination as leader and his subsequent parting of company with the Khalsa is very illustrative. The Khalsa agreed to follow Banda only on the condition that he would not aspire to sovereignty.[39] The Guru instructed Banda to abide by the Khalsa and appointed select Sikhs as his advisers.[40] After his military successes, Banda aspired to become Guru and a sovereign. The *Tat Khalsa* (the genuine Khalsa) parted company with him and his followers, because the Guru had given :

> 'Banda service and not sovereignty;
> The sovereignty had been given to the Panth by
> the Guru (*Sacha Padshah*) himself.'[41]

After Banda, Kapur Singh was elected as the leader of the Khalsa. He was elected, because he was, in those days, engaged in doing the humble services like fanning the daily congregations of the Khalsa. Kapur Singh showed his preference for the humble service he was engaged in and entreated that he should be spared the honour that was being conferred upon him. But, the leadership was virtually imposed upon him. Kapur Singh, on becoming the leader, did nothing without consulting the Khalsa.

> 'Showed great respect towards the Singhs;
> Did nothing without taking the Panth into confidence.
> (He) engaged himself in humble service with even greater vigour;

Great humility came to his mind.'[42]

With the end of Kapur Singh's era, the revolutionary spirit started waning. His successor was Jassa Singh 'Kalal', who was accepted leader by the Khalsa on the advice of Kapur Singh. Jassa Singh had very humble beginnings. 'He joined the Panth as a beggar and became its *Patshah*.'[43] Here '*Patshah*' does not mean sovereign ruler; it means only a supreme leader. Jassa Singh struck a coin in his own name when the Khalsa conquered Lahore for the first time. This was so much against the spirit of collective leadership of the Khalsa, that a special convention was held, where it was decided to withdraw the coin from circulation.[44] In its place, another coin struck in the name of the Guru was substituted. Polier (1780) observed, 'As for the Government of the Siques, it is properly an aristocracy, in which no pre-eminence is allowed except that which power and force naturally gives; otherwise all the chiefs, great and small, and even the poorest and most abject Siques, look on themselves as perfectly equal in all the public concerns and in the greatest Council or *Goormatta* of the nation, held annually either at Ambarsar, Lahore or some other place. Everything is decided by the plurality of votes taken indifferently from all who choose to be present at it,'[45] Forster also gives a similar account. 'An equality of rank is maintained in their civil society, which no class of men, however wealthy or powerful, is suffered to break down. At the periods when general councils of the nation were convened, which consisted of the army at large, every member had the privilege of delivering his opinion, and the majority, it is said, decided on the subject in debate.'[45a] This shows how strong the original spirit of equality and fraternization of the Sikh revolution must have been so that it could still reveal its glimpses even in the post-Khalsa period.

The leadership of the collective Khalsa or the Panth, did not mean that any majority decision taken by it had an automatic religious sanctity. The supreme consideration was that such decisions had to conform to the Sikh ideals. So long as the Gurus were there, they saw to it that there was no deviation from the Sikh principles. When the Sikhs of Lahore proposed to pay the fine on his behalf, Guru Arjun strongly turned down the proposal. Similarly, Guru Gobind Singh brushed aside the views of those Sikhs who advised him to make peace with Aurangzeb. It was the Sikh principles which were to be supreme. The Guruship was conferred on Guru Granth Sahib, and leadership on the collective Panth. These steps were taken to ensure that after the Gurus, the collective leadership of only those who were ideologically oriented, prevailed.

8. ITS ROLE

The creation of the Khalsa was not an idle dream. The Khalsa proved its mettle by passing through the ordeal of fire. It is unnecessary to go into details of the struggle, because these are writ large on the pages of Sikh history. But, it is relevant to emphasize the revolutionary mission which inspired and sustained the movement during its critical periods.

The Khalsa had to carry on its armed conflict all along in the heart and the citadel of the Mughal Empire. It had none of the advantages of terrain and a secure base that the Marathas had. It had no forts. The only fortification, if this could be called a fort at all, which Guru Gobind Singh had built at Anandpur, was lost to the movement for ever in the last battle there. After that, not to speak of a base or a fort, the Khalsa had not a foothold or land which it could call its own. It appeared from and disappeared into the villages, hideouts, jungles, and areas which were under the firm control of the governors of Sirhind and Lahore. This area was close to Delhi and was on the life-line of the Mughal Empire which connected its capital with Kabul. The Rajputs and the Marathas had found to their cost that it was not feasible.to fight the Mughal might in the plains. Bhao, the Maratha Commander in the battle of Panipat, 'judged himself to be unequal to cope with the Shah in the open field.' The Khalsa had no alternative. Moreover, the area had a large Muslim population whose hostility to the movement was very natural.

The Sikh movement was virtually crushed a number of times.[46a] It suffered many serious reverses. But each time, like the proverbial phoenix, it rose from its ashes. The first setback took place when Guru Gobind Singh had to leave Anandpur, Chamkaur and finally Mukatsar. But, within an year and a half of the Guru's death, the Khalsa under Banda had conquered Sirhind and humbled the government of Lahore. It was a miracle wrought. The Guru had sent messages to the Singhs to join Banda in his campaign. He had instructed Banda especially to put the revolutionaries from Majha in the forefront of the struggle.[47] Supreme sacrifices were made by the Khalsa. Guru Gobind Singh was no more, but the 'Promethean fire' that he had kindled was all ablaze.

The second occasion, when the Sikh movement was practically crushed, was when Banda was defeated, captured and executed. It may not be out of place to point out that Banda's defeat was in no small measure due to the *Tat Khalsa* having parted company with him. The Khalsa forces had already been weakened by this split in their ranks. The defeat of Banda was the final blow and the signal for a general persecution of the Singhs by the Mughal administration. The Khalsa was no longer in a position to take the field against the Mughals. Under the relentless persecution launched by Emperor Farrukh Siyar, they were forced to split into small bands. This was the beginning of the heroic guerilla warfare.

The time of the guerilla struggle was the most trying for the movement. We would like to quote Hari Ram Gupta rather extensively. 'The Emperor then issued a general edict which was applicable to all parts of the Empire. According to it, every Sikh wherever seen was to be immediately arrested. He was to be offered only one alternative, either Islam or the sword. It was to be executed there and then without any hesitation or loss of time. A schedule of valuable rewards was proclaimed. For every Sikh head Rs. 25/- was to be given, and for a Sikh captive a sum of Rs. 100/- was to be awarded.'[48]

'The Emperor's orders were strictly obeyed. The Governors of Sirhind, Lahore and Jammu tried to surpass one another in presecution of the Sikhs in order to win the goodwill of Farrukh Siyar. Abdul Samad was entrusted with the supervision of this work. They took written undertaking from the headmen of villages in their jurisdiction not to allow any Sikh to live there. If there were some Sikhs, they were to be arrested and sent to the neighbouring police station. In case they could not capture them, a report was to be lodged with Government officials about their presence. Scouts roamed about everywhere to see that the *lambardars* or village headmen obeyed the Government orders. Local intelligencers were appointed to report in secret at the nearby police or military posts. Connivance on their part resulted in imprisonment and confiscation of property.

They declared their own lists of prizes; Rs. 10/- for supplying information about the presence of a Sikh, Rs. 20/- for actually showing a Sikh, Rs. 40/- for helping in his capture, and Rs. 80/- for bringing every Sikh head.'[49]

Forster writes : "Such was the keen spirit that animated the persecution, such was the success of the exertions, that the name of a Sicque no longer existed in the Mughal dominion. Those who still adhered to the tenets of Nanock, either fled into the mountains at the head of the Punjab, or cut off their hair, and exteriorly renounced the profession of their religion."[50]

'The faithful followers of the Guru experienced the worst possible time in their history. Hunted like hare and pursued like wild beasts, they wandered from place to place seeking shelter to save themselves from the fury of the government, from the revenge of the hostile Muslim population, and from the greed of the toady Hindus.'[51]

'If anybody enquired of a Hindu woman how many sons she had, she would reply that she had three sons, but one of them had become a Sikh. Thereby she meant that the converted one should be considered among the dead.'[52]

'Majha, the homeland of the Sikhs, was completely ruined.'[53] "A wonderful and terrible trial indeed, from which the weak came out strong, from which the strong came out sublime. There were many great deeds done in the small struggles of life. There was a determined though unseen bravery, which defended itself foot to foot in the darkness, noble and mysterious triumphs which no eye could see.'[54]

It has been estimated that the number of these guerillas was at one time reduced to about two thousand men.[55] From this small force, they grew from strength to strength and not only challenged the Mughal Empire, but became the masters of the country right up to the bank of the Jamuna. To quote Gupta again : "Thus had the Sikhs emerged triumphant from their deadly struggle of the past thirty years; and the long-drawn agony of their subjection came to an end, and the dream of their independence was realised. They had admirably succeeded in holding their own and in steadily pursuing their course, notwithstanding the hosts of terrors and disasters that gathered themselves together, not only to check their ardour and to intercept their progress, but also to bring them to the verge of annihilation. Surging floods of opposition rose and increased : the impetuous rains of consternation descended and fell; the rending storms of desperation blew and raged; and all these opposing elements struck and beat upon them; but they could not shake the sturdy Sikhs standing on the steel-like rock of faith and freedom. The internal vigour consisting of their dogged faith in themselves and in the prophecy of Guru Gobind Singh that they would one day become a nation, their determined courage and unconquerable spirit of resistance, not only sustained them against the bloody persecution of a great Government determined to suppress them, but also raised them up again with greater strength after every attempt to annihilate them ......"[56]

Gupta is so much impressed by the achievements of the movement that he asks the question, "Readers! have we not witnessed a miracle ?[57] The struggle waged by the Khalsa was so glorious that any people in any culture would be proud of it."

What was the secret of this miracle ? Was it wrought about by the 'marauding instinct' which is associated with the *Jats* ? The *Jats* no doubt played a significant role, but which *Jats* ? There was Bhai Taru Singh who preferred his scalp to be removed rather than let his hair be cut; and there were *Jats* who cut their hair with their own hands in order to desert the Khalsa. One has to separate the grain from the chaff. Non-*Jats* or *Jats*, it was those elements who had fully imbibed the Sikh ideology who worked this miracle. It is they who were the steel-frame of the movement. It was not an ordinary warfare. It tested to the farthest human limit a person's faith in his cause, his tenacity of purpose, his courage and his endurance. 'The story of the Sikhs' deeds opens up the great difference between head and heart, between knowledge and action, between saying and doing, between words and works, and between a dead and a living faith.'[58] As Bhangu has put it :

> 'The Singhs had no resources;
> Were without arms and clothes.
> Were naked, hungry and thirsty;
> Had no ammunition with them.
> Had no access to shops or markets;
> Those who fell sick died for lack of medicine.
> They were sustained by the hope of the Guru's benediction;
> This was the only treasure they had.'[59]

Only those could come out successful through this fiery ordeal who had in full measure faith in God, the Guru and the ultimate triumph of the righteousness of the cause. During this long period of trial, only the best could face the challenge. The question of any weak person joining the movement for mundane considerations did not arise. Those who did, left the faith on the first sign of crisis, as all they had to do was to cut off their hair and join the common populace around them.

The Khalsa guerillas were dispersed into very small bands, sometimes of twos and fours, and in widely separate areas like those of the Siwalik hills, Lakhi jungle and the desert wastes bordering Rajputana. They had no common centre and no common leader. Contacts among the guerilla bands were rare. The only sentiment that held them together and made them converge for collective action was attachment to a common cause and the deepest commitment to the faith. Arjun Dass Malik writes that sustained guerilla warfare is not possible without an ideological inspiration. "As early as the very origin of the term guerilla, Napoleon had observed that 'in Spain, moral considerations made up three quarters of the game and the relative balance of military power accounted only for the remaining quarter.' T.E. Lawrence stresses the same point when he says : 'We have won a province, when we have taught the civilians in it to die for our idea of freedom.' Guerilla warfare thus has been ideological from the very outset." Again, "a guerilla is not an ill-trained, badly armed civilian-soldier, as he appears to be; he is, rather, an intensely motivated and highly dedicated soldier who has a keen sense of issues at stake and understands the nature of war he is fighting. His strength lies inside, in the moral considerations which make three-fourths of him." And, "his objective lies not in the field of battle but elsewhere, among the people ...... Guerilla warfare is essentially a form of people's war, in which a revolutionary vanguard, relying upon the support of the people, initiates limited armed action to gradually weaken the enemy and to bring about a situation of mass involvement culminating in the final defeat of the enemy and the attainment of peoples' political objective."[60]

REFERENCES

1. Macauliffe, M.A. : *The Sikh Religion,* Vol V, Low Price Publications, 1909, 1990, p.286.
2. Ibid., p. 280.
3. Ibid., p. 289.
4. *Guru Granth Sahib,* p. 15.
4a. Macauliffe, M.A. : op.cit. p. 299.
5. Ibid., p. 310.
6. Forster, Vol. I, p. 330.
7. *Rahatname,* pp. 88-89; Malcolm, p, 221; Hugel, p. 263.
7a. Latif, p. 261; Macauliffe, M.A. : op.cit.
8. Bhangu, p. 47.
9. *Rahitname,* p. 47.
10. Bhangu, Rattan Singh : *Panth Parkash,* p. 42.
11. *Sri Gur Sobha,* p. 21.
12. Koer Singh, p. 130.
13. *Rahitname,* p. 47.
14. Ibid., p. 117.
15. *Sarb Loh Granth,* part 3, p. 532.
15a. *Haqiqat, I.H.Q.,* March 1942, sup., p. 5.
16. Koer Singh, p. 202.
17. Ibid., p. 203; *Sri Gur Sobha,* p. 80.
18. *Guru Granth Sahib,* p. 918.
19. *Ibid.,* pp. 647 648.
20. Bhangu, Rattan Singh : op.cit. p. 80.
21. Macauliffe, M.A. : op.cit. p. 66.
22. *Sarb Loh Granth,* part 3, pp. 531-2.
23. Bhangu, Rattan Singh : op.cit. p. 215.
24. Malcolm, Brigadier General : *Asiatic Researches,* Vol. II (1812), pp. 252-256; Cunningham, pp. 99-100.
24a. Scott, G.B : *Religion and Short History of the Sikhs,* p. 90.
25. Ibid., p.35.
26. *Sarb Loh Granth,* part 3, p. 531.
27. *Sri Gur Sobha,* p. 24.
28. Ibid., p. 128.
29. *Rahatname,* p. 47.
30. Ibid., p. 56.

31.   Ibid., p. 111.

32.   *Guru Granth Sahib*, p. 1427.

33.   Ibid., p. 85.

34.   Macauliffe, M.A. op.cit. p. 66.

35.   Bhangu, Rattan Singh : op.cit. p. 214.

35a. Ibid., p. 326.

36.   Gupta, Hari Ram : *History of the Sikh Gurus*, p. 189.

37.   *Sri Guru Sobha*, p. 33; Koer Singh, pp. 132-133; Latif, p. 264.

38.   Narang, Gokal Chand : *Transformation of Sikhism,* p. 81.

39.   Bhangu, Rattan Singh : op.cit. p. 82.

40.   Ibid., p. 81.

41.   Ibid., p. 131.

42.   Ibid., p. 215.

43.   Ibid., p. 217.

44.   Budh Singh Arora : *Risala-i Nanak Shah,* cited by Gurbax Singh *Punjab History Conference* (Nov. 27-28, 1976), Proceedings, p. 79.

45.   Polier, *Early European Accounts of the Sikhs,* edited by Ganda Singh p. 197.

45a. Forster, Vol. i, p. 329.

46.   Prinsep, H.T. : *Origin of the Sikh Power in the Punjab,* p. 15.

46a. *Calendar of Persian Correspondence,* Vol, ii, p. 85; Malcolm; *Asiatic Researches* (1812), p. 246; Forster, i, pp. 312-3; Gupta : *History of the Sikhs,* I, pp. 8-10, 27-32 71-72, 82-83, 176-7, 261; Bhangu, Rattan Singh : op.cit. pp. 232-235; Polier (P.P.P.,Oct. 1970, p. 237).

47.   Bhangu, Rattan, Singh : op.cit. p. 81.

48.   Gupta, Hari Ram : *History of the Sikhs,* Vol. II, p. 39.

49.   Ibid., pp. 39-40; Bhangu, p. 235.

50.   Forster, Vol. 1, 312-313.

51.   Gupta, Hari Ram : *History of the Sikhs,* Vol. II, p. 40.

52.   Ibid., p. 41.

53.   Ibid., p. 45.

54.   Ibid., p. 41.

55.   Sita Ram Kohli : Foreword to *Umdat-ut-Tawarikh* of Sohan Lal Suri, Daftar iv, p. ii; *Haqiqat,* I.H.Q., March 1942 sup, p. 17.

56.   Gupta, Hari Ram : *History of the Sikhs,* Vol. I, p. 281.

57.   Ibid., p. 283.

58.   Ibid., p. 282.

59.   Bhangu, Rattan Singh : op.cit.pp. 394-305.

60.   Malik Arjan Das : *An Indian Guerilla War,* pp. 2-4.

18

MARTYRDOM IN SIKHISM

Kharak Singh

I. Introduction

1.1 Martyrdom in Sikhism is a fundamental concept and represents an important institution of the faith. In the Sikh form the institution is a complete departure from the Indian tradition, and for that matter radically distinguishes the whole-life character of Sikhism from the earlier dichotomous or pacific Indian religious traditions. It is significant that the concept was emphatically laid down by Guru Nanak, and the history of the Guru period as well as the subsequent history of the Sikhs is an open expression, in thought and deed, of this basic doctrine.

II. The Goal And Concept Of Martyrdom

2.1 In Sikhism, Guru Nanak in the very beginning of his famous hymn 'Japu Ji', while rejecting the paths of ascetic one point meditation or withdrawal, emphatically prescribes carrying out or living according to the Will of God as the goal of man. "How to become the abode of Truth and how to demolish the wall of falsehood ?" he asks, and then proceeds to answer, "Through following His Will." He then defines the Will to be the 'Ocean of Virtues' (*gunigahira*) or Altruistic. The Gurus' basic perception of this Will is that it is Loving or Love.

2.2 It is in this context that Guru Nanak proclaims that life is a 'game of love', and gives a call to humanity to follow this path. He says : "Shouldst thou seek to engage in the game of Love, step into my street with thy head placed on thy palm : While stepping on to this street, ungrudgingly sacrifice your head" (G.G.S., p. 1412), Repeated emphasis is laid on this goal of following the Will of God, Who is directing the universe, in Guru Granth Sahib :

"Through perception of His Will is the Supreme State attained." (p. 292)

"With the perception of His Will alone is the Essence realised." (p. 1289)

"By perceiving the Lord's Will is Truth attained." (p. 1244)

"By His Will was the world created as a place for righteous living." (p. 785)

"Profoundly wondrous is the Divine Will. Whoever has its perception, has awareness of the true praxis of life." (p. 940)

2.3 It should be clear that in Sikhism the goal is not to attain personal salvation or *moksha* or 'eternal bliss.' It is, instead, the perception or recognition of His Will and working in line with its direction. This state is in fact synonymous with Godrealisation.

2.4 The concept of martyrdom was laid down by Guru Nanak. In fact, his was an open challenge and a call. His hymn calling life 'a game of love' is of profoundest significance in Sikh thought and theology. It has five clear facets. It expresses in clear words the Guru's spiritual experience of God. While he repeatedly calls Him unknowable, his own experience, he states, is that He is All Love. Second, He is Benevolent and Gracious towards man and the world. Third, since He expresses His Love in the world, the same, by implication, becomes real and meaningful. Further, the Guru by giving this call clearly proclaims both the goal and the methodology of religious life in Sikhism. The goal is to live a life of love which is in line with His expression of Love and Grace in the world. Simultaneously, the methodology of whole-life activity and commitment for the goal is emphasized. The significant fact is that in the entire Guru Granth Sahib it is these principles of the Sikh way of life, that are repeatedly emphasized. There are innumerable hymns endorsing one or the other of the above principles of Sikh theology. It is this couplet of Guru Nanak that forms the basis of martyrdom in Sikhism. For, the commitment desired is total, and once on that Path the seeker has to have no wavering in laying down his life for the cause. In his hymn Guru Nanak has defined and stressed that the institution of martyrdom is an essential ingredient of the Path he was laying down for man.

III. UNDERSTANDING OF THE CONCEPT

3.1 As explained above, this is exactly the meaning that the subsequent Gurus themselves have conveyed about Guru Nanak's thesis and thought. It is on record that one *Bhai* Manjh who was a *Sakhi Sarvaria*, a system which enjoins only ritualistic living, came to the fifth guru, Guru Arjun, and sought his advice as to whether or not he should become a Sikh of the Guru. The latter gave a very clear answer. He advised him to continue with his old system and remain a *Sakhi Sarvaria*, until he was ready for the total commitment demanded in the Guru's system. He explained that to be a Sikh is to tread an extremely difficult path, and one has not only to risk his wealth and property, but the commitment requires even the laying down of one's life also. Thus, the institution of martyrdom is in-built in the Sikh way of life, proclaimed in the call of Guru Nanak. We have quoted Guru Arjun's amplification of the hymn, lest it should be understood that our interpretation is in any way not central to the Sikh way of life. Again it is important to understand that the same test was applied by the tenth guru, Guru Gobind Singh, when he finally initiated the system for the selection of the Five *Piaras* and the creation of the Khalsa through the institution of *amrit* on Vaisakhi Day, 1699 CE. At that time too, the call he gave was for total commitment and willingness to lay down one's life for the cause. The important fact is the unity of meaning and method of the system as laid down by Guru Nanak, as understood and explained by the Fifth Guru, and as finally formalised by the Tenth Guru for the creation of the Khalsa. No ambiguity had been left as to the requirement of the commitment and the quantum of sacrifice demanded from the Sikh or the Khalsa way of life. The above explanation of the Sikh path by three Gurus dispels the naive notion held in some quarters that the first five Gurus were only pacificist or introvertive in their outlook and method, and that they did not recommend militancy or martyrdom.

IV. INDIAN TRADITION OF SACRIFICE AND SIKH CONCEPT OF MARTYRDOM

4.1 Because of the practice of offering sacrifices, including human sacrifices, in some old cults, martyrdom has sometimes been traced to that institution. This requires clarification. True, not only in primitive religions, but also in religions like Judaism and some Hindu, *Devi* and *Nath* cults the method of sacrifice of animals stands accepted. In Judaism sacrifice of animals is a part of the Torah. Similarly, in *Devi* cults sacrifice is an approved mode of propitiating the deities. This concept is based on the rationale that expiation of sins of man is necessary, and that this can be secured only by the method of sacrifice of blood, including sometimes human blood, in order to secure one's future in heaven or on the Day of Judgement. In some of these religions life is considered a suffering or sinful, and release from it, or *mukti* or salvation of man is the goal. It is, perhaps, in this context of salvation from sin that Christ's sacrifice on the Cross is considered an event of redemption for all those who enter his fold. It is extremely incongruous, at least from the Sikh point of view, that while many of the Indian cults of *Devi*, *Naths* and other traditions, accept *ahimsa* as a cardinal virtue, they indulge in large scale sacrifice of animals. For example, at the temple of Bhairon at the annual fair at Devi Pattan, hundreds of buffaloes, goats and pigs are sacrificed, and the mark of blood is applied to the *Nath* and other devotees. 'Kalki Purana', which is a scripture of the Sakatas, has a chapter on human sacrifice also. *Nath* practices, too, are similar. Gorakhnath's contribution is said to be that he substituted animal sacrifice for human sacrifice. And yet the *Nath* has to take on initiation, a vow to observe *ahimsa* throughout his lifetime.

4.2 It, therefore, needs emphasis that the Sikh institution of martyrdom is entirely alien to the method of sacrifice referred to above. In Guru Granth Sahib there is a clear condemnation of the sacrifice of animals to propitiate gods. Guru Granth Sahib records : "Slaughter of animals you dub as religion — Then brother ! Tell what is irreligion ? Each other you style as saints — Then who is to be called butcher ?" (p.1103). The Sakata cult and its practices have been particularly deprecated. In Guru Granth Sahib the very system of gods, goddesses and incarnation has been rejected. There is not a trace of any event of such animal sacrifice on the part of the Gurus or the Sikhs in the entire Sikh history. Thus, the Sikh concept of martyrdom is unrelated to the system of animal sacrifices, or expiation through blood.

4.3 The rationale of the Sikh concept is entirely different. Since human life is an opportunity and its goal is to carry out the Altruistic Will of God, the very concept of release from life is rejected. It is so in all whole-life religions or *miri-piri* systems. As the Guru's hymn states, one has to live a life of commitment to the cause of love, and in pursuance of it one has to struggle against oppression by the powerful. *Mukti*, salvation or 'release' means freedom from egoism, selfishness and individualism, says the Guru. Two objectives have to be sought simultaneously, namely, release from self-centredness, living a life of love, and struggle against the forces of injustice. It is this kind of love of God that a Sikh strives for. The Bible also says that one should love God with all one's heart and, simultaneously, love one's neighbour as well. Guru Nanak says, "He who is fond of God, what cares he for *mukti* or heaven ?" The goal is to fall in line with God's love for man and practise virtues in fulfilment of His Altruistic Will. On the one hand, the Guru rejects *ahimsa* as a creed, and states that those who indulge in debate over meat eating do not know what sin is. On the other hand, he lays down that love integrally involves struggle for the oppressed and against the tyrant, God himself being the 'Destroyer' of the evil and demonical. This was very clearly explained by the Sixth Guru to *Sant* Ramdas, when he stated that he was distinctly following the path of Guru Nanak, and that his sword was for destruction of the tyrant and help to the weak. Accordingly, while the institution of martyrdom is entirely unrelated to the method of blood sacrifice, prevalent in India and outside, it follows clearly from Guru Nanak's system of love and help to the oppressed and struggle against Evil, as instrument of God's Love. Explanation for the institution of martyrdom was given by Guru Arjun to *Pir* Mianmir, when the Sufi Saint came to meet him in prison. "I bear all this torture to set an example. The true test of faith is the hour of misery. Without example to guide, ordinary persons' minds quail in the midst of suffering. And, if he, who possesses power within him, defends not his religion by open profession thereof, the man who possesses no such power will, when put to torture, abjure his faith. The sin will light on the head of him who has the power but showeth it not; and God will deem him an enemy of religion"

V. EXPRESSION OF THE INSTITUTION

5.1   The first landmark in this field is the sacrifice by the Fifth Guru. The compiler of Sri Adi Granth, himself became the first martyr of the faith. Here is a coincidence which most scholars from the pacific or social science group have missed. Today, many Christian theologians like Moltmann, Metz, Liberation theologians, and Black theologians, emphasize and interpret Christ's martyrdom on the Cross as a fundamental political act of confrontation with the state or the Forces of Oppression. Historically it is well-known now that Guru Arjun's martyrdom was an open act of confrontation with the state, initiative for which was taken by the Guru. There is ample evidence to indicate that Guru Arjun had created a 'state within a state.' This is recorded by contemporary Mohsin Fani and other historians like H.R. Gupta. Today even scholars like Juergensmeyer concede that the Mughal military state considered the early Sikh Gurus to be heading a separate community. Jehangir's autobiography is clear as to how he felt disturbed about the Guru and why he ordered the extreme step of his execution by torture. Heads of state are never concerned about pacificists. On the other hand, Mughal Emperors many a time sought their blessings. Facts about Guru Arjun's martyrdom are too glaring and open to leave any ambiguity in their interpretation. Beni Parsad, historian of Jehangir, records that Guru Arjun gave an amount of Rs. 5,000 to Khusro who was heading his army of revolt against Emperor Jehangir. The Guru blessed him. It was an open support to a rebel claimant for the throne. Obviously, the news was conveyed to the Emperor. He records in his autobiography that he had been observing this new socio-religious development and thinking of putting an end to it. He records with obvious rancour the incident of the Guru's meeting with rebel Khusro, his rival, and blessing him with a *tilak*. Political and military leaders are concerned only with the political potential of a move or movement. It is this potential as adjudged by the Emperor, that forced him to take the extreme step of ordering the Guru's execution and confiscation of his property. Evidently, the Fifth Guru's martyrdom, and confrontation with the state was the result of positive initiative taken by the Guru himself, both because of his organisation of the *Panth* and his help to rebel Khusro. It is important to know why the Guru took this step. A number of facts clarify the issue. Significantly, while he gave to Khusro a substantial sum of Rs. 5,000, collected by the system of *Daswandh* introduced by him, he refused to give even a penny towards the fine imposed on him by the Emperor. Not only that. He also forbade the Sikhs or anyone to make a collection for payment of the fine. He explained, as noted earlier, the role of a Sikh or a martyr, to Mianmir, who came to see him in prison. The Guru's statement embodies three elements, viz., the need for open profession, fearlessness, and readiness to die for the faith. The above is the story of the martyrdom of the Fifth Guru. The initiative for it proceeded from the Guru. It would thus be idle to suggest that the first five Gurus were pacificists, and that the militant turn in Sikhism arose because the Mughal Administration executed Guru Arjun Dev Ji.

5.2   From the Sixth Guru onwards preparations for militancy were undertaken with mounting vigour. The Guru clearly stated two things. First, that what he was doing, namely, confrontation with tyranny and help to the oppressed, was in pursuance of the thesis of Guru Nanak, as explained in his hymns. Second, the Guru clarified that those who lay down their lives while fighting for a cause in the Sikh struggle, perform a religious duty. Contemporary Mohsin Fani says, "The Guru told him that on Doomsday his disciples would be asked to give an explanation for their deeds." He adds, "The Sikhs believe that all disciples of the Guru go to Heaven." It needs to be stated that the concepts of Doomsday and Heaven are not Sikh concepts, but they represent the way Mohsin Fani interprets the words of the Guru in terms of his own theology. It is on record that dying for a cause in the Sikh armies has always been considered dying a martyr's death. Thus, the lead given by the Fifth Guru became a major institution of the Sikh *Panth*, resulting in heroism and martyrdom of thousands for the cause of the Guru and the *Panth*. This role of the *Panth* and the institution of martyrdom continued throughout the later Sikh history.

5.3   Here the martyrdom of the Ninth Guru also needs mention. It was reported to the Emperor that Guru Tegh Bahadur was heading a new nation, and that he had virtually raised the banner of revolt with his military preparations. On this the Emperor is reported to have conveyed to the Guru that if he gave up his political and military activities, and confined his mission to preaching and praying, he would be given state grants. The Guru declined the offer, and thus followed his martyrdom. Three things are clear. The Imperial perception was that the Guru was creating a nation in opposition to the state. Yet, despite the clear offer of grant the Guru declined to give up his political role. The consequences of rejecting the offer were clear to the Guru and everyone. But the choice was very emphatically made by him. Governor Timur Shah also mentions the offer made to the Guru. Evidently, both for the state and the Sikh Movement, confrontations between the two, with its logical consequences of struggle and martyrdom, were known continuing events. This is the part of martyrdom the Gurus laid down and led. The Sikhs have since followed it. Ultimately, Guru Tegh Bahadur, and his companions, Bhai Mati Das and Dyal Das, suffered martyrdom in reference to the oppression in Kashmir for conversion of Hindus to Islam. The subsequent struggles of Guru Gobind Singh, Banda and the Sikhs are well-known. At Chamkaur Sahib the Guru himself asked his two sons to go in for the unequal battle : "My sons, you are dear to me. You are born to destroy the tyrants (*Turks*). Only if you sacrifice yourselves in the battle, can the tyrants be eliminated. There can be no better opportunity than the present one. Both of you go and join the battle." And, when his elder son died fighting there, the Guru said, "Today he has become the chosen Khalsa in God's Court." Thus, the concept of martyrdom for a righteous cause was explained, demonstrated and sanctioned by the Guru.

5.4   In the Sikh tradition all the forty who died to a man in the battle at Chamkaur Sahib, and all the forty who died fighting at Muktsar are called '*Muktas*', or the 'Released Ones', or martyrs by the Sikh religious definition. In fact, it is also known that with Guru Gobind Singh were a number of Sikhs called '*Muktas*', who belonged to the Khalsa Order and had made a commitment to sacrifice their all for the cause of God and the Guru. They were considered Live *Muktas*. In contrast, the concept of *Videhi Mukta* in the Vedantic system is entirely different. Swami Sivananda writes about them, "Such a *Videhi Mukta* who is absolutely merged in Brahman, cannot have the awareness of the world which is non-existent to him. If his body is to be maintained, it has to be fed and cared for by others. The *Videhi Mukta* is thus not in a position to engage himself for the good of the world." It is also known that the two very young children of the Guru were executed, but refused to embrace Islam. The contribution of *Pir* Budhu Shah in the militant struggle of Guru Gobind Singh, is an extremely revealing event. Here is a *Pir* or a divine of another religion, who joins the armies of the Guru with hundreds of his followers, involving even the loss of life of two of his sons in the battles. This outstanding and unique event could never happen, unless *Pir* Budhu Shah had complete ideological affinity with the goal of the Guru, and the institution of martyrdom. That institution, it is well-known, is also a significant factor in the ideology of Islam. The only slight difference is eschatological. In the case of Islam the inspiration is hope of a pure life in Heaven. In Sikhism it means discharging one's responsibilities towards God and partaking in His Love for all human beings and life. On no other assumption can we explain *Pir* Budhu Shah's and the Sikh sacrifices in their struggle against evil. It also explains clearly that the Sikh institution of martyrdom has no historical or ideological relation with human or animal sacrifices common in some religions or cults.

5.5   Actually, in the post-Guru period there was a *misl* of Sikhs called *misl Shahidan* (living martyrs). They were the most respected group of Sikhs. It is Guru Gobind Singh who weaned away Banda from his ascetic life, and asked him not to die a coward's death, but to die a brave man's death, which was the real secret of life. Banda and his 700 companions faced death without flinching, and refused conversion to Islam. Even a young boy whose mother had obtained pardon for him refused to give up his faith and instead contradicted the statement of his mother that he was not a Sikh, and courted martyrdom. Sikh history of the 18th century is full of deeds of martyrs. Thousands of them refused to give up their faith, but courted torture and death boldly because the administrative orders were to destroy all Nanak-*panthis* or Sikhs, root and branch.

5.6   In sum, in Sikhism the institution of martyrdom is an integral part of the system enunciated by Guru Nanak, and the lead in the matter was given by the Fifth Guru. The Sixth Guru explained how destruction of the tyrant and protection of the weak were parts of the religion of Guru Nanak, and the dictates of God.

5.7   Here it is not just incidental, but very logical in Sikh religion and the Sikh tradition, to state that during the period of Independence Movement, of the 121 persons hanged, 2,644 imprisoned for life, and 1,300 massacred in the Jallianwala Bagh protest meeting, 93, 2,047, and 799, respectively, were Sikhs. Also, of the soldiers who fought under Subhash Chander Bose in the Indian National Army, 60% were Sikhs. Again, in 1975, when Prime Minister Indira Gandhi imposed the Emergency Laws curtailing all human rights and liberties, the Sikhs were the only people who sustained an organised struggle against this invasion on human freedom, involving the arrest of over 40,000 Sikhs, when in the rest of India not even one tenth of that number offered arrest as a protest. The movement was run from the Golden Temple, meaning thereby that for Sikhs the struggles against injustice and oppression and consequent martyrdom are a religious responsibility and have religious sanction.

VI INDIVIDUAL V/S COMMUNITARIAN RIGHTS

6.1   It has often been said that ideologies that lay emphasis on rights of the community, the state or the nation, are far more concerned about the society as a whole than the individual, and for that reason tend to sacrifice individual rights. This tendency is there in all national states, whether secular or religious. True, in modern states in the West there is an increasing emphasis on securing individual rights. But patriotism everywhere continues to be an important social virtue, although the right of the conscientious objector is being increasingly recognised. The main criticism of dictatorships by Western democracies has been on this score, suggesting that the excesses committed by secular rulers like Hitler and Stalin are really due to their concern for the community and not the individual. The Sikh understanding on this issue is entirely different. It is evident that the working of free market economies or capitalism can be equally oppressive, both for the individual and the community. The increasing gaps between the rich countries and the poor countries, and the rich and the poor in the same countries are, as lamented by the authors of the *Limits of Growth*, due not to any lack of concern for the individual or the community, but follow squarely from ego-centricism of man, which needs to be curbed. The Sikh understanding is that no amount of external pressure or even freedom of the individual can secure over-all justice for all, until man's sense of morality and self-discipline is awakened and developed. And there is no reason to believe that Enlightenment, Science or Technology or individual freedom has in any way enhanced his sense of self-control or morality. In fact, it has often been argued that over emphasis on individual rights has only loosened man's moral brakes, instead of strengthening them. The phenomena of Hitler, Stalin, and Hiroshima could never happen, if there had been any real rise in the level of moral discipline either in Secular Democracies or in Secular Dictatorships.

6.2   In Sikhism the villain of peace is the egoism of man, which, it is believed, is due to his present level of development, and not due to any in-built deficiency or sin. Hence, while Sikhism has been the foremost in emphasising equality between man and man, and between man and woman, it has been equally emphatic on two other scores. First, that there is hope for improvement and that this improvement towards a higher level is man's destiny. This gives abundant optimism or '*Charhdi Kala*', which is a Sikh religious doctrine. Second, that a balance is necessary and the individual sense of internal discipline has to be developed. The institution of martyrdom, the Sikhs believe, is a distinct step towards creation of that internal discipline. Since God loves one and all, all individual effort, howsoever seemingly expensive to the individual, only serves God's Love for the individual and all. This is the lesson Guru Arjun and Guru Tegh Bahadur gave by their martyrdoms, and Guru Gobind Singh demonstrated when he sent his two sons to die in the battle at Chamkaur.

VII. CONCLUSION

7.1   The above narration makes it plain that in a whole-life religion, where the spiritual perception is that God is Love, and Destroyer of the evil, martyrdom is an essential institution. For, life is a game of love; and in helping and protecting the weak from oppression, confrontation with the unjust and tyrants, as explained by the Sixth Guru himself to *Sant* Ramdas of Maharashtra, becomes a religious responsibility, in the discharge of which martyrdom of the religious man or seeker sometimes becomes inevitable. It is, therefore, no accident of history that Guru Arjun was the first prophet in the religious history of India to be a martyr of faith. Nor is it an accident that Guru Tegh Bahadur and the Tenth Guru sacrificed their all for the cause of truth or religion. Similarly, it is no accident that for over a hundred years, the Gurus kept an army and struggled with the oppressive Empire involving the loss of life of thousands of Sikhs who are considered, as in the case of Islam, another whole-life religion, martyrs. Secondly, the Sikh Gurus have demonstrated that not only is martyrdom a religious and essential institution, but it is also the most potent method of education and training a people for making sacrifices for the cause of righteousness, love and truth. This is amply proved by the capacity of the Sikhs to make maximum sacrifices for the cause of religion and man. Thus, the prominence of this institution in Sikhism not only shows its whole-life character; but also clearly distinguishes it from dichotomous, quietist or pacific systems where this institution is conspicuous by its absence. Hence, the institution of martyrdom in Sikhism, on the one hand, forms its fundamental feature, and, on the other hand, proves its class and character.

19

SIKH RAHIT MARYADA AND SIKH SYMBOLS

GOBIND SINGH MANSUKHANI

Sikhism is a dynamic and practical religion. Sikh *Rahit Maryada* started with Guru Nanak's *sangat* and *pangat*. In their compositions, the Gurus not only formulated the tenets of the Sikh faith, they also gave us guidelines for a Sikh way of life, known as the *Rahit Maryada*. The word *Rahit* means 'how to live' and *Maryada* means tradition and practice of the faith. The words *Rahit* and *Jap* are used in Guru Granth Sahib; for example :

(i) *Sewa surt sabad veechar, jap tap sanjam haumai mar. Jiwan mukt ja sabad sunae, sachi rahat sacha sukh pae.*   (G.G.S., p. 1343)

(ii) *Kahat mukt, sunat mukt, rahit janam rahate.*   (G.G.S., p.1230)

(iii) *Ghal khai kichu hathau dei, Nanak rah pachhanai sei.*   (G.G.S., p. 1245)

(Earn your living with honest work and share your earnings with others. This is the way of truthful living).

(iv) *Baba hor khana khushi khuwar,*

Jit khade tan peerie, mun mah chale vikar.   (G.G.S., p. 16)

The Gurus warned the Sikhs against the use of alcohol and wine and also emphasised the dangers of alcohol, i.e. alcohol destroys one's sense of discrimination.

(i) *Jit peete mutt door hoi, baral pave wich ai.*   (G.G.S., p. 554)

(Drinking wine takes away sense, and dementia results).

(ii) *It mud peete Nanaka, bahute khateeah bikar.*   (G.G.S., p. 553)

(By drinking such wine numerous sins are earned).

Guru Ram Das laid down a Sikh's routine as under :

"*Guru satguru ka jo sikh akhave, so bhalke uthh Har nam dhiave,*

Udam kare bhalke prabhatee, isnan kare amritsar nave"   (G.G.S., p. 305)

Bhai Gurdas also wrote many verses in his *Vars* on the Sikh way of life :

"*Kurbani tina Gur sikhan, pichhal ratee uthh bahande*"   (*Var,* 12-2)

"*Dekh paraian changeean, mavan bhainan, dheean jane*   (*Var,* 12)

When Guru Gobind Singh created the Khalsa, he defined the goal of the Khalsa as :

"Jagat jot japai nis basar, ek bina mun naik na ane, Pooran prem parteet saje, birt gor marhi mutt bhool na mane."   (Dasam Granth, p. 712)

(Only they who keep alight the unquenchable torch of Truth,

And never swerve from thoughts of One God,

Do not thus believe, even by mistake,

In fasting, monastic life or worshipping forebears,

May be recognised as True members of the Khalsa).

Guru Gobind Singh issued the following *Hukamnama* (Guru's Proclamation) to the *sangat* (congregation) of Kabul on 26th Jeth, 1756 Bikrami (23rd May, 1699 A.D.) soon after the founding of the Khalsa. In this, he mentioned the *Rahit* and especially, the five symbols, as under[1] :

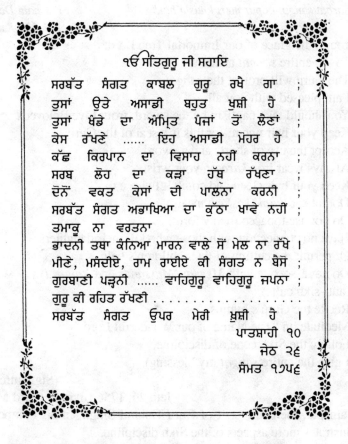

Copy of the letter written by Guru Gobind Singh to the *sangat* of Kabul (Afghanistan). The original manuscript can be seen in the S.G.P.C. Library, Amritsar (Punjab, India).

" *Sarbat sangat Kabul Guru rakhe ga*
  Tusa ute asadee bahut khusi hai
  Tusi Khande da Amrit Panjan ton lena
  Kesh rakhne ...... ih asadee mohur hai;
  Kachh, Kirpan da visah nahee karna
  Sarab loh da kara hath rakhna
  Dono vakat kesan dee palna karna
  Sarbat sangat abhakhia da kutha Khave naheen,
  Tamakoo na vartana
  Bhadni tatha kanya-maran-vale se mel na rakhe
  Meene, Massandyei, Ramraiye ki sangat na baiso.
  Gurbani parhni ...... Waheguru, Waheguru japna.
  Guru kee rahat rakhnee.
  Sarbat sangat oopar meri khushi hai."   *Patshahi Dasvin*
                                            Jeth 26, Samat 1756

(Through the grace of our Immortal True Lord,
    To the entire *sangat* at Kabul.
    The Guru will protect the *sangat*,
    I am pleased with you all.
    You should take baptism by the sword, from Five Beloveds
    Keep your hair uncut, for this is a seal of the Guru,
    Accept the use of shorts and a sword.
    Always wear iron *kara* on your wrist,
    Keep your hair clean and comb it twice a day.
    Do not eat *halal* (*kosher*) meat,
    Do not use tobacco in any form,
    Have no connection with those who kill their daughters
    Or permit the cutting of their children's hair.
    Do not associate with *Meenas*, *Massands* and *Ram-raiyas*
    (anti-sikh cults)
    Recite the Guru's hymns.
    Meditate on "The Name of our Wonderful Lord,"
    Follow the Sikh code of discipline,
    I give the entire *sangat* my blessing).

                                      (Signature of 10th Guru)
                  Jeth 26, 1756 Bikrami (23rd May, 1699 A.D.)

Kavi Sainapat, the court poet of Guru Gobind Singh, in his composition entitled *Gur Sobha* illustrates more aspects of the Sikh discipline.

    "*Aisee reet rahat bataee, santan sunee adhik mun bhaee*"   (26-141)
    "*Panch kee ku-sangat taj, sangat so preet kare,*
      Daya aur Dharam dhar, tiyage sabh lalsa,
      Huka na peevai, sis dharee na mundae,

So to Waheguru, Waheguru, Waheguru ji ka Khalsa." (31-147)

Bhai Desa Singh emphasises the importance of *Rahit* in his *Rahitnama* :

"Rahat bina nah Sikh kahave, Rahat bina dar chotan khave."

Rahitnamas : The *Rahitnamas* were written by some of the Guru's devoted Sikhs. They contain details of the Sikh code of discipline. H. McLeod in his latest attack on Sikhism writes, "The Sikh code of discipline — *Rahit Maryada* and the Sikh symbols were evolved during the 18th century as a result of gradual growth, though the tradition declares they were definitely settled by a pronouncement of Guru Gobind Singh and were part of the Baisakhi day proceedings in 1699 A.D."[2] The *Hukamnama* to the *sangat* of Kabul, issued seven weeks after the Vaisakhi (1699), quoted above, is a plain rebuttal of McLeod's insinuations. The *Rahitnama* of Bhai Prahlad Singh mentions the five K's (*Panj-kakkars*) :

"Kachha, kesh, kangha, kirpan, kara, aur jo karay bakhan
Ih kakay panj tum mano, Guru Granth ko sach tum mano."[3]

So also the *Rahitnama* of Chaupa Singh gives the names of the five K's :

"Kachh, kara, kirpan, kangha, kesh ki,
Ih panj kakaree rahat dhare Sikh so."[4]

According to Bhai Nandlal, the poet laureate of Guru Gobind Singh's court, five K's were the definite marks of the Khalsa :

"Sikhi nishani panj haraf ast kaf,
Hargiz na bashad arzi panj maf,
Kara, kardo, kachha, kangha bidan,
Bina kesh, hech ast jumle nishan."[5]

Giani Gian Singh, the author of *Panth Prakash*, also confirms the Sikh symbols :

"Rakhah kachh, kesh, kara, kirpan, singh nam ko iho nishan,
Kangha, kesh ke sung rahe, iho panj kakar dareh." (*Panth Prakash*, p. 233)

Piara Singh Padam has mentioned the authors of 14 compositions along with their dates which contain details of *Rahit Maryada*.[6] Pandit Tara Singh Narotam, in his book entitled *Sri Guru Tirath Sangrah* written in 1884, has listed 21 *Rahitnamas* by different authors. It is possible, that some of these *Rahitnamas* may have later interpolations, but to reject all outright is an error. McLeod himself translated Bhai Chaupa Singh's *Rahitnama* and has given its details along with the three versions.

There is, therefore, overwhelming and irrefutable evidence to prove that the *Rahit* and the five symbols of the Khalsa were proclaimed by the Tenth Guru. The traditional records of these facts cannot be later creations.

Following are the principles on which the *Rahit Maryada* is based :

(i) Symbols or commandments, which promote virtue and discourage vice. For example, *kachha* and *kara*. *Kachha* symbolises chastity and moral purity in thought and action. *Kara* acts to warn against forgetting God and, in so doing, being overtaken by wrong or evil desires.

(ii) Emphasis on those symbols or actions which promote cohesion and co-operation among Sikhs. For example, the five K's are not only tokens of identity, but also of fellowship and *espirit de corps*, which is further ensured by the use of a standardised greeting : "*Waheguru ji ka Khalsa, Waheguru ji ki Fateh.*"

(iii) There are also those symbols which encourage a concern for the poor and the helpless. The *kirpan* (Sikh sword) is meant to defend the victims of tyranny, injustice or exploitation. It emphasises the need to defend the weak, the downtrodden and the helpless.

(iv) Further, there is a series of injunctions against indulging in evil habits or association with vicious persons. The prohibition against tobacco, and adultery is to encourage personal well-being and social health. The dissociation with anti-Sikh cults, like the *Meenas* (followers of Baba Prithichand), *Dhirmalias*, *Ram-rayas* and other anti-Sikh sects, is to discourage apostasy and maintain purity in the Khalsa brotherhood.

Some say that the Khalsa *Panth* was created by Guru Gobind Singh to meet the challenge of his times, to resist oppression and to undo the erosion of human rights. But, Guru Hargobind on his accession to the guruship, started wearing two swords, one of *piri*, or spiritual power and the other of *miri*, or temporal power. This was more than 90 years before the creation of the Khalsa ! Guru Hargobind trained his Sikh soldiers in martial arts and fought four battles against tyranny and its Moghul perpetrators. Guru Hargobind clearly told Sant Ramdas that his sword was for the protection of the weak and destruction of the tyrant. Even Guru Gobind Singh, when in his teens, fought the battle of Bhangani and the battle of Nadaun against the oppressors before he had created the Khalsa in 1699.

The creation of the Khalsa was a historic event unrelated to any local situation. It was in fulfilment of the Guru's mission to propagate righteousness and to destroy evil. This two-fold purpose became achievable with the creation of the Khalsa *Panth*. The Khalsa describes an ideal man's intent in the support of goodness and morality and the protection of basic human rights. As such, they have an external uniform and inner vision. The external uniform included the five K's and the practice of virtuous and gallant deeds. Inner inspiration was achieved by a constant recall of and reflection on *Gurbani* coupled with meditation or *Naam-simran* on God's Name. Both functions were succintly summed up by Guru Gobind Singh as under :

"*Dhan jeo tah kau jug mai,*

Mukh te Hari, chit main judh bichare"   (Dasam Granth)

(Blessed are those of this world, who invoke God's Name in their minds and fight against the evil in their hearts).

Khalsa Symbols : Let us examine the five K's one by one and consider their significance in the context of the Khalsa *Panth*.

1. *Kesh* : Reference to *kesh* or *keshas* (uncut hair) is to be found in many places in Guru Granth Sahib. Hair is not only regarded as a symbol of saintliness or holiness, but also as a proof of one's living in harmony with the Will of God. All the Sikh Gurus and most of the saints of India left their hair intact. God was described by Guru Arjun as

under :

> *"Teray bankay loen dant reesala,*
> *Sohne nuk jin lambray vala."*   (G.G.S., p. 567)

(You have adoring eyes and sparkling teeth, You have a beautiful nose and long hair.)

While speaking to the Muslims about their faith, Guru Nanak stressed the need to maintain natural hair covered with a turban.

> *"Nanak pak kar hadon hadeesa, sabit soorat dastar sira"*   (G.G.S., p. 1084)

The Guru was not introducing something new. In India, hair was kept naturally by all sorts of persons. Hair was cut on the death of a relative as an expression of grief, or as a punishment for a sin. The Sikhs believe if hair is provided by God, with its peculiar distribution over our bodies, then we should respect this. Trimming or shaving only emphasises the futility of human effort, when opposing the natural law. To maintain hair is an article of Sikh faith; it is regarded as the seal of the Guru. The head of a devout Sikh is also an offering to the Guru as a proof of his devotion. In the past, Sikhs have made tremendous sacrifices to safeguard the sanctity of their hair.

Another explanation for the prescription of unshorn hair is that a Khalsa should look like his Guru and wear a natural uniform which is both inexpensive and dignified, i.e., to keep the Guru's form. Thus, the keeping of uncut hair and wearing a turban are both necessary. Guru Gobind Singh gave his own form to the Khalsa :

> *"Khalsa mero roop hai khas, khalse mai hau karon nivas."*   (Sarab Loh Granth)

During the first half of the 18th century, the Moghal rulers of the Punjab offered rewards for the head of a Sikh. As a result, the Sikhs receded into the jungles, but still did not cut their hair. Bhai Taru Singh faced death rather than allowing his hair to be cut. Sardar Mehtab Singh was sawn alive, but he too retained his hair and refused to give up his faith. Giani Gian Singh wrote :

> *"Mai Gursikhi nah tajohon, kesan swasan sang nibahon"* (Panth Prakash, p. 752)

Instructions regarding the care of hair are mentioned in the *Rahitnama* of Bhai Chaupa Singh :

> *"Guru ka Sikh kesan dee palana kare ...... Maila Hath na lae, joon na paven de,*
> *suchet rahe. Guru ki Mohar Nishani Sikhi hi jane."*   (92)[7]

(Sikhs of the Guru should look after their hair. They should not touch their hair with dirty hands or allow lice to get into them. They should always regard their hair as the seal of the Guru.)

Bhai Koer Singh in *Gur Bilas* (1752) wrote :

> *"Shastra mel, Gur sabad se, kachh, kesan sud prem,*
> *karad rakhani panche eh, taje na kabahi nem."*   (40)

Bhai Sukha Singh in *Gur Bilas Patshashi Dasvin* (1797) wrote :

> *"Bina Shastra kesan nare bhai janeo; Gahe kan tia ko kit loi sidhano Ihe more agia*
> *sun lai piyare, bina teg kesan divo na deedare."*

Rattan Singh Bhangu in *Prachin Panth Prakash* (1841) observed :

> *"Kesan ki kijoh pritpal, na ustran (razor) se katiyo bal."*   (18)

Almost all the *Rahitnamas* lay special emphasis on the maintenance of unshorn hair, for it is not only the most obvious symbol of the Sikhs, but also a sign of their commitment and devotion to the Guru.

> *"Kesh bahar di Sikhi, nishani Sikhi di hai,*
>> *Sikhi andar hovai, dono sikhia barabar rahe."*   (Chaupa Singh)[8]

> *"Kesan dhoop dei such pavan, Hai it Gur ki Mohur suhavan."*   (69)

There are details of how to keep one's hair clean by washing it with curd, soap-nuts (*areethha*) and Fuller's earth (*gachni*). It should be regularly combed so that it does not get entangled or matted. Hair should not be nibbled, cut, plucked or dyed.[9] The facial hair, specially the beard and the moustache, should receive extra care. According to Desa Singh's *Rahitnama* :

> *"Dahra, muchh, sirr kesh banaee,*
> *hai ih kirt ja prabhoo rajaee,*
> *met rajai jo sees mundave,*
> *kah te jag kaise Har pave ?"*   (70)[10]

(Beard, moustache and hair should be properly maintained, because these are the tasks assigned under the Divine Will. One who shaves his head against the Divine Will, how can he attain salvation ?)

2. *Kangha* : *Kangha* or the comb is a necessary adjunct for the hair. It should be on hand to keep the hair neat and tidy. It is, therefore, fixed in the hair knot. According to Bhai Kahn Singh, the best way to clean the hair with a *kangha* is to spread out a handkerchief and to collect the dead skin and fallen hair on to it. Then later burn it. It is wrong to fix a miniature sword on the *kangha* as is done by some Sikhs. We may as well put a miniature *kachha* and a *kara* or its drawing on the *kangha*. That would be ridiculous! Bhai Nandlal observed that the hair should be combed twice daily and a turban neatly tied on the head.

> *"Kangha donah vakat kar, pug chunah kar bandhaee'*   (13)[11]

3. *Kara* : *Kara* is a circular bangle made of steel. It reminds us of the iron will of the Khalsa. *Kara* tinkles and reminds us of fulfilling the Khalsa vows. *Kara* is worn on the right or the left wrist according to being right or left handed. *Kara* is not an ostentatious ornament. It should not be made of gold or other precious metal.

4. *KACHHA OR KACHHAHRA* : *Kachha* or underwear is meant to cover the private parts of the body. It is a symbol of moral restraint and conjugal fidelity. It keeps the wearer covered at all times. It also enables the wearer to move with briskness and agility. In the *Rahitnamas*, it is given as much importance as the other symbols.

> *"Kachh, kirpan na kabahoo tiyage."*[12]   (Desa Singh *Rahitnama*)

Bhai Daya Singh mentions that the underwear should remain above the knees so as not to restrict freedom of movement.

> *"Goday walee Kachh na pahane"*[13]   (Daya Singh *Rahitnama*)

Kachh along with *kesh* and *kirpan* are called *Tra-mudra* (The three emblems)

> *"Kachh, kesh, karad, Guru ki teen mudraih,*
> *Pas te na door karay, sada ang sung dhar"*   (Sarab Loh Granth)[14]

5. *Kirpan* : *Kirpan* means sword. It is generally suspended from a belt across the chest. According to Kahn Singh, *kirpan* literally means a 'house of compassion,' which implies that it is an instrument of compassion for helping victims of injustice and oppression. Others say that it is a combination of two words : *kirpa* and *aan*, *kirpa* means grace or compassion, *aan* means honour or dignity. That is, the *kirpan* is an instrument of compassion to protect and safeguard dignity or honour of others. *Kirpan* is also called *karad, tegh, shamsher, bhagauti.*

Guru Gobind Singh regarded the sword as an emblem of power or *shakti*. He refers to God as *Bhagauti* and *Sarab Loh* (All Steel).

KURAHITS :

Kurahits are prohibitions to be observed by *amritdhari* Sikhs. There are four *kurahits* (major lapses) as under :

(i) *Not To Cut One's Hair/s* : This is both a positive command, as also an injunction. Chaupa Singh states :

"*Guru ka Sikh bhadan na kare.*"

This is a prohibition against cutting or destroying body hair. On the positive side, the Guru wants his Sikhs to come to him in a way that he approves; Sukha Singh wrote :

"*Ihe mor agia suno he piare,*
  Bina tegh Kesan divo na deedare   (*Gur Bilas, Patshahi Dasvin*)

Chaupa Singh emphasises the prohibition against the cutting of hair :

"*Guru da Sikh dehi de rom na luhae.*"   (54)
                                               (*Rahitnama* Chaupa Singh).[15]

Sukha Singh also warns the Sikhs against shaving their hair :

"*Bikhia Kirya bhadan tiagah, jata joot rahbo anuragah.*"   (*Gur Bilas*)

(ii) *Prohibition On Use Of Tobacco* : The use of tobacco in any form is forbidden. Whether smoking a *biri*, a cigarette, a pipe or a *huka*. Snuff-taking is also forbidden. Giani Santokh Singh wrote :

"*Ganda dhoom bans te tiagah, ut gilan is te dhar bhagah.*   (*Suraj Prakash*-1-44)

Bhai Desa Singh's *Rahitnama* mentions :

"*Bhang tamakoo nikat na jave, Tin te bhi such degh karave.*"   (154)

Sainapat states in *Gur Sobha* :

"*Huka tiyage Har gun gavai, achha bhojan Har ras pavai, Bhadhan tiyag karo re*
  bhaee, tah sikhan yah bat sunaee."[16]   (21-137)

(iii) *Halal Meat* : The Tenth Guru prohibited the eating of *halal* meat, because the Muslim rulers had prohibited the sale of any meat except *halal* (*kosher*). The reason for this ban is that *halal* or *kutha* meat involves a lot of cruelty to the animal by gradual bleeding from the jugular vein. Secondly, it was a symbol of slavery as one had no choice but to take the prescribed meat from the Muslim vendors. According to the Guru, if meat was to be eaten, Sikhs should kill the animal with a single sword blow. This meat called *jhatka* is permitted to the Sikhs.

"*Bakra jhatka chhake ta chhakay, avar mas val kabi na takay*"

                                                              (Desa Singh *Rahitnama*)

Bhai Chaupa Singh wrote against the use of *kutha* meat :

"Jo kutha khave so neech tankhaiya.   (372)[17]

Kesar Singh Chibber cautions against eating dead animals :

   "Singh Ji hai, murdar na khae."   (*Bansawalinama*)

   (iv)   *Prohibition Of Adultery* : Guru Gobind Singh banned adultery. Sex within marriage is allowed, but any other sexual activity is prohibited. He wrote in *Bachittar Natak* :

   "Par nari ki sej, supne mool mut jaeeo."

(Do not even in a dream visit the bed of another woman).

When asked by the Sikh soldiers whether they could take female enemy prisoners as booty as the Muslim soldiers did, Guru Gobind Singh told them not to retaliate, for he wanted the Sikhs to set a good example. Kazi Noor Mohammed, one of the Muslim chroniclers of Ahmed Shah Durrani, who accompanied Abdali during three of his invasions of India, wrote approvingly about the high moral character of the Sikh soldiers in their treatment of the women of the opponents. When Jahan Khan's army was defeated by Sikh troops, he ran away and left his female retainers. These women were escorted to their homes by the Sikhs soon after the battle.[18] Desa Singh wrote in his *Rahitnama* :

   "Par beti ko beti jano, par istri ko mat bakhano
      Apnee istri so rat hoee, rahatwant Singh hai soee."   (13)[19]

Bhai Nandial also confirms the ban on adultery :

   "Par istri siu neh lagavai, Gobind Singh vah Sikh na bhavai."   (22)[20]

Bhai Chaupa Singh wrote :

   "Par istrian da sung na kare."   (11)

Besides the above four major *kurahits*, there are some other lapses which attract *tankhah*. Some of them are mentioned in the *Rahitnama* of Bhai Chaupa Singh; for example gambling, theft, consulting astrologers, observing omens and superstitions, use of intoxicants, giving and taking of dowry, and following Hindu rituals. The *Tankhahnama* of Bhai Nandlal also mentions some of the lapses which the Khalsa should avoid.[21] Some of them pertain to the relations between Sikhs and Muslims.

Dr McLeod objects to some of the points made in the *Rahit* which are adverse to the Muslims. He writes :

   "The prominence given in the early *rahit* to renunciation of Muslim contacts, as an example, indicates another major element. In this period of strife, Muslims came to be identified as the prime enemies of the Khalsa and injunctions which reflect this hostility find their way into the evolving *rahit*. Some are subsequently shed or modified as changing circumstances affect attitude towards the *rahit*; others survive to the present day. The clearest of all examples is provided by the ban on *halal* meat. Another major precept, which evidently reflects antagonism towards Muslims, is the strict ban on the use of tobacco."[22]

These conjectures of McLeod are quite misplaced and contrary to facts. Guru

Gobind Singh had not only good relations with Muslims, but he commanded their respect for his spiritual stature. It speaks volumes for his godliness that a Muslim saint, *Pir* Budhu Shah, should be so impressed by the spirit of the Guru's mission that he should not only send hundreds of his followers to join the army of the Guru, but two of his sons should also die fighting for the Guru's cause. It is a fact of history that the Hindu hill princes, besides being hostile and inimical to the Guru for his anti-caste crusade, were instrumental in inviting the Mughal forces to attack the Guru. Muslims like Nabi Khan, Ghani Khan and General Said Khan also admired him. Even in the *Zafarnama*, he has not condemned Emperor Aurangzeb, but has only exposed his fanaticism and cruelty. With regard to *halal*, the reason for its prohibition to the Sikhs have already been given under the section of *kurahits*. McLeod's other contention that the ban on the use of tobacco for the Sikhs is antagonistic to the Muslims is unreasonable. Tobacco was smoked by both Hindus and Muslims. It was a pernicious addiction for all people and was condemned as such. The Guru had created a dynamic community with a mission and a goal. Tobacco creates laziness, lethargy and disease, and was thus a hurdle in the pursuit of an active and constructive life by the *Panth*. The ban on tobacco cannot, thus, be taken as an example of Sikh hostility to Muslims.

Guru Gobind Singh wanted the Khalsa to follow the *Rahit* suictly. There could be no exception to it. It is said that he wanted the Sikhs to be vigilant.

> "*Jab lag Khalsa rahe Niyara, Tab lag tej dio mai sara,*
> *Jab ih gahay bipran ki reet, Mai na karo in ki parteet.*"

(Sarab Loh Granth)

Bipran-ki-reet implies generally Brahminism or 'Brahamanvad.' Some of the things which can be included under it are listed below :

(i) *Varna Ashram Dharma*, caste ideology, concept of pollution, superiority of Brahmins in society, and the monopoly of Brahmins for conducting religious and social ceremonies, etc.

(ii) That Brahmins alone are entitled to charity. The Guru says :
"*Sabhna noo kar dan.*" (G.G.S., Barah Mah)

(iii) Belief in the theory of pollution (*sutak*) at time of birth, death, etc. The Guru says :
"*Sabho sutak bharm hai*" (G.G.S., p. 472).

(iv) Ancestor worship and idol worship along with the ceremonies connected with it.

(v) Sanctity of cooking and enclosed space (*chauka*) for it.

(vi) Incarnation, that God assumes human birth.

(vii) Rituals like *yagna, sanskar, havan, tap*, pilgrimage and fasting.

The Guru rejected all superstitions and taboos :
"*Phoota unda bharam ka, manah bhaiyo pargas,*
Kati beree pagah te, Gur keeni bund khalas" (G.G.S., p. 1002)

(Superstition is overcome. The mind is illumined. The shackles are broken, the Guru has liberated me.)

Penalties : Infringements of the *Rahit Maryada* or the Sikh Code of Discipline involve penalties, with the clear intention of reforming the defaulter. The *Tankhahnama* of Bhai Nandlal and some other *Rahitnamas* mention certain penalties for infringements. The penalties differ according to the nature and seriousness of the lapse of misdemeanour. The infringements of the *Rahit Maryada* may be classified under three heads, along with the procedure for punishments :

(i) *Tankhah* : Some other lapses are mentioned in the *Rahitnamas*. *Tankhah* or the penalty imposed is the verdict or the decision of the local *sangat* or congregation after due deliberation and considering the explanation of the offender. The procedure may be set in motion by any Sikh in the form of a complaint against the offender. Some of the lapses include taking of dowry, use of intoxicants, associating with anti-Sikh cults, or some violation of the Sikh Code of Discipline. The *sangat* may accept the offender's apology and/or impose admonition, penitence, some sort of *sewa* (service) like cleaning the shoes, serving in the *langar* or reading of some sacred compositions, or the entire Guru Granth Sahib, and/or a fine. After the offender has carried out the penitence/ punishment, he has to appear before the *sangat* again, and then *Ardas* is offered which restores the penitent to his Sikh status.

(ii) *Patitism* (Apostasy) : This is a serious violation of one or all the four *kurahits* done by an *amritdhari* Sikh. These are cutting of hair, eating of *halal* meat, smoking and adultery. The offender has to appear before the *Panj Piaras*, render an apology and accept whatever punishment is prescribed by them. After he has gone through the punishment, he has to appear again before *Panj Piaras* and take *amrit* again, when he is restored to his former status.

(iii) *Excommunication* : This is the most serious punishment given for a very grave offence or misdemeanour which may affect the whole Sikh community. The punishment and penance is awarded by any of the five *Takhts* to those accused of grave error or insult to the Khalsa *Panth*. The *Jathedar* of the *Takht,* who after due consideration of the explanation of the offender, prescribes a severe punishment/ penitence of any kind. After the person has undergone the punishment and penitence, he appears before the *Takht* for restoration to his status as a Sikh.

Authorised Rahit Maryada : The Shiromani Gurdwara Parbandhak Committee, Amritsar, — An All India Sikh Institution — constituted a sub-committee in 1936 to consider the formulation of a universal Sikh *Rahit Maryada*. As a result, representatives of Sikh Associations and *Takhts* deliberated for a long time and formulated an authorised version which was published in 1945. The original publication is in Punjabi. Its English edition is also available.[23] This booklet is divided into six sections as under :

    I. Sikh Defined
    II. Aspects of Sikh Living
    III. Gurdwaras, Congregational Etiquette, Rites
    IV. Beliefs, Observances, Duties, Taboos and Ceremonies
    V. Altruistic Work
    VI. Panthic (Corporator Sikh) Life

CONCLUSION

The Sikh ideology and ethics have unambiguously been laid down in the Sikh scripture, Guru Granth Sahib. Similarly, our discussion makes it plain that the injunctions of the Gurus and the *Rahitnamas* have clearly specified the rules of Sikh conduct and *Maryada*. Should at any stage there be need of any clarification of an issue, the matter can be decided only at the *Panthic* level, the yardstick[24] provided being the teachings of the Gurus enshrined in Guru Granth Sahib.

REFERENCES

1. Sikh Research and Reference Library, Amritsar (Mss) Quoted by Sardar Kirpal Singh in *Sikh Symbols*, Sikh Missionary Society, Southall, U.K., 1971, p. 23.
2. H. McLeod : *Evolution of the Sikh Community*, p. 18. Also see his book - *The Saints*, p. 243.
3. *Gurmat Parkash*, monthly journal, April/May 1980 (S.G.P.C.) Amritsar, p. 158.
4. Ibid., p. 158.
5. Ibid., p. 50.
6. Piara Singh Padam : *Rahitname*, Patiala, 1974, p. 30.
7. H. McLeod : *The Chaupa Singh Rahitnama*, Otago Univ. Dunedin, 1987, p. 68.
8. Jodh Singh : *Gurmat Nirnae*, Ludhiana, p. 291.
9. H. McLeod : *op. cit.* p. 103.
10. Piara Singh Padam : *Rahitname*, p. 140.
11. Ibid., p. 68.
12. *Gurmat Parkash*, op.cit. p. 88.
13. Ibid., p. 88.
14. *Gurmat Parkash*, op. cit. p. 89.
15. McLeod : op. cit. p. 64.
16. *Gurmat Parkash*, op. cit. p. 54.
17. McLeod : op. cit. p. 104.
18. *Gurmat Parkash* op. cit. p. 137.
19. Piara Singh Padam : *Rahitname*, p. 135.
20. Ibid., p. 46.
21. Ibid., p. 44.
22. K. Schomer & W.H. McLeod : *The Saints*, Motilal Banarasidass, Delhi, 1987, p. 243.
23. *Rahit Maryada*, a guide to the Sikh way of life, S.G.P.C., Amritsar.
24. G.S. Mansukhani : *Aspects of Sikhism*, p. 212.

20

THE CASTE SYSTEM AND SIKHS

JAGJIT SINGH

BACKGROUND

The Sikh social revolution has not drawn the attention it deserves, probably for two main reasons. Max Weber has differentiated three systems of stratification based on class, status and power; but, prior to his clarification, economic stratification was "emphasised to the point of neglecting or confusing the role of other forms of stratification."[1] "For revolutions before the middle of the nineteenth century, the search for class struggle can lead to grave confusion;"[2] because, "Classes in the Weberian sense clearly emerge out of market relationships", and as these market relationships were weak before the growth of capitalism, "these failed to erupt out of their isolation and reshape whole societies in their image."[3] "Today, it is a fashion to interpret every insurrection, rebellion, or revolt in terms of class conflict. Yet, this is absolutely incorrect from a historical point of view. This is a firmly established fact : revolts and revolutions prior to the end of the eighteenth century are really not expressions of the class struggle ...... It is difficult today to understand that the social issue of exploitation never played an important part in revolts prior to the eighteenth century."[4] Therefore, it is wrong to minimize the Sikh social revolution in the light of later historical developments of the capitalist era; especially so, because in India, a Chhaturpati King was lower in 'caste-status' than his own priest *purohita*, who was economically dependent on the prince, and the wealthiest *Bania* was lower in 'caste-status' than the poorest *Kshatriya*. In short, caste circumscribed the limits within which Indian social, political and economic activities were to flow, and also set the direction these were to follow.

The second reason is that, even within the feudal set-up, the social and political context differed from society to society. Islam was lucky that it had to encounter at its birth primitive heathenic beliefs which it was easier to pierce than the hard shell of the elaborate dogma and religious philosophy (*Varna Ashrama Dharma*), the caste in India had spun around itself. Moreover, the Arabian society at that time was quite close to the level of primitive communism.[5] The Sikh movement, on the other hand, had to face the uphill task of overcoming not only caste, but an elaborate caste system.

THE CASTE AND THE CASTE SYSTEM

A good deal of misunderstanding is caused by confusing caste, as such, elements of which are present in most societies, with the caste system, which developed in India alone. We have to emphasise this distinction because it is vital to the clarification of our subject.

"The laws of the Anglo-Saxons laid down that none was to seek in marriage a mate outside one's class ...... Well-marked status-groups within a society, distinguished from one another by rights and disabilities, separated from one another by the absence of freedom of inter-marriage, may, therefore, be considered to be a common characteristic of the mental background and social picture of the Indo-European cultures."[6] "Neither race, nor occupation or function is by itself enough to cause a caste system to come into being, or to account for its restrictions on commensality and marriage."[7] Hereditary functionalism does not constitute caste.[8]

It is very important, therefore, to understand that elements of caste exclusiveness, common to many other societies, assumed special significance in India only because these got welded into a system that gave them added power, momentum and thrust.

Hutton has given a number of examples where the parallel to the excreableness attached to our outcastes is very close. In Burma, "pagoda slave is such for life, and his children and descendents are pagoda slaves in perpetum. If a person, who is not a pagoda slave, marries or be married to a pagoda slave even unwillingly, such a person and all her or his children, even by a former marriage, also become automatically pagoda slaves perpetually. Pagoda slaves cannot be employed in any other capacity than that of a pagoda servant. It will be observed that in the last two respects, the disabilities suffered are even more severe than those of outcastes in India, though the element of untouchability is not stressed at all to the same degree."[9] In Japan, "So strong is the prejudice against them (Eta) that they were considered sub-human ...... lived in separate quarters in the village; had to wear distinct dress; could only marry among themselves; had no social intercourse with other classes, and could go abroad between sunset and sunrise ......"[10]

What is pertinent to our purpose in these examples is that although there was common ground in these countries and in India for the origin of caste, in India alone it developed into an organic structure covering the whole society. In other countries, elements of even extreme social exclusiveness (such as in the case of pagoda slaves and Eta) became stabilized in an undeveloped form, or even degenerated, so as to affect only a limited part of society, leaving the main body of the people untouched. "For, the Burmese as a whole are as free from the working of the caste system as are other peoples among whom analogous institutions have been pointed out."[11] In India alone, the elements of caste exclusiveness developed into an elaborate system covering the whole society.

A system is qualitatively different from a casual or unmotivated get-together or assortment of factors or forces. It is what distinguishes philosophy, religion or science from an unintegrated mass of doctrines, tenets or data. It is what distinguishes an army from a rabble, as it involves organization, arrangement, method and well-thought out principles of procedure. Above all, a system assumes a purpose, an objective, a direction, a plan, towards the fulfilment of which the functioning of the different constituents of the system is coordinated and harmonized. Moreover, a system acquires its own cumulative power, thrust, momentum and grip.

Why the caste system developed in India and no where else is a complicated question not easy to answer. But, broadly speaking other societies lacked an elaborate caste ideology and a human agency which could harness the functioning of the different caste elements towards a set purpose and a fixed direction. In India, the Brahmin Lavite caste was consciously committed and devoted to the preservation of primarily its own 'caste-status' and, to a lesser degree, that of other 'twice-born' castes. Towards that end, economic status was lowered than 'caste-status', and political power was made subservient to the Brahmin priesthood.[12] The preservation of the caste order, based on 'caste-status', became the overriding compulsion of the caste society to such an extent that all liberal and egalitarian socio-religious values and trends were either engulfed in the caste ideology, or so distorted as to blunt their liberal import.[13]

THREE PILLARS OF THE CASTE SYSTEM

There are three main factors responsible for constituting and consolidating the castes into the Indian caste system, namely, the caste ideology, Brahmins, and the caste-society.

The fundamental assumption of the caste ideology is that "Men were not — as for classical Confucianism — in principle equal, but for ever unequal."[14] They were so by birth, and some of them "were as unlike as man and animal."[15] This ideology of human inequality was sought to be reinforced through a number of channels, but mainly through the religious sanction of Hindu scriptures, Hindu *dharma* and the taboos of pollution.

The *Purushua Sukta* hymn in the *Rig Veda* was regarded as a divine ordinance sanctioning the origin of the four castes.[16] Gita sanctified hereditary functionalism ("Congenital duty, O son of Kunti, though defective, ought not to be abandoned.");[17] and Lord Krishna claims himself to be the author of castes.[18] What is even more significant is that in the huge corpus of orthodox literature, there is not a single line which specifically condemns the *Varna Ashrama Dharma*. This scriptural sanction of the *Varna Ashrama Dharma* and the castes, bears major responsibility for consolidating the castes; because, "To acknowledge the authority of the Vedas, as demanded of the Hindu, means *fides implicita* in a more fundamental sense than that of the Catholic Church ......";[19] and "Brahminical and caste power resulted from the inviolability of all sacred law ......"[20]

The concept of Hindu *dharma* came to be very closely interwoven with the social order of Brahminism, as the caste became a part and parcel of the *Varna Ashrama Dharma*, the religiously sanctioned caste system. The Hindu law books were significantly named as *Dharam Shastras*. "In contrast to the orthodox sects, the heresy of theophratries consists in the fact that they tear the individual away from his ritualistic duties, hence from the duties of the caste of his birth, and thus ignore or destroy his *dharma*. When this happens, the Hindu loses caste. And since only through caste one can belong to the Hindu community, he is lost to it."[21]

The taboos about pollution played the biggest role in extending the range of the caste system and in projecting it in day to day life. The idea of pollution associated with the effects of childbirth and the monthly period of women had much to do with the undermining of their social position. The peasants were downgraded because ploughing involved the killing of worms;[22] and, "The lowest caste strata was considered to be absolutely defiling and contaminating ...... This stratum comprised services which Hinduism had come to consider ritually impure; tanning, leather work."[23]

What we have cited above should be enough to leave no doubt that the caste ideology was altogether different from the loose bundle or combination of social prejudices such as we meet in other societies. The caste ideology raised social exclusiveness and hierarchy to the level of a religious principle by stamping it with the sanction of Hindu scriptures, *Shastras*, and Hindu *dharma*; and this was the ideological base on which the super-structure of the caste system was reared and maintained.

The Brahmins, as a levite caste, were the all-time standing kingpin of the caste system; they were both its ideologues and the human focal point around which the system revolved. Almost all authorities agree that practically all the orthodox literature is the work of, or inspired by, the Brahmin hierarchy,[24] and the Brahmins were its sole interpreters. The Brahmins came to occupy the central position in Hindu society because caste is essentially a social rank, and the social rank of the castes is determined with reference to the Brahmins.[25] In the political sphere too, : "Whereas in other countries the rivalry between the nobility and the sacerdotal class generally resulted in the triumph of the temporal power over the spiritual ...... in India reverse has been the case ...... The supremacy of the Brahmins has now become one of the cardinal doctrines of Hinduism."[26]

The role of caste ideology and Brahmin levite caste in initiating and consolidating the caste system has been widely discussed and understood. What we want to emphasise here is the role of the third main pillar of the caste system, its social frame-work, i.e. the caste society itself.

Although the caste ideology, its codes and rules, were laid down by the Brahmins, the adherence to these rules and usages was ensured by the caste members of the locality, who knew one another intimately, through caste councils (*Panchayats*) or otherwise. The very constitution of the caste society, its every cell, was built on the principle of social inequality and hierarchy, and the caste society was inexorable in its operational efficiency to uphold that principle. The irony of it is that "the lower the caste in the social scale, the stronger its combination and the more efficient its organization."[27] In other words, the lower castes were more prone to tighten their own caste shackles.

To what extent the caste governs every member of the caste is detailed by Wilson, who sums up : "It (caste) interferes, in short, with all the relations and events of life, and with what precedes and follows life ......"[28] And, the inexhorable working of the caste mechanism is illustrated by Abbe Dubois, who describes the fate of an ex-communicated man. "It renders him, so to speak, dead to the world. With the loss of caste, he loses not only his relations and friends, but sometimes even his wife and children, who prefer to abandon him entirely rather than share his ill-fortune."[29]

Each salient element of the caste ideology (i.e. caste hierarchy; scriptural sanction; sanctions of Hindu *dharma*, ritualism, custom and tradition; caste connubial and commensal restrictions; the taboos of pollution; the theory of *karma* as applied to justify caste, etc.) fastens each and every individual of a sub-caste with its own ideological strand of human inequality and social exclusiveness. In other words, a member of a sub-caste was bound down, not by one or two, but by several such ideological bonds or chains. If one keeps in view how difficult it has been to erase social prejudices even where these were operating as a single factor (e.g. as colour bar in U.S.A., or as taboos in Burmah and Japan, or as endogamy in class societies), the improbability of overcoming the multiplicative power of so many different strands of caste ideology, acting in unison, becomes quite apparent.

What made the problem of the caste system still more intricate and intractable was that this composite ideology of caste hierarchy and social exclusiveness was fused with every fibre of the social texture of the caste society. Every individual in the caste society was not only himself entangled by several tentacles of the caste ideology, but he was fastened to other similarly bound individuals within a sub-caste to form a rigid horizontal social network. In fact, the caste-bounds were the most predominant, if not the only, social bonds that united the members of a sub-caste. On top of it, this horizontal social net-work of each sub-caste was tied vertically, layer upon layer, both ideologically (as the ritual, the ethical code, and the penal code were all hierarchically graded)[30] and organizationally, to other similarly constituted higher and lower sub-castes. In short, the social fabric of the caste society and the caste ideology were interlocked around each and every social unit of the caste society. This is what made the caste system synonymous with the Hindu society. In Risley's somewhat graphic phrase, the removal of the caste system would be "more than a revolution : it would resemble the removal of some elemental force like gravitation or molecular attraction." In any case, the caste system could not be tackled without tackling the caste society; it was imperative and could not be bypassed. This perspective is of great importance for understanding the social significance of the Sikh movement.

THE CASTE SYSTEM AND THE SIKHS IN THE PERIOD OF IDEOLOGICAL ASCENDENCY

The Sikh movement attacked all the three (and other) pillars of the caste system.

Guru Nank directly condemned caste ideology and called it as the wisdom of the perverse.[31] The Sikh Gurus also rejected the Hindu scriptures;[32] and, since Guru Arjun established Guru Granth Sahib as the Sikh scripture, Sikhs have never owned any other. *Varna Ashrama dharma* was integral part of the Hindu *dharma*, but Guru Nanak rejected it and "made *dharma* perfect by blending the four castes into one."[33] Discarding pollution taboos, all the members of the Khalsa Dal (including Rangrettas drawn from outcastes) dined together,[34] which fact was vouchsafed by two Muslim historians in 1733.[35]

Although the Brahmins were the third numerous caste in the Punjab, out-numbering all but Jats and Rajputs,[36] there were only about 7,000 Sikh Brahmins in the Census of 1881. Even these Brahmins did not constitute a priestly class, as it is a well-known fact that the Sikhs have no hereditary levite caste. By eliminating the Brahminical influence in the *Panth*, the Sikh society eliminated the human kingpin of the caste system from within its ranks.

Break from the caste ideology and getting rid of Brahmin levite caste were no doubt vital steps for undermining the caste system. But, what we want to emphasise is that the greatest hurdle was the social framework of the caste system, i.e. the caste society. The anti-caste movements could survive only if these divorced themselves from the caste society.

Max Weber writes "Once established, the assimilative power of Hinduism is so great that it tends even to integrate social forms considered beyond its religious borders. The religious movements of expressly anti-Brahminical and anti-caste character that were contrary to one of the fundamentals of Hinduism, have been in all essentials returned to the caste order ...... Unless the sect is able to abolish the caste system altogether, instead of simply tearing away some of its members, it becomes, from the stand point of the caste system, a quasi-guest folk, a kind of confessional guest community in an ambiguous position in the prevailing Hindu Order."[37]

As the abolition of the system at one stroke could happen only through a miracle, the only practical way was to form a society outside the caste society and use it as a base for attacking the caste system from outside. This lesson of Indian history is of the utmost importance for grasping the social significance of the Sikh movement. The contaminative power of the caste system was so great that it did not spare Indian Muslims and Christians,[38] whom the caste society was not prepared to assimilate even if they wished it. Then, how could those anti-caste movements, whether be of Lingayats, Chaitanyites, or of other radical *Bhakats* like Namdev, Kabir, and other Saints, despite all their radical anti-caste innovations, remained as mere sects of Hinduism, or as mere appendages of the caste society. None of these came to be enumerated in census operations as distinctly non-Hindu social units like the Muslims, Christians and Sikhs. It was because these anti-caste protests did not develop, for one reason or another, into sustained movements which worked consistently over a period to establish and maintain their separate social identity from the caste society in the manner the Sikh movement did in the revolutionary period of about 275 years (approximately from 1486 A.D., when Guru Nanak started his mission, to the establishment of the *missls* in 1764). Even the ideological anti-caste distinctiveness of such movements tended to fade after the inspiration provided by their founders began to wane after their death, and they became more and more vulnerable to the "assimilative power of Hinduism." In other words, mere ideological gap between the caste ideology and the anti-caste ideology of these movements, howsoever wide, was not enough. The chances of success of any anti-caste movement were in direct proportion to the extent it established and retained a separate social identity from the caste society. A very important achievement of the Sikh movement, therefore, is that it marked a clear break from the caste society.

The *Vars* of Bhai Gurdas link the creation of the *Panth* with the abolition of caste and sects.[39] A contemporary Muslim historian of Guru Hargobind (1595-1644) testifies that the "Sikhs do not read the *Mantras* (i.e. Vedic or other scriptural hymns) of the Hindus, they do not venerate their temples or idols, nor do they esteem their *avtars*."[40] The creation of the Khalsa made the final break with the caste society. For joining the Khalsa brotherhood, one had to take five solemn vows of *Dharam Nash*, *Kul Nash*, *Karam Nash*, *Bharam Nash* and *Krit Nash* which cut at the roots of the cardinal principles of the caste system.[41]

The newswriter of the area sent to the Mughal Emperor a report of the Guru's address at the time of the creation of the Khalsa (1699). "Let men of the four castes receive my baptism, eat out of one dish, and feel no disgust or contempt for one another."[42] This is also corroborated by the near-contemporary Koer Singh (1751), who records that the Guru "blended the four castes into one", had rejected both the Hindu and Muslim religions and created a new noble Khalsa, wherein Sudra, Vaishya, Khatri and Brahmin eat together.[43]

The later Sikh literature of the 18th century, written by different persons and at different times, is agreed on this issue that the Khalsa broke away from the caste ideology and the caste society. *Rahitnamas*, which contain mostly precepts, take a very strong line on this issue. "He who abides by the six *Darshnas*, drags along with him his whole family into hell."[44] "If any baptized Sikh puts on *Janeo*, he will be caste into hell."[45] "A Sikh should sever connection with Musalmans and Hindus (Mussalmans Hindu *ki aan mete*)."[46] Kesar Singh Chibber (1769) writes that "the Guru created a new Third *Panth* (Khalsa *Panth*) by breaking with both Hindus and Mussalmans."[47] Sukha Singh (1797) states the same fact more explicitly : "Sudra, Vaish, Khatri and Brahmin all ate together. The religion of Vedas was rejected ...... All the religions of Hindus were discarded and one pure, 'Khalsa' was established."[48] One Bhai Gurdas Singh wrote about the same time : "Ved, Puran, six Shastras and Kuran were eliminated ...... The third religion of Khalsa became supreme."[49] We have already referred to non-Sikh sources of Dabistan and the Mughal newswriter (1699). In order to appreciate this 'striking and complete break' from caste society, we have to remind that no one could be a Hindu unless he was born Hindu and also not without belonging to one caste or another;[50] and that restrictions on inter-caste commensality were fundamental to the caste system.[51]

All the evidence given above belongs to the 17th and 18th centuries. It clearly demonstrates that the separation of the Khalsa from the caste society was not an accident or an expediency. It was a regular movement which continued without a break during its revolutionary phase. But, a preposterous proposition continues to be persistently repeated that the separate identity of the Khalsa from the caste society was a creation of the Singh Sabha movement in the late 19th and early 20th centuries under the influence of the divide and rule policy of the British. The Singh Sabha movement was a revival, no doubt, but by no means an innovation.

A NEW SOCIO-POLITICAL ORDER

The Khalsa not only broke away from the caste society, but also succeeded to a remarkable degree in giving an egalitarian socio-political orientation to its own polity. This was both an acid test and a proof of its separate identity from the caste society as well as its *raison d'etre*.

(a) *Social Structure* : The unit of the Sikh *Panth* was *sangat* (i.e. a congregation of Sikhs) and not sub-caste or caste. Bhai Gurdas in his *Var* eleven has given account of some of the prominent *sangats* of his time, from which it is clear that almost all the *sangats* were composed of Sikhs drawn from all castes, including the Sudras and outcastes, without any distinction.

(b) *Mass Base Of The Khalsa* : The Khalsa had not only an egalitarian socio-political mission, but it had also a plebeian composition. This mass base of the Khalsa reinforced the execution of the Khalsa missions as the downtrodden became both the architects and masters of their own destiny.

The plebeian base of the Khalsa is testified to by Sikh historical literature.[52] Non-Sikh sources of history also confirm that scavengers, leather-dressers, and such like persons were very numerous among Banda's forces.[53] The mass base of the *Panth* continued even in the later period.[54]

(c) *The Spirit Of Equality, Brotherhood And Fraternization* : More than the form or its composition, it is the spirit which prevails within a movement which reflects its real character. The prevalence of the spirit of equality, brotherhood and fraternization is attested to by Sikh sources of history,[55] and is confirmed by Ghulam Mohyy-ud-Din (1722-23), who writes that the low caste Hindus swelled the ranks of Banda, and everyone in his army "would address the other as the adopted son of the oppressed Guru (Guru Gobind Singh) and would publicize himself with the title of *sahibzada*."[56]

(d) *Political Power* : The Sikh movement not only raised the social status of the people drawn from the lower castes into the *Panth*, but also shared political power with them.   There cannot be a permanent footing for a social revolution without a corresponding political set up.[57] The Khalsa shared political power with scavengers and leather dressers, "the lowest of low in Indian estimation", under Banda.[58] Even in the *misl* period, ordinary peasants, village menials (Jassa Singh Ramgarhia), and distillers (Jassa Singh Ahluwalia), whom the caste society rated very near the outcastes, became the leaders. What is even more significant is that there was no one else from castes higher than these. "...... the whole country of the Punjab ...... is in the possession of this community (the Khalsa) and most of their exalted leaders are of low origin, such as carpenters, animal-skin treaters and Jats."[59] As against it, "None of the revolutions (English, American, French or Russian) quite substituted a brand new ruling class for the old one, atleast not unless one thinks of a class without bothering about the human beings who make up the class ......"[60]

The capture of political power by the commoners had a great social impact. It was on this account that the Sikhs in general (drawn from all castes) have come to be addressed as Sardars upto this day by the non-Sikhs. It was the taste of political power which made the Sikh Jat feel prouder than the Rajput,[61] and the Ramgarhias (Carpenters) and Ahluwalias (distillers) feel as equals to the Jat.[62]

THE CASTE SYSTEM AND THE SIKHS IN THE LATER PERIOD

"It would also seem that most men cannot long stand the strain of prolonged effort to live in accordance with very high ideals ...... Thermidor (i.e. return to less hectic time) comes as naturally to societies in revolution as an ebbing tide, as calm after a storm, as convalescence after fever, as the snapping back of a stretched elastic band."[63]

This slide towards Thermidor, common to all revolutions, was compounded in the case of the Sikh movement by another development. The Sikh *Panth* had no sectarian, ethnic, or regional loyalty as a base of its own. With the exception of stray Muslims, all its recruits came from those Hindus who were drawn towards it by its ideological appeal; and, who were, in addition, during the period of the revolutionary struggle, prepared to suffer for its practical fulfilment. The number of Khalsa guerillas was for this reason, at one stage, reduced to about 2,000 persons.[64] Thus the ideologically qualitative content of the movement during the revolutionary phase came to be regulated so to say, automatically. But, with the prospects of political power in sight, the number of Singhs suddenly rose, as estimated by Khushwaqt Rai in 1811, to be about 200,000.[65] It is said that this number swelled further during the *raj* of Ranjit Singh, but what can be said for certain is that the number of Sikhs increased a good deal in the British period. Between 1881 and 1931, the total number of Sikhs increased from 1,853,426 to 4,33,771.[66] As such, conversions were, by and large, not so much a matter of conviction as of convenience, these proselytes retained in varying degrees some elements of their heritage from their previous connection with the caste system. What is of consequence, therefore, for our study in this background is to examine in what manner, or to what extent, the revolutionary heritage of the *Panth* has affected the abolition or retention of the caste heritage of these proselytes at various levels of the Sikh society during the modern period, about which alone we have authentic information regarding the post-revolutionary period.

(a)   *At The Panthic Level* :   (i)   At the *Panthic* level, there is no discrimination agaisnt Sikhs drawn from any caste. Sikhs from the outcastes have been the priests (*granthies*) of Harimandar Sahib, Amritsar, the most sacred place to the Sikhs; and, by an unwritten convention, vice-Presidents of S.G.P.C. (the constitutional body which controls all the major historic Gurdwaras in the Punjab) have been elected from Sikhs drawn from the outcastes. As against this, the Shankracharya has publicly declared very recently that free entry of Sudras into the premier Hindu temples would lead to the destruction of Hinduism.

The institution of *langar* (as distinct from taking *prasad* in a temple) has been a very important factor in keeping alive, at the *Panthic* level, the anti-caste heritage of the earlier period. In the *langars* attached to the gurdwaras and at the time of *Jor Melas* (Sikh religious gatherings), Sikhs drawn from all castes, including the outcastes, dine together and no body bothers by whom the food is cooked or served. This fact can be verified at any time. But "it is one of the constitutive principles of the castes that there should be atleast ritually inviolable barriers against complete commensalism among different castes."[67]

(ii)   *Jat Sikhs Vis-a-vis Khatri Sikhs, Arora Sikhs And Ramgarhia Sikhs* : These categories do not constitute a hierarchy, as is wrongly supposed, atleast in the Brahminical sense. A hierarchy pre-supposes fixation of higher and lower grades, and, what is more, their acceptance by the categories concerned voluntarily or otherwise. As a consequence of the Sikh Revolution, the Jat Sikhs do not recognise anybody as their social superiors;[68] on the other hand, "Khatri Sikhs probably considred themselves above the Jat Sikhs in status."[69] This apparent contradiction in these two statements is resolved if one faces the reality that none of the two groups regards itself as inferior to the other — the Jat Sikh because of the elevation of his social position by the Sikh Revolution, and the Khatri Sikh because of his wealth, education and the lingering consciousness that the Jats had once been his inferiors in the caste hierarchy. In this respect, we bracket the Arora Sikhs with Khatri Sikhs, as the former claim Khatri origin and are socially, more or less, similarly placed.

Similarly, ever since the formation of Ramgarhia *misl*, the Ramgarhia Sikhs have regarded themselves as peers to the Jat Sikhs; and their recently acquired phenomenal prosperity,[70] as compared to the Jat Sikhs, has added to their pride and social status. Ramgarhia Sikhs have never been denied access to gurdwaras, but sometimes they build their own just to assert their independent status. In short, the Ramgarhia Sikhs do not accept at all that the Jat Sikhs are superior to them.

Ramgarhia Sikhs are not, as wrongly alleged, a sub-caste of Tarkhan Sikhs, because there are no commensal or connubial barriers between the two as evidenced by extensive family ties between them. Any Tarkhan Sikh, who leaves his village surroundings and chooses to call himself a Ramgarhia, automatically becomes one.

There are, therefore, no grounds for inferring that the Jat Sikhs, Khatri Sikhs, Arora Sikhs and Ramgarhia Sikhs constitute a hierarchy, because stratification "implies that a zero-sum of I-win-you-lose relationship exists between higher and lower strata."[71] In no case do they constitute a hierarchy in the Brahminical sense; as they freely interdine, and whatever inhibitions there might be regarding intermarriages between them, belong to the type of group prejudices common to most societies, as there are absolutely no religious or ritual barriers.

(iii)   *Artisans And Menials* : Out of a total of 1,853,426 Sikhs in 1881, the number of artisan and menial castes among the Sikhs, other than the Tarkhans, was Lohar Sikhs 24,614; Jhinwar Sikhs 21,754; Nai Sikhs 21,500; Chimba Sikhs 17,748; Sunar Sikhs 14,046; Kumhar Sikhs 11,947, and Kalal Sikhs 8,931.[72] In other words these categories do not constitute any caste problem of major social significance. Of these, Kalal Sikhs, although assigned a lower position than most of the artisan castes, raised their social status considerably, like the Ramgarhia Sikhs, by capturing political power when they formed the Ahluwalia *misl*. Since then they have taken to service, primarily in the army and the police,[73] and have shaken off their dependence upon any social hierarchy. The other artisan castes of the Sikhs migrated to the cities in large numbers,[74] where, being in small numbers and being widely dispersed, they can hardly be treated as compact groups. In the villages, too, they are similarly dispersed. As already noted, Sikhs derived from all castes, excepting the Mazhbis, interdine. Therefore, the Sikhs from artisans and menial categories face no social discrimination excepting that they find reluctance on the part of Jat, Khatri, Arora and Ramgarhia Sikhs to intermarry with them. Such intermarriages are not so common, but they are not insignificant either, the writer himself having attended such marriage ceremonies on a number of occasions. The important point to note, however, is that intermarriages are prevented by sentiment and not by hard and fast rules. "Marriages outside the class in Europe might be rare and invalid, but in India, if it is contracted outside the caste, it is a sacrilege."[75] Such marriages are neither a sacrilege in the Sikh society, nor are these visited by penalties such as those imposed by the caste ideology.

(b) *At The Village Level* : It is at the village level that we find remnants of the social hierarchy operating among the Sikhs, as it does, more or less on similar lines, in Muslim villages. In both cases, the peasantry, whether Jat, Baloch or Pathan, is at the top of the hierarchy, and the artisans and menials are arranged in different lower grades, though under different labels in some cases (e.g. Mashki for Jhiwar, Mochi for Chamar, and Mussali for Chuhra). Our subject is confined to the position of the Sikhs vis-a-vis the Indian caste system, but it is pertinent to point out that most of the artisans and menials got coverted to Islam long ago under the Muslim rule and their social and occupational status remains much the same as it was before conversion. This fact suggests two important implications. One, that the social hierarchy in the village hierarchy could not be overhauled during the long impact of Islam and Muslim rule, it is too much to expect drastic changes in the hierarchy of Sikh villages which embraced Sikhism at a very late date during the post-revolutionary period.

To come to our main thesis, let us find out in what respects and how far the social gradings in the Sikh village compare with the corresponding hierarchy of the Indian caste system. The very fact that quite a large number of Sudras and outcastes left Hindu ranks and embraced Sikhism during the British period (when there could be no political pressure by the Sikhs) shows that there was a clear advantage in doing so. "Between 1901 and 1911 there were large scale conversions to Sikhism among the *chuhras* and *chamars*. Hinduism lost some 151,806 *chuhras* and 189,103 *chamars* in this period."[76]

Chimba Sikhs, Jhiwar Sikhs and Labana Sikhs (all from exterior castes) had hypergamous relations with their Hindu counterparts,[77] and the practice of this hypergamy was a step for breaking off from the parent castes.[78] Hutton points to the low position of the Dhobis and Chimbas who washed clothes.[79] The fact that a washerman's pursuit brings him into contact with menstrually polluted clothes is enough to make him an outcaste no less than the scavenger who removed night soil or dead bodies.[80] The Sikh Chimbas are not at all treated as out-castes. In another important field, the Sikhs from artisan castes have clearly improved their social position in the villages, because all the Sikhs in the village, except the Mazhabis, interdine.[81] Secondly, the Sikh Jats have hypergamous relations with the lower castes of the village. These are two basic departures from the two 'Constitutive principles' of the Indian caste system. Also, these Sikhs share religious equality with the Jat Sikhs, whether in the village or outside it. The *granthi* in the village gurdwara, from whatever caste drawn, whether Mazhbi or any other, is respected as much as any *granthi* drawn from whatever level of society.

These facts are enough to show that the Sikhs from artisan and menial castes have travelled a long distance away from the corresponding social position of their counterparts in the caste-society.

The real tough problem at the village level is that of Chamar and Mazhabi Sikhs. We do not want to minimise that this problem is the darkest social blot on the Sikh society, but for the sake of our comparative study we have to point out : "No Miasma of touch pollution is attributed to them (i.e. Mazhabi Sikhs drawn from the sweeper caste)."[82] This is a major advance from the position of the Hindu untouchables (among whom Hutton counts *chamar, dhobi, dom* and sweeper castes) in the caste society, where, "Some castes themselves low are especially strict in keeping untouchables at a distance ......"[83] But, the greatest advantage to these castes is that since Sikhism rejects the Hindu system of *Varn Ashram Dharma*, there is no religious prejudice, or bar against their moral, religious or spiritual progress. This is evidenced by the fact that Sudra Saints, whose *bani* (hymns) is in Guru Granth Sahib are as much respected as the Sikh Gurus and a Sudra *granthi* or President of the S.G.P.C. or the *Jathedar* (head) of the Akal Takhat has the same authority and commands the same respect among the Sikhs as any other Sikh *granthi*, President or Jathedar.

"They (Mazhabi Sikhs) sit among others in the temple."[84] On the other hand, we have already mentioned Shankracharya's public declaration that the free entry of Sudras in the premier Hindu temples would lead to the destruction of Hinduism.

"All Sikh Jats, excepting the Mazhabis, interdine."[85] Since I.P. Singh conducted his investigations in 1959, 1961, we have not come across any other scientific sociological field study on this subject, but it is a widely held opinion that the commensal prejudice against the Mazhabi Sikh among the Sikh Jats in the villages has almost disappeared. Secondly, the reluctance of the Sikh Jats to dine with the Mazhabi Sikhs in their own village, although they do so knowingly at the *langars*, appears to be more a question of maintaining their social prestige in the locality, rather than, unlike the caste society, of ritual taboos sanctified by the *Varna Ashrama Dharma*. Thirdly, there is readiness among Jat Sikhs to accept Mazhabi brides.[86] This automatically means preparedness to abrogate commensal barriers with respect to atleast their Mazhabi brides, and this fact further supports the view we have expressed above.

The Ramdasias or the Sikh Chamars "occupy a much higher position than the Hindu Chamar."[87] The workers in leather (Chamars) "are looked upon in detestation by orthodox Hindus" and the sweepers are "regarded as the very dregs of impurity."[88] Marenco points out that the Chamar and Chuhra Sikhs had more literates than the Chamar and Chuhra Hindus;[89] and "the Chuhra Sikhs were more frequent in dropping their traditional occupation than the Chuhra Muslims or the Chuhra Hindus."[90] "The

Chuhra Hindu occupies the lowest place in the social scale. He was avoided by all, and his touch was considered as pollution. When converted to Sikhism, he was still a village menial but he was no longer the remover of night soil. By taking the *Pahul* (baptism), the Chuhra convert might change his standing in the hierarchy."[91]

CONCLUSION

The revolutionary and post-revolutionary phases of a revolution are two differently motivated periods. In the former case, "virtue was the order of the day."[92] Whereas in the latter period what prevails is "self-seeking at the expense of revolutionary idealism."[93] Therefore, these two periods should not be so confused as to judge one in the light of the other.

The anti-caste achievements of the Sikh movement during the period of the Gurus and the Khalsa Dal stand out in bold relief. No Indian movement succeded, to the extent the Sikh revolution did, in making the Khatries, Aroras, Jats, artisans, village menials and the outcastes (Chamars and sweepers), forego their caste hierarchy and merge on equal terms into a genuine brotherhood of the Khalsa; or shared political power with 'the lowest of low in Indian estimation', as was done under Banda; or enabled the Jat (on the border line of Vaisyas and Sudras) to regard his social status as higher than that of the Brahmin and the Rajput; or raised Jats, shepherds, artisans (carpenters) and the despised caste of Kalals to be the rulers of the land. These achievements compare favourably even on the world map, if it is kept in view that the social stigma attached to the Sudras and the outcastes in the Indian society was far worse than that from which the Negroes in the U.S.A. or the slaves suffered elsewhere.

As regards the post-revolutionary period, any assessment of the problem of caste vis-a-vis the Sikhs would remain lopsided unless viewed in the proper perspective. Owing to human failings and environmental hurdles, the progress of human society in terms of its ideological aspirations has been so slow and inperceptible[94] that many sceptics doubt whether there has been any transformation of human motivation at all.[95] Hence, it is the overall contribution, even if small, which a revolutionary movement makes towards humanitarian progress that matters more than its shortcomings. The social discrimination against the Negroes prevailing in the U.S.A. should not blind us to the ennobling spirit of Christianity that opened a new chapter in the political liberation of Negroes there. Though slaves survived in the Muslim world, but one must not on that account overlook one of the greatest egalitarian social revolutions in the history of the world brought about by Islam. For a similar reason, it is no mean achievement of the Sikh Revolution that the Sikh *Panth*, despite all the counter-revolutionary forces at work in the post-revolutionary period, remains cut off from the most rigid social system known to mankind. All other Indian radical movements have reverted, or have remained as appendages, to the caste society, and hence to the caste system.

Secondly, the residuary progress that revolutionary movements leave behind is so impalpable that it is measurable only in comparative terms and not by absolute standards. Whereas the Hindu temples and Maths are the strongholds of the caste ideology and practices, there are no religious, commensal, or other social discriminations at the

Panthic level. At the village level too, the Sikhs drawn from artisan, menial and outcaste categories are decidedly well-placed socially when compared to their counterparts in the caste society. These contrasts are, indeed, significant.

REFERENCES

1. Hagopian, Mark N. : *The Phenomenon of Revolution*, p. 52.
2. Ibid., p. 83.
3. Ibid., p. 81.
4. Ellul, Jacques : *Autopsy of Revolution*, pp. 17-22.
5. Nizami, Khaliq Ahmed : *Some Aspects of Religion and Politics in India during the Thirteenth Century*, p. 15.
6. Ghurye, G.S. : *Caste and Race in India*, pp. 157-159.
7. Hutton, J.H. : *Caste in India*, p. 173.
8. Ibid., p. 139.
9. Ibid., p. 144.
10. Ibid., p. 147.
11. Ibid., p. 147.
12. Ghurye, pp. 57-58, 90-91; Max Weber : *The Religion of India*, p. 60.
13. *The Sikh Revolution*, Chap. V.
14. Max Weber, p. 144.
15. Ibid.
16. Ya'jnik, J.U. : J.R.A.S.B. (1872), pp. 100-12; Phear, I.A. (1875).
17. Bhagavadgita, XVIII, 48.
18. Ibid., IV, 13; Bharatiya Vidya Bhavan : *The History and Culture of the Indian People*, Vol. II, p. 441.
19. Max Weber, p. 28.
20. Ibid., p. 48.
21. Ibid., p. 24.
22. Senart, Emile : *Caste in India*, p. 69.
23. Max Weber, p. 100.
24. Crooke, W. : *E.R.E.*, Vol. 6, p. 695.
25. Max Weber, p. 30; Senart, pp. 18-19.
26. Gait, E.A. : *E.R.E.*, Vol. 3, p. 236.
27. Hutton, p. 99; Gait, *E.R.E.*, Vol. 3, p. 239.
28. Quoted by Hutton, pp. 90-91.
29. Quoted by Senart, p. 71.
30. Max Weber, p. 144; Crooke W. : *E.R.E.*, Vol. 6, p. 712; Bannerji P. : *Journal of Asiastic Society*, Vol. XIX (1953).
31. Macauliffe, Max Arthur : *The Sikh Religion*, i, p. 379.
32. Ibid., p. 310.
33. Bhai Gurdas, *Var One, Pauries*, 23, 25; *Var 23, Pauries*, 19, 20.
34. Bhangu, Rattan Singh : *Prachin Panth Parkash*, pp. 202, 216, 436.
35. *Siyar-ul-Mutakharin*, trans, by John Briggs, p. 73; Haqiqat, *Indian Historical Quarterly*, March 1942, sup. p. 5.
36. Ibbetson, Sir Denzil : *Punjab Castes*, Sec. 512.
37. Max Weber, pp. 18-19.
38. Gait, E.A. : *E.R.E.*, Vol. 3, p. 239; Hutton, p. 121.

39. *Var 23, Pauri* 19.
40. *Dabistan* trans. by Ganda Singh : *The Panjab Past and Present* (1969),   p. 51.
41. Hari Ram Gupta : *History of the Sikh Gurus,* p. 189.
42. Macauliffe, V, pp. 93-94.
43. Koer Singh : *Gurbilas Patshahi Das,* p. 136.
44. (Prahlad Singh), *Rehatnama,* edited by Piara Singh Padam, p. 55.
45. *Rehatnama* (Daya Singh), p. 64.
46. Ibid.
47. *Parakh* (Panjab University, Chandigarh), Vol. 11 (1972).
48. Sukha Singh : *Gurbilas,* p. 133.
49. *Varan* Bhai Gurdas, Var 41.
50. Max Weber, p. 29.
51. Max Weber, p. 36.
52. Koer Singh, p. 90; Bhangu, pp. 50, 58, 104, 236, 244, 262, 268, 368, 469.
53. Irvine, William : *Later Mughals,* pp. 94, 96, 98-99; *Fatuhat Name-i-Sandi,* p. 28; *Asrar-i-Sandi,* trans. in Punjabi, p. 7; *Haqiqat,* p. 6; Khafi Khan, *Eliot & Dowson,* Vol. vii, pp. 419-420; *Haqiqat,* l.H.Q., March 1942, sup., p. 6.
54. Ganda Singh : *Early European Accounts of the Sikhs,* (Folier, 1780), p. 192.
55. Mehma Parkash, II, p. 136; Bhangu, pp. 212, 261, 436, 86, 215.
56. Cited by Gurbax Singh, *Punjab History Conference* (Dec. 1973), Proceedings, pp. 55-56.
57. Hagopian, Mark N : *The Phenomenon of Revolution,* p. 51.
58. Irvine, pp. 98-99.
59. Syed Ghulam Ali Khan : *Imdad Saadat,* p. 71.
60. Brinton, p. 270.
61. Ibbetson, Sir Denzil : *Punjab Castes,* Sec. 437.
62. The terms such as "Jat Sikhs", "Khatri Sikh", "Mazhabi Sikhs", etc. are invalid according to Sikhism, but we are using them for the sake of brevity and should be taken to mean Sikhs drawn from such castes.
63. Brinton, Crane : *The Anatomy of Revolution,* p. 224.
64. *Haqiqat,* l.H.Q. (1942), Sup., p.17.
65. *Tarikh-i-Punjab-i-Sikhan,* pp. 63-64.
66. Marenco, E.K. : *The Transformation of Sikh Society,* p. 140.
67. Max Weber, p. 36.
68. Marenco, E.K. : op. cit., p. 121.
69. Ibid., p. 114.
70. Marenco, p. 172.
71. Hagapian, p. 79.
72. Marenco, pp. 176-77.
73. Ibid., pp. 200-204.
74. Ibid., p. 89.
75. Ketkar, S.V. : *History of the Caste in India,* p. 117.
76. Marenco, p. 256.
77. Ibid., pp. 210, 273.
78. Ibid., p. 273.
79. Hutton, p. 129.
80. Ibid.
81. I.P. Singh, cited by Mandebaum, D.G. : *Society of India,* II, pp. 539-543.
82. Ibid., II, pp.539-543.
83. Bingley, A.H. : *History, Caste and Culture of Jats and Gujars,* p. 102.
84. I.P. Singh, op. cit.
85. I.P. Singh, op. cit., pp. 539-43.

86. Ibid.
87. Ibbetson, p. 300.
88. Crooke, W. : *The North-Western Provinces of India,* etc., p. 206.
89. Marenco, p. 279.
90. Ibid., pp. 285-286.
91. Ibid., p. 130.
92. Brinton, Crane : *The Anatomy of Revolution,* pp. 199, 207.
93. Hagopian, pp. 228-230; Brinton, pp. 233-44.
94. Brinton, pp. 209, 271.
95. Ibid., pp. 290-91.

21

GURU GRANTH SAHIB — GURU ETERNAL FOR SIKHS

HARBANS SINGH

Guru Granth Sahib — some of the variations on the title being Aad Granth, Sri Aad Granth or Aad Sri Guru Granth Sahib — is the religious Scripture of the Sikhs as well as Guru Eternal for them. The basic word in the expressions listed is *granth* meaning a book, *sahib* and *sri* being honorifics, *guru* indicating its status as successor in the guruship after Guru Gobind Singh and *aad,* literally original, first or primary.

Guru Granth Sahib is an anthology of the sacred compositions of the Gurus and of some of the medieval Indian saints. The latter came from a variety of class and creedal background — Hindu as well as Muslim, high-caste as well as low-caste. One criterion for choosing their verses for Guru Granth Sahib apparently was its tone of harmony with the teachings of the Gurus. The anthology was prepared by Guru Arjun, the fifth Guru, in 1603-4. To it were added by Guru Gobind Singh, the tenth Guru, the compositions of Guru Tegh Bahadur, the ninth Guru.

Even before the time of Guru Arjun, *pothis* or books in Gurmukhi characters existed containing the holy utterances of the Gurus. A line in Bhai Gurdas, Var I.32 suggests that Guru Nanak during his travels carried under his arm a book, evidently comprising his own compositions. According to the *Puratan Janamsakhi,* he handed over such a manuscript to Guru Angad as he passed on the spiritual office to him. Two of the collections of hymns, or *pothis* are still extant. They are in the possession of the descendants of Guru Amar Das. One of the families in the line lives at Pinjore and the *pothi* it has inherited is on view for the devotees in their home on the morning of the full moon day every month. A collateral family, which is in possession of the second *pothi,* lives in the village of Darapur in Hoshiarpur district of the Punjab.

The *bani,* or word revealed, was held in great veneration by the Sikhs even before Guru Granth was compiled. It was equated with the Guru himself. "The *bani* is the Guru and the Guru is *bani*," sang Guru Ram Das in Rag Nat Narain. The *bani* echoed the Divine Truth; it was the voice of God — "the Lord's own word", as said Guru Nanak in Guru Granth Sahib. Guru Amar Das says :

Vahu, vahu bani nirankar hai,
  tis jevad avar na koe

Hail Hail, the word of the Guru, which is the Formless Lord Himself,
  There is none other, nothing else to be reckoned equal to it.

The compilation of the Aad Granth, a momentous event in Sikh history, is generally described in the briefest terms. The Sacred Volume was prepared by Guru Arjun (A.D. 1563-1606) and the first copy was calligraphed by Bhai Gurdas (1551-1636) at his dictation — this is all we learn from most of our sources. The amount of planning, minute attention to detail and diligent and meticulous work it involved is slurred over. An old text which gives some detailed information is the *Gurbilas Chhevin Patshahi*. Written in A.D. 1718, this, in fact, is the oldest source. Although it does not go into the technical and literary minutiae, it narrates the entire process from the beginning of the transcription of the Aad Granth to its installation in the newly-built Harimandar at Amritsar.

Why Guru Arjun undertook the task is variously explained. One commonly accepted assumption is that the codification of the Gurus' compositions into an authorized volume was begun by him with a view to preserving them from garbling by schismatic groups and others. According to the *Mahima Prakash* (A.D. 1776), he set to work with the announcement : "As the *Panth* (Community) has been revealed unto the world, so must there be the Granth (Book), too." By accumulating the canon, Guru Arjun wished to affix the seal on the sacred word. It was also to be the perennial fountain of inspiration and the means of self-perpetuation for the community.

Guru Arjun called Bhai Gurdas to his presence and expressed to him the wish that the composition of the Gurus as well as those of some of the saints and sufis be collected. Messages were sent to the disciples to gather and transmit to him the hymns of his predecessors.

To quote the *Gurbilas* again, an attractive spot in the thick of a forest on the outskirts of Amritsar was marked out by Guru Arjun. So dense was the foliage that not even a moonbeam could pry into it. The site was peaceful and picturesque. A tent was hoisted in this idyllic setting. Here Guru Arjun and Bhai Gurdas started work on the sacred volume.

The making of the Granth was no easy task. It involved sustained labour and a rigorous intellectual discipline. Selections had to be made from a vast amount of material. Besides the compositions of the four preceding Gurus and of Guru Arjun, who himself was a poet with a rare spiritual insight, there were songs and hymns by saints, both Hindu and Muslim. What was genuine had to be sifted from what was counterfeit. Then the selected material had to be assigned to appropriate musical measures and transcribed in a minutely laid out order.

Guru Arjun carried out the work with extraordinary exactness. He arranged the hymns in thirty different *ragas,* or musical patterns. A precise method was followed in setting down the compositions. First came *shabads* by the Gurus in the order of their succession. Then came *chhands, vars,* and other poetic forms in a set order. The compositions of the Gurus in each *raga* were followed by those of the *bhaktas* in the same format. Gurmukhi was the script used for the transcription.

According to Bhai Gurdas' testimony, the text had been transcribed by Bhadon Vadi Ekam 1661 B.K. At the head of the index he recorded : *"Sammat 1661 miti bhadon vadi ekam pothi likh pahuche",* i.e., on Bhadon Vadi Ekam 1661 he had reached this spot where the index was to begin after completing the writing of the book. The index, giving the opening words of each *shabad* or hymn and its pagination, is itself a marvel of scholarly fastidiousness. A genius, unique in spiritual intuition and not unconcerned with methodological design, had created a scripture with an exalted mystical tone and a high degree of organization. It was large in size — nearly 7,000 hymns, comprising compositions of the first five Sikh Gurus and fifteen *bhaktas* and *sufis* from different parts of India, including Shaikh Farid, Kabir and Ravidas. The Sacred Volume consisted of 974 leaves, or 1948 pages, 12"x8", with several blank ones at the end of a *raga* when there were not *shabads* enough to fill the section assigned to it. The site of these marvellous labours is now marked by a shrine called Ramsar.

The completion of the Granth Sahib was, says the *Gurbilas,* celebrated with much jubilation. In thanksgiving, *karahprasad* was prepared in huge quantities. Sikhs came in large numbers to see the Aad Granth. They were rejoiced in their hearts by the sight of it and bowed before it in veneration. The Guru enjoined the Sikhs to own the Granth equal with the Guru and make no distinction between the two. "He who wishes to see the Guru, let him see the Granth. He who seeks the Guru's word, let him read the Granth with love and attention."

Guru Arjun asked the Sikhs where the Granth Sahib should be installed. Bhai Budha spoke, "You are omniscient, Master. But there is no place more suitable than the Harimandar." The Guru was happy to hear these words "like one who has sighted the new moon." He then recited the praise of the Harimandar : "There is nothing like it in all the world. Harimandar is like the ship — the means for the people to cross over the worldly ocean triumphantly. A new joy pervades here every day. A sight of it annuls all sins."

It was decided to spend the night at Ramsar and return to Amritsar the next morning. The Granth Sahib rested on a seat under the canopy, whereas the Guru and the Sikhs slept on the ground.

A disciple had to be chosen to take charge of the Granth Sahib. As says the *Gurbilas,* Guru Arjun lay awake through the night reflecting on the question. His choice finally fell on Bhai Budha whose devotion was universally applauded. As they awoke, the Guru and his Sikhs made ablutions in Ramsar. The former thereupon practised his wonted meditation. At dawn, the entire *sangat* marched towards Harimandar. Bhai Budha carried the Aad Granth on his head and Guru Arjun walked behind swinging the *chaur* over it. Musicians sang *shabads.* Thus they reached the Harimandar. The Granth Sahib was ceremonially installed in the centre of the inner sanctuary on Bhadon Sudi 1,

1661 B.K./August 16, 1604. Bhai Budha opened it with reverence to obtain from it the divine command, as Guru Arjun stood in attendance behind. The following hymn was read as God's own pronouncement for the occasion :

He Himself hath succoured his saints in their work,
 He Himself hath come to see their task fulfilled.
 Blessed is the earth, blessed the tank,
 Blessed is the tank with *amrit* filled.
 Amrit overfloweth the tank : He hath had the task completed.
 Eternal is the Perfect Being,
 Vedas and Puranas sing His praise.
 The Creator hath bestowed on me the nine treasures,
 and all the supernatural powers,
 No lack do I suffer now,
 Enjoying His largesse, bliss have I attained,
 Ever-expanding is the Lord's bounty.

Guru Arjun directed that during daytime the Aad Granth should remain in the Harimandar and by night, after the *Sohila* was read, it should be taken to the room he had built for himself in Guru-ka-Mahal. As evening advanced by two watches, Bhai Budha recited *Sohila* and made the concluding *Ardas* or supplication. The Granth Sahib was closed and wrapped in silks. Bhai Budha held it on his head and marched towards the chamber indicated by Guru Arjun. The Guru led the *sangat* singing hymns. The Granth Sahib was placed on the appointed seat, and the Guru slept on the ground by its side. Daily in the small hours of the morning as the stars twinkle in the pool below, the Aad Granth is taken out in state to the Harimandar and brought by night to rest — now, in a room at the Akal Takht. The practice continues to this day. But the volume is not the same. That original copy was taken to Kartarpur, when Guru Arjun's successor, Guru Hargobind, left Amritsar in 1634. There it passed into the possession of his grandson, Dhir Mall. It has since remained in that family.

In the Sikh system, the word *Guru* is used only for the ten prophet-preceptors — Guru Nanak to Guru Gobind Singh, and for none other. Now this office of Guru is fulfilled by Guru Granth Sahib, the Sacred Book, which was so apotheosized by the last Guru, Guru Gobind Singh, before he passed away in 1708. No living person, however holy or revered, can have the title or status of Guru. For Sikhs, Guru is the holy teacher, the prophet under direct commission from God — the ten who have been and Guru Granth Sahib which is their countinuing visible mainfestation.

Guru Gobind Singh created the Khalsa in 1699. In 1708, he supplied another permanent and final feature in the evolution of the Sikh faith when he installed the Aad Granth as Guru. This is how the *Bhatt Vahi Talauda Parganah Jind* describes the event :

Guru Gobind Singh mahall dasman beta Guru Tegh Bahadur ka pota Guru Hargobindji
ka parpota Guru Arjunji ka bans Guru Ram Dasji ki Surajbansi Gosal gotra Sodhi
Khatri basi Anandpur parganah Kahlur muqam Nander tat Godavari des dakkhan
sammat satran sai painsath Kartik mas ki chauth shukla pakkhe budhvar ke dihun

Bhai Daya Singh se bachan hoya Sri Granth Sahib lai ao. bachan pai Daya Singh Sri Granth Sahib lai aya. Guruji ne panch paise narial age bheta rakha matha teka, sarbatt sangat se kaha mera hukam hai meri jagah Sri Granthji ko janana jo Sikh janega tis ki ghal thaen paegi Guru tis ki bahuri karega sat kar manana.

Guru Gobind Singh, the Tenth Master, son of Guru Tegh Bahadur, grandson of Guru Hargobind, great-grandson of Guru Arjun, of the family of Guru Ram Das, Surajbansi Gosal clan, Sodhi Khatri, resident of Anandpur, parganah Kahlur, now at Nanded, on the Godavari bank in the Deccan, asked Bhai Daya Singh, on Wednesday, *Shukla Chauth* of the month of Katik, 1765 B.K. (October 6,1708) to fetch Sri Granth Sahib. The Guru placed before it five pice and a coconut and bowed his head before it. He said to the *sangat*, "It is my commandment : Own Sri Granthji in my place. He who so acknowledges it will obtain his reward. The Guru will rescue him. Know this as the truth."

According to Gaini Garja Singh to whom we owe the discovery of this entry, the author was Narbud Singh Bhatt, who was with Guru Gobind Singh at Nanded at that time.

Bhatt Vahis are a new source of information discovered by Gaini Garja Singh (1904-77), a dogged searcher for materials on Sikh history. The Bhatts were hereditary panegyrists, genealogists or family bards. (A group of them were introduced to Guru Arjun by Bhatt Bhikkha who himself had become a disciple in the time of Guru Amar Das. According to Bhai Gurdas, Var XI. 21, and Bhai Mani Singh, *Sikkhan di Bhagatmala,* he had earlier visited Guru Arjun with the *sangat* of Sultanpur Lodhi). Those of them who came into the Sikh fold composed hymns in honour of the Gurus which were entered in Guru Granth Sahib by Guru Arjun.

These Bhatts also recorded events of the lives of the Gurus and of the members of their families in their scrolls called *vahis.* Some of these *vahis* are preserved to this day in the descendant families, especially at the village of Karsindhu, in Jind district of Haryana. The script in which they are written is called *bhatakshri* — a kind of family code like *lande* and *mahajani.* The only known scholar to have worked with these materials is Giani Garja Singh.

Apart from this new testimony culled by Giani Garja Singh from the Bhatt Vahis, another contemporary document which authenticates the fact of Guru Granth Sahib having been invested with the final authority is a letter issued by reference of Guru Gobind Singh's wife, Mata Sundari. To quote from the original, which is now in the possession of Bhai Chet Singh of the village of Bhai Rupa, in present day Bhatinda district, to whose ancestors it was addressed :

Ikk Oankor Wahguru ji ki fateh. Sri Akalpurkji ka Khalsa yak rang jina ditha Wahguruji chit avai. Bhai Sahib Dan Singhji Bhai Duni Singhji, Bhai Jagat Singhji Bhai Gurbakhsh Singhji, Ugar Singhji, Bhai Ram Singhji, sarbatt Khalsa Wahguru Akal-purkhji ka pase likhtam gulam Khalsa ji ka Kahn Singh, Nival Singh, Mul Singhji, Sujan Singh, Gaja Singh, Mahan Singh sarbatt Khalsa, Wahguru Akalpurkh ka Wahguru ji ki fateh vachani

*khusha karna ki Wahguru Akalpurkhji har dam chit avai sukh hoe Khalse ji
ka bol bala hoi ardas tusadi marfat Bhai Dulcha Singh ke hath pahuti
parhkai Khalsa ji bahut khuswaqat hoiya tusade bab Khalsaji dayal ho kai
hath jore hai jo rakhya hove. "Jo jan harika sevako hari tiske kami," Guru
Granth japna Wahguru ang sang hai fajal karkai rakhia hovegi Khalsaji
Bhai Kahn Singhji kau Mata Sahibji ne gumastgiri Amristar ji ki mukarar
kiti hai Khalsaji ne gurmata karke Harimandir ate bagh die murammat
imarat ka kam shuru kita hai, Sri Mata sahibji ne likha hai ki Wahguru
Akalpurkh ji ke nagari mei langar jarur karna ...... Khalsa Sri Wahguru ji
ka suchet bibek budh chahie jo sivai Akalpurkh duje no janai nahi. Dasam
patshahian tak jamai paihne yarvin barvin Banda Chaubanda Ajita vagaire
te aitkad lai avana hatiya hai. Hor hatiya Guru japan nal dur hosan, par
ih hatyia gunah bakhshiaiga nahi jo manmukh ke jame upar aitkad
Karenge. 'Mukh (mohi) pheriai mukh (mohi) jutha hoi.' Khalsa ji tusan
sivai Akal duje no mannana nahi. Sabad dasvin patshahi tak khojna.
"Shabad khoji ihu gharu lahai Nanak taka dasu." Guru ka nivas shabad
vich hai."Guru mahi ap samoi shabad vartaiya." "Jian andar jiu shabad
hai jit sahu milava hoi." Wahguru ji ki fateh. Bhai Mehar Singh tahlia
Bhai Bule ke pattar ko khasmane vich rahina Guru nal gandh paisi.*

Ikk Oankar Wahiguru ji ki Fateh

The Khalsa, of the Timeless Himself, immersed in the One, and whose sight brings
Wahiguru to mind. Addressed to Bhai Sahib Dan Singhji, Bhai Duni Singhji, Bhai
Jagat Singhji, Bhai Gurbaksh Singhji, Ugar Singhji, Bhai Ram Singhji, the entire
Khalsa of Wahiguru, the Timeless One. From the slaves of the Khalsaji, Kahn
Singhji, Nival Singhji, Mul Singhji, Sujan Singh, Gaja Singh, Maha Singh,
Wahiguruji Ki Fateh to the entire Khalsa. May you be rejoiced in constant
remembrance of the Timeless Wahiguru. May prosperity prevail; may supremacy
belong to the Khalsa. Having received your missive through Bhai Dulcha Singh,
Khalsaji is highly pleased. Khalsaji happily prays with folded hands for your security.
"He who to the Lord surrenders himself, his affairs the Lord will set right." Repeat
always the name of the Guru. Wahiguru is by your side. He will extend to you His
grace and protection. Khalsaji, Mata Sahibji has appointed Bhai Kahn Singhji to the
superintendence of Amritsarji. The Khalsaji, through a *gurmatta,* has taken in hand
the construction and repair of the Harimandar and the garden. Sri Mata Sahibji has
written that *langar* must be run in that place which is the abode of God Himself ......
Wahiguru's Khalsa must always be alert, possessed of discriminating wisdom. The
Khalsa must believe in none other than the Timeless One. There have been only Ten
Masters in human form; to believe in the eleventh and twelfth, Banda (Banda Singh
Bahadur), Ajita (Ajit Singh, adopted son of Mata Sundariji), etc. is a mortal sin.
Every other sin can be forgiven by repeating the Guru's name, but this sin of believing
in human form will not be pardoned. "The faces turned away from the Guru are faces
perverted." Khalsaji, you must believe in none other except the Timeless One. Go

only to the Ten Gurus in search of the Word. "Nanak is the slave of him who by seeking the Lord's Name obtains his goal." The Guru resides in *shabad*. "The Lord hath merged His own Self in the Guru through whom He hath revealed His Word." "The Word is the life of all life, for, through it, one experiences God." Victory to the Lord. Bhai Mehar Singh, the messenger, son of Bhai Bula; keep the letter secure in your custody. You will gain the Guru's favour.

From this letter it is clear how the Sikhs after Guru Gobind Singh believed that the guruship had passed to the *shabad*, i.e., the Word as contained in Guru Granth Sahib. None in the human form after the ten Gurus was to be acknowledged by the Sikhs as Guru. Those who, like some of Banda Singh's or Ajit Singh's followers, called their leaders gurus were committing a mortal sin. All their sins, says the letter, could be forgiven by repeating the Guru's name, but not the sin of believing in a living Guru after the Ten Masters of the Sikh faith.

Several other old Sikh documents also attest the fact of succession having been passed on by Guru Gobind Singh to Guru Granth Sahib. For instance, the *Rahitnama* by Bhai Nand Lal, one of Guru Gobind Singh's disciples remembered to this day for his Persian poetry in honour of the Gurus. In his *Rahitnama,* or code of conduct, Bhai Nand Lal, who was at Nanded in the camp of Emperor Bahadur Shah as one of his ministers at the time of Guru Gobind Singh's passing away, thus records his last words in his Punjabi verse :

He who would wish to see the Guru,
Let him come and see the Granth.
He who would wish to speak with him,
Let him read and reflect upon what says the Granth.
He who would wish to hear his word,
He should with all his heart read the Granth,
    or listen to the Granth being read.

Another of Guru Gobind Singh's disciples and associates, Bhai Prahlad Singh, records in his *Rahitnama* the Guru's commandment :

By the word of the Timeless One,
Has the Khalsa been manifested.
This is my commandment for all of my Sikhs :
Thou shalt acknowledge Granth as the Guru.

In *Gurbilas Patshahi* 10 (author Koer Singh; the year of writing 1751), Guru Gobind Singh is quoted as saying :

This is no more the age for a personal Guru to be anointed.
I shall not place the mark on anyone's forehead
All *sangat* is owned as Khalsa now, under the shelter of the Almighty Himself,
They are now to the Word attached.
He who believes is the Sikh par excellence.
On Guru Granth should he put his reliance,
To none else should he direct his adoration.

All his wishes the Guru will bring to fulfilment
This he should believe,
Casting away all dubiety.

Another authority that may relevantly be quoted is Devaraja Sharma's *Nanaka candrodaya mahakavyam,* an old Sanskrit manuscript which has recently been published by Sanskrit University, Varanasi. It records Guru Gobind Singh's proclamation that the Scripture would be the Guru after him. "While the Master lay on his deathbed, Nand Lal (?) came forward and asked the following question : 'Who shall be our teacher now ? Whom shall we salute and see, and what shall be the object of our discourses ?' The Master replied, 'The Granth, which itself is the doctrine of the Guru, shall be your teacher. This is what you should see; this is what you should honour; this is what should be the object of your discourses'." The original, in Sanskrit, reads as follows :

Nandalalas tadaprchat ko asmakam adhuna guruh kam namena ch pasyema kasmai varta vadema ca uce gurutu yusmakam grantha eva gururmatah tam nameta ca pasyeta tasmai varta vedeta ca.

Nanaka chndrodaya mahakavyam, XXI, 227-229

This point has been laboured somewhat lengthily for the reason that objections are sometimes raised. Certain cults among Sikhs still owning personal gurus ask for authentic evidence to the effect that Guru Gobind Singh had named Guru Granth Sahib his successor. No archival testimony can be presented, unless the Bhatt Vahi entry be included in that category. But, evidence bequeathed through tradition, written as well as oral, supports this fact. This is what has come down through Sikh memory. Had there been the 11th Guru, the name could not have been effaced from the pages of history. Guru Gobind Singh brought to an end the line of personal Gurus and declared the Holy Granth Guru after him.

Along with Guru Granth Sahib, the Khalsa was now the visible person of the Guru. The word *khalsa* is derived from the Arabic *khalis*, meaning pure or pious. Guru Gobind Singh used the term in its symbolic and technical sense. In official terminology, *khalsa* in Mughal days meant lands or territory directly under the king. Crown-land was known as *khalsa* land. As says a contemporary poet, Bhai Gurdas II, Guru Gobind Singh converted the *sangat* into the Khalsa. Sikhs were the Guru's Khalsa, i.e., directly his own, without any intermediary or local *sangat* leader. On that point, we have the evidence of *Sri Gur Sobha* by Sainapat, a contemporary of Guru Gobind Singh, and Guru Gobind Singh's own *hukamnamas.* To quote from the former :

A day preceding the event (i.e. passing of Guru Gobind Singh),
The Sikhs gathered together,
And began to ask :
"What body will the Lord now take ?"
The Guru at that moment spoke :
"In the Khalsa wilt thou see me;
With the Khalsa is my sole concern :
My physical form have I bestowed upon the Khalsa."

Guru Gobind Singh, in his *hukamnama* issued on Phagun 4, 1765 B.K./February 1,1700, to the *sangat* of Pattan Farid, modern Pakpattan, refers to the *sangat* as "his own Khalsa." *Hukamnamas* are letters written by the Gurus to *sangats* in different parts of the country. Some of them have been traced in recent years and two collections were published in 1967 — one by Dr Ganda Singh (Punjabi University, Patiala) and the second by Shamsher Singh Ashok (Shiromani Gurdwara Parbandhak Committee, Amritsar). Most of the *hukamnamas* are common to both anthologies. These *hukamnamas* are another valuable source of information on the lives of the Gurus and on the Sikh communities living in far-flung places.

That Guru Granth Sahib is Guru Eternal has been the understanding and conviction of the Sikh community since the passing away of Guru Gobind Singh. In their hard, exilic days soon afterwards, when they were outlawed and had to seek the safety of the hills and jungles, the Sikhs' most precious possesssion which they cherished and defended at the cost of their lives was the Guru Granth Sahib. Guru Granth Sahib was their sole religious reference, and they acknowledged none other. In the time of Maharaja Ranjit Singh, who established sovereignty in the name of the Khalsa, personal piety and court ceremonial centred upon Guru Granth Sahib. As contemporary records testify, Ranjit Singh began his day by making obeisance to Guru Granth Sahib. On festive occasions, he made pilgrimage to Amritsar to bow before Guru Granth Sahib in the Harimandar. For the Sikhs in general, Guru Granth Sahib was the only focus of religious attachment. None other existed, either in human form or symbolically. In all Sikh literature after Guru Gobind Singh, the Holy Book is uniformly referred to as Guru Granth.

The personal guruship was ended by Guru Gobind Singh himself. Succession passed to Guru Granth Sahib in perpetuity. This was a most significant development in the history of the community. The finality of the Holy Book was a fact rich in religious and social implications. Guru Granth Sahib became Guru and received divine honours. It was acknowledged as the revelation descended through the Gurus. It was for the Sikhs the perpetual authority, spiritual as well as historical. They lived their religion in response to it. Through it, they were able to follow their faith more fully and more vividly. It was central to all that subsequently happened in Sikh life. It was the source of their verbal tradition and it shaped their intellectual and cultural environment. It moulded the Sikh concept of life. From it the community's ideals, institutions and rituals derived their meaning. Its role in guaranteeing the community's integration and permanence, and in determining the course of its history, has been crucial.

The Word enshrined in Guru Granth was always revered by the Gurus as well as by their disciples as of Divine origin. The Guru was the revealer of the Word. One day the Word was to take the place of the Guru. The line of personal Gurus could not have continued for ever. The inevitable came to pass when Guru Gobind Singh declared Guru Granth Sahib to be his successor. It was only through the Word that the Guruship could be made everlasting. This object Guru Gobind Singh intuitively secured when he pronounced Guru Granth Sahib to be Guru after him. Guru Granth Sahib was henceforth

— for all time — the Guru of the Sikhs.

Since the day Guru Gobind Singh vested succession in it, Guru Granth Sahib has commanded the same honour and reverence as would be due to the Guru himself. It is the focal point of Sikhs' devotion. The object of veneration in Sikh *gurdwaras* is the Guru Granth Sahib. *Gurdwara* is in fact that place of worship wherein the Guru Granth is seated. No images or idols are permitted inside a *gurdwara*. The Holy Volume is opened ceremonially in the early hours of the morning after *ardas* or supplication. It must be enthroned, draped in silk or other pieces of clean cloth, on a high seat on a pedestal under a canopy. The congregation takes place in the presence of the Guru Granth Sahib, with the officiant, who could be anyone from among those present, sitting in attendance, with a *chavar* or whisk in his hand which he keeps swinging over it in veneration. The singing of hymns by a group of musicians will go on. All the time devotees keep coming and bow low to the ground before Guru Granth Sahib to pay homage and take their seats on the ground. The officiant or any other learned person, who will take his place behind Guru Granth Sahib, will read out a hymn and expound it for the audience. At the end of the service, the audience will stand up in the presence of Guru Granth Sahib with hands folded in front in reverence and one of them leading the *Ardas* or prayer. At the end of the evening service Guru Granth Sahib will be closed, again after a short prayer, and put to rest for the night. Guru Granth Sahib is similarly kept in some Sikh homes, where a separate room is set apart for it. It is opened in the morning and put to rest in the evening in the same style and manner. Before starting the day's work, men and women will go into the room where Guru Granth Sahib has been ceremonially installed, say a prayer in front of it and open the book at random and read the first hymn which meets the eye to obtain what is called *vak* or the day's lesson or order (*hukam*). Breviaries contain stipulated *banis* from Guru Granth Sahib which constitute the daily offices and prayers of a Sikh.

An old custom which is coming more and more into vogue is that of *akhand path* or uninterrupted recital of Guru Granth Sahib from beginning to end. Such a recital must be completed within 48 hours. The entire Guru Granth Sahib, 1430 large pages, is read through in a continuous ceremony. This reading must go on day and night, without a moment's intermission. The relay of reciters who take turns at reading the Scripture must ensure that no break occurs. As they change places at given intervals, one picks the line from his predecessor's lips and continues. When and how the custom of reciting the canon in its entirety, in one continuous service began, is not known. Conjecture traces it to the turbulent days of the 18th century when persecutions scattered the Sikhs to far-off places. In those exilic, uncertain times, the practice of accomplishing a reading of Guru Granth Sahib by continuous recital is believed to have originated.

Important days on the Sikh calendar are marked by *akhand paths* in *gurdwaras*. Celebrations and ceremonies in Sikh families centre around *akhand paths*. The homes are filled with holiness for those two days and nights as the Guru Granth Sahib, installed with due ceremony in a room especially decorated for the occasion, is being recited. Apart from lending the air of sanctity, such readings make available to listeners the entire text. The listeners come as they wish and depart at their will. Thus they keep picking up snatches of the *bani* from different portions at different times. Without such ceremonial recitals, Guru Granth Sahib, a very large volume, would remain generally inaccessible to the laity except for *banis* which are recited by Sikhs as part of their daily devotion. In bereavement, families derive comfort from these *paths*. Obsequies in fact conclude with a completed reading of Guru Granth Sahib and prayers are offered in its presence at the end for the departed soul.

There are variations on *akhand path* as well. A common one is the *saptahik path* wherein the recital of the text is taken in parts and completed within one week. A *sahj* or slow-reading *path* may continue for a longer time, even for months. At such *paths* Guru Granth Sahib is recited or intoned, not merely read. This brings out tellingly the poetic quality of the *bani* and its power to move or grip the listener. But it must be listened to in silence, sitting on the floor in front of it in a reverent posture.

The *bani* of Guru Granth Sahib is all in the spiritual key. It is poetry of pure devotion, lyrical and moral. Guru Granth Sahib is the basis of Sikh practice as well as of Sikh devotion. It is the living source of authority, the ultimate guide for the spiritual and moral path pointed out by the Gurus. Whatever is in harmony with its tenor will be acceptable; whatever not, is rejected. Guidance is sought from it on doctrine, or the tenets of the faith.

The Sikh *Panth* as a whole will resort to Guru Granth Sahib as will the individuals in moments of perplexity or crisis. Instance comes to mind of the early days of the gurdwara movement aiming to reform the ritual in Sikh places of worship. On October 12, 1920, a meeting of Sikh backward castes, sponsored by the faculty and students of the Khalsa College at Amritsar, was held in the Jallianwala Bagh. The following morning some of them were taken to the Golden Tample, but the *granthis* in control refused to accept *karahprashad* or sacrament they had brought as an offering and to say the *Ardas* on their behalf. There was an outburst of protest against this discrimination towards the socalled low-caste Sikhs, totally contrary to the Sikh teaching. A compromise was at last reached, and it was decided that the Guru's direction be sought. The Guru Granth Sahib was, as is the custom, opened at random and the first verse on the page to be read was :

> He receives the lowly into grace,
> And puts them in the path of righteous service.

The Guru's verdict was clearly in favour of those whom the *granthis* had refused to accept as full members of the community. This was a triumph for reformist Sikhs. The *karahprasad* brought was accepted and distributed among the *sangat*.

Singly or in groups, in their homes or in congregations in their places of worship, Sikhs conclude their morning and evening prayer, or prayer said at any other time as part of personal piety or of a ceremony, with a supplication called *Ardas*. *Ardas* is followed by the recitation of these verses :

> *Agya bhaei Akal ki tabhi chalayo Panth,*
> *Sabh sikkhan kau hukm hai Guru manio Granth.*

Guru granth ji maniyo pragat Guran ki dehi
Jo Prabhu ko milibo chahai khoj shabad main lehi.

By the command of the Timeless Creator, was the *Panth* promulgated!

All Sikhs are hereby charged to own the Granth as their Guru.

Know the Guru Granth to be the person visible of the Gurus.

They who would seek to meet the Lord,

In the Word as manifested in the Granth shall they discover Him.

This is the status, the significance of Guru Granth Sahib in the Sikh way of life.

IV

SIKH HISTORY

22

THE GURUS LIVE THEIR IDEOLOGY[1]

DALJEET SINGH

By the very nature of our psyche we can take only a partial, relative and selective view of things and events. That is a human frailty. There will, therefore, always be differences in the interpretation of various hymns in Guru Granth Sahib and the system they lay down. But the best way to reduce and eliminate these differences and to clarify the issues is to make a close study of the lives of the Gurus. Evidently their lives are the best interpretation of their hymns. They are the true index to the kind of life they recommend. Conversely, no study of their lives can be fruitful, and no conclusions about them valid, unless seen in the light of their hymns. The right interpretation of the system embodied in Guru Granth Sahib is the one illustrated and exemplified by the lives of the Gurus themselves, since their words and deeds match each other.

From the hymns in Guru Granth Sahib we have drawn some conclusions on various issues, like, their world-view, the reality of the physical world, the goal of man, the ideal life, the role and ethics of the mystic, especially concerning social and political problems, freedom and necessity. The lives of the Gurus will clarify and testify whether the inferences drawn by us about their ideology are cogent and correct. That is why we are separately studying their lives in order to understand and interpret their views on different aspects of their religion.

We do not propose to write a detailed account of the lives of the Gurus, nor shall we try to evaluate their contribution to history. That is beyond the scope of our study. Our object is to state only those activities which elucidate and illustrate the Sikh ideology. Secondly, we shall, for obvious reasons, accept facts, views and sources that are authentic. Evidently, contemporary and near contemporary views have a weight of their own. In addition, they furnish a reliable evidence of the image the Gurus left about their views on the contemporary society and on those who came into contact with them.

GURU NANAK (1469-1539)*

Guru Nanak was born in 1469 in Talwandi, a village in the Sheikhupura district, 65 kms. west of Lahore. His father was a village official in the local revenue administration. As a boy, Guru Nanak learnt, besides the regional languages, Persian and Arabic. He was married in 1487 and was blessed with two sons, one in 1491 and the second in 1496. In 1485 he took up, at the instance of his brother-in-law, the appointment of an official in charge of the stores of Daulat Khan Lodhi, the Muslim ruler of the area at Sultanpur. It is there that he came into contact with Mardana, a low caste (*Mirasi*) Muslim minstrel who was ten years senior in age.

By all accounts, 1496 was the year of his enlightenment when he started on his mission. His first statement after his prophetic communion with God was "There is no Hindu, nor any Mussalman." This is an announcement of supreme significance. It declared not only the brotherhood of man and the fatherhood of God, but also his clear and primary interest not in any metaphysical doctrine but only in man and his fate. It means love your neighbour as yourself. In addition, it emphasised, simultaneously, the inalienable spirituo-moral combination of his message. Accompanied by Mardana, he began his missionary tours. Apart from conveying his message and rendering help to the weak, he forcefully preached, both by precept and practice, against caste distinctions, ritualism, idol worship and the pseudo-religious beliefs that had no spiritual content. He chose to mix with all. He dined and lived with men of the lowest castes and classes. Considering the then prevailing cultural practices and traditions, this was something socially and religiously unheard of in those days of rigid Hindu caste system sanctioned by the scriptures and the religiously approved notions of untouchability and pollution. It is a matter of great significance that at the very beginning of his mission, the Guru's first companion was a low caste Muslim. The offerings he received during his tours, were distributed among the poor. Any surplus collected was given to his hosts to maintain a common kitchen, where all could sit and eat together without any distinction of caste and status. This institution of common kitchen or *langar* became a major instrument of helping the poor, and a nucleus for religious gatherings of his society and of establishing the basic equality of all castes, classes and sexes.

Despite the hazards of travel in those times, he performed five long tours all over the country and even outside it. He visited most of the known religious places and centres of worship. At one time he preferred to dine at the place of a low caste artisan, Bhai Lallo, instead of accepting the invitation of a high caste rich landlord, Malik Bhago, because the latter lived by exploitation of the poor and the former earned his bread by the sweat of his brow. This incident has been depicted by a symbolic representation of the reason for his preference. Guru Nanak pressed in one hand the coarse loaf of bread from Lallo's hut and in the other the food from Bhago's house. Milk gushed forth from the loaf of Lallo's and blood from the delicacies of Bhago. This prescription for honest work and living and the condemnation of exploitation, coupled with the Guru's dictum that "riches cannot be gathered without sin and evil means," have, from the very beginning,

---

* The years noted against the name of each Guru relate only to the period of his Guruship.

continued to be the basic moral tenet with the Sikh mystics and the Sikh society.

During his tours, he visited numerous places of Hindu and Muslim worship. He explained and exposed through his preachings the incongruities and fruitlessness of ritualistic and ascetic practices. At Hardwar, when he found people throwing Ganges water towards the sun in the east as oblations to their ancestors in heaven, he started, as a measure of correction, throwing the water towards the West, in the direction of his fields in the Punjab. When ridiculed about his folly, he replied, "If Ganges water will reach your ancestors in heaven, why should the water I throw up not reach my fields in the Punjab, which are far less distant ?"

He spent twentyfive years of his life preaching from place to place. Many of his hymns were composed during this period. They represent answers to the major religious and social problems of the day and cogent responses to the situations and incidents that he came across. Some of the hymns convey dialogues with Yogis in the Punjab and elsewhere. He denounced their methods of living and their religious views. During these tours he studied other religious systems like Hinduism, Jainism, Buddhism and Islam. At the same time, he preached the doctrines of his new religion and mission at the places and centres he visited.

Since his mystic system almost completely reversed the trends, principles and practices of the then prevailing religions, he criticised and rejected virtually all the old beliefs, rituals and harmful practices existing in the country. This explains the necessity of his long and arduous tours and the variety and profusion of his hymns on all the religious, social, political and theological issues, practices and institutions of his period.

Finally, on the completion of his tours, he settled as a peasant farmer at Kartarpur, a village in the Punjab. Bhai Gurdas, the scribe of Guru Granth Sahib, was a devout and close associate of the third and the three subsequent Gurus. He was born 12 years after Guru Nanak's death and joined the Sikh mission in his very boyhood. He became the chief missionary agent of the Gurus. Because of his intimate knowledge of the Sikh society and his being a near contemporary of Guru Nanak, his writings are historically authentic and reliable. He writes that at Kartarpur Guru Nanak donned the robes of a peasant and continued his ministry. He organised Sikh societies at places he visited with their meeting places called *Dharamsalas*. A similar society was created at Kartarpur. In the morning, *Japji* was sung in the congregation. In the evening *Sodar* and *Arti* were recited. The Guru cultivated his lands and also continued with his mission and preachings. His followers throughout the country were known as *Nanak-panthies* or Sikhs. The places where Sikh congregation and religious gatherings of his followers were held were called *Dharamsalas*. These were also the places for feeding the poor. Eventually, every Sikh home became a *Dharamsala*.

One thing is very evident. Guru Nanak had a distinct sense of his prophethood and that his mission was God-ordained. During his preachings, he himself announced. "O Lallo, as the words of the Lord come to me, so do I express them." Successors of Guru Nanak have also made similar statements indicating that they were the messengers of God. So often Guru Nanak refers to God as his Enlightener and Teacher. His statements clearly show his belief that God had commanded him to preach an entirely new religion, the central idea of which was the brotherhood of man and the fatherhood of God, shorn of all ritualism and priestcraft. During a dialogue with the Yogis, he stated that his mission was to help everyone. He came to be called a Guru in his lifetime. In Punjabi, the word Guru means both God and an enlightener or a prophet. During his life, his disciples were formed and came to be recognised as a separate community. He was accepted as a new religious prophet. His followers adopted a separate way of greeting each other with the words *Sat Kartar* (God is true). Twentyfive years of his extensive preparatory tours and preachings across the length and breadth of the country clearly show his deep conviction that the people needed a new prophetic message which God had commanded him to deliver. He chose his successor and in his own life time established him as the future Guru or enlightener of the new community. This step is of the greatest significance, showing Guru Nanak's determination and declaration that the mission which he had started and the community he had created were distinct and should be continued, promoted and developed. By the formal ceremony of appointing his successor and by giving him a new name, Angad (his part or limb), he laid down the clear principle of impersonality, unity and indivisibility of Guruship. At that time he addressed Angad by saying, "Between thou and me there is now no difference." In Guru Granth Sahib there is clear acceptance and proclamation of this identity of personality in the hymns of *Satta-Balwand*. This unity of spiritual personality of all the Gurus has a theological and mystic implication. It is also endorsed by the fact that each of the subsequent Gurus calls himself Nanak in his hymns. Never do they call themselves by their own names as was done by other *Bhagats* and mystics. That Guru Nanak attached the highest importance to his mission is also evident from his selection of the successor by a system of test, and only when he was found perfect,[2] was Guru Angad appointed as his successor. He was comparatively a new comer to the fold, and yet he was chosen in preference to the Guru's own son, Sri Chand, who also had the reputation of being a pious person, and Baba Budha, a devout Sikh of long standing, who during his own lifetime had the distinction of ceremonially installing all subsequent Gurus.

All these facts indicate that Guru Nanak had a clear plan and vision that his mission was to be continued as an independent and distinct spiritual system on the lines laid down by him, and that, in the context of the country, there was a clear need for the organisation of such a spiritual mission and society. In his own lifetime, he distinctly determined its direction and laid the foundations of some of the new religious institutions. In addition, he created the basis for the extension and organisation of his community and religion.

The above in brief is the story of the Guru's life. We shall now note the chief features of his work, how they arose from his message and how he proceeded to develop them during his lifetime.

(1) After his enlightenment, the first words of Guru Nanak declared the brotherhood of man. This principle formed the foundation of his new spiritual gospel. It involved a fundamental doctrinal change because moral life received the sole spiritual

recognition and status. This was something entirely opposed to the religious systems in vogue in the country during the time of the Guru. All those systems were, by and large, other-worldly. As against it, the Guru by his new message brought God on earth. For the first time in the country, he made a declaration that God was deeply involved and interested in the affairs of man and the world which was real and worth living in. Having taken the first step by the proclamation of his radical message, his obvious concern was to adopt further measures to implement the same.

(2)   The Guru realised that in the context and climate of the country, especially because of the then existing religious systems and the prevailing prejudices, there would be resistance to his message, which, in view of his very thesis, he wanted to convey to all.   He, therefore, refused to remain at Sultanpur and preach his gospel from there. Having declared the sanctity of life, his second major step was in the planning and organisation of institutions that would spread his message. As such, his twentyfive years of extensive touring can be understood only as a major organisational step. These tours were not casual. They had a triple object. He wanted to acquaint himself with all the centres and organisations of the prevalent religious systems so as to assess the forces his mission had to contend with, and to find out the institutions that he could use in the aid of his own system. Secondly, he wanted to convey his gospel at the very centres of the old systems and point out the futile and harmful nature of their methods and practices. It is for this purpose that he visited Hardwar, Kurukshetra, Banaras, Kanshi, Gaya, Ceylon, Baghdad, Mecca, etc. Simultaneously, he desired to organise all his followers and set up for them local centres for their gatherings and worship. The existence of some of these far-flung centres even up-till today is a testimony to his initiative in the organisational and the societal field. His hymns became the sole guide and the scripture for his flock and were sung at the *Dharamsalas*.

(3)   Guru Nanak's gospel was for all men. He proclaimed their equality in all respects. In his system, the householder's life became the primary forum of religious activity. Human life was not a burden but a privilege. His was not a concession to the laity. In fact, the normal life became the medium of spiritual training and expression. The entire discipline and institutions of the Gurus can be appreciated only if one understands that, by the very logic of Guru Nanak's system, the householder's life became essential for the seeker. On reaching Kartarpur after his tours, the Guru sent for the members of his family and lived there with them for the remaining eighteen years of his life. For the same reason his followers all over the country were not recluses. They were ordinary men, living at their own homes and pursuing their normal vocations. The Guru's system involved morning and evening prayers. Congregational gatherings of the local followers were also held at their respective *Dharamsalas*.

(4)   After he returned to Kartarpur, Guru Nanak did not rest. He straightaway took up work as a cultivator of land, without interrupting his discourses and morning and evening prayers. It is very significant that throughout the later eighteen years of his mission he continued to work as a peasant. It was a total involvement in the moral and productive life of the community. His life was a model for others to follow. Like him all

his disciples were regular workers who had not given up their normal vocations. Even while he was performing the important duties of organising a new religion, he never shirked the full-time duties of a small cultivator. By his personal example he showed that the leading of a normal man's working life was fundamental to his spiritual system. Even a seemingly small departure from this basic tenet would have been misunderstood and misconstrued both by his own followers and others. In the Guru's system, idleness became a vice and engagement in productive and constructive work a virtue. It was Guru Nanak who chastised ascetics as idlers and condemned their practice of begging for food at the doors of the householders.

(5) Another important aspect of the moral life which the Guru emphasised was the sharing of one's income. He said, "property could be gathered only by vice." It obviously meant that while doing productive work and earning one's livelihood were moral, the amassing of wealth was evil. In this context, he introduced the new practice of sharing one's income. We have already quoted his dictum that "he knows the way who works hard and shares his earnings with others." He insisted that his disciples should share their income with others and divert it for common purposes. Every Sikh home, as enjoined by him, became a centre for helping the weak and the poor. Here, too, the Guru gave a personal lead. During his tours, whatever he received was given to feed the poor and finance the common kitchen. Similarly, at Kartarpur he created the institution of a free common kitchen (*langar*) and started the practice of everyone eating at one place (*pangat*).

(6) According to the Guru, moral life was the sole medium of spiritual progress. In those times, caste, religious and social distinctions, and the idea of pollution were major problems. Unfortunately, these distinctions had received religious sanction. The problem of poverty and food was another moral challenge. The institution of *langar* had a twin purpose. As every one sat and ate at the same place and shared the same food, it cut at the root of the evil of caste, class and religious distinctions. Besides, it demolished the idea of pollution of food by the mere presence of an untouchable. Secondly, it provided food to the needy. This institution of *langar* and *pangat* was started by the Guru among all his followers wherever they had been organised. It became an integral part of the moral life of the Sikhs. Considering that a large number of his followers were of low caste and poor members of society, he, from the very start, made it clear that persons who wanted to maintain caste and class distinctions had no place in his system. In fact, the twin duties of sharing one's income with the poor and doing away with social distinctions were the two obligations which every Sikh had to discharge. On this score, he left no option to anyone, since he started his mission with Mardana, a low caste Muslim, as his life long companion.

(7) The greatest departure Guru Nanak made was to prescribe for the religious man the responsibility of confronting evil and oppression. It was he who said that God destroys 'the evil doers' and 'the demonical'; and that such being God's nature and will, it is man's goal to carry out that will. Since there are evil doers in life, it is the spiritual duty of the seeker and his society to resist evil and injustice. Again, it is Guru Nanak

who protests and complains that Babur had been committing tyranny against the weak and the innocent. Having laid the principle and the doctrine, it was again he who proceeded to organise a society. Because political and societal oppression cannot be resisted by individuals, the same can be confronted only by a committed society. It was, therefore, he who proceeded to create a society and appointed a successor with the clear instructions to develop his *Panth*. Again, it was Guru Nanak who emphasised that life is a game of love, and once on that path one should not shirk laying down one's life. Love of one's brother or neighbour also implies, if love is true, his or her protection from attack, injustice and tyranny. Hence, the necessity of creating a religious society that can discharge this spiritual obligation. This is the rationale of Guru Nanak's system and the development of the Sikh society which he organised.

(8) The Guru expressed all his teachings in Punjabi, the spoken language of Northern India. It was a clear indication of his desire not to address the elite alone but the masses as well. It is recorded that the Sikhs had no regard for Sanskrit, which was the sole scriptural language of the Hindus. Both these facts lead to important inferences. They reiterate that the Guru's message was for all. It was not for the few who, because of their personal aptitude, should feel drawn to a life of a so-called spiritual meditation and contemplation. Nor was it an exclusive spiritual system divorced from the normal life. In addition, it stressed that the Guru's message was entirely new and was completely embodied in his hymns. His disciples used his hymns as their sole guide for all their moral, religious and spiritual purposes. Thirdly, the disregard of the Sikhs for Sanskrit strongly suggests that not only was the Guru's message independent and self-contained, without reference and resort to the Sanskrit scriptures and literature, but also that the Guru made a deliberate attempt to cut off his disciples completely from all the traditional sources and the priestly class. Otherwise, the old concepts, ritualistic practices, modes of worship and orthodox religions were bound to affect adversely the growth of his religion which had wholly a different basis and direction and demanded an entirely new approach.

The following hymn from Guru Nanak and the subsequent one from Sankara are contrast in their approach to the world.

"The sun and moon, O Lord, are Thy lamps; the firmament Thy salver; the orbs of the stars the pearls encased in it.

The perfume of the sandal is Thine incense, the wind is Thy fan, all the forests are Thy flowers, O Lord of light.

What worship is this, O Thou Destroyer of birth ? Unbeaten strains of ecstasy are the trumpets of Thy worship.

Thou has a thousand eyes and yet not one eye; Thou hast a thousand forms and yet not one form;

Thou hast a thousand stainless feet and yet not one foot; Thou hast a thousand organs of smell and yet not one organ. I am fascinated by this play of Thine.

The light which is in everything is Thine, O Lord of light.

From its brilliancy everything is illuminated;

By the Guru's teaching the light becometh manifest.

What pleaseth Thee is the real worship.

O God, my mind is fascinated with Thy lotus feet as the *bumble-bee* with the flower; night and day I thirst for them.

Give the water of Thy favour to the *Sarang* (bird) Nanak, so that he may dwell in Thy Name."[3]

Sankara writes : "I am not a combination of the five perishable elements. I am neither body, the senses, nor what is in the body (*antar-anga* : i.e., the mind). I am not the ego-function : I am not the group of the vital breathforces; I am not intuitive intelligence (*buddhi*). Far from wife and son am I, far from land and wealth and other notions of that kind. I am the Witness, the Eternal, the Inner Self, the Blissful One (*sivo-ham;* suggesting also, 'I am Siva')."

"Owing to ignorance of the rope the rope appears to be a snake; owing to ignorance of the Self the transient state arises of the individualized, limited, phenomenal aspect of the Self. The rope becomes a rope when the false impression disappears because of the statement of some credible person; because of the statement of my teacher I am not an individual life-monad (*jivo-naham*), I am the Blissful One (*sivo-ham*)."

"I am not the born; how can there be either birth or death for me ?"

"I am not the vital air; how can there be either hunger or thirst for me ?"

"I am not the mind, the organ of thought and feeling; how can there be either sorrow or delusion for me ?"

"I am not the doer; how can there be either bondage or release for me ?"

"I am neither male nor female, nor am I sexless. I am the Peaceful One, whose form is self-effulgent, powerful radiance. I am neither a child, a young man, nor an ancient; nor am I of any caste. I do not belong to one of the four life-stages. I am the Blessed-Peaceful One, who is the only Cause of the origin and dissolution of the world."[4]

While Guru Nanak is bewitched by the beauty of His creation and sees in the panorama of nature a lovely scene of the worshipful adoration of the Lord, Sankara in his hymn rejects the reality of the world and treats himself as the Sole Reality. Zimmer feels that "Such holy megalomania goes past the bounds of sense. With Sankara, the grandeur of the supreme human experience becomes intellectualised and reveals its inhuman sterility."[5]

No wonder that Guru Nanak found the traditional religions and concepts as of no use for his purpose. He calculatedly tried to wean away his people from them. For Guru Nanak, religion did not consist in a "patched coat or besmearing oneself with ashes"[6] but in treating all as equals. For him the service of man is supreme and that alone wins a place in God's heart.

By this time it should be easy to discern that all the eight features of the Guru's system are integrally connected. In fact, one flows from the other and all follow from the basic tenet of his spiritual system, viz., the fatherhood of God and the brotherhood of man. For Guru Nanak, life and human beings became the sole field of his work. Thus arose the spiritual necessity of a normal life and work and the identity of moral and spiritual functioning and growth.

Having accepted the primacy of moral life and its spiritual validity, the Guru proceeded to identify the chief moral problems of his time. These were caste and class distinctions, the institutions, of property and wealth, and poverty and scarcity of food. Immoral institutions could be substituted and replaced only by the setting up of rival institutions. Guru Nanak believed that while it is essential to elevate man internally, it is equally necessary to uplift the fallen and the downtrodden in actual life. Because, the ultimate test of one's spiritual progress is the kind of moral life one leads in the social field. The Guru not only accepted the necessity of affecting change in the environment, but also endeavoured to build new institutions. We shall find that these eight basic principles of the spirituo-moral life enunciated by Guru Nanak, were strictly carried out by his successors. As envisaged by the first prophet, his successors further extended the structure and organised the institutions of which the foundations had been laid by Guru Nanak. Though we shall consider these points while dealing with the lives of the other nine Gurus, some of them need to be mentioned here.

The primacy of the householder's life was maintained. Everyone of the Gurus, excepting Guru Harkishan who died at an early age, was a married person who maintained a family. When Guru Nanak, sent Guru Angad from Kartarpur to Khadur Sahib to start his mission there, he advised him to send for the members of his family and live a normal life. According to Bhalla,[8] when Guru Nanak went to visit Guru Angad at Khadur Sahib, he found him living a life of withdrawal and meditation. Guru Nanak directed him to be active as he had to fulfill his mission and organise a community inspired by his religious principles.

Work in life, both for earning the livelihood and serving the common good, continued to be the fundamental tenet of Sikhism. There is a clear record that everyone upto the Fifth Guru (and probably subsequent Gurus too) earned his livelihood by a separate vocation and contributed his surplus to the institution of *langar.* Each Sikh was made to accept his social responsibility. So much so that Guru Angad and finally Guru Amar Das clearly ordered that *Udasis*, persons living a celibate and ascetic life without any productive vocation, should remain excluded from the Sikh fold. As against it, any worker or a householder without distinction of class or caste could become a Sikh. This indicates how these two principles were deemed fundamental to the mystic system of Guru Nanak. It was defined and laid down that in Sikhism a normal productive and moral life could alone be the basis of spiritual progress. Here, by the very rationale of the mystic path, no one who was not following a normal life could be fruitfully included.

The organisation of moral life and institutions, of which the foundations had been laid by Guru Nanak, came to be the chief concern of the other Gurus. We refer to the socio-political martyrdoms of two of the Gurus and the organisation of the military struggle by the Sixth Guru and his successors. Here it would be pertinent to mention Bhai Gurdas's narration of Guru Nanak's encounter and dialogue with the Nath Yogis who were living an ascetic life of retreat in the remote hills. They asked Guru Nanak how the world below in the plains was faring. "How could it be well", replied Guru Nanak, "when the so-called pious men had resorted to the seclusion of the hills ?" The Naths commented that it was incongruous and self-contradictory for Guru Nanak to be a householder and also pretend to lead a spiritual life. That, they said, was like putting acid in milk and thereby destroying its purity. The Guru replied emphatically that the Naths were ignorant of even the basic elements of spiritual life.[9] This authentic record of the dialouge reveals the then prevailing religious thought in the country. It points to the clear and deliberate break the Guru made from the traditional system.

While Guru Nanak was catholic in his criticism of other religions, he was unsparing where he felt it necessary to clarify an issue or to keep his flock away from a wrong practice or prejudice. He categorically attacked all the evil institutions of his time including oppression and barbarity in the political field, corruption among the officials and hypocrisy and greed in the priestly class. He deprecated the degrading practices of inequality in the social field. He criticised and repudiated the scriptures that sanctioned such practices. After having denounced all of them, he took tangible steps to create a society that accepted the religious responsibility of eliminating these evils from the new institutions created by him and of attacking the evil practices and institutions in the social and political fields. This was a fundamental institutional change with the largest dimensions and implications for the future of the community and the country. The very fact that originally poorer classes were attracted to the Gurus, fold shows that they found there a society and a place where they could breathe freely and live with a sense of equality and dignity.

Dr H.R. Gupta, the well-known historian, writes, "Nanak's religion consisted in the love of God, love of man and love of godly living. His religion was above the limits of caste, creed and country. He gave his love to all, Hindus, Muslims, Indians and foreigners alike. His religion was a people's movement based on modern conceptions of secularism and socialism, a common brotherhood of all human beings. Like Rousseau, Nanak felt 250 years earlier that it was the common people who made up the human race. They had always toiled and tussled for princes, priests and politicians. What did not concern the common people was hardly worth considering. Nanak's work to begin with assumed the form of an agrarian movement. His teachings were purely in Punjabi language mostly spoken by cultivators. They appealed to the downtrodden and the oppressed peasants and petty traders as they were ground down between the two mill stones of Government tyranny and the new Muslims' brutality. Nanak's faith was simple and sublime. It was the life lived. His religion was not a system of philosophy like Hinduism. It was a discipline, a way of life, a force, which connected one Sikh with another as well as with the Guru."[10] "In Nanak's time Indian society was based on caste and was divided into countless watertight compartments. Men were considered high and low on account of their birth and not according to their deeds. Equality of human beings was a dream. There was no spirit of national unity except feelings of community fellowship. In Nanak's views men's love of God was the criterion to judge whether a person was good or bad, high or low. As the caste system was not based on divine love, he condemned it. Nanak aimed at creating a casteless and classless society similar to the modern type of socialist society in which all were equal and where one member did not exploit the other. Nanak insisted that every Sikh house should serve as a place of love and devotion, a true guest house (*Sach dharamshala*). Every Sikh was enjoined to welcome a traveller or a needy person and to share his meals and other comforts with him."[11] "Guru Nanak aimed at uplifting the individual as well as building a nation."[12]

Considering the religious conditions and the philosophies of the time and the social and political *milieu* in which Guru Nanak was born, the new spirituo-moral thesis he introduced and the changes he brought about in the social and spiritual field were indeed radical and revolutionary. Earlier, release from the bondage of the world was sought as the goal. The householder's life was considered an impediment and an entanglement to be avoided by seclusion, monasticism, celibacy, *sanyasa or vanprastha*. In contrast, in the Guru's system the world became the arena of spiritual endeavour. A normal life and moral and righteous deeds became the fundamental means of spiritual progress, since these alone were approved by God. Man was free to choose between the good and the bad and shape his own future by choosing virtue and fighting evil. All this gave "new hope, new faith, new life and new expectations to the depressed, dejected and downcast people of Punjab."[13]

Guru Nanak's religious concepts and system were entirely opposed to those of the traditional religions in the country. His views were different even from those of the saints of the Radical Bhakti movement. From the very beginning of his mission, he started implementing his doctrines and creating institutions for their practice and development. In his time the religious energy and zeal were flowing away from the empirical world into the desert of otherworldliness, asceticism and renunciation. It was Guru Nanak's mission and achievement not only to dam that Amazon of moral and spiritual energy but also to divert it into the world so as to enrich the moral, social the political life of man. We wonder if, in the context of his times, anything could be more astounding and miraculous. The task was undertaken with a faith, confidence and determination which could only be prophetic.

It is indeed the emphatic manifestation of his spiritual system into the moral formations and institutions that created a casteless society of people who mixed freely, worked and earned righteously, contributed some of their income to the common causes and the *langar*. It was this community, with all kinds of its shackles broken and a new freedom gained, that bound its members with a new sense of cohesion, enabling it to rise triumphant even though subjected to the severest of political and military persecutions.

The life of Guru Nanak shows that the only interpretation of his thesis and doctrines could be the one which we have accepted. He expressed his doctrines through the medium of activities. He himself laid the firm foundations of institutions and trends which flowered and fructified later on. As we do not find a trace of those ideas and institutions in the religious milieu of his time or the religious history of the country, the entirely original and new character of his spiritual system could have only been mystically and prophetically inspired.

Apart from the continuation, consolidation and expansion of Guru Nanak's mission, the account that follows seeks to present the major contributions made by the remaining Gurus.

NANAK II (1539-1552)

Guru Angad invented the present form of the Gurmukhi script. It became the medium of writing the Punjabi language in which the hymns of the Gurus are expressed. This step had a far-reaching purpose and impact. First, it gave the people who spoke this language an identity of their own, enabling them to express their thought directly and without any difficulty or transliteration. The measure had the effect of establishing the independence of the mission and the followers of the Guru. Secondly, it helped the community to dissociate itself from the Sanskrit religous tradition so that the growth and development of the Sikhs could take place unhampered and unprejudiced by the backlog of the earlier religious and social philosophies and practices. This measure, as shown by the subsequent growth of Sikhism, was essential in order to secure its unhindered development and progress as it required an entirely different approach to life.

Dr Gupta feels that this step, to a certain extent, kept the upper classes among Hindus, to which the Guru belonged, away from Sikhism, partly because they were steeped in the old religious and Brahminical tradition and partly because the Sanskrit tradition fed their ego by giving them a superior caste status to that of the other castes. But, the idea of equality of man was fundamental to the Sikh spiritual system. The Guru knew that its association with traditional religious literature would tend to water it down. The matter is extremely important from the point of view of the historical growth and study. Actually, the students of Sikh history know that over the centuries the influence of these old traditions has been very much in evidence. It has sometimes even given a wrong twist to the new thesis and its growth. The educated persons were almost entirely drawn from the upper castes and classes. They had a vested interest, visible also in their writings, in introducing ideas and practices which helped in maintaining their privileges and prejudices of caste superiority, even though such customs were opposed to the fundamentals about the equality of man laid down by the Gurus. For example, the Jats, who were themselves drawn from classes branded as low by the Brahminical system, started exhibiting caste prejudices *vis-a-vis* the lower castes drawn from the Hindu fold.

Earlier, the Punjabi language was written in the *Landa* or *Mahajani* script. This had no vowel sounds, which had to be imagined or construed by the reader in order to decipher the writing. Therefore, there was the need of a script which could faithfully reproduce the hymns of the Gurus so that the true meaning and message of the Gurus could not be misconstrued and misinterpreted by each reader to suit his own purpose and prejudices. The devising of the Gurmukhi script was an essential step in order to maintain the purity of the doctrine and exclude all possibility of misunderstanding and misconstruction by interested persons.

The institution of *langar* was maintained and developed. The Guru's wife personally worked in the kitchen. She also served food to the members of the community and the visitors. Her devotion to this institution finds mention in Guru

Granth Sahib.[14]

The Guru earned his own living by twisting coarse grass into strings used for cots. All offerings went to the common fund. This demonstrates that it is necessary and honourable to do even the meanest productive work. It also emphasises that parasitical living is not in consonance with the mystic and moral path. In line with Guru Nanak's teaching, the Guru also declared that there was no place for passive recluses in the community.

Like Guru Nanak, Guru Angad and the subsequent Gurus selected and appointed their successors by completely satisfying themselves about their mystic fitness and capacity to discharge the responsibilities of the mission.

NANAK III (1552-1574)

Guru Amar Das, though born in 1479, became the Guru in 1552 when he was in his seventies. All the same he took many significant steps. He established new centres for conveying to the people the message of Guru Nanak. Twentytwo such centres were created in different areas where persons, approved by the Guru, performed extension work. They administered both to the religious and the temporal needs of the disciples; for, in the Guru's system legitimate temporal needs were included in the religious needs. They collected offerings from the disciples and sent them to the Guru for the common use of the community. The Guru himself earned his living as a small tradesman.

He started the system of holding two annual gatherings of his disciples from all over the country. At his headquarters, he undertook the construction of a *baoli* (a well with a perennial source of spring water). For the Sikhs the headquarters of the Guru and this *baoli* became a holy place of pilgrimage.

Guru Angad had collected the hymns of Guru Nanak. To these Guru Amar Das added the hymns of the former as well as his own.

As an anti-caste and anti-pollution measure, he made it incumbent that no one, irrespective of his status or caste, could see him unless he had first partaken, along with others, of the food cooked at the common kitchen. Emperor Akbar had also to dine at the *langar* before he met the Guru.

In his time, ascetics and recluses again made an attempt to enter the Guru's flock. But the Guru issued a final injunction that no recluse or ascetic could be a Sikh. He also denounced the system of *sati* and of *purdah* among women.

According to the Guru, the human body was the temple of God. He, therefore, laid emphasis on keeping it healthy and sound to the end. For the same reason, he denounced the ascetic practices of torturing the body. The Guru felt that the health of the body could not be divorced from moral and spiritual well-being.

NANAK IV (1574-1581)

Guru Ram Das was Guru for a short period. After obtaining land for the purpose, he founded the town of Amritsar which continues to be the centre of Sikhism till today. He dug a tank which became the principal place of pilgrimage. Traders and artisans were invited to settle at the town so that its growth could be rapid. In due course it became the largest commercial centre in northern India. It was a landmark in the life of the community, because the Guru established a central place that was quite distinct from that of the Hindus and the Muslims. Since then Amritsar is for the Sikhs what Mecca is for the Muslims. All this indicates that the Guru had a distinct sense of his mission and did everything to establish it as a separate religious system and entity.

NANAK V (1581-1606)

Guru Arjun's multifarious activities, apart from making a very major contribution to the organisation of the mission, demonstrate, as laid down by Guru Nanak, that no field of life, whether temporal, social or political, is excluded for the operation of a mystic. Slowly but surely the movement came out with a distinct identity of its own and with clear-cut religious and socio-political facets.

The system of voluntary offerings for the common cause and the sharing of one's earnings was made regular. Every Sikh was supposed to contribute 10% of his income to the common fund maintained by the Guru. The representatives of the Guru collected contributions from their respective areas and sent them to the common treasury.

The construction of the temple at Amritsar was started by the Guru and its foundation stone was laid by the reputed Muslim Sufi Saint, Mian Mir. He built another tank and temple at Taran Taran. These temples had doors on all sides, indicating that these were open to all castes and communities.

The Guru had a well-organised central establishment which included the maintenance of a contingent of horses and elephants. He encouraged his followers to trade in horses from Central Asia. For his personal maintenance, the Guru also took up the trade. As such, the Sikhs became good horsemen and formed later the nucleus of military power. All these features were important developments because they were clear preparation for the military organisation that was to follow from the time of the Sixth Guru. It was in the lifetime of Guru Arjun that his son, Hargobind, started learning to wield the sword and hunting.[15]

In 1598, the Guru interceded on behalf of the local peasantry with Emperor Akbar to get the excessive levy of land revenue reduced. These activities of the Guru gave him a new status. It was at this time that the Guru came to be called by the Sikhs as *Sacha Patshah* (True Emperor). The Guru had come to guide, govern and influence the lives of the Sikhs both in the temporal and the spiritual fields. It was a significant development. The organisation of the community, according to Gupta, became a state within a state.[16]

An important step in the separate consolidation of the religion was the compilation of the *Adi Granth* as the sole and authentic scripture of the Sikhs. It has a significant feature. Besides the hymns of the five Gurus, it contains the hymns of Hindu and Muslim saints. The *Adi Granth* was formally installed at the Amritsar temple on the annual gathering of the Sikhs. From the very start it was recognized as the Sikh scripture. Emperor Akbar made an offering of 51 gold coins to the *Adi Granth*. Its installation at the only Sikh temple constructed then by the Guru and the appointment of the most venerated Sikh as its *Granthi* (minister) show that it was meant to be the exclusive scripture of the Sikhs and the embodiment of the Gurus' system and thought. In this way conjectures about links with the other systems or scriptures were set at rest for ever. This is an important step, especially when we find that in Guru Granth Sahib no status or sanctity has been given to any gods, goddesses or *avatars*.

This compilation is a landmark in the history of Sikhism. It is a clear testimony of the fact that the Guru took this vital step to emphasise that their message and mission were prophetic. This fact comes out in all its glaring singularity when we see that, in the entire religious history of man, no other prophet felt it essential to authenticate his message so as to secure its purity and exclude the possibility of interpolation and misinterpretation. In fact, in most cases the utterances of the prophets were compiled by their devotees long after their ministry. This authentication of the scripture by the Guru himself once and for all ensured its separate identity and purity. In the case of other prophets, their opponents can say that the prophets themselves never meant to declare any new truths, but their overzealous followers made it into a separate system not intended by the prophets. Nothing of that kind can be asserted about the Gurus and Guru Granth Sahib.

It is something very extraordinary that, in line with Guru Nanak's hymn that 'with the help of other God-conscious beings he would help every one to be a God-centered person', the Guru included in the *Adi Granth* hymns of twentytwo Muslim and Hindu saints. It is a singular example of the Guru's sense of personal anonymity. He truly felt that in accomplishing this task he was working only as an agent of God's mission. We also find that contemporary saints like Mian Mir and Pir Budhu Shah, irrespective of religion and race, remained closely associated with the mission of the Gurus.

Owing to the growing religious and political influence of the Gurus, the Sikhs had got a clear consciousness of their religious and socio-political identity. Consequently, the position of the Gurus had naturally given rise to hostility, both in the religious and political quarters. Saikh Ahmad, the head of the *Naqashbandi* order at Sirhind and a leader of the revivalist movement of Islam in India, got upset at the influence of the Guru among men of both the communities. He had access to the court of Jahangir. But, probably the chief reason that upset the Emperor was that the Guru had blessed Khusro and helped him monetarily while the latter had rebelled against Jahangir. The local administration was naturally aware of the growing socio-political strength and influence of the Guru. That this incident rankled in the mind of Emperor Jahangir, is evident from his own statement recorded in his autobiography. He wrote that he had ordered the execution by torture of Guru Arjun unless he embraced Islam, because the Guru had raised aloft the standard of holiness and many Hindus and Muslims had foolishly become his followers.

The Guru was ordered to be executed. In addition a fine of Rupees two lakhs was imposed on him. Some historians say that, as a measure of clemency at the intervention of Mian Mir, this fine was imposed in lieu of the sentence of death. The Sikhs offered to pay the fine themselves but the Guru forbade them to do so. He replied to the Emperor, "Whatever money I have is for the poor, the friendless and the stranger. If thou ask for money thou mayest take what I have; but if thou ask for it by way of fine, I shall not give thee even a *Kauri* (penny)."[17] The Guru accepted death by torture and suffered the first great martyrdom. His sacrifice further steeled the faith of the community in the mission of the Gurus. Gupta, who considers the views of all other historians as relevant material, concludes that it was principally a political execution.

A ruling administration never takes notice of a religious institution, unless it has a political complexion and potential. The Mughal emperors never bothered about any saint of the Bhakti school. The Sikh movement was growing into a clear socio-political body, fired with a religious and moral zeal. It constituted a disciplined people who were being guided and led towards their ideals by a prophetic mystic. It was this socio-political growth which no ruler or administration could fail to take note of as a potential danger and challenge to its existence and rule. It is evident that the Sikh growth was of such dimensions that it attracted the attention of the administration and also of the Emperor. In addition it is a political fact that the Guru, as recoded by Beni Prasad (the historian on Jahangir), had given a very substantial aid of Rs. 5,000/- to Khusro, leading a rebel army and claimant to the throne. Further, this organisation was of such size and importance that the Emperor not only took the extreme step of the execution of Guru Arjun, so as to stop altogether this unwanted growth (as recorded by the Emperor), but also found the movement and the episode as significant enough for mention in his autobiography. Jahangir was undoubtedly right that the organisation and the movement posed a political threat to the Empire. But he was mistaken in his belief that by the execution of the Guru he had nipped this growth in the bud. In this background and the context of future developments, it would surely be naive for anyone to say either that Jahangir, by this execution of Guru Arjun, converted a simple, peaceful and innocuous movement into a military organisation, or that the reaction of the Sixth Guru to his father's execution was overzealous, especially when we know that by the very nature of the Gurus' thesis, socio-political developments and activities were an integral part of their spiritual life. The Fifth and the Sixth Gurus had done nothing beyond the extension and development of the foundations laid and the organisation built by Guru Nanak.

Gupta calls Guru Arjun "an original thinker, an illustrious poet, a practical philosopher, a great organiser, an eminent statesman and the first martyr of the faith. He completely changed the external aspect of Sikhism."[18]

NANAK VI (1606 -1644)

While in prison, before his execution at Lahore, Guru Arjun had sent a message to his son, Guru Hargobind, then aged only eleven, that he should henceforth maintain an army. At the very time of his installation as Guru, he insisted that he should wear two swords, one representing his spiritual leadership and the other his temporal and political leadership. Soon after it, he constructed in front of the Amritsar temple, another building called the Akal Takht (God's throne) as the seat of temporal power. This place continues to the present day as the centre of every socio-political deliberation and power of the community. There, like the two swords he wore, he raised aloft two flags representing the two aspects of his activities. He told his followers, "My rosary shall be my sword-belt and on my turban I shall wear the emblem of royalty."[19] The Sikhs were already engaged in the trade of horses and the Guru advised every Sikh to keep a sword and maintain a horse, wherever possible. He started recruiting a regular army. He had a personal bodyguard of 57 horsemen and kept 700 horses, 60 gunmen and 500 infantry men. Thus a state within a state, started and developed by the earlier Gurus, was consolidated by him. When this news reached the Emperor, he demanded from the Guru the fine imposed on his father. The Guru was imprisoned in the Gwalior fort along with other political prisoners of high status. Later he was released.

There is an important incident which brings out the religious policy of the Gurus. One Ram Das, a Maharashtra saint, met Guru Hargobind. He questioned him as to how he reconciled his being a successor to the spiritual seat of Guru Nanak with his living as a soldier, maintaining an army and calling himself a true Emperor. The Guru replied that Guru Nanak had given up mammon (greed for money). He had not renounced the world, and that the sword was for the double purpose of protecting the poor and destroying the tyrant.[20] These words of the Guru most clearly bring out the religious and spiritual philosophy of Sikh mysticism, its originality and its break with the past. Persons brought up in the tradition of old beliefs and ideas of dichotomy between the religious and the temporal life find it difficult to understand and grasp the significance of the Gurus' system. The problem of comprehension that confronted saint Ram Das was the same as arose with the Nath Yogis in their dialogue with Guru Nanak. It arises even now with some of our present-day academicians. But, for the Sikh mystic, participation in life is spiritually essential. Consequently, the defence of moral life, reaction and responses to challenges from the environment form an integral part of the Gurus' mystic system. The reply of Guru Hargobind is an unambiguous clarification of the system of Guru Nanak as understood by the Gurus themselves. This also explains the various empirical steps taken by the first five Gurus in order to develop their religious system and organise the Sikhs in the way they did. Saint Ram Das's meeting with the Guru had a great historical consequence, for he was so impressed by the Guru's thesis that he later trained Shivaji, the great Maratha leader, in the same manner.[21]

Guru Hargobind sponsored the cause of the downtrodden Hindus and provided leadership to the oppressed people of Punjab. In this struggle, he fought six battles with the Mughals in the plains of the Punjab. People came to him and joined his forces because they felt that no one else had the power to stand against the Emperor. In one of these battles he defeated 7,000 Mughal soldiers. Finally, he settled at Kiratpur. His reputation as a military leader spread and ambassadors of the hill Rajas waited upon him.

The organisation of the Sikhs into a separate socio-religious group with political implications had started from the time of the very first Guru. This close and integral combination of the temporal and the spiritual life was a thesis which was foreign to the Indian tradition. No wonder that some of the people around the Sixth Guru, including his own followers, could not understand the spiritual character of these military developments. This explains two points. First, that the transformation of the community into a spirituo-political organisation could only be gradual, because the Gurus had to carry the people with them. Unfortunately, they had all been conditioned by the old traditions. The full understanding and acceptance of the new thesis could only be slow.

The Gurus, naturally, had to wait till their followers fully realised the implications of the new doctrine and owned its responsibilities. Secondly, it also confirms the view that the object was to organise a mission and a movement in the empirical world and not merely to deliver a message and embody it in a scripture or a mythical tale. The scriptural thesis had to be lived among the people and not in the seclusion of a monastery for the training of a few. The aim was to uplift everyone irrespective of caste and creed and to show that each one, howsoever placed, could tread the spiritual path. This choice was open to everyone and the Guru was there to organise and lead the movement. Hence, the progress could only be gradual both in the education of the people and in the pace of the movement. The latter could not outstrip the former. The task was stupendous. For, it had to take place in the face of the understandable opposition of one of the greatest empires of all times.

One incident is very significant of the socio-political climate in the Guru's camp. During a hunt being carried out by the Imperial party in a jungle, the Sikhs also entered the same area in pursuit of game. The Sikhs got hold of a falcon, which was claimed by the official party. A clash took place and the Imperial forces were beaten off. But, what is important is the approval of the Sikhs who stressed, "you are talking of the return of the *baz* (falcon), we are after your *taj* (crown)." It clearly shows the independence of political status claimed by the Guru and his Sikhs.

The number and areas of sub-centres of preachings were extended. The Guru himself controlled both the religious centres and the temporal centre at Amritsar. The Guru, thereby, only brought out visibly and symbolically what, in view of the steps that had already been taken by the earlier Gurus, was inherent in the integrated spiritual thesis of Guru Nanak. In fact secure and clear foundations had already been laid by him. While the Gurus, and those engaged in these developments, were fully aware of their responsibility to maintain the original spiritual purity of the religion and the entire movement, to some outsiders, including historians conditioned and committed to different doctrines and systems of religion and polity, the Sixth Guru's work has seemed to show a departure from the original growth. But, a departure, as we have seen, it was not.

NANAK VII (1644-1661)

Guru Har Rai continued to maintain regular soldiers and military preparations. It was a masterly stroke of Guru Hargobind that he built a viable military organisation under the very eye of the Mughal rulers and without serious intervention by them to throttle the rising movement. Finding that the battle of succession was about to begin, Dara Shikoh met Guru Har Rai. But, later Dara was defeated by Aurangzeb and he moved towards Lahore. At Rupar, Guru Har Rai met him again with his troops, but Dara was in no mood to offer resistance and renew the fight with Aurangzeb. This incident, as Khusro's incident in the case of Jahangir, was, it seems, never forgotten by Aurangzeb. After ascending the throne, he called Guru Har Rai to Delhi. The Guru sent his son Ram Rai to represent him. Ram Rai, perhaps, in deference to his host, while reciting a couplet from Guru Granth Sahib misquoted one word of the text. This apparent display of fear was reported by the Delhi Sikhs to the Guru. He was very unhappy about it. He not only disowned him but directed him not to appear before him at all. This event is of considerable importance. The Guru knew that he was preparing his people for a moral and military struggle with the Empire. In this battle any doubt or fear in the mind of a soldier for the cause of the mission would have been a disastrous handicap. It was fear from the minds of the people that the Gurus were trying to eradicate. They had to be taught to react boldly against every wrong or injustice, whatever be the authority which should inflict it. This new conditioning was essential for the health and strength of the community the Gurus were trying to build. The subsequent history of the struggle shows that they succeeded to a large extent. Hence, the drastic action by the Guru against his own son at the latter's seeming display of fear.

NANAK VIII (1661-1664)

Guru Harkishan as head of the faith led the Sikhs only for three years. As soon as Aurangzeb found time, he sent for Guru Harkishan to Delhi and Raja Jai Singh was sent to escort him. But before the meeting at Delhi could take place, he fell ill and died.

NANAK IX (1664-1675)

After Guru Arjun, all the Gurus maintained regular military forces and equipment. Guru Tegh Bahadur himself had fought and distinguished himself in the battles against the Mughal forces.

Aurangzeb followed a policy of religious persecution. He imposed a tax on the Hindus and demolished and defiled their temples and religious places. Persecution was more severe in Kashmir and thousands were forcibly converted to Islam.

The Guru toured the Punjab and exhorted the people to live courageously and fearlessly. He helped them in their vocations. During this time, a deputation of Kashmiri Pandits came to the Guru and complained to him of their sad plight and the threat of their being forcibly converted to Islam. The Guru considered the matter. The crucial issue of human and religious freedom was at stake and had to be faced. The Guru finally advised them to convey to the ruler that if Guru Tegh Bahadur were converted to Islam, they would follow suit. Naturally, all this was conveyed to the Emperor. The Emperor asked the Guru to desist from political involvements and keep to religious pursuits only, and that if he did so, he could also be given official grants.[22] It is very significant to note that had the Guru's thesis and intentions admitted of this bifurcation, he would have readily obliged the Emperor. But he did not do so. Later, the Guru was arrested and taken to Delhi. Under the orders of the Emperor, he was asked to embrace Islam. He naturally refused. He was put in an iron cage and asked to show a miracle. His companions were hacked to pieces or executed in his presence. The only miracle he showed was that he tied a piece of paper round his neck when he was ordered to be executed. The paper was found to contain the words that he laid his head but had not forsaken his freedom and his mission.[23] The Guru invited martydom to uphold the freedom of religion and the dignity of man. This generated a wave of resentment and set the hearts of the people in the country ablaze with anger. It emboldened every honest man to be ready to face with determination the oppression that had been launched against the people. A great challenge had been posed to the religious movement started by Guru Nanak. After the martyrdom of Guru Arjun, followed the military activities of the Sixth Guru. Now, the second crucial stage had been reached for taking yet another major step. The organisation had been built and the military preparations made. A community bound in a common faith and cohesive social ideas and ideals had been formed. The people as a whole had suffered acutely under oppressive bigotry. Though helpless themselves, they were eagerly looking forward to one who should espouse their cause and relieve them of their continuing anguish and suffering. At that time, Guru Tegh Bahadur voluntarily came forward to suffer one of the greatest martyrdoms of history. He stood for man. He invited execution in order to awaken the spirit of the people and the moral and spiritual consciousness of man. So far as his own people were concerned, the leader's obvious object was, by his own example, to prepare and steel his men for the moral and grim struggle ahead, and enthuse them to make sacrifices for the cause of the faith and man. The Guru by his supreme sacrifice gave a glorious lead.

NANAK X (1675-1708)

In the life of Sikhism and the Sikh community, the period of Guru Gobind Singh is the most crucial one. Momentous decisions had to be made and steps taken concerning the religion. In addition, the community faced serious challenges from the Empire which had become openly hostile to the Sikhs. All these problems had to be solved and measures taken to secure the progress of the mission. Because of the extreme complexity of the situation, there is, among historians ignorant of the ideology of the Gurus, a general lack of understanding of the issues involved, their implications and the solutions devised. In order to have a proper appreciation of the events and the role of the Tenth Guru, it is necessary for us to have a rapid look at the system developed by the Gurus.

Guru Nanak believes that *haumain* corrupts and destroys both the personal and the social life of man. The only remedy for it is the path of God. He envisages a two-fold moral or spiritual progress. One is the establishment of the kingdom of God. This involves the creation of a society where all are treated alike. Second is the constitutional conversion of man into superman. He works for the fulfilment of a free and creative society so as to eliminate aggression and encroachments on the freedom of man. In the Gurus' system, tyranny is an evil, but it is no smaller evil to suffer tyranny and not to stand up against it. This two-fold progress of man has to take place side by side, both aspects being inalienably linked with each other. It is, in fact, a single integrated development. One could neither become God-conscious, nor be tested as such outside the main stream of life. It is the Gurus' way of living a total life. A Sikh was being moulded as a complete man. That was his training and ideal of life. His orientation was not for being a mere worshipper of the deity, nor for seeking personal salvation. His living embraced all phases of life, moral, socio-political and spiritual.

This ideal explains why Guru Nanak is so profuse in condemning evils in all aspects of life, religious, social and political. He stressed and commended the spiritual necessity of work, production and the sharing of one's earnings with the needy, and, what was most important, of treating all men and women as equal in every respect. Further, he felt that the evils should not only be resisted and eliminated, but, simultaneously, the society should be so reorganised that these do not re-appear and grow again. He started the establishment of a community wedded to new spirituo-moral ideals. He himself laid the foundations of these four-fold developments and new organisations. Such institutions take time to come into shape and develop because they are contrary to the instinctive and egoistic urges of man.

Guru Nanak had laid down a mystic thesis in which moral life in the world had the highest priority. His ethical system clearly envisaged the use of force and the change of the environment in order to serve righteous cause. He organised all over the country a separate community of people. In short, he had accepted and implemented the principle of environmental, organisational and institutional changes in order to gain moral ends in all fields of life. A real sense of equality between man and man was created among his followers.

It is important to bear this context in mind. For, it enables us to understand the two pronged development of Guru Nanak's religion. On the one hand, he created a new society with new aims and objectives. On the other hand, he tried to remove the ills of the environmental situation to the extent his new society could tackle them. The goal was the same, but the problem could be solved only by this two-directional approach. Obnoxious socio-political institutions could be fought out and eliminated only by a community or society wedded to new ideals. Major environmental changes cannot be brought about by individuals alone. The organisation of a separate community was essential for the Gurus' task of reorganising the socio-political structure of the society. The Sikhs were not a sect of any religion. They were a people with an entirely new way of life. Their social outlook and views had changed radically. The Sikh response to the military challenges from the rulers was not a temporary expedient, nor a way devised to meet any ephemeral, local or historical situation. It was a total way of life for which the Gurus had prepared them.

The Gurus continued to build and organise a classless and casteless society based on the principles laid down by Guru Nanak. The object was first to organise such a society and then to employ it for socio-political purposes. Later, along with the necessary training and orientation for moral and spiritual progress, environmental and social issues were also taken up for solution. As soon as the social base and standing of the community became consolidated, the Fifth Guru began to grapple with the socio-political problems. This involved confrontation with the Empire. From then on the Gurus started military preparations for the purpose.

There were two distinct issues before Guru Gobind Singh. The foremost issue was the final organisation and consolidation of his people into a well-knit and self-governing religious community so that it could shoulder the responsibilities of the mission. The second issue related to the impending struggle against the Empire. With the vision of a prophetic mystic, the Guru assessed the situation and took steps for the solution of both the problems.

The Guru had a distinct sense of his mission. He wrote, "For this purpose I came into the world; God sent me for the sake of *dharam* (righteousness); wherever you are, spread *dharam*; root out the oppressors and the wicked." God's own words were conveyed by him like this : "I have cherished you as my son, I have created you to preach righteousness; wherever you are promote righteousness; restrain the people from evil deeds." Again he said, "For this purpose I was born, bear this in mind all ye saints; to propagate *dharam*, to protect saints, to annihilate the tyrants."[24]

The Guru continued the development of his religious organisation. He created, among his people a spirit of equality, adventure, and disregard for personal possessions and accumulation of worldly goods. The following rules were prescribed for the service of food to the Sikhs and the visitors (*pangat*).

(a) The Guru's *langar* should be considered as belonging to God.

(b) All Sikhs and visitors should eat there.

(c) Anyone who objected to eating there for considerations of caste should be deemed a non-Sikh.

(d) A prayer to God should be offered before taking the food. Similarly, after completion of meals, prayers from the hymns in the *Adi Granth* should be recited.

(e) After eating to one's fill, no one should take any food along with him.

(f) Invitation for food from a Sikh should not be declined nor should the guest criticise the food offered by the host.

(g) A hungry Sikh should be fed and treated respectfully.[25]

The Guru inspired the extreme devotion of his Sikhs. Writing in 1696, a historian describes the love of the Sikhs for the Guru and their faith in Guru Nanak : "They cherish such faith in the Guru as is not found in other communities. They utter his name at all times, and consider serving him as one of the most meritorious acts. If a wayfarer arrives at midnight and takes the name of Guru Nanak, he is treated as a friend and brother, no matter if he is an utter stranger or even a thief, or a robber, or an evildoer."[26] This statement is of great significance. It was recorded when Guru Gobind Singh had already clashed with the hill princes and the Empire. And yet, even then for the Sikhs, it was Guru Nanak and not Guru Gobind Singh, who was deemed to be the pioneer prophet of the entire movement. It was his name that was for the Sikhs the sole point of reference and not that of any subsequent Guru.

The process of socio-spiritual development and self-identification of the Sikh society had been in progress since the time of Guru Nanak. It had been a gradual growth, the landmarks of which were distinctly discernible. Guru Nanak had started the spiritual struggle and had prepared his men for it. The subsequent Gurus had nurtured the growth of the community by the sacrifice of their lives. It was now for Guru Gobind Singh to live the final scene of this glorious drama. It was a drama in the sense that the Guru was carrying out the Will of God and not his own. But it was, at the same time, the greatest reality, for it was the final phase of the Sikh society under the Gurus. The Guru knew that his mission was to spread righteousness. He was aware of the immediate tasks he had to accomplish in the furtherance of his mission. He understood fully well the might of the Empire he had to face and contend with. It would have been entirely different, if the ideal had been mere personal salvation. But, a spiritual society with an ideology like that of the Gurus has to prepare itself for a perpetual war against the forces of evil. These are always well equipped. They can be surmounted only by the blood of the martyrs and the mystics. The Guru, as the leader of the community, was ready for the extreme sacrifices he had to make. But, he had also to prepare his men, whom he had to lead to victory.

For the Guru, the matter of the highest priority was to prepare his people to be self-reliant, self-governing and capable of leading themselves. The Sikh Gurus wanted to raise the community to the level of responsible self-direction. The Sikhs had to carry out the spiritual mission of the Gurus. They had to perform the role not only of maintaining their internal cohesion but also of reacting to the environment in the manner the community had done under the leadership of the Gurus. This was the dual role for which the Gurus had been preparing them. It is for this purpose that the tenth Guru created the institution of the Khalsa and baptised the five beloved ones as their leaders. He gave new symbols and shape to the community. The superhuman sacrifices of the Guru, unparalled in human history, and the *amrit* ceremony should be deemed a part of this final stage of self-identification of the community. It was the culmination of a gradual process of development and maturity. It is clear that the primary object of the Guru in creating the institution of the Khalsa and *amrit* was to put his formal seal on an integrated, responsible and independent community that the Gurus had planned to build. The Guru wanted to evolve a system for creating the leaders of the community when he left his mortal coil. It was at this time that the Guru decided to test his men who were to be the future leaders of the mission. It was not a kingship to be conferred. It was the stage set to select leaders who could make sacrifices and defy death without flinching. Let us explain how the Guru started the *amrit* (baptism) ceremony. On the Vaisakhi day in 1699, the Guru appeared with a drawn sword in the annual gathering of the Sikhs. In a resonant voice he declared that he wanted a human head for sacrifice and enquired if any Sikh could offer it. There was silence in the congregation. Then arose a Sikh announcing his readiness to sacrifice his life. The Guru took him aside in a tent. After a while, he appeared again with the same naked sword red with blood. Again he called for a head. This time the consternation was even greater than before. The timid started slipping away. Some thought the Guru had gone crazy. But, another brave Sikh rose and made the offer. The Guru took him to the tent. Similarly, the Guru reappeared the third, the fourth and the fifth time. On each occasion he made the same demand and took the volunteer into his tent. Finally, he brought out all the five Sikhs, hale and hearty. They were robed in a new Sikh uniform. He performed the *amrit* (baptism) ceremony and declared them to be the first five beloved ones (*piaras*).

Four of these five belonged to the Shudra class and the fifth was a Khatri. As a token of their leadership and in order to set the seal on the tradition of equality, he got himself baptised at the hands of these five chosen ones. This, apart from signifying his extreme humility, established them as the future leaders of the community. The Guru called this community Khalsa, which means the purified people or God's own. At this ceremony, the Guru made a most stirring speech exhorting his men to be prepared to lay their lives for the continuous struggle in the cause of the mission. He declared that he was in the Khalsa and the Khalsa was in him.

There is a recorded incident which is relevant to the creation of the Khalsa. At the time of the martyrdom of Guru Tegh Bahadur, the Sikhs of Delhi had displayed fear and weakness. Instead of taking care of the body of the Guru, they had left the scene. Actually, it was some so-called low-caste Sikhs who boldly took charge of the head of the Ninth Guru and brought it to Anandpur. It was reported to Guru Gobind Singh that apprehending trouble, the local Sikhs had slipped away and disappeared in the crowd around the place. The Guru thought over it and then observed, "I will give them such shape and form that a Sikh can be spotted and identified even from among thousands present."[27]

It is important to understand the five freedoms a person gained on receiving the *amrit*. A mention of these five freedoms is being repeated even up-till today at the time of every *amrit* ceremony.

(1) Freedom from all previous religions, customs and practices.

(2) Obliteration of and freedom from the effect of past bad deeds.

(3) Freedom from the influence of previous caste or family.

(4) Freedom from the stigma or distinction attached to a calling or a hereditary profession.

(5) Freedom from all rituals, prejudices and inhibitions.

It is significant that none of these freedoms has any reference to the impending struggle with the Empire. Each one of these freedoms has only a socio-spiritual or theological implication. The emphasis is on the identity of the religion, the independence of its character and of one's complete break with the past. The fundamental nature of these freedoms is concerned with the doctrine and the socio-religious cohesion of the community and not with any temporary or immediate objective. The creation of the Khalsa has, essentially and primarily, to be viewed as the final step in the consolidation of the Sikhs as a religious community. It was the formal founding of a new society. All traditional bonds inhibiting the progress and freedom of the individual were broken. It was a salvation from the diehard customs of the past. The individual was freed from the stigma of caste, race and profession. The shackles imposed by the old traditions, religious and social practices and prejudices were shattered. He was rescued from his past and a new freedom dawned on him.

Accordingly, we conclude that the objective of the Guru in creating the Khalsa was purely to serve the mission of Guru Nanak. Our conclusion is further supported by a very important writing of a companion of the Tenth Guru. He records that by the creation of the Khalsa, the Tenth Guru revealed and made known what till then had been the secret goal of the Gurus and the Sikh movement. This incontrovertible contemporary evidence is a complete rebuttal of any ignorant suggestion that the Guru's step was directed by any consideration other than those of the mission itself; much less was the step a departure from the message and thesis of the earlier Gurus. There is twice an emphatic assertion in this book that this step was revelatory of the original plan of the Gurus and was the epitome of the entire movement.[28]

It was, indeed, the most momentous decision in the history of the mission. Internal and external disciplines were prescribed for the Sikhs. Basically, one had to eliminate the ego and accept the path of *Naam*. Externally, one had to fulfil moral duties to the society and to the entire world. Every prayer of the Sikhs ends with the words "May God bless the whole world." The duties towards the society were, in fact, an aspect of the duties to the world. One's duties to the world cannot be performed as an individual. These can be discharged only as a community.

The Gurus not only uplifted the individual but did it through the medium of the society. Simultaneously, the Khalsa tackled the social and political problems of the time. It was only incidental that the challenges from the political field coincided with the creation of the Khalsa. The community was meant for the purpose. It was for this role that the Gurus created and nurtured the community with their own blood.

We record the views of Dr Gupta on the significance of the *amrit* ceremony.

(1) It created an inalienable spirit of brotherhood and comradeship among his men. As soon as one joined the Khalsa, all were equal. People who had lived for centuries under servility turned into doughty warriors, whose deeds of valour were sung by the whole world, even by their bitterest enemies.

(2) Each one of the Sikhs was equal in status and had the same rights and privileges. Thus 100 years before the French Revolution, principles of liberty, fraternity and equality were enunciated and became the bedrock of the Khalsa life.

(3) By his selection on merit of the five representative leaders, the Guru destroyed the theory of divine rights of kings and established the supremacy of the common man in the political field.

(4) The doctrine of collective responsibility was proclaimed. The five beloved ones — in the presence of the Holy Granth — were to be obeyed by the entire community.[29]

The second problem before Guru Gobind Singh was of confrontation with the Empire. The time for it had arrived.

For any military preparation three things are fundamentally important; the first is to create the wherewithal of organisation and equipment. But far more important are a strong sense of cohesion and loyalty among the fighting forces and a deep and abiding faith in the righteousness of the cause for which the battles are fought. For the last two items of moral equipment, Guru Nanak had laid a sound organisational basis. The succeeding Gurus developed it further. Guru Arjun took tangible steps both in the field of moral and military equipment so as to face the anticipated clash with the Imperial forces. On the organisational side, he persuaded his men to trade in horses and become good horsemen. The Guru was not unaware of what the consequences would be of his aiding and blessing Khusro, a rebel fighting against the Emperor. One of his greatest contributions was his confrontation with the Emperor and courting martyrdom. Nothing could be more potent to inspire the people and prepare them morally and spiritually for the mighty struggles ahead, which were indeed the struggles of the spiritual man.

From the very beginning of his Guruship, Hargobind openly started to build a military organisation. He created separate spiritual and temporal centres, both headed by himself. It would be quite idle to suggest that on the very first day of his Guruship, Guru Hargobind could take these major steps as his own innovation without instructions from his father. After making his preparations and testing the mettle of his men with the Mughal armies, he shifted the venue of his organisation to the out-of-the-way hill areas, where the mightly Mughal could not throttle the young nation in its infancy. The military preparations continued unabated even in the time of the succeeding Gurus. For obvious reasons they did not come into direct clash with the Empire; though, when the opportunity presented itself, the Seventh Guru did not miss it and sided with Dara Shikoh, Aurangzeb's rival to the throne.

Then followed the oppressive persecutions by Aurangzeb that set a seething wave of suffering amongst the people. From the time of Guru Arjun, the Sikh Gurus had come to be the spokesmen and saviours of the poor and the oppressed. For they alone had the capacity and courage to intervene on their behalf with the rulers and stand up for all righteous causes against the might of the Mughals. So it was quite natural for the hard-pressed Kashmiris to come to Guru Tegh Bahadur, who was their only hope, especially because he was maintaining a military organisation. In view of the developing crisis and demoralisation in the country, the Guru felt that the situation was ripe to offer a second martyrdom for the cause of moral and spiritual freedom and regeneration of man. It was a calculated step to invite confrontation with the Delhi Emperor.

The principles of the Gurus' ethics and morality discussed earlier have essentially to be borne in mind in order to fully understand and appreciate the growth and development of the Sikh organisation and institutions. We find that whereas all the fundamental doctrines about the mystic thesis had been specified and clarified by Guru Nanak, the other Gurus worked only within the spirituo-moral limits laid by him. Seen in the light of the historical context, Guru Arjun, Guru Hargobind, Guru Tegh Bahadur and finally Guru Gobind Singh did take what seemingly were major and momentous decisions, but they were all pursued strictly within the ambit of the original thesis of Guru Nanak. The Tenth Guru created the Khalsa and had direct military confrontation with the Mughal Empire, involving the sacrifice of all his four sons and his mother. Throughout, it was, indeed, the religious plan of Guru Nanak that was being unfolded and implemented. Nay, it was the plan of God which the God-conscious men carried out.

To some people these changes may look kaleidoscopic and appear in different colours, but it was the same light that shaped everything. Whatever be the apparent form or area of activity, it was the barriers and the chains of man that were being broken.

Aurangzeb intensified his policies of religious persecution. It had for long been clear to the Gurus that the Mughal Empire had to be faced if the seed of moral and spiritual life had to grow. The call had been given by Guru Tegh Bahadur. In view of the impending clash with the Empire, Guru Gobind Singh speeded up his military preparations. The Guru had thought that the hill chiefs would join him in his struggle against the Empire. In the ranks of the Guru a complete sense of brotherhood prevailed. Low castes from the Hindu fold, who had swelled his organisation, got a treatment of equality. But, this did not suit the caste-ridden and feudal hill Rajputs. The spirituo-moral ideals of equality and fraternity affected their vested interests. Many of them, instead of co-operating with the Guru in the common cause of man he was espousing, became openly hostile to him. But it is of great significance that all good persons, including Muslim saints, were friendly to him. In the battle of Bhangani, Pir Budhu Shah, a local Muslim saint, came to his aid at the head of a contingent of 700 soldiers. Two of his sons fell on the battlefield.

The defeated hill chiefs reported the growing military power of the Guru to the Muslim Rulers. Mughal expeditions sent by the local Governors under the orders of the Emperor had failed to curb him and were repulsed. The Guru fortified Anandpur Sahib. On receipt of these reports, the Emperor asked his Governors to crush the Guru.

Now another stage in the history of the moral struggle had been reached. The Governors of Lahore, Sirhind and Jammu, along with the alliance of the hostile hill chiefs, failed to subdue the Guru. He knew the next stage would be a direct confrontation with the Emperor and the Imperial forces. He felt that as a leader of the mission, he had to set a still more glorious example to his men and train them to rise to still greater heights of sacrifice and glory.

Ten thousand men under Painda Khan were sent to attack Anandpur. This army was defeated. Five times the hill Rajas and the Imperial forces attacked the Guru but were repulsed with losses. Ultimately, Anandpur was besieged by the Mughal forces from Delhi, Sirhind, Lahore and Jammu. The army of the hill chiefs joined them. On the first day, the attacking army lost 900 men. The siege continued. Finally, because the supplies had completely been cut off, the Guru had to leave Anandpur. He was pursued. At Chamkaur Sahib he was again besieged. There his two sons, aged 14 and 18, voluntarily went to the field and died fighting.

Latif, the Punjab historian, writes the following story depicting the spirit of the Guru's son even on the last day of the siege. A person from the besieging commander brought a message that as the Guru had practically no army and was pitted against the mighty Imperial forces, he should surrender and seek conversion. At this the Guru's son spoke, "Utter another word and I will smite your head from your body and cut you to pieces for daring to so address our chief."[30] Even at this time of peril, the Guru was not inclined to leave the place but the leaders of the community asked him to move out of the fort so as to reorganise his men. In the darkness of night the Guru left almost alone.

All his men left behind lost their lives. The party in which the mother and the two younger sons of the Guru had left from Anandpur was betrayed. His sons aged 8 and 10 were executed at Sirhind. Within a span of a week, the Guru lost his mother, all the four sons and everything. But the Guru was not dismayed. The letters he wrote to

Aurangzeb, called the Epistles of Victory, are a testimony to the loftiness of his spirit. He continued the struggle. Aurangzeb died. The Guru met Bahadur Shah, his successor, so that the brutalities, tyranny and oppression of the people by the Governor of Sirhind should stop. The Emperor did not respond. As negotiations to bring about peace in Punjab failed, the Guru picked up Banda, a Bairagi Saint, and sent him to undo the barbarian misrule in Punjab. Five chosen Sikhs were deputed to advice him and organise the attack. About 200 Sikh soldiers were to accompany them and orders were sent to the Sikhs in Punjab to join the expedition. The Guru, as Dr Gupta writes, gave Banda Singh his sword, a bow and five arrows as insignia. He died in 1708 as the result of treacherous stabbing by an agent of the Nawab of Sirhind. Within one and a half years of his death, the Mughal forces were humbled. The Sikhs became supreme in all the areas.

That was the miracle the Guru had wrought. Dr Gupta writes : "There are in this world men who are endowed by nature with infinite capacity for attaining perfection. In the days of peace they work for the solace of mankind, and strive to smooth the way for the chariot of progress. In times of calamity they suddenly rise up to guide the people, and give them an ideal, great and glorious. While putting that ideal into execution, they remain stoic to the shocks of adverse fortune. They endure untold mortifications and sufferings, but stick fast to their ideal, and cheerfully make supreme sacrifices. The grateful world would point to Guru Gobind Singh as one of such men.

"His dream and deeds wrought a wonderful change in his own generation in the religious, military and political life of the people. His personality was so fascinating, so bewitching, so dynamic, so momentous and so unforgettable that we are seized with wonder at the changes which took place in Panjab within one year and half of his death. He was the greatest genius of his age. Whenever we touch that short life, as he died at the age of forty-two, we are at once brought into contact with a live wire. He was a meteor that consumed itself to light the world. He was luminous like the sun, and had conquered death.

"He possessed a rare combination of so many excellences, supreme self-denial, marvellous intellect, super-human will-power, great heart and limitless energy. He examined life and sought its real meaning and true goal. He came to grips with this fundamental question. He realised his deep bond to humanity. He was moved by the sufferings he saw around him. He decided to help men find freedom.

"Guru Gobind Singh was not destined to have peace in his lifetime. He was born in conflict. He was brought up in conflict. He lived in conflict, and he died in conflict. This conflict was not of his own making. It was an age of conflict. Conflict was thrust upon him by the force of circumstances, and he had a full measure of it. It was a holy conflict. It aimed at regenerating a decaying people. It endeavoured to create a new nation. It planned to lay the foundation of a new society based upon justice and freedom of conscience. It sought to promulgate the principles of liberty, equality and fraternity.

"At the age of nine, Gobind Singh had his father sacrificed in the cause of religious freedom. Between the age of nine and thirty-nine, in the thirty years he had to fight as many as twenty battles, nine before the creation of the Khalsa and eleven afterwards. He had enemies all round. He had little resources in men, money and material. Within a week in December 1704, he laid at the altar his mother and all the four of his sons. Besides, thousands of his devoted followers were launched into eternity. Eventually at the young age of forty-two, he shuffled off this mortal coil in the cause of freedom and in the service of humanity. Can there be a greater and nobler sacrifice than this ? The legacy left behind by him was that of sacrifice, service, self-support and self-respect."

Bulleh Shah, a celebrated Sufi Muslim saint of Punjab, was a contemporary of Guru Gobind Singh. He pays a tribute to the Guru thus :

"I neither say of the past; nor do I speak of the future; but I talk of the time of Guru Gobind Singh and declare openly :
That but for him all the Hindus would have been converted to a foreign culture and religion."[31]

"Victory deserves the applause of the people; but a heroic defeat deserves their compassion. One is magnificent, the other is sublime. Martyrdom is more glorious than success. The martyrs struggle for the great work with the inflexible logic of the ideal. They give their life, a pure gift, for progress. They accomplish the will of providence. They perform a religious act. At the appointed hour, obedient to the divine will, they enter into the tomb. In this stoical disappearance they leave behind a landmark on the path of progress."[32] "As a brave soldier and leader, Gobind Singh is undoubtedly amongst the greatest saviours of mankind."[33]

Dr Gupta concludes that the creation of the Khalsa and the bestowal of political sovereignty on the Khalsa are two of the Guru's acts of crowning glory.[34]

REFERENCES

1. This chapter is based mainly on *History of the Sikh Gurus* by Dr H.R. Gupta.
2. Guru Granth Sahib, p. 967.
3. Macauliffe, i, p. 259.
4. Zimmer, pp. 462-463.
5. Ibid., p. 463.
6. Guru Granth Sahib, p. 730.
7. Ibid., pp. 1028, 224.
8. Sarup Das Bhalla : *Mehma Parkash*, i, p. 326.
9. *Bhai Gurdas*, first *Var*.
10. H.R. Gupta, op. cit. p. 57.
11. Ibid., pp. 67-68.
12. Ibid., p. 73.
13. Ibid., p. 59.
14. Guru Granth Sahib, p. 967.
15. *Gur Bilas Patshahi Chevin*, p. 85; *Mehma Parkash*, ii, p. 395.
16. H.R. Gupta, op. cit. p. 110.
17. Ibid., p. 102.
18. Ibid., p. 90.

19. Sarkar : *A Short History of Aurangzeb*, p. 156.
20. H.R. Gupta, op. cit. p. 114.
21. Ibid.
22. Timur Shah, Ahmad Shah Abdali's son, quoted by Banerjee, A.C. : *Journal of Sikh Studies*, Amritsar, Vol. III, No. 1 (Feb. 1976), p. 61.
23. H.R. Gupta, op. cit. p. 143.
24. Ibid., pp. 177-178.
25. Macauliffe, V, p. 109.
26. H.R. Gupta, op. cit. p. 177.
27. Chaupa Singh Chibber : *Rehatnama*.
28. *Gur Sobha* (ed. Ganda Singh), pp. 21, 32.
29. H.R. Gupta, op. cit. pp. 193-195.
30. Ibid., p. 207.
31. Ibid., pp. 148-149.
32. Ibid., p. 245.
33. Ibid., p. 246.
34. Ibid.

GURU GOBIND SINGH : CREATION OF THE KHALSA

HARI RAM GUPTA

AURANGZEB'S RELIGIOUS POLICY

In Islam, the "true king is God, and earthly rulers are merely His agents bound to enforce His law on all. The civil authorities exist solely to spread and enforce the true faith. In such a state, infidelity is logically equivalent to treason, because the infidel repudiates the authority of the true king and pays homage to his rivals, the false gods and goddesses. Therefore, the toleration of any sect outside the fold of orthodox Islam is no better than compounding with sin. And the worst form of sin is polytheism, the belief that the one true God has partners in the form of other deities. Islamic theology, therefore, tells the true believer that his highest duty is to make exertion (*jihad*) in the path of God[1], by waging war against infidel lands (*dar-ul-harb*) till they become a part of the realm of Islam (*dar-ul-Islam*) and their populations are converted into true believers. After conquests, the entire infidel population becomes theoretically reduced to the status of slaves of the conquering army. The conversion of the entire population to Islam and the extinction of every form of dissent, is the ideal of the Muslim State. If any infidel is suffered to exist in the community, it is a necessary evil, and for a transitional period only. Political and social disabilities must be imposed on him, and bribe offered to him from the public funds to hasten the day of his spiritual enlightenment and the addition of his name to the roll of true believers."[2]

Aurangzeb was a true believer in this Islamic theory. His reputation had suffered greatly in the Muslim world for having executed all his brothers and their sons and for imprisoning his father. To improve his image, he became a ruthless puritan. He wished to show that his aim was to restore Islam to its original glory. He adopted the policy of persecution of non-Muslims as well as non-Sunni Muslims.

Aurangzeb decided to use all the resources of a vast empire in suppressing Hinduism and converting the infidels to Islam. During his viceroyalty of Gujarat in 1644, he "desecrated the recently built Hindu temple of Chintaman in Ahmadabad by killing a cow in it and then turned the building into a mosque. He had at that time also demolished many other Hindu temples in the province."[3]

In the beginning of a his reign, Aurangzeb ordered the local officers in every town and village of Orissa from Katak to Medinipur "to pull down all temples, including even clay huts, built during the last 10 or 12 years, and to allow no old temple to be repaired."[4] In 1661-62, a big temple was demolished at Mathura and a Jama Masjid was erected in its place in the heart of Hindu population.[5] From April, 1665, Hindus were charged double the customs duty of that paid by Muslims on all articles brought for sale.[6] In May, 1667, Muslims were exempted from payment of customs duty altogether, while Hindus had to pay at the old rate of five percent.[7]

In 1668, Hindu fairs and festivals were stopped.[8] On April 9, 1669, a general order applicable to all parts of the Mughal Empire was issued "to demolish all the schools and temples of the infidels and to put down their religious teaching." In January, 1670, the biggest temple of Keshav Rae at Mathura was destroyed and the city was named Islamabad.[9] "The destruction of Hindu places of worship was one of the chief duties of the *Muhtasibs* of Censors of Morals who were appointed in all the sub-divisions and cities of the empire."[10]

Hindus employed in public service including clerk and accountants were dismissed in 1671.[11] The post of Qanungo could be retained by a Hindu on embracing Islam.[12] Others who became Muslims received stipends, rewards, government jobs, release from jails, right to ancestral property and other privileges. The new converts riding on elephants followed by bands and flags were paraded through the streets and bazars.[13] *Jazia* was charged from all Hindus from April 2, 1679. "*Jazia* meant for the Hindus an addition of fully one-third to every subject's direct contribution to the State.[14] The contemporary European traveller Manucci observed : "Many Hindus who were unable to pay turned Muhammadan, to obtain relief from the insults of the Collectors. Aurangzeb rejoices."[15] In June, 1680, the temples of Amber, the capital of Jaipur State, the most loyal Hindu State, were demolished.[16] In March, 1695, all the Hindus except Rajputs were ordered not to ride on elephants, fine horses and in palanquins or to carry arms.[17]

Syed Muhammad Latif in his *History of Punjab* on pp. 176-77 writes :

> "He discouraged the teaching of the Hindus, burnt to the ground the great Pagoda near Delhi, and destroyed the temple of Bishnath at Benares, and the great temple of Dera Kesu Rai at Mathura, said to have been built by Raja Narshingh Deo at a cost of thirty-three *lakhs* of Rupees. The gilded domes of this temple were so high that they could be seen from Agra. On the site of the ruined temple, he built a vast mosque at a great cost. The richly decorated idols of the temples were removed to Agra and placed beneath the steps leading to the mosque of Nawab Begum. The name Mathura was changed into Islamabad, and was so written in all correspondence and spoken by the people. Aurangzeb had resolved that the belief in one God and the Prophet should be, not the prevailing, but the only religion of the empire of Hindostan. He issued mandates to the viceroys and governors of provinces to destroy pagodas and idols throughout his dominions. About three hundred temples in various parts of Rajputana were destroyed and

their idols broken. The emperor appointed *mullahs*, with a party of horse attached to each, to check all ostentatious display of idol worship, and, sometime afterwards, he forbade fairs on Hindu festivals, and issued a circular to all governors and men in authority prohibiting the employment of Hindus in the officers of state immediately under them, and commanding them to confer all such.offices on Mahomedans only. About the year 1690, the emperor issued an edict prohibiting Hindus from being carried in palanquins or riding on Arab horses. All servants of the state were ordered to embrace the Mahomedan religion, under pain of dismissal, those who refused were deprived of their posts. A large number of *jogis, saniasis* and other religious men were driven out of the king's dominions. The emperor reduced the duty on merchandise belonging to Mahomedans to one half the amount paid by Hindus and remitted a number of other obnoxious taxes. Following the tradition of his house, he, in 1661, married his son, Moazzam, to the daughter of Raja Rup Singh. In the 22nd year of his reign, he renewed the *Jazia*, or poll-tax, on Hindus, throughout his dominions. The Hindus of Delhi gathered in large numbers beneath the *jharoka* window, on the bank of the river, and implored his majesty to remit the obnoxious tax; but the emperor was inexorable. The Hindus adopted the expedient of closing the shops in the city, and all business came to a standstill. They thronged the bazaars from the place to the grand mosque, one Friday, with the object of seeking relief. The crowd increased every moment, and the king's equipage was interrupted at every step. He stopped for a while to hear them, but the multitude held their ground. At length, under orders from the emperor, war elephants were directed against the mob, and, the retinue forcing its way through, numbers were trodden to death by horses and elephants. After this, the Hindus submitted without further demur."

HINDU REVOLTS SUPPRESSED

1. *The Jats* : Gokal, a Jat of Tilpat, revolted against the bigoted governor of Mathura, Abdu Nabi, and in an encounter shot him dead in May, 1669. Aurangzeb sent a strong force against him. After a fierce resistance, Gokal was defeated and hacked to piece. His womenfolk were given away to Muslims. Five thousand Jats were killed and 7,000 were taken prisoners.[18]

2. *The Satnamis* : Satnamis were living at Narnaul and in its neighbourhood. Khafi Khan, the contemporary historian of Aurangzeb, writes : "Though they dress like faqirs, most of them follow agriculture or trade on a small capital. Following the path of their own faith, they wish to live with a good name and never attempt to obtain money by any dishonest and unlawful means."[19] One day in 1672, a Mughal soldier picked up a quarrel with a Satnami and broke his head with his baton. Other Satnamis beat the soldier in return. The local officer sent a party of footmen to punish the Satnamis who gathered in a body, seized their arms and drove them away. Thereafter, about 5,000 Satnamis gathered in arms. Small parties of troops sent by local officers were repulsed. The rebels plundered Narnaul and demolished mosques. Aurangzeb sent a force of 10,000 strong with artillery. "After a most obstinate battle, two thousand of the Satnamis fell on the field, while many more were slain

during the pursuit."[20] All the Satnamis were wiped out, and no trace of them was left.

3. *The Sikhs* : Aurangzeb dealt with the Sikhs in the same manner. In November, 1675, Guru Tegh Bahadur was called upon to embrace Islam, and on his refusal was beheaded. His companions were most brutally murdered.

4. *The Rajputs* : In December, 1678, Maharaja Jaswant Singh of Jodhpur, the *thanedar* of Jamrud at the Khaibar Pass, passed away. Aurangzeb immediately proceeded to annex his kingdom to the Mughal empire, and himself went to Ajmer in January, 1679. Jaswant Singh's two widows give birth to two sons on their way back at Lahore. One of them died soon afterwards. The other child, Ajit Singh, was detained at Delhi to be brought up in the imperial *harem*. "The throne of Jodhpur was offered to Ajit on condition of his turning a Muslim."[21] On the Rani's refusal, Aurangzeb ordered them to be taken under a strong escort to the prison fortress of Nurgarh. Before the Mughal troops could arrive, their residence in Delhi was besieged by Raghunath, a noble of Jodhpur, with one hundred devoted soldiers. There were a few Mughal troopers guarding the mansion. In the melee, Durgadas, "the flower of Rathor chivalry,"[22] "slipped out with Ajit and the Ranis dressed in male attire, and rode away direct for Marwar."[23] Raghunath and his men "dyed the streets of Delhi with blood,"[24] and then all met hero's death. The Mughal army went in pursuit of Durgadas. Small bands of Rathors turn by turn, at intervals, barred the path of Mughal forces, and thus allowed time to Durgadas to escape. These terrible conflicts every two or three hours, dismayed the Mughals who gave up the pursuit late in the same night. Ajit and Ranis reached Marwar territory safely. Then ensued a regular war between Aurangzeb and the Rathors." But for Durgadas's twenty-five years of unflagging exertion and wise contrivance, Ajit Singh could not have secured his father's throne."[25] Jodhpur and all the great towns in the plain fell and were pillaged; the temples were thrown down and mosques erected on their sites."[26]

The annexation of Marwar was followed by the conquest of Mewar. Aurangzeb's artillery manned by Europeans easily defeated Maharana Raja Singh of Udaipur. Chitor was seized and 63 temples in the town were razed to the ground. At Udaipur, 173 temples were demolished.[27]

5. *The Marathas* : Aurangzeb then turned his attention towards the Marathas. He reached Aurangabad on March 22, 1682, never to return to the north, and died at the same place 25 years later. The great Shivaji had passed away at the age of 53 on April 4, 1680. His eldest son, Shambhuji, succeeded him. Aurangzeb decided to destroy him. An Englishman who was living at Karwar wrote about the Emperor on July 30, 1682 : "He is so inveterate against the Raja that he hath thrown off his *pagri* and sworn never to put it on again, till he hath either killed, taken, or routed him out of his country."[28] Aurangzeb succeeded in his object. On February 1, 1689, he was captured and dragged by his long hair.[29] Twenty-five of his leading chiefs along with their wives and daughters were also seized. Shambhuji and his Prime Minister Kavikalash "were dressed as buffoons with long fool's caps and bell placed on their heads, mounted on camels, and brought to Bahadurgarh with drums beating and trumpets pealing. Hundreds of thousands of spectators lined the roads, to gaze at Shambhuji as at new kind of wild beast or demon. Thus degraded, the

captives were slowly paraded through the entire camp and finally brought to the Emperor who was sitting in full darbar for the occasion. At the sight of the prisoner, Aurangzeb descended from his throne and kneeling down on the carpet bowed his head to the ground in double thankfulness to the Giver of this crowning victory."[30]

Khafi Khan, the contemporary historian of Aurangzeb's region says that at this, Kavikalash shouted to Shambhuji :

"O Rajah ! even Aurangzeb dare not sit on the throne in thy presence, but must kneel to do thee homage."[31] Shambhuji did not bow before the Emperor though pressed hard by the courtiers to do so. On the other hand, he asked for the hand of one of Aurangzeb's daughters. He was immediately blinded and the tongue of Kavikalash was cut off. They were tortured for a fortnight. On March 11, 1689, their limbs were hacked to pieces, one by one, and dogs were fed on their flesh. Their heads were fixed on spears and exhibited in all the major towns and cities of the Deccan with the beat of drums and blowing of trumpets.[32] Aurangzeb then seized the surviving widows of Shivaji, wives of Shambhuji and of his younger brother Rajaram and their sons and daughters including seven year old Shahu."[33]

THE MARATHAS HARASS THE EMPEROR

Now there being no head of the Marathas, hundreds of Maratha chiefs at the head of their small bands began to harass the Mughals anywhere and everywhere. It became a people's war. Aurangzeb and his Generals could not be present at all places. The Emperor had to face "an enemy all pervasive from Bombay to Madras across the Indian Peninsula, elusive as the wind, without any headman or stronghold whose capture would naturally result in the extinction of their power."[34] The Empire's leading chiefs and men suffered terribly. "Porters disappeared; transport beasts died of hunger and overwork; scarcity of grain was ever present in his camp. The endless war in the Deccan exhausted his treasury; the Government turned bankrupt; the soldiers starving from arrears of pay (usually three years overdue) mutinied."[35] The Marathas were supreme. They plundered the Mughal territory and camp mercilessly. "There was an exultant and menacing Maratha army always hanging three or four miles behind the Emperor's camp wherever it marched or halted."[36] This happened during the regime of Raja Ram, the younger son of Shivaji who died at the age of thirty on March 2, 1700.

After him, the leadership of the Marathas was taken over by Raja Ram's 25-year-old widow, Tara Bai. This young woman worked wonders. She created a new and vigorous Maharashtra in a few years. "The Maratha queen flew from camp to camp and from fortress to fortress, sharing the hardships of a trooper, exposed to the sun, sleeping on the ground. Tara Bai seemed to multiply herself to be everywhere and always encouraging her officers, and planning campaigns on a wider front. So clear was her vision, unerring her judgement, that she was equally welcome on the battlefield and in the council chamber by the war-worn soldiers and astute politicians of the older generation. Within a short time, the Maratha counter-offensive, at first halting and ineffective, assumed alarming proportions and began to threaten the very heart of the Mughal Empire."[37]

The enormous losses sustained by the Emperor are thus described by Sir Jadunath :

"The wastage of the Deccan war which raged intensely for nearly twenty-years, was one hundred thousand soldiers and followers and three times that number of horses, elephants, camels and oxen on the Mughal side every year."[38]

About the appalling economic devastation of the Maratha country, the European traveller Manucci wrote :

"The fields are left devoid of trees and bare of crops, their places being taken by the bones of men and beasts. The country was so entirely desolated and depopulated that neither fire nor light could be found in the course of a three or four day's journey."[39]

GURU GOBIND DAS'S CONTEMPLATION

The Guru knew that he had a definite mission and duty to perform. The time had come and the hour had struck. The circumstances were favourable and the opportunity was at hand. Delay might be dangerous. If the Emperor, the mightiest of the mighty, could be defied while commanding in person, there was no reason why he should not succeed against the Emperor's governors.

A moment's reflection reminded him that Guru Nanak had described the rulers of his time as tigers and dogs. That situation had not changed even after 200 years. The policy of non-violence, submission and surrender had produced no effect upon these ferocious tigers and mad dogs. Appeals, protests and representations were treated as treasons, punishable with death. Agitation was followed by disastrous consequences. Should this situation be allowed to continue till eternity ?, the Guru thought. Musketry and gunnery were the only remedies, he realised.

After the most determined meditation on this sad state of affairs, the Guru came to the conclusion that to tyrannise was bad, but to bear tyranny patiently was worse. The country did not belong to the king. The king belonged to the country, and the country belonged to the people. If the king was bad, people must rise in revolt. Without political liberty, religious, intellectual, social and economic freedom could not be achieved. Political freedom could be won by armies. The armies of the suppressed people were non-existent. The spirit of the brave Jats of Agra and Delhi had been crushed. The heroic Satnamis had been completely wiped out of existence. The Rajput resistance was broken. The noble Shivaji had died young. His eldest son Shambhuji had been hacked to pieces. His only son Shahu was in captivity. The Guru's own house was no exception. His great grandfather, Guru Arjun, was tortured to death. His grandfather Hargobind had suffered twelve years' imprisonment. His father Guru Tegh Bahadur was executed. His most faithful follower, Bhai Matidas, was sawn across from head to loins, while others were boiled or skinned alive.

Gobind Das did not feel dismayed. He did not lose heart. He knew that human mind when properly inspired was capable of rising to the loftiest heights, and when rightly guided and controlled could work wonders. He also realised that he would have to depend entirely on his own resources. The hill Rajputs whom he wanted to use in the national cause had failed. He set about planning and preparing himself for the struggle to win freedom. His army was to be based on social justice. There could be no discrimination in the name of caste, creed and colour. His soldiers unpaid, ill-armed, poorly equipped, untrained were to be inspired with feeling of patriotism and nationalism.

In *Krishna Avtar* the Guru Says :

Kou Kise ko raj na de hai
   Jo lai hai nij bal sit lai hai.

(No people can have self-rule as a gift from another. It is to be seized through their own strength.)[40]

WAS GURU GOBIND SINGH AN ENEMY OF ISLAM ?

Guru Gobind Das was determined to exterminate the religious oppression of the Mughal Government. He concentrated against the cruel Government and not against Islam. There is not a word in his speech and writings to prove this baseless charge. Nor does history offer any event or incident in proof of it. He was an embodiment of love and affection for all. His instructions to his Sikhs were to treat everybody with courtesy and consideration. It was for this reason that both Hindus and Muslims were attracted towards him. Muslim Sufi saints and Muslim commanders of note, and hundreds of Muslim soldiers fought under his banners. Pir Budhu Shah of Sadhaura, together with his sons and seven hundred followers fought hard in the battle of Bhangani in 1688, in which the Muslim saint lost two of his sons and hundreds of his disciples. In the battle of Anandpur in 1702 Mir Beg and Mamun Khan commanded the Guru's forces in fighting against the Mughal troops. At the same place in 1704, General Sayyid Khan of the Mughal army considered it improper and unjust to wage a war against the Guru. He deserted his post and joined the Guru. Nabi Khan and Ghani Khan saved him from capture by the Mughal army. Qazi Pir Muhammad did not confirm the Guru's identity, while Rae Kalha offered him a refuge and entertained him generously.

In *Akal Ustat*, the Guru says :

1. "Some are Hindus while others are Muslims. Of the latter, some are Shias and others are Sunnis. Man's caste should be considered as one." (*Manas ki jat sabhi ekai pahchanbo.*)

2. "*Karta, Karim Rajak Rahim* is the same. No other distinction should be recognised at all."

3. "Temple and mosque are the same. Hindu worship and Muslim prayer are the same. All men are alike, but they are under delusion."

4. "Gods, demons, heavenly dancers, singers, Muslims, Hindus wear different dresses under the condition of their countries. But they possess eyes, bodies, made of the same elements, composed of earth, air, fire and water."

5. "Allah, the unknowable, the Puranas and the Quran are the same. All are manifestations of One, and One is the Creator of all."[41]

In the *Jap,* Guru Gobind Das has given 735 names to God. Of these 30 are of Islam.

He declared Ram and Rahim were the same, Ishwar, Allah were the same. *Barat* and *Roza* were the same. *Puja* and *Nimaz* were the same. *Pandit* and *Qazi* were the same. *Brahman* and *Mullah* were the same.

Sujan Rae Bhandari, while describing the Sikhs wrote in 1696 :

"In their eyes, their own people and others as well as friends and foes are all alike. They love their friends, but they do not ill-treat their enemies."[42]

THE GURU'S MISSION

Guru Gobind Das decided to create national awakening in Punjab as it had been done in Maharashtra by Shivaji. The time chosen was opportunate. Aurangzeb was involved in the life and death struggle in the Deccan with Marathas. Punjab was in charge of Prince Muazzam who lived in Kabul. The Governors of Lahore, Jammu and Sarhind had failed to crush him. The Government at Delhi was in a state of disorganisation. The hill *rajas* were in revolt against the Mughals. A better time could not be expected to fulfil his life's mission, and the Guru was not the man to miss it. He had first tried to plant his ideas in the mind of the warrior class of Rajputs of the Shivalik Hills. He soon discovered that the caste-ridden and class-dominated feudal lords would not respond to his appeals and they would not fit in his ideology. They had grown flabby possibly because of comforts enjoyed by them. He therefore turned his attention to the downtrodden masses. He believed that he would be able to achieve his objective by stirring the latent faculties of the human will, which possessed the elasticity of rising to the tallest heights as well as of sinking to the lowest depths. The Guru made full use of the strong sentiment which had been expressing itself in the Sikh community in the form of sincere devotion and loving obedience for the person of the Guru. Sujan Rae in 1696 described the devotion of the Sikhs to their Gurus thus :

"They cherish such faith in their Guru as is not found in other communities. They utter his name at all times, and consider serving him as the most meritorious act. If a wayfarer arrives at midnight and takes the name of Guru Nanak, he is treated as a friend and brother, no matter he may be an utter stranger, or even a thief, or a robber, or an evil-doer."[43]

The Guru realised that God was the wielder of arms to punish tyrants and destroy evil-doers. He was also bestower of gifts and fountain-head of mercy. Further, the Guru had been deeply struck by the idea that God had been sending a saviour at critical times to save the virtuous and destroy the wicked. He knew that he had been sent to this world for the same purpose. In *Bachitra Natak*, the Guru says :

1. *Ham eh Kaj jagat mo ae*
   Dharam het Gur Dev pathae
   Jahana tahan tum dharam bitharo
   Dusht dokhian pakar pachharo

(For this purpose did I come into this world.
   God sent me for the sake of *dharam*;
   Wherever you are, spread *dharam*,
   Root out the oppressors and the wicked.)

2. *Yahi kaj dhara ham janmam*
   Samajh leho sadhu sab manmam
   Dharam chalawan sant ubaran
   Dust saban ko mul uparan.[44]

(For this purpose was I born,

    Bear this in mind all ye saints;

    To propagate *dharam,* to protect saints,

    To annihilate all the tyrants.)

In order to seek divine approval of his mission, he entered into a blissful communion with Almighty and received the following reply :

Main apna sut tohe niwaja

    Panth prachur karbe kaho saja

    Jahan tahan tai dharam chalae

    Kabudh karan te lok hatae.[55]

(I have cherished you as my son,

    I have created you to preach righteousness;

    Wherever you are promote righteousness,

    Restrain the people from evil deeds.)

The Guru then prays to God to give him strength of mind to fight valorously to a finish for victory in the cause of right and justice. He says :

Deh Siva bar mohi ehai

    Subh karman te kabhun na tarun,

    Na darun ar so jab jae larun,

    Nishche kar apni jit karun,

    Aru Sikh hau apne hi man kau

    Eh lalach hu gun tau uchrun

    Jab av ki audh nidhan bane,

    At hi ran mai tab jujh marun.[46]

(O God ! give me the boon that I may not deter from righteous deeds,

    Nor may I fear from any enemy, when I go to fight,

    I must have determination for victory;

    And I may guide my mind to aspire after uttering your attributes;

    When the end of my life comes, then I may die fighting heroically.)

The Guru then invokes for the long life of all those who ever remember God and fight in the righteous cause. In *Krishna Avtar,* he writes :

Dhan joyo tih kau jag main

    Mukh te Hari chit main yudh bichare.

(Blessed are they in this world,

    Who have Hari on their tongue and war in their heart.)

THE FOUNDATION OF THE KHALSA, MARCH 30, 1699

The Guru declared that his mission would be proclaimed at Anandpur on the first of Baisakh, the New Year Day, March 30, 1699. He invited the entire audience to attend the grand function.[47] I was then on a visit to the shrine of Naina Devi.

The Guru remained busy in meditation and contemplation. On the morning of 30th March, he sought God's blessing :

Thad bhao main jor kar bachan kaha sar naye

Panth chale tab jagat men jab tum ho sahae.

(I stood up with folded hands and head bent down and said,

   Panth can flourish in the world only with Your help.)

He entered a specially constructed canopy where a huge congregation was seated. Behind it there was a small tent which was closed on all sides and it could be entered from the canopy alone. The Guru asked them to utter the following call after him :

Jo bole so nihal, Sat Sri Akal !

(Whoever utters 'The Immortal God is true' will be blessed.)

The Guru narrated the stories of Government's tyranny, humiliation, tortures, forcible conversions, destruction of temples and schools, and brutal persecution of those who protested. He depicted the miseries they had suffered from and presented pictures of fresh horrors and tribulations which lay in store for them at the hands of the Emperor and his officials. He aroused their enthusiasm to get ready to fight against those who trod upon their beliefs and on their very existence. He expressed great faith in the power of common people. They were many and their oppressors were few.

The Guru then made the most stirring oration on saving religion which was in great peril, and about his divine mission. The discourse first excited the whole audience, then enthralled and terrified them and eventually thrilled them. He criticised the Hindu view of life. They believed in non-violence (*Ahimsa parmo dharam*). They would do no wrong to others. If anybody else oppressed them they would not oppose. They thought that the oppressor would get the punishment of his evil deeds in the next world. Instead of self-help and resistance they practised patience, non-violence and renunciation. For want of organisation, the Hindus could not resist the onslaught of the invaders and government. They called Hindus sparrows and themselves hawks, meaning thereby that they could cut up Hindus as a hawk mutilated sparrows.[48]

The Guru explained that in order to safeguard their spiritual and temporal rights, the people should not depend on fate. They ought to entrust this duty to themselves. They should individually feel any national wrong done, and collectively organise means to resist it. "The Kal age had reached such a stage that success would come only if a brick could be returned with a stone." Humility and service alone were out of place in this age. To goodness was to be added not only condemnation of evil, but also destruction of the evil-doers. Love of a neighbour must accompany the punishment of the trespasser. Service of saints implied annihilation of tyrants as well. Helping friends meant harming enemies too. *Degh, Tegh* and *Fateh* formed the Holy Trinity in place of Brahma, Vishnu and Shiv, to lead to victory. *Degh* or cooking cauldron meant food for all, and it was put in place of Brahma. *Tegh* was the only means of preserving this life in those days, and it stood for Vishnu. *Fateh* or victory destroyed [49] the enemy and it represented Shiva. The age when salvation was needed after death had passed. Salvation was to be obtained in this very life, here and now.

In this ecstasy, the Guru sang the praises of the Sword. "God subdues enemies, so does the Sword, therefore the Sword is God, and God is the Sword."[50] Addressing the Sword he said :

"I bow with love and devotion to the Holy Sword.

Assist me that I may complete this work.

Thou art the subduer of countries,

The destroyer of armies of the wicked in battlefield.

Thou greatly adornest the brave.

Thine arm is infrangible,

Thy brightness in refulgent,

Thy radiance and splendour dazzle like the sun ......

I bow to the Sword, spotless, fearless, and unbreakable ......

I bow to the Sword, and Rapier which destroy the evil ......

In this *Kal* age and at all times, there is great confidence in the powerful arm of the Sword ......

The demons who could not be drowned in the sea, and who could not be burnt by fiery arrows,

On beholding Thy flash, O Sword, cast aside shame and fled ......

Thy greatness is endless and boundless;

No one hath found its limits.

Thou art God of gods, King of kings,

Compassionate to the poor, and cherisher of the lowly."[51]

Addressing the fighting weapons, the Guru said :

Jite shastar nam

Namaskar tam

Jite astar bhen

Namaskar ten.[52]

Namaskaryan more tiran tufang,

Namo Kahg,

Gadaer grishtan, namo saithiyan,

Khag, adong abhen abhang,

(Like them no other hero is born.)

He made a stimulating appeal in the name of the country and nation. He placed great emphasis on the love of the mother country and loyalty to *dharam*. He dwelt on the necessity of subverting the Mughal Empire and building a new nation. He presented a picture of a new class of men and women ready to sacrifice everything in the service of the nation. He put forth the belief that the time was ripe for action.

After this exciting oration, the Guru flashed his sword and said that every great deed was preceded by equally great sacrifice. The Holy Sword would create a heroic nation after supreme sacrifice. He said that the *Dharam* thirsted for sacrificial blood. The Guru demanded a devotee in whose heart he would plunge his sword. This sent a thrill of horror in the audience. He repeated it in a sterner and more sonorous voice. All were terror-stricken and there was no response at the first and second call. At the third call, Daya Ram, a Khatri of village Dalla in district Lahore, rose in his seat and expressed willingness to lay down his life. He was led into the adjoining tent and asked to sit there quietly. He dipped his sword blade into a vessel full of goats' blood. The general belief is that the Guru had tied five goats, and he killed them one by one with a single stroke. This assertion does not appear to be plausible. At the first killing, the goats would have bleated loudly which could have been easily heard in the open ground where the Guru was conducting the meeting. He came back with the sword dripping with blood, and asked for another head. Dharam Das, a Jat of Jatwara village in district Saharanpur, offered his life. He was also taken to the same place. The blade was again immersed in blood. The sword was gleamed again and the Guru said : "Is there any other Sikh who will offer me his head ? I am in great need of Sikhs' heads."[54] Sahib Chand, a barber, stood up. The Guru acted similarly. At the call for a fourth Sikh, the audience was horrified. Some fled away, while others bent down their heads in despair. Himmat Chand Kahar or water carrier by caste offered himself for the sacrifice. The fifth to volunteer was Mohkam Chand Chhimba, or a calico-printer.[55] The Guru stopped at five. He then ordered the curtain separating the tent from the canopy to be removed. All were wonder-struck to see the five men standing hale and hearty. The whole area rang with loud applause and thunderous clapping of hands.

All the five men were robed in similar new dresses and garlanded and then brought into the assembly. The Guru declared that Baba Nanak had found only one devoted Sikh in Guru Angad, while he had found five such Sikhs. Through the devotion of one true disciple Sikhism had flourished so well. By the consecration of five Sikhs his mission was bound to succeed beyond measure. He further said that since the time of Guru Nanak, the newly initiated Sikhs had taken *charanpahul* or water in which the Gurus had dipped their toes. It developed spirit of humility and meekness. The times had changed. In place of humility and meekness, boldness and pluck were required. He would therefore change the form of baptism, and would administer to his warrior Sikhs water stirred with a double-edged dagger in an iron vessel, and would change the name Sikh to Singh or lion. This title previously was exclusively confined to the noble Rajputs. His Singhs would look upon themselves as inferior to no other. Every man was a sworn soldier from the time of his baptism. His Singhs would fight against the enemies of their faith and freedom like lions. They would be rulers in this life and would attain salvation and bliss hereafter.[56]

The Guru's wife did not like that the five Sikhs who had offered their heads to the Guru should be given plain water. She immediately brought a plate full of sugar cakes (*patashas*), and with the approval of the Guru put them into water. The Guru observed : "We filled the *Panth* with heroism (*bir-ras*), you have mixed with it love (*prem-ras*)."[57] While stirring water, the Guru recited the sacred hymns of the holy Granth. The following five *banis* were recited by the Guru while preparing the *amrit* or nectar : Guru Nanak's *Japji*, Guru Amar Das's *Anand*, and his own *Jap*, *Chaupai* and ten *Swayyas*. The five Sikhs were asked to kneel down on their left knees and look into the eyes of the Guru. In this way, the Guru's soul power penetrated into their souls. The Guru then gave everyone of them five palmfuls of sweet water called *amrit* or nectar to drink, and five times was the holy water sprinkled over their heads and faces. The Guru said that the five beloved ones were his sons.[58] Individually, each was called a Singh and collectively they were given the name of Khalsa.

After administering baptism, the Guru stood before these five beloved ones and requested them to baptise him in the same manner. They pleaded their unfitness for such a performance. The Guru replied that he was not superior to his devoted disciples. His superiority lay in one thing. The Guru had attained salvation, *nirwan* or *sachkhand*, while his disciples were in the process of attaining it. The Guru said : "The Khalsa is the Guru and the Guru is the Khalsa. There is no difference between you and me." They baptised him, everyone of the five giving one palmful of nectar and sprinkling it on his head and face turn by turn. He also added Singh to his own name in place of Das and henceforth came to be called Gobind Singh.

Somebody in the congregation observed : *"Wah Guru Gobind Singh, ape Guru te ape Chela."* (Bravo Gobind Singh ! himself divine as well as disciple.)

The Guru's Khalsa consisted of four *Shudras* and only one *Kshatriya* .

Guru Gobind Singh then addressed the Five Beloved Ones :

> You are now of one creed, followers of one path. You are above all religions, all creeds, all castes, and all classes. You are the immortal soldiers of true *dharma*. You are the messengers of God. This country's honour and liberty is entrusted to you by Waheguru. Mix freely with the world, but remain of one soul, one ideal, and one aim. As Baba Nanak and his successors possessed one soul and one mind, so you possess one soul and one mind in the service of Waheguru, *dharam* and country. You are the soldiers of God. Today you have taken new birth in the home of the Guru. You are members of the Khalsa brotherhood. Anandpur is your birthplace. Gobind Singh is your father. You are the citizens of Bharatvarsha. Its independence and security is entrusted to you. Work for it with one mind. Success is sure. From today your salutation will be : Waheguru Ji Ka Khalsa, Waheguru Ji Ki Fatah.

Koer Singh in *Gur Bilas Patshahi Das* says :

> *Char barn ik barn pukara*
> *Nam Khalsa panth sudhara*

MEANING OF KHALSA

There are different views about the meaning of Khalsa. Some say that in Persian the word means pure and sincere, and that the Guru had purified his Sikhs after a certain ceremony by a test of steel and called them Singhs or lions. This is the general view which is accepted by almost all historians.

As a matter of fact, the Guru wished to inspire his Singhs with the conviction that while engaged in the service of the *Panth* (community) and the country, God was always present with them. For this purpose, he made full use of the number five.

The number five has always been sacred in India from time immemorial. The best form of self-government provided by ancient sages was *Panchayat* or a council of five. *Panchon men Parmeshwar* (God is present in the council of chosen five) was the famous saying in those days. The village administration in this country based on this principle survived unpolluted through all the upheavals of history. Guru Nanak laid emphasis on number five. In *Japji* he says :

> *Panch parwan,panch pradhan,*

Panche pawen dargah man,
Panche so hain dar rajan,
Panchan ka Gur ek dhayan.

Guru Gobind Singh made the best use of this spiritual sentiment. According to Giani Kartar Singh Kalaswalia in *Sri Guru Dashmesh Prakash*, page 106, Guruji sent from Paonta five Sikhs to Kashi to study Sanskrit. He built five forts at Anandpur. He selected five beloved ones at Anandpur. He read five *banis* while preparing *amrit*. He administered to each of them five palmfuls of *amrit* or holy water.

With a view to giving the Singhs an optimistic view of life in the midst of trails and tribulations which lay ahead of them, the Guru gave them a unique form of salutation :

Wahe Guru ji ka Khalsa, Wahe Guru ji ki Fatah.[59]

(The Khalsa is Thine, O Lord ! So does the Victory belong to You.)

Each half of this salutation again consist of five words. By this mode of salutation a strong link was established between the Khalsa and Victory, these two being the offspring of the Lord.

Guru Gobind Singh was in search of a word which could have the sanctity of five and the presence of God. Persian was the language of the elite and the Guru was himself a great scholar of Persian language and literature. He adopted the word Khalsa for his Singhs, because it fulfilled both the conditions in the most appropriate manner. Besides this word had already been used by Guru Hargobind for his Sikhs. In Persian Script Khalsa consists of five letters :

  (i) *Khe* or Kh stands for *Khud* or oneself.
 (ii) *Alif* or A represents *Akal Purkh*, *Allah* or God.
(iii) *Lam* or L signifies *Labbaik.* The News Royal Persian-English Dictionary by S. C. Paul, 1925 edition, Allahabad, page 357, gives its meaning as follows : "What do you want with me ? Here I am. What would you have ?"
 (iv) *Swad* or S alludes to *Sahib* or Lord or Master.
  (v) It ends with either A or H. *Alif* or A points to *Azadi* or freedom. If written with *he* or h, as it is generally the case, it refers to *huma*, a legendary bird. Every head it overshades, in time wears a crown.

The word Khalsa, therefore, has the sacredness of number five as well as the presence of God with his Singhs both engaged in a pleasant conversation. God Himself asks the Singhs :

"What do you want from me ? Here am I. What would you have ?" The Singhs reply : "Lord ! give us liberty and sovereignty."

THE FORMULA OF FIVE INTO FIVE

For the guidance of his Singhs, Guru Gobind Singh prescribed a formula consisting of five principles each governed by five rules. The five principles were : Five beliefs, five symbols, five vows, five deliverances and five rules of conduct.

(I) FIVE BELIEFS

The Khalsa were enjoined to have fivefold belief in God (*Akal Purkh*), Guru, Granth, Greeting — *Wahe Guru ji ka Khalsa, Wahe Guru ji ki Fateh, and Guru Nanak's Japji.*

(II) FIVE SYMBOLS

In those days, Hindus of respectable families wore five ornaments : gold earrings, a necklace, gold or silver bangles, finger ring and a waist belt of gold or silver or a *tagri*. The wearer felt proud of displaying his superior social position. At the same time, he ran the risk of losing these articles as well as his life into the bargain.

Guru Gobind Singh provided to his followers five jewels which were within reach of everybody down to the poorest peasant and the lowest labourer. Instead of creating fear in the mind of the wearer, his five jewels made his Singh bold, brave and awe-inspiring. These jewels were *kesh* or long hair, *kangha* or comb, *kirpan* or dagger, *kara* or steel bangle and *kachha* or a pair of knickerbockers. These symbols gave the Khalsa a semblance of unity, close brotherhood and equality. They developed group consciousness.

Several arguments are advanced in favour of unshorn hair, beards and moustaches :

1. That it was a general practice with Hindu sages and ascetics to keep long hair tied in a knot on top and flowing beard, and that Guru Gobind Singh wanted his disciples, in spite of their being householders, to be *karam yogis* or practical saints like Rama, Krishna and Bharata or the Five Pandavas.

2. That the warlike tribesmen of the North-West Frontier kept long hair though trimmed, and that the Guru wished his followers to have a similarly impressive and alarming appearance.

3. That the Guru adopted the practice of Goddess Durga of preserving long locks unshorn.

4. That the previous Gurus also kept long hair and Gobind Singh did not introduce any innovation.

5. The most reasonable explanation is that Guru Gobind Singh desired to provide his Khalsa a natural military uniform, the least expensive and most impressive permanent costume. Besides, he deemed it necessary that their heads should be properly guarded from sword cuts and *lathi* blows by means of long hair and turbans.

Comb indicated cleanliness. Steel bangle developed an iron will and destroyed the evil effects of misfortune. It was a permanent substitute of *rakhri*, a thread tied by sister on the wrists of brothers, reminding them of their duty to help and protect them. Similarly, the *kara* served as a reminder to the Sikhs that they had promised to be true to the Guru and the *Panth* and that promise must be kept at all cost.

Dagger depicted power and prestige. The pair of knickerbockers aimed at agility. It was more convenient for fighting than the long *dhoti* of Hindus and loose trousers of Muslims. Thus, the five symbols of Guru Gobind Singh gave strength to the body, mind and soul and developed an integrated personality of the wearer.

(III) FIVE VOWS

The Khalsa were required not to do five things : (a) to shave or cut hair, (b) to smoke,[60] (c) to eat *halal* meat of the animal killed in the Muslim style, (d) to wear a cap (*Jo Sikh sar topidhare, sat janam kushti hoe mare*) and, (e) to worship tombs, graves and relics of cremation and cherish superstitions.[61]

(IV) FIVE DELIVERANCES

Guru Gobind Singh declared the following five deliverances for his disciples :

1. *Dharam Nash* or freedom from previous religious practices and customs.[62]
2. *Karam Nash* or the obliteration of the past bad deeds.
3. *Janam Nash* or giving up the family influences and caste effects. The Guru explained that all the four Hindu castes had been blended into the Khalsa like the betel leaf. When mixed with *supari* (betel nut), *Katha* (catechu) and *chuna* (lime), the leaf reddened lips, strengthened gums, gave flavour to mouth and added heat to the body. Individually, none of these things could produce this effect. Similarly, the four Hindu castes when united would change them into a flower possessing beauty, bloom, fragrance and freshness. All the castes were blended on a democratic basis in which all were equal, and nobody was higher or lower.
4. *Sharam Nash* or the disappearance of hereditary professional distinctions, as all the callings like those of priests, soldiers, traders, weavers, tailors, barbers, cobblers and sweepers were given equal respect and status.
5. *Bharam Nash* or discarding the rituals prescribed by previous practices.

(V) FIVE RULES OF CONDUCT

Five rules were laid down for the general observance of the Sikhs :

1. Before beginning every work or enterprise, prayer should be offered.
2. The Sikhs should help one another and serve the *Panth*.
3. They should practise riding and using arms.
4. A Sikh coveting another's property would go to hell.
5. Regarding sexual matters the Guru said that his father Guru Tegh Bahadur had given him these instructions which should serve as a guide to the Sikhs :

"O son, as long as there is life in the body, make this thy sacred duty ever to love thine own wife more and more. Approach not another woman's couch either by mistake or even in a dream. Know, that the love of another's wife is a sharp dagger. Believe me death entereth the body by making love to another's wife. They who think it great cleverness to enjoy another's wife, shall in the end, die the death of dogs."[63]

The Guru Declared :

"Par nari ki sej, bhul supne hun na jaiyo."

(Go not ye, even in dream to the bed of a woman other than your own wife.)

ABOLITION OF THE INSTITUTION OF MASANDS

Immediately after the creation of the Khalsa, Guru Gobind Singh took another momentous decision in regard to the institution of *masands*. The third Guru, Amar Das, 1552-1574, had organised his Sikhs territorially into twenty-two districts. They were called *manjis*, because the priest in charge of the district sat on a cot, while all others were seated on the floor. These missionaries were called *Sangatias*. During the pontificate of Guru Ram Das, 1574-1581, they were called Ramdas after the name of the Guru. The fifth Guru, Arjun, 1581-1606, put a Sikh of status in charge of each district. He called him by the dignified term of *masand*. It was the Punjabi form of the Persian word *musannad* or an elevated man of grace and dignity. The *masands* collected one-tenth or *daswandh* of the income of each Sikh living in the area of their jurisdiction, and presented it to the Guru on the occasions of Baisakhi and Diwali, twice a year.

The *masand* system worked well in the beginning at least up to the time of the sixth Guru, Hargobind. The seventh Guru, Har Rai, died at the age of thirty-one. Out of this short life, he lived at Nahan for twelve years. The eighth Guru, Har Krishan died at the age of eight. The ninth Guru, Tegh Bahadur lived outside Punjab for many years, and when he came back he was involved in a conflict with the Government and was shortly afterwards executed. The central control having been loose and weak, the *masands* became independent to all intents and purposes. They began to gather riches and power for themselves, and became corrupt.

Ram Rai, the eldest son of Guru Har Rai, had been excluded from succession for misinterpreting the holy Granth. He established his own institution of guruship at Dehradun. Many people became his followers. To collect their offerings, he also appointed *masands*. He failed to control them. Guru Gobind Singh in his early days was living at Paonta, not very far from Dehradun. He sought Guru Gobind Singh's help. He said : "My *masands* are getting too powerful and headstrong. When I am gone, do protect my family and property from being ruined at their hands."[64]

A little later, Ram Rai was in a trance. The *masands* said he had died. Ram Rai's wife protested that it often happened before and he was alive. The *masands* cremated him and seized his property. At her request, Guru Gobind Singh went to Dehradun and punished them. This was the first experience by the Guru of their arrogance and effrontery.

The Guru's own *masands* had become corrupt, selfish, profligate and cruel. Frequent complaints were pouring in against their misbehaviour. They treated the Sikhs with scorn, and persecuted them. They had courtesans in their *harems*. They demanded the hands of the daughters of the Sikhs for their servants and sycophants. They extorted from them good food, good beds and full service. They let loose their horses into the green and ripe fields of the Sikhs.[65]

They were also adopting a defiant attitude towards the Guru. They retained a larger part of the offerings for themselves. They opposed the Guru's Ranjit Nagara, the huge kettledrum beaten every morning and evening at Anandpur. They exerted pressure upon Gobind Singh to lend his elephant and the tent to the Raja of Bilaspur. They often boasted that the Guru's power and prestige was mainly due to their work of preaching and procuring money.[66]

In *Bachitra Natak*, the Guru condemns the *masands* thus :

> *Jo Babe ke dam na dai hain*
> *Tin te gah babar ke lai hain*
> *Dai dai tin ko bari sajai*
> *Pun lahen greh loot banai.*[67]

(Those who do not pass on the offerings received for Baba,
   They would be seized by the successors of Babar;
   Severe punishment would be inflicted upon them,

Then their houses would be ransacked.)

On this occasion, Guru Gobind Singh abolished this institution. Most of the *masands* were present there. The notorious ones were severely punished, while others had to pay fines.

The *Akhbarat-e Durbar-e-Mualla* or a newsletter of the Mughal court dated May 13, 1710 stated : "Guru Gobind Singh had summarily dismissed the *masands* long ago."[68] This measure not only freed the Sikh from humiliation, but also restored a close personal contact between the Guru and his disciples.

He issued strict instructions to the Sikhs not to pay anything to the *masands*, but make their offerings to the Guru directly while visiting him. Those Sikhs who gave money to *masands* were placed under a curse :

> *Jab hawai hai bemukh bina dhan*
> *Tab charhi hain Sikhan kah mangan*
> *Je je Sikh tin ain dhan dai hain*
> *Loot Malechh tin u hau lai hain.*[69]

(When these disloyal persons become paupers,

> They go to the Sikhs to beg;
> Those Sikhs who gave them money.
> Shall be plundered by the Muslims.)

In *Chaupais* 12 to 15, the Guru says he will not forgive them, and God also will not own them.

ADMONITION TO PRINCES

Besides the Sikhs, a large number of hill Rajputs and the Rajput princes of the neighbourhood had gathered there to see what the Guru was doing. After creating the Khalsa, the Guru addressed them :

"How has your religious, political and social status deteriorated ! You have abandoned the worship of the true God and addressed your devotions to gods, goddesses, rivers, trees, etc. Through ignorance, you know not how to govern your territories; through indolence and vice, you disregard the interests of your subjects. You place over them officials who not only hate you, but are besides your mortal enemies. You despise and loath one another through your narrow prejudices, and you act contrary to the wishes of the great Almighty Father. Your morals have become so perverted that through fear and with a desire to please your Mussalman rulers, you give them your daughters to gratify their lust. Self-respect hath found no place in your thoughts, and you have forgotten the history of your sires. I am intensely concerned for your fallen state. Are you not ashamed to call yourselves Rajputs when the Mussalmans seize your wives and daughters before your very eyes ? Your temples have been demolished and mosques built on their sites; and many of your faith have been forcibly converted to Islam. If you still possess a trace of bravery and of the ancient spirit of your race, then listen to my advice, embrace the Khalsa religion, and gird up your loins to elevate the fallen condition of your country."[70]

PARABLE OF DONKEY

After the creation of the Khalsa, a large number of Sikhs stayed at Anandpur to get baptism and to enjoy the company of the youthful Guru who was then 32. A Sikh presented a tiger's skin to Guru Gobind Singh. In the evening stroll, the Guru saw a donkey grazing in a field. He left two Sikhs to keep a watch on the donkey's movements. In the night, the tiger's skin was fastened on the donkey. Early next morning people raised an alarm. The whole population was terrified. Nobody dared to stir out of his house. The Guru collected his Sikhs, approached the donkey and removed the tiger's skin. The Guru then said : You should be Khalsa from within and without and should not behave like the disguised donkey. Your persecutors are outwardly like lions, but inwardly they are cowards. Face them boldly, and they will be beaten.

SIGNIFICANCE OF THE CREATION OF THE KHALSA

1. The creation of the Khalsa was an epoch-making event in the religious and political history of the country. It marked the beginning of the rise of a new people, destined to play the role of hero against all oppression and tyranny. The severities of the high caste people over their brethren, the Shudras, were set at naught as soon as one joined the ranks of the Khalsa, where all were equal and ready to render one another every help and useful service. Their only difficulty lay in destroying the organised oppression of tyrannical despotism of the Mughal Government. It was a gigantic task for the small community of the Khalsa. Under the direction of the Guru, the Khalsa took up the profession of arms and the results were most surprising. The people, lowliest of the low, who had lived for centuries under complete servility now turned into doughty warriors, the praises of whose physique and valour were sung by the whole world including their bitterest foes. The Guru's assertion made on this occasion was fully justified :

    "Chiryan kolon baz marawan,
    Tan main Gobind nam kahawan."

    (Call me by the name of Gobind only if I succeed in making sparrows kill hawks.) Its implication was that his Khalsa who were poor and unarmed and who were as docile and innocent as sparrows would destroy the hawks meaning the Mughal Empire and the foreigners whose constant stream was running from the north-west across the Punjab to Delhi and other places.

2. The Guru declared himself equal with his five beloved ones. He considered them even superior to himself when he took baptism at their hands. It was pure and genuine democracy. It represented the spirit of the Glorious Revolution in Britain which had taken place ten years earlier in 1689. It had demolished the theory of the divine rights of kingship.

3. Further, the foundation of the Khalsa implied that the people had the divine right to overthrow a tyrannical government, and establish in its place a government of their own choice. In this doctrine, the Guru anticipated the Declaration of Rights by the thirteen American colonies in 1776.

4. The Guru gave the Khalsa the social ideal of equality and close brotherhood. There was to be no distinction of birth, caste, class or colour. All were equal in social status, and had the same rights and privileges. He, thus, enunciated ninety

years earlier the principles of liberty, equality and fraternity which formed the bedrock of the French Revolution.

REFERENCES

1. *The Quran,* ix, 29 quoted by Sir Jadunath Sarkar in his *A Short History of Aurangzib* (1954), p. 140.
2. Sir Jadunath Sarkar, *A Short History of Aurangzib* (1954), pp. 140-41.
3. Ibid., p. 147.
4. Ibid.
5. Ibid., p. 152.
6. Ibid., p. 150.
7. Ibid.
8. Ibid., p. 151.
9. Ibid., pp. 147-18.
10. Ibid., p. 148.
11. Ibid., pp. 150-51.
12. Ibid., p. 151.
13. Ibid., p. 150.
14. Ibid., p. 149.
15. Ibid., p. 150.
16. Ibid., p. 151.
17. Ibid.
18. Ibid., p. 152.
19. Ibid., p. 153.
20. Ibid., p. 154.
21. Ibid., p. 161.
22. Ibid., p. 162.
23. Ibid.
24. Ibid.
25. Ibid., p. 162.
26. Ibid., p. 163.
27. Ibid., p. 164.
28. Ibid., p. 277.
29. Ibid., p. 293.
30. Ibid., p. 294.
31. Ibid., f.n.
32. Ibid., p. 295.
33. Ibid., p. 296.
34. Ibid., p. 300.
35. Ibid., p. 302.
36. Ibid., p. 303.
37. Rajware, xvi, document no. 35, quoted by Brij Kishore, in his *Tara Bai and Her Times,* p. 70.
38. *A Short History of Aurangzib* (1954), p. 303.
39. Ibid.
40. Narain Singh, *Guru Gobind Singh,* Guru Gobind Singh Foundation, Chandigarh, 1967, p. 16.
41. *Akal Ustat,* Swayyas 15, 85; Pt. Narain Singh Giani, *Dasam Granthi Stik,* published by Buta Singh Pratap Singh, Amritsar, pp. 82-83.
42. *Khulasat-ut-Twarikh,* p. 70.

43. Ibid.

44. *Bachitra Natak,* Section vi, Chaupais 42-43.

45. Ibid., Section vi, Chaupai 29.

   In the translation from *Bachitra Natak, Chandi Charitra* and *Akal Ustat* my friend and colleague
   Professor Nirbhai Singh has given me great help.

46. *Chandi Charitra,* Part I, p. 231.

47. Sainapat, *Sri Gur Sobha,* Harnam Singh, Lahore, 1925, pp. 18-19.

48. *Bachitra Natak,* Nanak Chand Naz, Jullundur, 1952, No. 140, p. 126.

49. *Gur Bilas,* quoted by Banerjee in *Evolution of the Khalsa,* ii, p. 95.

50. Macauliffe, *The Sikh Religion,* V, p. 83.

51. Ibid., pp. 286, 287, 289.

52. *Bachitra Natak,* Raswal Chhand.

53. *Bachitra Natak,* Bhujang Paryat Chhand.

54. Macauliffe, op. cit. V, p. 92.

55. Ganda Singh, *Makhiz-e-Twarikh-e-Sikhan,* i, p. 8.

56. Macauliffe, op. cit. V, p. 93.

57. Kalaswalia, p. 203.

58. W. L. M'Gregor draws a ludicrous conclusion : "The term Singh, applied by Gooroo Govind to his
   followers, may have had reference to the great number of lions infesting the Punjab even in his
   time." *History of the Sikhs,* i, p. 23.

59. The word 'Wahe Guru' is used in *Puratan Janam Sakhi* on p. 23. It says Guru Nanak used it.

60. The Guru Said : "Wine is bad, bhang destroyeth one generation.   But tobacco destroyeth all
   generations."   (Macauliffe, op. cit. V, p. 153).

   Santokh Singh says that the tobacco leaf resembles the ear of a cow, and so the Guru prohibited its use.
   Suraj Prakash, 5571, f. n.

61. Bhai Nandlal, *Rahit Namah,* published by Bhais Partap Singh Sunder Singh, Amritsar, p. 2 *"Gor marhi
   mat bhul na mane."*

   (Worship not even by mistake a tomb or a relic of cremation.)

62. *Phokat dharam na kauri kaman.* Bhagat Lakshman Singh, *Guru Gobind Singh,* 1963, p. 3.

63. Macauliffe, op. cit. V, p. 110.

64. Kartar Singh, *Life of Guru Gobind Singh,* pp. 70-71.

65. Bhagat Lakshman Singh, *Guru Gobind Singh,* 1963, pp. 24-25.

66. Macauliffe, op. cit. IV, pp. 316-17; V, pp. 5, 11, 12, 23, 84, 86.

67. *Bachitra Natak,* Section xiii, Chaupai 10.

68. Ganda Singh, *Makhiz-e-Twarikh-Sikhan,* i, p. 84; *Kalgidhar Chamatkar,* pp. 293-65.

69. *Bachitra Natak,* Section xiii, Chaupai ii.

70. Macauliffe, op. cit. V, pp. 100-101; *Kaligidhar Chamatkar,* pp. 217-24.

24

GURU GOBIND SINGH DESIGNATES SRI GRANTH SAHIB TO BE GURU

Ganda Singh

The two historical facts that Guru Gobind Singh, the Tenth and the last personal Guru of the Sikhs, died at Nanded in the Deccan, now in Maharashtra, on October 6-7, 1708, and was cremated there have been substantiated not only by contemporary and semi-contemporary evidence, but also by other authorities of undeniable historical importance. It has also been authenticated beyond doubt that Guru Gobind Singh did not appoint any one of his followers to succeed him as Guru and that he commanded his Sikhs to look upon the Word of the great Masters, as embodied in their holy book, the Granth Sahib, as their Guru, thenceforward known as Guru Granth Sahib.

Guru's Personality

Like all his predecessors, from Guru Nanak to Guru Tegh Bahadur, Guru Gobind Singh was a historical person who lived in this world. He was born at Patna in the eastern province of Bihar. He travelled throughout the length of the Uttar Pradesh on his way to Anandpur and spent the greater part of his life in the Punjab. He was neither a renunciatory recluse nor an ultra-spiritualistic saint given to slumbering meditation, and thus beyond the reach of his fellow beings. He was, no doubt, a godly being. But his godliness was not otherworldly. He believed and declared that he had come to the world with the mission to protect, encourage and help the good, and to chastise and uproot the evil-doers. This could be done only by leading an active life in the world, not in the hiding retreats of mountains and jungles, far away from the people, but by living amongst them, teaching and guiding them both by precept and example, leading them at every step of their worldly lives, protecting them from aggression and oppression, ready to lay down his life in the cause, if need be. This was Guru Gobind Singh, both a teacher and a disciple — the real Khalsa — a saint and a soldier, a man of the world and yet detached.

As the son of a martyred father, he was the subject of the attention of both the oppressed people and of the oppressive rulers. While his people looked up to him as their saviour and socio-political guide, the power-mad rulers looked upon him as a dangerous enemy, who was inspiring their meek and submissive subjects with a spirit of freedom and resistance. The latter, therefore, were ever watchful of his programmes and vigilant of his activities.

As a scholar of many languages and a writer of soul-stirring poetry, practising the use of arms and training his men in it, he always acted in the open and kept himself in close and constant touch with those around him. As a commander of his armies fighting either against the Hill Rajas of the Shivaliks or Mughal levies of Sirhind and Lahore, he always occupied a prominent place within the sight of his men. Those were the days when it was *darshan* of the leader that inspired and sustained them in the field of action. He created out of the indistinguishable common people the distinct order of the Khalsa, with an uncommon form and symbols that helped distinguish them easily in a crowd of millions.

The Guru knew no despondency and did not give way to frustration under the most adverse circumstances. He lost not his heart at the death of his four young sons and aged mother. Two of his sons he had himself sent into the battlefield at Chamkaur. He heard the news of cold-blooded murder of his younger sons at Sirhind with complete resignation to the Will of God. His letter addressed to Emperor Aurangzeb from Dina, popularly known as the *Zafarnamah* or *Epistle of Victory*, evidently in reply to one from the Emperor, in its style and content, bespeaks volumes for the unruffled and evercalm state of his mind.

With the cessation of war, Guru Gobind Singh again engaged himself in literary pursuits, and completed and edited the Sikh's holy Book at Talwandi Sabo, now known as Damdama Sahib, in the Bathinda district of Punjab.

GURU'S MAGNANIMITY

In spite of the long-standing animosity and continued persecution by the Mughal Emperor, the Guru favourably responded to the invitation of Aurangzeb for a meeting and set out for the Deccan where the Emperor then lay encamped. But the Emperor died on February 20, 1707, while the Guru was on his way to the South. He received the news near Baghaur in Rajasthan. He immediately marched back towards the Punjab and was in the neighbourhood of Delhi when the emissaries of the heir-apparent Prince Muhammad Muazzam appealed to him for assistance. He was then face to face with a great trial of his life. And he was able to meet it boldly and in the right way. He was not to be deflected from the right decision by memories of past bitter relations with the Prince's ancestors. For him, the bitter past had died with the past. He rose above the weaknesses of revengeful mortals and, like the true Guru and the chivalrous soldier that he was, helped him with a detachment of men in the battle of Jajau in June, 1707. He met the new Emperor, Shah Alam Bahadur Shah (the old Prince Muhammad Muazzam) at Agra in a public *darbar* on July 23, 1707, when the royal host publicly acknowledged the Guru's assistance in the war of succession, and in token thereof, presented to him, a rich dress of honour, including a *dhukh-dhukhi* worth sixty thousand Rupees. The Guru was then accompanied by a number of Sikhs. He kept his people in the Punjab and elsewhere fully informed through formal letters not only of his important activities, but also of his future intentions and programme. He kept nothing secret from the Khalsa, whom he had openly, and on many occasions, declared to be his very image — *Khalsa mero rup hai khas, Khalse men hau karaun nivas*. Nor did he ever, throughout his normal life, travel or move about incognito. In the company of Emperor

Bahadur Shah moving to the Deccan, he was accompanied by a number of Sikhs and availed himself of the opportunity of visiting the various Sikh *sangats* on the way. The *Tarikh-i-Bahadur Shahi* tells us that, when accompanying the royal camp, "He was in the habit of constantly addressing assemblies of worldly persons, religious fanatics and all sorts of people." (Elliot and Dowson, *History of India*, vii, p. 566).

HIS LAST DAYS

At Nanded, where he arrived in the last week of August, 1708, he performed the normal duties of life and regularly attended and addressed the assemblies of the Sikhs and other people both in the morning and afternoon when the *dhadis* headed by Nath Mall and his companions recited ballads on Sikh themes. He was in the best of spirits throughout his stay there. Although warned on his way to the Deccan by the *Dadupanthi* saint Jait Ram of the sorceries of the *bairagi* ascetic Madho Das, the Guru visited his hermitage on the bank of the river Godavari on September 3, 1708, the day of the solar eclipse and successfully reclaimed him to a normal life in the world. He then baptized him into a regular Khalsa and relumed him with Promethean fire to play in the Punjab the historic role of a valiant hero and a great martyr. Even after he had been stabbed near the heart and his imperfectly healed wound had burst open as the result of his bending a stiff bow, he maintained his usual cheerfulness and told his sorrowful Sikhs not to give way to mourning on his death.

In his last farewell message, he told the Khalsa :

"I have entrusted you to the Immortal God ...... I have infused my mental and bodily spirit into the Granth Sahib and the Khalsa ...... Obey the Granth Sahib. It is the visible body of the Guru." (Macauliffe, *The Sikh Religion*, Vol. V, p. 244.)

HISTORIC STEP

It is a very significant thing indeed from the historical point of view that he did not nominate anyone of his followers to succeed him as Guru of the Sikhs. Those who have studied the story of his life know that at the institution of the baptismal ceremony and, through it, of the creation of the Khalsa, on the Vaisakhi day of 1756 *Vikrami*, 30th March, 1699, he had not only presented himself to be formally initiated into the fraternity of the Khalsa, but had also submitted himself to the discipline which had been prescribed by him for the new order of the Singhs (the Khalsa). This virtually meant the surrender of his high office of guruship to the will of the Khalsa and its merger into the body politic of the new order. And this is what he reaffirmed and declared from his deathbed. In the words of Sainapat, who was not only a contemporary of the Guru, but was also one of his trusted courtiers at Anandpur and who wrote his *Sri Gur Sobha* in 1711, within three years of the Guru's death :

"A day before his death, the Singhs asked him as to the form he was adopting (or the person whom he was nominating to succeed him). In reply, he said that the Khalsa was his very self and that to them he had granted his robe — his physical self, and that the Eternal and the limitless Word uttered with the Lord's light is our Supreme Master — *Satguru hamara*" (XVIII. 40-44, 805-809)."

This is supported by Bhai Nandlal, a devoted disciple, who was present at Nanded at the time of the Guru's death. He tells us in the *Rahitnama* that the Guru had told him that his one form is the formless Supreme Spirit and the other the Granth *Ji* — the *Gur-Sabda*, the Word of the great Gurus incorporated in the holy Granth Sahib — *Dusar rup Granth ji jan, ... mera rup Granth ji jan, is men bhed nahin kuch man* (have no doubt about it). The visible form, is the Sikhs, the Khalsa, absorbed in *Gurbani* (the Word of the Guru, Guru Granth Sahib), night and day.

GURU'S COMMANDMENT

Another close associate of the Guru and the author of a *Rahitnama* is Bhai Prahlad Singh who has also recorded the Guru's commandment in this respect saying :

"With the order of the Eternal Lord has been established the (Sikh) *Panth* : All the Sikhs are hereby commanded to obey the Granth as the Guru." (*Rahitnama Bhai Prahlad Singh*).

Similarly, Bhai Chaupa Singh, another associate of the Guru, has mentioned this commandment in his *Rahitnama*.

PERSONAL GURUSHIP ABOLISHED

Thus, Guru Gobind Singh abolished for all time to come the nomination of any one person as the Guru of the Sikhs. After him, the Khalsa, with Guru Granth Sahib as their Eternal Guru, became the Guru-*Panth*, believing in the unity and uniqueness of the One Formless, Self-existing, All-pervading and Eternal God.

With this, the historical life of Guru Gobind Singh came to an end and he departed from this world on *Katik Sudi* 5, 1765 *Bikrami*, October 6-7, 1708 A.D.

There is abundant reliable, original, contemporary and semi-contemporary evidence available for comparative study of different versions of controversial events and for sifting fact from fiction. It is in the light of such material that we propose to examine here the last event of the earthly life of Guru Gobind Singh, i.e., his death at Nanded and the appointment of his successor.

It will greatly help us to understand the various points of this study if we know the different types of scholars who have written about the last days of Guru Gobind Singh at Nanded.

EYEWITNESSES

First of all there are those who were then present at Nanded or had been in its neighbourhood and had unmistakable knowledge of his death. To this type also belong those who had known the Guru personally, had met his companions and had received first-hand information about the end of his life.

IMPARTIAL SCHOLARS

The second type comprises the unattached scholars who have written on this topic purely from a historical point of view. Only such of them have taken notice of his last command and farewell message as have studied the growth and development of the Sikh movement from the time of Guru Nanak and were interested in the religious life of the Sikh people after the demise of Guru Gobind Singh. They are mostly non-Sikhs — Hindus, Muslims and Christians.

ACTUAL FACTS

To come to the story of the death of Guru Gobind Singh. It is agreed on all hands that, while at Nanded, he was one evening stabbed by a Pathan, and that his wound was stitched and bandaged by a surgeon sent by Emperor Bahadur Shah. It is also accepted, without doubt, that his imperfectly healed wound burst open when the Guru bent a stiff bow presented to him by a visitor.

The news of the death of Guru Gobind Singh finds a prominent mention in the Royal Court News, *Akhbarat-i-Darbar-i-Mualla*, of October-November, 1708 A.D. and the *Bahadur Shah Nama* in a number of places. Emperor Bahadur Shah had crossed the river Godavari on October 7, 1708, to quell the rebellion of his younger brother Kam Bakhsh before the news about the death of the Guru was reported to him. For the next three weeks, he was extremely busy preparing for the coming struggle. On October 28, the Emperor ordered the grant of a dress of honour to the son of Jamshed Khan Afghan who had died at the hands of the Guru. Apparently, he was the same person who had, under the assumed name of Gul Khan, stabbed the Guru at Nanded and had fallen under his sword before he could escape. Or, he might have been the companion of Gul Khan killed by the Sikhs while he was trying to run away after the death of Gul Khan.

On *Ramazan 9, 2nd Bahadurshahi* (November 11, 1708), the Emperor's orders were solicited about the movable property of the deceased Guru, which according to the Mughal practice ought to have been confiscated. The Emperor, however, commanded that "These goods will not add to the affluence of the royal treasury. It is the property of saintly people. It should not be interfered with" — *hukm shud as-in amwal khazanah-i-Badshahan ma'mur na-mi-shawad, mal-i-darveshan ast, mazaham nami shawand —*

(Cf. *Bahadur Shah Nama*, Irvine Later Mughals, i. 90.)

BALLAD VERSIONS

Dhadi Nath Mall was present in the camp of the Guru at Nanded and used to recite ballads in the afternoon assemblies of the Sikhs there. One such ballad known as the *Amar Namah*, composed under the name of the Guru himself in the first person, has come down to us through the son of Bhai Fatta, the seventh descendant of Nath Mall. According to its colophon, it was completed in the month of *Katik* 1765 *Bikrami* after the death of the Tenth Guru. As the 30th of *Katik* of that year corresponded to 31st October, 1708, the *Amar Namah* was evidently completed within twenty-four days of the Guru's death. Describing it in the first person in the words of the Guru, the *Amar Nama* says in lines 61-62 :

"I then resolved to set out for the lasting abode in heaven, which is the place of all peace and divine blissfulness. My Singhs (the Khalsa) shall remain firm, listening to *vars* from *dhadi* singers."

In keeping with the tradition of the ancient balladists, Nath Mall did not enter into the details of the painful event. Except in the case of deaths occurring in the thick of battle, the reciters or writers of *vars* generally skipped over the mention of deaths or made a casual reference to them in a prose sentence. In support of this observation, we have the example of Bhai Gurdas. He was one of the closest relatives of Guru Arjun on the mother's side, and was also one of the most revered and knowledgeable Sikhs of his time. In his *Varan*, he has, in a systematic manner, given brief accounts not only of the Gurus from the time of Guru Nanak to Guru Hargobind, but also of the various *sangats* and important Sikhs in the Punjab and outside. But, he does not make any clear and direct statement on the martyrdom of Guru Arjun which gave a sharp turn to the development and transformation of the Sikh movement. He has quietly passed over the event with only a casual reference to his death in a line or two.

In his *Ibrat Namah* or the *Swaneh*, 1705-19 A.D., Mirza Muhammad Harisi had devoted some thirteen pages to the contemporary account of the Sikhs, with particular reference to Banda Singh. He tells us that Guru Gobind Singh had travelled in the train of Emperor Bahadur Shah to the Deccan and was killed there in 1120 *al-Hijri*, 1708 A.D., by an Afghan, an old enemy of his, and his body was cremated.

FIRST RELIABLE BIOGRAPHY

The *Sri Gur Sobha* by poet Sainapat, mentioned as Saina Singh by Bawa Sumer Singh in his *Pothi Gur-Bilas ki*, was completed in 1768 *Bikrami*, 1711 A.D., i.e., within three years of the Guru's death. He was an old Sikh of his and had lived with him at Anandpur. His is the first book which could be said to have been a reliable biography of the Guru. His narrative was evidently based on first-hand information received from the Sikhs who had returned from Nanded and had been eyewitnesses to what they related to Sainapat. As far as we can see, the purity of his account, though brief in many places, is not muddied with the mixture of imaginary myths introduced later into the life of the Guru, beginning with the *Gur-bilas Patshahi Das* by Koer Singh, written in 1751, forty three years after the death of the Guru.

Mentioning the death of the Guru (XVIII. 34-37) without any poetical embellishments, the *Sri Gur Sobha* tells us that a day before the event, the Guru had, in reply to a question of the Sikhs, said that he had bestowed his physical form upon the Khalsa — *bakhsh dio Khalis ko jama* (XVIII-41), and that the Limitless and the Eternal Word was the *Satguru* — *Satguru hamara apar apara Shabad bichara ajar-jaran* (XVIII-43). This was Guru Gobind Singh's last message and his final commandment saying in unmistakable language and clear words that he was not appointing any particular individual as the succeeding Guru and that the Khalsa under the guidance of the Divine Word — *Gurbani* — was to be the future physical and spiritual representative of the Guru.

SIKHS' ACCEPTED CREED

This has since become the accepted creed of the Sikhs as inculcated by Bhai Nandlal in his *Rahitnama* or the *Rules of Conduct*. Bhai Nandlal, as history knows, was a devoted Sikh of Guru Gobind Singh and had stayed with him for some time at Anandpur. According to the *Amar Namah*, line 42, Bhai Nandlal was present in the Emperor's camp at Nanded as one of his ministers during the Guru's stay there. He was a distinguished scholar of Persian and Punjabi and, out of his ten works known to us, eight — five in Persian and three in Punjabi — are commentaries on Sikh life and teachings. One of them, the *Rahitnama*, which is written in the form of a dialogue between the Guru and the Bhai, lays down the rules for Sikh conduct. Therein, as already mentioned in one of the previous paragraphs, the Guru had told Bhai Nandlal that his two forms were the Granth — *mera rupa Granth ji jan* — embodying *Gurbani* and the Sikhs (the Khalsa) deeply absorbed in it. This not only clarifies but also supports the Guru's last message and commandment to the Khalsa mentioned in *Sri Gur Sobha*.

The *Gur-bilas Chhevin Patshahi* leaves no doubt about the recognition by the Sikhs of the guruship of Guru Granth Sahib after the death of Guru Gobind Singh. The *Gur-bilas* was begun by its author, poet Sohan, in May 1717 and was completed on July 22, 1718 (*Sawan* 22, *Sudi* 5, 1775 *Bikrami*), within ten years of the Guru's death. Its fourth chapter is devoted to the compilation of the holy book by Guru Arjun and the first twelve verses of the fifth chapter to its formal installation in the *Darbar Sahib*, Amritsar. Therein, the author has invariably used the then accepted prefix Guru to the Granth and has called it Guru Granth. The following verses of chapter IV are very significant indeed.

"Hear ye all, this precept of mine as true and certain.

Recognise the Granth to be the same as the Guru, think not of any difference (between the two).

In the *Kali-yuga*, Guru Granth has assumed the form of Sri Guru.

Recognise Guru Granth to be the very self of the Ten Gurus. (412)

He who wishes to see the Guru, let him see Guru Granth.

And, he who wishes to speak to the Guru, let him read the Granth with a devoted mind. (413)"

(Chapter IV old ed., p. 75; new ed., p. 90.)

FURTHER TESTAMENTS

We have available to us in a collection of manuscripts the accounts of Guru Gobind Singh's meeting with Emperor Bahadur Shah in 1707 (*Bahadur Shah ki Mulaqat ka Prasang*), of his last days and death at Nanded in the Deccan in 1708 (*Guru Sahib Daswen Patshah ji ke Joti Jot Samawane ka Prasang*) and of the first battle of the Sikhs at Amritsar with the Mughal forces of Lahore in 1709 (*Var Amritsar ki*) during the governorship of Aslam Khan. Copies of the first two manuscripts are also available in the *Amrit Gutka* preserved in the Punjab State Archives, Patiala. According to the *Guru Sahib Daswen Patshah ji ke Joti Jot Samawane ka Prasang*, which is based on the information received from the companions of the Guru himself — *Hazur ke khas Sikhan di rasna thin* —, the Guru, before his death, told the Sikhs that he was not appointing anyone to succeed him as Guru, and that he was entrusting them to *Sri Sahib* and the *Sabda*, the great Word, as given in Granth Sahib which should be accepted by them all.

The *Parchian Sewa Das*, according to the date mentioned in the manuscript preserved in the Punjab University, Lahore, was written in 1798 *Vikrami*, 1741 A.D., while the manuscript in the Central State Library Patiala, bears 1896 *Vikrami*, 1839 A.D. as the date of its transcription. Sewa Das was an Udasi Sadhu. Writing in the style of a mystic, he tells us that the Guru had his funeral pyre prepared under his own supervision. He mounted it fully dressed and armed, sat on it cross-legged and that his light blended with the Divine Light — *Joti meh jot samane*. Heaps of flowers and scent were then showered on the pyre. After pouring plenty of *ghee* thereon, the pyre was set alight — *bahur baisantar lagava diya*. The Sikhs standing there started crying loudly. Several of them tried to jump into the flaming pyre, but they were not allowed to do so. When the pyre was all reduced to ashes, they found no trace of the dead body or of the Guru's arms. "All then so thought that the

Guru Baba had gone (to heaven) bodily."

BIRTH OF MYTHOLOGY

It is here for the first time, thirty-three years after the death and cremation of the Guru, that a suggestion has been made by a mystical minded Sadhu of the Guru having ascended to heaven bodily. This is only a reflection of the thinking of an ultra-devotional mind of an ascetic fed on the mythology of ancient Hindu *Puranas* full of supernatural fables added to the lives of their *avtars* — and also of the Gurus including Guru Nanak and his sons.

COHERENT ACCOUNT

Ten years later, in 1808 *Vikrami*, 1751 A.D., Koer Singh wrote his *Gur-bilas Patshahi Das*, making a liberal use of the *Sri Gur Sobha*. He has, however, covered a broader canvas and given an extensive and a coherent picture of the Tenth Guru's life. In his twenty-first chapter devoted to the death of the Guru, *Pyan Gur ker* based on the commentaries of Bhai Mani Singh, as mentioned in the colophon, Koer Singh tells us that in reply to a question of the Sikhs, Guru Gobind Singh had said that he would (always) be with the Sikhs and that he had raised his worthy sons (the Khalsa) to wreak vengeance (XXI, 60-61).

This is clearly a reflection of the mind of Koer Singh under the influence of the brutal treatment that had been meted out to Bhai Mani Singh, his preceptor, during the latter's captivity and martyrdom at Lahore in 1734, when he was hacked to pieces limb by limb under the orders of Nawab Zakariya Khan, the Governor of Lahore. Koer Singh has also made some very disparaging observations on the lowering standard of morality of the so-called religious teachers of his time moving about from house to house and begging for alms. "Without meditation, these immoral people", says he, "call themselves saints, while in their minds, they think of other people's women. As such, in the dark age of *Kali*, the real saints have disappeared like sun in the clouds." "Therefore, my virtuous Sikhs", says Guru, "should acknowledge the Guru Granth as supreme and worthy of worship" (and not any pretender saint of the type mentioned above) (XXI, 89-93). Koer Singh then goes on to say in the next verses that Guru Nanak had himself told Baba Budha of Ramdas :

"Recognise Ten of our incarnations then your family will be supreme." (94-95)

He then goes on to say :

"When the Ten incarnations disappear (from this world with the death of the Tenth one), then the ancestral line *Kul* will not continue."

"It is no longer the time for guruship : I will not anoint anyone (now)."

"Consider the entire Khalsa to have been entrusted to the protection (*lap*) of the Wielder of the Sword (*Asi Ketu*) — the Divine Protector."

"I have given to you to hold the sheet of the embodiment of the Word (*Shabad ka rup*). He who accepts it shall be an incomparable — really true Singh."

Recognise Sri Granth *Ji* as ever-ready (readily available), ever-present *darshan* (sight, appearance or embodiment) of the Guru. "Bring it here to this place." (96-98)

HOW GRANTH BECAME GURU

The Guru had by then grown very weak, as has been mentioned in verse XXX-56. The Holy Book was, therefore, brought to him. Coming to know of it, he said : "Let us go to the *Adi Sat-Guru* (the great Adi Guru Granth Sahib)". Evidently, he could then see that his end was fast approaching. He got up along with all of his Sikhs; took five *paise* and a coconut with him; offered them himself (to the Holy Book), bowed down, circumambulated it with all reverence and said :

> 'He who wishes to talk to me should read the Guru (Granth Sahib) and receive the peace of mind.

> 'There is no other Guru equal to it. Without any hesitation, I utter this truth.'

> 'There is no other Guru like it anywhere. Therefore, it should be accepted as the True Guru.'

> 'With its study (*darshan*) sins disappear. And by realising its Word in practice, salvation is obtained.' (XXI, 90-102)

Saying this, he calmly prepared himself for the end and desired a funeral pyre to be raised with the sandalwood worth five thousand Rupees previously purchased from a Labana Sikh. He told his wife Sahib Devi not to immolate herself on his pyre and sent her to Delhi. He then consoled the sorrowful Sikhs explaining to them the inevitableness of the end of human life saying : 'He who has full faith in Guru Granth and does not place his reliance on anything else shall have his wishes fulfilled by the Guru. With full faith in it, all suspicions will disappear.' He then bowed to Sri Granth, prayed in all reverence, made offerings to *rababi* musicians and was absorbed in the Word of the Granth Sahib" (XXI, 124-37).

The Guru died a little before midnight and was cremated in a place enclosed by a tent-wall, a Sikh setting fire to his dead body. The Sikhs then went out of the enclosure and stood there. Flames went up and the body of the Guru became all ashes. "Then came all the Gods (from Heaven) blowing conches and showering flowers and, amidst shouts of victory, took the Master away with them, with all the Heavens (*lokas*) singing his praises." (Ibid., 140, 142 and 143).

On the fourth morning, they searched the ashes, washing them with diluted milk, and found only a dagger therein. The Sikhs were all drowned in sorrow. At that time appeared on the scene an Udasi Sadhu and said that it was not becoming of the Sikhs to be sorrowful, for he had met the Guru in full dress on horseback and the Guru had told him (the Sadhu) to convey his message to the Sikhs not to go into mourning (Ibid., XXI, 144-5).

BEST INFORMED AUTHOR

Better accomplished in the art of writing, Koer Singh has not only supplied more details to his story but has also given clarity to it. He tells us in explicit language that Guru Gobind Singh discontinued the line of personal guruship and did not appoint anyone to succeed him as Guru. In fact, he had surrendered his personality to the Khalsa when he became one of them at the baptismal ceremony and he publicly declared this merger on many an occasion afterwards, and especially a little before his death at Nanded. Entrusting the Khalsa to the care of the Divine Protector, as declared by the great Master, Koer Singh narrates at some length the formal installation of Guru Granth Sahib as the Guru. He had been in close touch with Bhai Mani Singh who was a contemporary and close associate of Guru Gobind Singh and was the first person to be appointed as the reader of Guru Granth Sahib in the *Darbar Sahib* at Amritsar by Mata Sundri after the Guru's death. As such, he was the best informed person on the subject in addition to being the most qualified to explain the significance of Guru Granth Sahib to Koer Singh.

ANOTHER RELIABLE VERSION

Another work of the last quarter of the eighteenth century, which we may refer to here, is the *Bansawali Nama* of Kesar Singh Chhibar completed in 1826 *Bikrami*, 1769-70 A.D. Kesar Singh's ancestors had been in the service of Guru Gobind Singh as *dewans*. He claims to have seen and consulted in his early days a *bahi* or account book of the house of the Guru. The tenth *charan*, or chapter of the book, deals with the life of Guru Gobind Singh. Towards the end of it, in stanzas 678-83, he mentions the death of the Guru and his last commandment saying in reply to the questions of the Sikhs : "The Granth is the Guru; you hold the garment (seek the protection) of the Timeless God — *bachan kita Granth hai Guru, lar pakro Akal* (679). Two hours (*ghari*) later, the Guru went to heaven; his light blended with the Eternal Light. The same night, he was cremated after he had been bathed in rose water." (653)

Kesar Singh makes no mention of any heavenly reception or anything else of the kind.

MOST TRUTHFUL VERSION

The account of the death of Guru Gobind Singh as given in *sakhi* 27 of *Sakhian Patshahi Das* chapter of the *Mehma Prakash* by Sarup Das Bhalla, pp. 891-93, may on the whole be said to be nearest the truth and may be accepted as objective and historical. Written by a descendant of Guru Amar Das and based, apparently, on reliable evidence, it was completed in January, 1801. The first part of the chapter regarding the incitement to the Pathan who attacked and wounded the Guru seems to have come from earlier writers. But, the second part is based entirely on independent evidence. In the absence of any poetical embellishment and unnatural, mysterious or supernatural element introduced into it, the account may be accepted as historically correct. According to the *Mehma Prakash* :

"When the Guru took the bow in his hand and wished to pull it, the Sikhs submitted that the wound had not yet completely healed. The Guru said that there was no cause for fear. He then pulled the bow, and the stitches gave way. At this time, the Guru said that the time for his death had come. He called the Sikhs to his presence and he was pleased to see them. The Sikhs then asked him where they would have the *darshan* (of the Guru). The great Guru, merciful to the lowly, said : 'Our Ten forms have come to end. Now recognise Guru Granth Sahib in my place. He who wishes to talk to me should read the Adi Granth Sahib. This will be like talking to me. I have entrusted you to the lap of the Almighty.' Having said this, he desired them to prepare the *biban* (the wooden board to carry the dead body to the cremation ground). After this was done, he lay down and covered himself with a sheet and liberated himself from human existence (or merged himself in the Divine). Neither did he come anywhere nor did he go anywhere. Seeing this spectacle, all people fully believed that the great Guru was a part of the Divine Light. The Guru's body was then cremated and Sri Guru Granth Sahib was recognised in place of the Guru."

This is a simple and straightforward account of the death of Guru Gobind Singh with no mystery or embellishment enshrouding it. And it agrees, in all its essentials, with the contemporary and the earliest known accounts.

MOST RELIABLE AUTHORITY

Munshi Sant Singh, a lawyer of the Bedis, wrote an account of the Bedi family of the Una under the title of the *Bayan-i-Khandan-i-Karamat Nishan-i-Bedian* from the time of Guru Nanak to that of Baba Sujan Singh. It was completed in May, 1865. The first sixty-five pages of the work are devoted to the account of the Ten Gurus which ends with the death of Guru Gobind Singh at Nanded in 1765 *Bikrami*, 1708 A.D. According to it :

> "When on *Katik Sudi* 5, 1765 *Bikrami*, Guru Gobind Singh was about to die at Nanded in the Deccan, all the Singhs and disciples asked as to who would be the future Guru. The Guru then said : 'Guru Khalsa, Khalsa Guru. He who shall observe the Sikh *rahit* or the rule of conduct and morality and meditation, him know ye to be my very Self.' Then thinking that there should be a difinite centre of faith for all the Sikhs, the Guru with five paise and a coconut in his hand (as offering) bowed before Guru Granth Sahib and said : 'Ye all community should recognise Guru Granth Sahib as the Guru after me and obey the commandments contained therein.' And then he uttered the following couplet :
>
> 'Recognise the Guru Granth as the visible body of the Guru.
>
> The Sikh who wishes to meet me should find me therein.'"

In this, the author of the *Bayan* has reiterated the last commandment of Guru Gobind Singh in the words of his contemporary and well-known disciple Bhai Nandlal who was present at Nanded at the time of the Guru's death. There could be no better and more reliable authority than him on the subject.

The author of the *Bayan* is all devotion and praise for Baba Sahib Singh Bedi of Una, whom he has called 'Guru Sahib', throughout his book. He also tells us that, according to Guru Gobind Singh's promise, he was reborn in the house of Baba Kaladhari Bedi as his grandson — Sahib Singh (pp. 57-58, 66). But in spite of it, Munshi Sant Singh does not claim formal guruship for him in place of the Tenth Guru, who, he says, had formally declared Guru Granth Sahib to be the Guru after him. Born in 1756, A.D., within forty-eight years of the Tenth Guru's death and being the most respected Sikh of his time, commanding overwhelming influence with the Sikh Sardars, Rajas and Maharaja Ranjit Singh, he had a better chance than all the later pretenders. Baba Sahib Singh, however, preferred to be a humble disciple, a Sikh of Guru Gobind Singh — a Khalsa — than to pretend to be an equal of his. In 1780, he presented himself at Dera Guru Tegh Bahadur at Anandpur and received *Khande ki Pahul*, the *amrit* of the Khalsa, there. According to the *Bayan*, Baba Sahib Singh was the first of the Bedis to receive the Khalsa baptism, which he himself later on administered from time to time to a large number of Sikhs throughout the country.

HISTORICAL WORKS

Having referred to official records, contemporary works and hagiological literature, we now come to historical works of the eighteenth and nineteenth centuries based on the information available to, or collected by, professional historians. They are either in Persian or in English. The works written by Indian scholars, both Hindu and Muslim, are in Persian while those of the Europeans are in English. As almost all the Indian writers belonged to the Punjab or its neighbourhood, they had either lived amongst the Sikhs as neighbours or had close associations with them in day-to-day life. As such, most of them had first-hand knowledge of the prevalent beliefs, practices and ceremonies of the Sikhs and could, therefore, speak with a certain amount of authority. Some of them might have differed with the Sikhs in matters theological or might as well have had political prejudices against them, but about the broad facts of their history, there could be no misgivings. Moreover, as writers, they are expected to be impartial and objective. And to be as near the truth as possible, they must have relevant sources. As the subject under our immediate study here belongs to the prevalent beliefs of the Sikhs through the centuries and is purely historical, their mention in the historical works of the eighteenth and nineteenth centuries carries special weight with students of history and cannot be ignored by serious scholars.

IMPORTANT MUSLIM ACCOUNTS

We have already referred to the contemporary accounts of Mirza Muhammad Harisi's *Ibrat Namah* (1705-19 A.D.). To almost the same period belongs Sayyed Muhammad Qasim Husaini Lahauri's *Ibrat Namah* (1135 al-Hijri, 1722 A.D.) and *Ibrat Maqal* (1144 A.H., 1731 A.D.) written within fourteen and twenty-three years, respectively, of the death of Guru Gobind Singh. Giving the usual account of the Guru having died of the wound inflicted on him with a dagger by a Pathan at Nanded, Muhammad Qasim tells us that the Guru's body was cremated by his disciples with aloe and sandal wood according to the necessary Sikh rites (p. 36).

Muhammad Ali Khan Ansari has to his credit two very important historical works, the *Tarikh-i-Muzaffari* (1225 A.H., 1810 A.D.) and the *Tarikh-i-Bahr-ul-Mawwaj*, carrying the history of the Mughals to the beginning of the reign of Akbar Shah II (1806-37 A.D.). These works deal extensively with the struggles of the Sikhs against the Mughals and Durranis, and are considered to be important sources on the history of the Punjab during the eighteenth century. Before the end of Guru Gobind Singh's account, Muhammad Ali Khan writes that "after him (Guru Gobind Singh), according to the faith of these people (the Sikhs), the descending of guruship and of internal spiritualism came to end and the book, the Granth, was established in place of Guru" (*Tarikh-i-Muzaffari*, p. 152; *Tarikh-i-Bahr-ul-Mawwaj*, p. 208).

At the same time in 1810 A.D. (1225 A.H.) was completed Ahmed-bin-Muhammad Ali's *Mirat-ul-Ahwal-i-Jahan Numa*. According to it, "the sons of Guru Gobind had been killed in the battle of Alamgir. After him there is no *Khalifah* (successor, Guru)."

SUPPORTERS OF CONVENTIONAL VERSION

Rai Chatarman, the author of the *Chahar Gulshan Akhbar-un-Nawadar*, also known as the *Chatar Gulshan* or *Khulasat-un-Nawadir*, compiled his work in 1759 soon after the death of Mata Sundri about whom, and about Ajit Singh, her adopted son, and Mata Sahib Devi, he seems to be well-informed. According to him, the Pathan's dagger put an end to the Guru's life. "As declared by Guru Nanak", says he, "there are Ten persons (to be recognised). These Ten *Khalifahs* (Gurus) are called *Das Mahal*. Anyone else sitting on the *gaddi* after them is not acceptable to them (the Sikhs). Some recognise him (Ajit Singh, the adopted son of Mata Sundri). He was later disowned by Mata Sundri" (pp. 35-36).

In the *Maima-ul-Akhbar* (1214-20 A.H., 1799 A.D.), its author Har-Sukh Rai says about Guru Gobind Singh that "He is the Tenth *Mahal* and is the last *Zahur* (appearance or successor) of Guru Nanak" (p. 481).

EUROPEAN VERSIONS

This was the time when Maharaja Ranjit Singh had been on the throne of Lahore for some eleven years. He had occupied the traditional capital of the Punjab in 1799 A.D. and had fully established himself as the undisputed Maharaja of the Land of the Five Rivers. He had not only been accepted as such by a number of Muslim, Hindu and Sikh chieftains, but had also been recognised by the greatest foreign power in India, the British East India Company, which had entered into a political treaty with him. This attracted the attention of a number of British and Indian scholars, who wrote historical works devoted exclusively to the Sikhs. A few pamphlets, it is true, had also been written on the Sikhs in the eighteenth century by men like Antoine L. H. Polier (1780), William Franklin (1798-1803), etc., but they were too sketchy to contain any detailed account of the Sikh Gurus. George Forster alone has referred to the Gurus in his Letter No. XI in 1783 in his *A Journey from Bengal to England* and says :

> "Govind Singh was assassinated during this expedition (of Emperor Bahadur Shah to the Deccan) by a Pathan soldier and he died of his wounds in 1708 at the town of Nanded without leaving any male issue; and a tradition delivered to the *Sicques*, limiting their priests to the number of ten, induced them to appoint no successors to Govind Singh" (Vol. I, pub. 1798, p. 263).

Talking about the change in the inscription on the Sikh coins, Major James Brown has casually referred to Guru Nanak and Guru Gobind Singh as the first and the last Gurus of the Sikhs, respectively, and has indirectly given us the confirmed belief of the Sikhs of about 1787-88. He says in his *History of the Origin and Progress of the Sikhs*, published in 1788 :

> "...... but after they had been current about fifteen years, the grand Diet of the Sikh chiefs (called *Goormutta*) determined to call in all those Rupees, and to strike them in the names of Gooroo Nanuck and Gooroo Gobind Singh, the first and last of their Gooroos or religious leaders (pp. vi, viii)."

RELIABLE INDIAN WRITERS

In referring to the historians of the nineteenth century, we would prefer to mention at first the Indian writers who should presumably be better informed about the Sikh Gurus than Europeans. It may, however, be mentioned that some of the Indian writers wrote their books at the instance of Europeans, who were at this time feeling interested in the history and religion of the Sikhs, with whom they expected to come in close political contact in the near future. For this purpose, they desired to obtain as correct and reliable information as possible.

Khushwaqt Rai's *Tarikh-i-Sikhan*, also called the *Kitab-i-Tawarikh-i-Punjab*, was written in 1811. Therein he says that, "at Afzal (Abchal) Nagar (Nanded) the Guru purchased a piece of land and moved in all happiness from this transitory world to the world Eternal. The disciples of the Guru collected from all sides and cremated his body with aloe and sandalwood with all the necessary rites ...... This event, that is his death, took place on *Katik Sudi 5, 1765 Bikrami*. The generation (of Gurus) of Guru Nanak up to Guru Gobind Singh came to an end" (pp. 36b-37a).

In 1233 *al-Hijri*, 1817-18 A.D. was completed Ahmad Shah Batalia's *Tawarikh-i-Hind : Bayan-i-Ahwal-i-Mulk-i-Hind wa Maluk-i-an az Zaman-i-qadim ta 1233 Hijri*, a part of which, the *Zikr-i-Guruan wa ibtida-i-Singhan wa Mazhab-i-eshan*, forms an appendix to *Daftar* I and II of the *Umdat-u-Tawarikh* by Munshi Sohan Lal Suri. In it, Ahmad Shah tells us that Guru Gobind Singh, who had accompanied Emperor Bahadur Shah to the Deccan, died at Nanded in 1756 *Bikrami*, 1708 A.D. and that the place was known as Abchal Nagar. He says that some Sikhs also lived there and that the Nizam of Hyderabad had fixed a daily allowance for them. In addition to it, Maharaja Ranjit Singh also made handsome donations for the upkeep of the sanctuary and the maintenance of its custodians (p. 11).

OUTSTANDING WORK

The *Umdat-u-Tawarikh* of Lala Sohan Lal Suri is a very important work on the reign of Maharaja Ranjit Singh and his successors up to 1849. Although its first volume dealing with the Guru and the *misl* period was published in 1885, it was originally begun in the form of notes somewhere in the middle of the eighteenth century during the time of Sohan Lal Suri's grandfather and father, Lala Hakumat Rai and Lala Ganpat Rai. It tells us that during the last moments of Guru Gobind Singh's life, a disciple of his asked him as to whom he had appointed as Guru after him. Thereupon, the Guru replied, "the Guru is Granth *Ji*. There is no difference between the Granth and the Guru. From the *darshan* of Granth *Ji*, one shall have the happy *darshan* of the Guru Sahib" (Vol. I, pp. 64-65).

So intense was the faith of Maharaja Ranjit Singh in Guru Gobind Singh and so ardent was his desire to raise a befitting memorial on his last resting place at Nanded, that he occasionally sent large sums of money and a number of his men for the purpose all the way from the Punjab. The name of one Sardar Chanda Singh is mentioned in the *Umdat-u-Tawarikh* (Vol. III, part iii, p. 355) as having been deputed by him on the Ist of *Magh*, 1893 *Bikrami*, to proceed to Abchal Nagar with twenty-five thousand Rupees, with promise to remit more money, for the renovation and construction of buildings of the Sachkhand gurdwara there. (Also see Ibid. III, iii, pp. 77, 187, 267, 455).

Ratan Chand Bal, the author of the *Khalis Namah* (1846 A.D., p. 13b. 14a) and Ganesh Das Badehra of the *Char Bagh-i-Punjab* (1855 A.D., p. 118) also confirm the information about the death of the Guru.

MUSLIM CONFIRMATION

Ghulam Muhy-ud-Din alias Bute Shah in his *Tarikh-i-Panjab* (1848, p. 206) and Mufti-Ali-ud-Din in his *Ibrat Namah* of 1854 (Vol. I, p. 178) have both recorded the death of the Guru as an historical fact. Bute Shah in his abridged recension of the *Tarikh-i-Panjab* (preserved in the Punjab Public Library, Lahore) has followed Lala Sohan Lal's *Umdat-ut-*

Tawarikh in recording the last commandment of the Guru regarding the Granth being the Guru after his death and that "there is no difference between the Guru and the Granth" (p. 62).

The last Persian work to furnish a reference on the subject is Kanhaiya Lal Hindi's *Zafar Namah-i-Ranjit Singh* published in Lahore in 1876. In the introductory pages, he has given a sketch of the Gurus at the end of which he says that "Guru Gobind Singh died at Abchal Nagar (Nanded in the Deccan) in 1765 *Bikrami* and that no one (of his disciples) succeeded him to the *gaddi* (throne of Guruship). With him ended the *gaddi* of leadership (*masnad-i-sarwari* and with him came to end the custom of the (succession of) Gurus (*shewa-i-rahbari*)" (p. 52).

OBJECTIVE EUROPEANS

European writers on history are generally more objective and precise, and those who have written on the Sikhs in the first half of the nineteenth century were seasoned scholars like Sir John Malcolm, the Hon'ble W. G. Osborne, Dr W. L. M'Gregor and Captain Joseph D. Cunningham. The last of them incurred the displeasure of his superiors and lost his political appointment for his frank and honest observations in his *History of the Sikhs*. All of them had been in close contact with the Sikhs in the Punjab and may be safely relied upon for their information on the historicity of Guru Gobind Singh's death, of his being the Tenth and the last living Guru of the Sikhs and of his declaration and commandment regarding Guru Granth Sahib being the Guru after him. We would, therefore, quote here only the relevant passages from their works without going into any particulars about them, following only the chronological order of their publication.

Malcolm Lt. Col., *Sketch of the Sikhs*, London, 1812.

Osborne, W. G., *The Court and Camp of Ranjeet Singh*, London, 1840.

"The Tenth and the last of their spiritual leaders was called Gooroo Govind, whose plans of ambition were different from those of his predecessor Nanak ......" (p. xiv).

"We accordingly set the old Faqueer Uzeezoodeen to work with him, and much to our satisfaction, heard, in the course of the evening, that on his mentioning our wishes to the Maharaja, he had consulted the *Grunth*, or sacred volume of the Sikhs, and that, as the oracle was propitious, we might be prepared to set off for Lahore in four days' time." (p. 121)

"Ranjeet Singh rarely undertakes any expedition of importance without consulting this holy book ......" (p. 122)

"Guru Govind was the last acknowledged religious ruler of the Sikhs. A prophecy had limited their spiritual guides to the number of ten : ......" (p. 76).

"This sect, as has been before stated, have never admitted a spiritual leader since the death of Guru Govind." (p. 89)

M'Gregor, W. L. *The History of the Sikhs*, London, 1846, Vol. I.

"The wound was sewed up, and to all appearance, healing, but Govind was determined to die. He called for a strong bow, which he bent with all his force, and in doing so, the stitches of his wound gave way, his bowels again protruded, and he died almost immediately ".

"This event occurred in the year of the *Hijera* 1132, *Samwat* 1765, and A.D. 1708, at the city of Nadshur (Nanded) in the reign of Buhadoor Shah." (p. 100)

"Aware that since the death of his brave sons there was none among his adherents capable of following up his views and conquests, he fixed upon a *Byragee fukeer*, named Bunda who became his successor, though not as Gooroo. That title died with Gobind Singh, the Tenth and last." (p. 104)

Cunningham, J. D. *History of the Sikhs*, 1849.

"The expiring Gooroo was childless, and the assembled disciples asked in sorrow who should inspire them with truth and lead them to victory when he was no more. Govind bade them be of good cheer; the appointed Ten had indeed fulfilled their mission, but he was about to deliever the Khalsa to God, the never dying. 'He who wishes to behold the Gooroo, let him search the Granth of Nanak. The Gooroo will dwell with the Khalsa : be firm and faithful; wherever five Sikhs are gathered together, there will I also be present.'" (p. 88)

"Govind was killed in 1708 at Nuderh on the banks of the Godavery." (pp. 88-89)

Trumpp, Ernest, *The Adi Granth*, 1877.

"The Guru felt that his dissolution was near at hand, and ordered his Sikhs to keep ready wood (for cremation) and shroud. Having done so, they all joined their hands and asked : 'O true Guru, whom will you seat, for the sake of our welfare, on the throne of the Guruship ?' He answered : 'As the nine Kings before me were at the time of their death seating another Guru on their throne, so shall I now not do; I have entrusted the whole society (of the disciples) to the bosom of the timeless, divine Male. After me, you shall everywhere mind the book of the Granth Sahib as your Guru; whatever you shall ask, it will show to you. Whoever be my disciple, he shall consider the Granth as the form of the Guru.'

...... Having uttered these verses he closed his eyes and expired A.D. 1708." (p. xcvi)

WELL-KNOWN BOOK

The last important writer of the ninteenth century on the history of the Punjab in English is Syed Muhammed Latif of the Punjab Judicial Service. His well-known book *History of the Punjab* was published in 1891 and is still one of the best books on the subject. Some time before the death of Guru Gobind Singh, when Sikhs asked him as to who would be Guru after him, the dying apostolic hero, according to Syed Muhammad Latif, told them :

"I entrust my Khalsa to the bosom of the everlasting Divine Being. Whoever wishes to behold the Guru, let him offer *karah parshad* worth Re 1-4 or less, and bow before the Granth and open it, and he shall be given an interview with the Guru. The Granth shall support you under all your troubles and adversities in this world, and be a sure guide to you hereafter. The Guru shall dwell with the society of disciples, the Khalsa, and wherever there shall be five Sikhs gathered together, there shall the Guru be also present."

"The Guru also gave them sundry warnings, telling them that there were impostors in the world who would try to dissuade them from the right path, but that his disciples should be on their guard against them and give no ear to what they say. They must have belief in One God and look on the Granth as His inspired law ...... He then closed his eyes and began to pray, and expired in the performance of his devotions." (p. 269)

MACAULIFFE'S STANDARD WORK

Of the writers of the twentieth century, we would refer only to M. A. Macauliffe, whose book *The Sikh Religion*, in six volumes published in 1909, was begun in the eighties of the nineteenth century and is considered to be a standard work on the lives of the Gurus and of the *bhagtas,* whose hymns are incorporated in Guru Granth Sahib. In the compilation of this work, Macauliffe was assisted by a number of well-known Sikh scholars of his time, like Bhai Hazara Singh, Bhai Sardul Singh, Bhai Dit Singh and Bhai Kahan Singh of Nabha, who was closely associated with it up to the last stage of its publication at Oxford in England. The views expressed in *The Sikh Religion*, therefore, represent the views and beliefs not only of the orthodox section of the Sikh community, but also of their reformist intelligentsia in the beginning of the twentieth century. Writing about the last commandments and the death of Guru Gobind Singh, he says :

"When the Sikhs came again to take their last farewell of the Guru, they inquired who was to succeed him. He replied, 'I have entrusted you to the Immortal God. Ever remain under His protection, and trust to none besides. Wherever there are five Sikhs assembled who abide by the Guru's teachings, know that I am in the midst of them. He who serveth them shall obtain the reward thereof the fulfilment of all his heart's desires. Read the history of your Gurus from the time of Guru Nanak. Henceforth, the Guru shall be the Khalsa and the Khalsa the Guru. I have infused my mental and bodily spirit into the Granth Sahib and the Khalsa."

"After this, the Guru bathed and changed his dress. He then read the *Japji* and repeated an *ardas* or supplication. While doing so, he gave instructions that no clothes should be bestowed as alms in his name. He then put on a muslin waistband, slung his bow on his shoulder and took his musket in his hand. He opened the Granth Sahib and placing five paise and a coconut before it solemnly bowed to it as his successor. Then uttering *Waheguru ji ka Khalsa; Waheguru ji ki Fateh*, he circumambulated the sacred volume and said, 'O beloved Khalsa, let him who desireth to behold me, behold the Guru Granth. Obey the Granth Sahib. It is the visible body of the Guru. And let him who desireth to meet me, diligently search its hymns.'"

USEFUL SOURCE OF INFORMATION

There is another class of evidence which is particularly relevant to our study here. It is known as the *Gur-parnalian* or Genealogies of the Gurus. As they deal mainly with the parentage, births, deaths, descendants and successors of the Gurus, they are a very useful source of information for determining the order of succession of Guruship. Six of these *Gur-parnalis* by Bhai Kesar Singh, Poet Saundha, Bhai Gulab Singh, Kavi Ram Singh, an anonymous poet and by Kavi Gulab Singh, are available, and all of them, without exception, accept the death of Guru Gobind Singh at Nanded in 1708 as an indisputable historical fact.

GRANTH IS GURU

Under the heading *Guru Granth Sahib* in his well-known book the *Gurmat Martand*, Vol. I, p. 411, Bhai Kahan Singh refers to the holy book as *Sri Guru Granth Sahib* and tells us on page 415 that the use of the word 'Guru' with Granth Sahib began in *Samvat* 1766 BK., (A.D. 1708) when Guru Gobind Singh invested the Granth, the basic scripture of the Sikh faith, with guruship at Abchal Nagar (Nanded in the Deccan).

Bhai Kahan Singh has also answered the question of those who at times asked about the volume which was invested with guruship. He writes on page 415 of the book mentioned above :

"We believe that it was that volume which the Tenth Guru had compiled at Damdama Sahib after including therein the compositions of the Ninth Guru and which was lost during the great holocaust (*Wadda Ghalu-Ghara*) and of which Baba Dip Singh had previously prepared several copies. But, even if no volume was available at the time of the death of the Tenth Guru, could there be any difficulty in the investiture ? Was Guru Tegh Bahadur present at Delhi at the time of the death of Guru Har Krishan (Who invested Guru Tegh Bahadur with guruship) ? The Guruship could be entrusted by mental contemplation or through word (of mouth)."

These statements and writings of Bhai Kahan Singh leave no doubt about his belief that :

(i)   Guru Gobind Singh did not appoint any person to succeed him as Guru, and

(ii) The Tenth Guru had invested Guru Granth Sahib with guruship, and commanded the Sikhs to accept it as their Eternal Guru.

Recently, a contemporary Narbud Singh Bhatt has been traced by Giani Garja Singh, his book *Bhatt Vahi Talauda Parganah Jind* also contains an entry regarding the succession of Sri Guru Granth Sahib as future Guru of the Sikhs ending the personal line of succession. It reads, "Guru Gobind Singh, the Tenth Master, son of Guru Tegh Bahadur, grandson of Guru Hargobind, great-grandson of Guru Arjun, of the family of Guru Ram Das, Surajbansi Gosal clan, Sodhi Khatri, resident of Anandpur, parganah Kahlur, now at Nanded, on the Godavari bank in the Deccan, asked Bhai Daya Singh, on Wednesday, *shukla chauth* of the month of *Katik*, 1765 BK. (October 6, 1708) to fetch Sri Granth Sahib. The Guru placed before it five *pice* and a coconut and bowed his head before it. He said to the *sangat*, 'It is my commandment : Own Sri Granth *Ji* in my place. He who so acknowledges it will obtain his reward. The Guru will rescue him. Know this as the truth.'"

25

BANDA SINGH BAHADUR*

Tharam Singh

Banda Singh's Early Exploits

The period of eight years after the demise of Guru Gobind Singh in October 1708 is essentially centred around the activities of Banda Singh, as far as the Sikhs are concerned. It is unfortunate that there are hardly any authentic records of this short but lively episode in Sikh history. There are many disjointed accounts of certain incidents in the life of Banda Singh, some written in appreciation of the man, others written in ridicule of him. There is no complete and truly balanced account of his life and doings, written by the early historians, but one fact emerges very clearly out of all these contradictory stories. The Sikhs of the Punjab were waiting anxiously for the return of their Guru from the South. They then heard the sad story of his assassination, and with Wazir Khan still waging war on them in spite of the Imperial amnesty, they were sorely in need of a leader — one who could fill the vacuum left in their hearts by the departure of their Guru. This vacuum was ably filled by Banda Singh Bahadur.

He was born in October 1670, to a well-to-do Rajput family living in Rajauri in Western Kashmir. He was named Lachman Das. He had a happy boyhood, showed little love for learning, and a great deal for riding and hunting. It is possible that his father rarely pressed him to sit down at his books. By the age of 15, he was a good marksman with the bow and arrow.

In one of these hunting exercises, he brought down a female deer, which appeared to be pregnant. When he slit open the carcass, he found in its womb two young calves, still alive. These little creatures kicked about for a while and then died. This pitiful sight so upset Lachman Das, that he gave up hunting and the eating of meat. A short while later, he gave up all worldly pursuits and became a *sanyasi* (recluse), and left home to become the disciple of one *sadhu* Janki Das. He was about 16 years old then and was re-named Madho Das.

---

* Based on *History of the Sikhs* by H. R. Gupta.

As other *sanyasis*, he wandered from house to house for his daily needs — but could get no peace of mind. He later joined the company of another *sadhu*, Ram Das, wandered down into the present Maharashtra State and reached a place called Panchbatti, near Nasik. He found this place very peaceful, and decided to make it his home. Here, he came in contact with one famous yogi called Amar Nath. This man showed Madho Das a book he had written on the control of man over his bodily organs (yoga) and further the science of mesmerism and spiritualism.

When he had attained some degree of perfection in this science, Madho Das left Panchbatti and followed the river Godaveri downstream until he arrived at Nanded, where he set up his permanent *ashram* (home of *sadhus*). It was here that he was then taken in hand by Guru Gobind Singh, in early 1708, administered the *amrit*, and named Banda Singh.

Banda Singh's imagination was fired by the stories of the siege of Chamkaur, the cowardly execution by Wazir Khan of the Guru's young sons, Fateh Singh and Zorawar Singh, and of the feats of the small band of the prodigals at Muktsar who were posthumously blessed by the Guru as the *mukte* (released from all transmigration). When the Guru realised his own end drawing near, and that the task of re-uniting the Sikhs in the Punjab must be entrusted to another man, he found Banda Singh waiting only for his command to proceed.

He was conferred the title *Bahadur* by Guru Gobind Singh, who then handed him the war-drum, the Khalsa flag, and five arrows from the Guru's quiver. Five Sikhs were appointed to go with him as his Council-of-War, and Banda was ordered to consult them in all major campaigns. Their names were Binod Singh, Kahn Singh, Baaj Singh, Daya Singh and Ran Singh. His objective was to punish all who were responsible for the execution of the Guru's true Sikhs, like Pir Budhu Shah, and for the protection of God-loving men. He was further enjoined to remain a good Sikh of a clean and strong character, and never to lay claim to the title of a Guru. Banda acquiesced to all these commands with bowed head, and asking for the Guru's blessing, he set out northwards on about the 4th October, 1708.

On leaving Nanded, Banda Singh headed for Delhi, which he reached in about 60 days. From Delhi, he then started moving westward through the district of Sonipat. He now began to show the Sikhs there the orders *(hukumname)* of Guru Gobind Singh, requesting all to muster under Banda's command. The sad news had already reached them about the manner in which the Guru had been attacked, and they were all fuming with rage, and were anxious to punish the person they assumed to be responsible for that deed — Wazir Khan, the Governor of Sirhind. As soon as one villager read the *hukamnama*, he passed the word round throughout the village, and volunteers came pouring in to join Banda's camp. He needed funds for his army, and for that he devised the simple plan of robbing the rich landlords, who had oppressed the tillers of the soil for so long, and who were easily singled out by the poor peasants. As for weapons, his men had brought anything that had been laid up — old swords, spears, axes, poles — anything that came to hand. The Sikhs from Bathinda district led by Fateh Singh, one of the descendants of Bhai Bhagtu, came up bringing a lot of provisions with them. The brothers Karam Singh and Param Singh of Bhai Rupa (founded during Guru Hargobind's time) also brought many volunteers with them. The sons of Phool, Bhai Ram Singh and Tirlok Singh, who had fought for Guru Gobind Singh during the siege of Anandpur, now sent men and money to Banda Singh. Ahli Singh and Mali Singh, two brothers who served in Wazir Khan's court, were taunted one day by their master thus :

"I hear that a new Guru has arisen amongst you. He will soon be dragged down the streets of Sirhind, as easily as I disposed of your Guru Gobind Singh in Nanded."

The two Sikhs promptly left Sirhind to join Banda, taking 22 more men with them and carrying useful information about the defences of the town. Messengers from Banda had reached beyond the river Satluj, but the Sikhs around Amritsar and Jalandhar were prevented from crossing the river by the posting of guards by Wazir Khan at all river crossings. A good number of them, however, had reached Keeratpur and here they received word from Banda that they should await orders from him before they advanced further. Meanwhile Banda made his plans for the capture of Samana.

He had now an army of about 500 gathered at Sehri, a village in the district of Kharkhod near Sonipat. As he neared Sonipat, the garrison commander there took fright and fled towards Delhi leaving the town at the mercy of the Sikhs. Banda then moved further into the Punjab. As he rested near Kaithal, he was informed about a small troop of horsemen carrying the district town's revenue towards Delhi. He fell upon that group and obtained sufficient funds for the pay of his army for some months. The commander of Kaithal came out to put up a show of resistance, but was quickly overcome, and made to contribute a large number of horses for the Sikh soldiers.

Banda's men were thus gaining material, experience and morale, as they approached their first big battle at Samana. This town lies about 35 miles south of Sirhind. It was the town of Jalalluddin, the executioner of Guru Tegh Bahadur. The two executioners who built the brick walls that buried alive the young *sahibzade* of Guru Gobind Singh, also belonged to this ill-fated town. On 25th November, 1709 Banda had reached Samana at the head of a force of 3,000 horsemen and 5,000 foot-soldiers. The commander of Samana had his walled town well-defended, and never for a moment imagined Banda capable of carrying it. But Banda advanced swiftly during the night and reached the gates of the town at dawn on the 26th November. Once the gate-keepers were killed, the whole army poured into the town and there was little the Mughals and Sayads could do to stem the tide. The three executioners were tracked down and dispatched. There were many wealthy Muslim families in this town, who tried saving themselves behind bolted doors. But the soldiers of fortune who formed a part of Banda's army gathered all the wealth that had been amassed in this town, and Banda appointed Fateh Singh Governor of Samana leaving a small force with him to administer the town. He marched eastward passing by Shahabad which offered his men whatever provisions they needed. He then reached Mustafabad (near Jagadhri) whose commander put a small fight before allowing the Sikhs access to food, horses and rifles.

Banda now turned north-east towards Sadhaura, (about 20 miles from Ambala) the

home-town of the late Pir Budhu Shah. This was the man who had gone to the aid of
Guru Gobind Singh at Bhangani, with his four sons and 700 followers. For that crime
Aurangzeb had ordered the commander of Sadhaura, Usman Khan to capture and execute
the good Pir, and this news had saddened Guru Gobind Singh. He had expressly ordered
Banda Singh to mete out a just punishment for the culprit. The Sikhs fell upon Sadhaura
with intense fury, and killed almost all its males. Some of the rich Sayads took shelter in
the late Pir's mansion hoping to escape death there, but none were spared. In their zeal
some of the raiders had set fire to a mausoleum, but this was quickly extinguished on the
orders of Banda Singh. Usman Khan was killed and his body was allowed to hang by the
feet from a tree.

News of the sack of Samana and Sadhaura reached Wazir Khan, and he was now
more afraid than ever of the danger of the Sikhs of Keeratpur joining forces with Banda
Singh. To forestall that, he requested the brothers Sher Mohammed Khan and Khizar
Khan of Malerkotla to march towards Ropar to block the Sikh advance from Keeratpur.
They engaged the Sikhs somewhere between Ropar and Keeratpur and appeared to push
them back some distance. During the night, however, fresh reinforcements of Sikhs from
the Jalandhar-Amritsar areas arrived in Keeratpur, and in the fight that erupted the next
morning, Khizar Khan was hit by a bullet and fell dead. With his fall the Malerkotla
force lost heart and retreated towards Sirhind. The Sikhs then thought it right to follow
up their victory by advancing towards Ropar and Sirhind.

On the other side, Banda had circled around by the east of Sirhind, captured
Banoor on the way, and was awaiting the arrival of his allies at a spot between Banoor
and Kharar. The two forces joined up here to the loud hail of the Khalsa war cry
accompanied by the liberal distribution of the Guru's *krah-parshad* (sweet made from
equal proportions of ghee, flour and sugar).

THE CAPTURE OF SIRHIND

Wazir Khan now knew he could not stem the tide, and he, therefore, tried his hand
at treachery. He bribed one of his Generals, a nephew of Sucha Nand, to take a thousand
Hindu and Pathan soldiers over to Banda and pretend to offer allegiance to the Sikh
leader. In the heat of battle, they were to desert from there to re-join the Mughal army,
thereby dealing a blow to the morale of the Sikhs. Banda could not see through this
scheme and accepted this unusual offer of aid.

Meanwhile Wazir Khan decided to meet the Sikhs in the open, and he himself took
command ordering his heavy guns, elephants and horsemen into the line of battle,
followed by his well-equipped foot-soldiers, a force of 20,000 men all told. On the other
side, there were hardly any rifles, leave alone artillery and elephants. But they had tasted
victory many times by now, and remembering the atrocity committed by this town on
Mata Gujri and the two young *sahibzade* (sons), they had immense fanatic zeal to make
up for the lack of proper weapons. The two armies made contact at a spot known as
Chhapar Chhiri about 10 miles from Sirhind. Banda Singh divided his forces into 3
groups sending ahead two of them, one under the command of Fateh Singh, Karam
Singh, Param Singh, and the other made up of the new arrivals who were commanded by

Baaj Singh, Binod Singh and Sham Singh. He kept a third group with him on a nearby hillock from where he could follow the whole action, and send aid wherever needed.

With the first sound of fighting, the thousand men under the nephew of Sucha Nand fled to the other side. Banda promptly brought his men down to take their place, and with that the Sikhs began attacking with fresh heart. Casualties were heavy on both sides, but the men under Fateh Singh kept advancing towards the heavy guns which were soon silenced. Baaj Singh and Binod Singh were also showing their mettle, and cutting down their foe in hand to hand fighting. Sher Mohammed Khan and his brother Khuaja Ali of Malerkotla were killed in this battle. Then Baaj Singh came face to face with Wazir Khan who was on horseback, and who was mowing down the Sikhs with his sword. Baaj Singh would have been killed there, had not Fateh Singh rushed up in time to bring Wazir Khan down with a shot from his rifle. With his fall, the Mughals lost heart and scattered in all directions, leaving a rich booty of cannon and rifles in the hands of the Sikhs.

This action took place on 22nd May 1710. Banda's army then advanced on Sirhind, whose remaining defenders could put up only a half-hearted resistance. On the 23rd May, Banda's men entered Sirhind. The Sikhs were assisted by a mob of Hindu peasantry from the surrounding villages also, whose person and property had been outraged by the rich landlords of this town.

The Sikhs had waited for this moment for six years. They had vowed in their daily prayers to tear this town of ill-repute down to the ground. For Sucha Nand, the Brahmin adviser in the court of Wazir Khan, the Sikhs bore a severe hatred. This man had urged his master not to spare the young sons of the Guru, as according to him, "the snake's young ones deserve no mercy." So the invaders went straight to this man's house, killed all its occupants, and grabbed all its treasures. As a contemporary writer puts it, "It seemed as if Sucha Nand had amassed all his wealth merely to keep it ready for the arrival of the Sikhs." His empty house was then literally demolished.

The eldest son of Wazir Khan had fled to Delhi. The general slaughter was halted on the orders of Banda Singh, when a deputation of Hindus came to him begging for mercy. The town was, therefore, saved from being razed to the ground, as the Sikhs had vowed in their resolution passed at the Akal Takht at Amritsar. This fate was to befall it later at the hands of Jassa Singh in the year 1763.

Banda's immediate objective had been attained. Next came the task of setting up a new administration. Baaj Singh was appointed the Governor of Sirhind. Fateh Singh retained his post at Samana. Ram Singh, a brother of Baaj Singh, was made a District Officer at Thanesar. Binod Singh assisted him there. Sirhind occupied a central post in the lines of communication between Delhi and Lahore. Its location enabled it to exercise control over all the territories between the rivers Jamuna and Satluj. Banda Singh was now acknowledged master of this area, even by the smaller Muslim Commanders, a few of whom even chose to be converted to Sikhism. Nazir Khan, the keeper of Records at Sirhind, was one of these to avow Sikhism. Banda's successes had spread terror amongst the Muslim Commanders at Jalandhar and at Lahore, where the Sikhs were now openly raiding the countryside. They passed resolutions at Amritsar and marched upon Batala and Kalanaur, which were easily occupied. The Commander of Lahore, Aslam Khan dared not venture out of his fortified town in order to aid any of his Subordinate Commanders. Hearing about the successes of their friends in the *Majha* districts, the Sikhs of the *Doaba* also sent a challenge to Shamas Khan, the Commander of the Jalandhar Doab.

Coming back to Banda Singh's doings, his first job was the establishment of his own headquarters at Mukhlispur, a few miles north of Sadhaura. Being in hilly land it was easier to defend against an enemy. There was a half-built fort already there. Banda completed it and called it Lohgarh.

Then he learnt about the burial in Malerkotla of a Sikh girl Anup Kaur, who had served in the Guru's household at Anandpur, and who had fallen into the hands of Sher Mohammed Khan during the crossing of the river Sirsá. This Commander had brought the girl to Malerkotla intending to make her his mistress. But, the brave girl had stabbed herself to death, and the Nawab had hastily buried her close to the palace compound, afraid of adverse publicity.

Banda Singh Bahadur marched on Malerkotla, with the intention of digging up the body and giving it a cremation as approved by Sikh rites. He remembered too well, the affection the Sikhs had for the same Sher Mohammed Khan, who was the only one of the Muslim leaders present at the trial and condemnation of the two sons of Guru Gobind Singh, who had raised his voice in dissent over the cruel sentence. So Banda Singh's orders to his men were to search for the grave without any harm to the inhabitants of Malerkotla. The body had lain in the ground for over a year, and it took a deal of exhumation of nearby graves, before the correct one was identified. Some Muslim historians have picked on this incident as an excuse to paint Banda Singh in the goriest of pictures that they could imagine. But if they could see the motive behind this action, they would have better appreciated the lofty ideals and the true character of the man.

With the cremation completed, he returned to Sirhind, to quell any dissident groups that still remained in the regions surrounding this town. He then impressed his stamp of authority over the whole region by minting a special coin. He remembered Guru Gobind Singh's advice to consider himself the caretaker and the servant of the Khalsa, and not to assume Guruship. His coin bore evidence of his great respect for the house of Guru Nanak.

While Banda was away in Malerkotla, Baaj Singh had to take action against Ghurani, a village occupied mainly by the Ram Rai sect. These people had abused a Sikh musician who had sung *Gurbani* and had mentioned Guru Gobind Singh in his *ardas*. Ahli Singh was dispatched with a small force westward, and he soon put matters right, setting up a guard post at Chawa Pail. Ahli Singh received tribute from the local landlords and then proceeded southward through Sunam, and Mansoorpur, exacting tribute as he moved, until he reached Kaithal. The Baloch tribe of Kaithal were proud and had refused to acknowledge the authority of the Sikhs. Ahli Singh made a surprise attack on the town and after subduing the Muslim defenders, he made them pay up a heavy tribute and to promise a regular payment of revenues in future. Ahli Singh then returned to Sirhind.

As mentioned earlier, quite a number of the Muslim Chiefs had embraced Sikhism for personal security. There were a great many Hindus especially those of the untouchable caste, who took to this faith because of the status and equality it gave to its members. If a low-caste villager joined a Sikh band and took baptism from its leaders, he would return to his own village to find its landlords bowing to him in utmost respect. Banda also abolished the system of landlordism, making the tenants the direct owners of the land they tilled, and collecting revenues direct from the tenants. This had liberated large areas between Sirhind and Panipat from the cruel oppression of the rich landlords, and was another factor in favour of a large-scale conversion to Sikhism. This movement had spread to the Deoband district across the river Jamuna, much to the annoyance of Jalal Khan, the Commander of Jalalabad. He arrested any new Sikhs around his town, and one day he threw Kapoor Singh, a Sikh preacher into prison. This incident was reported to Banda Singh, who immediately set out across the Jamuna and headed for Saharanpur, the divisional headquarters for 24 smaller districts, including Deoband.

Sayad Ali Khan, the Commander of Saharanpur, was sorely afraid, and could not be persuaded by the rich citizens of the town to take to the battlefield. He had vivid memories of the massacres at Samana and Sirhind. During the night, he collected all his valuables and fled with his family towards Delhi. As the Sikhs approached the town, only a small force set out to offer a token resistance, and the Sikhs were soon swarming all over the city's rich mansions.

From there, Banda headed for Jalalabad. Nanauta, a town owned by the Sayads, came on their way and Banda set upon that on 11th July, 1710. A sharp encounter took place here, but the Sheikhs and Sayads were heavily out-numbered and overcome. Jalalabad lay about five miles away. It was strongly fortified by the Pathan Commander, who had made full preparations for the attack. The fort was built on a hillock with a small stream flowing by it. Jalal Khan sent a force under his son Dindar Ali Khan, and his nephews Jamal Khan and Pir Khan to engage the Sikhs as they neared the fort. The fighting was fierce and losses heavy on both sides. But the Pathans retreated after this encounter and decided to stay within their fort. The Sikhs could not force an entry into the fort. They laid a siege that lasted 20 days, but to no avail. Meanwhile Banda received urgent calls for help from the Punjab, and decided to lift the siege, much to the relief of Jalal Khan. He re-crossed the Jamuna and reached Karnal which was easily taken. He then left Ram Singh and Binod Singh in charge of all this territory up to Panipat and headed for Sirhind.

THE ACTION IN THE TERRITORY WEST OF THE SATLUJ

The lands between the river Beas and Satluj are known as the *Doab*. Those further west are broadly described as the *Majha*, though here again there used to be further sub-division into the *Bari Doab* and the *Rachna Doab*.

News of the victories of Banda Singh at Samana and Sadhaura had spread to these areas, and the uncommitted peasantry here eagerly espoused Sikhism with the double aim of gaining self-respect and of revolting to throw off the Mughal yoke. They had suffered heavy taxes, and persecution at the hands of the landlords, and Banda Singh was promising lower taxes and personal ownership to all. So the *Majha* peasants stopped paying revenue to their landlords. Instead they assembled at Amritsar and passed a resolution at the Akal Takht that the Khalsa would henceforth drive the foreigners out of the Punjab, and would try to bring into reality the saying of Guru Gobind Singh, *"Raj Karega Khalsa."*

They decided that Lahore and Qasoor (a Pathan stronghold) were too well defended against assault. They turned their attention first to the territory along both banks of the Beas river known as the *Riarki*. These villages were easily subdued and their headmen removed from their posts. The new headman of each village was instructed to hand all future revenues to the Sikh Commanders.

Batala, a rich trading centre, was their next target. This town was easily taken. Kalanaur, a hillside town where the Emperor Akbar had been crowned, was captured next, and then followed the subjugation of the inhabited area around the Kahnuwan woods. A party of Sikhs had marched as far north as Pathankot and taken that district under their control.

Aslam Khan, the Governor of Lahore, had watched all these proceedings with a sinking heart. He was urged by the rich merchants and the priests of Lahore to do something, but he refused to leave the town, or to send a force out to meet the enemy, for fear of an attack on Lahore, should things go wrong. The merchants, *maulvis*, and landlords, in desperation raised the *Haideri* flag for a holy war, and called for volunteers to gather at the *Id Gah* (prayer place) just outside the town gates. (*Haideri* is the name given to the flag after Haider Ali, the son-in-law of Prophet Mohammed).

Those who are prepared to sacrifice themselves in a holy war or *jehad* are called *Ghazis*, and these volunteers gathered in thousands from the countryside around Lahore. They appointed Mohammed Taqi, Haji Sayed Ismail, and Pir Mohammed Waiz as their leaders. The Governor was at last moved to contribute 500 horsemen and 1,000 infantry under Mir Ataullah Khan and Muhib Khan, to re-inforce the *Ghazis*. So the martyrs dressed in bright green and holding green flags in their hands marched by the side of the royal forces, and this made quite a pretty sight for the inhabitants of Lahore who came out to give them a good send-off.

The Sikh force nearest to Lahore consisting of about 200 men was stationed inside a big brick house at Bharath village, on the bank of the Ravi. It had been converted into a fortress, and it was for this that the *Ghazis* headed with much cheering and the beating drums. They found the defenders well prepared, and on the first charge, a hail of bullets and arrows knocked down a large number in the front rows. An equal number stepped up to take their places, and they met the same fate. The attackers were too numerous to be easily disheartened, and they continued their series of charges on to the brick walls of the fort until nightfall, even though hundreds of dead bodies lay piled up around. The defenders, on the other hand, were safe behind their defences, but were now feeling exhausted after a continuous action of 12 hours. They did not have sufficient men to allow one party to take rest.

During the night they opened the gate and charged out along the weakest point in the enemy lines. They thus escaped into the darkness with minimum loss in lives.

The next morning the *Ghazi* army, overjoyed at their victory began looting the Hindu families of Bharath and turned back towards Lahore, abusing and robbing all the villagers that came in their way. They then held a big celebration at the *Id Gah*. A few days later, the Sikhs assembled about 700 strong at Kotla Begum, near the village Chamiari. The *Ghazi* force set out at once, joined this time by many bad characters who hoped to secure some easy loot. True enough, this army robbed all the innocent villagers that came their way and quite a few women were outraged. Their leaders were shocked over these happenings, and did their best to punish the offenders, but the general tone of this army was far from disciplined. They came face to face with the well prepared Sikhs at Kotla, and both armies began discharging their muskets and arrows. These soon gave way to the sword in hand to hand fighting, and it was here that the discipline of the Sikh and his firm conviction in the justice of his cause really told. The sky was overcast, but the steel blade flashed in the hands of the Sikhs like lightning and the *Ghaziz* bit the dust in large heaps everywhere. Towards noon, the Government cavalry began to give way, retreated, and as if with one intent they fled the battleground.

That took the heart out of the *Ghazis*. They began running in all directions, and the Sikhs pursued them a short distance. Then a dust-storm arose, reducing visibility and the victors thought it prudent to return to collect all the weapons thrown away by the running *Ghazis*. They then returned to their fort to rest for the night.

This battle had taken place at about the time when Banda was marching upon Jalandhar (July 1710). The routed *Ghazis* had tried to follow the trail of the retreating Government troops, and they finally converged upon Bhilowal by night-fall the following day. Here they lay down to rest, in the open, completely broken in spirit, and careless about all regards for their safety during the night. Unfortunately for them, the Sikhs at Kotla Begum woke up refreshed, the morning after their victory, and decided to follow the retreating foe. They reached Bhilowal towards midnight and immediately fell upon the unguarded *Ghazis*. The Government troops sleeping within the village heard the commotion outside, but dared not come out to the aid of their comrades. Only a few hundred *Ghazis* outside the village escaped this slaughter. The Sikhs captured more weapons and some horses, and left before day break. The remnants of this once proud band of *Ghazi* fighters reached Lahore in tears, and no further attempts were made to raise the *Haideri* flag at the *Id Gah*.

Following the early successes of the *Majha* Sikhs, those in the *Doab* were encouraged to try their fortunes in war. Moreover, they were joined by a number of fighters from the Sirhind bands of Banda Singh. So the *Doaba* peasants mustered an army of one to two thousand and fell upon Rahon (near Sultanpur). Enayat Khan, the landlord of this town, had robbed many of the surrounding villages, was notorious for his greed and lust, and had usurped the powers of the Commissioner of that district. He was quickly disposed off and a Sikh Commander was set up in his post, to collect all future revenues from the farmers. The Sikhs then set their sights on Sultanpur.

Sultanpur was then the military headquarters for the whole of the Jalandhar division. Shamas Khan, the son of Mir Khan, had been appointed its Governor by Bahadur Shah in return for the services both father and son had rendered him in his campaigns against his brothers. The Sikhs sent two of their men to Shamas Khan with an ultimatum for submission or war. Shamas Khan was a good tactician. He received the two messengers with all courtesy, and sent them back with a small gift of food and some ammunition, with a promise of more supplies in a few days time. He then summoned his military chiefs, along with the *maulvis* and rich merchants and obtained their promises of loyalty and speedy action to raise an army. Messengers were sent out to the villages to recruit fighters (*Ghazis*) for a holy war. In this manner, he was able to muster a force of 5,000 horsemen and over 20,000 foot-soldiers, before the Sikhs at Rahon realised what was happening. As he began his march on them, the Sikhs sent urgent messages to Banda Singh (then at Jalandhar), and prepared to dig themselves in at an abandoned brick kiln outside the Rahon fort. They raised its walls higher with sacks of old bricks and earth. As Shamas Khan drew near, led by eager bands of *Ghazis*, ill trained and armed with ineffective scythes and cudgels, the Sikhs fired volley after volley of arrows and bullets killing or wounding the vanguard by the hundreds. Even when *Ghazis* came close enough for hand to hand fighting they were no match for the Sikh swordsmen. As the Sikhs tired of this slaughter, they decided on a rearguard action, slowly retreating into the fort. Shamas Khan decided to lay siege, as a direct assault would be too costly. This began on 11th October, 1710.

Seeing no advantage in holding this fort against such an overwhelming force, this band of about a thousand men waited for midnight before charging out into the darkness, and the woods nearby. Shamas Khan was glad to be rid of them, and he returned to Sultanpur, leaving a small guard in charge of Rahon. But the Sikhs had not gone far. They waited till the Khan reached Sultanpur, and re-occupied the fort, compelling the residents of Rahon to pay tribute to them. Shamas Khan had no heart for a second attack on Rahon, but had meanwhile sent a report of his action to the Emperor, Bahadur Shah.

The Sikhs next advanced upon Jalandhar, met no resistance there, collected tribute money, and moved north towards Hoshiarpur. The District Officer here also agreed to pay his collections to the Sikh representatives. In this manner, practically the whole of the *Doab*, with the exception of Sultanpur and its neighbourhood, was under Sikh control.

Their next target was Bilaspur, the capital of Kahloor, the hill-state around Anandpur that had marshalled all the other hill Rajas against Guru Gobind Singh, and had even repaid with treachery the Guru's timely aid against the Raja's enemies. The Sikhs advanced on Bilaspur under Sardar Baghar Singh, Bajjar Singh, Kehar Singh and others, and as was their custom, they sent the Raja an ultimatum to accept allegiance or fight. The Raja summoned aid from other hill Rajas, and stored up enough supplies in his fort for a siege. He had mustered about 1,500 Rajput fighters by the time the Sikhs charged. They cut down his guard of elephants first and then broke through the main gate of the fort. They made quick work of the 1,500 defenders. Not a soul was spared; so fierce was their desire to punish this sworn enemy of their beloved Guru.

After this action, the Sikhs had unchallenged control of all the *Majha* and *Doaba* lands with the exception of two pockets — one at Lahore and the other at Sultanpur. Banda himself was in command of the *Malwa* territories from Sirhind to Panipat, and also of some of the areas beyond the Jumuna river. For a brief period in the history of the Punjab, the Sikhs were masters of their own land, with Banda Singh Bahadur as their uncrowned king (May - October 1710).

THE TIDE TURNS AGAINST BANDA

Whilst Banda Singh was capturing Samana and Sirhind, Emperor Bahadur Shah was engaged in a war in the Deccan against one of his brothers. He received news of the Sikh victories on 30th May, 1710. Asad Khan, his Governor at Delhi had been sending frequent reports of the events around Panipat, Saharanpur, and Sultanpur. He had planned to spend some time in Rajputana to punish the Rajas there for siding with his brother, but the worsening situation in the Punjab compelled him to forsake those plans and to march at once northward. He wrote to the Governors of Oudh, Moradabad and Allahabad to send their troops to Delhi, where they were to join the forces already stationed under Asad Khan, who was ordered to despatch his army against the Sikhs. He himself bypassed Delhi and reached Sonipat on 22nd October. He had an advance force under his trusted General Feroze Khan, and as this force neared Panipat they found an army under Bazid Khan of Qasoor already camped there, but afraid to proceed further on their own. Bazid Khan had been appointed Governor of Jammu when Bahadur Shah had defeated one of his own brothers in the Punjab some time back, but this General had never been able to reach his province from Delhi, because of the Sikhs.

This combined force under Bazid Khan and Feroze Khan now marched into the territory controlled by Sardars Ram Singh and Binod Singh. The latter had only a token force under their command. In fact the whole Sikh army was scattered over distant areas, and each unit itself was no match against the advancing Mughal army. The two Sikh Generals were, however, determined to take the most out of the enemy. They retreated towards Thanesar, and concealed themselves in the woods on both sides of the main road near the village of Amingarh.

Muhabat Khan, the son of the Minister Munim Khan, led the vanguard. As they came within range they received a sudden hail of arrows and bullets, were too shaken to recover, and retreated in complete rout. Then Feroze Khan brought up his horsemen. As the cavalry were hampered by the thick growth of trees, he ordered his foot-soldiers forward and the vastly superior numbers of Mughals pushed the Sikhs back. They lost a large number in this action but succeeded in sending the dreaded Sikhs away into the deep jungle. The Sikhs had lost 300 men in this action. The heads of the dead were cut off and sent in a cart as trophies to the Emperor. Feroze Khan was rewarded with a large sum in cash and the post of the Commissioner of Sirhind. This took place at the end of October 1710.

This Sikh force retreated through Thanesar to Shahabad with Feroze Khan in pursuit. Meanwhile, the army under Bazid Khan advanced towards Sirhind. Here he was joined by his nephew Shamas Khan who had now ventured out of Sultanpur. Baaj Singh, the Commander of Sirhind, happened to be away on some business, and his two brothers, Sham Singh and Sukha Singh, came out to offer a spirited resistance, but were pushed back into the fort. Sukha Singh was killed in this action which took place about the 20th November. Bahadur Shah now ordered another famous General Mohammed Amin Khan to lay siege to Sirhind on 27th November. But before he could reach Sirhind, the fort had already fallen to the combined armies of Bazid Khan and Shamas Khan. The Sikhs had seen the impossibility of holding out against such enormous odds, and after a couple of days fighting, they had vacated it, during the night and retreated to Lohgarh.

The Emperor had meanwhile reached Sadhaura, and on 4th December, 1710 he received a number of Sikh heads as trophies sent by Shamas Khan from Sirhind. At about the same time he received a report from the jealous Mohammed Amin Khan, which said that Shamas Khan had collected a very large force under his command, and was showing signs of mutiny against the Emperor. So instead of rewarding the energetic Shamas Khan, the Emperor relieved him of his Command at Sultanpur, and appointed in his place, the Deputy Commander Isa Khan who had been left in charge there. Isa Khan had been a notorious bandit along the highways of the *Doab*, and had come to Sultanpur only when the Sikhs took charge of the countryside. With his official appointment as Commander, and with the return of the defeated Sikhs from Samana and Sirhind, this man began a reign of terror in the *Doab*, ordering the execution of all Sikhs on sight.

After a brief resistance, the Sikhs had retreated from Sadhaura, and joined the main party about 7 miles away at the fort of Lohgarh. The forces under Bahadur Shah were too powerful for the scattered groups of Sikhs. The Emperor's son Jahandar Shah commanded 30,000 cavalry, Muhabat Khan commanded 7,000 cavalry and Feroze Khan, Rustum Dil Khan and other Generals had over 20,000 cavalry and at least 30,000 foot-soldiers.

At their best of times, the Sikhs could have had 10,000 cavalry, and about twice as many foot-soldiers. At this particular moment Banda Singh had with him no more than 5,000 fighters all told, at Lohgarh. He had failed to store much food for a long siege, but he had made the best use of the location of the fort. It was situated on a hillock surrounded by smaller mounds, with numerous ravines running between them, some of which were now in flood. To reach the fort, the Mughal troops had to pass by a number of these mounds, which had Sikh soldiers perched atop of them, ready to rain down arrows and bullets into the enemy below.

What with such treacherous terrain, the rain and winter cold, and the stories then going round their camp about the supernatural powers of Banda Singh, and his ability to transform himself into the shape of various beasts, the Mughal Generals were sorely afraid to take the lead in the attack. The Emperor had actually forbidden his Generals making a frontal attack. He had given his son Prince Rafi-ul-Shah the overall command. His minister Munim Khan, Generals Feroze Khan, Rustum-Dil Khan, Hamid-ud-Din Khan, and two Rajput Rajas were to take orders from the Prince.

Feroze Khan and Rustum Dil Khan were ordered to take up positions a little closer to the fort. On 4th December, they advanced a mile or so and were set upon by the Sikhs entrenched atop the mounds. The Mughals were losing a large number of men, and more reinforcements under Munim Khan and his son Muhabat Khan arrived and the Sikhs were dislodged from the mounds and pushed back into the main fort. Rustum Dil Khan then advanced cautiously for another half a mile until he reached the bank of the Som rivulet near the fort. He encamped there for the night. The Emperor too brought his main army up to this bank by the 9th December, and he had his first look at the fort from there.

The next day Prince Rafi-ul-Shan took his 30,000 troops to the foot of the fort on the left. Munim Khan advanced with his two sons and with General Hamid-ud-Din'd forces towards the right of the fort. Munim Khan then asked the Emperor's permission to move closer to probe the defences on the right. As he neared the main hillock, his army received a hail of bullets and arrows from the mounds still in the way, and it took the Mughals the whole day to reach the walls of Lohgarh. It had cost them heavily to reach there, and the Emperor was watching this advance from the other flank, still undecided whether he should give his troops the order for the assault. Towards nightfall Munim Khan had ordered a slight withdrawal to rest for the final assault the next day.

Inside the fort, Banda's men had run short of food and ammunition. All roads to the fort had been blocked by the enemy for nearly a month now. They knew they could not hold out any longer against such an enormous force, and so they prepared to vacate the fort. In the middle of the night they charged out through the weakest point in the enemy circle, and escaped into the hills of Nahan behind them. So when the forces of Munim Khan stormed the fort the next morning and forced an entry into the main gate, they were confronted by only a dozen or so wounded Sikhs led by one Gulab Singh who had donned Banda's robes, with the intention of playing a fatal prank on the invaders. He had thought nothing of offering himself in place of his master, so that the Sikhs could have the last laugh over Bahadur Shah. The fort had fallen on 11th December, 1710.

Munim Khan, as expected, was overjoyed to capture these men alive and to lead his prisoners in procession, with the beat of drums, to the royal camp. Over there someone had whispered to the Emperor that the bird had flown away. The Emperor's command to Munim Khan was brief and incisive. He was told to keep out of his sight until he had captured Banda Singh. The poor minister was deeply hurt, and his health declined rapidly from that day. He died two months later, while the royal army was marching across the *Doab* towards Lahore.

Orders were sent immediately to the Rajas of Nahan and of Srinagar to arrest the fugitive Banda Singh. Hamid Khan was also sent to Nahan to arrest the Raja if he could not produce Banda Singh. This man brought back Bhoop Prakash the son of the Raja, as prisoner, and this boy was sent along with Gulab Singh to be locked into prison at Delhi. The Emperor then began his leisurely march across the *Doab* stopping at Bhadoli, Ropar, Hoshiarpur, Kalanaur, and Chamiari until he reached Lahore in April, 1711.

Banda Singh had to separate from his Generals during their escape from Lohgarh.

He reached Keeratpur and Anandpur in two days, and as if these towns had infused the Guru's spirit and a new life into him, he began writing letters to various towns in the *Doaba* and the *Majha* regions asking the Sikhs there to collect whatever weapons they could and join him at Keeratpur. One of these letters dated 12th December, 1710 is reproduced in its original form by Dr Ganda Singh in his book, *Banda Singh Bahadur*. The stamp of office that he had used when he began his administration of the Punjab from Lohgarh, is used still in this letter, and is indicative of the humility of the man. The words are translated as follows :

"The iron kettle, the sword, and the victory are all under the gracious patronage of Guru Nanak Guru Gobind Singh."

The letter itself gives an insight into the sterling character of this brave man. It runs as follows :

"The one Lord of Creation, victory to a glimpse of You.

It is the wish of the true Guru Gobind that the entire assembly of Jaunpur shall be saved. You are the Khalsa (warriors) of the Almighty. On reading this, take up five weapons and come to join me. Adhere to the precepts of the Khalsa. Refrain from the use of *bhang* (a narcotic), tobacco, opium, the brew from poppy pods, or liquor. Do not eat meat, fish, or onion. Do not commit theft or adultery. We have tried to spread the rule of the truth and love on this earth. My orders to all are to adhere to the precepts of the Khalsa to earn the Guru's protection."

His injunction against the consumption of meat sprang from the hunting mishap he had in his youth, and the subsequent compunction he felt for meat for the rest of his life. The Sikhs had not lost heart over the defeats at Sirhind, and they answered this call from Banda with alacrity. He gathered a few hundred men at Keeratpur, and then moved on towards Pathankot to gather more forces before challenging the Emperor again.

Bazid Khan had marched into the Punjab along with the Emperor's forces. He and his nephew Shamas Khan had participated in the capture of Sirhind, but Shamas Khan had been dismissed from his post at Sultanpur, as a result of court intrigues, and Bazid Khan had asked for the Emperor's permission to proceed to Jammu, the post that had been assigned to him almost two years back. Bazid Khan was joined by his discomfited nephew Shamas Khan, and together these two men neared Rajpur at about the time that Banda was collecting his Sikhs around Pathankot. Uncle and nephew were out in the woods near Brahampur one day, when they learnt that a party of Sikhs was in the neighbourhood. They had about 900 horsemen with them, a strong enough force to challenge the Sikh party. So they followed the trail of the fugitives until they saw them a short distance away. Shamas Khan immediately ordered his men to charge, without waiting for his uncle's advice. Strangely enough the Sikh horsemen took to flight. This encouraged Shamas Khan to give chase, and he had followed the retreating Sikhs for a mile or so, when suddenly he saw them turn round in good formation, and with swords drawn ready for battle. His men were too surprised to give much fight, and were quickly cut down. Baaj Singh was leading his men in the attack, and he soon came up against

Shamas Khan, who tried to pierce him with a lance thrust. Baaj Singh moved aside and before the Khan could recover, he slashed him across the body with his sword cutting him into two.

The forces of Bazid Khan had meanwhile come up to help his nephew, and when he saw the boy fall, he rushed up to attack Baaj Singh. Both men parried each other's blows for a while, until Fateh Singh came up from one side and wounded Bazid Khan so severely that he fell off his horse. The Pathans now concentrated only on charging for the bodies of their fallen Generals, which they managed to carry away to Rajpur. Bazid Khan died two days later, and both bodies were sent for burial to their ancestral town, Qasoor. This battle fought in March 1711, gave great heart to Banda's men. They took complete charge of the territory around Kalanaur, Rajpur and Pathankot.

When news of this defeat reached the Emperor, in April, he despatched 5,000 men under Hamid Khan. Then in May, he sent Rustum Dil Khan and Mohammed Amin Khan with 10,000 more men. By the time the last two Generals arrived in Rajpur, Banda's forces had crossed the river Ravi and entered the *Rachna Doab*. He plundered the district of Jammu. But the Mughal forces caught up with him near Parol and Kathooha, and finding himself encircled on three sides by the enemy, with the hills of Jammu behind him on the fourth side, Banda decided to charge through the sector guarded by Rustum Dil Khan. This escape so enraged Rustam Dil that he fell upon the poor peasantry around Kathooha and plundered the whole countryside.

Mohammed Amin Khan sent a report of this escape to the Emperor putting the full blame for it on Rustum Dil Khan's head. The Emperor summoned Rustum to Lahore and clapped him behind prison bars. He was freed only 4 months later. Amin Khan meanwhile continued chasing Banda Singh all over western Punjab. The Emperor found the city of Lahore in great turmoil. The officers of Aslam Khan and the *maulvis* of the city were oppressing all Hindus who gave aid or shelter to Sikhs. With the arrival of the Emperor the order went out that all Hindus should crop their heads and shave their beards, otherwise they were to be executed. Towards the end of January, 1712, the Emperor began losing his health and his sanity. Towards the end of February, he was ordering the killing of all dogs and donkeys in the city. He died on the night of the 26th February.

The struggle for the throne of Delhi between the four sons of Bahadur Shah had begun in January 1712 with the Generals siding one or the other of the brothers. By March 1712, Rafi-ul-Shah, Azim Shah and Jahan Shah had been killed, along with some Generals and the eldest brother Jahandar Shah had ascended the throne. Mohammed Amin Khan had given up the pursuit of Banda Singh and returned to Lahore to side Jahandar Shah. Rustum Dil Khan, Mukhlis Khan, Muhabat Khan, Khan Zaman, and many more Generals were either executed or imprisoned. In April 1712 Zabardast Khan was appointed Governor of Lahore, and the new Emperor left for Delhi.

While this internecine war was raging at Lahore, Banda Singh was consolidating his position in the hills of Jammu. He travelled to and fro between Jammu and the states of Mandi and Chamba. These hill Rajas had been won over to the Sikh cause mainly through Banda's personality and his reputation for blessing his admirers with wealth and offspring. At this time, Banda Singh was pressed to take in marriage the daughter of the Raja of Chamba. By this marriage, a son named Ajai Singh was born. At about the time that Jahandar Shah left for Delhi, Banda had reached Sadhaura, and occupied it after a brief fight. Lohgarh was once again made the capital of the Sikh state in May 1712.

On reaching Delhi, Jahandar Shah despatched Mohammed Amin Khan to the aid of Zain Khan the Govenor of Sirhind, who was trying to recapture Sadhaura. These two armies tried to storm the fort first, but failing that they surrounded it and bided their time. The Sikhs would often venture out at night, to raid one side, collect as much supplies of food as they could, and return as swiftly as they had come. Sometimes Banda would send fresh men and weapons from Lohgarh, and this would add to the frustration of Zain Khan. The siege lasted till December 1712, and then Amin Khan was called back to Delhi to help the Emperor in another emergency.

During the upheaval at Lahore, practically all the blood relatives of Jahandar Shah had been liquidated. Farukh Syar, the son of Azim Shah, happened to be a Commander over the eastern area at that moment, and so escaped the slaughter. This man now enlisted the aid of the Sayad brothers, Hussain Ali and Abdulla, who had garrisons at Allahabad and Patna, and this army marched towards Delhi. Jahandar Shah was joined by Mohammed Amin Khan and moved out to meet the rebels at Agra. He was killed in this battle on 11th February, 1713, and Farukh Syar ascended the throne. He immediately removed Zabardast Khan and appointed Abdus Samad Khan as Governor of Lahore, with orders for the suppression of the Sikhs at Sadhaura. One of the Sayad brothers became the Chief Minister and the other the Commander-in-chief at Delhi. Zakaria Khan, the son of Abdus Samad, was appointed Governor of Jammu.

With the arrival of Abdus Samad and his son at the head of a large army at Sadhaura, the Sikhs were hard pressed for fresh rations, and after holding out a couple of months they vacated Sadhaura in the early part of October 1713. They joined Banda Singh at Lohgarh, which was also vacated after a few days with the Sikhs disappearing into the hills behind. Zakaria Khan was sent to Delhi to inform the Emperor about this and to offer him the heads of Sikhs killed in the fighting. Abdus Samad then proceeded to consolidate his position at Lahore.

Banda Singh had now reached his old haven in Jammu, known later as Dehra Baba Banda Singh. It is a place on the bank of the river Chenab, about 28 miles from Jammu town, and well concealed in the hillside. Here he stayed in relative peace till February 1715, receiving news of the happenings in the Punjab. Perhaps he was awaiting a suitable moment to mount the next offensive.

BANDA SINGH'S LAST BATTLE

With the disintegration of Banda's forces after his evacuation of Sadhaura and Lohgarh, the garrison Commanders of the smaller towns had begun a reign of suppression of the Sikhs all over the countryside. Abdus Samad Khan had ordered their execution on sight. Even the Hindus who were suspected of aiding them were robbed and beaten up. Some prominent Sikhs in Kahnuwan had been forced to fight back, and in March 1714, they had mustered under Sardar Jagat Singh and attacked the Pathans of Kahnuwan, burning and looting their rich mansions. But this was only an isolated case of organised resistance.

By February 1715, Banda Singh had got his forces together again near Jammu, and came down upon Kalanaur, the rich holiday resort of Mughal Emperors. He was given a fight by the Commander Sohrab Khan and his Khatri employees, but these defenders wilted before the furious onslaught of Banda's horsemen, and quickly left the town at the mercy of the Sikhs.

After plundering Kalanaur and resting the night at Achal, Banda then advanced upon Batala, a very rich trading centre, occupied by Sayads, Qazis, and other rich noblemen. Sheikh Mohammed Daim, the Commander, put up a spirited fight, but was overcome and killed after a short engagement. This town was partly burnt down, and those who could, escaped to Lahore or into the hills.

Farukh Syar heard about these disorders, and on 20th March, 1715 sent orders to Kamar Din Khan (son of Mohammed Amin Khan), Muzaffar Khan and some Hindu Rajas to take their forces to Lahore to join the army of Abdus Samad Khan in hunting down Banda Singh. The Commanders of Gujrat, Aurangabad, Kalanaur, and a few more also brought their forces up to join in the hunt.

Banda had some information about these preparations, and ordered his men to build a mud-walled fort at Kot Mirza Jan, a village midway between Batala and Kalanaur. He was still busy building this wall when Samad Khan's army appeared in sight and began to attack. Banda Singh ordered the charge, and this was so ferocious, that the imperial troops began to lose their foot-hold. The royal Commanders had to shout themselves hoarse to give their men courage and to urge them to counter-attack. The tide gradually turned against the Sikhs who were after all heavily outnumbered. (Mohammed Qasim, the author of the *Ibratnama*, who was present in this action, puts the Mughal forces at 24,000). The 2,000 to 3,000 Sikhs began to retreat holding the enemy at bay at the same time. In this manner, they reached the large mansion of Duni Chand in the village of Gurdas Nangal. This mansion had a low brick wall round it, and it also had a ditch further outside. Banda spent the night digging the ditch deeper, and then turning water into it from a stream flowing nearby. That made the crossing extremely muddy and well-nigh impossible for men on horseback. (This mansion is nothing but a mound of earth and bricks now, and is a mile outside the present village of Gurdas Nangal, which is 4 miles west of Gurdaspur).

The royal army had brought small cannon along, with which they could bombard the wall, but Banda spent the next two days and nights raising its height with the help of mud and stone. Abdus Samad Khan dared not try a crossing anywhere, because of the deadly fire he received from the well-manned walls. Banda, on the other hand, had to send out parties of horsemen for provisions. Even the grass for their horses had to be collected from the growth outside the fortress, and it is difficult to believe the daring displayed by those Sikhs. Lest the reader should think this story an exaggeration, here is a translation from the *Ibratnama* of Mohammed Qasim :

"The deeds of reckless bravery of the accursed Sikhs were astounding. At least twice each day parties of 40 to 50 of those infidels would emerge from their fortress, to cut grass for their animals. When challenged by our men this group would discharge their arrows and bullets and then cut their way so quickly through our soldiers, that within a few minutes they would disappear from sight. These raids were spreading terror throughout our camp."

Quite apart from the daring exploits of the ordinary Sikh soldier, there were strong rumours in the Mughal camps that Banda Singh had magical powers, and could transform himself into many shapes to escape captivity. Most of the Mughal Commanders were afraid of a face to face encounter with Banda, and were constantly pushing their *Qazis* and *Mullas* to the front to offer prayers to counter the spells of the enemy. Abdus Samad Khan openly prayed that Banda escaped from there, so that the whole business could be disposed off on any excuse. Only fresh orders from the Emperor to capture Banda dead or alive kept him at his task. He was taking new measures everyday to tighten the siege, to starve the defenders to submission. Kamar-ud-Din's forces were holding one half of the circle and his own forces were on the other half.

This siege dragged on for eight months. Towards the end, an unfortunate dispute arose between Banda Singh and one of his most trusted advisers Baba Binod Singh. This man along with Baaj Singh and three others made up the war council that Banda was supposed to consult in any difficult situation. Binod Singh advised the evacuation of the fortress, but for some reasons of his own, Banda wished to fight it out there. Binod Singh was senior in age, and when this difference of views flared up into an open quarrel, Banda agreed to let Baba Binod Singh take his men out of the fortress. Binod Singh and his supporters then charged out of the fortress and escaped.

Towards the end of November 1715, the remaining defenders were running out of ammunition and food. They were trying to exist on boiled leaves and the bark of trees, and were gradually reduced to mere skeletons. Then on 17th December, 1715, Abdus Samad shouted across the separating moat, that he would not allow any killing by his men, if Banda opened the gate to the fortress. When Banda ordered the gate be opened, the Mughals rushed in to spear or stab as many as three hundred of the half-dead and helpless defenders. About 200 were captured alive and handcuffed in twos. Banda Singh had chains round his ankles and his wrists, and was then locked in an iron cage. The Mughals were still afraid that he might escape and so they placed a guard on each side of the cage with swords drawn and the cage was placed aloft an elephant, which led the procession, which paraded through Lahore, before proceeding towards Delhi. Zakaria Khan, the son of the Lahore Governor, then took charge, and in order to give the Emperor a bigger present, he ordered his men to lop off more heads of Sikhs that they caught on the way, and he loaded them on to the carts that carried the 300 from Gurdas Nangal.

On 26th February, 1716, this procession neared Delhi, and Farukh Siyar ordered his Minister Mohammed Amin Khan to go out to receive them and to prepare them for a suitable display in the town. On the 29th February, the citizens of Delhi had lined the streets in full force, to get a good sight of the show. First marched 2,000 soldiers each holding a Sikh head impaled on his upright spear (so many extra had been collected on the way). Next followed Banda Singh's elephant. A gold-laced red turban was placed on his head, and to add further mockery to his plight, a bright printed scarlet shirt was slipped on his body. Then came 740 prisoners (500 had been collected on the way). These men were chained in pairs and thrown across the backs of camels. Their faces were blackened, and pointed sheepskin or paper caps were clapped on their heads. Behind this line came the Mughal Commanders, Mohammed Amin Khan, his son Kamar-ud-Din Khan, and his son-in-law Zakaria Khan. Their army men lined both sides of the streets.

However humiliating their plight, there were no signs of dejection or remorse on the faces of these Sikhs. In the words of Mohammed Harisi, author of the *Ibratnama*, who was on the spot that day : "The crowds were pressing forward to get a better view. Many were enjoying the sight and taking hillarious jibes at them. But nothing changed the air of calm and resignation on the faces of those Sikhs. There were no signs of bitterness or dejection anywhere. They appeared to be happy with their lot, and were actually joined in groups singing their Guru's hymns. If anyone remarked that they were being punished for their sins, their retort was : 'No, it is all according to God's Will ?'"

When we see the list of weapons captured from them at Gurdas Nangal we are really amazed at what they could do with so little. This is the list as supplied by Kanwar, the author of the *Tazkrah* :

1,000 swords, 217 small swords, 114 daggers, 278 shields, 173 bows, and 180 rifles. In spite of this scanty material they could have continued defying the Mughal might a long long time, if only their supplies of food had not run out.

The procession finally entered the famous Red Fort, where Farukh Siyar passed the sentence of death by public execution on all of them. Only those who were prepared to avow Islam could be pardoned. All were locked into cells, and on 5th March, 1716 the executions began. Parties of 100 were led out of prison each day to the open square in front of the Chabutra Jail. As the executioner called out for one man to come forward, the latter shouted his greeting : "The Khalsa belongs to God, and victory is also His", and lowered his head for the sword to strike. The head rolled away, and before the executioner could call out, the next prisoner had already stepped forward. Some were actually trying to beat the queue to receive what they termed their salvation as quickly as possible. Often had they heard *Gurbani* describe Death as the Bride, and meeting it as a marriage. Khafi Khan who was an eye-witness at this show, makes special mention of the astonishing cheerfulness, eagerness and sheer bravado displayed by those martyrs. All the historians of that period were amazed at the way those captives appeared to be laughing in the face of death. Gulam Hussain writes :

"The most noticeable feature about them was their sheer unconcern about their fate. They were vying with each other to be in front, and some were even trading jokes with the executioner."

Khafi Khan illustrates the resolute will and complete devotion to their cause displayed by those Sikhs by telling us about one young prisoner who was about to be called up from the line. This boy had been newly married and had been hauled in by Zakaria Khan's soldiers on the way, only to swell the number of captives for the pleasure of Farukh Siyar. He was the only son of his widowed mother, who had hurried to plead her case before the Emperor. She said that her son had been beguiled into joining the Sikh bands, but was not a Sikh at heart. On that ground, the Emperor wrote out the order of pardon for the boy, and the mother had hurried with that note and handed it to the officer-in-charge of the executions. The officer read out the pardon and the youth shouted out, "My mother has lied. I am a Sikh of my Guru in body and soul. Do not separate me from my departed friends. Please hurry so that I can join them now."

Saying that he left the guards dumbfounded and rushed away to the front of the queue again. He lowered his head before the executioner and refused to budge until the sword had descended and cut him into two.

That gory scene was enacted for seven days until all the ordinary captives had been disposed off. According to Mohammed Harisi, their bodies were loaded on wagons and taken out of town to be thrown to the vultures. The heads were hung up on trees or on poles near the market-place to be a lesson to all rebels. Not one from the 700 odd men had asked for pardon.

The jailors next turned their attention to the 20 odd *sardars*, including Baaj Singh, Fateh Singh, Ahli Singh and Gulab Singh (of Lohgarh fame). These men were tortured to the extreme and were asked to divulge the place where they had buried all the treasures that had been looted from Sirhind, Batala and other towns during their better days. These cruelties are described vividly in a letter dated March 1716 written by two representatives of the East India Company at Delhi — John Surman and Edward Stephenson.

Failing to get any clues after three months, they prepared to put an end to their lives on 19th June, 1716. Banda's cage was again hoisted on top of an elephant, and he was dressed in mock attire of an emperor, with a colourful red pointed turban on his head. His 4 year old son Ajai Singh was placed in his lap. The twenty odd *sardars* marched behind the elephant and this special procession then passed through the streets of Delhi, and headed for the Kutub-ud-Din mausoleum of Bahadur Shah, near the present Kutab Minar. On reaching that graveyard, the captives were again offered a choice of two alternatives : conversion to Islam or death. Needless to say all chose death. The Sikh *sardars* were subjected to tortures before being executed. Their heads were then impaled on spears and arranged in a circle round Banda who was now squatting on the ground. There were hundreds of spectators standing around watching this scene.

Banda Singh was then given a short sword and ordered to kill his own son Ajai Singh. As he sat unperturbed, the executioner moved forward and plunged his sword into the little child cutting the body into two. Then pieces of flesh were cut from the body and thrown in Banda's face. His liver was removed and thrust into Banda Singh's mouth. The father sat through all this without any signs of emotion. His powers of endurance were to be tested still further. But before that, Mohammed Amin Khan, who was standing near spoke as follows : "From your manner so far you appear to be a man of virtue, who believes in God, and in doing good deeds. You are also very intelligent. Can you tell me why you are having to suffer all this here ?"

Banda's reply was, "When the tyrants oppress their subjects to the limit, then God sends men like me on this earth to mete out punishment to them. But being human, we sometimes overstep the laws of justice, and for that we are made to pay whilst we are still here. God is not being unjust to me in any way."

The executioner then stepped forward and thrust the point of his dagger into Banda's right eye, pulling out the eyeball. He then pulled out the other eyeball. Banda sat through all this as still as a rock. His face gave no twitch of pain.

The cruel devil then took his sword and slashed off Banda's left foot, then both his arms. But Banda's features were still calm as if he was at peace with his Creator. Finally they tore off his flesh with red-hot pincers, and there being nothing else left in their book of tortures, they cut his body up into a hundred pieces, and were satisfied. (These details of the torture are given in full, by the following writers : Mohammed Harisi, Khafi Khan, Thornton, Elphinstone, Daneshwar and others).

BANDA SINGH'S CHARACTER AND HIS ACHIEVEMENTS

With Banda's death in June 1716, we close a short but hectic chapter in Sikh history, a chapter that evolves entirely around the achievements of this man.

It is necessary now to correct some of the opinions given on his character by the Muslim historians of those days. They are all agreed on his good judgement and great bravery in battle, but nearly all the Muslim writers have painted him in gory colours as a merciless animal in victory. They can be excused for holding this view because to them, as to the Muslims of Lahore, every battle fought by the Sikhs was a religious war. They failed to appreciate the philosophy taught and practised by Guru Gobind Singh :

Hindu Turuk Kou, Rafze, Emam Shaffi,

manas ki jaat sabhai ekai pehchaanbo.

which emphatically states "men may call themselves Hindus, Muslims, Emams and Shaffies, but I see them all belonging to one race — mankind."

Guru Gobind Singh had given Banda specific orders to punish those who had persecuted good saints like Pir Budhu Shah. He had not mentioned any revenge on those who had executed his own young boys at Sirhind. He had expected Bahadur Shah to fulfil his promise to punish those who had committed atrocities on good men, but had parted company from the Emperor completely disappointed. Banda Singh was then taught to bring to reality the Guru's own dream :

Dharam Chalawan, sant ubaaran

Dust sabhon ko mool upaaran.

which simply says : "To propagate justice, to uplift the righteous, and to uproot their oppressors."

That Banda Singh had kept this injunction in mind throughout his campaign, is apparent from the specimen copy of the letters (*hukumnama*) he wrote to the Sikhs, in which he mentions his ambition to establish "the rule of truth and love on this earth."

One can understand the error in judgement made by all these Muslim writers, when one recalls the gross misjudgements committed by their Emperors on such peace loving saints as Guru Arjun Dev and Guru Tegh Bahadur. When writers are blinded by the cry of a religious war (jehad), they can never discern between truth and falsehood. Guru Gobind Singh never waged a war on any religion. In fact, he was always on the defensive. If his wars had any religious tint in them, then he could never have had leaders like Budhu Shah and Said Beg fighting for him. Indeed no writer can ever pass wrong judgement on any of the Sikh Gurus if he has only once read a few lines of their poetical compositions and grasped their message to all mankind. Unfortunately for them, no Muslim historian cared to look into the writings of Guru Gobind Singh. And so, when it came to judging Banda Singh, they were looking at him from the viewpoint of the Muslim inhabitants of Lahore, who had raised the *Haideri* flag and called for a *jehad*.

To understand all this, we must recall that Banda's army was made up of three different types of men. Firstly, there were the true Sikhs of Guru Gobind Singh who had given up home and hearth for his sake, and who were anxiously awaiting his return from the Deccan. These men threw in their lot with Banda as soon as he read out the Guru's *hukumnana* to them. They were true Sikhs who fought only for the defence of the weak and the oppressed. The accumulation of wealth was not part of their creed. Secondly, there were those who were in the pay of the Chiefs of Phool Mehraj, whose elders had been blessed with rich states of their own during the days of Guru Har Rai. These men needed no share in the loot as their families were already provided for by their Chiefs. The third category consisted of the peasantry recruited from around the countryside, who had been exploited by their landlords, and who now found an opportunity to recover their losses. In this group also were some from the towns whose families had been outraged by the Mughal officers. So wherever there was looting and unnecessary killing, it was committed by such men who had once been looted themselves or whose families had been raped. A man who writes orders to his Sikhs to "adhere to the precepts of the Khalsa. Refrain from the use of ...... Do not commit theft or adultery", would be the last person to allow them freedom to loot the population.

Banda himself never enjoyed killing. His orders were strict against any killing of women and children. At Sirhind the killing had been more severe than usual, mainly because of the pent-up wrath of the Sikhs over the wanton slaying of Baba Fateh Singh and Baba Zorawar Singh. But even here Banda gives us an indication of his true character by ordering a halt to all killing, when a deputation of Hindus pleaded for mercy. This was done in spite of the resolution which had been passed by the Sikhs at Amritsar to have Sirhind razed to the ground. No Muslim historian of those days cares to mention such incidents. Nor do they mention the fact that during the short period of his reign over Sirhind, all Muslim employees were given time off to say their noon prayers. Nor were any mosques destroyed by his men. Not a soul in Malerkotla suffered any harm when Banda Singh went there to search for the grave of Anup Kaur.

The truth is that all the historians of that period were either employees of the Emperor or were writing from a religious viewpoint. In his *History of the Punjab*, Mr. Thornton makes a cute remark, when he says, "One cannot believe everything said by these Muslim writers."

Mills also sees the point when he says that those writers had to make Banda responsible for all the atrocities committed on their co-religionists in order to arouse their emotions for a religious war.

All that has been said above applies also to the history written by Mohammed Latif. His assessment of Banda Singh is ludicrous to the extreme, and can be dismissed with the statement that his views suffer from the additional defect of being second-hand, since he is of a much later period (late 19th century).

To appreciate Banda's nature, one has to remember how he turned away from all killing when his arrow struck down a mother deer and her young kids. He shunned meat from that day. How could a man of such sensitivity be ever portrayed as a man who killed with cruelty; that he seemed to relish shedding blood ? And, yet this is what Latif and the rest have said of Banda.

The charge levelled against him, that his was a communal war of Sikhs against Muslims, is refuted by the following report submitted to Emperor Bahadur Shah by one of his courtiers on 28th April, 1711.

"The wretched disciple of Nanak has his camp in the town of Kalanaur up to 26th April, 1711. During this period, he has promised and proclaimed, 'I do not oppose the Muslims.' Accordingly, for any Muslim who approaches him, he fixes a daily wage, and looks after him. He has permitted them to read *Khutba* and *Namaz*, with the result that 5,000 Muslims are in his service. They are free to shout their call and say their prayers in the army of the wretched (Sikhs)."

— Akhbar-i-Darbar-i-Mualla

There is no doubt about Banda's extraordinary bravery when he attacked. This great strength had been instilled into him from the *amrit* he received from Guru Gobind Singh. But his ferocity in battle was channelled only towards one goal — the destruction of tyranny. This bravery in battle was well controlled. He knew exactly when the odds against victory were too heavy, and on such occasions, he chose to retreat.

The Mughal General Amin Khan himself bears witness to Banda's bravery in the face of death. He is so astonished at the calmness with which Banda watches his little son die before him, that he cannot help asking why God is so unjust to an apparently benign soul. Little did Amin Khan or the historians of those days know about Banda Singh's powers of meditation and deep attachment to the-Almighty. That attachment which had enabled Guru Arjun Dev to bear without flinching the tortures of the red hot iron plate below him, was now helping Banda to take without flinching the thrust of the dagger in both his eyes and the lopping off of both his arms and his left foot. Such bravery could only be displayed by a conscience that was clear, and in complete harmony with God.

To close this account of Banda Singh's character, let us now look at his achievements. When he arrived from Nanded in the Punjab he had neither an army, nor weapons, no horses and no cannon. All he had was a dream of an ideal — a reign of peace and justice. That dream had drawn the three or four types of men under his banner, and had taken the shape of a revolution, which spread across the whole of the Punjab, and into the states of the Rajas. The Mughal forces at Lahore, Sultanpur, Sirhind and Jammu were unable to stem the flow of this revolution. Until the royal might at Delhi moved, this revolution had grown unabated, and every menial villager had the right to espouse Sikhism and hold his head high in society. The serfs had become the equals of their erstwhile masters. Guru Gobind Singh had sown the seed, and Banda Singh saw it sprout into a healthy sapling.

From the military viewpoint, Banda Singh stands out as a General of outstanding talent. He realised the need to join forces with the Sikhs at Keeratpur before attacking the mighty fort of Sirhind, and to that end he made a detour around the north of the town to meet his friends near Kharar. He saw how strategic Sirhind was for the control of the whole of the Punjab. Then again from the defensive point of view he realised he needed a safer retreat, and to that end he made Lohgarh his own headquarters. He strengthened this fort by posting small parties on the numerous mounds along the valley that led up to the fort. All these are proof of his extraordinary powers of judgement and leadership. After Guru Gobind Singh, the Sikhs had found in Banda another leader who could inspire them and provide some unity to their divided forces. He could achieve all this only on the basis of his own strong character. He was a complete Sikh in every sense, and exhorted all who came to him to partake of the Guru's *amrit*, and then retain the Sikh symbols and continue reciting the Name. At the commencement of any action he was seen to go into meditation to make his *ardas* before God.

All his letters bear testimony to his personal humility and his firm belief that all his achievements were through the grace of Guru Nanak and Guru Gobind Singh. He never assumed kingship as is sometimes alleged by our historians. His seal of office and his coins are all in the name of his master.

In conclusion it can be said that under Banda Singh the serfs of the Punjab had their first taste of freedom from their Mughal masters, though only for a brief period. This was the first real blow to the organised exploitation of the Punjab. It laid the foundation for the real conquest of the Punjab by the Sikhs, forty years later.

26

SIKH STRUGGLE AFTER BANDA

Tharam Singh

June, 1716 marks the end of a short but glorious chapter in Sikh history. It also marks the beginning of a critical phase, when the Sikhs were almost wiped out of existence. After Banda, the Sikhs had nobody who could rally their divided and disheartened groups into any sort of a united force. Bhai Mani Singh was there no doubt, but his was a peaceful and religious role, and this was a time when force had to be met with force, as explained by Guru Gobind Singh in his *Zafarnama* to Aurangzeb.

A big division had taken place in the Sikh nation, when Baba Binod Singh disagreed with Banda Singh and had vacated the fortress of Gurdas Nangal. This cleavage widened after the death of Banda, when a group of his admirers under Mahant Amar Singh of Khem Karan, calling themselves the Bandai Sikhs, assumed to themselves the control of the organisation of the Golden Temple. This squabble was settled only in 1721.

In addition to this big division, there were minor splinter groups setting up their own gurus. One such false guru was Gulab Rai, the son of Suraj Mal, one of the brothers of Guru Tegh Bahadur. Another such guru was Kharak Singh, a descendant of a Sikh of Guru Amar Das called Gangoo. So this sect came to be known as Gangoo Shahiay. Yet another section called Hindaliay set up their own guru, one Niranjan Das, a descendant of a Sikh of Guru Amar Das called Baba Hindal, who was made the Guru's preacher in Jandiala. One of Hindal's sons had turned apostate, and the Sikhs had condemned his whole clan for this transgression. Niranjan Das became a tormentor of all Sikhs, informing upon them to the Muslim authorities at Lahore.

To add to their woes, the Hindu landlords also turned against the Sikhs, and for material rewards, they gave full information about the movements of Sikhs to the Mughal Commanders. So, when Farukh Siyar gave Abdus Samad Khan full authority to hunt down all the Sikhs in the Punjab, the latter set about his task with great eagerness. All Hindus were ordered to cut their hair short and to shave their beards, otherwise they stood the risk of capital punishment. Orders were sent throughout the Punjab that nobody should supply food or shelter to any Sikh on pain of death, and further that those who gave information on Sikhs or who arrested them would be suitably rewarded. A price was put on each Sikh head. They were hunted down like wild animals. They had no sanctuary except in flight. Some fled to the marshy jungle in Kahnuwan, some to the jungles in the Malwa region, others to the hills in the north or to the sandy barren lands of Rajasthan. Their families that remained were quickly exterminated, thanks to the information supplied by their neighbours. Soon there was no Sikh to be seen in the Punjab in daylight. This inhuman persecution lasted for almost five years from 1716 to 1721.

Then, for one thing, Abdus Samad got satiated with the killing, and for another, the situation in Delhi took a change. The Sayad brothers, Hussain Ali and Abdulla Khan, who had helped Farukh Siyar ascend the throne in 1713, were soon scheming to wield power on their own. They enlisted the aid of the army officers and in 1719, had Farukh Siyar thrown into prison and later had him blinded and put to death. Prince Rafi-ud-Darjat was installed Emperor, but as he did not exactly comply with their wishes, he was poisoned to death after only three months. His brother Rafi-ud-Daulah was more amenable to their instructions, but he too met the fate of his brother after a reign of a few months. Roshan Akhtar, a son of Jahan Shah, one of the murdered sons of Bahadur Shah, was next selected for the unenviable post of Emperor of Delhi. The boy's mother pleaded with the king-makers to leave her son alone, but to no avail. He was enthroned with due ceremony in September 1719, and re-named Mohammed Shah. His Minister, Mohammed Amin Khan contrived to keep him safe from the clutches of the Sayad brothers, and he managed to remain on the throne for 26 years, albeit as Emperor in name only. The Commanders in the outlying provinces looked after their interests, each in his own way.

It was under such circumstances that Abdus Samad Khan loosened his iron grip on the Sikhs, and the latter began to visit their own villages again, and to gather on festive occasions at Amritsar. By 1720, some Sikhs could be seen in the plains on the banks of the river Beas.

On returning to their former villages, those who had left their families behind came to hear about their cruel fate. There were many again whose lands had been confiscated or handed over to their neighbours. The able-bodied amongst all these Sikhs bought or grabbed a horse, formed into small groups and took to highway robbery. These raiders were the founders of the famous Sikh *misls* (confederacies) that were to control the Punjab for almost 50 years.

These roving bands were soon raiding the towns for their daily needs of food and clothing, and Abdus Samad Khan was too tired to take any action. With the return of some of the Sikhs to their former occupation of tilling the soil and raising their families in the remote and more sheltered areas, the practice of celebrating the Divali and Vaisakhi festivals at the Golden Temple was revived. The more devoted followers of Banda had taken to his advice on the renunciation of meat. They were called Bandais and distinguished themselves from the others (the Tat Khalsa) by wearing crimson coloured shirts. Their greeting to each other was also different. They called out *Fateh Darshan* instead of the usual Khalsa greeting. The martyrdom of Banda Singh had raised his status in their minds, and they headed for Amritsar during the Divali season in 1720, with the aim of organising all the celeberations and of taking charge of all the offerings that the faithful would be making at the Harimandar Sahib.

On the other side, the followers of Kahn Singh, the son of Baba Binod Singh, had obtained approval from Lahore to celebrate the festival at Amritsar. So his *Tat Khalsa* also closed in on the Harimandar Sahib to take charge of all the celebrations. The leaders of both the sides were persuaded to make a joint organisation on this occasion so that trouble could be avoided. The festival passed off without incident, but tempers were high and the mood was explosive, and the Sikhs sent a report of this situation to the Guru's widow, Mata Sundri, at Delhi.

At the time of Guru Gobind Singh's demise at Nanded, Bhai Nand Lal had already passed away (1705) in his hometown Multan. The remaining Sikhs and scholars had returned to the Punjab. Foremost amongst those scholars was one Bhai Mani Singh. In the year 1720, he was with Mata Sundri at Delhi, when the Sikhs appealed to her for help. She wisely chose Bhai Mani Singh, sending him to Amritsar, as the head-priest of the Harimandar Sahib. This man reached there in January, 1721, and immediately set about his duties regulating the *kirtan* sessions, and organising the use of the collections for the benefit of the needy. He also sent invitations to all the Sikhs of the Punjab to attend the next Vaisakhi festival there (April, 1721).

At this gathering, he announced to the leaders of both parties, his plan to settle their differences once and for all. He proposed to write down on two slips of paper the greetings of both parties, *Fateh Darshan* on one and *Waheguruji ka Khalsa* on the other, to fold them up and drop them into the pool at the same spot at the small steps behind the Golden Temple. The party whose paper surfaced first would be accepted as the true leaders of the Sikhs and the other party must merge themselves into the winning party. When both sides had signified acceptance of this plan, Bhai Mani Singh wrote out the two slips of paper and dropped them into the pool. Both slips sank below the surface and there was a long wait, and that made the Sikhs very apprehensive. If neither slip came up to the surface it would mean the loss of the Sikh hold on Amritsar to the Mughals. Then slowly one slip emerged, and on picking it up they read the words *Waheguruji ka Khalsa*. The Tat Khalsa gave a loud cheer, and the majority of the Bandais present gave up their rituals and their separate identity.

With this problem solved, Bhai Mani Singh devoted all his energies to the preaching of *Gurbani,* and the consolidation of the unity of the Sikh nation. He was gaining fresh recruits into Sikhism everyday. After Banda, he took on the task of keeping the Sikhs together and in high spirits. For a brief spell, the Sikhs were going about their daily chores unmolested by the Mughal police.

Then the Minister at Delhi, Mohammed Amin Khan, decided to act to strengthen his grip over the Punjab. In 1726, he appointed Zakaria Khan, the son of Abdus Samad and his own son-in-law, as the Governor of Lahore. Samad Khan was posted as Governor of Multan. From 1726 to 1745, Zakaria Khan gave all his attention to the suppression of the Sikhs. He was energetic and he was skilful in battle. A new round of iniquities descended upon the Sikhs who were just beginning to enjoy their well-earned freedom. Zakaria Khan had learnt from his father's failure that the Sikhs could not be finished off by the sword. He adopted a double-edged weapon. He executed the able-bodied, but offered land to their families or the aged, to settle down under his rule. He offered government posts to Sikhs only to liquidate them later, on some charge or the other. He would allow peace loving farmers to till the soil, but he would kill any Sikh caught in the jungles.

BHAI TARA SINGH WAN

Those who saw through this scheme continued their life in their jungle sanctuaries. The *choudhris* (headmen) of the villages seized upon this opportunity to exercise their power over the peasants. Many peace loving innocent Sikhs were martyred at the instigation of the *choudhris*. One such Sikh was Bhai Tara Singh of village Wan next to Dal, almost on the present border between India and Pakistan. His father Gurdas Singh had been initiated by Guru Gobind Singh and had fought in the Guru's wars. Tara Singh had been initiated by Bhai Mani Singh, and had commenced a life of service to all travellers who passed through the village. There grew a thick hedge of thorny bushes all round his compound, and there was a small pit inside that compound in which logs were kept burning during the winter months, to give warmth to those who rested there. Many a weary traveller stopped at this hermitage and enjoyed the free food and a comfortable bed before resuming his journey the following day. In addition to being good-natured, and a truthful Sikh, Tara Singh was an accomplished swordsman and a good rider. During the hunt down of the Sikhs by Abdus Samad, he had provided sanctuary to large groups of refugees.

In a nearby village Naushehra, the *choudhry* Sahib Rai displayed his arrogance by letting loose his horses in the grain fields of the Sikh farmers. The poor men appealed to him to control the animals, but the *choudhry* angrily retorted, "You should be glad I am not reporting on you to Zakaria Khan. Otherwise the hair on your head would be made into ropes for these horses."

On hearing this taunt Sardar Baghel Singh and Amar Singh of nearby village captured the *choudhry's* horses and had them transported and sold to Sardar Aala Singh of Patiala. This outrage was duly reported by the *choudhry* to Zakaria Khan who sent a strong force of a thousand horsemen to punish the occupants of the hermitage. Needless to say the small band of about 20 Sikhs with Tara Singh died fighting to the last man.

NEW RESOLUTIONS AT AMRITSAR

News of the martyrdom of Tara Singh spread fast, and the Sikhs assembled in large numbers at the Akal Takht at Amritsar. They passed a *gurmata* (resolution) approving the purchase of horses for all fighting men, and their use in plunder of Government convoys carrying treasure to the towns. All those Sikhs who had gone into the Kahnuwan and the Lakhi jungles emerged now to carry out these raids. Instead of being frightened into submission, the Sikh bands turned bolder than ever. One party attacked a convoy carrying revenue from Multan to Delhi, and seized 400,000 Rupees. Another party seized the treasure being carried from Chawinda to Lahore. In the same manner, the convoys from Qasoor and Chunia were plundered. In 1727, one Murtaza Khan was robbed near Jandiala of a herd of horses he was taking from Kandhar for the Emperor at Delhi.

Zakaria Khan had deputed over 20,000 soldiers all over the Punjab for the control of this lawlessness, but the Sikhs could not be repressed. Their raids came up to the outskirts of Lahore, right up to the gates of the fort. They had the knack of attacking a government force near wooded territory, and then melting away into the bushes and trees. In the course of these disturbances, the peasantry suffered the most. They were in no position to pay revenues to Zakaria Khan, who naturally had gone into arrears at Delhi. In the year 1730, he was owing several millions for the past three years. The Emperor sent a force of 2,000 Rohelas to Lahore to demand the overdue revenue. Zakaria Khan packed two million Rupees in money-bags and loaded these on carts, saying the whole sum due was in the bags. In order to cover up his underpayment, he sent one of his Sikh employees Subeg Singh to inform the Sikhs about this convoy. As the Rohelas neared the river crossing near Goindwal, they were set upon by a force of 8,000 Sikhs, who found no difficulty in relieving them of their treasure.

Emperor Muhamed Shah despatched an army of 20,000 into the Punjab to punish the Sikhs for the last outrage. By the time this force reached Lahore, the Sikhs had retired into the hills or the jungle. They came down to their former haunts the moment this army returned to Delhi in 1731. They set about plundering the rich *choudhries* with greater boldness. Those who had told upon them, to the Emperor's men, were also given special attention. And all this while, their ranks were swelling with fresh converts from those Hindus who had been forced into Islam by Zakaria's men, and who were refused re-admission into Hinduism.

These Robin Hood style bands proved to be the training ground for the future leaders of the Sikhs. Only those with great endurance, self-sacrifice, grit and dare-devilry could aspire to the responsible post of a leader of men who were all self-disciplined and cast in the image of Guru Gobind Singh. The harsh measures adopted by Zakaria Khan only added to the challenge. The dangers they faced and overcame proved to be the forge from which men of proper steel were produced. It was during these days that men like Sham Singh, Kapur Singh, Darbara Singh, Hari Singh Hazoori, Deep Singh Shaheed, Jassa Singh Ramgarhia, Budha Singh Sukerchakia and Garja Singh showed up as outstanding leaders of men. Of these men, Deep Singh, Darbara Singh, Kapur Singh, Budha Singh and Sham Singh had personally seen Guru Gobind Singh.

THE HAND OF FRIENDSHIP

Zakaria Khan had tried all ways of holding down the Sikhs, but failed. He then deputed a government contracter Subeg Singh to offer them a *jagir* (largesse) of one *lakh* Rupees together with the title of *Nawab* to any one leader of their choice. This offer was made at the Vaisakhi gathering of all the *sardars* at Amritsar in 1733. It was rejected by each one of the leaders there, but the largesse was accepted in the name of the *Panth*. When they looked around as to who should receive the title of *Nawab,* they heard the words of *Gurbani* that was being read at the *Akal Takht* :

> *"Tahil mahil tako milai ja-ko sadh kirpal."*

And they spotted Sardar Kapur Singh fanning the assembly with a large hand-fan. From that day, he was known as Nawab Kapur Singh.

THE BIRTH OF THE SIKH MISLS

With the receipt of the handsome largesse from Zakaria Khan, the Sikhs enjoyed comparative peace for two years, under the leadership of Sardar Darbara Singh, who was a sort of Chief Minister and Cashier, with Nawab Kapur Singh as the Commander-in-Chief. Bhai Mani Singh's duties were confined to the maintenance of the Golden Temple. A large number of Sikhs left for their farm lands, and set about initiating others into Sikhism. Many of these recruits joined the roving bands of the *sardars*, after taking a little training in horsemanship. The majority of them collected at Amritsar. By July 1734, Sardar Darbara Singh died, and Nawab Kapur Singh became the acknowledged leader of the *Panth*. All the other *sardars* gathered at Amritsar one day and advised Kapur Singh to reorganise the fighting force into smaller groups for ease of management. Initially Nawab Kapur Singh split the army into two large groups, the *Budha Dal* (Senior Division) and the *Tarna Dal* (the Young Division). The Tarna Dal was later split into five *jathas* or camps, each stationed at one of the smaller tanks in Amritsar. Their leaders were Sardar Deep Singh Shaheed, Sardar Karam Singh, Sardar Kahn Singh Bhalla, Sardar Dasaundha Singh of Kot Budha, and Sardar Madan Singh Ranghreta. Each one of the generals was given a flag and a drum, and the individual soldiers were asked to join the general of their choice. Each camp had from 500 to 1,000 men, who sat down to eat from the common kitchen. All the goods they acquired in their raids were paid into the common fund, whose account was kept with the Budha Dal.

The Budha Dal, with Nawab Kapur Singh in overall charge had the following Chiefs under its wing : Gurbaksh Singh, Sham Singh Naroke, Bagh Singh Ahluwalia, Bhoomia Singh and Kubher Singh. This group occupied the territory around the Akal Takht. Jassa Singh Ahluwalia was then in his teens and helped Nawab Kapur Singh by looking after the stores and accounts.

This strange truce lasted throughout 1734, with the Sikh forces relying mainly on the largesse for their sustenance. They soon found the largesse insufficient as their numbers grew quite rapidly. The *Tarna Dal* Chiefs then started moving eastwards out of the Punjab, into Hissar and Hansi territory. Wherever they obtained their simple needs, they left the farmers unharmed. If anyone refused to comply, then force had to be used on him, but their women and children never came to any harm. The only sufferer in this exercise was the Emperor. The revenues due to him were now going into Sikh hands, and he put the blame entirely on Zakaria Khan. When the latter saw that the Sikhs at Amritsar were quite small in number, he reverted to his former policy of suppression. In 1735, he withdrew the *jagir*, and that drove the *Budha Dal* too back to their old Robin Hood style of raids on the rich landlords or on the government convoys. They also forced the village *choudhris* to hand over their half-yearly revenues to Sikh *sardars* who patrolled those areas.

PERSECUTION IS RENEWED

Zakaria's Chief Minister Diwan Lakhpat Rai was assigned the special job of subduing the Sikh rebels. The Budha Dal was then forced out of the *Majha* territories by a force of 10,000 Pathans and Mughals. They headed east and reached Barnala, where they were received by Sardar Aala Singh, who was then the Chief of a large territory that would later form the State of Patiala. Aala Singh was most courteous to the Sikh *sardars*. He was administered *amrit* by Nawab Kapur Singh. The Dal helped Aala Singh capture some towns up to Sunam. Kapur Singh then attacked Sirhind, exacting tribute from the Muslim Chiefs of that area. He brought the Budha Dal back across the Satluj from there and began collecting revenues from the towns of the *Doaba*. They were joined here by the groups of the Tarna Dal, and feeling more confident of facing the government forces now, they decided to celebrate the Divali festival of 1736 at Amritsar. They crossed the Beas at Goindwal, and moved up to Khadur, and then to Taran Taran, donating large sums out of their collections to the temples at these towns. The Tarna Dal encamped around Taran Taran, and the Budha Dal proceeded towards Basarkay.

Lakhpat Rai, with an army of 7,000, surprised the Budha Dal at Basarkay. Although the Mughals lost two of their generals, Salabat Khan and Qutub-ud-Din, they heavily outnumbered the Sikhs, who had to fight a retreating action towards Choonia. Just about there, they were joined by some groups of the Tarna Dal and they then began organising themselves into a line of battle at Hujra Shah Muqeem. A pitched battle was fought here, and the Mughals were routed. The Budha Dal was still bitter over their defeat at Basarkay, and they now pursued the Mughals with a vengeance, killing many of their generals, like Duni Chand (nephew of Lakhpat Rai), Tatar Khan and Jamal Khan. Lakhpat Rai brought the remnants of his army back to Lahore and the Sikhs celebrated Divali as arranged, at Amritsar in November, 1736.

Zakaria Khan was quite mad over this defeat, and immediately despatched Samund Khan at the head of a large army. The Sikhs avoided a new clash and withdrew into the Riarki (the plain of the Beas) plundering Kalanaur, Gurdaspur and Pathankot, crossed the Ravi westwards and captured Sialkot and Wazirabad.

Zakaria Khan decided to occupy Amritsar and posted Qazi Rahman and another general at the head of 2,000 men around the holy tank at Amritsar, with orders to kill any Sikh coming to bathe there. A fresh round of atrocities began on Sikh families. They had to flee to the hills again. Thousands were put to the sword. Bhai Mani Singh continued running *langar* for all nationalities. He preached *Gurbani*, which applied to all, and there were many Hindus and Sufi Muslims in his audience. Therefore, he was left unharmed.

Then in December 1738, on a charge of failing to pay up Rs. 5,000/- for holding the Divali celebrations at Amritsar that year, the good Bhai was ordered to be executed by dismemberment joint by joint in an open place in front of the fort of Lahore in full view of the citizens of the town.

The round of persecution did not cease with the killing of Bhai Mani Singh and the retaliatory execution of the Qazi by the Sikhs. Zakaria Khan passed stricter laws, which forbade any assistance to Sikhs or their families. They could not visit their holy tank at Amritsar for fear of being shot down. Any unfortunate ones caught by the government forces were submitted to various forms of torture before death. Tying them on to spiked wheels which turned against each other in pairs, was a favourite method in those days. The women were not spared. They had their children cut up before their eyes, and the pieces dropped into their laps. They were made to work the hand mills to grind wheat for the soldiers. Soon there was not a Sikh to be seen in the *majha* (territory west of the Beas). They took to the Kahnuwan and Lakhi jungles and into the *Malwa* regions and to Rajasthan. Only the very brave still moved about at night near the Taran Taran and Amritsar areas. One such pair of Sikhs have cut a niche for themselves in our annals. Bhai Bota Singh of village Bharana and his comrade Bhai Garja Singh, a fresh initiate from the scheduled castes, were one night moving towards Amritsar, when they were spotted by two Muslims. One of them said to the other, "There are no Sikhs left any more in the Panjab. These must be some actors in disguise."

These words cut the Sikhs to the quick. They immediately came out into the open road near Sarai Nur Din, and with heavy poles in hand they held up all carts or laden mules going towards Lahore and exacted toll from their drivers. Bota Singh also wrote out a short note in native doggerel, addressed to Zakaria Khan, which said :

Letter written by Singh Bota,
    cudgel in hand, *(sota)*
    standing in the road, *(khalota)*
    charging an *anna* per cart and a cent per donkey *(khota)*
    Addressed to Khano, my sister-in-law, so says Singh Bota.

This saucy letter turned Zakaria Khan livid with rage. He dispatched one hundred horsemen under Jalal Din to bring back Bota Singh alive. As they drew near, they saw the two Sikhs waiting in the road, back to back, and with swords drawn. Jalal Din shouted to Bota Singh to give himself up as it was futile to fight so many against him; but the two replied that they were there to die fighting. So Jalal Din ordered four of his men to attack first. When all four were killed, he sent eight more, and then another eight until both the Sikhs were killed. They had knocked out ten horsemen to prove a point — that the Sikhs were still very much alive.

Whilst Zakaria Khan and his general Lakhpat Rai were engaged in this game of hunting down the Sikhs, events were taking place in Afghanistan that were to have a profound effect on both Lahore and Delhi. For a moment, Zakaria Khan's attention was diverted to thoughts of his own preservation.

NADIR SHAH'S INVASION - 1739

Both Kabul and Delhi have had a share in shaping the history of the Sikhs. Persecution from one of them made the Sikhs take up arms, and the intervention of the other, gave them the opportunity to grasp and to consolidate their power over large tracts of land in the Punjab.

Babar was the first of the Mughals to invade India in 1521, and seize power at Delhi by defeating the army of the Lodhi Sultan Ibrahim at Panipat in 1526. Towards December 1719, Mohammed Shah Rangila was placed on the throne inspite of the protestations of his widowed mother. Power slowly passed from the hands of the Sayad brothers into the hands of Mohammed Amin Khan. He died in 1721 and was replaced by his son Qamar-ud Din Khan. Mohammed Shah remained an Emperor in name only till his death in 1748. During all these years Afghanistan (then known as Kabul) had been a part of the Mughal Kingdom, and at the time of Mohammed Shah it was under Governor Nasir Khan. This man's control over his province was as weak as that of the Delhi Emperor. There was hardly any collection of state revenues. The soldiers had not been paid for several years, which in fact was happening in Delhi too.

Such conditions of unrest and frustration provided an energetic outsider like Nadir Shah a golden opportunity to seize power. A son of a poor shepherd in Khurasan, a province of Iran, Nadir had joined a robber band when he was still a boy. He grew up to be its leader at about the time in 1717, when the Afghans occupied Khurasan and later the capital of Iran. Nadir's patriotic zeal was roused and he rallied a strong band of horsemen who helped him regain Khurasan. By 1725, he had become a national hero, who drove the Afghans out of Iran, and who became a sort of regent with a boy of the royal family as King of Iran. In 1736, when the boy King died, Nadir assumed the title of Emperor of Iran.

The Afghans had invaded Iran several times, and to avenge these raids, Nadir Shah advanced upon Ghazni and then Kabul, both of which were occupied in May, 1738. The Governor Nasir Khan was then in Peshawar. As Nadir Shah rode out towards the Khyber Pass in November 1738, Nasir tried to block his passage with a force of 20,000 ill trained Afghans, who were just no match for the fierce Khurasani horsemen. By December 1738, Nadir Shah had crossed the river Indus, and the lush plains of the Punjab stretched before him, literally beckoning him on. Zakaria Khan had made frantic requests for aid from Delhi, but without success. When he himself came out to oppose the invaders at the banks of the river Ravi, his army was just brushed aside (January, 1739).

Nadir Shah was an able General and a wise administrator. He accepted a gift of two million Rupees and retained Zakaria Khan as his governor at Lahore. He then took as hostages a son of Zakaria and a son of the minister Lakhpat Rai, and thus secure against revolt, he proceeded towards Delhi. As his whole army was on horseback, his advance was rapid. Leaving Lahore on the 26th January, he reached Sirhind on the 5th February, Ambala on the 7th, and Karnal on the 12th February. The Delhi army had been alerted in November on the fall of Kabul. The generals dragged their feet in moving out of Delhi. Every fresh report of Nadir's advance struck terror into them. They took two months to move their large army and their heavy guns up to Karnal, a distance of 75 miles. Here, they decided to give battle. They heavily outnumbered the attackers, but had no discipline and hardly any heart for a fight. On the 13th February, 1739, within three hours they had lost, over 20,000 killed or wounded, and the rest just scattered in all directions.

Nadir Shah entered Delhi as a victor on 9th March, 1739. He demanded 2.5 million Rupees as retribution, but the *Rangila* Emperor had nothing in his government treasury. He threw open his personal safe of jewels, and Nadir availed himself of all the diamonds and rubies of the Peacock Throne, and also the famous Koh-i-noor.

He left Delhi at the beginning of May 1739, taking with him a few thousand Indian girls (both Hindu and Muslim), a large number of boys as slaves and thousands of elephants, horses and camels loaded with the booty his men had collected. The hollow shell that made up the Mughal empire had been smashed open by Nadir Shah with one sweep, and the Sikhs quickly moved in to collect the broken pieces.

During his stay at Delhi, the Sikhs had come out of their jungle retreats and had no difficulty in looting all the countryside from the river Chenab to the areas around Karnal. Zakaria Khan's police forces were too demoralised to offer resistance. So Nadir's arrival was most opportune for the Sikhs in the replenishment of their depleted stores. Again when people learnt about his departure from Delhi, the rich landlords and noblemen promptly evacuated the cities and headed for the hills, only to be relieved of their gold by the long-suffering bands of Nawab Kapur Singh.

These bands got together and passed a resolution : Nadir Shah must deliver a part of the booty he was carrying away from Delhi. Nadir, on the other hand, felt that his reputation was a sufficient deterrent to anyone attacking him on the way. He had chosen the route along the foothills of the northern mountains to escape the heat of the plains. His baggage train being heavy-laden, lagged well behind his main force, and it was quite a shock for him to hear on reaching Akhnoor by the river Chenab, that all his slaves had been freed by Sikh bands, who had also seized a large share of his gold. Sardar Jassa Singh Ahluwalia who had just turned 21, showed a glimpse of his greatness as a leader by planning those raids, and by escorting the freed maidens to responsible homes from where they could return to their families.

Zakaria Khan had accompanied Nadir Shah to Akhnoor, and Nadir asked Zakaria Khan who those Sikhs were. On being told that they were all bands of poor *sadhus*, without clothing or riches, he asked;

"Then why don't you burn their houses down to punish them ?"

To that Zakaria replied,

"Their only homes are the saddles of their horses. They can last long periods without food and rest. They are known to sleep on horseback. We have put prizes on their heads, but their numbers keep increasing. They are never despondent, but are always singing the songs of their *Pirs*."

With a sigh, Nadir admitted that in that case the Sikhs would one day rule the land. Then he obtained a promise of a tribute of 2 million Rupees annually from Lahore, and confirmed the appointment of Zakaria Khan at Lahore and of his son Shah Nawaz Khan at Multan (where Abdus Samad Khan had just died).

MORE PERSECUTION

With the departure of Nadir Shah, Zakaria Khan took stock of his household and saw it all in ruins. He decided to take full revenge on the Sikhs for all his misfortunes, and issued a fresh proclamation :

"No Sikh shall remain alive in the Punjab. It would be no offence to murder a Sikh or to loot his house. Anyone giving information on a Sikh will be given ten Rupees. If he brings the head of a Sikh, he earns fifty Rupees. Anyone caught helping a Sikh with shelter or provisions will be converted to Islam."

So, the full machinery of the State was put to work to root the Sikhs out of the Punjab again. They stayed a while in the Jalandhar Doab, but here also the new governor Adina Beg was compelled to take action. So, for the next five years till 1745, the Sikhs went into hiding again in the hills or the jungles of the Malwa regions or in Rajasthan.

SUKHA SINGH AND MEHTAB SINGH PUNISH MASSA

Zakaria Khan knew that Sikhs would always try to visit their fountain of Truth — the Golden Temple. The *choudhry* of Mandiala was one Mir Musalul Khan, commonly known as Massa Ranghar. In 1740, Zakaria Khan assigned this man the task of watching around Amritsar for Sikh devotees. His guard was augmented by government soldiers. Massa needed no further prompting from the authorities. He placed his cot in the centre of the temple, and set about desecrating it to his heart's fill. Street girls danced before him while he dined and wined in the holiest of the Sikh shrines.

There would always be one or two Sikhs in hiding near the temple, waiting for nightfall, when they could steal in for a dip in the tank. Sardar Bulaka Singh happened to be around when Massa was in occupation. He hurried away with his painful secret and headed straight for Bikaner, where he unburdened himself before the band of Sardar Sham Singh. From the assembly of Sikhs stood up one Mehtab Singh of Meerankot, who declared his resolve to go and kill Massa or be killed himself. Another very brave man Sukha Singh of Mari Kamboki also stood up and asked permission of Sardar Sham Singh to accompany Mehtab Singh. The whole gathering said their *ardas* for the success of the mission, and the two rode away in the hot month of August disguised as two landlords bringing the revenue into Amritsar. They hung their hair loose behind their necks (as the Pathans do), and held a cloth bag each filled with chips of broken pottery.

They reached the entrance to the Harimandar Sahib towards noon, when the guards were resting, half asleep because of the heat. They tied their horses to the *Elaichee Ber*, at the right of the *Darshani* doorstep, and nobody suspected them of being anything other than revenue collectors.

As they entered the Temple, they saw Massa sitting on his cot smoking a pipe, with a girl dancing before him, and a few of his companions reclining half-drunk along the walls. Sukha Singh threw down his bag at Massa's feet and as the latter bent down to pick it up, Mehtab Singh pulled out his sword and cut his head off clean with one stroke. Sukha Singh had meanwhile drawn his sword and made quick work of the few men inside the Temple. They placed Massa's head in a cloth bag and came away to their horses, and rode away before the guards could get ready to challenge them. They reached Bikaner safely and placed the head before Sardar Sham Singh. The gathering congratulated them and ordered that the head be consigned to the flames.

Zakaria Khan summoned all the *choudhries* of the district of Amritsar and threatened them with severe punishment if they did not find out all about the two Sikhs. Harbhagat Das (Niranjania) came forward with the names and the villages of the two, and orders were immediately given for the arrest of the family of Mehtab Singh. He had left his 7 year old son Rai Singh in the care of the village headman Natha Khehra. As soon as he heard about the approaching soldiers, he took flight towards the jungles taking with him the boy, his own son, a nephew and two friends. They were overtaken by the soldiers and all the men were killed except the nephew who escaped during the fighting. Rai Singh was given three sword thrusts as he lay clinging to Natha's leg. The blade passed through his shoulder, his collar-bone and the side of his neck, but he was later picked up by a village woman and nursed back to health. He was to grow up to be the father to Rattan Singh Bhangoo, a famous Sikh historian.

BHAI TAROO SINGH BECOMES A MARTYR

What with such deeds of defiance by Sukha Singh and Mehtab Singh, and with an empty state treasury, and the soldiers clamouring for their pay, Zakaria Khan grew daily more desperate and short-tempered. He once had his Minister Lakhpat Rai locked up, and sent threatening notes to Adina Beg, his deputy at Jalandhar to pay his arrears. Finding no fugitives on whom he could vent his wrath, Zakaria Khan now turned to persecuting the peace loving citizens. Harbhagat Das of Jandiala was always active in his spying duties. He mentioned the help that Bhai Taroo of Pulla (Amritsar District) was giving to those in hiding.

Bhai Taroo was a model Sikh, just turned 22, who lived by tilling the soil, and sharing his meals with all who travelled through his village. He had a sister and a widowed mother, both of whom had the same spirit of service. Often had they gone out towards the jungle to supply food to the Sikh fighters in hiding there. In 1745, an order for the arrest of the Bhai was issued and he was taken in chains to Lahore. In a fit of rage Zakaria Khan ordered his scalp to be removed as he would not allow his hair to be cropped and this cruel sentence was executed in full view of the public at Nakhas Chowk (now known as Shahid Gunj). He remained alive for 22 days, and during this period Zakaria Khan was taken seriously ill with diseased prostate gland. He died on 1st July, 1745 and Bhai Taroo Singh breathed his last a few days later.

A SHORT BREATHING SPELL

With the death of Zakaria Khan, a tussle arose for the post of Lahore between his three sons, and this was not settled till January, 1746. Attention was, thus, diverted from the Sikhs, who once again returned to Amritsar, and began to fan out all over the countryside in parties of a hundred or more, exacting food or cash, and gaining more recruits into their ranks. During the Divali celebrations in October 1745, Nawab Kapur Singh reorganised the whole army (called the Dal Khalsa) into about 25 autonomous units, each under its own *Sardar*, with full powers to carry out their own raids and to share their booty amongst their members. These independent bands were to unite under their leader Nawab Kapur Singh in times of national emergency.

These bands halted all the machinery of government for about three months. One of them was so bold as to enter the city of Lahore in January 1746, towards nightfall, and to begin looting the shopkeepers just as they were closing up for the day. When the government soldiers appeared they were riding away into the jungle along the banks of the Ravi. By January, the fraternal dispute had been settled, with the eldest Yahya Khan, son-in-law of Qamar-ud-Din Khan, as Governor of Lahore. He yielded a part of his father's collection of precious stones to Shah Nawaz Khan, who retained his old command of Multan. There is some uncertainty as to what the third brother Mir Bagi was allotted, but Adina Beg continued as Commander of Jalandhar.

Yahya Khan now gave his minister Lakhpat Rai firm orders to take personal charge of the army to drive the Sikhs out of the area around Lahore. Lakhpat Rai chased those bands up the river Ravi and across it into Eminabad district. He then returned leaving about 2,000 Sikhs settling down to camp at a site now known as Rori Sahib (a temple in Eminabad).

The Commander of Eminabad was Jaspat Rai, the brother of Lakhpat Rai. This man was no friend to the tired Sikhs, who requested nothing but a night's rest there. Jaspat Rai ordered his army out and led the attack from atop an elephant. The Sikhs withdrew as they fought until they reached Badoki Gosaian. Here, they turned round and fell with great fury upon the government army. One Nibahu Singh Rangretta took hold of the elephant's tail and climbed up to cut off the head of Jaspat Rai. With his end, the soldiers fled the battlefield.

Lakhpat Rai vowed he would not rest till all the Sikhs had been eliminated. He obtained Yahya Khan's consent for a general massacre of Sikhs, the peaceful as well as the fighters. So all Sikh government employees or other inhabitants of Lahore were arrested. Amongst these were Subeg Singh, the contractor, later appointed *kotwal* of Lahore, and his son Shahbaz Singh. On 10th March, 1746, both father and son were tortured to death on the spiked wheels.

Lakhpat further ordered that the use of the word *Granth Sahib* was forbidden, and that the word *Pothi* could be used instead. The word *gur* for raw sugar was to be replaced by *rori* or *bheli*, because the former reminded people of their Guru. Sikh scriptures were seized and committed to the flames.

THE SMALLER HOLOCAUST, APRIL 1746

Finding himself free after the massacre of all the Sikhs in and around Lahore, Lakhpat set out in early April at the head of a strong army, with some pieces of artillery, in pursuit of the groups of the Dal Khalsa, sheltering along the banks of the Ravi. These bands were led by Jassa Singh Ahluwalia, Naudh Singh Sukerchakia, Deep Singh, Sukha Singh Mari Kamboki, Gordial Singh Dallewalia, and Nawab Kapur Singh.

Lakhpat brought his guns to bear on the thickets where the Sikhs were hiding and so forced them out and to retreat northwards. They had kept to the right bank of the river, and gradually retreated towards the hills of Basoli. They had been charging into the enemy time and again while retreating, and by the time they reached the hills, all their ammunitions were used up. They were thus hoping to scale the hills into safety, but their hopes were shattered when a shower of bullets and stones greeted them from the hill slopes. The hill *rajas* had been forewarned by Lakhpat Rai against sheltering any Sikh there. Apart from this hail of missiles from the top, their horses were simply not used to scaling the steep slopes.

It was now decided to split into two parties. Those on foot should try scaling the hills and go on through Kangra and Mandi towards Keeratpur. This they accomplished in about four months, with great loss of life. The rest were to charge back into the enemy, and cut through them, to reach a river crossing further downstream.

Kapur Singh, Jassa Singh and Sukha Singh came down upon the Lahore forces, with swords and spears, and a bloody encounter took place, with heavy losses on both sides. A son of Lakhpat Rai was killed, as also a son of Yahya Khan. Sukha Singh headed straight for Lakhpat Rai's elephant, and would have got there if not for a cannon ball that went straight through his thigh. He tore off a piece from his turban and bandaged his leg to the saddle to keep the bones in position. Jassa Singh had meanwhile come to his aid, and together they rode off through the enemy lines to the safety of the woods.

The bands had all joined up now, leaving Lakhpat Rai in great chagrin over their escape, and in deep pain over the loss of his son. As they halted for the night, Jassa Singh and Sukha Singh addressed their men thus :

"We have left the enemy behind us, but he is not far. Tomorrow he will come hard on us again, and we are without weapons or good horses. Let us strike again and get what we need from them. This is the moment to do it, as they will be asleep free of all care, thinking that we have run away from them."

This was the spirit that fired new hope into disheartened men, and that made such leaders truly great. True enough they found Lakhpat Rai's camp unguarded, and so they gathered all the horses and weapons they needed and came away into the woods again.

The next day, they were up and moving before dawn and so came down to where the waters were slow and rafts could be used to cross over to the left bank. They then rode out across the plains towards Hargobindpur where they crossed the river Beas into the *Doaba*. Here they were molested by the forces of Adina Beg, who obeyed the commands from Lahore, but never quite whole-heartedly. So these Sikh survivors crossed over the Satluj near Alipur and entered the *Malwa* regions some time in June 1746. This engagement had dealt the Sikhs a crippling blow, costing them at least 10,000 fighting men. The leaders took their men to various districts to recuperate and within 6 months they were ready to unite for further action.

AHMED SHAH ABDALI'S INVASIONS BEGIN

In November 1746, Shah Nawaz Khan attacked Lahore and defeated his brother Yahya Khan and threw him into prison together with his general Lakhpat Rai and Moman Khan. Yahya Khan later escaped and reached Delhi.

These disturbances at Lahore were just what the Sikhs needed for their revival. But, there was more good fortune coming their way. Nadir Shah had been consolidating his rule over Afghanistan, since his return from Delhi in 1739. The general at the head of his army was one Ahmed Shah, a Sadozai Pathan of the province of Herat. Nadir Shah had grown extremely short-tempered and suspicious of late. On the night of 9th June,

1747 he was assassinated by his own servants and Ahmed Shah ascended the throne.

Ahmed Shah had accompanied Nadir Shah to Delhi in 1738, and had seen the weakness of the ruler there. To pay for the maintenance of the army, he had to conquer new lands. His own country had no resources at all, compared with the vast wealth of India. Apart from that, he wished to enhance his own reputation in Afghanistan by capturing a neighbouring country. He attacked Peshawar and drove out its Mughal governor Nasir Khan in October 1747.

Just about then, he received an invitation from Shah Nawaz Khan to invade and annex the provinces of Multan, Kashmir and Lahore, saying that he would co-operate fully in this campaign in return for his own confirmation as governor of Lahore.

In December 1747, Ahmed Shah set out from Peshawar, and arrived at the Indus river-crossing at Attock. From there, he sent his messenger to Lahore, but the man was given a rough reception by Shah Nawaz, who was then a different man. He had been won over by the Delhi minister with an offer of confirmation in his appointment of Governor of Lahore. Thus, when Ahmed Shah reached the bank of the Ravi on 8th January, 1748, the Lahore army of 70,000 prepared to oppose the invader. The Pathans crossed over on the 10th of January and the battle was joined on the 11th. Ahmed Shah had only 18,000 horsemen, and no artillery. But during the battle, a force of 5,000 Pathans of Qasoor under Jamal Khan defected to his side, and he was able to crush the poorly trained forces of Lahore. Shah Nawaz fled to Delhi, and Adina Beg was equally fast in running away to the Jalandhar area.

Ahmed Shah entered the city on the 12th January 1748, and set free Moman Khan and Lakhpat Rai. He then ordered a general massacre. Towards evening, the prominent leaders of the city including Moman Khan, Lakhpat Rai and Surat Singh collected a sum of three million Rupees and offered it as expenses to Abdali, requesting him to halt the looting and slaughter.

Ahmed Shah appointed Jamal Khan of Qasoor Governor of Lahore, and Lakhpat Rai his minister, and restoring law and order around the town by February 18, he set out towards Delhi.

Meanwhile Qamar-ud-Din Khan collected an army of 200,000 and marched towards Sirhind which was reached on 25th February. Here he found that the Rohela commander of Sirhind, Mohammed Khan had fled into the hills on hearing about the advance of Ahmed Shah. Qamar-ud-Din left his baggage and his *begums* under the protection of 1,000 men at Sirhind, and advanced towards Machhiwara.

Ahmed Shah crossed the river Satluj at Phillaur on the 1st March at night, and reached Sirhind the next day to find it almost undefended. On hearing about the capture of his *begums,* Qamar-ud-Din hastened back, and on the 11th March, 1748, the two armies clashed in battle at Manupur. Qamar-ud-Din was killed in one of a series of skirmishes that went on for some days. His son Muin-ul-Mulk (Mir Manu for short) took over the lead, and he made such a furious charge that Abdali's men gave way, and fled. By 17th March, Abdali was crossing the Satluj and heading towards Lahore, with Mir Manu following him, but at a safe distance behind.

This train of events seemed to have been specially designed by Providence for the benefit of the Sikhs, who lost no time in making the most of their good fortune. Yahya Khan had tried his best to annihilate them during his short stay of 15 months as Governor of Lahore. But after October 1746, his energies were diverted to his own welfare on account of the activities of Shah Nawaz and Adina Beg. Shah Nawaz Khan was too preoccupied with the confirmation of his command over the Punjab by the Minister at Delhi, to give the Sikhs much trouble. Then when the Afghan threat loomed in January 1748, he had called up Adina Beg from Jalandhar, leaving the Sikhs completely free to raid and occupy large tracts of land in both the Jalandhar and the Bari *Doabs*. During the two months that Abdali spent marching down from Lahore to the battle at Manupur, the Sikhs were busy taking control over the countryside, and chastising those *choudhries* who had informed on them. Rama Randhawa of Ghanayan, Harbhagat of Jandiala, Dharamdas of Jodh Nagar, Sanmukh Rai of Wadali, the Khatris of Patti, and the Ranghars of Sheikhupura were amongst those that were put to the sword. Village headmen would inform on Sikhs in future only at their own peril.

Whilst Abdali was engaged at Manupur, Jassa Singh's band swooped upon Amritsar, which was then under the charge of one Salabat Khan. This Commander was slain in the fight and his troops fled, leaving the city and its holy tank in the hands of the Sikhs. The partly earth-filled tank was cleaned up, and the masses were once more able to take their ablutions there.

When Abdali began his retreat from Manupur in March 1748, the Sikh bands under Jassa Singh, Charhat Singh and Karora Singh gave him a taste of the same guerilla raids that had been applied on Nadir Shah. Mir Manu was coming too far behind to bother Ahmed Shah. The Sikhs would swoop down on Abdali's camp at night and make away with baggage and horses. They continued with this harassment till he reached the banks of the Chenab. Here they stopped because Vaisakhi day that year fell on the 29th March, and they wished to celebrate it at Amritsar.

This was the first Vaisakhi they had celebrated after many years, in complete freedom, and it also marked a new phase in the organisation of the Dal Khalsa. The holocaust of 1746 had shown up the weakness of small groups or *jathas* fighting under separate leaders. Nawab Kapur Singh proposed the organisation of the army under one Commander, who would have a council of 10 *sardars* to advise him. The whole Dal Khalsa was, thus, reconstituted from a federation of eleven *misls* or confederacies. When the question of the leader was raised by the Nawab, all eyes turned to Jassa Singh Ahluwalia, who had by then amply proved his qualities of judgement, daring and fighting prowess. The eleven *misls* and their leaders were :

1. *Misl* Ahluwalia   (Jassa Singh Kalaal)
2. *Misl* Faizalpuria or Singhpuria   (Nawab Kapur Singh)
3. *Misl* Sukerchakia   (Naudh Singh)
4. *Misl* Nishanwali (or flag-bearer)   (Dasaundha Singh)
5. *Misl* Bhangi   (Hari Singh of Panjawar)
6. *Misl* Kanhaya   (Jai Singh of Khalra)

  7. *Misl* Nakai   (Hari Singh of Bahirwal)
  8. *Misl* Dallewal   (Gulab Singh of Dallewal)
  9. *Misl* Shaheed   (Baba Deep Singh)
10. *Misl* Karoria   (Karora Singh of Paijgarh)
11. *Misl* Singhania or Ramgarhia   (Nand Singh of Singhani)

Sikh soldiers were free to join the *misl* of their choice. All initiated Sikhs could be members of the Dal Khalsa, and equal partners in the Dal.

A second important decision was taken at this Vaisakhi. They felt the need for a good fortress for purposes of defence. They chose a site in Amritsar by the side of Ramsar, and immediately set about laying mud-bricks into a wall six feet wide and ten feet high. This enclosure was called Ram Rauni (later Ramgarh). There was room for 500 horsemen within this fortress, and 500 were accordingly posted there in April 1748.

Mir Manu had made leisurely progress to reach Lahore in April 1748. In his father's post at Delhi was now installed an Irani Shia named Safdar Jang. After Mir Manu had established himself firmly at Lahore, he despatched his minister Diwan Kaura Mal to Multan, which had passed into the hands of Zahid Khan. Diwan Kaura Mal overpowered Zahid Khan without much difficulty.

Mir Manu now turned to the suppression of the Sikhs. His patrolling units began capturing them, with the result that the Sikh bands moved out of the *Majha* areas into the Jalandhar *Doab*. Here, so far, Adina Beg had been fairly accommodating. The Sikhs caused no disturbances in this area, and he left them alone. But, when he received a strict order from Mir Manu in June 1748, he gathered a large force and attacked those assembled at Anandpur, killing about 500 and losing the same number in the operation. The Sikh bands dispersed into the *Malwa* regions beyond the Satluj. Shortly after this, Adina Beg made peace with the Sikhs on his own. He wanted them around to prove how indispensable he himself was to the Lahore government. He even engaged a band of 100 men under Jassa Singh of Icho Gill in his army. This Jassa Singh had somehow fallen out with the Dal Khalsa.

There was comparative peace in the Punjab till the Divali month of October 1748, when the Dal Khalsa again assembled at Amritsar. Mir Manu immediately sent Diwan Kaura Mal with a large force to surround the city. Adina Beg was also ordered to bring his army to join the Lahore force, and Jassa Singh's one hundred Sikhs were in this force. By the time Adina Beg's army reached Amritsar, the Dal Khalsa had stationed 500 men in the Ram Rauni and the rest had dispersed into the neighbouring jungles. A siege of the fortress had been laid for over 30 days, and about 200 of the defenders had died while making their foraging excursions out of the fortress to replenish their stock of food. At last, when all their supplies were used up, the remaining 300 Sikhs resolved to make a final charge out of the fortress and to die fighting.

That night, one of the defenders, disguised himself as a Pathan and came out into the camp of Jassa Singh of Icho Gill. He had not expected to see Sikhs amongst Adina Beg's forces, and he said in surprise, "It looks as if Sikhs are murdering the Sikhs inside."

Jassa Singh decided to join his Sikh brothers and during the night he stole into the Ram Rauni bringing in a large stock of food and weapons.

News had reached Kaura Mal that Abdali was coming into the Punjab again. Mir Manu was further disturbed when he learnt that the new Minister at Delhi, Safdar Jang had appointed Shah Nawaz as Governor of Multan. Diwan Kaura Mal, who at heart was a good Sikh, advised Mir Manu to come to terms with the Sikhs to meet the twin threats to the State, and the Governor readily agreed. So the siege of Ram Rauni was lifted in November 1748, and at the further request of Diwan Kaura Mal, the revenue from the 12 villages attached to Harimandar Sahib since the days of Akbar, was restored. For such deeds of affection for the Sikh cause, Diwan Kaura Mal is remembered amongst Sikhs as Diwan 'Mitha' Mal, the new word meaning 'sweet' as opposed to the original word 'bitter.'

THE SECOND INVASION

Ahmed Shah Abdali came to know about the intrigues at Delhi, and that Mir Manu could expect no aid from there. So in December 1748, he crossed the Indus again and began plundering all the villages along his route, until he reached a place called Sohdra on the bank of the river Chenab. From there, he wrote a note to Mir Manu, "Char Mahal, the districts of Gujrat, Pasrur, Sialkot and Aurangabad have been part of the Kingdom of Kabul since the days of Nadir Shah. Pay up the arrears due and promise to pay future revenues yearly."

Mir Manu had moved his army half-way up between the Ravi and the Chenab, but had not had to fight. He kept negotiating with Abdali, while he sent his courtier to Delhi to ask for advice. The Emperor promptly agreed to pay the revenue of Char Mahal to Kabul. Mir Manu then paid 1.4 million Rupees as the current revenue and promised to pay the same amount yearly. Abdali was highly pleased with this outcome and retired to Kabul. His aim had been only to size up the strength of the victor of Manupur. Mir Manu, on his part, felt quite free now to give his full attention to his domestic problems, and he had two big ones to face. On the one hand, Nasir Khan who had been appointed Commander of the Char Mahal territory by Mir Manu, was now instigated by Safdar Jang to rebel and take over Lahore also. On the other hand, Shah Nawaz had reached Multan by April 1748, with a letter of appointment from Safdar Jang. He found no difficulty in recruiting the army Generals there to his cause, and was gradually building up a large force of about 20,000 in preparation for the capture of Lahore.

Mir Manu marched upon Sialkot at the head of a large army and routed Nasir Khan in July 1749. He then despatched Diwan Kaura Mal to seize Multan. With Mir Manu's consent, Kaura Mal invited a Sikh force of about 5,000 men under Jassa Singh Ahluwalia to join him in this campaign. The two armies met in battle in September 1749 about three miles out of Multan, and the Sikhs were of great help in the complete defeat of Shah Nawaz, who was himself killed in this battle.

Mir Manu bestowed the title of Raja Bahadur on Kaura Mal and appointed him Governor of Multan. The Sikhs stopped all harassing raids for the next 12 months and occupied themselves in repairing their shrines.

THE THIRD INVASION

In October 1751, Abdali's courtier Harun Khan arrived at Lahore demanding payment of 2.5 million Rupees as revenue due from the Char Mahal. Ahmed Shah himself was already on the move, leaving Peshawar in November. Mir Manu tried to buy more time. He paid a sum of 900,000 and promised to send the balance in a few month's time if Abdali would only retire to Kabul. He sent an urgent appeal to Delhi for a large force, and at the same time, he summoned the armies of Adina Beg and Kaura Mal. As expected, Delhi ignored his appeal. Abdali received this cash offering, but continued to advance across the Jhelum and the Chenab. He had 50,000 horsemen this time, with Generals Jehan Khan, Abdus Samad Khan and Abdulla Khan in charge. By the 30th November, he was camped at Shahdra, and the Lahore armies faced him on the opposite bank of the Ravi.

The Sikhs were persuaded by Kaura Mal to send a force of 20,000 men to help the Lahore army, but suspecting the intentions of Adina Beg, they engaged only in one skirmish and withdrew.

Abdali spent over a month on the other side of the Ravi, ravaging the countryside for miles around Shahdra, and sending all the rich *choudhris* flying with their families to the hills. Then one night, he moved his army a few miles upstream, and took them across the river at Shah Daula. Before dawn the next day, he was in camp at the Shalamar Gardens, within easy range of the walls of Lahore.

Against all advice, Mir Manu came out of his position on 12th April, and made a furious charge. He almost succeeded in dislodging the Pathan forces, but just then misfortune struck. The good Kaura Mal was leading his horsemen atop an elephant, when the animal's foot rested on an old grave and sank into the soft earth. He stumbled and fell, and just then a stray bullet hit Raja Kaura Mal in the head, killing him on the spot. Seeing him fall, that wing of the army lost heart and ran, and Abdali's forces rushed up to disperse the Lahore army, which quickly withdrew into the town. It is said that Adina Beg had bribed one of his men to fire on Kaura Mal. Thus ends the story of one of the staunchest of friends of the Sikhs. His name has lived in the hearts of the Sikhs over the centuries.

Mir Manu sued for peace, and Abdali having a high regard for his bravery and general ability, retained him as his Governor over Lahore and Multan. He had this acquisition of the two provinces ratified in the form of a treaty, which was signed by the Delhi Emperor.

With the dangers from both Kabul and Delhi removed, Mir Manu was now a free man to enforce law and order in the Punjab. His advisers were now the *qazis* and *mullahs*, who quickly put all blame for his defeat on the Sikhs who had deserted him at Lahore. One of his first acts was the withdrawal of the largesse for the Golden Temple. He was further advised that the stability of his rule depended on the destruction of the Sikhs, and to that end, he ordered their wholesale capture and execution. So from May 1752 till his death in November 1753, he let loose on the Sikhs all the barbarities he knew. A price of 10 Rupees was placed on the head of a Sikh. His orders applied to

Sikh men, women and children. According to the historian Nur Ahmed Chishti, "Mir Manu had ordered one thousand and one hundred Sikhs to be killed at the Nakhas Chowk on Id Day", and further "Mir Manu was fanatic to his fingertips. He would have a kilogram of the holy threads of Hindus taken off and burnt, before he had his dinner."

His cruelty to women and children is given special prominence in the daily *Ardas* of Sikhs today. Mir Manu's troops roamed the countryside like demons looking for victims, and the Sikh fighters who had taken to the hills, came back to take away those of their families who had survived this carnage. They came back in parties of fifty or more and often clashed with the troops.

Mir Manu met his end during one of these encounters. In November 1753, he was leading his troops in the chase of a group of Sikhs near Tilakpur, on the banks of the Ravi, and about 10 miles from Lahore. He was suddenly taken ill and died. According to his page Tahmas Miskin, he had been poisoned by one of his own officers. Thus ended the career of a vigorous and capable Governor. From the Sikh viewpoint, it was a timely end to a reign of 18 months of terror. Aziz-ud-Din, a grandson of Bahadur Shah, was put on the throne in June 1754. He called himself Alamgir the 2nd.

The new Emperor appointed Moman Khan as Governor of Lahore in October 1754, but Murad Begum used all her womanly wiles to entice the other Generals to her cause. There was constant unrest in the city, and in December, the citizens invited Khwaja Mirza Khan of Eminabad to take over Lahore, which he did without much opposition. The Begum then sent her uncle Abdulla Khan to appeal to Ahmed Shah Abdali, who sent Jehan Khan at the head of 10,000 infantry and cavalry to defeat Mirza Khan in April 1755. The Durani soldiers looted the town to their heart's content, and left the Begum as the Governor, with her uncle as her deputy. These two soon fell out when the latter usurped authority. The Begum then wrote to Ghazi-ud-Din at Delhi, offering her daughter in marriage to the Minister. This man secured aid from Adina Beg, who had been expanding his dominion from the Jalandhar to the Cis-Satluj area around Sirhind. A force from Sirhind attacked Lahore and drove out Abdulla Khan in March 1756, but the Delhi Minister, knowing the immoral character of the Begum, had her taken prisoner and brought to him at Sirhind. The Minister appointed Adina Beg in charge of Lahore and Multan in return for a yearly tribute of 3 million. Adina Beg appointed Jamil-ud Din as his Lieutenant at Lahore. With these arrangements completed, the Minister returned to Delhi in May 1756.

Abdulla Khan had fled to Abdali at Kandhar. He now returned with Abdali's General Jangbaz Khan at the head of a strong force, and Jamil-ud Din hastily retreated to join Adina Beg in Jalandhar. This Afghan army plundered Lahore once again, and installed Abdulla Khan as its Governor in October 1756. Soon after this, Abdali himself invaded India for the fourth time.

THE FOURTH INVASION

From 1752 onwards, the Punjab was in turmoil. Whilst Mir Manu was busy pursuing the Sikhs and killing them, their numbers increased. The peaceful Hindus found it more profitable to take up Sikhism and join the bandits than stay at home to be fleeced by both the soldiery and the Sikhs. Thus, the Sikh replacements were faster than their losses. A common saying amongst them those days was :

"Manu is our scythe and we are his weeds,

As he keeps mowing, fourfold we increase."

Then after Mir Manu's death, the unsettled conditions in Lahore gave the Sikhs full freedom to consolidate their hold over vast territories. They imposed on the farmers the system called *Rakhi*, whereby they guaranteed them immunity from government or other interference, in return for the payment of a fifth of the produce of the land at each harvest. Theirs was the only organisation that could give protection to the oppressed, and large numbers, who had suffered at the hands of the soldiery, or who had other grievances, turned to the Sikhs, who admitted them as equals into their fraternity. It was during this period that Jassa Singh of Icho Gill, who was a carpenter by trade, undertook the rebuilding of the Ram Rauni with red baked bricks. He named it the Ramgarh. He was known as Jassa Singh Ramgarhia from that day.

So when Ahmed Shah advanced through the Punjab in November 1756, he had no opposition on the battlefield. Adina Beg had nimbly moved out of the *Doab* and taken to the northern hills. The Sikh bands hung on Abdali 's flanks, harassing any stragglers and cutting off all his supplies. Abdali swore he would punish them when he returned. He reached Delhi without further trouble and set about plundering the city with a will. In this job, he was ably abetted by Murad Begum, who pointed out the houses of all the rich nobles, and even the location of their secret vaults. Abdali's soldiers not only seized valuables, but also satisfied their lust on the women of the town.

Abdali moved down through Mathura to Agra, desecrating the temples and plundering the cities. Having enjoyed approximately three months of revelry in and around the precincts of Delhi, Ahmed Shah set out for Kabul on the 2nd of April, 1757. He had a train of 28,000 mules, camels and trucks laden with booty, and each one of his 80,000 soldiers and horsemen was loaded with spoils. The setting was near perfect for the Sikh marauders, who set to work on this helpless target from Karnal, and who carried on their nighty raids on his camp right up to the river Chenab. Abdali could do nothing but watch himself slowly relieved of more than half his treasure. He stopped a few days at Lahore, setting up Nasir Ali as Governor in Jalandhar, and Timur Shah as Governor of Lahore with General Jahan Khan as his deputy. He left strict orders with Jahan Khan for the chastisement of the Sikhs. Murad Begum did not get what she had worked for.

Abdali returned to Kandhar leaving 10,000 troops under Jahan Khan. This General quickly organised the administration of Lahore, and then attacked Amritsar. The Sikhs had vacated the city and gone into the *Malwa* regions. Jahan Khan killed the caretaker of the Golden Temple and about 20 of his comrades who had stayed on. The smaller shrines were pulled down and the tank was filled with earth. The fort of Ramgarh was razed to the ground, and the residents of the city were plundered.

News of the desecration of the Harimandar Sahib reached the Shaheed *misl* which was camped at Damdama Sahib (in Talwandi). Baba Deep Singh was then engaged in writing out a copy of the Granth Sahib. He entrusted this job to his nephew Sadda Singh, and led his *misl* on the march through Mehraj, Lakhi Jungle, Ferozepur, and reached Taran Taran on 10 November, 1757. By this time, this band had increased to 5,000 men. As he moved closer to Amritsar on 11th November, 1757, the number had risen to 10,000.

On the other side, Jahan Khan had called up all his horsemen from Lahore, and other forces from the towns of Patti and Qasur. At the first clash, the Pathans were driven back. Jahan Khan then ordered his Generals to fight a retreating action, moving towards Amritsar. Near the tank of Ramsar, Aman Khan, the brother of Jahan Khan, and Deep Singh came face to face. Both these men received slicing wounds in the neck and died there. (The Shaheed Ganj of Baba Deep Singh stands there now). The Sikhs continued pressing the enemy inspite of sustaining severe losses, and pushed them right up to the banks of the tank, and to the walls of the Akal Takht. Thousands had died on both sides by nightfall. During the night, the Sikhs withdrew leaving Jahan Khan in possession at Amritsar.

The Sikhs entered into an alliance with Adina Beg, who was then in the hills, and both armies came down upon Jalandhar, killed Nasir Ali, and sent the other Generals Murad Khan and Sarbuland Khan, flying back to Lahore (30th December, 1757).

Shortly after this, Timur Shah agreed to retain Adina Beg as Commander of Jalandhar on payment of 3.5 million Rupees a year. The Lahore forces were sent out in many directions against the Sikhs in 1758, but they came back always thoroughly defeated. The prestige of the Afghan armies disappeared. The number of Sikh horsemen rose to 10,000 at this time. Had Adina Beg continued in alliance with the Sikhs, their combined forces would have driven the Afghans out of Lahore and the whole Punjab.

Adina Beg was a craftly politician, well accomplished in the art of manoeuvring for a position of advantage. He approached the Mahratha Chiefs Raghu Nath and Malhar Rao in January 1758, to aid him, promising to pay them 100,000 Rupees a day when they were on the march. He also invited the Sikhs to join him, but only to keep them happy temporarily.

The Mahrathas joined Adina Beg at Sirhind on 8th March, 1758. Abdus Samad fought bravely, but his army fled and he himself was captured. The Sikhs knew Sirhind well, and they were ahead of the Mahrathas in looting.

As the Mahrathas crossed the Satluj, Timur Shah and Jahan Khan collected their belongings and left Lahore. Lahore was occupied by Adina Beg and his allies on 11th April, 1758. The Sikhs were invited by him to join in the pursuit of the Durani army, which was overtaken at the crossing of the river Chenab. Timur and Jahan Khan escaped, but their camp was seized and a number of Pathans captured by the Sikhs, and brought back to Amritsar, to clean up the mud from the holy tank. The Mahrathas returned to the Deccan in June 1758.

The Sikhs spent these months building mud fortresses, the most notable one being the one built by Sardar Charhat Singh at Gujranwala. They knew that a clash with Adina Beg was imminent. Adina Beg appointed his son-in-law Khwaja Mirza Khan as Commander of Lahore, and made Batala, his own capital. Sadiq Beg was appointed over

Sirhind.

As expected, Adina Beg deputed his minister Hira Mal and all the *choudhris* to gather forces to destroy the Sikhs, and for the next four months, he and Sadiq Beg of Sirhind kept a hot pursuit of the Sikh bands across both Amritsar and the *Doaba* regions. But this harassment did not last long. In September 1758, Adina Beg was taken ill at Batala and died.

Even when Adina Beg was alive, the Sikh *misls* were steadily asserting themselves over large areas. Charhat Singh in the Bari *Doab*, and Jassa Singh Ramgarhia in the Jalandhar *Doab* were very successful indeed. But when Adina Beg died, there was nothing to hold these *misls* in check. They met for the Divali, at Amritsar on 30th October, and passed a resolution that they were to occupy all areas in the Punjab. The Dal Khalsa marched into the Jalandhar *Doab* and was met by Bishambar Das the *Diwan* of Hassan Beg (son of Adina Beg) at the head of his army. The *Diwan* was killed and his army dispersed leaving the Sikhs masters of the whole *Doab*. They then overran all the countryside between the Beas and the Ravi.

THE FIFTH INVASION : SIKHS RISE TO OPPOSE THE INVADER

In October 1759, with a force of 60,000, Abdali reached Lahore, which he occupied with little opposition. The Mahrathas had withdrawn before him towards Delhi, and the Sikhs applied only their usual harassing tactics. Abdali appointed Karim Dad Khan at Lahore and leaving Zain Khan in charge at Sirhind, he advanced towards Saharanpur. The Mahrathas had raised the siege of Sakartal, and Najib-ud-Daula joined Abdali there in December 1759.

Abdali moved into Aligarh and the Oudh regions, winning over their Commanders to join him in his plan to oust the Mahrathas from Delhi. After a few minor skirmishes, he crossed the Jamuna and camped opposite the Mahratha forces at Panipat.

At last on 14th January, 1761 was fought the decisive battle of Panipat, in which the Mahrathas were completely routed. They lost at least 100,000 men in this battle, which sealed their future in Delhi and the Punjab.

Having captured booty in this battle and a large number of Mahrathas as slaves, Abdali entered Delhi and looted that city as before. He stayed on for two months and left for Kabul in March 1761.

Whilst Abdali had been waging his protracted wars around Delhi, utmost disorder had prevailed in the Punjab. On the Divali of November 1760, the Sikh Chiefs assembled at Amritsar and passed a resolution to attack Lahore. Jassa Singh Ahluwalia, Hakikat Singh Kanahya, Hari Singh Bhangi and Lehna Singh mustered 10,000 men and occupied the suburbs. They then started plundering the town, but Mir Mohammed shut himself up within the fort. He sent them an offering of 30,000 Rupees to buy them off the attack on the state treasury. The Sikhs withdrew, but when Ahmed Shah arrived there, and heard the full story, he transferred Sarblund Khan to Multan, and appointed Khwaja Ubed Khan at Lahore. He promised to return from Kabul in six months time, to punish the Sikhs.

When Ahmed Shah had crossed the Satluj, his army was subjected to the usual guerilla raids by the Sikh bands, and since his men were loaded with spoils he was helpless to retaliate. He would put up some sort of a barricade round his camp at night, but some quarters would always be attacked, and a share of his booty taken away. At the river crossing at Goindwal, a large number of the prisoners he was taking with him were liberated by the Sikhs under Jassa Singh Ahluwalia. These nightly raids continued after Lahore. At the Jehlum crossing, Sardars Jassa Singh Ahluwalia and Charhat Singh Sukerchakia were particularly active in releasing all the remaining women and children from Abdali's hands, and in arranging for their return to their families. These two intrepid Sardars kept raiding Abdali's camp right up to the crossing at Attock.

On their return from this mission in June 1761, the Sikh force of about 30,000 attacked and captured Gujrat and Wazirabad. From there, they advanced upon Sialkot and captured that town after killing its Commander Khwaja Mirza Jan in battle. They then moved down along the Riarki and into the Jalandhar area, whilst Charhat Singh returned to his fort at Gujranwala. Jassa Singh and other leaders then moved down the Sutlej, capturing Sirhind, Malerkotla and the Muslim pocket at Patti.

Ahmed Shah was still very sore over the losses he had sustained at the hands of the Sikhs during his last retreat, and so in August 1761, he equipped a Durrani force under Nur-ud-Din Khan which entered the Punjab and was promptly challenged by Sardar Charhat Singh at the Chenab river crossing. A battle was fought there, and the Durranis gave way and fled towards Sialkot, actively pursued by Charhat Singh's men. He laid siege to the town, and when Nur-ud-Din escaped from there in disguise, the Durrani soldiers laid down arms. Charhat Singh captured a great deal of war supplies, and carried them to his fort at Gujranwala.

All the other Sikh Sardars were busy now securing lands for themselves. Jai Singh Kanahya took Batala, Jassa Singh Ramgarhia took Kalanaur and a large tract in the Jalandhar *Doab*. The Governor Ubed Khan at Lahore decided he would try to control Charhat Singh who was too close to him for comfort. So, he marched upon Gujranwala with a force of 20,000 and laid siege to the fort. As soon as the other Sardars received a call from Charhat Singh, they set out for Gujranwala with their detachments. Within 13 days, Jassa Singh Ahluwalia, Jai Singh Kanahya, Hari Singh Bhangi, Jhanda Singh and Gujjar Singh had arrived and surrounded the besieger. Ubed Khan abandoned a great deal of ammunition and stores in his hurry to get back to Lahore.

The Sikhs had now grown too numerous and too strong for any of the local Commanders in the Punjab. They were now ready to take on the great Abdali, and the real tussle for the Punjab was about to begin. In the words of Prof. N.K. Sinha, "The most glorious chapter of Sikh history, and one of the most glorious chapters of Indian history was now to begin."

THE SIXTH INVASION AND THE GREAT HOLOCAUST

On 27th October, 1761, the Khalsa assembled at Amritsar for the Divali festival, and a resolution was passed at the Akal Takht to say that the Sikhs should punish the enemies of the nation, in particular the Niranjanias of Jandiala. This sect which was founded by a good Sikh of Guru Amar Das, had turned apostate during the days of Banda

Bahadur. They had persistently informed against the Sikhs to the Lahore Governors, and had been instrumental in the capture of the family of Mehtab Singh in 1740, of Mehtab Singh himself in 1745 and Taroo Singh the same year, and then of a prominent Sikh, Sukha Singh in 1753. Their current leader was one Aakil Das. His town was surrounded by the Sikhs, in January 1762, but he had shut the gates, and was safe for some time. He wrote an urgent appeal to Abdali, who himself marched ahead of his troops to reach Lahore on 3rd February, 1762.

The Sikhs had received information of his approach and had lifted the siege and withdrawn into the Cis-Satluj areas of the *Malwa*. They plundered the regions around Malerkotla, and intended moving into the Bikaner regions after that. They were then 40,000 strong, but had with them a baggage train of about 10,000 women and children, who were being escorted to safety in Bikaner. Ahmed Shah had been informed about their position by Zain Khan of Sirhind, and he had immediately ordered this General to engage the Sikhs, promising to come up with the main Afghan force to help him. Zain Khan was joined by Bhikhan Khan of Malerkotla. They encountered the Sikhs at Kupp, six miles north of Malerkotla. The baggage train of the Sikhs was then about four miles away and moving in the direction of Barnala.

The battle was joined on the morning of 5th February, 1762. The troops under Zain Khan numbering about 20,000 with artillery, attacked first, and the Sikhs had never expected Abdali to join them so soon. So when he turned up later with his 30,000 horsemen, the attackers had a decisive edge over the Sikhs. But, to add to their difficulties, this time Abdali had at last caught the Sikhs in the same predicament in which they had been wont to harass him on previous occasions. He also had the advantage of artillery and superior rifles.

Jassa Singh and Charhat Singh realised what was happening and immediately ordered their men to form a human wall around their women and children, and to keep moving with them towards Barnala. They were successful in this manoeuvre, but at a heavy cost in lives. A large number of women and children had been killed, but the bravery and example set by Charhat Singh Sukerchakia saved many more. Towards dusk, the human shield formed by Charhat Singh's men had enabled their families to reach Barnala and safety. The Durranis were too tired after their long march and the day's fighting to pursue.

This action had cost the Sikhs at least 25,000 in dead, and is remembered as the Great Holocaust. Sardar Jassa Singh Ahluwalia was almost killed in this action. He had 22 wounds on his body, and Sardar Charhat Singh sustained 19 wounds. This gives us an indication of how much of the action these leaders carried on their own shoulders.

There was hardly any Sikh soldier who did not carry a scar from this action. Practically all their goods had been lost. But the Sikh spirit was undaunted. As one *Nihang* Sikh remarked, "Only the soft and unbaked ones have fallen off." Hardly four months had passed, before they were up again and attacking Sirhind, and by July 1762, they were raiding the country around Lahore. They had dispersed into the villages around Bathinda, and we will leave them there to recuperate over the next three months, and follow the course taken by Abdali.

Ahmed Shah rested a while at Sirhind.   He had noted that Aala Singh, the powerful Cheif of Patiala, had helped the Mahrathas with provisions when they were preparing for the battle at Panipat in 1761.   He had not taken any part in the last Sikh battle, but his fort at Barnala had obviously given shelter to the Sikhs.   Abdali sent an army that attacked Barnala, but Aala Singh had moved out, and eluded capture.   Later, he turned up at Sirhind of his own accord, and Abdali had him thrown into prison.   Aala Singh used the good offices of Abdali's minister Wali Khan to purchase his freedom by paying 300,000 Rupees.   Not only was he released, but Abdali conferred on him the title of Raja.   Aala Singh had all along advanced in life by bending to the wind.   He had remained on the best of terms with the Sikhs of Jassa Singh, and with the Mahrathas when they were around Delhi and Sirhind.   Abdali on the other hand showed good statesmanship in retaining the friendship of a Chief who was already the most powerful in the *Malwa* region.   He knew that he would have his hands full in managing the rest of the Punjab and Kashmir and Multan.   He was at the same time employing the policy of widening the rift between the *Majha* and the *Malwa* Sikhs.   Aala Singh died three years later, (in 1765).

In February 1762, Abdali reached Amritsar, with cartloads of Sikh heads for display to the population.   He placed cans of gunpowder beneath the foundations of the Harimandar (Golden Temple), and blew the temple up.   He filled the tank up with the rubble from all the demolished buildings.   On reaching Lahore, he appointed Kabuli Mal as Governor there, and sent an expedition into Kashmir under Nur-ud-Din.   During June, July and August, Abdali moved out into the cooler regions of Kalanaur.

SIKHS RISE AGAIN

In May 1762, the *misl* leaders met near Barnala and decided on a surprise attack on Sirhind.   Though very much short of weapons, they had nevertheless a large enough force to frighten Zain Khan into submission.   He bought them off for 50,000 Rupees, but as they were retiring, he came out of his fort with his General Lakshmi Narayan to surprise them from behind.   The Sikhs turned back and charged so ferociously that both Zain Khan and his Lieutenant fled for their lives, leaving a most welcome haul of arms and ammunition in Sikh hands.

During the months of July and August, the Sikh bands were visiting Amritsar and then raiding the Jalandhar *Doab* for cash.   From August to September 1762,   they encamped in the Karnal-Panipat region purchasing arms from that area.   By October, they were back at Amritsar fully prepared for their revenge on the great Abdali, for whom they now had as little regard as for his appointed Commanders.   They now had an army of 30,000 fully armed men.   Abdali learnt about this development, and despatched Jahan Khan at the head of an equally large force on the evening of 16th October.   The next morning was Divali day, and the Sikhs fell upon the enemy as if this was their only chance for salvation.   By evening, Jahan Khan realised he was beaten.   Thousands were dead and many had given up the fight.   He himself fled during the night, leaving hundreds of his men prisoners in Sikh hands.   These Pathans were made to work the next day, to remove the debris from the holy tank. The battle had been fought near the temple Pipli Sahib.

After the last battle, Abdali made another attempt to engage the Sikhs in a pitched battle, but the latter had by then withdrawn into the *Malwa* region known as the Lakhi jungle.

As soon as Abdali left Lahore, the Dal Khalsa met at Amritsar and was reorganised into two sections again. The senior Dal headed by Jassa Singh Ahluwalia, comprised the following *misls* : Ahluwalia, Singhpuria, Dallewalia, Karoria, Nishanwali and Shaheedi. This Dal's duty was to punish the enemies of the nation and to subjugate all to the rule of the Khalsa. The junior Dal headed by Hari Singh Bhangi, comprised the following *misls* : Bhangis, Ramgarhias, Kanhayas, Sukerchakias, and Nakai. Their assignment was the protection of Amritsar and the temples. In April 1763, the second Dal met at Amritsar and a Brahmin of Qasur appeared at the Harimandar Sahib to appeal to the Khalsa for the recovery of his wife, who had been abducted by Usman Khan, the Commander of Qasur. Hari Singh Bhangi, at the head of the Dal Khalsa of 15,000 men, attacked this well-defended town, and rescued the lady from Usman's grasp. They then looted the town and came away with a haul of gold jewellery.

Jassa Singh's Dal then cleaned up the Jalandhar *Doab* of all opposition to its sway. It stayed in this territory till the Divali of 1763 in November, when the Sarbat Khalsa held its customary reunion at Amritsar. The Dal had a mission at Dina Nagar, where Adina Beg's son, Jafar Beg was entertaining dreams of a Mughal resurgence in the Punjab. In July, he had called up the Commanders of Pasrur and Kalanaur to join him near Batala, where the detachments of Hari Singh, Charhat Singh and Jassa Singh Ramgarhia came up to give him a crushing defeat. Jafar Beg fled to save himself.

When the two Dals met in November 1763 at Amritsar, the Sarbat Khalsa passed a resolution to rebuild the Golden Temple. The foundation stone was laid anew on the 17th November by Sardar Jassa Singh Ahluwalia. Just about then, news was received that Jahan Khan had entered India, and was moving towards Wazirabad. The Sikhs rushed up to meet him at Wazirabad, where a sharp action took place and the Afghans were routed. Jahan Khan was seen to fall off his horse and to flee towards Rohtas.

In December 1763, the combined Dal Khalsa set out to punish Zain Khan of Sirhind. They attacked Malerkotla first, killing its Commander Bhikhan Khan, and then had Aala Singh of Patiala joining them in the atack on Sirhind. The Patiala Chief felt he had to give some proof of his loyalty to the Khalsa, who were still very sore over his failure to come to their aid at the hour of need during the Great Massacre. Zain Khan was baited by the Tarna Dal into leaving his fort, and when he found himself cut off from Sirhind by the units of the Budha Dal, he had to make a fight of it. He was slain and his army just threw away their weapons and fled.

The town of Sirhind was then turned upside down for loot. No male Muslim was spared. The fort was completely razed. This happened in January 1764. The wall that had taken the lives of the young sons of Guru Gobind was identified by the older residents of the town, and the building of the gurdwara of Fatehgarh Sahib was commenced at that spot. Only then was the Khalsa *Panth* satisfied that justice had been done. They had fulfilled their vow to pull that city down brick by brick.

Nur Mohammed, the author of the *Jangnama*, who was with Abdali in March 1765 writes, "No man, not even a bird was to be seen there except the owl ...... the royal palaces of the city and its gardens, orchards and water tanks were all lying in ruins."

After its destruction, the city was assigned by the Sikhs to Budha Singh of Bhaika. Later, Aala Singh purchased it from him for a sum of Rs. 20,000. The town controlled the province of the same name, which extended for 200 miles between the Jumuna and the Satluj, and which had a revenue of over five million. The leaders of eight *misls* divided this territory and took charge of its revenues for themselves.

The method they used in this division is most amusing. Each Sardar or his deputy would ride into a village, and leave some article of his dress or equipment with the headman as a sign of ownership. He would repeat this excercise at the next village, leaving a shirt here, a saddle there, a head-cloth at the next, until by nigh-fall he would finish up quite naked. There was never any dispute, if any other rider turned up later at the village that had already been 'acquired.'

After the capture of Sirhind and its outlying villages, the Budha Dal crossed the Jumuna and ransacked Saharanpur, Ambli, Miranpur, Deoband, Muzaffarnagar, Jawalapur, Kankhal, Najibabad, Nagina, Muradabad, Garhmukteshar. Karora Singh was lost in this action. They then turned back towards Lahore, to await Abdali, who was said to be coming into India on his seventh invasion.

The Junior or Tarna Dal had come back to take control of the Jalandhar *Doab*, and then laid siege to Lahore. Kabuli Mal shut himself up in the fort. Only after he had agreed to cut off the noses and ears of the cow-killing butchers of the town, and to pay a large sum in tribute did they retire. Hari Singh Bhangi also left behind a Sikh representative Tek Chand to advise the Governor in his administration.

THE SEVENTH INVASION

In March 1764, Ahmed Shah advanced towards Sialkot and Kalanaur, and then turned towards Batala and entered Lahore. There were some minor harassing engagements on the way near Batala. After two weeks in Lahore, Abdali received news of an uprising in Kandhar, and had to hurry back to Afghanistan. Charhat Singh's band followed Abdali all the way up to the Jehlum river inflicting their usual nibbling attacks on his rear. Then this band came back and joined up with Gujjar Singh Bhangi to capture the fort of Rohtas from Sarblund Khan. These two *misls* then occupied most of the territory between the Indus and the Jehlum.

Meanwhile the Nakai *misl* moved from the Lahore precincts towards the southwest, to occupy the lands between the Ravi and the Satluj, known as the Naka. The Bhangis went further to plunder the territory around Multan and then crossed over to the right bank of the Indus to capture Dehra Ismail Khan and Dera Gazi Khan. From there, they returned to the other bank to capture Khushab, Jhang and Chiniot. These Bhangi raids made Nasir Khan of neighbouring Baluchistan cancel all his plans to go on a pilgrimage to Mecca, and to join Abdali in his next invasion of India.

The Kanhayas were now in charge of the lands between Pasrur and Gurdaspur. The Ramgarhias had established their control over Hargobindpur and the *Riarki* (along both banks of the Beas river).

The Ahluwalias and Dallewalias were in control of the whole of the Jalandhar *Doab*. With the exception of the cities of Lahore and Jalandhar, the whole of the territory between the Jumuna and the Indus rivers was in Sikh hands, and all these conquests had been completed by the middle of 1764.

THE EIGHTH INVASION

Ahmed Shah Abdali had already made up his plans to invade India during the winter of 1764. Nasir Khan Baloch was equally eager to join in. Abdali now received an urgent appeal for help from the Rohela Commander of Delhi, Najib-ud-Daulah.

Abdali had set out with 18,000 men as soon as Najib's courier arrived in December 1764. At Eminabad, he was joined by Nasir Khan at the head of 12,000 Baluchis. Qazi Nur Mohammed was a member of Nasir Khan's army, and he has given a good description of the march, in the *Jangnama*. On reaching Lahore, Abdali held his council of war to decide on a plan to engage the enemy, who was said to be 100 miles away, in the Lakhi jungle. To his intense surprise, he heard next morning that a Sikh detachment under Charhat Singh Sukerchakia was attacking his provision camp just outside the town. Nasir Khan Baloch brought his men out, and the hit and run tactics of the Sikhs continued the whole day. Towards nightfall, the Sikhs disappeared, and Nasir Khan brought his men back into the fort.

Hearing that the Sikhs had retreated to Amritsar, Abdali equipped himself lightly and rode quickly to that city. But the Sikh bands had moved away from there, and Abdali found himself challenged by only 30 of the Sikhs who had stayed on in the Golden Temple. Their leader Sardar Gurbaksh Singh and his devoted band raised their war cry *Sat Sri Akal* and charged into the army of 30,000 and offered themselves at the altar of their Guru. According to Nur Mohammed, "They showed not the slightest fear of death."

Abdali again destroyed a large part of Amritsar and returned to Lahore, from where he set out for Batala, which was plundered. He encountered little opposition so far, but when he entered the Jalandhar *Doab*, his advance columns were set upon by Jassa Singh Ramgarhia's bands. Jahan Khan was already experienced in Sikh tactics and he refrained from any attempt at pursuit, but the Baluchi Chief Nasir Khan had to be checked by Abdali from that course of action. His orders to his Generals were strict, that they should remain on the defensive only. As this army progressed through the well-cultivated lands of the *Doab*, they seized whatever provisions of meat, sugar-candy, and oils they needed from the deserted villages.

This army crossed the Satluj at Machhiwara, where again the Sikh bands fell upon them to inflict some damage. Abdali reached Kunjpura, via Pinjore towards the end of February 1765. Here he learnt that Najib-ud-Daula had made peace with Jawahar Mal, and although Nasir still suggested that he should proceed to Delhi, and gather all the forces together to come back "to fall upon the heads of these dogs (the Sikhs)", Abdali decided to return. His Durani soldiers were not quite happy with their successes so far, and were anxious about their prospects on the return journey.

Abdali stopped at the deserted city of Sirhind, where Aala Singh arrived to pay his respects to the Shah. Abdali expressed a desire to conciliate the Sikh Chiefs. He was willing to forgive their past sins, if they submitted to him. He then made a grant of the province of Sirhind to Aala Singh for an annual tribute of 300,000 Rupees, and also conferred on him the rank of Maharaja.

Abdali crossed the river Satluj at Ropar in March 1765, and came face to face with the main Sikh army which had by then returned from Delhi and joined up with Charhat Singh and the rest. It was no longer mere skirmishing, but a frontal attack in regular battle formation. Abdali's formation was : Shah Wali Khan and Jahan Khan on his right, and Nasir Khan's Baluchis on his left. On the Sikh side, Jassa Singh Kalal (Ahluwalia) stood like a mountain in the middle together with the other Jassa Singh. On their right were Charhat Singh, Jhanda Singh Bhangi and Jai Singh Kanhaya, and on the left were the Bhangi Chiefs Hari Singh, Gulab Singh and Gujjar Singh.

The Sikhs pressed hard on Abdali's right, and Nasir Khan was asked to go to the relief of that side. As he approached, the Sikhs fell back, and Nasir Khan gave chase, thinking he had won the day. He had gone only a short distance away from the main army, when the Sikhs wheeled round and began mowing down his men like corn. Nasir Khan had to order a quick retreat to join the main army to save himself.

On the second day, Abdali had advanced only three miles, when the Sikhs came again. They are described by Qazi Nur Mohammed as "stone-hearted and strong-armed *kaffirs*." This time the Sikh left formed their right wing, and their right had become their left. As soon as Abdali's men attacked, the Sikhs fell back. But this time Abdali's orders were obeyed by all. They did not attempt any pursuit, with the result that the Sikhs came again and again to discharge their muskets into the enemy.

On the third day, the Sikh *misls* took turns at riding up to a reasonable distance in front of the Durani army, discharging their muskets, and then riding away "without any shame or modesty" (Nur Mohammed).

For seven days, this daylong confrontation continued, until Abdali crossed the Beas, with great care to avoid any surprise raid by the Sikhs on his rear. Then near Batala, according to the historian Rattan Singh Bhangoo, a pitched battle is said to have taken place. But no such encounter is mentioned by Qazi Nur Mohammed. Abdali did not stop at Lahore, but continued marching towards Kabul, reaching Rohtas towards the end of March 1765. At Gujrat, the Sikhs had abandoned pursuit and had returned to Amritsar to celebrate the Vaisakhi festival.

The Sikhs stayed on, repairing their temples at Amritsar for about a month. They then departed to their respective territories to exert proper control over them. The Bhangi Chiefs Lehna Singh and Gujjar Singh camped outside the fort of Lahore with 2,000 troops. Kabuli Mal had gone to see Abdali off at Rohtas leaving his nephew in charge of the fort. The Sikh Sardars persuaded the Muslim gardeners employed in the fort, to show them the easiest point of entry through the encircling wall. They secured an opening there at night and took the nephew of Kabuli Mal completely by surprise. Sardar Sobha Singh Kanhaya who had stationed himself at Niazbagg, eight miles south of Lahore, and had been collecting octroi there, now joined his two comrades in the fort, and the three Sardars set about apportioning the town amongst themselves. The eastern part was allotted to Gujjar Singh. The fort itself and the central area were given to Lehna Singh, and the southern and western sectors of Lahore came under Sobha Singh.

The prominent citizens of the town waited in a deputation on the three Sardars, requesting only a rule of peace. That was duly enforced by proclamation and the three Chiefs went round in person to see to the proper execution of justice. On learning about these developments, Sardar Charhat Singh also arrived at Lahore, to demand his share of the city. The three occupants could only offer him the famous Zamzama gun. Charhat Singh saw no prospect of getting anything more, and so he accepted it and carried it away to his own fort at Gujranwala.

Between April and July 1765, the *misls* were busy occupying as much land as they could, and this is how they stood after that exercise :

Bhangis : The suburbs of Amritsar and Taran Taran under Karam Singh. This Sardar also held Firozke, Kaleke and Bajra in the Sialkot district. Here Sardar Hari Singh held Kalewal, Chak Ramdas, Chaubara. Sialkot was occupied by Tara Singh and Sahib Singh. Further west Gujjar Singh, with the aid of Charhat Singh captured Gujrat and the lands of Waraich. Midh and Moosa Chula were taken by Ganda Singh and Jhanda Singh; Miani was taken by Tara Singh Bhangi.

Ahluwalias : Areas along the lower section of the river Beas river — Jandiala, Sathiala, Bandala, Jalalabad, Varowal, and large tracts in the Jalandhar *Doab*.

Ramgarhias : Hargobindpura, Qadian, Matewal, and large tracts on the other side of the Beas.

Kanhayas : Batala, Fatehgarh, Gilwali and Panjgraian.

Nakai : The territory of Naka and Lamma.

Singhpurias : Singhpura, Khaparkheri, Saurian and Sainsara.

Sukerchakias : Most of the lands between the Ravi and the Chenab, and half the district of Gujrat; also the salt mines at Miani, for which Charhat Singh opened his own salt-market at Ramnagar. Beyond the Jehlum, Dhani, Chakwal, Pothohar, Sayidpur were all under his control.

After the Divali of 1765, the Sikhs asserted their full sovereignty over the Punjab by striking their first coin of good silver with the inscription *Degh Tegh Fateh*. During the rainy months from July to September, they stayed in their own territories and consolidated their positions. Between September and December 1765, the two Dals met at Amritsar and moved eastwards in a combined operation into the territories of Najib-ud-Daula, the agent of Ahmed Shah at Delhi, and came back with much booty. The Budha Dal went further down towards Dhaulpur to help Jawahar Mal in March 1766, and then came back to Delhi. In April 1766 it had an encounter with Najib-ud-Daula on the left bank of the Jumuna, across Panipat and suffered a reversal. But the Dal shrugged off this defeat and continued moving across to the right bank of the Jumuna river to plunder more towns belonging to Najib-ud-Daula. The Sikhs moved fast, and it was not possible for Najib-ud-Daula to be everywhere to guard his territory from their depredations.

THE NINTH AND THE LAST INVASION OF AHMED SHAH

In December 1766, Abdali crossed the Indus with an army of 30,000. As he neared Rohtas, he was challenged by a force of 7,000 Bhangis and Sukerchakias, who were easily defeated and dispersed. He was joined here by the forces of some Muslim Chiefs of Gujrat district, and proceeded towards the Chenab crossing. Here, he was again challenged by the local Sikh bands aided by the re-grouped force from Rohtas. This attempt proved equally futile, and Abdali marched on to the districts around Sialkot. Here, he summoned all the landlords of Sialkot, Pasrur, and Aurangabad and extracted a levy of 150,000 Rupees from them for harbouring the "infidel Sikhs" and providing food to them.

As he neared Lahore on 21st December, the Sikh Chiefs vacated the town, Lehna and Gujjar proceeding to Qasur, whilst Sobha Singh took his men to Pakpattan. On the request of the leading citizens of Lahore, Abdali agreed to appoint Lehna Singh Governor of the town. He accordingly sent his emissary with a gift of dried fruit and a letter offering the command of Lahore to Lehna Singh Bhangi. The Sikh returned the fruit and sent a sample of gram together with a letter saying, "Fruit is for Kings like you. I prefer a simple meal of gram. As for the governorship, my Guru has already bestowed on me the rule of the three kingdoms." Lehna Singh would not accept any post under a foreign master.

Abdali stayed on at Lahore, sending detachments under his Generals to plunder or subdue the Sikh leaders in the neighbourhood. He attacked the fort of Fatehabad, 20 miles south of Amritsar, on 28th December, but while he was busy there, a Sikh force under Charhat Singh and Lehna Singh attacked Lahore and plundered Abdali's provisions.

On 17th January, 1767, Jahan Khan, with an army of 15,000 went towards Amritsar. Here, he was engaged by Charhat Singh, Lehna Singh and Gujjar Singh's bands, and in the battle that lasted 3 to 4 hours, a large number of Duranis were killed and Jahan Khan retired wounded. Abdali himself arrived to his aid, but the Sikhs had by then retreated. Another group meanwhile attacked his baggage at Lahore and he had to hurry back there. Once again to his frustration, the attackers had moved out to a distance of 15 miles by the time he arrived there.

Ahmed Shah finally departed for Sirhind on the 17th January after appointing Dadan Khan Govenor at Lahore. As he crossed the Satluj, the Sikhs attacked him again near Machhiwara. They could do this with ease now, because the whole countryside was helpful to them as regards supplies and concealment.

Abdali advanced as far as Ismailabad, 30 miles south of Ambala, where he was met by Najib-ud-Daula, who advised him against proceeding further towards Delhi. So he turned back from there reaching Ambala on the 18th March and Sirhind on the 20th

March, 1767. Abdali then came back to Machhiwara, where he stayed for about a month. Some of the Sikh bands under Baghel Singh and others were active during this period raiding Ambeta, Nanauta, Shamli and other places under Najib's rule.

Abdali now prepared to leave for Kabul for good. He knew he had failed to subdue the Sikhs, but worse than that, his own troops were on the point of mutiny. They had not received the loot they had expected and had not even received the normal pay for some time. He was now getting old and tired of war. The cancer of the nose that had set in during 1762, was causing him acute misery. The man who had never been defeated in battle, whose very name spread fear amongst his men and terror amongst his enemies, was returning now broken in spirit, to live his last years in Kandhar. His General Jahan Khan died in 1770 and Abdali himself died in 1772.

No sooner had Abdali crossed the Ravi in June 1767, than the three Sikh rulers of Lahore, returned to camp outside the walls of the fort. Dadan Khan appeared before them together with the leading citizens of the town. He was treated with courtesy, was sanctioned an allowance of 20 Rupees a day, and the management of the town was taken over by the three as before, and without any disturbance to the citizens.

The other Sardars also set about extending their territories. Gujjar Singh Bhangi occupied Rawalpindi and its suburbs and left Sardar Milkha Singh in charge there.

Budh Singh Singhpuria drove Sheikh Nizamudin out of Jalandhar, and acquired Behrampur, Nurpur, Haibatpur and Patti.

Desu Singh, son of Gurbaksh Singh Bhaika, snatched Kaithal from two brothers Bheekh Baksh and Niamat Khan.

Towards the end of 1767, the Sikhs were again plundering the territories of Najib-ud-Daula, who engaged them first at Nanauta, again at Islamnagar in January 1768, and finally around Panipat Karnal in March 1768. He was defeated in the last action, and the Sikhs were thereafter in control of all the territories of the present state of Haryana up to Delhi.

From 1708 when Banda Singh Bahadur set out for the Punjab, to the end of 1768, the Sikhs had been locked in a life and death struggle, first with the Mughal power, and then with the powerful Afghan invader. It had taken them 60 years of blood and toil and an unshakable faith in their ultimate success (*Raj Karega Khalsa*), to emerge finally as masters of their own destiny in the land of the five rivers. To what did this nation owe such success ? What advantages did they have over the brilliant General Ahmed Shah, who thought in 1762 that he had finished them off, and who yet left the country six years later knowing he was beaten ? A brief analysis of these factors follows :

1. The strong religious character of the Sikh fighter and his intense faith in his Guru which gave him great moral support in times of adversity.
2. Their self-denial and their ability to survive in the open.
3. Their good guerilla tactics.
4. The difference in calibre between the Sikh leaders and the Mughal Generals. The latter were mere mercenary soldiers. Sikh leaders, on the other hand, followed the Sikh precepts to the letter. Their integrity was beyond doubt, and they

treated their men as equals and were always ready to die for the Guru's cause. Guru Gobind Singh says :

"Dharam chalaavan sant ubaaran
dusht sabhan ko mool upaaran."

27

SIKH RULE AND RANJIT SINGH

GURDARSHAN SINGH DHILLON

The reign of Maharaja Ranjit Singh has been the subject of abiding interest for scholars and historians, but, by and large, they have concentrated their attention on the military and political achievements of the Maharaja. There is no doubt that he was a great military genius. His political objectives could not have been achieved without his outstanding military ability, but this is an incomplete epithet to describe him adequately. For, considering the times, the Indian background and the historical circumstances in which he appeared, the great edifice which he created and the manner in which he fostered it, were, we believe, primarily due to the religious background, approach and tolerance, and the catholicity of Sikh ethos in which Ranjit Singh was born and brought up. Otherwise, he would have remained a mere war-lord and an adventurer. Nurtured in the Sikh tradition and unequalled for the daring and originality of his many-sided genius, the Maharaja gave the Punjab four decades of peace, prosperity and progress, the benefits of which were enjoyed equally by all the communities. This paper is an endeavour to study the salient features of the Khalsa Raj under Ranjit Singh, and to evaluate his place in the history of this region.

The character and the nature of his polity is a subject of controversy among scholars. Many writers like J.D. Cunningham[1] and Sita Ram Kohli[2] ascribe to Ranjit Singh high and noble objectives on the basis of which he carved out his kingdom, which became the source of power and pride for the Sikhs. Many others like Prinsep[3] and N.K. Sinha[4] have characterized his polity as absolute despotism, which was the just outcome of his military enterprise.

Kingdoms and empires have almost invariably been founded and maintained on the strength of arms. Ranjit Singh had as good a right to carve out a kingdom for himself and his people through the exercise of arms as any other ruler before or after him. In the ultimate analysis, the fundamental criterion to measure a ruler's greatness should be the manner in which he wields his authority. To what end does he use his power, for the furtherance of his own personal ambitions or for the welfare of his subjects through the projection of eternal values of truth, goodness, justice and freedom ? This is the fundamental criterion which we shall use, and which we feel should be the only criterion for any kind of modern historiography. In short, our test should be not how an Ashoka or a Changez Khan gets his power but how he uses it and the net result which he achieves.

Both Carlyle[5] and Macaulay[6] lodged their protest against history being a mere record of 'court and camp', of royal intrigue and state rivalry, of pageants and processions. According to Carlyle, the essence of history does not lie in laws, senate houses or battlefields, but in the tide of thoughts and actions — the world of existence that brightens, glooms, blossoms and fades. What gives meaning to history is not merely the exploits and aggressive enterprises of the conquerors and kings, but how the victorious sword is used during the times of peace. A ruler's greatness lies in the vision he projects for the future, the message he leaves for posterity, and the direction and dimension that he imparts to history. What mankind needs is peace, progress, prosperity and a harmonious social order. A ruler can best be judged in terms of Arnold Toynbee's well-known historical formula of 'Challenge and Response.' The correct measure of a ruler is the vision — in terms of initiative, depth and sincerity — that he has in responding to the need of the times, whether he is an Ashoka or a Changez Khan, a Lenin or a Stalin.

In view of the above criterion we shall explain in this study how Ranjit Singh employed his power and how other rulers of his times, great or small, directed their power to different ends. For this purpose we shall also indicate very briefly the ideological background, which shaped his character and governed his perceptions and personality. According to Lepel Griffin, "Ranjit Singh was so completely a product of the Sikh theocracy and so embodied the spirit of the Khalsa, that no account of his character and career would be complete without a description of the religious system of the Sikhs."[8]

IDEOLOGICAL BACKGROUND

Sikhism arose in the sixteenth century as a new revolutionary ideology opposed in its fundamentals to the contemporary and earlier religions. It challenged, on the one hand, the fanaticism and religious hypocrisy of the priestly class,[9] and, on the other hand, the religio-political oppression of the contemporary rulers.[10] Guru Nanak's rejection of the *Varna Ashrma Dharma* and of the cult of gods and goddesses[11], his emphasis on the unity of mankind[12] and the oneness of God,[13] constituted a daring and a glaring departure from orthodox Hinduism. He challenged the conventional yardsticks of religion and society of his times by denouncing asceticism,[14] idolatry,[15] ceremonialism and the role of the intermediary agency between God and man.[16] He exhorted people not to shun the battle of life, not to renounce their hearths and homes, not to retreat to the private solitude of the hills and caves, but to live their life as householders. He introduced a conspicuous note of world- and life-affirmation in his teachings by bridging the gulf between the spiritual and the empirical realms of human existence.[17] The significance of the Guru's message lies in emphasising the role of religion as an instrument of liberation, personal as well as social. In the integrated vision of the Guru, religion became a potential basis of freedom for man — freedom from tyranny, freedom from injustice and freedom from ruthless religious conversion. The Guru thus laid the foundations of a catholic or liberal religion, which was not a mere system of philosophy or a set of abstract ideas, concerning God and the mystery of life and death. It was a discipline, a way of life which infused spiritual and social vitality in its followers, and brought about a far-reaching transformation in their outlook. The Gurus believed religion to be an effective vehicle of promoting the values of social harmony, love, equality, freedom and brotherhood of man. They aimed at a social revolution that would lead to the emergence of an egalitarian, forward-looking and a just social order.[18]

The Sikh movement was not only an egalitarian social order; it was a plebeian political revolution as well; but the pressure of circumstances prevented it from assuming spectacular dimensions. Nevertheless, the rise of the Khalsa, the martyrdom of the Gurus, the saga of Sikh resistance to the Mughals and Afghan invaders, carried a new message of hope, and kindled that spark in human nature which impelled men to seek out a better and saner path for mankind. People looked with eager eyes to the rise of a messiah who would finally deliver them from socio-political persecution of the contemporary rulers, and from tyranny and oppression of the invaders.

The first bid for establishing the Khalsa Raj was made by Banda Singh Bahadur, but without much success. Banda had an indomitable spirit, but faced with the over-whelming might of the Mughal empire, he could not succeed in liberating the country from the oppressive rule. He and his 740 followers were tortured to death.[19] However, Banda deserves credit for laying down the foundations of the political sovereignty of the Sikhs. On the Divali day of October 27, 1761, the Sikhs assembled at Amritsar, and passed a national resolution, called *gurmatta*, to liberate Punjab from the foreign invaders and seize all their strongholds.[20]

The Sikh *misls*, which emerged on the scene, no doubt, had a great political potential, but through their internecine quarrels, they had reduced each other to a state of political importence. George Forster, a traveller, who was a keen observer of things, remarked; "We may see some ambitious chief led on by his genius and success and absorbing the power of his associates display from the ruins of their commonwealth the standard of monarchy."[21]

Ranjit Singh was a characteristic product of the Sikh tradition, and was also the leader, who had come to deliver the goods. Thus the emergence of the Khalsa Raj under him was neither an accident nor a freak of history. It was a unique historical phenomenon, the outcome and the flowering of a prolonged struggle for capturing political power, and must be understood in its true perspective. Bir Singh, a contemporary of Ranjit Singh in his poetical composition, *Bara Maha Guru Gobind Singh Ji Ka*, refers to the period of socio-political turmoil gone through by the peasant-soldiers or the *Singhs*, who had become *Sardars* (rulers) with the Guru's grace.[22]

RANJIT SINGH'S CAREER

Ranjit Singh became the chief of the *Sukerchakia misl* at the age of eleven years in

1791. In his young days, he was an excellent soldier and the beau-ideal of youth. One of his ancestors, Budh Singh, had been one of the Khalsas initiated by Guru Gobind Singh.[23] He found the Punjab strife-ridden and chaotic, a loose confederacy of powerful misl chiefs, lacking the corporate spirit, and indulging in petty intrigues and dissensions. In the absence of a strong central authority, the state had become a prey to the Afghan invaders on the one hand and to the Maratha and the British designs on the other. Ranjit Singh brought the *misl* chiefs into submission, fired his people with a corporate zeal and led them from victory to victory so as to galvanise a whole people with a sense of collective triumph. 'He avenged the innumerable defeats, humiliations and depredations suffered by India over the centuries at the hands of the Afghan invaders, by conquering a part of the Indian territory wrested by them and more than that, by being an arbiter in the fate of Afghanistan herself.'[24] He rose to be the ruler of a powerful state extending from Tibet to Sind and from Khyber pass to the Satluj. With his capture of Peshawar, he sealed the Khyber pass for ever, thus putting an end to the tyranny and oppression of the invaders. He was both feared and respected by the British, who ruled over the rest of the sub-continent. It has been acknowledged that in fulfilling his ambitions, Ranjit Singh used the barest minimum of force necessary. Baron Charles Hugel records, "Never perhaps was so large an empire founded by one man with so little criminality; and when we consider the country and the uncivilised people with whom he had to deal, his mild and prudent Government must be regarded with feelings of astonishment."[25] Similarly, Captain Murray says, "It is difficult to suppress admiration in contemplating the career of such a man, who, with so many disadvantages, succeeded, with so few crimes in elevating himself from a simple *Sardar* to be the sovereign of a large kingdom, including Hindus and Mohammadans, as well as the Sikhs, the only state in India, not substantially under British domination."[26] Even Henry T. Prinsep, who is a critic of Ranjit Singh, acknowledges that the Maharaja's career was "stained by no bloody executions and by much fewer crimes."[27]

THE SIKH RAJ

In Sikhism, the inward and the outward, the spiritual and the empirical, are inextricably interwoven.[28] The Gurus believed that a combination of religion and politics was essential to achieve the ethical ideals of human equality, freedom and justice. This combination is essential to abolish the evils of society and open new vistas of peace, progress and harmony. A sound social order could be built and preserved only through moral and ethical imperatives, and by abiding values of tolerance, humility, charity and compassion that constitute *dharma*.

Ranjit Singh built his rule on religious foundations. He referred to his Government as *Sarkar-i-Khalsa*, which derived its legitimacy from the Khalsa or the Commonwealth — the mystic entity in which resided all sovereign powers pertaining to the Sikh community. He referred to his *Darbar* as *Darbar-i-Khalsa*. He never arrogated to himself the title or powers of a despot. He never wore a crown, and never sat on a throne. He attributed every success to the favour of God, and he styled himself and the people collectively as the Khalsa or Commonwealth of Gobind. Everything was meant for the benefit of his subjects, including the Sikhs, Hindus and Muslims, because the Khalsa aims at 'Sarbat da Bhala' (welfare of entire humanity). His state salutation was Wahe Guru Ji Ka Khalsa, Wahe Guru Ji Ki Fateh (Khalsa belongs to God and its victory is the victory of God). He was often heard saying that he was nothing more than a mere Nagara (drum) of Guru Gobind Singh. He would say that while the literal meaning of Ranjit — the meaning which his father had apparently intended while choosing his name in preference to his original name, 'Budh Singh' — was victorious, its real significance to his mind lay in that it had been the name of one of the drums of Guru Gobind Singh.[29] Both the Guru's drum and he himself announced the victory of the Khalsa, but were in themselves nothing but instruments. On every Vaisakhi, he would go to Amritsar and make his salutations at the hallowed centre, where the Gurus had inspired their followers, and had laid the foundations of the Sikh society.

His official seal bore the words — Akal Sahai (May God help). The term also indicated that the Khalsa did not owe its allegiance to any earthly power, and that he acted in total devotion to Akal (The Timeless Reality). Similarly, the coin of Ranjit Singh does not mention any particular person or king, except Guru Nanak as the true emperor of both the worlds, spiritual and empirical. His coinage which was called Nanak Shahi bore the inscription, which means, "Prosperity, power, victory and patronage, unfailing received from Guru Nanak and Guru Gobind Singh." He never struck any coin in his own name. He listened daily to the readings from Guru Granth Sahib. On one occasion when the Akal Takht took exception to a moral lapse on the part of the Maharaja, he humbly surrendered to the dictates of the Supreme Sikh Authority, the Akal Takht, and readily bared his back for receiving public flogging as chastisement for the offence.

Born and brought up in the Sikh faith, Ranjit Singh was fully conversant with the catholicity of the Sikh tradition, which left its visible impact on his outlook and policy. Religious bigotry, he knew, was incompatible with Sikhism. The ideas of unity of God, universal brotherhood and welfare of all (Sarbat Da Bhala), which summed up the basic tenets of Sikhism, enabled him to restore complete religious harmony in his kingdom. Here, it will be worthwhile to compare him with the great Maratha ruler Shivaji, who had directed his power to the patronage of Brahmins, cow and caste, and was known by the title of Gou Brahman Pritpalika (Defender of Orthodox Hindu faith).[30] All his ministers, except the Commander-in-Chief, belonged to the Brahmin caste. His reign marked the triumphant establishment of an aggressive Hindu Swarajya (militant political expression of orthodox Hinduism).[31]

Ranjit Singh did not proclaim Sikhism to be the state religion, nor did he make any conscious efforts to propagate his own religion. His catholicity of religious outlook was reflected in his according due respect to all religions. This was fully in consonance with the principle of universal love and equality propounded by the Sikh Gurus. Sikhism did not have an ordained priestly class that could rule in the name of Sikh religion. But the religio-political views of the Gurus could be inferred from Gurbani and the lives and deeds of the Gurus. In the vision of the Sikh Gurus, a sane human society was essentially a plural one in which each community was afforded the opportunity to work out its genius to the fullest possibilities and potentialities. The Sikh Gurus, who suffered martyrdoms to uphold the religious liberties of the people, laid repeated emphasis on the unity of mankind in their *bani*. Ranjit Singh held fast to the values of justice, freedom and human dignity, not through any defined statements or religious vows or policy pronouncements, but through stark deeds. There is no denying the fact that it was because of his Sikh religious background, that he proved to be a more enlightened exponent of humanitarianism and tolerance than his contemporary emperors and kings, or even some of the so-called modern, secular or democratic rulers.

The spirit of forbearance and moderation displayed by Ranjit Singh was in sharp contrast with the inhuman practices of the Mughal rulers, their plunder, greed, devastations and forced conversions. The Muslim state in India, being entirely subordinate to the Church, had believed in waging a religious war (*Jehad*) against the 'infidels.' It aimed at stamping out all forms of pluralism, whether political, religious or social, and demanded total conformity in faith, belief, form and action. The ideal of the Muslim state was conversion of the entire population to Islam and extinction of every form of dissent. Accordingly, non-Muslims were not looked upon as equal citizens of the State. In order to secure the right of exercising their religion, they had to suffer political and social disabilities and pay toll tax (*Jazia*). Under Aurangzeb there was large scale destruction of non-Muslim religious temples and other religious institutions in northern India.

The Muslim rule in Europe was, without doubt, liberal as compared to the contemporary Christian states, but its limitation was that it had to abide by the strict rules of the *Shariat*, which was sometimes interpreted arbitrarily by bigoted Mullas, resulting in serious socio-political discrimination. Of course, the imposition of *Jazia* on non-Muslims was an accepted principle under the *Shariat*. The crusade or *Jehad* against the non-believers or non-Muslim states with a view to spreading Islam, was also an accepted principle of Islamic polity.

In pre-Muslim India, the four fold division of Hindu society was looked upon as divinely ordained. Manu laid down that a king should zealously guard and uphold this caste-based division. As a result, Brahmins came to enjoy a special status, and laid claim to various immunities from the working of the common law, even in matters of taxation and justice. In addition to those immunities, they enjoyed the right to collect from the masses a regular tax called *Brahman Avimasti*, the only logic behind it being their claim to divine favour as a reward for their good deeds done in their past lives.[32] Evidently, there was no equality before law. The state, too, became a party to the various discriminations made against the lower castes in the name of a divinely ordained caste system.[33] Not only the perpetuation of acute and serious caste discrimination against the *Shudras* and lower castes, and maintenance of the supremacy of Brahmins as the sole interpreters of *dharma*, was the primary duty of a Hindu king, but the manner in which the Buddhists were treated, involving their virtual elimination from the Indian sub-continent, is a part of history.[34] It is very relevant to point out that in contemporary

Europe of the seventeenth and eighteenth centuries, the Jewish ghetto, like the discrimination against the untouchables, was an established institution.

In the times just preceding the Muslim invasion of India, the Hindu orthodoxy was seen launching a religious crusade against the Buddhists. The holy Boddhi tree at Gaya was burnt.[35] A Hindu temple was erected on the ruins of a Buddhist monastery. A large scale massacre of Buddhists was ordered. Such a policy resulted in the alienation of the Buddhists from the Hindus and eventually led to their virtual disappearance from India.[36]

As against what we have stated about the Muslim rulers and Hindu kings, the most striking feature of the policy of Ranjit Singh was the equal respect shown to all faiths. He did not treat the Sikhs as a privileged class, and did not place any disabilities on his non-Sikh subjects. Nor did he interfere with the religious and cultural life of other communities. They were allowed to freely practise their religions without payment of any special tax. There were no discriminatory tariffs. His policy was free from bigotry or any kind of narrowness of outlook and racial arrogance, inherent in the traditional Hindu system of caste. His contemporary rulers, the Peshwas, could not be entirely free from the shackles of casteism and Brahaminical chauvinism. Between one caste and another they could not always maintain the balance evenly.[37]

Ranjit Singh gave complete freedom of expression and worship to all his subjects. Under him, careers were thrown open to men of talent, irrespective of their religion, caste or class. Even when he bestowed his favours, he endeavoured to maintain an even balance among Hindus, Sikhs and Muslims. Far from demolishing the religious places of Muslims or Hindus, he was in fact generous in his endowments to Hindu and Muslim places of worship. He gave liberal grants to Muslim places of worship. He gave generous help to learned Muslims, and paid due respect to the *fakirs* and *derveshs* of his kingdom. He repaired the Muslim monuments. The Sunehri Masjid in Kashmiri Bazar of Lahore, which had earlier been in the possession of the non-Muslims, was restored to Muslims, and the tombs of Hazrat Data Ganja and Monj-i-Darya were repaired at state expense. A Muslim calligraphist, who had transcribed the *Quran* in an exquisite hand and did not find a buyer to pay the price of his life long labour and was ready to leave for Hyderabad to sell the Quran to the Nizam, was paid Rupees one *lakh* by the Maharaja. He got the holy books of Muslims and Hindus translated into other languages. He participated in the festivals of *Id, Holi, Dusshehra, Vaisakhi* and *Basant* with the same enthusiasm as others. His Hindu, Muslim and Sikh subjects reciprocated these gestures by praying for him on important occasions — when he launched a new campaign, when he won a new victory, when he had a hair-breadth escape, when he was ill, or when he recovered from illness.

The minority status of the Sikh ruler was no handicap in commanding allegiance from his Muslim and Hindu subjects. Surjit Hans's argument that the Maharaja on account of his minority status per force had to strengthen his bonds with the Hindus and pacify the Muslims[38] is untenable. Invaders, who came too often, always imposed their minority rule through sheer force. In the background that the Sikhs had suffered immensely and immediately before the Sikh rule, and the community had gone through one of the worst persecutions at the hands of the Muslim rulers, it is extremely creditable for the Maharaja not only to give equal treatment to his Muslim subjects, but also fully to trust his Muslim employees manning the highest posts in his administration. In the medieval period, monarchs were not dependent on the votes of their subjects, and the question of majority or minority was hardly relevant. The Muslim rulers, when they chose, could be cruelly intolerant and oppressive towards the majority of their subjects. In this context it is idle to indicate that Ranjit Singh's policies towards the Muslims were influenced by any consideration of pacification of the majority community who were mostly converts and were only marginally a majority.[39] Besides, fake postures towards the Muslims could never beget their trust in a manner and to the extent that Ranjit Singh obtained. The revolts of Muslim generals during the Muslim history in India have been a common feature. It, therefore, speaks volumes for the humaneness of Ranjit Singh that none of his Muslim generals revolted. Even his fallen foes, once forgiven by him, gave him loyal service, and fought for the Sikh kingdom to the last. In this context, the observation of Surjit Hans looks so meaningless and puerile. Ranjit Singh solved the problem of multiple faiths by a policy of large-hearted liberalism. This liberalism, it may be reiterated, had its roots in the Sikh faith. As a matter of fact, Ranjit Singh's faith and Sikh ethos guided him inevitably along this path.

During his reign, there were no outbursts of communal fanaticism, no forced conversions, no attempts at bloody revenge, no language tensions, no second class citizens, no repression, no bloodsheds, no executions and no tortures. Punishments were humane. There was no capital punishment which even modern governments have not been able to abolish. It was not awarded even when there was an attempt on the life of the Maharaja himself. Such a thing is unknown in monarchical history, much less in the rule of a despot. It is, therefore, both incorrect and unfair to call his rule autocratic, despotic, or personalised, when it is seen that in modern India Mahatma Gandhi's assassin was hanged. W.G. Osborne says that, "except in actual open warfare he has never been known to take life, though his own has been attempted more than once, and his reign will be found freer from any striking acts of cruelty and oppression than those of many more civilised monarchs."[40] It is to his credit that during his reign of forty years, he did not sentence even one person to death. He bore no rancour against his Muslim predecessors, who were responsible for the persecution of the Sikh Gurus, and had unleashed a reign of terror on the Sikh community.

Ranjit Singh's employment policy reflected the basic liberal and humanitarian teachings of Sikhism. The highest posts in his Government were as open to Muslims as to Sikhs and Hindus. Fakir Aziz-ud-Din was his most trusted minister. Fakir Aziz-ud-Din was the Governor of Lahore, and was one of the closest confidants of the Maharaja. There were many Muslims occupying high positions as Governors of provinces and forts, and commanders of the armies.[41] Muslims on their part proved worthy of the trust. Poet Shah Muhammad shed tears over the fall of the Sikh kingdom.

Similarly, the Maharaja bore no malice towards the Hindus. He overlooked so many past instances of Hindu betrayal of the Sikhs, whether it be that of Chandu Shah, who had played a role in the persecution of Guru Arjun[42] or the Hill Rajput Rajas, who had invited the imperial forces to suppress Guru Gobind Singh and his followers,[43] or the role of Gangu in betraying the two younger sons of Guru Gobind Singh and passing them to the custody of the ruler of Sirhind. This execution later invited the wrath of Banda involving the sack of Sirhind. The other instances were that of Diwan Lakhpat Rai, who along with Yahiya Khan, was instrumental in the destruction of Darbar Sahib,[44] and Kabli Mal, who in his capacity as Governor of Lahore had defiled the sanctity of the sacred tank of Darbar Sahib on the instructions of Ahmed Shah Abdali.[45] The Sikhs had resented the hostility of the Pathans and the Mughals and the treason of the Hindus, who often became willing partners of Imperial forces and invaders in suppressing and oppressing the Sikhs. Ranjit Singh forgot all this and entrusted talented Hindus with the highest responsibilities of the State. Misr Beli Ram was the Revenue Minister of the State, while Diwan Bhawani Das, Diwan Ganga Ram and Diwan Dina Nath were, respectively, Pay Master General, Accountant General and Comptroller General of the Lahore Darbar. Hill Dogras Dhian Singh, Khushal Singh and Gulab Singh were appointed to the positions of supreme authority in the civil apparatus of the Maharaja's Government. Brahmins like Tej Singh and Lal Singh were granted such influence as eventually raised them to the supreme command of the Sikh army. Diwan Mohkam Chand was made the Commander of the Khalsa army. In fact, historians have strongly criticised Ranjit Singh's overindulgence towards the Hill Dogras and the Purbia Generals, and his misplaced trust in them. These men subsequently betrayed the Sikhs and became the principal cause of the fall of the Sikh kingdom.[46]

TREATMENT TO FALLEN ENEMIES

In dealing with his fallen enemies, Ranjit Singh displayed unexampled generosity. Not only the Sikh nobles and *Sardars,* but also the deposed Muslim and Hindu nobles were provided with *Jagirs* and treated equally and generously. In fact, the Maharaja's treatment of the fallen Muslim foes was unprecedented. The defeated Afghan Governor Sultan Muhammad Khan was given a *Jagir* of Rupees three *lakhs* as revenues of the areas comprising Kohat and Hashat Nagar. When he conquered Kasur from Nawab Kutab-ud-Din, he gave him the *Jagir* of Mamdot which brought a revenue of 190,000 Rupees a year. In the same way, when he conquered Multan he granted a big *Jagir* in Sharakpur and Naulakhe to the Nawab's sons.[47] He honoured the sentiments of his Muslim subjects, and maintained the established Muslim tradition of State-grants to Ulemas and holy men. There is an important entry in the Diary — News of Ranjit Singh's court — 25th August, 1825, "The Qazis, Sayads, Alamas and Fakirs of Peshawar were given good *khilats,* and each was given a *Jagir* for his maintenance, when the Maharaja annexed Peshawar."[48] When the victory procession of the Maharaja passed through the streets of Peshawar, he issued strict instructions to his *Sardars* to observe ethical restraint in keeping with the Sikh tradition, not to damage any mosque, not to insult any woman and not to destroy any crops. The Muslim priests were so pleased, that they blessed the victor.[49] No wonder the Muslim Generals of the Maharaja were responsible for carrying his flag across the Punjab borders. In this connection, observations made by Sir Henry Lawrence are noteworthy; "Members of the deposed ruling families may be seen in Delhi and Kabul in a state of penury, but in the Punjab there is not to be seen a single ruling family whose territories may have been conquered by Ranjit Singh, and which may have been left unprovided by him. Not only the Sikh ruling houses, but those of other faiths too, were provided for by him with equal munificence."[50] A similar observation is made by Lepel Griffin : "With all his rapacity, Ranjit Singh was not cruel or blood-thirsty. After the victory or the capture of a fortress he treated the vanquished with leniency and kindness, however stout their resistance might have been, and there were at his court many chiefs despoiled of their estates but to whom he had given suitable employ."[51]

Here it will not be out of place to compare Ranjit Singh with the Marathas who had allowed the Mughal Emperor Shah Alam II to languish in his palace with a niggardly allowance. By propping up the Imperial edifice the Marathas had derived considerable advantage, but it was rather sad that they did not mitigate the King's pecuniary distress. This sordid policy had not only disgusted the royal house of Timur, but had also roused the indignation of many Muhammadans in the country who did not approve of the treatment meted out to the Imperial family. It was, therefore, not surprising that in September, 1803, the hapless Mughal Emperor welcomed the English as deliverers.[52] Similarly, the treatment meted out by Governor-General Dalhousie to the royal house of Sikhs, reflected no credit on the British. The minor Maharaja Dalip Singh was converted to Christianity, given a meagre pension of Rs. 13,000 per annum and after separating him from his mother, was sent to England. Maharani Jindan, called the 'mother of the Khalsa,' was also treated very shabbily, and was forced to leave the country. In pursuance of his Imperial policies, Dalhousie abolished all military grants to the Sikh *Sardars*. Henry Lawrence, as head of the Board of Control, responsible for the administration of Punjab, recommended slight leniency towards the Sikh nobility. But Dalhousie insisted that *Jagirdars* deserved "little but maintenance."[53] Henry Lawrence tendered his resignation over this issue.

Among the notable traits of Ranjit Singh's character were his kindness and the total absence of malice, cruelty or vindictiveness. These being so uncommon in the context of his times, were evidently due to the Sikh tradition and ethos in which he had been nurtured, conditioned and motivated. His regime was not stained by such dark blots as was the Mughal rule. For, there are numerous instances like the cruel death of Dara Shikoh at the hands of his own brother, or the diabolical murders of twenty one captains of Ali Wardi Khan, or the degradation and blinding of Emperor Shah Alam II.

The Marathas knew how to conquer, but not how to govern. Though they were the strong exponents of Hindu *Swarajya*, yet outside the Swarajya they plundered Hindus as ruthlessly as Muslims so that their claim to be serving the cause of Hinduism was falsified.[54] Here it will be worthwhile to give another historical analogy of the British Governors Clive and Warren Hastings, both of whom had to face disgrace and degradation on account of their involvement on charges of corruption, bribery and extortion.[55] Both of them were impeached. Clive who is regarded as the founder of the British Empire in India, committed suicide in disgrace and frustration.

Similarly, Alfanso Albuquerque, the founder of the Portuguese Empire in India, tried to establish Christianity in his territory with sword and fire.[56] In its religious zeal, the Portuguese power became ruthless, and issued charters from time to time making invidious distinctions between Christians and non-Christians and subjecting the latter to untold disabilities. An enactment was passed debarring all non-Christians from holding any public office. In pursuance of another enactment, the property of non-Christian orphans was confiscated if they refused to be converted to Christianity. Under pain of being proceeded against by the law of the land, the people of Goa were prohibited from using their native language Konkani, and were forced to learn the Portuguese language within a period of three years. The aim of all these enactments was to compel the natives either to accept Christianity or to leave the state.[57]

To describe Ranjit Singh's rule as military despotism is to do a great injustice to him. A comparative study of the contemporary Governments in the West reveals that Ranjit Singh's rule was more humane and popular. Contemporary rulers in the West were known for their highly centralised and despotic rule, whether it was that of autocratic Napoleon Bonaparte (1804-15), or of the inglorious Louis XVIII (1814-24), or of the vindictive Bourbon Charles X (1824-30), or of the self-centred Louis Phillippe (1830-48) in France, or of George III, IV and William IV in England, or for that matter, of the tyrant Czar Nicholas I (1826-55) in Russia. Let us amplify the point in respect of Napoleon. The French Revolution was the flower of the centuries following the Reformation and the Renaissance. And yet, Napoleon buried that flower before it could fructify into a tangible fruit. It is not in doubt that he virtually destroyed the ideas and ethos of the Revolution that produced him. But the point for study is whether the ideas that led to the Revolution and which were easily smothered and distorted by Napoleon, an upstart, were really so great. Factually, Reformation in one sense belittled the Christian ethos, and its supremacy over the political life came to an end. The states came to be governed by the whims of the rulers, political elites or the nobles. Ultimately it revived, as Toynbee laments, the parochial Greek idea of the national state being the goddess, thereby involving the gradual erosion of Christian ethos, even in the social life. Rational concepts and dry ideas have no meaning, unless they influence human and social behaviour. To us it appears a contradiction to say that the French Revolution was a great event of history, even though it was destroyed in the country of its birth within half a dozen years. As against it, Sikhism was a movement that changed the life and motivations of a people, with the result that even an unlettered person, when he came to power, created a socio-political administration that was remarkably humane and just, even though, he belonged to a community that was in a microscopic minority. Ranjit Singh's conquests were not to bring glorification to his person, community or people but to give peace to Punjab by stopping, once and for all, a thousand year wave of invaders that had subjected Punjabis to perpetual loot, massacres, butchery and disgrace. As stated above, Ranjit Singh won the hearts of his people, including Muslims and Hindus, by giving them peace, security and justice, and not by any sense of glorification or threat or terror. What we mean to stress is that religious thought and ethos that permeate and affect the moral life, behaviour and sentiments of a people, are far more enduring and meaningful than rational concepts that generally remain ethereal and short-lived, and fail to influence human motivations. So, to us the inference is obvious enough that, in comparison, it is not that Napoleon was a villain and Ranjit Singh a saint, but that the ideology that produced Ranjit Singh was far superior to the ideas and thinking that preceded Napoleon and the French Revolution.

Ranjit Singh's rule was, on the whole, humanitarian and compassionate. In fact, his clear attempt at self-effacement and avoidance of any personal elevation, while giving credit to God, Guru and the Khalsa, would suggest a kind of rule, beneficient, free from wanton atrocities, and solicitous of the public zeal.[58] In its contemporary world it is the most inspiring example of a just state. That rule is, thus, full of lessons even for present day politics. Captain Murray pays the most befitting tribute to the Maharaja in these words, "Ranjit Singh has been likened to Mehmet Ali and to Napoleon ...... There are some points in which he resembles both; but estimating his character with reference to his circumstances and positions, he is perhaps a more remarkable man than either ...... There was no ferocity in his disposition, and he never punished a criminal with death, even under circumstances of aggravated offence. Humanity indeed, or rather tenderness for life, was a trait in the character of Ranjit Singh. There is no instance of his having wantonly imbued his hands in blood."[59] Similar observations were made by Jawahar Lal Nehru in his book 'Discovery of India' : "He (Ranjit Singh) was remarkably humane at a time when India and the world seethed with callousness and inhumanity. He built up a kingdom and a powerful army and yet he disliked bloodshed ...... He abolished the death sentence for every crime, however heinous it might be, when in England even petty pilferers had to face death."[59-a]

The habitual meekness of spirit which the Maharaja displayed even at the peak of his glory, the sympathy which he showed to the fallen foes and the compassion he had for animals demonstrated the breadth of his vision and the catholicity of his temper. It was quite in keeping with Sikh tradition and the Scriptural injuction, "To exercise forbearance in the midst of power, to be humble in the midst of honour."[60] G.L. Chopra believes that considering the social and political conditions of the country over which he ruled, the Government of Maharaja Ranjit Singh was "surprisingly mild and merciful."[61] On one occasion he is said to have punished one of his generals for killing a *Koel* (nightingale) when she was warbling. Nobody was allowed to hurt a swan, a parrot or a sparrow. Cow slaughter was banned throughout the Empire in deference to the wishes of his Hindu subjects.

SIKH ADMINISTRATION

A distinguishing feature of the Khalsa Raj was an orderly system of administration based upon territorial divisions like that of *Subas, Parganas, Tapas* and *Mauzas* (village). The administrative hierarchy of the *Nazim*, the *Kardar*, the *Chaudhary* and the *Muqaddam*, linked the far flung villages of the Sikh Empire to the capital city of Lahore.[62] Thus, Ranjit Singh exercised his authority on the basis of the willing co-operation of indigenous socio-political institutions. He made no innovations in the civil administration of his dominions, but tried to improve the old arrangements. The stability of Ranjit Singh's regime also rested upon moderation in what the state expropriated from the peasantry as its share of the agricultural produce. According to one source, the Government's share varied between two-fifth to one-third of the gross produce.[63] An agricultural tax of this order was in keeping with what the state could legitimately demand from the peasantry. The revenue could be paid in cash or kind and in easy instalments. A notable achievement of the Maharaja was that the ownership of the land was vested in the cultivator,[64] from whom the revenue was collected directly without the intervention of the middleman, an institution he summarily dispensed with. During the course of war or the movement of troops, any damage to the standing crops was severely dealt with. The soldiers had to dismount from their horses while passing through the villages and the pathways leading to the corn fields. Punjab peasantry, suppressed for centuries, was put on the road to prosperity, and given a new dispensation. Gardner's observations about the *Khalsa Sarkar* are noteworthy : "The Maharaja was indeed one of those master minds, which only require opportunity to change the face of the Punjab. The Punjab was not the same, semi starving, terrified, looted by the rulers, and poorly clothed during his reign. It was a prosperous, homogeneous and peaceful state with all the communities, Hindus, Muslims and Sikhs, fully satisfied partners in the Government, in military and civil administration, and it was the happiest State communally in Asia. The Maharaja visited the Hindu, Sikh and Muslim places of pilgrimage. It was the only state in India, which was the most prosperous, the most flourishing and the most contented."[64a]

The administration of justice under Ranjit Singh was, by the standards of the times, simple, well-organised and suited to the needs of the people. In villages, the disputes were settled by the arbitration of *Panchayats*, who had to decide cases according to the custom prevailing in each locality. In the towns the function was entrusted to the *Kardars, Nazims* or sometimes to officials called *Adaltis* (judges). An *Adalt-i-Ala* or High Court was set up at the capital. Above them all was the Maharaja himself to hear appeals and petitions made against the decisions of the above mentioned authorities. He was in the habit of receiving petitions and listening to complaints even during the course of passing through the streets. Decisions were speedy and justice was quick. With the Maharaja justice was a passion. He believed that the only divine element in kingship was justice. He sent instructions to the *Chief Kotwal* of Lahore that he should not spare the Maharaja himself or any member of his family, should they be found guilty of any offence. It was a unique instance where the king had accepted equality with his subjects. A protector of the poor and the weak, the Maharaja established a state where the strong were just and the weak secure.

Though cruelty, killings, injustice and oppression practised and the wars fought in the current century have raised a serious question mark in the minds of many thinking persons about the form of government best suited for a people, many persons conditioned by the western education are still sold to the ideal of a democratic structure of government being the best to secure justice among the people. On the other hand, the concept of kingship at once raises the idea of despotic and unjust rule. It is, perhaps, in this context that Fakir Syed Waheduddin has quoted two orders of Ranjit Singh to ensure justice among the people and the application of secular laws of each community to its members through courts presided over by persons of the community concerned. These orders emphasize two things. First, that equality before the law and equity in administration were the fundamental criteria of Ranjit Singh's administration. Second, that because of the actual humane manner in which justice was administered, it was never felt necessary by him to give the extreme punishment of death so as to secure respect for the law. And, in this respect, he ensured the sanctity of this principle by not punishing with death even those who had attempted to kill him. We give below the two orders issued by Ranjit Singh.

I. *"Sincere Well-wisher, Fakir Nuruddin Ji, May you be happy.*

It is hereby decreed by His Highness with the utmost emphasis that no person in the city should practise high-handedness and oppression on the people. Indeed, if even His Highness himself should issue an inappropriate order against any resident of Lahore, it should be clearly brought to the notice of His Highness so that it may be amended. Protector of Bravery, Malwa Singh should always be advised to dispense justice in accordance with legitimate right and without the slightest oppression and, furthermore, he should be advised to pass orders in consultation with the Panches and Judges of the city and in accordance with the Shastras and the Quran, as pertinent to the faith of the parties; for such is our pleasure. And should any person fail to act in accordance with your advice or instructions, you should send him a formal letter so that it may serve as a proof on the strength of which His Highness may punish him for disobedience.

Despatched from the Court of His Highness.

31 Bhadon, 1882 Sambat

For repairs to the old ditch an expenditure of two thousand Rupees is hereby sanctioned.

For the present the salary of Fakir Sahib, Rs.1500/-. After expenditure on the said ditch, the salary of Sher Dyal, Rs. 500/-."[65]

II. *"Ujjal Didar Nirmal Budh Sardar Amir Singh Ji and our sincere well-wisher, Fakir Nuruddin Ji, May you live long by the grace of Sri Akal Purakh and enjoy the protection of Sri Akal Budh.*

By the grace of Sri Sat Guruji, the exalted command is issued to you that, deeming yourselves to be responsible for the security of Lahore, you should take care of the duties pertaining thereto. Sri Sat Guruji forbid, if His Highness, his beloved son Kharak Singh Ji, Kanwar Sher Singh Ji, the Raja Kalan Bahadur, Raja Suchet Singh Ji, or Jamadar Ji should commit any inappropriate act, you should bring it to the notice of His Highness. Secondly, you should send your trusted representative to the Sardars with instructions to refrain from committing inappropriate acts. If the Sardars act according to your instruction, well and good; otherwise, you should send word to them that you will bring the matter to the notice of His Highness. Moreover, you should not permit forcible possession to be taken of any person's land or any person's house to be demolished. Nor should you allow any high-handedness to be practised upon woodcutters, fodder-vendors, oil-vendors, horse-shoers, factory owners, etc. In such case also you should prevent the oppressor from oppression. You should administer matters in the same way as Sardar Desa Singh Ji, should not permit anybody to be treated harshly and should forward to His Highness any petitions intended for him. Furthermore, you should daily send for Chand Mall, Kotwal of the Royal Court, and Babu Panda, and obtain from them news of all happenings so that every person's rights are secured and no person is oppressed. The frames of the city gates should be caused to be repaired from the revenue of the Court. Hazara Sawars should be appointed to watch the roads and, considering the security of the whole of Lahore city as your responsibility, you should act in accordance with this decree.

Dated Lahore, 19 Pos, 1888 Sambat."[66]

Waheeduddin concludes that these orders are "unique in one respect : they throw overboard the time-honoured legal fiction upon which the fact of kingship is based — that the king can do no wrong. It was characteristic of Ranjit Singh to acknowledge that, both as a man and as a king, he was fallible and to provide against any possible adverse effects of his fallibility upon the rights and well-being of his people."[67]

Students of history are well aware of the presence of racial, religious and ethnic discrimination and even riots in modern states, as also of the need for the use of drastic force to maintain law and order. In this context, three things are important and speak for themselves. First, Ranjit Singh never tried to convert Muslims or Hindus to Sikhism, even though his community remained a permanent minority in the State. Second, there were hardly any communal riots· in his times. This background and the actual administration of justice and equality was so impressive and evident to the people, that respect for law was spontaneous, and he never had to use strong or brutal measures to maintain or enforce the law.

Third, the cases of bribery and corruption in his kingdom were rare. The Maharaja's frequent and unexpected tours kept the local officials in check. While crime had been rampant under his immediate predecessors, it was reduced practically to the point of abolition during his reign. The cases of theft and highway robberies were uncommon. George Keene, an observer of the Punjab scene during the Maharaja's regime stated : "In hundreds and in thousands the orderly crowds stream on. Not a bough is broken from a way side tree, not a rude remark addressed to the traveller as he treads his horse's way."[68] As a result many people from the Cis-Satluj states migrated to the Maharaja's territories, where there was more security for life and property, where their rights and privileges were better protected. The Maharaja provided to his subjects all the fundamental rights and basic freedoms supposed to be enshrined in any modern constitution of today.

Ranjit Singh was an enlightened ruler. He trained his armies on modern lines through his European Generals like Allard, Ventura and Avitabile. A trained and disciplined army was the principal instrument that had led to western supremacy over the east in the seventeeth and eighteenth centuries. Among Indian princes, Ranjit Singh was the first to train his army to a level at par with western armies. It was this training and discipline coupled with the Sikh ethos that his armies even in his absence, and though betrayed by its Generals, proved a match for the British. So much so that, though vanquished, it commanded the unstinted praise of its opponents like General Gough. The Maharaja had a remarkable capacity for inspiring loyalty among the soldiers, who were imbued with national sentiments. They showed pride in their profession and valour, faith and righteousness, in their cause and conduct. This made them fight like brave soldiers against the British, even after the Maharaja's death. Empire builders have often used the army as an instrument of State policy. The invariable result in all such cases is disintegration in the ranks of the army after the ruler's death. But Ranjit Singh's army undertook the responsibility of defending Punjab from the British encroachment in accordance with the Khalsa tradition. They could not save the Sikh State, but even in their defeat won applause and admiration of their friends and foes. The poet Shah Muhammad in his *Jangnamah* extols the virtues of the Khalsa soldiers in the Anglo-Sikh Wars.

Though himself unlettered, the Maharaja knew the importance of education. The Gurus had bade their followers to be progressive in their outlook, always to be Sikhs or learners, to take increasing advantage of opportunities to improve their condition and knowledge as men free from the shackles of earlier prejudices, conventions and dogmas and the stranglehold of the priestly class who claimed monopoly of knowledge. The Maharaja was very liberal and impartial in the matter of making endowments for education. There were about four thousand schools belonging to different communities scattered over the length and breadth of his kingdom, with about one *lakh* and twenty thousand students. These schools were mostly attached to gurdwaras, mosques and temples. The Maharaja was most generous in helping the custodians of these places of learning. He also stood for modern knowledge and is said to have encouraged the learning of English and French. He also procured the services of a Christian missonary to set up English medium schools at Lahore, though without allowing him to propagate Christianity or introduce Bible lessons in the curriculum of the schools. Maharaja Ranjit Singh's department of Charity cost the State exchequer one tenth of the total revenues amounting nearly to twenty *lakh* Rupees a year. This is an extremely important fact of Ranjit Singh's administration that highlights its Sikh character. The Fifth Master had prescribed for the Sikh a contribution of *Daswandh* or one tenth of his earnings towards a charitable fund of the Society. It is indeed outstanding of Ranjit Singh's administration that he ear-marked one tenth of the total revenue towards expenditure on charities and other public causes.

RANJIT SINGH'S PLACE IN HISTORY

The Maharaja gave to his citizens a consistent and uniform system of administration and a greater amount of peace and prosperity than they had enjoyed for over a century. The Mughal and the Maratha rulers in the country had been marked by bigotry, corruption, degradation, persecution, treachery, confusion, disorder, extravagance and pomp. Ranjit Singh's claim to greatness lies in the fact that he successfully faced the historical challenge of abuse of power and religious bigotry by restoring communal harmony in his State. He endowed politics with a moral purpose. His State was governed and sustained by values and attitudes that characterised the Sikh tradition. The Gurus had envisioned an egalitarian social order based on justice and freedom. With the Sikh ethos governing his psyche, Ranjit Singh translated this vision into practice.

For the first time in Indian history a landmark was created. Mazhabhis, the centuries old untouchables of the Hindu society, far from being discriminated against, became a regular component of Ranjit Singh's army. The Hindu hill *Rajputs*, who had refused to co-operate with the Tenth Master on account of his giving equality to the lower castes ceased to have any compunction in working and fighting side by side with them. And his greatest achievement was the unstinted and uncommon loyalty he commanded from all sections of his men, whether Muslim, Hindu, Sikh, *Rajput* or European. The miracle was that a sense of comradeship was achieved just in a period of four decades, most of which time was spent in fighting and consolidation. Unlike the Muslim invaders or contemporary rulers of his times, another uncommon feature of his rule was that while he spent long periods in fighting far away from his capital, there never was a local uprising to challenge his authority. This indicates an incontrovertible belief and assessment of the people he ruled that he was not fighting for any personal aggrandisement nor was he or his armies out for gathering any booty or loot.

CONCLUSION

From our narration of facts about the rule of Ranjit Singh it is evident that in all aspects of its functioning and administration, Ranjit Singh's rule was in sharp contrast to the rule, not only of his contemporaries, but also of many modern secular administrations. Moses and Mohammed were both spiritual and political leaders. Moses was followed by kings, David and Solomon, well-known for their fairness and wisdom. Similarly, the Muslim rule in Europe, in contrast with the ghetto, repeated massacres and pogroms perpetrated by Christian monarchs, was remarkably tolerant, mild and humane towards its non-Muslim subjects. It is the lesson of history that a healthy combination of religion and politics is bound to lead to a harmonious socio-political order. It is well-known that Ashoka's rule, coloured by Buddhist ethics, was a shining light among the Empires of the earlier millenia. Even among modern secular rulers at least two of the despots are notorious for their inhumanity. We refer to Hitler's elimination of six million Jews and Stalin's liquidation of his twelve million countrymen in order to make their people safe and secure for peace, prosperity and equality. Hence, the inevitable conclusion that Ranjit Singh's rule, being a product of the Sikh tradition and ethos, was outstandingly humane, liberal and tolerant towards his people, including his erstwhile opponents and enemies. His rule was, undoubtedly, benign and fair, and why it was so, is explained by the background of the whole-life religious thesis and ethos which conditioned and influenced it, and of which Ranjit Singh was a shining product.

Ranjit Singh's rule epitomises and demonstrates a very important principle of religion and human history, namely, the comparative role and impact of dichotomous or pacificist religions and of whole-life or *miri-piri* religion, on the life of man. So far as the Indian contemporary life was governed by dichotomous Hinduism, there was little doubt that the discriminatory system of caste, pollution and untouchability, and the dominance of the upper castes remained a fact of life in the Indian society, including the times of Shivaji. At no time could the untouchables think of working shoulder to shoulder with the upper castes. The position in the matter of social discrimination was no different in the rule of Christian monarchs up to the nineteenth century, where the ghetto for the Jews remained a cursed institution, and the treatment of Muslim subjects was no less discriminatory. Arnold Toynbee finds himself caught in a web of self-contradiction, and perhaps bias as well, when, on the one hand, he condemns the diversion of religion to empirical and mundane tasks and seeks to justify and extol the pacificism and other-worldliness of the Christian mission, and, for that matter, condemns the *miri-piri* or the whole-life character of Islam; and, on the other hand, he is constrained to concede that "by contrast with the treatment of subject Jews and Muslims in the Christiandom, the treatment of subject 'People of the Book' in Dar-Ul-Islam has been honourably distinguished by its comparative tolerance."[69] This shows that it is a whole-life or a *miri-piri* system that alone is capable of fostering a harmonious progress and development of man and society. Consequently, dichotomous or pacificist religions to the extent they keep confined to what Toynbee calls their spiritual mission (as divorced from a whole-life mission), remain historically and socially barren in their influence and impact. The phenomenon of Ranjit Singh is not just a rule of a monarch. It demonstrates very clearly the role and impact of a whole-life or *miri-piri* religion on the society of its times.

REFERENCES

1. Cunningham, J.D. : *History of the Sikhs* (Reprint, New Delhi, 1966), p. 120.
2. Kohli, Sita Ram : *The Organisation of Ranjit Singh's Army; Maharaja Ranjit Singh* (ed.) Teja Singh and Ganda Singh (Reprint, Patiala, 1970), pp. 60-61.
3. Prinsep, H.T. : *Origin of The Sikh Power in The Punjab and Political Life of Maharaja Ranjit Singh* (Reprint, Patiala, 1970), pp. 142-43.
4. Sinha, N.K. : *Ranjit Singh* (Reprint, Calcutta), pp. 189-92.
5. Bentely, Eric : *Century of Hero-Worship* (Boston, 1957), pp. 3-8.
6. Macaulay, J.B. : *Lord Macaulay's Legislative Minutes* (London, 1946), pp. 2-3.
7. Toynbee, J. Arnold : *A Study of History* (Oxford, 1951), p.79.
8. Griffin, Lepel : *Ranjit Singh* (Reprint, Delhi, 1967), p. 39.
9. "You wear necklaces, put sacrificial marks on your foreheads, carry two *dhotis*, and put towels on your heads; If you know God's designs, you would know that yours is verily a vain religion :" Macauliffe, M.A. : *The Sikh Religion*, Vol. I (Delhi, 1963), p. 237.
   "The Qazi telleth lies and eateth filth. The Brahmin taketh life and then batheth. The ignorant jogi knoweth not the way of union with God. The whole three ruin the world." Macauliffe, M.A. : Ibid., p. 338.

10. Dhillon, G.S. : *Researches in Sikh Religion and History* (Chandigarh 1989); p. 2.
11. "Nanak, the Formless One is without fear; All the Rams dust; How many stories there are of Krishna! How many Veds and religious compositions! Afflicted are Brahma, Vishnu and Shiva : Yea, afflicted is the whole world." *Guru Granth Sahib*, p.1153, Trans. by Gopal Singh, Vol. IV, p. 1102.
12. "O Whom shall we call good or evil, When all creatures belong to Thee."*Guru Granth Sahib,* p. 383.
13. "God is self-existent; so is His Name; Beside Himself He made Nature, wherein He has His seat and looks on with fondness." *Asa-di-Var,* Trans. Teja Singh; *Essays in Sikhism* (Lahore, 1944), p.17.
14. "Householders and hermits are equal, whoever calls on the name of the Lord." *Asa Ragni,* Trans., Cunningham : *op.cit.,* p. 334.
15. "O Hindus, how shall the stone which itself sinketh carry you across ?" Macauliffe, Vol.I., p. 326.
16. *Guru Granth Sahib,* p. 1046.
17. Ibid., p. 463.
18. Dhillon, G.S. : *op.cit.,* p. 9.
19. Irvine, William : *Later Mughals* (Reprint, New Delhi, 1971), pp. 317-18.
20. Archer, John Clark : *Sikhs* (Princeton, 1946), p. 232.
21. Forster, George : *A Journey from Bengal to England,* Vol. I (Reprint, Patiala, 1970), p. 340.
22. 'ਜਪਦੇ ਜਾਪ ਗੁਰੂ ਦੇ ਪੂਰੇ, ਰਹਿੰਦੇ ਸਤਿਗੁਰੂ ਪਾਸ ਹਜ਼ੂਰੇ।
  ਕੇਸਾਧਾਰੀ ਸੁੰਦਰ ਸੂਰੇ, ਕੀਤੀ ਟਹਿਲ ਪਈ ਮਨਜ਼ੂਰੇ।
  ਬਖਸੀ ਰਿਯਾਸਿਧ ਭਰਪੂਰੇ, ਖੇਤੀ ਕਰਨ ਹੰਢਾਵਨ ਤੁਰੇ।
  ਅਬ ਸਿਰਦਾਰ ਹੈਂ।'

  Bir Singh : *Bara Maha Guru Gobind Singh Ji Ka* (ed.) Piara Singh Padam (Patiala, 1959), p. 143.
23. Waheeduddin, Fakir Syed : *The Real Ranjit Singh* (Karachi, 1965), p. 57.
24. Ibid., Intorduction, pp. 7-8.
25. Hugel, Baron Charles : *Travels in Kashmir and Punjab* (Reprint, Patiala, 1970), p. 382.
26. Murray (Captain) : *History of The Punjab,* Vol. II. (Reprint, Patiala, 1970), p. 175.
27. Henry, T. Prinsep : *Origin of The Sikh Power in the Punjab* (Reprint, Patiala, 1970), p. 148.
28. Dhillon, G.S. : *op.cit.,* pp. 2-3.
29. Waheeduddin : *op.cit.,* p. 57.
30. Sarkar, S.C. and Datta, K.K., *Modern Indian History* (Allahabad, 1957), p. 180.
31. Segal, Ronald : *The Crisis of India* (Bombay, 1968), p. 79.
32. Macrindle, J.W. : *Ancient India As Described by Magasthenes and Arian* (Calcutta, 1926), p. 214; Al-Bairuni, Al-Hind (Punjabi Trans. Yog Dhyan Ahuja) (Patiala, 1970), p. 362; Elliot and Dowson : *History of India as Told by its Own Historians,* Vol. I (Allahabad, 1969), p.184.
33. Ibid.
34. Elliot, Charles, *Hinduism and Buddhism,* Vol. II (Reprint London, 1962), p. 211. Joshi, L.M. : *Studies in the Buddhistic Culture in India,* (Delhi, 1967 L, pp. 395-403.
35. Ibid.
36. Parkash, Buddha : *Aspects of Indian History and Culture* (Agra, 1965), p. 215.
37. Qanungo, S.N. : *Decline and Fall of The Maratha Power* in Majumdar, R.C. (ed.) *The History and Culture of The Indian People : The Maratha Supremacy* (Bombay, 1971), pp. 515-16.
38. Hans, Surjit, 'The Gurbilas in The Early Nineteenth Century' in the *Journal of Regional History,* Vol. II, 1981, Guru Nanak Dev University, Amritsar, p. 56.
39. "The position was further complicated by the minority status of the rulers. Thus the bonds with the Hindu constituency had to be strengthened. The Muslim population had to be pacified not only administratively but also doctrinally." *Ibid.*
40. Obsorne, W.G. : *The Court and Camp of Runjeet Singh* (London, 1840), pp. 94-95.
41. Hugel, Baron Charles, *op.cit.,* pp. 292-93.
42. Cunningham, J.D. : *op.cit.,* pp. 48.
43. Ibid., p. 70.
44. Bhangu, Rattan Singh, *Prachin Panth Parkash* (ed.) Bhai Vir Singh (Amritsar, 1962), pp. 291-96.

45. Cunningham, J.D., *op.cit.,* p. 92.
46. "He (Ranjit Singh) raised the alien hill Dogras, Dhyan Singh, Khushal Singh and Gulab Singh, almost from the gutter to positions of supreme authority in the civil apparatus of his government, and Tej Singh, an insignificant Brahmin of the Gangetic-Doab and Lal Singh another Brahmin from Gandhara valley, were granted such influence which eventually raised them to the supreme command of the Sikh Army, and thus he dug his own grave, the grave of his descendents, and paved the way to the eventual enslavement of the Sikh people." Kapur Singh, *Parasaraprasana* (ed.)

Madanjit Kaur and Piar Singh (Amritsar 1989), p. 239.
47. Teja Singh, *op.cit.,* p.103.
48. Sinha, N.K : *op.cit.,* p. 149.
49. Khullar, K.K : *Maharaja Ranjit Singh* (New Delhi, 1980), p.185.
50. Lawrence, H.M.L. : *Adventures of an Officer in Punjab,* Vol. I (Reprint, Patiala, 1970), pp. 30-31.
51. Griffin, Lepel : *Ranjit Singh* (Reprint, Delhi, 1970), pp. 98-99.
52. Sen, S.N. : *'Marathas and North Indian States'* in Majumdar, R.C. (ed.), *The History And Culture of The Indian People : The Maratha Supremacy,* Vol. III (Bombay, 1977), p. 419.
53. Hunter, W.W. : *The Marquess of Dalhousie* (Oxford, 1895), p. 99;
Yadav, Kirpal Chandra, 'British Policy Towards Sikhs, 1849-57' in Harbans Singh and Barrier; N. Gerald (ed.), *Essays In Honour of Dr Ganda Singh* (Patiala, 1976), pp. 189-91; Khushwant Singh : *A History of The Sikhs,* Vol. 2; 1839-1964 (Delhi, 1977), pp. 94-95.
54. Segal, Ronald, *op.cit.* p. 80.
55. Datta, K.K., *Destruction of The Mughal Empire* in Majumdar, R.C. (ed.), *The History And Culture of The Indian People,* Vol.VIII (Bombay, 1977), pp. 117-18, 352-53.
56. Parekh, Manilar C., *Christian Proselytism In India* (Bombay, 1947), pp. 12, 20, 36-37; Report of the Christian Missionary Activities Inquiry Committee, Madhya Pradesh, 1956, p. 66, Quoted by Patel, Baburao : *Footprints of Christ* (Bombay, 1979), pp. 4-5.
57. Ibid.
58. *Guru Granth Sahib,* p. 74.
59. Murray (Captain), *op.cit.,* p. 174.
59-a. Nehru, Jawaharlal : *The Discovery of India* (New Delhi, 1964), p. 298.
60. *Guru Granth Sahib,* p. 85.
61. Chopra, G.L. : *The Punjab As a Sovereign State* (Hushiarpur, 1960), p. 137.
62. Banga, Indu : *Agrarian Systems of The Sikhs* (New Delhi, 1978), pp. 63-64.
63. Sinha, N.K., *op.cit.,* p. 142.
64. Banga, Indu, *op.cit.,* p. 191.
64a. Quoted in Diwan Singh's : *The Revolution of Guru Nanak* (Chandigarh, 1993), p. 227.
65. Waheeduddin : *op.cit.,* pp. 31-33.
66. Ibid.
67. Ibid.
68. George Keene, quoted by Khullar, K.K., *op.cit.,* p. 198.
69. Toynbee, Arnold : *An Historian's Approach To Religion* (London, 1956), p. 90.

28

ANGLO-SIKH WARS

KARNAIL SINGH

During the six thousand years of recorded history, there has been a war every third year.[1] There were short and long wars, community and religious wars, inter-state and world wars. While some of these wars were for loot, arson and mere aggrandizement, others were for establishing political and economic hegemony and building empires. Also, there were peaceful crusades involving persistent and monumental efforts and unique sacrifices for general uplift of the suffering humanity, which left their imperishable impact in the area of their happening. The Sikhs have had to go through both these types of human struggles again and again throughout their brief span of life of five hundred years, for the Sikh Gurus had established a religion which was to meet spiritual and temporal needs of the people everywhere and for all times. Such a religion had had Godly sanction.[2]

It is well-known that during a near century of warfare by the British in India from Plassey (1757) to Chillianwala (1849), they had met the most formidable resistance during the Sikh Wars. At Ferozeshah, at the failure of their attack, while retiring upon Ferozepur, they were destroying state papers and contemplating measures for unconditional surrender to save the wounded, even when the Governor-General Sir Henry Hardinge and the Commander-in-chief Lord Gough were themselves leading the attack against the Sikhs.[3] To fully grasp the background of the Anglo-Sikh Wars (1845-49) wherein such hard-fought battles took place, we will have to peruse brief history of Sikh religion and its people.

SIKH RELIGION AND ITS PEOPLE

The most important centre of spiritual regeneration in Asia has always been India. It is here that the teachings of Buddha profoundly influenced the culture of the whole of eastern Asia. About two thousand years thereafter, was born yet another great mystic, Guru Nanak (1469), when Hindu society was rife with caste and ritualism, and the ruling

Muslim community deviating from the essence of religion, practised fanaticism and tyranny of forcibly imposing their faith on others. Guru Nanak established a revealed religion based on principles of equality still unknown in the West. Its spiritual tenets are suitable for all mankind under all circumstances of modern life. He declared the common fatherhood of God and brotherhood of man. For the first time, he brought about equality between man and woman. He bitterly attacked the fundamentals of Hinduism such as caste, idol-worship, ritualism and asceticism. He welded the spiritual and temporal life of people into a harmonious whole.

His concern for the material world was as great as his pre-occupation with the spiritual one. He also laid down not to practise compromise with tyranny, whether from state or individual. Unlike the Hindus who chanted Vedic *shalokas* in Sanskrit, the Sikhs were to recite religious hymns composed by the Gurus in their spoken language. He brought about a far-reaching transformation among the people through the institution of *shabad, sangat* and *pangat*. Remembering God, earning of livelihood through honest and hard work, sharing income with the needy, and service of humanity were the cardinal principles of this new religion. He also forbade the use of intoxicants of all kinds. Little wonder then, that this new practical religion caught the imagination of the suppressed masses. With Guru Nanak's and his three successor Gurus' extreme exertions and preachings, it spread far and wide even beyond India. This excited religious jealousy and political suspicion in Emperor Jehangir, who ordered the fifth guru's, Guru Arjun's execution. This martyrdom (1606) changed the course of Indian history. His son and successor, the sixth guru, Guru Hargobind, girded up his loins to face the state onslaught and fought four successful battles against the state forces, thus infusing confidence among the Sikhs that they could themselves challenge the state fanaticism and injustice, religious or cultural. When Mughal Emperor Aurangzeb (1658-1707) resolved to turn Dar-ul-Harb (Hindu India) into Dar-ul-Islam (Muslim State) by force[4], the ninth Sikh guru, Guru Tegh Bahadur, offered himself for martyrdom (1675) to save the Hindu religion, in which he himself did not believe. When this unique sacrifice failed to bring about change in the state policy of forcibly converting Hindus, the tenth guru, Guru Gobind Singh, in keeping with the basic Sikh tenets of fighting oppression, himself fought sixteen battles against state forces and created a class of self-sacrificing saint-soldiers, who during the dark century of Mughal and Afghan onslaughts (1658-1764) struck again and again against the citadel of state fanaticism, until they established a benevolent political hegemony in the areas between the rivers Sindh and Ganges (1765-99). Besides, during this period, these early freedom fighting pioneers inflicted exemplary punishments on all those who had robbed and oppressed the masses during the last century, and also established a benign and righteous regime.

For this purpose, they crossed the river Yamuna seventeen times, thus bringing home to the people in northern India the true essence of Sikh religious principles of fighting and punishing the tyrants. Then appeared on the political scene the legendary Maharaja Ranjit Singh (1799-1839), who with amazing astuteness, established an era of peace, prosperity and dignity much beyond the borders of Punjab as far away as Sind,

Kashmir, Ladakh, Baltistan and Tibet. Donovan Williams, Prof. of South Asian and African History, University of Calgary, Alberta, Canada, records, "There is room for toying with the idea that this great leader (Maharaja Ranjit Singh) was born too late in the history of India to realise his full potential. Who knows what that history would have been if fate had presented him with an earlier opportunity to carve out an empire which conceivably might have delayed the British advance." (Prof. Bikramajit Husrat, *Life and Times of Ranjit Singh*, V.V.R.I. Press, Hoshiarpur, 1977, p. VI). There had been seventy one foreign invasions of India by then, which had bled people white physically, religiously and socially.[5] Sikh domination in the region dispelled the shadow of persistent Afghan menace of rape, loot and arson for all time to come. But, this happy state of affairs could be brought about only after this young nation had sacrificed two hundred thousand of its religiously soaked freedom fighters in defending *dharma* and honour of its people. It was thus, that the Punjab and its people were described as, "The country on the line of invasion — the people — a race nurtured in storm."[6] Prof. Stanley Wolpert, the California University expert on South Asia, describes Sikh power of those days thus : "Maharaja Ranjit Singh's standing army of the pure (Khalsa) numbered nearly a hundred thousand Sikhs, a mighty force forged in the fires of Mughal oppression, tempered with constant conflict with Afghans and welded into a weapon of righteous action by their faith in the scripture left to them by their ten Gurus. Thus by 1820, his kingdom embraced a quarter million square miles of south east Asia's richest and strategically the most significant domain."[7] It was such a Sikh military force which the British had to contend with in extending their power to the north west of India. But before we describe the actual fortunes of Anglo-Sikh wars, we may briefly explain the origin and manner of expansion of the British power *vis-a-vis* the Indian political scene of those days.

INDIA DURING MID-NINETEENTH CENTURY

Nadir Shah's invasion of India in 1739 greatly damaged the already weakened Mughal empire. Thereafter, Abdali's nine further onslaughts (1748-69) crippled what was left of this once magnificent kingdom. Abdali had also humbled the Mahrattas at Panipat in 1761, where one hundred thousand of their soldiers fell. As a result, several local chieftains formed independent principalities throughout India, but accepted one after another the British hegemony between the years 1757-1849, sometimes because of misrule, occasionally through the jealousy of a neighbouring chief, often as a result of British greed for expansion, but always accompanied by shameless treachery and intrigues by the British.

ADVENT OF THE BRITISH IN INDIA

The British under Capt. Hawkins came to India in 1608 as a trading Company. He brought presents of 25,000 gold coins from King James I for Emperor Jehangir and obtained some trade concessions at Surat (Gujarat). In 1639, a site in Madras was granted to another Englishman, Mr. Day, where they built Fort St. George. In 1690, they acquired a swampy area in Bengal, founded Calcutta and built Fort William. In 1757, Clive defeated Siraj-ud-Daula, Nawab of Bengal, with the help of traitor Mir Jafir and after putting him on the throne extracted heavy political and financial price from him. After three years, the British deposed Mir Jafir with the help of his son-in-law Mir Kasim, whom they put on the throne and again received further concessions for the Company and gifts for its employees. Besides, Kasim had undertaken, through a treaty, to pay £ 1,02,000 to the members of Calcutta council alone in addition to five hundred thousand Rupees for the Karnatic wars.[8] When Kasim tried to improve the state administration and check the Company and its servants from illegal private trade, the British went to war with him. Even before Kasim could be worsted in battle, the British again declared Mir Jafir as the future Nawab of Bengal, who again offered free trade to the Company and its servants in addition to other financial advantages and gifts. This pattern of encouraging traitors and of putting one Indian chief against the other, and obtaining political and private benefits, went on unabated till the end of the eighteenth century. Later, Lord Macaulay was to record this disgraceful plunder, "Such parts of India as were under the Company were subjected to a land tax of 50% of the produce and to other requisitions so numerous and severe that two thirds of population fled, while others sold their children to meet the rising rates. Enormous fortunes were rapidly accumulated at Calcutta, while thirty millions of human beings (in Bengal, Bihar and Orissa) were reduced to the last extremity of wretchedness. They had been accustomed to live under tryanny, but not under tryanny like this."[9] With the fall of Shujah-ud-Daula of Oudh in 1764, the Mughal Emperor, Shah Alam II, became a suppliant of the British camp. Under the fiction of grant of 'Diwani' from the Emperor in 1765, the British became a territorial power, and began to play a more active part in the Mysore, the Maharatta and Ruhela wars, always employing the usual tactics of deceit and betrayal along with the force of arms. By the turn of the century, they had virtually replaced the great Mughals, and their political policies thereafter were dictated by their desire for further expansion and consolidation.

BRITISH POLICY TOWARDS SIKHS WHEN THEIR HELP WAS NEEDED

There were rumours of yet another Afghan march on India in 1771, when General Robert of the Company's service wrote to Sardar Jhanda Singh Bhangi and another Sikh Sardar, "That he (Abdali) cannot cross the Attock for fear of the Khalsa Army", adding, "It is clear that as long as the Khalsa army is on the watch, no one can march on Hindustan unopposed."[10] The fear of Afghan invasion in the closing years of the eighteenth century and political designs of Napoleon on India in the beginning of the nineteenth century, drove the British to enter into a treaty of friendship with Ranjit Singh in 1806. Upto 1805, the British had decided to keep their western boundary at river Yamuna. But, with the signing of the Peace Treaty of Tilsit in 1807 between Nepoleon and Russia and their intended march on India, the British decided to extend their boundary to river Sutlej. Accordingly, the British, through prolonged and persistent negotiations, cajoled and even coerced Ranjit Singh into signing the treaty of Amritsar in 1809, fixing river Sutlej as the boundary between the two states. Having once signed the treaty, the Sikhs faithfully observed its terms. J.D.Cunningham records, "To one friendship the Maharaja remained ever constant, from one alliance he never sought to shake himself free. This was the friendly alliance with the British."[11] At times, there were temptations too alluring to be resisted when the British suffered reverses in their campaigns for expansion. Also, there were provocations from the British side of political interference in his affairs which were too great to be tolerated. For instance, in the early stages of the Nepal War (1816-18), the British suffered some military setbacks, when, with the death of British General Gillespie, the myth of their invincibility was broken. During the first Burmese War (1824-26), British soldiers suffered heavily in the jungles of Burma. In 1820, the Bhonsla *raja* of Nagpur appealed to Ranjit Singh for help. Four years later, Nepal government sought his co-operation in a defensive alliance. Next year, the Maharaja of Bharatpur asked for his help, but Ranjit Singh never wavered and remained firm to his plighted word of friendship. On the other hand, the British did not abide by the terms of the treaty of Amritsar. To them, friendship was only a matter of expediency. When engaged in consolidating their power in Hindustan, they kept up the facade of friendship with the Sikhs. But, as soon as they found themselves secure in their possessions and none to oppose their might there, they turned their attention to the north of the Sutlej, nay, even beyond the Indus.

BRITISH HOSTILITY TOWARDS SIKHS

Hari Ram Gupta records, "In the twenties of the nineteenth century, the British Government of India was planning expansion both to the east and the north-west. From their capital at Calcutta, they conquered lower Burma in 1825, and began penetration into China, resulting in the declaration of the Opium War in 1839, and the occupation of Hong Kong in 1842."

"For the extension of the British Empire in the north-west, a second capital was established at Shimla in 1828. In October 1831, Lord William Bentinck, Governor-General of India, met Ranjit Singh at Ropar to obtain first-hand knowledge of Ranjit Singh, his successor and the court, and to deceive the great Maharaja over Sind. The general impression left on his mind was that in a decade or so, the Sikh state after Ranjit Singh would fall into their hands like a ripe mango with a slight stroke. On the very field of the cloth of gold at Ropar, William Bentinck decided to build supremacy over Punjab, Sind, Afghanistan, Turkistan and Khorasan up to the borders of Russia. Punjab was entrusted to Wade with a Hindu spy at Lahore, Sind to Pottinger with Maulvi Azam-ud-din Husain, Kabul to Masson, Munshi Karamat Ali at King Kamran's court at Herat, and Alexander Burnes to study the situation at Bokhara."

He adds, "As planned by Wily Wade, his agents immediately started surveying every inch of the Sikh kingdom up to Gilgit, Kashmir, Ladakh, trans-Indus and Bahawalpur and to win over Muslim masses by portraying the attractive picture of British justice and fairplay."[12] "But in order to cover up the evil design to dismember a friendly kingdom with whom it had a treaty of friendship since 1809, Lord Ellenborough, President of the Board of Control of East India Company, sent a dispatch to Bombay in 1830 enclosing a personal letter of compliment for Maharaja Ranjit Singh together with a batch of horses to be forwarded to Lahore, under the charge of a British officer, as present from the King of England."[13] Yet on his appointment as Governor-General of

India in 1842, Lord Ellenborough while still in England was requesting Duke of Wellington for his opinion as to the general principles upon which a campaign against the Punjab should be conducted.

In 1826, Sayyed Ahmed of Bareilly, a British subject raised standard of *Jehad* in the Pathan area against the Sikh rule. He collected his funds and recruits mainly from the British Indian territory. He even obtained written consent of the British government for his anti-Ranjit Singh struggle. The *Jehad* continued with full vigour for four and a half years and ended only after the defeat and liquidation of the Sayyed and his principal deputy, Ismail, in 1831, when the Punjab heaved a sigh of relief. The British could not interfere in the affairs of Sind, according to the treaty of 1809, being on the north-western side of Sutlej and adjacent to the Sikh province of Multan. Also, as the Sikhs were the natural successors of Abdali's possessions of Punjab, Multan, Peshawar, Derajat and Sind, Ranjit Singh had every right to interfere in the affairs of Sind. But this was not acceptable to the British, who themselves hastily concluded a commercial treaty of navigation with the Emirs of Sind in 1832. It was a mere pretext for its future conquest of this province in 1843. Besides, Ranjit Singh was forestalled from occupying Shikar Pur, which was close to the areas already under his domain. The town of Ferozepur, barely 40 miles from Lahore, was recognized by the British to be in the sovereignty of Ranjit Singh, but the place being of strategic importance was occupied by the British in 1835, on the death of Sardarni Lachhman Kaur and converted into a cantonment. Such intrigues and duplicity had shaken Ranjit Singh's faith in the British. He bluntly expressed his disgust when he told a Christian missionary, the Rev. Dr Joseph Wolff, "You say you travel for the sake of religion; why then do you not preach to the English in Hindustan who have no religion at all." When the missionary tried to divert the subject from politics to religion and enquired, "How may one come nigh unto God." The Maharaja replied with biting sarcasm, "By making an alliance with the British Government as I lately did with the Laard Nawab Sahib (Governor-General) at Ropar."[14]

With the death of Hari Singh Nalwa in the battle of Jamrod, Dost Mohd Khan saw a ray of hope in recovering Peshawar from Ranjit Singh through mediation of the British. But when the latter failed to bring this about inspite of their best efforts, Dost Mohd began to look for greater co-operation with Persia and Russia. The British made this a pretext for removing him and instead putting the refugee Shah Shujah on the throne of Kabul, which they did with the help of Sikhs after signing the Tripartite treaty of 1838 among the British, Maharaja Ranjit Singh and Shah Shujah. But the Afghans were loathe to accept someone brought in the baggage of a foreign power. Thus, resentment against Shah Shujah exploded into violence in various parts of the country. On November 3,1841, an angry mob surrounded the house of the British envoy at Kabul and slaughtered every inmate. General Elphinstone lost his nerve and surrendered to Mohd Akbar, son of fugitive Dost Mohd, with 4,500 troops, including 700 Europeans, and his guns and stores. Leaving at his mercy the old and the sick, women and children, he made an exit from Kabul on 6th Jan.,1842. The Afghans fell on the retreating foreigners. Two days later, only 800 were left alive. Hunger, frost and Afghan bullets accounted for most of the others.   Out of the 16,500 men, almost the sole survivor, Dr Brydon, "fainting from wounds, hunger and exhaustion", arrived at Jallalabad to tell the tale of disaster.[15]

Sir Herbert Edwardes records, "The rash Governor-General who, without even consulting his Council, had been capable of marching a British army into Afghanistan, 400 miles from the British frontier, to dethrone a reigning Prince, and set up an exile, was now paralysed at the first rumour of disaster to his troops, and could with difficulty be brought to move a single regiment to their succour.' He adds, 'The Commander-in-Chief had been against the policy of Cabul war from the beginning and foretold disaster for a war carried on without a base, and seemed incapable of drawing the soldier's sword to succour his subordinates."[16]

There remained hundred and twenty British prisioners in Kabul; a British garrison at Kandhar under General Nott; another at Ghazni under Colonel Palmer; one at Kelat-i-Ghilzai under Captain Craigie, and a fourth at Jalalabad under Robert Sale, but all in desparate need of help.   The Khyber route was the shortest, easiest and safest for a relieving force to take.   Sir George Clerk, the British agent at Ludhiana went to Lahore to request assistance.   Maharaja Sher Singh readily agreed to render this in every possible way.

Sir George Clerk despatched four native regiments under Brigadier Wilde for the relief of Jalalabad and Maharaja Sher Singh sent orders to General Avitabile, Governor of Peshawar, to supply them with a few pieces of artillary and render any other help which they may require.   After obtaining four guns from the Sikhs, Wilde forced his way through the Khyber Pass when his force was ambushed by the Afghans and forced to retire to Jamrud with heavy casulties, Wilde himself being among the injured.   Thus the first attempt to relieve Jalalabad failed in January 1842.   In the meantime another force under General Pollock was proceeding to Peshawar to take part in operations.   Sir Herbert Edwards records, "Lord Auckland's last instructions to Pollock before giving up his disastrous government in February were to "withdraw" the garrison from Jalalabad, and then do what seemed best to "procure the safe return of our troops and people detained beyond the Khyber Pass", whatever that might mean.   Four days after this ambiguous order, Lord Auckland was relieved by Lord Ellenborough, and with him it rested to decide what policy should be pursued; — whether it were worthier, or even safer, for the English in India to put up with defeat, withdraw at once from Afghanistan and leave their captive countrymen to their fate; or to turn the whole resources of the Empire to the retrieval of the national honour, and re-assertion of supremacy in arms.

He adds, "On the 15th of March, Ellenborough pronounced for war.   But the tidings of disaster of Brigadier England at Hykulzye on March 26, in attempting to reinforce General Nott in Kandhar, made him forthwith the hand that a month ago was clenched to 're-establish our military reputation by the infliction of some signal and decisive blow upon the Afghans', now scrawled instructions to Nott to withdraw from Kandhar and to Pollock to withdraw from Jalalabad.   Not a word was said about English captives."

Further, "While the Governor-General was issuing orders to his Generals in Afghanistan to withdraw; Clerk was submitting opinon to the Government that General Pollock was in a position to judge how to act impressively upon the Afghan nation for the recovery of our fame." He adds, "The Sikh Government proposed now to unite with British in setting up a Vizeer at Kabul to represent them both."[17]

This position became possible only after the Sikh Government provided a contingent of 15,000 men against the stipulated 6,000 to take part in the campaign. Also when the stark conspiracy of the British in corrupting Gulab Singh Dogra and Governor Avitabile, who were ordered by their government to help the British, was completed with the offer of Kashmir to the former and the guaranty to aid the latter to retire with his vast property through the British territory.

Thus strengthened by the additional force of ten Sikh regiments under General Avitabile, Pollock left Peshawar on April 5, fighting Afghans throughout the 35 miles long narrow defiles of Khyber Pass reaching Jalalabad on April 15, and relieved the garrison. According to Sir Herbert Edwards, "Great was the relief to every Englishman and woman in the country by Pollock forcing of the Khyber and junction with Sale at Jalalabad, but the political crisis by no means was over. On the contrary, the five long months of April, May, June, July and August 1842 were probably as critical a period as the British Indian Empire ever passed through, except the great Mutiny of 1857, for Pollock had repeatedly declared that he would not stay above the Pass unless his communications could be maintained."[18] The task to keep open the communications to Jalalabad through the treacherous Pass was left to the Sikh contingent engaged in the campaign. "Ellenborough had even decided to hand over the valley of Jalalabad to the Sikhs after British withdrawal from Afghanistan before November 1842."[19]

"The Sikhs were only bound to employ a contingent of 6,000 men, but they did the work with not less than 15,000," wrote Henry Lawrence to J. C. Marshman on April 11,1842.[20] And in the words of Major General Sir Herbert Edwards and Merivale, "If at this moment when one British force had been annihilated at Kabul and two others were beleaguered at Jallalabad and Kandhar, the Sikhs had turned against us, the year 1857 (Mutiny) would have been anticipated in 1842 under circumstances of far greater aggravation."[21] General Pollock commanding this army felt that the support of the Sikh government was indispensable, "Firstly, because we wanted all the soldiers we could bring in the field; and secondly, because it was of vital consequence to show our enemies in Afghanistan that the Sikhs were with us."[22] After successful close of the campaign, when the British flag was replanted at Bala-Hissar Fort in September, 1842 with the active help of the Sikhs, "Lord Ellenborough was also desirous of an interview with Sher Singh and as gratitude was uppermost for the time and added a grace even to success, it was proposed to thank the Maharaja in person for proofs which he had offered of his continued friendship."[23]

THE BRITISH INGRATITUDE

"But, O ingratitude, thy name was the British Government in India. While a Sikh contingent of 15,000 men was fighting their (British) battles in the blood thirsty defiles of Khyber Pass, the British were assembling a third army at Ferozepur to keep the Sikhs in check and act if necessary."[24]   Far worse was the intriguing conduct of some British officers accompanying the Sikh force in this campaign. Sir Herbert Edwards records, "It occurred to Henry Lawrence that a consideration should be offered to the Rajahs Dhian Singh and Gulab Singh for their assistance, they alone in the Punjab being now able to give aid. We need such men as the Rajahs and Avitabile and should bind them to us by the only tie they recognize, self-interest."[25]   This formed the beginning of all future betrayals in the coming Anglo-Sikh wars three years later. Even earlier, when the British Commander-in-Chief Sir Henry Fane came to Lahore in March, 1837 to attend the marriage of Prince Nau Nihal Singh, "He formed an estimate of the force which would be required for the complete subjugation of Punjab and got prepared by his Quarter-Master-General complete maps which formed the ground work of all the maps used, when hostilities did at last break out with the Sikhs."[26]

BRITISH AND DOGRAS PLAN SUBVERSION OF SIKH KINGDOM

"The proposals of Henry Lawrence at Peshawar to entice some Sikh Chiefs and the negotiations of Sir George Clerk at Lahore served a double purpose of the British. They secured active support of the Sikh Government for operations in Afghanistan and bound Gulab Singh and Avitabile to their own political interest in the Punjab. They also drove a wedge between the ruler and his Chiefs. The seeds of division and dismemberment of the Sikh kingdom were thus sown with the Dogras already dreaming of accession of their family to the throne of Lahore. This ultimately led to the murder of Maharaja Sher Singh, his son Partap Singh and Dhian Singh Dogra on the same day (September 15,1843) at the hands of Sandhanwalia Sardars." Sita Ram Kohli records, "Dhian Singh was responsible for a policy whereby the more violent elements in the army, very often Sikhs, were transferred from important military stations to others, where scope for making trouble was slighter, and of recruiting new men, mostly non-Sikhs, from Jammu and the other Punjab hills. Between the months of June, 1841 and February, 1842, some six thousand of these hill men were formed into 8 battalions of infantry and 3 units of light artillery. This, very naturally, aroused suspicion of him, both as disciplinarian and a Dogra."[27] This version is also supported by Dr Ganda Singh. "This has been confirmed by the *Memoirs of Alexander Gardner*, edited by Major Hugh Pears, 1898. Gardner was a confidant of Raja Dhian Singh, who had given him a wife out of his own house. Through her and living always among the Dogras, he knew and had heard a great deal about the intrigues then afoot." According to his Memoirs, pp. 212-13 :

> 'This dream was that Hira Singh, the heir of their family, or at least the most promising of its rising generation, might eventually succeed to the throne of Ranjit Singh. Those to be swept away were the male members of the Maharaja's family, and all those ministers, advisors and chiefs who would not join the Dogra party ...... All these murders were brought about directly or indirectly by the Dogra brothers, Dhian Singh and Gulab Singh, for the eventual aggrandizement of their family in the person of Hira Singh.'[28]

Hari Ram Gupta says, "The perusal of these news-letters (Abstracts of Intelligence from the Punjab, Lahore, December, 1843 — October, 1844, about 300 reports in all) discloses a well-laid-out plot to seize the Sikh Empire on the part of the Jammu Rajahs, in particular by Gulab Singh. During the later years of Ranjit Singh's rule, Dhian Singh had been almost a dictator ...... Was it then too bold an ambition to hope that some day he (Hira Singh) might rule the Punjab as king; with Dhian Singh, his father as Prime Minister and Chief Advisor, with one uncle (Suchet Singh) as Commander-in-Chief and the other, Gulab Singh, ruling all the hill country. Then in firm alliance with the Kabul Amir and the Court of Nepal, the Dogra family might become the most powerful in India, and found a dynasty for itself. Even after assassination of Dhian Singh, Gulab Singh wrote to Hira Singh early in February, 1844, that he should declare himself the Maharaja of Punjab, take Suchet Singh as Prime Minister, Rai Kesri Chand as Commander-in-Chief and appoint Misr Jalla manager of Jasrota and of the town duties of Lahore and Amritsar. He himself desired to be invested with more territories including Kashmir, Peshawar, Multan, Dera Ismail Khan and Hazara. Another reference in these newsletters states that Raja Hira Singh was the king of Punjab."[29]

General Sir Charles Gough records, "It is probable that the Jammu brothers designed to share the rule of the whole of Punjab between them, the plan being that Gulab Singh was to acquire the whole of Jammu, Kashmir and the North East generally; while Dhian Singh rule at Lahore. There was also a third brother, Suchet Singh."[30]

THE REGIMENTAL PANCHAYATS

It is significant to state that after the death of Maharaja Kharak Singh and Nau Nihal Singh in November, 1840, and the dispute for the throne between Sher Singh and Chand Kaur having been resolved, the relation of the army to the state had become wholly altered. By the middle of 1841, according to Cunningham, "It was no longer the willing instrument of an arbitrary and genial government, but it looked upon itself, and was regarded by others, as the representative body of the Sikh people, as the Khalsa itself assembled by tribes for centuries to take its part in public affairs. The efficiency of the Army as a disciplined force was not much impaired, for a higher feeling possessed the men, and increased alacrity and resolution supplied the place of exact training. They were sensible of the advantages of systematic union, and they were proud of their array as the visible body of Gobind's commonwealth. As a rule, the troops were obedient to their appointed officers, so far as concerned their ordinary military duties, but the position of a regiment, of a brigade, of a division, or of the whole army, relative to the executive government of the country, was determined by a committee called Regimental *Panchayat* composed of men selected from each battalion, or each company in consideration of their general character as faithful Sikh soldiers, or from their particular influence in their native villages."[31]

An example of how these Regimental *Panchayats* acted when things went wrong, may be quoted with advantage. During the period Hira Singh was the minister at Lahore (September 1843 — December 1844) with Misr Jalla as his chief advisor, great harassment was caused to princes Pashaura Singh and Kashmira Singh (sons of Maharaja Ranjit Singh) besides many other Darbar dignitaries opposed to the Dogra hegemony.

This roused the Khalsa against the Dogras. Army *Panchayats* held meetings on 21st — 23rd March,1844, when Hira Singh's administration was subjected to a searching examination. They decided, therefore, that unless Hira Singh conceded certain demands, he must be forced to resign. Four representatives of these *Panchayats* appeared before him in the open *Darbar*, claimed that they had come on behalf of the Sarbat Khalsa, and conveyed to him the *hukam*. It said that he must release Jawahar Singh (brother of Maharani Jindan), remove the guard placed on the house of Misr Beli Ram, set free his relations and dependents, raise the siege of Sialkot and Kuryanwala, both garrisons of Princes Pashaura Singh and Kashmira Singh and give an undertaking that the princes will not be ill-treated in future. They also demanded the surrender of Misr Jalla, Sheikh Imam-ud-Din and Lal Singh. "If he hesitated or refused", the delegates added "The order was that Hira Singh himself be seized."[32]

Again, when Maharani Jindan collected a number of articles of gold and silver to give in charity on the first day of new month, as was the custom, Misr Jalla questioned her right for such charitable actions. He is said to have even used abusive language for her. The Maharani thus extremely troubled at heart, appealed to the Khalsa for protection. Besides this, Hira Singh and Misr Jalla's actions had greatly offended the Sikh psyche beyond toleration in more than one way, such as the brutal massacre of the highly venerated Sikh Saint Bhai Bir Singh and his devoted associates in thousands in May, 1844, when the Saint was reciting the holy scripture, which brought matters to a speedy climax. Accordingly, some of the Khalsa regiments moved out of the cantonment to an open space near the fort. Once more, they demanded the surrender of the hated and wily Jalla. This was refused. Instead, according to Sohan Lal Suri, the court chronicler, "In the early hours of December 21,1844, Hira Singh and party loaded with cash and jewellery on elephants stealthily left their residence for Jammu. But hardly had they passed the Taxali Gate, when they were noticed by a company of Sikh soldiers." The news was flashed to the military lines and a body of 6,000 troopers led by Sham Singh Attari went in pursuit. They overtook the fugitives. Hira Singh and his companions put up a fight, but the odds against them were heavy. Among the 1,000 slain were Hira Singh, Jalla, Mian Sohan Singh, son of Gulab Singh Dogra, Mian Labh Singh, responsible for the massacre at Bhai Bir Singh's centre, and many others.[33]

According to Cunningham, "That the Regimental *Panchayats* sincerely aimed at maintaining discipline among the soldiers and protecting national interest is further provided by the fact that as soon as the decision to mobilize against the British was made, they voluntarily stopped functioning by an agreement with the executive head of the state, realizing the necessity of unity of counsel in the affairs of war."[34]

According to Hugh Pears (Memoirs of Alexander Gardner, pp. 265-66) "The resolve of their rulers anyhow and by whatever means to destroy them was known even to the Sikh army itself; but such has been the stern discipline of the *Panches* ...... such the real belief that the intentions of the British were aggressive ...... and such their devotion to their mystic faith that one single dogged determination filled the bosom of each soldier. The word went round, 'We will go to the sacrifice.'" (*Panth Lai Shahidi*)[35]

BRITISH PREPARATIONS FOR THE WAR

Having secured their hold on almost the whole of Hindustan by the late twenties of the nineteenth century and after the death of Maharaja Ranjit Singh in 1839, the British resolved at actual dismemberment of the Sikh Empire. Lord Auckland was recalled after the Kabul massacre and Lord Ellenborough was sent to India as Governor-General in 1842. While still in England, he wrote to the Duke of Wellington on Oct.15,1841, "I am most anxious to have your opinion as to the general principles, upon which a campaign against the Punjab should be conducted."[36] In collusion with the Duke in England, Ellenborough again started the bogey of 'French intrigues' with the Lahore *Darbar* with a view to prejudicing the British public mind against the Sikhs. In this process, they also involved General Ventura of the Sikh service who regularly informed the British of political happenings at Lahore. About this time, the Sandhanwalia Sardars, who on resumption of power by Maharaja Sher Singh had either escaped to the British territory or were put in jail, were called to return to Lahore through the intervention of the British Resident. Their old status and *Jagirs* were restored. After some time, when they killed Sher Singh, his son Partap Singh, and Raja Dhyan Singh, it raised Ellenborough's hopes of the British soon becoming masters of the Punjab. He wrote to Queen Victoria on Oct. 20, 1843, "It is impossible not to perceive that the ultimate tendency of the late events at Lahore is, to bring the plains first and at somewhat later period, the hills under our control."[37] The Governor General was regularly informing the Duke and the Queen through his letters of Sept. 20, and Nov. 20, 1843 and again on July 2, and July 14, 1844, saying that, "There does not seem to be any feeling against us", that, "The Sikh army has remained tranquil and no indication has been given of the least desire to provoke the resentment of the British Government", that, "In the Punjab, there is more of pacific appearance than at any time since the murder of Sher Singh", and that, "There is much less apprehension than there has been at any time since the death of Sher Singh that this tranquillity will be disturbed on the side of Punjab."[38] Yet, the British continued war preparations. Writing to the Secret Committee on February 11, 1844, twenty two months before the actual war, Ellenborough said, "I must confess, that when I look at the whole condition of our army I had rather, if the contest cannot be further postponed, that it were at least postponed to November, 1845."[39] On Feb.15, 1844, he wrote to the Duke, "I earnestly hope that we may not be obliged to cross the Sutlej in December next. We shall not be ready so soon. The army required a great deal of setting up after five years of war. I am quietly doing what I can to strengthen and equip it ...... I know it would be of protracted character. I should be obliged to remain at Lahore myself more than a year."[40] He again wrote to the Duke on April 20, 1844, "We are altogether very ill-provided with officers for the higher commands. The whole army requires a great deal of teaching and I am satisfied the eighteen months I ask are not more than enough to make it what it ought to be."[41] Major Basu in his, *Rise of Christian Power in India*, asks, "Does it not show conclusively the deep scheme of the British in bringing on the war with the Sikhs ?"[42] Ellenborough was so sure of the means he was adopting for creating the war and of the efficiency of his secret agents that he wrote to the Duke, "Depend upon it, I will not engage in such an operation hastily or unnecessarily, and I will do all I can beforehand to secure certain success if ever I should be obliged to undertake it."[43] When in his efforts to capture the Prime Ministership at Lahore from his nephew Hira Singh, Raja Suchet Singh Dogra was killed, the Governor-General informed the Duke on May 9, 1844, "Everything is going on there as we could desire if we looked forward to the ultimate possession of Punjab."[44]

As the Afghan fiasco by Auckland and military preparations for war by Ellenborough had caused the English Company great expenditure and losses, the latter was recalled in 1844. Sir Henry Hardinge was sent to India as Governor-General. He was a great soldier and a veteran of the Peninsular War and had participated in the Battle of Waterloo. His passion for military glory was as great as that of his predecessor. There was not going to be any change of policy with regard to the Punjab war. The appointment of a person as Governor-General, who had been a distinguished soldier, a mature parliamentarian and a statesman, clearly pointed towards future plans for the Punjab. At his farewell banquet at London, the Chairman of the Court of Directors conveyed a similar indication, when he said, "It has always been the desire of the Court that the Government of East India Company should be eminently just, moderate and conciliatory, but the supremacy of our power must be maintained, when necessary, by the force of our arms."[45] On Sir Henry's arrival in India, "He found the attention of Ellenborough had been turned seriously towards the North Western Frontier; that all towns from Delhi to Karnal were filled with troops, that the Commander-in-Chief had already surveyed the whole extent of the Protected States with a view to making choice of military positions, and that the advanced parts of Ludhiana and Ferozepur had been strengthened."[46] (Viscount Hardinge, pp 74-75). During the next sixteen months before the war, Sir Henry constantly added to the forces already assembled at the Punjab frontier and raised them from 17,612 to 40,523 men and from 66 to 94 guns, exclusive of hill stations.[47]

THE BRIDGE OF BOATS

On instructions from the Duke, Ellenborough had got prepared seventy pontoons at Bombay and brought them to Ferozepur for transporting troops and military supplies and the formation of a bridge over the Sutlej to cross into the Punjab 'for an offensive plan.'

MAJOR BROADFOOT

Major Broadfoot, a war monger diplomat and a man of boundless ambition, after serving in the Kabul expedition, was transferred to Burma. He intimately knew about preparations being made for the Punjab war. He, therefore, applied on the basis of feigned ill-health to be brought to the North-Western side, so that his health might be restored. He also added, "I could not recover if the Army were in the field, and I am idler elsewhere."[48] Ellenborough informed him, "If there should be, at any future time, a prospect of our having more important operations, I will, if possible, have you with me."[49] Consequently, Sir Henry, who himself wanted a warlike diplomat at Ludhiana, appointed him resident to the Lahore *Darbar*. His arrival added fresh vigour and speed to the war preparations already at an advanced stage. To provoke hostilities, one of his first acts was to declare the Cis-Sutlej possessions of Sikhs as under the British protection. According to Cunningham, "It was generally held by the English in India that Major Broadfoot's appointment greatly increased the probabilities of war with the Sikhs; and the impression was equally strong that had Mr. Clerk, for instance, remained as Agent, there would have been no war. Had Mr. Clerk again or Col. Wade been the British representative in 1845, either would have gone to Lahore in person and would have remonstrated against the selfish and unscrupulous proceedings of the managers of affairs as obviously tending to bring upon a rupture. They would have also taken measures to show to the troops that the British Government would not be aggressors; they would have told the chiefs that a war would compromise them with the English, nor would they have come away until every personal risk had been run, and every exertion used to avert resort to arms."[50] George Campbell records, "Several accounts agree that in the period immediately preceding the war when matters were becoming very serious and the Sikh army had, for the most part, taken affairs into their own hands, they maintained for a while wonderful order at Lahore and through their *Panches* exercised an almost puritanical discipline in the military republic ...... The immediate collision however was, I think, hastened by imprudence on the part of British Frontier Agent Major Broadfoot. I knew of some things done by him which it would be difficult to defend. But he paid the penalty by his death in the actions which followed."[51]

ARMY PANCHAYATS AND PUNJAB CHIEFS

The Sikh Army, and the population generally, were convinced that war was inevitable. When moved as much by jealousy of one another as by a common dread of the army, the Chiefs of the Punjab had clung to wealth and ease rather than honour and independence. Gulab Singh Dogra, Lal Singh, Tej Singh and many others all felt incapable to control the troops. They considered their only chance of retaining power was through a contest with the British which they believed would end in their dispersion, and pave the way for their own recognition as ministers more surely than if they did their duty by the state. According to Cunningham, "Had the shrewd Army *Panchayats* observed no military preparations on the part of the English, they would not have heeded the insidious exhortations of such mercenary men as Lal Singh and Tej Singh, although in former days, they would have marched uninquiringly towards Delhi at the bidding of their great Maharaja."[52] Even a *gurmata* was passed by the *Panchayats* on Sept. 21,1845, saying, 'They wanted peace rather than conflict' with the British, adding, 'If the English forces advanced towards Ludhiana and Ferozepur from the east, only then they will proceed towards Sutlej.'[53] This information was conveyed to his Government by Maj. Broadfoot vide his letter of September 26, 1845. Maharani Jindan was also not in favour of war. "But, the advice of the Rani and many of the Sardars was disregarded"[54], says Dr M'Gregor in his *History of the Sikhs*, (ii. 39).

According to Lahore court historian, Sohan Lal Suri, "On the report of Rai Kishan Chand, the Court Vaikil, that the British intend to occupy the Cis-Sutlej territories of the *Darbar*, lot of excitement was created."[55] The anti-British party proposed military action, but the Maharani cautioned the courtiers against such a step saying that, "In the event of clash with the British, the Govt. of Maharaja Dalip Singh was likely to suffer, Diwan Dina Nath and Faqir Aziz-ud-Din supporting her views."[56]

According to Lt. Col. R.G. Burton, "while the Army declared they desired peace, there was a strong party backed by traitors who urged them to war and the Army men would assemble in groups in their camps and cantonments and meet round the tomb of Ranjit Singh to talk of the battle in prospect and to swear fidelity to the Khalsa."[57]

THE BRITISH WITHOUT A PLEA FOR WAR

Although British preparations for war were complete, yet in the absence of any provocation from the Sikhs and also in view of their *gurmata* for peace, the English were unable to find an excuse for war. Sir Henry Hardinge wrote to Ellenborough on January 23, 1845, "If the hills and plains weaken each other, on what plea could we attack the Punjab ? How are we to justify the seizure of our friend's territory, who in our adversity assisted us to retrieve our affairs."[58] A month and a half before the war, Hardinge again wrote to Ellenborough on October 23, "We must bear in mind that as yet no cause for war has been given."[59] Even five days after the declaration of war by the British, Hardinge was not convinced of its moral justification. Robert Cust wrote on December 18, "I rode behind the Governor-General. He remarked : Will the people of England consider this (crossing the Sutlej by the Sikhs) an actual invasion of our frontier and a justification of war ?"[60] But peace was not the policy of the British at this stage. Time fixed by Ellenborough and confirmed by Hardinge was coming to a close. The Commander-in-Chief Lord Gough had already arrived near the border and fixed his headquarters at Ambala. Gulab Singh Dogra had fulfilled his promise to 'Divide the Lahore Govt., the army and the people.' The Sikhs had been sufficiently provoked and irritated. The only thing that remained to be done to start the war was to give the Sikhs the final provocation by marching troops towards the Sikh frontier, so that they might as well march and cross the Sutlej to protect their territories to the south east of the river. This, the British did on December 6, 1845, when the Commander-in-Chief Lord Gough marched with his troops from Ambala towards the Sikh frontier. The Sikhs patiently watched the situation for a week. It was only on December 12 that the first Sikh detachment crossed the Sutlej and encamped in their own territory. The passage of their artillery was not completed till December 16. Inspite of the fact that the Sikhs were camping in their own area across the river, and had violated no provision of any treaty or committed any aggression against the British, yet the Governor-General issued his proclamation on December 13, declaring war on the Sikhs, and confiscating and annexing to the British territories the Sikh possessions on the left bank of the Sutlej.[61]

FIRST SIKH WAR

We may now briefly tell the tale of the battles fought during the first Sikh War and the part played by the traitors Gulab Singh Dogra, Misr Tej Singh, Misr Lal Singh and their henchmen. "Their services had been secured beforehand by the British. The former had been assured the provinces of Jammu and Kashmir and the latter, both mercenaries from Uttar Pradesh and Rohtas, had been guaranteed their offices of Commander-in-Chief and Prime Minister respectively."[62]

THE BATTLE OF MUDKI

Lal Singh was unwilling to cross Sutlej, but when forced by his zealous soldiery to do so, he wrote to Capt. Nicholson, Assistant to Maj. Broadfoot at Ferozepur, "I have crossed the river with the Sikh Army. You know my friendship for the British. Tell me what to do." Nicholson replied, "Do not attack Ferozepur. Halt as many days as you can. And then march towards the Governor-General."[63] About this incident, Cunningham says, "The object, indeed of Lal Singh and Tej Singh was not to compromise themselves with the English by destroying an isolated division at Ferozepur, but to get their own troops dispersed by the converging forces of their opponents."[64] John Ludlow says, "Had he attacked, our garrison of 8,000 men at Ferozepur would have been destroyed and the victorious 60,000 would have fallen on Sir Henry Hardinge, who had then but 8,000. So utterly unprepared were we, that even this treachery of one of our enemies scarcely sufficed to save us."[65]

According to Col. Mouton of the Sikh Service, "Lal Singh robbed the ardour of the Sikhs a great deal by assuring them of the defection of 4 Indian battalions in the English army which would surely join them."[66]

About the general temperament of the Sikh soldiers, Cunningham writes; "Every Sikh considered the cause as his own, and he would work as a labourer as well as carry a musket; he would drag guns, drive bullocks, lead camels, load and unload boats with a cheerful alacrity, which contrasted strongly with the inept and sluggish obedience of mere mercenaries, drilled indeed, and fed with skill and care, but unwarmed by one generous feeling for their country and their foreign employers."[67]

Lal Singh's force comprised of 18,000 infantry, 16,000 cavalry and 85 guns. Leaving about 7,000 men with 20 guns to watch over Ferozepur, he moved towards Mudki on the afternoon of December 17, 1845. During their march, whether by design or by accident, the troops lost their way. After a whole night's wandering, they arrived not at Mudki but at Ferozeshah in the morning. It was here that he got the message that the Governor-General had reached Mudki. Lal Singh moved from Ferozeshah with only half the force with him on the false plea that Tej Singh might require the remainder. Under such circumstances of intrigue and treachery, began the battle of Mudki on the afternoon of December 18, 1845.

Cunningham describes the battle, "Lal Singh headed the attack, but in accordance with the original design, he involved his followers in an engagement, and left them to fight as their undirected valour might prompt."[68] The battle lasted less than two hours, during which, in the words of Lord Gough, "The Sikhs fought as if they had everything at stake."[69] Considering the brevity of the action, the British losses were deemed heavy, General Sir Robert Sale and Sir Joseph Macgaskill and two aides of the Governor-General being amongst the 215 killed. On close of the battle, the Sikhs withdrew to Ferozeshah by midnight.

BATTLE OF FEROZESHAH

There was no movement of troops on 19th and 20th, although the adversar remained at a very close range of each other. The Sikhs used this respite to their best ability by throwing up earthwork without guidance from senior officers or expert technicians. Lal Singh conveyed this position to the British through emissary Shams-ud-Din. The Governor-General ordered Sir Littler to bring assistance from Ferozepur. He also sent his available transport at Mudki to bring the European hilly troops already on the march to the scene of battle. Relinquishing his senior civil status as Governor-General, he decided to take part in the battle as Second-in-Command to Lord Gough. In view of what he saw of the fighting spirit of the Sikhs at Mudki, he overruled Gough and ordered that the attack be deferred till Littler's force from Ferozepur joined the main army. On the other hand, Tej Singh with a force of ten thousand under him remained idle in the neighbourhood of the battlefield absurdly pretending that he was guarding Ferozepur although Littler's force had left the place in broad daylight.

Lord Gough opened the attack at 3:30 P.M. on December 21. He himself led the right, the Governor-General the centre and Sir Littler the left wing of the assailing force. As the British forces came in sight, the Sikh gunners opened fire. Such were the quick volleys of this fire that within ten minutes two hundred British soldiers were either killed or crippled and Sir Littler retired with his force. General Harry Smith who tried to take a Sikh position, was also repulsed. Sir Walter Gilbert and General Wallace showed tremendous daring with some success, losing 270 men in the exploit. The British now found themselves in a grave position. Half their force under Littler and Harry Smith was outside the Sikh entrenchments, but the other half within, unable to advance. Cunningham, who was present in the battle gives a graphic description of the battle scene, "Darkness and the obstinacy of the contest threw the English in confusion; men of all regiments and arms were mixed together; Generals were doubtful of the fact or of the extent of their own success and Colonels knew not what had become of the regiments they commanded or of the army of which they formed a part."[70]

He adds, "On that memorable night, the English were hardly masters of the ground on which they stood; they had no reserves at hand, while the enemy had fallen back upon a second army, and could renew the fight with increased numbers. The not imprudent thought occurred of retiring upon Ferozepur. On the morning of December 22, the last remnants of the Sikhs were driven from their camp; but as the day advanced, the second wing of their army approached in battle array, and the wearied and famished English saw before them a desperate, and perhaps a useless struggle. This reserve was commanded by Tej Singh, who had been urged by his sincere soldiery to fall upon the English at daybreak, but his object was to have the dreaded army of the Khalsa overcome and dispersed, and he delayed until Lal Singh's force was everywhere put to flight, and until his opponents had again ranged themselves around their colours. Even at the last moment, he rather skirmished and made feints than led his men to a resolute attack, and after a time, he precipitately fled, leaving his subordinates without orders and without an object, at a moment when the artillery ammunition of the English had failed, when a portion of their force was retiring upon Ferozepur, and when no exertions could have prevented the remainder from retreating likewise, if the Sikhs had boldly pressed forward."[71]

Lal Singh had spent the day hidden in a ditch and at night stole away to Amritsar.

Col. G. B. Malleson writes, "Then among many panic set in. The cry of 'India lost' was heard from one Commanding Officer who tried in vain to rally his men. The left attack on the Khalsa had failed so signally that it could not be renewed. The Sikh army had repulsed the British attack. They had driven back Littler, forced Smith to retire, compelled even Gilbert to evacuate the position he had gained, and had thrown the whole British army into disorder. What was more, they had still 10,000 men under Tej Singh. Had a guiding mind directed the movements of the Sikh army, nothing could have saved the exhausted British."[72]

Sir Robert Cust records in his diary, "December 22. News came from the Governor-General that our attack of yesterday had failed, that affairs were desperate, that all state papers were to be destroyed, and that if the morning attack failed, all would be over; this was kept secret by Mr. Currie and we were concerting measures to make an unconditional surrender to save the wounded, the part of the news that grieved me the most."[73]

General Sir Hope Grant, who fought in the Anglo-Sikh wars says; "Sir Henry Hardinge thought it was all up, and gave his sword, a present from the Duke of Wellington and which once belonged to Napoleon, and his Star of the Bath to his son, with directions to proceed to Ferozepur, remarking that, 'If the day were lost, he must fall."[74]

William Edwards writes, "Had the Sikhs advanced during the night, the result must have been very disastrous to us, as our European regiments were much reduced in number and our ammunition both for artillery and small arms almost expended."[75]

Cunningham records, "As regards Tej Singh's treachery, it may be stated that according to a reliable tradition, that officer discovered early in the operations that his artillery ammunition had been tampered with and much of it rendered useless. Such treachery on the part of his own side doubtless had considerable effect on his subsequent conduct."[76]

William Edwards, Under Secretary to the British Govt., who followed the Governor-General in the thick of these battles, mentions having been told by Lord Hardinge, "That the fire of Sikh artillery was even more terrible than at Albuera, for the Sikhs had guns in position of treble the calibre ever used in European warfare."[77]

GULAB SINGH DOGRA'S TREACHEROUS NEGOTIATIONS WITH THE BRITISH

According to Ahluwalia and Kirpal Singh, "More dangerous than the treachery of Tej Singh and Lal Singh in the battlefield, were the political intrigues of Gulab Singh Dogra, who was then conducting negotiations with the Governor-General. As the plenipotentiary of the Lahore Darbar, Gulab Singh did not hesitate to sell his country. He had already agreed to the following conditions dictated by the British, (i) that the Sikh Army should be attacked by the British, (ii) that after being defeated, it should be abandoned by its own Government, and (iii) that the passage of the Sutlej should be unopposed and the road to the capital laid open to the victor."[78]

Luckily for the Sikhs, the main hitch still remained : the dispersal of the Sikh

Army. Gulab Singh had shown his inability to accomplish this, and had left it entirely to the British, whose immediate aim was to drive the Sikhs across the Sutlej and secure the unconditional submission of the chiefs and delegates of the army. But a single defeat could not completely disperse so large and well-equipped an army of the brave Khalsa.

SHAM SINGH ATTARI ARRIVES ON THE SCENE

Sardar Sham Singh Attari was in Ludhiana District when the hostilities began. As soon as the Sikh forces crossed the Sutlej, he returned to his village Attari. When the news of the defeat reached Maharani Jindan, she dispatched ten horsemen to the Sardar with an urgent message. The Attari Chief hurried to the scene of battle to find the shameful part played by the traitors in the hope of being upheld as Ministers of a dependent kingdom. When he fully apprised himself of the situation, he hesitated for a while to take command. But in view of the delicate political situation then existing, he decided to follow the course which the legendary Maharaja had taught them to take when honour and duty to their faith and country were involved. Accordingly, he declared his resolve to resist the British and stop them from occupying the Punjab.

The Sikhs dejected at their defeat at Ferozeshah again took heart and were inspired anew by his noble example. Cunningham again describes the scene, "The dangers which threatened the Sikh people pressed upon their mind and they saw no escape from foreign subjection. The grey bearded chief, Sham Singh of Attari, made known his resolution to die in the first conflict with the enemies of his race and so to offer himself as a sacrifice of propitiation to the spirit of Gobind and to the genius of his mystic Commonwealth."[79]

BATTLE OF SABRAON

By the close of the first week of February, 1846, the Sikh Army had constructed formidable entrenchments about two and a half miles long on the left bank of the Sutlej near Sabraon. Their batteries were placed about six feet high protected by deep trenches. These defensive works were connected with the right bank by a bridge of boats. Some twenty to twenty five thousand men and seventy guns were placed behind these entrenchments. Nevertheless, the traitors were determined once again to see the Khalsa Army beaten. Lal Singh was again re-imposed on the Army. Two days before the battle, Lal Singh again sent Shams-ud-Din to Major Lawrence with details of its defensive plan. The weakest point in the Sikh line was its right flank where the loose sand made it impossible to build high parapets for heavy guns. It was to be protected by the *ghorcharas* and light camel guns which only fired balls one or two pounds in weight; moreover, the command of this wing was reserved by Lal Singh for himself. On the basis of this intelligence, Cunningham writes, "it was arranged that the whole of the heavy ordnance should be planted in masses opposite particular points of the enemy entrenchments, and that when the Sikhs had been shaken by a continuous storm of shot and shell, the right or weakest point of their position should be assaulted in line by the strongest of the three investing divisions, which together mustered nearly fifteen thousand men."[80] Sir Robert Dick's Division was ordered to commence the attack on the right flank with Sir Walter Gilbert's Division in immediate support on the right. Sir Harry Smith's Division was to be close to Gilbert's right to support him.

Sardar Sham Singh, knowing that 10th February was going to be the day of battle, rose early in the morning, dressed himself in white, and mounting his white mare proceeded to address the Sikh Army. He reminded the assembled Khalsa about their glorious traditions of bravery and sacrifices in the past and begged them, as true sons of the soil, to die rather than turn their backs on the enemy. Since he had himself dedicated his life to the sacred cause, his words had the desired effect.

Dick's Division advanced according to plan and found the defenses weak and easily surmountable, as Lal Singh's emissaries had reported. The 10th Queen's Regiment broke through totally unopposed, but when the entire division had penetrated some way, it was suddenly fallen upon by the Sikhs and driven back. Sir Robert Dick was himself mortally wounded. "Rally those men", the Governor-General shouted.[81] Colonel Wood, his Aide-de-Camp, galloped to the centre of the line and seizing the colours from the hands of an ensign carried them to the front. In a moment, the wavering British troops had rallied and stormed the breastworks simultaneously with the Brigade of Gilbert's Division, who had also experienced a similar check, but had soon recovered their lost ground. Now both Gilbert's and Dick's Divisions engaged in what may be called the deadliest hand-to-hand encounter with the Sikh infantry.

During the first British attack, Sardar Sham Singh had been present almost everywhere. He did not allow his men to lose heart, as he moved from column to column urging the men to fight on. His action stirred the Sikhs to greater efforts and the British were eventually repulsed. William Edwards, who was present during the attack, has described the scene most graphically. "Gilbert's troops immediately advanced, but finding the centre of the works from their height perfectly impregnable, were driven back with very heavy loss. Sir Harry Smith's Division, instead of being near the right of Gilbert, was on the extreme left of the Sikh position. It also advanced on the works in front, and was driven back with great loss."[82]

For some time, the issue of the battle of Sabraon was hanging in the balance as the conflict raged fiercely. Cunningham describes the contest, "The round shot exploded tumbrils or dashed heaps of sand into the air; the hollow shells cast their fatal contents fully before them, and the devious rocket sprang aloft with fury to fall hissing amid a flood of men but all was in vain; the Sikhs stood unappalled and flash for flash returned and fire for fire."[83] According to Kapur Singh, "The ill-equipped, ill-fed and ingloriously betrayed Sikh soldiers fought the enemy with such bravery and ferocity that the enemy had to make hurried special contacts with Generals Lal Singh and Tej Singh to save the situation for them, who readily obliged by retreating with munitions, guns and the battalions of Dogra and Gorkha soldiers across the Sutlej, from where they trained a formidable battery of guns at the back of the fighting Sikh Army, after destroying the boat bridge on the river. Thus, the sure defeat of the enemy was again converted into years of occupation of Lahore by the British and consolidation of their hold on the country."[84]

Hesketh Pearson says, "A British defeat was again turned into a victory by the convenient flight of Tej Singh, who damaged the bridge of boats over the Sutlej on his way, and so helped to drown a large number of his countrymen."[85]

Lord Gough described Sabraon as the Waterloo of India. Writing to Sir Robert Peel, the British Prime Minister, he paid glowing tribute to the Sikhs. "Policy precluded me publicly recording my sentiments on the splendid gallantry of our fallen foe, or to record the acts of heroism displayed, not only individually, but almost collectively by the Sikh *sardars* and the army, and I declare, were it not from a deep conviction that my country's good required the sacrifice, I could have wept to have witnessed the fearful slaughter of so devoted a body of men." Lord Gough then told the whole truth when he added, "Certain it is that there would have been a different story to tell if the body of men had not been commanded by traitors."[86]

Out of the once 54 European officers in the Khalsa army, only two, namely Col. Mouton and Col. Harbon took part in the First Anglo-Sikh War. Col. Mouton, a Commander of Regular Cavalry and a French officer, published a report in Paris in 1846, which *inter-alia*, records, "Very little was needed to conquer the British, at least in the north of India. The English were almost conquered. If the outcome of these first encounters were favourable, then three kingdoms, an infinite number of Rajas and Musalmans of Kabul, numbering about a hundred thousand men more would have come out of the Punjab to their succour. Without treason a campaign of one month would have lead us to Delhi. Shame, therefore, to all those who enriched by the great Maharaja or his successors, preferred dishonour and the breaking up of the kingdom to a glorious war and the sharing of its perils."[87]

The self-sacrifice of Sardar Sham Singh, the hero of Sabraon, had an inspiring effect. According to Cunningham, "No Sikh offered to submit and no disciple of Govind asked for quarter. They everywhere showed a front to the victor and stalked slowly and sullenly away, while many rushed singly forth to meet assured death by contending with a multitude." According to Lord Hardinge who was present in the battle, "Few escaped; none, it may be said, surrendered. The Sikhs met their fate with the resignation which distinguishes their race."[88]

Sardar Sham Singh's courage and determination had turned Sabraon into the Waterloo of India, as according to Malleson, 'Victory for the Sikhs would have meant to the English the loss of India.'[89] The Sardar's devotion to his country's cause was unique in an era of betrayals, and his fidelity and self-sacrifice shone like a beacon amidst the treachery and selfishness of his contemporaries who sold their country to the foreigners. Indeed Sardar Sham Singh proved himself a prince among patriots and martyrs.

According to the secret understanding with the Governor-General, no opposition was offered to the British troops who arrived at Lahore on 20-2-1846. Two days later, a portion of the fort was garrisoned by the British Regiments.

SETTING UP A PLIANT GOVERNMENT AT LAHORE

According to Sita Ram Kohli, "Lord Hardinge now addressed himself to the task of setting up a pliant government at Lahore. The Khalsa were made to vacate the citadel and its immediate vicinity. These were occupied by British and the Muhammedan battalions in the service of the *Darbar*. Sikh troops were ordered to move across the river

Ravi and camp at Shahadara, and no Sikh soldier was to enter the city without a permit"[90], for the Governor-General knew them as, "The finest soldiers in Asia, bold and daring Republicans," as he wrote in a private letter dated March 19, 1846 to Ellenborough in England. (Hardinge Family Papers, Penhurst, Kent, England.)[91]

Sita Ram Kohli adds, "The Sikh soldiers who had fought so valiantly, posed a major problem. About 20,000 of them though vanquished were not without fight. Some were encamped at Raiwind, half-way between Lahore and Ferozepur; a few thousand near Amritsar. In addition, there were strong garrisons at Peshawar, Multan and various points in the kingdom. On the other hand, British troops had suffered considerably in the campaign; for instance, besides every member of Lord Hardinge's personal staff having been either killed or severely wounded during the war, the Governor-General himself, as a result of a fall from a horse, was almost a cripple during the battle of Sabraon. He came to the field in a carriage and mounted his horse only when guns opened fire."[92] The season was advancing into summer. The British-Indian treasury was depleted. The idea of an immediate annexation of the Punjab had, therefore, to be deferred. But Lord Hardinge was determined to make the state so weak that its eventual absorption into the British empire would present no major problem. He wrote to the Secret Committee : "A diminution of strength of such a war-like nation on our weakest frontier seems to me imperatively required. I have, therefore, determined to take a strong and fertile district between the Sutlej and Beas. This will cover Ludhiana, and will bring us within a few miles of Amritsar, with our backs to the hills. In a military sense; it will be very important it will weaken the Sikhs and punish them in the eyes of Asia. I shall demand one million and a half in money as compensation, and if I can arrange to make Gulab Singh and the hill tribes independent, including Kashmere, I shall have weakened the war-like republic. Its army must be disbanded and reorganized. The numbers of the artillery must be limited. The Maharaja himself must present the keys of Gobindgarh and Lahore, where the terms must be dictated and signed."[93]

THE TREATY OF LAHORE MARCH 9, 1846

On March 9, 1846, was signed the treaty of Lahore imposed by the British upon the young Maharaja Duleep Singh, aged seven and a half years. By this treaty, among other things,

(a) *the British Government took possession of all the territories of the Lahore Government lying to the south of Sutlej and of the Doab, hill and plain situated between the rivers Sutlej and the Beas, and :*

(b) *also the territories of Jammu and Kashmir between the Beas and the Indus to be alienated to Gulab Singh as a sovereign ruler in lieu of his services to the British Government, and :*

(c) *the British Government will not exercise any interference in the internal administration of the Lahore State, but in all cases or questions which may be referred to the British Government, the Governor-General will give the aid of his advice and good offices for the furtherance of the interests of the Lahore Government.*

On the third day, March 11, another Agreement was dictated to the Lahore *Darbar*, whereby, in addition to other terms,

(a)   *British force was to be stationed at Lahore, which force shall not be detained at Lahore beyond the expiration of the current year(1846);*

(b)   *the British Government had the choice to retain any part of the State property in addition to what had been confiscated paying for it at a fair valuation.*

In addition to Maharaja Duleep Singh, who was only a helpless child of seven and a half years, both of these treaties were signed by seven chiefs. The first of them, Bhai Ram Singh (real brother of traitor Tej Singh's father) had been an agent of Gulab Singh Dogra in his treacherous negotiations with the British. The next two were the notorious Lal Singh and Tej Singh, whom the British had recognised as the chief men of the State. The other four were associated with them to keep up the appearance of the representative character of the signatories. "These ready instruments of our policy and the betrayers of their country", wrote Sir Claud Wade, "were not representing the nation", yet it suited the British authorities to place them in privileged positions.

About this, Cunningham says : "The transaction scarcely seems worthy of the British name and greatness, and the objections became stronger when it is considered that Gulab Singh had agreed to pay sixty-eight *lakhs* of Rupees as a fine to his paramount ruler before the war broke out, and that the custom of the East as well as of the West requires the feudatory to aid his lord in foreign wars and domestic strife. Gulab Singh ought thus to have paid the deficient million of money as a Lahore subject instead of being put in possession of the Lahore provinces as an independent prince."[94]

Lal Singh, as a reward for his services was raised to his old office of Prime Ministership, while Tej Singh in a formal *Darbar* was raised to the status of a Raja.

Thus we have seen the circumstances under which the Sikhs were forced to cross the boundary river Sutlej, and were repulsed through sheer intrigue and treachery of its own so-called leaders, Lal Singh and Tej Singh, as also Gulab Singh Dogra who was then empowered by the *Darbar* to negotiate a treaty of peace with the British.

INSTALLATION OF REGENCY

We may now examine the installation of the Regency. According to Article I of the Agreement of March 11, 1846, the British troops were not to be retained in the Punjab beyond the end of December, 1846. The Lahore *Darbar* had, therefore, begun to initiate measures for the administration of the country after the departure of the British. But the latter, on the other hand, wished to stay on in the Punjab with a strong force and to hold it in a tight grip with unlimited powers given to a Resident representative of the Governor-General. To this, the Lahore *Darbar* was not willing to agree, still less to request the British Government for it, as desired by Sir Henry Hardinge.

Sir Henry Hardinge wrote to Frederick Currie, his Secretary, on December 10, 1846, "The coyness of the *Darbar* and the *Sardars* is very natural, but it is very important that the proposal should originate with them, and in any document proceeding from them, this admission must be stated in clear and unqualified terms, our reluctance to undertake a heavy responsibility must be set forth."[95]

But as the *Darbar* could not be easily brought round to make the desired request, the Governor-General wrote to his Secretary again on December 12, to, "persevere in your line of making the Sikh *Darbar* propose the condition or rather their readiness to assent to any conditions imposed as the price of the continuance of our support. In the preamble of the supplementary Articles, this solicitation must clearly be their act."[96]

The Governor-General wrote to Currie on 7-12-1846, "In any agreement made for continuing the occupation of Lahore, Maharani's deprivation of power is an indispensable condition."[97] He again wrote on the 10th, "If the *Sardars* and influential Chiefs, and especially the Attariwala family, urge the British Government to be the guardian of the Maharaja during his minority, the Rani's power will cease silently and quietly, the admission being recorded that the British Government as the guardian of the boy and administering the affairs of the state, is to exercise all the functions and possess all the powers of the Regent acting on behalf of the Prince"[98]

Henry and John Lawrence were assiduous in implementing Hardinge's policy. On the one hand, they sought to exacerbate a feeling of helplessness that prevailed in the Lahore *Darbar*, and emphasised the fact that the time agreed upon for the withdrawal of British troops was at hand; on the other, they set themselves to foster in the minds of the individual *Sardars* hopes of obtaining favour with the British if they remained loyal. They were given to understand that in their doing so, lay the only chance of retaining their estates and privileges. This would serve in the words of Lord Hardinge, "as a powerful stimulus to ensure their adhesion to the conditions imposed." As indeed it turned out to be.

The Rani's goodwill was not so easily to be gained. As soon as the Governor-General's proposals came up for consideration in the *Darbar* (December 9), she made a counter-proposal, that she be formally recognised as head of the government and be lent by the British two regiments of infantry, one of cavalry and a battery of artillery. This was not acceptable to the British, nor did they encourage the *Sardars* to fall in with it .[99]

In December, 1846, Lord Hardinge was encamped at Bharowal, a few marches from Lahore, and there planned an elaborate charade to stimulate the *Darbar* into decision. He began to send instructions to Currie on December 12 with a view to creating an impression of military arrangements afoot. He wrote, "I send this by express to desire that the Regiment of Native infantry, the 2 guns and the Irregular Cavalry, escorting Lal Singh may not return to Lahore ...... these troops will cross the Sutlej and encamp at Ferozepore till further orders, and the troops ordered from Ferozepore to Kasoor will be countermanded ...... my object is to give the Lahore *Darbar* a hint that the garrison is on the move ...... it also authorizes you to send another regiment of native infantry from Lahore to Ferozepore, there to encamp till further orders and not to be relieved by any other regiment from Ferozepore ...... H.M. 80th Regiment will receive orders to march to Meerut at any moment. H.M. 10th at Ferozepore are ready to relieve them, but will not move till ordered, nor will it transpire that they are intended to relieve the 80th. These announcements will be made to accelerate the *Darbar's* decision."[100]

Two days later, he wrote, "This day (14 December) and tomorrow will enable you to form a pretty accurate judgement of the progress you are likely to make. I authorize you to desire Sir John Littler (in command of the British garrison at Lahore) to move all the troops out of Lahore by the end of a week, on the day you may judge to be the most expedient, encamping them as near as may be convenient, to the citadel. If this hint should be unnecessary by the temper of the chiefs to assent to our views, it will not be made."[101]

Lord Hardinge's stratagem was effective. The *Sardars* sent messages to Lawrence pledging their support to the Governor-General's scheme. Henry Lawrence, keeping in view the Rani's counter-proposal, wished matters to be arranged in a constitutional manner. An assembly of people, with more than fifty *Sardars* among them, was to decide the future administrative set-up of the state during the minority of the ruler. This meeting was held in Henry Lawrence's tent on 15th December, and "was more fully attended than any state meeting I have yet seen at Lahore; the momentous importance of the occasion to the Khalsa having, in addition to the Ministers and principal *Sardars*, drawn many petty chiefs, officers, and yeomen to the spot. An Akali, in the full costume of his order, with high blue turban, wreathed with steel quoits and crescents, was quite a new figure in this deliberative assembly, and showed that all ranks took an interest in the business of the day."[101] Sir Frederick Currie had been Foreign Secretary to Government of India for six years from 1842 to 1847, during which period a number of independent states had been annexed to the British dominions in India and had thus become an expert in manipulating circumstances to serve as a pretext for hostilities and ultimate annexation. He then explained to the members of the *impromptu* constituent assembly, clause by clause, the terms on which the Governor-General would consent to keep the British troops in the Punjab, and at the same time, place at their service, a senior British officer to advise in matters of administration. They were then left to discuss the matter among themselves, while Currie and Lawrence went to another tent. After a while, a deputation of six *Sardars* arrived, asking by way of change in the Governor-General's proposal, only that the amount required in return for the loan of British troops, Rs. 2,600,000, be reduced. After an amicable talk, this was done and the sum fixed at Rs. 2,200,000. Currie then sent an express letter to the Governor-General at Bharowal, informing him that agreement had been reached, to which the reply was immediate and most gracious : "The result deserves my most unqualified approbation, and I shall be happy to record another instance of the approved ability, zeal, temper and judgement you have shown, aided by the local experience, reputation and well-established influence of Lieutenant Colonel Lawrence. It is quite impossible to have brought this affair to a more satisfactory conclusion. Your intimate knowledge of my sentiments and the concurrence of our views in Punjab politics have enabled you, most successfully, to realise all the objects I had in view, not only in the substance of the arrangements made, but in the form of the proceedings, for, you have conducted this matter so judiciously that the truth and sincerity of our policy cannot be brought into doubt, or the honour of the British Government suffer any impeachment."[103]

"The moral effect of the Sikh chiefs entreating the British Government to become the guardian of the prince, by the continuance of a British garrison at Lahore, and our consent to undertake the responsible charge, must be felt throughout Asia in raising the reputation and extending the influence of the British character."[104]

"Personally I may regret that it has not been my fate to plant a British standard on the banks of the Indus. I have taken the less ambitious course, and I am consoled by the reflection that I have acted right for the interests of England and India."[105]

Thus was the treaty of Bharowal manoeuvered on 16.12.1846, again through intrigue, in utter disregard of some important provisions of earlier treaties of March 9 and 11 of the same year. The treaty of Bharowal provided for the installation of a Council of Regency with Tej Singh at its head. But actually the Regency was a body of executive officers who were to carry out the orders of the British Resident at Lahore, who in the words of the Governor-General, "Can change them and appoint others, and in military matters his power is as unlimited as in the civil administration; he can withdraw Sikh garrisons replacing them by British troops and in every part of Punjab."[106]

The British Government also became the self-appointed sole guardian of the person and property of Maharaja Dalip Singh. In the words of Sir Herbert Edwardes, "The beginning of the year 1847 thus found Henry Lawrence in peaceful possession of viceregal authority over the province."[107] The annual allowance of Maharani Jindan was fixed at Rs. one *lakh* and a half. This arrangement was to continue during the minority of Maharaja Dalip Singh until Sept. 4, 1854.

Henry Lawrence, though fully equipped with powers and prestige as Resident to rule the state, felt nervous and reported to the Governor-General on 9.4.1847, "The national independence of the Sikh character may dictate the attempt to escape from foreign yoke, for, however benevolent be our motives and conciliating our demeanour, a British army cannot garrison Lahore, and the fiat of a British functionary cannot supersede that of the *Darbar* throughout the land, without our presence being considered a burden and a yoke."[108] The members of the Regency headed by traitor Tej Singh and some others having been enticed to their individual interests, the Resident considered the Maharani to be the only stumbling block to be removed for smooth annexation. Thus recommending her "expulsion from the Punjab for ever", he wrote to the Secretary of the Governor-General on 9.8.1847, "I don't disguise for myself, nor do I wish the Governor-General to be ignorant of the fact that the Maharani is the only effective enemy to our policy that I know of in the country." The Governor-General replied on 23.10.47, "In all our measures taken during the minority, we must bear in mind that by the Treaty of Lahore, March 1846, the Punjab never was intended to be an independent State. By the clause I added, the chief of the State can neither make war or peace, or exchangè or sell an acre of territory or admit of a European Officer, or refuse us a thoroughfare through his territories, or, in fact, perform any act without our permission. In fact, the native prince is in fetters, and under our protection, and must do our bidding."[109]

Thus further strengthened with the authority from the Governor-General, the Resident Sir Henry Lawrence and later Sir Currie cooked up excuses first to intern her in the Samman Tower of the Lahore Fort, then transferred her to Sheikhu Pura Fort and finally banished her to the British territory (Chunar Fort) in Uttar Pradesh. The Maharani, at this near loss of the kingdom and separation from her son, only 9 years old, now under protection of traitors and foreigners, with her monthly allowance of Rs. 12,500 under the treaty, reduced first to Rs. 4000/- p.m. and on banishment to U.P. to Rs. 1,000/- p.m. and all her communications with the outside world completely cut off, broken and subdued in spirit, was deeply smitten at heart. She vehemently protested to the Resident, "I had entrusted my head to your care", the Maharani wrote to John Lawrence, then acting Resident, from her place of confinement. "You ought to have instituted an enquiry, and then charged me with what you found against me ...... Why do you take possession of my kingdom by underhand means ? Why do you not do it openly ? ...... Do justice to me or I shall appeal to London headquarters." Without her son, the Maharani was without power and wrote passionate letters to Lawrence begging to be re-united with him, "You have been very cruel to me!" she wailed, "You have snatched my son from me. For ten months I kept him in my womb ...... In the name of the God you worship and in the name of the King whose salt you eat, restore my son to me. I cannot bear the pain of this separation. Instead, you should put me to death."[110]

Lawrence wrote a conciliatory reply, assuring her that her son was perfectly happy and in good hands. "I am very glad to hear from your letter that the Maharajah is happy", she answered on August 30, 1847, "Whatever you write may be true. But my mind does not believe that the Maharajah is happy. How can he, whose mother has been separated from him, be happy ? ...... Weeping, he was torn away from his mother and taken to Shalamar Garden, while the mother was dragged out by her hair. Well has friendship been rewarded."[111]

"You had been kept for the protection of our honour and dignity. But the traitors have robbed us of these also. It is a matter of sorrow," she continued, "that you did not weigh things before accusing me. You have exiled me on the instigation of traitors. Whatever you have done has earned a good name for you. I have lost my dignity and you have lost regard for your word. This treatment that you have given to me is not given even to murderers. Having renounced everything, I had become a faqir, but you have not allowed me to live even like a faqir."[112]

The gentlemanly Lawrence was moved to pity, and possibly to shame, by such maternal pleas, but Hardinge, who had motivated and taken full responsibility for her removal, was little more than cynical. "We must expect these letters in various shapes, which a woman of her strong mind and passions will assume as best suited either to gratify her vengeance or obtain her ends."[113]

The installation of the Regency was thus a means to an end, in the words of Lord Hardinge, as he wrote to Ellenborough on 23.1.1845, "Devouring an ally in adversity."

CIRCUMSTANCES LEADING TO THE BATTLE OF CHILLIANWALA

And now we may give an account of circumstances leading to the battle of Chillianwala and the final annexation, in some detail.

With the banishment of Maharani Jindan from Punjab in May 1848, whom Lord Dalhousie, while writing to Brigadier Mountain, on January 31,1849, described as being, 'the only person having manly understanding in the Punjab', the stage for annexation was finally set by the British.

The Governor-General Sir Henry Hardinge on retirement and Sir Henry Lawrence on sick leave, both returned to England together in January, 1848. They were replaced by the young lowland Scot, Lord Dalhousie, then only 35, as Governor-General and by John Lawrence and later by Sir Currie as Resident. Dalhousie expected his authority to be unquestioned as he wrote, "There can be only one master in all India and while I am here I have no mind that it should be anybody else than the Governor-General in Council."[114] On assumption of office as Governor-General, he wrote in one of his official minutes, 'In the exercise of a wise and sound policy, the British Government is bound not to put aside or neglect such rightful opportunities of acquiring territories or revenue, as may from time to time present themselves.'

Lord Hardinge had assured his successor, 'It would not be necessary to fire a gun in India for seven years to come.' This wishful forecast was disproved within three months, when towards the end of April, 1848, the spark set off at Multan. A succession fee of Rs. 30 *lakhs* was demanded from Governor Mool Raj and the annual revenue of the province of Multan was raised from about Rs. 20 *lakhs* to Rs. 30 *lakhs*, although his territory was reduced. Mool Raj resigned and Kahn Singh Mann was appointed Governor. Two British Officers assisted him in taking over the charge. When on 19.4.1848 they were coming out of the fort, an ugly incident took place, and the two British Officers were wounded and later killed in an assault by the local troops. Thus did Mool Raj, driven by circumstances, rather than design, come to be placed at the head of a local revolt.

Major Evans Bell, a contemporary of these events, in his *The Annexation of the Punjab and Maharaja Duleep Singh,* (pp. 46-47) quoting extensively from *The Blue Book Official Documents* and other private papers records, "Everything tends to prove that the original outbreak at Multan was equally unpremeditated. The Diwan Mool Raj was rich, in infirm health and without children, timid, unpopular with the army and people; and the Resident reports that immediately before the catastrophe he had 'only five or six field guns' and 'had discharged almost all his regular troops, preparatory to resigning his government.' The attack on the two British officers sent to relieve him of his post, was caused by a sudden impulse of discontent and fanaticism, in the results of which, after a vain attempt to quell it, Mool Raj felt himself irretrievably compromised. With hope of scant mercy from the British government and certain of death from the mutinous soldiery, if he trusted to that mercy, he yielded to circumstances and accepted the lot that fate flung before him."

It could be suppressed by timely action as strongly advocated by Herbert Edwardes, then Assistant to the Lahore Resident, by deploying a little force. But this incident, the Governor-General, wanted to use as a pretext and give it the appearance of a general rebellion by the Sikhs and then annex the state of Punjab.

Edwardes wrote on May 24,1848 to Major Hodson, the political Assistant of the Resident at Lahore :

"You express a hope in your letter that the British Government will act for itself, and not prop up a fallen dynasty. In other words, you hope we shall seize the opportunity to annex the Punjab. In this I cannot agree with you, for I think, for all that has yet happened, it would be both unjust and inexpedient. The treaty we made with the Sikh Government and people cannot be forfeited by the treachery of a Gorkha regiment in Multan, the rebellion of a discharged kardar or the treasonable intrigues of the queen mother who has no connection with the Sikh Government of her son."[115]

He again wrote to the Resident on June 29, 1848 :

"I am afraid considerable mischief has been done by an idea of annexation getting abroad. It is my opinion that you are certainly running a great and unnecessary risk in waiting for the cold weather, and giving the Sikh army the temptation to rise, when by a mere march, the rebellion would now be settled." He added, *"I fancy the dodge is that all these senior officers want to come marching up themselves at the head of Brigades and Divisions and don't care two brass farthings whether Whish is able or unable to maintain his position at Multan."[116]*

And again, after eleven days, he wrote : *"I think it will be most culpable supineness if we allow a rebellion, which may be settled by a brigade or two, to rise again into a meet foe for the British army."[117]* When Lord Dalhousie snubbed Edwardes for his criticism of 'Policy of Delay', in harsh and insulting words, Edwardes wrote back to Currie, then Resident at Lahore, *"I certainly did not expect to be insulted. He may command my services to their fraction, but to his censure and praise, I feel indifferent for the future."*

Maharaja Dalip Singh was betrothed to the daughter of Sardar Chattar Singh Attariwala, then Governor of Hazara in the North-West. Sardar Chattar Singh asked his son, Raja Sher Singh, who had been sent alongwith others to suppress the so-called Multan revolt, to enquire from the Resident, through Herbert Edwardes, his close friend, a firm date of the Maharaja's marriage which the Resident was persistently postponing for one reason or another. Edwardes, therefore, wrote, "The request seems strange at the present moment. The secret motives of men are difficult to divine, but there can be no question that an opinion has gone very prevalently abroad and been carefully disseminated by the evil disposed that the British meditate declaring the Punjab forfeited by the recent troubles and misconduct of the troops." He, therefore, suggested, "It would, I think, be a wise and timely measure to give such assurance of British good faith and intention to adhere to the Treaty, as would be involved in authoritative preparations for providing the young prince with a Queen. It would, no doubt, settle men's minds greatly."[118] The Governor-General Lord Dalhousie, was greatly upset to read the suggestions and wrote to Sir Currie on 22.8.1848, 'It would be a friendly act if you or some of his well-wishers would point out to him that for an assistant to the Resident to transmit to his Government a volunteer opinion that they would be guilty of breach of faith if they adopt a particular policy, which the Governor-General of India, Her Majesty's Ministers, and the Secret Committee, all contemplate as probable, is hardly discreet, quite un-becoming and altogether unnecessary. I don't intend to take any notice of this and mention it privately to you because I wish well to Mr. Edwardes."[119] On the other hand, Captain Abbot, the British representative at Hazara and a subordinate to Sardar Chattar Singh Attariwala, excited the local Muslims against the Sardar and wrote to the Resident on 19.8.1848, "I on my part, assembled the chiefs of Hazara, explained what had happened, and called upon them, by the memory of their murdered parents, friends and relatives, to rise, and aid me in destroying the Sikh forces in detail. I issued *purwanas* to this effect throughout the land and marched to a strong position."[120] Thus disappointed and harassed, Sardar Chattar Singh wrote to his son, Raja Sher Singh, on 23.8.1848, "complaining bitterly of Abbot, whose suspicions and treachery had driven him to adopt military measures to guard his life and honour, and asked him to join in defending the family honour and independence of his country."[121] Raja Sher Singh, therefore, decided to throw in his lot with the rebel leader Mool Raj of Multan.

Mool Raj didn't trust Sher Singh and thought it was a ruse and, therefore, refused him admission to the fort. Thus again disappointed, Sher Singh left Multan to meet his old father somewhere in the North-West. Sardar Chattar Singh also left Hazara, captured Peshawar and Attock and wanted to reinforce the army of Sher Singh. But luck willed it otherwise. He was still on his way, when the famous battle of Chillianwala took place on 13.1.1849 between Raja Sher Singh and the British Commander-in-Chief, Lord Hugh Gough.

Major Evans Bell again succinctly records, "When Sardar Chattar Singh was fully committed beyond all possibility of retreat or redemption — when redress was refused and he was sentenced without judgement — his sons threw in their lot with their father, and the second Sikh war began. Until they took that step, the Multan rebellion was isolated, — confined indeed, within the walls of the fortress; although its importance was enhanced and dangers attending it were aggravated by the Maharani's removal, by our military vacillation and delay, and by the rumour of impending annexation. Upto the middle of September 1848, no Chief of note or distinction had joined the insurrection. Capt. Abbot's notion of a general conspiracy throughout the Punjab, in which all the members of the Durbar and Gulab Singh Dogra of Kashmir were implicated, as well as his charge against Sardar Chattar Singh of having been accessory before the fact to the Multan outbreak, are conclusively disproved by the dates and incidents of each successive convulsion." (p. 43)

The Governor-General wrote to the Resident on 8.10.1848, "The rebellion of Raja Sher Singh, followed by his army, the rebellion of Sardar Chattar Singh with the *Darbar* army under his command, the state of the troops and of the Sikh population everywhere, have brought matters to that crisis, I have for months been looking for, and we are now not on the eve but in the midst of war with the Sikh nation and the kingdom of the Punjab."[122]

The Resident wrote to the Governor-General on 12.10.1848, "Now if that be the case, I with my assistants, am in an anomalous position, as superintending and aiding the · administration of the Lahore State and if I were to withdraw from the Government and to declare the Treaty violated and all amicable relations between the two States an end, we should have the whole country up at once as one man to destroy us, if possible. There is no doubt that all, with a very few exceptions, are, at this time, chiefs, army and people, inimical, aye hostile to us in their hearts and desire to get rid of us."[123] He, therefore, suggested, "This declaration regarding the 'State of Lahore being directly at war with the British Government' should not be made till the Commander-in-Chief is in a commanding attitude at Lahore ...... I think the declaration to be made by the Government should be to the purport ...... setting forth that the British Government will now occupy the Punjab Province ...... that all consideration will be paid to the interests of Maharaja Duleep Singh who, from his tender years, cannot be held personally responsible for the misconduct of Lahore State ...... I think in the first instance nothing more explicit of the Government intentions need be proclaimed, and that this proclamation should not be made till we are in circumstances to follow it up ...... I think we may quietly annex the Punjab districts to the British Provinces, making a suitable provision for the state and comfort of Maharaja Duleep Singh."[124]

A grand army was then constituted at Ferozepur in November, 1848 and the Commander-in-Chief, Lord Gough, reached Lahore on 13th November, and three days later on the right bank of Chenab where Raja Sher Singh's army was then encamped. In the absence of any declaration of war by the British, "It was not till after leaving Lahore that Lord Gough came to know that the war was to be against and not in support of the Darbar." He, therefore, wrote on 15.11.1848, "I do not know whether we are at peace or war, or who is it we are fighting for."[125] At long last a proclamation was addressed to all loyal subjects of the Maharaja to assure them that the British had come not as an enemy to the Constituted Government, but to restore order and obedience.

THE BATTLE OF CHILLIANWALA

The Commander-in-Chief Lord Hugh Gough, who had enough experience of the Sikh valour at Ferozeshah and Sabraon, felt nervous and stuck to his camp for five weeks only ten miles away from that of Raja Sher Singh. It was a period of inaction on both sides. According to Burton, "Lord Gough was himself of the opinion that he was not strong enough, and that it would be best to await the fall of Multan, which would release the troops there engaged, before attacking the Sikhs."[126] But the news of fall of Peshawar and Attock to Sardar Chattar Singh had reached the British Camp and the Commander-in-Chief was forced by the Governor-General to engage Sher Singh before he was reinforced by the army of his father. Thus, Lord Gough, assisted by the Darbar troops and Jammu soldiers under Colonel Steinbach, moved up on 13.1.1849 and was received by the Sikh artillery under General Ilahi Bakhsh.

Chillianwala was one of the hardest-fought battles. There was a feeling of consternation, both in British India and in England, over the battle of Chillianwala which was considered to be a disaster worse than that in Afghanistan, as more than three thousand British lay dead or wounded in the ravines and brushwood, and the camp was overspread with a funeral gloom. "Chillianwala was not a victory," says Dr Adams. "When the news of Chillianwala reached England, the nation was stricken with profound emotion. A long series of military successes had ill fitted it to hear with composure of

British guns and British standards taken, of British cavalry flying before the enemy, and of a British army scarcely able by the most desperate exertions to snatch a victory from a wild Indian people. It was felt that our fame and influence in India had undergone a heavy blow; and a disaster was attributed very generally to the blunders of the Commander-in-Chief."[127] The battle paralyzed Lord Gough, and Lord Dalhousie lost confidence in him. Writing to Sir John Hobhouse on 21.2.1849, the Governor-General said, "If he again fights an incomplete action with terrible carnage as before, you must expect of my taking a strong step; he shall not remain in command of that army in the field."[128] *The Times of London* woefully declared that Lord Gough was playing with the lives of our soldiers.[129] Sir John Hobhouse, the President of the Board of Directors, observed on March 7, 1849, "The disaster has thrown the success into the shade and the impression made upon the public mind is stronger than that caused by the Kabul Massacre. The result has been that in eight-and-forty hours after the arrival of the mail, it was determined to send Sir Charles Napier to command the Indian Army."[130] Even the eighty year old Duke of Wellington, conqueror of Napoleon, offered to go out to India to fight against the Sikhs, if Napier hesitated. He said to the latter, "If you do not go, I must."[131] The English poet, George Meredith wrote a poem in commemoration of the battle :

Chillianwallah, Chillianwallah !
> *When the night set in with rain,*
> *Came the savage plundering devils*
> *To their work among the slain;*
> *And the wounded and the dying*
> *In cold blood did share the doom*
> *Of their comrades round them lying,*
> *Stiff in, the dead skyless gloom.*

The British Subaltern wrote, "The Sikhs fought like devils ...... Such a mass of men I never set eye on and as plucky as lions they ran right on the bayonets of the 21st. (Regiment) and struck at their assailants when they were transfixed."[132]

Kapur Singh records, "When the remnants of Sikh soldiers, without any backing from their state, challenged in battle the British army at Chillianwala on 13th January, 1849, the rout of British was so decisive and complete that even patriotic British historians are obliged to admit that they were defeated. The great grand-father of the writer of these lines, who fought in this battle, used to narrate that the Sikhs, for full twelve hours pursued the scattered British soldiers in all directions, who when overtaken would fall on their knees to beg for mercy, saying *"ham tumhara gai"* (I am like a defenseless cow to you), on the sight of a Sikh soldier."[133]

Even Sir Winston Churchill, after describing the Afghan massacre in 1841, records, "Another defeat (Chillianwala) soon followed in the Punjab, the most northernly state of Indian provinces."[134]

Next morning Sikh guns boomed a twenty-one gun salute to their victory. The British also claimed the battle as a victory. However, writing secretly to the Duke of

Wellington on 22.1.1949 Lord Dalhousie said, "In public I make, of course, the best of things, I treat it as a great victory. But writing confidentially to you I do not hesitate to say that I consider my position grave."

LOSS OF BATTLE OF GUJRAT AND ANNEXATION

Mool Raj having got his magazine in the fort containing 400,000 lbs. of gun powder blown up by a shell from the besieging troops, became helpless and surrendered on 22.1.1849 at Multan to General Whish, who was assisted by the *Darbar* troops. And Raja Sher Singh who had three horses killed under him in this action, lost the battle of Gujrat on 21.2.1849. Writing about this battle, General Thackwell, who was present, wrote, "In this action as well as at Chillianwala, Sikhs caught hold of the bayonets of their assailants with their left hands and closing with their adversaries, dealt furious sword blows with their right. This circumstance alone will suffice to demonstrate the rare species of courage possessed by these men."[135] He added, "The fidelity displayed by the Sikh gunners is worthy of record : the devotion with which they remained at their posts, when the atmosphere around them was absolutely fired by the British guns, does not admit description."[136]

The fight at Gujrat was a disaster though, the *coup de grace* was, however, delivered again by the Arch Traitor, Gulab Singh Dogra. He helped Abbot to cut off Sher Singh Attariwala's retreat towards the frontier. The prospect of continuing the fight with Afghan help was thus obviated. He also arranged for the supply of boats for the British Army to cross the Jhelum. Thus driven by adverse circumstances, the Attariwalas, both father and son, came to the British Camp with their faces covered under their shawls and formally surrendered their swords to General Gilbert at Hurmuck on March 11,1849. Three days later, the Sikh soldiers with tears in their eyes, kissed their swords and laid down their arms. General Thackwell has again vividly described the scene, "The reluctance of some of the old Khalsa veterans to surrender their arms was evident. Some could not restrain their tears, while on the faces of others, rage and hatred were visibly depicted." The remark of one grey-bearded veteran as he put down his gun summed up the history of the Punjab : '*Aj Ranjit Singh mar gaya*' (today Ranjit Singh has died)."[137]

HENRY LAWRENCE NOT ALLOWED TO ACT IN PUBLIC CAPACITY

Henry Lawrence had returned to England on long sick leave on 18.1.1848. When he heard of the Multan rebellion, Lawrence got his remaining leave cancelled, landed at Bombay and reached Multan, hoping to conciliate Mool Raj. While there, he was prevented from acting in any public capacity under instructions from Lord Dalhousie. He received a letter from Currie, then Resident at Lahore, which said, "There are strong rumours that if you should arrive anywhere near Multan, Diwan Mool Raj means to surrender to you. I have no doubt whatever that you would not receive him."[138] Thus Lawrence reached Lahore in the first week of January, 1849, after staying at Multan for two days only, and resumed his charge as Resident on 1.2.1849. He drew up a proclamation to be issued on conclusion of the Multan affair, and submitted it to Lord Dalhousie for approval. It was in accordance with the practice, policy and tone in force under Lord Hardinge. But Dalhousie found them utterly unsatisfactory and conveyed his rejection in harsh and unbecoming language, to which Sir Lawrence replied in a dignified tone on 5.2.1849, "My own opinion, as more than once expressed to your Lordship in writing, is against annexation. I did think it unjust; I now consider it impolitic. It is quite possible I may be prejudiced and blinded, but I have thought over the subject long and carefully."[139]

THE FINAL TRANSACTION

Thus finding Sir Henry Lawrence unhelpful in his designs of annexation, Lord Dalhousie selected his Foreign Secretary, Elliot, for the final transaction. How he managed this delicate task, Elliot himself describes in his report of March 29,1849, "Immediately on my arrival, I communicated to Sir Henry Lawrence and John Lawrence the instructions with which I was charged, and regretted to find that both these officers were fully persuaded that the Council of Regency would, on no account, be induced to accede to the terms which were offered for their acceptance, in as much as they had already incurred great odium amongst their countrymen for what were considered to be their former concessions."[140]

Elliot was disheartened at first, but his resourcefulness did not fail him. He then hit upon the more artful device of working separately on the personal interests of each member of the Council and studying their reaction. He requested Henry Lawrence immediately to send for the two most influential members of the council as he wanted to talk to them. Raja Tej Singh and Diwan Dina Nath were accordingly summoned. The Raja at first excused himself on the ground of sickness. But the messenger was sent again and was told to inform him that the mission on which Sir Henry Elliot had come was urgent and could not be accomplished without him, so he should come to the Residency unless he was really very seriously ill. Upon this Tej Singh came. His looks, Elliot's report states, gave no warrant for his excuses. Diwan Dina Nath came with him.

How the talks went on and ended is again explicitly stated in Mr. Elliot's report. He writes : *"I explained to them the purpose for which I had come, that the Punjab would be annexed to the British dominions at all events, but that it was for them to decide whether this should be done in an unqualified manner, or whether they would subscribe to the conditions which I was about to lay before them."*[141]

"The Rajah opened out in a strain of invective against Sher Singh and all the rebellious Sardars acknowledged that the British Government had acquired a perfect right to dispose of the country as it saw fit, and recommended that it should declare its will without calling upon the Council to sign any conditions. I replied that if they refused to accept the terms, which the Governor-General offered, the Maharaja and themselves would be entirely at his mercy, and I had no authority to say that they would be entitled to receive any allowance whatever."[142]

"The Diwan commented on the severity of the conditions and particularly on the exile of the Maharaja. I promised that the Maharaja should not be sent anywhere to the east of the Ganges, pointing out Hardwar, Garhmukteswar, Bithoor, and Allahabad as being all of them places of high sanctity in their religion. They seemed to be thankful for this as a concession ...... they seemed fully satisfied with the personal allowance

assigned to the Maharaja, which I told them would be about 10,000 Rupees per mensem."[143]

"Other subjects were then discussed, and they enquired anxiously about their own future position; I told them it was not intended to deprive them of their jagirs or salaries, and that, for this indulgence they would be expected to yield the British Government the benefit of their advice and assistance whenever called upon to do so, that if they did not subscribe to the conditions, I could not promise that any consideration would be shown to them."[144]

"After much more parley, during which ...... I convinced them of my resolute determination to yield to no point, they expressed their willingness to sign the paper, and signed it accordingly, not without evident sorrow and repugnance on the part of the Diwan."[145]

Having succeeded with Tej Singh and Dina Nath, Elliot next summoned Bhai Nidhan Singh and Fakir Nur-ud-Din, the only other members of the regency Council who were residing in Lahore at the moment. Nidhan Singh was the doyen of the celebrated priestly family of Bhai Basti Ram, and Fakir Nur-ud Din that of the most influential Muhammadan family of Lahore. "When they came and were told what had passed," writes Sir Henry Elliot, "they said they would abide by whatever their colleagues were prepared to do. They then affixed their seal and signatures to the paper in duplicate and Sir Henry Lawrence and myself then added our counter-signatures. The members then took their leave after the conference had lasted about two hours." The remaining two members of the Regency Council, namely, Sardar Shamsher Singh Sandhanwalia and Sardar Attar Singh Kalianwala not being present in Lahore, their accredited agents (*vakils*) signed the documents on their behalf. The question of the dissolution of the kingdom of the Sikhs and of the confiscation of its property including the world famous gem Koh-i-Noor, was thus finally decided, and agreed upon.

That the destiny of a ruling Prince and of his twenty million subjects should have been decided by four of his timid and selfish councillors and this, too, within the brief space, of two hours, is one of the very grim facts of history. Even the deal over the sale of a flock of sheep, between a shepherd and a butcher, perhaps, takes longer time than was taken by Mr. Elliot and Raja Tej Singh and Co, in making over to the British, the fortunes of the two crores of people of the Punjab.

PROCLAMATION OF MARCH 29, 1849 AND THE ANNEXATION

All that now remained to be done was the formal ratification of this business by the minor Prince and Mr. Elliot, which the latter desired should be done in a public *Darbar*. A *Darbar* was accordingly arranged for the next morning, viz. 29th March at 7 A.M. At the appointed, hour Sir Henry Elliot arrived at the *Darbar* Hall accompanied by the Lawrences (John and Henry) and other officials of the Residency. The party was escorted by a squadron of the Governor-General's bodyguard which Lord Dalhousie had specially sent for the occasion from his Ferozepore Camp. The *Darbar* Hall in the Lahore Fort was suitably decorated, English and Indian spectators lining the walls on either side. The Maharaja and his Ministers who were waiting at the gate of the citadel to receive the Governor-General's representative, then joined the small cavalcade which together moved to the audience hall. The boy-king was conducted to the throne at the end of the Hall (being the last time he occupied this seat) and the British envoys with the members of the Regency Council sat on either side. A deep silence prevailed in the Hall. The proceedings began with the reading aloud of the fatal 'edict' in English by Henry Elliot, which said, "The British have faithfully kept their word and have scrupulously observed every obligation which the treaties imposed upon them. But the Sikh people and their Chiefs have, on their part, grossly and faithlessly violated the promises by which they were bound. Finally, the army of the state, and the whole Sikh people, joined by many of the *Sardars* in the Punjab, who signed the treaties, and led by a member of the Regency itself have risen in arms against us and have waged a fierce and bloody war, for the proclaimed purpose of destroying the British and their power."[146]

Upon the conclusion of the Manifesto, the paper was passed on by the Chief Minister, Raja Tej Singh, to the Maharaja who affixed his signature "by tracing the initials of his name in English letters." This completed the ratification of that farcical transaction which formally and finally transformed the sovereign state of the Punjab into a British province and its ruler, Duleep Singh, into a throneless pensioner of the British Government. Elliot concludes his report with a feeling of pride and exultation over his achievement. "As I left the place," says he, "I had the proud satisfaction of seeing the British colours hoisted on the citadel under a royal salute from our own artillery, at once proclaiming the ascendancy of British rule, and sounding the knell of the Khalsa Raj."[147]

FULL CO-OPERATION OF THE PEOPLE AND LAHORE DARBAR

Thus, despite Henry Lawrence's threats to resign, the British succeeded in their plans of annexation of the Punjab on the flimsy ground of Sikh rebellion. Otherwise the troops commanded by General Gortlandt, Sardar Fateh Singh, Missar Sahib Dyal, Diwan Jawahar Mal, Shaikh Imam-ud-Din, Sardar Jhanda Singh, Colonel Bhup Singh, Colonel Bahadur Singh, Colonel Budh Singh, Babu Pandey, Colonel Nur-ud-Din, General Sultan Mahmood, and other military Officers, remained faithful and obedient to Lieutenants Edwardes and Lake, and Captains Abbot and Nicholson in accordance with the orders of the Lahore Darbar. As late as November 15, when the British Commander-in-Chief, Lord Gough, had entered the Punjab territories and was encamped at the capital of the state, the Lahore *Darbar*, as desired by the British Resident, ordered two of its chief officers, Sardar Boor Singh and Diwan Kishan Lal, to accompany and guide the Commander-in-Chief and his force to Ram Nagar (against Raja Sher Singh), to look after their comforts and supply them with food and fodder.

There was no rising either of the army or the people in the central Sikh districts of the State; not a single British Officer was attacked or molested. The British Resident continued to stay at the capital of the kingdom, issuing orders to the Council of Regency, the *Darbar*, and receiving their fullest co-operation. Only one member of the Regency, out of eight, Raja Sher Singh, had joined the rebels and that too, as a result of Captain Abbot's mean instigations and provocations against his father Sardar Chattar Singh, then Governor of Hazara, and his family. The remaining members were perfectly faithful and obedient. In addition to the great majority of the army who took no part in the revolt, "at least 20,000 subjects of the Lahore State," according to Major Bell, "enrolled in its service, fought on the side of the Government, and assisted in suppressing the rebellion, not knowing that at the end of it, their country would be annexed and permanently occupied by the British Government."[148]

TREATIES VIOLATED BY THE BRITISH

Major Bell adds, *"Having conducted the administration of the Lahore State for two years and three months ...... by means of his own Agent and his own nominees, in the name of his Ward and Ally, the Maharaja, under a treaty which he upholds and enforces to the last, he (Lord Dalhousie) turns round, when the rebellion is over, declares the Treaty to have been violated, and therefore null and void, and explains that the successful campaign, ostensibly carried on for the suppression of a rebellion against the Government of Maharaja Duleep Singh, really constituted a war against the Maharaja and the State of Lahore, by which the British Government has 'conquered' the Punjab"*(Retros. and Pros. of Ind. Policy,157-8).[149] *"But during the period prescribed by the treaty for the Maharaja's minority, no crisis, no second struggle, could absolve the British Government from the obligations of guardianship and management, so long as it professed to fulfil those duties, and was able to do so without interruption"* (Ibid., 152-3), Lord Dalhousie has, as such, *"violated treaties, abused a sacred trust..and (made) an acquisition as unjust as it was imprudent ...... This, I believe, will be the verdict of posterity and history, upon the transactions which have just passed under our review"* (Ibid.,179).[150]

"This is perhaps the first instance on record in which a guardian has visited his own misdeeds upon his ward," says John Sullivan. *"The British Government was the self-constituted guardian of the Raja and the regent of his kingdom, a rebellion was provoked by the agents of the guardian, it was acknowledged by the guardian to be a rebellion against the government of his ward, and the guardian punished that ward by confiscating his dominions and his diamonds to his own use."* (Are We Bound by our Treaties, p. 52)[151]

According to John M. Ludlow : *"Duleep Singh was an infant; his minority was only to end in 1854. We were his declared protectors. On our last advance into his country, we had proclaimed (18th Nov., 1848) that we came to punish insurgents, and to put down all armed opposition to constituted authority. We fulfilled that pledge by annexing his whole country within six months."*[152]

"The duty of a Lord Paramount is to protect, and we assume this title with a view to destroy. We are bound by treaties to 'protect' the states, which we are now employed in annihilating." (Ibid., p. 54). *"The verdict against us must be, that in matters Oriental this nation has no conscience."* (Ibid., 78).[153]

In the words of William S.R. Hodson, *"All our history shows that sooner or later connection with us is political death. The sunshine is not more fatal to a dew-drop than our friendship or alliance to an Asiatic kingdom."* (Trotter, Hodson of Hodson's Horse, p. 150).[154]

In utter contrast, one is sadly reminded of the chivalrous standards of yore in the field of battle. Alexander the Great is said to have spurned the suggestion of a surprise night attack in the battle of Albela against King Darius of Persia in 331 B.C. remarking, "No, I will not steal a victory."[155]   But it is pretty clear that the British during their battles in India heartlessly employed low conspiracy, vile treachery and rank betrayal more than the noble principles of warfare, in founding and consolidating an eastern empire.

DALHOUSIE'S PATHETIC CONFESSION OF MORAL GUILT

But Lord Dalhousie was indifferent to what history might record. He never perhaps realised to what a pitiable condition he had reduced the ten-year old innocent fatherless boy, Maharaja Duleep Singh, forcibly separated from his mother at the age of nine and heartlessly driven out of his kingdom, until, with the death of his (Dalhousie's) wife, his own children were rendered motherless, though not fatherless. Writing to Colonel Mountain in the last week of June,1853, after the death of Lady Dalhousie on the 13th, he said :

"God, and those on whom he places it, alone can tell how heavy it is and how hard to bear this burden and every circumstance both to me and to her poor children that could sharpen the anguish of such a lash has been added. I try to submit and I hope I may."[156]

Dalhousie added :

"God's ways are not as our ways. It is no right of ours to enquire His reasons. If we had such right, I should be quick to admit that He had abundant cause, if it seemed to Him good, to inflict this punishment and chastisement upon me."[157]   But alas, this realisation had come all too late.

CONFISCATION OF LAHORE TOSHAKHANA

The first important act of Lord Dalhousie after annexation was the confiscation of property in the Lahore Toshakhana. In addition to jewels and treasures in gold, silver, and precious stones, dishes, plates, cups, cooking pots, many valuable curiosities and relics of all kinds and vast store of Kashmir shawls, chogas, etc., and the swords of Persian hero Rustam and Wazir Fateh Khan Barakzai of Kabul and the wedding garments of Sardar Mahan Singh, father of Maharaja Ranjit Singh, there were :

(a) The *kalghi* or aigrette of Guru Gobind Singh,
(b) The Koh-i-Noor diamond,
(c) Maharaja Ranjit Singh's golden chair, silver summer house, gold and silver poled tents and equipage of rich Cashmere and his magnificient arms and armour.
(d) Shah Shuja's pavilion, gorgeously embroidered.[158]

On November 28,1849, Lord Dalhousie inspected the Toshakhana articles and decided not only on the sale of most of the property, but also on the removal of certain valuables to England for presentation to the Queen and for preservation in official museums there. The Maharaja was allowed to take with him only a very small part of his things to Fatehgarh in the United Provinces, where he was removed in February, 1850.

Thus we have seen, how fraudulently the Punjab lost its independence, which it had won after eight weary centuries of foreign rule, by going through numberless holocausts for nearly a century by the virile young Sikh nation and how the eleven year old innocent Maharaja Duleep Singh was deprived not only of a magnificient kingdom, but also of such national and personal unique marvels as the *kalghi* of Guru Gobind Singh, the matchless jewel Koh-i-Noor, along with many other world famous marvels and even the wedding garments of his grandfather, the great Sardar Mahan Singh.

These gory and machiavellian episodes bring to mind the maxim in his, *The Kingdom of God* (pp. 25-26) quoted from the *Book of Faith* by the saintly Tolstoy, "Christ by means of his disciples caught the whole world in his net of faith, but the big fish burst the net and escaped from it, and through the holes they made the other fish got out so that the net has been left almost empty. The big fish that burst the net are the rulers, emperors, popes and kings, who without renouncing power, accepted not Christianity but only its mask."

There can be no better finale to this blood-dripping tale than what Sita Ram Kohli, the doyen of Punjab historians, has given to his *Sunset of Sikh Empire.*

"How inscrutable is the way of the working of destiny! Could any English statesman at that time imagine that within ten decades his people would also have to wind up their empire and erase the red from the political maps of Asia and Africa. So turns the cycle of Time. Verily has a Persian poet observed :

Dar en wurta kashti fro sudd hazar

   Ki paeda na shudd takhta ra ba kinar

In the whirpool of time, thousands of boats were drawn in and sank. Not a plank
   (splinter) of any one of them came up to the surface, to tell its sad tale.

Again,

Ae Sikander na rehi teri bhi alamgiri

   Kitne din aap jiya kis liye Dara Mara.

O Alexander the Great, even your dream of world hegemony didn't last long. Why
   then didst thou kill Darius ? For you yourself lived only for a short while."

One wonders, then, if the present-day so-called modern governments, with evil designs and wicked machinations would ever take a leaf out of this universal truth.

REFERENCES

1. Lt. General Kaul, *The Untold Story.*
2. Gurtej Singh, *Recent Researches in Sikhism,* Punjabi University Patiala, 1992, p. 62.
3. Ganda Singh, *The British Occupation of the Punjab,* Sikh History Society, Amritsar, Patiala, 1955, p. 81.
4. Sir Jadu Nath Sarkar, *History of Aurangzeb,* Vol. III, Orient Longman Ltd., 1972, pp. 164, 174.
5. Hari Ram Gupta, *History of Sikh Gurus,* U.C. Kapur and Sons, New Delhi, 1973, pp. 1, 18.
6. N.K. Sinha, *Ranjit Singh,* III Edition, p. 2.
7. Prof. Stanley Wolpert, *A New History of India,* Oxford University, 1982, p. 216.
8. R.R. Sethi & V.D. Mahajan, *India Since 1526,* S. Chand & Co. Delhi, 1957, p. 28.

9. Sir Penderel Moon, *Strangers in India,* Greenwood Press, Publishers, Westport, Connecticut, U.S.A., 1971, p. 12.

10. Ganda Singh (ed.), *History of the Freedom Movement in the Punjab,* Vol. III, Punjabi University, Patiala, 1977.

11. Ibid., p. 6.

12. Hari Ram Gupta, *Punjab, Central Asia, and the First Afghan War,* Panjab University, Chandigarh, 1987, p. (vii)

13. Sir John Kaye, *Lives of Indian Officers,* Vol. II, A. Strahan and Co. Ludgate Hill, London, 1867, pp. 17-18.

14. Ganda Singh (ed.), *History of the Freedom Movement in the Punjab,* op. cit., p. 69.

15. Karnail Singh, *Anglo-Sikh Wars,* S.G.P.C., Amritsar, 1984, p. 3.

16. Sir Herbert Edwards and Merivale, *Life of Sir Henry Lawrence,* Vol. I, Smith Elder & Co., 15 Waterloo Place, London, 1872, pp. 267-68.

17. Ibid., pp. 365-67.

18. Ibid., pp. 365-77.

19. Ibid., p. 371.

20. Ganda Singh (ed.), *History of the Freedom Movement in the Punjab,* op. cit., p. 15.

21. Ibid., p. 15.

22. Ibid., pp. 14-15.

23. Cunningham, J. D., *A History of the Sikhs,* (ed.) H.L.O. Garret., S. Chand & Co., Delhi, 1955, p. 227.

24. Ganda Singh, *The British Occupation of the Punjab,* op. cit., pp. 31, 35.

25. Ibid., pp. 32-33.

26. Cunningham, J. D., *A History of the Sikhs,* (ed.) H.L.O. Garret., S. Chand & Co., Delhi, 1955, p. 227.

27. Sita Ram Kohli, *Sunset of the Sikh Empire,* (ed.) Khushwant Singh, Orient Longmans, New Delhi, 1967, p. 41.

28. Ganda Singh (ed.), *History of the Freedom Movement in the Punjab,* op. cit., pp. 18-19.

29. Hari Ram Gupta, *Punjab on the Eve of First Sikh War,* Panjab University, Chandigarh, 1975, pp. 60-61.

30. General Sir Charles Gough and Arthur D. Innes, *The Sikhs and the Sikh Wars,* Language Department, Punjab, 1970, p. 50.

31. Cunningham, J. D., *A History of the Sikhs,* (ed.) H.L.O. Garret., S. Chand & Co., Delhi, 1955, p. 227.

32. Sita Ram Kohli, op. cit., p. 47.

33. Ibid., p. 74.

34. Karnail Singh, op. cit., p. 21.

35. Kapur Singh, *Parasara Prasna* (ed.), Piar Singh and Madanjit Kaur, Guru Nanak Dev University, Amritsar, 1989, p. 224.

36. Ganda Singh (ed.), *History of the Freedom Movement in the Punjab,* op. cit., p. 19.

37. Ibid., p. 23.

38. Ibid., p. 24.

39. Ibid., p. 25.

40. Ibid., p. 25.

41. Ibid., p. 25.

42. Ibid., p. 25.

43. Ibid., p. 25.

44. Ibid., p. 26.

45. Ibid., p. 27.

46. Ibid., p. 27-28.

47. Ibid., p. 28.

48. Ibid., p. 31.
49. Ibid., p. 31.
50. Cunningham, J. D. op. cit., p. 255.
51. Ganda Singh, *The British Occupation of the Punjab,* op. cit, p. 68.
52. Cunningham, J. D. op. cit, p. 257.
53. Sita Ram Kohli, Sewa Singh Giani (ed.), *Var Shah Mohd. Jang Hind-Punjab,* Punjabi Sahit Academy, Ludhiana, 1988, p. 60.
54. Ganda Singh (ed.), *History of the Freedom Movement in the Punjab,* op. cit., p. 69.
55. Ibid., p. 69.
56. M.L. Ahluwalia and Kirpal Singh, *The Punjab's Pioneer Freedom Fighters,* Orient Longmans Ltd., New Delhi, 1963, pp. 83-84, F.N. 4.
57. Ganda Singh (ed.), *History of the Freedom Movement in the Punjab,* op. cit., p. 36.
58. Ganda Singh, *The British Occupation of the Punjab,* op. cit, p. 60.
59. Ibid., p. 60.
60. Ibid p. 77.
61. Ganda Singh (ed.), *History of the Freedom Movement in the Punjab,* op. cit., p. 38.
62. Ibid., p. 33-34.
63. Ibid., p. 42.
64. Cunningham, J. D. op. cit., p. 263.
65. Ganda Singh, *The British Occupation of the Punjab,* op. cit., pp. 77-78.
66. Ibid., p. 79.
67. Cunningham, J. D. op. cit., p. 264.
68. Ibid., p. 265.
69. Sita Ram Kohli, *Sunset of the Sikh Empire,* op. cit., p. 109.
70. Cunningham, J. D. op. cit., p. 266.
71. Ibid., p. 267.
72. M.L. Ahluwalia and Kirpal Singh, op. cit., pp. 21-22.
73. Ganda Singh, *The British Occupation of the Punjab,* op. cit., pp. 81.
74. Ibid., p. 81.
75. Ibid., p. 82.
76. Cunningham, J. D. op. cit., p. 263 F.N. 1.
77. M. L. Ahluwalia and Kirpal Singh, op. cit., p. 8.
78. Ibid., p. 23.
79. Cunningham, J. D. op. cit., p. 281.
80. Ibid., p. 281.
81. M. L. Ahluwalia and Kirpal Singh, op. cit., p. 26.
82. Ibid., p. 27.
83. Cunningham, J. D. op. cit., p. 282.
84. Kapur Singh, *Parasara Prasna* op. cit., pp. 248-249.
85. Ganda Singh, *The British Occupation of the Punjab,* op. cit., pp. 89.
86. *The Life and Campaigns of Viscount Gough,* p. 108.
87. Dr Ganda Singh, (ed.) *The First Anglo-Sikh War* (1845-46). Panjab Past and Present, Serial No. 29, April 1981, p. 127
88. Cunningham, J. D. op. cit., p. 284.
89. M. L. Ahluwalia and Kirpal Singh, op. cit., p. 28.
90. Sita Ram Kohli, op. cit., p. 117.
91. Kapur Singh, op. cit., p. 246.
92. Ibid., p. 115 and 118.
93. Ibid., p. 118.
94. Cunningham, J. D. op. cit., p. 288.
95. Ganda Singh, *The British Occupation of the Punjab,* op. cit., pp. 95.

96. Ibid., p. 95.
97. Ibid., p. 95.
98. Ibid., p. 95-96.
99. Sita Ram Kohli, op. cit., p. 128.
100. Ibid., p. 129.
101. Ibid., p. 129.
102. Ibid., pp. 129-130.
103. Ibid., pp. 130-131.
104. Ibid., p. 131.
105. Ibid., p. 131.
106. Ganda Singh (ed.), *History of the Freedom Movement in the Punjab,* op. cit., p. 50.
107. Ibid., p. 50.
108. Ibid., p. 50.
109. Ibid., p. 55.
110. Ibid., p. 51-52.
111. Ibid., p. 100.
112. Ibid., p. 100.
113. Michael Alexander and Sushila Anand, *Queen Victoria's Maharaja Duleep Singh,* Vikas Publishing House, N. Delhi, 1979, p. 8.
114. Ibid., p. 9.
115. Ganda Singh, *The British Occupation of the Punjab,* op. cit., pp. 115.
116. Ibid., p. 115-116.
117. Ibid., p. 115.
118. Ibid., p. 120.
119. Ibid., p. 120-21.
120. Ibid., p. 123.
121. Ibid., p. 127.
122. Ibid., p. 129.
123. Ibid., p. 129.
124. Ibid., p. 130.
125. Ibid., p. 132.
126. Ibid., p. 133.
127. Ibid., p. 133-34.
128. Ibid., p. 134.
129. Ibid., p. 134.
130. Ibid., p. 134.
131. Ibid., p. 134.
132. Sita Ram Kohli, op. cit., p. 175.
133. Kapur Singh, *Parasara Prasna* op. cit., p. 249.
134. Sir Winston Churchill, *History of the English Speaking Peoples,* Vol. IV, Cassel and Co. Ltd., London, 1962, p. 65.
135. Sita Ram Kohli, op. cit., p. 178.
136. Ibid., p. 178.
137. Ibid., p. 179.
138. Ganda Singh (ed.), *History of the Freedom Movement in the Punjab,* op. cit., p. 66.
139. Ibid., p. 131.
140. Sita Ram Kohli, op. cit., pp. 180-181.
141. Ibid., p. 181.
142. Ibid., p. 181.
143. Ibid., pp. 181-182.
144. Ibid., p. 182.

145. Ibid., p. 182.
146. Ganda Singh (ed.), *History of the Freedom Movement in the Punjab,* op. cit., p. 68.
147. Sita Ram Kohli, op. cit., p. 184.
148. Ganda Singh, *The British Occupation of the Punjab,* op. cit., pp. 147-148.
149. Ganda Singh (ed.), *History of the Freedom Movement in the Punjab,* op. cit., p. 75.
150. Ibid., pp. 76-77.
151. Ibid., p. 76.
152. Ibid., p. 76.
153. Ibid., p. 76.
154. Ibid., p. 77.
155. Kapur Singh, *Parasaraprasna,* op. cit., p. 223.
156. Ganda Singh, *The British Occupation of the Punjab,* op. cit., p. 150.
157. Ibid., p. 150.
158. *John Login and Maharaja Duleep Singh,* pp. 182-83.

29

SINGH SABHA MOVEMENT — A REVIVAL

GURDARSHAN SINGH DHILLON

INTRODUCTION

In recent years some writings have appeared, which suggest that the Singh Sabha Movement was a reformist movement that made innovations in Sikh thought and practices. Academically speaking, the method to determine whether a religious movement (Singh Sabha in this case) is reformist or revivalist, is to study four aspects of it. The first aspect is the ideology of the original movement (Sikhism), and especially whether the movement under study created changes in that ideology, or only invoked the original ideology of the system to bring about changes in the then existing practices. Second is the level of achievement in practices which the original movement (Sikh religion in this case), had made during its hey day and whether the leaders of the movement under study had invoked those achievements and the tradition as a model to follow. Thirdly, what was the fall, if any, in the state of things in the life of the community that was sought to be changed, and how it measured with the earlier high mark of the tradition, i.e., what was the then state of affairs and practices that were sought to be changed. Fourthly, how the changes brought about by the leaders of the new movement (Singh Sabha in this case) compare with the earlier tradition, and whether or not those were in consonance with it or entirely variant from it.

We are dividing our present paper into four parts so as to make a proper assessment of the Singh Sabha Movement. Side by side we shall be considering some variant views in the light of our discussion of the subject. We shall first state the fundamentals of the Sikh ideology, especially those where Sikhism radically departed from the earlier Indian traditions.

SIKH IDEOLOGY

Sikhism arose in the 16th century as an entirely new ideology, opposed in its fundamentals to those of the contemporary religions. It challenged fanaticism and religious hypocrisy of the Brahmins and political oppression of the contemporary rulers. Guru Nanak, the first Sikh Guru, stressed the oneness of God, Immanent, Creator, "Who is Timeless, Eternal Reality, Formless, Unborn, Unincarnated and Self-existent without Fear and Rancour, and Who is realised by the Enlightener's Grace." These attributes are incorporated in the *Mul Mantra* of Guru Nanak's *Japji*, which is the "fundamental primal text expounding the beliefs of Sikhism." He explicitly denounced all those religious traditions which denied the unity of God. He declared that "the belief in gods and goddesses was the source of *maya* (great illusion),"[1] which led people astray. The Gurus accept *Ek Onkar* as a declaration of the unity of God. In *Asa Raag*, the Guru says : "Six are the (Hindu) *Shashtras* and six their authors who have laid down six different philosophical concepts. But the Guru of these groups is God Himself."[2]

Guru Nanak led a crusade against the caste system, idolatry, ritualism, asceticism and the Brahmin's claim to superiority. He put an end to the role of middle-men (Brahmins) in man's relation with God. He advocated that man can be one with Him through his own good deeds. He emphasised moral virtues and considered rituals to be a hindrance in the salvation of man. He denounced idol worship of gods in most explicit terms : "The ignorant fools take stones and worship them, O Hindus, how shall the stone which itself sinketh carry you across ?"[3] He rejected asceticism and emphasised truthful living based on good deeds and righteousness. He impressed upon his followers that salvation could be attained through fulfilment of one's duties towards family and society. For Guru Nanak, social responsibility forms an integral part of the spiritual attributes of the ideal man. It is this element that constitutes one of the essential tenets of the Sikh faith. It is this element that gives Sikhism its distinctive and historic character, role and personality.

Guru Nanak laid emphasis on the brotherhood of man and strongly condemned social inequality. He declared : "The sense of high and low, and of caste and colour, such are the illusions created in man."[4] He raised his voice against economic exploitation and political despotism of his times. "This *Kal* age is a knife and kings are butchers; justice has taken to wings. The moon of Truth is invisible in the black night of falsehood."[5] "Rulers are turned beasts of prey, their offices hounds; None do they allow in peace to rest. The subordinates wound the people with their claws."[6] According to Guru Nanak, the world is not only real, but it is also a meaningful place where alone God's Creative and Attributive Will works. That is, "God being riches to the poor, milk to the child, and eyes to the blind,"[7] the seeker has to follow the ethical path of values and virtues laid down by the Guru. It is clear that in Guru Nanak's mission of love, two objectives become logically uppermost; and these he emphasised unambiguously in his *bani*, namely, that he was to establish equality and fraternity among men, and that it was the duty and responsibility of the religious man and the religious society he was creating, to resist oppression and safeguard human rights and values. The life-affirming faith founded by Guru Nanak attracted a large number of followers who found in it a welcome escape from the debasing caste discrimination, Brahminical domination and empty ritualism. It is a revolutionary system in which the dichotomy between the spiritual life and the empirical life of man was emphatically broken for the first time in the East. It was Guru Nanak who laid and led the path of universal love and emancipation of man without distinction of caste and creed. The call for this mission was given by him in these terms :

"If thou art zealous of playing the game of Love,
  Then come upon my path with thy head on thy palm.
  Yea, once thou settest thy foot on this way,
  Then find not a way out, and be prepared to lay down thy head."[8]

It is in this context that the importance of Guru Nanak's criticism of the doctrine of *ahimsa* should be understood. "Men discriminate not and quarrel over meat eating, they do not know what is flesh and what is non-flesh, or what is sin and what is not sin."[9] "Life", he said, "is in every grain of corn or seed."[10]

LEVEL OF ACHIEVEMENT

It is in this background that we have to charter the course of Sikh history from Guru Nanak to Guru Gobind Singh. After Guru Nanak, the period of the next three Gurus relates mainly to the creation, expansion, and organisation of the cohesive society or *Panth,* which Guru Nanak had started. With each succeeding Guru, Sikhism became increasingly crystallised and institutionalised into a distinct faith and society.

The next major landmark was the time of the Fifth Guru, who not only compiled the scripture of the new society, thereby weaning it away from all earlier beliefs, risked confrontation with the empire, and made the supreme sacrifice of his life, but also created in his lifetime what Dr H.R. Gupta calls "a state within a state." No wonder Emperor Jahangir took note of this mounting challenge, and attacked the Sikh society.[11] From this time onward, the Sikhs had to make tremendous sacrifices and undergo sufferings to preserve their faith.

Further, it is important that the doctrine of *miri* and *piri* proclaimed by Guru Hargobind, is the natural and inevitable corollary of the path of love and true service of man, of the rejection of asceticism and monasticism, the acceptance of a householder's life and responsibility, and of securing justice, equality and freedom for all men preached by Guru Nanak. The Guru justified use of force to uphold justice and righteousness, and to defend the oppressed. Guru Tegh Bahadur, carried on the Sikh tradition of martyrdom for the cause of justice and emancipation of man.

Guru Gobind Singh laid down an initiation (*amrit*) ceremony for the Sikhs, admitting them into the Khalsa Order and prescribed the wearing of five K's. Those who went through this ceremony, became members of the Khalsa brotherhood. The organisation was committed to pursuing the right path and resisting and undoing injustice, tyranny and aggression, since in the Sikh society it was a religious duty and social responsibility to promote and maintain righteousness. The Guru also furnished the Order of the Khalsa with the institutions of *Panj Piaras* (Five beloved ones or leaders) and *daswandh* (voluntary contribution of one tenth of one's income to the exchequer of the *Panth*), thereby bestowing upon the organisation the character of a self-contained community. It is significant to note that of the five beloved ones initiated by the tenth

Guru, four belonged to what the Indian society then regarded as the Shudra caste. The Guru's object was to obliterate all distinctions of caste and creed, and to weld his followers into a cohesive society. The Sikhs and the five beloved ones were amazed when the Guru requested them to initiate him into the Khalsa brotherhood in exactly the same manner as he had initiated them. By this symbolic act, the Guru invested the Khalsa with leadership of the *Panth* and the authority of his personality. Henceforward the Guru was the Khalsa and the Khalsa was the Guru. Sikhism, thus, emerged as the most democratic religion in the world.

The Gurus categorically rejected all such beliefs, rituals or ceremonies as implied the recognition of anything but one true Lord. In order to emphasise the complete independence and separateness of Sikh ideology, Guru Gobind Singh introduced the *Nash* doctrine, involving *Kirtnash, Kulnash, Dharamnash, Bharamnash,* and *Karamnash* i.e. giving up of all those beliefs, prejudices and traditions that stood in the way of the sole worship of the Supreme Being.[12] In this way they made a complete break of the Sikh society with the past religious systems, traditions and customs. The Guru accomplished this many-sided transformation in bold defiance of the age-old beliefs, dogmas and conservatism of the traditional Indian religions. The Khalsa created by Guru Gobind Singh was unique, both in its internal features and external form and was to play a vital role in Indian history. In the words of J. D. Cunnigham, "A living spirit possesses the whole Sikh people and the impress of Gobind has not only elevated and altered the constitution of their minds, but has operated materially and given amplitude to their physical frames."[13]

Let us here record the relevant and clear injunctions of Guru Gobind Singh, "He who keeps alight the torch of Truth and with love, has faith only in One Supreme Being, and does not believe, even by mistake, in fasting, monastic life, or worship of graves or ancestors, is the true Khalsa."[14] Further, a few extracts from the report of a Muslim chronicler, Ahmad Shah Batala, as given in his book *Twarikh-i-Hind,* of the speech by Guru Gobind Singh given at the time of the *amrit* (initiating) ceremony are as follows : "I wish you all to embrace one creed and follow one path, obliterating all differences of religion. Let the four Hindu castes, who have different rules laid down for them in the *Shastras,* abandon them altogether, and mix freely with one another. Let no one deem himself superior to another. Do not follow the old scriptures. Let none pay heed to the Ganges and other places of pilgrimage, which are considered holy in the Hindu religion, or adore Hindu deities, like Rama, Krishna, Brahma and Durga, but all should have faith only in Guru Nanak and his successors. Let men of four castes receive my *amrit,* eat out of the same vessel and feel no disgust or contempt for one another."[15]

The spirit of Guru Gobind Singh was carried on by Banda Singh Bahadur and his men, who fought against the Mughals under most adverse circumstances. But they stuck to their faith and principles until the end of their lives. The Sikh devotion to their religion and their spirit is evident from the fact that out of 740 Sikh prisoners of war, who were executed in Delhi, along with Banda, not one deserted the faith, even while given the choice to do so.[16]

SIKHISM IN THE 19TH CENTURY

Here it is necessary to give a demographic picture of the Sikh community from the 18th to the 19th century. The struggle and the persecution of the Sikhs were severest during the mid 18th century. A price was put on every Sikh head, and three times it was reported to the authorities that the Sikhs had been exterminated root and branch.[17] During this period of struggle, it is reported that at one time barely two thousand guerillas were left.[18] This was the spirit and character of the Sikhs, when they gained power in the later half of the 18th century. The establishment of the Khalsa commonwealth, naturally, gave opportunity both to Muslim and Hindu populations to seek conversion for reasons which were obviously mundane. The Sikhs never started any proselytising campaign, because it is not sanctified in their religion. Obviously, these new entrants were slow in shedding some of their old personal, family or customary prejudices and beliefs, which included faith in local gods and goddesses, saints, *fakirs* and *pirs*. In the time of Ranjit Singh the number of Sikhs, thus, rose to 10-11 *lakhs*.[19] The first census in 1881 reports that the number of Sikhs was 17 *lakhs*.[20] It is evident that this large scale increase in the number of Sikhs was certainly not due to the natural increase in the members of the faith, who had struggled to power in the 18th century. Regarding the Sikhs in the second half of the 19th century, Ibbetson reports that with the exception of the Akalis, who still adhered to the ordinances of the Khalsa, many of the original observances of the Sikhs had fallen in disuse but for the five external signs and abstinence from tobacco.[21] Similarly, the *sehjdhari* group of the Nirankaris, who were sixty thousand at the time of the census of 1891, never believed in any god or goddess and adhered strictly to faith in Guru Granth Sahib as the sole scripture and guide.[22]

A demoralising effect of the annexation of the Punjab was that some of the Sikh *gyanis*, who were very learned in their special departments, did not find jobs for their talents. They, therefore, went over to the Hindus and taught their religious books. Apart from neglecting the dissemination of Sikh thought, they, in order to please their employers, started giving a Hindu tint to the Sikh doctrines and beliefs, causing thereby great harm to Sikhism. Secondly, it is also true that many of the Hindu entrants to the Sikh faith who had naturally curbed or shed Hindu rituals and customs during the Sikh rule, reverted to their old prejudices and practices.

Before the advent of the Singh Sabha Movement in 1873, the Sikh society was, thus, passing through a lean phase. With their uncertain political future, Sikhs had become a prey to Brahminical Hinduism, and the socio-religious fabric of the community was being damaged. Owing to the weakness of some of the neo-Sikhs, the number of Sikhs embracing other faiths was increasing steadily.[23] A contemporary observer noted, "Just as we do not see any Buddhist in the country except in images, in the same fashion, the Sikhs, who are now here and there, visible in their turbans and their other religious forms like wrist-bangles and swords, will be seen only in pictures and museums. Their own sons and grandsons clad in coats and trousers and sporting mushroom-like caps will go to see them in museums and say in their pidgin Punjabi, 'Look, that is the picture of a Sikh — the tribe that inhabited this country once upon a time.'"[24]

The proselytising activities of the Christian missionaries also alarmed the Sikhs. The historic conversion of Maharaja Dalip Singh (son of Maharaja Ranjit Singh) and Raja Harnam Singh of Kapurthala to Christianity came as a rude shock to the Sikhs.[25] The British sponsored Christian Missions had started schools at Batala, Amritsar and Taran Tarn. When in 1873 some Sikh students of the Mission school at Amritsar were preparing to crop their heads and openly accept Christianity under pressure from the missionaries, the Sikhs of Amritsar had a rude awakening. They moved quickly to check this apostasy. In 1874 some important leaders got together to form the Amritsar Singh Sabha. They had taken a laudable step but they had in the forefront of this movement a few self-centred men such as Baba Khem Singh Bedi and the Raja of Faridkot. The former expected to be paid homage for his Bedi lindage and always demanded seat on a special dais in Sikh congregations. He also accepted offerings from followers, like *pujaris*. At about this time the Sikhs were being duped into an offer of assistance in their anti-Christian campaign by an artful Arya Samajist preacher — Swami Dayanand. His thesis was the abolition of idol worship, as he explained that God can be seen in all His Creation. He believed in the primacy of the Vedas but carefully concealed this view in his initial lectures in Punjab. He found an excellent ally in Giani Ditt Singh, who was just finding his feet under the able guidance of the Principal of the Oriental College, Lahore — Prof. Gurmukh Singh. Both these gentlemen had very humble beginnings — the former being a Ramdasia from Patiala, and the latter being the son of a cook of the Raja of Kapurthala.

Giani Ditt Singh had a sharp intellect, and after taking *amrit* and going through the full 'Giani' course in Divinity at the Oriental College, gained so much knowledge and mastery on the art of public speaking that he was able to hold his own against the best exponents of religious thought of those times. Swami Dayanand appreciated his talents and joined hands with him in the initial stage of their challenge to Christian preaching. But when the Swamy began extolling the Vedas and criticising Guru Nanak, calling him an uneducated man, ignorant of Sanskrit, etc., the Giani parted company. The Swamy published all his derogatory comments on the Gurus and their teachings in a treatise called *The Satyarath Parkash*. He was challenged to a public debate by Giani Ditt Singh and the latter was able to justify all the tenet of Sikhism and to prove the Swami wrong in all his surmises of the Creation.

As there was hardly any preaching of Sikhism amongst the masses either in the villages or in the towns, most of the new converts accepted the view of the Swami that Sikhs were only a part of the Sanatan Hindu fold. We must remember that the main gurdwaras at Nanakana Sahib, Taran Tarn, Lahore and Amritsar were in the hands of *mahants* and *pujaris*, who had no knowledge of *Gurbani*. They were in fact Hindus at heart, and had been given custody of gurdwaras under the policy of the British to keep the Sikhs away from their main source of inspiration and spiritual strength.

So a large number of Sikhs, especially the recent converts of convenience, shed their Sikh symbols, and reverted to Hinduism. And the Amritsar Singh Sabha, led by Baba Khem Singh and other landed gentry, did nothing to preach true Sikh principles but rather encouraged the cult of personal worship and collection of offerings. This practice, though in consonance with the old Hindu culture, was violative of Sikh doctrines, wherein the Gurus "had prohibited touching the feet of so-called pious men, and had stated that the religous path lay in working hard and sharing one's earnings with others."[26] But, these wealthy Sikhs had got a vested interest in these cults, because personal worship brought them offerings from both their Sikh and non-Sikh followers.[27] Out of sheer self-interest of maintaining their income and offerings from their Hindu followers, they started saying that the Gurus had preached the same religious system as in the Vedas, even though the Gurus had called 'the Vedic doctrines to be misleading concerning caste, heaven, hell, etc..'[28] So to blunt the onslaughts of the Christian Missions and of the Arya Samajs and to counter the wrong interpretation of the Sikh tenets by the leaders of the Amritsar Singh Sabha, Prof. Gurmukh Singh and Giani Ditt Singh founded in 1879 the Lahore Singh Sabha, which immediately set about the preaching of equality of man regardless of race, caste or economic status. They stressed the need for Sikh Rahit and faith only in the *Akal Purakh*, rejecting *devis, devatas* or any places of pilgrimage, etc. In other words, it was a revival of the teachings of the Gurus as contained in Guru Granth Sahib and in the Rahitnamas of Guru Gobind Singh. The first newspaper in Punjabi was out in 1880 under the editorship of these two stalwarts. When their message reached every village of Punjab, a new life was breathed into the followers of the Sikh way of life. Branches of the Lahore Singh Sabha sprang up in *scores* all over Punjab, and the earlier Amritsar Sabha lost its following.

Recently some scholars in the West have presented a distorted version of the nineteenth century Sikhism. For example, H.S. Oberoi, in his paper entitled *Re-reading Sikh Experience in the Nineteenth Century*, read recently at a seminar at Berkeley (U.S.A.), observes, "The word Sanatan derives from Sanskrit, and has connotation of something that is ancient, almost as if out of secular time. The Sanatanist Sikhs, therefore, believed that these customs, rites and rituals had origins in the beginnings of time, when the universe came into existence and were beyond the pale of diachronic time.' ...... 'The fact that the Sikhs took part in the myths, worship and cults of miracle saints, goddesses and village gods, does not imply that Sikhism was in a state of decline or irrational. These practices were an integral part of a coherent way of life, and should not be judged from standards which were invented at the turn of the century."

Let us now examine the position stated by Oberoi in his paper. He mentions four practices which he claims to be ancient and native to Sikhs of the times. These are the worship of Sakhi Sarvar, Guga Pir, Seetla Devi and village ancestors. A close examination of Oberoi's paper reveals that he has merely tried to conceal the reality by resort to vague generalisations, and by giving unnecessary details of the concerned practices, without specifying the extent of their prevalence in the Sikh society.

We first take up the case of the worship of Sakhi Sarvar which is the only practice of which he has indicated some data in support of his argument by saying that less than 3% Sikhs had faith in Sakhi Sarvar. Otherwise, about twenty pages of his paper are filled with irrelevant verbiage giving just a journalistic description of the four practices. The entire structure of Oberoi's argument is based on the flimsy premises that these practices were native and ancient, and that no one ever prohibited them. He writes, "It was Sikh reformers in the 19th century who for the first time labelled many of the current beliefs and practices among the Sikhs as acts of deviance and expressions of a superstitious mind." This observation of Oberoi is a clear misstatement. Guru Granth Sahib is full of hymns rejecting the spiritual character of *devis, jogis, pirs,* etc. "Afflicted are Brahma, Vishnu and Shiva; afflicted is the entire world."[29] "The Vedas do not know His greatness. Neither Brahma, nor Shiva have any clue of Him. The *devis* and *devatas* have sought to know Him, but failed."[30]

In the Sikh tradition there are four stories concerning the futility of Sakhi Sarvar worship. The first story is of a Sakhi Sarvaria, Bhai Manj, coming to Guru Arjun for religious guidance. The Guru's reply is very revealing of the Sikh thesis. He said, "You may go on with the easy path of Sakhi Sarvar worship, because Sikhism is a very difficult path, and unless you are willing to be dispossessed of your wealth and to sacrifice your very life, it is no use coming to me." But, Bhai Manj did become a Sikh.[31] The second story also concerns Guru Arjun when he deprecated the Sakhi Sarvar practice of preparing a big cake and presenting it before the priest who read Durud (a verse from Quran), and then kept the cake, giving only a marginal part to the devotees. The Guru says, "Without the true Guru they must sit and watch without eating until the Durud is read."[32] The Guru, thus, denounced the practice of seeking benediction of the priest, for, only a true Guru could lead one to the right path. The third story is of a Sikh's daughter having been married to the son of a Sakhi Sarvaria. The bride seeks the blessings of Guru Hargobind, and her husband also becomes a Sikh. A tussle develops between the groom and his father, when the former demolishes the family shrine of Sakhi Sarvar. But the groom continues to be a Sikh. Later, his handsome son founds a village now called Bhai Rupa in Nabha State.[33] A similar story concerning the futility of Sakhi Sarvar worship relates to the time of Guru Tegh Bahadur, when he visited Patiala area.[34] In fact, Sikh writings and *Rahitnamas* categorically prohibit the worship of *devi, devtas,* saints etc.[35] Even Bhangu in his *Panth Parkash* (mid 19th century) specifically condemns the worship of Sakhi Sarvar. He says that the Sikhs did not believe in ghosts, spirits and graves, nor did they have any faith in Guga and Sakhi Sarvar. He rather refers to the "frequent clashes between the Sikhs and the Sarvarias in the villages and towns of Punjab."[36] Therefore, in the face of a clear rejection of the Sakhi Sarvar practice by the Guru, the Sikh religious literature, and the traditions, the existence of a marginal 3% residue of the Sakhi Sarvarias among the new Hindu entrants to Sikhism, only shows how insignificant is its value in drawing a correct picture of the Sikh society in that period. In fact, it is creditable that under the Sikh influence all except about 3% of the new entrants had given up their old Hindus practices.

In this context, Rose clearly endorses Bhangu's view, "comparatively few Sikhs are followers of Sarvar, and there is in fact a sort of opposition in the central districts between Sikhs and Sultanis. You hear men say that one party in a village worships the Guru, the other worships Sarvar; that is that one party are Sikhs, the other ordinary

Hindus who follow Sarvar. It has been suggested that the worship of Sarvar probably spread eastward among the Jats in the 15th and 16th centuries, and was the prevalent cult at the time of the great development of Sikhism in the days of Guru Gobind Singh; and that most of the conversions to the Khalsa faith were from the worshippers of Sultan. This appears a very probable account of the origin of such opposition as does exist between these two forms of faith. As between the Hindus generally and the Sultanis there is no sort of opposition; there are instances in the popular legends of men opposing the cult of Sarvar, but in the present day the Sultanis are looked on as ordinary Hindus."[37] Oberoi, while he gives irrelevant details of the miraculous powers attributed to Sakhi Sarvar and lavishly quotes Rose as evidence, seems to have deliberately concealed the above mentioned conclusion drawn by Rose and, instead, made the distortion that Singh Sabha leaders were the first to object to such practices. Such clear misstatements are generally made by partisan propagandists, but never, we believe, by any academician. This indicates either a lack of indepth study or a conscious attempt to suppress facts with a view to misrepresenting Sikhism.

There is another misstatement when Oberoi says, "Historians cannot simply reproduce these value judgements and employ categories invented by a section of the Sikh elite." We have seen that prohibition of these practices was neither the invention of the Singh Sabha, nor was it the first to object to them. Nor is it true that leaders of the Singh Sabha formed a section of the Sikh elite. In fact, the pioneers of the Singh Sabha, namely, Bhais Ditt Singh and Gurmukh Singh were persons of extremely humble beginnings. Ditt Singh belonged to a poor Ramdasia family of a small village (Nandpur Kalaur) of district Ropar.[38] Gurmukh Singh's father was just a cook in Kapurthala.[39] As against that, the persons with vested interests in personal worship were Baba Sir Khem Singh Bedi, Baba Sir Gurbakhsh Singh Bedi and the Raja of Faridkot. Men like Vehiria were the proteges of wealthy persons, whom they had kept to propagate their point of view, even though clearly opposed to the Sikh doctrines in Guru Granth Sahib, and who constituted the elite, and who represented the voice of the people and the Sikh culture, is evident from the fact that in the tussle between them, all the local and base Singh Sabhas in the country shifted their loyalty to the Ditt Singh group, except three which belonged to the towns or places of these feudal kings.[40] It is, therefore, just naive to suggest that these persons of small beginnings could achieve the tremendous success they did achieve by just innovations or inventions, unless what they promoted or preached had the clear sanction of the scripture and the Sikh tradition. As pointed out earlier, the Singh Sabha of 1899 had quite a hard time in countering the inroads into Sikhism from both the Christian missions and the Arya Samaj. The onslaught still continues. One of the ex-missionaries has recently tried to create doubt and disbelief on every aspect of the Sikh tradition and history. His efforts include sponsoring bogus research by his own students, and promoting the appointments of non-Sikhs to certain Chairs of Sikh Studies in Canada. One of those incumbents is Dr Harjot Oberoi, who also suggests that the real background of Sikhs is Sanatani Hinduism and that present Sikhism is a later development that came up only in the later half of the 19th Century, under the influence of the Singh Sabha Movement. His stress on Sanatani origin of Sikhism and of peasant practices of the cults of Sakhi Sarvar and idol worship smacks so strongly of the Arya Samaj preachings of Swami Dayanand, that one begins to wonder if he is not from the same school himself. W. H. McLeod did well in picking such an enemy of Sikhism for the Chair of Sikh Studies at the University of British Columbia. It serves his grand design of undermining the Sikh religion by posing as one of its great promoters, and looking around for any schismatic literature such as the obscure manuscript 1245 to promote doubt and confusion among Sikhs.

Regarding Guga, Sitla and ancestor worship, Oberoi has given no data at all in support of his argument, meaning thereby that the extent of these practices was even less significant than the practice of Sakhi Sarvar worship. Oberoi instead of being precise has written page after page of a journalistic account of the practices without suggesting the extent of these practices, their sanction by the Sikh tradition, or their existence during any earlier period of Sikh history. Every student of Hindu religion knows that in that system, especially under *Purva Mimansa,* spiritual and other benefits can be obtained by the practice of Yajnas, sacrifices, mantras, etc. On the other hand, even the most elementry student of Guru Granth Sahib is aware that all such practices and worship of *devi, devatas* and the like are regarded as futile in Sikhism. Let us here just indicate two instances. Every scholar of Sikhism and Sikh history knows that the basic reason why the Hindu Hill Rajas refused to cooperate with the tenth Guru was his rejection of *devi* worship and their rituals and caste observances.[41] The second instance is of a complaint made to Guru Hargobind about a Sikh having broken an idol of a *devi*.[42] The Sikh explained as to what was the worth of a *devi* idol if it could not protect itself. It indicates that no one respected the *devi* or *devatas* in the Sikh society.

Without indicating any statistical evidence, Oberoi makes another assertion saying that "the popularity of Sakhi Sarvar among the Sikhs was matched by another *pir* called Guga Pir." It is necessary to understand that in the old Punjab, Sikhs were less than 14% and the Hindus were more than double the number of Sikhs; and even among the Sikhs about three fourths were 19th century Hindu converts of convenience. It is, therefore, highly misleading to talk in vague terms about some Hindu practices current among Punjab Hindus and then to relate them to the Sikhs on the mere ground that the Singh Sabha had also preached against them as being contrary to the Sikh tradition.

Regarding Sitla worship too, Oberoi is equally irrelevant and vague. The Sikh position about *devi* worship both in precept and practice, has already been indicated. In the article of the *Khalsa Akhbar* of March 6, 1896, it is the entire Punjab population that has been addressed to give up Sitla worship, without even mentioning the word Sikh therein. And the advice to the people is to have themselves inoculated instead of suffering the disease.

About ancestor worship among Sikhs, Oberoi's observations are even more far-fetched. He cites Dube's *Indian Village* and Brubaker's *A Study of South Indian Village Goddesses and their Religious Meaning.* The only reference to the Sikhs is a manual by an army officer mentioning that Satnamis, Hindus and Sikhs had a practice of ancestor worship.

From Oberoi's own paper, it is evident that Sitla, Guga and ancestor worship among the Sikhs were even less significant than the worship of Sakhi Sarvar prevalent among less than 3% Sikhs. It is suggested by Oberoi that though the practice of Sakhi Sarvar worship was insignificant in 1911, it must have been wide-spread and native to the Sikh society before the Singh Sabha propaganda. The argument is quite meaningless. If in the earlier four hundred years of preaching by the ten Gurus themselves and others, the Sikh tradition could not eliminate these Hindu practices entirely, how could the Singh Sabha workers, with humble beginnings, work this miracle in about one generation ? It is quite significant that in order to prove his point that in the 19th century there was not much of an ideological difference between the Hindus and the Sikhs, Oberoi has quoted neither Guru Granth Sahib nor any *Rahitnamas,* nor any earlier Sikh literature or traditions, but only A.S. Vahiria and Gulab Singh, both spokesmen of the Bedi group with vested interests in maintaining the cult of personal worship. So far as the loyalist Gulab Singh is concerned, his propagandist statement that the four Vedas are also the religious books of the Sikhs is quite understandable. But for Oberoi to quote him approvingly shows either poor scholarship and a gross ignorance of the contents of Guru Granth Sahib, the *Nash* doctrine of Guru Gobind Singh, the *Rahitnamas* and the Sikh religious literature and practices, or a deliberate attempt at distortion by his avoiding all references to Guru Granth Sahib and Sikh literature. Even in the article of the *Khalsa Akhbar*, dated March 29, 1901, it had clearly been argued by the Sikh paper, by quoting Guru Granth Sahib, that the Gurus had specifically repudiated the doctrine of the Vedas. Oberoi has also failed to record the categoric contemporary evidence that the Akalis, the core of the Panth, were fully adhering to the norm prescribed by the Gurus. If his conclusions were correct, and Sikhs, like the Hindu peasantry, were mere superstitious worshippers of *devi, devatas* and Guga and Sakhi Sarvar Pirs, how does Oberoi explain that (i) the Sikhs, an insignificant section of the population, were able to supplant the Mughal Empire in the entire north-west and stem once for all the wave after wave of invaders that had plagued India for a thousand years, (ii) a leaderless community gave to the British the toughest fight, almost to the point of their defeat and annihilation, on the Indian soil, (iii) the Sikhs were predominantly the people who organised and manned the first rebellion (Ghaddar rebellion) against the British, (iv) of the 121 persons executed and 2646 sentenced to life imprisonment during the entire freedom struggle during the 20th century, 93 and 2047, respectively, were Sikhs[43] and (v) during the period of Emergency from June, 1975 - March, 1977, involving the suspension of the Indian Constitution and abrogation of all human rights and individual liberties, it was only the Sikhs who conducted a regular civil disobedience movement (Save Democracy Morcha) suffering imprisonment of over forty thousand persons,[44] while in the rest of India, not even half that number courted arrest or imprisonment.[45]

CHANGES MADE BY SINGH SABHA

Now, considering the fourth aspect of the Singh Sabha Movement, namely, the revival it brought about in the Sikh society, we find that every step they took and change they made, had full sanction of the Sikh scripture and tradition. One has only to read *Ham Hindu Nahin* by Bhai Kahn Singh, and *Nakli Sikh Prabodh* by Ditt Singh, to find that almost every page quotes the *bani* of the Gurus in support of their suggestions.[46] The only new step they took, was the establishment of educational institutions on modern lines and the publication and propagation of religious literature, not available earlier, because the services of the Printing Press had not been fully established yet.

Oberoi denies that Sikh resurgence in the 19th century derived its inspiration from the teachings of the Gurus and the Sikh scripture. The greatest contribution of Singh Sabha lies in projecting Sikh religion in its traditional perspective. Sikhism is a revealed religion and has a recorded scripture authenticated by the Guru himself. Oberoi looks upon Sikhism as a rural religion, which "by definition is a part of the oral culture of people, and it is always difficult to reconstruct and recover all the elements which go into its making." Such statements prove the dishonesty of the writer in so far as there is a clear blackout of the writings of the Gurus, of Sikh tradition and practices, and of Sikh history in the earlier three centuries. In his entire paper, Oberoi has not quoted even one line from Guru Granth Sahib, indicating the principles of the Sikh faith; nor has he mentioned any of its fundamentals on which the Gurus insisted. The only conclusion one can draw is that Oberoi has not read and fully grasped a single page of our sacred scripture Guru Granth Sahib. To talk of the characteristics of the Sikh faith and beliefs without reference to the Gurus, Guru Granth Sahib, and the Sikh tradition and history, is something completely incomprehensible, if not deliberately biased. One wonders how Oberoi found a free and easy access to the so-called 'Oral tradition' to the exclusion of the actual Sikh history.

The burden of Oberoi's thesis is to highlight the points of deviation and departure from the Sikh tradition. In analysing the nature of Sikhism he forgets the historical perspective and the Sikh ideology. Marked by descriptive profusion and meaningless rhetoric, his thesis betrays an obvious ignorance of the basic tenets of the Sikh faith. By characterising the aberrations in the 19th century Sikh society as the original or ancient Sikhism, he has identified Sikh norms with the Hindu practices of the neo-converts. He has made a particular blackout of the Sikh history and the Sikh literature and injunctions that specifically prohibited pre-Sikh Hindu beliefs and practices. The author has taken it upon himself to select or reject any opinion; thus completely ignoring the traditional model and negating the original sources and opinions of many earlier or contemporary scholars. His contention that 'Sanatan Sikhism', (a term used by Swami Dayanand) constituted real Sikh tradition, is self-contradictory and deceptive. This term has had no place or relevance in the entire history of Sikhism or any earlier writings pertaining to Sikhs. A Sikh movement, Singh Sabha or any other, should be judged in terms of what the Gurus had taught and the Sikhs had practised in the Guru or the revolutionary period. Any attempt virtually to legitimize the Hindu practices or the aberrations against which the Sikh Gurus, the *Rahitnamas* and Sikh writings had launched a crusade, is nothing but misleading. Apart from the clear injunctions of Guru Gobind Singh quoted earlier, a near-contemporary source also records that "Guru Gobind Singh rejected the paths of both the Hindus and the Muslims, and created his own *Panth*."[47] The *Rahitnamas* emphasised that "the Sikhs should maintain their separate identity from the caste society."[48] Rattan Singh Bhangu, in his *Prachin Panth Prakash*, talks of "separate identity of the *Panth*, its egalitarian character, and the plebeian political objectives and character of the Khalsa."[49] The testimony of earlier injunctions, writings and contemporary observers cannot be ignored. Therefore, to designate the lean period of Sikhism, when Hindu practices had crept into it, as Sanatan Sikhism is a misnomer. To assess and measure the significance of an aberration in the period of decline of the Sikh movement, without reference to the norm, the long standing tradition or the injunctions in the scripture or Sikh writings, suggests a lack of sense of proportion or an attempt at distortion.

The Singh Sabha leaders aimed at "restoring the pristine purity of Sikhism,"[50] without propounding any philosophy of their own or introducing a new practice unsanctioned by the ideology or the tradition. Any Sikh, who adhered to the injunctions of the ten Gurus, and was ready to serve the community, could be admitted to the fold of the Singh Sabha.[51] There was no ceremony to be gone through for this purpose, nor was there any distinctive dress, badge or mark to be worn. The movement was not a new cult. It retained its democratic character, despite the efforts of some persons to style themselves as Gurus and to wield control over its affairs. Baba Khem Singh Bedi introduced a new cult, and tried to gain supremacy over the activities of the Sabha. Being a direct descendant of Guru Nanak, he virtually aspired to become a Guru.[52] He wanted a well-furnished seat (*gadella*) for himself, even in the presence of Guru Granth Sahib.[53] Baba Khem Singh Bedi wished his authority to be regarded as paramount and absolute in religious matters and himself to be looked upon as Guru in succession to Guru Nanak.[54] Bhai Avtar Singh Vahiria was a chosen associate of Baba Khem Singh Bedi. In his books, *Khalsa Dharam Shastar, Sikh Dharam Tat Darshan and Gurdarshan Shastar,* he writes that the Sikh Gurus did not prohibit the worship of gods and goddesses, and that it was wrong to remove caste distinctions.

Actually, it was such obvious misstatements that Prof. Gurmukh Singh, Giani Ditt Singh, Bhai Mayya Singh and Bhai Jawahar Singh of the Lahore Singh Sabha were out to controvert. They aimed at checking "outside influences and undesirable elements which had crept into Sikhism, and thus to restore it to its former purity."[55] Whereas the appeal of the Khem Singh Bedi and the Vahiria group, who had their own vested interests, was mostly confined to their personal circles, that of the Lahore Sabha went further and touched the hearts of the general mass of the community.[56] Missionaries (*Parcharaks*) were sent even in the interior of the province to spread the message of Sikhism among hundreds and thousands of the village folks, who constituted the backbone of the Sikh community, and without whose co-operation no movement could acquire a mass base. They made them aware of the fundamentals of Sikh religion, thereby removing all doubts regarding the identity and practices of the Khalsa. In the words of Giani Ditt Singh, "Having sprung from the Hindus, the Sikhs are yet a separate community clearly distinguished from them in outward form, religious and social outlook, conception of God and Gurus, mode of worship, language of the scriptures and their ideas regarding caste, pilgrimage and priesthood."[57]   In fact, the pamphlets and writings of the Singh Sabhaites profusely quote the scripture and religious writings in support of their views, exhorting Sikhs to shed the wrong practices that had crept in the Sikh fold following the political confusion after the defeat of the Khalsa.   Bhai Kahan Singh's book, *Ham Hindu Nahin* (We Are Not Hindus) was a conscious reaction against the propaganda by some of the Hindus and Sikhs like the Khem Singh and Vahiria group. Giani Gain Singh's *Panth Parkash,* Naurang Singh's *Sikh Hindu Nahin,* Jodh Singh's *Sacha Dharmi* and many others also quoted several passages from the Sikh scripture to prove that the Sikh religion was an independent religion, and had nothing to do with Hinduism.   In fact, Sikhism had controverted almost every fundamental of Hinduism.

Such writings inspired the Sikhs with self-confidence and gave them a renewed sense of distinctiveness and direction.[58]   The masses became sufficiently enlightened not to be misled by the Sikh vested interests and the Arya Samajists, who tried to say that Sikhs were a part of Hindus.   The Singh Sabha leaders had a clear and firm grasp of the issues facing the Sikhs.   They rightly realised that the form and spirit of the Khalsa could be kept intact only if the Sikhs conformed to the code of conduct prescribed by Guru Gobind Singh.   Any laxity in maintaining the five symbols (the five K's), they knew, would mean a fall from the faith and would lead to gradual erosion of the basic Sikh ideals.[59]   Bhai Kahn Singh in his books, *Gurmat Prabhakar and Gurmat Sudhakar,* quoted several passages from the Sikh scripture in order to prove that the worship of images was contrary to the teachings of the Gurus.

The Singh Sabha leaders laid emphasis on the inculcation of such virtues as love of God, service of one's fellow beings, purity of living, charitableness and truthfulness. They made it clear, as the Gurus had emphasised in their *bani*, that the way to one's moral and spiritual uplift lay through good deeds and not through miracles, mystries and *mantras*.   "The worship of the Almighty in homes is the best of all to obtain eternal happiness, rather than going to pilgrimage, where one was bound to be misled by selfish and greedy priests."[60]   Misguided notions regarding the worship of graves, tombs, *samadhs* and cremation marks, which were contrary to Sikh religious injunctions and tradition, were clearly condemned in the preachings of the Singh Sabha.[61]   Giani Ditt Singh's booklet *Durga Parbodh,* was written primarily to dispel the belief in *pirs* and *fakirs* which was of no avail and diverted man's attention from the path of righteousness. That is why, as indicated already, all the thirty seven Singh Sabhas, except the three Sabhas of Rawalpindi, Faridkot and Amritsar, which were personally connected with Khem Singh and Raja of Faridkot group, followed the lead of the Ditt Singh-Gurmukh Singh group.[62]

As a result, the period of diffidence was over, and Sikhism regained its self-confidence in its historic mission.   The Census Report of 1921 noted : "Sikhism is a religion with a very distinct worship of its own and having attained a position of independence, is fully entitled to rank as a separate religion."[63]

The passing of the Anand Marriage Act in 1909, legalising the Sikh form of marriage, was a significant achievement of the Singh Sabha. Various Sikh organisations and Singh Sabhas sent telegrams and petitions signed by *lakhs* of Sikhs, demanding the passing of the Act.[64] The Government was impressed by this demonstration of Sikh unity in favour of this legislation which involved a separate Sikh entity. It was an important step forward because the State was forced to accept the self assertion of the will of an independent socio-religious community.

The Sabha periodicals, the *Khalsa,* the *Khalsa Akhbar,* the *Khalsa Samachar,* the *Khalsa Advocate* and the *Sikhs and Sikhism* helped a great deal in projecting the true image of Sikhism. The influence of these periodicals was tremendous, and they greatly helped in quickening the pace of revival. They succeeded in counteracting the attack of the Arya Samajists and the Christian Missionaries, who were misrepresenting the teachings of the Sikh Gurus. These periodicals were run by persons like Giani Ditt Singh, Bhai Gurmukh Singh, Bhai Mayya Singh, Bhagat Lakshman Singh, and Bhai Vir Singh, who had been nurtured in the Sikh tradition.

People came in large numbers to receive *amrit.* A major plank of the Singh Sabha was a crusade of *Amrit Parchar,* because to revive the institution of initiation and the connected doctrine of *Nash,* making a complete break with all earlier religious and social traditions, was the best means of eliminating the Brahminical practices that had appeared among the Sikh ranks.[65] The Singh Sabha preachings being in line with the earlier tradition, and having the sanction of the Gurus and the scripture, were accepted and acted upon by all true Sikhs. In fact, the tremendous success the Singh Sabha revivalists had in bringing back dynamism in the Sikh life, was entirely due to their ability to invoke the authority of the Sikh Gurus, Guru Granth Sahib and the Sikh tradition in support of everything they said and preached. The chief pillars of the movement, workers like Giani Ditt Singh, Bhai Gurmukh Singh, Bhai Mayya Singh, Bhai Jawahar Singh and Bhagat Lakshman Singh, were very ordinary persons of hardly any consequence in the socio-economic or the political life of the community. There was nothing to recommend them except their devotion to the cause of the great tradition which the mass of the people understood very well.[66] It would, therefore, be naive to suggest that these simple Singh Sabha workers could have the capacity to impose on the community a new system, or make innovations in the Sikh ideology or even a major reform, without their suggestions and programme being strictly in line with the thesis of the Gurus, especially when many socially and politically influential persons in the Sikh community continued to oppose them.[67]

The Chief Khalsa Diwan formed a sub-committee to suggest ways and means to reform the gurdwaras that had gone into the hands of Brahminical priests and vested interests.[68] But it could not take effective measures because *mahants* and *pujaris* who controlled the gurdwaras enjoyed the support of the Government.[69] After this tussle, the *mahants* and the *pujaris* became hostile to the Singh Sabha leaders.[70] The Sikh public was rudely awakened to the evil designs of the *pujaris* when they condemned the *Komagata Maru* Sikhs at the Akal Takht, and presented a robe of honour to General Dyer after the tragedy of *Jallianwala Bagh.*[71] This made the Sikhs furious. It took the

Sikhs quite some time to get their shrines liberated from the *mahants* and the *pujaris*.

Nevertheless, the Singh Sabha succeeded in renewing a sense of self-awareness among the Sikhs. The movement, which derived its inspiration from the great spiritual heritage of the Gurus, did not 'invent' any standard of its own. It is highly incorrect, rather misleading, to attribute innovations to a movement which was wholly revivalist in its nature and character. In fact, to propound a new ideology was against the very basic principles of the Singh Sabha. A scholar, who sets out to study and understand the true nature of Sikhism, should do so in the context of the Sikh scripture and the historical background of the emergence of Sikhism. Oberoi's assertion that Sikhism is first and foremost a peasant faith or rural religion, displays a complete lack of knowledge and understanding of Guru Granth Sahib and the fundamentals of Sikhism. This deficiency is common with those who use social-science methodology in studying a religion and its history. Nowhere in the history of India or elsewhere in the world is there any evidence to suggest that the peasantry could, on its own, devise a radically new religious system or sustain a social revolution of the kind that took place in the Punjab.

Throughout the ages, Sikhism has shown a remarkable potency and will to grapple with all crises, without compromising the basic and enduring values of its faith. It is through tremendous sacrifices and sufferings, that the Sikhs have maintained their identity, ideals and ethos, and carried out the mission entrusted to them by their Gurus. Their birth, training, tradition and history have marked them out as a people separate from the rest. It is quite idle to draw simplistic conclusions about the Sikh religion and its history without an in-depth study and analysis of the Sikh scripture and the role of each doctrine and institution in shaping the Sikh movement and the revolutionary changes it brought about.

The study of the Singh Sabha Movement in isolation, and in complete disregard of the Sikh ideology and the earlier Sikh history, apart from being methodically inadequate and faulty, shows very clearly the failings of a narrow and lopsided approach. Lloyd has drawn a very interesting caricature of an anthropological view which would first magnify a very narrow aspect of a social phenomenon and then try to draw inferences therefrom. The social anthropologist who views religion as a social institution, quite often, fails to take into account the socio-cultural complex, "constituted by institutions, rules, beliefs and intentions", and arrives at erroneous conclusions.[72] Lloyd has provided a rather amusing account of what a tribal anthropologist might see, if he visited the Brighton beach in the middle of summer. The anthropologist's account, he says, may read somewhat like the following :

"The people of England are religious and devout worshippers of the sun. Each year they leave their homes and travel to the coast for the purpose of worship, and often take up small accommodation in tents, or in what they call caravans, or live with other people during their short stay. Each day they begin worship by prostrating themselves on the shingle in the heat of the sun, which is often so hot that they wear shields over their eyes. Their bodies become burnt and some become ill, but few are deterred by this, such is their devotion. At various times people will baptise themselves in the waters, calling to each other and waving their arms in ecstacy. At midday, families group together when a symbolic ceremony takes place. Three-cornered pieces of bread, known to the natives as 'sandwiches' are passed around and eaten. During the afternoon they throw symbolic, large, inflated, multi-coloured orbs to one another, illustrating the dominance of the sun in their lives. Throughout all this, elders lie motionless in their canvas seats with their faces covered, in deep and prolonged meditation. These observances may continue for a family for upto fourteen days, when they return to their work until the following year."[73]

Lloyd says that such an interpretation of what the people of Brighton beach were doing, seems quite consistant with their physical movements. That is to say, if these people really were sun-worshipping, instead of sun-bathing and enjoying themselves, their bodily movements may be no different. The difference lies in how they saw their movements. What the anthropologist did not do, was to see things the way the natives did, to entertain the ideas they had, to understand the significance that these things had for them. If we wish to understand what a person is doing we have to understand not only his beliefs and intentions, but also the socio-cultural context and institutions, norms and rules which provide the framework within which he forms his purposes in terms of appraisal of his situation. Oberoi's study is equally narrow and inept in its vision.

CONCLUSION

A lop-sided or isolated study of a few rituals and beliefs prevalent in a very small section of the community during a particularly lean period cannot form the basis of a study of Sikhism and its ideology. The worshipping of a 'Sakhi Sarvar' by less than three percent of ignorant and illiterate villagers or a similar local aberration, cannot be regarded as the views and practices of the entire Sikh community, especially when the Sikh scripture, tradition and writings had specifically and repeatedly condemned them, and when there was hardly a trace of them in the Sikh community of the Guru period or of the 18th century.

People of different religions are quite often found harmonising together in social life and mutually respecting, understanding and taking part in each other's cultural activities. For example, *Purdah* system which crept into the Hindu society bore the stamp of Muslim culture. It is misleading to draw inferences about the form and dynamics of a religion on the basis of socio-cultural practices and usages, which are local and temporary in character. A visitor to a Christian Sunday worship in a Punjabi village observed that "many aspects of the worship were strongly influenced by Punjabi village culture, e.g., the timing of worship, taking off shoes outside the church, the separation of the men from the women, the noise and informality of worship, the music and musical instruments."[74] If some Sikhs and Muslims worshipped the Sakhi Sarvar, it does not mean that Islam and Sikhism are not independent religions, or that such worship is native to the two religions. "Saturnatia, the Roman winter festival of 17-21 December, provided the merriment, gift-giving and candles typical of later Christmas holidays. Sun worship hung on in Roman Christianity, and Pope Leo I in the middle of the fifth century, rebuked worshippers who turned round to bow to the sun before entering St. Peter's basilica, some pagan customs which were later Christianised, ... In short, many pagan customs continued in Christianity in one form or the other for centuries on end."[75]

There are features which are particular to Punjab, and there are practices derived from the surrounding culture, which give it a particular flavour not found in other parts of the world. Popular legends of *Heer-Ranjha, Sassi-Punnu* and *Sohni Mahiwal* (mentioned by Oberoi) which found mention in the Punjabi literature placed no impediments in the recognition of Sikhism as an independent religion.

There are certain features of a culture which are local and temporal and cannot by any stretch be deemed to be a part of the prevailing religious system. Just as the pop music that is a common feature of the urban life of the Indian community today could not be called an integral part of the Brahminical religion, in the same way, it would be wrong to characterise folk fables and love stories of *Heer Ranjha, Sassi Punnu*, etc. as a part of the Sikh religion.

Our discussion of the four related aspects of the Singh Sabha Movement shows that while it played an important and significant regenerative role during a lean period of Sikh history, it was wholly a revivalist movement, working strictly within the parameters of the Sikh religion and its tradition. In fact, the very reasons that it invoked the authority of the Gurus and Guru Granth Sahib, and placed before the public examples of the Sikh society and Sikh heroes who had suffered and sacrificed for the principles of Sikh religion, account for the success of the Singh Sabha leaders in safely and creditably steering the Sikh community towards its goals.

REFERENCES

1. Guru Granth Sahib : p. 129.
2. Ibid., p. 357.
3. Ibid., p. 556.
4. Ibid., p. 1243.
5. Ibid., p. 145.
6. Ibid., p. 1288.
7. Ibid., pp. 830.
8. Ibid., pp. 1412,
9. Ibid., pp. 1298.
10. Ibid., p. 1290.
11. Gurdev Singh : *Sikh Tradition,* (Chandigarh, 1986), p. 328.
12. Cunningham, J. D. : *A History of the Sikhs* (Delhi, 1966); p. 64.
    Bannerjee, Indubhushan : *Evoultion of the Khalsa,* Vol. II (Calcutta, 1962), p.116.
    Also Daljeet Singh : *Sikhism* (New Delhi, 1979), pp. 285-286.
13. Cunningham, J. D. : op. cit., p. 75.
14. Guru Gobind Singh : *Dasam Granth, Kabit Swayia,* p. 712.
15. Ahmad Shah Batala : *Tawarikh-i-Hind,* A.H. 1233/A.D. 1818, pp. 405-6; Also printed in *Zikar-i-Quruan-Ibtida-i-Singhan-Wa-Mazhab-i-Eshan-Twarikh-Daftri-Sohan,* Sohan Lal Suri.
16. Cunningham, J. D. : op. cit., pp.79-80.
    Ganda Singh : *Early European Accounts of the Sikhs* (New Delhi, 1974), p.188.

17. Gupta, Hari Ram : *History of the Sikhs,* Vol. II, pp. 39-45; Also Vol. I, p. 281.
18. Kohli, Sita Ram : Foreword to *Umdat-Ut-Tawarikh* of Sohan Lal Suri, Daftar IV, p. ii.
19. Devi Prasad, Pandit : *Gulshan-i-Punjab* (Lukhnow 1872), p. 224.
    See also Cunningham : op. cit., p. 301.
20. *Census of India,* 1921 (Punjab and Delhi), Vol. XV, Part I. p. 184.
21. Ibbeston, Denzil : *Punjab Castes* (Reprinted) (Patiala, 1970), p. 228.
    Similar views are also expressed by Major R. Leech. For details see Leech, R.(Major) : *Notes on the Religion of the Sikhs and Other Sects Inhabiting the Punjab;* Foreign Secret Proceedings, Vol. 590, 6-20, December 1845, 3712.
22. Nirankari, Man Singh : *The Nirankaris As Harbinger of Sikhs Renaissance,* article published in the book entitled *A Prophecy Fulfilled* (Amritsar, 1984), edited by the same author, p. 48.
23. Sahni, Ruchi Ram : *The Gurdwara Reform Movement and the Sikh Awakening* (Jullundur, 1922), p. 34.
    Also Bingley, A. H. : *The Sikhs* (Reprint) (Patiala, 1970), p. 56.
24. *The Khalsa Akhbar,* Lahore, May 25, 1894.
25. Clark, Robert (Revd.) : *Thirty Years of Missionary Work in Punjab and Sindh* (Lahore, 1883), pp. 219-20, 224 and 246.
26. Guru Granth Sahib : p.1245.
27. Gurmukh Singh, Bhai : *My Attempted Ex-communication From the Sikh Temples and the Khalsa Community at Faridkot in 1897* (Lahore, 1898), pp. 2-3.
28. Macauliffe, M. A. : *The Sikh Religion,* Vol. I, pp. 310 and 379.
29. Guru Granth Sahib : p. 1153.
30. Ibid., p. 310.
31. Macauliffe, M. A. : op. cit., Vol. III, pp. 7-8.
32. Ibid., p. 419.
33. Ibid, Vol. IV, pp. 147-49.
34. Ibid., pp. 339-40.
35. (Prahlad Singh), *Rahitnama,* edited by Piara Singh Padam, p. 55. Also *Rahitnama* (Daya Singh), p. 64.
36. Bhangu, Rattan Singh : *Prachin Panth Parkash* (ed.) Bhai Vir Singh, Amritsar, 1962 pp. 42 and 47.
37. Rose, H. A. : *A Glossary of the Tribes and Castes of the Punjab and North-West Frontier Province* Vol. III (Reprint 1970, Patiala), pp. 436-437.
38. Daljit Singh : *Singh Sabha de Modhi Giani Ditt Singh Ji,* (Amritsar, 1951), pp. 72-73.
39. *The Khalsa Akhbar,* Lahore, September 30, 1898.
40. Petrie, D. : *Memorandum on Recent Developments in Sikh Politics* (Simla, August 11, 1911), *The Panjab Past and Present,* Vol. IV, Part II (Patiala, October, 1970), pp. 310-11.
41. Koer Singh : *Gurbilas Patshahi Das,* p. 137; Macauliffe : op. cit., Vol. V, pp. 99-100. Also Jagjit Singh : *The Sikh Revolution* (Chandigarh, 1981), p.177.
42. Macauliffe : op. cit., Vol. V, p. 218; Jagjit Singh : Ibid., p. 278.
43. Bharat Mukti Morcha, *Punjab : The Sikh Case* (Chandigarh, 1988). They have quoted Maulana Abdul Kalam Azad as an evidence in support of these figures.
44. Akbar, M. J. : *India : The Siege Within* (London, 1985), pp. 307-8.
45. Ibid.
46. For details see Kahn Singh, Bhai; *Ham Hindu Nahin* (Reprint, Amritsar, 1973) and Ditt Singh, Giani; *Nakli Sikh Parbodh* (Reprint, Amritsar, 1974).
47. Koer Singh : *Gurbilas Patshahi Das* (Patiala, 1968), pp. 136,143.
48. Padam, Piara Singh (edited), *Rahitnama* (Patiala, 1974), pp. 68-69.
49. Jagjit Singh : op. cit., pp. 291-92.
50. Ganda Singh : *A History of the Khalsa College Amritsar,* (Amritsar, 1949), p. 2.
51. Ibid.
52. Khem Singh Bedi's followers called him *Avtar* (incarnation of God). For details see Avtar Singh

Vahiria, Bhai; *Shok Pattar* (Lahore 1905), p. 38.

53. *The Khalsa Akhbar,* Lahore, April 14, 1899.

54. Petrie, D. op. cit., pp. 310-311.

55. Jagjit Singh : *Singh Sabha Lehr* (Tarn Tarn, 1941), pp. 16-17.

56. *The Civil and Military Gazette,* Lahore, April 30, 1888; Petrie, D; op. cit., p. 311.

57. *The Khalsa Akhbar,* Lahore, November 18, 1898.

58. Jodh Singh, Bhai; *Guru Sahib Ate Ved* (Amritsar, n.d.) pp.15-20.

59. Gian Singh, Giani; *Panth Parkash* (Patiala, 1970), reprint, pp. 233-34.

60. Macauliffe's Lecture, delivered at Simla and published in the *Khalsa Akhbar,* Lahore, August 14, 1903.

61. Teja Singh, Babu; *Singhan Da Panth Niyara* (Amritsar, 1900), pp. 1-5.

62. Lakshman Singh, Bhagat; *Autobiography* (edited by Ganda Singh), (Calcutta, 1965), pp. 142-143.

63. *Census of India, 1921, Punjab and Delhi,* Vol.XV, p. 171.

64. Talwar, K.S. : *The Anand Marriage Act. The Panjab Past and Present* (October, 1968), Vol. II, p. 407.

65. Teja Singh : *Sikhism Its Ideals and Institutions* (Calcutta 1938), pp. 38-39.

66. *The Civil and Military Gazettee,* Lahore , April 30, 1888.

67. Ibid.

68. Caveeshar, Sardul Singh : *The Sikh Studies* (Lahore, 1937), pp. 189-90.

69. Ibid.

70. Ibid.

71. Ibid.

72. Gautam, Satya P. : *On Understanding Human Action,* Paper read at a Seminar on *Philosophical Theory and Social Reality*, January 18-22, 1982 available at Nehru Memorial Museum and Library, New Delhi.

73. Lloyd, D. L : *Nature of Man, in Philosophy and the Teacher* edited by D.L.Lloyd, (London; Routlege and Kegan Paul 1978), p. 36.

74. Caleb, Maqbul : *Chrisitan Sunday Worship In a Punjabi Village,* an article published in a book entitled, *Popular Religion In the Punjab Today* edited by Johan C. B. Webster (Delhi, 1974), p. 125.

75. Richard A. Todd. : *Eerdsmans' Handbook to the History of Christianity* (Michigan, 1987) pp. 131-32.

30

SIKHS AND THE BRITISH

GURDARSHAN SINGH DHILLON

Recently many scholars, especially in the West, have contended that the assertion of a distinct Sikh identity in the mid-nineteenth century was very largely due to advertent support extended by the British. W. H. McLeod holds that "there were several Sikh identities available during the period immediately following the 1849 annexation and one such identity (the militant Khalsa version) was vigorously promoted by the British in order to serve their own military purposes. The same identity was accepted by the stronger[1] of the Singh Sabha leaders and became the focus of their reforming activities late in the nineteenth century."[2] Richard Fox refers to the Sikhs in the Indian army "transmuted into Singhs by the British."[3] Scholars like N. G. Barrier and Rajiv Kapur have also referred to the recruiting and organisational policy of the British Indian army as the instrument for fostering the distinct Sikh identity. Rajiv Kapur observes : "Recruitment into the army provided strong encouragement for the development and maintenance of a separate Sikh identity."[4] Barrier[5] and Fox[6] both find themselves caught in an intricate and incoherent analysis of the British motives in dealing with the Sikhs.

The Relevant Questions Are : Did not the Sikh leaders invoke the Sikh doctrine in the Guru Granth ? Was it not inevitable for a Sikh movement, aimed at restoring the purity of Sikhism, to remove outside accretions, including Hindu influences and make the Sikhs stand on their own ground un-encumbered ? Was it not necessary for the Sikhs to go through a discipline of education in order to equip themselves for participation in the political life ? Is it right to brand the Singh Sabha leaders as loyalists and accuse them of misguiding the community to serve the ends of the British in India ? Did not the Sikhs have to wage a long battle to maintain their religious institutions and practices and free their gurdwaras from the control of the *mahants* and *pujaris*, who enjoyed the patronage and backing of the British ? Is it right or misleading for the historians to talk of the role of the British military policy in promoting the Sikh identity and to make a complete blackout of the Sikh ideology and four hunderd years of the Guru period and

Sikh history ? How can they turn a blind eye to the patronage extended by the British to the *mahants* (Priests) at the Sikh temples who because of their background opposed the Sikh identity tooth and nail ?

In deriving some of their hasty and ill-conceived inferences, the writers fail to study the subject methodically and to see the *Singh Sabha* Movement and its work in the background of (a) the Sikh ideology, (b) the method and history of the Sikh Gurus and the Sikh movement in the preceding three hundred and fifty years, and (c) the general and overall historical perspective of ideological movements during their lean periods. Therefore, in order to make a comprehensive and methodical study of the subject, we shall divide our paper under the following heads :   (i) the Sikh ideology, (ii) the preparatory period of educating and motivating the masses, (iii) reviving institutions and centres of the faith to rebuild the Panth and its distinct identity and the final stage of political preparation and struggle, (iv) realities of the situation after the annexation of Punjab and factors hostile to Sikh identity, (v) the *Singh Sabha* Movement and its plan of work, activities and achievements, (vi) the preparatory stage leading to the second stage of Gurdwara Reform Movement and participation in political struggle, (vii) general historical perspective, and (viii) conclusion.

First of all we shall take up the salient features of Sikh religion, especially where Sikhism made a radical departure from the earlier religious traditions.

SIKH IDEOLOGY

Sikhism is a revelatory religion, which revolted against the religious hypocrisy of the Brahmins and the political oppression of the contemporary rulers. Guru Nanak, the founder of the Sikh religion, stressed the unity of God[7] and the brotherhood of man.[8] He attacked such pillars of the Hindu society as caste,[9] idolatry,[10] ritualism,[11] asceticism[12] and intermediary role of the priests[13] in man's relations with God. His spiritual thesis, with an inalienable social content, sought to establish equality, not only between man and man, but also between man and woman. He welded the spiritual and the temporal planes of human existence into a harmonious whole, and brought about reconciliation between the religious and the secular means for achieving the best results in human affairs.[14] The Guru's followers were not required to chant Sanskrit *salokas* before stone idols but sang hymns composed by the Guru himself in their mother tongue. They came to have different places and modes of worship. It was not an easy task to confront the dogmatism of the priest-dominated and caste-ridden Hindu society. The Guru brought about a far-reaching transformation in the minds of the people through the institutions of *Shabad, Sangat, Pangat, Guru-Ka-Langar,* Guru and *Dharamsal.* The three cardinal principles of Guru's teachings were : *'Kirt Karo'* (earn your bread through hard labour), *'Vand Chhako'* (Share your earnings with others) and *'Naam Japo'* (always remember God). This resulted in building a separate and self-reliant community with new beliefs and institutions.

The process of separation of identity was carried forward by the second Sikh Guru Angad. He introduced the Gurmukhi script, in which he compiled Guru Nanak's and his own compositions. The Guru was opposed to mendicancy and parasitical living. He earned his own living by twisting coarse grass strings used for cots. The third Guru Amar Das took many steps which tended to break further the affiliations of the Sikhs with the Hindus. He introduced new forms of ceremonials for birth, death and marriage. He deprecated the practice of *'Purdah'* and *'Sati'*; encouraged inter-caste alliances and re-marriage of widows. He declared that the Sikhs who were active householders were wholly separate from the passive and recluse *'Udasis'* whom he excluded form the Sikh society. The Guru established twenty two new centres or parishes (*Manjis*) for conveying the message of Guru Nanak to the people.

These centres were supposed to cater both to the religious and the empirical needs of the people. Guru Ram Das, who succeeded him as the fourth Guru, acquired the site of the present city of Amritsar which became the religious capital of the Sikhs. He had a tank dug, around which bazars or trading centres were established.

Guru Arjun Dev, the fifth Guru, took some very important steps for fortifying the Sikh identity. He raised the Harimandir, and gave to the Sikhs a central place and shrine of their own. This was to wean away Sikhs from Hindu institutions like those at Hardwar, Varanasi, etc. He also gave the Sikhs a scripture of their own in the form of Guru Granth Sahib, which they could read and understand. They did not require the help of Brahmin priests to read out Sanskrit texts from the Vedas or the Upanishads, which they did not understand. It was Guru Arjun, who very clearly and emphatically declared that the Sikhs were an independent community :

> *" I do not keep the Hindu fast,*
> *nor the Muslim Ramadan;*
> *I serve Him alone who is my refuge,*
> *I serve the one Master who is also Allah,*
> *I have broken with the Hindu and the Muslim,*
> *I will not worship with the Hindu, nor like*
> *The Muslim go to Mecca,*
> *I shall serve Him and no other,*
> *I will not pray to idols nor say the Muslim prayer;*
> *I shall put my heart at the feet of the One Supreme Being;*
> *For we are neither Hindus nor Mussalmans"*[15]

The Guru made, for the principles of his religion, the supreme sacrifice of his life, and became the first martyr in Sikh history. Guru Arjun's son and successor Guru Hargobind started military preparations. His resort to arms was in keeping with the last instructions of his father. Guru Nanak too had rejected *Ahimsa* as an inviolable religious doctrine. Facing the Harimandar, Guru Hargobind built the Akal Takht, a seat of the temporal authority as distinct from Harimandar Sahib, clearly signifying that the Sikhs owed their primary allegiance to God. He also hoisted two flags before it as visible symbols of *miri* and *piri*, i.e., the temporal and the religious authorities. The concept of *miri* and *piri* was the natural and inevitable outcome of the doctrine of the combination of the spiritual and the empirical, laid down by the first Guru. That this combination is fundamental to the Sikh doctrine, is clear from the fact that in Sikhism the insignia for

Piri or spiritualism is a sword, and not a rosary. Many of the misunderstandings by scholars of Sikhism or its history are due to their failure to have an adequate knowledge of the Sikh ideology. This lack of knowledge, or sometimes bias, is quite apparent among scholars drawn from pacificist or dichotomous religions.

The ninth Sikh guru, Guru Tegh Bahadur suffered martyrdom to counter the forces of tyranny and injustice and to uphold the freedom of man to practise his religion. He demonstrated that to lay down one's life in defence of righteousness was a paramount religious duty. When a report was sent to Emperor Aurangzeb that the Guru was organising a people (*millat*), he offered to the Guru that if he confined his activities to prayers and preachings, he would be given grants for the purpose, provided he gave up his political activities. But the Guru declined the offer.[16] The inspiration stemming from the creative vision of Guru Nanak reached its climax under the tenth Guru, Gobind Singh. The ideal of Saint-Soldier implicit in the *Miri-Piri* doctrine of Guru Nanak fructified in the creation of the Khalsa of Guru Gobind Singh. It was the objective of the Sikh society or Khalsa to restore justice and harmony in the prevailing state of affairs. He created the Khalsa, a disciplined body of Sikhs, and conferred upon them a distinct personality. He gave them a martial name 'Singh' (Lion), and prescribed five *kakar* including *kirpan* and unshorn hair. In fact, the rule about keeping unshorn hair started a debate, and those wanting to cut their hair and to follow Hindu customs were automatically excluded from the Sikh society.[17] The symbols strengthened religious discipline, gave external uniformity to the Sikh faith, and served as aids to the preservation of the corporate life of the community. It is very important to remember that the egalitarian principle was an accepted and practised norm of Sikh society. It is noteworthy that four out of the five *Piaras* (Beloved ones), who offered their heads to the Guru, and were initiated were Shudras. He intended to make a complete break with the past religious tradition through the introduction of the *nash* doctrine involving *Kirtnash, Kulnash, Dharamnash, Bharamnash* and *Karamnash*,[18] i.e., the giving up of all those beliefs, ideologies and practices that came in the way of the sole worship of the One Supreme Being. The creation of the Khalsa was a unique phenomenon in the annals of mankind. It was the epitome of the Sikh movement. There is no evidence, whatsoever, to suggest that there was any other Sikh identity or society promoted by the Gurus or in existence in the seventeenth or eighteenth century. The Guru raised the Indian spirit from servility, interiority, fatalism and defeatism to the dynamic ideal of responsible reaction and resistance against tyranny and injustice. The supreme acts of martyrdom of the Guru, his father, mother and four sons for the cause of righteousness left an indelible stamp on the Sikh way of life. It is sheer idleness and mischief to think or suggest that the deep seated moral conditioning created by the longest chain of martyrdoms and conscious struggles, could just be re-created or affected by any wishful self-interest of the British or any other ruler. Such artificial creation of religious identity is unknown to history.

During his lifetime Guru Gobind Singh chose Banda Singh Bahadur to conduct the final phase of the Sikh struggle against the Mughal Empire. It was under his leadership that the Khalsa armies won decisive victories and shook the very foundations of the mighty Mughal Empire. Banda struck coins in the name of the Khalsa Panth. The inscriptions on the coins are significant :

"This coin is struck as a token of our sovereignty here and hereafter. This divine bounty flows from the sword of Nanak (*Tegh-i-Nanak*) and the victory and felicity is the gift of Guru Gobind Singh, the king of kings, the true master."[19]

This coin itself clearly signifies that in the consciousness of the Sikhs of those times, there was complete unity of spirit and ideology between the first and the last Guru and in fact, among all Gurus. It clearly shows that the concept about differences in the ideologies of the first and the tenth Guru is due to the ignorance of some of the biased writers of the present day. Banda Bahadur's seal also depicted similar thought, i.e., "*Degh*, the kettle for service; *Tegh*, the strength of the sword; and *Fateh*, the resultant victory, received from Guru Nanak and Guru Gobind Singh."[20]

Under Banda's inspiration, Sikhism became popluar with the people of Punjab. About one lac persons embraced Sikhism. Banda and several hundered soldiers of the Khalsa army who were arrested, kept their cool even in the face of death. None of them renounced his faith to save his life.[21] They carried on the glorious traditions of sacrifice and martyrdom for the cause of righteousness handed down to them by the Gurus. Their blood created fertile soil for sprouting the seeds of Sikh glory. The Sikhs confronted the hordes of Persian and Afghan invaders with the same religious spirit. This was a time when a price was put on every Sikh head, and thrice it was reported to the authorities that the Sikhs had been exterminated root and branch.[22] The imperial order for the elimination of the Sikhs was directed at the destruction of the *Nanakpanthis*.[23] It did not declare them as Sikhs or *Singhs* or the *Khalsa*. This clearly indicated that there was no question of any multiple identities among the Sikhs in the eighteenth century. The clear teachings of the ten Gurus and the fire of suffering and persecution had welded the Sikhs with a unity of ideals, ethos and practices entirely different from those of the Hindu society with which they were surrounded. The *Bani* and the *Nash* doctrine created the wall of division betweem them, and persecution and suffering cemented the internal cohesion of the community as a distinct society. For the followers of the Gurus and their opponents, there was only one community of *Nanakpanthis*, Sikhs or Khalsa whose sole founder was Guru Nanak. The definition of a Sikh was very clear, without any scope for ambiguity. There was no question of any multiple identities among the Sikhs.

After a long period of turmoil, suffering and persecution, the Sikhs rose to political power under Ranjit Singh, who ruled under the banner of Sarkar-i-Khalsa. It was at this time that Hindus swelled the ranks of the Khalsa in the hope of temporal gains. The population of the Sikhs, which at one time was reported to be not more than twenty thousand in the 18th century now rose to the peak figure of 10-11 *lakhs* in the times of Ranjit Singh.[24] It was not so easy for these converts of convenience to shed some of their beliefs and practices. Ranjit Singh had to spend most of his time in conquering and consolidating territories. The result was that the Sikhs had hardly any time to set their house in order. It is evident that the large scale increase in the Sikh population was due to the new entrants who had flocked to the new faith not out of conviction but to put up an appearance of closer ties with the people in power.[25] There began a new phase of Sikhism with new entrants to the Sikh fold. Their ways and customs were still overlaid with Hinduism. It was very easy for them to slide back into their old faith when power did not rest with the community. This was the first time in their history that the Sikhs could be divided into two categories, the first consisting of those who nursed their traditional culture and carried in them the spirit to suffer and sacrifice for a righteous cause, and the second comprising the new lot with hardly any strong commitment to the faith. During the Guru and the post-Guru period there is no evidence, whatsoever, of the so called "multiple identities." During the phase of struggle and persecution in the 18th century, when to be a Sikh was to invite death, the Sikhs never had any ambiguity about their identity or ideals created by the ten Nanaks. And both for the insiders and outsiders there was a single community of society they had created. They kept the torch of Sikhism ablaze through tremendous suffering and sacrifice.

POST-ANNEXATION PERIOD

With the fall of the Sikh kingdom, the new entrants to the Sikh fold started wavering in their loyalty to Sikhism. The Sikhs had hardly had peace for one generation, when some of these new entrants reverted to Hinduism and its old prejudices and practices.[26] Still there were many for whom the border line between Hinduism and Sikhism became very thin and vague, and they kept unsurely on the border line. In their outlook, character and behaviour they stood clearly apart from the main segment of the Sikh society who had a clear identity. The latter traced their lineage from the Guru period and had inherited the glorious tradition of martyrdom for the cause of righteousness. With the emergence of the British as the new rulers, the relationships between Muslims, Hindus and Sikhs underwent a complete change. In Punjab the Hindus, who had looked upon the Sikhs as their protectors against the Muslims and were partners in power during the years of triumphs under Ranjit Singh, showed hardly any commitment towards Sikhism that had successfully fought battles for liberty and freedom of the land and its people. With both the Muslim threat and the Sikh kingdom gone, the external pressures that had held them seemingly close to Sikhism disappeared. They had to redefine their mutual relationship. Apart from this, the role of some members of the Hindu elites during the period of annexation, a point which we shall detail later on, was far from creditable, and created some gap between the two communities. It is note-worthy that the Hindu *Dogras* and *Purbias* during the crucial Anglo-Sikh wars deserted the Khalsa army. On the other hand, the Muslim part of the Khalsa army fought against the British till the end.[27] Tears at the defeat of Sarkar-i-Khalsa were shed by Shah Muhammad, the celebrated Muslim poet.

The British looked upon the Sikhs as enemies, and initiated a policy aimed at the suppression of the "War-like Sikhs", with the help of an army of occupation comprising 60,000 soldiers and a police force of 15,000, largely manned by the Punjabi Muslims.[28] Special precautions were taken in policing the Majha area, where Bhai Mehraj Singh and Narain Singh were reported to be active.[29] The royal house of the Sikhs was completely destroyed. It is well-known that Maharani Jindan, called the "mother of the Khalsa," whom the British considered to be the root cause of all trouble, was treated very shabbily and was forced to leave the country.[30] The minor Maharaja Dalip Singh was made to resign "for himself, his heirs and successors, all rights, title and claim to the sovereignty of the Punjab or to any sovereign power whatever."[31] The 'Koh-i-Noor' considered by Dalhousie as a historical emblem of conquest in India, was 'presented' to the Queen of England.[32]

The Government confiscated all the valuables, including the antiques of the Sikh Raj from the Toshakhana of the Maharaja, and also the estates of all those chiefs who had fought against the British in the two Anglo-Sikh Wars.[33] Some of them were exiled from the Punjab, and others were kept under surveillance in their own houses. They were not allowed to keep arms in their possession.[34] Forts and defensive fortifications — practically every Sikh village had defensive bastions — were levelled. All military grants to the Sikh Jagirdars were abolished.[35] Henry Lawrence, as head of the Board of Control, responsible for the administration of Punjab, recommended slight leniency towards the Sikh nobility. He thought and argued that it was most impolitic and dangerous to deprive them of their rights unfairly. But, he was overruled by Governor General Dalhousie, who in pursuance of his Imperialistic policies, thought that the "Jagirdars deserved little but maintenance."[36] Henry Lawrence tendered his resignation over this issue.

Nearly 50,000 Sikh soldiers were disbanded.[37] Hardly a tenth of the old army of Punjab was taken into the British pay. Although the term 'Sikh' was used for the re-employed soldiers, few were in fact Sikhs. They were largely Punjabi Muslims, Gurkhas and Hindustanis of the Durbar army. The British officers looked upon the Sikh soldiers with suspicion. They were called, "dirty sepoys"[38] and many officers wished them to cut their hair "forgetting that the very essence of Sikhism lies in its locks."[39] D. Petrie, an Assistant Director, Criminal Intelligence, Government of India, in a Confidential report on the 'Development of Sikh Politics (1900-1911)', wrote :

"The British adopted a very strict and rigid policy detrimental to the growth of Sikhism. After annexation, the Golden Temple, Amritsar, alongwith 6 other gurdwaras and the gurdwara at Taran Taran, were practically controlled by the British authorities through a Manager of these gurdwaras appointed by the British Government. The Waqf Act of 1861 gave the control and management of the holy places of the Hindus and Muslims to the communities concerned, but in the case of the Sikh gurdwaras, the Act was not applied on political grounds. The properties of Sikh places of worship were transferred and given over to the *Udasi mahants* and others, throughout the Punjab."[40] A significant blow was given by the British to the Sikh religion when they conferred proprietory rights on the temple *mahants,* Brahmins, *Udasis* or *Nirmalas,*[41] most of whom had Hindu leanings and hardly understood or had faith in Sikh religion and its practices. This was an extremely subtle method by which the British sought to secure the undoing of the ideological base of the Sikhs. A committee of nine Sikhs with a Government nominated *Sarbrah* or Warden as its head was appointed. After 1883, however, the Committee was quietly dropped, and the whole control came to be vested in the *Sarbrah* who received his instructions from the Deputy Commissioner.[42] The government wanted to maintain the gurdwaras as channels of indirect control over the Sikhs.

The British rule dealt a severe blow to the socio-economic condition of the Sikhs. Thousands of Sikh soldiers were rendered jobless. Because of earlier wars and consequent disturbances, the lot of the peasantry was no better. Instead of the Sikhs, Hindus were preferred in the civil services. Most of the jobs in military and police were given to the Punjabi Muslims. Out of the eleven Extra Assistant Commissioners, appointed by the Board of Control, only one was a Sikh.[43]

One wonders how in the face of all above historical facts, W. H. McLeod can make such a wild statement as that "one Sikh identity was vigorously promoted by the British to serve their military purposes."

The Christian missions which came to be established in Punjab, also generated a feeling of hatred and hostility towards Sikhs. The Charter granted in 1600 by Queen Elizabeth of England to a Colonising Company spoke of "duties higher than those of Commerce."[44] If merchants must buy and sell, they must also convert. Religious imperialism was the first phase of British Colonial imperialism. Christian Missions worked under British political wings. The Missionaries established their centres at Amritsar, Tarn Taran, Batala,[45] Ludhiana and Lahore.[46] Many Sikh students studying in Missionary schools began to despise the religion of their forefathers.[48] Some of them cut their hair and beards. The conversions of Maharaja Dalip Singh and Raja Harnam Singh of Kapurthala were serious and deliberate blows at the roots of the community. Further, the growing success of Missionaries in their evangelical work, with the support of the government, was an overt measure against the Sikhs. Sir John Lawrence used to make annual contribution of Rupees five hundred towards Missionary activities.[49] Some of the Missionaries openly condemned the Sikh institutions, tradition and the Gurus. They called the Guru Granth a "heathen scripture."[50] The Administrative Report (1849-51) noted : "The Sikh faith and ecclesiastical policy is rapidly going where Sikh political ascendency has already gone ...... These men joined (Sikhism) in thousands and they now desert in equal numbers ...... The sacred tank of Amritsar is less thronged than formerly, and the attendance at annual festivals is diminishing yearly. Initiatory ceremony for adult persons is now rarely performed ...... Gurmukhi is rapidly falling into desuetude. The Punjabi as a spoken language is also losing its currency and degenerating into a merely provincial and rustic dialect."[51] A series of discreditable manouevres, interference with the local customs, feverish activity of the Christian missions, and the attempts to westernise the Sikh culture filled the Sikhs with alarm.

SIKHS AND THE MUTINY

During the Mutiny of 1857, the Muslims sought restoration of the rule of Muslim princes and rulers, and the Hindus hoped to put the Maratha rulers back into power. The princes of the two communities had a unity of purpose in putting up a common front against a common enemy, the British. Because of the earlier British repression of the Sikhs, they were too disorganised to think of putting up a united leadership to reclaim their lost kingdom. The community was leaderless.[52] Moreover, the situation in the Punjab was quite different from the one that prevailed in the rest of India. An important and the main factor was that the Sikhs had nursed a serious grudge against the *Purbias* who, despite the Sikhs having never given them any cause for offence, had by their betrayal and other overt and covert acts, helped the British during the Anglo-Sikh wars and later in the annexation of Punjab. The British used the Sikh grievance and the consequent "natural hatred" towards the *Purbias*. Kavi Khazan Singh in his work, 'Jangnama Dilli', written in 1858, mentions that the Sikh participation against the *Purbia* soldiers was in reaction to their boast that they had vanquished the Sikhs in 1845-46 and in 1848-49.[53] Another contemporary observer noted : "The animosity between the Sikhs and the *Purbias* is notorious. The former gave out that they would not allow the latter to pass through their country. It was, therefore, determined to take advantage of this ill-feeling and to stimulate it by the offer of rewards for every Hindostanee sepoy who should be captured."[54] The bitter memories of *Purbia* co-operation with the British were so fresh in Sikh minds that any coalition between the two became impossible. The people who now claimed to be fighters for freedom were the same who, eight years earlier, had actively helped the British to usurp Sikh sovereignty. The pleas of *Purbias* were so hollow and incongruous with their earlier conduct, that they fell on deaf ears of the aggrieved Punjabi Sikhs and Muslims whose independence they had helped the British to rob. Besides, it is a well-accepted view that the risings in 1857 were just revolts by the princes to regain their feudal or territorial rights. It was far from being any ideological struggle for any common Indian interest. In this context, the Sikhs in the background of their rule in Punjab and egalitarian tradition could harldy be expected to side with Mulsim and Hindu princes to regain their kingdoms, nor could religious taboos which affected Hindu and Muslim sentiments, against many of which the Sikh Gurus had led a crusade, in any measure inflame Sikh sentiments. It was on account of all this that the Punjab was not affected by the rebellion which convulsed the rest of northern India. Punjabi Mussalmans turned a deaf ear to their Hindustani co-religionists' exhortation of *'jihad'* against the pig-eating despoilers of Islam. Punjabi Hindus and, with greater reason, the Sikhs refused to listen to the belated appeal to save Hindu Dharma from beef-eating foreigners who used cow fat to grease their cartridges.[55] However, there were stray cases of Sikhs joining the mutineers. It was reported that a large number of Sikhs gathered at Ropar and declared the Khalsa Raj for which the leader of the band was immediately put to death. A Sikh Chief, Raja Nahar Singh, was executed for supporting the cause of the rebels. After annexation Bhai Maharaj Singh had moved from village to village in Majha region and incited the people to rebel.[56]

The Cis-Satluj chiefs of Patiala, Malerkotla, Kalsia, Nabha, Faridkot and Jind, alongwith their mercenary forces, rendered full help to the British in suppressing the rebellion. These chiefs owed their existence to the British and were always outside the main Punjab, being hostile to Ranjit Singh. They still remembered with gratitude the support extended to them by the British against Maharaja Ranjit Singh. But for the British protection, Ranjit Singh would have overpowered them long ago. The British had guaranteed them full protection ever since the proclamation of 1809 (Treaty of Amritsar). Very few scholars have studied the role of the Sikhs in the Mutiny in its true historical perspective. In the opinion of M.A. Rahim : "Disarmament of people, dismantling of fortifications, disbanding of the Khalsa Army, suppression of the Sikh gentry, stationing of a large army and police in the Punjab, and various other measures were taken to cow down the brave militant and turbulent Khalsa nation into humble submission ...... so that the Khalsa may not be allowed to recover its prestige and reconstitute its army."[57] Similarly, Evans Bell believes that the Khalsa was bound to feel discomfited, for their Gurus had been discredited and their union had been dissolved.[58]

Although the Mutiny did not spread to the Punjab, the British did not look upon the Sikhs as trustworthy. They knew that Punjab was still seething with disaffection. Therefore, they kept a strict vigil over their fallen enemies. A big force consisting of 60,000 soldiers and 15,000 police personnel was stationed in Punjab to exercise control in the event of an emergency. There was one soldier for every forty persons. Thus, peace in Punjab was preserved at the point of the bayonet. A Government report of this time noted : "A spirit of nationality and military ambition still survives in the minds and hearts of thousands among Sikhs. It was vain to suppose that thoughts of future triumphs and future independence did not cross the imagination of these people or that aspirations of restoring the Khalsa Raj were not excited during the summer of 1857. Universal revolt in the Punjab would have broken out if Delhi had not fallen soon into our hands."[59] Despite recruitment from Punjab, during and after the revolt, the total number of Sikh soldiers by May, 1858 stood at 13,344 as against 20,027 Mohammandans.[60]

As detailed above, it is evident that the Sikh soldiers who had joined the British army in 1857 were, by and large, drawn from the cis-Satluj states, whose rulers during Ranjit Singh's rule owed their very existence to British bayonets, and who even during the Anglo-Sikh Wars were obviously sympathetic to the British and not to the Sikhs. In fact, the Sikhs of Punjab were virtually segregated from the rest of India by the intervening cis-Satluj states and the adjacent Hill and Dogra rulers, who had been traditionally pro-Delhi. So far as the Hill-Rajas were concerned, their hostility towards the Gurus and the Sikhs dated from the Mughal period.

BRITISH POLICY AFTER THE MUTINY

With the transfer of authority from the East India Company to the Crown, it had become the declared policy of the British to give due respect to the religious sensibilities of each community, to raise army regiments on communal lines, to ensure that every community, and not the Sikh community alone, observed its separate religious discipline. The immediate cause leading to the Mutiny had been the greased cartridges smeared with the fat of cows and swines. This had outraged the feelings of both Hindus, to whom the cow was sacred, and Muslims for whom the swine was unclean. The British Government had learnt a good lesson, and its policy, in reference to Indian religions was radically altered. While deciding to raise regiments on communal lines, the British also kept in view the prejudices of the caste Hindus, especially in matters pertaining to eating from a common mess and living together under the same roof in military barracks. Government not only maintained the religious identity of the units but also respected the religious taboos of the soldiers, and even allowed each Brahmin to cook his food separately.[61]

In the new native army the number of high castes was reduced. A soldier in each regiment was required to take the oath of allegiance on his respective scripture by the help of his own priest at his own place of worship. Soldiers were allowed to use their own communal war-cries. This new policy was in no way designed to further one religion at the cost of the other. A notable decision was taken to reduce the number of native sepoys in the Indian army and to increase the strength of the European soldiers. There was an overall decrease of 40 per cent in the total strength of the native soldiers but an increase of 60 per cent in the number of European troops. It was an established principle of British policy for the period since 1858 that the native troops should not exceed more than 40 per cent of the total army.

Many scholars like Fox, Mcleod, Rajiv Kapur and Barrier have wrongly highlighted the recruiting policy of the British in maintaining religious neutrality and freedom, as if this policy had only related to the Sikhs. Actually as we have stated, it was a general policy regarding the maintenance of religious neutrality and status quo concerning each community. It is, therefore, incorrect that the British policy either in any manner related only to the Sikhs, or that it had introduced any religious practice that had not been in existence earlier in the 18th and 19th centuries. It is, therefore, an idle prejudice to suggest that the British chose any particular or Khalsa identity. In relation to every community the British accepted what was the authentic and the typical. In fact, any partiality or prejudice in the choice of any sect would unnecessarily have raised criticism, which the British wanted to avoid, being contrary to their new religious policy of neutrality. Here it is relevant to give the statement of Henry Lawrence quoted by Barrier in his article, 'The Punjab Government and Communal Politics, 1870-1908' : "My men are expected to extend equal rights to all native religions and to align with none."[62] On the basis of the above statement and other facts Barrier concludes that "the first Punjab administration thus responded to a communal problem with religious impartiality."[63] In fact the burden of his entire article is to suggest British neutrality towards different religious communities in the Punjab and defend them against the charge of creating communal divisions. It is difficult to understand what climatic change has occurred or what interests have over-weighed with the same author that later he writes that, "the British also played an important role by supporting the maintenance of separate Sikh identity for military purposes."[64] Because, it is normally unusual for an author to give on the one hand a clean chit to the British for their avowed and practical neutrality towards the three communities in Punjab, and, on the other hand, strongly to endorse the oft-repeated charge of Hindu politicians that the Hindu-Sikh divide in the Punjab is a British creation to serve their partisan interests. Besides, this religious policy regarding various communities had been formulated by the British long before the publication of pamphlets by the Singh Sabha at the fag end of the 19th century. Here it is very important to mention that the British religious policies regarding communal practices in the army were strictly governed by their own self-interest, so as to maintain the loyalty of the soldiers. The important and authentic fact is that both for the Muslim rulers of the 16th to 18th centuries and the British rulers of the 19th century, there was only one reality or identity, namely the Sikhs, *Nanakpanthis* or Khalsa with which they battled or dealt with. Any other identity existed neither in the field of religion, society, politics nor even in fiction or imagination. The religious realities the British found, were dealt with uniformly by their new religious policy; they did not choose any one, ignore anyone, or promote any one. It is only the split vision of some interested modern writers that raises the phantoms of plural images, which, for the rulers and historians of the time, were non-existent.

But the British knew full well that the centres of Sikh strength and inspiration were their scripture, ideology and gurdwaras. In fact, the British were very vigilant and particular in ensuring that the Sikh gurdwaras were kept in the hands of the Hindu *mahants* and *pujaris,* so that the Sikhs who were traditionally known to draw their religious vigour, vitality and inspiration from their holy places, (some of which were associated with the martyrdoms and struggles of the Gurus against the rulers) were, through their appointed managers, segregated from these centres of inspiration.

Recruitment to the army was made, keeping in view, the qualities of fine physique and a military background and tradition. The British, no doubt, had preference for martial races, but the Sikhs were not the only martial race recruited in the Indian army. There were many Muslim tribes and Hindu castes like the Pathans and Dogra Rajputs with martial traditions, who provided good recruiting grounds for the British. This is amply borne out by a contemporary report in the Army Book :

"At present the Sikhs, together with the other inhabitants of the Punjab, whether Hindu, as the Dogra (Rajputs), or Mohammadan as the Punjabi Musalmans, and the Pathan Musalmans, the latter being descendants of Afghan or other Asiatic invaders of India, are reckoned among our best and most willing soldiers."[65] M. S. Leigh observes : "Although the Sikhs produced a percentage of recruits during the First World War greatly in excess of their percentage in the population of Punjab, the fact remains that out of the 370,609 combatants recruited from Punjab, 190,078 (51.4%) were Moslems and "only" 97,016 (26%) were Sikhs."[66]

In fact, the lower Hindu contribution to recruits is not due to any selective policy of the Government, but is due to the Hindu population in Punjab being largely urban and well-off in trading and business, and, for that matter, being reluctant by tradition to accept risks and hazards of a military career.

ATTACK ON SIKH IDENTITY

The Government of India Act of 1858, which transferred the authority from the East India Company to the Crown, brought the Sikhs directly under the Imperial rule. After the loss of political power, a sense of despair pervaded the Sikh society. An editorial in the *Khalsa Advocate* sums up the situation :

"False Gurus grew up in great numbers whose only business was to fleece their flock and pamper their own self-aggrandisement. Properly speaking, there was no Sikhism. Belief in the Guru was gone. The idea of brotherhood in the *Panth* was discarded."[67]

Under the circumstances the discerning Sikh mind knew full well that while the chances of engaging themselves successfully in a political battle with the British were slim, it was essential to invoke and strengthen its religious base which was their very source of zeal and vigour.

The advent of Christian missions and spread of western education and science also provoked self-understanding. Naturally, the Sikh mind looked back on its history and ideology with a clear self-discerning eye.

The ideologically and politically conscious wing of the Sikhs was being calculatedly curbed and kept under virtual surveillance. It was a tremendous task to revive the purity of the Sikh doctrine and to rid the faith and its institutions of wrong accretions and adulterations in order to maintain their independence. It was under great difficulties that the Sikhs started their struggle for survival in the mid-nineteenth century. They rightly realised that before they could consciously and usefully start any political struggle with the British masters, they had to revive and reinvigorate their religious understanding and discipline. Like the Sikh Gurus, who had undone the social and religious trammels of Hindu dogmatism, and created new motivations and traditions in the Sikh society before preparing and taking up the struggle against political oppression, the Sikhs at this time decided first to reinforce their socio-religious base and strength before taking up the political challenges.

Contrary to what is generally imagined, the fall of the Sikh kingdom was an episode in the turbulent history of the Sikhs, rather than the close of an epoch. The proudest outcome of the apparent disaster was that it forced Sikhism to exist on the strength of its own ideology and tradition. The period between 1849 and the rise of the Singh Sabha was a time of acute pain, trauma, distress, confusion and even of some despair in the Sikh society, which had to face multifarious problems. The British were too conscious to ignore the political potential of their foe that had given them the greatest challenge. Obviously, they were keen that the political objectives of the community should be kept permanently frustrated. To this end, they had taken away and converted the Sikh Maharaja Dalip Singh and virtually exiled the entire family of Ranjit Singh. Similarly, the principal political Sardars were also curbed or hunted out. Such a step was natural for an erstwhile victor and the Sikhs had no illusions in this regard. The British knew very well that the entire vigour and strength of the Sikhs lay in their religious zeal, and that it was their religion from which they derived their entire inspiration and power. Therefore, with their uncanny understanding they made sure that the Sikh religious places were kept in hands that were hostile to the thesis of the Gurus and which sought to divert them to the ritualistic maze of Hinduism.[68]

The contrast is very significant. Whereas the British restored the territory and kingdoms of some princes and persons who had revolted during the British rule, they made sure that none from the family of the Maharaja or the Sikh Sardars were allowed to have an opportunity to regain the leadership of the Khalsa, because in the case of the Sikhs, they knew, they were dealing not with individuals, but with a people or a nation imbued with an ideology of liberty and independence. The Sikh princes left intact were those who had always been non-leaders of the community and outside the pale of Sarkar-i-Khalsa.

The second part of the attack on the Sikh religion was the arrival of Christian missionaries in the heart of Central Punjab under the political wings of the British. Their activites and propaganda as already indicated, were significantly subversive to the Sikh religion. In fact, the Missionaries sought in every way to facilitate the colonial expansion of Britain by objectively acting as agents for their country's big capital. They were often unoffical consuls.

Third is the process and thinking that starts at the time of a ship feared to be sinking. As the bulk of converts of convenience were from Hinduism, most of whom had neither shed their old practices and prejudices nor their socio-ritual connections with their parent community, they started reversion to that fold as also revival of their affinities with the Hindus. That this trend took the form of a serious attack on Sikhism, is evident from the virulent activities of Pt. Sharda Ram Phillauri, a top *Sanatanist* Hindu leader considered to be an agent of the British. He spoke even from the precincts of the Darbar Sahib,[69] with the cooperation of British nominees in charge of it. With the rise of the Arya Samaj he also started propaganda against the Sikh religion and vicious personal attacks on the Gurus. Phillauri delivered a series of lectures at Jallianwala Bagh, Amritsar, in which he made disparaging remarks against all the Sikh Gurus.[70] He also published a book entitled *Sikhan De Raj Di Vithya,* in which he misinterpreted the teachings of the Sikh Gurus.[71] The book was prescribed in the Oriental College, Lahore, as a subject of study.[72] Such distorted accounts of Sikhism and Sikh history undermined the prestige of the community. And all this could not happen without the British patronage. Though the British were on the one hand claiming a policy of neutrality towards Indian religions, they were fully and approvingly aware of this multi-pronged attack on the Sikh source of strength, their religious places and their ideology.

The reality is that both the Mughal and the British rulers were well aware of this intimate connection between the life-affirming moral zeal of the Sikhs and their religion and places of worship. In the past too, with this awareness[73] in mind, the Afghan invaders led by Ahmed Shah Abdali sought to destroy the Darbar Sahib and fill up its sacred tank.[74] Similarly, Massa Ranghar tried to have his indulgent orgies at the sacred centre of Sikhism.[75] The British also tried to weaken the religious base of the Sikh community by extending support to the pro-Hindu *mahants* and *pujaris* of the Sikh gurdwaras.[76]

In the beginning of 1873 four Sikh students of the Mission High School, Amritsar, under the influence of the Missionaries, offered themselves to be converted to Christianity.[77] There were protest meetings all over the province and prominent Sikh leaders persuaded the boys not to abandon their faith. But the incident served as an eye-opener to the Sikhs. In this state of affairs the traditional Sikh ethos was bound to react.

BIRTH OF THE SINGH SABHA

With a view to mustering forces for an all round Panthic uplift, some prominent

Sikhs including Harsha Singh Dhupia, Thakur Singh Sandhawalia, Baba Sir Khem Singh Bedi and Raja Bikram Singh Kapurthala, convened a meeting in Amritsar in July, 1873. The meeting was attended by leading Sikh chiefs, Sardars, Gianis, *pujaris* and *mahants* of the Sikh gurdwaras of Amritsar and the adjoining districts.[78] The new association, Sri Guru Singh Sabha, Amritsar, was formed on July 28,1873.[79] The object of the Singh Sabha was to take up social, religious and educational programmes.[80] But most of the leaders of the Amritsar Singh Sabha being drawn from the rich, the upper, the privileged and the British supported strata of Sikh society, were not ready to shed their old prejudices against the low-caste Sikhs. They sided with the *mahants* and *pujaris* in discriminating against them. This created a gulf between the high and the low-caste Sikhs and, thus, the movement failed to gain the support of the masses because this behaviour of the *mahants* and *pujaris* was clearly contrary to the basic tenets and practises of Sikhism.[81] Baba Khem Singh Bedi tried to wield absolute control over the activities of the Sabha. Being a direct descendant of Guru Nanak, he aspired after reverence due to a Guru, and claimed some privileges. His followers called him *avtar* (Incarnation of God).[82] He wanted a well-furnished seat (*gudela*) for himself even in the presence of the Holy Granth.[83] This shocked Sikh sentiments.[84]

The Amritsar group adopted and approved anti-Sikh practices like discrimination, and personal worship, and made ideological distortions.[85] Naturally, persons conversant with the Sikh tradition objected to all such aberrations resulting in a schism and the formation of the Lahore Singh Sabha in November 1879.[86] It is significant to say that the chief organisers of this Sabha Prof. Gurmukh Singh and Giani Ditt Singh were devoted Sikhs with humble beginnings, whereas the Amritsar group was clearly British backed. The Lahore Singh Sabha developed a broad and comprehensive outlook, making no distinction between the high and low-caste Sikhs and extending its activities both to the urban and rural masses of Punjab. They preached and practised Sikh value systems as required by Guru Granth Sahib. They strongly opposed the institution of human worship and regarded all men as equals.[87] They judged a man by his worth and not by his birth. Prof. Gurmukh Singh made an appeal to the Sikhs of all castes and classes, to enlist themselves as volunteers of the newly formed Sabha and to carry its message to every nook and corner of the Punjab.[88]

The religious revival under the Singh Sabha was a protest against forms and ceremonies and class distinctions based on birth. It was ethical in its preference for a pure heart, the law of love, and good deeds. This religious revival was the work of the people, of the masses, and not of the classes. At its head were leaders like Ditt Singh, Gurmukh Singh and others, who sprang chiefly from the lower orders of the society — Ramdasias, weavers, cooks, clerks, shopkeepers and peasants, rather than the gilded gentry. Thus, the gulf between the privileged and British-backed, and the Sikh oriented groups started and continued. And, it is this basic difference which some of the scholars ignore.

Whereas the appeal of the Amritsar Singh Sabha was mostly confined to the personal pockets of influence of its leaders, that of the Lahore Singh Sabha went further and touched the hearts of the general mass of the community. The Lahore party sent its *Parcharaks* (preachers) even in the interior of the State to spread the message of Sikhism among hundreds and thousands of the village folks, who constituted the backbone of the Sikh community and without whose cooperation no movement could acquire a mass base. Simultaneously, the Lahore Singh Sabha opened branches in many towns. By 1882, the Singh Sabhas sprang up at places like Peshawar, Bannu, Kohat, Abotabad, Jullundur, Gujranwala, Lyallpur, Patiala, Simla, Jhelum, Ludhiana, Ambala, Quetta, Multan and Jind.[89] Lahore Singh Sabha served as a model for all these Sabhas. Since the Lahore Singh Sabha was working in line with the Sikh tradition, and the Amritsar Singh Sabha office bearers were concerned only in maintaining their own personal position and privileges,very soon, except for three Singh Sabhas, all rural and urban Singh Sabhas joined the Lahore Sabha.[90]

McLeod calls the section of the Singh Sabha that promoted the Sikh identity the "stronger" one. This statement begs the question. The real question to answer, which McLeod avoids, is why it proved to be the stronger, the better and the wiser leadership. For there is no reason to assume that the Lahore Singh Sabha was in material respects more influential. In fact, from the angle of social status, and available resources, the Lahore Singh Sabhaites were men of meagre means, and belonged to the lowest class and castes. On the other hand, the Amritsar Singh Sabha belonged to the gilded gentry including Knights and Princes, who looked to the British as their patrons. Thus, if the British had their way they would have their designs executed through their own and rich loyalists who looked up to them both for their gained strength and future prospects. By none of the normal socio-economic factors can the Lahore Singh Sahba be called the stronger one. What McLeod seems to conceal by calling them stronger is the moral strength and sap which they drew from Guru Granth Sahib and the lives of the Gurus. Hence McLeod's own reluctant admission of the strength of the Lahore Singh Sabha demolishes the very basis of his argument that the Sikh identity which the Lahore party espoused was either a created or a planted one, and not the only original one. Mcleod seems to conceal the fact, of which he could not be unaware, that originally the only Singh Sabha with all its branches was headed by the rich and gilded gentry. It was only later that, on ideological grounds, some juniors and unprivileged members broke away from it and formed the Lahore Singh Sabha.

No political, economic or social factor in any sense contributed to its growth, and spread, except its ability to invoke the Sikh doctrines in Guru Granth Sahib. It is still later that all except three branches of the old Singh Sabha shifted their affiliation from the old to the new Singh Sabha. We do not think it is fair for a scholar to suppress or omit such a fact and to suggest to the reader that the British supported the Lahore Singh Sabha because it was the "stronger" one. The Lahore Sabha's appeal to the masses lay in the Sikh doctrines and not in any material, British or social factor. It appears the author has been unable to shed the conditioned bias that is naturally associated with long years of functioning in Christian organisations in Punjab.

Again, there arose a schism in the first meeting of the newly constituted Khalsa

Diwan (on April 11, 1883), when Baba Khem Singh Bedi suggested that the title of the Singh Sabha should be changed to Sikh Singh Sabhas.[91] The object was to include the *Sehjdhari* Sikhs. But the proposal was considered motivated, being only a method to include under this garb Hindu followers of the gilded Bedis. It was straightaway opposed and rejected outright. At this time, these Bedis along with Thakur Singh Sandhawalia and their followers were inspired by their personal interests.[92] As things were, it would have been naive to hope that any worthwhile political rebellion could be organised in the State. For, the British with their experience of 1857 were quite cautious and alert.

The Baba desired to assume the role of a spiritual guide and the Raja aspired to become the temporal head of the whole community.[93] The Baba was, therefore, ready to allow some laxity in maintaining the five symbols.[94] The Lahore group maintained that Sikhism was, as proclaimed by the Guru Granth, the Gurus and the Sikh tradition. They laid emphasis on *Rahit* prescribed by the Tenth Guru. They did not tolerate any attempted ideological compromise with Hinduism.[95]

The activities of the Singh Sabha were focussed on the eradication of un-Sikh like customs and social evils and the encouragement of modern education of both men and women. The revivalist impulse stirred the Sikhs to an awareness of their faith, and impelled them to resuscitate the essential contents of Sikh beliefs. It was a trying time for the Sikhs, because their religion was under serious attack from the resurgent Arya Samaj section of the Hindus.[96] In this context, the move of the Amritsar Singh Sabha to own and promote Hindu practices among their followers had to be repelled as a serious departure from the Sikh tradition. Hence, the Lahore Singh Sabha had to fight on many fronts, against the Arya Samaj, against the Christian missionaries, against the British-backed elite of their own community, and against the corruption of the British patronised *mahants* and *pujaris* who practised anti-Sikh rites at the sacred Sikh shrines. The Sikh literature was collected, scanned, edited and compiled. Amongst these was Bhai Kahn Singh's well-known work *Mahan Kosh* and the *Ham Hindu Nahin* (We are not Hindus) as a rejoinder to the Arya Samaj propaganda that the Sikhs were a branch of the Hindus.

The British government at this time was also ready to "encourage freedom of thought, ideas of reforms on modern lines and even social revolt so long as these did not touch the dangerous ground of politics."[97] The Government appreciated the diversion of people's attention from politics to religious and social reform. It refrained from adopting any such policy as would further antagonise the Sikhs, arouse their military instincts, and remind them of their lost glory. The following remarks of Lord Lawrence are note-worthy in this connection : "The Sikhs were the bravest and the most chivalrous race in India and they now seemed disposed to submit with manly self restraint to our superior power, if only we use it with equity and toleration."[98]

The British were extra cautious in dealing with the Sikhs and this is borne out by the observaion of Sir Richard Temple : "Sikhism, though quiet and loyal at present, is one of those inflammable things of which a spark might kindle into a flame. Its idiosyncrasy and susceptibilities are thoroughly understood by the Punjab authorities and its fidelity to the Empire is well preserved. It would stand proof against many trials and temptations, but if tried over much, it would re-assert itself and would assume the leadership of a national movement."[99] This emphasizes two important realities of the day. First, that Sikhism was not an amorphous, ambiguous or confused and dispersed reality. Because of its ideology and a community having been welded into a society of religious heroes, and its history of suffering and martyrdoms, under the severest trials, it was a society with the greatest potential. This is the assessment of an important erstwhile adversary. Secondly, his objective which is clear enough, is to see that the enormous potential does not get to be used or exploited against them. For that matter, while it was natural, as we shall see, for the adversary slowly to erode that potential, Temple suggests that it would be unwise unnecessarily to provoke the Sikhs regarding minor issues, lest the inflammable material should explode against them. Accordingly, it would be naive for any historian not to understand the British policies and the course of events or ignore the assessment of the chief British actors of the time.

Sir Richard Temple's expression of British policy is extremely revealing of the British mind. So far as the Sikhs were concerned they very well understood the natural and logical basis of that policy, namely, that while the British would not mind helping and placating the Sikhs on minor and non-essential issues, they would never tolerate any subversion of their political interests. It is for this reason that both the Singh Sabhas had incorporated a clause in their constitutions that they would not indulge in political matters.

POLITICAL SUPPRESSION OF THE SIKHS

The last quarter of the nineteenth century was primarily devoted to reviving the strength of the community by educating them in their religion and tradition. The main emphasis was in social and religious fields. Having discreetly reconstructed these aspects of Sikh society, slowly and surely the Singh Sabha Movement took up the political problems as well. With the formation of the Chief Khalsa Diwan in 1902, there came a significant change in the attitude of the Singh Sabha leaders towards politics. In the beginning of the twentieth century, the rising tide of political consciousness and the new born awareness arising from the regeneration brought about by the Singh Sabha Movement, prompted the leaders of the Chief Khalsa Diwan to play their role in the political life of the province. They took it upon themselves "to safeguard the political rights of the Sikhs."[100]

The passing of the Universities Act, in 1904, which required greater official control over the management of the Khalsa College, Amritsar, made the Diwan leaders sceptical of British intentions.[101] Even the proposal of the Government to give an annual grant of Rupees ten thousand to the College, which provided that the constitution of the managing body was to be maintained according to the wishes of the Government, was viewed to be fraught with mischief. In 1907, a fresh controversy erupted when the Government forced Sardar Dharam Singh, who was working in an honorary capacity as the Engineer-in-charge of the college, to be replaced by a European engineer, Major Hill. The College Managing Comittee dissociated itself from the activities of this Government appointed Engineer. This resulted in a direct confrontation between the College

Governing Council and the Government. *The Punjab,* Lahore, in its issue dated May, 1, 1908, observed : "one can imagine the plight of stuoents studying in Khalsa College whose management is going to be dominated by the Christians." The government authorities handed over the management of the College to a nominated body with the Commissioner as Chairman, and later on June 10, 1908 forced a new constitution on the Governing Body.[102]

In November 1908, one member of the House of Commons raised a question in the British Parliament, whether the Government of India was aware of the fact that the new management of the Khalsa College had created resentment among the Sikhs and whether the government was doing anything to remove this resentment.[103] Master Sunder Singh of Lyallpur wrote a book, *Ki Khalsa Kalaj Sikhan Da Hai* ? in which he clearly stated that the government control over the Khalsa College had hurt the national pride of the Sikhs. He accused the British of having taken over the college in the same dishonest manner as it had annexed the Punjab.[104] D. Petrie, Assistant Director, Criminal Intelligence, mentions the sentiments of a Sikh student of Khalsa College, who after the Amritsar Educational Conference expressed himself as follows :

> "I am not afraid to die. All life is sacrifice. If I had been allowed to live, I might have done great things by sacrifice. Until the nation realises that, lives must be sacrificed, it will never come to anything."[104-a]

Petrie also stated that a Khalsa College student had been openly advising people in his village not to serve the British Government any more.

The year 1907 saw the beginning of a political agitation in the Punjab in connection with the Colonisation Bill of 1907, which was considered to be unduly oppressive to the Punjabi agriculturists. The Bill was passed on the assumption that the land was the property of the Government and the farmer was a mere tenant. This was contrary to the prevailing notions of peasant-proprietorship, continuing from the times of Banda Bahadur. The districts most affected by the new measure were Lyallpur and Rawalpindi, mainly colonised by the Sikhs. Some Singh Sabha preachers (*Updeshaks*) like Jagat Singh Updeshak and Harbans Singh Attari, were accused by the Government of instigating the agriculturists against the authorities.[105] The students of Khalsa College Amritsar also organised a protest demonstration against Sir Charles Rivaz, the Lt. Governor of the Punjab.[106] The agitation over the Colonisation Bill was an important event. The chief strength of the Sikhs was a bold peasantry that possessed proprietory rights in their lands. This was an important Sikh reform different from the *Zimindari* system in most other parts of India. Under the Colonisation Bill, the British proposed that the peasants would not have the proprietory rights which they had during the Sikh rule. This was felt to be an important step to reduce the economic, social and political strength of the colonists, most of whom were Sikhs. They reacted against this contemplated erosion of their socio-economic base. This reaction of the Sikh colonists is significant, because it was based on the Sikh tradition that it was Banda Bahadur, who had introduced the system of peasant proprietorship and created among the masses a real consciousness of equality and the strength to defend their rights.

The founding of the Sikh Education Conference by the Chief Khalsa Diwan, in 1908, was also viewed by the Government to be fraught with political motives.[107] It was alleged that "the Conference was founded by the Chief Khalsa Diwan, which resenting Government's interference in Khalsa College affairs in 1908, resolved to build a new Sikh College independent of Government control and devised in the Conference a means of collecting funds for this object."[108] Though declared to be a non-political institution, the Sikh Educational Conference did provide a forum to the Singh Sabha leaders to express their views on day-to-day affairs — religious, social, educational and even political. Some of the speeches delivered at various conferences by the Chief Khalsa Diwan leaders were thought to be marked with strong political bias. At the third Sikh Educational Conference held at Amritsar in 1910, Professor Jodh Singh of the Khalsa College Amritsar was charged with giving a 'seditious talk' in connection with the government system of education.[109] The British Government also began to view the activities of Sunder Singh Majithia, Tarlochan Singh (Pleader), Professor Jodh Singh and Harbans Singh Attari with suspicion.[110] The authorities also noticed that teachers like Nihal Singh, Sunder Singh, Niranjan Singh, Hari Singh Cheema and others were openly provoking the students against the British.[111]

It was said that in the course of their lectures these teachers, quite often, referred to the days of Sikh ascendancy, their past glory and their present subjugation.[112] The students were so much excited that, in 1910, when R. G. Wright took over as the Principal of the Khalsa College, they expressed their resentment against an Englishman's appointment by pasting handbills on the College walls.[113] On another occasion, when Gopal Krishan Gokhale came to Amritsar, he was given a hearty welcome by the students of the Khalsa College. Their enthusiasm was reflected in the fact that they even unyoked his horses and themselves pulled his carriage to the College, where his lecture was listened to with thunderous applause.[114]

The British acted in defiance of the Sikh sentiments and interests. The Minto-Morlay Reforms, of 1909, were discriminatory against the Sikhs. The Muslim minority was conceded separate representation and weightage in the State where they were a minority, as well as at the Centre. Similar consideration was not shown to the Sikhs in Punjab. This shows that the British were always niggardly, when it was a question of promoting Sikh political interests. Hardly were they given the same treatment as the Muslim minority. The series of events outlined above show that the British were most reluctant to adopt policies that would build the real strength of the community.

The Khalsa Advocate, Amritsar, which was the chief spokesman of the Chief Khalsa Diwan, was administered warning three times, between 1911 and 1922, for printing 'objectionable matters.'[115] Khalsa Samachar, Amritsar, in one of its issues, delivered the following message to the Sikhs on the occasion of Guru Gobind Singh's birthday : "The founder of the Khalsa, Guru Gobind Singh, fought against tyranny and oppression and expelled darkness. He sacrificed his life for the cause of justice and righteousness. O'brave Khalsa ? Wake up! Follow in the Guru's footsteps. The country is again in the throes of tyranny and needs sacrifices."[116]

It was not an easy task for the Singh Sabha to restore the values and objectives of the Sikh faith, in view of the stern posture adopted by the British at every step. The Arms Act of 1878, had placed a check on the rights of the Sikhs to wear *kirpan* (Sword), which is one of the five essential symbols of the Sikh faith. The movement for emancipation of the *kirpan* was started in 1913, when Baba Nihal Singh was arrested for wearing a *kirpan.*[117]

The incident sent a wave of indignation among the Sikhs. The Chief Khalsa Diwan and the Singh Sabha held hundreds of meetings. Consequently, an agitation was launched. After some Sikhs had suffered arrests, the Government exempted these Sikhs from the Arms Act, allowed them the possession and the wearing of the *kirpan* on June 25, 1914.[118] In spite of the exemption of wearing the *kirpan,* the Sikh soldiers were still not allowed to wear it in the army. Three soldiers at Roorkee were punished and dismissed for wearing it. The Singh Sabhas held protest meetings, but they were not taken back. Bhai Mangal Singh of the 34th Sikh Regiment, who was afterwards martyred at Nankana Sahib, was dismissed and sentenced to one year's rigorous imprisonment (R.I.) for the same fault. It was only after the First World War, that the Government sanctioned the wearing of *kirpans* by Sikh soldiers, both in uniform and plain clothes, while serving on the active list.[119] McLeod seems unaware of the *kirpan* agitation, when he states that the British required the "Sikh recruits to observe the full regalia of the orthodox Khalsa identity."[120] Fox, too, suffers from a similar mis-conception, when he says that the Sikh identity and their religious values were subsidised by the British.[121] In this context N. G. Barrier's opinion that the British played an important role in maintaining Sikh identity[122] looks so odd, especially when it contradicts his own observations in defence of British neutrality towards the three Punjab communities. Want of indepth study has led these scholars completely to overlook the overwhelming evidence relating to the Singh Sabha struggle for their religious rights, whether it be the Anand Marriage Act (1909), or the right to wear *kirpan*, or the control over the shrines and other institutions. The lack of clear perception has led them to make confusing and contradictory statements regarding the British motives and policies. The confusion arises mainly because the general policy of the British, after the Mutiny, was not to disturb the religious norms of the soldiers. So far as the British policy in the state was concerned, it was obviously directed against the promotion of the Sikh ideological identity, a far cry from "vigorous promotion" as alleged by McLeod.

The Chief Khalsa Diwan preachers consciously mingled politics with religion in the course of their speeches. The tone of their speeches clearly reflected their dissatisfaction with the British Government. Social and economic backwardness of the community was attributed to the loss of political power. The preachers quite often referred to the days of political ascendancy of the Khalsa and tended to compare their political subjugation with the bitter experiences of the past under the Mughals. The preachers argued that the Sikhs suffered under the Mughals because of the tyranny of the rulers. As a corollary, the responsibility for the then existing state of affairs was attributed to the British. The Government began to suspect the motives and designs of the Singh Sabha preachers.[123] Many cases were reported to the Government in which Sikh preachers were found instigating the people against the Government.[124] In spite of their handicaps, in the earlier stages, the Singh Sabha *parcharaks* (preachers), through their emphasis on religion, were able to make a successful appeal to the Sikh mind and to awaken the Sikh consciousness to its religio-political entity. The organisation of festivals, prayer-meetings, *Nagar Kirtans* (religious processions) and *Kavi Samelans* (Religio-political recitations) was attempted to escape the notice of the intelligence authorities who normally prohibited political activities and gatherings. This role of the Singh Sabha preachers in awakening the Sikh masses from religion to politics is important. A contemporary Government report noted : "The Chief Khalsa Diwan keeps a staff of paid preachers *(Updeshaks)* who tramp the country and lecture on various topics- social, educational, religious, political, and more often than not, all four are inextricably intermingled."[125]

Sikh militancy assumed alarming proportions with the Rikabganj Gurdwara affair in 1913.[126] The Government thoughtlessly acquired some land attached to the Gurdwara, and domolished its outer wall, so that a road could be built to the nearby Secretariat.[127] "Bitter agitation arose among the Sikh masses."[128] The Sikhs agitated and threatened to launch a *Morcha,* but it was abandoned because of the outbreak of the First World War.[129]

It is well-known that the translation of the Sikh scripture, which the British had commissioned the Christian missionary, Dr Trumpp, to undertake was full of derogatory references to the Sikh Gurus and was offensive to Sikh sentiments. On the other hand, scholars like J. D. Cunningham, Evans Bell and John Sullivan had to suffer extreme penalties of dismissal from service for writing honest accounts, but what Government considered to be pro-Sikh. M. A. Macauliffe, who produced a monumental work on the Sikh religion in six volumes, also did not find favour with the British, and was not given the benefits and advantages enjoyed by Dr Trumpp, who wrote against the Sikhs.

REBELLION IN PUNJAB

The failure of the Government to protect the rights of the Sikh immigrants living in Canada and America, who were the victims of racial discrimination, led to the formation of a revolutionary organisation known as the *Hindustan Ghadr Party*. The object of the *Ghadar Party* was to spread an armed rebellion and free India from the foreign yoke.[130] War was considered a good opportunity to cause the rebellion, especially because early British reverses involving large scale casualties of the Sikh soldiers from the rural areas seemed to the *Ghadrites* a ripe stage for achieving their objective.[131]

Ghadar Party was virtually a Sikh organisation, and Sohan Singh Bhakna was its President. These persons came to Punjab and started their subversive activities both in rural central Punjab and among the Sikh soldiery. By the end of 1914, the *Ghadrites* succeeded in sending one thousand revolutionaries to India out of the total membership of ten thousand. Some of the Singh Sabhas, were said to be sympathetic to the *Ghadrites*. Bhai Takhat Singh entertained the delegates of the *Ghadar Party* when they visited Ferozepur. Daljit Singh, assistant editor of the *Punjabi Bhain*, a monthly publication of the *Sikh Kanya Maha Vidyala*, Ferozepur, joined the *Ghadrites* and became a Secretary of Baba Gurdit Singh, leader of the *Komagata Maru* affair.[132] "The methods to be employed by the delegates (of the *Ghadar Party*) in pushing campaign in India appeared to have been discussed in the weekly meetings of the Singh Sabha at Lahore ...... A member of the Singh Sabha in advocating these measures spoke of creating a spirit of awakening among Hindus and Sikhs."[133] However, the Government succeeded in crushing the rebellion before it could assume bigger dimensions. Before the appointed date when large scale rebellion in the army or the state could be started, information leaked out at Lahore. A widespread hunt for the rebels in the state was made and scores were hanged and sent to transportation for life.

The *Ghadrites* to their chagrin, discovered that the Congress leaders were more sympathetic to the British than to the *Ghadrite* revolutionaries.[134] Tilak, the so called 'militant' Congressite, had expressed his strong disapproval of the activities of the *Ghadrites*. Gokhale is said to have openly told the Viceroy that he would like the British to extend their stay in India.[135] There is no denying the fact that the *Ghadar Movement* received a set-back on account of lack of support from the Congress leadership, and their persecution evoked no sympathy from these quarters. This is an important political event which influenced the Sikhs and their psyche. For Sikh independence Kartar Singh Sarabha is as great a hero as, if not greater than, Bhagat Singh. In his memory the first statue was raised in Ludhiana, though statues of other heroes, including of Bhagat Singh, were raised much later.

In this regard three things are extremely significant. The rebellion was by and large a Sikh affair, and took place mostly in rural Punjab. Nothing of this sort or extent appeared in the rest of the country. Ninety per cent of the participants and the sufferers were Sikhs. The second point is that two of the noted Sikh mystics, Baba Wasakha Singh and Bhai Randhir Singh were the participants, who were sentenced to life imprisonment.

This indicates that in Sikhism there is a basic and inalienable ideological link between religion and righteous political activity. Third, it is noteworthy that, while the Sikh masses were politically awakened to sustain a rebellion, persons who later became political leaders of the Congress for Indian independence, were whole-heartedly cooperating with the British war effort during this period, and the idea of liberation was beyond their ken, if not foreign to them.

Here it is relevant to quote the confessional statement of Mewa Singh in 1914 who had eliminated William Hopkinson recruited from India for suppressing a ferment among Canadian Sikhs and whose agent Bela Singh had murdered two Sikhs in the Gurdwara. Prior to his execution, he stated; "My religion does not teach me to bear enmity to anybody, no matter what class, creed or order he belongs to, nor had I any enmity for Hopkinson. I heard that he was suppressing my poor people very much ...... Being a staunch Sikh I could no longer bear to see the wrong done both to my innocent countrymen and the Dominion of Canada ...... And I, performing the duty of a true Sikh and remembering the name of God, will proceed towards the scaffled with the same amount of pleasure as the hungry babe does towards its mother. I shall have the rope around my neck thinking it to be a rosary of God's name ......"[136]

Now, who had taught Mewa Singh an ordinary Sikh coming from a remote Punjab village and migrating to Canada for earning his living, an essential principle of the Sikh religion, namely, to react against social injustice. It would be naive to say that Mewa Singh or the *Ghadrites* were the product of British policy. What the Singh Sabha did was to revive and invoke the teachings, training and traditions of the Gurus. For, the history of Sikhism and other whole-life religions clearly demonstrates that it is the blood of the martyrs that alone can create a healthy and sound moral conditioning of the masses and not any artificial administrative attempts in pursuance of colonial interests.

When the war came to an end in 1918, the Sikhs launched a strong agitation under the leadership of Harchand Singh of Lyallpur and Sardul Singh Caveeshar. They appealed to the Sikhs to volunteer themselves for the *Shaheedee Jatha* (band of martyrs) and to join a march to Delhi to re-erect the demolished wall of the Gurdwara Rakkab Ganj. However, the timely intervention of Maharaja Ripudaman Singh of Nabha saved the situation from getting worse. The Government acceded to the Sikh demand by restoring the Gurdwara wall.[137]

The tragedy of Budge Budge Ghat came as a bolt from the blue for the Sikhs. A group of Sikh immigrants returning from Canada became the victims of the British high-handedness. Eighteen men were killed and another twenty five were injured.[138] However, Gurdit Singh, their leader, along with twenty eight of his companions escaped. The rest were rounded up and sent to Punjab, where over two hundred of them were interned under the Ingress Ordinance. This incident was universally condemned and Sikh public opinion was greatly mobilised against the British. "Several Sikh papers notably the *Khalsa Akhbar* (of Harchand Singh of Lyallpur) and *Sher-i-Punjab,* both started in 1914, attacked the Government in connection with the *Budge Budge Ghat* incident.."[139]

Sardul Singh Caveeshar, an important contemporary writes, "The *Komagata Maru* tragedy at Budge Budge was another cause of estrangement between the Sikhs and the Government. Through the foolishness of some police officers, a tragedy was enacted at Budge Budge that threw the whole of India into consternation ...... The subsequent ruthless punishment of the returned emigrants by Sir Michael O'Dwyer did not allow the sores to heal; and the injustice done to India and the Sikhs by the Canadian Government became a permanent cause of grievance against the British."[140]

Thus the post-war policy of the British resulting in such like incidents, created both resentment and anger among the Sikhs in Punjab. Caveeshar observes; "The Sikhs were in this attitude of mind, when they were thrown in the vortex of Martial Law as a consequence of agitation against the Rowlatt Act."[141]

The Sikh mind was seriously disturbed. Agitation against the Rowlatt Act started while the Sikh feelings were already aggrieved at the treatment of the Canadian Government and of the returned immigrants from there at *Budge Bhdge Ghat*. This led to violent reaction as reported in the government communique : "The last communique issued brought the history of events in Lahore and Amritsar, as then known, down to the afternoon of the 12th of April (1919). The information in the possession of Government was not complete at the time of its issue. The morning train from Ferozepur on the 12th was held up outside Kasur Station and looted by a mob of about 1,000; of whom many were armed with lathis. Two Europeans, honorary Lieutenant Selby of the Ordnance and Sergeant Mostyn, R.A., were killed and another was injured. After looting the train and doing a great deal of damage in the Station, the crowd burnt the post office and attacked the Tehsil. Here, however, they were driven off by the police with a loss of one killed and about six wounded. Some arrests were made. Several stations on the Kasur and Amritsar line were attacked the same day. Khem Karan station was looted and treasury at Tarn Taran was assaulted unsuccessfully. As the result of these disturbances it was decided to march a movable column with a gun from Kasur through the Majha to Amritsar. The column started on the morning of Sunday, the 13th, and arrived at Khem Karan.

"On Sunday, the 13th, the Prevention of Seditious Meetings Act, 1911, was applied to the districts of Lahore and Amritsar which were declared to be proclaimed areas under the Act. The result of this action is to make it illegal to hold, without permission, a public meeting for the furtherance or discussion of any subject likely to cause disturbance or public excitement without permission."[142]

The events mentioned above clearly explain why, unlike in the rest of the country, the agitation against the Rowlatt Act took a serious rebellious trend in the central districts of Punjab where the Sikh population was predominant. This also explains why despite the prohibitory order in the districts of Lahore and Amritsar, thousands of Sikhs came to Amritsar on the Baisakhi, and later thronged at the Jallianwala Bagh in defiance of the local order banning the holding of any meeting in the city. That this defiant agitation was predominantly a rural Sikh reaction is evident from the fact that out of the total casualties of 1300 more than sixty per cent were Sikhs, when it is well-known that the Sikh population in the city was just marginal.[143]

An important fact which has often been ignored is that in Punjab most agitations have been mass upsurges and movements, unlike those in the rest of India, where those have generally been either among the literate classes or in the urban areas. In Punjab since the *Ghadar* rebellion, the trial and sentences of death and transportation of life to *Ghadrites*, following it, and the events preceding and following the Budge Budge Ghat tragedy, were a chain of occurences that never allowed the enlivened and agitated Sikh spirit to rest in peace. From the time of the *Ghadar* rebellion upto the Jallianwala Bagh firing, the Sikh Punjab had remained in continuous ferment. As against it, the position in the rest of India, had been very different, and one fact alone indicates the climate, namely, that Mahatma Gandhi had earned during that period two Medals, Kaiser-i-Hind and Zulu War Medal.[144] As stated already, the Congress leaders like Gokhale, Tilak and Lajpat Rai were sympathetic to the British and condemned the *Ghadrite* revolutionaries, whose activities, they openly disapproved.[145] It is difficult to deny that this reaction of Indian political leaders gave support to the British and caused a setback to the movement of the *Ghadrites*.

The *Ghadr* unrest in central rural Punjab leading to the Sikhs' gathering at

Jallianwala Bagh, and the oppression indulged in by the British administration in the rural Punjab, are primarily and fundamentally a continuous episode in the Sikh struggle for independence. In fact, it is only incidentally a part of the Indian political movement which till then was living in a cooperative mood and enjoying the benefits of the Raj. Much less had it gained any momentum to make any confrontation and suffer large scale oppression. Another fact which indicates the Sikh character of the agitation is that it was G. A. Wathen, the Principal of the premier Sikh educational institution in Punjab, who felt so deeply concerned at the inhuman activities of General Dyer that he ran on a motor-cycle from Amritsar to Lahore and woke up Governor O'Dwyer to request him not to approve Dyer's action.[146] It is very relevant and important to understand the complexion of events in Punjab. The fact is that the pre-Jallianwala Bagh rebellion was a Sikh affair in the Punjab and for that matter the reaction and the repression perpetrated by Dyer and O'Dwyer were directed against the Sikhs. K. F. Rustamji writes : "The people of Punjab are a vibrant, vigorous lot ...... Like all brave, warlike races they are ready for a fight whenever they feel they have been ill-treated or misled. The Punjabis who participated in *satyagraha* and violence against the British were so strong in the vanguard that the majority of the British in India felt at that time that making an example of them at Jallianwala Bagh was unnecessary. The wisest believed that in the process General Dyer was reckless and overdid it. Few saw it as a setback to British rule. The British never recovered from the effects of that mistake till the end."[146-a] That explains how the rural mind of Udham Singh remained deeply agitated and aggrieved to prompt him to act against O'Dwyer, the person responsible for the Punjab tragedies of the period. Here it is also significant to state that the basic inspiration that sustained or inspired Udham Singh to attack O'Dwyer was religious. This is also evidenced by his letters and his demand for *Gutka*, the Sikh prayer Book of *Gurbani*.[147] It is also relevant in this connection, that whereas the non-Sikh Indian communities in U.K. disowned him, he was supported only by the Sikhs of a Gurdwara of West London.[148]

The above narration of facts shows that following the Singh Sabha movement side by side with the religious awakening, the British measures against political awakening became increasingly open and firm. It is also clear that the British had always been vigilant in this regard and never failed to suppress, to the extent possible, the growth of Sikh political consciousness. The important fact is that under the Sikh ideology religious consicousness, socio-political consciousness and consequent responsibility and reaction go hand in hand. The net result was that in 1919 the Sikh religious and socio-political consciousness had reached, because of its tradition and history, a distinctly higher level of commitment and activity than that among the people in other parts of the country. This is clearly borne out by a contemporary Government Report : "the Home Rule Agitation and Rowlatt Bills exercised an undesirable effect on the whole Press. The Sikh Press ventilated petty grievances that the Government was unmindful of the true interests of the Sikhs."[149] Thus, it is this that explains the role of Sikhs in the Ghadr revolution and that of Mewa Singh in Canada. Significant as it is, at that time the Indian political leaders had mostly been cooperating with the British war efforts. This clearly explains, as we have seen, that when Gandhi after giving up his role of cooperation during the War, gave the call against the Rowlatt Bills, the response and reaction in Punjab were more significant as compared with other parts of the country where also the call had been given. For the Sikhs, it was only a continuation of the socio-political struggle which the Singh Sabha had initiated.

The brutal massacre of Jallianwala Bagh in 1919, in which hundreds of Sikhs were killed and wounded, added fuel to the fire. After the Singh Sabha Movement had helped the Sikhs to regain their strength and cohesion, the Sikhs felt that it was time they cleared their gurdwaras from the non-Sikh *mahants* and their adverse influence which had the clear backing of the British. So far as the political consciousness is concerned, it has always been a part of the Sikh ethos, as has been evidenced by the *Kuka* and the *Ghadr* Movements. With the Singh Sabha, as we shall see, it was only a tactical move when they for some decades remained quiet on the political front. In order to remove the confusion and despondency, which followed annexation, they wanted first to rebuild their socio-religious cohesion. Tempers rose very high, when the Manager and priests of the *Darbar Sahib* condemned the *Komagata Maru* and the *Ghadrite* Sikhs at the *Akal Takhat*. Later on, they also presented a robe of honour to Brigadier-General Dyer, who was responsible for the Jallianwala Bagh massacre.[150]

It was such suicidal policies of the British that Principal Wathen had rushed to stop. As a saying goes, it is human blunders that sometimes change history. During these days, there spread an unfounded rumour among the Sikh masses, as well as the Sikhs in the British Indian army, that since the Sikhs were involved in the Anti-Rowlatt Act agitation and had used the Golden Temple complex as their hide out, the British authorities had resorted to aerial bombardment of the Golden Temple.[151] This infuriated Sikhs all over Punjab. To quell this unrest the army took over the administration, and whatever vestiges of a civilised government had remained, also vanished. The British Government's actions at Amritsar set the tone of "Dyerarchy" for the rest of the province, in which the Sikhs were the worst sufferers of the ruthless repression carried on by the Government. Many Sikh villages were subjected to bombing and machine-gunning from the air; one of the targets successfully hit was the Khalsa High School at Gujranwala, where many people were killed and wounded.[152] In the seven weeks that the Punjab was administered by martial law, nearly 1200 were killed, and at least 3600 were wounded.[153] All this brutal repression came as a shock to the Sikh masses. Winston Churchill made the most scathing criticism of General Dyer's action. He described it as "an episode which appeared to be without parallel in the modern history of the British Empire ...... an extarodinary event, a monstrous event, an event which stood in singular and sinister isolation."[154]

In this context and the known misuse of the gurdwaras, the Sikhs became acutely conscious that they could no longer afford to permit their own sacred shrines to become places of corruption, and to be used to destroy the very roots and the sap that in the past had given them such strength and vigour. Thereafter started the Gurdwara reform movement and the peacefully organised confrontation with the British. For, the cover had been lifted, and it had become clear that behind the priests and the *mahants* stood the strength and might of the British. Consequently and logically as a second important step, the Sikhs did the greatest mobilisation against the Government for regaining the control of their gurdwaras from the corrupt *pujaris*.

The Chief Khalsa Diwan had, no doubt, formed a sub-committee to suggest ways and means to reform the gurdwaras, but it could not take effective measures owing to the stiff opposition of the *mahants* and *pujaris* who enjoyed the support and protection of the Government. In 1919, the Central Sikh League was established at Amritsar, with a view to protecting the political interests of the Sikhs.[155] The League passed a resolution of non-cooperation with the British Government in October, 1919. Its meeting was attended by Harbans Singh Attari, Baba Kharak Singh and Master Tara Singh. In 1920 the Shiromani Gurdwara Prabandhak Committee was established and undertook to 'take over' all the Shrines including the Darbar Sahib.[156] The establishment of this committee brought the issues to a wider notice. Thus "a movement which was religious in origin rapidly acquired a political character."[157] The Sikhs now began to realise that a clash with the Government was inevitable in order to secure justice and to safeguard their interests.

Thus the Singh Sabha movement, after the period of reconstruction, naturally, gave birth to the Akali movement which was equally motivated by religious as well as political considerations. The following remarks of V. M. Smith, a contemporary observer, are illuminating in this respect : "All Sikh traditions, whether national or religous, are martial. In times of political excitement the militant spirit reasserts iteslf."[158] It was, therefore, natural that at that stage of history, the Sikhs should come into direct clash with the British policies which, as we have explained earlier, were hostile to their political and ideological interests.

CONCLUSION

The above narration of events shows that two aspects of the British policy towards the Sikhs have been clear and consistent, namely : their comparative political suppression as evidenced in the Minto-Morley (1909) and Montague-Chelmsford Reforms (1919); and the Sikh ideological erosion by a studied patronage of Hinduised *mahants* and *pujaris,* and control of their shrines through Government nominated Managers.

The *Ghadr* Rebellion under the Presidentship of Sohan Singh Bhakna and the leadership of religiously oriented *Ghadrite* Babas and the martyrdoms of Kartar Singh Sarabha and his associates had politically inflamed the Sikhs in Punjab. Extremely painful was the fact that the Government had managed to have disowned and declared persons of the religious eminance of Baba Wasakha Singh and Bhai Randhir Singh of the *Ghadr* Movement as non-Sikhs by a *Sarbrah* (custodian appointed by the Government) of the Golden Temple. Because of the *Ghadr* Rebellion, suppression of the Sikhs continued to be severe during the War. These events, however, made it evident that a political struggle with the British with the dual objective of political freedom and removal of Government control over Sikh gurdwaras, would become inevitable. It was clear that more than any other area in the country, the Sikhs in Punjab were ready for a confrontation with the British.

We have already recorded that Sikh religious ethos is both the foundation and the strength of their urges and aspirations for socio-political liberty. The Sikh shrines, particularly the Darbar Sahib, Amritsar, continue since the times of the Gurus to be the fount of Sikh power and inspiration.

Under the leadership of the Akalis, the Sikhs came into an open clash with the Government, first for the liberation of their shrines, and then for the liberation of their motherland. The struggle for the liberation of their shrines has been given the appellation Third Sikh War. The two Anglo-Sikh Wars had already been fought in the middle of the last century. In the Third Sikh War the stakes were the freedom of their gurdwaras and their religion. It was fought on the basis and strength of their religious identity and institutions. For a Sikh the freedom of his religion and the freedom of his motherland are synonymous. This is not a recent or a post-facto interpretation of the Sikh religion. We record below the actual understanding of a contemporary who partook in the Sikh struggle. Sardul Singh Caveeshar writes, "A Sikh wants to fight his country's battles from the vantage ground of his religion. Being of a religious trend of mind, he finds everything subordinate to his *Dharma*; politics is nothing for him but a promising child of religion. A Sikh has not yet developed that fine sense of doubtful value that divides life into watertight compartments and makes of religion in the west something different from one's social and political life. For the Sikhs, politics and religion are one. He wants the freedom of his religion, he wants the freedom of his country, but he knows that he cannot have one without the other. If religion is safe, he is sure to get back, sooner or later, the freedom of his country. In fact he regards religion as the strong post, from which one should start to get back the lost liberty, as, in his opinion, the religious spirit alone can keep the freedom of a country safe when once that has been won."[159]

Still among scholars who talk of the British promotion of the Khalsa identity, there is a clear lack of understanding of the Sikh ideology, the realities of the situation, Sikh history and the general historical perspective. As already explained, the Sikh ideology laid down by Guru Nanak and the Guru Granth involves a combination of the spiritual and the empirical elements of life. The history of Islam and Judaism that make a similar ideological combination furnishes very helpful analogies. It is, therefore, sheer misinterpretation, misrepresentation or misunderstanding of the Sikh ideology to talk of two Sikh identities, namely, the Khalsa and the *Nanakpanthis*. Scholars drawn from pacificist or dichotomous religions, involving divorce between religious and empirical lives and recommending *Sanyas*, on the one hand, and *Varna Ashram Dharma,* on the other hand, not only misunderstand the unity of the Sikh doctrine, but tend sometimes to measure the Sikh ideology and history by the standards of their own religions. Often such basically conditioned vision is inclined not to take an objective or over-all view. We have made it very clear how Guru Gobind Singh's creation of the Khalsa was the epitome of Guru Nanak's mission, and how Khalsa and *Nanakpanthis* were synonymous terms and were taken and treated as such by the Muslim rulers, their contemporaries or successors.

It is also important that the first coin struck by Banda Singh Bahadur in 1710 clearly recognises his victory to be due to the grace of the sword of Guru Nanak. Similarly the coin of Ranjit Singh does not mention any particular person or king except Guru Nanak as the true Emperor of both the worlds, spiritual and empirical. Contemporary Mufti-Ali-ud-Din, author of *Ibrat Nama*, makes a significant statement, about Sikh identity of the first half of the nineteenth century, "the Sikhs as belonging to a class highly conscious of the need of shaking off meaningless rituals that the Brahmins had fostered on the Hindu society ...... They observed no formalities in the matter of dress and social intercourse also. *Ram-Ram* and *Salam* had given place to *Waheguru ji Ki Fateh.* They had also done away with the Brahmanic practice of reading the *Vedas*, the *Shastras* and the *Puranas,* and recited only Guru's *Bani*. The morning prayer consisted of the recitation of the *Japji* and the *Sukhmani*. They were particularly careful of their personal cleanliness and purity. A regular daily bath before offering prayers was considered essential, but there were sometimes deviations, and those who preferred to wash their mouth, hands and feet alone, were permitted to do so, and the practice was known as *panjishnana*. *Ardas* was an indispensable and prominent feature of their prayers. It was through *Ardas* that the Sikhs solicited help from the Almighty for the efficient performance of their daily life and duties."[160]

The Sikh identity was founded by Guru Nanak, it was nurtured by the subsequent Gurus. When mature, the final seal in the form of the *amrit* ceremony was put on it by the tenth Master. The Sikh Gurus themselves have been emphasising the unity of the Sikh doctrine. This is evidenced by the use of word 'Nanak' in every hymn of the Gurus in Guru Granth Sahib. Thus, ideologically, scripturally, traditionally, and in the eyes of the community and its opponents, there was only one identity, namely, the followers of the Gurus. The history of the struggle and persecution in the 18th century, and the way the companions of Banda got beheaded at Delhi, make for singularity of identity and not for its plurality. Identities are built on the ideology, motivation, the blood of the martyrs, tradition, suffering and sacrifice, and not by the juxtaposition of material facts or by verbal argumentation. Therefore, the two components that constitute Sikh identity, namely, Sikh ideology and the Sikh history during the time of the Gurus and the periods of their struggle for survival, have to be taken into view and not just ignored. That is why the Singh Sabha leadership used *Gurbani* and the Sikh history, especially the armed resistance to the Mughals, as a rallying symbol for the Sikh revival.

The second factor is the reality of the situation in the post-annexation (1849) period. The Khalsa army's strength and power had been annihilated. The British in power were extremely conscious of the Sikh capacity for resurgence, and they sought to ensure in every manner, as indicated earlier, that there was no political uprising in the State. After the 1857 experience they were doubly conscious and particularly vigilant to take all measures against any sign of political unrest or uprising. This is clear from the known tyrannical manner in which the minor Namdhari uprising was suppressed. As we have noted, the British allowed, under the protection of their wings, free play to the Christian missionaries to attack the identity and ideology of the Sikh religion, its history and institutions. These missions were located in the heart of Sikh areas like Amritsar and Batala. The purpose and work of these missions are well-known. The journalistic work of McLeod, who has for long years been a functionary of the Batala Christian centre, can be taken to be typically representative and revealing of the aims and objectives of such Centres. Further, in order to destroy the very roots of Sikhism, the British gave charge of Sikh Shrines to Hinduised Managers, *mahants* or *pujaris*, who did their best to suppress Sikh practices and tradition, and instead to introduce Hindu ways and customs. For example, whereas Jassa Singh, the head of Sikh leadership, when he struck the coin after his victory of Lahore in 1761, felt no stigma in calling himself a Kalal, a low *Shudra* in the Hindu caste hierarchy, the *mahants* and *pujaris* introduced the practice that *Mazhabi* Sikhs would not be given *parshad* at Darbar Sahib, Amritsar, even though *Mazhabi* Sikhs formed a part of Ranjit Singh's army. In short, had Jassa Singh been alive in the British period, he would have been debarred from doing any ceremonial service at that shrine.

This was the state of affairs after the annexation, which the leaders of the Singh Sabha had to battle against. Therefore, they decided, and very wisely, that it would be suicidal to fight on two fronts, namely, the poltical front and the socio-religious front. Here it is necessary to mention that the first step the Sikhs took, after they had revived the religious understanding, cohesion and consciousness of the community and dispelled its sense of shock at the loss of empire, was to free the gurdwaras from the *mahants* and *pujaris*. And it is well-known that the agitation which was only directed against these private priests (*mahants* and *pujaris*), involved the Sikhs in a confrontation with the Government which was really the power behind them and was interested in their continuance as instruments of erosion of the religious base, the real strength of the community. Thus, the realities of the situation were such that, if the Sikhs had tried to fight on both the fronts, failure would have been inevitable. It speaks volumes for their wisdom that they first strengthened their ideological understanding and foundation. And in this they succeeded to a large extent.

Thirdly, these scholars also ignore the general historical perspective. For example, referring to the period of Jewish history after A.D. 70, when consequent to the fall of Jerusalem and the total annihilation of the political elite and the Temple by the Romans, the Rabbis started the intensive work of religious reconstruction. These religious leaders represented the community both in the religious and the political spheres. This period of scholars and Rabbis, historian, Cecil Roth, calls the work and time of 'The Rule of the Wisest.' Ideologically, Judaism too combines the spiritual life with the empirical life of man. After A.D. 70 it was socio-politically a very lean period of Jewish history. It was a time when "Jerusalem, and the Temple, lay in ruins, and their rebuilding was forbidden ...... It is true that the people as a whole sat in mourning for those who had fallen in the War, and for the glory that was gone from Israel ...... The spokesmen of the Jewish people had hitherto been the rulers of the house of Herod; but the last male representative of that family, Herod Agrippa II, was estranged from his people, and had not much longer to live. The High Priest had been hardly less prominent, but with the destruction of the Temple, the High Priesthood itself had come to an end. But, even, before the fall of

Jerusalem, there had been a category which enjoyed almost equal, if not superior consideration. The Rabbis — the scholars who expounded the Holy Writ — had always been looked up to by the people with reverence. Now, there was no one else to revere. It happened that, before Jerusalem fell, one of the outstanding scholars of his generation, Johanan ben Zakkai, had managed to escape from the city — according to legend, in a coffin borne by his disciples. Titus had permitted him to settle in the township of Jabneh (Jamina), on the coast near Jaffa, used as a concentration camp, where he opened a school for the study and exposition of the traditional Jewish lore. The most eminent of contemporary scholars gathered around him there. The Sanhedrin, formerly the highest Council of State, became reconstituted from members chosen for their erudition rather than for political influence or wealth. During the subsequent long period it is this syndrome constituted of scholarly persons that steered the Jewish people to safety over a period of three and a half centuries. With this scholarly group, its president or Nasi slowly acquired semi-official status, and in due course came to be recognised as the representative of the Jewish people in its relation with the Roman authorities. With the fall of the Temple, the Sadducees, who were the religious heads, and whose existence was bound up with the essential Temple worship, lost their separate identity or influence. The Pharisee scholars were left masters of the field. These persons developed the educational system, and became the centres of local life everywhere. These scholars even went on missions to Rome, discharging duties pertaining to political matters as well. In A.D. 115 the work of reconstruction was interrupted by a terrible catastrophe. The reason was a political revolt which was put down with an excess of cruelty and bloodshed. Another insurrection took place in A.D. 182. This too was mercilessly suppressed, followed by intense religious persecution. A harrow was drawn over the site of Jerusalem, and a new city erected, under the name Aelia Capitolina, into which no Jew was allowed to set foot save once a year when they were suffered to 'buy their tears' at the Temple site."[161]

The lessons of this period of Jewish history are too obvious to be ignored, by any perceptive historian. When a community suffers political defeat, respite for reconstruction is essential; and during this period the fruitful work has to be a stress on ideology, tradition and the rebuilding of morale and the personality of the community. It involves fight only on one front, namely the religious, the socio-cultural and the educational. Emotional or sporadic political revolts during such a lean period are suicidal and become catastrophic and may put the clock of regeneration back. That is why Roth calls this period of reconstruction by the scholars, Rabbis and others the "Rule of the Wisest." No historian dubs these Jewish religious scholars as stooges or loyalists of the Romans or creation of Roman rulers; nor does any historian ignore centuries of earlier Jewish history to call the Jewish cohesion and identity revived by these scholars to be the work done at the instance of the Roman masters.

Like the efforts of the Jewish Rabbis and scholars, the work of Singh Sabha scholars is so strikingly reconstructive of the life of the Sikh community, that it would be sheer prejudice and distortion to call them the tools or creation of the British Masters.

Any course of revival, political or military, other than the one taken by Singh Sabhaites, would have been suicidal. Politically and militarily, the British were too strong to be taken on directly. Just as the catastrophic result of the two Jewish rebellions crushed by the Romans after the fall of the Temple and Jerusalem, we are well aware of the dismal fate of the sporadic Kuka uprising and the unorganised plans of the Sandhawalia group that were speedily destroyed with a heavy hand. The British power in India then was too well entrenched and alert to be shaken by such flee bites. Considering the work and achievements of the Singh Sabha and the Akali Movements from 1873 onwards, it is evident that the Singh Sabhaites and the later Sikh leaders had been politically more wise, alert and conscious than the urban leaders of the Congress like Gokhale and Tilak. In fact, the Congress leaders, it is well-known, later only made use of the Sikh struggle, which in its consistency and mass base had taken a clear lead over the subsequent Congress movement. This is also evident from the fact that the *Ghadrites* and other heroes of the struggle whom these leaders had condemned, were later accepted as the martyrs of the Indian freedom movement. And yet no one dubs the Congress leaders as the creation of the British.

Our statement about the Sikh ideology and the entire narration of events from the annexation of Punjab to the start of the Third Sikh War, the Gurdwara Reform Movement, makes a number of issues extremely explicit. The Sikh world view is different from the systems of dichotomous, pacificist, or salvation religions. The Gurus embodied their thesis in the Guru Granth, and structured the Sikh *Panth* and its institutions during a period of over two hundred years. The creation of the Khalsa by the Tenth Master and its struggle during the eighteenth century are a part of its glorious tradition and its history. We have recounted that after annexation two historical forces were working with fixed directions and objectives. The British, as explained, were clear about their political interests and in a studied manner used all means to serve them. For obvious reasons, one of their aims was to erode the religious base of the Sikhs, which gave them their power and vigour. They were fully aware of the potential of their erstwhile adversaries, and while they were keen to divert their energies to other ends, they were equally careful to ensure that the Sikhs were neither unnecessarily provoked nor allowed to regenerate or develop their socio-political strength.

Our analysis shows that the objectives which the British Government, on the one hand, and the Singh Sabhaites, on the other hand, continued to pursue were clearly divergent. This made an ultimate clash between them inevitable. It also explains why the Sikh mass struggle for liberation started much earlier than such an urge in the rest of the country. But the scholars who assume a community of interests and objectives between the British and the Sikhs simply fail to suggest, much less explain, why the clash and the Third Sikh War took place and why it happened in Punjab much earlier than elsewhere.

On the other hand, the Singh Sabhaites knew full well that their only source of inspiration, regeneration and strength was to draw upon their religion, tradition and history. As it is, the course they were to traverse, the lines on which they were to work and the institutions which were to be revived, stood clearly defined and chalked out for them in the Guru Granth and their history. The wisdom of the Singh Sabha leaders lies in their clear understanding of their past and the situation they were to face. While they never wavered from the ideals and objectives that had been laid down for them, they, according to the needs of the times, limited their efforts to the task of regeneration and revival of the spirit of the community, without directing initially its struggle to the political front. We have also seen that having reconstructed and secured their socio-religious base, slowly the Singh Sabhaites started pursuing their political objectives. It is not an accident or just a coincidence that the first tangible rebellion against the British which was mass-based took place in Punjab.

It is significant that it happened in the later part of the Singh Sabha period, and at a time when in the rest of India there were hardly any signs of any such uprising or even a preparation for it. In fact, the Indian leaders and the politically conscious elite were openly co-operating with the British war effort in those times. Equally contrasted was the reaction of the Sikhs in the Punjab to the Rowlatt Act and similar reaction in the rest of India. The agitation against the Rowlatt Act, culminating in the Jallianwala Bagh massacre and the subsequent imposition of Martial Law and the Akali struggle for the liberation of their shrines, were the two off-shoots of the religious base that had been securely revived by the Singh Sabha. It is a part of history that between 1919 and 1925 no mass based political struggle was conducted outside Punjab.

It is just idle to suggest that any religious identity, or the Sikh religious identity that had been created by an ideology, new institutions, and a four-hundred year tradition of martyrdoms and unparalleled sacrifices, could be demolished by the British rulers, as they wished to do, through the *mahants*; or that such a vigorous identity could be created by the British, as some writers suggest. Religious ideologies or identites cannot be created either by wishful thinking or by fiats of the rulers. The fate of Din-i-Ilahi of Akbar, an Indian Emperor, seeking to change the established tradition and religions is well-known.

Three features of the British Sikh relations are significant. In the annexation of India, the leaderless Sikh armies had given to the British the hardest resistance. Second, the Sikhs were a people capable of rebounding after defeat, as they did after Abdali's blow at Kup. Third, that the entire Sikh strength lay in their religious base. It is in this context that we have to interpret the two worst massacres of peaceful agitators during the British period. The first was the killing of hundreds of Sikhs gathered on the Baisakhi day at Jallianwala Bagh by General Dyer, who felt that he had nipped in the bud another mutiny. The second was the cold-blooded murder and burning of the entire *jatha* of 130 peaceful Sikhs who had gone to Nankana Sahib to hold a gathering there to free the shrine. And it is the British machine guns which under the direction and guidance of the Punjab Administration threatened to shoot thousands of Sikhs who collected to lift and cremate the bodies of the dead Sikhs at the Gurdwara. It is no accident or coincidence that in both these tragedies the victims were predominatly or wholly Sikhs against whom the assaults were directed. Both these tragedies followed the Singh Sabha Movement;

the first as a part of the continuing political activity as evidenced by the Kuka Movement, *Ghadr* rebellion and the pre-Jallianwallah risings in rural Punjab. The second was an overt British intervention when the Sikhs tried to free their Shrines from the Hinduised *mahants*. These two greatest political massacres in Indian colonial history were logical results of the British policy towards the Sikhs. However, it is correct that knowing full well the potential of a difficult adversary, the British were careful enough to placate them on minor issues without unnecessarily provoking them into a bitter opposition. It is indeed strange that a perceptive scholar like Richard Fox, who calls the Akali struggle, the Third Anglo-Sikh War, is misled into saying that the Sikhs were transmuted into Singhs by the British. Such a misreading happens, when scholars study a narrow period of events, without viewing them in their long and true perspective, including the Guru period, when the Sikh society was created, matured and its targets fixed.

From the foregoing account it should be clear that the attitude of the British Government was far from patronising or sympathetic. Rather, it was visibly hostile, as should be clear from the following :

1. On the defeat of the leaderless Sikh army the British confiscated the estates of all the Sikh Chiefs who had fought in the two Anglo-Sikh Wars.
2. All military grants to the Sikhs Jagirdars were abolished.
3. Hardly a tenth of the old army of Punjab was kept under British pay. Almost 50,000 soldiers were disbanded.
4. In the words of Dr Petric, a Director of Criminal Intelligence, Government of India : "After annexation, the Golden Temple and about six other gurdwaras were controlled by the British Government through a manager directly appointed by the Government."
5. The gurdwara properties were given over to *Nirmalas*, *Udasis* and *mahants* all of whom had Hindu leanings.
6. The struggle that the Sikhs had to put up and their immense suffering in regaining control of their gurdwaras to retain their genuine identity is very well-known.

That the Sikhs came out victorious in the end is due only to their ideology of fighting injustice and their readiness to lay down their lives to save the sanctity of their gurdwaras and religion.

REFERENCES

1. Uncalled for assumption which we shall discuss in detail at a later stage.
2. McLeod, W.H. : *The Sikhs : History, Religion and Society* (New York, 1989), p. 37.
3. Fox, G. Richard : *Lions of the Punjab : Culture in the Making* (New Delhi, 1987), p. 143.
4. Kapur, Rajiv A. : *Sikh Separatism : The Politics of Faith* (London, 1986), p. 25.
5. Barrier, N. Gerald : *The Sikhs and Their Literature* (Delhi, 1970), Introduction, p. xl.
6. Fox : op. cit., pp. 140-145.

7. "One, *Self-existent, Himself the Creator,*
    O Nanak! One continueth, another never was and never will be."
    Guru Granth Sahib; *Gauri Rag*, Trans.
    Cunningham, J. D. *A History of the Sikhs* (Delhi, 1966), p. 330.

8. "Religion consisteth not in mere words; He who looketh on all men as equal is religious."
    Trans. Macauliffe, M. A. : *The Sikh Religion*, Vol. I (Delhi, 1963), p. 60.

9. "The sense of high and low, and of caste and colour; such are the illusions created in man."
    Guru Granth Sahib, Trans. Gopal Singh : *Shri Guru Granth Sahib*, Vol. IV (New Delhi, 1987),
    p. 1188.

10. "The ignorant fools take stones and worship them. O Hindu, how shall the stone which itself
    sinketh carry you across."
    Trans. Macauliffe M.A., Vol.I, p. 326.

11. "O Brahmin, thou worshippest and propitiatest the Salagram, and deemest it a good act to wear a
    necklace of sweet basil. Why irrigate barren land and waste thy life."
    Trans., Macauliffe M.A., Vol. I, p. 61.

12. "Householders and Hermits are equal, whoever calls on the name of the Lord."
    Guru Granth Sahib, Asa Ragni. Trans., Cunningham, p. 334.

13. "In this age few Brahmins are Brahm." *Guru Granth Sahib*, 'Bilawal', Trans., Cunningham, p. 335.

14. Dhillon, G.S. : *Researches in Sikh Religion and History* (Chandigarh, 1989), pp. 2-4.

15. *Guru Granth Sahib, Bhairo*, Trans., Teja Singh, *Essays in Sikhism* (Lahore, 1944). p. 111.

16. *Haqiqat-i-Banau-i-Firqa-i-Sikhan* (1783 A.D.) quoted in Sher Singh's article, *Guru Tegh Bahadur
    gave His Head* for Millat-i-nau, in *The Sikh Review* Vol. 39. 2, No. 446, February, 1991.

17. Ganda Singh (ed.), Senapat, *Shri Gur Sobha* (Patiala, 1967), pp. 32-33.

18. Cunningham, J.D. :   op. cit., p. 64; Bannerjee, I.B. : *Evolution of the Khalsa*, Vol I (Calcutta,
    1963), p.116.

19. Kapur Singh, *Parasaraprasna* (Amritsar, 1989), (ed.) Piara Singh and Madanjit Kaur, p. 233.

20. Khushwant Singh : *A History of the Sikhs*, Vol. I (New Delhi, 1977), p. 107.

21. Ganda Singh (ed.) : *Early European Accounts of The Sikhs* (New Delhi, 1974), p. 188.

22. Bhangu, Rattan Singh : *Prachin Panth Parkash* (ed.) Bhai Vir Singh (Amritsar, 1962), p. 235;
    Forster, George; *A Journey from Bengal to England*, Vol. I (Patiala, 1970) pp. 312-313; Gupta,
    H.R. : *History of The Sikhs*, Vol. II (Delhi, 1978), p. 39.

23. Ibid.

24. Devi Prasad, Pandit : *Gulshan-i-Punjab* (Lucknow, 1872), p. 224; Cunningham : *op. cit.,* p. 301.

25. Dhillon, G.S. : *op. cit.,* p. 77.

26. Khushwant Singh : *op. cit.,* Vol. II, p. 137.

27. Khullar, K.K. : *Maharaja Ranjit Singh* (New Delhi, 1980), p. 185.

28. Government Records, VIII-II, p. 328; *Punjab Administrative Report*, 1851-53, pp. 41-42.

29. *Lahore Political Diaries*, Vol. III, p. 260; *Secret Consultation*, 7 October, 1848, No. 621;
    Fauja Singh : 'Presidential Address' in *Punjab History Conference, Proceedings* (Punjabi
    University, Patiala, November, 1965), p. 139.

30. Khushwant Singh : *op. cit.,* Vol. II, p. 70-71.

31. *Foreign Secret Consultation*, No. 21, April 28, 1849.

32. Ibid.

33. Yadav, Kripal Chandra : '*British Policy Towards Sikhs*, 1849-57' in Harbans Singh and Barrier, N.
    Gerald (ed.) : *Essays in Honour of Dr Ganda Singh* (Patiala, 1976), p. 189.

34. Ibid.

35. Khushwant Singh; op. cit., Vol. II, p. 88.

36. Hunter, W.W. : *The Marquess of Dalhousie* (Oxford, 1985), p. 99.

37. Yadav, Kirpal Chandra : op. cit., p. 190.

38. Ibid., p. 191.

39. Ibid.

40. Petrie, D. (Assistant Director, Criminal Intelligence, Government of India) : 'Development in Sikh Politics (1900-1911) (A Report)' in Shiromani Gurdwara Prabandhak Committee; gurdwara *Gazette* (Amritsar, April 1969), p. 11.

41. Khushwant Singh : *op. cit.*, Vol. II, p. 195.

42. Teja Singh : *op. cit.*, p.161.

43. Khushwant Singh : *op. cit.*, Vol. II, p. 94n.

44. Maunier, Rene : *The Sociology of Colonies,* Vol. I (London, 1949), p. 171.

45. Dr W. H. McLeod, a protagonist of some obviously odd and incongruous and superficial formulations about Sikh history has lived and worked at this centre.

46. Clark, Robert : *A Brief Account of Thirty Years of Missonary Work in the Punjab and Sind* (Lahore, 1883) pp. 18-19, 66.

47. The most notable of these Missionaries societies were the American Presbyterian Mission, the Church of England, the Cambridge Mission, the Baptist Mission and the Church of Scotland.

48. Government of India : Census of India, 1921, Vol. I, p. 117.

49. Clark, Robert : op. cit., pp. 44-45; *Letters of Queen Victoria 1837-1861*, Vol. III (London, 1908), pp. 68-69.

50. Archer, John Clark : *The Sikhs* (Princeton, 1946), p. 266.

51. *Selections From the Records of the Government of India*, Foreign Department, No. VI, *General Report on the Administration of the Punjab Territories*, 1852-53, p. 498, in, Yadav, Kirpal Chandra; op. cit., p. 196.

52. In the Central Punjab, there was a dispossessed aristocracy which had "been brow beaten and rendered inert by a calculated official policy of intimidation and suppression with the beginning of the British Rule in the Punjab."

    Fauja Singh (ed.) : *History of Punjab*, Vol. VIII, See article by the editor on *Kuka Movement*.

53. Khazan Singh : 'Jangnama Dilli' in Ashok, Shamsher Singh (ed.) *Prachin Varan Te Jangname* (Amritsar, 1971), pp. 324-48.

54. Punjab Government Records : *Mutiny Reports*, Vol. VIII, Part I, p. 237.

55. Khushwant Singh : *op. cit.*, Vol. II, p. 109.

56. Fauja Singh : 'Presidential Address', *Punjab History Conference*, First Session November 12-14, 1965, (Punjabi University, Patiala), pp. 138-139.

57. Rehman, M. A. : *Lord Dalhousie's Administration of Conquered and Annexed States* (Delhi, 1963), pp. 47-48, 67.

58. Bell, Evans : *The Annexation of the Punjab and Raja Daleep Singh,* (London, 1882), pp. 82-83.

59. Fauja Singh : 'Presidential Address', *op. cit.,* p. 139.

60. Payne, C.H. : *A Short History of The Sikhs* (London, n.d.), p. 216.

61. Ellinwood, C.De Witt (Jr.) : *An Historical Study of the Punjabi Soldier in World War I*, in Harbans Singh and Barrier; op. cit., p. 348.

62. Barrier, N. Gerald : *The Punjab Government and Communal Politics 1870-1908* in *The Journal of Asian Studies*, Vol. XXVII, November 3, May 1968, p. 525.

63. Ibid., p. 526.

64. Barrier, N. Gerald : *Sikh Emigrants and Their Homeland in Dusenbery*, Verne A. and Barrier, N. Gerald (ed.), *The Sikh Diaspora* (Delhi, 1989), p. 51.

65. (Lt. General) Goodenough, W. H. and (Lt. Col.) Dalton, J. C : *The Army Book For the British Empire* (London, 1893), p. 447.

66. Kerr, J. Ian : *Fox and the Lions; The Akali Movement Revisited* in O'Connel, T. Joseph, Isral, Milton et. al. (ed.) : *Sikh History and Religion in the Twentieth Century* (Toronto, 1988), p. 216.

67. *The Khalsa Advocate*, December 15, 1904.

68. *File No. 942-1922, Home-Political, The Sikh Question in the Punjab, Section 7 (N.A.I.); Ludhiana Gazetteer 1888-89, Chapter IIIC, p. 72*;

    Punjab Legislature Concil Dabates - 8th January to 16th April, 1921, Vol, I, p. 546.

69. Phillauri, Sharda Ram (Pandit) : *Sikhan De Raj Di Vithya* (Jallandhar, 1956), p. 42 (ed.) Pritam

Singh;

Gill, Harbans Kaur, *Sharda Ram Phillauri* (Patiala, 1976), p. 19.

70. Pritam Singh. Ibid., p. 43;

Balbir Singh; *Charn Hari Visthar* (Amritsar, n.d.). Part I, pp. 63-64.

Gurdwara Gazettee, Amritsar, August 1953, p. 9.

71. Court, Henry : *Sikhan De Raj Di Vithiya* (Patiala, 1970), p. 8.

72. Ganda Singh : *A History of the Khalsa College, Amritsar* (Amritsar, 1949), p. 2; *The Khalsa Advocate*, Amritsar, September 20, 1903.

73. Bhangu, Rattan Singh : *op. cit.*, pp. 372-75; Latif, Syed Muhammad : *History of the Punjab* (Calcutta, 1891) p. 213.

Khuswant Singh : *op. cit.*, Vol. I, p. 129.

74. Khuswant Singh : Ibid. P. 145.

75. Ibid., p. 127 (n)

76. *Ludhiana Gazetteer*, 1888-89, Chapter III-C, p. 72.

77. *Report of the Singh Sabha*, Patiala, 1880, pp. 5-6.

78. *Shri Gurmat Parkash*, Rawalpindi, September, 1885.

79. Dhillon, G.S. : *Origin and Development of the Singh Sabha Movement; Constituional Aspects'* in Ganda Singh (ed.) : *The Singh Sabha and other Socio-Religious Movements in the Punjab* 1850-1925; *The Panjab Past and Present*, Vol. VII, Part I, April, 1973, Serial No. 13, Punjabi University, Patiala, pp. 50-51.

80. Singh Sabha Amritsar; *Niyam* (Amritsar, 1890), p.1; Report on the Administration of The Punjab and Its Dependencies For 1897-98 (Lahore, 1898); No. 62, p. ccxix;

Ganda Singh : op. cit., p. 2;

Dhillon,G.S. : *Character and Impact of The Singh Sabha Movement on the History of the Punjab* (Ph.D. Thesis, Punjabi University, Patiala, 1973), p. 54.

81. Sahni, Ruchi Ram : *The Gurdwará Reform Movement and the Sikh Awakening* (Jullundur, 1922), p. 150.

82. Vihiria, Avtar Singh (Bhai) : *Shok Pattar* (Lahore, 1905), p. 38.

83. Ibid.

84. *Khalsa Akhbar*, Lahore, April 14th, 1899.

85. Sahni, Ruchi Ram : *op. cit.,* p. 150;

Vihiria, Avtar Singh (Bhai) : *Gurdarshan Shastar* (Amritsar, 1916), pp. 12-13; Vihiria; *Shok Pattar*, p. 38.

86. *Khalsa Akhbar*, Lahore, September 30, 1898.

87. Chief Khalsa Diwan : *Seva De Panjah Sal* (Amritsar, 1952), p. 2;

Dhillon G.S. : *op. cit.*, p. 58.

88. *Khalsa Akhbar*, Lahore, September 30, 1898.

89. *Report of the Singh Sabha*, (Patiala, 1906), pp. 1-5.

90. Gurmukh Singh (Bhai) : *My Attempted Ex-Communication From The Sikh Temples and The Khalsa Community at Faridkot in 1897* (Lahore, 1898), p. 12.

91. Ibid.

92. Ibid.

93. Patrie, D. *op. cit.* in *The Panjab Past and Present,* Vol. IV Part II (Patiala, October, 1970);

Sahni, Ruchi Ram *op. cit.*, p. 15;

Gurmukh Singh (Bhai) : *op. cit.*, pp. 2-3.

94. Ibid.

95. Ibid.

96. Durga Parsad : *An English Translation of the Satyarth Parkash* (Lahore, 1904), pp. 361-363; Ganda Singh : *'The Origins of the Hindu-Sikh Tension in the Punjab'* in *The Journal of Indian History*, Vol. XXIV, April 1961, pp. 121-23; *The Khalsa Akhbar,* Lahore, July 7, 1899;

Lakshman Singh, Bhagat; *Autobiography* (Calcutta, 1965), p. 58;

Vaid, Mohan Singh (Bhai) : *Arya De Dhol Da Pol* (Taran Taran, 1915), p. 14.

97. Majumdar, R.C (ed.) : *History and Culture of the Indian People*, Vol. X (Bombay, 1965), p. 103.

98. Smith, R. Bosworth : *Life of Lord Lawrence* (London, 1883), Vol. I, p. 287.

99. Temple, Richard : *India in 1880* (London, 1881), p. 120.

100. Chief Khalsa Diwan : *Rules and Regulations of the Chief Khalsa Diwan* (Amritsar, 1904), p.1.

101. "I had come to regard the Khalsa College, Amritsar, as Government College minus Government discipline. No member had a free hand in it, hence it was idle to think of doing any constructive work without the previous sanction of the Government." Lakshman Singh, Bhagat : *op. cit.*, p. 203.

102. Ahluwalia, M. L. (ed.) : *Select Documents — Gurdwara Reform Movement 1919-1925* (New Delhi, 1985), Introduction, p. xxiii.

103. *Khalsa Advocate*, Amritsar, (November 14, 1908.)

104. Sunder Singh, Master : *Ki Khalsa Kalaj Sikhan Da Hai* ? (Amritsar, 1909), pp. 30-37.

104-a. Petrie D. : *op. cit., in Gurdwara Gazette*, p. 45; Isemonger. F.C. and Slattery, J. : *An Account of the Ghadr Consipracy*, 1913-15 (Lahore, 1919), p. 19.

105. Petrie, D. : *op. cit.*, pp. 37-39.

106. Ibid., Dhillon : *op. cit.*, p. 284.

107. Petrie, D. : Ibid., p. 46.

108. Ibid.

109. Ibid., pp. 46-48.

110. Ibid.

111. Talwar, K.S. : *Early Phases of the Sikh Renaissance and Struggle for Freedom* in *Panjab Past and Present* (Patiala, October 1970), p. 295.

112. Ibid.

113. Ibid.

114. Ibid.

115. Barrier N. Gerald : *The Sikhs and Their Literature* (Delhi, 1970), p. 79.

116. *Khalsa Samachar*, Amritsar, December 23, 1908.

117. Sahni, Ruchi Ram : *op. cit.*, p. 466; Narang, Gokul Chand : *Transformation of Sikhism* (Lahore, 1946), p. 321.

118. Government of India, Home Department, *Judicial No. 950,* June 25, 1914, Simla; Government of India; Home Department, *Judicial No. 1118,* July 17, 1914, Simla; Government of India; Home Department *Judicial No. 2248*, October, 1914, Simla (N.A.I.);

Teja Singh : *op. cit.*, p. 208;

Ganda Singh : *Exemption of kirpan from Restrictions under the Arms Act* in *Panjab Past and Present,* Vol. VII, part I (Punjabi University, Patiala, April 1973), pp. 162-172.

119. Teja Singh : Ibid., p. 209.

120. McLeod, W. H. : *The Sikhs : History, Religion and Society* (New York, 1989), p. 8.

121. Fox, Richard : *op. cit.*, pp. 208-210.

122. Barrier, N. Gerald : *Sikh Emigrants and Their Homeland* in Dusenbery, Verne A, and Barrier N. Gerald (ed).) : *The Sikh Diaspora* (Delhi, 1989), p. 51.

123. Semonger, F.C. and Slattery, J. : *op. cit.*, pp. 2-4.

124. Talwar, K.S. : *op. cit.*, pp. 293-94.

125. Patrie, D. : *op. cit.*, p. 325.

126. *Punjab Administrative Report* (1921-22).Vol. I. p. 238.

127. Caveeshar, Sardul Singh : *The Akali Movement* in *Panjab Past and Present*, Vol. VII, Part I (Punjabi University, Patiala, April 1973), p. 120.

128. Ibid.

129. Ibid.

130. Jagjit Singh : *Ghadar Party Lehr* (Delhi, 1976), pp. 47, 204.

131. Ibid., pp. 51-52.

132. Isemonger, F.C. and Slattery, J. : *op. cit.,* pp. 2-3, 37.
133. Ibid.
134. Ibid.
135. Hardinge, Charles : *My Indian Years, 1910-16* (London, 1947), p. 115.
136. Khushwant Singh : *op. cit.,* Vol. II. p.179 (28n).
137. Caveeshar, Sardul Singh : *op. cit.,* pp. 120, 137.
138. Government of India : *Home-Political-*A-November, 1914-Pro. No. 100; Caveeshar : *op. cit.,* p. 121.
139. *Punjab Administrative Report* (1921-22), Vol. I, pp. 238-239.
140. Caveeshar; *op. cit.,* p. 138.
141. Ibid.
142. Ahluwalia : *op. cit.,* p. 87.
143. Puri, Rajinder : *Rediscovery of India* (New Delhi, 1984), pp. 112-13.
144. Mittal, S.C. : *Freedom Movement in Punjab (1905-29)* (Delhi, 1977), pp. 82, 143.
145. Puri, Rajinder : *op. cit.,* p. 110.
146. Datta, V.N. : *Inaugural Address At the 24th Session* of Punjab History Confrence, Punjabi University, Patiala, 15-17 March, 1991.
146-a. Rustamji, K.F. : *Revenge Not the Answer* in the *Tribune,* February 20, 1992.
147. Grewal, J.S. and Puri, H.K. : *Udham Singh Dian Chithian* (Amritsar, 1974), pp. 58, 60-61.
148. Ibid., 66-67.
149. *Punjab Administrative Report* (1921-22), Vol. I, pp. 238-39.
150. Mohinder Singh : *The Akali Movement* (Delhi, 1978), p. 14.
151. Ahluwalia, M.L. : *op. cit.,* p. 89.
152. Khushwant Singh : *op. cit.,* Vol. II, pp. 165-66.
153. Ibid.
154. Ibid.
155. Josh, Sohan Singh : *Akali Morchian Da Itihas* (Delhi, 1972), p. 28.
156. Mohinder Singh : *op. cit.,* pp. 87-88.
157. *Punjab Administrative Report,* 1921-22, Vol. I, p. 351.
158. Smith, V.M. : *The Akali Dal and Shiromani Gurdwara Parbandhak Committee* (1921-22), A Confidential Memorandum in *Panjab Past and Present* (Punjabi University, Patiala, October, 1967), Vol. I, part II, p. 279.
159. Caveeshar : *op. cit.,* p. 141.
160. Gurbax Singh : *Society in The Punjab Under Ranjit Singh*; Mufti-Ali-Ud-Din's analysis in *Punjab History Conference Proceedings,* February 28-29, 1976 (Patiala, 1976), pp. 135-37.
161. Roth, Cecil : *Short History of the Jewish People* (Glasgow, 1948), pp. 110-112.

V

CONTROVERSIES

31

FUNDAMENTALISM, MODERNITY AND SIKHISM :
A TERTIUM QUID

NOEL Q. KING

"Fundamentalism" in its strictest technical use refers to a movement within American Protestant Evangelicalism of fairly recent origin. The word has come to be linked with various literalist, evangelical and charismatic groups and televangelists. Thence it has been applied to religous extremists who claim to be returning to fundamentals.[1] We find the media and some scholars using it of the Pire pinis cargo cultists of yesterday in Sepik River, New Guinea, onwards to the *Babri masjid/Ram janam bhoomi* folk in today's India. Recently in his Defenders of God, *the Fundamentalist Revolt against the Modern Age,* Bruce B. Lawrence with great scholarly care and erudition defines terms and deals mainly with what he considers prime examples-American-style. Protestant Fundamentalists, the Ithna-ashariya Shia of Iran and such defenders of "The Jewish collectivity" as Gush Emunim.[2] He refers the movements back to some of the major concepts of modern world history as it has developed since World War 1. We will turn back to this shortly.

"Modernity" and "Modernism" refer to a tendency among religions to update themselves by accepting concepts and techniques from the modern secular world around them. The words are sometimes used as a kind of second part in a dichotomy-"Fundamentalism versus Modernity/Modernism." They easily fit into the academic discussion on the "Modernization" of religions like Islam or the influence of modern America or the Third Republic in France on their own Roman Catholicism early in the century.[3] But, easily the concepts elide towards association with Western dominance and the Great Western Transmutation (abbreviated to GWT) by which the world was transformed between 1492 and 1947.[4]

Here it is necessary for our purposes to interject that the word "fundamentalist" has been applied to Sikhism too by both media and scholars especially in the time leading up to and since the tragic Operation Blue Star. Recent examples include Angela Dietrich's "The Khalsa Resurrected : Sikh Fundamentalism in the Punjab."[5] In this article which struggles to be sympathetic and respectful, the essay on the Sikhs rubs shoulders with those on Fundamentalist Muslims in West Africa, Iran and Egypt, Secularists in Turky, Sri Lankan Hindus in Britian, Protestant Tamils in Madras, as well as the American Moral Majority. Again, late in 1989 at a meeting of the American Academy of Religion at Anaheim in California, a panel discussed these issues in connection with Sikhism. A paper which has not to date been published and which requests it be not quoted for it had not been finalized, was read by Professor Harjot Oberoi of Vancouver. It was entitled "Sikh Fundamentalism : Ways of Turning Things Over ?"

In the discussion generated, it became clear that though a religion which used a *Mul Mantra* and was given to *mulvad* obviously got down to fundamentals, the word "Fundamentalist" could hardly be used in the same way as it was of American Fundamentalists. There was also considerable objection to the way in which by the use of social science and Marxit historical methods it was to be supposed that Sikhs were mainly peasants who were led along by a few people who drew them out from the main body of Hinduistic Indians. The idea was also hotly contested that deep changes in Sikh History from 1699 onwards came in response to outer stimuli on the part of a body in which it was alleged increasingly *Jats* had taken over leadership from *Khatris*. If we reject such explanations of evolution into modernity and other similarly based arguments and hypotheses, what better propositions can we put forward to explain the Sikh situation today ? In answering it, it is necessary to note that modernizing thought since the so-called Enlightenment, a European movement especially reflected in philosophy of the eighteenth century, has tended to discount any use of hypotheses of explanations which include the supernatural or that which passes human understanding. Recently some cracks in this carapace have begun to show.

It is now possible to tune back and take up our consideration of the position of Fundamentalism, Modernity and Sikhism against their background in some major trends of thinking about World History. World History is not a modern western invention. In the eighth century before the Common Era strata of the Jewish Torah, building on much older West Asian and Egyptian ideas, and the Jewish Scriptures as a whole give us a *schema* of how the nations came to be and how they interact and the plan of their history. In the *Puranas, Indic* thinkers give us concepts of world ages and world movements. In the eighth/fourteenth century, Ibn Khaldun gives us in his *Muqaddimah* a pattern which looks back to the earlier thinking of Arabs and Jews.

It is impressive how many older Sikhs of my generation read at High School H.G. Wells' *Short History of the World,* which originally came out in 1924. I have also met a good number who had read Toynbee. Although Karl Jaspers wrote in German, many of his ideas have come to be known to users of English. Thus a number of us take it almost for granted that there is a kind of intellectual spirit of the age (*Zeitgeist*) which seems mysteriously to affect thinkers across the world with the same kind of ideas just as it is said, new bird songs will spread from bird to bird across an island. Jaspers especially juxtaposes the Athenian philosophers, the Hebrew prophets, the Upanishadic seers and the Chinese sages in an Axial Age.[6]

Joseph Needham in his eighty-eighth year remarked that if he had time to carry the implications of his *History of Science and Technology in China* into World History, he would very much desire to trace Taoist ideas and techniques, for instance, with regard to chemistry and the use of gun powder in their influence upon Muslim scientists such as the alchemists.[7] One could follow this up to try to postulate a transmission of thinking even in a perverted way between the original Chinese invention of gunpowder and the Portuguese floating fortress. There are many such transmissions which suggest themselves but lack of sound historical evidence interdicts even their formulation. We turn back to trying to trace some factors in History of Religion which, if not transmitted, naturally overtake or take place in an ecclesiastical body or corpus at a certain point in her life.

At Chicago, William McNeill and Marshall Hodgson formulated ideas which have deeply affected Bruce Lawrence, whose book was mentioned above. In her years of Empire, Muslim civilization was, according to this hypothesis breathed through and through by a religion which was its conscience and shaper. But, during the time of "the Great Western Transmutation" of world history, religion was apparently not a predominant controlling factor or an effective conscience.[8] However, when some thinkers in great cultures and civilizations, including Western culture, see their societies disintegrating, their young being lost to them, their best traditions destroyed, they turn desparately to their religions as a means of hope and a way of working for survival, recovery and resurgence. This is a comparatively late movement which of its own nature must come after the modernisers have brought the threatening outside influences into their own most cherished holy of holies. As a movement it too will use the language and methods of the enemy in its attempt to recover the fundamentals as it imagines them. It too will invent tradition. It too will use science and technology and be dependent on them and indeed be transformed by them. Broadly and approximately, Fundamentalism may be considered such a movement or a manifestation of this tendency.

Let us turn back to Sikhism. Sikhism was presented to the world by the first Guru, who lived from 1469 to 1539. The tenth occupied the *takht* from 1675 to 1708. During those centuries, the Punjab faced yet more of the Muslim invasions which had gone on since the days of Mahmud of Ghazni, and the Europeans arrived and began to weave India into their world web. In the nineteenth century they broke in with full force bringing their world diseases, economics, their philosophical, religious and political ideals and failures. They brought their ways of education, science and technology. Everywhere the local product seemed to be swept away. Even their intellectual history with its tale of revolutions in politics, literary critical method, social and gender structure, its divorce between religion, ethics, philosophy and poltics found local supporters and exponents and some partial acceptance. But the response in Sikhism was not just one of meeting one emergency after another, or the evolution of an overall response by any one person nor of a committee nor of a group of leaders. Rather at base it was the continued unfolding of the enseeded, encoded nature of Sikhism as originally propounded by the first Mahala and the other nine. After the tenth, it was vested in the Book and in the *Sangat* and the same Spirit held forth the same truths as they applied to that stage of life. Let us give but one brief example. It was not one person, however brilliant, saying *Hum Hindu nain hai* late in the nineteenth century, but the First Teacher coming up from the Three Day Waters saying, *Hai nain Hindu, Hai nain Mussulman,* which is basic. The nineteenth century remark is but a working out of the early teaching. In that dichotomy we find posited a third something (the *tertium quid* of our title) : Sikhism.

In the debate about Fundamentalism and Modernity, other buzz words are appearing. These include "primitivism," that is, the seeking for a primitive pure state and the attempt to imitate it under present day conditions. This may be called the restoration ideal or a quest for a return to the primordial, a seeking for a renewal of a primal vision. At the same time many are talking of ours as a post-modern age. There is growing suspicion of western ways just as they penetrate more and more places. A colleague brought back from former East Germany a copy of a poster which shows an attractive young western woman giving a cigarette in a packet labelled "West" to a Russian official who is choking on his own cigarette. The caption in Russian says "Try out the West" or more snappily "Test the West." A caption in German says "This applies in East Germany too." On the packet there is a printed warning in English about Life in the West with "its banal culture and brutal extremes of poverty."

In their day, thinkers both Eastern, Western and from Africa and the Pacific have done their best. We test their best, each time the teachings of Sikhism may seem to be fitted into their categories. Then we find it escaping their fingers and passing on its way. Young Sikh scholars thoroughly grounded in their own inheritance, who are encouraged and enabled to devote the years of detailed and disciplined study to the age-long international debate from China to California via the Punjab and Olduvai Gorge will contribute much to a genuine theory of World History.

REFERENCES

1. For dictionary definitions see for instance any recent edition of Webster's *College Dictionary*. Compare also handbooks like Roger Scruton's *A Dictionary of Political Thought,* London : Pan Books 1982. These works do not really attempt to define so much as to sum up current usage. However, the article on *Fundamentalism* in edited *Mircea Eliade : Encyclopedia of Religions,* Free Press and MacMillian : New York 1988 volume gives some definitions and bibliography. (This *Encyclopedia* is disgracefully inadequate on Sikhism.) The works of James Barr culminating in his *Fundamentalism* (London, 1977), though written from a British point of view, have an exactness of scholarship and originality which make fascinating reading.

2. Published by Harper and Row : San Franciso, 1989.

3. Again for bibliography see in edited Mircea Eliade : *Encyclopedia of Religion,* Volume 10, the artticles on *Modernism and Modernity.*

4. G.W.T. is a term used by Marshall Hodgson whom we mention below which has come into jargon use in American Universities. Like the Ninja Mutant Turtles of present day fame, it is by no

means purely Western. The British would not have got far in India in any of their enterprises without widespread and gifted local help and co-operation. The GWT is a world achievement even as it is a world tragedy.

5. Essay number 6 in a collection edited by lionel Caplan : *Studies in Religious Fundamentalism,* London : Macmillan Press, 1987.

6. With Karl Jaspers it is impossible to pick out few titles but ed. Edith Ehrilch, etc. Basic Philosophical *Writings, Selections,* Athens : Ohio University Press, 1986 and *Man in the Modern Age,* London : Routledge and K.Paul, 1959, give an inkling.

7. The writer had the privilege of two visits with Dr Joseph Needham in July 1988. He made the remarks quoted in conversation. When I asked after his middle name "Noel", he said he was born on the first Christmas of the century. Volumes 1 and 2 of his *Science and Civilization in China.* Cambridge (England) : University Press, 1956 and 1958, are the most relevant to our purpose.

8. On William Hardy McNeill see his *Readings in World History,* New York : Oxford University Press, 1968 and *A World History,* 1967, subsequently re-edited. On Marshall G.S. Hodgson see *The Venture of Islam : Conscience and History in a World Civilization,* Chicago : University Press, 3 volumes, 1974. Other "display options" as the bibliographical retrieval systems say, include Sir Herbert Butterfield, Christopher Dawson and a host of others.

32

MISREPRESENTATION OF SIKH TRADITION IN WORLD RELIGIOUS TEXTBOOKS

JAMES R. LEWIS

(Genuine) knowledge of another culture is possible (but) the student must feel he or she is answerable to and in uncoercive contact with the culture and the people being studied. (In the past), most of what the West knew about the non-Western world it knew in the framework of colonialism; the European scholar therefore approached his subject from a general position of dominance, and what he said about this subject was said with little reference to what anyone but other European scholars had said.[1]

Over the course of the past few decades, academics have invested increasing amounts of energy into analysing the scholarly discourse of previous eras, particularly the scholarship that was carried out by colonialist nations with respect to subject peoples. The focus of most of this relatively recent work has been to point out how the images of non-European peoples presented in such discourse were shaped by the (often unconscious) presuppositions of European scholars, as well as how this scholarship ultimately fed back into, and helped to legitimize imperialistic attitudes. Within Sikh studies, a fair amount of analysis along these lines has been carried out with respect to the semi-scholarly works produced by British officials during the period of time leading up to the annexation of the Punjab.

As someone professionally involved in teaching of general courses on world religions, I became interested in examining how non-Western people were presented in contemporary survey treatments of world religions, especially the representations found in world religion textbooks. What follows is a short report of my findings in this area with respect to the Sikh community. The focus of the discussion will be on the misrepresentations of Sikhism that are present in survey treatments of world religions, as well as an analysis of the factors responsible for such misrepresentations.

The paper has been divided into three major sections. The first section looks at simple errors of fact. The second and third sections examine two themes that surface over and over again in Western treatments of Sikhism : Sikh "syncretism," and the contrast between the supposed "pacificism" of early Sikhism and the militancy of later Sikhism.[2] Unlike the first set of errors, which are due largely to carelessness, the second two misrepresentations ultimately have their roots in the less objective scholarship of the British Raj. Hence, we will find that, despite the good intentions of present-day scholars, discussions of these latter two themes often subtly slander the Sikh tradition.

ERRORS OF FACT

If one just glances through a half dozen or so world religion textbooks at random, the first thing that strikes one about their treatment of Sikhism is the wide diversity in the amount of space devoted to the Sikh religious tradition. This diversity ranges from whole chapters on the Sikh religion to complete absence in some texts. More often than not, Guru Nanak is at least mentioned, although usually in the form of a passing reference to the "impact" of Islam on Hinduism. The incidence of misrepresentations seems to bear no relationship either to date of publication or to length of treatment. In other words, contrary to what one might anticipate, lengthier or more recent treatments of the Sikh religion do not appear to contain fewer mistakes than shorter or older treatments. For example, in the 1987 edition of *Many Peoples, Many Faiths,* Robert Ellwood mistakenly asserts not only that Guru Nanak spent the *entire* later part of his life as an "itinerant poet and minstrel" but he also remarks that Guru Gobind Singh was "killed in battle." Another curious error is when Ellwood says that the Tenth Master slew a chicken rather than a goat on the occasion of the formation of the Khalsa.[3] Hence, proximity in time to the present is no guarantee of accuracy.

As for more extended recent treatments of Sikhism, in the 1987 edition of *Religions of the World,* Lewis M. Hopfe asserts that Guru Gobind Singh "introduced into Sikhism the worship of the terrible Hindu goddess of death, Durga."[4] Hopfe appears to have fallen into this error by taking an item of historical fact, the Tenth Guru's employment of the martial symbolism associated with the Hindu goddess, and misconstruing it so that (at least in Hopfe's statement) it appears that the Sikh community as a whole actually adopted the ritual worship of Durga — a portrayal that is manifestly false. Hence, extended treatment of the Sikh religion (i.e., devoting an entire chapter to Sikhism) is no more a guarantee of accuracy than a recent publication date.

Other mistakes that occasionally crop up are the long-refuted position that the First Master was a "disciple of Kabir,"[5] and the rather unusual item of misinformation that the Sikh community made an abortive attempt to form a country of its own during the 1947 partition of India.[6] One will also occasionally find statements to the effect that Guru Nanak "accepted the gods of the Hindu pantheon,"[7] without adding the important qualification that the First Master regarded the deities of Hindu mythology as demi-gods unworthy of religious devotion.[8]

It is all too apparent that the source of every one of these misrepresentations is superficial acquaintance with the Sikh tradition. In the bibliographies of these works, one rarely finds more than one or two book-length references on Sikhism. While one can sympathize with the difficult position of an author who takes on the Herculean task of writing a world religious text, and can understand the temptation to consult as few references as absolutely necessary, there are enough Sikhs in the English speaking world that, with relatively little expenditure of energy, an author could *at least* have sent a draft of his or her chapter on the Sikh religion to a responsible member of the Sikh community for comment and correction.

Although one might justifiably be irritated with the sloppy scholarship of these various authors, their mistakes pale in comparison with the lamentable tendency of some academics who are irresponsible enough to make negative, evaluative remarks about a religious tradition that they have all too obviously neglected to study with care. Thus, for instance, in *A Guide to the World's Religions,* David G. Bradley remarks, in language that seems to heap ridicule on the Sikh community, that the Guru Granth Sahib is "not comprehensive to most Sikhs; despite that fact, they hold it sacred."[9] Similarly, in a multi-authored work, *The Religious World,* Hyla S. Converse asserts that, "with the intention of achieving religious unity, the Sikhs, in their fight for survival against Islam, became instead a symbol of religious intransigence and hatred."[10] And lastly, in a statement made by an otherwise reputable contemporary scholar (in the context of an edited work, *Religion and Man*), Robert D. Baird asserts that "Whereas for Nanak, the ultimate matter was devotion to the True Name, for the present community, self-preservation appears to be somewhat more important."[11] When contrasted with statements such as these, which constitute errors of judgement as well as errors of fact, the non-evaluative mistakes of other authors appear more forgivable.

Before leaving this section of the paper, it should be noted that not all surveys of world religions misrepresent Sikhism. There are, in fact, at least six texts containing a full chapter on the Sikh religion that appear to be free from misrepresentations. Not by coincidence, all of these general works are multi-authored volumes, ¾ an approach which, although, by no means capable of guaranteeing accuracy (as we have already noted with respect to the books in which Converse's and Baird's remarks appear), at least guarantees that the people composing individual chapters have adequate opportunity to read more than one or two books on Sikhism. Three of the acceptable treatments that I found were composed by recognized scholars of the Sikh tradition : Christopher Shackle, W. Owen Cole, and W. H. McLeod.[12] (Although Sikhs have often criticized McLeod's more specialized studies, they will find nothing objectionable in his chapter in Parrinder's *Man and His Gods).* Hilda Wierum Boulter, who authored the chapter on Sikhism in the comparatively old 1961 *Living Schools of Religion,* was able to construct an accurate picture by consulting a learned Sikh (Dr Anup Singh) about his own tradition.[13] Niels C. Nielsen, Jr., who authored the Sikhism chapter in *Religions of the World,* appears to have avoided error by sticking rather closely to the presentation of the Sikh religion found in Cole and Sambhi's *The Sikhs : Their Religious Beliefs and Practices.*[14] And finally, S. Vernon McCasland, who authored the Sikhism chapter in an older survey of religion that was also entitled *Religions of the World,* managed to portray the Sikh faith accurately.[15] He seems to have accomplished this by following the sympathetic treatments of Sikhism found in such works as Max Arthur Macauliffe's *The Sikh Religion.*

SYNCRETISM

While it should be self-evident that every emergent religion relies on prior religious traditions as points of reference for a new vision of spiritual reality, the relationship between early Sikhism and its religious environment appears to have captured the attention of observers of the Sikh religion more so than other religions. In particular, the question of the relative impact of Hinduism and Islam, and more especially the notion of a "syncretism" of these two traditions, has constituted almost an obsession in Western treatments of the Sikh religion. One of the most peculiar aspects of this phenomenon is that although the majority of authors of world religion texts are willing to rely on the syncretism category in their interpretation of the Sikh religion, there is widespread disagreement as to the precise nature of this blend of Hinduism and Islam. For example, while some authors confidently portray Sikhism as being more of a "reformed Hindu religion",[16] other authors assert, with apparently equal confidence, that in Sikhism "there is little doubt that the Muslim source predominates."[17] Similarly, whereas some scholars argue that "Nanak's doctrine is more a reform of Hinduism,"[18] one can find other scholars who see no difficulty in asserting that Guru Nanak "leaned rather more to Islam than to Hinduism."[19] Yet other writers appear to argue for an equal admixture of Islam and Hinduism."[20] Finally, while some advocates of the syncretism interpretation are willing to go so far as to assert that the Sikh religion "is not in any absolute sense new"[21] (i.e., that *everything* in Sikhism can be traced to a source in either Hinduism or Islam), other scholars, particularly those who criticize the syncretism interpretation, have stressed "originality of Guru Nanak."[22] Thus Hindu/Muslim syncretism, which the majority of authors of general surveys of world religions seem to accept uncritically as the starting point for their interpretation of Sikhism, turns out to be far more ambiguous that one might at first assume. This peculiar state of affairs should lead the careful observer to ask broader sorts of questions about the syncretism interpretation, such as, why has so much scholarly energy been invested in this particular question ? And, what, ultimately, does it mean for one religion to be a "syncretism" and another not ?

The answers to this line of questioning are complex because there is more than one factor at work here. The widespread influence of the syncretism interpretation is partially attributable to the writings of certain Sikhs who advocate the idea in order to portray Sikhism as an inherently ecumenical religion. Another factor contributing to the pre-eminence of the idea in surveys of world religions is the tendency of authors to over-emphasize Sikhism's syncretic character "due to the attractiveness of a syncretistic religion in a textbook on the great world religions."[28] There is, however, an often unrecognized problem with the label "syncretism," which is that the term was traditionally utilized to denounce groups that had deviated from the dominant religion, and who were consequently portrayed as having polluted the true faith by "grafting on foreign elements."[24] From this perspective, it is reasonable to hypothesize that the syncretism appellation probably originated with English missionaries or some other group of colonial officials who regarded the Sikh religion as spurious.

If someone were to argue that "syncretism" has lost its negative, judgemental connotations, we can ask, why, then, are the major religions of the West never described as "syncretisms" ? In other words, there is basically nothing wrong with the observation that both Muslim and Hindu influences are evident in the Sikh religion, as long as one does not fail to note that the same state of affairs exists in other religious traditions. Christianity, for example, was shaped by Judaism, Mithraism, Neoplatonis, and other Hellenistic religions. And, not just during the period of their birth, but also over the course of later contact with other peoples, all of the major world traditions have been influenced, to some extent, by other religions. Why, then, is it appropriate to refer to Sikhism as a "syncretism," but not appropriate to thus refer to other religions ? In other words, if a faith like Christianity cannot appropriately be called a "syncretism," then what term would apply to Christianity's particular blend of influences that could not apply to Sikhism ?

With a little reflection, it should be apparent that there is no clear criterion for distinguishing Sikhism from other religious traditions on this point. The covert judgement, and here we are finally in a position to state the evaluation implicit in this seemingly neutral term, is that Sikhism can be understood entirely in terms of its constituent religions, whereas other traditions are somehow "more," or that they somehow "transcend," the religions from which their constituents are derived. To restate this value-judgement as bluntly as possible, the founders of other traditions were somehow able to provide a special (creative ? revealed ?) element to their new spiritual synthesis that was somehow missing in the case of Guru Nanak.

I am, of course, exaggerating the point, but it needs to be made perfectly clear that the characterization of the Sikh tradition as a "syncretism" is a holdover from the days when all of the other world religions were compared with Christianity for the purpose of demonstrating Christianity's superiority. Although I recognize that present-day scholars do not consciously intend to pronounce such a judgement against Sikhism, the fact that "syncretism" continues to be used differentially — to describe some religions but not others — indicates that this judgement has not ceased to shape interpretations of the Sikh tradition.

PACIFICISM / MILITANCY

Next to Hindu/Muslim syncretism, the most frequent misinterpretation of the Sikh religion to appear in world religion textbooks is the contrast between the supposed "pacificism" of Guru Nanak and the militancy of Guru Gobind Singh. Although a few authors of general surveys have recognized that the difference between the First Master and the Tenth Master on this point lay more in the circumstances of the time during which they lived rather than in their basic orientations (the First Nanak's attitude was no more "passive" than the Tenth Nanak's was "violent" — both forcefully preached the truth and asserted the rights of the oppressed), more often than not such authors have seen it fit to exaggerate the contrast until it appears that there is an actual contradiction between early and later Sikhism. To cite just a few such misrepresentations :

Another element in the religion of Nanak was his pacificism. This man, in all his travels and with all the rejection that he received, maintained the stance of a pacificist. He never struck out at his enemies, and apparently he taught his disciples to follow this pattern. In contrast to the teachings of Nanak, Sikhs, in their later history, became known as the most militant of warriors.[25]

Although the teachings of Nanak himself set forth a quietistic religion that laid stress upon the individual and his relationship to God, the religion, which developed after Nanak, became highly political, leading to a religious state in the Punjab. Also, the original emphasis on individual virtues and piety became in time a faith that emphasized strength, combativeness, and even militarism.[26]

Guru Gobind Singh built up Sikh fighting strength, and what had begun as a group of believers in brotherly love turned into a formidable military brotherhood which waged war against Muslims, and which believed, as Muslims did, that death in battle was a passport to paradise.[27]

These negative judgements constitute only the most recent manifestations of a biased interpretation of Sikhism that was first articulated by some of the British scholar-administrators of the Nineteenth Century. W. L. McGregor, for example, in a book originally published in 1846, observed that, "Nanak, as the founder of the Sikhs, is greatly venerated by that nation, though they appear to have entirely forgotten his tenets of peace."[28] In a more sharply worded statement, H. H. Wilson, in an article first published in 1848, asserted that,

(Guru Gobind Singh) changed the whole character of the community, and converted the Sikhs of Nanak, the disciples of a religion of spirituality and benevolence, and professors of a faith of peace and goodwill, into an armed confederacy, a military republic. The worship of "steel" was combined with that of the "book", and instead of attempting to unite Muhammadans and Hindus into one family fraternity, he made his disciples vow implacable hatred to the followers of Mohammed.[29]

Although we might be inclined to be somewhat forgiving toward these Nineteenth Century figures, who were, after all, writing around the period of the Anglo-Sikh wars as well as engaged in the difficult task of legitimating British imperialism, we have to wonder what issue is at stake behind the very similar statements of contemporary scholars. Rather than tackle this problem directly, let us ask the same type of question about the early pacificism/later militancy contrast that we asked about Hindu/Muslim syncretism — the question of differential treatment. In the case at hand, the proper way to pose the question is; Are there other religious traditions in which the founder preached (or at least appeared to preach) a pacificist message that later followers disregarded ?

Of the established world religions, Jainism has been the most faithful to its founder's pacificism, whereas Buddhism's historical record is somewhat uneven. However, indisputably the religion with the worst history of violence — a violence totally at odds with the teachings of its founder — is Christianity. Hence, while all of the above citations are more or less inaccurate evaluations of Sikhism, in many instances a little substitution of terms would transform them into highly accurate evaluations of

Christianity. For example, if one substitutes relevant Christian terms for a few of the corresponding terms in McGregor's statement cited earlier, one obtains an entirely appropriate description of the Christian tradition :

> Jesus, as the founder of Christianity, is greatly venerated by the members of that religion, though they appear to have entirely forgotten his tenets of peace.

One could do much the same with the passages cited earlier from contemporary world religion textbooks.

Considering the applicability of such statements to the Christian tradition, one might be surprised to learn that the same authors who are willing to pronounce judgement on Sikhism fail to voice similar criticisms of Christianity. Given the peculiarity of this state of affairs, it would not be inappropriate to postulate some kind of unconscious repression-projection mechanism at work that might explain these scholars' lack of even-handedness. One does not have to be a psychoanalyst to perceive that guilt about the gap between one's ideals and one's behaviour can be pushed out of the light of full awareness only to re-emerge as a projection. In lieu of a better explanation of the one-sided treatment of the Sikh religion by Westerners, it appears to the present writer that the relevant scholars are uncomfortable with the contradiction between theory and practice in their own religious tradition, but have repressed the problem and have projected the contradiction onto Sikhism, a tradition that *apparently* (but not actually) contains the same contradiction. Thus, their condemnation of Sikh militancy is really a projection of their own (unexpressed, repressed) condemnation of the Christian tradition. The point here is not to criticize Christianity, but rather to once again point out the differential treatment that the Sikh religion has received at the hands of Western scholars; these kinds of evaluative statements would have been less objectionable had similar criticism been levelled against other religious traditions as well.

CONCLUSION

To bring this discussion to a close, I should like to remark that I found it highly distressing that a relative amateur in the field of Sikh studies such as myself could uncover so many errors of fact and judgement in the academic productions of religion scholars — the great majority of whom are my countrymen. While many of the misrepresentations I have indicated result from sloppy scholarship, in these writers' defense we should take into account that the Sikh religion is one of the most understudied traditions in the American Academy. If one glances at the structure of the American Academy of Religion, for instance, one finds program units devoted to such tiny traditions as alive American Religions, Baha'i and Zorastrianism, but no unit focusing on the relatively larger Sikh tradition.[30] The poverty of American scholarship on Sikhism is a self-perpetuating situation that prevents an American school of Sikh studies from emerging. For example, to speak from personal experience early in my graduate work, I was discouraged from focusing on the Sikh tradition because, it was said, such a speciality would limit my employment prospects. As a consequence, I set aside my original interest for a different speciality and have only sporadically been able to put my energies into Sikhism.

I know that I have painted an extremely dismal picture of the state of Sikh Studies in the American Religion Academy, but there are indications that this situation could change. Americans as a group, and consequently the American Academy, have become increasingly interested in the Sikh community, although unfortunately, the primary cause of this new interest in Sikhism is the series of tragic events that have taken place in the Punjab during the eighties. It was in the same way that Islam became an important area of study in the wake of upheavals in Islamic countries. We can anticipate the emergence (though on a smaller scale) of Sikhism as a recognized area of study.

REFERENCES

1. Edward W. Said : *Covering Islam* (New York : Pantheon, 1981), p. 155.
2. Much of the basic analysis in the latter two sections repeat the analysis found in certain parts of my earlier paper, "Some Unexamined Assumptions in Western Studies of Sikhism" *Journal of Sikh Studies* 13 : 2 (August 1985), although many of the examples in the present paper are new. In the section on the pacificism-militancy contrast, one will also find a few continuities with my "Images of Sikhism in the Writings of Early Orientalists" *Studies in Sikhism and Comparative Religion* 6 : 2 (October 1987).
3. Robert St. Ellwood, Jr. : *Many Peoples, Many Faiths* (Englewood Clffs, New Jersey : Prentice-Hall, 1987, 3rd ed.), p. 93, p. 102, and pp. 101-102.
4. Lewis M.Hopfe : *Religions of the World* (New York : Macmillan, 1987, 4th ed.), p. 184.
5. Ward J. Fellows : *Religions East and West* (New York : Holt, Rinehart & Winston, 1979), p. 82.
6. "The Sikhs rose in arms to claim a state of their own, and the Muslims and Hindus retaliated." Geoffrey Parrinder : *The Faiths of Mankind* (New York : Thomas Y. Crowell, 1965), p. 60.
7. Kenneth W. Morgan, (ed.) : *The Religion of the Hindus* (New York : Ronald Press, 1953), p. 41.
8. "Nanak says in the *Japji* that the Hindu gods and goddesses, including Shiva, Brahma, and Devi, adore the True One," S. Vernon McCasland : *Religion of the World* (New York : Random House, 1969), p. 506.
9. David G. Bradley : *A Guide to the World's Religions* (Englewood Cliefs, New Jersey : Prentice-Hall, 1963), p. 128.
10. Kyle M. Yates, Jr., (ed.) : *The Religious World : Communities of Faith* (New York : Macmillan, 1988, 2nd ed.), p. 98.
11. W. Richard Comstock, (ed.) : *Religion and Man : An Introduction* (New York : Harper & Row, 1971), p. 217.
12. These works are, respectively, Stewart Sutherland et al., (ed.) : *The World's Religions* (Boston, Mass. : Mass G.K. Hall, 1988), Peter Bishop & Michael Darton, (eds.) : *The Encyclopaedia of World Faiths* (New York : Facts on File, 1988), and Geoffrey Parrinder, (ed.) : *Man and His Gods* (London : Hamlyn, 1971).
13. Vergilius Ferm : *Living Schools of Religion* (Paterson, New Jersey : Littlefied, Adams & Co., 1961).
14. Neils C. Nielsen, Jr., (ed.) : *Religions of the World* (New York : St. Martin's, 1983).
15. McCasland : *op. cit.*
16. Wing-tsit Chan, Ismal'il Ragi al Faruqui, Joseph M. Kitagawa, and P.T. Raju : *The Great Asian Religions : An Anthology* (New York : Macmillan, 1969), p. 5.
17. Johan A. Hutchison : *Paths of Faith* (New York : McGraw-Hill, 1969), p. 200.
18. Bradley : *op. cit.,* p. 127.
19. Ninian Smart : *The Religious Experience of Mankind* (New York : Charles Scribner's Sons. 1976), p. 150.

20. E.g. Denise Lardner Carmody & John Carmody : *The Story of World Religions* (Mountain View, California : Mayfield, 1988), p. 253; Mithrapuram K. Alexander : *World Religions* (Dubuque, Iowa : Wm. C. Brown. 1968), p. 78; and Hans-Joachim Schoeps : *The Religions of Mankind* (Garden City, New York : Anchor, 1968), p. 167.

21. John B. Noss & David S. Noss : *Man's Religions* (New York : Macmillan, 1984, 7th ed.), p. 221.

22. McLeod in Parrinder's : *op. cit.*, p. 212.

23. Mark Juergensmeyer : *The Forgotten Tradition : Sikhism in the Study of World Religions*, in Mark Juergensmeyer & N. Gerald Barrier, (eds.) : *Sikh Studies* (Berkeley, Graduate Theological Union, 1979), p. 15.

24. Paul B. Courtright : *Syncretism and the Formation of the Sikh Tradition*, in Harbans Singh & N, Gerald Barrier, (eds.) : *Panjab Past and Present : Essays in Honour of Dr Ganda Singh* (Patiala : Punjabi University, 1976), p. 417.

25. Hopfe : *op. cit.*, p. 183.

26. Herbert Stroup : *Founders of Living Religions* (Philadelphia : Westminster , 1974), p. 104.

27. Richard Cavendish : *The Great Religions* (New York : Arco, 1980), p. 49.

28. W.L. McGregor : *The History of the Sikhs* (Patiala : Languages Dept., Punjabi Univ., 1970; orig. pub. 1946), p. 41.

29. H.H. Wilson : *Civil and Religious Institutions of the Sikhs*, in M. Macauliffe et. al. : *The Sikh Religion : A Symposium* (Calcutta : Sushil Gupta, 1958), p. 58. Originally published in the *Journal of the Royal Asiatic Society* (1848).

30. A small group of interested scholars recently attempted to form a new program unit of the Sikh tradition. This proposal was rejected. (Letter from James E. Wiggins, Executive Director of the AAR, to James R. Lewis, December 13, 1988, author's files.)

33

MISREPRESENTATION OF SIKHISM IN WESTERN ENCYCLOPAEDIAS

KHARAK SINGH

I. INTRODUCTION

1.1   The purpose of this paper is to draw the attention of the Sikh public in general, and scholars in particular, to the treatment of Sikhism in encyclopaedias and books on comparative religion published in the West since the beginning of the present century. There is a wide diversity in the amount of space devoted to the Sikh religion, varying from whole chapters to complete absence in some texts. Treatment of Sikhism as an independent religious system is rare. Frequently, Sikhs are described as a sect of Hindus and Sikhism mentioned in a passing reference, as an impact of Islam on Hinduism. As compared with other major religions of the world, like Christianity, Islam, Judaism, Hinduism, etc., the space provided for Sikhism should be considered insignificant.

1.2   Factual errors are common. For example, many publications show Guru Nanak as a disciple of Kabir. Guru Nanak's mention of some Hindu gods and goddesses has been given as his acceptance of these deities, although he has repeatedly asserted that they are not worthy of religious devotion. One author has made the frivolous suggestion that Guru Hargobind (the Sixth Guru) was an employee of Emperor Jehangir. In some texts, worship of the Hindu goddess Durga has been attributed to Guru Gobind Singh, although there is overwhelming evidence that he was an uncompromising monotheist, and that he recognized no other deity except the *Akal Purakh* or the Timeless Lord.

1.3   Other features are misinterpretation of Guru Nanak's system as a syncretism of elements borrowed from Islam and Hinduism, and the alleged 'pacificism' of Guru Nanak and 'militancy' of Guru Gobind Singh, questioning the unity of thought of the ten Gurus. Such views are obviously based on a very superficial study of Sikhism.

1.4   The authors of entries on Sikhism were invariably non-Sikhs. It is hard to believe that no Sikh scholars were available for this purpose. The publishers could at least show the entries to some followers of the Sikh faith, who could point out the obvious mistakes. Guru Nanak is the only Prophet whose original writings are available. In his numerous compositions, he has explained his religious philosophy and world-view unambiguously, leaving little scope for misinterpretation. The obvious handicap of the Western non-Sikh scholars was that they did not have the time or patience to study the original literature, a large part of which had not yet been translated into English or some other Western language. In a few cases, their views also appear to be visibly influenced by their own chauvinism and bias in favour of their own faith, which makes it difficult for them to see merit in another faith.

1.5   Misrepresentations started appearing as early as the beginning of the present century in the encyclopaedias. These were, by and large, ignored and it was hoped that in subsequent publications the entries would be entrusted to more knowledgeable scholars. The hope has unfortunately not materialised, and errors continue to be repeated even in recent publications of the eighties. Sikhs are no more confined to a few districts in the Punjab. A Sikh with a beard and turban is now a common sight almost anywhere in the world. People are curious to know about their faith and culture. The information available in the encyclopaedias is highly misleading, and this affects their image. An exercise has, therefore, been undertaken to examine the version of Sikhism in major publications. It is proposed to take up the matter with the Publishers with a view to helping them present a correct picture of the Sikh religion, its founder and its followers. This paper is a part of that exercise, covering relevant extracts from selected texts, with suitable comments. This might, as it should, stimulate interest of scholars in this almost completely neglected area, for the benefit of Sikhs in particular, and the world community in general.

II.   ENCYCLOPAEDIA OF RELIGION AND ETHICS, VOL. IX & XI

Ed. James Hastings : T. & T Clark, 38 George St. New York : Charles Scribers Sons, 153-157, Fifth Av.

2.1   This is the oldest among the encyclopaedias examined, and was published as early as 1917. There are two entries, one on Nanak by J.W. Youngson (pages 181 to 184 of Vol. IX), and the other on 'Sikhs' by H.A. Rose (page 507 to 511 of Vol. XI). The authors draw heavily on Ernest Trumpp, who is known more for his hostility towards Sikhism than his contribution as a scholar. Another source, M.A. Macauliffe is also mentioned, but is used selectively only where it endorses the biased opinion of Trumpp. For example, while following Trumpp, the *Janamsakhis*, as a source of historical information about the life of Guru Nanak, are summarily rejected as 'rubbish', the following remarks of Macauliffe are also quoted as implicit support of the conclusion : "We must premise that several of the details of this and of all the current *Janamsakhis* appear to us to be simply settings for the verses and sayings of Guru Nanak. His followers and admirers found dainty word pictures in his compositions. They considered under what circumstances they could have been produced, and thus devised the framework of a biography in which to exhibit them to the populace."

2.2   Referring to the compositions of the *bhagats* included in the Adi Granth, the note records :

"It shows to what extent Nanak was indebted to his predecessors in the Indian field of thought within those limits of time, and how much their influence tended to bring about the remarkable reformation that took place. The Reformation had begun before his day. Nanak was fourteen years older than Luther, and died eight years before him, and when that great reformer took his stand for truth at the Diet of Worms, Nanak was in his humble way seeking to guide the Indian people to the recognition of a personal God. The Indian reformation was salvation from atheism, and we may see in Nanak the highest and the best it reached."

2.3   The implication of the above is that Guru Nanak merely carried forward a reformation that had been set in motion by earlier *bhagats*, and that its scope was limited to salvation from atheism as compared with the much broader and higher Reformation of Luther. Unfortunately, the author has failed to see, much less understand, the full content of Guru Nanak's message and the revolution brought about by the religion revealed through him, as discussed in this paper.

2.4   But, it does not appear to be the intention of the author to give accurate information about Guru Nanak and the Sikh religion. He appears to be more keen to prove the superiority of his own faith. He writes :

"He (Nanak) fearlessly attacked idolatry, and, if he did not rise to a high degree of spiritual enlightenment, we can only say that Christian truth had not been conveyed to him."

And again,

"Although it is the fashion among the Sikhs to regard all their Gurus as true Guru (*sat gur*), yet, when pressed, they tell us that the true guru is God, and the true guru of the Granth Sahib is not Nanak, but is the supreme, the *gur-dev*, the incarnation of God, the sinless one, and it cannot fail to strike the least observant reader of the Granth that the only religion that can satisfy the aspirations of the Sikhs, and disclose the identity of the *sat gur* and that claims to do so, is the Christian. Whether Nanak was acquainted with the Christian truth is a debated question, but, whether he was or not, we must allow that, being in some degree conversant with the Mohammadan faith, he may have known something of the revelation of God in His Word, the true teacher, God-incarnate, the Lord Jesus Christ."

2.5   Such remarks about a Prophet of the stature of Guru Nanak, based on ignorance as they are, and the arrogance of the above claims, are certainly not in good academic taste, and are in fact un-Christian. The suggestion that Guru Nanak did not realise the Christian truth, whatever that means, is meaningless. The logic behind the conclusion as to who is true guru, is also difficult to accept.

2.6   There are a couple of other errors in the section relating to Sikhs, contributed by Young. On page 508, Gurditta is described as having entered the Udasi order. Gurditta was a householder. In fact, he was a soldier, married twice and had children. Also, his death was a sequel to a hunting accident. These two facts hardly conform to the cult of the Udasi sect.

2.7   On the same page, the author records of Guru Tegh Bahadur as saying that, "he was unworthy of wearing his father's sword, he proclaimed his ambition to be styled Degh Bahadur, or 'Lord of the Vessel', the *degh* which symbolises the world." One would like to see any reliable historical evidence in its support. For, 'Tegh Bahadur' was the title or name given to him much earlier by his great father Guru Hargobind, when he displayed extraordinary skill in wielding the sword in an encounter with the Mughal forces.

2.8   Describing the *amrit* ceremony, it is stated that "a Sikh who is regualr in observing Sikh rules of conduct, stirs with a dagger some sugar in water in an iron basin, while chanting verses from the Granth." As a matter of fact, five Sikhs are required to perform the ceremony. No single Sikh can prepare or administer *amrit* to himself or any one else.

III.   MODERN RELIGIOUS MOVEMENTS IN INDIA

J.N. Farquhar : The Macmillan Company, New York, 1918, pages 338-343.

3.1   This commentary is important for the purpose of this paper, since it is among the earliest ones recorded in the beginning of this century, and it causes some basic mis-statements about Sikhs and their faith, which have persisted in most of the subsequent publications. The very first paragraph is as follows :

"Nanak (1469-1538), the founder of the Sikh Sect, was a disciple of the famous teacher Kabir. Except in two matters, his system is practically identical with that of many Vaishnava sects. It is theism, and the main teaching of the founder is highly spiritual in character. Yet, the whole Hindu pantheon is retained. The doctrine of transmigration and *Karma* and the Indian social system remain unaltered." Let us examine the above statement briefly in the following paragraph :

3.2   *Was Guru Nanak a Disciple of Kabir ?* : The answer is an emphatic No. And no disrespect is meant to the great Saint who is held in highest esteem by all Sikhs. Here we are trying to ascertain a historical fact. As it is, Kabir and Guru Nanak were not contemporaries. There is no historical evidence to suggest that they ever met each other, much less that they had a teacher-disciple relationship. Kabir was a resident of Benares, while Guru Nanak lived at Talwandi (now Nankana Sahib) and Sultanpur Lodhi in the Punjab, until he set out on his divine mission around 1500 A.D. Guru Nanak did visit Benares during his sojourn to the East. Kabir had died earlier. None of the reliable *Janamsakhis* mention a meeting between the Guru and Kabir. During the time of Guru Arjun Dev, approximately 60 years after the death of Guru Nanak, Bhai Gurdas wrote a *var* giving a brief biographical account of Guru Nanak. Later, Bhai Mani Singh wrote a biography of the Guru at the behest of Sikhs who felt concerned over the interpolations in *Janamsakhis* by interested parties. Neither of these two writings mention any meeting between Kabir and Guru Nanak. In the Guru's own writings, we do not find any reference to a dialogue with Kabir, nor has Kabir or any of his successors ever made such a claim.

3.3   A fundamental difference between Kabir's system and that of Guru Nanak is in their attitude towards women and pacificism (*ahimsa*). Religions like Islam, Judaism and Sikhism accept total social responsibility and reject celibacy and *ahimsa*. Kabir, however, was a misogynist, and accepted *ahimsa*. This is exactly contrary to the fundamentals of Guru Nanak, who recommends a householder's life and equality of man and woman. He also accepts total social participation and responsibility, and clearly rejects *ahimsa*. True, they are both monotheists, but their over-all world-views are clearly at variance. Evidently, a person rejecting *ahimsa* could never be a disciple of Kabir.

3.4   The question that remains to be answered is that in spite of overwhelming evidence to the contrary, how did this view as to Guru Nanak being a disciple of Kabir gain currency ? Fortunately, apart from the warnings of Bhai Gurdas and Bhai Mani Singh against distortion of the life history of Guru Nanak, the question has been examined in detail by M.A. Macauliffe.[1] Acccording to him, "There were three great schisms of the Sikh religion which led to the falsification of old, or of the composition of new *Janamsakhis*. The schismatics were known as the Udasis, the Minas and the Handalis. The first schism of the Sikhs began immediately after the demise of Guru Nanak. Some of his followers adopted Sri Chand, his elder son, as his successor, and repudiated the nomination of Guru Angad." .... "The second schismatical body of the Sikhs were the Minas. Ram Dass, the fourth guru, had three sons, Prithi Chand, Mahadev and Arjun. Prithi Chand proved unfilial and disobedient, Mahadev became a religious enthusiast, while Arjun, the youngest, followed in the steps of his father. To Arjun, therefore, he bequeathed the Guruship. Prithi Chand is stigmatised as Mina or deceitful, a name given to a robber tribe of Rajputana. Prithi Chand, however, succeeded in obtaining a following, whom he warned against association with the Sikhs of Guru Arjun." .... "The Handalis, the third schismatic sect of the Sikhs, were the followers of Handal, a *Jat* of Manjha, who had been converted to the Sikh religion by Guru Amar Das, the third Sikh Guru. Bidhi Chand, a descendant of Handal, was a Sikh priest at Jandiala, in the Amritsar district. He took unto himself a Muhammadan woman, whom he attached to him rather by ties of love than of law, and upon this he was abandoned by his followers."

3.5   "He then devised a religion of his own, and compiled a Granth and a *Janamsakhi* to correspond. In both, he sought to exalt to the rank of chief apostle his father, Handal, and degrade Guru Nanak, the legitimate Sikh Guru. For this purpose, creative fancy was largely employed."

The motive behind this is clear, viz., degrading Guru Nanak. The suggestion that Guru Nanak was a disciple of Kabir, is a part of the same conspiracy.

3.6   Kabir is, and will continue to be held in very high esteem in the Sikh world. The Gurus respected Kabir's teachings, and common areas in their preachings are by no means inconsiderable. That is why Guru Arjun incorporated selected compositions of Kabir in the Adi Granth. Here it is necessary to add that not all his works form a part of Guru Granth Sahib. Only such compositions as conform to the system of Guru Nanak's thought, have been included.

3.7   With regard to the Hindu pantheon, which, in the author's view, is retained by Guru Nanak, it must be understood that the deities of Hindu mythology are mentioned in the Guru's compositions only to say that they are not worthy of religious devotion.

3.8　*Was Guru Nanak's System Identical with Vaishnavism ?* :　Very often Guru Nanak's system is confused not only with the system of Vaishnavas, but also with that of Kabir and other *bhagats*. Under the superficial identity, however, there is a divergence of a far-reaching consequence, which is frequently missed. The subject has been examined in detail by Daljeet Singh.[2] In the limited space available here, the best thing will be to quote his conclusion :

"Our discussion reveals that the so-called devotional systems may be divided into three clear-cut categories. To the first category belong Vaisnavism and Nathism where devotion is purely formal and confined mainly to image worship or Yogic, meditational and ascetic practices. The value of ritualism is recognized. In the social field, the caste system forms the sanctified spiritual basis of man's social and moral ethics and duties; or the world is renounced and a monastic life of asceticism and celibacy is taken up ...... The second devotional system is of men like Plotinus, Sufis, Christian mystics and Saints like Kabir, Ravidas and Namdev. The history of this devotional system in India and outside shows that saints of this group, while they accept the principle of human equality, resort primarily to a system of faith and meditation for spiritual attainments. They, as stated by Niharranjan Ray, work just as individuals, purely for their own salvation or personal religious and spiritual aims and aspirations. Their love or devotion is directed towards God with the goal of union with Him as an end in itself. Here, in the words of Ray, 'there is absolute surrender as much to the personal God as to the established social order.' In this category, man's love of God does not move in the field of social concern, responsibility or involvement. The methodology adopted is of meditation and interiority. In the third group, to use the inimitable words of Bergson, man's love of God is transformed into 'God's love for all men', Here, the sole religious path, both for the seeker and the superman, is through deeds prompted by the love of man and God's attributive Will. Just as Vaishnavism falls into the first category, Sikhism belongs to the third category."

3.9　In Vaishnavism, like other earlier Indian traditions, the world is considered a misery or suffering, or *mithya*, and for liberation, *sanyasa*, asceticism, celibacy and yogic practices enjoy high spiritual value. The religious or spiritual aims and aspirations are personal, with little or no concern for society or the established social order. "In Sikhism (according to Guru Nanak), the world is real. In fact, it is the abode of the True Lord, and birth as a human being is a great privilege, since it gives one the great opportunity of not only knowing the truth, but also the more glorious privilege of living it; of not only understanding the Creative Will, but also of carrying it out. For, God works not through miracles, but through man whose resources and capacity are enormous. Therefore, in Sikhism the ideal is not only to know the truth, but to live truth. Realisation of truth is not an end in itself, but only a means to the highest end of creative living, the latter alone being the correct test and index of the former. In fact, such an effort is not optional but obligatory, it being the sole measure of spirituality."[3]

3.10　The cults of Vaishnavism and Bhakti are much older than Sikhism. Guru

Nanak came on the scene much later. A look at the history would indicate that while the Saints and the Vaishanavites carefully avoided involvement in the socio-political field, Guru Nanak, his successors and followers were repeatedly involved in defence of righteousness and confrontation with the forces of oppression and injustice. The Fifth and the Ninth Guru made supreme sacrifices for this cause. The last personal guru (Guru Gobind Singh) sacrificed his all including his four sons, and inspired the entire community of his followers to leap into the struggle which lasted for several decades, and effectively ended the regular tide of invasions from the north-west, that had plagued India for over a thousand years. This contrast in the historical record is not merely incidental. "It represents the compulsive consequences of the ideologies and objectives of the different religious systems."[4]

3.11   This should be enough to show that Guru Nanak's system was not identical with that of the Vaishnava sect or Kabir.

3.12 *Indian Social System* : The author says that the Indian social system remains unaltered in Guru Nanak's system. As everyone knows, the Indian social system was and still is based on caste system. There are four main castes and hundreds of sub-castes in the social hierarchy. The lowest ones are *Sudras* who are untouchable. Even their shadow is enough to cause pollution, and they have no other rights except to perform menial jobs that the higher castes will not look at. Women also are given a lower status. Guru Nanak's crusade against the caste system is well-known. There are numerous verses in which he decries discrimination between man and man on the basis of caste. Examples are :

"I consider all men high and I acknowledge none as low.
   One God hath fashioned all the vessels,
   One Light pervades the whole creation."[5]
"Appreciate the Light, do not ask for caste.
   There is no caste hereafter."[6]
"Vain chatter is the boast of caste
   Vain chatter is the boast of fame."[7]
"Caste can gain nothing,
   Truth within will be tested."[8]
"Of no avail is the caste by birth, ...
   A man's caste or faith is determined
   by the works he performs."[9]
"(it is said) The *dharma* of Jogis is to acquire gnosis,
   The *dharma* of Brahmins is what is ordained in the Vedas.
   The *dharma* of Kshatriyas is the *dharma* of the brave,
   And the *dharma* of Sudras is to serve others.
   But, a universal *dharma* should be one for all.
   Nanak is a slave to one who understands this secret.
   For, he is the image of the God impeccable."[10]
"There are the lowly among the low castes,

And there are the lowliest among them.
Nanak stands by their side.
Why should he look to the higher castes ?
Where the lowly are cared for,
It is there that the Grace of the Lord is showered."[11]

3.13   The other major area of inequality in the Indian society was the status of woman. Even in higher castes under certain circumstances, women were treated like Sudras. Woman was considered deceitful, a temptress, and a hindrance to spiritual progress. Guru Nanak's was the first great voice raised in favour of equality of sexes. Towards the end of a long stanza written to plead the cause of equality for women, he demands :

"How can you call her inferior, who gives birth to kings ?"[12]

3.14   Guru Nanak attacked social vices like *suttee* (burning of widows), female infanticide and slavery. He opened the door of religious, social and material development to all human beings irrespective of caste, creed, sex or social status. He practised every word of what he preached. He chose for his companion a low caste Muslim (Mardana). During his travels, he preferred to stay with low caste people over the high castes. At Kartarpur, where he settled eventually, he started a community kitchen where everybody ate together. Everybody worked and was required to do all kinds of duties. His successors continued and even intensified the reforms. Guru Amar Das never granted audience to anybody who was reluctant to eat from the common kitchen. He assigned responsible positions to women in the missionary set-up organised by him. Guru Gobind Singh completely abolished the caste system among his devotees by making them drink *amrit* from a common bowl at the *amrit* ceremony. He declared that everybody joining the order was his son.

3.15   It should be abundantly clear from the above that in Guru Nanak's system, the Indian social order received his attention and he materially altered it. In fact, what the Guru and his successors achieved, amounts to a complete revolution. The point has been more completely elaborated by Jagjit Singh in his book *The Sikh Revolution*.[13]

3.16   *Other Comments* : Comments are necessary also on a few other points in the author's note. Some of these are :

(a)   On pages 335-336 he writes :

"This volume is called the Adi Granth or 'Original Book.' The Tenth Guru added a great deal of fresh material; and the result is the Granth Sahib, or Noble Book of the Sikhs." The correct position is that Guru Gobind Singh did not add any of his compositions to the Adi Granth. The hymns of his father, Guru Tegh Bahadur, were, however, incorporated in the volume compiled by the Fifth Guru. His own compositions, were collected much later. The Guruship was conferred only on the Adi Granth, which alone embodies the Canon.

(b)   At the bottom of page 336 is the following remark :

"The Khalsa became strong to resist the Mughals, but their organisation cut them off from their fellow-countrymen, and made them practically a new caste." The Khalsa can never become a caste, since it is a voluntary order open to everybody. The caste, on the other hand, is determined by birth. The Khalsa was highly respected by the common man because of the sacrifices made by them for the cause of the *dharma,* righteousness and the poor people. In fact, Khalsa provided an ideal, and ordinary people, particularly among the Sikhs, aspired to become its members.

IV.   HINDU WORLD : AN ENCYCLOPAEDIC SURVEY OF HINDUISM, VOL.II.

Benjamin Walker : George Allen & Unwin Ltd.,

Ruskin House, Museum Street, London, 1968.

4.1   The more important among the points in the section relating to Sikhs in this publication which need comments are briefly reproduced below :

4.2   Sikhs have been described as a "sect of reformist Hindus founded by Nanak ...... who was greatly influenced by the reformer Kabir ...... who owes much to Kabir" (pp. 396 and 398). On page 121 it is stated :

"Early in life he (Guru Nanak) came under the influence of the great religious reformer Kabir to whom he was indebted for some of his later doctrines."

The question of Sikhism as an independent religious system has been discussed in detail earlier, and needs no repetition. The mere fact that the Guru was born of Hindu parents and that the majority of his initial followers were of Hindu origin, does not make his religious system a part of Hinduism. Similarly, the position of Guru Nanak *vis-a-vis* Kabir has been explained in an earlier section. The existence of some common areas in the religious beliefs of the two, does not make one indebted to or a disciple of the other.

4.3   *Guru Tegh Bahadur :* The author records on page 396 :

"It is said that during his imprisonment, he (Guru Tegh Bahadur) was charged with looking in the direction of the Emperor's harem, to which the Guru replied, 'Emperor, I was not gazing at your queens' apartments. I was looking in the direction of the Europeans who are coming from beyond the western seas to tear down your *purdah* and destroy your empire.'"

The story is ridiculous and highly improbable, since it assumes (a) that the prison was located in the vicinity of Aurangzeb's harem, (b) that his prisoners awaiting death sentence were free to move out and gaze at the Queens' apartments, and (c) that Guru Tegh Bahadur who gave his life for human rights and religious freedom of his own people, could think of replacing the Mughals with Europeans as rulers. The story was obviously planted by an interested party of the East India Company to justify and perpetuate its foreign rule over India. A parallel is found in the story invented during the Mughal rule that when Babur met Guru Nanak, the latter blessed him with the Indian Empire for seven generations. It is needless to say that this and such stories are baseless.

4.4   *Guru Gobind Singh :* the book acknowledges that "Guru Gobind Singh knew Sanskrit, Persian and Arabic, wrote inspiring poetry of great literary excellence in Punjabi and was also the author of what is known as the *Dasam Granth*" (p. 396).

4.5   It may be added that his works written in Punjabi, available to us, are limited. Bulk of his compositions are in Braj Bhasha, and their literary excellence is also unquestionable. However, the *Dasam Granth* in the extant form(s) was not compiled by the Guru. In fact, the collection appeared decades after his demise, with large sections attributed to anonymous authors. Apart from this, the author has made some remarks about the Guru, which are damaging and without basis, for example,

"He is said to have introduced into Sikhism the worship of the terrible goddess, Durga."

"There is no doubt that the violent philosophy he preached was far removed from the gentle philosophy of pacificism of Guru Nanak. Gandhi referred to him as 'a misguided patriot'." Bhai Vir Singh, the great Sikh scholar, published a book *Devi Pujan Partal*[14] in Punjabi, in which he has examined the alleged worship of the goddess Durga by Guru Gobind Singh. He has concluded that the story is a pure fabrication. The Guru was at Paonta Sahib during the period when the *Hom* to please the goddess is alleged to have been performed. In all his known authentic works, the Guru praises only One Supreme Lord, the *Akal Purakh*. He accepts no other deity including gods, goddesses or even the *avtars*. The same injunction was issued to the Khalsa at the time of *amrit* and this has been handed down by tradition to the present-day. He taught his disciples not to depend upon gods or goddesses, but be self-reliant. They must wage the fight against evil forces themselves taking the sword in hand and lay down their lives in the battlefield, if necessary. If still the story of the worship of the goddess has persisted, it is because it has been planted in a most subtle manner by Brahmins, the challenge to whose authority started with Guru Nanak and reached a climax, when Guru Gobind Singh opened the doors of the Khalsa Order to one and all who believed in One *Akal Purakh* and were prepared to fight for the cause of *dharma* or righteousness.

4.6 The alleged discrepancy between the philosophies of Guru Gobind Singh and Guru Nanak results from a superficial look and a lack of understanding of Guru Nanak's thesis. In fact, it does not exist. Guru Nanak never preached a philosophy of pacificism. Realising that the root-cause of people's misery was spiritual degeneration, he emphasized the need for their spiritual uplift. But, he did not neglect the worldly aspect of life. He exhorted the people to uphold their honour and self-respect and fight the tyrant. He says :

    "Should one's honour be violated, while living,
        He does not deserve the food he eats."[15]

Again

    "To what avail are worship without honour,
        Sanyas without truth, and the sacred thread
        Devoid of moral restraint ?"[16]

He founded a society that would face aggression like heroes. His challenge was :

    "If you want to play the game of love,
        come to my path, holding your head on your palm."[17]

Again, he calls God 'Destroyer of the evil', 'Annihilator of the devilish', and

    "If God wills, He brandishes the sword
        to cut the head of the enemy."[18]

4.7   When Babur invaded India and his troops plundered cities and temples and murdered countless innocent men, women and children, Guru Nanak could not remain silent and content with his rosary. His famous composition *Babur Vani*[19] expresses his deep anguish over the atrocities committed by the 'Horde of Sin', as he calls the army of Babur. He not only condemned the aggressor, he also took to task the local rulers for their unpreparedness and failure to protect their subjects. "If a powerful lion attacks a herd of cattle, the master is squarely responsible," he said. He shared the intensity of his feelings with God thus : "O Lord, did you not experience any pain over the suffering of such magnitude ?" In the light of the above views, who would say that Guru Nanak preached a philosophy of pacificism ?

4.8   The fifth Guru, Guru Arjun Dev, affirms Guru Nanak's philosophy. In the same vein this apostle of peace says :

"First accept death, forget the desire to live,
    and then with humility come to me."[20]

Guru Gobind Singh's philosophy was no different. He declares, "When all other means fail, it is justified to take the sword in hand in the cause of righteousness."[21] Thus, when Guru Gobind Singh launched the Khalsa Order, he simply carried out something that was envisaged in Guru Nanak's plans. In the words of Dr Gokal Chand Narang, 'the steel required for the sword of Guru Gobind Singh was provided by Guru Nanak.'[22] The complete unity, consistency and continuity of the message of all the Ten Gurus, including Guru Nanak Dev and Guru Gobind Singh, are expresed in the Guru Granth Sahib : "*Ika bani Ik Gur Iko sabad veechar.*"[23] (Trans. : The Revelation is one, the Guru is one, the interpretion or contemplation of the Word is also the same.)

4.9   Reference to Guru Gobind Singh as a 'misguided patriot' could only result from a lack of study of the Guru's life and philosophy and from ignorance of political, social and religious conditions of his times. In *Bachittar Natak,* the Guru has stated the purpose of his birth very clearly. It was to propagate *dharma*, protection of the saints and to end oppression and tyranny, both political and religious. He had come to guide humanity out of superstition, political subjugation and misery. His was a divine mission. Who could misguide him ? He had studied the history of previous centuries during which all non-violent means had been tried without success. He realised what should be obvious to any impartial student of Indian history that adherence to *ahimsa* in all situations had done incalculable harm to the society, and was responsible for its misery. He reached the most carefully considered conclusion that "for a righteous cause, when all other means fail, it is justified to take to arms."[24] That is what he did. He inspired the people to fight for their honour and freedom. He organised them and trained them. He taught them to make sacrifices for a noble cause and to overcome the fear of death with his personal example. The humble people, who had been treated worse than animals, saw in him their saviour, and responded to his call. Under his guidance and inspiration, the people shed the fear of the mighty Mughal Empire, and after a prolonged struggle succeeded in bringing about its downfall and establishing their own government. It was due to Guru Gobind Singh that freedom dawned in the country after centuries of slavery.

How could Guru Gobind Singh be called an innovator, when five out of the Ten Gurus maintained an army and wielded the sword, and when the Fifth of them had created a 'state within a state'; and, apart from organising the wherewithal for militarisation, had left instructions for his young son, Guru Hargobind, to raise an army. The subsequent gurus, including Guru Gobind Singh, only continued the tradition.

4.10   For Mahatma Gandhi, *ahimsa* or non-violence was a creed and a cure for all ills. Let us take one incident out of Indian history reported by the official reporter of Mahmud Ghaznavi, who invaded India several times during the eleventh century. He records that when Mahmud's troops were plundering the famous Hindu Temple of Somnath and breaking the images of the deities, people from the neighbouring 300 villages collected and sat chanting *mantras*. Not one of them resisted or raised a little finger to stop the soldiers from desecrating the Temple. Probably they had received the traditional pacificist 'guidance' from some *mahatma*. Anybody who would fight or ask others to fight, would be dubbed as 'misguided.' *Ahimsa* or pacificism has its votaries, but the Sikh Gurus are not among them. It is both self-righteous and narrow for Toynbee to measure Prophet Mohammad by the pacificist standards of his own religion and criticise him severely. It is equally myopic for pacificist Gandhi to see Guru Gohind Singh through the lens of his own prejudices, especially when it is well-known that he gave up pacificism, when it suited his interests. In Sikhism, the ideal is a saint-soldier, *sant-sipahi* or *gurmukh*, and not a pacificist recluse who is considered escapist.

4.11   *Ranjit Singh* : It has been stated that when Maharaja Ranjit Singh died, four of his wives and seven slave women were burnt with him in accordance with the Hindu practice of *suttee*. While this may be a historical fact, it needs to be pointed out that the practice was strongly condemned by the Gurus. The Sikh religion does not approve of it. The Maharaja had died. He cannot be held responsible for the act of *suttee*. The fact is that it were his Hindu wives, who did the *suttee* according to their own beliefs.

4.12   *Guru Granth Sahib* : The remarks regarding Guru Granth Sahib include the following :

"The Granth does not quite escape polytheism, as it practically assumes the Hindu pantheon, and it accepts the doctrine of *karma* and transmigration."

"In the course of time the Granth suffered many doctrinal modifications and has yielded much to Hinduism. The teachings of Guru Gobind Singh were again of a different character, being militant, in accordance with the needs of the age in which he lived."

The above observations show complete ignorance of Guru Granth Sahib and Sikh history. No doubt, the Sikhs accept the doctrine of *karma* and transmigration. However, Sikhs believe strictly in One God, and Guru Granth Sahib clearly rejects polytheism. Guru Granth Sahib starts with the *Mul Mantra* beginning with *Ik Onkar*, which means that there is only One God who is immanent. According to the Sikh Gurus, God is a Being to be approached and loved as a fond and faithful wife loves her spouse. Guru Nanak calls Him *Nirankar*, that is, without form. Bhai Gurdas spoke of Him as formless, without equal, wonderful and not perceptible by the senses. At the same time, all the

Gurus believed that He is immanent in His creation. In fact, the Guru emphasizes that "God is One, brother, He is One Alone."[25]

4.13   There has not been even the slightest change, doctrinal or otherwise, in the text of Guru Granth Sahib. In fact, any attempt to make a change would be regarded as heresy. The authenticity of the present *Bir* of Guru Granth Sahib was earlier established by Bhai Jodh Singh[26] and has been confirmed by Daljeet Singh.[27] The *bani* of Guru Gobind Singh was never incorporated in the Adi Granth, which alone is the scripture and Guru or Sole Guide. So, the question of modifications on this account does not arise. With regard to militancy of Guru Gobind Singh, it has been shown earlier that this was no innovation of the Guru. Four earlier Gurus had maintained an army and Guru Nanak had himself rejected *ahimsa* as a creed.

4.14   *Other Remarks* :   Some of the other remarks in this entry that deserve attention, are reproduced below :

"Critics have frequently pointed out that while Sikhism ostensibly dropped many features of Hinduism, it has itself adopted similar features in a disguised form."

"Nanak is regarded as an incarnation of God. It is believed that Nanak performed miracles ...... The other Gurus are regarded as incarnations of Nanak, assuming his divinity upon their formal installation."

"Sikhism set its face against ceremonial and meaningless repetition of the name of God, although Sikhs now lay great emphasis on the Name."

4.15   Sikhs do not believe in the theory of *avtarhood* or incarnation. Guru Nanak declared in the *Mul Mantra* that God is *Ajuni*, i.e., He never takes birth. The so-called *avtars* or prophets are His creation. "Cursed be the tongue that says 'God incarnates'",[28] records Guru Granth Sahib. Guru Nanak never claimed that he was God incarnate, nor did any of his successors do so. They considered themselves His servants. Guru Gobind Singh warns :

"He who calls me God, shall fall into the fire pit of hell. I am the servant of the Supreme Lord, come to see the wonderful *dharma* of this world."[29]

After having initiated the five *piaras*, he, in all humility, requested them to initiate him. No knowledgeable Sikh has ever claimed that the Gurus were incarnations of God. They are given profound reverence for the Lord's Word delivered through them.

4.16   Neither Guru Nanak nor any other Guru ever claimed any miracles, and there is no mention of these in the Adi Granth. Bhai Gurdas has quoted Guru Nanak as saying, "Apart from the Word of the Lord and the holy congregation, there is no other miracle."[30] The stories invented by some ignorant or interested people should not be confused with the spirit of Sikhism or the Gurus' teachings.

4.17   The doctrine of *Naam* in Sikhism is not mere repetition of a name. In fact, Guru Granth Sahib clearly says, "Everyone repeats God's name. But such repetition is not the way to God."[31] "With guile in the heart he practises guile, but mutters God's name. He is pounding husk, and is in darkness and pain."[32] "One mutters God's name, but practises evil daily. In this way the heart is not purified."[33] *Naam* is realisation of the immanence of God in everything, and expresses itself as love and service of humanity, following the examples of the Gurus themselves. For, Guru Granth Sahib says that it is by "one's deeds that man is assessed in His Court", and "by our deeds alone we are near or away from God."

V. ASIAN RELIGIONS

Geoffery Parrinder; Sheldon Press, London (1977)

5.1   The author has made the following observations :

"Nanak did not intend at first to found a sect, but disciples were attracted by his teaching. The word Sikh means 'disciple.' He declared, 'There is no Hindu and no Muslim.' This bold utterance and his songs attracted considerable attention. He passed his life partly in teaching and partly in retirement.

"As a poet, Nanak differs from Kabir, but as a social and religious reformer, he did much to bring Hindus and Muslims together. He strongly opposed formalism in worship, and inculcated devotion to one God."

"Persecution under the Mughals caused the Sikhs to take up arms, and henceforth, they have regarded themselves as a military brotherhood, more akin to missionary Islam, usually distasteful to Hindus. Distinctive features were adopted for Sikhs which have remained as their badge : the hair must not be cut, a steel comb, a bangle must be worn, together with shorts and a sword."

5.2   There is one factual error in the above statements. A 'steel' comb is mentioned in the five distinctive features for Sikhs. While a comb is one of the five K's, it need not be of steel. More often and almost aways the comb worn by Sikhs is wooden. It is believed that the combs adopted by the five *piaras*, when they were initiated by Guru Gobind Singh, were wooden. There could, however, be no objection against a steel comb either.

5.3   *The Other Mistaken Suggestion Is* : "Persecution under the Mughals caused the Sikhs to take up arms." There is no doubt that the Sikhs resisted persecution. But it was not merely a reaction to circumstance. It was in accordance with the doctrines laid down by the founder of the Sikh faith, Guru Nanak, who had enjoined upon his followers to resist oppression and injustice not only on themselves, but even on others who were weak and poor. The Guru protested strongly against tyranny of the invaders and oppression of the local rulers. The Guru preached a whole-life philosophy that involved defence of self and society and full development of the individual and the society, socially, spiritually and economically. His successor, Guru Angad did not neglect any of these aspects. He took concrete steps to develop the physical fitness and fighting qualities of his disciples. There is a gurdwara at Khadur Sahib, called Mal Akhara (literally, Wrestler's Ring) at the spot where he used personally to supervise wrestling and other physical fitness activities of his disciples. Diet in the *langar* or the common kitchen received personal attention of the Guru's wife, Mata Khivi. This was continued during the Third and the Fourth Gurus' period. The Fifth Guru, Arjun Dev, gave special military training to his son, Hargobind, who became the Sixth Guru after the martyrdom of his father in Mughal captivity. Guru Hargobind formally donned two swords, one, the insignia of *miri* (empirical life), and the other of *piri* (spiritual life). Following instructions of his father, he organised a regular army, and actually fought and won several battles with the local Mughal chiefs or rulers. The two swords meant that the *miri* aspect, which had always been there, became more visible than it had been earlier, because of the increased numerical strength and better organisation of the Sikhs. The two swords also demonstrated that the *piri* aspect was equally important and that it was not neglected or discarded, as some critics would have us believe. In Sikhism, the strength for physical resistance to evil or oppression and injustice derives from spiritual development. So, emphasis on the spiritual aspect continued undiminished. There was no doctrinal change involved in wearing two swords by Guru Hargobind. It is very important to understand that in Sikhism, the insignia for *piri* is also a sword, and not a rosary, showing the basic combination of the spiritual with the empirical in Guru Nanak's system.

5.4   Another statement that needs to be contradicted is that "He (Guru Nanak) passed his life partly in teaching and partly in retirement." This indirectly suggests that the Guru became a recluse and gave up interest in life and the world. This is absolutely incorrect. He never retired, but actively carried on his mission upto the last day of his life. He made sure that the mission continued even after his death by appointing a worthy successor like Guru Angad Dev, who was selected after a very rigorous test.

5.5   It is incorrect to say that Guru Nanak at first did not intend to found a society, or that he passed his time partly in retirement, or that it became a military brotherhood because of Mughal persecution.   Guru Nanak's system is based on a whole-life philosophy, involving full development of the individual and society in their spiritual, social and economic aspects. Since his religion accepts combination of the spiritual and empirical aspects of life, or the *miri-piri* doctrine, he organised a fraternal society, recommending total participation and responsibility in all walks of life and making reaction against injustice an essential duty of the religious man. It was in this context that militarisation of the society took place, since Sikhism permits the use of force as a last resort for a righteous cause. The Indian society suffered from two major maladies, viz., caste discrimination in the social field and injustice and oppression in the political field. The Sikh society created institutions and succeeded to a large extent in solving both of these problems. Guru Nanak founded a classless community of his followers, in which everybody like himself, worked, and ate together from a common kitchen in a *pangat*, regardless of caste or origin. His concept of equality between man and woman was revolutionary. Most Indian traditions regarded her as a 'temptress', a '*nagini*', a 'gateway to hell','polluted' and unworthy of spiritual pursuits. Elaborating the crucial role of woman in society and in life, Guru Nanak asked, "How can you call one, who gives birth to kings, inferior ?" Guru Nanak's concept of perfect equality arises from the immanence of God in all creatures. His love and concern for the common man expressed itself in protests against exploitation of the poor and the weak. He condemned the brutalities and barbarities perpetrated by the invaders, whom he described as 'horde of sin.' He took to task the local rulers for their unpreparedness to face the invading armies and called them 'man-eating beasts', and their officials as 'hounds' for their exploitation of the poor, innocent and helpless subjects. He attacked the hypocrisy of the religious leaders, who had become a party to the plunder and the exploitation. He criticised the *yogis* and the ascetics for their parasitism and escapism. He raised a strong voice against oppression and injustice and exhorted the people to resist these. In fact, he founded a society to resist evil in society and to fight injustice. Thus was laid the foundation of the doctrine of *miri-piri*, which became a fundamental element in the Sikh philosophy.

VI.   DICTIONARY OF COMPARATIVE RELIGION

Ed. S.G.F. Brandon; Charles Scribner's Sons, New York, 1970 (Ninian Smart)

6.1   *An Extract From The Entry On Sikhism Is Reproduced :* "Sikhism : the Sikhs (literally 'Disciples'), though belonging originally to a movement designed to see unity between best in Islam and best in Hinduism have evolved a distinctive religion and culture of their own ...... The tendencies towards unified devotionalism were crystallised in the life and teachings of Nanak, first of the ten Gurus or leaders of Sikh community. He preached unity of God ......, centrality of devotion *bhakti*, summed up in the repetition of divine name, equality of men of different castes, evils of image worship, importance of brotherly love and need of a guru as a guide. None of these elements was precisely original to Nanak." (page 576).

6.2   The above interpretation of Sikhism as a blend or amalgam of selected features drawn from Hinduism and Islam, denying any originality to Guru Nanak, has been repeatedly advanced by some Western scholars. This notion of syncretism is obviously based on a superficial study of Sikhism or the doctrines of Guru Nanak. No religion has survived on borrowed ideas in history. Din-i-llahi of Akbar is a well-known example. Sikhism is a revealed religion based on the mystic experience of its founder, Guru Nanak, of the Reality or God. He saw God as 'All Love, the rest He is ineffable.'[34] He saw God as 'Creator who is immanent in His creation, loves it and looks after it.' He saw God as 'Ocean of Virtues.' He Saw God as Self-existent and as One who never takes birth. The roots of Guru Nanak's religious life lie in his unique experience of Love of God. Guru Nanak's *bhakti* is not mere repetition of a name. His *bhakti* is an intense love of God and His creation which expresses itself in the service of mankind and carrying out His altruistic Will. In fact, the goal in Sikhism is to recognise and carry out the altruistic Will of God. Most religions are a search for Truth. Guru Nanak went a step further. He said : 'Truth is higher than everything; Higher still is True Living.'[35] Virtuous deeds based on morality and ethics form the crux of Guru Nanak's system. 'It is one's deeds that determine one's closeness to God.'[36] He believed the world to be real, as God's creation and decried its rejection as *mithya*. He rejected monasticism and ascetic ways of life and insisted upon a householder's life, accepting all domestic and social responsibilities as a part of the practice of religion. He said, "He alone recognises the way to God, who earns an honest living and shares it with others in need."[37] His notion of equality crossed all previous boundaries and assumed dimensions which can never be surpassed. He not only condemned the thousands year old caste system, but took practical steps to abolish it. His companion during his famous journeys was a low-caste Muslim, Mardana. At Kartarpur, he continued his mission, created a society in which everybody worked and ate together from a common kitchen or *langar*.

6.3   Evidently, Guru Nanak gave a completely new system of religious thought based upon his own mystic experience. Its concept of the Ultimate Reality, nature of the Reality, its goals, the methods prescribed to achieve the goal, its world-view and approach to life, its emphasis on moral and ethical deeds, its activism, its acceptance of social responsibility, all point towards its uniqueness and independent status as a religion. It is failure to grasp these elements that has led to suggestions of syncretism in the interpretation of Sikhism. There are scores of hymns in Guru Granth Sahib, in which Guru Nanak criticises the old traditions. How could he borrow anything from those traditions ? Of course, whatever was true in the old religions, and conformed to his own spiritual experience, was included in the Guru's system, since, as the Third Nanak says, "Truth never becomes obsolete."[38]

6.4   Common areas are bound to exist amongst all religions; particularly monotheistic religions. Sikhism is no exception. A few common features with Hinduism or Islam do not justify a syncretic interpretation. In fact, there are more common features between Judaism and Christianity, than between any other two religions. Hence, the suggestion is irrelevant and indicates the Christian missionary's zeal, rather than a factual reality.

VII.   THE ENCYCLOPAEDIA AMERICANA INTERNATIONAL EDITION, VOLUME 24

   American Corporation. International Headquarters 575 Lexington Avenue, New York. copyright Philipines, 1977

   7.1   *The Entry Includes The Following Observations* :   "Sikhs, seks, are followers of the Sikh religion, particularly of Guru Gobind Singh and, by extension, a communal group of East Punjab, India ...... The religion combines elements of Islam and Hinduism."

   "When Nanak began teaching in 1499, there was almost complete lawlessness under the weak Lodi dynasty and the government was taking active measures to repress Hinduism. Nanak's doctrines in large part were a response to these chaotic conditions. The core of his belief was Hindu, but he was undoubtedly greatly influenced by Islam." (page 808)

   7.2   The above views do not show any serious study or knowledge of Sikhism and are apparently based on the 'syncretic' interpretation of Sikhism, which has been adopted by some Western writers without carefully studying the origin and the doctrines of Sikhism or the teachings of its founder, Guru Nanak. This view has been repudiated and correct position explained in an earlier section. The conclusion may, however, be repeated that Sikhism is a revealed religion based on the mystic experience of Guru Nanak with the Ultimate Reality or God who is the Creator of the universe. God is ineffable. He is All Love. He is immanent in His creation, loves it and looks after it. A Sikh must express his love for God through service of mankind. He should, therefore, stay in the world and discharge all his domestic and social responsibilities. He should not reject the world as *mithya* or unreal. He should not take to monasticism or asceticism, which, in the Guru's opinion, are tantamount to parasitism and escapism.

The goal of a Sikh is to carry out the altruistic Will of God, which inevitably involves resistance to oppression and injustice. The Guru's doctrines have an eternal relevance, and it is wrong to call them a response to one particular situation that prevailed under Lodi rule during the times of Guru Nanak. In fact, Guru Nanak's system is a whole-life or *miri-piri* system that in its essentials is opposed to the earlier Indian systems that are dichotomous, suggesting withdrawal from empirical life and its responsibilities.

VIII.   CONCLUSION

8.1   It should be clear from the preceding examples that many encyclopaedias published in the West contain serious errors of fact as well as understanding of Sikh religion. The list given in this paper is by no means exhaustive. It is only a sample. However, it should not be difficult to imagine the damage done to the cause of Sikhism and the image of its followers by such wrong views being propagated in the numerous encyclopaedias and other such publications in circulation. It is necessary, therefore, as indicated in the beginning of this paper to examine all the enteries on Sikhism, contradict misrepresentations and take up the matter with the publishers and editors concerned to ensure necessary corrections in future editions. The present alarming situation demands strict vigilance on the part of scholars in particular and followers of Sikhism in general.

REFERENCES

1. Macauliffe, M.A. : *The Sikh Religion*, Vol. I, Introduction; S. Chand & Co. New Delhi, 1963 edition, p. LXXIX.
2. Daljeet Singh : *The Sikh Ideology*; Guru Nanak Foundation, New Delhi, 1984, pp. 126-128.
3. Ibid., pp. 128-129.
4. Ibid., p. 128
5. Guru Granth Sahib : Sri Rag M-1, Astpadi 14.6., p. 62.
6. Ibid., M-1, Asa 1.3.
7. Ibid., Var Sri Rag M-1, Sloka 1, Pauri 3.
8. Ibid., Var Majh M-1, Pauri 10.
9. Ibid., Rag Parbhati 4.10.
10. Ibid., Sloka Sahaskirti 4.
11. Ibid., Sri rag, p. 15.
12. Ibid., Var Asa, p. 473.
13. Jagjit Singh : *The Sikh Revolution*, New Delhi, 1984.
14. Bhai Vir Singh : *Devi Pujan Partal* (Punjabi), Khalsa Samachar, Amritsar.
15. Guru Granth Sahib : Var Majh, M-1, p. 142.
16. Ibid., Ramkali M-1, p. 903.
17. Ibid., Sloka 1, p. 1412.
18. Ibid., M-1, p. 145.
19. Ibid., Tilang M-1, p. 722.
20. Ibid.,Var Maru, M-5, p. 1102.
21. Guru Gobind Singh : *Zafarnama*.
22. Gokal Chand Narang : *Transformation of Sikhism*.
23. Guru Granth Sahib : Var Sorath, M-4; p. 646.
24. Guru Gobind Singh : *Zafarnama*.

25. Guru Granth Sahib : Asa, M-1, p. 350.

26. Jodh Singh : *Kartarpuri Bir de Darshan* (Punjabi), Punjabi University Patiala, 1968 edition.

27. Daljeet Singh : *Authenticity of Kartarpuri Bir*, Punjabi University Patiala, 1987.

28. Guru Granth Sahib : Bhairon M-5, p. 1136.

29. Guru Gobind Singh : *Bachittar Natak.*

30. Bhai Gurdas : *Varan*, Var 1.42.

31. Guru Granth Sahib, p. 491.

32. Ibid., p. 1199

33. Ibid., p. 732.

34. Ibid., Asa, M-1, p. 459

35. Ibid., Sri Rag M-1, p. 62.

36. Ibid., Japu Ji, p. 8.

37. Ibid., Var Sarang M-4, p. 1245.

38. Ibid., Var Ramkali, p. 946.

THE PUNJAB PROBLEM AND FUNDAMENTALISM

Kharak Singh

Introduction

A view is being propagated in some quarters that fundamentalism among the Sikhs today is apparently the basic cause of the current political unrest in the Punjab. Without giving any evidence in support of this contention, one such writer proceeds to describe it as 'primarily a movement of resistance' and 'a universe that is characterised by incoherence and disorder.' And then 'as a social scientist' he seeks to provide 'meaning and shape to what appears to be chaotic and meaningless' or to discover 'what may be termed as theory and practice of the Sikh fundamentalist', although on the authority of Jurgen Habermas, quoted by him in the epigram, he maintains that 'Meanings ...... can be made accessible *only from the inside.*'[1] Incidentally, one would like to know whether he is interpreting the movement as an insider or outsider.

The author points out that 'Sikh fundamentalists have not succeeded in articulating their vision of the world in any great detail.' He attributes this 'lack of an elaborate model' to the 'social origins of Sikh activists.' He says, 'A great majority of them come from the country side and would be classified as peasants by social anthropologists. Historically, peasants have not been known to come up with grand paradigms of social transformation. Peasant societies are by definition made up of little communities and their cosmos is invariably parochial rather than universal.' This is his favourite theory which can explain all major questions relating to Sikhs and Sikhism. In an earlier paper read at Berkeley,[2] the author wrote : 'if there is any such thing as a key to a historical problem, in case of the Sikh tradition it is to be found in its social constituency. Sikh religion is first and foremost a peasant faith. Sociologists have often spoken of how Islam is an urban religion. Sikhism may be spoken of as a rural religion. When dealing with beliefs, rituals and practices of the Sikhs — be they religious or political — it is always worthwhile to constantly remind ourselves that we are fundamentally dealing with the peasantry.'

The above explanation is obviously unsatisfactory and inadequate. So the author also looks at 'correlations between Punjab's political economy and the nature of dissent in Sikh society, the demand for a new personal law for the Sikhs, and finally the famous Anandpur Sahib Resolution, a document that may be considered as the *Magna Carta* of Sikhs.'

The discussion of political economy revolves around the size of holdings, which is not of much help, since their distribution and size are not significantly different from those in other states. The Green Revolution is also prominently mentioned, particularly its social costs and the 'polarisation of Punjabi society over the last two decades.' Some of the inferences are difficult to accept. For example, it has been stated that small holdings, ranging from 2 to 5 hectares have become increasingly less viable. The Green Revolution entails adoption of high yielding varieties and modern farming techniques, which raise productivity per unit of land. So, if at all, the Green Revolution should make small holdings more viable than before. This enabled even the subsistence farmer to spare something for the market after meeting his family requirements. Also, the author has not explained why the Green Revolution occurred only in the Punjab, while the two major requirements, viz., better varieties and modern technique of farming, were available in all the countries of South Asia, including other states of India. Is it not due to the more progressive attitude of the Sikh peasants of Punjab towards modern methods of farming ? However, in the author's judgement using Weber's litmus test for modernity, Sikh fundamentalists 'badly fail.'

In the entire discussion of the political economy and the Green Revolution, the author has not suggested anything with fundamentalist connotations on the part of the Sikhs. Nor has he been able to point out any such thing while dealing subsequently with the other two major topics that fill the body of his paper, viz., the demand for Sikh personal law and the Anandpur Sahib Resolution. Hindus have a personal law. So have the Muslims. They are not dubbed as fundamentalists on that score. Then how could Sikhs turn fundamentalists by merely making such a demand ? The suggestion that the Sikhs do not have a uniform code at the present moment, is no disqualification for making such a demand. Similarly in the Anandpur Sahib Resolution the author himself does not find anything wrong, which is no more than a demand for greater provincial autonomy, already voiced in several other states. The author himself concedes that it is, like 'an election manifesto of a political party' in India or any other country.

The author's own discussion lends little support to his thesis of Sikh fundamentalism. He is, however, determined to put this tag on the Sikh struggle. Therefore, in the conclusion he formulates three new 'arguments', which convince nobody except himself. These are : First, 'in the Punjabi word *moolvad* Sikhs possess a term that exactly corresponds to fundamentalism.' Is it an agrument ? Second, 'many orthodox Sikhs have no patience for textual analysis of Sikh scriptures.' The statement is baseless. But even if it were correct, how could views of a few orthodox Sikhs expressed today, impart a fundamental character to a demand made over 40 years ago ? Third, 'the current Sikh movement manifests many tendencies like millenarianism, a prophetic vision, revivalism and puritanism, trends that are commonly associated with fundamentalism.' No evidence is given in support of this contention. The statement appears to be a product of the author's own 'prophetic vision.'

In the quest for material to support his unsustainable thesis, the author (who is probably an anthropologist) has wandered into areas of religion and politics where he does not belong. That is why he has wasted his scholarship on matters which are completely irrelevant to the Sikh struggle. He has obviously missed the real issues.

A few other scholars have also ventured to make uncalled for and ignorant observations concerning the Punjab problem, it appears necessary to give a perspective historical account of the major issues underlying this crisis. In this paper we shall mainly confine ourselves to the paper of Harjot Oberoi read at Anaheim. In his paper there appears an evident attempt to camouflage the realities of the situation by introducing unrelated matters like Sikh ideology, the *miri piri* concepts, modernity, Sikh pluralism, secularism, the Nirankari issue, Turner's theory of social structure, etc.

For our discussion we shall first take up the Punjab Problem and its genesis, which the author has carefully avoided, and then discuss his observations to show their irrelevance, except as an attempted cover to hide the realities in Punjab.

COMMITMENTS WITH SIKHS BEFORE 1947

In 1929 when Shri Jawahar Lal Nehru was the President, a formal resolution was passed by the Indian National Congress at Lahore that no constitution of India would be finalised, until it was acceptable to the Sikhs. The second assurance was the clear statement of Nehru in 1946 that there was nothing objectionable in the Sikhs having an area demarcated in the North West of India, where they could enjoy the 'glow of freedom.' It was a significant statement, since it was given in the context of Jinnah's offering to the Sikhs consitutional guarantees in a separate state in the Eastern part of the contemplated Pakistan. Third, there was the statement of Mahatma Gandhi[6] saying that his words should be accepted and that the Congress would never betray anyone, and that if they did, the Sikhs knew how to use their *kirpan*. Finally, there was the statement of Nehru[7] in the Constituent Assembly in December 1946. While proposing a federal system with autonomous states, he moved the executive resolution, which envisaged "The Indian union as an independent sovereign republic comprising autnomous units with residuary powers, wherein the ideals of social, political and economic democracy would be guaranteed to all sections of the people, and adequate safeguards would be provided for minorities, backward commmunities and areas." Nehru described the resolution as a "Declaration, a pledge and an undertaking before the world, a contract of millions of Indians, and therefore in the nature of an oath which we want to keep." These were some of the commitments regarding an autonomous area in a federal system, which the Congress had solemnly given to the Sikhs, on the basis of which they had agreed to throw their lot with India.

COMMITMENTS VIOLATED

Unfortunately, after 1947 the Congress completely changed its views and stand. The Sikhs were aghast, when the draft of the proposed Indian Constitution was circulated to the State Assemblies in 1949, because, instead of autonomous states and a federal constitution, the draft was for a purely unitary type of structure. Unanimously, all the Sikhs of the Punjab Assembly objected to the draft and wrote as follows :[8] "It has been the declared policy of the Congress that India is to be a union of autonomous states, and each unit is to develop in its own way, linguistically, culturally and socially. Of course, Defence, Communications and Foreign Affairs must remain the Central Subjects. To change the basic policy now, is to run counter to the oft-repeated creed of the Congress." "In the considered opinion of the Akali Dal the residuary powers should be with the states." "The list distributing legislative powers should be based on the principle that the Centre or the Union Parliament should be limited to Defence, Communications and Foreign Affairs only." But in 1950 the Congress, violating the earlier assurances and policies, framed a constitution, leaning heavily towards a unitary form of Government. In protest the Akali members declined to sign it. It is evident that the Anandpur Sahib Resolution of 1978[9] is just a reiteration of Nehru's commitments in the Constituent Assembly in 1946 and of the reminder the Sikh Legislators unanimously gave in 1949 to the Central Government, that it was violating its repeated assurances. Hence it is sheer ignorance on the part of the author to suggest that it is a "document of secession." Neither was Nehru a secessionist, nor would he or the Congress have made a commitment that could be detrimental to the interests of the country. Is it the function of a scholar just to be the mouthpiece of the Establishment and echo its voice, or to detail and examine the problem ? The latter the author has failed to do either out of ignorance or design. In fact, while the Sikhs in 1949 suggested three subjects for the centre, the Anandpur Sahib Resolution proposed Currency, too, to be a Central subject. Thus, factually, it is the Congress and the Central Government who have shifted their stand. The Sikhs are obviously not asking for anything new and unreasonable.

A DIAMETRIC CHANGE

It was soon after Independence that the Sikhs felt that the Centre or the Congress had diametrically deviated in their approach and policy towards them. The major indication was its framing a unitary form of constitution, with Sikhs to be kept a permanent minority in the State. A very significant indication of the biased Central approach to the Sikhs is what Patel conveyed to Master Tara Singh, when he wanted a Punjabi Suba to be carved out. No less a person than the Prime Minister Charan Singh has described it thus :[10] "When Master Tara Singh was there, he was talking of Pubjabi Suba. Then he had a talk with Sardar Patel. Sardar Patel said : I am ready to concede it. But you will have only that much land that falls to your share on grounds of population. So Punjab area will be halved. Now you form 17% of the Army. They will have to be dismissed. Are you prepared for it ?"

The above made it plain what would thereafter be the Central approach towards the Sikhs.

The Sikhs are known for their love and struggle for freedom. This new policy, the Sikhs feel, is aptly described by Machiavelli's observations,[11] "Those states which have been acquired or accustomed to live at liberty under their own laws, there are three ways of holding them. The first is to despoil them; the second is to go and live there in person; the third is to allow them to live under their own laws, taking tribute of them, and creating within the country a government composed of a few who will keep it friendly to you. Because this government, being created by the Prince, knows that it cannot exist without his friendship and protection, will do all it can to keep them." We shall see if the events of the subsequent years, justify the feelings and apprehensions of the Sikhs.

THE STRUGGLE STARTS

Following this complete change in the Central policy and disregard of its commitments, the Sikhs started an agitation for creation of a Punjabi speaking linguistic state in the North West. The Congress had been committed to creating homogenous linguistic states in the country and reorganising provincial boundaries. Accordingly, a State Reorganisation Commission was set up to propose boundaries of new linguistic states. But strangely enough, while it recommended the formation of other linguistic states, it specifically suggested that Punjabi linguistic state should not be formed. Another indication of Central policy was that in 1956, instead of forming a Punjabi linguistic state, as in other areas, it merged the Pepsu State, in which the Sikhs were in a majority, in the East Punjab, thereby reducing the Sikhs to a minority in the new state. The struggle for Punjabi speaking linguistic state continued for over a decade. In 1965 the war with Pakistan broke out, and against all apprehensions, the Sikhs suspended their agitation and whole-heartedly supported the war effort. This they did in the national interest, merely on a promise of the Prime Minister that their demand would be considered later on. The Sikh contribution to the war was so impressive, both by the people and the soldiers, that after the War, the Prime Minister appointed a Parliamentary Committee to report regarding the formation of a Punjabi speaking state. At the same time the Congress Party also resolved that a linguistic Punjabi speaking state should be carved out of the then Punjab. But it is very interesting and revealing to know the mind of Mrs. Indira Gandhi, the then Information Minister, and Sh. Gulzari Lal Nanda, the then Home Minister to the Government of India, who was at the Government level to give effect to the proposal of the Parliamentary Committee. Hukam Singh[12], then Speaker of the Lok Sabha writes :

"The Prime Minister was reported to have observed on November 26, 1982, when releasing some books published by the Delhi Sikh Gurdwara Management Committee (HT. Nov. 27), that 'When the Punjabi speaking State was formed, the suggestion made by the Committee headed by Sardar Hukam Singh had been accepted.' This was not so, according to her statements in *My Truth* (p.117). Unfortunately, Mr. Shastri had made Sardar Hukam Singh, the Speaker of the Lower House, Chairman of the Parliamentary Committee on Punjabi Suba although he was very biased in favour of Punjabi Suba ......

'I went to Mr. Chavan and said, I had heard that Sardar Hukam Singh was going to give a report in favour of Punjabi Suba, and that he should be stopped ......'

'Once the Prime Minister's appointee had declared himself in favour of Punjabi Suba, how could we get out of it.'

"Mrs. Gandhi along with Mr. Chavan, could see Mr. Shastri with much difficulty, and when they did, Mr. Shastri just said that he was fully in touch with the situation and that they need not bother. (Ibid. p.118). 'But I was very bothered, and I went around seeing everybody. Of course, once the report came, it was too late to change it."

"Lal Bahadur Shastri continued the policy of Jawahar Lal Nehru, and was as dead against the demand of Punjabi Suba as was Nehru. So, when he was urged upon by Mrs. Gandhi to stop Hukam Singh, he did not waste any time. Mr. Shastri called Mr. Gulzari Lal Nanda, then Home Minister, to his residence, and conveyed to him the concern about the feared report. I was contacted on the telephone. Mr. Shastri disclosed that Mr. Nanda was with him, and had complained that he had suggested my name (Hukam Singh, for the Chairmanship of the Parliamentary Committee under the mistaken impression, which he had formed during a casual talk with me, that I believed that Punjabi Suba would not be of any advantage to the Sikhs ultimately, but that now I appeared determined to make a report in its favour."

"I answered that the facts were only partly true. I had told Mr. Nanda that Punjabi suba would not ultimately be of much advantage to the Sikhs. But I had also added that the issue had by then become one of sentiment and had roused emotions. Therefore it was not possible to argue with, much less to convince, any Sikh about the advantages or disadvantages of Punjabi suba. Every Sikh considered the denial as discrimination. I further enquried from Mr. Shastri, whether I had not expressed the same opinion to him and his answer was in the affirmative. I myself offered to confront Mr. Nanda by immediately rushing to Mr. Shastri's residence, but he said there was no need. This disillusioned me. The intention of the Government then was to use me against my community, secure an adverse report, and then reject the demand."

"The Govt. has never seen merit in any Sikh demand. The Das Commission in 1948 recommended postponement of reorganisation on the plea, *inter alia*, that if once begun in the South, it might intensify the demand by Sikhs in the North. The J.V.P. committee (Jawaharlal, Vallabh Bhai Patel and Pattabhi Sitaramayya), when reviewing the Das report, gratuitously remarked that no question of rectification of boundaries in the provinces of Northern India should be raised at the present moment, whatever the merit of such a proposal might be."

"And this became the future policy. Nehru struck to it. Shastri continued the same, and Indira Gandhi has made no departure."

"Every effort was made by Mrs. Gandhi, Mr. Shastri, and Mr. Nanda to stop me from making my report."

Why the government had been so strongly against the Parliamentary Committee making a report in favour of Punjabi Suba and why Mrs. Gandhi had felt bothered and ran about seeing everybody to stop Hukam Singh, has been explained by Mrs. Gandhi herself. "The Congress found itself in a dilemma, to concede the Akali demand would mean abandoning a position to which it was firmly committed and letting down its Hindu supporters in the Punjabi Suba (p.117, *My Truth*)." The Government has always been very particular about not "letting down its Hindu supporters." The Congress could not depend upon Sikh voters and out of political considerations could not suffer losing Hindu votes also. Therefore, the Congress failed to do justice to the Sikhs.

"The first schedule of the Regional Committee Order 1957 contained Ropar, Morinda and Chandigarh assembly constituencies in Ambala district in the Punjab region."

"The subsequent reference to the Shah Commission was loaded heavily against Punjab. Making the 1961 census as the basis and the tehsil as the unit was a deliberate design to punish the Sikhs. The language returns in the 1961 census were on communal lines.

"Therefore the demarcation had to be on a communal rather than on a linguistic basis."

"Consequently merit was again ignored and justice denied. Naturally, tensions between the two communities increased. If the Sachar formula, worked out in 1949 had been accepted, there would not have been any further conflict, if the Regional Formula had been allowed to be implemented, there would not have been any further discontent. And if Punjabi Suba had been demarcated simply on a linguistic basis, and not on false returns in 1961, there would not have been any extremist movement."

It clearly shows that the demand for a linguistic state, a policy which was an old one with the Congress and which had been implemented in the rest of India, was to be denied in the Punjab, because Sikhs would become a majority there and come into power under the democratic process. Henceforward, it would seem that the Central Government has been following the three pronged policy of despoiling Punjab, ruling it by stooge governments, and imposing President's rule, if and when, by the democratic process, a non-Congress government came into power in the state. The subsequent history of the Punjab has been just a struggle between the Sikhs, historically known for their love of liberty, and the Centre pursuing the above policy. Both Mrs. Indira Gandhi and Shri Nanda were concerned and worried about the proposal for a Punjabi Suba being accepted by the Congress. The proposal was conceded only after over fifty thousand Sikhs had courted arrest, and scores had died during the peaceful agitation.

A SUB-STATE CREATED

The Parliamentary Committee having recommended the creation of a Punjabi Suba, the Home Minister got passed an Act, the Punjab Reorganisation Act, 1966, which in its implication was not only a denial to Punjab of a status equal to that of other states in the country, but also involved a permanent ceiling on the economic, social and political growth of the state and its people. The Act had the following crippling provisions and limitations :

1. For the development of every state in India two things are basic, namely, water and energy. As it is, Punjab, because of its rivers and very great hydel power potential, is fortunate. Under the Constitution of India, and everywhere under international law and practice, Irrigation and Power are state subjects (Item 17 of the State List read with Article 246 of the Constitution). These are under the exclusive executive and legislative jurisdiction of the states. But by the provision of Section 78 to 80 of the Reorganisation Act, the Centre

unconstitutionally kept to itself the power of control, maintenance and development of the waters and hydel power of the Punjab rivers. This was a clear violation of the Constitution. In other words, Punjab became a state which could do nothing for the control and development of its rivers, utilisation of their waters and exploitation of their hydel power potential. Thus Punjab became administratively and legislatively an ineffective and inferior state, which could do nothing for the economic development of its people. The question of political growth could not arise, because it had permanently been reduced to a sub-state without scope for regaining control of its waters and hydel power. Hence, progress towards autonomy became out of question.

2. The second limitation concerned the territorial boundaries of the states. In 1949 under the well-known Sachar Formula the state government indicated, upto a village, the boundaries of Punjabi speaking and Hindi speaking areas. Later, under an Act of Parliament, known as the Regional Formula, Punjabi speaking and Hindi speaking areas of the old Punjab were demarcated and separate legislative Committees representing the two areas were constituted. The Sachar Formula and the Regional Formula had been accepted and worked without any objection from the people, legislators or Ministers of the areas concerned, until 1966. Instead of accepting the settled boundaries, as had been recommended by the Parliamentary Committee proposing the formation of the Punjabi Suba, the Government appointed a Commission to redetermine the boundaries and thus to reopen and make controversial a settled issue. In fact, areas which were Punjabi speaking or were under the functional control of Punjab, were excluded from the Punjabi Suba, and the Commission excluded not only settled Punjabi speaking contiguous areas, but also the State capital from the Suba, even though it had been consituted by acquiring Punjabi speaking villages, and in every other reorganised state the capital had remained with the parent state. An area almost equal to half of the present Himachal Pradesh, was transferred from the Punjab to Himachal Pradesh though they were known Punjabi speaking areas. Even the site of the Bhakra Dam which was constructed solely by the Punjab Government and had always been under its functional control, was kept out of Punjab, although the area is Punjabi speaking. At the same time, Simla and other hill stations were transferred to Himachal Pradesh.

DEMANDS AFTER 1966

The new state being basically handicapped, an agitation for redressal of the grievances started soon after 1966, because it was anticipated that its future under the created discriminations would be ruinous for the people. The salient demands of this agitation were as follows :

(a) Satluj, Ravi and Beas, being purely Punjab rivers, and their waters and hydel power being indispensable for the economy of the State, no water or hydel power should be allotted to non-riparian states like Rajasthan, Haryana or

Delhi, because such an allocation would be unconstitutional. The issue could, therefore, be referred to the Consitution Bench of the Supreme Court. In no other state at the time of reorganisation had the provisions of the Consitutions been violated to deprive it of its wealth of water and hydel power as in Punjab.

(b)   The boundaries that had been accepted by all concerned, including the people and the legislators, should not be disturbed to deprive the new state of known Punjabi speaking areas, through a Centrally-appointed Commission.

(c)   The Central Government's order that recruitment to Defence Services should be based on the population of a state, was unconstitutional, being violative of Articles 15 and 16 of the Indian Constitution, which state that in the matter of recruitment to Public Services no distinction could be made on the basis of place of birth of an individual. The object of this order could evidently be to reduce the strength of Sikhs, which was originally about 20%, to below 2% which was to be the share of Punjab on the basis of its population during future recruitment to Defence Forces. Actually, the strength of the Sikhs in the Defence Forces had already been reduced to about 8%, and the Sikhs apprehended that the new policy would further reduce their strength to 2% or less. This unconstitutional policy of the Government has been a major cause for distress in the rural areas of the Punjab. As *lakhs* of families were dependent on the profession of soldiery for their livelihood, and since the percentage of the Sikh soldiers in the army became increasingly reduced, this caused serious economic dissatisfaction among the youth in rural areas of Punjab, especially when they found that in other states candidates with lower physical fitness standards were accepted. As this policy related only to the Defence Services, where Sikhs, because of their tradition, aptitude and fitness were eminently suitable for selection, it created a serious sense of discrimination against them in the policy of the Central Government.

(d)   Even before Independence, the keeping of *kirpan* (sword) was accepted as a religiously prescribed wear for Sikhs. Its wear by a Sikh has been guaranteed under the Law and the Indian Constitution. During British days there had been a specific agitation for this freedom. But now the Central Government issued an order placing restrictions on the carrying of *kirpan* in certain situations. This order was considered violative of the Indian Constitution. Hence the demand was for withdrawl of the unconstitutional restrictions.

Apart from the Anandpur Sahib Resolution, which will be discussed separately, the above were the four major demands of the Sikhs after 1966. These demands were reasonable and legitimate, and since the Constitution provides a specific forum for their solution, the Government, if it intended, could have lawfully settled them without the least objection from any party or State. No one could say that the constitutional issues should not be referred to the Constitutional Bench of the Supreme Court, which was the body to give a verdict on them, and once the decision had been made, no party could raise any objection. So far as the territorial matter was concerned, the demand was equally valid, because it required that the borders that stood settled and accepted by the people of the areas, and the decision embodied in an Act of Parliament, should not be arbitrarily altered through a Commission. But what could be settled in one day, has been made to linger on for decades, and the Congress dominated Central Government has consistently failed to follow the constitutional path or to maintain the status quo on a settled issue. Instead of giving the long history of the Akali agitation over the last about a quarter of a century, we shall, for the sake of brevity, confine our discussion mainly to the two issues of river waters and the Anandpur Sahib Resolution.

RIVER WATERS AND HYDEL POWER ISSUES

After Independence roughly 38 MAF of river waters fell to the share of East Punjab in India. Of these, about 32 MAF were carried by the three Punjab rivers, Satluj, Beas and Ravi, and the remaining 5.6 MAF were carried by the Jamuna in Haryana area or the Jamuna Basin. Excluding 5.6 MAF of Jamuna (only part of which was utilised in Haryana area of erstwhile Punjab), of the remaining over 32 MAF, about 9 MAF were being utilised in the Punjabi Suba area, and one MAF was used in the Gang Canal for the Bikaner State, which had an agreement with Punjab for a limited period, on payment of royalty to Punjab for the use of that water. In short, about 22 MAF of Punjab waters were still available for use of the State. Actually a considerable part of the 22 MAF was being used in the Pakistan area, before 1947. But after the Partition these waters fell to the share of Indian Punjab.

The second essential point is that Punjab is short of water. As Dr Lowdermilk[13] has pointed out, sweet water is going to be a scarce commodity and a limiting factor in the development of an area or state in the coming century. Agricultural experts have estimated that 5 to 6 acre feet of water are the annual rquirements of an acre for growing two crops like wheat and paddy, the recommended rotation in the state. The cultivable area in Punjab being 105 *lakh* acres, the annual requirements of surface water come to about 52.5 MAF. But the available waters are only 32 MAF, of which about 0.6 MAF have to go the co-riparian Jammu and Kashmir. In sum, Punjab is woefullly deficient in the availability of river waters to meet the requirements of its cultivated area. Here we should like to state two points :

First, we cannot for want of space give the entire history of the allotment of the river waters. We shall record only the result of the decision made by the Central Government. Second, we shall give only approximate figures, because these have been marginally changed by different assessments and are still under controversy. The figures given will be the accepted data during the period before 1970.

The Reorganisation Act has a provision that in case of any dispute between Punjab and Haryana regarding the Beas Project, the Centre would be the arbitrator. Apart from the provision being considered violative of the Constitution, it was really unnecessary, because the Beas Project had been framed and finalised long before 1966, and envisaged the allotment of only about 0.9 MAF to the Haryana area. Such projects are always drawn in great detail, including plans for utilisation of water, channels, commanded area, and water to be supplied to each channel, distributary or water course. As such, the very provision in the Act was superfluous, except as a lever for its unwarranted use, as has been revealed later. After 1966, Haryana drew up a project, Satluj Yamuna Link Canal, which is supposed to carry 5 MAF of water from Punjab rivers. The Central Government approved of it. Punjab did not accept its validity, being a post-Reorganisation project and not a part of the Beas Project. Because of the dispute the Centre gave an award, and the final result broadly is that out of the 22 MAF, only about 5 MAF have been allotted to the Punjab, while 8 MAF go to Rajasthan and the remaining to Haryana. In short after 1947, about three fourths of the available waters of the Punjab state have been allotted to non-riparian areas of Haryana, Rajasthan and Delhi.

We shall briefly mention the three stages of this long controversy. The first stage is the arbitration award by the Prime Minister, Mrs. Indira Gandhi, in 1976 allotting, excluding flow of Satluj waters of the Bhakra Project, 3.5 MAF each to Punjab and Haryana, 0.2 MAF to Delhi, leaving the remaining for Rajasthan which had been earlier earmarked under an executive order of the Centre. Following the defeat of Mrs. Indira Gandhi in the 1977 elections, an Akali-cum-Jan Sangh Ministry was formed in the Punjab. After obtaining expert legal advice, they filed a case in the Supreme Court questioning the award of the Prime Minister and the *vires* of the Punjab Reorganisation Act of 1966. The third stage is that soon after Indira Gandhi returned to power at the Centre, she dismissed the Akali Ministry in Punjab, and later called a meeting of the three Congress Chief Ministers of Rajasthan, Haryana and Punjab, and made them sign an agreement virtually endorsing the earlier award. It gave 8.6 MAF to Rajasthan, 3.5 MAF to Haryana, 0.2 to Delhi, and 4.2 MAF only to riparian Punjab. Following the agreement, the case pending before the Supreme Court was withdrawn by the Punjab Government, and the Prime Minister, Mrs. Gandhi laid the foundation of the SYL Canal. Thus a constitutional attempt to have a decision of the Supreme Court on the fundamental constitutional issue was frustrated, following executive decisions. The conclusion is incontrovertible that the diversion of Punjab's water and hydel power resources to non-riparian states has been done by the Centre by resort to extra-judicial measures and by frustrating the constitutional process, which the Akali Ministry had sought to follow. It only shows that all through the Centre was aware that the allotment was not constitutional and the Supreme Court would not endorse the validity of the unconstitutional provisions of the Reorganisation Act, 1966, and what it had decided regarding the allotment of Punjab waters and hydel power to non-riparian states.

Here, two other points need to be mentioned. There is a provision in the Reorganisation Act, that hydel power from Punjab rivers will go to Haryana in proportion to the allotment of water. Second, the agreement of 1981 among the three states only related to water of Punjab rivers. The constitutional issue about the provision concerning hydel power of these rivers was outside the scope of that agreement. Accordingly, it was still open to a future Punjab Government to raise before the Supreme Court the constitutional issue about the validity of the Reorganisation Act concerning hydel power. As such, the entire Reorganisation Act could be got declared unconstitutional, thereby upsetting the apple cart of all allotments of water and hydel power to non-riparian states.

The Centre's consciousness about its unconstitutional course appears evident from the fact that in May 1984 during the President's Rule the Punjab Governor entered into the extra-judicial agreement with Haryana and Rajasthan, providing that future disputes, if any, among them shall not be referred to the Supreme Court, but shall be decided through a nominee or a Tribunal appointed by the Central Government.

Without going into the history of such decisions regarding the Narmada and other river waters in India, we shall quote only one decision made by a California Court[14] in February 1988. The case related to a petition by the Federal Government that its lands situated in California be allowed some irrigation from a stream in South California. Until then the private land owners on the basis of their riparian rights were not allowing the use of the river water to even Government lands in the State. The Court decided that while the Federal lands might be allowed waters, the water use for State lands would be subordinated to the needs of the current water users in the State. This is to emphasise that, not to speak of allowing water to non-riparian states, the priority of private water users is so strong and universal that until Feb. 1988 the private land owners were not allowing water to even Government lands. This priority is evidently based on the principle that since for centuries on end, it is the people of a state that suffer loss in property, land and life from the floods and vagaries of rivers, they alone in equity have the corresponding right of having benefits from the waters or hydel power of those streams.

In no democratic country in Europe, America or India is there a decision contrary to the riparian principle which is also embodided in the Indian Constitution. One fact alone will show the equity of the riparian law. In 1988 the Punjab floods caused a havoc. The loss in erosion and silting of land, damage to crops, houses, property and cattle, apart from the loss of scores of human lives, was estimated at over a billion Dollars[15] in that single year. Neither Rajasthan, nor Haryana, nor Delhi suffered even a penny worth of loss or damage from Punjab rivers of which they had been made the principal beneficiaries. The above highlights the contradiction and evident injustice that while riparian Punjab continues to suffer such damages, the non-riparian states reap each year benefits and production of over a billion Dollars.

In India, too, there is a clear cut decision in the Narmada waters case,[16] saying that Rajasthan being a non-riparian state has no rights to its waters whatsoever. In that case Rajasthan itself pleaded that even though non-riparian, it was getting Punjab waters, and on that analogy it should be allowed waters from the Narmada. But it was held that Rajasthan was non-riparian vis-a-vis Punjab rivers, and Punjab's committment to Rajasthan was that it would supply water, only if it was surplus to its needs. This is to stress that knowing full well all this and other judicial decisions and rulings of the Indian Courts on the subject, the Congress dominated Central Government has consciously violated the riparian principle, and when challenged, avoided a judicial verdict on this constitutional issue.

DISASTROUS EFFECT OF DRAIN OF PUNJAB WATERS AND POWER

The ruinous and despoiling effects of Central decisions are large scale both in the fields of agriculture and industry. At present out of 105 *lakh* acres of cultivated land in the Punjab, about 92 *lakhs* are irrigated including about 37 *lakhs* by canals and the rest by tubewells. This indicates that the major part of irrigation and Punjab prosperity and production are due to private effort and enterprise. First, the capital cost and maintenance and running costs of these over 8 *lakh* tubewells are a heavy burden on the production costs of crops in the state. Current cost of tubewell irrigation is 3 to 10 times more than canal irrigation, depending upon the source of power. Apart from the fact that uninterrupted suppply of power from diesel or electricity is hardly assured, the heavy overdrawal of subsoil water exceeds the annual recharge by rains, seepage, etc. This is lowering the water table each year by one to ten feet. The present position of tubewell irrigation is that between 80 to 90 percent of the Community Blocks in the state have been branded as unsuitable for irrigation by tubewells. The clear warning given is that by the close of the century, the majority of these tubewells would become non functional because of the continuous fall of the water table. The second point is that available estimates suggest that ten *lakh* acres of existing canal irrigated areas especially from the Sirhind Canal area, would lose facility of canal water because water at present used in the state will have to be diverted to Haryana and Rajasthan under the present decision. In short, because of the lowering water table and diversion of canal waters, about 60% of the area or about 50 *lakhs* acres would become *barani* or unirrigated. Under the present cropping system, the question of dry farming does not arise. The holdings of small farmers being what they are, the resultant misery of a major part of the rural population can well be imagined. Its very serious effects on economic and social conditions in the state and their disturbing influence on the political life should be obvious. The annual loss of agricultural production would be of the order of 1.2 billion Dollars. The loss in consequential industrial production and in the diversion of hydel power to other states would be still greater. The unfortunate part is that whereas hydel power from Punjab is being allotted to other states, thermal power plants are being installed in Punjab. These being dependent on coal from distant states, the electricity generated by them is obviously several times more expensive than hydel power.

ANANDPUR SAHIB RESOLUTION

As explained, the basis of the Anandpur Sahib Resolution is not any snap decision or secessionist trend in Punjab politics. It simply asks for implementation of the assurances given by the Central leadership before 1947. Since 1949, the Akalis have been pressing the Central Government to give effect to their earlier policies and assurances. Since then the following additional factors have arisen to make it necessary that states should have autonomous power :

(a) In 1971 the Tamil Nadu Assembly adopted the Rajmanner Report, which requires that the Centre should have only four subjects as in the Anandpur Sahib Resolution, and in addition, there should be a consultative committee of Chief Ministers of states presided over by the Prime Minister to advise the Centre regarding the four Central subjects. Such views have also been expressed by West Bengal and other non-Congress Ministries.

(b)   In the preceding 40 years the Centre has amended the Constitution a number of times to make it more centralised. For example, Education, Administration of Justice and Constitution of Courts, have been made either concurrent or Central subjects. The percentage of discretionary grants to be given to the states from the Central revenue has been raised very considerably, thereby enabling the Centre to favour or punish any state it may like to do.

(c)   The Centre has created non-statutory or extra-constitutional bodies like the Planning Commission, the Water and Power Commission, the University Grants Commission, etc., which have great powers not only to make financial allocations, but also have unfettered discretion to approve or disapprove state schemes which fall exclusively within the sphere of state functioning. By this method, the Centre could completely throttle all development in a state, should it choose to do so. A classic case is the construction of the Punjab Project of the Thein Dam which was to cost originally only 70 crores, but Punjab failed to receive final approval from the Power Commission even though in the mean time its cost has risen to over 800 *crores*.

(d)   Another factor is the frequent Central intrusion in state affairs by creating instability in a state and introducing President's rule. For example, whenever a non-Congress Ministry was constitutionally formed in the Punjab, it was destabilised, followed by the President's rule. This was felt to be a negation of the democratic will of the people.

(e)   As the disastrous shackle of the Punjab Reorganisation Act makes Punjab a sub-state, the only way to promote socio-political progress in the state was to have full autonomy in the sphere of all development, planning and administration including control of water and hydel power of Punjab rivers.

(f)   Under the existing political set-up, as in the Punjab Reorganisation Act, the Centre has insisted on the construction of the Rajasthan Canal despite all expert advice to the contrary. International experts from the World Bank and other institutions clearly emphasised that the Project was economically unjustifiable and wasteful, and that at far less expense the use of Punjab river waters could be far more productive if utilised within the state. It shows that the Central decision neither served the national interests nor those of the Punjab.

(g)   Economic exploitation of Punjab in other fields has also been going on. Over 75% of the savings in Punjab Banks are diverted outside the state in order to develop other areas. Industrial licensing and approval of projects being in Central hands, it has not allowed more than 2% of the cotton produced in the Punjab to be processed within the state. Similarly, while Punjab is a major sugarcane producing area, large scale imports of sugar still take place from other states. Another way of serious curtailment of the wealth of rural Punjab, which sustains about 80% of the population, is by low pricing and monopoly procurement of wheat and rice which are in Central hands. Punjab suffers the most because about 60% of wheat and a large part of rice are procured from

Punjab by the Centre for distribution in deficit or urban areas in other states.

We have indicated above some of the Central measures that have seriously curtailed Punjab's Agricultural and Industrial growth. In fact, the Reorganisation Act has put a permanent ceiling on the economic, social and political development of the state. It is in this context that the assurances of the Congress leaders, and the Akali demand of 1949 were revived in 1973, because it became evident that in the existing set-up economic and social growth of the people of the Punjab stood completely arrested. Hence the need of autonomy in the field of development and administrative subjects, as envisaged in the Anandpur Sahib Resolution, became inevitable.

Evidently it is sheer bias on the part of a scholar to make a complete black-out of the context, the steps taken by the Centre and the political events in the Punjab and other states that have given rise to the Anandpur Sahib Resolution demanding state autonomy, and approvingly to endorse the Anandpur Sahib Resolution 'as a document of secession.' In the current political thinking both in the world and in India, it looks so incongruous for even a journalist, much less for a scholar to brand a simple demand for autonomy as secessionist. We give below by way of a sample a recent statement of a Central Minister, George Fernandes, who observed at a seminar on Indian nationalism, Problems and Challenges, that [17] "The growing militancy by the youth was a clear indication that the politicians had failed to solve the problems of the country. The only answer was to have a new constitution, providing a genuine decentralised state with development activity being the responsibility of the people." "If the country had adopted decentralisation instead of going in for centralised planning, there would not have been a single village in the country with a drinking water problem."

The author H. Oberoi has unnecessarily and illogically raised the issue of Sikh personal law, and tried to relate it to so-called Sikh fundamentalism. First, there is nothing fundamentalist in making a political demand. Second, Sikhs have undoubtedly a separate religion, a separate scripture and a separate socio-political identity and world-view. Accordingly, there is nothing abnormal or irrational, if the Sikhs, like the Muslims or the Hindus, want to have a separate personal law; it is the right of every ethnic community to make such a demand.

It is ridiculous for anyone to suggest, as has been done by Oberoi, that after the grant of autonomy the Sikhs would ban tobacoo, drugs or alcohol. Nothing of this sort was done by Ranjit Singh even in the nineteenth century. The Punjab Assembly has power even today to ban tobacco or alcohol, but nothing of the kind has happened, although some other states have introduced prohibition. It appears hardly rational to raise such a bogey. It reminds one of the fears expressed by some politicians that hens would stop laying eggs, if the steam locomotive invented by Stephenson was introduced. As explained earlier, the real object of Oberoi appears to be political, and the aim seems to be to misrepresent the justification and political necessity of the demand for state automomy. For, otherwise, it is difficult to accept that he is absolutely unaware of the basic importance of water and hydel power, territorial, recruitment and other issues in reference to Punjab and the demand for autonomy in many other parts of the country.

FUNDAMENTALISM

From the point of view of academic studies the point is completely irrelevant to the subject under consideration, because fundamentalism is related only to the literal acceptance of many of the stories and assertions in the Bible, which under modern conditions are not accepted by many. For example, it has been stated that the world is only a few thousand years old. There is nothing in the Sikh scripture or the Sikh ideology, which appears in any way illogical to modern thought. In fact it is the modernity that is its basic feature and is the reason for its departure from the earlier Indian religions. It is not our intention to give offence to any old relgion, but we all know that they have their statements which are questioned even by men of the faith. Hence, it appears necessary to give the Sikh world-view, so that Oberoi's contentions could be assessed in the correct ideological perspective.

Sikhism is free from any historical or mythical assumptions. It is a monotheistic faith with the belief that the basic Force or God is Love, and He is both transcendent and immanent in His creation. Love being dynamic, the mother of all values, and directive, God is deeply interested in His creation, and operates through His altruistic Will. As such, the seeker's goal is to carry out His Will. This makes for the reality of the world, instead of its being an illusion *(mithya)* or a suffering, as is considered by some other religions. Hence, Guru Nanak emphasises four things : First, that in life the spiritual dimension must be combined with the empirical dimension in order to live a full and fruitful life. This forms the basis of the *miri-piri* doctrine laid down by him. Second, that the ideal of man is not personal salvation or merger in Brahman, but working in tune with the altruistic Will of God. Our present malady is that we live an egoistic life, and remain alienated from the real force of Love, that is operative in the world and forms the base of all moral life. Third, in pursuance of the above logic Guru Nanak rejected the system of monasticism, asceticism, other-worldliness, caste ideology and the prevaling concepts of pollution, and woman being a temptress. No prophet in the world has made such radical changes in the then contemporary religious thought as did Guru Nanak. Fourth, he prescribed that man's assessment would be made on his deeds alone. It is in this context that he stated that "Truth is higher than every thing, but truthful living is higher still." A major corollary of his system of truthful living, which is its central element, is man's duty to participate in social life and accept total social responsibility. For that end he suggested that for the religious man, work, production and equitable distribution are essential, as also the responsibility of confronting or resisting injustice and oppression. Because he calls God the Destroyer of evil-doers and the demoniacal. In order to enable the religious man to discharge the responsibility of resisting oppression, he rejected the doctrine of *ahimsa* or pacificism, which had been an integral part of all Indian religions. And it is in this context he gave the call that whosoever wanted to join his society, should be willing to scarifice his all. For that end he organised a society, and created the institution of succession to enable his successors to develop and mature the *Panth*. Finally, it is this society which the Tenth Guru created as the Khalsa, again giving the call for total sacrifice, and breaking completely with the earlier religious systems, traditions, customs, etc. Hence it is sheer ignorance of Oberoi to relate Guru Granth Sahib and its system to something of the kind of Christian fundamentalism in order to create a prejudice in the minds of those who have no knowledge of Sikhism. Guru Granth Sahib or its ideology can be summed up as was done by Guru Nanak thus : Give up egoism and live a life of love, virtue, equality and justice. Accordingly there is no obscurantism or pluralism in the ideology of Guru Nanak. To make such a statement is to display gross ignorance of the basic ideology of Guru Nanak. As to the *miri-piri* doctrine, it is the fundamental of Guru Nanak's thesis to combine the empirical life with the spiritual life of man. It is the same principle as was accepted by Moses and Prophet Mohammad, both of whom were simultaneously religious and political leaders.

As to the Nirankaris, he has again completely misrepresented the position either out of ignorance or otherwise. The Nirankaris are neither a Sikh sect nor a break-away group, nor do the Nirankaris themselves make any claim to be Sikhs. The clash between the Nirankaris and the Bhindrawale group might well have been a created problem in order to sidetrack the Sikh political struggle for its rights. In any case, such a conflict could be between the two ideologies. Further, it is a mis-statement that the death of Gurbachan Singh was followed by mass killings in the Punjab. Nothing of the kind happened and Oberoi has not given any evidence to support this unfounded statement. The alleged clash had nothing to do with the political problems of Punjab and the issues involved therein. A minor clash between two communities can hardly be a reason for denying autonomy to a state.

Oberoi has also incongruously introduced the point of the Green Revolution, which is chronologically a baseless assertion. The Sikh agitation for Punjabi Suba and autonomous status, is a political issue of pre-Independence days and even the demand of Punjabi Suba and its autonomy arose in the life of Sardar Patel. Long before the Green Revolution, the agitation for the Suba had started. Over fifty thousand went to jail and suffered imprisonment and other hardships. All this happened before the onset of the Green Revolution. As every student of Punjab agriculture is aware, the first import of high yielding seeds from Mexcio took place in 1966, and the impact of the Green Revolution was not felt before the mid seventies. By that time the agitation for Sikh demands including the fasts of Sant Fateh Singh and Darshan Singh Pheruman, as also the death of the latter, had taken place. Second, the occurrence of the Green Revolution in Punjab is an accomplished fact. But the important question is why it took place in the North West corner of India among the rural Sikhs and not anywhere else in India or Asia, which had been deficient in food. It is the life-affirming ideology of Sikhism that is the sole explanation for it as has been explained by Upinderjit Kaur in her publication. Oberoi's difficulty appears to be his complete ignorance of the spirituo-empirical life combination or the *miri-piri* system of Guru Granth Sahib. That is why he seems to be beating about the bush. As to the subdivision of holdings, he has again made a contradiction. Subdivison is a natural consequence of the system of succession. The Green Revolution has not in any way accentuated it, but it has made small holdings more productive and life sustaining than before. Higher yields and greater production have relieved the economic situation, and this is supported by no less a person than Subramaniam, the Agriculture Minister of India.

Oberoi has harped a lot on modernity and secularism, and has only displayed an ignorance of the broad forces that are involved in the current century. It is Toynbee, who laments that for the last three hundred years religion has been driven out of the cultural life of man and instead parochialism of the worship of the national state as a goddess has started. He also laments that the Western technologist has lost his self-confidence and is in confusion, whether the technological genii which he has released would not destroy all human culture and whether his "professional success may not have been a social and moral disaster." For him "the great world religions have been replaced in modern times by three post-Christian ideologies — nationalism, communism and individualism. All three are equally impersonal and dehumanising." Similarly, Pierard believes "Secularism in the nineteenth century aided by Marxism, Darwinism and Positivism chipped away the Christian underpinning of Western thought." This thinking considers that secularism and nationalism eventually will give rise to militarism, imperialism, racism and despotism. The history of the current century hardly seems to suggest that secularism leads to cultural or moral progress. In fact, the indications, both historical and current, seem to be quite different. For, in Europe and the USSR millions were destroyed by Hitler and Stalin both of whom were secularists without any belief in religion. It is in this context that the American Churches have raised the voice that secularism is a major danger to life and that Christianity should co-operate with other religions in order to avoid the present decline in moral values of our culture. It is doubtful, whether Hegel, as Oberoi suggests, can be associated with the thinking of divorce between religion and politics. But whatever be his belief, he is certainly associated with German militarism and is considered to be the precursor of Kaiser, Hitler and despotism. In fact it is the post modern thinking of men like Huston Smith[18] that suggests the recognition of the role of religion against the limitation and potential harm that is contained in the power-over-nature approach to life that governs much of our modern culture. This philosophy appears to lead towards "only a dead end; annihilation of mythology, religion, all value system, all hope."

REFERENCES

1. Harjot Oberoi : *Sikh Fundamentalism : Ways of Turning Things Over*. Paper presented at the annual Meeting of the American Academy of Religion, Anaheim; November, 1989.
2. *Popular Saints, Goddesses and Village Sacred Sites : Re-reading Sikh Experience in the Nineteenth Century*. Read at Conference held at Berkeley, USA, Feb., 1987.
3. *Young India*, Bombay, March, 1931.
4. *The Statesman*, Calcutta, July 7, 1946.
5. Kapur Singh : *Sachi Sakhi*, Navyug Publishers, 1973, pp. 32-33.
6. *Young India*, Bombay, March 19, 1931.

7. Duggal, Devinder Singh : *The Truth about the Sikhs*, Amritsar, N.D., page 14.

8. The Council of Sikh Affairs, Chandigarh : *The Anguish of Punjab : Sikhs Demand Justice*, N.D., page 5.

9. Dhillon, G.S : *Researches in Sikh Religion and History*, Chandigarh, 1989, page 134-135.

10. *Illustarted Weekly of India*, June 10-16, 1984 : The Man Everyone Loves to Hate.

11. Machiavelli, Niccolo : *The Prince*, page 46, Oxford University Press; Reprint, A Mentor Book : New Amercian Library; A Division of Penguin Books, USA, New York, Revised Trans. 1935.

12. Dhillon, G.S. : *Researches in Sikh Religion and History*, op. cit., pp. 114-115.

13. The Council of Sikh Affairs; Chandigarh : *Punjab River Waters Dispute*, page 12.

14. *Los Angeles Times,* LA (USA), Feb., 1988, pages 1 and 32.

15. *The Tribune,* Chandigarh, dated Aug. 3, 1990.

16. Govt. of India : The Report of the Narmada Water Dispute Tribunal, Vol. III, pages 25, 26 and 30, New Delhi, 1930.

17. Fernandes, G., Rly Minister, Govt. of India.

18. Huston Smith : *Beyond the Post-Modern Mind*, The Theosophical Publishing House, Wheaton (III), USA, A Quest Book, 1985.

35

SIKH MILITANCY AND THE JATS*

Jagjit Singh

Some historians have expressed the view that the initiation and development of militarization within the Sikh movement was due to the cultural patterns and traits of the Jats who joined it in large numbers. We shall here discuss this theory (which we label as Jat Theory for the sake of brief reference to it), and show that it is based on factually wrong assumptions and premises. For instance, there is no data to infer that the Jats were the predominant element among the Sikhs when Guru Hargobind militarized the movement, or in the battles of Guru Gobind Singh and those of Banda. Rather, all the available historical evidence points to the contrary. To argue that, "a comparatively light representation in a list of prominent members does not necessarily imply a corresponding proportion of the actual adherants",[1] indicates how unsure the advocates of the Jat Theory themselves are about the factual basis of their main premise. Even this is a presumption that the Jats were the only people who bore arms, in case the population was not disarmed, and the Khatris and the castes lower than the Jats did not. Anyway, we are here attempting to draw attention to those substantive factors which the protagonists of the Jat Theory blackout, but which make it quite clear that it was the Sikh ideology, and not Jat constituency of the *Panth*, that was responsible for the initiation and development of Sikh militancy. Rather, the question whether or not the Jats were the dominant partners in the *Panth* is irrelevant; because, without the Sikh ideology, the Sikh social and political revolution would not have materialized even if the *Panth* had been composed entirely of Jats, and been left to their own native character and mores.

1. REVOLUTIONARY AND NON-REVOLUTIONARY MOVEMENTS

As the differences between revolutionary and non-revolutionary movements are

---

* It is against the Sikh religion to differentiate Sikhs in terms of castes, but we are constrained to do so in order to meet the argument from scholars who have tried to explain militarization of the Sikh movement due to "Jat cultural patterns." Therefore, wherever we indicate the caste of a Sikh, it should be taken to mean the original stock from which he was derived.

"qualitative, marked by differences in kind, not just in amount,"[2] the militancy of the Sikh movement should not be confused with that of non-revolutionary movements, or for that matter with that of such a period of this movement itself. It is not just militancy that leads to a revolution. For this reason, the significance of the militancy of a mass movement cannot be understood without relating it to the purpose it wants to achieve. Mere elan or magnitude of the militancy of a movement, howsoever intense, should not obscure the vital condition as to distinction whether or not it is yoked to serve a revolutionary purpose. "Thus, though in terms of their physical quality, there is little to choose between the burning of Newgate prison in 1780 and the fall of the Bastille in 1789, in terms of historical significance it is abundantly clear that the latter was a revolutionary act and the former was not."[3]

Near at home, there are few instances in world history which compare with the reckless courage shown by Rajput men and women who committed the suicidal *Johars*, in thousands at a time, just to preserve Rajput honour and polity. The most successful Hindu revolt against Muslim domination was that of the Marathas, who re-conquered a major part of the country; but their militancy was geared mainly to feudal ends, and, at its best, to some measure of Maratha-cum-Hindu nationalism allied to social reaction.[4]

At a later period, the Pindars overran the country for sheer loot a number of times; but would on each occasion retire to their homes to indulge in sensuous pleasures, and never bothered to carve out a dominion of their own which was within their easy reach. Similarly, the Rajasthan Jats showed exemplary courage and tenacity in defending the Bharatpur fort against Lord Lake, but their militancy either ended, like that of the Satnamis, in sporadic revolts, under Gokala and Raja Ram, against the Mughals, or later served the feudal-cum-dynastic objectives of the Bharatpur principality. None of these militant enterprises even conceive of revolutionary objectives; because non-revolutionary movements are "virtual prisoners of the reigning set of social values, and, therefore, cannot mount a full-scale attack on the institutional systems of stratification that are both cause and effect of these values."[5]

In addition to the "Jat cultural patterns", the second major factor assumed to have prompted a military response in the Sikh movement is the "economic problems." Here, again, the revolutionary character of the Sikh militancy is lost sight of. It is "wrong to assume that the latent conflict produced by the various modes of social stratification will automatically reach revolutionary proportions."[6] Trotsky writes : "In reality, the mere existence of privation is not enough to cause an insurrection; if it were, the masses would always be in revolt."[7] There were always in the French and Russian societies sub-marginally poor people, but the important thing to note is that French history and Russian history are filled with famines, plagues, bad harvests, many of which were accompanied by sporadic rioting, but by only one revolution.[8]

So in India, there was only one plebeian political revolution, the Sikh Revolution; and, quality-wise, it was no less significant. Whereas, none of the English, American or French revolutions "substituted a brand-new ruling class for the old one, at least not unless one thinks of class without bothering about the human beings, who make up the class."[9] "The lowest of low in Indian estimation" shared political power under Banda,[10] and none higher than the Jats (on the border-line of Vaishyas and Sudras), carpenters (Sudras), and distillers (on the border-line of Sudras and outcastes) did so in the *Misl* period. Other Indian peasants, particularly the Jats, were no less subject to the kind of economic, political or social stresses that the Jats of the Sikh tract were, but none of them even conceived, much less attempted, to achieve revolutionary objectives. The nearest approach to a revolutionary movement were the Jat uprisings under Gokala and Raja Ram, and the Satnami revolt, but, these partook the character of sporadic revolts. The fact is that revolutions do not just happen; they are made. And, there are a number of factors which contribute to the making of a revolution, of which we will consider here briefly a few important ones.

2. GOAL, PURPOSE OR STAKES AND IDEOLOGY

A revolution, by its very definition, has to have a stake no less than that of abolishing, or radically reconstructing, one or more of the traditional systems of stratification, based on class, status, or power,[11] in favour of the downtrodden. The last qualification is an overriding one, since any change in the reverse direction becomes counter-revolutionary. As the whole dynamics of a revolutionary movement revolves around its humanitarian motivation and stakes, the foremost question to be probed is the ideological source of such a motivation. About the Sikh ideological stand on this vital issue, there is no ambiguity.

Guru Nanak declared : "Call everyone exalted; let no one appear to thee low."[12] He laid down specifically : "O unwise, be not proud of thy caste. For, a myriad errors flow out of this pride",[13] and identified himself with the lowliest of the low castes. "There are lower castes among the low castes and some absolutely low. Nanak seeketh their company; what hath he to do with the high ones. For, where the lowly are cared for, there is Thine (God's) Benediction and Grace."[14]

The Guru did away with not only 'caste-status' consciousness, but also with the status consciousness gaps of every kind. "To treat the king and the pauper on equal footing, and while greeting to touch the feet of the other (i.e., to regard oneself humble as compared to others) was made the rule of conduct;"[15] because, "He who thinks himself to be the lowest of the lowly; Yes, he alone is the highest of the high."[16] In fact, the Gurus carried their egalitarianism to such an extent that they tried to bridge the gap between the Guru and the disciple. When Guru Nanak appointed Angad as his successor Guru, he literally laid his head on the latter's feet as a mark of paying respect; and Guru Gobind Singh beseeched, with folded hands, the Five Beloved, whom he had initiated earlier, to do him the honour of initiating him. This is the highest limit of humility and egalitarianism to which a religious teacher can go.

This ideology was the motivative fountain-head of the Sikh socio-political revolution. The Jat Theory suggests no alternative source of this ideological inspiration. For one thing, Jats, on their own, have rarely shown any proclivity for idealistic or deeply religious pursuits.[17] "The only distinctive Jat cults are tribal. ...... Among the Hindu and Sikh Jats, especially in the north-central and central districts, a form of ancestor-worship, called *Jathera*, is common."[18] It passes one's comprehension how this ancestor-worship gave rise to the Sikh revolutionary ideology ? Sikhism is against ancestor-worship;[19] therefore, *Jathera* worship could not be reconciled with it.

Nor can the Jat social egalitarianism be equated with the Sikh idea of brotherhood. Jats partake some of the traits of both a tribe and a caste. Their social equality is tribal, confined to their Jat *bhaichara*; and does not extend to castes lower than them. They, whether Hindu, Muslim or Sikh, dominated and exploited the Sudras and the outcastes in their own villages.[20] How did such tribal social exclusiveness square up with or lead to the brotherhood of the Khalsa (drawn from all castes including the Sudra and the outcastes) wherein the spirit of equality was a vital principle, and a Brahmin had no higher claim to eminence than the lowest Sudra who used to sweep his house ?[21]

It is only in the Jat uprisings under Gokal and Raja Ram that we find the Jats motivated by considerations higher than those of personal or tribal gain. Even these outbursts were not based on Jat traits or sentiments, but were born of the wrath directed against the destruction by the Mughals of Hindu temples at Mathura, which outraged the local religious feelings in particular. In any case, these were by no means revolutionary movements. Because, "The essence of revolt is angry, violent expression of the refusal of an individual or group to continue in its present condition....Revolt lives in the immediate; it is in the immediate that it needs someone accountable. ......"[22] "It is the very concreteness and specificity of revolt that prevents it from calling the whole social order in question. It is concerned with men and measures, not with fundamental institution. That is what separates it from revolution."[23] Neither these Jats in revolt challenged the caste social order, nor did they conceive of capturing political power for the masses. On the contrary, a little later they came in handy to Churaman and Suraj Mal, who exploited their restiveness to build the feudal and dynastic principality of Bharatpur.

In short, what the Jat Theory avoids to tackle is the most important issue that mere militancy of any kind, or extreme discontent alone based on economic or social disparities, is not enough to produce a revolution. What is missing is some extra-push of a revolutionary ideology : "a dynamic of a genuinely spiritual and religious kind."[24] "While ideology is not the whole of revolution, it is a characteristic and a partly autonomous part of it."[25] It is the revolutionary ideology that infuses a sense of a universally valid humanitarian purpose and direction to the revoltuionary movement. Revolts and other non-revolutionary upheavels also have some sort of purpose in view, but "the limited stakes and backward glance of revolt are associated with its low level of ideology."[26]

It is obvious that the Sikh revolutionary motivation could not be born of *Jathera* worship or of the tribal equality of the Jats, who on their own, never challenged or opted out of the caste society. Its mainspring was the Sikh view of religion : "Religion consisteth not in mere words; he who looks upon all men as equals is religious."[27] It is this inspiration which alone could unite into a genuine brotherhood of the Khalsa those disparate elements of the caste (drawn from Brahmins and Khatris down to the untouchables), separated by the three tendencies of repulsion, hierarchy and hereditary specialization."[28] The abolition or submergence of narrow sectional interests and sentiments takes place on a mass scale only if these are displaced or overshadowed by shared loyalty to a higher cause. How could the proselytes drawn from disparate, even hostile, castes be welded into the Sikh *Panth* and the Khalsa, with a feeling of oneness and brotherhood, if not by the Sikh faith ? It could not be done on the basis of the tribal and caste loyalties and mores of the Jats.

While ideology is not the whole of revolution, one finds that its other main features also hinge on its ideology, in one form or the other; at least it is so in the case of the Sikh revolutionary movement. Not only have these features of Sikh militancy no link with Jat traits, but they are also unique when considered in the Indian context as a whole. The foremost unique feature is that all other anti-caste movements remained pacific, and not even one conceived of capturing political power by the masses.

3. IDEOLOGY AND LEADERSHIP

The second pre-requisite of a revolution is leadership committed and devoted to its revolutionary goal. As a revolution cannot be conceived without a humanitarian goal, so it cannot be accomplished without a leadership committed and devoted to that ideology. It is the leadership which maintains the purpose and direction of a movement; and leadership and co-ordination form two related aspects of any directed action. Because a revolution has to have a revolutionary goal and direction, it is seldom the product of spontaneous mass upsurge. The risings of the peasants under Gokala and Raja Ram, and that of the Satnamis, which attracted so much attention, illustrate this point. Collective spontaneity is, moreover, not really capable of devising specific forms of revolutionary organization.[29] Without leadership, a revolutionary situation remains an unrealized potential.

It, is, therefore, obvious that the leaders of a revolutionary movement must be conscious of their mission and devoted to it. "Doctrine must subdue spontaneity", wrote Lenin.[30] "What seems to typify a revolution in contrast to revolt is the phenomenon of verbalization and conceptualization in advance it is not a random venture." ...... "In addition to the ideological factor, revolution implies an orientation toward organization and institutionalization."[31]

The role of leadership thus provided another major point of difference between revolutionary and non-revolutionary movements. "It is not that revolts are leaderless, while revolutions are led. All collective violence involves leaders of some sort. The question is rather the role played by the leadership. The leaders of revolts are often skilled tacticians with occasional charismatic qualities. Yet, they are not charged with the inspiration of a higher ideal, which only a clear-cut ideology can provide. The leaders of revolts, therefore, continue to move within a groove determined by their narrow objectives. Without guidelines of an ideology, they cannot see beyond their limited horizons and evolve plans for accomplishing some higher mission."[32] The leaders of a revolution, on the other hand, are ideologically oriented. In fact, they are the products of an ideology. This was one of the reasons why at the time of initiation into the Khalsa, the entrants were made to take solemn vows of *Dharam Nash, Kul Nash,* etc., which cut at the roots of the caste ideology and society. The Sikh militancy was thus wedded to the overthrow of the caste order, in addition to capturing political power for the masses. The Khalsa carried on a life and death guerilla warfare for 30 years, and guerilla warfare "has been ideological from the very outset."[33] A guerilla is "an intensely motivated and highly dedicated soldier who has a keen sense of issues at stake and understands the nature of war he is fighting. His strength lies inside, in the moral considerations, which 'make three-fourths of him.'"[34] And, the final measure of the depth of convictions is martyrdom. The Sikh movement was virtually crushed a number of times,[35] but each time, like the proverbial phoenix, it rose from its ashes.[36] The only thing that sustained the Khalsa was their religious faith. The English ambassadors in Delhi at the time reported to their head that about 750 prisoners were executed alongwith Banda. "It is not a little remarkable with what patience they undergo their fate, and to the last it has not been found that one apostatized from his new found faith.[37]

Forster writes, "Such was the keen spirit that animated the persecution, such was the success of the exertions, that the name of a *sicque* (Sikh) no longer existed in the Mughal dominion. Those who still adhered to the tenets of *Nanoch,* either fled into the mountains at the head of the Punjab, or cut off their hair, and exteriorily renounced the profession of their religion."[38] Who were the steel-frame of the Khalsa struggle ? Those who stuck to their faith and paid a heavy price for it, or those who 'cut off their hair ?' Like the charged (ions) and uncharged atoms of the same element, there were Jats and Jats. Those who were charged by the Sikh ideology played a magnificent role in the Sikh movement, but those who were not, either stayed back or renounced it in adverse circumstances. It is not the Jat traits that changed the character of the Sikh movement; it is the Sikh ideology that transformed the Jats who joined it. Latif writes : "It is acknowledged on all hands that the conversion of a band of undisciplined Jats (given to rapine and plunder or to agricultural pursuits) into a body of conquerors and a political corporation, was entirely due to the genius of *Govind,* whose history is closely interwoven with that of the Sikhs as a nation."[39]

It has to be made clear that we are concerned only with the Sikh revolutionary movement; because, the fallacy of those, who argue that the militarization of the Sikh movement was initiated and reinforced by the influx into it of a large number of Jats, arises in no small measure from their failure to distinguish between the revolutionary and post-revolutionary phases of the movement. They seem to judge the former in the light of the latter. There is a world of difference between the Jats who joined the Sikh movement, under the inspiration of the Sikh ideology and made an outstanding contribution to its struggle, and those who did not; or between the behaviour patterns of the same group, whether Jat or non-Jat, when, at different periods, it had the ideological inspiration and when it lost it. We have purposely quoted, here and there, eminent scholars of political science to substantiate our argument that the differences between the characteristics of revolutionary and non-revolutionary movements (and for that matter between those of the two such phases of the same movement) "are qualitative, marked by differences in kind, not just in amount."[40] In the revolutionary phase of a movement, the primary and dominant factor is its ideological content and not its ethnic composition. Without the ideological surcharge, inspiration and direction, how helpless or rudderless the peasants the world over, or the Jats in India (or for that matter the other downtrodden sections of society), have been, is writ large on the pages of history.

It has been a consistent fact of history that none of the revolutions have been initiated or led by the downtrodden themselves in whose favour the abolition or reconstruction of stratification took place. The French Revolution formally liberated the peasants from feudalism, but it was the middleclass which dominated the revolution, and the peasantry played only a secondary role limited to localized action against landlords. One of the main reasons for the failure of the German Peasant Wars, stated by Engels, is that these peasants were not indoctrinated enough, with the result that the bulk of the peasants were always ready to come to terms with the lords who exploited this weakness of theirs,[41] and were also readily demoralized when they met a strong resistance or a reverse.[42] About the Russian Revolution, Lenin observes : "While workers left to their own devices could only develop trade union consciousness and peasants only petty bourgeois demands for land, it would be the guiding intellectuals who would lead the revolution on behalf of the workers and the peasants."[43] Marx likens the peasants to a bag of potatoes. All the leaders of the Chinese Communist Party, which led the Communist Revolution in China, had higher education and most of them had studied abroad.[44] Troong Chinh points out that the great majority of the cadres and the militants in the Communist Party of the revolutionary period of Vietnam originated in the petty bourgeoisie.[45] Similarly, the Cuban Revolution was a great gamble by a group of determined, educated revolutionaries which paid off.[46]

Therefore, what is crucial to movements, besides the role of ideology, is initiative and leadership. It is the existence of a revolutionary purpose and direction, which ideology and leadership provide, that distinguishes a revolution from a mere riot or revolt. A very glaring example, which clarifies the distinction between revolution and revolt, is the well-known rebellion of the Gladiators. The capital of Rome lay at their feet, but they did not occupy it because they did not know what to do with it. As regards peasants, Eric R.Wolf gives weighty reasons for his conclusion that, "The peasant is especially handicapped in passing from passive recognition of wrongs to political participation as a means of setting them right."[47] The Jats form the majority in Sindh, and are approximately equal to the number of Rajputs in Bikaner, Jaiselmer and Marwar. They are three times more than the Rajputs in the Punjab (inclusive that of Pakistan), yet only fragmentary notices of the Jats occur in the accounts of Mohammadan historians, whereas the pages of Indian history are full of Rajput exploits. It could only be because the Jats were politically inconsequential.

It has got, therefore, to be explained : how the Jats of the Punjab, who dominated and exploited the Sudras and the outcastes in their own villages,[48] initiated and developed the militarization of a movement, whose political stake, as made explicit by Guru Hargobind to Samarath Ramdas, was to protect the poor; a movement which did not serve sectional interests, Jat or non-Jat; a movement which was not clannish, regional, feudal or dynastic; a movement which strove to capture political power by the Khalsa, a militant brotherhood drawn from all castes without discrimination ? It was for this purpose that the Guru *Panth* was placed subordinate to Guru Granth Sahib. How does all this fit in with the tribal egalitarianism of the Jats ? The problem is not as simple as that of merely identifying the ethnic composition and traits of the participants. Unless it is established, to what extent, and in what manner, the Jat character and mores moulded the ideology, leadership and organization of the Sikh revolutionary movement to their own pattern, it leads nowhere. Because, as we know, the Sikh ideology was laid down by Guru Nanak and never changed even by the succeeding Gurus. The leadership of the movement remained in the Gurus' hands during their lifetimes, devolving afterwards on the whole *Panth* (Guru *Panth*) as a corporate body. And, the organizational institutions of the *Panth* like *sangat*, Khalsa, *Panj Piaras, Dals* and *Sarbat Khalsa*, etc., do not bear the remotest resemblance to the Jat *gotras* and *Khaps*.

4. OTHER FEATURES

Two other features of a revolutionary movement, though related to the roles that ideology and leadership play, are mentioned here separately, because these serve to distinguish it from non-revolutionary upheavals.

"Revolution begins with an idea. It is specifically the infusion of an idea into a historical situation, whereas revolt is simply a movement leading from individual experience to an idea."[49] "A revolt does not have any idea (*pensee*) at the origin; it is visceral, immediate. A revolution implies a doctrine, a project, some kind of theory. ...... An idea may be expressed occasionally in the course of revolt, but is always incidental and emerges from the developing revolt itself."[50]

The Sikh movement began with an ideal. To be precise, Sikh humanitarianism was born of the deep religious experience of the founder guru, Guru Nanak, whose very first expression of his experience was that, "There is no Hindu, no Mussalman" (i.e., humanity is one). Further, as already seen, he identified himself with the lowest of the low castes.

Secondly, a revolutionary movement is not a chance development or a sporadic phenomenon. Not only has it a definite revolutionary goal or purpose, but it is a sustained movement with a fixed direction towards the achievement of that goal. "It is the goal of a movement that fixed its direction, and it is the existence of direction. ...... that makes revolution a political act and distinguishes it from riot."[51] And, it goes without saying that it is the quality of leadership committed and devoted to the goal which maintains the direction of a revolutionary movement. The very fact that the Sikh movement succeeded in establishing an egalitarian casteless *Panth* and in capturing political power for the masses, as a result of a long period of protracted armed struggle, is in itself a strong proof that it did not swerve from its revolutionary purpose or direction. One major contributory factor to this end was that it was loyalty to the principles of the movement, and not to individuals or groups, that was stressed. The *Tat Khalsa* did not hesitate to part company with Banda when he showed an inclination towards deviation from the democratic principles of the Khalsa. Even at a later period, although they were struggling for their very survival, the leaders of the *misls* spurned Abdali's several offers of negotiated settlement, and preferred that the Khalsa should capture political power in its own right.

How is this loyalty to a higher mission related to Jat character and traits ? And, where elsewhere, is a similar tenacity of purpose over a long period shown by Jats, as such ?

5. SIKH IDEOLOGY AND SIKH MILITANCY*

It is a historical reality that entrenched systems of stratification might be amenable to reform, but would not surrender without an armed struggle when their very existence is at stake. As all social, political or economic systems get entrenched, in the last analysis, on the basis of political and military sanctions, a revolution necessarily involves an armed struggle, especially when the system concerned is sought to be abolished within a short time. "Finally, our definition of revolution considers recourse to violence as essential rather than accidental to it. The magnitude and the abruptness of change involved in revolution always produces violence in some form. Revolution must be distinguished from reform, however radical, and from long-term evolutionary development such as the so-called industrial revolution and the growth of certain religious movements. The factor of violence helps to do this."[52]

Thus, the militarization of the Sikh movement was not accidental, but was an essential part of its development, because, "The issue of subordination is more pervasive than that of exploitation...[53] Therefore, to undo subordination to the Mughals, an armed struggle was indispensable. But, what made it doubly necessary was that the goal of the Khalsa armed struggle was to capture political power for the masses themselves.

What is, however, not generally appreciated is that the Sikh militancy was equally necessary for bringing about the Sikh social revolution, because even a social radical change cannot have a permanent footing without a corresponding political change. "In character and position there is nothing to distinguish the tribes I am about to notice, save that they have never enjoyed the political importance which distinguished the Sikh Jats under the Khalsa. ...... In the Sikh tract, the political position of the Jat was so high that he had no wish to be called Rajput; under the hills (i.e., adjoining the Sikh tract), the status of the Rajput is so superior that the Jat has no hope of being called Rajput."[54] How is it that the Ramgarhias (artisans) have come to regard themselves as peers to the Sikh Jats, and the Ahluwalias have raised their social status to be equal to that of Khatris and Brahmins, from that of distillers in the caste society (on the border-line of the Sudras and the outcastes), if not for having tasted political power by establishing their own *misl* ? It is again the legacy of the Sikh Raj that Sikhs derived from all castes are addressed by non-Sikhs as *Sardars* even to this day. In fact, the probability is that the Sikhs would have been engulfed by the caste society in the same manner as the other radical anti-caste

---

* The term ideology is used here in a restrictive sense to denote such an integrated system of ideals and values, allied to corresponding sentiments, as plays a positive role in the formulation and furtherance of a humanitarian purpose.

movements were, had not the Khalsa established its political sway. In short, it is political power which lends permanence to a radical social change;[55] and political power for a revolutionary purpose can neither be gained nor retained without armed might.

Sikh Values and Militancy : Sikh militancy was in no way linked to ethnic, sectional, regional, dynastic or fedual interests. While ethnic or group mores might help or retard a revolutionary process, revolutionary movements are mothered only by revolutionary ideologies and values which clash with the prevailing unjust social and political order. This clash was inherent in Guru Nanak's declaration :

"The kings are like leopards, the courtiers like dogs;
    Kings's servants tear (the docile subjects) with their nails;
    And, like curs, lick up all the blood they spill."[56]

Guru Arjan wrote :

"The bear that vents his wrath on the poor of the world,
    Is burnt in the fire by the Transendent Lord."[57]

Again :

"Power swells our heads and we tyrannize over others. ......"[58]

The Sikh view of religion does not permit any dichotomy in life, or of any divorce of the individual from his society. Nor does it visualize that true religion and morality can operate unconcerned beside an unjust social and political order; nor that spiritual freedom can co-exist with religious dictation and political slavery. A Sikh has to take up all the challenges which are irreligious and unethical; there cannot be a neutral position.

As stated earlier, no system of stratification has been known to yield without an armed conflict when its very existence is at stake. Hence, an armed struggle is inherent in those values which challenge stratification, provided those are pursued to their logical end. The modalities of this clash, of course, depend upon the circumstances. Guru Arjun could have saved his life by allowing his followers to pay the fine imposed on him, but he preferred, as he told Saint Mian Mir, to suffer torture and death rather than forsake a principle.

Ahimsa : This clash of values with the status-quo was inherent also in Christianity when Christ declared that a rich man could not enter heaven, and in Buddhism when it discarded status based on birth. But, the odium that somehow came to be attached to the use of force even for a just and noble cause proved a great hurdle in their way to taking to the revolutionary path. Sikhism had no such problem, because Guru Nanak, in a long hymn, emphasizes that no life process or animal life is possible without the use of flesh in one form or the other. He points out the fallacy of those who make a fetish of eating meat, but have no scruples in 'devouring' (exploiting) men.[59] God is : "Destroyer of the tyrant and benefactor of the downtrodden."[60]

Miri-Piri : It was Guru Arjun who instructed Guru Hargobind to take up arms when he felt that that was the only alternative to surrendering faith. The very first act of Guru Hargobind, when he initiated the militarization of the Sikhs, was to don two swords, which he specifically called of *miri* and *piri*, one symbolizing temporal authority and the other religious authority. In this manner, Sikh militancy began in pursuance of the concept of combining temporal and religious realms. At that very time two separate flags were also hoisted, side by side, to emphasise the confluence of the two principles. It was, again Guru Hargobind who explained to Samarath Ramdas (believed to be Shivaji's preceptor) that his sword was meant 'for the protection of the poor !'[61] This is how the seeds of the Sikh military struggle were sown. The naming of the headquarters of the Sikh militant movement as Akal Takht (the throne of God), too, meant that Sikh militancy was from its very inception linked to an eternal (*Akal*) universal principle and a moral cause. The creation of the Khalsa was a continuation of the ideological line of *miri-piri*, and "*Waheguru ji ka Khalsa and Waheguru ji ki Fateh*" was a continuation of the concept of Akal Takht. In this manner, the Sikh revolutionary militancy was wedded all along to an eternal principle embodying a humanitarian cause.

Soldier-Saints : The use of force becomes essential rather than accidental to a revolution, but misdirected and uncontrolled violence tends to destroy the community itself. As Camus has put it : "Absolute non-violence is negative basis of slavery and its acts of violence; systematic violence positively destroys the living community and the existence we receive from it. To be fruitful, these two ideas must establish their limits."[62]

Guru Gobind Singh wrote to Aurangzeb, 'when other means fail it is legitimate to have recourse to the sword.'[63] Qazi Nurud-Din testifies that the Sikhs would not strike at an enemy who laid down arms or fled from the battlefield.[64] The Mohammadan author of *Fatuhat Nama-i-Samdi* corroborates that, "if a woman falls into their hands (i.e., of the Khalsa), they look upon her as their mother."[65] Polier writes of the *misl* period that, "it is true they seldom kill in cold blood or make slaves."[66] Griffin opines that, "There are few stories in Sikh history of outrage to women and torture to men such as stain the pages of Indian history.."[67]

It is not at all suggested that the Sikh movement achieved or maintained that desired optimum balance. In fact, it is problematical whether or not humanity would be able to achieve such a target in the forseeable future. What is pertinent here is that : (i) the Sikh movement made a serious effort in this direction, even in the face of barbaric tortures to which they were subjected by the Mughals; (ii) this standard of Sikh conduct was not incidental. During their struggle, the Sikhs made the maintenance of ethical standards an integral part of their militant programme; because, the Gurus had laid down the ideal : "To exercise forbearance in the midst of power; to be humble in the midst of honour;"[68] (iii) the Sikh conduct as exhibited, could not be born of the mores of Jats who were given to 'rapine and plunder', and who were notoriously lax in those very qualities[69] for which the Qazi and others have praised the Sikhs.

6. CONCLUSION

The significance of the militancy of any mass movement cannot be grasped by divorcing it from the purpose to which it is yoked; but, the Jat Theory ignores altogether the motivational gap between an ideological struggle and the one for power, or the demarcation between the behaviour of the same individuals or groups, when they are charged and when not charged by a religio-moral ideology. The Jat Theory does not even attempt to explain how the prowess of Jats, left to their tribal mores, led to the Sikh political revolution in which political power was shared by Sudras and distillers; or how Jat cultural traits gave rise to such concepts as *Sache Patshah, Miri-Piri, Akal Takht, Waheguru ji ka Khalsa and Fateh* ? Nor does it explain as to what was the need of creating the Khalsa at all. Unless these questions, and other related ones, are answered, no conclusion would be logical or valid.

Brinton, who has studied in depth the English, American, French and Russian revolutions, has shown that revolutionary movements, while they last, rise above the mundane interests and normal mores of the participants.[70] Therefore, the postulate "that if a distinctive social group secures dominant status within a particular society it will inevitably exercise upon that society an influence which reflects its own mores,"[71] is not valid for the revolutionary period of the Sikh movement atleast. As it is accepted that "the sanctified will of the Guru was beyond challenge,"[72] why could the Sikh ideology and faith not be the driving force of the Sikh struggle and movement in following the course chartered for them by the Guru ? In fact, Le Bon has shown that : "Among the most important factors of history one was predominant. ...... the factor of belief."[73]

REFERENCES

1. E. Schomer and W.H. McLeod : *The Saints*, p. 240.
2. Mark N. Hagopian : *The Phenomenon of Revolution*, p. 10.
3. Ellul, Jacques : *Autopsy of Revolution*, pp. 43-44.
4. "It is recorded that under the rule of the Marathas and the Peshwas, the Mahars and Mongs were not allowed within the gates of Poona after 3 p.m. and before 9 a.m. ......" (Ghurye, G.S. : *Caste & Race in India*, p. 11).
5. Hagopian : op. cit., pp. 10-11.
6. Ibid., p. 99.
7. Quoted by Brinton, Crane : *The Anatomy of Revolution*, p. 34.
8. Ibid., p. 34.
9. Ibid., p. 270.
10. Irvine, William : *Later Mughals*, I, pp. 98-99.
11. Hagopian : op. cit., pp. 10-11.
12. Macauliffe, Max Arthur : *The Sikh Religion*, I, p. 274.
13. Guru Granth Sahib : p. 1128.
14. Ibid., p. 15.
15. Bhai Gurdas : *Var* One, *Pauries* 23, 25, *Var* 23, *Pauri* 20.
16. Guru Granth Sahib : p. 266.
17. Crooke, W. : *The N.W. Provinces of India*, etc., p. 93; *Jallandur Distt. Gazetteer* (1904), part A, p. 721; *Gurgaon Distt : Gazetteer* (1883-4), p. 41.
18. Rose, H.A. : *A Glossary of Tribes*, etc., II. p. 371.
19. Guru Granth Sahib : p. 332.
20. Crook, W. : op. cit. pp. 206, 244; *Settlement Report*, Ludhiana Distt. (1978-83); *Census Report* (1891), p. 202; Rose, III, p.75.
21. Malcolm, Brigadier General : *Asiatic Researches* (1812), pp. 219, 292.
22. Ellul, Jacques : *Autopsy of Revolution*, p. 27.
23. Hagopian : op. cit., pp. 10-11.
24. Edwards, L.P. : *The Natural History of Revolution*, p. 90.

25. Hagopian : op. cit., p. 280.
26. Ibid., p. 12.
27. Macauliffe, Max Arthur : op. cit. i, p. 60.
28. Celestin Bongle : *Essays on the Caste System* (trans. D.F. Peacock), p. 9.
29. Hagopian : op. cit., p. 2.
30. Quoted by Ellul : op. cit., p. 124.
31. Ellul : op. cit., pp. 47, 49.
32. Hagopian : op. cit., pp. 12-13.
33. Malik Arjan Das : *An Indian Guerilla War*, pp. 2-3.
34. Ibid., p. 3.
35. *Calendar of Persian Correspondence*, Vol. II, p. 85; Malcolm : op. cit., p. 246; Forster, I, pp. 312-3;
Polier, *Panjab Past & Present*, Oct. 1970, p. 237.
36. Malcolm : op.cit. (1812), pp. 246-7,
37. Ganda Singh : *Early European Accounts of the Sikhs*, p. 188.
38. Forster, George : *A Journey from Bengal to England*, Vol. I, pp. 312-13.
39. Syed Muhammad Latif : *History of the Punjab*, p. 271.
40. Hagopian : op. cit., p. 10; Brinton, Chap. VII.
41. Frederic Engels : *The Peasant War in Germany*, pp. 101, 102, 129.
42. Ibid., pp. 100-101, 105-6, 108.
43. Quoted by Eric R. Wolf : *Peasant Wars of the Twentieth Century*, p. 83.
44. Ibid., p. 150.
45. Ibid., p. 185.
46. Ibid., p. 269.
47. Ibid., pp. 289-90.
48. Crooke, W. : op. cit., pp. 206, 244; *Census Report* (1891), p. 202; Rose, III, p. 75.
49. Camus, Albert : *The Rebel*, p. 77.
50. Ellul : op. cit., pp. 43-44.
51. Peter Calvert : *A Study of Revolution*, p. 97.
52. Hagopian : op. cit., p. 3.
53. Bernard de Jouvenal cited by Ellul : op. cit., p. 108.
54. Ibbetson, Sir Denzil : *Punjab Castes*, sec 437.
55. Hagopian : op. cit., p. 51.
56. Guru Granth Sahib : op. cit., p. 1288.
57. Ibid., p. 199.
58. Ibid., p. 255.
59. Ibid., pp. 1289-90.
60. *Jap*.
61. Ganda Singh : *The Panjab Past & Present* (April 1979), pp. 240-42.
62. Camus : op. cit., p. 255.
63. *Zafarnama*.
64. *Jangnamah*, cited by Hari Ram Gupta : *History of the Sikhs*, I, p. 290.
65. Cited by Gurbax Singh : Punjab History Conference Proceedings (Sept. 1972), p. 50.
66. Ganda Singh : *Early European Accounts of the Sikhs*, p. 197.
67. Griffin, Lepel : *Rajas of the Punjab*, p. 17.
68. Guru Granth Sahib : p. 85.
69. Ibbetson : *Punjab Castes*, sec. 424; *Gazetteer of Lahore Distt.* (1883-84), pp. 66-68.
70. Brinton : op. cit., Chapter VII;
71. E. Schomer and W.H. McLeod : op. cit. p. 242.
72. Ibid., p. 244.
73. Le Bon Gustave : *The Psychology of Revolution*, p. 14.

SIKHISM AND TEMPORAL AUTHORITY

Sikhism is a whole-life religion laying emphasis on discharging one's socio-moral responsibilities as a part of the spiritual progress of the individual. Since the former cannot be performed without, at times, confrontation with an unjust termporal authority, such activity and pursuits have always been considered a legitimate and vital function of a Sikh and Sikh society. In short, Sikhism is a *miri-piri* or a *sant-sipahi* religious system. This conviction is so deep-rooted among the masses, that any argument in its support or justification would appear wholly superfluous. This is evidenced and clear from the following couplet which is a part of the litany sung by every Sikh at all congregational prayers for the last three centuries :

"*Raj Karega Khalsa, aki rahe na koe*;
Khwar hoe sabh milenge, bache sharan jo hoe."[1]

This slogan has constantly reminded the followers of the Gurus of their social commitment, and has inspired Sikhs all through their history to struggle against injustice and oppression, and to make extreme sacrifices, unparalleled in history for the cause of bringing about a humanitarian socio-political order, based on equality and justice, as preached by the Gurus.

Yet, occasionally a voice to the contrary is heard. From a non-Sikh, it could be understood, and even partly appreciated as an expression of concern over the seeming threat to his sovereignty, although, as would be explained later, it cannot be justified. But, when the objection issues from a member of the Sikh community itself, it questions the very philosophy of Sikhism, expressed through the doctrine of *miri-piri*, preached by Guru Nanak, symbolised by Guru Hargobind in two swords, and enjoined upon the Khalsa as a creed to be practised, by the Tenth Master. The opposition to investing the Khalsa with any degree of temporal involvement, springs from the alleged desire of the critics to prevent the "pure stream of religion" from entering into the "muddy waters of politics", borrowing the phrases from Jadu Nath Sarcar. There are a large number of hymns in the Guru Granth Sahib, emphasising merit of *Naam*, out of which they pick up a few, and misinterpret them to support their stand. They forget that Sikhism is not a personal salvation religion, and that, apart from *Naam simran*, *Gurbani* lays repeated stress on deeds and service to mankind. A few isolated incidents from history are sometimes picked up to show that the Gurus never approved of setting up a state for their followers. It is further argued that since the Gurus did not carve out any empire for themselves, they deprecated any such move for the Sikhs also. On the basis of such arguments, although with different motives, some of the critics have even expressed the view that the couplet *"Raj Karega Khalsa ......"* should be excluded from the litany sung by every Sikh, *sahjdhari* or *keshdhari*, ever since the creation of the Khalsa.

Their advice is that "Politics must be insulated from religion." Some even go to the extent of saying that any struggle for an honourable political status for the Sikhs or to ensure their identity, is against the teachings of the Gurus, and should, therefore, be eschewed. Impression is sought to be created that the Sikh Gurus preached a religion of 'interiority' aimed at personal salvation only, and that worldly pursuits, particularly temporal powers, are a taboo, to be abjured by the Sikhs. Such a view, unless contradicted, could mislead an unwary reader. Hence, the following discussion.

Late Sirdar Kapur Singh, the erudite Sikh scholar, has referred to the slogan *"Raj Karega Khalsa ......"*, and its opponents' reaction in the following words :

> "The startlingly tall and audacious claim, has been publicly proclaimed by the Sikh people during the last three centuries firmly and defiantly, and it has moved many to sheer ridicule, others to resentment and boiling-head anger, many Sikhs themselves to chicken-hearted, craven fear or shameless apologia, and the political Hindus of the post-1947 euphoria. It has, almost invariably moved them to greater contempt for those, whom they see as already in their last death-throes."[2]

Before dealing with the criticism, it seems necessary to understand the meaning of the couplet *"Raj Karega Khalsa ......"*, its origin and role in history. Since it pronounces a clear-cut position on the issue of temporal authority. Freely rendered into English, it would mean :

> "The Khalsa shall exercise temporal authority,
> unchallenged; Eventually everyone will accept this
> position, and whoever seeks, shall get protection."

According to tradition, the couplet first followed from the *Tankhahnama* of Bhai Nand Lal, whose *Granthavali*, collected from his family records, was edited by Dr Ganda Singh, the eminent Sikh historian. This Question-Answer series also records the words of Guru Gobind Singh, "Listen, Nand Lal to this truth — the revelation of sovereign rule." "(*Sune* Nand Lal *eho sach* : *Pargat Karoon apna Raj*"). On the same page after the above statement appears this couplet "Raj Karega Khalsa ......"[1] which had already become a part of the Sikh prayer by the time of Banda Singh's expedition to Sirhind. With this slogan, and the blessings of the Guru that went with it, Banda Singh succeeded in the mission entrusted to him by the Guru, capturing Sirhind, and established the

Khalsa Government in 1710 A.D., within two years of the demise of Guru Gobind Singh.

Three historical episodes recorded by Rattan Singh Bhangoo in his epic work *Sri Guru Panth Parkash* throw a flood of light on, and testifty to, the conviction of the Sikhs regarding bestowal of sovereignty on the Khalsa by the Guru, and its inevitability.

1.   Nawab Aslam Khan of Lahore, sent his emissary, Subegh Singh, to the Khalsa for peace, offering Nawabship. The title was offered to Darbara Singh, whose reaction, as recorded by Bhangoo, was : "When did we ask for it ? The Satguru has promised us Sovereign Rule. In comparison to that, the title of Nawab appears to be a lump of clay. We claim Sovereignty, which is sure to come sooner or later. What the Satguru has promised, is bound to materialise. The Guru's word can never go unfulfilled, although *Dhruva* (the Pole Star) or the *Dhawal* (the legendary Bull supporting the Earth on its horns), may shift their positions. How can we exchange our sovereignty with this insignificant title of *Nawab* ? Accursed be the servility." Similarly, a number of other Sikhs refused the title, adding, "How can sovereignty be had by begging ?"[3]

2.   Captain Murray, Charge-de-Affairs of the East India Company at Ludhiana, was obsessed with the question of the legitimacy of the Sikh Rule. He had a dialouge with the author of the *Panth Parkash* himself, which is recorded as follows :

"Murray :   Explain to me how the Sikhs attained power, and who gave them sovereignty.

Answer :   Sovereignty was bestowed upon the Khalsa by the True Lord.

Murray :   Who is the True Lord ?

Answer :   He is Satguru Nanak."[4]

3.   According to a government proclamation, in the 18th Century, Sikhs had been completely exterminated. No Sikh had been seen for four months. When Bota Singh was noticed by some people, they were surprised. Their remarks were : "How could it be that a Sikh has survived ?" "He must be an impostor. Sikhs have all been done to death." "He must be a coward, a bogus Sikh who saved himself by hiding, for, a Khalsa is one who is never afraid of death, and is ever ready to stake his head in battle." When Bota Singh heard this, he was dumb-founded. The remarks had stung him like a scorpion. He decided "the situation demands sacrifice of my head in a battle. That is the only way to give a lie to the claim of the Mughals regarding extermination of the Sikhs. Then only, will people talk of the Khalsa who have always claimed sovereignty."[5] What followed is history. Bhai Bota Singh challenged the Imperial authority, proclaimed the Khalsa rule, and started collecting toll, assisted by a single Ranghreta associate. Eventually, they both laid down their lives, fighting the Imperial forces. The thing to note in this account is the motivation of a common Sikh during that period to make the supreme sacrifice in defence of the claim to sovereignty.

From the above, it is clear that during their struggle with the Mughal Rulers, in the eighteenth century, the Sikhs had no doubt about the social goal of bringing about a revolution and the political goal of their sovereignty which are expressed in the couplet *Raj Karega Khalsa*. No body, Hindu or Sikh, ever objected to the singing of this couplet during that period, or even long after that. In fact, earlier, Hindus also supported this. Reaction changed only with the transfer of Power.

Dr Ganda Singh wrote a brief scholarly article on this subject, which appeared in the Sikh Review of July, 1987. He deprecated some of the earlier attempts to twist the meaning of the couplet *Raj Karega Khalsa* thus :

"The dread of Feringees suggested to some of the loyalists, afraid of being listed as rebels, a compromise in giving to the word 'Khalsa' an alternate meaning as 'pure.' They wished to convey to the new rulers that the Khalsa had then no political ambitions or aspirations to rule in the country, and that the couplet, appended to their prayer, only meant that the 'Pure' shall rule."

His conclusion was that the couplet "is a permanent and inseparable part of the Sikh prayer, and should be recited as such on all occasions of prayer by all Sikhs and Sikh congregations, wherever they might be, and in all Gurdwaras, historical or others."[6]

Motives like the ones indicated by Dr Ganda Singh, continue, and so do, therefore, the controversy and effort to misinterpret *Gurbani* and Sikh history, to suit the particular view. The basic question is as to what is the Sikh ideology, or what the Gurus had been aiming at. Is Sikhism a church of worship alone ? Or is it a church of social policy also ? This is a fundamental question. It is the difference on this issue that leads to misconception, especially in the interpretation of history. Picking up a few isolated incidents from a history of two centuries, and trying to relate them to a hymn or two from the *bani*, without regard to the total ideology of the Gurus and their lives, can yield only half truths and wrong conclusions.

Sikhism is not an extension of the *'Bhakti* Movement', nor were the Gurus merely *Bhakti* Saints, who started their own cult. Sikhism is a revealed religion and a mission, indeed the only whole-life religion or *miri-piri* system, native to India. Outside India also, except Judaism and Islam, no whole-life system combining spiritual and empirical life, has arisen. It is not an accident that the last five out of ten Gurus, maintained an army, and the Fifth Guru created a 'state within a state', much to the annoyance of the Emperor of the day, who later ordered his execution. It is Guru Nanak who calls God 'Destroyer of the evil-doers and the demonical.' Again in *Babar Vani,* he unambiguously states that oppression of the weak is violative of the order of the Lord, and that the rulers are responsible to see that they are not oppressed. This would mean that *gurmukh* who is committed to carry out the Will of God, must work for the creation of a society, in which aggression, oppression and injustice are eliminated. This is a requirement in all whole-life religions. Thus, social responsibility extends to the political field as well.

It is undeniable that the rulers have to ensure justice among their subjects, and that it is righteous to confront oppression and injustice. Also, when kings or rulers fail to be virtuous, injustice and oppression are invariably the result. To fight these evils, for over a hundered years, the Sikh Gurus maintained an army, for which purpose initially even mercenaries had to be employed. This militarisation was progressive, until the Tenth Guru created the Khalsa on *Vaisakhi* Day, 1699, and prescribed the *kirpan* as one of the five *Kakars*. It is important to understand that in a whole-life system, monasticism, asceticism, celibacy, *ahimsa*, pacificism, and all kinds of negativism, are rejected. This is a common characteristic of all whole-life systems, and these fundamentals explain why this category of systems accepts socio-political responsibility, and others do not. The *kirpan*, it has to be understood, is not just a symbol; it is a *hukumnama*, emphasizing two things, viz., that the Sikh society is both permitted and enjoined upon to use force as a last resort, for a righteous cause, and second, that Sikhism should never turn monastic or resort to withdrawal. The *kirpan* as a weapon, may not be of much public use today, but the injunction it represents, is fundamental and eternal.

Pleading against Political activities, a writer recently said, "They (The Gurus) were ready to take to the sword, but always in self-defence, and only as a last resort. For the *zulum* (tyranny) of the Governor of Sirhind, Guru Gobind Singh tried to seek redressal from Aurangzeb and Bahadur Shah, and waited for four long years before sending Banda Bahadur to punish the culprits and transgressors. It is also significant that when Banda Bahadur started establishing a State with the help of the Khalsa, a *hukamnama* was issued by Mata Sundri asking the Khalsa to disassociate themselves from the objective, which did not have the approval of the Tenth Guru, and they did so, which led to the defeat of Banda Bahadur."[7]

The first point is what was the *zulum* that the Governor of Sirhind had committed. Was it during the general course of administration over the years he had done it, or was there any specific act that was wrong or tyrannical ? So far as the general administration of the Governor is concerned, there is nothing to suggest that he did anything in violation of the orders or wishes of the Emperor in Delhi. In any case, there is nothing known to have happened to which the Emperor could have taken offence, as being contrary to his instructions, or for which only the Governor was responsible, and not the Emperor. If, however, the reference is to martyrdom of the two younger *Sahibzadas*, we wonder if this could be the real or even a laudable reason, for the Guru to depute Banda Singh Bahadur. Is it the writer's suggestion that while there was nothing wrong with the administration of the Emperor or the Governor, it was only the execution of the two *Sahibzadas* that furnished a good reason to the Tenth Guru to seek revenge by directing Banda and the Sikh armies to do so ? Also, can we accept the suggestion that the Gurus who were always the first to sacrifice their person, would, in this case, seek revenge ? For, we know full well that no military reaction was made after the martyrdom of the Ninth Guru, except the general preparation for confrontation with the empire or the establishment as a whole, for its misrule over the decades. The Tenth Guru could not be unaware that the attack on the Governor meant full scale war involving the death of thousands of Sikhs as well as their opponents. Is it suggested that revenge, involving death and devastation on such a vast scale, was justifiable ? And if that had really been the reason, would it serve as a good moral precedent or lesson for the Sikhs or the people ? Further, even assuming that only the Governor was to be punished, the Tenth Guru knew that it could not be accomplished without a major war, in which the Emperor at Delhi would not remain unconcerned. And in the event of Banda's victory and death of the Governor and other transgressors, to whom was the rule of Sirhind to be handed over ?

It is known to every historian that one of the greatest humanitarian acts of the Sikh rule, was Banda's distribution of land among the poorest tillers. It was he who created "The Bold Peasantry" which continues to be the backbone and the fundamental strength of the Punjab and the Sikh society. It is on the basis of this precedent and tradition that, when the British Government wanted to turn the clock of socialisation back, by granting only tenancy rights to settlers in the new Canal Colonies of the Punjab, that Sikhs and others agitated and forced the Government to confer proprietory rights on them. Against this, it may be recalled that Martin Luther, the great Christian reformer, called the peasants 'mad dogs', when they agitated for their rights against the princes with whom he had sided. Equally significant is the fact that, in the French Revolution, which took place eight decades after Banda, the peasants and the poor, or the Fourth Estate, had no place in the leadership, which rested with the privileged middle classes. Nor were they among its beneficiaries. Jagjit Singh in his book, *In the Caravan of Revolutions* has made a detailed comparison of the work of the Sikh Gurus with the French Revolution, and has shown convincingly that the characteristics, ideals and achievements of the Sikh Revolution, were in every respect, superior to, and more enduring than those of the French Revolution.[8]

Now let us consider the alleged *hukamnama* issued by Mata Sundri asking the Khalsa "to disassociate themselves from the objective which did not have the approval of the Tenth Guru." It has been difficult for us to locate the *hukamnama* of Mata Sundri, referred to in the above quotation. According to Dr Ganda Singh, three writers have narrated the role of Banda Singh Bahadur, namely, Chhibar, Sarup Dass Bhalla, and Rattan Singh Bhangoo. The first two make no mention of the *hukamnama*. In Bhangoo's *Panth Parkash,* there is a brief reference to the letter, said to have been written by Mata Sundri to the Khalsa. In that letter, there is nothing to suggest that the objectives of the attack by Banda Singh, excluded establishment of Khalsa rule in the land, or that the Khalsa was forbidden to rule. In fact, on the contrary, there is a clear statement that the Guru had bestowed *Patshahi* (Rule or Sovereignty) on the *Panth* and not on any individual. Thus, the letter, by implication and otherwise, far from denouncing the objective of temporal sovereignty, clearly records in the words of Mata Sundri, that *Patshahi* was granted to the Sikhs (*Banda Ko Khijmat dei, dei patshahi nahei. Dei patshahi Panth nij, aap Sache Patshah.*)[9]

The above, we feel, explains, both the reason for the Tenth Master's deputing Banda Singh, and the letter written by Mata Sundri to clarify that objective.

The writing of Tamur Shah should also be revealing to everyone. He says that the Emperor conveyed to the 'Apostle of Tranquility and Harmony', the Ninth Guru, that if he desisted from political activities, and confined himself only to spiritual prayers and preaching, he would have no trouble, and, in fact, would be given considerable grants.[10] But, the offer was spurned, with results that are a part of history. Quoting Ghulam

Hussain Khan in *Siyarul Mutakharin*, Sher Singh concludes that there were clear apprehensions of revolt by the Guru, which would lead to the setting up of a Sikh State within the State.[11] Further, quoting *Hiqiqat-i-Bina uruj-i-firqa-i-sikhan* he states that the Emperor feared that the people gathering around Guru Tegh Bahadur, were emerging as a "new nation" (*Millat-i-nau*).[12]

The unfortunate part is that often persons conditioned by pacificist influences, fail to understand the Saint-Soldier concept. The Ninth Guru embodied it as much as the Tenth Guru. The establishment has generally used aggression and oppresssion as the means to perpetuate its power, and the Saint-Soldier, as the instrument of God's Will, must inevitably come into clash with it. This is the eternal equation. For, 'the earth belonging to the 'Saint', is being usurped by robbers.' Hence, the struggle for its liberation. The lesson of history is that the series of martyrdoms initiated by the Fifth Guru, the Ninth Guru, the *Sahibzadas*, and the Tenth Guru, is a single historical process, and it would, we feel, be a sheer distortion, to reduce this glorious spiritual marvel to the level of personal revenge, as we egoist humans do or conceive under the cover of morality.

With regard to the critics' argument that the Gurus did not establish a political state for themselves to rule,[14] and that, therefore, the Sikhs should also not entertain any such ambition, it must be noted that no state could be established without a direct clash with the Mughals during the Gurus' time. A state could be governed either by becoming a vassal of Delhi and paying tribute to it, or by snatching a territory from the Empire after an inevitable clash with it. Thus, the choice was between becoming a subordinate of Delhi and a military confrontation with the Empire. The question of the first alternative did not arise. The second was, therefore, the alternative for which preparations were already afoot. The community was being motivated, and the Khalsa created. Evidently, confrontation could not be undertaken effectively before Vaisakhi, 1699, when the Khalsa appeared as the climax of the Sikh religious movement. The Khalsa was to spearhead the struggle against the forces of the Establishment, which indulged in oppression and repression against the helpless subjects. Even the Rajas were invited to join in, but, as is well-known, they declined. It was only after the organisational and preparatory work was completed, that the Guru deputed Banda Singh Bahadur to lead the Expedition to Sirhind.

It may be added that the Gurus never wanted an empire for themselves. Their aim was organisation of a community with trained motivations and aspirations to live as fraternal people with a sense of independence and capacity to discharge complete socio-political responsibilities, including struggle against oppression of the invaders and the Establishment.

Opponents of temporal authority for the Khalsa, often quote verses from Guru Granth Sahib, that eulogise *Naam Simran* and decry hankering after worldly power and personal redemption. The most often quoted and misinterpreted verse is : "*Raj na chahon, mukt na chahon, man preet charan kamlare.*"[15] Commenting upon critics who draw upon this verse, Sirdar Kapur Singh says that "they do not understand that these are not injunctions or commandments of Sikhism, nor statements of a doctrine."[16] These are mere clues to mood inducement with emphasis on the love of the Lord. Here '*raj*' referes to the lust for power for the individual for personal aggrandisement, which is deprecated. It does not mean that a community or a society shall not manage its socio-political affairs itself, or that it shall leave these things to outsiders. If that argument is stretched a little further, no effort should have been made to end the foreign rule of the Mughals or the British in India, for we do not want to rule (*Raj na chahon*). Secondly, the emphasis of the verse is on the Love of the Lotus Feet of the Lord (*Preet Charan Kamlare*). It says that the bliss of love is greater than the pleasures of autocratic authority or despotism. This does not amount to condemnation of *raj* or the act of ruling, even indirectly. When we want to stress the real merit of something, we compare it with something that is cherished, and not with something that has no value. For example, when we want to stress the sweetness of something, we say it sweater than honey; the sweetness of which is universally acknowledged. In this comparison we are not condemning honey. Another example to prove the same point is the widely quoted verse of Guru Nanak, '*Sachon are sabh ko, upar sach ovchare,*' which means 'Truth is higher than everyting; higher still is true living.' The Guru stresses the practice of truth by calling it even higher than truth. No stretch of imagination can construe it as rejection of truth. The society placed a high value on both *raj* and *mukti*. Through the verse, quoted earlier, the Guru places the Love of the Lord above everything else. If, however, we interpret this verse to mean that *raj* is being forbidden to the society of the Gurus' disciples, it would mean that the Gurus are condemning the society to perpetual subjugation and slavery. This is unthinkable.

The Gurus never missed an opportunity to stress the importance of *Naam* on their Sikhs. This finds expression in Guru Granth Sahib so frequently, that often Sikhism has been described as *Naam Marg*. Such verses are often invoked to plead that Sikh religion preaches 'interiority', and that the only thing that a Sikh should do is *Naam Simran*, which is further explained as muttering of a name, and no more. This is a grossly partial and inadequate view of the Gurus' teachings. In Sikhism, *Naam* has much wider scope, and expresses itself in the love for the creation of God, or mankind. It is the realization of the immanence of God, or the presence of the Creator in all His creation, a recognition of His altruistic Will, and a call to carry it out. *Naam* is the ability to see the Lord in every fellow being, which would determine the nature of man's dealings with them. This can by no stretch of imagination lead to neglect of social responsibilities and obligations. Rather, the Gurus have repeatedly emphasized deeds, which alone, in their opinion, determine man's closeness to or distance from the Lord.

Another aspect of this slogan "*Raj Karega Khalsa* ......", which is frequently missed, is the emphasis on its democratic character. It means that the authority to rule vest in the 'Khalsa' or the collectivity of the people, and not an individual. Monarchy or autocracy are completely ruled out. Following this, the Sikh rule in the 19th century over North India was called '*Sarkar-i-Khalsa.*' Maharaja Ranjit Singh who was head of the state never donned a crown or sat on a throne. Even the affairs of the army were controlled by an Army Panchayat.

Before we close, it may be proper to look at the couplet *"Raj Karega Khalsa"* affirming the need for temporal authority, again. It is simply an announcement of the determination of the Khalsa to look after its own affairs, including exercise of temporal authority and setting up of a government. Now, what is wrong with it ? It is a democratic resolve, and in these days, all political parties openly declare their intention to provide a government, and nobody objects. In fact, governments organise this exercise regularly. How could the same thing be a taboo in Sikhism ? It is also understood that Sikhs will exercise authority only in areas largely populated by them. And if the Sikhs are forbidden to rule in such areas, which are theirs, who will do it for them ? Will they hire outsiders for this purpose ? And if the outsiders do not run it properly, what will they do ? Will they not revolt ? Is perpetual revolt their destiny ? Why cannot they discharge this legitimate responsibility themselves, which is enjoined upon them by the Gurus ? It should be clear that exercise of temporal authority is a perfectly legitimate aspiration, which does not infringe upon the sovereignty of others. It is a resolve to discharge a fundamental and vital responsibility. There is no reason why anybody, much less Sikhs themselves, should object to it.

REFERENCES

1. Ganda Singh (ed.) : *Bhai Nand Lal Granthavli,* Punjabi University, Patiala, p. 285.
2. Kapur Singh : *Raj Karega Khalsa,* S.G.P.C. Amritsar, 1987, page 3.
3. Jit Singh Sital (ed.) : *Sri Guru Panth Parkash* of Rattan Singh Bhangoo, S.G.P.C., Amritsar, 1987, p. 285.
4. Ibid., p. 41.
5. Ibid., p. 319.
6. Ganda Singh : *The True Import of Raj Karega Khalsa,* The Sikh Review, Calcutta, July 1987, pp. 7.
7. Dhanoa, S.S. : *The Meaning of Raj Karega Khalsa,* The Sikh Review, Calcutta, December, 1990, pp. 24-26.
8. Jagjit Singh : *In the Caravan of Revolutions,* 1987.
9. Jit Singh Sital (ed.) : *Sri Guru Panth Parkash* of Rattan Singh Bhangoo, S.G.P.C., Amritsar, p. 1891.
10. A.C. Banerjee : *Journal of Sikh Studies,* February, 1976, p. 61 G.N.D. University, Amritsar.
11. Anonymous : *Haqiqat-i-Bina,Uruj-i-Firqa-i-Sikhan* 1783 A.D. p. 3-6, quoted by Sher Singh, *The Sikh Review,* Calcutta, Feb., 1991.
12. Ibid., p. 22.
13. Guru Granth Sahib : p. 965.
14. Dhanoa, S.S. : op. cit.
15. Guru Granth Sahib, p. 435.
16. Kapur Singh : *Sikhism and Politics,* S.G.P.C., Amritsar, 1987, p. 17.

37

AUTHENTICITY OF KARTARPURI BIR

DALJEET SINGH

INTRODUCTION

It is Guru Arjun Dev who made the important and sagacious decision to compile the Aad Granth as the Sikh scripture so that the spiritual and ideological identity of the Sikh Religion and *Panth* is established. An additional reason for the Guru to undertake the task was that it had come to his notice that persons outside the *Panth* were writing devotional hymns and giving them currency as the production of the Gurus. It is a settled and accepted tradition that the Fifth Guru compiled the Aad Granth with Bhai Gurdas as the scribe; and that the original Aad Granth is present with the Sodhis at Kartarpur. After the study of this *Bir* by Dr Jodh Singh and the publication of his book, *Kartarpuri Bir De Darshan*, it was considered that the authenticity of the *Bir* had been firmly established; but some oblique and incorrect observations by McLeod tended to throw doubt on its authenticity. It was, therefore, considered necessary to make a detailed study of the issue after a close examination of the *Bir* at Kartarpur. This article comprises the result of that examination.

CUSTODY

After its preparation, the *Bir* was installed at Harimandar Sahib, Amritsar, on Bhadon Sudhi Ist Samat 1661. The tradition and historical writings are unanimous that from Amritsar the Aad Granth was shifted to Kartarpur when the family of the Sixth Guru moved to that place. It is accepted that the original Aad Granth remained with the family of Dhirmal, the great grandson of the Guru, and his descendants at Kartarpur, even after the Gurus had shifted from there. Historical writings are also clear that during the time of the Ninth and Tenth Gurus, the Aad Granth was with the successors of Dhirmal. For, many copies of the Aad Granth, in which the *bani* (hymns) of the Ninth Guru had been recorded in the time of the Ninth or the Tenth Guru, show that those had been corrected by comparison with the Granth of the Fifth Guru.[1] It is not in doubt that all through the subsequent period, the Aad Granth at Kartarpur remained the Granth of reference for authenticating the *bani* of the Gurus and the *bhagats*.[2] And, it remained in the custody of the Sodhis of Kartarpur. After 1708 A.D., the Sikhs passed through an extremely difficult time. In that period, the question of the change of the custody of the Aad Granth could not arise. After Ranjit Singh came into power, he procured the Granth for himself and kept it with him as a national treasure of the Sikhs. After the British conquest of the Punjab, the *Bir* passed into the hands of the Indian Government. Thereafter, the *Bir* became the subject of a civil suit and it was restored to the descendants of Dhirmal. Therefore, its custody first with the Sodhis of Kartarpur, then with Ranjit Singh, and again with the Kartarpur family, is an important piece of evidence. Because, the presence and recovery of a manuscript, document, or book from its natural and proper custody and environment is a relevant and weighty factor in showing its originality.

CLAIM OF ORIGINALITY UNDISPUTED

We are not aware of any other copy of Aad Granth on behalf of which any claim of originality has ever been made. In India where there is an unfortunate tendency to make false claims about the presence of sacred places, scriptures, documents, manuscripts, etc., the singular absence of any claim of originality for any other *Bir,* is a very remarkabale fact to show that the authenticity of the Kartarpuri Bir has never been in doubt. Before we record the internal evidence showing the authenticity of the *Bir*, we shall indicate the method adopted in writing the Kartarpuri Bir.

METHOD OF WRITING

The knowledge of this method is necessary for understanding why the original Aad Granth has certain unusual features and incongruities and why those could never occur in a Granth which had been copied from the original or another Granth. The *bani* of Aad Granth has been classified *rag*-wise, and in each *rag* the *bani* has been recorded Guru-wise, *bhagat bani* being at the end. A particular sequence in regard to *shabads*, *saloks*, *ashtpadis*, *chhants*, *vars* has been observed. In *bhagat bani*, the *bani* of Kabir comes first, then of Namdev, and thereafter of *bhagat* Ravi Das and others. In order to eliminate any chance of interpolation the couplets or verses (*padas*) have been numbered. In addition, the *shabads*, *saloks*, etc.,of a particular Guru or *rag* have also been numbered serially. Further, reference of these numbers of *shabads* is given in the table of contents, along with the quotation of the first words of each hymn. Hence, there cannot be any chance of interpolation without it being detected. The scribe had also to devise a method by which the task could be accomplished easily and speedily. It is important to understand that while the *bani* was being recorded in the Granth, the work of collection of *bani* of the first four Gurus and the *bhagats* was also going on simultaneously. Therefore, the scribe had to take care of two things, first, that an adequate number of leaves were allotted to a particular *rag*, and within a *rag* to each Guru or *bhagat*, so as to enable the scribe to write within the allotted space the related *bani* anticipated to be available. Secondly, the *bani* under each *rag* was being written simultaneously, and, while the *bani* of one Guru, *bhagat*, or author was being collected, it was also being sorted out and recorded separately at appropriate places under each *rag* in accordance with the set scheme that had been devised. There being a single scribe for this gigantic task, sometimes this anticipation went wrong and many of the incongruities, as we shall see, are due to wrong anticipation, or late collection of *bani*. We also find that the numbering of the leaves of the book had been done in advance. The pages of the Kartarpuri Bir show two things. If the book is opened, the number of the page stands given only to the page on the left hand side; the page facing on the right hand side is deemed to be a part of it. We might call the page on the left 15/1, and the one on the right 15/2. However, in the Kartarpuri Bir, the number given to the page on the left is 15 and not 15/1. Secondly, after making a rough guess about the *bani* likely to be available for each section or *rag*, one or more clusters or bunches of eight or sixteen leaves each, numbered in advance, were allotted for each *rag* or section of the *bani*. And, as and when the *bani*, or part of it, of a particular *rag*, section, Guru, or *bhagat* was available, it was sorted out and copied out at the appropriate place in the concerned packets or sections, in proper sequence. In addition, totals of *padas*, *shabads*, or *shaloks* of each Guru or the totals of the *shabads* of each *rag* are also serially given. We shall hereafter record pieces of internal evidence into two parts : (i) those that are individually conclusive, and (ii) those that are, coupled with other evidence, conclusive in showing the authenticity of the *Bir*.

Individually Conclusive Factors : (1) The *Japu* of Guru Nanak was recorded by the Fourth Guru. In all the handwritten *Birs* the practice was to record either the words "*Japu Nisan*", or "Copy of the Copy of the *Japu* recorded by Guru Ram Das." If the *Bir* was a third copy of the original *Bir* of the Fifth Guru, it would say "Copy of the copy of the copy of the *Japu* recorded by Guru Ram Das." As the Fourth Guru was the person who collected and wrote the *Japu*, and the Fifth Guru was the first person to compile Aad Granth and copy *Japu* therein, in the Kartarpuri Bir alone it is written "Copy of the *Japu* recorded in the hand of Guru Ram Das." No other *Bir* records these words, for, Bhai Gurdas was the first person to copy the *Japu* from the collection and writing by the Fourth Guru.

(2) Secondly, in this *Bir* at page 45, the dates of the demise of the first four Gurus alone are with the same pen and ink and in the hand of the original scribe of the *Bir*. The date of the demise of the Fifth Guru is in the hand of the original scribe but with a different pen and shade of ink. No other *Bir* fulfils this test. It is also very significant that while writing the dates of the demise of the first four Gurus, the day of the week is not mentioned. But in the case of the Fifth Guru, apart from the date, the day of the week is also mentioned though the scribe is the same. This shows clearly that the date of the demise of the Fifth Guru was written by Bhai Gurdas on a later day, otherwise had all the five dates been wirtten at one time, either the day would have been mentioned in all the case or been absent from all the five entries.

(3) Thirdly, the words "*Sudh*" or "*Sudh Keeche*" ("It is correct" or "correct it") appear at so many places in the *Bir*. These are supposed to be in the hand of the Fifth Guru since these are in a different hand and not in the hand of the scribe of the *Bir*, and the handwriting of these marginal observations resembles the handwriting of the *Nishan*

of the Fifth Guru in the *Bir*. These words appear in other handwritten *Birs* as well. But those are in the same hand as of the scribe of the concerned *Bir*, showing that the *Bir* is a copy and not the original.

(4) The historical writings of Bhai Santokh Singh, Bhai Gurdas, Gur Bilas Chhevin Patshahi and others,[3] and the tradition assert that the Fifth Guru completed the Aad Granth in Bhadon Samat, 1661. The Kartarpuri Bir is the only *Bir* which records that it was completed in Bhadon, 1661 "*Samat 1661 Miti Bhadon Vadi ekam I pothi likh pouhnche.*" There is no handwritten *Bir* the record of which claims the same to have been completed on Bhadon Samat, 1661 or near about. In fact, this dated volume being the earliest, it is a good piece of evidence not only to show the authenticity of the Kartarpuri Bir but also to fix the date of the preparation of the *Bir* by the Fifth Guru.

(5) We have explained the method of allotment of clusters of papers for a *rag* or a proposed section of the Granth. For the expeditious completion of the work, the adoption of this method was natural and necessary, especially when the work of copying the collection of *bani* from different sources was going on side by side. This prior allotment of pages for a section had to be very liberal, so as to ensure that the available *bani* should not exceed the allotted space, nor thereby upset the entire system and sequence of *rags* and sections. But, evidently, this liberal allotment of leaves, based on rough anticipation of the *bani* likely to be available, was, in practice, bound to lead to a large number of pages remaining blank between different sections of the Aad Granth. And, this is what has actually happened in the case of the Kartarpuri Bir. The total numbered leaves of the Kartarpuri Bir are 974, comprising 1948 pages. Of these pages, 453 are entirely blank, hundreds of other pages are partly blank, and, considering that a fully utilized page accommodates 24 lines, the total space available on these partly blank pages comes up to another 133 full pages. Thus, of the total 1948 pages of this volume, the space of 586 of them remained unused. It is evident that this state of affairs could only arise in the originally written Aad Granth; it could never have happened in an Aad Granth which had been copied from the original. It is a fact that none of the writers like Jodh Singh, Harbhajan Singh and others, who have seen numerous handwritten *Birs*, state that any of the old handwritten *Birs* contains any blank pages or spaces. Obviously, in a copy, the very question of hundreds of pages being left blank does not arise, especially when it is copied by a single scribe. Because, in such a case the copyist has the entire material, ready and in proper sequence, before him for copying. The Banno Bir, which is supposed to be a copy of it, has only 467 folios. It is, therefore, out of question that the Kartarpuri Bir with 974 folios could be a copy of a Granth which had material that could be accommodated in about 467 folios. Generally, all the old handwritten *Birs*, including the Kartapuri Bir, are in one hand. Therefore, this internal evidence in the Kartarpuri Bir is both incontrovertible and singly conclusive to show its originality.

(6) There are many *shabads* of *bani* which have originally been written twice but later this duplication has either been erased by *hartal* (a chemical used in those days to remove the writing), or scored out with the observation in the margin that the *shabad* was

a duplication. In a copied *Bir* this duplication could never arise. This could happen only in the original in which case either the scribe himself or the compiler has on revision found the error and got the same removed by scoring out the duplicate *shabad* or *shalok*. This duplication has happened at pages 96/2, 186/2, 483/1, 511/1, 550/2, 836/1, 943/2, etc. Thus these duplications, too, are conclusive to prove its authenticity.

(7) There is another set of corrected incongruities which shows conclusively the authenticity of Kartarpuri Bir. At page 778/1 there is a marginal note that *shalok* No. 22 of *Mahila* 1 which is recorded at page 799 and is correct should be read there at that page after *shalok* No. 21. It is also indicated at page 778/1 that *shalok* "*Maru Mahila* 3" "*Agam Agochar Ve-Parwaha*" which is there on this page should be read at page 788. Further, at page 788 there is a corresponding note that the 23rd *shalok* of *Mahila* 3 *Agam Agochar Ve Parwaha* which is at page 778 should be read there. At page 799/2 *Maru Mahila* 1, the *shalok* of which the correct place is at page 778, after *shalok* No. 21 of *Mahila* I , stands recorded. Now, these inadvertent incongruities are such as could not be rectified except by cross-references, especially as *shalok* of *Mahila* 3 is long and could not be accommodated in the margin at page 788, nor could *Maru Mahila* 1 at page 799/2 be accommodated at page 778 and scored out at page 799/2. In the *Tatkara* (contents of *shaloks* and *shabads*), too, these incongruities are reflected but rectified. At page 16/1 of the *Tatkara*, the first lines of all the *shaloks* of *Mahila* are written with their serial numbers 1 to 21. But in the margin, against *shalok* No. 21 of *Mahila* 1, the first line of *shalok Kudrat Karnekar Apara* of *Mahila* 1, is vertically recorded. Its number is noted as No. 22 and page 799.

Further, at page 16/1 of the *Tatkara*, since in the text *shalok* of *Mahila* 3 *Agam Agochar Ve-Parwaha* actually, but incongruously, starts at page 778 immediately after *shalok* No. 21 of *Mahila* 1, its reference number and the first line of the *shabad* are recorded in the beginning, but its number is correctly given as *shalok* No. 23 of *Mahila* 3. Again, at this page 16/1 after the number and the first line of *shalok* No. 22 of *Mahila* 3, the number and line is of *shalok* 24 of *Mahila* 3. This is so because in the actual text *shalok* No. 23 of *Mahila* 3 comes between *shalok* 21 of *Mahila* 1 and *shalok* No. 1 of *Mahila* 3 at page 778 and not between *shalok* Nos. 22 and 24 of *Mahila* 3 at page 788. Another important feature of page 16/1 of the *Tatkara* is that the original *shalok* numberings of the first 23 *shaloks* of *Mahila* 3 on this page have been rubbed with *hartal* and thereafter these very 23 *shaloks* have been re-numbered, the first one as 23 and the remaining 22 numbers as 1 to 22. This clearly shows that originally the incongruity in the placement of *shaloks* 23 of *Mahila* 3 and *shalok* No. 22 of *Mahila* 1, that occurred in the text, was, actually reflected in the *Tatkara* by the scribe. But, when the out-of-sequence placements of these *shaloks* were later detected, the incongruities in the text were rectified by giving cross-references in the margin of the text at the appropriate pages, and, the errors in the *Tatkara* were corrected by rubbing with *hartal* the numbers of the first 23 *shaloks* of *Mahila* 3 and re-numbering them as numbers 23 and 1 to 22 of *Mahila* 3, and, in the case of, *shalok* No. 22 of *Mahila* 1, by writing its page and number correctly in the margin of page 16/1.

We have detailed these connected sets of corrections in the text and the *Tatkara* because these incongruities could happen only at the time of the original writing and never in the case of copying from the original text compiled by the Fifth Guru. It is also important to mention that on examination, no other *Bir* has revealed this set of incongruities at pages 778, 788 and 799 of the text and in the corresponding portions of the *Tatkara*. By itself this set of corrections alone is conclusive in proving the authenticity of the Kartarpuri Bir.

(8)   Here we shall record a number of other corrected mistakes which in their character, implication and importance are similar to the ones described above.

(a)   At page 804/2 it is recorded in the margin that instead of the 21st *Pauri*, 22nd has been written. Correspondingly on page 805/1 there is a note in the margin that the *Pauri* there should be sung and written as 21th *Pauri*. This error of sequence could never occur in a copy.

(b)   There are numerous instances where *shabads, shaloks* and a part of *bani* have been written in the margin, evidently, because in each case the *bani* appears to have been found or collected later on and there being no place on the relevant page it had to be recorded in the margin. In some cases the *bani* has been given the proper serial number and the numbers of the subsequent *bani* re-numbered. But, in some cases, numbers following them have remained uncorrected and the *bani* in the margin has been given the same number as to the *shalok* or *shabad* after which it has to be read. These incongruities are so large in number and the *bani* has been written in the margin at so many places that all this could happen only in the original, either because of the late collection of *bani* or because the scribe, Bhai Gurdas, had not recorded it in its right sequence. For example, at pages 154/2, 252/1, 364/1, 694/1, 945, 182, 946,1, 148/2, 374/2, etc. additional *bani* has been written in the margins. At pages 940/1, 940/2, etc., the *bani* recorded in the margins has been given the same number as borne by one of the *shabads* on the page. Again, on pages 251/1, 265/2, 266/2, 399/2, 252/1, 499/2, 689/2, 690/1, 842/2, 841/2, etc., portions of the *bani* have been written in the margin and a mark given at the relevant place on the page to show where the marginal portion should be read.

(c)   We know that at the end of each *shabad* or *shalok* the total of Pads, the total of *shabads* of each Guru, total of *shabads* of each *rag*, etc., have been recorded. The number of *Mahila* is also invariably given in addition. But, in the Kartarpuri Bir in scores of cases the number, totals, etc. were missed originally but were written later in small letters either in between or above the lines or in the margins, e.g. this has happened at pages 154/2, 164/2, 174/1, 240/2, 257/1, 267/1, 269/1, 270/1, 270/2, 399/1, 455/2, 802/2, etc. Apart from that, in quite a large number of cases, these totals have not been given or given incompletely. This incongruity and its rectification as mentioned above are very common. There is a very clear reason for this feature of the Kartarpuri Bir. As the job of collection of *bani* and its recording was being done simultaneously, the scribe was never sure whether more *shabads* or *bani* of a Guru, requiring precedence of sequence over the *shabads* of *bani* already written, would or would not be available.

As such, he had, as a necessary precaution and in order to aviod repeated scoring out and alterations of the totals, to leave the work of totalling to a later date. Therefore, this task of recording the totals had to be done as one of the last jobs to be completed. Perforce, the totals had to be squeezed in between or above the lines in small sized figures or in the margins. But such a position, too, could never arise in a copied Granth where the numbering would be complete and form a part of the line itself. The scribe could never fail to copy or record them in appropriate lines, even if in the original the numberings had been missing or been recorded in between or above the lines. In other handwritten *Birs* these incongruities do not occur. Even in the Banno Bir, totals are given in the lines themselves. Hence this feature of the Kartarpuri Bir, especially the large number in which these incongruities or omissions appear, proves its authenticity and originality.

(d) There is another kind of discrepancy in serial-wise numbering. On a number of pages the *bani* or the *shabad* has been scored out or removed by the use of *hartal*. But, the old serial numbering has remained uncorrected, e.g., this has happened at pages 186/2, 970/1. In some cases, the incongruity even stands reflected in the *Tatkara*, because as the numbering has remained uncorrected in the Granth, it could evidently not be corrected in the *Tatkara* which records only the state of numbering or sequence in the Granth, e.g. mention of *shalok* number 94/1 in the *Tatkara* at page 7 has been scored out, and the numbering of subsequent references stands uncorrected. The large number of cancellations and uncorrected numberings in this *Bir* prove its originality since such a state could never occur in a copy.

(e) As noted already, within the *bani* of a *rag* or section, the sequence of *shabads* or *shaloks* is Guruwise. After it, normally comes the *bani* of Kabir, Namdev, Ravidas and then other *bhagats*. But, the sources of the *bani* of *bhagat* Kabir and other *bhagats* being quite scattered, its collection and selection for incorporation in the Granth must have taken quite long, since the same involved in the case of each part a scrutiny and decision by the Guru himself. The result was that in many instances the *bani* of *bhagat* Kabir appears in between, and that also not at one place, or after the recorded *bani* of *bhagat* Namdev. It might be argued that such an abnormal sequence being in the original, it would also be there in a copy of it; therefore, the Kartarpuri Bir, cannot claim any originality on this account. But, it is significant that the *bani* of *bhagat* Kabir, which is not in proper sequence has, evidently, been written on different occasions. This is clear from the fact that though the writing of these hymns is by the same scribe, in each case the writing differs in the size and shape of letters and the shade of ink. Had the Kartarpuri Bir been a copy, these differences in the shades of ink and the size of the letters that are there, could not have occurred, even though the break in sequence would have been there, because of the corresponding break being present in the original, e.g. at pages 842/2, 810/1 and 863/2, though the scribe is the same, the shades of ink and size of writing are different even in the case of the *bani* of the same *bhagat* or Guru. Therefore, while variations in sequence can be explained, variations in pens, shades of ink, and size of letters of the *bani* of the same *bhagat* cannot be explained in a continuous writing, except on the assumption that the Kartarpuri Bir is the original and these variations occurred because of the variant timings of collection, selection and recording of the *bani* of a particular *bhagat*. Besides, because of this noncontinuous writing of *bhagat bani*, the totals of the *shabads* of a *bhagat* have not been given as has been done in other cases. The fact is that in the Kartarpuri Bir, the *bani* of *bhagat* Kabir, and even some other *bani*, when found and selected later on have not at many places been recorded in the normal serial sequence of the *Bir*. But, these hymns have been wirtten wherever space was available and even in the margin or between the *bani* of other *bhagats*, e.g. at pages 885/2, 945/1. But, the shades of ink and pens used for such *bani* are different showing clearly variant times of its original collection and recording in the Kartarpuri Bir.

(f) Another feature of the Kartarpuri Bir is the large number of pages where the original writing has been obliterated by *hartal* and later at those very places *bani* has been written. Sometimes the space accommodating a whole *shabad* or hymn has been cleaned with *hartal* and new *bani* written at the place e.g. at pages 840/1, 870/2, 966/1, 966/2. Had the Kartarpuri Bir been a copy of the original, such a large number of places requiring the need of scoring out or rubbing or cleaning with *hartal* could never have arisen.

(g) Another significant feature of the Kartarpuri Bir is that at numerous places the headings and words like *Ek Onkar* or the *Mahila*, or name of the *rag* are written, but below these headings there is no *bani* or *shabad* and the place is blank. This is so at pages 279/2, 297/2, 248/1, 528/1, 520/2, 348/1,468/2, 607/2, 617/1, 621/2. This writing of the heading like *Mahila*, *rag* etc., by the scribe clearly indicates that it was thought that the *bani* of that Guru or *bhagat* would be available for being written there, but actually it was either not available or not approved by the Fifth Guru. In a mere copy of the Aad Granth, such a thing could never happen, because where the original has no *bani* the question of recording the heading of a *shabad* or *bani* could never arise. Such recording of headings only, without being followed by related *bani*, is not present in any other handwritten *Bir*. It is also significant to mention that almost all these headings relate to the Fifth Guru who was alive at that time, e.g. pages 297/2, 248/1, 348/1, 418/2, 469/2, 528/1, 530/2, 607/2, 610/2, 617/1, and 621/2. Presumably, Bhai Gurdas' anticipation was that more *shabads* of the Guru were likely to be available under those *Rags*. This is also an important proof to show the originality of the Kartarpuri Bir. Because in a copy the occurrence of all these extra or lone headings, involving wrong anticipation, relating mostly to the Fifth or the living Guru could not arise.

(9) *Other Important Factors* : (a) The originality of the Kartarpuri Bir is also established by the Nishan or mark of the Fifth Guru. This mark, in those days meant, according to the accepted practice and tradition, the writing of the *Mul Mantra* of the *Japuji* in the hand of the Guru, the Fifth Guru in this case. This Nishan appears on page 29/1 of the *Bir*. As a mark of adoration, the page has been profusely decorated. The presence of the Nishan of the Fifth Guru is also noted in the *Tatkara*.

(b) At page 415/1 in the margin are written the words "The *shabad* is right." This *shabad* does not find mention in the *Tatkara*. But, this observation in the margin shows that for this *Bir*, there was a supervisor or editor, other than the scribe, who alone could record such an observation of approval regarding the *shabad* on the page. This observation shows the original character of the Kartarpuri Bir. Otherwise, if the *Bir* had been copied from another *Bir*, the question of such an obeservation by the scribe or some other person would not arise.

(c) In the *Tatkara* of *shabads* only the references of *shabads* 1 to 58 of *Ramkali Mahila* 5 are given. But, on page 681/2 of the *Bir*, which starts with *shabad* 59 of *Ramkali Mahila* 5 and ends with *shabad* 60 of *Ramkali Mahila* 5, two additional *shabads* of the Fifth Guru are written. Both these *shabads* are in a different hand from that of the scribe and their reference in the *Tatkara* of *shabads* is missing. This means that these two *shabads* were added or got added there by the editor or the compiler. Here again, the absence of the reference of these two *shabads* in the *Tatkara* and their text being in a different hand from that of the original scribe suggest that this feature could be only in the original and not in a copy. Because in a copy all the 1 to 60 *shabads* would normally be in the same hand. Similarly, *Ramkali Mahila* 5 *Chhand* No. 21 has no reference in the *Tatkara*, but the *Chhand* is present at its proper place, though it is in a different hand. This, too, supports the earlier inference drawn in the case of *shabads* 59 and 60. In both cases, the *bani* being of the Fifth Guru, it is very likely that he created it after 1604 A.D. and got it added at the appropriate places in the Aad Granth later on. The position is similar in the case of *Basant ki Var* composed by the Fifth Guru. This *Var* is recorded on page 854/2 in the middle of this page. But, there is no reference of this Var in the *Tatkara*, showing that the Fifth Guru composed it and got it included after Bhadon 1604 A.D. Hence, it could not find mention in the *Tatkara* that stood already completed. It is significant that in all other handwritten *Birs*, including the Banno *Bir*, reference of the *Var* is present in the *Tatkara*.

(d) At page 540 of the *Bir* the *Nishan* of the Sixth Guru is present. Its presence is also mentioned in the *Tatkara*. In the circumstances of the case, this is a very significant and natural thing to do. During the time of the Fifth Guru it had become abundantly clear that Guru Hargobind would succeed him. In fact, from the very start the Sixth Guru was associated with the task of the collection of the *bani* and preparation of the scripture. Some writers have even suggested that some of the *dhunnies* were got recorded by the Sixth Guru. They derive this inference from the fact that it is in the Kartarpuri Bir alone that we observe that the *dhunnies* of some *Vars* are recorded in a different hand or in small letters in between or above the normal written lines. In other copies of the Granth, including the Banno Bir, these have been wirtten in the lines and in the same manner as the *bani* itself. It evidently suggests that in the Kartarpuri Bir the *dhunnies* were written on some later date, and presumably at the instance of the Sixth Guru.

CONCLUSION FROM INTERNAL EVIDENCE

We have detailed above the various pieces and types of internal evidence most of which are individually and incontrovertibly conclusive in proving that the Kartarpuri Bir is the original Aad Granth compiled by the Fifth Guru in 1604 A.D. The other pieces of evidence we have recorded are cumulatively, or coupled with the other evidence, equally conclusive in proving the authenticity of the Kartarprui Bir to be the original production of the Fifth Guru.

EXAMINATION OF CRITICISM BY MCLEOD

Before we deal with the criticism of McLeod, let us record the present position and academic findings about the Banno Bir. This *Bir* is at present with the successors of Bhai Banno at Kanpur. It has been carefully seen by Bhai Mahan Singh, who examined the Kartarpuri Bir as well as a team of scholars from the Guru Nanak Dev University, Amritsar, Prof. Pritam Singh, who has written a paper on the subject, and Principal Harbhajan Singh of Sikh Missionary College, Amritsar. All of them have concluded that this *Bir* was recorded in Samat 1699 (thirty eight years after the preparation of the *Bir* by the Fifth Guru) and this is the year written in the *Bir* itself. Secondly, in this *Bir* the controversial *shabad*, "*Ranjhunara gao Sakhi*", is clearly a later interpolation because it is written in very small letters in a different shade of ink from the original writing of the *Bir*. These two conclusions about the Banno Bir are academically accepted and are not in doubt.

We now record the criticism by McLeod. He writes :

"First, there is the universal agreement that the important differences distinguishing the Kartarpur manuscript from the Banno version consist exclusively of material included in the latter which is not to be found in the former. Secondly, there is the testimony of those who have inspected the Kartarpuri manuscript concerning the obliteration of portions of its text."

"A third factor is the presence in the standard printed editions of two fragments, corresponding to two of the three additional Banno hymns. In Ramkali *rag* there occurs a single couplet where there should apparently be a complete hymn. The remainder of the hymns in the same section indicate that the couplet must be either the first two lines of a *chhant*, or a *shalok* introducing a chhant. The second fragment corresponds to the *Sur Das* hymn in *Sarang rag*. In this instance the standard printed text contains only the first line. There seemed to be only one possible reason for the appearance of these two fragments. The bulk of the hymn in each case must have been deleted, leaving a small remainder which was faithfully copied into the standard printed text."

"A fourth point seemed to clinch the issue. The Banno text of the missing portions indicated good reasons for later deletion, particularly in the case of the Ramkali hymn by Guru Arjun. This hymn describes the puberty rites conducted by Guru Arjun at the initiation of his son Hargobind. The rites follow a standard Hindu pattern and in the third stanza there is a reference to the manner in which the boy's head was shaved. This feature is an obvious contradiction to the later prohibition of hair cutting. When the prohibition became mandatory, not merely for Jat Sikhs but also those of other castes, the reference in the hymn could only be regarded as intolerable."

"Finally, there was ample evidence that others had already formed the same suspicions concerning the Kartarpur manuscript and were seeking alternative explanations. One writer has declared that the present Kartarpur manuscript is a Banno version, adding that the original manuscript of the Aad Granth must have been lost. Another has suggested that the present manuscript must be a first draft, subsequently amended by the Guru himself. Their evident uneasiness strengthened a hypothesis which already seemed firmly founded."

"By this time the hypothesis will have become obvious. The conclusion which seemed to be emerging with increasing assurance was that the widely disseminated Banno version must represent the original text; and that the Kartarpur manuscript must be a shortened version of the same text. A few portions must have been deleted because they could not be reconciled with beliefs subsequently accepted by the *Panth*. This much appeared to be well established and another point could be added as a possibility. It seemed likely that the amendments had originally been made by omitting the problem passage from later manuscripts rather than by deleting them from the Kartarpur manuscript. These later manuscripts reflected the distinctive pattern of Khalsa belief. The omission of the problem passage together with the addition of compositions by Guru Tegh Bahadur constituted the Damdama version of the Aad Granth. Later still, portions of the Kartarpur manuscript (the orginal manuscript written by Bhai Gurdas) were rather ineptly obliterated in order to bring the two versions into line."[4]

It appears that McLeod is unaware of the work done by Sahib Singh who disbelives the Banno story and the statements of Mahan Singh and others who have recorded the two findings mentioned earlier. For, had it been known to him, he would certainly have tried to verify the factual position by an examination of the Banno Bir. And this, evidently, he never did. Nor has he, it appears, examined the Kartarpuri Bir. Whether or not McLeod was aware of the views of Sahib Singh about the Banno story and of Mahan Singh and others about the year of completion of the Banno Bir, is not our present concern. It is now well established that the Banno Bir was prepared not earlier than 1699 and the Banno story is a myth. As such, the very basis of the argument about the Kartarpuri Bir being a copy of the Banno Bir is knocked out. McLeod's argument that the additional *bani* of Surdas and Ramkali *Mahila* 5 that was present in the Banno Bir, had been copied in the Kartarpuri Bir, but deleted later on is equally baseless. For, we have seen that in both these cases the addtional *bani* in the Banno Bir is either an interpolation or a later writing; and these verses, which are not present in the Kartarpuri Bir, had neither been copied there nor deleted. Therefore, McLeod's other agruments that the Kartarpuri Bir, which according to him had been copied from the Banno Bir, contained the so-called puberty hymn (additional 8 verses), but being incongruous with the later Khalsa belief was deleted, is also factually incorrect and fallacious. Kartarpuri Bir which was prepared in 1604 A.D. could not be copied from the Banno Bir prepared in 1642 A.D.; nor was the puberty hymn originally present even in the Banno Bir of *samat* 1699, it being a clear later interpolation. In fact, it was never recorded in the Kartarpuri Bir. Therefore, the question of its deletion from the Kartarpuri Bir could not arise. Every student of the Kartarpuri Bir knows that it has the largest number of blank pages and deletions. These two facts are one of the strongest points in favour of its originality. Apart from the fact that the Banno Bir was prepared 38 years after the Kartarpuri Bir, it is ridiculous that a copyist given the task of copying the Banno Bir comprising 467 folios, or any *Bir* with such material as could be accommodated on about 465 leaves, would copy it out on 974 folios. McLeod knows, since he is aware of the work of Jodh Singh, and has even quoted it, that in the case of the puberty hymn and *bhagat* Surdas verses, there is no deletion in the Kartarpuri Bir (as also seen by us). Yet, knowing all this, he has, on the one hand, tried to build the argument about deletion on the basis of the use of hartal elsewhere, and, on the other hand, has made the equally misleading argument of the deletion of the puberty hymn from the Kartarpuri Bir because of the later Khalsa beliefs.

Here it is also pertinent to state that McLeod's suggestion that the so-called Ramkali hymn was deleted from the Kartarpuri Bir because of later Khalsa beliefs displays his ignorance both of the history of the Sikhs and of the Dhirmalias. The latter became a splinter group and they went to the extent of making a murderous assault on the Ninth Guru. They never recognized him or the Tenth Master as Guru. As such, there was no love lost between the Khalsa, a creation of the Tenth Guru, whom the Mughals wanted to destroy, and the Dhirmalias who were Pro-Establishment. Therefore, there is not the remotest possibility that the Dhirmalias would ever tamper with the *Bir* in their possession in order to oblige the Khalsa, and bring it in accord with the *Rahit* or symbols prescribed by the Tenth Guru. Rather, their avowed hostility towards the Khalsa would prompt them to highlight the hymn if it had ever existed in that *Bir*. On the other hand, the Banno people formed a part of the main-stream of the Sikhs and if Sikhs would have been interested in a deletion, they might have done that in their *Bir*. But, nothing of the sort happened in that *Bir*. McLeod's conjecture about the deletion of the so-called puberty hymn because of the Khalsa beliefs is, thus, not only impossible, but is also controverted even by the very facts and circumstances of the situation as it existed then.

Besides, we find that Principal Harbhajan Singh who made a detailed survey of the handwritten *Birs* in the Sikh Reference Library, Golden Temple, Amritsar, (since destroyed in the Blue Star Attack) and some other *Birs,* writes that in numerous of the old handwritten *Birs* he examined, this additional *bani* was no where present. He gives details of it in his book : *Gurbani Sampadan Nirne.* A statement about some of them is as follows :

"1. *Bir* No. 97 in the Sikh Reference Library : It was produced in *Samat* 1739 (1682 A.D.), some two decades before the creation of the Khalsa, and bears the *Nishan* of the Ninth Guru. It has no additional *bani* as is contained in the Banno *Bir*. 2. Pindi Lala (Gujrat) Wali *Bir* : It was produced in *Samat* 1732 (1675 A.D.). It bears the *Nishan* of Ninth Guru, but, unlike the Banno Bir, it contains no additional *bani*. 3. *Bir* No. 14 in the Sikh Reference Library : It was completed in *Samat* 1748 (1691 A.D.). It contains no additional *bani* as is present in the Banno Bir. 4. *Bir* written by Pakhar Mal Dhillon, grandson of Chaudhri Langahia Dhillon, a known devout Sikh of the Fifth Guru : It was written, in *Samat* 1745 (1668 A.D.). Unlike the Banno Bir, it contains no additional *bani*."[5]

At Berkeley, McLeod raised two points : "One is the obscurity which envelops a significant period of the text's actual history. The other is the presence within the manuscript of numerous deletions."[6] On the issue of deletions we have already found that these large number of deletions are a good proof of its originality, especially when there is no other *Bir* with deletions in such a large number and when at most of those places where *bani* has been written again by the same scribe, showing thereby that the writing rubbed off was not correct or approved by the Guru. Actually, it stands established that not only was the Banno Bir prepared in *Samat* 1699, but the puberty hymn itself was clearly a later interpolation even in the Banno Bir of 1699. McLeod has been lamenting his frustration in not being able to serve academic interests, because he was not allowed necessary access to the Kartarpuri Bir. He even went to the extent of recording that non-availability of Kartarpuri Bir to him suggested that there was something to conceal therein.[7] But one wonders why his academic keenness never led him to see the Banno Bir, which was available all these years for his examination. Had he cared to see, he would have found that the year of its production was *Samat* 1699. Does all this not suggest that his motives in making unwarranted statements were quite different and unbecoming a scholar.

In view of the above, it is clear that the suggestion about the Kartarpuri Bir being non-authentic or its being a copy of the Banno Bir is both baseless and untenable.

On the second issue about the custody of the Kartarpuri Bir, the doubts of McLeod are equally without any basis. Here, too, the position had been made clear by Mahan Singh. The historical writings show that Bidhi Chand and other Sikhs were very well aware of the great value of the *Bir*. They held it in the highest esteem. Actually, this was the real reason that Bidhi Chand and others, despite the wishes of the Guru, initially failed to return the *Bir* to the Dhirmalias towards whom they were hostile for their having attacked the Ninth Guru to kill him. Therefore, for understandable reasons, when again directed by the Guru to return the *Bir,* they were reluctant to meet the Dhirmalias face to face. And all they did was that they deposited the *Bir* at a safe place and sent a message to the Dhirmalias to pick it up, and this they did.[8] Further, there is little doubt that when the Tenth Guru at Anandpur Sahib wanted to prepare the Damdami version, it was to the Dhirmalias that he sent the message for loan of the *Bir* of the Fifth Guru.[9] So, whatever be the facts of the earlier part of the story, at the time of the Tenth Guru, the original authentic *Bir* was certainly with the Dhirmalias. After that, the *Bir* always remained in safe hands. Had the *Bir* been lost, it is imposible to imagine that Ranjit Singh who had waged a war for obtaining a horse, would not be aware of it and recover this venerable treasure, or that he would be satisfied with a spurious version of the original *Bir*.

Here it is not our purpose to ascertain whether McLeod made his observations out of sheer ignorance of the available facts and materials, or of his anxiety to suppress known but awkward facts, or of his conscious or unconscious bias because of his thirteen years of working and association with a Christian Mission in Punjab. But in either case, it does little credit to his credibility as a scholar to suggest tampering with a Scripture without having examined it or the connected literature on the issue. In view of the above, we conclude that McLeod's criticism is factually incorrect, and untenable, and even less than responsible.

An observation was made by McLeod that in order to remove scholarly doubts, access to the Kartarpuri Bir would need to be allowed and "the alternative may well be a growing conviction that there is something to hide." The Kartarpuri Bir is private property and we do not hold any brief for its custodians. True, the Sodhis of Kartarpur while they do not permit access to every person who claims to be a scholar, yet, by all standards, their policy to allow access to the Kartarpuri Bir has been very liberal. In fact, during the current century there has been an extremely profuse exposure of the Kartarpuri Bir before genuine scholars and theologians. In the twenties, Master Isher Singh of the Sikh Vidyala, Tarn Taran, sent a team of scholars, who for many months made a detailed page by page and line by line study in order to prepare a standard version of Guru Granth Sahib. Second, is an equally major attempt of the S.G.P.C. to prepare a meticulously accurate version of Guru Granth Sahib from the Kartarpuri Bir. A team consisting of two scholars, namely, Giani Piara Singh Sukhi and Sant Harbhajan Singh Nirmla worked from day to day for six months at Kartarpur. In addition, other scholars also regularly visited Kartarpur so as to supervise the work of the team. Leaf by leaf comparison of an unbound *Bir* of Guru Granth Sahib was made with the Kartarpuri Bir. Every variation in the unbound *Bir* was corrected in accordance with the Kartarpuri Bir. Thereafter, calligraphists prepared another faultless copy of the Granth. This having been done, printing blocks of this new version were made. A committee of scholars was again appointed to verify and approve the corrected version. Actually, about 733 variations, major or minor, were found in the old printed version and these were all corrected. Finally, a faultlessly accurate version of Guru Granth Sahib copied from the Kartarpuri Bir was approved and printed through the Punjabi Press, Hall Bazar, Amritsar. These versions have been printed a number of times and these printed copies of the Kartarpuri Bir are there for every scholar to see and study. Dr Jodh Singh's rejoinder recorded after the publication of McLeod's lectures states that the printed version today tallies completely with the Kartarpuri Bir. Apart from that, many times groups of scholars, individual scholars, both foreign and Indian, have been allowed access to the Kartarpuri Bir. Many reports of the committees of scholars who examined the Kartarpuri Bir for general and specific purposes are available. Jodh Singh's *Kartarpuri Bir De Darshan* is a detailed page by page record of the Kartarpuri Bir giving an account of every feature on each page, including variations in words, spellings, *lagmatras*, use of *hartal*, blank spaces, size of margins, obliteration by use of *hartal*, over-writing on *hartal*, scoring-out, writing in-between lines, above the lines and in the margins, variations in the size of letters, handwriting, ink, etc., etc.. Among individual records of examination, these notes by Jodh Singh (recorded by Giani Mahan Singh) are the most detailed and give a scrupulously accurate picture of the Kartarpuri Bir. In this background, it would be both unfair and incorrect to blame the custodians of the *Bir* that they have barred scholarly study or exposure to genuine scholars. The difficulty is that wild conjectures of some scholars like G.B. Singh and others have raised the suspicions of the custodians of the *Bir*. At present the Kartarpuri Bir is the property of the Dhir Mal family, and no one can be blamed if the custodians want to be sure of the bonafides of a scholar before allowing him access to it for a study of the Kartarpuri Bir. Their exercise of such discretion is natural, understandable and unobjectionable. But, McLeod continued with his misleading and incorrect statements. In a lecture at Berkeley published in 1978 he said, "The earliest representing nearest approach to Guru Arjun's dictation would be Banno, the second an intermediate recension bearing the actual marks of a later revision through the excision of unaceptable material would be Kartarpuri."[10] In 1989, he published his book *The Sikhs*, in which he wrote, "This comparision suggests that the Banno recension may actually represent the original text by Bhai Gurdas", but he adds, "if this is indeed the case, the original version has subsequently been amended by obliterating occasional portions of the text."[11] Four Sikh organisations, the Institute of Sikh Studies, Chandigarh, the Council of Sikh Affairs, Chandigarh, the Academy of Sikh Religion and Culture, Patiala, and the Khalsa Diwan, Ludhiana, worte to the Toronto University complaining about the misconduct of McLeod in making wrong statements about the Sikh Scripture, especially when he had made no serious effort to examine the Banno Bir or the Kartarpuri Bir. Probably, in response to these allegations against him, McLeod published a letter in the *India Abroad*, dated 14 December 1990, saying that he had abandoned his doubts about the Kartarpuri Bir after reading Jodh Singh's book, *Kartarpuri Bir de Darshan*. Since McLeod had made all his incorrect statements of 1975, 1978 and 1989 after accepting knowledge of Jodh Singh's book in his publication of 1975, Dr Dhami of New York published all the statements of McLeod suggesting that the letter of McLeod in the *India Abroad* was another misstatement by him. All this indicates the level of scholarship, motivation and ethics at which McLeod has been working.

So far as the Kartarpuri Bir is concerned, it has since been examined by G.S. Mann of the Columbia University, USA,[12] and Pashaura Singh of the Toronto University, Canada,[13] and both of them have testified to its authenticity.

In sum, our analysis and examination of the *Bir*, the available material on the subject, and the statements of various authors lead us to the conclusion that the Kartarpuri Bir is incontrovertibly the authentic Aad Granth prepared by the Fifth Guru.

REFERENCES

1. Sahib Singh : *Adi Bir Bare*, pp.168,197; Harbhajan Singh : *Gurbani Sampadan Nirnai*, pp. 137,160.
2. Harbhajan Singh : *Gurbani Sampadan Nirnai*, pp.130-31, 135, 137-140.
3. Sahib Singh : op.cit., pp. 119-122.
4. McLeod, W.H. : *Evolution of the Sikh Community*, pp. 76-78.
5. Harbhajan Singh : op. cit., pp.121-126, 128-129.
6. Mark Juergensmegyer, and N.G. Barier, (eds.) : *Sikh Studies*, Berkeley, 1979, p. 100.
7. Ibid., p. 100.
8. Mahan Singh : *Parm Pavitar Adi Bir da Sakalan Kal*, pp. 43-44.
9. Harbhajan Singh : op. cit. pp. 135-138.
10. M. Juergensmegyer, and G. Barier : op. cit., p. 101.
11. McLeod, W.H. : *The Sikhs*, Columbia University Press, New York, 1989, p. 88.
12. Wawley, J. S. and G. S. Mann : *Studying the Sikhs*, State University of New York Press, 1993.
13. Pashaura Singh : *Ph.D. Thesis*, Tronto University, 1991, p. 232.

38

GURUS AND THE BANI — THE BASIC MESSAGE

DALJEET SINGH AND KHARAK SINGH

Some questions which are frequently asked by persons not adequately familiar with Sikh ideology and history are :

1. Does the *bani* of the *bhagats* and *bhatts* raise any ideological problems, namely, does it accept Lords Krishna and Rama as *avtars* ? And is their religious system binding on the Sikhs ?

2. Is the world-view of the *bhagats,* whose *bani* has been incorporated in Guru Granth Sahib, binding on the Sikhs ? And, are the *bhagats* also Gurus for Sikhs ?

3. Do the references to some stories or Hindu myths mean that the Gurus accept their historicity ?

These questions are indeed basic, and are in essence, and by implication, linked with the very independence and identity of the religion of the Gurus. We shall try to answer these questions in two parts. The first part deals with the rationale, and the second part with the related hymns.

I

On scrutinising the entire religious history of man, we do not find a single instance, where a religious system has had more than one prophet. Sikhism has the singular distinction of having ten prophets with an unrivalled unity of their spiritual thesis, a Scripture authenticated by the Prophet himself, and the prophets having demonstrated the principles of their religion with their lives and martyrdoms over a period of about 240 years. The Tenth Guru formally organised the *Panth*, and gave the Sikhs their *kakkas*, declaring Guru Granth Sahib as their sole Scripture and Guru. Further, he made a complete break with the past by his *Nash* doctrine of *dharam nash,* *karam nash, bharam nash, kul nash* and *krit nash*. It is indeed painful that we still find Sikhs quibbling about what is Sikhism and what are its principles and injunctions. The very fact that ten Gurus have lived and preached with singularity of purpose, their system for 240 years, emphasises three things : that the traditional systems had ceased to be helpful to the people, that there was need of a new and independent system; and that their religion was radically so different, that the Gurus had again and again to demonstrate its principles, so as to explain and bring home to the people the essence of their system. As such, the Gurus' lives are of fundamental importance in order to understand their *bani*. The Guru says, "Those who know His Will, carry it out" [1, p. 991]. "Wonderful is His Will. If one walks in His Will, then one knows how to lead the life of Truth" [1, p. 940]. Accordingly, for the understanding and control of our egoistic consciousness, it is important that we accept the historical lives of the Gurus as a model of those who are imbued with His Will. It is in this background, and with humility, we approach the issues.

1. The first point to study of the *bani* of the Gurus is to find if there is any contradiction in it. In Guru Granth Sahib, there is repeated emphasis on the unity of thought of the Gurus. The very use of the name Nanak for the hymns of all the Gurus indicates this. Second, there are many hymns of *bhatts* which declare the different Gurus one in spirit [1, p. 966]. Third, there is the statement of the Tenth Guru that there can be no spiritual understanding or success, unless the unity of spirit of all the Gurus is realised [2, p. 295].

As to Vaishnavism, the system of Lords Rama and Krishna, even a casual student of religion knows that their system and Sikhism belong to different categories of religion, and that in most of their basic principles they are poles apart. Vaishnavism is a salvation religion that believes in monasticism, *sanyasa*, withdrawal, celibacy, downgrading of women, *ahimsa* and rigid adherence to the caste ideology in the empirical field. For, it is unquestioned that Lord Rama cut the head of Shambuka, a Sudra, for having violated the caste prohibition against the study of Vedas by a Sudra. Similarly, Lord Krishna proclaims that he is the creator of the four *varnas*, and that it is more meritorious for a Sudra to follow, even though inefficiently, the duties of his own caste, than for him to do efficiently the duties of another caste. Sikhism does not accept any of these principles. Besides, the Gurus clearly reject *avtarhood*, by calling God *Ajuni* (who does not incarnate). The Fifth Guru says, "cursed be the mouth that states God incarnates" [1, p. 1136]. Therefore, the ideology of Lords Rama and Krishna has no relevance for us, nor can they be regarded as Sikh Gurus. All this emphasises the independence of Sikhism and explains clearly where we have to seek and search for the truths laid down by the Gurus, namely, in their *bani* as lived by them.

2. A considerable part of what we have said above, is also relevant in giving the answer to the second question, namely, whether the world-view of the *bhagats* whose *bani* is in Guru Granth Sahib, is binding on us. There is little doubt that the *bhagats* had variant faiths. For the Muslim saints, Qoran and the Islamic *Shariat* were binding and Prophet Mohammad was the seal of prophets. Similarly, the Hindu Vaishnavites like Jaidev and Ramanand, believed in *sanyasa*, caste, ritualism, celibacy, downgrading of women, *ahimsa*, etc. It is well-known that Ramanuja, the chief exponent of Vaishnavism, would not admit a woman as a Vaishnava [3, pp. 201-202]. *Bhagats* like Namdev, Kabir and others, had their own separate ideologies. Without meaning any

criticism, all these saints were quietists, and had faith in withdrawal and *ahimsa*, and they did not believe in the equality of man and woman. Without going into details, it can be broadly affirmed that the *bhagats* were quietist saints in the sense that none of them accepted social responsibility, or advocated the use of force for a righteous cause or as resistance against aggression, nor did they organise any society or *Panth*.

All students of religion know that there is a clear demarcation between whole-life religions and what may be called quietist or salvation systems. In the whole-life religions of Judaism, as laid down by Moses, or Islam, as laid down by Prophet Mohammad, or of Sikhism, as lived by the Gurus, a householder's life is accepted, as also social responsibility, for the discharging of which a society is organised. The use of minimum force to help the weak and oppressed is sanctioned. For over a period of a hundred years, five Gurus have demonstratively wielded the sword for righteous causes, and a sword has been prescribed as one of the *kakkas* for a Sikh. It is well-known that monasticism, *sanyasa*, celibacy, withdrawal, a lower status of woman, and non-violence, are integral values in quietist systems. The Gurus prescribe complete equality between man and woman, social responsibility, both for the sustenance of life, involving work and fair distribution of wealth, and confrontation of those who oppress or are unjust to the weak. In Sikhism, these are essential values. In a whole-life system, apart from the sanction of force for a righteous cause, the prophets organised societies, since social and political aggression cannot be resisted by individuals. It is extremely relevant and meaningful that whereas quietist prophets, saints or mystics only cater for individual salvation, whole-life religions lay down not only the spiritual principles of their systems, but simultaneously organise a *Panth* or society, as did the Sikh Gurus. The world over, no quietist saint has ever recommended the use of force for a righteous cause. This clear distinction between quietist systems and whole-life systems, with marked differences in their values, goals, ethics, approach to life and social responsibilities is too bold, glaring and well-known to be disregarded by any student of religion. In a whole-life religion, the love of God and the love of man are virtually synonymous. Thus, the love of man involves succour and sacrifice for those who are weak, oppressed, or discriminated against. For, "God showers His Grace where the weak are helped," [1, p. 15] and Guru Nanak's God destroys the 'evil' and the 'demoniacal' [1, pp. 224, 1228]. In *Japuji Sahib*, the execution of the Altruistic Will of God is the goal prescribed by Guru Nanak [1, p. 1]. Hence, in Sikhism, neither withdrawal, nor celibacy, nor *ahimsa* has been recommended as inviolable values. Again, it is Guru Nanak who complains to God, when there is oppression and butchery of the weak, meaning thereby that injustice and oppression violate the Order of God, and that the *gurmukh* cannot remain neutral or unconcerned about it. Sikh history is a clear and classic demonstration of the role God-conscious men have to play when oppression in society is rampant.

Undeniably, the world-view of the *bhagats* is different from that of the Gurus. Accordingly, as in the case of Lords Rama and Krishna, the question of Sikhs accepting their ideologies, outside Guru Granth Sahib, cannot arise. It is unthinkable that having started a new society and demonstrated their ideology, they would in their *bani* confuse us, or ask the Sikhs to follow systems which were well-known to be different. For, if the earlier ideologies had to be accepted, the entire Sikh history of the Gurus' period would become without purpose or aim. In fact, to us, the very suggestion of any identity with earlier systems would seem to be irrational and self-contradictory. Often, it is our own failure to understand the difference, or our incapacity to follow the Sikh path that creates the confusion. It is evident that the Gurus neither ask us to accept the variant and old ideologies, nor have they involved any contradiction by the inclusion of the *bhagat bani*. The *bhagat bani* in Guru Granth Sahib is a selection. It is a fact that most of the *bhagat bani* is outside Guru Granth Sahib, and expresses variant ideologies. The hymns of the *bhagats* were selected by the Guru to the extent that the ideas they convey were considered by the Guru to be congruous with their own *bani*. This is clear from the connected commentaries of the Gurus on those hymns, where they felt there could be a possibility of misunderstanding.

Just as it is unknown in human history to have ten successive prophets of a religion, it is equally unknown for a prophet to include the *bani* of another system in its own scripture. There is a reason for so doing. Sikhism is universal and non-exclusive in its approach. For that reason, it gives due respect to other systems, and is willing to co-operate with them. Ecumenical efforts or approach among religions is a very recent or modern phenomenon. But, Guru Nanak in *Sidh Gosht* clearly proclaims that his mission in life is, with the help of other God-conscious men, to steer man across the sea of life. It is in that spirit and with that purpose in view that the Fifth Guru has included the hymns of *bhagats* in Guru Granth Sahib. It does not at all mean an identity of ideologies; but, it is a step for co-ordination and co-operation with like-minded *bhagats*. Pir Budhu Shah sacrificed his sons for the righteous mission of the Tenth Guru, but that did not mean that he had lost faith in Islam or Prophet Mohammad. Therefore, the inclusion of the *bani* of *bhagats* is an ecumenical measure indicating the presence of like-minded strands in other faiths, thereby requiring the Sikhs to be co-operative and universal in their approach. This is the context which explains that when the Sikhs got power, there was no attempt at conversion or persecution of the Muslims.

Thus, while all reverence is due to *bhagats* and prophets of other religions, it would obviously be contrary to the *bani* of the Gurus and their lives, if we either call them God-incarnate or the Gurus of the Sikhs. While everything in Guru Granth Sahib is *bani*, the Gurus of the Sikhs are only the Ten Masters and Guru Granth Sahib, who represent a complete unity of spirit, thought, and deed.

3. The third question is about the Hindu myths and stories which find mention in Guru Granth Sahib. Without meaning any disrespect to anyone, it is known that *Ramayana* and *Mahabharata* are among the great epics of the world in which most of the stories are mythical and have hardly any historicity. And, yet, these stories being current, have their values for the purpose of clarifying religious propositions, and making them linguistically understandable to the people who were conversant with them and the concerned idiom. Their reference is mostly symbolic, idiomatic, metaphoric or allegoric, and involves no acceptance of their historical reality. For example, the Gurus who

repeatedly goad man to make moral decisions with a view to spiritual progress, certainly deny the concept of the determined fall or regression, from *satyug* to *kalyug*. In fact, they clearly convey the idea of evolution in their hymns, "God created first Himself, then *haumain*, third *maya*, and fourth the higher state of a *gurmukh* who lives truthfully."[10] Therefore, references to myths and stories do not, by implication or otherwise, accept their historical truth, or their literal meaning. All great teachers of the world have made use of the current myths, parables and stories to bring home to the people the truth of what they wanted to convey, which otherwise would have been difficult for the people to understand. In literature, and more especially in moral literature, where the purpose is to motivate and condition the emotions of the people, an effective means is by reference to examples, parables and tales, which are within the ken and experience of the masses. The stories in *Panch Tantra* and George Orwell's *Animal Farm* are tales of animals depicted to express human thoughts, sentiments, viles, failings and foibles. The importance of the stories is in the lessons they seek to bring home, and not in their historical or literal truth.

Guru Nanak's system was so radical, new and independent, that the Gurus felt that mere expression and communication of their doctrines in the *bani* could be misunderstood. Had this not been Gurus Nanak's assumption, there would hardly seem to be need for subsequent Gurus and their historical roles over the centuries. Actually, it is Guru Nanak in his spirit who has lived for 240 years. The Gurus very well felt that in view of the thousands of years old Indian tradition of *sanyasa*, monasticism, celibacy, downgrading of women, *ahimsa*, etc., it would not be enough to bring home to the people their revolutionary system by merely laying it down in a Granth. The fact is that even after the compilation of Adi Granth, five Gurus lived, kept armies, struggled and were martyred for over a hundred years. Later, the prescribing of a *kirpan* as a *kakka* represents a spiritual principle or a truth in the Sikh theology. It cannot be treated as a redundant remnant of what was once necessary.

The real difficulty is the human tendency to misconstrue, especially because of our own prejudices. It is for this reason that Guru Nanak, who lived in spirit for almost two and a half centuries, had to demonstrate its meanings and implications. The *kirpan* represents the principle of social responsibility, including struggle against injustice and oppression. By their examples and sacrifices, the Gurus have explained when and to what extent the *kirpan* or force is to be used. Had the Gurus not done it, the position could be the same as in the case of the Hindu scriptures, which are so variantly interpreted by K. Bhatt, Sankara, Ramanuja, Nimbarka, Madhava, Vallabha and Swami Dayanand. It was to avoid such a state, that the Gurus lived to demonstrate the meaning of their *bani*.

II

We have emphasised that by losing sight of the historical perspective and hastening to go by the literal interpretation, we may so often miss the very meaning of the *bani*. For this reason, the lives of the Gurus are of fundamental importance, so as to enable us to understand the real import of the words of the Gurus. For example, in *Asa di Var*, the

Guru sings :

> "*Sache tere khand sache brahmand,*
> *Sache tere loe sache akar.*"

And again :

> "*Kur raja kur parja kur sabh sansar.*"

To some, the two views might appear contradictory. In fact, they complement each other, contributing to a balanced world-view. The former regards the world as real, and pleads for responsible participation in its affairs. The latter reminds one of its evanescent nature to deprecate accumulation of power and wealth. The goal of life, prescribed by Guru Nanak in *Japuji*, is to carry out the Altruistic Will of God. This is properly understood only if we carefully study the lives of the Gurus, and see how they worked, struggled and made supreme sacrifices for the achievement of this goal. The Tenth Guru, almost from his childhood, was engaged in an intense strife involving pressures, anguish and tragedies of unprecedented magnitude, which would have crushed the spirit of any individual not inspired by that lofty goal. In the context of such an intense struggle, it would be naive to conclude that the Gurus considered life to be *mithya* or false and unreal. In the absence of a close study of the lives of the Gurus, it is not possible to be clear about so many subtle nuances and depths of the *bani*. Hence, the fundamental importance of the exemplary lives of the Gurus in Sikh hermeneutics. The *bani* says that those who know His Will, carry it out. It was His Altruistic Will that the Gurus were following in their lives.

It is in this background that we study the place of Lord(s) Rama, Krishna, and other gods and goddesses in Sikhism. In *Asa di Var*, the Guru writes that God alone is without fear, and that there are innumerable deities like Rama, as insignificant as the dust of His feet, numerous being the stories of Krishna [1, p. 464]. We need hardly labour the point. But, students of Guru Granth Sahib know what is the status of gods and goddesses in *Gurbani*, as well as in the hymns of the *bhagats* Namdev and Kabir [1, pp. 637, 894, 953, 954]. Many a time the word *Ram* or *Morari* in the *bani* only means God, and not any individual of that name. And, wherever there is a story of any Grace having been bestowed in response to any prayer, the Guru's real reference, despite the mention of a human name in the story, is to God's power, or His benevolent response to prayer. For example, the Ninth Guru, while referring to God's or Ram's graciousness in response to the prayer of Daropadi, writes, "*Panchali ko raj sabha mein Ram Nam sudh aai*" [1. p, 1008]. Evidently, the incident relates to the story of Lord Krishna and Daropadi. But, for the Guru the grace bestowed is by God, here named Ram. The absence of the word Krishna is very significant. It shows that statements in *Gurbani* of incidents of grace, as narrated in the current stories or myths, neither confirm their historicity, nor confine their meanings to particular individuals named therein, but those seek only to explain to the devotee the power of God through the medium of myths, parables or idioms with which he is familiar. In sum, both in the *bani* of the Gurus and that of the *bhagats*, the Power which answers the prayer, or is Gracious, is, in each case, God, and not any living being.

A related question could arise regarding the *bani* of *bhatts*. They want to praise and describe the Gurus as the greatest beings of all times. They regarded the *avtars* as the greatest they knew of. Accordingly, they use the then current idiom to extol the Gurus by calling them greater than anyone in any age. Their comparison with the mythical persons does not indicate, much less establish, the historicity of Janak, Paras Ram or the rest. For, *bhatt* Kall sings that Jogeshwar, Paras Ram with the mythical axe, many *avtars*, Kapil, Janak, Bidar, Mahadeo and others of all ages, are ever singing praises of Guru Nanak [1. pp. 1389-90]. This is just a poetic or allegoric way of expressing the *bhatt's* belief in the lofty stature of the Guru. It does not at all mean the historicity of the persons mentioned, nor that those who lived in ages gone by, were still living and singing the praises of the Gurus. Everyone knows the mythical character of Paras Ram and his axe, which is supposed to have killed all the *kshatriyas* in the land.

Now, a few words about Kabir Sahib's hymn, *"Ete aurat mardan saje eh sabha rup tumhare; Kabir pungra Ram Allah ka sabh gur pir hamare."* The hymn ends with the words, *"Kewal naam japo re prani tab hi nehchai tarna"* [1. p. 1349]. We wonder how a serious student who has gone through the entire *shabad* (which emphasises the immanence of God and salvation only through *Naam*) can conclude that the hymn means that everyone (which includes Sakhi Sarvar, Sitla Devi, Gugga Pir, and thousands of other *devis* and *devtas*, preaching diverse cults) is the guru or *pir* of a Sikh. It is the same Kabir who writes, *"Kabir Brahmin guru hai jagat ka, bhagatan ka gur nahi"* [1. p. 1377].

Equally unsustainable appears to be the observation "I do not consider any difference between Guru Nanak, Guru Gobind Singh, Krishna, Rama, Jesus or Mohammad, because they give me the message of the Lord." The statement could be only partly true, since the message in each case is not identical. For Guru Nanak, his Lord is also the Destroyer of the evil-doer, and the Sikh Gurus wielded the sword for 102 years, and a *kirpan* is prescribed as a part of the essential wear of every Sikh. Whereas the Sikh Guru prays to God to save the burning world by any way He may be gracious enough to do, the Christian message is of salvation only through Christ, and the Sermon on the Mount is strictly pacificist. Islam also shares this exclusivism. Similarly, Lord Krishna claims to be the author of the caste ideology, involving strict adherence to one's caste duties and prohibition against any mobility in caste profession. Logically, it gives sanction to the concept of pollution. It requires purification of a temple after a Sudra has happened to visit it, or the washing of the statue of Sampurananand with holy Ganges water after Jagjivan Ram, a scheduled caste Deputy Prime Minister of India, had unveiled it. The statement may be a good speech from a political platform. However, it is difficult to identify the ideology of the Gurus with the earlier preachings of *shastras* and other scriptures, and thus, to uphold the claim. Of course, respect for all religious leaders and scriptures is understandable, and has been amply demonstrated in the *bani*.

CONCLUSION

In the end, we should again like to re-emphasise the very special position of Sikh hermeneutics. We humans have no access to the actual spiritual experience of the Gurus, nor can we be aware of the deliberation consequent to that experience in the consciousness of the prophets. We are distantly aware only of the expression of the decisions made by the prophets. The expression is either in the form of words or deeds. Here comes the major difference. In the case of almost every other system, the scripture is a post-facto man-made construction, recorded decades or even centuries after the disappearance of the prohpets. Debate has continued as to how far the record could be true, considering the known human weaknesses to remain subservient to personal or social influences. This handicap does not exist in the case of Guru Granth Sahib, which stands authenticated by the Guru himself. The second point is that expression in the form of deeds has always been considered clearer than words. This is for two important reasons. The expression in words can at best be general or theoretical in nature. For, this expression for that very reason, must seek to cover all possible eventualities that may arise in the future, and which possibilities can never be guessed completely. In short, word is only the penultimate step in the expression of the spiritual perceptions of which the deed is a concrete, unambiguous and final step in a comparatively specific flux of events. For this reason, it is easier to understand and less liable to misinterpretation than the word. The second point about the word is that it is a borrowed mode of expression and for that matter, it can never be as clear and concrete as the deed. Language, at any time, is already an existing vehicle of expression. It has its own changing nuances and has its roots extending many a time to a distant cultural past. Obviously, language being a second-hand vehicle of expression, its truth is more liable to misinterpretation than the deed which is not only particular to the author, but is also closely related as a response to known or identifiable set of events. For this reason, it is simpler and easier to comprehend.

In the above context, let us see what Guru Nanak did for us to reduce all possibilities of misunderstanding or misinterpretation. In the case of the words, the Guru himself authenticated them. As to the clearly understandable expression of deeds, Guru Nanak lived for us for 240 years. He lived, worked, struggled, organised a *Panth*, sacrificed and was martryed, while facing all sets of events, eventualities and milieus, social and political. The above are the two unique steps Guru Nanak has taken to make his system clear to us and to solve our problems of hermeneutics.

REFERENCES

1. Guru Granth Sahib.
2. Macauliffe. M.A. : *The Sikh Religion* , Vol. V.
3. Murthy. H.V.S. : *Vaisnavism of Shankradeva and Ramanuja.*

39

TWO VIEWS ON DASAM GRANTH

GURTEJ SINGH

Ever since its compilation near about the fourth decade of the eighteenth century, authorship of the greater part of the *Dasam Granth*[1] has been fiercely disputed by scholars. That was in spite of the great prestige undoubtedly enjoyed by Bhai Mani Singh, to whom the original compilation was cleverly attributed. Even the contemporaries of the Guru held different views and objected to its compilation in one volume which hinted at single authorship. Within a decade, a strong sentiment in favour of dismembering it swelled up within the *Panth*. Decision in favour of its being kept in one volume was at best an interim one, made in a great hurry. It was also a result of a pure chance.[2] The controversy having been thus swept under the carpet, has never since been seriously addressed. Had the majority's view[3] been accepted then for maintaining it in the form of different volumes, as originally intended, it would have automatically solved the problem of authorship as the Guru's compositions were well-known. In this ongoing controversy, an attempt will be made to assess the value of the contributions of Dr D.P. Ashta[4] and Dr Rattan Singh Jaggi[5], who are prominent representatives of the two views on the subject of authorship.

At the outset, it may be mentioned that there is no controversy regarding the authorship of *Jap*, *Akal Ustat* (except from verses 201 to 230) and *Swayyias*.[6] These portions of the *Dasam Granth* are indisputably accepted as compositions of the Tenth Guru. It may also be observed that, strangely enough, both schools of thought appear to share the belief that whatever is written by the Tenth Guru, would *ipso facto* constitute a part of Sikh canon. The root-cause of the controversy is this underlying assumption, though it is clearly unsustainable. Since its compilation, Guru Granth Sahib is the only Sikh canon.

Though outwardly attempting to ward off the vital assumption by adopting an innocuous title for his work, Ashta is clearly drawing conclusions which are possible only if the entire *Dasam Granth* is accepted as canon. In the preface, he indicates that the *Dasam Granth*, "has a very important place in Sikh ...... theology" and decrees it an "excellent evidence of influence exercised by Hindu theology, mythology, philosophy, history and literature in the life and activities of Guru Gobind Singh."[7]   It is this baseless assumption which is fully revealed in the Foreword by S. Radhakrishnan who further widens the scope of the author's formulations to assert, "from a study of this work, we learn the profound influence which Hindu tradition and mythology has had on the development of the Sikh religion" and that, "Ashta's work ...... is exposition of the teachings of the 10th Sikh Guru, Shri Gobind Singh."[8] True import of the short foreword is that there is need of accepting "a religion which is spiritual and non-sectarian" (that is Hinduism) in prefernce to a "sectarian view"[9] (that is Sikhism). This work aims at making it easier for the Sikhs to accept the suggested transformation.

This underlying objective manifests itself in several subtle and not so subtle ways in Ashta's work. Quite often, he insinuates that the Sikh views are borrowed by the Gurus from Hindu *bhagats*. His statement that Guru Gobind Singh, "like other Hindu thinkers ...... uses negatives in describing Him" is repudiated in the same breath "confessing" that "to him God was not a mere abstraction."[10] It is indicative of the origin he would like to place on Sikh thought. That desire must explain another insinuation that the ideal of the transmigration of the soul in Sikhism is ultimately inspired by *Upanishads* and *Bhagwatgita*. This statement is made in the full knowledge of the Guru's clear injunction that, 'they who forsaking me adopt the ways of *Veds* and *Smrities*, shall fall into the pit of hell."[11] Ashta goes to absurd lengths while pursuing this course. For instance, he seriously holds that even the satire of Guru Nanak and Guru Gobind Singh is borrowed from Ramanand and Kabir.[12]

The self-created predicament obliges Ashta to take up untenable positions again and again. To bring the philosophy of Sikhism in unison with that of the Hindu *bhagats*, particularly Kabir, he states that the Gurus believed in Kabir's *Nirguna Brahma*.[13] While imposing *"vishishtadvaita* position" on the Sikh Gurus, he asserts that their God is "above ...... worldly entanglements."[14] Nothing could be further from the truth.

Facts, however, stare him in the face and he has to conclude that according to the Guru, "God is omnipotent as love.[15] ...... God is sublimest Love. He loves his creation."[16] He also accepts whole-heartedly the basic truth of the Sikh religion that, "God is Himself the Creator, the Preserver and Destroyer, all in one."[17] God of Sikhism is also accepted by him to be "the Punisher of the evil."[18] Surprisingly, in spite of all these realisations, he does not feel compelled to revise his earlier formulations regarding the *nirguna*, the *vishishtadvaita* and the non-involved nature wrongly attributed to God in Sikhism. He holds on to both points of view, though he himself has effectively refuted one.

Apart from the fact that he contradicts himself, he betrays ignorance of the overall position of Sikh theology and history which has always been clear to serious students. Discerning minds have always realised that the *Kabirpanthis* are "virtually submerged under the tide of Hinduism." In comparison, it is recognised that Guru Nanak's teachings conspicuously tended towards and eventually ended up providing "an entirely new environment which called for the reforms introduced by Guru Gobind Singh, while other medieval reformers ...... created sects which were swallowed up by Hinduism."[19] In view of the above, it must be said of Ashta that he ventures forth to study the *Dasam Granth* with a definite premeditated design in mind. That obliges him to give up objectivity and he abandons it without a second thought. It is, therefore, no surprise that he fails to see the significance of Guru Gobind Singh's formal recognition of *Adi Guru Granth* as the only Sikh canon. He also does not realise that the Tenth Master persistently refused to collect his compositions in a single volume and under a common heading. This approach also explains why Ashta enthusiastically accepts Ram, Shyam and Kal to be the pseudonyms[20] of Guru Gobind Singh on absolutely flimsy grounds. This is in spite of the fact that a previously existing work of Baba Sumer Singh testifies to the independent existence of these poets as pointed out by Jaggi. Jaggi has gone into the same question more deeply[21] and has not only noticed, Shyam[22] amongst the court poets of Guru Gobind Singh, but has also succeeded in unearthing some of their compositions which are not a part of the *Dasam Granth*.

In order to establish the authorship of the Tenth Guru, Ashta repeatedly asserts that the poet of the *Dasam Granth* "does not believe in incarnations, gods or goddesses of Hindu or Mohemmadan religious books."[23] That he also often contradicts himself[24] goes without saying. It is left to Jaggi to effectively bring out that several contributors to the *Dasam Granth* do regard goddesses, gods and incarnations[25] as objects of worship. Jaggi's argument that, therefore, the Guru is not the author of the bulk of it is more rational and cannot be controverted as it proceeds on the same basic premise as accepted by Ashta. It is strange how the deliberate non-use of "Nanak", the legitimate name of Guru Gobind Singh, in the *Dasam Granth* has not been noticed either by Ashta or by Jaggi. They have not worked out the implications of that ommission. Another fact that has been neglected is that the Guru insisted upon excluding his writings from the Adi Granth.[26] It is also quite significant that the entire schemata or grammatical representations used in the Adi Granth are almost completely missing from the *Dasam Granth*.[27] The significance of the fact that this book was originally known as *Bachittar Natak Granth* and has travelled arduously towards the present title has also been missed both by Ashta and Jaggi. These facts alone are sufficient to convince any scholar that Guru Gobind Singh did not wish to interfere with the previously settled Sikh canon beyond adding his father's (the Ninth Nanak) compositions to it.

In addition, the conclusion sought to be drawn by Ashta and emphasised by Dr Radhakrishnan, can only be sustained if the internal incongruities of the Hindu religious system are effectively ignored. Whatever may have been the earlier position, their gods were so jealous of each other as to promote mutual contempt amongst their mutually exclusive followers. "In all these respects, *Puranas* and *Tantras* were especially instrumental, and they not only taught their followers to assert the unapproachable superiority of gods they worshipped, but inspired them with feelings of animosity towards those who presumed to dispute that supremacy......."[28] Consideration of this aspect alone rules out any single authorship for the narration of various incarnations included in the *Dasam Granth*. Though in passing, Jaggi has at least noticed[29] the difficulty presented by such inclusions. They include the incarnations worshipped by Vaishnavites, Shaivites, Sakats, Sanyasis, Jogis and even Muslims, for, Mir Mehdi is also amongst them. Seven incarnations of Brahma are also included. In the context of the times in which it is written, it could only have been composed by several authors having differing views of Reality. This also explains the existence of at least three versions of the story of Chandi in the *Dasam Granth*.

Ashta's convenient argument that, "the diction, the rhythm and vigour of the lines are peculiarly Guru Gobind Singh's own"[30] sounds hollow when, in the latter part of his thesis, he compares the poetry of the *Dasam Granth* with that of other poets and hints that it is in strong measure influenced and inspired by the type of the diction, rhythm and vigour commonly found in the poetic compositions of the age.[31] This argument is further developed by Jaggi. He concludes that the poetry of most of the *Dasam Granth* is conventional and of common occurrence. He further states that most of the poets composing it exhibit themselves as humble supplicants who often pray for favours from their patron and seek forgiveness for the possible mistakes — living in constant dread that those would be detected and be laughed at.[32]

Jaggi, on the other hand, has proceeded scientifically and objectively. He has clearly delineated in detail the views of both parties to the controversy and has then set out to examine them thoroughly. His logic is scathing and whatever cannot stand scrutiny is discarded without hesitation. This constitutes the first three chapters of his present work. His scrutiny of the letter attributed to Bhai Mani Singh is quite thorough. One would wish that he had gone into the circumstances in which it was discovered. It is well worth knowing whether G.B. Singh discovered it when he was in the thick of the controversy about the authorship of the *Dasam Granth* stirred up mostly by G.B. Singh himself. It would also be relevant to know whether serious aspersions cast on the integrity and objectivity of G.B. Singh by Bhai Sahib Singh[33] are valid and whether any conclusion on that basis is warranted in the present context ?

The fourth and fifth chapters deal with the four well-known manuscripts of the *Dasam Granth*. After incisive enquiry done with extreme care, Jaggi comes to the conclusion that there are material differences in the four versions. These sometimes extend to including additional works not usually associated with the book.[34] He notices that the material put together represents diverse and scattered writings completely lacking a common theme. The conclusion that it would have been more homogeneous, had the Guru intended to put it in one volume is entirely warranted. The other conclusion that it was not compiled during the Guru's lifetime is obvious (It is only in the early nineteenth century Sikh literature that we find first mention of the volume). The very fact that such liberties have been taken by different compilers, clearly indicates that no particular sanctity was attached to the compilation. There is thus no doubt that it was not considered by them to be the Guru's word.[35]

An analysis of the portions supposedly in the handwriting of the Guru himself has been done with characteristic thoroughness by Jaggi. These pages have mostly been pasted later into the volumes pointing unmistakably to the very late origin of the compilations. It is also pointed out that these are often materially inaccurate which totally rules out their being written by the Guru.[36] Commonly used local script has been used for writing these pages. It is wrong to advertise it as the Guru's peculiar invention. Jaggi approvingly quotes Giani Gian Singh's assertion that these pages are forgeries made by Charat Singh, son of Sukha Singh, author of the *Gurbilas*. That perhaps reflects the true position.

Two chapters have been devoted by Jaggi to the analysis of the ideology of the rest of the *Dasam Granth*. By comparing it with the known writings of the Tenth Guru, he has conclusively shown that the two are poles apart. In this connection, it is highly significant that meat eating, drinking of alcohol and sex indulgence are profusely inducted in some writings, which are translations of other texts. This is in spite of the fact that the original texts of which these are translations, do not mention such activity.[37] That to Jaggi reasonably reveals an interested Sakat's hand in the composition. Serious anachronisms, which would discredit any ordinary man of moderate learning, have been pointed out.[38]

Concluding it can be stated without fear of contradiction that, in comparison, Jaggi's thesis is well-authenticated and balanced. Ashta, on the other hand, appears to be too keen to adopt a particular point of view. He is not thorough in his analysis, is quite often self-contradictory, and appears eager to gloss over material facts which are inconvenient and do not support his own point of view. On the whole, his work appears quite lacking in objective inquiry. If we relate it to the conclusions drawn from it by Dr Radhakrishnan, we cannot say that it is devoid of a motive or a predisposed desire to conform to certain pre-determined notions related to the position of Sikhs in the Indian polity.

REFERENCES

1. To begin with it was known as *Bachitter Natak* or *Bachittar Natak Granth*, then by various names including *Dasam Patshah ka Granth* until it was finally christened as *Dasam Granth* in this century.
2. Bhai Sukha Singh and Mehtab Singh, who passed through Damdama Sahib on their way to punish Massa Ranghar, desecrator of the Harimandar, proposed that it should be kept in one volume if they succeeded and returned, but should be kept separate if they died in the attempt. They were successful and returned.
   See Kahan Singh, Bhai, *Mahan Kosh* (Pbi) (Reprint) Bhasha Vibhag, Patiala, 1974, 616.
3. Ibid., 616.
4. Ashta, Dr Dharam Pal, *The Poetry of the Dasam Granth*, Arun Prakashan, New Delhi, pp. 312 + XXXXVIII + iv.
5. Jaggi, Dr Rattan Singh, *Dasam Granth Da Kartritav* (Pbi), Punjabi Sahit Sabha, New Delhi, 1966, pp. 237 + 1.
6. See conclusion by Jaggi, Dr Rattan Singh, loc. cit. p., 198. Jaggi has apparently kept his options open by using the word etc., at the end of his list.

7. Dr Ashta, loc. cit. X.

8. Ibid., VII.

9. Ibid., VII.

10. Ibid., 187.

11. Ibid., 188.

12. Ibid., 205-206.

13. Ashta, op. cit., 169.

14. Ibid., 171.

15. Ibid., 175.

16. Ibid., 178.

17. Ibid., 176 also "God not only creates but also provides for the sustenance of all" p. 180.

18. Ibid., 182.

19. Banerjee, A.C., *Guru Nanak and Problems of his Age*, *Journal of Religious Studies*, Vol. No. 1. September 1969, 45.

20. Ashta, op. cit., pp. 13-15.

21. Jaggi, Dr Rattan Singh, op. cit., pp. 21-22 see Appendix 3, and pp. 47 to 58.

22. Ibid., 173-175.

23. Ashta, op. cit, pp. 21-22.

24. Jaggi, op. cit., pp. 176-194.

25. The Sikh position is ably summed up by Mohsin Fani, a comtemporary of Guru Hargobind. See Ganda Singh's translation in *The Panjab Past and Present*, Vol. III, Punjabi University, Patiala, 1969, 5, wherein he says, 'disciples of Nanak condemn idol worship ...... they do not read the mantras of Hindus, They do not ...... esteem their Avtars.'

26. 'Guru did not allow it to be incorporated in the *Adi Granth*,' Chhibber, Kesar Singh, "Bansavalinama," *Parakh*, Panjab University, Chandigarh 1972.

27. For instance, had the system been followed, *ik chun chun jharon kadian* in *Chandi-di-var*, would have been written as : *ikki chuni chuni jharon kadiani*. cf. Gurdit Singh, Giani, *Shabdantik Lagan Matran*, Singh Sabha Patrika, August 1990, Chandigarh, 18.

28. Wilson, H.H., *Religious Sects of The Hindus*, (1861), (Reprint) Susil Gupta (India) Private Limited, Calcutta, 1958, 2.

29. A passing reference by Jaggi, op. cit., 181. Padam, Piara Singh, *Dasam Granth Darshan*, (Pbi.) Patiala April 1990, 81 is aware that no other work which includes these diverse incarnations, exists. Referring to love for Krishna, Ashta does affirm that "their devotion was so much that they could do away with all their deities and be devoted to him exclusively" Ashta, op. cit., p. 77.

30. Ibid., p. 168.

31. The following extracts are from Ashta, op. cit. :

"In the *Dasam Granth*, also descriptions of nature fall within this conventional category" p. 297.

"This form of poetry from the beginning of Hindi literature even to this day is still being attempted. The treatment is more or less conventional." p. 299.

"...... here too Guru Gobind Singh has employed the conventional style." p. 301.

He considers Gian Parbodh to be "an attempt at revival of the epic philosophy." p. 305.

"*Bachitra Natak Granth* follows the Puranic tradition ......" p. 306.

"The poetry of the *Dasam Granth*, like the Hindi poetry of the day has several elements of conventionality in it." p. 307. See also pp. 308, 309.

"In war poetry, Bhushan's *Shivraj Bhushan*, *Shiva Bhawani* and *Chhatarsal Dasak* get the precedence of *Dasam Granth* in time as well as in epic quality." p. 309.

"In variety of meter, *Dasam Granth* ranks next only to works of Keshavdas. ......" p. 310.

32. Jaggi, op. cit., pp. 166-168.

33. Cf. Sahib Singh, *Adi Bir Bare*, Singh Brothers, Amritsar, February, 1970, pp. 110-118.

34. Jaggi, Rattan Singh, op. cit., pp. 98-99.

35. Ibid., pp. 112, 125, 126.

36. Ibid., pp. 121, 138, 139.

37. Ibid., p. 151.

38. Ibid., p. 164.

40

DASAM GRANTH — ITS HISTORY

DALJEET SINGH

INTRODUCTION

Since the time the writings or *pothis*, to be later compiled and called the *granth* of the Tenth Master, were originally found, there has been a controversy about their authorship, authenticity and historicity. Very few persons have made a serious study about their genuineness. The issue is important, and writers like O'Connell and others have often made accusations like : "A conspicuous deficiency already mentioned is the general reluctance to grapple effectively with the *Dasam Granth*. The period whence it comes is absolutely crucial, and until it is adequately treated, we shall continue to grope in our efforts to trace the course of Sikh history or development of Sikh tradition." It is, therefore, necessary to assess the veracity of facts, and to indicate the probabilities of the issue, so that it is understood in its right academic perspective.

HISTORY — 18TH CENTURY CHHIBBER'S STORY

Most of the evidence about the present work called the '*Dasam Granth*' is negative. The earliest reference about some writings by the Tenth Master is by Chhibber in his *Bansavalinama*. Contemporary historians of the period of Guru Gobind Singh like Sainapat, Bhai Nandlal, Chaupa Singh, Sewadas, Koer Singh or Bhai Mani Singh, make no mention of the *Dasam Granth* or any such writing in the period. This negative evidence is quite significant and strong.

For, had there been any compilation like the *Dasam Granth*, these contemporary chroniclers could never have failed to mention it. The first reference to some writings by the Tenth Guru is in Chhibber's *Bansavalinama* written 71 years after the Guru's demise. This volume, as assessed by scholars like Jaggi, Kohli and others, has not been found to be very reliable as to its dates and other particulars. Besides, the author himself says that he is no chronicler, but has based the writing merely on hearsay, and just as a matter of his hobby : "I state what I had heard and what I could recollect." "This hearsay I record just by way of my hobby (*shauk*)."[1] Thus, Chhibber himself discounts the historical accuracy of his statements, for, he claims to belong only to the third generation of a Brahmin family whose head was a contemporary of the Tenth Master.

Further, two important points have also to be kept in view. First, most Brahmin writers always have a strong, natural and understandable bias to give a Brahminical colour to the Sikh religion and its history, even though all the Sikh Gurus were emphatic to proclaim the independence of their system and the *Panth*. The Fifth Master wrote :

"I keep not the Hindu fast, nor do I observe Muslim month of fast;

I serve only Him, who emancipates all; He is my Gosain;

He is my Allah; I have found release from the Hindus as from the Turks;

I visit not the pilgrim places of Hindus, nor go to Kaaba for Haj;

I serve only God, I serve not any other;

I worship not the Hindu way, nor say the Muslim prayers;

I bow to the one God within my heart;

I am neither a Hindu, nor a Muslim;

For, my body and life belong to Him, Allah and Ram."[2]

Second, Guru Gobind Singh had put the final seal on this complete separateness, by the creation of the Khalsa, the Nash Doctrine (Dharam Nash, Bharam Nash, Karam Nash, Sharam Nash and Janam Nash), and the declaration of Guru Granth Sahib as the sole Ideological Guide and Living Guru of the Sikhs. Yet, these writings have shown a subtle tendency to reshape and reframe Sikh events, so that these are accepted by the gullible as a part of the Brahminical tradition.

Following is what Chhibber records : "The Guru got written a Granth (book) called 'Samundar Sagar.' Later he got it thrown in a river." "Later still he composed other writings." "But, during the battles at Anandpur, the leaves of these writings or packets (*sanchian*) were scattered to the wind and lost."[3] Chhibber is vague about the contents or nature of these writings. Once he calls it 'Samundar Sagar', at another time 'Avtar Leela.' There is no reference at all to '*Dasam Granth*', 'Bachittar Natak', 'Chandi Charitar', 'Chandi di Var', 'Charitropakhyan' or 'Chaubis Avtar', as these are called now.

It is clear that it was peace time when the Guru had thrown the Samundar Sagar Granth in the river. Could it ever happen that he would destroy *Gurbani*, his own or that of earlier Gurus, or anything of value to Sikhs ? *Gurbani* has always been considered sacred, and been venerated more than even the Guru. Evidently, the writings were such as could conveniently be discarded. The argument applies doubly to the packets that were never completed or compiled, and were allowed to be scattered.

Thus, Chhibber's story adds nothing to our knowledge about the *Dasam Granth* writings, their compilation or loss. Therefore, the negative evidence of all contemporary chroniclers, coupled with the evidence of Chhibber's story, shows that till the end of the 18th century, there was nothing known about any *granth* of the Tenth Guru, or any writings now regarded as its chapters or contents. In fact, the only *granth* or compilation mentioned in the literature is 'Vidya Sagar' or 'Samundar Sagar Granth', the contents of which have no relation to the present *Dasam Granth*.

CHHIBBER'S STORY CONTRADICTED

Chhibber alleges three facts. First, that the Tenth Master initially created a *granth* called Samundar Sagar, and had it thrown into a river. Later, some papers (*sanchis*) were prepared, but these, too, were scattered to the wind and lost in the time of battles. Second, he records that in 1725 A.D. Bhai Mani Singh compiled a *granth* combining the *bani* of Aad Granth and the writings that subsequently came to be called *Dasam Granth*.[4] For doing this mix-up, and thereby violating the prescribed sequence or method of writing *gurbani*, a poor Sikh, when he saw the combined *granth*, cursed Bhai Sahib saying that just as he had disjointed the *gurbani* and mixed it up, he would also be cut to pieces.[5] Chhibber never writes chronologically. For example, in a still later couplet No. 389, he writes that in 1698 A.D. Guru Gobind Singh rejected the request of the Sikhs to combine the Aad Granth with his own writings.[6] It is very significant that the entire book of Chhibber is packed with his use and narration of Brahminical practices, and stories of demons, fairies, *Hom, mantras*, curses, etc., even though he knows that these are opposed to the doctrines in Guru Granth Sahib. In short, his Brahminical faith and prejudices are glaringly evident.

In addition, the above version of Chhibber, we find, is contradicted both by Gian Singh and Sarup Das Bhalla on all the essential points concerning *Dasam Granth* writings. Gian Singh never mentions that Samundar Sagar Granth or *sanchis* of Avtar Leela stories were prepared, thrown or lost. He also contradicts Chhibber that Sikhs at any time made a request to the Guru to combine his *bani* with the Aad Granth. All he states is that once Sikhs requested the Guru to compile his own *bani*, but he categorically declined to do so, saying that such a request should never be made again.[7] He also contradicts Chhibber's version that Bhai Mani Singh ever combined the two, and later suffered a 'curse' from a poor Sikh for doing so. He only states that in response to a suggestion by some Sikhs, he wrote *gurbani* in separate words for the purpose of explaining its meaning (*teeka*), and that the *sangat* disapproved of it, saying that he would suffer for it. But the *sangat* conceded that his faith in the Guru will remain unshaken. This satisfied Bhai Sahib.[8] However, he indicates that on the request of Sikhs, he collected the *bani* of Guru Gobind Singh.[9]

Mehma Parkash of Sarup Das Bhalla, a late 18th century or an early 19th century production, materially gives the same impression as does Gian Singh. Bhalla, a non-Brahmin, contradics all the three assertions of Chhibber, namely, the preparation or loss of any *granth* like Samundar Sagar or *sanchis* of other writings, the request of Sikhs to the Guru to add his *bani* to the Aad Granth, or any combined compilation by Bhai Mani Singh, and the curse by a poor Sikh. On the other hand, Bhalla gives the story that the Guru got prepared a *granth*, since lost, called Vidya Sagar, which constituted translations of Sanskrit literature.[10] He does not say that the Sikhs ever requested the Guru to include his *bani* in the Aad Granth, nor that Bhai Sahib ever produced any such compilation.

These being the realities, there is little doubt that Chhibber's version is not only unworthy of reliance, but is clearly the result of a prejudiced twist to facts as they really were. For, it is unthinkable that Bhai Sahib would ever combine the two, as alleged by

Chhibber and as now sought to be supported by the presence of the Delhi and Sangrur *birs*, when he knew full well that the Guru had clearly frowned upon such an idea. Had Bhai Sahib prepared any *bir*, it would be the authentic version, and there could never have been the possibility of such widely variant versions of the *granth*, as actually exist now. For, every *bir* would have been a copy of it. Nor is there any reason for the complete disappearance of it. Because, we find, that the Delhi *bir*, which has no history, is certainly not Bhai Sahib's production.

For the reasons and facts given above there is little doubt that the story of Chhibber stands belied, and that the version that Bhai Mani Singh compiled the *Dasam Granth*, is a distortion that has no historical, ideological or factual basis or possibility.

19TH CENTURY

The existence of *Dasam Granth* is mentioned for the first time in mid-nineteenth century by Bhai Santokh Singh, and later by Giani Gian Singh and others. Later, Bhai Kahn Singh and others repeat the story of Bhai Santokh Singh, suggesting that the *bir* of *Dasam Granth* was compiled by Bhai Mani Singh. It is also stated that there were many objections to the compilation in one volume of the various writings that had earlier existed separately. But, the final decision to do so or not, rested on the chance factor of the success or otherwise of the mission of Sukha Singh and Mehtab Singh against Massa Ranghar. The reality, however, is that none of these writers have given any shred of evidence to support the story of its compilation. In the absence of any authentic historical evidence, it is simply impossible to attribute the present collection, or any part of it, to Bhai Sahib. It is equally impossible to believe that if a respected contemporary of the Guru like Bhai Sahib had really compiled the *granth*, or any part of it, there could ever have been a controversy about it among the Sikhs so as to require them to resort to the chance decision depending on the success of Mehtab Singh and Sukha Singh. Bhai Mani Singh's position being pre-eminent as a trusted scribe and devout Sikh of the Guru, could any Sikh or *Panth* disregard or doubt his testimony about the *Dasam Granth*, if it had been there ? There is, thus, little doubt that the story of *Dasam Granth*'s compilation by Bhai Sahib has no historical basis. In fact, it is a motivated fabrication to give credence to the story of *Dasam Granth* compilation.

LETTER BY BHAI MANI SINGH

The supportive story of a letter written by Bhai Sahib, about the collection of *Charitropakhyan*, to Mataji at Delhi is another fabrication. Dr Jaggi has examined in detail the veracity of this letter and found it to be unreliable. The method of writing separate words, as in this letter, was not at all in vogue in the time of Bhai Sahib. Nor is the practice visible in the contemporary manuscripts. The words or language used also relates to a later period. Besides, the use of *bindi*, other features, *matras* and shape of letters are comparatively modern. Very probably the letter is written by a metallic nib which was not available in those times. The words used are rather unsophisticated and could not have been from a learned *gurmukh* like Bhai Sahib. It is also strange that the letter mentions 303 *charitars* or stories, whereas everywhere else the number is 404.[11] Nor has the letter been forthcoming from a natural custody. It was never heard of in the

18th or 19th centuries, and its appearance is only a mid 20th century phenomenon. It is strange that Dr Ashta who accepts it, has done so virtually without any examination of it. *Charitropakhyan* is a writing which no Sikh, *granthi*, or scholar has been willing to read or send to his mother, sister or daughter. No one has so far read it out in the open *sangat*. It is, indeed, unlikely that a *gurmukh* like Bhai Sahib would send its manuscript to venerated Mataji. It is, thus, historically baseless to connect Bhai Sahib or Mataji in any manner with the collection or compilation of *Dasam Granth* or any part of it.

The above rationale makes it plain that there is no evidence whatsoever of the existence of *Dasam Granth* or any part of it in the 18th or even the 19th century. All we now know is the later appearance of some manuscripts or *birs* of the *Dasam Granth*. Four of them are regarded as the oldest. We shall consider their reliability or authenticity.

BHAI MANI SINGH BIR

Raja Gulab Singh of Delhi purchased a *bir* in 1944-45, which is known as the Bhai Mani Singh Bir. Nothing historically verifiable is known about it, except a story given by him that a soldier of Ranjit Singh found or looted it during an attack on Multan in 1818 A.D. The soldier then shifted to and settled at Hyderabad. How the *bir* got to Multan and remained unknown for 125 years, is quite enigmatic and unexplained. External evidence about its history is completely missing. The *bir* is far from being a speaking manuscript. For, the authorship is unknown, as also the place or time of its compilation. In a corner of a page there is a slanting postscript, recording 1713 A.D. as the date of it. Jaggi's examination and its photocopy clearly show it to be a suspicious interpolation. The ink and writing of this entry are different from those of the original *bir*. The handwriting and shape of letters are also comparatively crude. Its introduction in slanting lines in a corner proves its belated character.[12] In fact, it is a thoughtless fabrication of the date. For, the story of Bhai Sahib's collection of its parts and the *Panthic* decision to have them in one volume following Massa Ranghar's death, relate to a time about two decades later.

All the internal evidence of the *bir* is against its authenticity. Jaggi finds that the writer of the *bir* does not seem to be a good scribe or to have a good knowledge of the Gurmukhi script or the Punjabi language.[13] Therefore, it is not at all possible to connect this *bir* with Bhai Sahib. On the other hand, the scribe is a Hindi-knowing person who is distinctly interested in distorting the Sikh doctrines and mixing up Sikh literature with *Puranic* literature. And this is, exactly what he has done. The *bir* comprises both the *bani* of the Gurus and that of the *Dasam Granth*. *Gurbani* has not been recorded as in Guru Granth Sahib, i.e., *raag*-wise. It is done Guru-wise and *Bhagat Bani* is mostly at the end of the combined volume. It shows conclusively that the scribe is a non-Sikh who, without any knowledge of the prescribed method of writing *Gurbani*, is out to do the heretical distortion of mixing-up *dhur ki bani* with *Puranic* myths about worship of *devis* and *avtars*. For, no Sikh, and much less a *gurmukh* like Bhai Sahib, could ever plan to combine the two and flout the sacred sequence of *Gurbani* (written *raag*-wise) laid down by the Gurus. The shape of writing and its language suggest that the distortion was done long after the demise of Bhai Sahib, when the Sikh world was engaged in its life and death struggle with the Empire and the invaders.

Thus, the lack of any history of the manuscript for over 200 years, its internal evidence of interpolation, shape of letters and language, together with the heretical change of method in writing *Gurbani*, and its mix-up with *Puranic* and *avtar*-worship literature, conclusively exclude the possibility of the *bir* being a production of Sikh quarters. On the other hand, the probability is that it is a compilation by those either unconversant with Sikh doctrines, tradition and literature, or those out to confuse the Sikh ideology. In any case, the manuscript has no historical or academic value as an authentic *bir*.

MOTI BAGH BIR

The *bir* of Moti Bagh is another manuscript that has no verifiable history. In 1959, one Natha Singh stated that his ancestor, one Hakam Singh had given this *bir* to Maharaja Mohinder Singh (1862-1876 A.D.), that earlier one Nahar Singh had obtained it from Charat Singh, son of Sukha Singh, and that the former had been obtaining for it a grant from Maharaja Ranjit Singh.[14] But, no part of its history is verifiable, or is otherwise corroborated. Nor is there anything in the internal evidence of the *bir* to support the story or any part of it. The *bir* shows that it had been compiled by more than one person. Jaggi opines that the age of the paper and the character of words and writing show that it could not have been compiled earlier than a hundred years after the demise of the Tenth Guru.

SANGRUR BIR

The *granthi* at gurdwara Deodi Sahib Dewan Khara, Sangrur, says that in 1857 A.D. the *bir* had been presented to the Raja by a *Pathan* of Delhi, when he had gone there in aid of the British. The *bir* was in two parts, pages 1 to 600 contained *Gurbani* from Guru Granth Sahib, and pages 601 to 1166 the chapters that form *Dasam Granth*. The first part stands lost. Its history before 1857 A.D. is unknown.[15] Internal evidence suggests that it is a combined collection of *bani* from Guru Granth Sahib and the chapters of *Dasam Granth*. Since the very system of combining *dhur ki bani* with *puranic* and *avtar* and other literature is opposed to the specific tradition laid down by the Gurus, the heretical mix-up has been done, as explained earlier, by non-Sikh elements. For, it is inconceivable that a composition like the *Charitropakhyan*, which even the SGPC, vide its letter No. 36672 dated 3.8.1972, has declared to be a composition from Hindu mythology and not by the Tenth Master, could have been combined with sacred *Gurbani* by any Sikh. This fact alone shows conclusively that the *Dasam Granth*, which contains *Charitropakhyan*, could never be a compilation of Sikh quarters, much less could it be by the Tenth Guru. The *bir*, thus, is of no historical or academic value.

PATNA BIR

The Patna Bir has also no historical value. Nothing worthwhile about it was narrated to Jaggi when he examined it there.[16] The writing is simple, except that red ink has also been used. The arguments against the authenticity of its compilation, production, and mix-up of the Tenth Gurus's *bani* with *Charitropakhyan*, as noted earlier, also apply to this volume. Jaggi feels that the condition of the paper, shape of letters, writing, etc., suggest that it is a production of the 19th century.

NO BIR IS AUTHENTIC

Dr Jaggi's detailed descriptions of these and other *birs* shows that in matters of contents, number of hymns and *chhands*, sequence of topics, list of writings, distribution of writings, or headings, etc., etc., there is no uniformity between any two *birs*. In fact, some of these contain additional material clearly known to be from non-Sikh sources. The conclusion is inevitable that these *birs* are odd, assorted and belated compilations or collections of unconnected and disjointed materials, made by individuals from non-Sikh quarters, who were neither conversant with the Sikh literature, nor with the method and sanctity of writing *Gurbani*. Their only interest was to mix-up Sikh literature with *puranic* and *avtar* literature so as to show both of them as parts of a single tradition. For, had the compilers been acquainted with Sikh practices and quarters, there would not have been such a variation in contents, combinations, sequence, number of hymns, as is evidenced by the different *birs*. Nor are these *birs*, for the same reasons, copies from one traceable or authentic source. This conclusion is fortified by the facts that not only have these *birs* virtually no known history, but the earlier ones relate to the period when struggle with the Empire was intense and there was a price on every Sikh head. And, later when peace came, in the late 18th or early 19th century, these writings containing mixed-up literature were quietly introduced and got copied without much scrutiny. Otherwise, how could it be that no *bir* bears any authentic date or name of a known Sikh scribe of the Guru, of the early Sikh period ? We also find that some of the errors are too gross to be committed by a person conversant with *Gurbani*. Jaggi has listed many of these errors in chapter six of his book. These errors and their repetition show their non-Sikh origin. These are very significant aspects of the old compilations, and in any serious assessment of their value, the importance of their import and implications cannot be ignored.

Here it is necessary to mention an unverified story that the Tenth Guru had initiated a move to translate into Gurmukhi some ancient literature. It is well-known that in his short life he was faced with colossal tasks, and his accomplishments, as declared by H.R. Gupta, were indeed superhuman in every field of his activities : "His dreams and deeds brought a wonderful change in his own generation in the religious, military and political life of the people. His personality was so fascinating, so bewitching, so dynamic, so momentous and so unforgettable, that we are seized with wonder at the changes which took place in Punjab within one year and half of his death. He was the greatest genius of his age. Whenever we touch that short life, as he died at the age of forty two, we are at once brought into contact with a live wire. He was a meteor that consumed itself to light the world. He was luminous like the sun and had conquered death. He possessed a rare combination of so many excellences, supreme self-denial, marvellous intellect, superhuman willpower, great heart and limitless energy ......"[17] It is quite apparent that whatever translations were done by Brahmins and Sikhs, were lost, and could not be suitably compiled or scrutinized about their utility in his time or even later. In any case, there is no historical evidence to this effect. Very probably it is only the Brahminical quarters who had later the time and interest to compile those translations and combine them with *Gurbani*. This view, we feel, explains all aspects of the *Dasam Granth* and what Jaggi considers its numerous inconsistencies and contradictions.

INTERNAL EVIDENCE

I. *Historical Contradictions* : There are, as detailed by Jaggi, many historical and other incongruities in the *Dasam Granth* which it would be naive to attribute to the Tenth Guru.[18] We give only two instances :

(i) In the story of Prithoo Raja, the author has shown that the legendary Shakuntala had connection not with Prince Dushyant, but with the mythical Prithoo. According to Bhagwat Puran, Prithoo was an *avtar* of Vishnu who appeared in Treta Yug. But Shakuntala's story of love with Dushyant in Bhagwat Puran is entirely different.[19] Thus, the writer who has joined Prithoo and Shakuntala, could not be concerned with the purity of *Puranic* stories. But his only interest appears to be to link the *bani* of Guru Gobind Singh Sahib with concocted Hindu legends, so that he is shown to be part of the Brahminical lore and legend.

(ii) Similarly, in the story of Raghu Raja, to say that Sanyasis regarded him as Dutt, Yogis as Gorakh Nath, Bairagis as Ramanand, and Muslims as Prophet Mohammad, shows that the interest of the story writer is not to narrate any rational history or myth.[20] He only seeks to represent that the Guru accepted Hindu mythology and tradition, and for the purpose to distort Sikh doctrines and ideas.

By no means can the authorship of such cock-and-bull stories be attributed to the lofty personality of the Guru. Obviously, the interest of the authors of these incongruities is quite extraneous to any faithful representation of events, doctrines, ideas, or even myths.

Another fact that seriously affects the historicity of these writings, is quite significant. Normally, the preparation, compilation or reproduction of a *granth* by a scholar is a great achievement, and the same is kept as a treasure, which the author or his family is always reluctant to part with. But, in the case of these manuscripts or *birs* not only their history and names or identity of compilers are unknown, but, we also find, that none of the compilers or custodians ever showed any reluctance to part with them. On the other hand, an apparent aim seems to have been that the compilation reaches an important place or a distinguished person, that could confer authenticity to it.

II. *Ideological Contradictions* : The unity of spirit of all the Ten Gurus is a fundamental of Sikhism, which stands emphasised and recorded in Guru Granth Sahib. The second basic and unalterable concept of Sikhism, as opposed to that of Brahminism, is that God does not incarnate. This concept is an integral element of the creedal hymn *Mul Mantra*[21] of Guru Nanak in the very beginning of Guru Granth Sahib. This concept is the corner-stone of Sikh theology. So much so, that the Guru says : "May that mouth burn which says that God incarnate."[22] "God alone is the one who is not born of a woman."[23] "God is self-existent, without form and incarnates not."[24] The Gurus clearly deny belief in the theory of incarnation of God. In order to dispel such ideas they state, "The Formless alone, Nanak, is without fear, many are Ramas as the dust of His Feet, many Krishnas. Many are their stories and many are the Vedas."[25] The Gurus write that He created countless Brahmas, Sivas and Vishnus.

The above is the categoric thesis of the Gurus and Guru Granth Sahib, the sole Ideological Guide of the Sikhs. We have to test any idea, doctrine or practice on the touchstone of *Gurbani*. For, it is unimaginable that any Guru or Sikh could approve of anything incongruous with the creedal statement of Guru Nanak. It is in the above context that we have to examine and test the authenticity of what is in any *granth*, not specifically authenticated by the Gurus.

DEVI AND AVTAR WORSHIP IN THE DASAM GRANTH

Dr Jaggi has made a detailed examination of the issue. He finds that except for about 70 pages of the *Dasam Granth*, including *Jap Sahib*, *Swayyas*, *Akal Ustat* (excluding hymns in praise of Durga), *Asphotak Chhand* and *Zaffarnama*, the other contents which involve worship of *avtars*, *devis* and *mahakal* are mostly from the *Puranic* literature. Following are some instances of *devi* worship. (For details see chapter 9 of Jaggi's book).

  (i) *Tribhangi Chhands* (201-220, In *Akal Ustat*) are clearly in praise of the *devi*.

  (ii) In *Shashtarnama* in the beginning there is a whole chapter (27 *chhands*) in praise of the *devi*.

 (iii) *Chandi Charitar* I & II, *Chaubis Avtar*, *Rudra Avtar* including parts of *Charitropakhyan*, all relate to the *Puranic* myths that are in praise of the *devi* and *avtars*.

 (iv) Similarly, in the above *Puranic* stories there are numerous hymns in praise of Maha Kal, who is a *Tantric* or *Sakat* deity, pages 55, 56, 57, 58, 73, 156, 157, 183, 185, 254, 310, 612, 613, 642, etc.

  (v) Worship of *devi* under the name of Kalika, Chandi, Siva or Durga is found at pages 74, 76, 99, 117, 255, 118, 309, 310, 116, 673, 675, etc., etc.

 (vi) Apart from the *Var* of Durga, there is the entire *Puranic* story of the *devi* coming to the rescue of the mythical Indra and fighting battles with demon Maikhasur, involving trillions of soldiers (*devi* worship *chhands* and narration of the myth).

 (vii) In *Chandi Charitar Ukat Bilas* the author mentions that he has virtually made the composition from 700 *slokas* of *Markand Purana*. He adds that whoever hears or recites the same for any specific boon, the *devi* would certainly grant it instantaneously (*Chandi Charitar, Ukat Bilas - sloka* 232).

(viii) In *Chandi Charitar* II in the *sloka* 261 the author writes that whoever remembers or worships the *devi* with devotion, shall attain salvation. Similarly, in the *Durga Var* the author writes that whoever recites the same, will achieve salvation and not be born again (stanza or *pauri* - 55).

 (ix) Whether it is *Rama Avtar*, *Parasnath Avtar*, *Krishna Avtar*, *Brahma Avtar*, or the other *Puranic* stories, these all relate to the worship to the *devi* and *avtars*.

(x) *Charitropakhyan*, too, involves worship of the *devi* and *Kal* or *Maha Kal* (*charitra* 405, *chhands* 52, 77, 126 and 132). The very facts that no Sikh is willing to read it in the presence of women or the *sangat*, and that the S.G.P.C. has called it a *Puranic* myth and not work of the Tenth Guru, show that it is no longer considered a part of the *Dasam Granth*.

The above few instances prove that, apart from the about 70 pages or so, the writings in the *Dasam Granth* positively accept and involve *devi* and *avtar* worship. Accordingly, these writings (*Chandi Charitra* and *Chandi Di Var* - 126 pages, *Chaubis Avtar* - 744 pages, *Brahm Rudra Avtar* - 383 pages, *Charitropakhyan* and *Hikayat* - 923 pages) are opposed to the doctrines of the Gurus and Guru Granth Sahib.

GURU GRANTH SAHIB ON DEVI AND AVTAR WORSHIP

About mythical writings and *devi* and *avtar* worship Guru Granth Sahib records :

(i) "O brother, fools worship gods and goddesses. They do not know that these imaginary deities can give nothing."[26]

(ii) "The Vedas, Brahma, gods and goddesses know not His secrets, and have no knowledge of the Creator."[27]

(iii) "The fools, the ignorant and the blind forget the Master Lord, and instead, worship His slaves, the goddesses and *Maya*."[28]

GURU GOBIND SINGH ON DEVI WORSHIP

Hereunder we give the *bani* of the Tenth Guru as in the *Akal Ustat* :

(i) "There are millions of Indras and incarnations of Brahma, Vishnu and Krishna. But, without worship of God none are accepted in His Court." (stanza 38).

(ii) "Millions of Indras are servants at His door. Countless are the insignificant Shivas, Ramas and Krishnas." (stanza 40).

(iii) "Some worship Shiva (Mahadev); some say Vishnu is master of the universe, and that by devotion to him, all calamities disappear. O, fool, think over a thousand times and understand that at the last moment everyone will leave you in the lurch to die alone. Remember only the One Lord who will never forsake you." (ibid).

(iv) "There was a Shiva; he was gone, and there appeared another and he was gone too. There are innumerable *avtars* like Rama or Krishna." "Countless are Brahmas, Vishnus, Vedas, Puranas and Simritis that have come and gone." (stanza 77).

These being the categoric hymns of Guru Granth Sahib and the clear statements of the Tenth Guru himself, does it make any sense that he approved of or could ever have accepted any of the writings mentioned earlier, which so clearly involve worship of *devis* and *devtas*, and some of which faithfully reflect and reproduce *Puranic* writings and myths in praise of *avtars* and the *devis*, suggesting faith in the efficacy of the mantra system discarded by Guru Granth Sahib ?

CHANGING NAME OF THE GRANTH

There is another important factor suggesting that the major part of the *Dasam Granth* is actually taken from some other sources, and has been mistakenly or deliberately combined with the *bani* of the Tenth Guru. For example, the writings were originally all separate and unconnected *pothis*, or compilations. For that reason these were first called '*Dasam Patshah Ka Granth.*' This name does not suggest any authorship of the Guru, but only seeks to link his name by way of reference to his period or quarters. Later, the *granth* was called *Dasam Granth* and still later Sri *Dasam Granth*, and so on. The frequent changes in name only reflect the interests of the writers or the publishers.

That this is a deliberate mix-up, is evident from the fact that originally most parts of the *granth* were called *Bachittar Natak Granth*. This name appears 151 times in the *Puranic* parts of the compilation. It is repeated at the end of each composition, story, chapter or poem. This name appears 19 times in *Rama Avtar*, 67 times in *Krishna Avtar*, 33 times at the end of the stories of other *Avtars*, etc.

The probability is that the mix-up has been done deliberately. For, *Puranic* verses, and *chhands* in praise of *devi* are interpolated in the midst of what is clearly the *bani* of the Tenth Guru, as seen in the light of Guru Granth Sahib. Similarly, some couplets, which are the *bani* of the Tenth Guru, as seen in the context of Guru Granth Sahib, stand introduced in the midst of *Puranic* stories.

The *bani* in Guru Granth Sahib is the Sole Guru and Guide of every Sikh. It is the Light that alone shows us the way to truth, especially when one may be wavering or in doubt. May we ask if there is any objection to accepting what is clearly in consonance with it and avoiding what is admittedly, theologically and logically, opposed to it ?

CONCLUSION

Our discussion makes it plain that such contents of the *Dasam Granth* as suggest worship of gods, goddesses and *avtars*, are opposed to the doctrines of Sri Guru Granth Sahib and the Gurus. These are also opposed to the unanimously accepted *bani* of Guru Gobind Singh, quoted above. By no stretch of reason can it be suggested that those writings are consonant with the *bani* and doctrines of Guru Granth Sahib. On the other hand, they clearly support the theory of *avtarhood* which the Gurus have emphatically rejected. Further, we find that there is not a shred of historical evidence to suggest that the Guru at any time approved of it. In fact, he had thrown away or permitted to be scattered, whatever was not worth presentation. On the other hand, Guru Granth Sahib was declared the Guru. *Gurbani* has been given to us to test what is valid or true and what is unacceptable or spurious. That test is final and unalterable.

It is also evident that none of the *devi* or *avtar*-worship writings are the collection of a Sikh or indicate the authorship of a Sikh as the original scribe or compiler. On the other hand, the manner in which this mix-up has been done, and the method of writing *Gurbani* laid down by the Gurus, grossly violated in the old *birs*, show that the author could not be a Sikh. Further, already the S.G.P.C. has accepted the position that 923 pages of *Charitropakhyan* are *Puranic* myths, unconnected with the Guru.

Many outside scholars have clearly stated that in the absence of clarification of the position about the *Dasam Granth*, the stand and history of the Tenth Guru cannot be clear. The oblique suggestion is that the Tenth Guru brought the *Panth* into the Hindu fold, and drew inspiration from the *Puranic* past and the *Shakti* cult, even though it is a historical fact that the hill princes, the staunch worshippers of the *Shakti* or *devi* cult, not only opposed the Guru, but also voluntarily accepted the supremacy of the mighty Mughal instead of confronting him. Another scholar, Ramji Lal, writes that Sikhs are Hindus, saying, "The Khalsa was constituted to emancipate the Hindu society from the contemporary evils including idolatry, caste system, superstition and ritualism." "Again at that time among the disciples of the Great Guru Gobind Singh — Bhai Nand Lal, Bhai Kanahya and Mohkam Chand, all were Hindus. Bhai Mati Das and Bhai Dayala who sacrificed their lives along with Guru Tegh Bahadur, were also Hindus." "Not only this, but Guru Gobind Singh himself revered Hindu Goddesses — Chandi and Durga and the Hindu *avtars* including — Sri Ram Chander and Lord Krishna."[29]

While it is well-known that views of many scholars like Bhai Ardaman Singh of Bagrian, Dr Jaggi, Shamsher Singh Ashok, Prof. Jagjit Singh, Principal Harbhajan Singh, Principal Jagjit Singh, Dr Rann Singh, Sardar Harnam Singh, Maj. Gen. Narinder Singh, Sardar M.S. Marco, Bhai Ashok Singh and others are the same as ours. Open attempts at ideological erosion, as quoted above, are being made. Hence the need of academic clarification. For, no Sikh can accept that anything opposed to the categoric rejection of the doctrine of *avtarhood* in Guru Granth Sahib, could ever be from an authentic Sikh source, much less from the Tenth Guru. It is undeniable that Guru Granth Sahib is our Living Guru, and its principles and doctrines are our Sole Guide to test the veracity or acceptability of any idea, concept, writing, suggestion or activity.

REFERENCES

1. Chhibber, Kesar Singh : *Bansavalinama*, p. 1.
2. Guru Granth Sahib : p. 1136.
3. Chhibber, Kesar Singh : op. cit., p. 135.
4. Ibid., p. 136.
5. Ibid.
6. Ibid.
7. Gian Singh : *Panth Prakash*, p. 320.
8. Ibid., pp. 688-689.
9. Ibid., p. 321.
10. Bhalla, Sarupdas : *Mehma Parkash*, p. 794.
11. Jaggi, Rattan Singh : *Dasam Granth da Karitartav*, pp. 38-45.
12. Ibid., pp. 92-93.
13. Ibid.
14. Ibid., pp. 93-95.
15. Ibid., pp. 95-97.
16. Ibid., pp. 97-98.
17. Gupta, H.R. : *The Sikh Gurus*, p. 245.
18. Jaggi, Rattan Singh : op. cit., pp. 152-154.
19. Ibid., p. 152.
20. Ibid., p. 153.

21. Guru Granth Sahib : p. 1.
22. Ibid., p. 1136.
23. Ibid., p. 473.
24. Ibid., p. 547.
25. Ibid., pp. 464, 1156.
26. Ibid., p. 637.
27. Ibid., p. 894.
28. Ibid., p. 1138.
29. Geholt, N.S. : *Politics of Communalism and Secularism*, Deep and Deep Publications, New Delhi, 1993, p. 67.

OUR CONTRIBUTORS

Dr AVTAR SINGH : Former Head, Department of Philosophy and Dean Academic Affairs, Punjabi University, Patiala. A distinguished scholar and author of *Ethics of The Sikhs*, and many other papers.

Justice CHOOR SINGH : Retired Judge of the Supreme Court of Singapore. Author of *The Sikh Gurus, Understanding Sikhism*, and a monograph on Sant Jarnail Singh Bhindranwale.

Sardar DALJEET SINGH : Author of *Sikhism — A Comparative Study of Its Theology And Mysticism, The Sikh Ideology, Authenticity of Kartarpuri Bir* and *Essentials of Sikhism*. Delivered Guru Nanak Dev Memorial Lectures, and Guru Tegh Bahadur Commemorative Lectures, at Punjabi University, Patiala; Contributor of several papers on Sikhism.

Dr GANDA SINGH : Ph.D., D.Litt., Well-known Sikh Historian and Research Scholar. Author of more than 50 books and over 175 papers in English, Urdu, Punjabi and Hindi.

Dr GOBIND SINGH MANSUKHANI : Author of *Introduction to Sikhism, Guru Gobind Singh, Life of Guru Nanak Dev*, and other books on Sikhism.

Dr GURDARSHAN SINGH DHILLON : Chairman, Department of Evening Classes, Panjab University, Chandigarh. Author of *Researches in Sikh Religion and History, India Commits Suicide*, and *Perspectives on Sikh Religion and History*. Is also the author of several research papers on Sikh History; Specialist in the Singh Sabha period.

Sardar GURTEJ SINGH : National Professor of Sikhism. Author of *Tandav of the Centaur : Sikhs and Indian Secularism* and several papers on Sikh Religion and History.

Professor HARBANS SINGH : Editor-in-Chief of *The Encyclopaedia of Sikhism*, Punjabi University, Patiala. His publications include *The Heritage of the Sikhs, Guru Nanak and Origin of the Sikh Faith, Guru Gobind Singh, Aspects of Punjabi Literature and Bhai Vir Singh*.

Dr HARI RAM GUPTA : Ph.D., D.Litt., Retired as Professor and Head of the Department of History, Panjab University, Chandigarh. Author of thirteen research volumes on the history of Sikhs and Punjab and a large number of papers and monograms. Honorary Head of the Post-graduate Department of History at Dev Samaj College for Women, Firozpur (Punjab).

Dr HARNAM SINGH SHAN : Formerly Professor and Head, Department of Guru Nanak Studies, Panjab University, Chandigarh. A known scholar of Sikhism, and author of many books on Sikh religion.

Sirdar KAPUR SINGH : Erudite Sikh scholar, author of *Parasaraprasna, Sikhism : An Oecumenical Religion* and several other books and research papers.

Sardar KARNAIL SINGH : A scholar of Sikh history, known for his book *Anglo-Sikh Wars*.

Dr KHARAK SINGH : Secretary, Institute of Sikh Studies, Chandigarh. Author of several research papers on Sikh Studies. Editor of *Abstracts of Sikh Studies*, and several books.

Sardar JAGJIT SINGH : Author of *The Sikh Revolution, Perspectives on Sikh Studies* and *In The Caravan of Revolutions*, besides other books and publications on Sikh Studies.

Dr NOEL Q. KING : Prof. Emeritus of Religion, University of California, Santa Cruz (U.S.A.). Author of several books on religion, and papers on Sikh Studies.

Dr JAMES R. LEWIS : Prof. of Philosophy and Religion, Appalachian State University, Boone, North Carolina, (U.S.A.). Author of several papers on religion and Sikh Studies.

Sardar THARAM SINGH : Retired Secondary Principal, Singapore. Wrote *The Story Of The Sikhs* for Singapore school-children.

GLOSSARY

AAD/ADI : First, original, e.g., Adi Granth, the original Sikh scripture.

AHIMSA : Hindu religious doctrine of non-injury.

AKAL : Eternal; immortal; a term used to describe God.

AKAL BUNGA : Lord's mansion; another name for Akal Takht.

AKALI : Worshipper of the Eternal God; usually refers to members of the Shiromani Akali Dal — a political party of the Sikhs.

AKALI DAL : Corps of volunteers originally organised for wresting control of gurdwaras from the corrupt Hindu *mahants*. Now a political party.

AKAL TAKHT : The throne of the Almighty, the highest seat of authority of the Sikh religion; the building erected by Guru Hargobind opposite the Golden Temple.

AMRITDHARI KHALSA : One who has been initiated as a Khalsa.

ARDAS : An important Sikh prayer recited at the conclusion of a service; the word itself means supplication; Petition to God invoking His Grace.

AVTAR : Incarnation of a deity, usually Vishnu.

BAISAKHI : See Vaisakhi.

BANI : See *Gurbani*.

BHAGAT/BHAKTA : Saint; exponent of bhakti; devotee who adores God.

BHAKTI : Devotion, worship, meditation, religious obervances.

BIR : Volume of Guru Granth Sahib.

CHARHDI KALA : The waxing mood; ever rising high spirits.

DARBAR SAHIB : The Lord's Court; used as a synonym for the Golden Temple, the Harimandar.

DASAM GRANTH : Lit. Tenth Book. An anthology of 1422 pages, compiled some two decades after the passing away of Guru Gobind Singh. Besides a few hymns of the Guru, the compilation includes contributions of a number of poets of his times.

DASWANDH : Tithe or one tenth of one's income; contribution towards common socio-religious development of society.

DHARAM KHAND : A hymn in the *Japji Sahib* of Guru Nanak. It gives the description of the earth, our planet, which according to the Guru, is the place for the practice of righteousness.

DHARMA : Righteousness; moral law.

DHARAMSAL : Hostel for pilgrims; sometimes used as Prayer Hall. Literally, a place for righteous actions.

DIVALI : Festival of lights celebrated by the Hindus. Sikhs celebrate it as the day on which Guru Hargobind, after release from prison, arrived at Amritsar.

GADDI : Throne of Guruship.

GRANTHI : One who recites from Guru Granth Sahib. Frequently he may look after the gurdwara also, but he is not a priest. There is no priest class among Sikhs.

GURBANI (OR BANI) : The Revealed Word; the utterances of the Gurus and *bhagats* recorded in the Adi Granth; the Divine word received from God. See *Gurshabad.*

GURDWARA : Literally, "Door of the Guru"; a building that houses the sacred Sikh scripture.

GURMATTA : The intention, resolution or will of the Guru expressed in a formal decision made by a representative assembly of Sikhs; a resolution of the *Sarbat Khalsa.*

GURMUKH : See *Sachiara.*

GURMUKHI : The script in which Guru Granth Sahib is written. Literally, "from the mouth of the Guru".

GURSHABAD : The divine word of the Guru; hymns from the sacred scripture of the Sikhs — Guru Granth Sahib.

GURU GRANTH SAHIB : The Adi Granth, the sacred scripture of the Sikhs on which Guruship was conferred by Guru Gobind Singh after adding the hymns of his father, Guru Tegh Bahadur.

GURU PANTH : The corporate Guru of the Sikhs.

GURU KA LANGAR : "The Guru's Mess;" food served from the community kitchen of a gurdwara.

HAUMAIN : Self-exaltation; self-centredness; ego.

HUKM (OR RAZA) : Divine Order; Command of God; Will of God.

JATHEDAR : Leader of a *Jatha* (contingent of Sikhs) : Chief or Head, e.g., *Jathedar* of the Akal Takht.

KACHI : Literally unripe; false; apocryphal.

KAKKAS : The five symbols enjoined on Sikhs, viz., *kachh* (breeches), *kara* (steel bangle) *kirpan* (sword), *kangha* (comb) and *kesh* (hair).

KHALSA DAL : The army of initiated Sikhs, the Khalsa; term used during the 18th century.

KHALSA PANTH : In the time of the Gurus, the Sikh *Panth* was a religious community. After the creation of the Khalsa by Guru Gobind Singh, the Khalsa became rulers of North India and the Khalsa *Panth* became the Sikh nation.

KIRPAN : Sabre which a Khalsa when initiated is enjoined to carry on his/her person always.

KIRTAN : Devotional singing in praise of deity.

LAKH : One hundred thousand, 100,000.

LANGAR : See *Guru ka Langar.*

MAHANT : Head of a Hindu *mandir* (temple)

MANJIS : 22 seats of religious authority (*manjis*) were established by Guru Amar Das, but abolished by Guru Gobind Singh because they had become corrupt.

MANMUKH : Guided by one's own mind, rather than by the Guru's advice; self-oriented, irreligious.

MIRI-PIRI : The Sikh doctrine of whole-life religion or complementarity and inseparability of spiritual and temporal aspects of life.

MISLS : Sikh confederacies in the eighteenth century which later consolidated to form the Sikh nation ruled by Ranjit Singh.

MITHYA : Illusion; Hindu doctrine that this earth is a place of suffering.

MOHURS : Former Indian gold coins.

MOKSHA : Return of the soul for merger in Brahman, or a state of bliss and union with God, without involvement in the world of man; Hindu doctrine of liberation in this life.

MORCHAS : Resistance or confrontation by unarmed *Jathas* (contingents) of Sikhs to wrest control of gurdwaras from corrupt Hindu *mahants*; anti-government agitation.

MUKTI : Liberation; salvation; end of transmigration of soul and its union with God.

MUL MANTRA : The basic belief or the fundamental doctrine of the Sikh faith enunciated by Guru Nanak in *Japji Sahib*; the opening words of Guru Granth Sahib.

NAM, NAAM : God and *Naam* are Real, Eternal and Unfathomable. *Naam* may be called the immanent or the qualitative aspect of God, working and directing the manifest world described by the Sikh Gurus as unmanifest (*nirguna*) and manifest (*sarguna*); the Highest Power, creating, informing, supporting and working the entire universe. Sikhs pray for the boon of *Naam,* i.e., linkage with God.

NAMSIMRAN : The daily worship or remembrance of God which Sikhs are enjoined to do.

NANAKPANTHIS : Guru Nanak's disciples. Before the creation of Khalsa, Sikhs were known as Nanakpanthis.

NIRGUNA SAMPRADAYA : The Sant tradition of Nothern India; a sect of Hinduism.

NIRVAN, NIRVANA : Liberation, salvation, redemption, Buddhist term for *mukti.*

PANGAT : A line of devotees sitting on the floor for a meal from the Guru's kitchen attached to every gurdwara.

PANJ PIARAS : Literally 'Five Beloveds'; the term originally used for the five Sikhs who offered to sacrifice their heads on a call from Guru Gobind Singh on the Vaisakhi day in 1699. Currently used to refer to five Sikhs chosen to represent the community.

PANTH : Literally path or way; Sikh *Panth* means the entire community following the Sikh way of life.

PARSAD : Kindness, grace, favour. *Karah prasad* is consecrated pudding distributed in a gurdwara, symbolising the Guru's kindness.

PATASHAHI : Political sovereignty.

POTHI : Book, *granth*.

PUJARI : A Hindu priest.

RAGIS : Hymn-singers who perform *kirtan*, the singing of devotional songs and hymns from Guru Granth Sahib.

RAHIT MARYADA : Disciplinary Code of the Khalsa issued by the Shiromani Gurdwara Parbandhak Committee.

RAHITNAMA : Book containing the original disciplinary Code of the Khalsa. There are several published in the eighteenth century.

RAJ JAATI : People of royal lineage; people destined to rule.

RAJ KAREGA KHALSA : The Khalsa shall rule.

RAZA : See *Hukm*.

SACHI : True.

SACH ACHAR : Truthful living enjoined by the Sikh Gurus.

SACHIARA (or GURMUKH) : One who lives truthfully; God-conscious man.

SAMSARA : The world, universe, the creation as a whole; mundane existence.

SANGAT : A Sikh gathering; assembly; congregation.

SANT MAT : Sant tradition of Nothern India; a sect of Hinduism.

SANT SIPAHI (or SAINT-SOLDIER) : Who is prepared to fight for justice or a noble cause as an expression of his devotion to God.

SARBAT DA BHALA : Welfare of all; peace and prosperity for all.

SARBAT KHALSA : An assembly of all the Khalsa. In the eighteenth century, the *misls* used to hold *Sarbat Khalsa* meetings.

SATGURU : Lit. true Guru; Eternal Guru or God; frequently used for the Sikh Gurus.

SAWAIYA : Religious text; panegyric; an eulogy; laudation, a form of poetry.

SEVADAR : Attendant.

SHABAD : Divine Word of the Gurus received from God; refers to the sacred word appearing in Guru Granth Sahib.

SHAKTI : Power; strength; might; energy; authority.

VAISAKHI : The harvest season festival observed on 13th April each year. It is also the day on which Guru Gobind Singh initiated the Sikhs as the Khalsa.

VARNA DHARMA : The Hindu caste system, which divides human beings into four major castes, based on the principle of inequality of human beings.

ZULUM : Persecution; tyranny; torture.